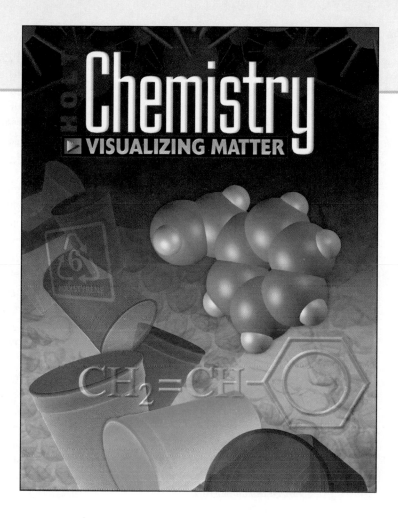

Chemistry
VISUALIZING MATTER

AUTHORS

R. Thomas Myers, Ph.D.
Professor Emeritus of Chemistry
Kent State University
Kent, Ohio

Keith B. Oldham, Ph.D.
Professor of Chemistry
Trent University
Peterborough, Ontario, Canada

Salvatore Tocci
Science Writer
East Hampton, NY

HOLT, RINEHART AND WINSTON
Harcourt Brace & Company

Austin • New York • Orlando • Atlanta • San Francisco
Boston • Dallas • Toronto • London

▼ Contributing Writers

Jeffrey D. Bracken
Chemistry Teacher
Westerville North High School
Westerville, OH

Robert Davisson
Science Writer and Editor
Delaware, Ohio

Dave Jaeger
Chemistry Teacher
Will C. Wood High School
Vacaville, CA

Mary Ellen Teasdale
Chemistry Reference Librarian
Texas A&M University
College Station, TX

Suzanne Weisker
*Science Teacher and
Department Chair*
Will C. Wood High School
Vacaville, CA

Jay A. Young, Ph.D.
Chemical Safety Consultant
Silver Spring, MD

▼ Staff Credits

Managing Editor
David F. Bowman

Editorial Staff
John Benner
Derika Hatcher
Cecelia B. Schneider
Amanda Tinsley

Copyediting Supervisor
Steve Oelenberger

Copyeditors
Suzanne Brooks
Brooke Fugitt
Denise Haney
Tania Hannan

**Senior Designer
Book Design**
Marta Kimball

Book Design Staff
José Garza
Cathy Jenevein
Amanda Marks
Bob Prestwood

Editorial Permissions
Jan Harrington

**Director
Image Services**
Debra Schorn

Image Services Staff
Elaine Tate
Sherry France
Linda Wilbourn
Leroy Dee Golden II

Photo Research Manager
Peggy Cooper

Photo Researchers
Jeannie Taylor
Diana Suthard
Jennifer Guidry

Senior Staff Photographer
Sam Dudgeon

Photo Studio
Victoria Smith
Lauren Eischen

**Media Design
Art Director**
Joe Melomo

Media Design Staff
Shawn McKinney

New Media Design Art Director
Susan Michael

Senior Production Manager
Mimi Stockdell

Production Coordinator
Beth Sample

**Production
Senior Secretary**
Sara Downs

Media Senior Production Manager
Kim A. Scott

Media Production Coordinator
Nancy Hargis

Production Assistant
Adriana Bardin

Manufacturing Coordinator
Jevara Jackson

**New Media
Associate Director**
Kate Bennett

**New Media
Project Manager**
Stacy Doolittle

Researchers
Mike Tracy
Joyce Herbert
Patty Kolar
Jennifer Swift

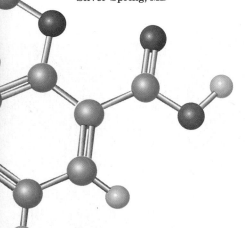

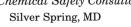

Cover: Design by Lawrence R. Didona. **Photos:** John Langford/HRW Photo.

Requests for permission to make copies of any part of the work should be mailed to the following address: Permissions Department, Holt, Rinehart and Winston, 1120 South Capital of Texas Highway, Austin, Texas 78746-6487.

For permission to reprint copyrighted material, grateful acknowledgment is made to the following sources:
*sci*LINKS is owned and provided by the National Science Teachers Association. All Rights Reserved.
Flinn Scientific, Inc., Batavia, IL: From *Latex, The Preparation of a Rubber Ball,* Publication Number 430.00. Copyright © 1993 by Flinn Scientific, Inc. All Rights Reserved. No part of this material may be reproduced or transmitted in any form or by any means, electronic or mechanical, including, but not limited to photocopy, recording, or any information storage and retrieval system, without permission in writing from Flinn Scientific, Inc.

Printed in the United States of America

ISBN 0-03-052002-9
345678 048 03 02 01 00

Contents

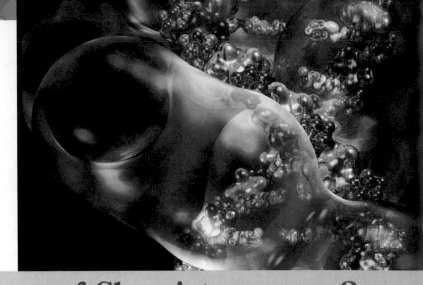

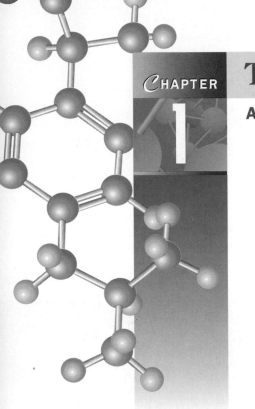

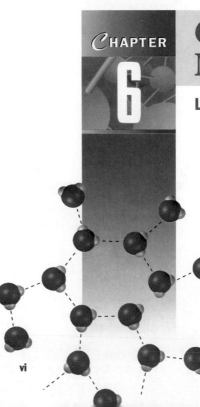

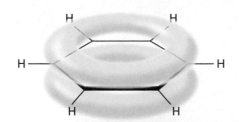

Copper-65

1997 American League Batting Average

Player	Team	Average
Frank Thomas	Chicago	.347
Edgar Martinez	Seattle	.330
David Justice	Cleveland	.329
Bernie Williams	New York	.328
Manny Ramirez	Cleveland	.328

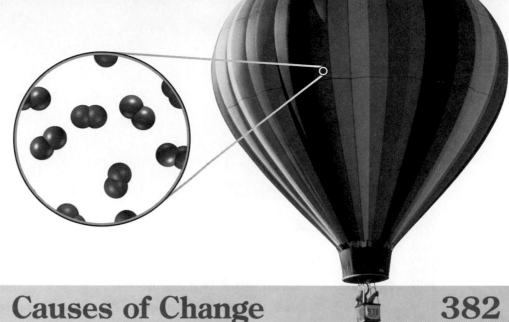

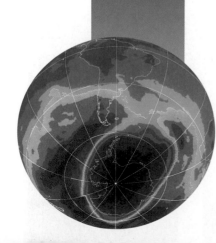

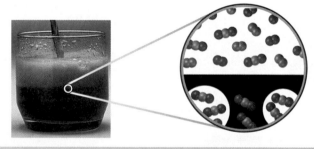

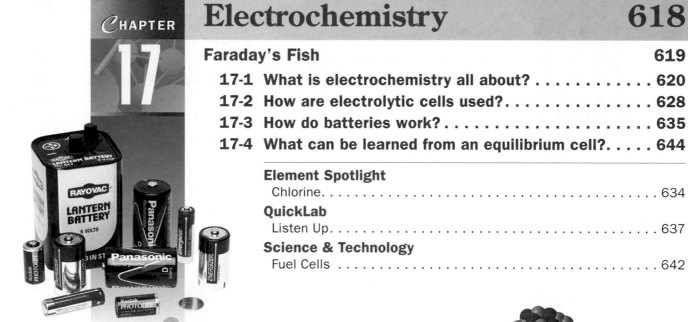
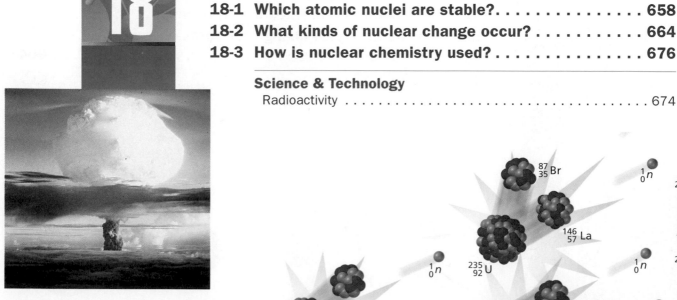

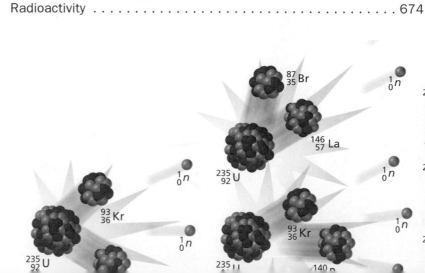

Appendices

Laboratory Program 688

Sample Problems

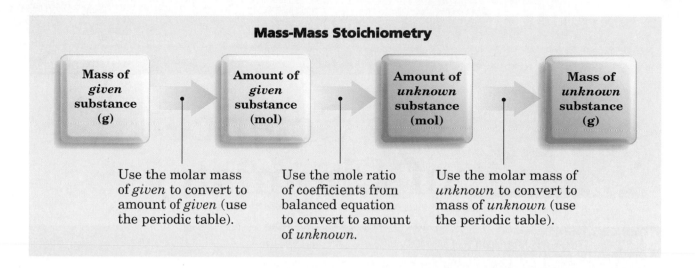

Mass-Mass Stoichiometry

Mass of *given* substance (g)	Amount of *given* substance (mol)	Amount of *unknown* substance (mol)	Mass of *unknown* substance (g)

Use the molar mass of *given* to convert to amount of *given* (use the periodic table).

Use the mole ratio of coefficients from balanced equation to convert to amount of *unknown*.

Use the molar mass of *unknown* to convert to mass of *unknown* (use the periodic table).

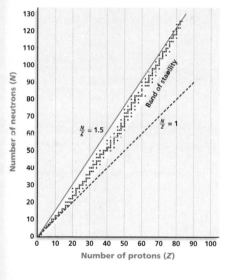

The Science
of Chemistry

A WONDER DRUG

2000 years ago, the Greeks and Romans relied on a substance extracted from plants, particularly the bark of willow trees, to relieve pain and reduce fevers. Plant extracts were used to treat various ailments in other parts of the world, including North America, where Native Americans used a bark extract to treat fever and pain.

In the 1760s, Edward Stone, an English clergyman and naturalist, wrote that he used "twenty grains of powdered bark dissolved in water, administered every four hours" to treat 50 people suffering from acute shiver-provoking illnesses. The results, he reported, were excellent.

Following up on Stone's report, German chemists in the early 1800s isolated a tiny amount of what they believed to be the active ingredient in the willow bark extract and called it salicin, from *Salix,* the scientific name for willow trees. French chemists improved on the extraction process and discovered that salicin could be converted to a substance called salicylic acid, the active form of the pain reliever.

Once salicylic acid was identified as the active ingredient, a related substance, sodium salicylate, was made available for public use. Unfortunately, sodium salicylate was extremely irritating to the lining of the stomach. People who took it often suffered stomach irritation or nausea and occasionally developed ulcers.

In the late 1800s, Felix Hoffmann, a German chemist, began looking for ways to reduce some of the unpleasant side effects of sodium salicylate. Although his research focused on the chemistry of dyes, Hoffmann became interested in sodium salicylate because he wanted to help relieve the pain his father experienced from arthritis. Hoffmann was able to synthesize another derivative of salicylic acid, acetylsalicylic acid—the compound we know today as aspirin. Little did Hoffmann or Stone know that their treatments would someday become a common prescription—take two aspirin every four hours to relieve pain or reduce fever.

Chemistry has enabled tremendous changes to be made in the way we live. These changes can lead to new challenges that we all must face and, at times, to problems that we have yet to solve and questions that we have yet to answer. However, there are some questions that you should be able to answer after reading this chapter.

CHAPTER LINKS

What type of chemical substance is aspirin?

How is aspirin similar to other widely used pain relievers?

How does name-brand aspirin differ from generic brands of aspirin?

What is chemistry?

OBJECTIVES

▶ **Describe** the characteristics of the three most common physical states.

▶ **Draw** models to represent solids, liquids, and gases.

▶ **Write** a word equation for a chemical reaction.

▶ **Identify** the reactants and products in a chemical reaction.

▶ **Distinguish** between exothermic and endothermic reactions.

Chemistry deals with the properties of matter

You probably think of chemistry as simply another subject that you study in high school. Or you may feel that chemistry is important only to people working in laboratories. But there is much more to chemistry than this. In fact, whether you are aware of it or not, chemistry is an important part of your daily life.

You depend on chemicals every day

chemical

any substance with a definite composition

Chemistry deals with the properties of chemicals. What is a chemical? A **chemical** is any substance with a definite composition. You will learn in this course that chemical reactions are taking place constantly all around you and that chemists are not the only people who work with chemicals. For example, the chef shown in **Figure 1-1** carefully controls

▶ **FIGURE 1-1**

The ingredients in your food are chemicals. A skilled chef understands how the chemicals interact in foods.

the many chemical reactions necessary to produce a delicious meal. A photographer uses chemicals to develop exposed film and to stabilize the images on photographic paper. A boat owner applies a paint containing chemicals that will retard the growth of organisms on the hull. A consumer buying aspirin scans the label for chemicals that might cause an allergic reaction. Obviously, chemists are not the only people who benefit from a knowledge of chemistry. Because chemicals are an integral part of our everyday lives, everyone needs some understanding of chemistry. This text will give you that understanding and will also show you the variety of ways that chemistry plays a role in your daily life.

Some people think of chemicals mainly in negative terms—as the causes of pollution, cancer, and explosions. Many of these people believe that chemicals and chemical additives should be banned. But think for a moment what such a ban would mean—after all, everything around you is a chemical. Imagine going to the supermarket to buy fruits and vegetables grown without the use of any chemicals at all. The produce section would be completely empty! In fact, the entire supermarket would be empty because all foods are made of chemicals.

Without chemicals, you would have nothing to wear. Much of your clothing is made from synthetic fibers that are the products of chemical reactions. Even clothing made from natural fibers, such as cotton or wool, is the product of chemical reactions. As you can see from **Table 1-1,** the production of chemical compounds is a major industry. The top five chemical producers in the United States might be familiar to you, especially if you live in one of the top 10 chemical-producing states, shown in **Figure 1-2. Table 1-2,** on the next page, lists the top five chemicals produced in the United States.

internet**connect**

SC*LINKS*
NSTA
TOPIC: Chemicals
GO TO: www.scilinks.org
KEYWORD: HW011

FIGURE 1-2 ▼

You can see that major chemical-producing states are clustered by region. Why do you think most chemical-producing states are located near the ocean or Great Lakes?

TABLE 1-1	Top Five Chemical Producers in the U.S.	
Rank	**Name**	**Sales (in millions of dollars)**
1	Dow Chemical	18 988
2	Du Pont	18 044
3	Exxon	11 430
4	Monsanto	7 267
5	Hoechst Celanese	6 906

Source: *Chemical and Engineering News,* May 1997

TABLE 1-2	Top Five Chemicals in the United States (production by weight)			
Rank	Name	Formula	Uses	
1	sulfuric acid	H_2SO_4	production of fertilizer, metal processing, petroleum refining	
2	nitrogen	N_2	packaging food, production of fertilizers	
3	oxygen	O_2	rocket propellant, production of steel	
4	ethene	C_2H_4	production of plastics	
5	calcium oxide (lime)	CaO	production of glass and cement	

Source: *Chemical and Engineering News*

Solids, liquids, and gases are physical states of matter

physical state

the form matter takes as a result of the arrangement of its particles

All matter is made of particles. The type and arrangement of the particles in a sample of matter determine its properties. A basic property of matter is its **physical state.** Most matter you observe is in one of three physical states: solid, liquid, or gas.

Figure 1-3 illustrates the solid, liquid, and gaseous states of water at the microscopic level. In this text *microscopic* refers to objects that are about the size of atoms. Contrast *microscopic* with *macroscopic,* which refers to objects large enough to be seen with the unaided eye.

▼ FIGURE 1-3

a Between 0°C and 100°C, water exists mostly as a liquid. In the liquid state, water particles are close together and can move about freely.

c At 100°C, water becomes a gas. Water molecules can move randomly over large distances.

b At 0°C, water exists as ice. In the solid state, water molecules are in a rigid structure.

Solids have fixed volume and shape. These properties result from the way solids are structured on the microscopic level. When matter is in the solid state, the particles that make up the matter are held tightly in a rigid structure. These particles are able to vibrate only slightly.

Liquids have fixed volume but variable shape. The particles in a liquid are not held together as rigidly as those in a solid. Like grains of sand, the particles of a liquid can slip past one another. Thus, a liquid as a whole is able to flow and take the shape of its container. But as with a solid, the particles of a liquid are held close to one another, and the adjacent particles are in contact most of the time. As a result, the overall volume of the liquid is constant.

Gases have neither fixed shape nor fixed volume, and they expand to fill any container they occupy. Even a few grams of a gas would become evenly distributed in a large room. This is because gas particles are not strongly attracted to one another. Instead, they are free to move about independently. The average distance between gas particles is always much greater than the average distance between particles in liquids or in solids.

Chemical reactions describe how matter behaves

You know from previous science courses that compounds, such as water, H_2O, and the sugar glucose, $C_6H_{12}O_6$, are made by **chemical reactions.** Acetylsalicylic acid, the active ingredient in aspirin, is also made by a chemical reaction. To produce acetylsalicylic acid in a laboratory, salicylic acid is mixed with a chemical called acetic anhydride and the mixture is heated. These two chemicals react to form acetylsalicylic acid in a reaction described by the following word equation.

salicylic acid + acetic anhydride $\longrightarrow$ acetylsalicylic acid + acetic acid

Salicylic acid and acetic anhydride, the starting materials in this reaction, are called **reactants.** Acetylsalicylic acid and acetic acid are called **products.** The arrow in the chemical equation separates the reactants from products and also indicates in which direction the reaction usually proceeds—from left to right. The equation above indicates that the two reactants form two new products.

Not all reactions involve reactants that combine. **Figure 1-4** shows a reaction that involves a single reactant breaking apart to form two or more products. This type of reaction is a decomposition. During the reaction, mercury(II) oxide decomposes to

chemical reaction

the process by which elements and/or compounds interact with one another to form new substances

reactant

a chemical that is present at the beginning of a chemical reaction and that takes part in the reaction

product

a chemical produced as a result of a chemical reaction

FIGURE 1-4 ◄

The chemical reaction in which mercury(II) oxide decomposes to form mercury and oxygen requires energy. The energy is supplied by the burner.

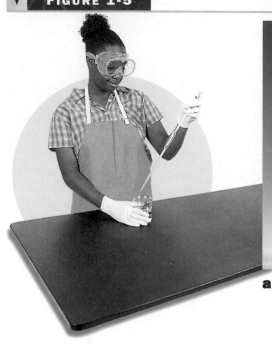

a The formation of silver chloride is an exothermic reaction because energy is released. The temperature of the matter in the beaker rises when the precipitate forms.

b The reaction of hydrated barium hydroxide and ammonium nitrate absorbs energy. The temperature of the matter in the flask drops as the product forms.

form mercury and oxygen gas. The word equation for this reaction is written as follows.

mercury(II) oxide → mercury + oxygen

Notice in Figure 1-4 that a burner is used to heat the mercury (II) oxide in the test tube. The burner supplies energy. Many reactions require some energy input for the reaction to begin. The energy needed to start a reaction is called *activation energy*. If there is insufficient energy present in the reactants as room temperature, heat, light, or some other source of energy must be used to supply activation energy.

There are two types of reactions, those that release energy overall and those that absorb energy overall. You can easily recognize a reaction that releases energy; light is given off or the temperature of the reaction system increases. If you add silver nitrate to hydrochloric acid, a precipitate like the one shown in **Figure 1-5a** forms. The beaker also feels warmer, indicating that the reaction releases energy. A reaction that releases energy is called an **exothermic reaction** (the prefix *exo-* means "outside").

Figure 1-5b shows what happens when you mix hydrated barium hydroxide with ammonium nitrate and shake the mixture. A reaction takes place because the two solids now form a liquid slush-like product. The reaction flask feels colder, indicating that this reaction absorbs energy. Reactions that absorb energy are called **endothermic reactions** (the prefix *endo-* means "within").

exothermic reaction

a reaction in which energy is released

endothermic reaction

a reaction in which energy is absorbed

CONSUMER FOCUS

ASPIRIN

The FDA and the safe use of aspirin

The FDA requires that every container of aspirin—the most widely used over-the-counter drug—have a warning label. This label warns not to give aspirin to children and adolescents with chickenpox or a severe case of flu. Some studies have shown that aspirin may cause liver malfunction and swelling of the brain, a condition known as Reye syndrome.

The label also warns that aspirin can cause side effects, such as nausea and vomiting, and can interfere with the clotting of blood. Aspirin should not be taken by pregnant women, hemophiliacs, or anyone who has recently had a tonsillectomy or oral surgery. Some people may also be allergic to aspirin.

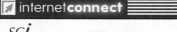 internetconnect

 SCI**LINKS**
NSTA

TOPIC: Aspirin
GO TO: www.scilinks.org
KEYWORD: HW012

Product warning labels

When you purchase a product, it is your responsibility as a consumer to check the warning label carefully for any warnings about the chemicals it contains.

> **WARNINGS:** Children and teenagers should not use this medicine for chicken pox or flu symptoms before a doctor is consulted about Reye syndrome, a rare but serious illness reported to be associated with aspirin. As with any drug, if you are pregnant or nursing a baby, see the advice of a health professional before using this product. **IT IS ESPECIALLY IMPORTANT NOT TO USE ASPIRIN DURING THE LAST 3 MONTHS OF PREGNANCY UNLESS SPECIFICALLY DIRECTED TO DO SO BY A DOCTOR BECAUSE IT MAY CAUSE PROBLEMS IN THE UNBORN CHILD OR COMPLICATIONS DURING DELIVERY.** Keep this and all medicines out of the reach of children. In the case of accidental overdose, see professional assistance or contact a poison control center immediately.

SECTION REVIEW

Total recall

1. What are the common physical states of matter?

2. How do the particle models for the states of matter differ?

3. What is the difference between an endothermic reaction and an exothermic reaction?

4. In what ways do the three fundamental states of matter differ?

Critical thinking

5. During photosynthesis, light energy is captured by plants to make sugar from carbon dioxide and water. In the process, oxygen is also produced. Write the word equation for photosynthesis.

6. What observation indicates that a reaction is exothermic?

7. Draw a picture to show what happens to atoms when a piece of lead is heated until it melts (turns from a solid to a liquid).

What is matter?

OBJECTIVES

▶ **Relate** mass, volume, and density.

▶ **Distinguish** between qualitative and quantitative properties.

▶ **Describe** the difference between a quantity and a unit.

▶ **Convert** measurements between SI units.

▶ **Distinguish** between physical and chemical properties.

▶ **List** four ways to determine if a chemical change has occurred.

Matter has mass and volume

Matter, the stuff all things in the universe are composed of, exists in a dazzling variety of forms. Chemistry is an ongoing investigation into the nature of matter. **Matter** is anything that has mass and volume. Even the air you breathe is matter. Consider what happens when you blow up a balloon. When inflated, a balloon has more mass and greater volume than it does when it is deflated. The increase in the mass and volume of the balloon comes from the mass and volume of air that you blew into the balloon.

matter

anything that has mass and volume

volume

the space an object occupies

The space an object occupies is its volume

An object's **volume** is the space the object occupies. For example, this book has volume because it takes up space. Volume can be determined in several different ways, depending on the nature of the matter being examined. The *graduated cylinder* is commonly used to determine the volume of a liquid in the lab. The volume of a liquid must be read the same way every time, as shown in **Figure 1-6.** Can you see why? Volumes of solids are generally expressed in cubic units based on length, width, and height.

▼ **FIGURE 1-6**

To read the liquid level in a graduated cylinder correctly, read the level at the bottom of the meniscus. The volume shown is 50 mL.

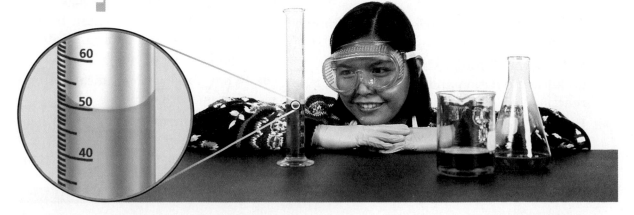

Mass is not weight

The **mass** of an object is the quantity of matter in that object. Scientists measure mass using a balance. A type of electronic balance often used in industrial-chemistry laboratories is shown in **Figure 1-7.** This balance gives a quick, digital readout of mass.

Balances differ based on the *accuracy* of the mass reading you can obtain. The balance often found in a school chemistry laboratory is the triple-beam balance. This balance can be used for measurements of less than 300 g. If the smallest scale on the triple-beam balance is graduated in 0.1 g increments, you can obtain mass readings that are estimated to the hundredth place. You can get a reading to a greater number of decimal places by using a more accurate analytical balance than by using a simple triple-beam balance.

Mass is related but not identical to weight. Recall that mass reflects the amount of matter in an object. As long as an object remains intact, it will have the same mass—no matter where in the universe it is. Thus, the mass of an object is constant.

The weight of an object depends on where it is. This is because weight depends on gravity, while mass does not. **Weight** is defined as the force produced by gravity acting on mass. Scientists measure force in *newtons*. Because gravity can vary from one location to another, the weight of an object can vary. For example, an astronaut weighs about six times more on Earth than on the moon because the effect of gravity is less on the moon. The astronaut's mass, however, remains constant.

Keep in mind the difference between mass and weight as you conduct laboratory activities that call for the use of a balance. Determining the weight of an object is not the same as determining its mass. Although the term *weigh* is not literally equivalent to "determine the mass of," these expressions are often interchanged. In chemistry, when you read the word *weigh* in a laboratory procedure, you probably will be required to record the mass. Check with your teacher to be sure.

mass

the quantity of matter in an object

weight

the force produced by gravity acting on mass

CONCEPT CHECK

1. What two properties are characteristic of matter?

2. What is the difference between mass and weight?

3. What units are used to express mass and weight?

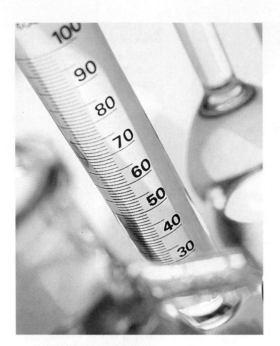

▲ **FIGURE 1-8**

A measurement instrument like this graduated cylinder gives us quantitative descriptions of the volume of a liquid. The scale on the cylinder is an agreed upon standard.

quantity

something that has magnitude or size

unit

a standard used when measuring a quantity

Units of measurement

Terms such as *light, heavy, large,* and *small* are *qualitative* descriptions of matter. Some properties of matter, such as color and texture, are best described in qualitative terms.

Many properties of matter, including mass and volume, are best described in *quantitative* terms. Quantitative terms include numbers, which make descriptions more exact. But numbers alone are not sufficient because the significance of numbers alone is unclear. Standard units are needed along with numbers for more accurate descriptions. For example, 15 grams of sugar is a more accurate description than a spoonful of sugar. Measurement instruments, like the one shown in **Figure 1-8,** are used to quantify descriptions.

When working with quantitative terms, be sure to distinguish between a quantity and a unit. A **quantity** is something that has magnitude or size. Volume, mass, and distance are quantities. A **unit** is the standard used to measure a quantity. For example, you can measure the *quantity* mass with the *unit* kilogram. What quantity can be measured in meters?

Scientists express measurements in SI units

In 1960, the scientific community adopted a subset of the metric system as the standard system of measurement units. This is the Système Internationale d'Unités (SI); it features the seven base units listed in **Table 1-3.** The five you will use extensively in chemistry are meter, kilogram, second, kelvin, and mole.

SI base units can be modified with the prefixes listed in **Table 1-4** to match the scale of the object being measured. For example, the base unit for length, meter, is suitable for expressing a person's height, but distances between cities should be measured in *kilo*meters.

internet**connect**

*SCI*LINKS
NSTA

TOPIC: SI units
GO TO: www.scilinks.org
KEYWORD: HW013

| TABLE 1-3 | SI Base Units |

Quantity	Symbol	Unit	Abbreviation
Length	*l*	meter	m
Mass	*m*	kilogram	kg
Time	*t*	second	s
Thermodynamic temperature	*T*	kelvin	K
Amount of substance	*n*	mole	mol
Electric current	*I*	ampere	A
Luminous intensity	I_v	candela	cd

TABLE 1-4	SI Prefixes				

Prefix	Unit abbreviation	Exponential multiplier	Meaning	Example using length
Giga-	G	10^9	1 000 000 000	1 gigameter (Gm) = 1×10^9 m
Mega-	M	10^6	1 000 000	1 megameter (Mm) = 1×10^6 m
Kilo-	k	10^3	1000	1 kilometer (km) = 1000 m
Hecto-	h	10^2	100	1 hectometer (hm) = 100 m
		10^0	1	**1 meter (m)**
Deci-	d	10^{-1}	1/10	1 decimeter (dm) = 0.1 m
Centi-	c	10^{-2}	1/100	1 centimeter (cm) = 0.01 m
Milli-	m	10^{-3}	1/1000	1 millimeter (mm) = 0.001 m
Micro-	μ	10^{-6}	1/1 000 000	1 micrometer (μm) = 1×10^{-6} m
Nano-	n	10^{-9}	1/1 000 000 000	1 nanometer (nm) = 1×10^{-9} m
Pico-	p	10^{-12}	1/1 000 000 000 000	1 picometer (pm) = 1×10^{-12} m
Femto-	f	10^{-15}	1/1 000 000 000 000 000	1 femtometer (fm) = 1×10^{-15} m

Conversion factors enable you to convert from one unit to another

Situations often arise in chemistry that require you to convert measurements from one unit to another. A **conversion factor** is a mathematical expression that relates two units that measure the same quantity. Conversion factors are based on statements of equality. For example, to convert a mass expressed in kilograms to grams, you need the equality that relates grams and kilograms.

$$1 \text{ kg} = 1000 \text{ g} \quad \text{or} \quad 1 \text{ g} = 0.001 \text{ kg}$$

These equalities can be written as the following conversion factors.

1 kg = 1000 g can be written as $\dfrac{1000 \text{ g}}{1 \text{ kg}}$ or $\dfrac{1 \text{ kg}}{1000 \text{ g}}$

1 g = 0.001 kg can be written as $\dfrac{1 \text{ g}}{0.001 \text{ kg}}$ or $\dfrac{0.001 \text{ kg}}{1 \text{ g}}$

How do you use conversion factors? Just multiply the original measurement by the appropriate conversion factor to convert the measurement to the desired unit. To convert 1.5 kg to grams, you need a factor that will allow you to cancel out kilograms, but will give grams in the final answer. The calculation looks like the following.

$$1.5 \text{ kg} \times \frac{1000 \text{ g}}{1 \text{ kg}} = 1500 \text{ g}$$

conversion factor

a mathematical expression that relates two units

What is the mass, in kilograms, of a 22 000 g bag of fertilizer?

1 **Write the equality that relates the units given in the problem**
Use Table 1-4 for data. The equality for grams and kilograms is the following.

$$1000 \text{ g} = 1 \text{ kg}$$

2 **Write the conversion factor that is the bridge between the units you have and the units you want in the answer**
The conversion factor must have grams in the denominator to give an answer of kilograms.

$$\frac{1 \text{ kg}}{1000 \text{ g}}$$

3 **Set up the problem and solve**
Cancel units that divide out.

$$22\,000 \, \cancel{g} \times \frac{1 \text{ kg}}{1000 \, \cancel{g}} = 22 \text{ kg}$$

Derived units can be obtained for any quantity

Units for the volume of a cube are derived from three length measurements.

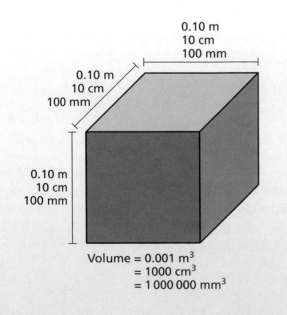

0.10 m
10 cm
100 mm

0.10 m
10 cm
100 mm

0.10 m
10 cm
100 mm

Volume = 0.001 m³
= 1000 cm³
= 1 000 000 mm³

SI base units cannot be used to measure every observable quantity, so *derived units* must also be used. Derived units are created from combinations of the seven base units. One derived unit for volume, for example, is cubic meters, m^3. This derived unit can be obtained by multiplying the length, width, and height of an object, which are measurements expressed in meters.

$$\text{volume} = l \times w \times h$$
$$\text{m} \times \text{m} \times \text{m} = \text{m}^3$$

The cube shown in **Figure 1-9,** has a length, width, and height of 10 cm each. Each of these dimensions has equivalent values in meters and millimeters. The volume of the cube in cubic centimeters is calculated as follows.

$$10 \text{ cm} \times 10 \text{ cm} \times 10 \text{ cm} = 1000 \text{ cm}^3$$
$$\text{or } 0.001 \text{ m}^3 \text{ or } 1\,000\,000 \text{ mm}^3$$

This volume—1000 cm³, or 0.001 m³ or 1 000 000 mm³—is 1 liter (1 L), which is a favorite unit of chemists. The liter and the milliliter, mL, are widely used in scientific work even though the cubic meter is the SI unit for volume. The prefix *milli-* tells you that there are 1000 mL in 1 L.

1. What are the five SI base units you will use in this chemistry course?

2. What is a conversion factor?

3. How does a quantity differ from a unit?

4. Write the equalities needed to make the following conversions:
   a. milliliters to liters
   c. kilometers to centimeters
   b. grams to micrograms
   d. milligrams to grams

5. Write conversion factors for each equality in item 4.

6. Convert the following:
   a. 50 mL to ? cm^3
   c. 25 mg to ? g
   b. 750 mL to ? L
   d. 3×10^5 cm to ? m

Properties of matter

The relationship between two properties can be represented by graphing. The masses and volumes of a set of aluminum blocks are listed in **Figure 1-10.** These values are plotted on the graph shown below. What do you notice about the line connecting these points?

The straight line rising from left to right indicates that mass increases at a constant rate as volume increases. As the volume of aluminum doubles, its mass doubles; as its volume triples, its mass triples; and so on. In other words, the mass of aluminum is directly proportional to its volume.

The slope of the line equals the ratio of mass, the value obtained from the vertical *y*-axis, divided by volume, the value obtained from the

FIGURE 1-10 ▼

The graph of mass versus volume shows a relationship of direct proportionality. Notice that the line has been extended to pass through the origin.

Mass and Volume Data for Samples of Aluminum

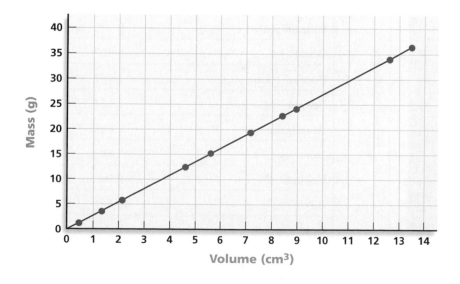

Volume (cm³)

Block number	Mass (g)	Volume (cm³)
1	1.20	0.443
2	3.59	1.33
3	5.72	2.12
4	12.4	4.60
5	15.3	5.66
6	19.4	7.17
7	22.7	8.41
8	24.1	8.94
9	34.0	12.6
10	36.4	13.5

horizontal x-axis. You may remember this as "rise over run" from math class. Slope is mathematically stated as follows.

$$\text{slope} = \frac{y_2 - y_1}{x_2 - x_1}$$

In this equation, x_1 and y_1 represent one ordered pair of values on the graph, and x_2 and y_2 represent another ordered pair.

Note that the slope of the graph shown in Figure 1-10 is constant. At any point on the line, if you divide the mass value by the corresponding volume value, you will get the value 2.70. This constant value showing the relationship between mass and volume has a special name—density. **Density** is the ratio of mass to volume.

density

the ratio of mass to volume

$$\text{density} = \frac{\text{mass}}{\text{volume}}, \quad \text{or} \quad D = \frac{m}{V}$$

Density is usually expressed in grams per cubic centimeter, g/cm^3. **Table 1-5** lists the densities of various substances. As you saw in the previous example, the density of aluminum is 2.70 g/cm^3. Osmium, a bluish white metal, is the densest substance on Earth. A piece of osmium the size of a football would be too heavy to lift.

Density can be used to identify substances

Because the density of a given substance is the same for all samples, density can be used to identify matter. For example, suppose you find

▼ **FIGURE 1-11**

Substances float in layers, and the order of the layers is determined by their densities. Dyes have been added to make the liquid layers more visible.

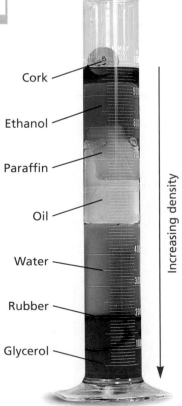

Cork
Ethanol
Paraffin
Oil
Water
Rubber
Glycerol

Increasing density

| **TABLE 1-5** | **Densities of Various Substances** |

Substance	Density (g/cm^3) at 25°C
Hydrogen gas*	0.000 824
Carbon dioxide gas*	0.001 80
Ethanol (ethyl alcohol)	0.789
Water	0.997
Sucrose (table sugar)	1.587
Sodium chloride	2.164
Aluminum	2.699
Iron	7.86
Copper	8.94
Silver	10.5
Gold	19.3
Osmium	22.6

*at 1 atm

a bracelet on the street that appears to be silver. To find out if it is pure silver, you can take the bracelet into the lab and measure its mass using a balance. Next you can measure its volume by measuring the volume of water the bracelet displaces. If the mass is 199.0 g and the volume is 20.5 cm^3, you can calculate the density of the bracelet.

$$D = \frac{m}{V}$$

$$= \frac{199.0 \text{ g}}{20.5 \text{ cm}^3} = 9.71 \text{ g/cm}^3$$

Because the density of silver is 10.5 g/cm^3, you can then deduce that the bracelet you found is not pure silver.

Density is a physical property of matter

To determine the density of the metal in a bracelet, you do not have to change any of the metal's characteristics or properties. Any property of matter that can be measured without changing its chemical nature is known as a **physical property.** You recognize your friends and family members by their physical properties, such as height, hair color, and the sound of a voice.

Quantities such as mass, volume, and density are physical properties of matter. Other physical properties of matter include color, texture, melting point, and boiling point. Keep in mind that matter can even be described in terms of the absence of a physical property. For example, a physical property of air is that it is colorless.

Matter can undergo **physical changes.** A physical change affects only physical properties of matter; chemical properties are not affected. For example, when you melt ice to get water, you still have the substance H_2O. When you boil water to get steam, it's still H_2O. Only the physical state of the substance has changed.

Physical changes can involve changes in energy. Melting and boiling are examples of endothermic changes because energy in the form of heat is transferred to the substance from its surroundings. Freezing and condensation are also physical changes. But in contrast to melting and boiling, freezing and condensation are examples of exothermic changes because heat energy is transferred from the substance to its surroundings.

QUICKLAB

Thickness of Aluminum Foil

Using the density of aluminum, you can determine the thickness of a piece of aluminum foil. You will need to design a procedure that will give you the data you need to determine thickness.

Materials   aluminum foil, balances, metric ruler, calculator, scissors

Problem   There are two brands of aluminum foil in the front of the classroom. Your job is to use the known density of aluminum (see Table 1-5 on page 16) to calculate the thickness of a sample from each of these two different brands of aluminum foil.

Analysis   Your report should include your experimental procedure, a data table with all of your measurements and the thicknesses of each brand of aluminum foil.

physical property

any property of matter that can be measured without changing its chemical nature

physical change

a change that affects only physical properties

Matter also has chemical properties

Matter cannot be fully described by physical properties alone. Left out of the description is how matter will behave when it is in contact with other types of matter. To describe this type of behavior, **chemical properties** of matter must be considered. Chemical properties are often observed when matter reacts.

You learned earlier that a word equation can be used to describe this reaction. The reaction between hydrogen and oxygen results in a new substance—water. Whenever one or more substances are changed into new substances, a **chemical change** occurs.

The reaction on page 7 shows mercury(II) oxide decomposing. **Figure 1-12** shows the same reaction along with a comparison of the physical and chemical properties of the substances involved. As you look at this diagram, think about the definition of a chemical reaction. You can see from comparing the properties that the products of the chemical reaction have distinctly different chemical and physical properties from the reactants. Many of the physical and chemical properties of substances can be found in chemical reference handbooks.

All chemical changes are accompanied by changes in energy. Therefore, all chemical changes can be classified as either endothermic or exothermic processes. **Figure 1-13** shows some common types of chemical changes. Evidence that a chemical change has occurred is easily observed and generally fits one of the following categories.

1. **The evolution of a gas.** The production of a gas is often observed by bubbling, as shown in Figure 1-13a, or by the emission of an odor.
2. **The formation of a precipitate.** A precipitate is an insoluble solid formed from a solution, such as that shown in Figure 1-13b.
3. **The evolution or absorption of heat.** An increase in temperature of a reaction system signifies an exothermic chemical change. Similarly, a lower temperature indicates an endothermic reaction.

chemical property

a property of matter that can be observed only when substances interact with one another

chemical change

a change that produces one or more new substances

▼ **FIGURE 1-12**

The physical and chemical properties of the components of this reaction system are shown. Decomposition of mercury (II) oxide is a chemical change.

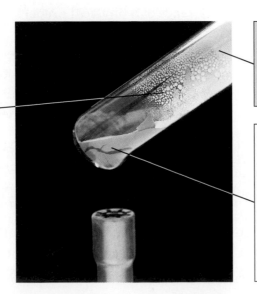

MERCURY
Physical properties: Silver-white, liquid metal; in the solid state, mercury is ductile and malleable and can be cut with a knife
Chemical properties: Combines readily with sulfur at normal temperatures; reacts with nitric acid and hot sulfuric acid; oxidizes to form mercury(II) oxide upon heating in air

OXYGEN
Physical properties: Colorless, odorless gas
Chemical properties: Supports combustion; soluble in water

MERCURY(II) OXIDE
Physical properties: Bright red or orange-red, odorless crystalline solid
Chemical properties: Decomposes when exposed to light or at 500°C to form mercury and oxygen gas; dissolves in dilute nitric acid or hydrochloric acid, but is almost insoluble in water

a When vinegar and baking soda are mixed, the solution bubbles as carbon dioxide forms.

b When solutions of sodium sulfide and cadmium nitrate are mixed, cadmium sulfide, a solid, forms.

c When aluminum reacts with iron oxide in the clay pot, heat and light are produced.

d When phenolphthalein is added to ammonia, a color change to pink occurs.

4. **The emission of light.** Some reactions will produce light, like that shown in Figure 1-13c.

5. **A color change in the reaction system.** The color change you noted during the decomposition of mercury(II) oxide is a clue that a reaction has occurred, producing new substances. Figure 1-13d shows the color change of an indicator in the presence of a base.

SECTION REVIEW

Total recall

1. What two physical properties characterize matter?

2. What SI unit is usually used to express the density of liquids?

3. How does mass differ from weight?

4. Why is density considered a physical property rather than a chemical property of matter?

Critical thinking

5. Classify the following as either a physical or a chemical property of matter: area, flammability, odor, temperature, oxygen changing into ozone.

6. When a piece of potassium metal is placed in water, a violent reaction occurs. But when a piece of copper metal is placed in water, nothing happens. Is this a physical or chemical property of the metal? Explain the reason for your choice.

7. **Interpreting Graphics** What evidence do you have that a chemical change has occurred in the reactions shown in Figure 1-5, on page 8?

Practice problems

8. **Interpreting Tables** Refer to Table 1-4. Perform the following conversions:
   a. milliliters in 21.59 L
   b. centimeters in 1.62 m
   c. nanometers in 0.064 mm
   d. kilograms in 2648 cg

SECTION 1-3

What is the nature of matter?

OBJECTIVES

- ***Use*** chemical tables to determine the names and symbols for various elements.
- ***Distinguish*** between atoms, elements, and molecules.
- ***Describe*** different forms of elements.

Atoms and elements

atom

the basic unit of matter

element

one of the 111 simplest substances from which more complex substances are made

All matter is composed of **atoms.** Atoms are microscopic particles; it would take nearly 4 million of the largest atoms to form a line 1 mm long. Atoms come in over 110 basic types called **elements.** Each element has a unique set of chemical and physical properties that distinguish it from all other elements. Aluminum, copper, oxygen, and silicon are some elements that may be familiar to you. Each atom of an element has similar chemical properties to every other atom of that element.

Each element has a unique symbol that is internationally recognized. Symbols for the elements are shown on the periodic table in **Figure 1-14.** The symbol for an element consists of one to three letters. Three-letter symbols are used for newly discovered unnamed elements. The first letter of the symbol is always capitalized. You can find a complete listing of symbols with the names of the elements in **Table 1-6,** on page 22.

FIGURE 1-14

This periodic table shows the symbols for all the known elements. The names are shown in alphabetical order in Table 1-6.

	Group 1	Group 2	Group 3	Group 4	Group 5	Group 6	Group 7	Group 8	Group 9	Group 10	Group 11	Group 12	Group 13	Group 14	Group 15	Group 16	Group 17	Group 18
1	1 H																	2 He
2	3 Li	4 Be											5 B	6 C	7 N	8 O	9 F	10 Ne
3	11 Na	12 Mg											13 Al	14 Si	15 P	16 S	17 Cl	18 Ar
4	19 K	20 Ca	21 Sc	22 Ti	23 V	24 Cr	25 Mn	26 Fe	27 Co	28 Ni	29 Cu	30 Zn	31 Ga	32 Ge	33 As	34 Se	35 Br	36 Kr
5	37 Rb	38 Sr	39 Y	40 Zr	41 Nb	42 Mo	43 Tc	44 Ru	45 Rh	46 Pd	47 Ag	48 Cd	49 In	50 Sn	51 Sb	52 Te	53 I	54 Xe
6	55 Cs	56 Ba	57 La	72 Hf	73 Ta	74 W	75 Re	76 Os	77 Ir	78 Pt	79 Au	80 Hg	81 Tl	82 Pb	83 Bi	84 Po	85 At	86 Rn
7	87 Fr	88 Ra	89 Ac	104 Rf	105 Db	106 Sg	107 Bh	108 Hs	109 Mt	110 Uun	111 Uuu							
					58 Ce	59 Pr	60 Nd	61 Pm	62 Sm	63 Eu	64 Gd	65 Tb	66 Dy	67 Ho	68 Er	69 Tm	70 Yb	71 Lu
					90 Th	91 Pa	92 U	93 Np	94 Pu	95 Am	96 Cm	97 Bk	98 Cf	99 Es	100 Fm	101 Md	102 No	103 Lr

Elements in Earth's Crust

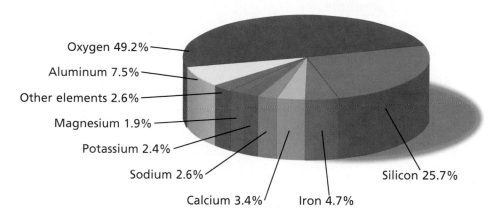

Oxygen 49.2%
Aluminum 7.5%
Other elements 2.6%
Magnesium 1.9%
Potassium 2.4%
Sodium 2.6%
Calcium 3.4%
Iron 4.7%
Silicon 25.7%

FIGURE 1-15 ◄

This pie chart shows the various elements in the Earth's crust and their abundances by mass.

It is easy to see how the symbols for hydrogen, H, helium, He, and silicon, Si, were chosen, but you may wonder about the symbols for tin, Sn, tungsten, W, and a few others. Both of these symbols come from languages other than English. Because Latin was the language of many early chemists, a number of symbols are based on the Latin names for the elements. For example, Sn is an abbreviation for *stannum,* the Latin word for "tin." The symbols for gold, silver, mercury, iron, and copper also come from the Latin names for these elements. Not all symbols come from English or Latin names—W stands for *Wolfram,* the German word for "tungsten."

Other elements have been named in honor of a person or after the place where the element was discovered. Curium, Cm, is a radioactive element named in honor of Marie and Pierre Curie, who first discovered radium and polonium. Berkelium, Bk, was first synthesized in Berkeley, California. Where do you think francium, Fr, was discovered?

Every element has its own unique set of physical and chemical properties. Once it is purified, gold mined in Africa today is indistinguishable from gold panned in California during the gold rush or gold discovered by the Aztecs of Mexico centuries ago. Pure gold is the same substance regardless of where it is obtained, and it is made up of the same type of atoms.

A small number of elements make up most common substances

There are 111 known elements. However, the elements are not equally common. By far the most common element is hydrogen. More than 90% of the atoms in the known universe are hydrogen atoms. The elements oxygen and silicon make up more than 70% of the mass of the Earth's crust. **Figure 1-15** shows the other elements whose masses contribute substantially to the Earth's crust. Living things are composed primarily of four elements: carbon, hydrogen, oxygen, and nitrogen. These four elements combine to create thousands of different chemicals needed to sustain life.

TABLE 1-6 **Element Names and Symbols**

Element	Symbol	Element	Symbol	Element	Symbol
Actinium	Ac	Hafnium	Hf	Promethium	Pm
Aluminum	Al	Hassium	Hs	Protactinium	Pa
Americium	Am	Helium	He	Radium	Ra
Antimony	Sb	Holmium	Ho	Radon	Rn
Argon	Ar	Hydrogen	H	Rhenium	Re
Arsenic	As	Indium	In	Rhodium	Rh
Astatine	At	Iodine	I	Rubidium	Rb
Barium	Ba	Iridium	Ir	Ruthenium	Ru
Berkelium	Bk	Iron	Fe	Rutherfordium	Rf
Beryllium	Be	Krypton	Kr	Samarium	Sm
Bismuth	Bi	Lanthanum	La	Scandium	Sc
Bohrium	Bh	Lawrencium	Lr	Seaborgium	Sg
Boron	B	Lead	Pb	Selenium	Se
Bromine	Br	Lithium	Li	Silicon	Si
Cadmium	Cd	Lutetium	Lu	Silver	Ag
Calcium	Ca	Magnesium	Mg	Sodium	Na
Californium	Cf	Manganese	Mn	Strontium	Sr
Carbon	C	Meitnerium	Mt	Sulfur	S
Cerium	Ce	Mendelevium	Md	Tantalum	Ta
Cesium	Cs	Mercury	Hg	Technetium	Tc
Chlorine	Cl	Molybdenum	Mo	Tellurium	Te
Chromium	Cr	Neodymium	Nd	Terbium	Tb
Cobalt	Co	Neon	Ne	Thallium	Tl
Copper	Cu	Neptunium	Np	Thorium	Th
Curium	Cm	Nickel	Ni	Thulium	Tm
Dubnium	Db	Niobium	Nb	Tin	Sn
Dysprosium	Dy	Nitrogen	N	Titanium	Ti
Einsteinium	Es	Nobelium	No	Tungsten	W
Erbium	Er	Osmium	Os	Ununnilium*	Uun
Europium	Eu	Oxygen	O	Unununium*	Uuu
Fermium	Fm	Palladium	Pd	Uranium	U
Fluorine	F	Phosphorus	P	Vanadium	V
Francium	Fr	Platinum	Pt	Xenon	Xe
Gadolinium	Gd	Plutonium	Pu	Ytterbium	Yb
Gallium	Ga	Polonium	Po	Yttrium	Y
Germanium	Ge	Potassium	K	Zinc	Zn
Gold	Au	Praseodymium	Pr	Zirconium	Zr

*Temporary names and symbols for elements greater than 109 will be used until the approval of trivial names by IUPAC.

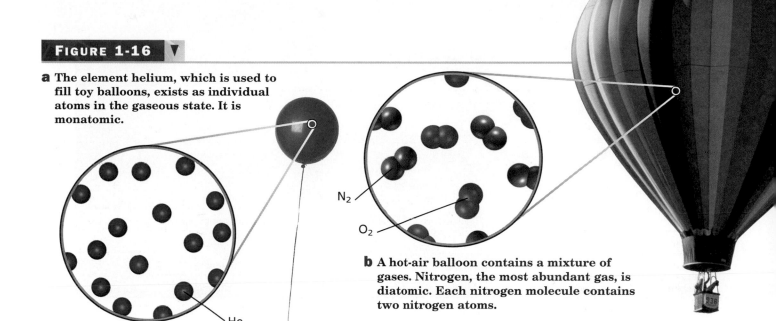

FIGURE 1-16 ▼

a The element helium, which is used to fill toy balloons, exists as individual atoms in the gaseous state. It is monatomic.

N$_2$

O$_2$

He

b A hot-air balloon contains a mixture of gases. Nitrogen, the most abundant gas, is diatomic. Each nitrogen molecule contains two nitrogen atoms.

Elements may exist as single atoms or as molecules

A **molecule** consists of two or more atoms combined in a definite ratio. The atoms in a molecule may be of the same element or of different elements. The nitrogen gas in the atmosphere is an example of a molecular element because it exists as two nitrogen atoms joined together. Acetylsalicylic acid, or aspirin, is made of molecules. Each molecule of acetylsalicylic acid consists of a set number of carbon, hydrogen, and oxygen atoms joined together.

Some elements exist as single atoms, others as molecules consisting of as few as two or as many as millions of atoms. For example, the helium gas in a balloon consists of individual atoms, as shown by the model in **Figure 1-16a.** Because it exists as individual atoms, helium gas is known as a *monatomic gas*. If an element consists of molecules, those molecules contain just one type of atom. For example, the element nitrogen, found in air, exists in the molecular state. Each nitrogen gas molecule consists of two nitrogen atoms joined together, as illustrated by the model in **Figure 1-16b.** Therefore, nitrogen is called a *diatomic gas*. Oxygen, another gas found in the air, is also diatomic.

Some elements have allotropic forms

A few elements, notably oxygen, phosphorus, sulfur, and carbon, are unusual because they exist as allotropes. An **allotrope** is one of a number of different molecular forms of an element. Oxygen has two allotropes, which are depicted in **Figure 1-17.** One is O$_2$, the diatomic oxygen gas you breathe. *Ozone,* O$_3$, is an oxygen allotrope that consists of three oxygen atoms.

The properties of allotropes can vary widely. Diatomic oxygen is a colorless, odorless gas essential to most forms of life. Ozone is a toxic, pale blue gas with a sharp odor. You can smell ozone after an intense

molecule

a neutral group of atoms held together by covalent bonds

allotrope

one of a number of different molecular or crystalline forms of an element

FIGURE 1-17 ▼

The allotropes of oxygen are oxygen gas and ozone.

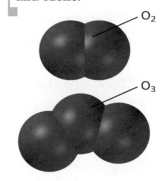

O$_2$

O$_3$

internet**connect**

SC*LINKS*
NSTA

TOPIC: Allotropes
GO TO: www.scilinks.org
KEYWORD: HW014

thunderstorm. Lightning provides the energy to convert diatomic oxygen to ozone in the lower atmosphere.

Carbon has several interesting allotropes in the solid state. One carbon allotrope is graphite, a soft gray solid with a slippery texture. Diamond, the hardest substance known, is another carbon allotrope. In the 1980s, a new carbon allotrope consisting of molecules with 60 carbon atoms was discovered. The atoms in this allotrope form a shape like the geodesic dome designed by the innovative American philosopher and engineer Buckminster Fuller. For this reason, the 60-carbon molecule, a model of which is shown in **Figure 1-18,** is called *buckminsterfullerene,* or, more informally, *buckyball.* Recently, another allotropic form of carbon, the *buckytube,* has been found. Combined with certain substances, fullerenes exhibit superconductivity, which is the ability to conduct electricity with no loss of energy.

$\mathcal{S}$ECTION REVIEW

Total recall

1. How does an atom differ from an element?

2. How is an atom related to a *molecule*?

3. What are allotropes?

Critical thinking

4. How do you think the symbols for newly discovered elements are determined?

5. **Interpreting Tables** List the symbols for the following elements.
   a. carbon   **c.** hydrogen   **e.** neon
   b. nitrogen   **d.** gold   **f.** astatine

6. **Interpreting Tables** Write the names of the elements with the following symbols.
   a. He   **c.** Cl   **e.** Mg
   b. Na   **d.** S   **f.** Sb

7. **Interpreting Tables** Why don't we use As as the symbol for astatine?

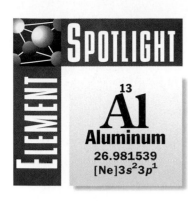

<table>
<tr><td>13</td></tr>
<tr><td>Al</td></tr>
<tr><td>Aluminum</td></tr>
<tr><td>26.981539</td></tr>
<tr><td>[Ne]$3s^2 3p^1$</td></tr>
</table>

Recycling just one aluminum can saves enough electricity to run a TV for four hours.

WHERE IS IT?

Earth's Crust
8% by mass

Sea Water
less than 0.1%

internet**connect**

SC*LINKS*
NSTA
TOPIC: Aluminum
GO TO: www.scilinks.org
KEYWORD: HW015

Aluminum's humble beginnings

In 1881, Charles Martin Hall was a 22-year-old student at Oberlin College, in Ohio. One day, Hall's chemistry professor mentioned in a lecture that anyone who could discover an inexpensive method for making aluminum metal would be rich. Working in a wooden shed and using a cast-iron frying pan, a blacksmith's forge, and homemade batteries, Hall discovered a practical technique for producing aluminum. Hall's process is the basis for the industrial production of aluminum today.

Industrial Uses

▶ Aluminum is the most abundant metal on Earth, but it is never found in nature as pure metal.

▶ The most important source of aluminum is the mineral bauxite. Bauxite consists mostly of hydrated aluminum oxide.

▶ In 1997, 3.6 million metric tons of aluminum was produced by the United States.

▶ Recycling aluminum by melting and reusing it is considerably cheaper than producing new aluminum.

▶ Aluminum is light, weather-resistant, and easily worked. These properties make aluminum ideal for use in aircraft, cars, cans, window frames, screens, gutters, wire, food packaging, hardware, and tools.

Aluminum's resistance to corrosion makes it suitable for many outdoor uses.

A BRIEF HISTORY

1824: F. Wöhler isolates aluminum from aluminum chloride.

1886: Charles Martin Hall, of the United States, and Paul-Louis Héroult, of France, independently discover the process for extracting aluminum from aluminum oxide.

1700   1800   1900

1827: F. Wöhler describes some of the properties of aluminum.

1854: Henri Saint-Claire Deville, of France, and R. Bunsen, of Germany, independently accomplish the electrolysis of aluminum from sodium aluminum chloride.

How is matter classified?

Classifying matter

Notice how the objects have been classified in **Figure 1-19.** What would it be like to shop in a store where there was no order or organization for the items on display? Shopping would be time-consuming and confusing. To study matter, chemists start with an order. They use the properties of matter—both physical and chemical—to classify matter.

Compounds consist of bonded atoms

Pure substances composed of atoms from two or more different elements are classified as **compounds.** Two types of compounds are created in chemical reactions—covalent compounds and ionic compounds.

The smallest particle of a covalent compound that has the properties of the compound is a molecule. Water, sugar, and oxygen are *covalent compounds.* Compounds that consist of ions, such as table salt, are called *ionic compounds.* An **ion** is an atom or group of atoms with an electrical charge. You will learn more about the differences between covalent and ionic compounds in Chapters 5 and 6.

Because a compound is a pure substance, it has a unique set of chemical and physical properties. Acetic acid, shown in **Figure 1-20,** is a clear liquid with a very strong odor. The term **acid** in the name sig-

compound

the product that results when two or more different elements are chemically combined

ion

an atom or group of atoms with an electrical charge

acid

a class of compounds whose water solutions taste sour, turn blue litmus paper red, and react with bases to form salts

▶ **FIGURE 1-19**

Just as consumer products are classified and sorted by properties and uses, chemists classify matter by chemical and physical properties.

FIGURE 1-20 ▼

a A strip of pH paper dipped in an acetic acid solution turns red, showing that the solution is acidic.

b A strip of pH paper dipped in a sodium hydroxide solution turns blue, showing that the solution is basic.

nifies that it belongs to a group of compounds that have certain chemical properties.

The degree to which an aqueous solution of compound shows the properties of an acid is expressed numerically as **pH.** In water, acids have pH values less than 7. For example, the pH of aspirin in water is 2.7. Compounds dissolved in water that have pH values greater than 7 are called **bases.** Bases have properties that are in some ways opposite those of acids, as shown in **Table 1-7.**

The pH of a solution is found by using a pH meter or by using special compounds called indicators. When the solution is tested by using an indicator, the color of the indicator often changes. Indicators are being used to test acidity in Figure 1-20.

Compounds can also be classified as organic or inorganic

Another way to classify matter depends on whether the element carbon is present in a compound. With some exceptions, compounds that contain the element carbon such as aspirin, with the formula $C_9H_8O_4$, are

pH

a numerical scale used to express acidity

base

a class of compounds that taste bitter, feel slippery in water solution, turn red litmus to blue, and react with acids to form salts

TABLE 1-7	Some Properties of Acids and Bases

Water solutions of acids . . .	Water solutions of bases . . .
taste sour	taste bitter and feel slippery
turn blue pH paper red	turn red pH paper blue
have pH values less than 7	have pH values greater than 7
react with bases and certain metals to form salts	react with acids to form salts

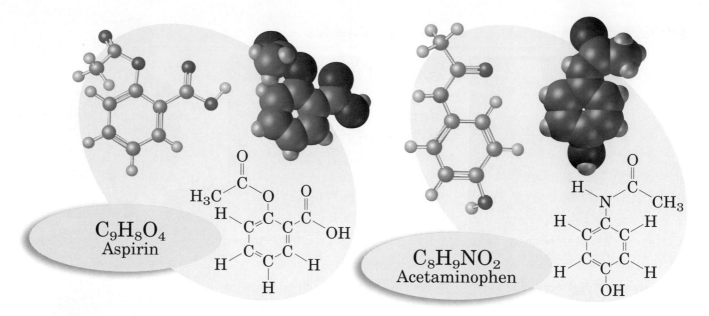

$C_9H_8O_4$
Aspirin

$C_8H_9NO_2$
Acetaminophen

▲ **FIGURE 1-21**

Formulas and models are used by chemists to represent acetylsalicylic acid (aspirin), acetaminophen, and ibuprofen. Acetaminophen is commonly known by the brand name Tylenol®; ibuprofen is commonly known by the brand name Advil®.

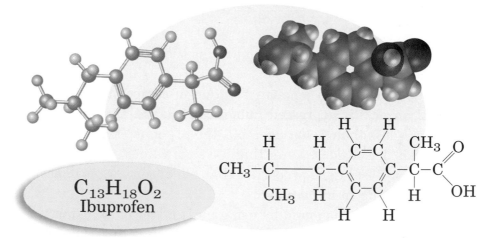

$C_{13}H_{18}O_2$
Ibuprofen

organic compound

any covalently bonded compound containing carbon (except carbonates and oxides)

inorganic compound

any compound outside the organic family of compounds

classified as **organic compounds.** Generally, those that lack carbon are referred to as **inorganic compounds.** Because organic compounds play an important role in your daily life, you will study them throughout this text.

Compounds are represented by formulas

Four different ways of representing three compounds used as pain-relievers are shown in **Figure 1-21.** The *molecular formula,* such as $C_9H_8O_4$, shows the numbers of atoms of each element present in a molecule but not how the atoms are bonded. The *structural formula* shows the exact number of atoms present in a molecule and how these atoms are bonded to one another. The lines represent the bonds between atoms. The *ball-and-stick model* shows the geometric arrangement of atoms in a formula. The *space-fill model* also shows the geometric arrangment and most closely represents the actual shape of a molecule. What do all three structural formulas in Figure 1-21 have in common? What is unique about the structural formula of acetaminophen compared with the other formulas?

Mixtures can be classified as homogeneous or heterogeneous

A collection of two or more pure substances physically mixed together is classified as a **mixture.** The proportions of different substances in a mixture can vary. For instance, chicken soup is a mixture. Different batches of chicken soup may contain different relative quantities of celery, carrots, chicken, pepper, water, and other ingredients, depending on the recipe.

The properties of mixtures can vary because the proportions of the substances in them can vary. For example, gold is mixed with other metals in various proportions to obtain materials suitable for different purposes. The pure gold shown in **Figure 1-22a,** which is also called 24-karat gold, is too soft to keep its shape in jewelry, so it is often mixed with other metals to achieve necessary strength. The *alloy,* or solid mixture, of gold used in much jewelry is 18-karat gold; it contains 18 parts gold out of 24 parts, or 75% gold by mass. The remaining six parts are usually copper, silver, or nickel. For even greater hardness and strength, 14-karat gold, shown in **Figure 1-22b,** is used.

Mixtures can be classified as homogeneous or heterogeneous. A **homogeneous mixture** is one in which the components are uniformly distributed at the microscopic level. Gasoline, syrup, air, and 18-karat gold are homogeneous mixtures. All regions of a homogeneous mixture are identical in their composition and properties. The most common type of homogeneous mixture is the *solution.* Vinegar, tea, and salt water are examples of solutions.

A **heterogeneous mixture** contains substances that are not evenly distributed. Some regions of a heterogeneous mixture have different properties from other regions. Heterogeneous mixtures can take many forms. **Table 1-8,** on the next page, summarizes the differences between heterogeneous and homogeneous mixtures.

mixture

a collection of two or more pure substances physically mixed together

homogeneous mixture

a mixture containing substances that are uniformly distributed

heterogeneous mixture

a mixture containing substances that are not uniformly distributed

---

FIGURE 1-22 ▼

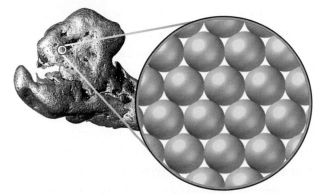

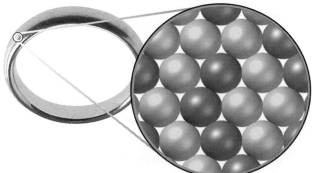

a The gold nugget is a pure substance—gold. Pure gold, also called 24 karat gold, is usually considered too soft for jewelry.

b 14-karat gold is 14/24, or 58.3%, gold. This homogeneous mixture is stronger than pure gold and is often used for jewelry.

TABLE 1-8   Examples of Mixtures

Heterogeneous	Homogeneous
Orange juice or tomato juice (suspension) uneven distribution of components; settles out upon standing	**Iced tea** (solution) uniform distribution of components; components cannot be filtered out and will not settle out upon standing
Chocolate chip pecan cookie uneven distribution of components	**Stainless steel** (alloy) uniform distribution of components
Granite uneven distribution of components	**Carbonated beverage** (solution) uniform distribution of components
Salad uneven distribution of components; can be easily separated by physical means	**Maple syrup** (solution) uniform distribution of components; components cannot be filtered out and will not settle out upon standing

Mixtures can be distinguished from compounds

There are two principal differences between mixtures and compounds.

1. The properties of a mixture reflect the properties of the substances it contains, but the properties of a compound often bear no resemblance to the properties of the elements that compose it.

2. Compounds have a definite composition by mass of their combining elements, while the components of mixtures may be present in varying proportions.

For example, the compound acetylsalicylic acid has a definite composition—by mass. It is always 60.0% carbon, 35.5% oxygen, and 4.5% hydrogen. In contrast, substances in a mixture can have any mass ratio. The sand in a sand-and-gravel mixture may make up 99% or 1% of the overall mass.

Separating mixtures may require physical or chemical means

One major task a chemist often undertakes is the isolation and analysis of the components of a mixture. This task can be likened to sorting materials in a recycling bin. Recyclable items can be separated into different piles based on one or more physical properties. For example, soft-drink cans can be placed in the aluminum recycling bin, while glass and plastics are placed in other bins.

Although chemists can use physical properties to separate components, separating chemical mixtures is not always that easy. Often the only way to remove a substance from a mixture is to react the mixture to form a substance that can be easily removed by filtration. Techniques for separating mixtures will be described in Chapter 13.

Stockroom chemicals may be mixtures

When is a substance pure? That's a difficult question to answer. When you drink water from the tap, you may think you are drinking pure water, but not likely. Even bottled water contains minerals that are impurities. Chemicals too contain impurities that can alter a reaction. For this reason, standards for chemical purity have been established so that chemists can control the effects of impurities in their work.

Figure 1-23 shows the label for a zinc compound that meets reagent-grade standards set by the Committee on Analytical Reagents of the American Chemical Society (ACS). *Primary-standard* grade chemicals are of higher purity than *reagent-grade* chemicals. You may be using *commercial* or *technical* grade chemicals in the lab because they are less expensive and because high-purity chemicals are not needed.

Figure 1-24, on the next page, summarizes the properties that characterize elements, compounds, and mixtures.

INQUIRYLAB

CONSUMER ACTIVITY

Using Physical Properties to Separate a Mixture

Observing physical properties, such as color, shape, texture, or mass, can be used to identify a substance. Chemists also use physical properties to separate the components of a mixture.

Materials distilled water, filter funnel, filter paper, magnet, paper towels, clear plastic cups, plastic spoon, sample of mixture

Problem Design an experiment using the given materials to separate the components of the sample mixture. Once you have separated the mixture, describe the components by their physical properties.

Analysis
1. What properties did you observe in each of the components of the mixture?
2. How did these properties help you to separate the mixture?
3. Did any of the components share similar properties?

FIGURE 1-23 ▼

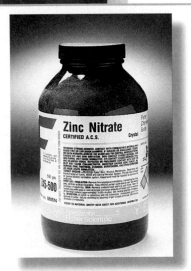

$Zn(NO_3)_2 \cdot 6H_2O$ F.W. 297.47

Certificate of Actual Lot Analysis

Acidity (as HNO_3)	0.008%
Alkalies and Earths	0.02%
Chloride (Cl)	0.005%
Insoluble Matter	0.001%
Iron (Fe)	0.0002%
Lead (Pb)	0.001%
Phosphate (PO_4)	0.0002%
Sulfate (SO_4)	0.002%

Store separately from and avoid contact with combustible materials. Keep container closed and in a cool, dry place. Avoid contact with skin, eyes and clothing.

LOT NO. 917356

FL-02-0588   CAS 10196-18-6

a This bottle of zinc nitrate would be considered a pure substance . . .

b . . . even though the label shows that it contains impurities.

This figure summarizes the relationships between different classes of matter.

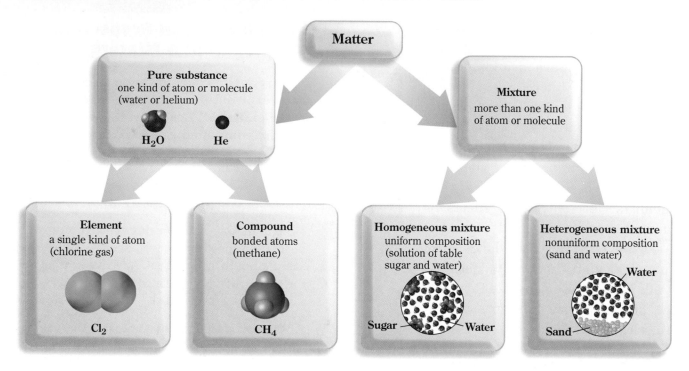

SECTION REVIEW

Total recall

1. Define the term *compound*.

2. What are some of the properties of an acid?

3. What element do all organic compounds contain?

4. What information is shown in a structural formula that is not shown in a molecular formula?

5. How is a homogeneous mixture different from a heterogeneous mixture?

Critical thinking

6. Compare and contrast molecular and ionic compounds.

7. Describe three properties of aspirin that classify it as an acid.

8. Identify each of the following as an element, compound, or mixture. If it is a mixture, classify it as homogeneous or heterogeneous.
   a. CH_4 d. distilled water
   b. S_8 e. salt water
   c. cup of coffee f. CH_2O

9. Which of the compounds in item 8, if any, are organic?

10. **Story Clue** If you have ever had difficulty swallowing aspirin, you know it has an unpleasant taste. To help a child swallow aspirin, a parent may crush the tablet and add it to apple sauce. Is the aspirin-apple-sauce combination classified as a compound or a mixture? Is it homogeneous or heterogeneous? Explain the reasons for your choices.

You read at the beginning of the chapter that Felix Hoffmann produced acetylsalicylic acid by reacting two organic compounds, salicylic acid and acetic anhydride. Today, acetylsalicylic acid can be made from several other organic compounds. No matter what the starting reactant is, each process involves a number of chemical reactions in which the product of one step is the reactant in the next step.

Having finished this introduction to chemistry, you should now be able to answer the questions that were posed at the beginning of the chapter.

LOOKING BACK

What type of chemical substance is aspirin?

Aspirin is the common name for acetylsalicylic acid. You can see from the structure on the right that acetylsalicylic acid is an organic compound containing the elements carbon, hydrogen, and oxygen. Acetylsalicylic acid has both physical properties (for example, white color) and chemical proper-

ties (for example, a water solution of aspirin turns litmus indicator from blue to red).

How is aspirin similar to other widely used pain relievers?

Acetylsalicylic acid, ibuprofen, and acetaminophen are organic compounds that have been made by chemical reactions. All three have structural similarities, including a ring formed by six carbon atoms.

How does name-brand aspirin differ from generic brands?

Aspirin is a pure compound. Therefore, there is no difference between the effect of named brands and that of a generic aspirin product in the body. But different brands of aspirin can vary in terms of dosage, buffering systems that control acidity, and the time they take to act.

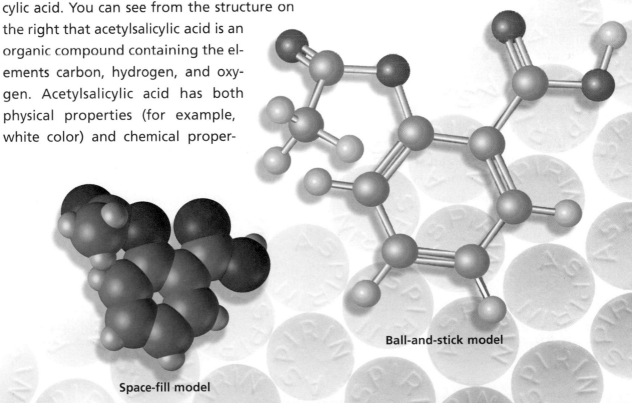

Ball-and-stick model

Space-fill model

$\mathcal{H}$IGHLIGHTS

KEY TERMS

1-1

chemical
chemical reaction
endothermic reaction
exothermic reaction
physical state
product
reactant

1-2

chemical change
chemical property
conversion factor
density
mass
matter
physical change
physical property

quantity
unit
volume
weight

1-3

allotrope
atom
element
molecule

1-4

acid
base
compound
heterogeneous mixture
homogeneous mixture
inorganic compound
ion
mixture
organic compound
pH

KEY CONCEPTS

1-1 What is chemistry?

▶ Chemistry is the study of chemicals, their properties, and the reactions in which they are involved.

▶ Matter can exist as a solid, liquid, or gas.

▶ The relative position and motion of particles in a substance determine whether the substance exists as a solid, liquid, or gas.

▶ A word equation can be used to describe a chemical reaction; an arrow separates the reactants on the left from the products on the right.

1-2 What is matter?

▶ Matter has both mass and volume; matter thus has density, which is the ratio of mass to volume.

▶ SI units are used in science to measure seven basic quantities: length, mass, time, electric current, thermodynamic temperature, amount of substance, and luminous intensity.

▶ Other quantities, including volume, are measured in derived units.

▶ Properties of matter may be either physical or chemical.

▶ Chemical properties are observed when one substance interacts with another or changes composition following an input of energy.

1-3 What is the nature of matter?

▶ All matter is made from atoms.

▶ All atoms of an element are the same.

▶ Elements may exist as single atoms or as molecules.

▶ Allotropes are different molecular or crystalline forms of an element.

1-4 How is matter classified?

▶ Matter can be classified as a pure substance or a mixture.

▶ Elements and compounds are pure substances; mixtures may be homogeneous or heterogeneous.

▶ Compounds can be classified as organic or inorganic.

KEY SKILLS

Review the following model before your exam. Be sure you can solve this type of problem.

How To Use conversion factors (p. 14)

REVIEW & ASSESS

TERM REVIEW

1. A change that produces one or more new substances is known as a ———.
(physical change, chemical change)

2. Examine the following word equation:

iron oxide + aluminum ⟶
                    iron + aluminum oxide

Aluminum is a ——— in this reaction.
(reactant, product)

3. The simplest pure substance is a(n) ———.
(molecule, element)

4. A ——— is used to measure a quantity.
(conversion factor, unit)

5. The ratio of mass to volume is defined as the ——— of matter.
(weight, density)

6. A property of matter that can be measured without changing its chemical nature is known as a ———.
(chemical property, physical property)

7. Two or more different elements that are chemically combined are known as a(n) ———.
(compound, mixture, allotrope)

8. Matter that is composed of only one kind of atom or molecule is known as a(n) ———.
(organic compound, pure substance)

9. A(n) ——— produces a solution with a pH value less than 7.
(acid, base)

10. Oil and water mixed for a salad dressing and left standing is an example of a ———.
(heterogeneous mixture, homogeneous mixture)

11. Cubic centimeter is a unit used to measure ———.
(mass, volume, weight)

12. Amount of substance is measured in ———.
(milliliters, grams, moles)

CONCEPT & SKILLS REVIEW

THE NATURE OF MATTER

1. Use particle-model descriptions to explain why liquids and gases take the shape of their containers.

2. Your friend mentions that she buys shirts made only of natural materials because she follows a chemical-free lifestyle. How would you respond?

3. Sodium salicylate is made by reacting sodium phenoxide with carbon dioxide in the presence of heat. Write a word equation for this reaction.

4. An astronaut plans to bring home a massive moon-rock collection. Mission control on Earth wants to know the weight of the collection in advance. What must the astronaut consider when sending the weight to mission control?

5. Pick an object you can see right now. List three physical properties of the object that you can observe. Can you also observe a chemical property of the object? Explain.

6. Compare the physical and chemical properties of salt and sugar. What properties do they share? Which properties could you use to distinguish between salt and sugar?

7. A student checks the volume, melting point, and shape of two unlabeled samples of matter and finds that the measurements are identical. From this he concludes that the samples have the same chemical composition. What is wrong with his thinking?

8. Describe how different substances can be distinguished by density.

9. For each pair below, indicate the substance with the greater density. Explain your answer.
   a. rubber stopper and cork
   b. ice cube and water

10. Substances A and B are colorless, odorless liquids that are nonconductors and flammable. The density of substance A is 0.97 g/mL; the density of substance B is 0.89 g/mL. Are A and B the same substance? Explain.

11. A forgetful student leaves an uncapped watercolor marker on an open notebook. Later she discovers the leaking marker has produced a rainbow of colors on the top page. Is this an example of a physical change or a chemical change? Explain the reason for your choice.

12. a. Why are measurements often more useful than word descriptions?
  b. There are two parts to every measurement. What are they?

13. a. Name the five most common SI base units used in chemistry. What quantities are measured by each unit?
  b. Explain what derived units are. Give an example of one.

14. What derived unit is appropriate for expressing the following?
  a. rate of water flow
  b. speed
  c. volume of a room

15. Complete the following equalities
a. 1 nm = ? m	**e.** 1 mL = ? L
b. 1 g = ? kg	**f.** 1 L = ? mL
c. 1 kg = ? g	**g.** 1 cm^3 = ? L
d. 1 m = ? nm	**h.** 1 L = ? cm^3

16. Convert the following measurements to the units specified.
  a. 357 mL = ? L
  b. 25 kg = ? mg
  c. 650 nm = ? m
  d. 35 000 cm^3 = ? L
  e. 2.46 L = ? cm^3
  f. 250 μg = ? g
  g. 250 μg = ? kg
  h. 1.5 L = ? mL
  i. 10.5 mol = ? mmol

THE COMPONENTS OF MATTER

17. What is an element?

18. How are atoms and molecules related to one another?

19. Give one example of a monatomic gas and one example of a diatomic gas.

20. Both diamond and graphite are allotropic forms of carbon. Why do their physical properties differ?

CLASSIFYING MATTER

21. Compare and contrast the properties of homogeneous and heterogeneous mixtures.

22. Differentiate between pure substances and mixtures.

23. Differentiate between compounds and mixtures.

24. Steel is an alloy of the elements iron and carbon. In the steel used to make nails, iron makes up 99.8%, while carbon constitutes only 0.2%. Is this steel a homogeneous mixture or a heterogeneous mixture? Explain the reason for your choice.

25. Explain why steel is not considered a compound of iron and carbon.

ALTERNATIVE ASSESSMENTS

Performance assessment

1. Outline a study strategy for learning the important facts and understanding the concepts for this course. One effective strategy is to get a study partner. Another is to approach your study by pretending that you have to teach someone the material you are expected to learn. Discuss your plans with your teacher, and use your method throughout the course.

2. Your teacher will provide you with a sample of a metallic element. Determine its density. Check references that list the density of metals to identify the sample that you analyzed.

Portfolio projects

1. Chemistry and you
Make a poster showing the types of product warning labels that are found on products in your home.

1. Magnesium dissolves in hydrochloric acid to produce magnesium chloride and hydrogen gas. Which of the following represents the reactants in this reaction?
   a. magnesium and magnesium chloride
   b. hydrochloric acid and hydrogen gas
   c. magnesium and hydrochloric acid
   d. magnesium chloride and hydrogen gas

2. Matter that has a definite shape and volume is a(n) ———.
   a. acid
   b. base
   c. solid
   d. gas

3. Which of the following are equal?
   a. 1.63 kg and 163 g
   b. 0.0704 m and 7.04 mm
   c. 0.015 mL and 1.5 L
   d. 325 mg and 0.325 g

4. A chemical property of matter ———.
   a. depends on how it reacts with other substances
   b. can be described when it undergoes a physical change
   c. cannot be quantitatively described
   d. cannot be qualitatively described

5. An SI base unit that is commonly used in chemistry is the ———.
   a. degree Celsius
   b. gram
   c. liter
   d. mole

6. Matter can be defined as anything that ———.
   a. has weight
   b. has mass and volume
   c. can be described in SI units
   d. exhibits both chemical and physical properties

7. Assume that you use time-lapse photography to film the rusting of a piece of iron. You then watch the film and observe the iron rust. What you see is both a ———.
   a. chemical change and a qualitative observation
   b. physical change and a qualitative observation
   c. chemical change and a quantitative observation
   d. physical change and a quantitative observation

8. Which of the following is classified as a heterogeneous mixture?
   a. bean burrito
   b. blood
   c. hot chocolate
   d. plastic wrap

9. A compound differs from a mixture in that the former ———.
   a. contains only one element
   b. varies in chemical composition depending on the sample size
   c. has a definite composition by mass of the elements it contains
   d. can be classified as either heterogeneous or homogeneous

10. Which of the following would be considered allotropes?
    a. CO and CO_2
    b. H_2O and H_2S
    c. C_2H_2 and C_6H_6
    d. S_6 and S_8

CHAPTER 2

Matter and Energy

THE LAST VOYAGE OF THE *GRANDCAMP*

On April 11, 1947, a cargo ship named the *Grandcamp* arrived in Texas City, a Texas port city of 50 000 people. The *Grandcamp* was carrying cargo destined for France—aid from the United States following World War II. Before departing for France, the *Grandcamp* had to be loaded with fertilizer.

Over the next few days, longshoremen loaded the ship with fertilizer, which consisted of a compound known as ammonium nitrate. Stored in 45 kg paper bags, 2300 metric tons of ammonium nitrate was loaded onto the ship. Also in the hold were 16 cases of ammunition, 380 bales of cotton, 9334 bags of shelled peanuts, 59 000 bales of twine, and some refrigeration and farm machinery. No one realized that with tons of ammonium nitrate on board the *Grandcamp* was a time bomb.

Soon after the last bags were loaded, one of the longshoremen noticed smoke coming from the ship's cargo hold. He alerted some co-workers, and they discovered flames coming from the bags of fertilizer. They tried to put out the fire, but it continued to spread and was soon burning out of control.

A little over an hour after the smoke was first detected, the *Grandcamp* exploded, causing a blast that was heard 240 km away. The blast created a 5 m wave of water that roared out of the harbor. Debris was tossed in every direction. An anchor from the ship flew 2.6 km through the air and created a 3 m wide hole in the ground where it landed. The blast triggered a series of explosions and fires throughout Texas City. When the catastrophe finally ended, 576 people were dead, 4000 were injured, and every building in the city was either destroyed or damaged. It was the worst industrial disaster in United States history.

The catastrophe on the *Grandcamp* was a direct result of a chemical process. As you will see, the explosion created by the ammonium nitrate was like all other processes in chemistry—it involved the interaction between matter and energy.

CHAPTER LINKS

Where did all the destructive energy that caused this catastrophe come from?

What happened in terms of energy when the Grandcamp exploded?

How much mass was converted to energy to produce the 350 gigajoules released by the explosion of the ammonium nitrate on the Grandcamp?

What is energy?

OBJECTIVES

▶ **Distinguish** between potential and kinetic energy.

▶ **Distinguish** between heat and temperature.

▶ **State** the law of conservation of energy.

▶ **Calculate** changes in heat energy.

▶ **Describe** the relationship between mass and energy.

Chemical energy

What comes to mind when you see or hear the word *energy*? Perhaps you think of a time when you were able to play an hour of basketball after taking two tests in school, wash the car when you got home, and then enjoy the school dance that night. Maybe the word *energy* brings to mind an image of a power plant. Or from what you have learned in previous science courses, you might associate *energy* with food or fuel.

Chemical energy involves chemical bonds

chemical energy

the energy that matter possesses because of its chemical makeup

chemical bond

a mutual attraction between different atoms that binds the atoms together

Chemical energy is the energy that matter possesses because of its chemical makeup. What does the chemical energy in an ordinary liquid compound like water involve? **Figure 2-1** shows the chemical structure of a water molecule. Notice that a water molecule consists of two hydrogen atoms that are connected to one oxygen atom. The electrons in each atom are moving, so they have energy. There is also energy associated with the force of attraction that holds hydrogen and oxygen atoms together. This force of attraction is known as a **chemical bond.** Water has chemical energy because of the atoms it contains and the bonds that hold them together.

▶ FIGURE 2-1

A water molecule consists of one oxygen atom attached to two hydrogen atoms. Chemical energy involves the chemical bonds holding the atoms together.

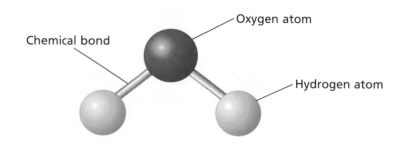

Chemical bond
Oxygen atom
Hydrogen atom

Water molecules and the atoms that compose them have both kinetic and potential energy. **Kinetic energy** is the energy an object possesses due to its motion. Atoms and molecules are in constant motion, so they have kinetic energy. This is true even in ice. Although fixed somewhat in position in the ice crystal, as shown in **Figure 2-2,** the molecules vibrate back and forth. However, this vibrational energy is small compared with the energy of chemical bonds.

Potential energy is the energy an object has due to its position relative to other objects. To understand how the position of atoms is connected to energy, consider the reaction between the elements hydrogen and oxygen to form water. This reaction is shown symbolically in **Figure 2-3.** The process of forming water releases a large amount of heat. Why? The answer is that the relative positions of atoms have changed. Before the reaction, hydrogen atoms are bonded together and oxygen atoms are bonded together. The reaction changes the relative positions of the atoms, and therefore potential energy changes. Specifically, the potential energy of the atoms bonded in H_2O is lower than when the atoms bond in H_2 and O_2. The decrease in potential energy becomes heat energy. **Table 2-1,** on page 42, gives an overview of the energy changes that occur in the process of reacting hydrogen and oxygen to produce water. When chemical bonds are formed or broken, the energy changes are considered chemical energy.

All physical and chemical changes involve a change in energy

Think about any familiar chemical or physical change. What causes the change to occur? For a solid to melt, energy must be added to the solid. For a liquid to evaporate, the particles in the liquid must have enough energy to move away from the surface of the liquid. When you activate

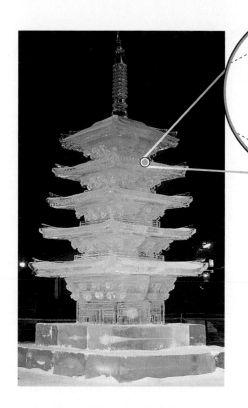

FIGURE 2-2 ▲

Ice consists of water molecules held in a rigid, regular structure. Although the molecules in ice are not able to move freely, they are able to vibrate and therefore have kinetic energy.

kinetic energy

energy a moving object has because of its motion

potential energy

energy an object has because of its position

FIGURE 2-3 ▼

Hydrogen and oxygen react in a 2:1 ratio to produce water.

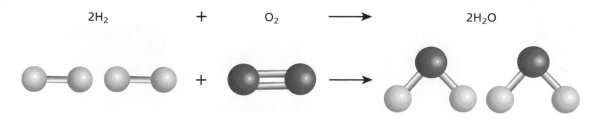

$2H_2$ + O_2 $\longrightarrow$ $2H_2O$

TABLE 2-1 **Forms of Energy in a Water Molecule**

Energy change	Process	Symbolic picture
Energy in	Breaking bond between H atoms	
Energy in	Breaking bond between O atoms	
Energy out	Forming bonds between H and O atoms	

internetconnect

SCiLINKS
NSTA

TOPIC: Physical/chemical change
GO TO: www.scilinks.org
KEYWORD: HW022

energy

the capacity to do work

law of conservation of energy

in any chemical or physical process, energy is neither created nor destroyed

a light stick, such as the one in **Figure 2-4,** chemicals inside must react to give off light. When wood burns, it gives off heat. Energy from the sun drives some of the reactions of photosynthesis to produce food for the plant. All chemical or physical changes involve energy changes.

The term *energy* represents a broad concept. One definition of **energy** is the capacity to do some type of work, such as moving an object, forming a new compound, or producing light. In Chapter 1 you read that exothermic processes release energy, while endothermic processes absorb energy. The term *release* may give you the impression that energy can be created, while the term *absorb* may convey the idea that energy can be destroyed. However, the **law of conservation of energy** states that in any physical or chemical change, energy can change form, but the total amount of energy remains constant. Therefore, energy can be converted from kinetic energy to potential energy, but it cannot be created or destroyed.

► **FIGURE 2-4**

When you activate a light stick, chemical energy is converted to light energy.

FIGURE 2-5 ◄

A chemical reaction taking place inside the heat pack releases heat. The heat is transferred from the heat pack to its surroundings.

Energy can be transferred

Energy can be transferred from one object or substance to another. The most common energy transfers in chemistry are transfers of heat energy. **Heat** is the sum total of kinetic energy of the particles in a sample of matter. To keep track of energy transfers, chemists define the system being studied. A **system** consists of all the components that are being studied at a given time. Everything outside a system is referred to as the surroundings. A system can be quite complex and include a variety of substances and objects, or it can be very simple, like the heat pack shown in **Figure 2-5.**

One type of heat pack consists of a bag containing a metal disk and a compound called sodium acetate that is dissolved in water. The heat pack and its contents can be considered a system. Clicking the metal disk inside the pack causes the sodium acetate to crystallize, or come out of the solution. Energy is involved in the change when sodium acetate dissolves or crystallizes. All you need to recognize at this point is that these reactions involve a transfer of heat energy. The crystallization process for sodium acetate is exothermic. Although we say that heat is "released," it is more accurate to say that energy in the form of heat is transferred *from* the system *to* the surroundings. In this example, the surroundings may be your hands on a cold day.

Heat energy can also be transferred in the opposite direction—from the surroundings to a system. You can recharge the heat pack by placing it in boiling water so that energy can be transferred from the hot water (the surroundings) to the heat pack (the system). As heat energy is transferred, the sodium acetate dissolves. As the sodium acetate dissolves, its chemical energy increases. Energy transferred as heat into the heat pack is converted into the chemical energy of dissolved sodium acetate. Reactions in which energy is

heat

the sum total of kinetic energy of the particles in a sample of matter

system

a specific portion of matter in a given region of space that has been selected for study during an experiment or observation

► **FIGURE 2-6**

Some of the heat that is transferred to the heat pack from its surroundings (the boiling water) is converted into chemical energy in the compounds inside the heat pack. Thus, the heat pack can be used over and over again.

transferred as heat from the surroundings into the system are endothermic processes. Thus energy is not really "absorbed" in an endothermic reaction—it is converted *into* chemical energy or some other form of energy. Once the energy transferred as heat is converted into chemical energy, the heat pack is ready to be used again. **Figure 2-6** shows the heat pack system after it has been recharged with heat energy.

CONCEPT CHECK

1. What is energy?
2. State the law of conservation of energy.

Energy transfer as heat

Temperature indicates how hot or cold something is. When energy is transferred to heat water, the temperature of the water increases. The more rapidly the water molecules move, the higher their average kinetic energy. As the average kinetic energy of the molecules increases, so does the temperature of the water. **Temperature** is a measure of the average kinetic energy of the random motion of particles in a substance.

temperature

a measure of the average kinetic energy of the particles in a sample of matter

Temperature is expressed using different scales

You know that a thermometer is a device used to measure temperature. The operation of most thermometers is based on the principle that matter expands as its temperature increases. Thermometers are usually marked with the Fahrenheit or Celsius temperature scales. However, the Fahrenheit scale is not used in chemistry. In Chapter 1 you learned that the SI unit for temperature is the kelvin, K. **Figure 2-7** shows a comparison of the Celsius and Kelvin temperature scales. The zero point on the Celsius scale is designated as the freezing point of water. The zero point on the Kelvin scale is designated as absolute zero, the lowest temperature theoretically possible. In chemistry, you will use both scales, and at times, you will have to convert between the two scales. Conversion between the Celsius and Kelvin scales simply requires an adjustment to account for their different zero points. The following equations show how to convert between these two temperature scales. The symbol t stands for temperature in degrees Celsius, and the symbol T stands for temperature in kelvins.

$$t(°C) = T(K) - 273.15 \text{ K}$$

$$T(K) = t(°C) + 273.15°C$$

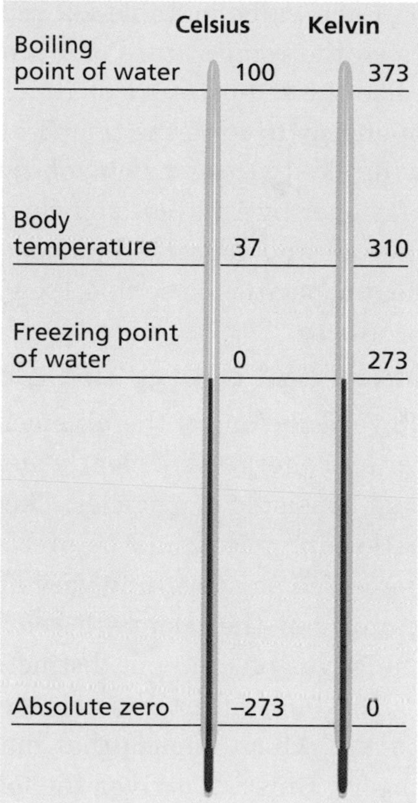

Specific heat capacity— changing the temperature of a substance

If you have done much cooking, you know that metal pans transfer heat to food faster than glass or ceramic pans do. If you add the same heat energy to similar masses of different substances, they don't all show the same increase in temperature. This relationship between heat energy and temperature change, which is unique to each substance, is called the specific heat capacity. The **specific heat capacity** (c_p) of a substance is the amount of heat energy required to raise the temperature of 1 g of the substance by 1 K. The SI unit for energy is the *joule* (J). One joule is approximately equal to the amount of energy you expend bringing a cheeseburger to your mouth. Specific heat capacity is expressed in joules per gram kelvin (J/g•K). You will find the specific heat capacity of some elements listed in **Table 2-2.** Specific heat capacities are calculated from experimental data.

	Celsius	Kelvin
Boiling point of water	100	373
Body temperature	37	310
Freezing point of water	0	273
Absolute zero	−273	0

FIGURE 2-7 ◀

You will encounter two temperature scales in your study of chemistry. The Celsius scale is part of the metric system; the Kelvin scale is the SI temperature scale.

specific heat capacity

the amount of heat energy required to raise the temperature of 1 g of a substance by 1 K

TABLE 2-2 | **Specific Heat Capacities at Room Temperature of Some Elements**

Substance	Specific heat capacity (J/g•K)	Substance	Specific heat capacity (J/g•K)
Aluminum	0.897	Lead	0.129
Cadmium	0.232	Neon	1.030
Calcium	0.647	Nickel	0.444
Carbon (graphite)	0.709	Platinum	0.133
Chromium	0.449	Silicon	0.705
Copper	0.385	Silver	0.235
Gold	0.129	Tin	0.228
Iron	0.449	Zinc	0.388

Each value in Table 2-2 represents the amount of energy needed to raise the temperature of 1 g of the substance 1 K. It takes 0.897 J to raise the temperature of 1 g of aluminum by 1 K. It takes only 0.385 J of energy to raise the temperature of 1 g of copper by 1 K. Of course, it will take twice as much energy, 0.770 J, to raise the temperature of 2 g of copper by 1 K. For a single atom, however, the heat capacities of aluminum and copper are almost identical. In fact, all metal atoms have heat capacities close to 4.1×10^{-23} J/K.

Mass and energy are closely related

Toward the end of the nineteenth century, scientists believed that matter and energy were clearly distinct. Matter was perceived as something that consisted of particles. These particles had mass, and their exact location in space could be precisely pinpointed. In contrast, energy was perceived as something very different from matter. However, by the beginning of the twentieth century, scientists had come to realize that there was no clear-cut distinction between matter and energy.

In 1905, Albert Einstein proposed his special theory of relativity, a part of which implies that mass and energy are equivalent. From his theory, Einstein derived the following equation.

$$E = mc^2$$

E is the energy equivalent of an object, m is its mass, and c is the speed of light in a vacuum (2.998×10^8 m/s). Einstein's equation shows that energy has a mass equivalent. Conversely, mass has an energy equivalent. This relationship becomes clearer when the equation is rearranged.

$$m = \frac{E}{c^2}$$

"*Now* that desk looks better. Everything's squared away, yessir, squaaaaaared away."

 ▶ FIGURE 2-8

Widely considered to have possessed one of the greatest scientific minds of all time, Albert Einstein gave the world theories that revolutionized how scientists look at the universe.

Mass and energy are no longer considered completely different quantities. Each can be transformed into the other. In such transformations, a small amount of mass corresponds to a huge amount of energy. In nuclear power plants, an extremely small fraction of the mass of atoms is converted to heat energy, a part of which is then transformed to electric energy. Einstein's equation reveals how much energy can be obtained from a given amount of mass.

Assume that all the mass of a 1.000 g object could be converted to energy. Substituting the appropriate values into Einstein's equation reveals how much energy can theoretically be obtained from a 1.000 g object.

$$E = (1.000 \text{ g})(2.998 \times 10^8 \text{ m/s})^2 =$$

$$8.988 \times 10^{16} \text{ g} \bullet \text{m}^2/\text{s}^2 \times \frac{1 \text{ kg}}{1000 \text{ g}} = 8.988 \times 10^{13} \text{ kg} \bullet \text{m}^2/\text{s}^2$$

One $\text{kg} \bullet \text{m}^2/\text{s}^2$ is 1 J. Thus, 8.998×10^{13} J of energy can be obtained from a 1.000 g object. Recall that 1 J is the energy you expend to bring a cheeseburger to your mouth. Thus, converting the mass of a 1.000 g object would give you enough energy to lift a cheeseburger to your mouth 90 trillion times! But converting mass to energy is not a simple task, as you will learn in Chapter 18.

SECTION REVIEW

Total recall

1. What is the difference between potential energy and kinetic energy?

2. What is the difference between heat and temperature?

3. Explain what the equation $E = mc^2$ signifies.

4. What energy changes are considered chemical energy?

5. What is a system?

6. Define *specific heat capacity.*

Critical thinking

7. What happens in terms of heat transfer when you hold a snowball in your hand?

8. **Interpreting Tables** Use Table 2-2 to determine the following.
   a. Which of the metals listed requires the most energy to raise its temperature by 1°C?
   b. If energy is added at the same rate to containers all of the same mass made of copper, chromium, and lead, which container will show the greatest rise in temperature after 10 minutes?

Practice problems

9. Convert the following Celsius temperatures to Kelvin temperatures.
   a. 100°C   c. 0°C
   b. 785°C   d. −37°C

10. Convert the following Kelvin temperatures to Celsius temperatures.
   a. 273 K   c. 0 K
   b. 1200 K   d. 100 K

11. **Story Clue** The formula for calculating kinetic energy is

$$KE = \frac{mv^2}{2}.$$

KE is the kinetic energy of an object, m is its mass, and v is its velocity. Recall that the explosion of the *Grandcamp* hurled the ship's anchor through the air. How much kinetic energy did the 1300 kg anchor have if it was traveling at a velocity of 50 m/s?

What is the process of science?

OBJECTIVES

▶ **Describe** the process used by scientists to study matter and energy.

▶ **Explain** the purpose of controls in an experiment.

▶ **Describe** the role of models in chemistry.

▶ **Distinguish** between a hypothesis, a theory, and a law.

The scientific method

The first scientists placed great reliance on rational thought and logic. They rarely felt it was necessary to test their ideas or conclusions and were not inclined to experiment. Gradually, experiments became the crucial test for the acceptance of scientific knowledge. Today, experiments are an integral part of research in all sciences, including chemistry. Science is distinguished from other fields of study in that it provides precise guidelines and includes specific procedures for conducting research. Scientists constantly challenge the work of other scientists to ensure that their results and conclusions are correct.

Experiments are part of the scientific method

The way scientists carry out investigations is referred to as the *scientific method*. The scientific method is not a series of exact steps; rather, it is a strategy for drawing sound conclusions. A scientist chooses various scientific procedures to use in an investigation. **Figure 2-9** lists some of these procedures. Which ones have you used in investigations that you have performed in previous science courses?

A chemist selects procedures that best fit the nature of the particular investigation. For example, a chemist who has an idea for developing a

▼ **FIGURE 2-9**

The scientific method is not a stepwise procedure. Scientists may repeat steps many times before there is sufficient evidence to formulate a theory. You can see that each stage represents a number of different activities.

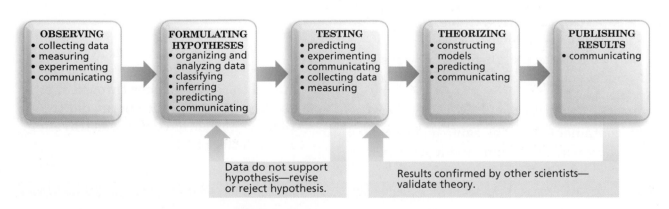

OBSERVING
• collecting data
• measuring
• experimenting
• communicating

FORMULATING HYPOTHESES
• organizing and analyzing data
• classifying
• inferring
• predicting
• communicating

TESTING
• predicting
• experimenting
• communicating
• collecting data
• measuring

THEORIZING
• constructing models
• predicting
• communicating

PUBLISHING RESULTS
• communicating

Data do not support hypothesis—revise or reject hypothesis.

Results confirmed by other scientists—validate theory.

better method to recycle plastics may research the literature, collect information, propose a method to separate the materials, and then test the method. This sequence of events forms the scientific method that will be used by this chemist.

In contrast, another chemist may be investigating the pollution caused by an incinerator. This investigation would follow a different procedure that might include collecting and analyzing samples, interviewing people, predicting the role the incinerator plays in producing the pollution, and conducting field studies to test that prediction. This approach would also constitute a scientific method.

Thus, the scientific method can be viewed as a logical approach to exploring a problem or question that has been raised through observation or mental reflection. No matter which procedures are selected, the scientific method used by a chemist consists of the fundamental activities outlined in Figure 2-9. Notice the last step in the figure. The research findings of any experiment or investigation must be reproducible by other scientists for those findings to be accepted as valid. Ultimately, the success of the scientific method depends on publishing what has been found so that others can repeat the procedures that were used and verify the results.

INQUIRYLAB

Applications of the Scientific Method

In this activity, you must design a successful experimental approach to solve four problems.

The first two problems involve studying the boiling point of a pure liquid. The boiling point of a substance can be defined as the temperature at which a liquid becomes a gas. The third and fourth problems involve observing how the addition of different substances affects the boiling point of the liquid.

Materials beakers, graduated cylinders, sugar, thermometers, Bunsen burners, salt, ring stands, ring clamps

Problems
1. Design an experiment to determine what happens to the temperature of a liquid after it has started to boil.
2. Design an experiment to determine if the volume of a liquid has an effect on its boiling point.
3. Design an experiment to determine what happens to the boiling point of water when table salt is added.
4. Design an experiment to find out which chemical, salt or sugar, has a more dramatic effect on the boiling point of water.

Analysis
1. Consider two beakers of boiling water. The water in beaker A has been boiling for 5 minutes, and the water in beaker B has been boiling for 10 minutes. Which water sample is at a higher temperature?
2. Antifreeze is added to a car's radiator in the summertime. Explain how antifreeze affects the boiling point of the water in a radiator.

Scientific discoveries can come from unexpected observations

Not all discoveries and findings are the result of a carefully worked-out plan based on the scientific method. In fact, some important discoveries and developments have been made simply by accident. An example is the discovery of the chemical compound commonly known as Teflon®. You are probably familiar with Teflon as the nonstick coating used on pots and pans, but it has many more applications. Teflon is used

► **FIGURE 2-10**

Tetrafluoroethene is an example of a *fluorocarbon,* an organic compound composed of carbon and fluorine atoms. Teflon is prepared using tetrafluoroethene.

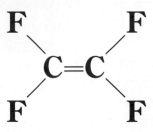

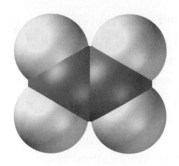

as thermal insulation in clothing, as a component in wall coverings and roofing materials, and as a protective coating on metals, glass, and plastics. Teflon's properties of low chemical reactivity and very low friction make it valuable in the construction of artificial joints for human limbs.

Teflon was discovered by chance

In 1938, Dr. Roy Plunkett, a chemist employed by DuPont, was working in his lab, trying to develop a new coolant gas to use as a refrigerant. At the time, a compound called dichlorotetrafluoroethene was the most widely used refrigerant. Plunkett's research had led him to believe that he could make a less expensive coolant by reacting a gas called tetrafluoroethene (TFE) with hydrochloric acid. A structural formula and model for TFE are shown in **Figure 2-10.** He cooled the canisters of TFE to liquefy the gas. Once everything was ready for the experiment, Plunkett placed a canister of TFE on a balance to record its mass. He then opened the valve to let the TFE flow into a container filled with hydrochloric acid. But no TFE came out of the metal canister.

Plunkett checked the valve to make sure it was open; it was. He then used a piece of wire to poke out anything that might be clogging the opening in the valve. Still nothing came out of the metal canister. Thinking that the TFE might have somehow leaked out of the canister, Plunkett noted its mass on the balance. Because the canister had the same mass as it did when it was filled with TFE, he knew that the TFE had not leaked out.

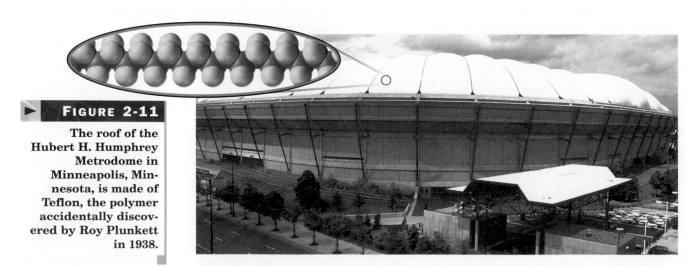

► **FIGURE 2-11**

The roof of the Hubert H. Humphrey Metrodome in Minneapolis, Minnesota, is made of Teflon, the polymer accidentally discovered by Roy Plunkett in 1938.

Puzzled, Plunkett removed the valve and shook the canister upside down. Only a few white flakes fell out. Curious about what had happened, Plunkett decided to analyze the white flakes. He discovered that he had accidentally created the proper conditions for TFE molecules to form a long chain known as a **polymer.** Further research revealed that the polymer he had made, called polytetrafluoroethene, was very slippery. In addition, the polymer was not affected by many of the chemicals that would normally break down a polymer. After 10 years of additional research and development, large-scale manufacture of the polymer, now known as Teflon, became practical.

polymer

a large organic molecule composed of smaller units bonded together

The anticancer drug cisplatin was discovered accidentally

Another accidental discovery was made some 30 years later. In this case, Dr. Barnett Rosenberg had been using platinum probes to study the effects of electric fields on living cells. He and his colleagues observed that bacteria did not reproduce near the platinum probes. After conducting extensive experiments, they were able to show that a platinum compound formed near the probes in an electrochemical reaction. This compound, called cisplatin, has the chemical structure shown in **Figure 2-12.** After a long series of carefully planned experiments, researchers showed that cisplatin, and not the electric fields, caused the changes in cell reproduction.

Rosenberg reasoned that because cancer involves uncontrolled cell growth, perhaps cisplatin would be effective in treating cancer. The results of another series of experiments showed that Rosenberg's reasoning was correct. Rosenberg's initial work spawned further research of the anticancer properties of cisplatin. After years of testing by independent sources to verify the effectiveness of the drug, cisplatin was approved by the Food and Drug Administration in 1979 for treatment of certain types of cancer.

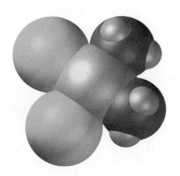

FIGURE 2-12 ◄

Cisplatin is a compound formed from platinum, chlorine, nitrogen, and hydrogen atoms.

This student is testing various food products claimed to be sugar-free for the presence of sugar. If the test reagent turns from blue to red after reacting with the samples, sugar is present in the product.

hypothesis

a reasonable and testable explanation of observations

A hypothesis is a testable explanation of an observation

Recognizing and defining a problem or question often stems from observing, as the student is doing in **Figure 2-13.** The discovery of cisplatin and its usefulness in treating cancer resulted from a simple observation—bacteria did not reproduce near the platinum probes. That observation led to further experiments and tests.

Once observations have been made, they must be analyzed. Scientists start by examining all the relevant information or data they have gathered. They look for patterns in the data that can suggest an explanation for their observations. This proposed explanation is called a hypothesis. A **hypothesis** is a reasonable and testable explanation for observations. Hypotheses are often written in an "if-then" format that describes a cause-and-effect relationship. A hypothesis for Rosenberg's work with cisplatin is as follows: *if* cisplatin can slow or stop cell reproduction, *then* it could be effective in treating cancer, which is caused by uncontrolled cell growth.

Experiments are used to test hypotheses

An *experiment* is a process carried out under controlled conditions, often to test the validity of a hypothesis, as shown in **Figure 2-14.** Rosenberg's work with cisplatin initially involved the question of what was inhibiting the growth of the cells. The most important part of his experimentation was documenting the effects of variables. A *variable* is any aspect of an experiment that can be changed to affect the outcome of the experiment. Before Rosenberg could come to the conclusion that cisplatin was indeed the reason that the growth of bacteria was slowed, he had to measure the effects of all other variables. How did he know the effect was not caused by a simple temperature change in the culture medium?

These students are experimenting to determine how to get the largest volume of popped corn from the fewest kernels.

How did he know the culture had not been contaminated? How did he know there weren't changes in the electric current? Because platinum is generally an unreactive element and the concentration of platinum compounds in the culture medium was very low, it initially seemed unlikely that platinum could be causing the cells to stop reproducing.

The researchers had to narrow the field of possible variables by keeping all of the variables constant except one, and that one was varied in each trial. Temperature, current, purity of the platinum, and the contents of the culture medium are some of the many variables that could change from experiment to experiment. When a variable is kept constant from one trial to the next, the procedure is called a *control experiment*. Control experiments allow researchers to isolate the key variable. It took many experiments over a two-year period for Rosenberg and his team to verify that the formation of cisplatin was the key factor that interfered with the growth of cells.

Data from experiments can lead to a theory

Any conclusion scientists make must come directly and solely from the data they obtain in their experiments. Many times, scientists discover that they are unable to arrive at a conclusion. In fact, they may discover that the data fail to support their hypothesis. In that case, they must re-examine the question and develop and test a new hypothesis.

Any hypothesis that withstands repeated testing may become part of a theory. A **theory** is a broad generalization that is based on observation, experimentation, and reasoning. Because theories are not facts, but rather explanations, they can never be completely proven. A theory is considered successful if it explains *most* of what is observed. When a theory is not successful, it may be modified or discarded as new information is discovered. An example of such a modification is the atomic theory, which you will learn about in Chapter 3. In the early 1800s, John Dalton collected data from experiments to support the idea that matter is made of atoms. Part of Dalton's atomic theory was that atoms are indivisible. This part of his theory had to be discarded after the discovery of subatomic particles. But much of Dalton's original theory is still valid.

Top Quark, Last Piece in Puzzle Of Matter, Appears to Be in Place

By WILLIAM J. BROAD

The quest begun by philosophers in ancient Greece to understand the nature of matter may have ended in Batavia, Ill., with the discovery of evidence for the top quark, the last of 12 subatomic building blocks now believed to constitute all of the material world.

An international team of 439 scientists working at the Fermi National Accelerator Laboratory will announce the finding today, bringing nearly two decades of searching to a dramatic conclusion.

The Fermilab discovery, if confirmed, would be a major milestone for modern physics because it would complete the experimental proof of the grand theoretical edifice known

in physics at Cornell University, said the finding was "a very big deal" that "makes the whole picture of subnuclear particles much more believable and better established."

"We've needed the top quark," he said. "It figures in all our calculations for further processes, and none of them would be right if it weren't there."

If the top quark could not be found, the Standard Model of theoretical physicists would collapse, touching off an intellectual crisis that would force scientists to rethink three decades of work in which governments around the globe had invested many billions of dollars.

All matter is made of atoms, but nearly a century ago physicists discovered that atoms, long considered the smallest units of matter, were composed of small...

FIGURE 2-15 ▲

The discovery of the subatomic particles called quarks forced a revision of the theory of atomic structure.

theory

a well-tested explanation of observations

CONSUMER ACTIVITY

QUICKLAB

Model of a Black Box

In this activity, you will construct a model of objects in a sealed box by making inferences about them.

Materials sealed box containing one or more objects

Problems
1. Carefully tilt, shake, or rotate the box.
2. Record all observations.
3. Use your observations to determine the number of objects in the box, their masses, general shapes, and sizes.
4. Compare observations and ideas about the objects in the box with others in your class. Make a hypothesis about the identity of each object.

Analysis
1. Provide a written description (model) of your objects. If you were able to infer the identity of the object, include its identity in your model.

FIGURE 2-16 ▼

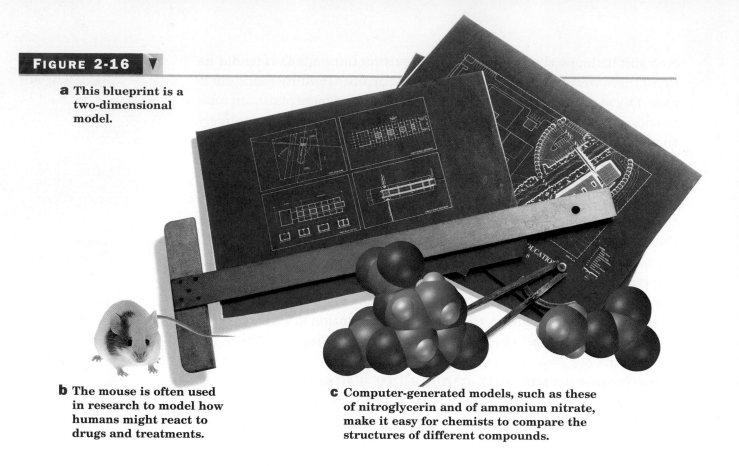

a This blueprint is a two-dimensional model.

b The mouse is often used in research to model how humans might react to drugs and treatments.

c Computer-generated models, such as these of nitroglycerin and of ammonium nitrate, make it easy for chemists to compare the structures of different compounds.

Theories can be models

Models play a major role in science. A model is a simplified representation of an object, a system, a process, or an idea. Models can take many forms, from actual replicas to written descriptions. **Figure 2-16** shows several types of models. Models can be used in various ways. One of the models represents ammonium nitrate, the compound that caused the *Grandcamp* explosion. Compare the model of ammonium nitrate with the model of nitroglycerin in Figure 2-16. Nitroglycerin is the explosive used in dynamite. What do the structures of ammonium nitrate and nitroglycerin have in common?

It is important to remember that models are simplified representations. The atoms making up ammonium nitrate and nitroglycerin are not hard spheres, nor are they the sizes and colors shown. However, the model does show the geometrical arrangement of the atoms and their relative sizes. An effective model clearly depicts a particular set of characteristics of what is being modeled. Models, like theories, are refined as new information becomes available.

Scientific laws are based on facts

Certain facts in science hold true consistently. Such facts are known as scientific laws. A **scientific law** is a statement or mathematical expression that reliably describes the behavior of the natural world. Note that a scientific law *describes* events in the natural world but does not attempt to *explain* them. For example, the **law of conservation of mass**

scientific law

a description of the natural world that has proven reliable over time

law of conservation of mass

the products of a chemical reaction have the same mass as the reactants states that the products of a chemical reaction have the same mass as the reactants. This law does not explain why matter in chemical reactions behaves this way; it simply describes this behavior.

In some cases, scientific laws are subject to reinterpretation based on the discovery of new information. For example, you learned in Section 2-1 that the law of conservation of energy states that energy can be neither created nor destroyed in any physical or chemical process. Similarly, the law of conservation of mass states that mass cannot be created or destroyed. Einstein's special theory of relativity connects these two laws. Through the equation $E = mc^2$, the theory of relativity explains that energy and mass are equivalent. Although neither can be created or destroyed, energy *can* be converted into mass, and vice versa. Einstein prompted a reevaluation of these two conservation laws by his assertion that energy and mass are interconvertible.

Because there are so few facts that are consistently reliable in describing the behavior of the natural world, there are a limited number of laws in science compared with the number of theories and hypotheses. Do not confuse a scientific law with either a hypothesis or a theory. A hypothesis *predicts* an event. A theory *explains* it. A law *describes* it.

$\mathcal{S}$ECTION REVIEW

Total recall

1. What activities are part of the scientific method?

2. How does a hypothesis differ from a theory?

3. State the law of conservation of mass.

4. What is a scientific law, and how does it differ from a theory?

5. Name two chemical compounds that were accidentally discovered, and describe what they are used for.

Critical thinking

6. Why does a scientist include a control in the design of an experiment?

7. Give two reasons why scientists publish the results of their experiments.

8. How do models help chemists acquire knowledge about matter and energy?

9. What variables would a chemist need to control when setting up an experiment to determine whether or not a low temperature is required for TFE to form a polymer?

10. Describe what is needed for a hypothesis to develop into a theory.

11. Why is there no single scientific method?

12. **Interpreting graphics** Refer to Figure 2-9 on page 48. Describe a sequence of actions that a chemist might take to develop a new drug to treat diabetics.

13. **Story Clue** What scientific processes listed in Figure 2-9 would you use to determine why the *Grandcamp* exploded?

SECTION 2-3

How do chemists measure quantities?

OBJECTIVES

▶ **Distinguish** between accuracy and precision in measurements.

▶ **Determine** the number of significant figures in a measurement.

▶ **Perform** calculations using measurements, and round the results to the correct number of significant figures.

▶ **Write** very large and very small numbers in scientific notation.

Measuring and calculating

When you measure some quantitative property of matter or calculate a quantity of energy, how close to the "true" value are these measurements and calculations? No experimentally obtained value is exact because all measurements are subject to errors—human errors, method errors, and instrument errors.

▼ **FIGURE 2-17**

In order to obtain meaningful data, it is important to choose the correct instrument for your measurements. All of these graduated cylinders measure volume, but each is calibrated for different capacities.

Measurements must be made with standard procedures and the correct measuring instruments

Errors can arise depending on the instrument that is used to make the measurement. You must keep in mind the limitations of your measuring instruments when deciding which instrument to use in a particular situation. In Chapter 1, you read that there are a number of different types of balances available to the chemist for measuring mass. A chemist who needs 0.155 g of a substance cannot use a balance that is calibrated only to the nearest 1 g. Which graduated cylinder shown in **Figure 2-17** would you select for measuring 8.6 mL of a liquid?

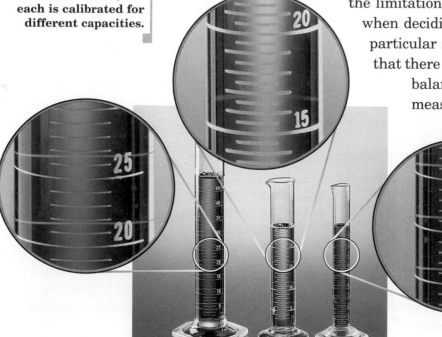

50 mL   25 mL   10 mL

FIGURE 2-18 ▼

The difference between accuracy and precision

a Darts within large area
= Low precision

Area covered on bull's eye
= High accuracy
(on average)

b Darts within large area
= Low precision

Area far from bull's eye
= Low accuracy

c Darts within small area
= High precision

Area far from bull's eye
= Low accuracy

d Darts within small area
= High precision

Area centered around
bull's eye
= High accuracy

Accuracy differs from precision

There are two things to consider when making and reporting a measurement: accuracy and precision. The **accuracy** of a measurement is how exact it is—how close it is to the true value. Suppose you measure the volume of a solution as 35.8 mL and your lab partner measures the volume of the same solution as 37.2 mL. If the true volume of the solution is 36.0 mL, your measurement is more accurate than your lab partner's measurement because 35.8 mL is closer to the true value of 36.0 mL.

Precision refers to how closely several measurements of the same quantity made in the same way agree with one another. For example, suppose you measure the mass of a substance four times using the same balance, and you record the measurements 110 g, 109 g, 111 g, and 110 g. These measurements are close to one another, so you can say that your measurements are precise. The precision of a single measurement depends on how finely graduated the measuring scale is and how easily you can make the measurement. Keep in mind that precise measurements are not necessarily accurate measurements. For example, if the balance was not reset to zero before the measurements are made, the measurements may be close to one another, but they will not be very accurate. **Figure 2-18** illustrates a way to visualize the difference between accuracy and precision.

accuracy

the extent to which a measurement approaches the true value of a quantity

precision

the extent to which a series of measurements of the same quantity made in the same way agree with one another

CONCEPT CHECK

1. Define *accuracy*.

2. Explain how a series of measurements can be precise without being accurate.

Significant figures

When making measurements or performing calculations, it is important to indicate how precise the values are. For example, if you report the mass of a sample as 10 g, it is not clear whether you mean that the mass of the sample is between 8 g and 12 g or that it is between 9.999 g and 10.001 g. In order to communicate the precision of their measurements and calculations, scientists report these values using significant figures. The **significant figures** of a measurement or calculation consist of all the digits known with certainty plus one estimated, or uncertain, digit. For example, a mass measurement of 10.7834 g is accurate to five places. The sixth place, 0.0004, is the estimated digit.

Measurements must be reported to the correct number of significant figures

It is necessary to report all measurements in an experiment to the correct number of significant figures in order to maintain the validity of the results. Suppose you are measuring temperature with a thermometer marked in intervals of 1°C. You can be certain of the temperature to the nearest degree. For example, the temperature may be slightly above 28°C, but it is definitely not less than 28°C nor greater than 29°C. However, by reading between the markings on the thermometer, you may be able to estimate the temperature to the nearest 0.2°C. For example, if the mercury in the thermometer appears to be slightly closer to 28°C than to 29°C, you may estimate the temperature as 28.4°C. Therefore, you can record the temperature to three significant figures—28.4°C. The first two digits you know with certainty; the third digit you estimated to the nearest 0.2°C. Therefore, the three significant figures in your recorded temperature of 28.4°C indicate that the actual temperature is between 28.2°C and 28.6°C.

Figure 2-19 shows two pieces of common laboratory equipment that you can use for measuring volumes. You are familiar with the first piece of equipment—a graduated cylinder. The other piece of equipment is known as a *buret*.

Suppose an experimental procedure requires 25.00 mL of water. A typical 100 mL graduated cylinder is calibrated to the nearest 1 mL; a typical buret is calibrated to the nearest 0.1 mL. Should you use the graduated cylinder or the buret to measure the water? If you use the graduated cylinder, your best measurement will be 25.0 mL with uncertainty in the tenths place. If you use the buret, your best measurement will be 25.00 mL with uncertainty in the hundredths place. Obviously, the buret is the best choice in this situation. Chemists often use a buret when precise volume measurements are essential.

Balances also allow for different degrees of precision. A microbalance can be used to determine mass to up to eight figures. A standard triple beam balance could provide precise readings to four figures.

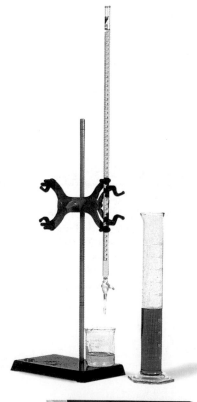

▲ **FIGURE 2-19**

Both the graduated cylinder and the buret are used to measure volumes of liquids. When would you want to use the graduated cylinder? When would you want to use the buret?

TABLE 2-3 **Rules for Determining Significant Zeros**

Rule	Example
1. Zeros appearing between nonzero digits are significant.	a. 40.7 L has three significant figures. b. 87 009 km has five significant figures.
2. Zeros appearing in front of nonzero digits are not significant.	a. 0.0095 87 m has four significant figures. b. 0.0009 kg has one significant figure.
3. Zeros at the end of a number *and* to the right of a decimal point are significant.	a. 85.00 g has four significant figures. b. 9.070 000 000 has ten significant figures.
4. Zeros at the end of a number with no decimal point may or may not be significant. If such a zero has been measured or estimated, it is significant. If a zero has not been measured or estimated and is just a place holder, it is not significant. A decimal point placed after zeros indicates that they are all significant.	a. 2000 m may contain from one to four significant figures, depending on how many zeros are place holders. **In this text, if the value does not contain a decimal point, assume that none of the zeros at the end of a measurement are significant.** b. 2000. m has four significant figures, indicated by the decimal point.

Rules for determining significant figures

How can you tell the number of significant figures in a measurement? Why does 25.00 mL have four significant figures, 25 mL have two, and 20 mL have only one? Scientists have agreed on rules for determining the number of significant figures in a value. **The first rule is that nonzero digits are *always* significant. Table 2-3** lists the rules for determining whether or not the zeros in a value are significant.

Calculations can exaggerate precision

You must pay special attention when calculating with significant figures to ensure that you get a meaningful result. The calculator in **Figure 2-20** was used to determine the density of isopropyl alcohol, commonly known as rubbing alcohol. The mass of a 32.4 mL sample of isopropyl alcohol was measured to be 25.42 g. In Chapter 1, you learned that mass and volume can be used to calculate density.

$$D = \frac{m}{V}$$

Notice that the calculator shown in Figure 2-20 reports the density of the liquid as 0.7845679012 g/mL. The mass was measured to four significant figures, while the volume was measured to three significant figures. Yet the calculator displays a density that is calculated to 10 significant figures. The

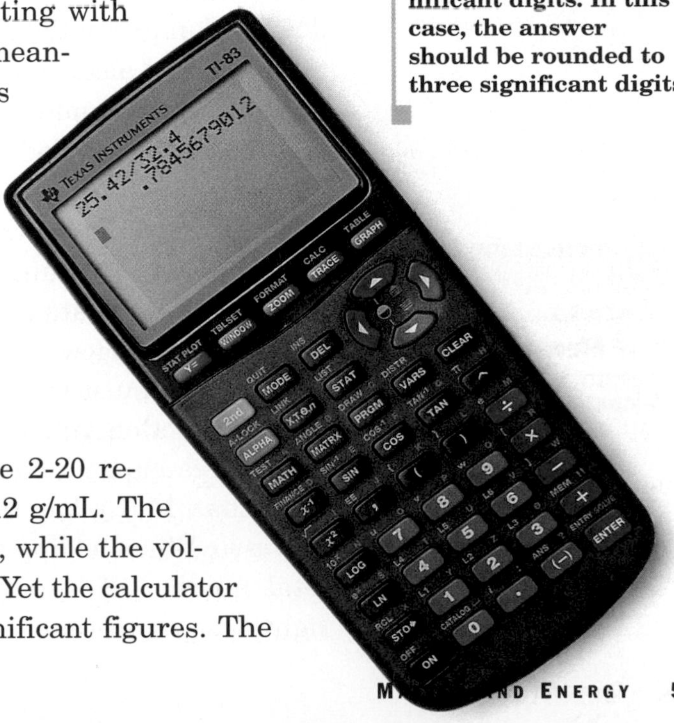

FIGURE 2-20 ▼

A calculator does not round the result to the correct number of significant digits. In this case, the answer should be rounded to three significant digits.

Operation	Rule	Example
Multiplication and division	The answer can have no more significant figures than there are in the measurement with the smallest number of significant figures.	12.257 × 1.162 ←—— four significant figures 14.2426340 —round off→ 14.24
Addition and subtraction	The answer can have no more digits to the right of the decimal point than there are in the measurement with the smallest number of digits to the right of the decimal point.	3.95 2.879 + 213.6 220.429 —round off→ 220.4

result provided by the calculator is misleading. It implies that we know the density of the isopropyl alcohol to a greater precision than we actually do.

To avoid exaggerating the precision of a calculated value, the result of the calculation must be rounded to the correct number of significant figures. The procedures for calculations involving multiplication and division are different from the procedures for calculations involving addition and subtraction. **Table 2-4** describes how to carry out each procedure.

Multiplication and division Round the calculated result to the same number of significant figures as the measurement having the least number of significant figures. If a sequence of calculations is involved, do not round until the end. In the example for calculating the density of the isopropyl alcohol, the answer must have only three significant figures, the same number as in the volume of the alcohol (32.4 mL). Thus, the density is rounded to 0.785 g/mL.

Addition and subtraction The answer can have no more digits to the right of the decimal point than there are in the measurement with the smallest number of digits to the right of the decimal point.

Consider the data shown in **Table 2-5**. The sum of the masses appears to be 14.592 g. However, to determine the correct number of significant figures, you must refer to the rule for calculations involving addition and subtraction. According to this rule, the result must be rounded to 14.6 g because 2.8 g has only one digit to the right of the decimal point. Note that 14.6 g has three significant figures even though 2.8 g has only two. When adding and subtracting, you are not concerned with the total number of significant digits; you are concerned only with the rightmost significant figure present in all values.

Mass Measurements

Measurement	Mass (g)
1	4.73
2	5.375
3	2.8
4	1.687

Exact values have an infinite number of significant figures

Some of the values you will use in your calculations are *exact values*. Exact values have no uncertainty, so they have an unlimited number of significant figures. The exact values you will encounter most often in your study of chemistry fall into two categories. The first category is count values. A count value is a value that is determined by counting, not by measuring. For example, a water molecule contains *exactly* two hydrogen atoms and *exactly* one oxygen atom. There is no uncertainty in this value—the number of hydrogen and oxygen atoms is counted, not measured.

The second category of exact values is defined conversion factors. You read about conversion factors in Chapter 1. For example, if you want to convert millimeters to meters, you use the following conversion factor.

$$\frac{1 \text{ m}}{1000 \text{ mm}}$$

There is no uncertainty in the values that make up the conversion factor because a millimeter is defined as *exactly* one-thousandth of a meter.

$$1 \text{ mm} = 0.001 \text{ m}$$

Watch for any exact values that may occur in your calculations, and remember that exact values always have more significant figures than any other value in the calculation. Therefore, you never use exact values, either counted values or conversion factors, to determine the number of significant figures in your calculated results.

INQUIRY LAB

U.S. Pennies Comparison

Though materials may look the same, subtle differences in their properties can be used to tell them apart. In this activity, you will look at the differences in properties of pennies that were minted at different times.

Materials
two sets of pennies (pre-1982 and post-1983), 100 mL graduated cylinder, balance, graph paper, colored pencils, ruler

Problem
Design an experiment to determine the relationship between the masses and volumes of the two sets of pennies provided by your teacher. Compare the masses and volumes of pennies minted before 1982 with the masses and volumes of those minted after 1983. **Your masses and volumes must contain at least three significant figures.**

Analysis
1. Prepare a data table (or tables) to record your experimental masses and volumes.
2. Construct a best-fit line graph (mass versus volume) to illustrate the relationship between the masses and volumes for each set of pennies. Both graphs (pre-1982 and post-1983) can be placed on the same piece of graph paper. Use colored pencils to distinguish the lines.

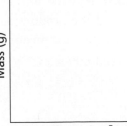

3. Calculate the slopes of your best-fit lines for each type of penny.
4. Calculate the average density value for each type of penny.
5. Compare the slope values from item 3 with your calculated densities from item 4. Are they similar?
6. Compare your density values with the known density of copper. If pennies are made of copper, why is there a difference?

1   Identify the limit of precision in each measurement given in the problem

A measurement expressed to the appropriate number of significant figures includes all digits that are certain and one digit that is uncertain.

▸ *Nonzero digits are always significant*

673 kg has three 1.45×10^5 km has three

2.8 m has two   3567 mg has four

▸ *Using rule 1 in Table 2-3*

506 g has three   5060 mg has three

$1.009 \ cm^2$ has four   10 900 kg has three

▸ *Using rule 2 in Table 2-3*

0.984 kg has three   0.067 mL has two

0.6 mm has one $0.004 \ cm^3$ has one

▸ *Using rule 3 in Table 2-3*

57.50 K has four   4.0 kg has two

2.90×10^3 km has three $61.00 \ m^2$ has four

▸ *Using rule 4 in Table 2-3*

34 800. mL has five   8900 kg has two

70 K has one   10 900. cm has five

2   Do not round any numbers in calculations until you reach a final answer

Addition and subtraction

Round the answer so that it matches the number of digits to the right of the decimal point in the measurement with the fewest digits to the right of the decimal point.

2.89 m + 0.00043 m = 2.89043 m (round to 2 places after the decimal point)

                  = 2.89 m

Multiplication and division

Round the product or quotient to the same number of significant figures as in the measurement with the fewest significant figures.

3.5293 mol × 34.2 g/mol = 120.70206 g (round to 3 significant figures)

                      = 121 g

CONCEPT CHECK

1. Why are significant figures important when reporting measurements?
2. How can calculations such as addition and division skew experimental results?
3. What digits are always significant?

Scientific notation

At times, chemists make measurements and perform calculations with very large or very small numbers. In Chapter 3, for example, you will calculate how many copper atoms there are in one penny—29 640 000 000 000 000 000 000 copper atoms, a very large number. You will also calculate the mass that is converted to energy during a particular chemical reaction—0.000 000 000 000 003 322 kg, a very small number. Very large and very small numbers such as these are written in *scientific notation*.

Each value expressed in scientific notation has two parts. The first part consists of a number between 1 and 10, but it may have any number of digits after the decimal point. The second part consists of a power of 10. To write the first part, move the decimal point to the right or left so that there is only one nonzero digit to the left of it. The second part of the number—the exponent—is determined by counting the number of decimal places the decimal point must be moved. If the decimal point is moved to the left, the exponent is positive. If the decimal point is moved to the right, the exponent is negative.

$$29\,640\,000\,000\,000\,000\,000\,000 \text{ g becomes } 2.964 \times 10^{22} \text{ g}$$

$$0.000\,000\,000\,000\,003\,332 \text{ kg becomes } 3.322 \times 10^{-15} \text{ kg}$$

Scientific notation not only takes up less space but also eliminates the need to count zeros. For example, in which of the following quantities is it easier to see that there are four significant figures, in 3.322×10^{-15} kg or 0.000 000 000 000 003 332 kg? **Tables 2-6** and **2-7** provide guidelines for using scientific notation in calculations.

TABLE 2-6   Rules for Calculations with Numbers in Scientific Notation

Rule	Example
Addition and subtraction All values must have the same exponent before they can be added or subtracted. The result is the sum or difference of the first factors, all multiplied by the same exponent of 10.	$4.5 \times 10^6 - 2.3 \times 10^5 =$ $45 \times 10^5 - 2.3 \times 10^5 = 42.7 \times 10^5$ $= 4.3 \times 10^6$
Multiplication The first factors of the numbers are multiplied, and the exponents of 10 are added.	$(3.1 \times 10^3)(5.01 \times 10^4) =$ $(3.1 \times 5.01) \times 10^{4+3} = 16 \times 10^7$ $= 1.6 \times 10^8$
Division The first factors of the number are divided, and the exponent of 10 in the denominator is subtracted from the exponent of 10 in the numerator.	$\dfrac{7.63 \times 10^3}{8.6203 \times 10^4} =$ $\dfrac{7.63 \times 10^{3-4}}{8.6203} = 0.885 \times 10^{-1}$ $= 8.85 \times 10^{-2}$

TABLE 2-7 — Rules for Expressing Scientific Notation with Significant Figures

Rule	Example
Use scientific notation to eliminate all placeholding zeros.	$2400 \longrightarrow 2.4 \times 10^4$ (both zeros are not significant)
Convert the number to scientific notation and eliminate zeros before an unwritten decimal point that are not significant figures.	$600 \longrightarrow 6 \times 10^2$ (both zeros are not significant) $750\,000. \longrightarrow 7.50000 \times 10^5$ (all zeros are significant)

SECTION REVIEW

Total recall

1. How does accuracy differ from precision?
2. What do the significant figures in a measurement indicate?
3. Explain the advantage of using scientific notation.
4. What is an exact value? Give an example.

Critical thinking

5. Describe a problem that may arise when you use a calculator to compute an answer.
6. Why is a buret rather than a graduated cylinder used when precise volumes are required in a lab procedure?
7. If you measure the mass of a liquid as 11.50 g and its volume as 9.03 mL, how many significant figures should its density value have?

Practice problems

8. How many significant figures are there in these expressions?
   a. 470. km
   b. 0.0980 m
   c. 30.8900 g
   d. 0.09709 kg
   e. 1000 g/1 kg

9. Perform the following calculations, and express the answers in significant figures.
   a. 32.89 g + 14.21 g
   b. 34.09 L − 1.230 L
   c. 3.45×10^5 g − 2.6×10^3 g
   d. 1.8940 cm × 0.0651 cm
   e. 24.897 mi/0.8700 h

   (handwritten:) 32.89 34.09
   14.21 −1.230
   47.10 32.860

10. Express the following calculations in the proper number of significant figures. Use scientific notation where appropriate.
    a. 129g/ 29.2 mL =
    b. (1.551 mm)(3.260 mm)(4.9001 mm) =
    c. 35 000 kJ/0.250 s =
    d. 0.367 L + 2.51 L + 1.6004 L =

11. A chemical process produces 653 550 kJ of heat in 142.3 min. What is the rate of heat production in kJ/min?

12. Express the following quantities in scientific notation.
    a. 277 088 000 000 000 atoms
    b. 0.000 000 000 000 839 602 g
    c. 700 004 mm

13. **Story Clue** The *Grandcamp* was loaded with 2300 metric tons of ammonium nitrate. Convert this mass to grams of ammonium nitrate. Express your answer in scientific notation to the correct number of significant figures (1 metric ton = 1000 kg).

SPOTLIGHT
ELEMENT

^{2}
He
Helium
4.002 60
$1s^2$

Deep diving with helium

Divers who breathe air while at great undersea depths run the risk of suffering from a condition known as nitrogen narcosis. Nitrogen narcosis can cause a diver to become disoriented and exercise poor judgment, leading to dangerous behavior. To avoid nitrogen narcosis, professional divers who work at depths of more than 60 m breathe heliox, a mixture of helium and oxygen, instead of air.

The greatest advantage of heliox is that it does not cause nitrogen narcosis. A disadvantage of heliox is that it removes body heat faster than air does. This makes a diver breathing heliox feel chilled sooner than a diver breathing air.

Breathing heliox also affects the voice. Helium is much less dense than nitrogen, so vocal cords vibrate faster in a heliox atmosphere. This raises the pitch of the diver's voice and makes the diver sound like Donald Duck. Fortunately, this effect disappears when the diver surfaces and begins breathing air again.

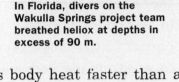

In Florida, divers on the Wakulla Springs project team breathed heliox at depths in excess of 90 m.

Industrial Uses

▶ Helium is used as a lifting gas in balloons and dirigibles.

▶ Helium is used as an inert atmosphere for welding very heavy sections and for high-speed machine welding of long seams.

▶ Helium liquefies at a temperature of −269°C. Liquid helium is used as a coolant in superconductor research.

▶ Helium is used as an inert atmosphere for growing high-purity silicon crystals for semiconducting devices.

Helium was discovered in the sun before it was found on Earth.

WHERE IS IT?

Universe
about 23% by mass

Earth's Crust
0.000001% by mass

Air
0.0005% by mass

internet**connect**

*sci*LINKS
NSTA

TOPIC: Helium
GO TO: www.scilinks.org
KEYWORD: HW023

A BRIEF HISTORY

1888: William Hillebrand discovers that an inert gas is produced when a uranium mineral is dissolved in sulfuric acid.

1908: Ernest Rutherford and Thomas Royds prove that alpha particles emitted during radioactive decay are helium nuclei.

1800   1850   1900

1868: Pierre Janssen, studies the spectra of a solar eclipse and finds evidence of a new element. Edward Frankland, an English chemist, and Joseph Lockyer, an English astronomer, suggest the name *helium.*

1894: Sir William Ramsay and Lord Rayleigh discover argon. They suspect that the gas Hildebrand found in 1888 was argon. They repeat his experiment and find that the gas is helium.

Based on what you have learned about matter and energy, you should now be able to answer the questions posed at the beginning of this chapter.

LOOKING BACK

Where did all the destructive energy that caused this catastrophe come from?
In Section 2-1 you read that chemical compounds contain chemical energy. The chemical energy in the ammonium nitrate that was loaded on the *Grandcamp* was the source of all the destructive energy in the Texas City explosion. In fact, ammonium nitrate is an excellent source of chemical energy that can be used for destructive purposes. Recall in the discussion of chemical energy that the formation of water is an exothermic process. The reason that ammonium nitrate is an explosive is because its decomposition is an exothermic process. The decomposition of water is endothermic—thankfully, it cannot explode. In 1995, a small truck filled with a mixture of ammonium nitrate and fuel oil was used to blow up a federal office building in Oklahoma City, Oklahoma. That explosion killed 168 people.

What happened in terms of energy when the Grandcamp exploded?
Recall that energy can be transformed into various forms. When the ammonium nitrate was ignited, an exothermic chemical reaction took place. In this exothermic reaction, the chemical energy possessed by the ammonium nitrate was transformed into heat, light, sound, and mechanical energy.

Billowing black smoke filled the sky over Texas City in the aftermath of the *Grandcamp* explosion.

How much mass was converted to energy to produce the 350 gigajoules released by the explosion of the ammonium nitrate on the Grandcamp?
When 2300 metric tons of ammonium nitrate is ignited, about 3.5×10^{11} J of energy is released. Using the equation $m = \dfrac{E}{c^2}$, you can calculate the mass equivalent of this energy.

$$m = \frac{3.5 \times 10^{11}\ \text{J}}{(3.00 \times 10^8\ \text{m/s})^2}$$

$$m = \frac{3.5 \times 10^{11}\ \text{J}}{9.00 \times 10^{16}\ \text{m}^2/\text{s}^2}$$

$$m = 3.9 \times 10^{-6}\ \text{kg}$$

Thus, only 3.9 mg of matter was converted to energy in the Texas City explosion. A much greater fraction of matter is converted to energy in nuclear reactions, but the Einstein principle applies equally to both.

HIGHLIGHTS

KEY TERMS

2-1
chemical bond
chemical energy
energy
heat
kinetic energy
law of conservation of
  energy

potential energy
specific heat capacity
system
temperature

2-2
hypothesis

law of conservation of
  mass
polymer
scientific law
theory

2-3
accuracy
precision
significant figure

KEY CONCEPTS

2-1 What is energy?

▶ Energy is the capacity to do some type of work.

▶ Potential energy depends on the position of an object; kinetic energy depends on its motion.

▶ Matter possesses chemical energy as a result of its chemical makeup.

▶ The law of conservation of energy states that the total amount of energy remains constant.

▶ Energy can be transferred between a system and its surroundings.

▶ The transfer of heat energy usually results in a change in temperature.

▶ The equation $E = mc^2$ shows that mass and energy are equivalent.

2-2 What is the process of science?

▶ The scientific method is a systematic approach to solving a problem or answering a question.

▶ Scientific discoveries are sometimes made accidentally.

▶ A hypothesis is a reasonable explanation of an observed phenomenon.

▶ A hypothesis that has been thoroughly tested can lead to a theory, which can take the form of a scientific model.

▶ A scientific law is a statement or mathematical expression that reliably describes the behavior of the natural world.

▶ The law of conservation of mass states that the total quantity of mass remains constant.

2-3 How do chemists measure quantities?

▶ The accuracy of a measurement reflects how close it is to the true or accepted value.

▶ The precision of a measurement reflects how closely several measurements of the same quantity agree.

▶ Measurements and the results of calculations must be reported to the correct number of significant figures.

▶ Scientific notation is used to write both very small and very large numbers.

KEY SKILLS

Review the following models before your exam. Be sure you know these rules.

Rules for Determining Significant Zeros (Table 2-3, p. 59)

Rules for Using Significant Figures in Calculations (Table 2-4, p. 60)

Rules for Calculations with Numbers in Scientific Notation (Table 2-6, p. 63)

Rules for Expressing Scientific Notation with Significant Figures (Table 2-7, p. 64)

How To Determine the number of significant figures (p. 62)

REVIEW & ASSESS

TERM REVIEW

1. All the digits known with certainty plus one estimated digit indicate a measurement's
   _____.
   (scientific notation, significant figures)

2. The energy an object possesses because of its motion is known as _____.
   (kinetic energy, potential energy)

3. _____ is a measurement of the average kinetic energy of the particles in a substance.
   (Specific heat capacity, Temperature)

4. A _____ is often included in an experiment to identify the variable responsible for the results.
   (control, scientific process)

5. Heat energy is transferred between a _____ and its surroundings.
   (system, chemical bond)

6. A _____ is a reasonable explanation of an observation that can be tested.
   (theory, law)

7. A mathematical statement concerning some natural phenomenon is known as a scientific
   _____.
   (model, law)

8. _____ refers to how closely several measurements of the same quantity agree with one another.
   (Precision, Accuracy)

CONCEPT & SKILLS REVIEW

NATURE OF ENERGY

1. Define *kinetic energy*, and give an example.

2. Define *potential energy*, and give an example of an object that possesses it.

3. Give an example of energy transfer that you witnessed today.

4. What is the relationship between mass and energy?

5. State the law of conservation of energy.

6. Explain how a skateboard resting on the ground contains energy. If the skateboard were moving, would it have more energy than it did at rest? Explain.

7. Water evaporates from a puddle on a hot, sunny day faster than on a cold, cloudy day. Explain this phenomenon in terms of interactions between matter and energy.

8. Beaker A contains water at a temperature of 15°C. Beaker B contains water at a temperature of 37°C. Which beaker contains water molecules with greater average kinetic energy? Explain your answer.

INVESTIGATING MATTER AND ENERGY

9. Identify the requirements of a good hypothesis.

10. How does the phrase "cause and effect" relate to the formation of a good hypothesis?

11. Classify the following statements as observation, hypothesis, theory, or law:
    a. A system containing many particles will not go spontaneously from a disordered state to an ordered state.
    b. The substance is silvery white, is fairly hard, and is a good conductor of electricity.
    c. Bases taste bitter and feel slippery in water.
    d. If I pay attention in class, then I will succeed in this course.

12. What components are necessary for an experiment to be valid?

13. Explain the purpose of an experimental control.

14. Explain the relationship between models and theories.

15. Explain the statement, "No theory is written in stone."

16. a. The table below contains data from an experiment in which an air sample is sub-

jected to different pressures. Based on this set of observations, propose a hypothesis that could be tested.

b. What theories can be stated from the data in the table below?

c. Are the data sufficient for the establishment of a scientific law. Why or why not?

The Results of Compressing an Air Sample

Volume (cm^3)	Pressure (kPa)	Volume × pressure (cm^3 × kPa)
100.0	33.3	3330
50.0	66.7	3340
25.0	133.2	3330
12.5	266.4	3330

17. Is a hypothesis that is rejected through experimentation of any value to scientists? Defend your position.

MEASUREMENTS

18. Why it is important to keep track of significant figures?

19. a. If you add several numbers, how many significant figures can the sum have?

b. If you multiply several numbers, how many significant figures can the product have?

20. Perform the following calculations, and express the answers with the correct number of significant figures.

a. $(12.4 \times 7.943) + 0.0064$

b. $\left(\dfrac{246.83}{26.3}\right) - 1.349$

c. $0.1273 - 0.000008$

21. Why can a measured number never be exact?

22. Is it possible for a number to be too small or too large to be expressed adequately in the metric system? Explain your answer.

23. Around 1150, King David I of Scotland defined the inch as the width of a man's thumb at the base of the nail. Discuss the practical limitations of this early unit of measurement.

24. Which of the following are exact numbers?

a. There are 12 eggs in a dozen.

b. Some Major League Baseball pitchers can throw a ball over 140 km/h.

c. The accident injured 21 people.

d. The circumference of the Earth at the equator is 40 000 km.

e. The cost of filling the gas tank came to $17.85.

f. The tank was filled with 54 L of gas.

g. A nickel has a mass of 5 g.

25. Express 743 000 000 in scientific notation to the following number of significant figures:

a. one significant figure

b. two significant figures

c. four significant figures

d. seven significant figures

LINKING CHAPTERS

1. Scientific method
What might have constituted the scientific method Felix Hoffmann used in his study of aspirin that you read about in Chapter 1?

2. Scientific laws
Why are the conservation of energy and the conservation of mass considered laws and not theories?

3. Theme: Conservation
How does Einstein's equation $E = mc^2$ seem to contradict both the law of conservation of energy and the law of conservation of mass?

ALTERNATIVE ASSESSMENTS

Performance assessment

1. Your teacher will provide you with a passage to read. Identify the scientific processes that were used in this passage.

2. Find a solid object with an irregular shape, such as a pencil or a small stone. Determine its density, expressing your answer with the correct number of significant figures.

3. Design an experimental procedure for determining the specific heat capacity of a metal.

Portfolio projects

1. Chemistry and you

For one week, practice your observation skills by listing chemistry-related events around you. After your list is compiled, choose three events that are especially interesting or curious to you. Label three pocket portfolios, one for each event. As you progress through the chapters in this textbook, gather information that helps explain these events. Put pertinent notes, questions, figures, and charts in the folders. When you have enough information to explain each phenomenon, write a report and present it in class.

2. Research and communication

Make a poster of scientific laws that you have encountered in previous science courses. What facts were used to support each of these laws?

3. Chemistry and you

Energy can be transformed from one form to another. For example, light (solar) energy is transformed into chemical energy during photosynthesis. Prepare a list of several different forms of energy. Describe transformations of energy that you encounter on a daily basis. Try to include examples that involve more than one transformation, i.e., light $\longrightarrow$ chemical $\longrightarrow$ mechanical. Select one example, and demonstrate the actual transformation to the class.

4. internet**connect**

SCI*LINKS*™ NSTA

TOPIC: Chance discoveries
GO TO: www.scilinks.org
KEYWORD: HW024

Research and communication

Check the Internet for information about a scientific discovery that was made accidentally. Prepare a report summarizing your findings. Be sure to include the scientific processes that were used in this discovery. Also include information about any technological impact this discovery has had.

1. The equation $E = mc^2$ shows that ____.
   a. chemical reactions are either exothermic or endothermic
   b. mass and energy are equivalent
   c. a hypothesis may develop into a theory
   d. the kinetic energy of an object relates to its motion

2. Which of the following measurements contains three significant figures?
   a. 200 mL
   b. 0.02 mL
   c. 20.2 mL
   d. 200.0 mL

3. A control in an experiment ____.
   a. is often not needed
   b. means that the scientist has everything under control
   c. is required only if the hypothesis leads to the development of a theory
   d. allows the scientist to identify the cause of the results in an experiment

4. A theory differs from a hypothesis in that the former ____.
   a. cannot be disproved
   b. always leads to the formation of a scientific law
   c. has been subjected to experimental testing
   d. represents an educated guess

5. All measurements in science ____.
   a. must be expressed in scientific notation
   b. have some degree of uncertainty
   c. are both accurate and precise
   d. must include only those digits that are known with certainty

6. If the temperature outside is 26°C, then the temperature would be ____ kelvins.
   a. 26
   b. 273
   c. 299
   d. −247

7. When numbers are multiplied or divided, the answer can have no more ____.
   a. significant figures than there are in the measurement with the smallest number of significant figures
   b. significant figures than there are in the measurement with the largest number of significant figures
   c. digits to the right of the decimal point than there are in the measurement with the smallest number of digits to the right of the decimal point
   d. digits to the right of the decimal point than there are in the measurement with the largest number of digits to the right of the decimal point

8. Which of the following is not part of the scientific method?
   a. making measurements
   b. introducing bias
   c. making an educated guess
   d. analyzing data

9. Chemical energy includes kinetic energy because ____.
   a. the atoms in a molecule remain in a fixed position
   b. all forms of energy include kinetic energy
   c. chemical bonds bend and stretch
   d. chemical compounds can release energy when they dissolve in solution

10. The accuracy of a measurement ____.
    a. is how close it is to the true value
    b. does not depend on the instrument being used to measure the object
    c. indicates that the measurement is also precise
    d. is something that scientists rarely achieve

11. A measurement of 23 465 mg converted to grams equals ____.
    a. 2.3465 g
    b. 23.465 g
    c. 234.65 g
    d. 0.23465 g

12. A metal sample has a mass of 45.65 g. The volume of the sample is 16.9 cm³. The density of the sample is ____.
    a. 2.7 g/cm³
    b. 2.70 g/cm³
    c. 0.370 g/cm³
    d. 0.37 g/cm³

Atomic Structure and Electron Configuration

EXCITED ATOMS AND THE FOURTH OF JULY

The national anthem blasts through loudspeakers, and the show is about to begin. It's the Fourth of July, and hundreds have come to watch the fireworks display. Crack! A rocket flares and red, white, and gold stars burst forth. Kaboom!

A dazzling, white chrysanthemum-shaped shower of light fills the sky. The show continues, but wait, something is missing. You've seen red and white fireworks, but what about blue?

The red, white, and gold stars are brilliant but any blue color is dull by comparison. The art of making fireworks is called pyrotechnics, and today's pyrotechnic technology can successfully create red, white, orange, green, gold, pink, and yellow displays but has not produced a bright blue. The search for bright blue keeps fireworks manufacturers scrambling.

Bill Page, the resident chemist at Astro Pyrotechnics fireworks manufacturing firm, is one of a number of chemists trying to produce a bright blue. Bill explains that a lit fuse supplies the energy to cause the fireworks to explode. When they explode, their chemical contents react to produce hot gases. The atoms and molecules in these gases absorb some of the energy released by the explosion. Almost as soon as this energy is absorbed, some of it is released in the form of light, producing spectacular displays of color.

Fireworks manufacturers control what colors are displayed by carefully mixing a variety of chemical compounds. Different elements, either in the elemental state or combined in compounds, produce different colors when heated to the right temperature. For example, compounds of strontium produce red light, aluminum compounds produce bright white light, barium compounds produce green light, and sodium compounds produce yellow light. A copper compound, copper(II) chloride, is the best producer of blue light to be identified so far. But copper(II) chloride is unstable at high temperatures.

A brilliant blue display may be achieved someday by Bill Page or some other pyrotechnic chemist, or maybe by someone who is studying chemistry today—maybe even by you.

CHAPTER LINKS

What is light, and how do various colors of light differ?

What is happening to atoms when fireworks produce colored light?

How does the instability of the copper(II) chloride molecule at high temperatures interfere with its ability to emit blue light?

How do we know atoms exist?

OBJECTIVES

▶ **State** the three laws that support the existence of atoms.

▶ **List** the five principles of Dalton's atomic theory.

▶ **Calculate** the masses of atoms in amu and gram units.

▶ **Describe** how the atomic mass unit was chosen.

Atomic theory

You probably take the existence of atoms for granted. You have never seen an atom, yet you undoubtedly believe they exist. In fact, until recently even scientists had never seen an atom. Without actually seeing them, scientists *theorized* the existence of atoms based on their observations of the properties of matter.

Evidence for the existence of atoms

In Chapter 2 you learned that as early as 400 B.C. Greek philosophers proposed the **atomic theory,** which is the theory that all matter is composed of atoms. These ancient philosophers were great thinkers, but they did not place much emphasis on testing their hypotheses. Experimental results supporting the existence of atoms did not appear until more than 2000 years later, in eighteenth-century Europe. There, early investigators—the first true chemists—noticed certain characteristics shared by all chemical compounds. You read in Chapter 1 that a com-

atomic theory

the theory that all matter is composed of indivisible particles called atoms

▶ **FIGURE 3-1**

The history of chemistry dates back to the work of alchemists who searched for methods to change common metals to gold. Historical evidence indicates that alchemy was practiced throughout the world during the Middle Ages.

pound is a pure substance composed of atoms of two or more elements that are chemically combined. These observations about compounds, and the reactions they undergo, led to three important laws: the law of definite proportions, the law of conservation of mass, and the law of multiple proportions.

The law of definite proportions

The **law of definite proportions** states that a given compound contains the same elements in exactly the same proportions by mass, regardless of the size of the sample or the source of the compound. This means that every molecule of ethylene glycol shown in **Figure 3-2** contains the same number and types of atoms, regardless of how or where the antifreeze was produced. If a sample of ethylene glycol is found to have the formula $C_2H_6O_2$, then the law of definite proportions tells you that all other samples will have the same molecular formula.

Another example to illustrate this law is table salt, sodium chloride. No matter where it is mined or how it is prepared, any sample of pure sodium chloride always consists of the following proportions.

39.34% by mass of sodium and 60.66% by mass of chlorine

As chemists of the eighteenth century began to quantify their study of matter, it became apparent to John Dalton, an English schoolteacher, that there was a way to explain the patterns that emerged. Though the idea of atoms had been proposed well before his time, Dalton could finally use experimental data to support his hypothesis.

law of definite proportions

any sample of a compound always has the same composition

FIGURE 3-2 ▼

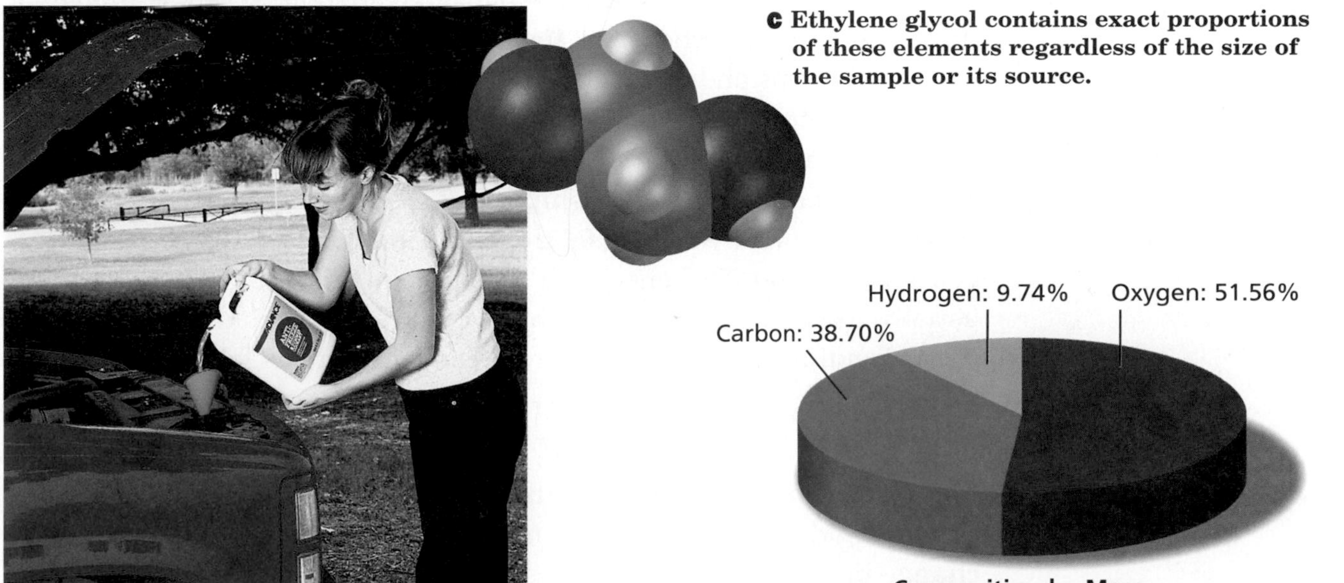

c Ethylene glycol contains exact proportions of these elements regardless of the size of the sample or its source.

Hydrogen: 9.74%   Oxygen: 51.56%

Carbon: 38.70%

Composition by Mass

a Ethylene glycol, the main component of automotive antifreeze, . . .

b . . . is composed of carbon, oxygen, and hydrogen.

For all practical purposes, the total mass of a system remains the same whether atoms are combined, separated, or rearranged. Mass is expressed here in atomic mass units, amu.

Combination of atoms

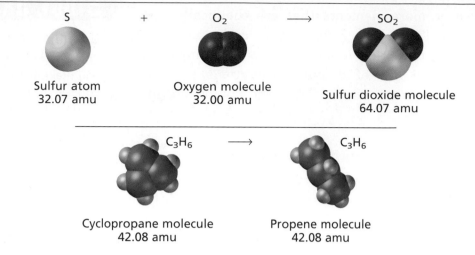

Separation of atoms

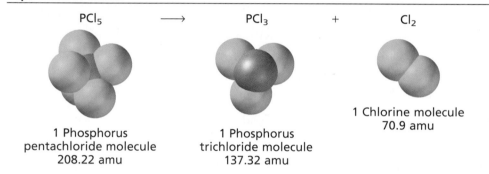

The law of conservation of mass

The law of conservation of mass states that the mass of the products of a reaction equals the mass of the reactants. This law applies when two or more elements combine to produce a compound, when a compound decomposes, or when the atoms in a compound are rearranged. Examples of these reactions are shown in **Figure 3-3.** Notice in Figure 3-3 that the masses of atoms and molecules are expressed in atomic mass units. You will learn more about atomic mass units later in this section.

From Einstein's equation $E = mc^2$, you know that mass and energy are equivalent. This relationship appears to contradict the law of conservation of mass. When 32.06 g of sulfur combines with 32.00 g of oxygen gas 296 800 J of energy is released in this exothermic reaction, usually as heat. Einstein's equation assures us that there must be a corresponding mass loss, which you can calculate as follows.

$$m = \frac{E}{c^2} = \frac{296\,800 \text{ kg} \cdot \text{m}^2/\text{s}^2}{(2.998 \times 10^8 \text{ m/s})^2} = 3.302 \times 10^{-12} \text{ kg}$$

The mass that is lost is so small compared with the masses of the reactants and products that scientists could never hope to detect any change in mass. In fact, the mass change in any chemical reaction is so small that it can be safely ignored. Thus, for all practical purposes, the law of conservation of mass is considered valid.

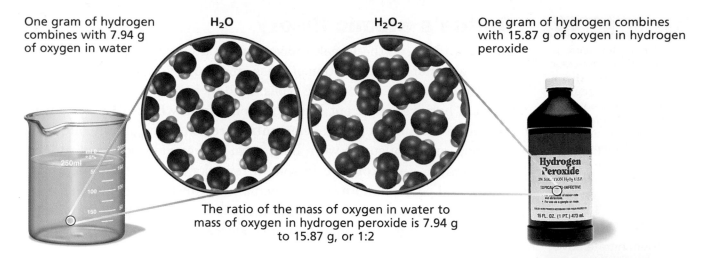

One gram of hydrogen combines with 7.94 g of oxygen in water

H₂O

H₂O₂

One gram of hydrogen combines with 15.87 g of oxygen in hydrogen peroxide

The ratio of the mass of oxygen in water to mass of oxygen in hydrogen peroxide is 7.94 g to 15.87 g, or 1:2

FIGURE 3-4 ▲

For water and hydrogen peroxide, the ratio of the masses of oxygen that combine with a fixed mass of hydrogen is 1:2.

The law of multiple proportions

The **law of multiple proportions** applies to different compounds formed from the same two elements. **Figure 3-4** and **Table 3-1** illustrate this important law. There are three different compounds made from the elements nitrogen and oxygen. All three compounds are gases, but each has its own physical and chemical properties. Table 3-1 shows the mass ratio of oxygen to nitrogen for each of these compounds. Notice that for a given mass of nitrogen, nitrogen dioxide contains twice as much oxygen as does nitrogen monoxide. In turn, nitrogen monoxide contains twice as much oxygen as does dinitrogen monoxide. The masses of oxygen that combine with a fixed mass of nitrogen are ratios of small whole numbers.

law of multiple proportions

the mass ratio for one of the elements in a compound that combines with a fixed mass of another element can be expressed in small whole numbers

TABLE 3-1 | Compounds of Nitrogen and Oxygen and the Law of Multiple Proportions

Name of compound	Description	%O by mass	%N by mass	%O/%N	Mass ratio	Formula
Nitrogen dioxide	poisonous brown gas in smog	69.56	30.44	2.285	4	NO₂
Nitrogen monoxide	colorless gas that reacts readily with oxygen	53.32	46.68	1.142	2	NO
Dinitrogen monoxide	anesthetic, "laughing gas"	36.35	63.65	0.571	1	N₂O

CONCEPT CHECK

1. What is the atomic theory?
2. State the laws of definite proportions, conservation of mass, and multiple proportions.

Black powder used in some fireworks is a mixture of the three components shown. Sulfur and carbon are elements. Potassium nitrate is an ionic compound.

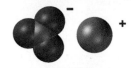

Potassium nitrate, KNO_3

Sulfur, S_8

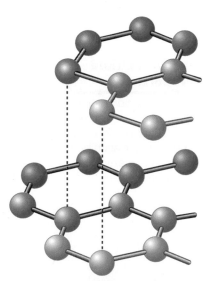

Graphite, C

Dalton's atomic theory

John Dalton used the Greek concept of the atom and the laws of definite proportions, conservation of mass, and multiple proportions to give the atomic theory a scientific basis. Dalton believed that there were about a hundred different kinds of atoms from which all matter was formed. According to Dalton, elements were composed of only one kind of atom and compounds were built from two or more kinds of atoms. For example, the explosive in some fireworks is a mixture of carbon, sulfur, and potassium nitrate. Carbon and sulfur are elements and consist of only one kind of atom. Potassium nitrate is a compound and consists of three different types of atoms. **Figure 3-5** shows models of these structures.

Dalton proposed that the properties of elements differ from one another because their atoms differ. He also recognized that even though they may share the same atoms, compounds have properties that bear no relationship to those of the elements of which they are composed. For example, potassium nitrate, a white salt formed from atoms of potassium, nitrogen, and oxygen, is quite unlike the element potassium, a silvery metal, or the elements nitrogen and oxygen, which are colorless gases found in air.

Dalton recognized that the laws of definite composition, conservation of mass, and multiple proportions could be explained by the existence of tiny particles that combine with one another in small whole-number ratios. Based on this inference, Dalton proposed a theory of the atomic stucture of matter. Dalton's theory includes the five principles shown in **Figure 3-6.**

Dalton's model explained the data chemists had collected about combinations of matter.

A Summary of Dalton's Atomic Theory

1. All matter is made of indivisible and indestructible atoms.

2. All atoms of a given element are identical in their physical and chemical properties.

3. Atoms of different elements differ in their physical and chemical properties.

4. Atoms of different elements combine in simple whole-number ratios to form compounds.

5. Chemical reactions consist of the combination, separation, or rearrangement of atoms.

Dalton's theory explained most of the chemical data of the day and was readily accepted by most of his fellow chemists. As you will learn later in this chapter, evidence gathered since Dalton's time has shown that the first two principles are not valid. A feature of atoms that Dalton overlooked is that most atoms will combine with others of their own kind. Oxygen, for example, is generally found as O_2, in which two oxygen atoms arc combined. Sulfur is S_8. However, Dalton's theory has not been discarded, only modified and expanded as more was learned about the atom.

CONCEPT CHECK

1. According to Dalton, what is the difference between an element and a compound?
2. What are the five principles of Dalton's atomic theory?

Atomic mass

You would not expect something as small as an atom to have much mass, and indeed atoms have a very small mass. For example, a copper atom has a mass of only

1.0552×10^{-25} kg, or 0.000 000 000 000 000 000 000 000 105 52 kg,

on average. That's pretty light! But isn't it remarkable that scientists have been able to measure such a small mass so precisely?

The mass of the copper atom given above, $(1.0552 \times 10^{-25}$ kg) is *an average* mass. Rccall that Dalton thought all atoms of an element had the same mass. But now chemists know this is not true for copper and many other elements. 69.2% of copper atoms have a mass of 1.04497×10^{-25} kg, and 30.8% of copper atoms have a mass of 1.07815×10^{-25} kg. You'll see why the masses differ in Section 3-2.

Each penny shown in **Figure 3-7** has a mass of 3.1276×10^{-3} kg and is made mostly of copper. How many copper atoms are there in one penny? Assuming the penny is pure copper, you can find the number of atoms by dividing the mass of the penny by the average mass of a single copper atom, or by using the following conversion factor.

$$\frac{1 \text{ atom Cu}}{1.0552 \times 10^{-25} \text{ kg}}$$

The number of copper atoms in the penny is

$$3.1276 \times 10^{-3} \text{ kg} \times \frac{1 \text{ atom Cu}}{1.0552 \times 10^{-25} \text{ kg}} = 2.9640 \times 10^{22} \text{ atoms Cu}$$

This huge number serves to illustrate how small atoms are and that they are usually encountered in vast numbers.

FIGURE 3-7 ▲

These pennies each contain 2.9640×10^{22}, or about 29 640 000 000 000 000 000 000, copper atoms.

Masses of atoms are measured in atomic mass units

Clearly, atoms are so light that the gram is not a very convenient unit for measuring their masses. Even the picogram (10^{-12} g) is unsuitable. A special mass unit is used to measure **atomic mass.** This unit has two names—the *atomic mass unit,* amu, and the *dalton,* Da. In this book, atomic mass unit will used. One atomic mass unit is equal to $1.6605402 \times 10^{-27}$ kg. The periodic table of the elements on the inside back cover of this book lists the atomic mass in atomic mass units. The mass of an atom in kilograms can be found by multiplying the atom's atomic mass in atomic mass units by the number of kilograms per atomic mass unit. For example, you can find the mass of a copper atom by performing the following calculation.

$$(63.546 \text{ amu})(1.6605402 \times 10^{-27} \text{ kg/amu}) = 1.0552 \times 10^{-25} \text{ kg}$$

This mass was reported on page 79 as the average mass of a copper atom. The periodic table lists the *average* mass of atoms for those elements that have atoms of different masses.

Chemists and physicists agree on the scale

You may wonder why 1 amu is equal to $1.6005402 \times 10^{-27}$ kg. After all, wouldn't it be more convenient if 1 amu were equal to 1.00×10^{-27} kg? Actually, the atomic mass unit has been defined in a number of different ways over the years. Originally atomic masses expressed the ratio of the mass of an atom to that of a hydrogen atom. Using hydrogen as the standard turned out to be inconvenient because hydrogen doesn't react with many elements. Early chemists determined atomic masses by comparing how much of one element reacted with another element. Because oxygen combines with almost all other elements, oxygen became the standard of comparison. The atomic mass of oxygen was defined as exactly 16, and the atomic masses of the other elements were based on this standard. But this choice also led to difficulties. Oxygen exists as three isotopes. Physicists based their atomic masses on assigning 16.0000 as the mass of the most common oxygen isotope. Chemists, on the other hand, decided that 16.0000 should be the average mass of all oxygen isotopes, weighted according to their abundances. Can you imagine the confusion that caused? To a physicist the atomic mass of fluorine was 19.0044, but to a chemist it was 18.9991. Finally, in 1962, a joint conference of chemists and physicists agreed on a scale based on an isotope of carbon, described in **Figure 3-8.** This scale, used by all scientists today, defines the atomic mass unit as exactly ¹⁄₁₂ the mass of one carbon-12 atom.

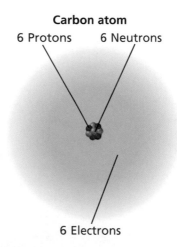

Carbon atom

6 Protons   6 Neutrons

6 Electrons

$^{12}_{6}\text{C}$

Carbon

▲ FIGURE 3-8

Carbon-12 is the standard for the atomic mass scale. 1 amu = ¹⁄₁₂ the mass of carbon-12.

The SI unit for amount is the mole

So far we have discussed atoms in microscopic amounts, usually at the level of individual atoms. But most chemistry is done on the macroscopic level, and chemists often find it useful to work with a unit that represents a large collection of atoms. Such a unit serves as a bridge between the invisible world of atoms and the macroscopic world of materials and objects. This unit is called a **mole,** mol, and is the SI unit for amount of substance.

How big is a mole? A mole is a collection of $6.022\,1367 \times 10^{23}$ particles. In this text, the mole is usually rounded to 6.022×10^{23} particles. What is so special about this number? The answer is that 1 mol of atoms of any element has a mass in grams numerically equal to the atom's mass in atomic mass units. For example, the mass of a fluorine atom is 19.9984 amu, while the mass of one mole of fluorine atoms is

$$19.9984\ \text{amu} \times \frac{1.660\,5402 \times 10^{-27}\ \text{kg}}{1\ \text{amu}} \times \frac{1000\ \text{g}}{1\ \text{kg}}$$

$$\times \frac{6.022\,1367 \times 10^{23}}{1\ \text{mol}} = 19.9984\ \text{g/mol}$$

In recognition of the value and importance of the number 6.022×10^{23}, scientists named it in honor of Amedeo Avogadro (1776–1856), shown in **Figure 3-9.** He was an Italian scientist whose ideas were crucial to the early development of chemistry. **Avogadro's constant** is the number of particles, $6.022\,137 \times 10^{23}$, in exactly 1 mol of a pure substance.

To appreciate how large Avogadro's constant is, imagine that all 6 billion people on Earth were to do nothing but count the atoms in 1 mol of an element. If each person counted at the rate of one atom per second, it would take over 3 million years to count all of the atoms in 1 mol!

FIGURE 3-9 ▲

Avogadro was a lawyer who later became a professor of physics and mathematics.

mole

the SI unit for measuring the amount of a substance

Avogadro's constant

the number of particles in 1 mol, $6.022\,1367 \times 10^{23}/\text{mol}$

SECTION REVIEW

Total recall

1. What laws provided evidence for the existence of atoms?

2. Which atom is used as the standard for the atomic mass scale?

3. State the law of definite proportions.

4. What is the SI unit for the amount of a substance?

Critical thinking

5. Which of Dalton's five principles still apply to the structure of an atom?

6. How does Einstein's equation $E = mc^2$ seem to contradict the law of conservation of mass?

7. What is the mass in grams of 1.00 mol of oxygen-16 atoms?

8. Three different compounds contain the elements sulfur (S) and fluorine (F). How do the following data support the law of multiple proportions?

   compound a: 1.188 g of F for every 1.000 g of S

   compound b: 2.375 g of F for every 1.000 g of S

   compound c: 3.563 g of F for every 1.000 g of S

9. Calculate the mass of a sulfur atom in kilograms using the atomic mass of sulfur.

What is the internal structure of atoms?

OBJECTIVES

▶ **Describe** the evidence for the existence of electrons and their presence in atoms.

▶ **Explain** how Rutherford's experiments led to the discovery of the nucleus.

▶ **Discuss** atoms of different elements in terms of the numbers of electrons, protons, and neutrons they contain.

▶ **Define** the terms *atomic number, mass number,* and *isotope.*

---

internetconnect

SCI LINKS

NSTA

TOPIC: Subatomic particles
GO TO: www.scilinks.org
KEYWORD: HW031

---

anode

an electrode through which electrons enter a metal

cathode

an electrode through which electrons leave a metal

Subatomic particles

Experiments by several scientists in the mid-1800s led to the first modification of Dalton's atomic theory. Atoms were found to be divisible after all. Scientists discovered that the atom was made of smaller particles, referred to as *subatomic particles.* While many types of subatomic particles have been discovered, only three are important to your study of chemistry. These particles are electrons, protons, and neutrons.

The first evidence that atoms consist of subatomic particles was obtained by researchers whose main interest was electricity, not atomic structure. One of these scientists was the English physicist J. J. Thomson. To study the flow of electric current, Thomson pumped most of the air out of a glass tube such as the one shown in **Figure 3-10.** He then applied a voltage to two metal plates placed at each end of the tube. These plates are called *electrodes.* One of these plates, called the **anode,** was attached to the positive terminal of the voltage source, so it had a positive charge. The other plate, called a **cathode,** carried a negative charge because it was attached to the negative terminal of the voltage source.

▶ FIGURE 3-10

Electric current flows through the cathode-ray tube when the electrodes are connected to a source of high voltage.

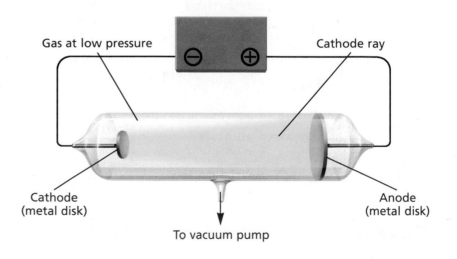

Gas at low pressure

Cathode ray

Cathode (metal disk)

Anode (metal disk)

To vacuum pump

Thomson observed that rays emerged from the cathode and struck the anode and the nearby glass walls of the tube. Because of their origin, these rays were called *cathode rays*. The apparatus shown in Figure 3-10 is called a cathode-ray tube (CRT). CRTs have become an important part of modern technology, being used in television sets, such as the one shown in **Figure 3-11,** computer monitors, oscilloscopes, and radar displays. For reasons that will soon be obvious, cathode rays are now usually called electron beams.

Cathode rays are composed of electrons

Thomson and other physicists observed that when a small paddle wheel was placed in the path of cathode rays, the wheel was set in motion. This observation suggested that the cathode rays consisted of tiny particles that were hitting the paddles of the wheel. The particles that made up the ray had mass. Because the rays originated at the negatively charged cathode, scientists reasoned that the particles, which they called **electrons,** were negatively charged. Thomson confirmed this prediction by observing the response of electrons to electric and magnetic fields, as illustrated in **Figure 3-12.** Subsequent experiments have shown that the mass of an electron is $5.485\,799 \times 10^{-4}$ amu, which is almost 2000 times smaller than the mass of the lightest atom. The charge of an electron was found to be $-1.602\,189 \times 10^{-19}$ C, where C stands for *coulombs,* the SI unit of electric charge.

Physicists soon found that the cathode rays were always identical, regardless of the metal used. Furthermore, the metal nor the gas was changed by the flow of current. The inescapable conclusion is that the cathode rays are electrons. It was later established that atoms of all elements contain electrons.

Electrons are negatively charged, but atoms are neutral. Therefore, atoms must contain positive charges that balance the negative charges of the electrons. Scientists could no longer view atoms as the simplest form of matter. The atom could be broken down into still smaller particles. Research continued to discover the nature of these particles. Dalton's theory that atoms were indivisible had to be abandoned.

FIGURE 3-11 ▲

The image on a television screen or a computer monitor is produced when cathode rays strike the special coating on the inside of the screen.

electron

small, negatively charged particle found in atoms

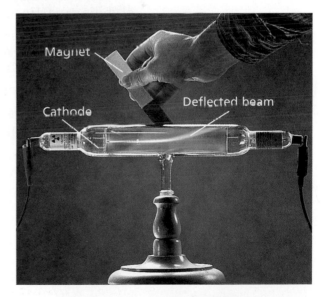

FIGURE 3-12 ▲

A magnet near the cathode-ray tube causes the beam to be deflected as shown. The deflection of the beam indicates that the particles that compose the beam have a negative charge.

CONCEPT CHECK

1. What observations led scientists to propose the existence of subatomic particles?
2. What type of electrical charge does an electron carry?

▲ **FIGURE 3-13**

Thomson's model of an atom featured negatively charged electrons embedded in a ball of positive charge.

alpha particle

a positively charged particle produced by some nuclear disintegrations

nucleus

the central region of an atom made up of protons and neutrons

The nucleus

Thomson proposed that the electrons of an atom were embedded in a positively charged ball of matter. His picture of an atom, which is shown in **Figure 3-13,** was named the *plum-pudding model* because it resembled plum pudding, a dessert consisting of a ball of sweet cake with pieces of fruit embedded in it. One of Thomson's former students soon replaced the plum-pudding model of the atom.

Rutherford discovered the nucleus

It was the work of New Zealander Ernest Rutherford that made the plum-pudding model obsolete. His team of researchers carried out the experiment illustrated in **Figure 3-14.** A beam of small positively charged particles, called **alpha particles,** was directed at a thin gold foil. The team measured the angles at which the particles were deflected from their former straight-line paths as they emerged from the foil.

Rutherford found that most of the alpha particles shot at the foil passed straight through undeflected. But a very small number were deflected, some even backward, as illustrated in Figure 3-14. This greatly surprised the researchers—nothing like that was predicted by Thomson's plum-pudding model. As Ernest Rutherford expressed it, "It was almost as if you fired a 15-inch shell into a piece of tissue paper and it came back and hit you." He went on to reason that only a very concentrated positive charge, localized somewhere within the gold atom, could possibly repel the fast-moving, positively charged alpha particles sufficiently to reverse their direction of travel.

In addition, Rutherford hypothesized that this localized region, called the **nucleus,** must have a large mass compared with the alpha particle, or else the incoming particle would have knocked the positive

▼ **FIGURE 3-14**

a In the gold foil experiment, small positively charged particles were directed at a thin foil of gold atoms.

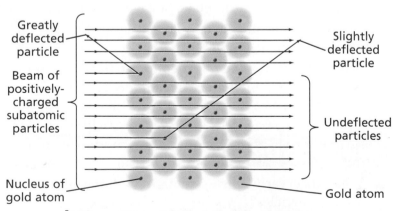

Gold Foil Micro View

Greatly deflected particle

Beam of positively-charged subatomic particles

Nucleus of gold atom

Slightly deflected particle

Undeflected particles

Gold atom

b The pattern of deflected alpha particles supported Rutherford's hypothesis that gold atoms were mostly empty space.

FIGURE 3-15

If the nucleus of an atom were the size of one of the marbles shown, then the whole atom would be about the size of a football stadium.

charge out of the way. The reason that most of the alpha particles were undeflected, Rutherford argued, was that most of the gold foil was almost empty space.

And so our modern picture of the nuclear atom emerged. The nucleus is the dense, central portion of the atom that contains all of the atom's positive charge and nearly all of its mass, but only a very small fraction of its volume. By measuring the fraction of alpha particles that were deflected and their angles of deflection, scientists calculated the radius of the nucleus to be less than $\frac{1}{10\,000}$ of the radius of the whole atom. **Figure 3-15** puts these relative sizes into perspective.

CONCEPT CHECK

1. How did the results of the gold foil experiment lead Rutherford to recognize the existence of atomic nuclei?

2. The fact that the vast majority of alpha particles passed undeflected through the gold foil indicates what about atoms?

Protons and neutrons

The positive charges that repelled the alpha particles in the gold foil experiments were present on subatomic particles named **protons,** found in all nuclei. The charge of a proton was found to be exactly equal, but opposite in sign, to the charge of an electron. The mass of a proton was determined to be 1.0073 amu, almost 2000 times the mass of an electron.

Because protons and electrons have equal but opposite charges, a neutral atom must contain equal numbers of protons and electrons. However, the masses of all atoms except for hydrogen were known to be

proton

a particle with a positive charge found in atomic nuclei

TABLE 3-2 Properties of the Three Fundamental Subatomic Particles

Particle	Symbol	Charge (C)	Common charge notation	Mass (amu)	Where found
Electron	e, e^-, or $_{-1}^{0}e$	-1.602×10^{-19}	-1	0.000 549	outside nucleus
Proton	p, p^+, or $_{1}^{1}p^+$	$+1.602 \times 10^{-19}$	$+1$	1.007 276	inside nucleus
Neutron	n or $_{0}^{1}n$	0	0	1.008 665	inside nucleus

greater than the combined masses of their protons and electrons. What could account for the rest of the mass? Hoping to find an answer, scientists began to search for a third subatomic particle.

About 30 years after the discovery of the electron, Irene Joliot-Curie (daughter of famous scientists Marie and Pierre Curie) discovered that when the element beryllium was bombarded with alpha particles, a beam of great penetrating power was produced. The British scientist James Chadwick found that this beam was made of particles that were not deflected by electric or magnetic fields. Logically, he concluded that the particles carried no electric charge. Further investigation showed that these neutral particles, which were named **neutrons,** have a mass of 1.0087 amu and are present in almost all atomic nuclei. **Table 3-2** summarizes the characteristics of the three fundamental subatomic particles.

neutron

a particle with no electric charge found in atomic nuclei

Atomic number is the number of protons in the nucleus

atomic number

the number of protons in the nucleus of an atom

The number of protons an atom contains is known as its **atomic number.** Because all atoms are electrically neutral, the number of electrons must equal the number of protons. Thus, if you know the atomic number of an element, you immediately know the number of protons and the number of electrons found in one of its atoms. **Figure 3-16** shows the relationship between atomic number and atomic structure for oxygen.

To date, scientists have identified a total of 111 elements, with atomic numbers from 1 to 111. Note that atomic numbers are always

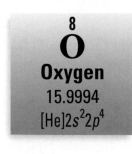

► FIGURE 3-16

The atomic number shown on the periodic table for oxygen tells you that the oxygen atom has eight protons and eight electrons.

Oxygen atom

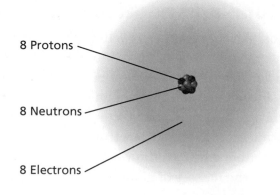

8 Protons

8 Neutrons

8 Electrons

whole numbers—an atom can't have 2.5 protons! In addition, each atomic number is unique to a particular element. For example, all atoms with the atomic number 8 are oxygen atoms; conversely, all oxygen atoms have the atomic number 8.

Mass number is the total number of particles in the nucleus

In addition to atomic number, every atomic nucleus can be described by its **mass number.** The mass number is equal to the total number of particles in the nucleus, which is the total number of protons plus neutrons. For example, a particular atom of boron has a mass number of 11. Therefore, this atom has a total of 11 protons and neutrons in its nucleus. Recall that the atomic number for an atom of boron is 5 because it has 5 protons in its nucleus. You can calculate the number of neutrons the boron atom has by subtracting its atomic number (the number of protons) from its mass number (the number of protons and neutrons). In our example, the boron atom has 6 neutrons.

$$\begin{aligned}
\text{number of protons and neutrons (mass number)} &= 11 \\
\underline{\textit{minus} \text{ the number of protons (atomic number)} = -5} \\
\text{number of neutrons} &= 6
\end{aligned}$$

How many protons, electrons, and neutrons are present in an atom of copper whose atomic number is 29 and whose mass number is 64?

Unlike the atomic number, which is the same for all atoms of an element, mass number can vary among atoms of a single element. In other words, all atoms of an element have the same number of protons, but they might have different numbers of neutrons. The atomic number of all oxygen atoms is 8, as shown in Figure 3-16, but oxygen atoms can have mass numbers of 16, 17, and 18. These atoms differ from one another in having 8, 9, and 10 neutrons, respectively.

Atomic structures can be represented by symbols

Each element has a name, and the same name is given to its atoms. For example, sulfur is composed of sulfur atoms, and tin consists of tin atoms. As you learned in Chapter 1, each element also has a symbol—S for sulfur, and Sn for tin—and the same symbol is used to represent one of its atoms. Thus, S represents a single atom of sulfur, 2S represents two sulfur atoms, and 8S represents eight sulfur atoms. However, chemists also write S_8 to indicate that the eight sulfur atoms are joined together as the molecule modeled in **Figure 3-17.**

Atomic number and mass number are sometimes written with an element's symbol. The atomic number always appears to the lower left of the symbol. For example, the symbols for the first five elements are written with atomic numbers as follows.

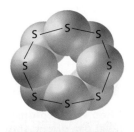

FIGURE 3-17 ▲

In nature, elemental sulfur exists as eight sulfur atoms joined to form a wreath-shaped molecule.

$$_1\text{H} \qquad _2\text{He} \qquad _3\text{Li} \qquad _4\text{Be} \qquad _5\text{B}$$

Note that these subscript numbers add no new information; they are simply reminders of what the atomic number of a particular element is. On the other hand, mass numbers provide information that specifies particular atoms of an element. Mass numbers are written at the upper left of the symbol. The following are the symbols of stable atoms of the first five elements.

$$^{1}\text{H} \quad ^{2}\text{H} \quad ^{3}\text{He} \quad ^{4}\text{He} \quad ^{6}\text{Li} \quad ^{7}\text{Li} \quad ^{9}\text{Be} \quad ^{10}\text{B} \quad ^{11}\text{B}$$

Both numbers may be written with the symbol. For example, the most abundant isotope of each of the first five elements can be represented by one of the following symbols.

$$^{1}_{1}\text{H} \quad ^{4}_{2}\text{He} \quad ^{7}_{3}\text{Li} \quad ^{9}_{4}\text{Be} \quad ^{11}_{5}\text{B}$$

It is important to keep in mind that all atoms of an element have the same number of protons, and therefore the same atomic number, but may have different numbers of neutrons, and therefore different mass numbers. You will find out about the variability in the number of neutrons later in this section.

CONCEPT CHECK

1. What three subatomic particles are important to chemistry? What is the electric charge of each?
2. One particular atom of calcium can be represented as $^{44}_{20}\text{Ca}$. How many of each type of subatomic particle does this atom have?

Neutrons, protons, and Coulomb's law

Coulomb's law

the force between two charged particles is inversely proportional to the square of the distance between them

Coulomb's law states that the closer two charges come together, the greater the force between them. In fact, the force increases by a factor of four as the distance decreases by a factor of two, as illustrated in **Figure 3-18.** If the charges have different signs, they attract one another; if both charges have the same sign, they repel one another. As a consequence of their like charges, two or more free protons cannot come close enough together to form an atomic nucleus.

▼ **FIGURE 3-18**

a When two protons are 0.020 pm apart, they repel each other with a force of 0.58 N.

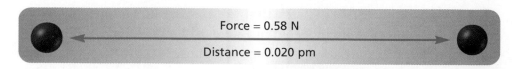

Force = 0.58 N
Distance = 0.020 pm

b The repulsive force quadruples to 2.32 N when the distance diminishes to 0.010 pm.

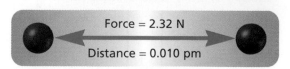

Force = 2.32 N
Distance = 0.010 pm

Keeping in mind Coulomb's law, it is easy to understand why—with the exception of some atoms of hydrogen—there are no atoms with nuclei containing only protons. All protons are positively charged, and at the close distances inside tiny nuclei, the forces of repulsion between particles of like charge are enormous.

Protons and neutrons can form a stable nucleus despite the repulsion between protons, due to the attraction of the *strong force*. This force is greater than the repulsive force at close distances. The simplest multi-proton atom, with a nucleus consisting of two protons and one neutron, is illustrated in **Figure 3-19.** This atom is called helium-3 because its mass number, the number of particles in its nucleus, is 3. Every atom of helium has 2 protons and therefore an atomic number of 2. But as you can see, not all helium atoms have a mass number of 3; in fact, 99.999% of helium atoms are helium-4.

Isotopes of an element have the same number of protons but different numbers of neutrons

All atoms of an element have the same atomic number and therefore the same number of protons. However, for many elements, the number of neutrons can vary. Atoms of the same element with different numbers of neutrons are called **isotopes.** The two atoms modeled in **Figure 3-19** are stable isotopes of helium.

The variation in the number of neutrons among isotopes is responsible for the average atomic masses of elements being far from whole numbers. A majority of the elements exist as mixtures of two or more isotopes. For example, the 82 protons in a lead nucleus are stable with 122, 124, 125, or 126 neutrons. When expressed in amu, the actual mass of each isotope is always very close to its mass number. **Table 3-3,** on the next page, lists lead's four stable isotopes, and all are present in natural lead. The abundance of lead isotopes varies a little depending on the source of the sample; chemists have therefore agreed on representative values. You can infer from the data in Table 3-3 that the average atomic mass for lead would be closer to 208 amu than to 204 amu.

isotope

one of two or more atoms of the same element with different numbers of neutrons

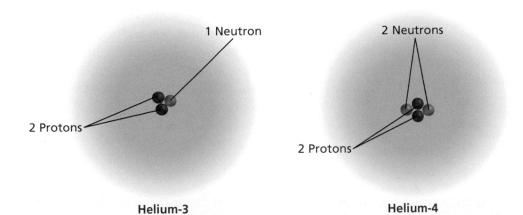

Helium-3   Helium-4

FIGURE 3-19 ◄

The two stable isotopes of helium are helium-3 and helium-4. The nucleus of a helium-4 atom is known as an alpha particle.

Name of atom	Number of neutrons	Symbol	Mass (amu)	Abundance (%)
Lead-204	122	^{204}Pb	203.973	1.4
Lead-206	124	^{206}Pb	205.974	24.1
Lead-207	125	^{207}Pb	206.976	22.1
Lead-208	126	^{208}Pb	207.977	52.4

TABLE 3-3 The Stable Isotopes of Lead—All Lead Atoms Have 82 Electrons and 82 Protons

Unlike lead, there are elements for which there is only one stable isotope. Beryllium is such an element. Outside nuclear laboratories, all the beryllium on Earth is ^9_4Be. Beryllium's four protons need five neutrons to form a stable nucleus. With four or six neutrons, or any number other than five, the beryllium atom is unstable, and sooner or later it will disintegrate in ways that are discussed in Chapter 18. Atoms having unstable nuclear configurations are called **radioisotopes** of an element.

Some elements have no stable isotopes. Technetium, element 43, is the lightest such element. There is no number of neutrons that will form a stable nucleus with its 43 protons. There are no known deposits of technetium on Earth. It was the first element to be artificially produced in a laboratory.

radioisotope

an unstable atom that undergoes radioactive decay

SECTION REVIEW

Total recall

1. How are isotopes of the same element alike? different?

2. Describe the major differences between electrons, protons, and neutrons in terms of size, mass, and location.

Critical thinking

3. Determine the number of electrons, protons, and neutrons for each of the following.

    a. $^{235}_{92}\text{U}$ **b.** $^{106}_{46}\text{Pd}$ **c.** $^{133}_{55}\text{Cs}$

4. How did a study of electricity contribute to an understanding of atomic structure?

5. Why did some of the alpha particles shot at the gold foil in Rutherford's experiment bounce backward?

6. What role does the strong force play in atomic structure?

7. **Story Clue** The element barium (Ba) is used in fireworks to produce a green color. All barium atoms contain 56 protons. One isotope of barium contains 74 neutrons, and another isotope contains 81 neutrons. Write the symbols for these two isotopes of barium.

CONSUMER FOCUS

ESSENTIAL ELEMENTS

Good health is elementary

Which of the 111 elements are needed for a healthful life? Four elements—hydrogen, oxygen, carbon, and nitrogen—account for more than 99% of all the atoms in the human body. These elements are the major components of the carbohydrate, lipid, and protein molecules that our bodies need for support, growth, and repair. Likewise, these four are the major elements in the food that you eat.

Another seven elements are used by our bodies in substantial quantities, more than 0.1 g per day. These are listed in the table below, together with the role that each plays in the body's struc-

internetconnect

SCI**LINKS** NSTA

TOPIC: Essential elements
GO TO: www.scilinks.org
KEYWORD: HW033

ture and chemistry. These elements are known as *macronutrients* or, more commonly, as "minerals."

Some elements, known as **trace elements** or **micronutrients,** are necessary for healthy human life, but each only in very small amounts. In many cases, less than 15 ng per day is required for good health. Remember that *ng* stands for "nanograms" and *nano* means 10^{-9}, so you can easily show that you need less than 0.0004 g of each of these elements during your entire lifetime.

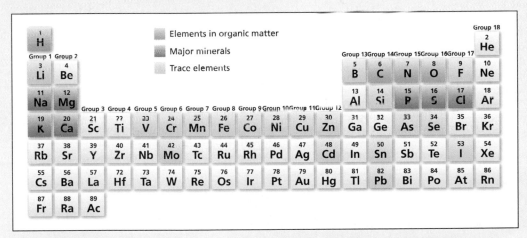

Elements Other Than H, O, C, and N Needed to Sustain Human Life

Element	Symbol	Role in human body chemistry
Calcium	Ca	bones, teeth; essential for blood clotting and muscle contraction
Phosphorus	P	bones, teeth; component of nucleic acids, including DNA
Potassium	K	present as K^+ in all body fluids; essential for nerve action
Sulfur	S	component of many proteins; essential for blood clotting
Chlorine	Cl	present as Cl^- in all body fluids; important to maintaining salt balance
Sodium	Na	present as Na^+ in all body fluids; essential for nerve and muscle action
Magnesium	Mg	bones, teeth; essential for muscle action

How are an atom's electrons configured?

OBJECTIVES

▶ **Describe** the nature of light and how it is produced.

▶ **Explain** how the wavelengths of light emitted by an atom provide information about electron energy levels.

▶ **Compare** the atomic models of Rutherford and Bohr.

▶ **Describe** the quantum mechanical interpretation of electrons in atoms.

▶ **State** Pauli's exclusion principle, the aufbau principle, and Hund's rule, and **describe** their roles in determining the electron configuration of atoms.

Electrons and light

To a chemist, electrons are the most important parts of an atom. Though they are an insignificant part of an atom's mass, electrons occupy most of an atom's volume and determine virtually all of its chemistry. Much of our knowledge of electrons in atoms comes from studying the light they emit, so this section starts with a review of some properties of light. **Figure 3-20** shows the range of wavelengths for visible light and some other radiations.

▼ **FIGURE 3-20**

The electromagnetic spectrum is composed of radiation with a broad range of wavelengths. Our eyes can detect only the visible spectrum.

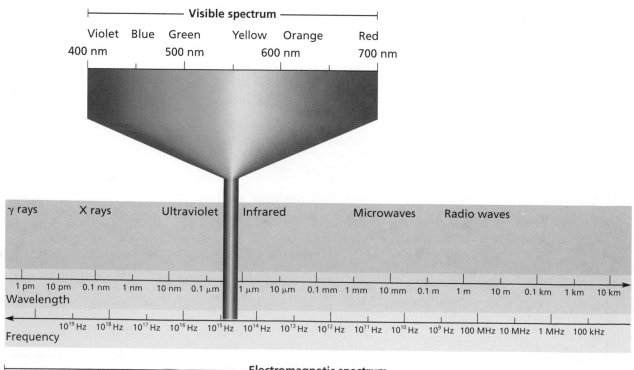

Light is an electromagnetic wave

Sunlight, when passed through a glass prism, produces the *visible spectrum*—all the colors of light that the human eye can perceive. You can see from Figure 3-20 that the visible spectrum is only a tiny portion of the **electromagnetic spectrum.** The electromagnetic spectrum also includes X rays, ultraviolet and infrared radiation, microwaves, and radio waves. The term *light* is often applied to regions of the spectrum that we cannot see, such as ultraviolet light.

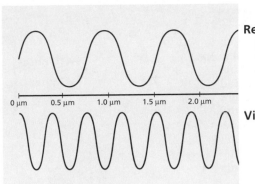
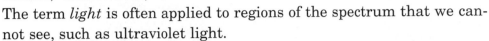

Red light
Low frequency
Long wavelength

Violet light
High frequency
Short wavelength

Light, and all other electromagnetic radiation, can be thought of as moving waves. These waves, illustrated in **Figure 3-21,** can be described by three characteristics: speed, wavelength, and frequency. Though they move a little more slowly through matter, all electromagnetic waves travel at the same high speed in empty space. This is the so-called *speed of light,* which, as you saw in Chapter 2, is 2.998×10^8 m/s. Light travels so fast that it takes only 500 seconds to travel the 150 million kilometers between the sun and the Earth.

The distance between two consecutive peaks or troughs of a wave is its *wavelength,* and it is measured in meters. The wavelengths of electromagnetic radiation range from less than 10^{-13} m for gamma rays to more than 10^5 m for radio waves. Wavelength is closely related to frequency. The *frequency* of a wave is the number of waves that pass a stationary point in one second. One wave per second is called a *hertz,* Hz, the unit in which frequency is measured. One hertz is equal to one event per second. The frequencies of electromagnetic radiation range from less than 1000 Hz to more than 10^{22} Hz.

There is a very simple relationship between speed, wavelength, and frequency of electromagnetic waves, as shown in the following equation.

$$frequency \times wavelength = speed\ of\ light$$

With this equation, you can determine the wavelength of an electromagnetic wave given its frequency, or determine its frequency given its wavelength. For example, if you know that red light has a wavelength of 7.6×10^{-7} m, the following calculation provides its frequency.

$$frequency = \frac{speed}{wavelength} = \frac{2.998 \times 10^8\ \text{m/s}}{7.6 \times 10^{-7}\ \text{m}} =$$
$$3.9 \times 10^{14}/\text{s} = 3.9 \times 10^{14}\ \text{Hz}$$

FIGURE 3-21

The frequency and wavelength of a wave are inversely related. As frequency increases, wavelength decreases. The higher the frequency of an electromagnetic wave, the shorter its wavelength.

electromagnetic spectrum

the total range of electromagnetic radiation, ranging from the longest radio waves to the shortest gamma waves

internet**connect**

SC*LINKS*
NSTA

TOPIC: Electromagnetic spectrum
GO TO: www.scilinks.org
KEYWORD: HW034

The Rutherford model of the atom could not explain line-emission spectra

In the late nineteenth century, scientists observed that a characteristic lavender light was produced when a high-voltage electric current was passed through hydrogen gas. When the lavender light was sent through

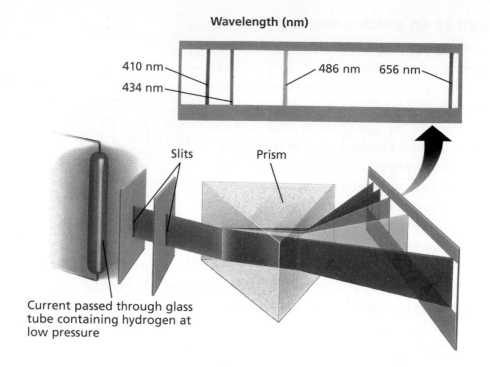

► FIGURE 3-22

Excited hydrogen atoms emit a lavendar glow. When the visible portion of the emitted light is passed through a prism, it is separated into specific wavelengths that are part of hydrogen's line-emission spectrum.

Current passed through glass tube containing hydrogen at low pressure

line-emission spectrum

distinct lines of colored light that are produced when the light produced by excited atoms of an element is passed through a prism

a narrow slit, then through a prism, it separated into distinct lines of different colors. The spectrum shown in **Figure 3-22** is known as a **line-emission spectrum.** Experiments with other elements in the gas phase showed that each element emits characteristic colors of light that produce a distinctive line-emission spectrum for that element.

Scientists suspected that line-emission spectra provided information about the basic structure of atoms. But how could these distinctive spectra be explained by the arrangement of protons, neutrons, and electrons in atoms? The answer was provided by a young Danish physicist named Niels Bohr.

Excited electrons emit light

In 1913, Bohr showed that line-emission spectra could be explained by assuming that an electron in an atom is able to exist in any one of a number of energy states. An electron could move from a low energy state to a high energy state by absorbing energy. Conversely, an electron could move from a higher energy state to a lower energy state by releasing energy.

ground state

the lowest energy state of a quantized system

excited state

the condition of an atom in a higher energy state than ground state

Normally, each electron in an atom is in a state of lowest possible energy, a **ground state.** If an electron acquires additional energy, then it is in an **excited state.** This unstable state is associated with a specific amount of energy that is greater than the ground state. The electron will quickly "fall" back to its ground state, and when it does, the excess energy is released as light. This light has a characteristic frequency (color) that reflects the energy released. It is the emission of characteristic frequencies of light that produces line-emission spectra.

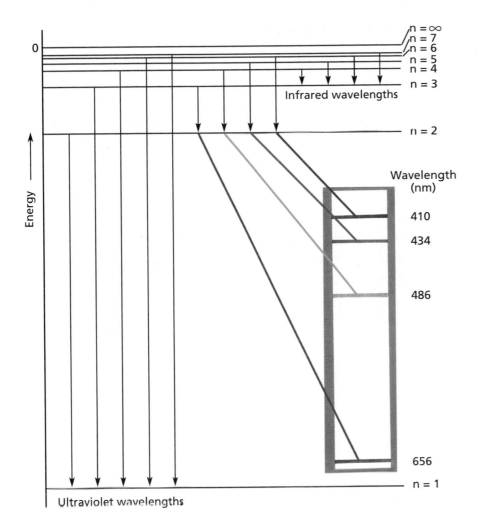

FIGURE 3-23 ◀

The seven lowest energy levels for the electron in the hydrogen atom are shown. When an electron in the $n = 3$ level falls to the $n = 2$ level, a flash of cherry red light, of wavelength 6.563×10^{-7} m, is emitted.

According to Bohr, the only possible energies for the electron in the hydrogen atom are defined by the following equation.

$$\text{energy of electron} = \frac{-2.179 \times 10^{-18}\,\text{J}}{n^2}$$

In the equation, n can be any positive whole number, such as 1, 2, 3, 4, and so on. **Figure 3-23** shows several of these energy levels. A number such as n, which can take on only certain definite values, is called a **quantum number.** Bohr's formula matched the spectroscopic data so well that there was little doubt his hypothesis was correct.

When energies can only adopt certain values, the energy is said to be *quantized.* The effects of quantized energies are apparent only at the atomic level.

quantum number

a number with certain definite values

CONCEPT CHECK

1. What is a line-emission spectrum?
2. What does it mean to say that energy is *quantized*?
3. Look at Figure 3-20. What wavelengths and what frequencies define light in the visible spectrum?

Orbitals replace orbits

The experiments of Rutherford's team led to the replacement of the plum-pudding model of the atom with a nuclear atom model. But Rutherford suggested that, like planets orbiting the sun, electrons revolve around the nucleus in circular or elliptical orbits. This was a very appealing explanation, and to this day, it is the model generally thought of by non-scientists. But Rutherford could not explain why the negatively charged electrons were not pulled into the positively charged nucleus as Coulomb's law would suggest. Thus, among scientists, the Rutherford model has been replaced by the Bohr atomic model, which describes electrons in terms of their energy states. Bohr postulated that electrons did not radiate energy while in orbit around the nucleus. But Bohr's model could not explain the spectra of larger atoms.

The present-day quantum model postulates that electrons have the properties of both particles and waves. According to quantum theory, each electron in an atom is assigned three quantum numbers, symbolized n, l, and m. Let's refer to an analogy again. If you have ever attended an event such as a concert, you know that your ticket specified your seat by a series of numbers and letters. For example, the ticket shown in **Figure 3-24** specifies seat number 20 in row U in section 3 of the south set of stands. These numbers are unique for this particular seat—no other seat shares this exact set of identifiers. Like section, row, and seat numbers, quantum numbers uniquely identify each electron in an atom.

orbital

a region of an atom in which there is a high probability of finding one or more electrons

In quantum theory, electrons are located in **orbitals,** regions of space in which you can expect to find electrons of specific energy. Despite the similar names, an orbital is very different from an orbit. An orbital is a region of high probability for finding a particular electron. It is as if the electron is smeared into a cloud, like the model in Figure 3-24b. The orbital is designated by a particular set of values of the quantum numbers n, l, and m in much the same way that a seat is identified by section, row, and seat numbers. Not every combination of the three quantum numbers is acceptable. Quantum theory provides rules for which combinations of n, l, and m are permitted.

▼ FIGURE 3-24

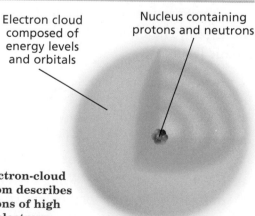

a A ticket for an event describes the location of a specific seat in much the same way a set of quantum numbers specifies where an electron is likely to be found.

Electron cloud composed of energy levels and orbitals

Nucleus containing protons and neutrons

b The current electron-cloud model of the atom describes orbitals as regions of high probability for electrons.

TABLE 3-4 Quantum Numbers of the First 30 Atomic Orbitals

n	l	m	Orbital name	Number of such orbitals
1	0	0	$1s$	one
2	0	0	$2s$	one
2	1	−1, 0, 1	$2p$	three
3	0	0	$3s$	one
3	1	−1, 0, 1	$3p$	three
3	2	−2, −1, 0, 1, 2	$3d$	five
4	0	0	$4s$	one
4	1	−1, 0, 1	$4p$	three
4	2	−2, −1, 0, 1, 2	$4d$	five
4	3	−3, −2, −1, 0, 1, 2, 3	$4f$	seven

Rules for assigning quantum numbers

Refer to **Table 3-4** as you study the descriptions of quantum numbers. The *principal quantum number, n,* can take the values 1, 2, 3, 4, and so on. In practice, n values greater than 7 are not encountered. The larger n is, the farther the orbital is from the nucleus and the higher its energy is.

The l quantum number can take any whole-number value from 0 to $n - 1$. For example, if $n = 3$, l can take the values 0, 1, or 2. When discussing the l quantum number, chemists use a letter code. A quantum number $l = 0$ corresponds to an s orbital; $l = 1$ corresponds to a p orbital; $l = 2$ corresponds to a d orbital; $l = 3$ corresponds to an f orbital. For example, an orbital with $n = 3$ and $l = 1$ is called a $3p$ orbital, and an electron occupying that orbital is called a $3p$ electron.

The m quantum number may take whole-number values depending on the value of l. In Table 3-4 you see that if $l = 1$, m can take any of the three values −1, 0, or 1. An $l = 1$ orbital is a p orbital, and so there are three p orbitals for each principal quantum number.

The l and m quantum numbers designate the shapes and orientations of the orbitals. **Figure 3-25,** on the next page, illustrates the shapes that are encountered. You might ask, "Where exactly are the electrons in these orbitals?" But quantum theory doesn't provide an answer to that question. Quantum theory tells us the *exact* energy of the electron, but only the *probability* that the electron will be in a particular region. The models in Figure 3-25 show regions where an electron is most likely to be. Picture the electron as a cloud of electric charge that is dense in regions of high probability and less dense in regions of low probability.

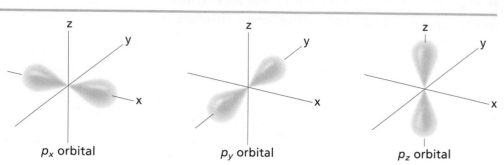

s orbital

p_x orbital

p_y orbital

p_z orbital

a The *s* orbital is spherically shaped. There is one *s* orbital for each value $n = 1, 2, 3 \ldots$ of the principal quantum number.

b For each of the values $n = 2, n = 3, n = 4 \ldots$, there are three *p* orbitals. Each is dumbbell shaped, but they differ in orientation.

c For each of the values $n = 3, n = 4, n = 5, \ldots$, there are five *d* orbitals. Four of the five have similar shapes, but differ in orientation.

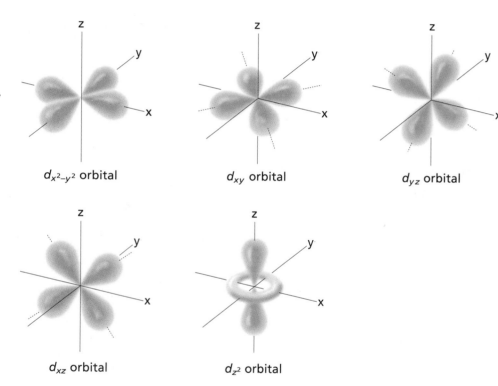

$d_{x^2-y^2}$ orbital

d_{xy} orbital

d_{yz} orbital

d_{xz} orbital

d_{z^2} orbital

No more than two electrons occupy an orbital

German chemist Wolfgang Pauli determined that two, but no more than two, electrons can occupy a single orbital. This rule is known as the **Pauli exclusion principle.** Thus, the occupancy of an orbital is 0, 1, or 2 electrons. Chemists imagine that electrons spin, and they believe that if two electrons are in the same orbital, they must spin in opposite directions. Electrons are assigned a *spin quantum number, m_s,* to describe the direction of their spin. There are only two possible values for the spin quantum number, $m_s = -\frac{1}{2}$ and $m_s = +\frac{1}{2}$. The spinning electron is a tiny magnet. Two electrons in the same orbital spin in opposite directions.

Scientists have found out exactly which orbitals are occupied, and by how many electrons, in all of the 111 elements. This information describes the **electron configuration** of an atom.

Pauli exclusion principle

a maximum of two electrons can occupy each orbital, and these electrons must have different spin quantum numbers

electron configuration

a description of the occupied electron orbitals in an atom

Electrons occupy lower-energy orbitals first

In the ground state, you would expect electrons to fill those orbitals with the lowest available energy first. And that's exactly what happens. According to the **aufbau principle** (*aufbau* is the German word for "building up"), the electrons in an atom will occupy the lowest available orbitals.

Recall that the smaller the principal quantum number, the lower the energy. But also, for elements with many electrons, the smaller the l quantum number, the lower the energy. So the order in which the orbitals are filled matches the order of energies, which starts out as follows.

$$1s < 2s < 2p < 3s < 3p$$

After that, however, the picture is less straightforward. The energy levels of the $3d$ orbitals are slightly higher than those of the $4s$ orbitals.

$$1s < 2s < 2p < 3s < 3p < 4s \approx 3d$$

After the $4p$ orbital is filled, there is another irregularity because the $5s$ and $4d$ orbitals are close in energy.

$$1s < 2s < 2p < 3s < 3p < 4s \approx 3d < 4p < 5s \approx 4d$$

Still more irregularities occur with the higher-energy orbitals. **Figure 3-26** illustrates the overlap of some of the energy levels schematically.

For example, the electron configuration of sulfur, whose atomic number is 16, is written as follows.

$$S = 1s^2 2s^2 2p^6 3s^2 3p^4$$

This line of symbols tells us exactly how the 16 electrons of a sulfur atom are configured. There are two in the $1s$ orbital, two in the $2s$ orbital, six in the $2p$ orbitals (two in each of the 3 p orbitals), and so on. To save space, this configuration is sometimes written using the configuration of a noble gas.

$$S = [Ne]\, 3s^2 3p^4$$

The neon atom's configuration is $1s^2 2s^2 2p^6$. Similarly, the electron configuration of manganese is

$$Mn = [Ar]\, 3d^5 4s^2$$

There are some exceptions to the aufbau principle. Chromium is one such exception, its configuration shows both an unfilled $3d$ and $4s$.

$$Cr = [Ar]\, 3d^5 4s^1$$

You will find a listing of all the configurations on the inside back cover of this book. It should be emphasized that these are the *ground-state* configurations of the *isolated* atoms in the *gas* phase. In other circumstances, atoms may adopt configurations different from those listed on that periodic table.

FIGURE 3-26 ▼

This diagram illustrates how the energy levels of orbitals can overlap, resulting in 4s filling before 3d.

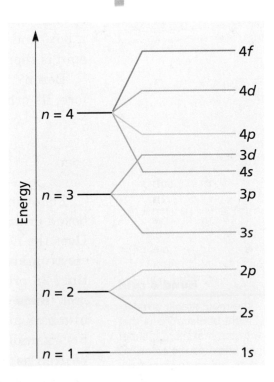

Write the electron configuration for fluorine.

1 **Determine the number of electrons the atom has**

The element's atomic number tells you how many electrons it has. An atom of fluorine has an atomic number of 9 and therefore has 9 electrons.

2 **Fill orbitals in order of increasing energy, and use the figure at right as a guide**

▶ Each s orbital can hold 2 electrons.

▶ Each p orbital can hold 2 electrons. 3 available p orbitals can hold a total of 6 electrons.

▶ Each d orbital can hold 2 electrons. 5 available d orbitals can hold a total of 10 electrons.

▶ Each f orbital can hold 2 electrons. 7 available f orbitals can hold a total of 14 electrons.

The electron configuration for fluorine follows.

$$1s^2 2s^2 2p^5$$

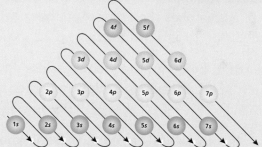

Electrons usually fill orbitals in the order shown by the arrows.

3 **Make sure the total number of electrons in the electron configuration equals the atomic number**

The total number of electrons shown in the fluorine electron configuration is $2 + 2 + 5 = 9$.

Orbital diagrams are models of electron arrangements

Orbital diagrams are also used to show how electrons are distributed within sublevels. In an orbital diagram, each orbital is represented by a box, and each electron is represented by an arrow. The direction of spin is represented by the direction of the arrow.

Boron's electron configuration can be written as $1s^2 2s^2 2p^1$; therefore, its orbital diagram is written as follows.

$$\boxed{\uparrow\downarrow}\ \underset{2s}{\boxed{\uparrow\downarrow}}\ \underset{2p}{\boxed{\uparrow}\boxed{}\boxed{}}$$
$$\underset{1s}{}$$

Following the aufbau strategy, let's think about constructing the boxed orbital diagram for carbon, the next element. A question arises: Does the next electron enter the first $2p$ orbital to pair with the single electron already there? Or does carbon have two electrons in two distinct $2p$ orbitals? According to Hund's rule, the second answer is correct. **Hund's rule** states that orbitals of the same n and l quantum numbers are each occupied by one electron, before any pairing occurs. For example, nitrogen has seven electrons. Its electron configuration is written as $1s^2 2s^2 2p^3$. This configuration is shown by the following orbital diagram.

Hund's rule

the most stable arrangement of electrons is that with the maximum number of unpaired electrons, all with the same spin quantum number

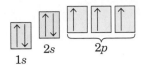

Recall that published configurations are for isolated atoms in the gas phase. But chemists seldom deal with monatomic gases. For example, the ground-state electron configuration of chromium is as follows.

$$[Cr] = 1s^2 2s^2 2p^6 3s^2 3p^6 3d^5 4s^1 = [Ar]3d^5 4s^1$$

Because the $4s$ and $3d$ levels are so close, it takes very little energy to excite a ground-state chromium atom by moving an electron to create the following configuration.

$$[Cr^*] = [Ar]3d^6 4s^0$$

Note that an asterisk is used to indicate an excited state. If it is to the energetic advantage of a chromium atom (to form stronger bonds, for example), the chromium atom can easily make the switch to the excited state. In such cases the gas-phase configuration is of little importance.

However, when dealing with electron levels that are energetically well separated, it is *very* important to know which orbitals are occupied by the electrons in the atom. Their configuration then affects both the properties and the reactions of the elements in question. This will be further explained in Chapter 4.

SECTION REVIEW

Total recall

1. How does Bohr's model of the atom differ from Rutherford's?

2. How does the quantum model of the atom differ from that suggested by Rutherford?

3. What happens when an electron returns to its ground state from its excited state?

4. What does n represent in the quantum theory of electrons in atoms?

Critical thinking

5. Use Pauli's exclusion principle or Hund's rule to explain why the following configurations are incorrect.

   a. $1s^2 2s^3 2p^6 3s^1$

b.

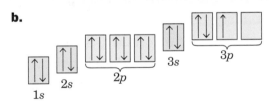

6. What information is provided by an electron configuration?

7. Calculate the maximum number of electrons that can occupy the fourth principal energy level.

8. **Story Clue** Write the electron configuration and draw the orbital diagram for an atom of aluminum, the element used in fireworks to produce a bright white light.

Now that you have completed the chapter, you should be able to answer the questions about how fireworks and light are related to atomic structure.

LOOKING BACK

What is light, and how do various colors of light differ?

From Figure 3-20, you can see that visible light consists of electromagnetic radiation having wavelengths between 4×10^{-7} m and 7×10^{-7} m. The longest visible wavelengths are red, and the shortest visible wavelengths are at the violet end of the spectrum.

What is happening to atoms when fireworks produce colored light?

Energy is supplied to a fireworks system when a fuse ignites the chemicals. The high temperature of the fireworks' explosion vaporizes the atoms or molecules and the abundant energy moves electrons to an excited energy state. The colors are generated by atoms or molecules in an excited state. A line-emission spectrum is produced by excited atoms as energy-rich electrons quickly return to the ground state, shedding their extra energy as light of one or more specific wavelengths.

Sodium atoms, in particular, are potent light emitters. Heated to more than 1800°C by the violently exothermic chemistry of the fireworks, atoms of sodium give off mainly yellow light which has a wavelength of 5.89×10^{-7} m. The reaction of sodium that emits light can be represented by the following equation.

$$Na^* \longrightarrow Na + \text{light energy}$$

Na on the products side of the equation represents a ground-state sodium atom.

$$Na = 1s^2 2s^2 2p^6 3s^1$$

Na* on the reactants side of the equation represents an excited sodium atom. The atom differs from a ground-state sodium atom by having its $3s$ electron elevated into a normally unoccupied $3p$ orbital.

$$Na^* = 1s^2 2s^2 2p^6 3p^1$$

This light-emitting process is so efficient that it tends to overwhelm other atomic or molecular light emissions in a fireworks explosion.

How does the instability of copper(II) chloride at high temperature interfere with its ability to emit blue light?

Copper(II) chloride is unstable because it decomposes into copper and chlorine atoms at a temperature only slightly higher than that at which it emits light. Therefore, if the temperatures generated by the exploding shell and reacting chemicals are not precisely controlled, copper(II) chloride crystals will absorb so much energy that they decompose before electrons reach the excited state. The decomposition products cannot emit blue light.

4
Be
Beryllium
9.012 182
[He]2s²

Beryllium has only one naturally occurring isotope, beryllium-9.

WHERE IS IT?

Earth's Crust
0.005%

internet**connect**

SCLINKS
NSTA

TOPIC: Beryllium
GO TO: www.scilinks.org
KEYWORD: HW035

A BRIEF HISTORY

Beryllium—An Uncommon Element

Although it is an uncommon element, beryllium has a number of properties that make it a very useful element. Beryllium has a relatively high melting point, 1278°C, and is an excellent conductor of heat and electricity. Beryllium transmits X rays extremely well and is therefore used to make "windows" for X-ray devices. All compounds of beryllium are toxic to humans. People who experience prolonged exposure to beryllium dust may contract berylliosis, a disease that can lead to severe lung damage and even death.

Industrial Uses

▶ The addition of 2% beryllium to copper forms an alloy that is six times stronger than copper. This alloy is used for nonsparking tools, critical moving parts in jet engines, and components in precision equipment.

▶ Emerald and aquamarine are precious forms of the mineral beryl, $Be_3Al_2(SiO_3)_6$.

▶ Beryllium is used in nuclear reactors as a neutron reflector and as an alloy with the fuel elements.

Crystals of pure beryllium look very different from the combined form of beryllium in an emerald.

1898: P. Lebeau discovers a method of extracting high-purity beryllium with an electrolytic process.

1828: F. Wöhler, of Germany, gives beryllium its name after he and W. Bussy, of France, simultaneously isolate the pure metal.

1942: A Ra-Be source provides the neutrons for Fermi's studies that lead to the construction of a nuclear reactor.

1700   1800   1900

1798: R. J. Haüy, a French mineralogist, observes that emeralds and beryl have the same optical properties and, therefore, the same chemical composition.

1926: M. G. Corson, of the United States, discovers that beryllium can be used to age-harden copper-nickel alloys.

HIGHLIGHTS

KEY TERMS

3-1

atomic mass
atomic theory
Avogadro's constant
law of definite proportion
law of multiple proportions
mole

3-2

alpha particle
anode
atomic number
cathode
Coulomb's law
electron
isotope
mass number

neutron
nucleus
proton
radioisotope

3-3

electromagnetic
  spectrum
electron configuration

excited state
ground state
Hund's rule
line-emission spectrum
orbital
Pauli exclusion principle
quantum number
aufbau principle

KEY CONCEPTS

3-1 How do we know atoms exist?

▶ Three laws support the existence of atoms: the laws of definite proportions, conservation of mass, and multiple proportions.

▶ Dalton's atomic theory contains five basic principles, some of which have been modified.

▶ The mass of atoms is measured in atomic mass units (amu); 1 amu is equal to 1.6605×10^{-27} kg.

▶ The mass of an atom of the carbon-12 isotope is defined as exactly 12 amu.

▶ The mole is the SI unit for amount of a substance.

▶ Avogadro's constant, 6.022×10^{23}/mol, is the number of particles in a mole.

3-2 What is the internal structure of atoms?

▶ Atoms consist of electrons, protons, and neutrons; protium is the only exception in that it consists solely of one electron and one proton.

▶ Protons, particles with a positive charge, and neutrons, particles with a neutral charge, make up the nucleus of an atom.

▶ Electrons, particles with a negative charge and very little mass, occupy the region around the nucleus.

▶ The atomic number of an atom is the number of protons it contains; its mass number is the number of protons plus neutrons.

▶ Isotopes are atoms that have the same atomic number but different mass numbers.

3-3 How are an atom's electrons configured?

▶ The electromagnetic spectrum spans a broad range of wavelengths of radiation, including those of visible light.

▶ Quantum theory places each electron in an atom into an orbital. The theory also describes the probability of locating an electron at any place.

▶ Each electron is assigned four quantum numbers that describe its orbital; no two electrons can have the same four quantum numbers.

▶ The electron configuration of an atom reveals which orbitals are occupied and how many electrons occupy each orbital.

KEY SKILLS

Review the following model before your exam. Be sure you can write electron configurations.

How To Write an electron configuration
  (p. 100)

REVIEW & ASSESS

TERM REVIEW

1. Atoms of the same element that have different masses are known as ——.
(radioisotopes, isotopes)

2. —— are the particles in the nucleus that have mass but no charge.
(Neutrons, Protons, Electrons)

3. The fact that no more than two electrons can occupy a single orbital is known as ——.
(Hund's rule, the Pauli exclusion principle, Coulomb's law)

4. The electrode from which electrons leave a metal is the ——.
(cathode, anode)

5. The total number of particles in the nucleus of an atom is its ——.
(atomic number, mass number)

6. A(n) —— is the positively charged particle emitted by a radioisotope.
(alpha particle, proton)

7. Information about the electronic energy levels in an atom can be obtained from its ——.
(line-emission spectrum, electromagnetic spectrum)

8. Light is emitted when an electron returns to its ——.
(excited state, ground state)

9. The branch of science that explains the behavior of electrons in atoms is called ——.
(atomic theory, quantum theory)

CONCEPT & SKILLS REVIEW

ATOMIC THEORY

1. What law is illustrated by the fact that ice, liquid water, and steam consist of 88.8% oxygen and 11.2% hydrogen by mass.

2. Identify the law that explains why the water molecules in a raindrop falling on Phoenix, Arizona, and the water flowing through the Nile Delta in Egypt both contain two hydrogen atoms for every oxygen atom.

3. Relate the law of definite proportions to the law of multiple proportions.

4. What is a mole? How is a mole related to Avogadro's constant?

5. How would you rewrite Dalton's fourth principle to account for such compounds as O_2, P_4, and S_8?

6. Calculate the mass of one atom of each of the following elements:
   a. gold
   b. neon
   c. uranium

7. Many elements exist as polyatomic molecules. Use atomic masses to calculate the molecular masses of the following:
   a. O_2 b. P_4 c. S_8

ATOMIC STRUCTURE

8. a. What flaws exist in Dalton's model of the atom?
   b. What flaws exist in Thomson's plum-pudding model of the atom?
   c. What flaws exist in Rutherford's model of the atom?
   d. What flaws exist in Bohr's model of the atom?

9. a. Which of Dalton's principles was contradicted by the work of J. J. Thomson?
   b. Which of Dalton's principles is contradicted by a doctor using radioactive isotopes to trace chemicals in the body?
   c. Do any of Dalton's principles still hold true today? If so, which ones hold true?

10. Identify the scientists who proposed each of the models illustrated below.

a.

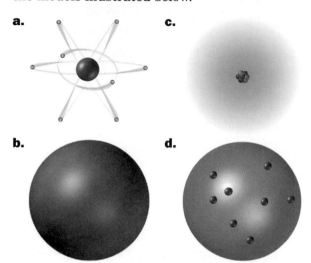

c.

b.

d.

11. If a lightning bolt strikes your power lines while your color television is running, your screen may become magnetized, causing the color to become unbalanced. This problem can be fixed with a magnetic instrument known as a degausser.

   a. Refer to the diagram below to explain how you know that the ray creating the picture on the screen is composed of charged particles.

   b. How is this related to the development of the plum-pudding atomic model?

TELEVISION AND DEGAUSSER

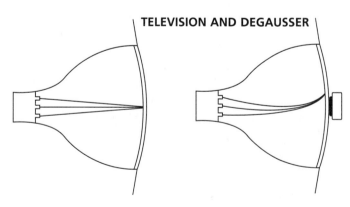

12. How were atomic models developed when no one had seen an atom?

13. Write nuclear symbols for isotopes of uranium with the following numbers of neutrons:
   a. 142 neutrons
   b. 143 neutrons
   c. 146 neutrons

14. Three isotopes of oxygen are listed below. Identify how many protons, neutrons, and electrons are in each atom.
   a. oxygen-16
   b. oxygen-17
   c. oxygen-18

15. Use the periodic table to complete the table below.

Isotope	Atomic number	Number of protons	Number of electrons	Number of neutrons
Carbon-12				
Carbon-14				
Lithium-7				
Sodium-23				

16. What would happen to poisonous chlorine gas if the following alterations were made?

   a. A proton is added to each atom.
   b. An electron is added to each atom.
   c. A neutron is added to each atom.

17. In the diagram below, indicate which sub-atomic particles would be found in areas *a* and *b*.

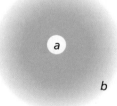

18. For hundreds of years, alchemists searched for ways to turn various metals into gold. How would the structure of an atom of $^{202}_{80}Hg$, have to be changed in order for it to become an atom of $^{197}_{79}Au$?

QUANTUM THEORY

19. How are quantum numbers like an address?

20. Complete the following table involving quantum numbers.

Type	Symbol	Values	Description
Principal			
Orbital shape			
Magnetic			
Spin			

21. What do the electron configurations of neon, Ne; argon, Ar; krypton, Kr; xenon, Xe; and radon, Rn, have in common?

22. The element sulfur has an electron configuration of $1s^2 2s^2 2p^6 3s^2 3p^4$.
  a. What does the superscript *6* refer to?
  b. What does the letter *s* refer to?
  c. What does the coefficient *3* refer to?

23. Why does the Pauli exclusion principle include the word *exclusion*?

24. Write the electron configuration for calcium, a nutrient essential to healthy bone growth and development.

25. Write the electron configuration for copper, which is used in pennies.

26. Identify the atomic numbers of elements with the following electron configurations:
  a. $1s^2 2s^2 2p^2$
  b. $1s^2 2s^2 2p^6 3s^2 3p^1$
  c. $1s^2 2s^2 2p^6 3s^2 3p^6 4s^2 3d^{10} 4p^6 5s^1 4d^{10}$

27. Identify the element that has each of the following electron configurations:
  a.

  1s   2s

  b.

  1s   2s   2p

c.

1s   2s   2p   3s

d.

1s   2s   2p   3s   3p

28. Hydrogen's sole electron occupies the $1s$ orbital but can be excited to the $4p$ orbital. List all the orbitals this electron might occupy on its way back to its ground state.

29. The next element to be synthesized is element 112. What would be its electron configuration? Show both the complete configuration and the abbreviated form.

30. Answer the following regarding electron configurations of atoms in the fourth period of the periodic table.
  a. Which orbitals are filled by transition metals?
  b. Which orbitals are filled by nonmetals?
  c. How do the configurations of elements in the fourth period differ from those in the fifth period?

31. The magnetic properties of an element depend on the number of unpaired electrons it has. Explain why iron, Fe, is highly magnetic but neon, Ne, is not.

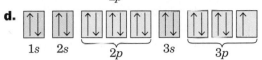

LINKING CHAPTERS

1. Theme: Conservation
A Japanese company recently developed a signboard that uses no wiring and no power source. The characters are illuminated by absorbing surrounding light and then radiating different colors. Explain how this sign can emit light with no power source.

2. Theme: Micromodels
Explain the different macroscopic observations that led to the following:
  a. the discovery of the nucleus
  b. the discovery of electrons

3. Theme: Classification and trends

Prepare a table of elements with atomic numbers 3 through 10. List the names in order of increasing atomic number down one side of the table. Write the electron configuration for each element alongside its name. What do all these electron configurations have in common? What trend is evident as you proceed from one element to the next?

ALTERNATIVE ASSESSMENTS

Performance assessment

1. Your teacher will provide you with an index card that lists the name, atomic number, mass number, and an incorrect electron configuration of an element. Make the changes necessary to correct the electron configuration.

2. Your teacher will provide you with an index card listing a principal energy level and the number of electrons that are present in that level. Draw an orbital box diagram to show how the electrons are arranged in that energy level.

Portfolio projects

1. **Research and communication**

So-called "Neon" signs actually contain a variety. Research the different colors used for these signs. Determine the substances that are used. Design your own sign on paper, and identify which gases you would use to achieve the desired color scheme.

2. **Cooperative activity**

Build your own model of a particular isotope of an atom. Be sure to use a wide-open area for this project. Look up the radius of the atom, and build the atom with relative sizes. Discover how far away another atom would be if the atoms existed in the solid state.

3. **Chemistry and you**

Select one of the essential elements listed in the table on page 91. Check your school library or the Internet for details concerning the roles the element plays in the human body. Contact the Food and Drug Administration for any guidelines and recommendations they have regarding the element.

4.

| internet**connect** |

SC*LINKS*
NSTA

TOPIC: Element names
GO TO: www.scilinks.org
KEYWORD: HW036

Research and communication

Research several elements whose symbols are inconsistent with their English names. Some examples include silver, Ag; gold, Au; and mercury, Hg. Compare the origin for these names with the origin for their symbols.

1. Which of the following represents an electron configuration for a calcium atom, Ca?
   a. $1s^2 2s^2 2p^6 3s^2 3p^6 4s^2$
   b. $1s^2 2s^2 2p^6 3s^1 3p^6 4s^2 3d^1$
   c. $1s^2 2s^2 2p^6 3s^1 3p^6 4s^3$
   d. $1s^2 2s^2 2p^6 3s^2 3p^6 4s^2 3d^1$

2. Isotopes of an element differ in their ——.
   a. atomic numbers
   b. electron configurations
   c. number of protons
   d. masses

3. The ratio of protons to neutrons in the nucleus affects the atom's ——.
   a. stability
   b. ground state
   c. line-emission spectrum
   d. ability to travel through a cathode-ray tube

4. The law of multiple proportions states that elements ——.
   a. combine in mass ratios that can be expressed in small whole numbers
   b. combine in the same mass ratio in a compound regardless of the quantity of sample or its source
   c. have different physical and chemical properties
   d. cannot be created, destroyed, or subdivided when they participate in a chemical reaction

5. How many neutrons are present in an atom of tin that has the atomic number 50 and a mass number of 119?
   a. 50   c. 119
   b. 69   d. 169

6. As an electron in an excited state returns to its ground state, ——.
   a. light energy is emitted
   b. energy is absorbed by the atom
   c. the atom is likely to undergo spontaneous decay
   d. the electron configuration of the atom remains unchanged

7. Atomic masses for elements shown on the periodic table are not expressed as whole numbers because ——.
   a. the number of protons in an atom of an element varies
   b. atoms may gain or lose electrons during a chemical reaction
   c. they represent weighted averages of the isotopes of that atom
   d. scientists cannot measure the masses of atoms with great precision

8. The maximum number of electrons with quantum numbers $n = 2$ and $l = 1$ in one atom is ——.
   a. 2   c. 8
   b. 12   d. 6

9. According to quantum theory, an electron ——.
   a. remains in a fixed position
   b. can replace a proton in the nucleus
   c. occupies the space around the nucleus only in certain, well-defined orbitals
   d. has neither mass nor charge

10. Which of the following could represent a pair of isotopes?
    a. $^{20}_{8}X$ and $^{20}_{9}X$ c. $^{32}_{15}X$ and $^{34}_{16}X$
    b. $^{44}_{23}X$ and $^{44}_{23}X$ d. $^{40}_{19}X$ and $^{42}_{19}X$

11. Among the phenomena that enabled scientists to infer the existence of atoms was the ——.
    a. Pauli exclusion principle
    b. law of conservation of mass
    c. relationship between mass and energy shown by the equation $E = mc^2$
    d. observation that each element differed in the number of protons present in one of its atoms

12. The significance of Rutherford's work was to establish that ——.
    a. atoms have mass
    b. electrons have a negative charge
    c. gold is an element
    d. the atom is mostly empty space

The Periodic Table

PERIODIC TRENDS AND A MEDICAL MYSTERY

George Decker seemed to be in perfect health. He was 35 years old, did not smoke, and had no history of serious illness. But one day, after cooking something on his stove, Decker began to cough, wheeze, and gasp for air. A friend rushed him to the hospital for treatment.

Tests revealed that Decker had acute pneumonia in both lungs. Pneumonia is an inflammation of lung tissue that causes the air sacs to fill with white blood cells and cellular debris, which makes breathing difficult. Most pneumonias are caused by organisms such as bacteria, fungi, or viruses. But tissue samples taken from Decker's lungs showed no evidence of microorganisms or viruses. Extensive tests turned up nothing. The cause of Decker's pneumonia was a mystery. In the meantime, Decker's condition became worse. His health faded, and Decker was dead in three months.

A pathologist was called in to perform an autopsy. The autopsy confirmed that Decker had died of pneumonia, yet there was still no trace of pneumonia-causing microorganisms. Baffled, the pathologist scrutinized Decker's hospital records and discovered that Decker had been cooking something just before he began having breathing problems. What Decker had been cooking turned out to be the cause of the pneumonia.

Decker had worked in a metal shop. By talking to Decker's employer, the pathologist discovered that Decker collected old gold dental fillings. Gold dental fillings are actually mixtures of gold, palladium, platinum and silver with small amounts of zinc, iron, and copper. Decker would take the fillings home and heat them on his stove to extract the precious metals. Upon melting, the zinc, copper, and iron formed oxides; these oxides rose to the top, where they could be skimmed off. Decker sold the remaining precious metals for a sizable profit.

Decker thought he could apply the same process to extract silver from silver fillings. Silver dental fillings are composed of silver and mercury with copper or other metals. Unfortunately, Decker's ignorance about certain physical and chemical properties of metals proved fatal.

CHAPTER LINKS

Which metal melts first in gold fillings? in silver fillings?

Why did Decker's process work for gold fillings but prove fatal with silver fillings?

What element was most likely the cause of Decker's death?

What makes a group of elements?

OBJECTIVES

▶ *Describe* the organization of the modern periodic table.

▶ *State* the periodic law.

▶ *Describe* characteristic properties of groups of elements.

▶ *Relate* the properties of the main-group elements to their electron configurations.

Elements are different yet similar

Some elements are gases, some are liquids, and still others are solids. Some are colored and some are colorless, as you can see in **Figure 4-1.** Yet there are similarities. For example, the elements lithium, sodium, potassium, rubidium, cesium, and francium can combine with chlorine in a 1:1 ratio to form the compounds LiCl, NaCl, KCl, RbCl, CsCl, and FrCl. All of these compounds are white solids, are soluble in water, and form solutions that are good conductors of electricity.

Similarly, fluorine, chlorine, bromine, iodine, and astatine combine with sodium to form white solids with the formulas NaF, NaCl, NaBr, NaI, and NaAt, respectively. All of these compounds are also white solids, are soluble in water, and form solutions that are good conductors of electricity. These examples highlight the similarities among the elements rather than differences.

▶ **FIGURE 4-1**

Though some elements may look dissimilar, they react similarly. Samples of the *elements* chlorine, bromine, and iodine show dissimilar physical characteristics. Samples of the *compounds* NaCl, NaBr, and NaI show similar physical characteristics.

Chlorine   Iodine

Bromine

Sodium chloride   Sodium bromide   Sodium iodide

John Newlands notices a periodic pattern

Elements vary widely in their properties, but in an orderly way. In 1865, the English chemist John Newlands arranged the first 16 elements known at the time (excluding hydrogen) in order of increasing atomic mass. When Newlands placed the elements in two rows, as follows, he observed that the elements in each column had similar chemical and physical properties.

Li	Be	B	C	N	O	F
Na	Mg	Al	Si	P	S	Cl

Because the chemical and physical properties repeated with the eighth element, Newlands called this pattern the law of octaves.

Dmitri Mendeleev invented the modern periodic system

In 1870, the Russian chemist Dmitri Mendeleev made use of this scheme and other information to produce the first orderly arrangement of all 63 elements known at the time. Mendeleev wrote the symbol for each element on a card along with its physical and chemical properties and its relative atomic mass. He arranged and rearranged the cards in various configurations until he arrived at the pattern shown in **Figure 4-2,** which places the elements in order of increasing atomic mass. In Mendeleev's table, elements with similar properties fall in vertical columns.

There are two interesting things to notice about Mendeleev's table. First, the elements do not always fit neatly in the order of increasing atomic mass. For example, Mendeleev had to reverse the order of tellurium and iodine to keep similar elements in the same column. At first he thought that their atomic masses were in error. But careful research by others showed that the values were correct. He had no explanation for this discrepancy.

The second noteworthy point is that there were gaps in his table where elements with a particular atomic mass should occur. Mendeleev was able to predict the properties of these undiscovered elements, which he called ekaaluminum, ekaboron, and ekasilicon (the prefix *eka-* is derived from a Sanskrit word meaning "one beyond"). These elements were discovered shortly thereafter, and their properties were

ПЕРИОДИЧЕСКАЯ СИСТЕМА ЭЛЕМЕНТОВ

ГРУППЫ ЭЛЕМЕНТОВ

РЯДЫ	I	II	III	IV	V	VI	VII	VIII		
I	H 1									
II	Li 7	Be 9,4	B 11	C 12	N 14	O 16	F 19			
III	Na 23	Mg 24	Al 27,4	Si 28	P 31	S 32	Cl 35,5			
IV	K 39	Ca 40	? 45	Ti 50	V 51	Cr 52	Mn 55	Fe 56	Co 59	Ni 59
V	Cu 63,4	Zn 65,2	? 68	? 70	As 75	Se 79,4	Br 80			
VI	Rb 85,4	Sr 87,6	Yt? 88	Zr 90	Nb 94	Mo 96	? 100	Ru 104,4	Rh 104,4	Pd 106,6
VII	Ag 108	Cd 112	In 113	Sn 118	Sb 122	Te 128?	J 127			
VIII	Cs 133	Ba 137	Di? 138	Ce? 140						
IX										
X			Er? 178	La? 180	Ta 182	W 186		Pt 197,4	Ir 198	Os 199
XI	Au 197?	Hg 200	Tl 204	Pb 207	Bi 210					
XII				Th 231		U 240				

FIGURE 4-2 ▲

Mendeleev's table grouped elements with similar properties into vertical columns called "groups" or "families." The elements highlighted in red in the table—fluorine, F, chlorine, Cl, bromine, Br, and iodine, I—constitute a group. Compare this periodic table with the modern periodic table on pages 114 and 115.

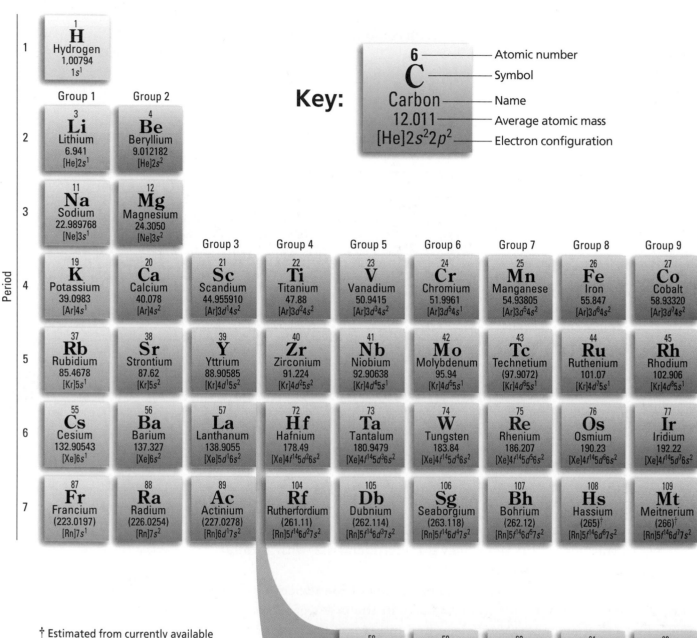

Key:

6 — Atomic number
C — Symbol
Carbon — Name
12.011 — Average atomic mass
[He]$2s^2 2p^2$ — Electron configuration

Period

| | Group 1 | Group 2 | Group 3 | Group 4 | Group 5 | Group 6 | Group 7 | Group 8 | Group 9 |

1

1
H
Hydrogen
1.00794
$1s^1$

2

3
Li
Lithium
6.941
[He]$2s^1$

4
Be
Beryllium
9.012182
[He]$2s^2$

3

11
Na
Sodium
22.989768
[Ne]$3s^1$

12
Mg
Magnesium
24.3050
[Ne]$3s^2$

4

19
K
Potassium
39.0983
[Ar]$4s^1$

20
Ca
Calcium
40.078
[Ar]$4s^2$

21
Sc
Scandium
44.955910
[Ar]$3d^1 4s^2$

22
Ti
Titanium
47.88
[Ar]$3d^2 4s^2$

23
V
Vanadium
50.9415
[Ar]$3d^3 4s^2$

24
Cr
Chromium
51.9961
[Ar]$3d^5 4s^1$

25
Mn
Manganese
54.93805
[Ar]$3d^5 4s^2$

26
Fe
Iron
55.847
[Ar]$3d^6 4s^2$

27
Co
Cobalt
58.93320
[Ar]$3d^7 4s^2$

5

37
Rb
Rubidium
85.4678
[Kr]$5s^1$

38
Sr
Strontium
87.62
[Kr]$5s^2$

39
Y
Yttrium
88.90585
[Kr]$4d^1 5s^2$

40
Zr
Zirconium
91.224
[Kr]$4d^2 5s^2$

41
Nb
Niobium
92.90638
[Kr]$4d^4 5s^1$

42
Mo
Molybdenum
95.94
[Kr]$4d^5 5s^1$

43
Tc
Technetium
(97.9072)
[Kr]$4d^6 5s^1$

44
Ru
Ruthenium
101.07
[Kr]$4d^7 5s^1$

45
Rh
Rhodium
102.906
[Kr]$4d^8 5s^1$

6

55
Cs
Cesium
132.90543
[Xe]$6s^1$

56
Ba
Barium
137.327
[Xe]$6s^2$

57
La
Lanthanum
138.9055
[Xe]$5d^1 6s^2$

72
Hf
Hafnium
178.49
[Xe]$4f^{14} 5d^2 6s^2$

73
Ta
Tantalum
180.9479
[Xe]$4f^{14} 5d^3 6s^2$

74
W
Tungsten
183.84
[Xe]$4f^{14} 5d^4 6s^2$

75
Re
Rhenium
186.207
[Xe]$4f^{14} 5d^5 6s^2$

76
Os
Osmium
190.23
[Xe]$4f^{14} 5d^6 6s^2$

77
Ir
Iridium
192.22
[Xe]$4f^{14} 5d^7 6s^2$

7

87
Fr
Francium
(223.0197)†
[Rn]$7s^1$

88
Ra
Radium
(226.0254)
[Rn]$7s^2$

89
Ac
Actinium
(227.0278)
[Rn]$6d^1 7s^2$

104
Rf
Rutherfordium
(261.11)
[Rn]$5f^{14} 6d^2 7s^2$

105
Db
Dubnium
(262.114)
[Rn]$5f^{14} 6d^3 7s^2$

106
Sg
Seaborgium
(263.118)
[Rn]$5f^{14} 6d^4 7s^2$

107
Bh
Bohrium
(262.12)
[Rn]$5f^{14} 6d^5 7s^2$

108
Hs
Hassium
(265)†
[Rn]$5f^{14} 6d^6 7s^2$

109
Mt
Meitnerium
(266)†
[Rn]$5f^{14} 6d^7 7s^2$

† Estimated from currently available IUPAC data.

* The systematic names and symbols for elements greater than 109 will be used until the approval of trivial names by IUPAC.

58
Ce
Cerium
140.115
[Xe]$4f^1 5d^1 6s^2$

59
Pr
Praseodymium
140.908
[Xe]$4f^3 6s^2$

60
Nd
Neodymium
144.24
[Xe]$4f^4 6s^2$

61
Pm
Promethium
(144.9127)
[Xe]$4f^5 6s^2$

62
Sm
Samarium
150.36
[Xe]$4f^6 6s^2$

90
Th
Thorium
232.0381
[Rn]$6d^2 7s^2$

91
Pa
Protactinium
231.03588
[Rn]$5f^2 6d^1 7s^2$

92
U
Uranium
238.0289
[Rn]$5f^3 6d^1 7s^2$

93
Np
Neptunium
(237.0482)
[Rn]$5f^4 6d^1 7s^2$

94
Pu
Plutonium
244.0642
[Rn]$5f^6 7s^2$

Metals
- Alkali metals
- Alkaline-earth metals
- Transition metals
- Other metals

Metalloids
- Semiconductors

Nonmetals
- Halogens
- Other nonmetals
- Noble gases

			Group 13	Group 14	Group 15	Group 16	Group 17	Group 18
								2 **He** Helium 4.002602 $1s^2$

Group 13	Group 14	Group 15	Group 16	Group 17	Group 18
5 **B** Boron 10.811 $[He]2s^22p^1$	6 **C** Carbon 12.011 $[He]2s^22p^2$	7 **N** Nitrogen 14.00674 $[He]2s^22p^3$	8 **O** Oxygen 15.9994 $[He]2s^22p^4$	9 **F** Fluorine 18.9984032 $[He]2s^22p^5$	10 **Ne** Neon 20.1797 $[He]2s^22p^6$
13 **Al** Aluminum 26.981539 $[Ne]3s^23p^1$	14 **Si** Silicon 28.0855 $[Ne]3s^23p^2$	15 **P** Phosphorus 30.9738 $[Ne]3s^23p^3$	16 **S** Sulfur 32.066 $[Ne]3s^23p^4$	17 **Cl** Chlorine 35.4527 $[Ne]3s^23p^5$	18 **Ar** Argon 39.948 $[Ne]3s^23p^6$

Group 10	Group 11	Group 12	Group 13	Group 14	Group 15	Group 16	Group 17	Group 18
28 **Ni** Nickel 58.6934 $[Ar]3d^84s^2$	29 **Cu** Copper 63.546 $[Ar]3d^{10}4s^1$	30 **Zn** Zinc 65.39 $[Ar]3d^{10}4s^2$	31 **Ga** Gallium 69.723 $[Ar]3d^{10}4s^24p^1$	32 **Ge** Germanium 72.61 $[Ar]3d^{10}4s^24p^2$	33 **As** Arsenic 74.92159 $[Ar]3d^{10}4s^24p^3$	34 **Se** Selenium 78.96 $[Ar]3d^{10}4s^24p^4$	35 **Br** Bromine 79.904 $[Ar]3d^{10}4s^24p^5$	36 **Kr** Krypton 83.80 $[Ar]3d^{10}4s^24p^6$
46 **Pd** Palladium 106.42 $[Kr]4d^{10}5s^0$	47 **Ag** Silver 107.8682 $[Kr]4d^{10}5s^1$	48 **Cd** Cadmium 112.411 $[Kr]4d^{10}5s^2$	49 **In** Indium 114.818 $[Kr]4d^{10}5s^25p^1$	50 **Sn** Tin 118.710 $[Kr]4d^{10}5s^25p^2$	51 **Sb** Antimony 121.757 $[Kr]4d^{10}5s^25p^3$	52 **Te** Tellurium 127.60 $[Kr]4d^{10}5s^25p^4$	53 **I** Iodine 126.904 $[Kr]4d^{10}5s^25p^5$	54 **Xe** Xenon 131.29 $[Kr]4d^{10}5s^25p^6$
78 **Pt** Platinum 195.08 $[Xe]4f^{14}5d^96s^1$	79 **Au** Gold 196.96654 $[Xe]4f^{14}5d^{10}6s^1$	80 **Hg** Mercury 200.59 $[Xe]4f^{14}5d^{10}6s^2$	81 **Tl** Thallium 204.3833 $[Xe]4f^{14}5d^{10}6s^26p^1$	82 **Pb** Lead 207.2 $[Xe]4f^{14}5d^{10}6s^26p^2$	83 **Bi** Bismuth 208.98037 $[Xe]4f^{14}5d^{10}6s^26p^3$	84 **Po** Polonium (208.9824) $[Xe]4f^{14}5d^{10}6s^26p^4$	85 **At** Astatine (209.9871) $[Xe]4f^{14}5d^{10}6s^26p^5$	86 **Rn** Radon (222.0176) $[Xe]4f^{14}5d^{10}6s^26p^6$
110 **Uun*** Ununnilium (269)† $[Rn]5f^{14}6d^97s^1$	111 **Uuu*** Unununium (272)† $[Rn]5f^{14}6d^{10}7s^1$							

63 **Eu** Europium 151.966 $[Xe]4f^76s^2$	64 **Gd** Gadolinium 157.25 $[Xe]4f^75d^16s^2$	65 **Tb** Terbium 158.92534 $[Xe]4f^96s^2$	66 **Dy** Dysprosium 162.50 $[Xe]4f^{10}6s^2$	67 **Ho** Holmium 164.930 $[Xe]4f^{11}6s^2$	68 **Er** Erbium 167.26 $[Xe]4f^{12}6s^2$	69 **Tm** Thulium 168.93421 $[Xe]4f^{13}6s^2$	70 **Yb** Ytterbium 173.04 $[Xe]4f^{14}6s^2$	71 **Lu** Lutetium 174.967 $[Xe]4f^{14}5d^16s^2$
95 **Am** Americium (243.0614) $[Rn]5f^77s^2$	96 **Cm** Curium (247.0703) $[Rn]5f^76d^17s^2$	97 **Bk** Berkelium (247.0703) $[Rn]5f^97s^2$	98 **Cf** Californium (251.0796) $[Rn]5f^{10}7s^2$	99 **Es** Einsteinium (252.083) $[Rn]5f^{11}7s^2$	100 **Fm** Fermium (257.0951) $[Rn]5f^{12}7s^2$	101 **Md** Mendelevium (258.10) $[Rn]5f^{13}7s^2$	102 **No** Nobelium (259.1009) $[Rn]5f^{14}7s^2$	103 **Lr** Lawrencium (262.11) $[Rn]5f^{14}6d^17s^2$

The atomic masses listed in this table reflect the precision of current measurements. (Values listed in parentheses are those of the element's most stable or most common isotope.) In calculations throughout the text, however, atomic masses have been rounded to two places to the right of the decimal.

Properties	Ekaaluminum (gallium, 1875)		Ekaboron (scandium, 1877)		Ekasilicon (germanium, 1886)	
	Predicted	Observed	Predicted	Observed	Predicted	Observed
Density	6.0 g/cm^3	5.96 g/cm^3	3.5 g/cm^3	3.5 g/cm^3	5.5 g/cm^3	5.47 g/cm^3
Melting point	low	30°C	*	*	high	900°C
Oxide formula	Ea_2O_3	Ga_2O_3	Eb_2O_3	Sc_2O_3	EsO_2	GeO_2
Solubility of oxide	*	*	dissolves in acid	dissolves in acid	*	*
Density of oxide	*	*	*	*	4.7 g/cm^3	4.70 g/cm^3
Chloride formula	*	*	*	*	$EsCl_4$	$GeCl_4$
Color of metal	*	*	*	*	dark gray	grayish white

(Data listed in parentheses indicate current name of element and year of discovery.)

very close to Mendeleev's predictions, as illustrated in **Table 4-1.** Other scientists had created tables of the elements, but Mendeleev had the genius to perceive the periodic system and to predict the existence of elements unknown at the time.

About 40 years after Mendeleev published his table, a young English chemist named Henry Moseley established a physical basis for the periodic arrangement. Moseley studied the lines in the X-ray spectra of the elements. He found that with a few exceptions the wavelengths of the lines in the spectra decreased in a regular manner as atomic mass increased. With further work, Moseley realized that the spectral lines correlated not to atomic mass but to atomic number. When the elements in Mendeleev's table were arranged in order of increasing atomic number, the discrepancies disappeared.

The most common periodic table, recommended by IUPAC (the International Union of Pure and Applied Chemistry), is shown in **Figure 4-3,** on page 114 and 115. It is based on the **periodic law,** which states that the physical and chemical properties of the elements are periodic functions of their atomic numbers. This periodic table contains a wealth of information about individual elements. Examine the key to Figure 4-3 for the information it gives about carbon: atomic number, symbol, name, atomic mass, and electron configuration. Notice that a shorthand form is used to show electron configurations.

periodic law

the physical and chemical properties of elements are periodic functions of their atomic numbers

CONCEPT CHECK

1. Mendeleev arranged the elements in his periodic table according to what property?
2. What is the periodic law?

Overview of the modern periodic table

The rows of the periodic table are called **periods.** Elements in a period have similar electron configurations. For example, the first period has two elements, hydrogen and helium, and the electrons of these elements occupy the 1s orbital. Similarly, the outer electrons of second-period elements occupy the 2s and 2p orbitals, and the outer electrons of third-period elements occupy the 3s and 3p orbitals. Although there are exceptions, similar patterns are found in the electron configurations of elements in Periods 4 through 7.

The columns of the periodic table are called **groups.** The elements within a group have properties in common but with some gradation. For example, all Group 1 elements are solid at room temperature, are good conductors of electricity, and combine with chlorine in a 1:1 ratio. Although the elements in Group 14 exhibit a wide variety of properties, all of them combine with chlorine in a 1:4 ratio to form the chlorides CCl_4, $SiCl_4$, $GeCl_4$, $SnCl_4$, and $PbCl_4$.

It is convenient to divide the periodic table into two distinct regions, metals and nonmetals. The **metals** include all members of Groups 1 through 12 as well as some elements of Groups 13 through 16. As you can see, most of the known elements are metals. All metals are good conductors of electricity, and their conductivity increases as temperature decreases. Except for mercury, all are solid at room temperature. Elements in Groups 3 through 12, including the two long rows below the main table, are called the **transition metals.** As you move from left to right across the transition metals, you will see that electrons are usually added to d orbitals. For this reason the transition metals are sometimes referred to as the d-block elements. The transition metals are generally not as reactive as the elements in Groups 1 and 2, and they have varied properties.

The second region of the periodic table contains the **nonmetals.** Differences in the physical appearance of metals and nonmetals are shown in **Figure 4-4.** The nonmetals include all of Groups 17 and 18 as well as some members of Groups 14 through 16. The characteristic shared by all nonmetals is that they are poor conductors of electricity, but their

period

a series of elements that form a horizontal row in the periodic table

group

a series of elements that form a vertical column in the periodic table

metal

an element that is a good conductor of electricity

transition metals

elements in Groups 3 through 12

nonmetal

an element that is a poor conductor of electricity

FIGURE 4-4 ▼

Tin has the physical appearance typical of metals. Boron is a semiconductor. Sulfur is a nonmetal. Nonmetals vary widely in physical appearance.

Tin (metal)

Boron (semiconductor)

Sulfur (nonmetal)

conductivity increases as temperature increases. In other respects, nonmetals exhibit a wide variety of properties. Nonmetals may be gases, liquids, or solids at room temperature.

Along the stair-step line separating metals from nonmetals are the elements known as **semiconductors,** or *metalloids.* As their name implies, these elements conduct electricity better than nonmetals but not as well as metals. The conductivity of semiconductors can be greatly enhanced by adding traces of selected substances. This makes semiconductors very useful in transistors and other electronic devices. Semiconductors are solid at room temperature.

semiconductor

a crystalline material with intermediate electrical conductivity

CONCEPT CHECK

1. What are the horizontal rows of the modern periodic table called? What are the vertical columns called?
2. What are the two main regions of the periodic table?

The main-group elements

main-group elements

elements belonging to Groups 1, 2, and 13 through 18 in the periodic table and having very regular electron configurations

Groups 1, 2, and 13 through 18 are referred to as the **main-group elements.** The electron configuration of elements within each group is quite consistent. For example, all the elements in Group 14 have four electrons in the outermost shell. Their configuration can be written as ns^2np^2, where n is the period number. The regular electron configuration of the Group 14 elements explains the regular formulas for the chlorides CCl_4, $SiCl_4$, $GeCl_4$, $SnCl_4$, and $PbCl_4$ mentioned earlier.

The main-group elements are sometimes called *representative elements.* Look at **Figure 4-5** to see the elements in this block. Their electron configurations are regular and consistent. The main-group elements include gases (the noble gases, for example), liquids, solids, metals, and nonmetals. The main-group elements silicon and oxygen account for four of every five atoms found on or near the Earth's surface.

Four groups within the main-group elements have special names. These are the *alkali metals* (Group 1), the *alkaline-earth metals* (Group 2), the *halogens* (Group 17), and the *noble gases* (Group 18).

▶ **FIGURE 4-5**

Main-group elements have diverse properties and uses. They are highlighted in the long columns on the left and right sides of the periodic table.

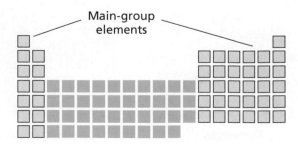

Main-group elements

Group 1: the alkali metals

Group 1 elements are called **alkali metals** because they react with water to produce alkaline solutions and because they have metallic properties. The term *alkali* dates back to ancient times, when people discovered that wood ashes mixed with water produce a slippery solution that can remove grease. In the Middle Ages such solutions were named *alkaline,* after the Arabic word for wood ashes, *al-qili.* Chemists now know that wood ashes contain compounds of Group 1 elements, especially potassium hydroxide, KOH.

The alkali metals are so soft that they can be cut with a knife. The freshly cut surface of an alkali metal is shiny, but it dulls quickly as the metal reacts with oxygen and water in the air. In the laboratory, alkali metals are usually stored in oil or kerosene to isolate them from the air. Alkali metals react vigorously with cold water, forming hydrogen gas and a very alkaline solution.

The high reactivity of alkali metals is the result of their electron configuration—a single electron in the highest energy level. By losing this outer electron and becoming a cation an alkali metal can achieve the stable electron configuration of the noble gas.

The physical properties of the alkali metals are described in **Table 4-2.** All of the alkali metals are excellent conductors of electricity. In the gaseous state at high temperatures, alkali metals become plasmas. **Plasmas** are the fourth state of matter and consist of an electrically conductive mixture of ions, electrons, and neutral particles. As electricity flows through the gas, some electrons are transferred to higher-energy orbitals. When a sodium plasma goes through this process, its electrons emit yellow light as they return to the ground state. This yellow light is of higher intensity, but it uses less energy than the light emitted from a normal light bulb with a tungsten metal filament. Light of this wavelength penetrates fog better than white light. Sodium-vapor lamps are used as fog lights and for street lighting.

alkali metals

highly reactive metallic elements in Group 1 that react rapidly with water to form hydrogen and alkaline solutions and that burn in air

TOPIC: Alkali metals
GO TO: www.scilinks.org
KEYWORD: HW041

plasma

a gas composed of ions, electrons, and neutral particles

TABLE 4-2 Physical Properties of Alkali Metals

Element	Flame test	Hardness (Mohs' scale)	Melting point (°C)	Boiling point (°C)	Density (g/cm^3)	Atomic radius (pm)
Lithium	red	0.6	180.5	1342	0.53	134
Sodium	yellow	0.4	97.7	883	0.97	154
Potassium	violet	0.5	63.3	759	0.86	196
Rubidium	yellowish violet	0.3	39.3	688	1.53	(216)
Cesium	reddish violet	0.2	28.4	671	1.87	(233)
Francium	—	—	(27)	(677)	(3.0)	(250)

Values in parentheses are estimated.

▶ **FIGURE 4-6**

The alkaline-earth metals are the second column of elements in the periodic table.

▲ **FIGURE 4-7**

Marble is used in sculptures. The pure forms have the formula $CaCO_3$.

Group 2: the alkaline-earth metals

The elements of Group 2, as shown in **Figure 4-6,** are called the **alkaline-earth metals.** Compared with the alkali metals, the alkaline-earth metals are harder, denser, stronger, and have higher melting points. The elements of this group are reactive, but less so than Group 1 elements. Beryllium is the least active of the alkaline-earth metals. In reactions with other elements, alkaline-earth metals often lose two electrons to become the M^{2+} ion and thus achieve the configuration of the preceding noble gas. Losing two electrons requires about twice as much energy as losing just one electron.

Consider the metal magnesium. If the surface of an object made from magnesium is exposed to air, the magnesium reacts with the oxygen in air to form the compound magnesium oxide, MgO. This reaction forms a protective coating of MgO that slows the corrosion of the magnesium metal underneath. Magnesium is lighter than other structural metals, yet it is still very strong, especially when alloyed with other metals. For all these reasons, magnesium metal has a wide variety of practical uses, especially in aircraft and aerospace applications, where materials must be strong but light.

Perhaps the best known alkaline-earth metal is calcium. Calcium compounds, such as those in limestone and marble, are common in the Earth's crust. Marble, shown in **Figure 4-7,** is almost pure calcium carbonate. Marble is hard and durable, but it is dissolved by acid rain.

The lanthanides and actinides

Part of the last two periods of transition elements are placed toward the bottom of the periodic table to keep the table conveniently narrow. The metals in these two rows, shown in **Figure 4-8,** on the next page, are referred to as the lanthanides and actinides. Moving left to right along these rows, electrons are added to the 4*f* orbitals in the lanthanides and to the 5*f* orbitals in the actinides. The **lanthanides** have atomic numbers from 58 to 71. The name of element 57 will give you a clue to how the lanthanides got their name. The lanthanides are shiny, reactive metals that have irregular electron configurations. Some have practical uses. For

mp = 1287°C
bp = 2467°C
density = 1.85 g/cm^3
4 Be Beryllium

mp = 649°C
bp = 1090°C
density = 1.74 g/cm^3
12 Mg Magnesium

mp = 839°C
bp = 1484°C
density = 1.54 g/cm^3
20 Ca Calcium

mp = 769°C
bp = 1384°C
density = 2.58g/cm^3
38 Sr Strontium

mp = 729°C
bp = 1637°C
density = 3.51 g/cm^3
56 Ba Barium

mp = 700°C
bp = 1737°C
density = 5.50 g/cm^3
88 Ra Radium

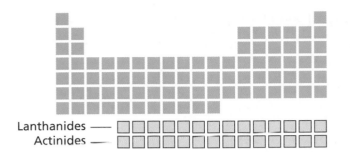

FIGURE 4-8

In order to keep the periodic table from becoming too wide, the lanthanides and actinides are placed below the rest of the table.

Lanthanides —
Actinides —

example, compounds of some lanthanide metals are used to make the phosphor dots in television tubes. When bombarded by a beam of electrons, the phosphors emit light of certain colors. The colors combine to create the brilliant images you see on a color television screen.

Elements 90 through 103 are the **actinides,** named for the first element in the series, actinium. Actinides are unique in that their nuclear structures are of more importance than their electron configurations. All actinides have an unstable arrangement of protons and neutrons in the nucleus, so actinides are *radioactive.* Perhaps the best-known actinide is uranium, which you will learn more about in Chapter 18. The nuclear disintegration of the uranium nucleus releases sufficient energy to run power plants, submarines, and aircraft carriers. Elements with atomic numbers 104 and above do not fall in the same category as the lanthanides or the actinides. These elements will be discussed further in Section 4-3.

Group 17: the halogens

The elements of Group 17, (fluorine, chlorine, bromine, iodine, and astatine) shown in **Figure 4-9,** are the **halogens.** The halogens combine with most metals to produce the compounds known as **salts.** The word *halogen* is derived from Greek and means "salt former." In common table salt, sodium chloride, the halogen chlorine has reacted with the alkali metal sodium to form sodium and chloride ions. You will learn more about salts in Chapter 5.

The halogens are the most reactive group of nonmetals and are members of the *p*-block elements. Electrons of elements in this group add to a *p* sublevel after the *s* sublevel in the same energy level is filled. Their electron configurations show why. Halogens have seven electrons in the outermost energy level,

actinides

shiny, metallic transition metals with atomic numbers 90 through 103 in which electrons are added to 5*f* orbitals

halogen

a nonmetallic element in Group 17 of the periodic table that has seven electrons in the outermost energy level and that combines with many metals to form salts

salt

a compound composed of positive and negative ions arranged in a regular three-dimensional pattern

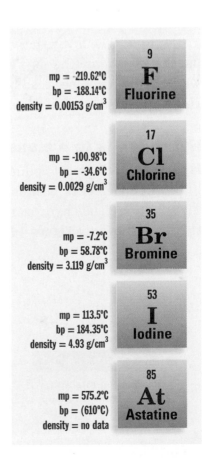

9
F
Fluorine
mp = -219.62°C
bp = -188.14°C
density = 0.00153 g/cm³

17
Cl
Chlorine
mp = -100.98°C
bp = -34.6°C
density = 0.0029 g/cm³

35
Br
Bromine
mp = -7.2°C
bp = 58.78°C
density = 3.119 g/cm³

53
I
Iodine
mp = 113.5°C
bp = 184.35°C
density = 4.93 g/cm³

85
At
Astatine
mp = 575.2°C
bp = (610°C)
density = no data

internet**connect**

SC*L*INKS
NSTA
TOPIC: Halogens
GO TO: www.scilinks.org
KEYWORD: HW043

FIGURE 4-9

The elements of Group 17 are called *halogens.* Halogens combine with metals to form salts.

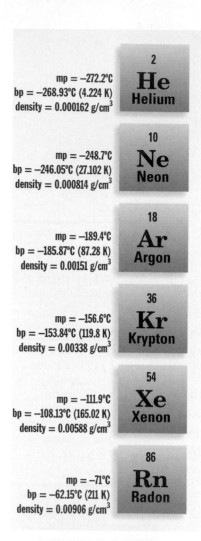

mp = −272.2°C
bp = −268.93°C (4.224 K)
density = 0.000162 g/cm³

2
He
Helium

mp = −248.7°C
bp = −246.05°C (27.102 K)
density = 0.000814 g/cm³

10
Ne
Neon

mp = −189.4°C
bp = −185.87°C (87.28 K)
density = 0.00151 g/cm³

18
Ar
Argon

mp = −156.6°C
bp = −153.84°C (119.8 K)
density = 0.00338 g/cm³

36
Kr
Krypton

mp = −111.9°C
bp = −108.13°C (165.02 K)
density = 0.00588 g/cm³

54
Xe
Xenon

mp = −71°C
bp = −62.15°C (211 K)
density = 0.00906 g/cm³

86
Rn
Radon

▲ **FIGURE 4-10**

The noble gases family consists of gaseous elements with extrememly low reactivity.

noble gases

elements in Group 18 of the periodic table that are characterized by low reactivity

so the highest energy level of a halogen atom is just one electron short of a noble gas structure. When halogen atoms react chemically they often acquire one electron to achieve the stable outer electron configuration of their closest noble gas neighbor in the periodic table.

Group 18: the noble gases

The Group 18 elements, shown in **Figure 4-10** are called **noble gases.** They were formerly called inert gases because they were thought to be completely unreactive. But in 1962, the first noble gas compound, XeF_2, was prepared. No compounds of helium, neon, and argon have yet been prepared.

Except for helium atoms, noble gas atoms are characterized by an octet of electrons, ns^2np^6, in the outermost energy level. From the low chemical reactivity observed in the noble gases, chemists infer that this *octet* of electrons makes these elements very stable. Although helium has only two electrons, the filled 1s shell of helium gives this gas the low reactivity characteristic of the other noble gases. Chemical reactions of the main-group elements show that these elements frequently achieve the stable outer electron configuration of the noble gases. For example, by losing an electron, lithium achieves the electron configuration of helium, $1s^2$, when forming compounds with most other elements.

A number of practical applications have been found for noble gases. Neon and argon, for example, are used in illuminated signs. The low reactivity of the noble gases leads to some special uses. Helium is the preferred gas in party balloons, blimps, and weather balloons because it is less dense than air but not flammable. Helium is also used to provide an inert atmosphere for welding.

Hydrogen is in a class by itself

Hydrogen is the most common element in the universe. It behaves unlike other elements because it has just one proton and one electron. This distinguishes hydrogen from all the other elements in the periodic table, as shown in **Figure 4-11.**

🔲 internet**connect**

SCI **LINKS**
NSTA

TOPIC: Noble gases
GO TO: www.scilinks.org
KEYWORD: HW044

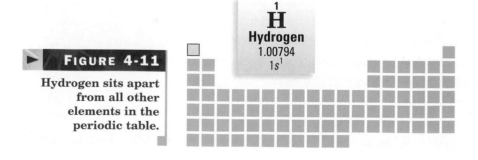

► **FIGURE 4-11**

Hydrogen sits apart from all other elements in the periodic table.

1
H
Hydrogen
1.00794
$1s^1$

Hydrogen can react with many elements, including oxygen. Hydrogen gas and oxygen gas react explosively to form water. Hydrogen is a component of all hydrocarbons as well as molecules that are essential to the chemistry of life, such as fats, proteins, and carbohydrates. The main industrial use of hydrogen is in the production of ammonia, NH_3. Large quantities of ammonia are used in the production of fertilizers. Elemental hydrogen is rare on the surface of Earth because free hydrogen is able to escape from Earth's atmosphere into space.

SECTION REVIEW

Total recall

1. State the periodic law.

2. What do elements in a period have in common? elements in a group?

3. What contribution did Moseley make to the development of the periodic table?

4. **Interpreting Tables** Write the atomic numbers and symbols for each of the following elements:
   a. silver   d. copper   g. palladium
   b. gold   e. zinc   h. radon
   c. mercury   f. platinum   i. radium

5. **Interpreting Tables** Which element in item 4 has the greatest atomic mass? the least atomic mass?

6. **Interpreting Tables** Round the atomic masses for each element listed in item 4 to the hundredths place.

7. What is the name of the elements located between the metals and nonmetals in the periodic table?

8. Give the group number and period number for each of the elements listed in item 4.

9. Which elements are considered the most stable? Why?

10. What is produced when halogens combine with alkali metals?

11. Why do groups of main-block elements display similar chemical behaviors?

12. What do you expect the electron configuration of element 112 to be?

13. Explain what the transition metals have in common with respect to their electron configurations.

14. What features do the halogens have in common? the noble gases?

15. Why is hydrogen placed in a group by itself?

Critical thinking

16. What characteristic of Newland's periodic table did Mendeleev incorporate into his periodic table?

17. How do the alkali metals differ from the alkaline-earth metals?

18. What led Mendeleev to predict that some elements had not yet been discovered?

19. Why are the nuclear configurations of the actinides more important than their electron configurations?

20. **Story Clue** To what groups do silver, gold, mercury, and copper belong?

21. **Interpreting Graphics** Use Figure 4-2 to answer the following questions.
    a. What do the question marks represent on Mendeleev's table?
    b. What does the comma represent in the entries for rubidium and strontium?

ELEMENT SPOTLIGHT

$\overset{8}{O}$ Oxygen
15.9994
$[He]2s^2 2p^4$

Every oxygen molecule in the atmosphere is a product of a living organism.

WHERE IS IT?

Earth's Crust
49% by mass

Air
23% by mass

Water
89% by mass

Rocks
45% by mass

internet**connect**

SC**LINKS**
NSTA

TOPIC: Oxygen
GO TO: www.scilinks.org
KEYWORD: HW045

Learning to live with oxygen

Paleontologists believe that life evolved in an environment free of oxygen gas but rich in carbon dioxide. Some early organisms developed the ability to use the energy of sunlight to drive chemical reactions that would otherwise be nonspontaneous. This process is called photosynthesis.

At this early point in the development of Earth's atmosphere, oxygen was a pollutant. Photosynthetic organisms kept releasing oxygen into the atmosphere. At the time, there were many minerals around for the oxygen to react with, so the amount of oxygen in the atmosphere did not change much. But as these photosynthetic organisms thrived and evolved, they released more and more oxygen into the atmosphere. This eventually exhausted the oxidizable minerals, and the oxygen level in the air began to climb. Over millions of years, organisms adapted to the rising level of oxygen in their environment. Now, many organisms depend on atmospheric oxygen, a waste product of photosynthesis, to carry out their essential life functions.

These photosynthetic plants release oxygen into the Earth's atmosphere.

Industrial Uses

▶ Sixty-five to eighty-five percent of oxygen produced in many countries is used to speed up reactions in steel making.

▶ Environmental and biomedical uses of oxygen include sewage treatment, river revival, paper/pulp bleaching, and submarine work.

▶ Liquid oxygen is used as an oxidizer of rocket fuels, which are essential to space exploration.

A BRIEF HISTORY

1773–1774: C. W. Scheele and J. Priestley independently discover oxygen.

1840: Ozone is detected and named by C. F. Schönbein.

| 1400 | 1700 | 1800 | 1900 |

15th century: Leonardo da Vinci notes that a component of air supports combustion.

1781: H. Cavendish establishes oxygen as a large component of water.

1775–1777: A. L. Lavoisier determines that oxygen is an element. He is also responsible for its name.

1963: Liquid O_2 and liquid H_2 are used to successfully launch a rocket at Cape Kennedy.

What gives metals their distinctive properties?

OBJECTIVES

▶ *Identify* the defining property of metals.

▶ *Describe* the varied properties of metals.

▶ *Explain* why metals are good conductors of electricity and heat.

▶ *Describe* how the atoms in most metals pack.

Characteristics of metals

Metals make up most of the periodic table, as **Figure 4-12** shows. But what exactly are metals? Often you can recognize a metal by its shiny appearance, but some nonmetals, plastics, and mineral samples can appear metallic. Conversely, some unpolished metals can look black and dull. Metals are good conductors of electricity and heat, although the nonmetal carbon, in the form of diamond, is the best conductor of heat, especially if it is composed only of carbon-12.

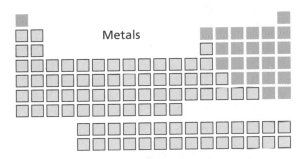
Metals

FIGURE 4-12 ▲

The majority of elements are metals, as this periodic table clearly indicates by its highlighted regions.

Metals are good conductors of electricity

One property distinguishes metallic elements from nonmetals: They are excellent conductors of electricity. Even the least conductive metal conducts electricity 100 times better than the best nonmetallic conductor. Surprisingly, metallic nature is *not* an innate property of an element. Instead, metallic nature appears to depend on temperature. *At room temperature* the stair-step line in the periodic table roughly divides the metals from the nonmetals. However, tin changes spontaneously into a nonmetal if it is kept for a long time below 13.2°C. Most nonmetals have been changed into metallic form by being placed under high pressure, especially at low temperatures.

The high electrical conductivity of metals is one reason why they are of such great importance. Gold is used extensively in electronic equipment despite its relatively high cost, especially in applications where resistance to corrosion is important. The metal most widely used to conduct electricity is copper, as shown in **Figure 4-13.** Copper conducts almost as well as gold, yet it is relatively inexpensive. It is used for everything from the wires in your home to the chips in your computer. For a while, aluminum was used for electrical wiring in homes, but its tendency to corrode caused many problems.

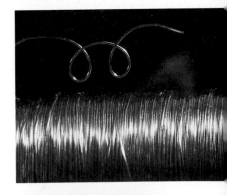

FIGURE 4-13 ▲

Copper, a transition metal, is used in wiring because it is an excellent conductor of electricity.

Metals that are good conductors of electricity are also good conductors of heat

In general, poor electrical conductors are poor heat conductors. What can you infer from that? Think about it. It indicates that the mechanism by which electricity is conducted must also be closely connected with the mechanism for conduction of heat.

You don't have to look far for the agent that causes conductivity in a metal. Ever since the discovery of electrons by J. J. Thomson and his colleagues, it has been known that electrons are responsible for the conduction of electricity by metals. Evidently, they are responsible for the conduction of heat as well. However, metals are the only elemental substances that are good conductors of electricity. It must be concluded that at least some of the electrons in metals must be in a different configuration than in nonmetals. These electrons are free to move through the metal in all directions.

CONCEPT CHECK

1. What is the single distinctive property of metals?
2. Explain the following statement: There is a relationship between high conductivity of electricity and high conductivity of heat.

Crystals and the conduction band

Consider the samples of carbon (diamond) and silicon shown in **Figure 4-14.** They are examples of matter in the form of crystals. A **crystal** is a substance in which atoms or molecules are arranged in an orderly, geometric repeating pattern in three dimensions.

crystal

a substance in which the atoms or molecules are arranged in an orderly, geometric, repeating pattern

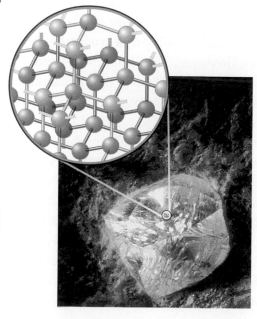 

> **FIGURE 4-14**
>
> **These samples of diamond and silicon are examples of matter in the form of crystals.**

FIGURE 4-15 ▼

Metals	Semiconductors	Nonmetals

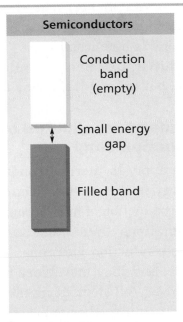
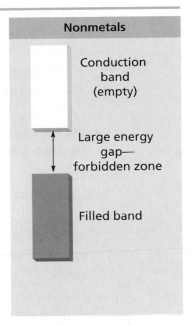

Energy

Conduction bands

or

Partially filled band | Overlapping bands

Conduction band (empty)

Small energy gap

Filled band

Conduction band (empty)

Large energy gap— forbidden zone

Filled band

a The forbidden gap is absent in many metals; very little energy is required to move electrons to the conduction band.

b The forbidden gap is smaller in semiconductors, so a few electrons are able to enter the conduction band.

c Electrons cannot occupy energy levels in the forbidden gap. This gap prevents practically all electrons from reaching the conduction band in insulators.

The outer electrons in the atoms of each element form the bonds that bind the atoms together in a crystal. In a crystal, each atom is bonded to all neighboring atoms. These electrons in the bonds exist in orbitals, just as electrons do in atoms. The electrons occupy the orbitals of lowest energy. However, just as in atoms, there are vacant orbitals of higher energy. Electrons in these higher orbitals are free to move about in three dimensions throughout the crystal, forming the **conduction band. Figure 4-15a** shows that in metals the orbitals of the conduction band actually overlap and are continuous with the bond orbitals in energy, so even at room temperature there are many electrons in the conduction band. Consequently, metals are very good conductors of electricity. On the other hand, the metal atoms are vibrating back and forth with thermal motion, interfering with the motion of electrons. The vibration increases as the temperature increases, so the conductivity of metals decreases as temperature increases.

In semiconductors, the energy of the higher (conducting) orbitals is not very high compared with the energy of the filled bonding orbitals, as shown in **Figure 4-15b.** It does not take much energy to excite electrons to these orbitals, so even at room temperature a semiconductor will carry a measurable current. At higher temperatures there are more electrons excited up to the conduction band, so the conductivity of semiconductors increases as the temperature increases.

conduction band

a band within which (or into which) electrons must move to allow electrical conduction

In typical nonmetals, such as carbon in the form of diamond, these orbitals have very high energy, as shown in **Figure 4-15c.** It is practically impossible to excite electrons to the orbitals of the conduction band, so diamond is a nonconductor. (There is no such thing as an absolute nonconductor. Extremely minute currents can be forced through any substance, but in practical terms they are nonconductors.)

In metals, heat is conducted by electrons in the conduction band

How does this apply to thermal conductivity? Recall from Chapter 2 that heat energy is the random motion of atom-sized particles. In a nonmetal, the conduction of heat is caused by the transfer of the energy of random vibrations from atom to atom. In metals the transfer medium is the conduction electrons. These electrons are of very low mass, of course, and they move very freely. Therefore, the transfer of heat energy is very efficient in metals. A high electrical conductivity will correspond to a high thermal conductivity.

It should be noted that high thermal conductivity does not always correspond to high electrical conductivity. For example, a diamond is the best known conductor of heat, yet it is a nonconductor of electricity. If electrons cannot move freely through a diamond crystal, how is heat conducted? The actual mechanism of heat conduction in diamond is complex, but it is related to the passage of vibration waves through the crystal, not to electrons.

The high thermal conductivity of metals explains why metals feel cold to the touch, even at room temperature. Your fingers are warmer than the metal, and when you touch the metal, it conducts heat away from your flesh, causing your fingers to sense cold. Which will feel colder to the touch, lead or aluminum?

Some other properties of metals

Aside from being good conductors of electricity and heat, metals exhibit a wide array of properties. Tungsten has the highest melting point, 3422°C, of any element. In contrast, mercury melts at –39°C. This low melting point, along with high density, makes mercury useful for barometers. Cesium is extremely reactive chemically, yet other metals, such as gold, are unreactive. This makes gold, along with copper and silver, invaluable in electronics and other sensitive applications. Many metals, such as iron, are very strong and durable. Aluminum and magnesium have a high strength-to-weight ratio, making them useful for many construction purposes where light weight is advantageous.

Some metals, such as manganese and bismuth, are very brittle, yet others, such as gold and iron, are ductile and

▼ **FIGURE 4-16**

Steel, a mixture of iron and carbon, is one of the most important industrial alloys. When heated, steel can be worked into many useful shapes.

malleable. The capacity to be squeezed out into a wire is known as *ductility*. Gold can be drawn into wires only a few micrometers in diameter. The gold wires can then be spun into fine cloth. A *malleable* substance can be hammered or rolled into sheets. Gold can be hammered out into gold leaves only 25 nm thick. Iron becomes malleable when heated to red heat, as shown in **Figure 4-16** on page 128. It can also be rolled into thin sheets for cans.

Adding to the versatility of metals is the fact that two or more metallic elements can be mixed together to produce an alloy. An **alloy** is a solution of metallic, and sometimes nonmetallic, elements. Stainless steel, an alloy of iron and chromium, and either nickel or manganese, is extremely resistant to corrosion.

alloy

a solid or liquid solution of two or more metals

CONCEPT CHECK

1. What is a crystal?
2. What is the conduction band? How is the conduction band related to the conductivity of electricity and heat?

The structure of metallic crystals

The attraction between metal atoms and the electrons accounts for the metallic bonding in metals. Even a tiny piece of metal may contain millions of identical atoms. How are these atoms arranged in a sample of metal? Metallic atoms adopt regular arrangements in crystals. To a chemist, a crystal is a solid characterized by a regular, orderly arrangement of its constituent particles. Some examples are diamonds, table salt, sugar, and metals in the solid state. A crystal structure is an orderly array, like the display in a fruit store, as shown in **Figure 4-17.**

How can the atoms pack together in the densest fashion? One layer of atoms is shown in **Figure 4-18a.** Exactly six atoms fit around any one atom. The next layer, shown in **Figure 4-18b,** is an exact copy of the first but displaced slightly so that it fits into the depressions between atoms in the first layer. If you look down on these two layers, half the spaces between atoms show atoms in the first layer and

FIGURE 4-18 ▼

The arrangement of atoms in metals is similar to the packing of spheres. As the illustration shows, there are two ways atoms can pack as densely as possible, between spaces or directly above atoms.

a   Layer 1

b   Layer 2

c   Layer 3
or

d   Layer 3

► **FIGURE 4-17**

The arrangement of oranges shows how spheres can be packed together to take up the least amount of space. You can think of the atoms in crystals as spheres that pack in the same pattern.

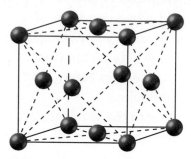

a The atoms in a lead crystal assume a cubic close-packed structure.

b This model shows that a cubic close-packed structure has an atom at each corner and at the center of each face of a cube.

half show spaces in the first layer. The third layer has two possible arrangements. It can fit directly above spaces in the first layer, as shown in **Figure 4-18c,** or directly above atoms in the first layer, as shown in **Figure 4-18d.**

If the atoms in the third layer are placed directly above spaces in the first layer and this process is repeated, the result is a *cubic close-packed* structure, also called *face-centered cubic.* This structure is shown in **Figure 4-19a.** Notice that the cube has an atom in each face. The unit structure is shown in **Figure 4-19b.** Repetition of this unit in three dimensions produces a macroscopic crystal of cubic shape.

If the atoms in the third layer are placed directly above the atoms in the first layer and this arrangement is repeated, the result is the *hexagonal close-packed* crystal structure, illustrated in **Figure 4-20a.** The unit structure is shown in **Figure 4-20b.** If this arrangement is repeated in three dimensions, the result is a macroscopic hexagonal crystal.

Most metals crystallize in one of these two structures, indicating that the atoms are essentially spherical in shape. The elements that do not crystallize in one of these two crystal forms have localized bonds between the atoms that force the crystal into some other shape.

▼ **FIGURE 4-20**

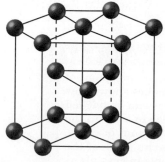

a The atoms in a magnesium crystal assume a hexagonal close-packed structure.

b This model shows the distinctive six-sided shape of a hexagonal close-packed structure.

Symbols for metallic elements

Some elements exist in nature as molecules. You read in Chapter 1 that hydrogen, nitrogen, and oxygen are diatomic gases. Therefore, we write the symbols of these elements as H_2, N_2, and O_2. The subscript on the symbol indicates the number of atoms in each molecule. However, metals as well as several nonmetallic elements, such as C and Si, form crystals of many atoms, all of which are bonded to one another. Thus a very small iron crystal might be $Fe_{1\ 236\ 459\ 028}$. This indicates a lot of atoms in a very small crystal of iron. If you chop this crystal in half, you will have two crystals, each having the same properties of the original crystal but with half the number of atoms. This property applies to all solid metallic elements, but because there is no set number of atoms in the crystals of these elements, it is convenient to write their symbols as if they were monatomic: Fe, Hg, Pb, and so on. Keep in mind that the only truly monatomic elements at room temperature are the noble gases: He, Ne, Ar, Kr, Xe, and Rn.

SECTION REVIEW

Total recall

1. What is the difference between a metal and a nonmetal?

2. Why is copper used in electrical wiring? Would gold or aluminum be a better choice? Explain.

3. Define what is meant by malleability and ductility.

4. Identify the one property that all metals share.

5. How is an alloy made?

6. What are crystals?

7. Explain the difference in the conduction bands of metals, nonmetals, and semiconductors.

8. Which electrons form the bonds that bind atoms of an element together in a crystal?

Critical thinking

9. The conductivity of semiconductors increases with an increase in temperature, while the conductivity of metals decreases. Explain why this is so.

10. Why is the symbol for a piece of aluminum foil, which contains billions of aluminum atoms, written simply as Al?

11. Give two reasons why iron is such a useful metal.

12. What element has the highest melting point?

13. Suggest a reason why high pressure can change a nonmetal into metallic form.

14. An element is shiny, can be squeezed to form a wire, and can be hammered to form a sheet. Can this element be classified as a metal? Explain the reason for your answer.

15. **Story Clue** Why are dental fillings classified as alloys?

SUPERCONDUCTORS

Saving Energy with Superconductors

When electric current passes along a wire, some of the energy of the flowing electrons is converted to heat as the electrons interact with the metal atoms in the wire. This effect, called *resistance,* is useful in a toaster, an electric heater, or a light bulb filament. In most cases, though, as in an electric motor, heat is an unwanted result of the resistance to flow of electrons and is wasted energy.

Superconductivity Discovered Since the nineteenth century scientists have known that a metal becomes a better conductor as its temperature is lowered. In 1911, a Dutch physicist was studying the decrease in resistance of mercury as its temperature decreased. When he used liquid helium to cool the metal to about 4 K, an unexpected thing happened—the mercury lost all electric resistance and became a *superconductor.*

Overhead power lines typically waste half the energy of the current that flows through them. If wires had no resistance at all, we could save a huge amount of energy.

Scientists were excited about this new discovery, but the use of superconductors was severely limited by the huge expense of cooling them to near absolute zero. Scientists began research to find a material that would superconduct at temperatures above 77 K, the boiling point of liquid nitrogen, which is cheap to produce.

High-Temperature Superconductors

Ceramic Conductors Finally, in 1987 scientists discovered materials that became superconductors when cooled to only 90 K. A surprise was that these "high-temperature" superconductors weren't metals at all. Rather, they were ceramics, usually copper oxides combined with elements such as yttrium or barium. These ceramic materials are brittle and difficult to form into wire-like strands. Since the discovery of ceramic superconductors, engineers have found ways to fabricate these materials into useful forms.

Electromagnets High-temperature superconductors are used in the construction of very powerful electromagnets that are not limited by resistance or heat buildup. These magnets can be used to build powerful particle accelerators as well as high-efficiency electric motors and generators. Electromagnets have already been used to levitate a passenger train above its guide rail so that it can move with minimum friction and thus save fuel. Engineers are now working to build a similar system that will use superconducting electromagnets.

Medical Tools Superconductors are being used to construct devices that can detect and measure the very faint magnetic fields of the heart and brain. The results allow physicians to diagnose and study heart disease and neurological disorders such as epilepsy. Similar devices can be used to detect flaws in the structure of an aircraft. This is a useful tool in the prevention of aircraft failure due to structural problems.

The strong magnetic field produced by these superconducting electromagnets can suspend this 8 cm disk. Such a disk could form a magnetically levitated bearing for a nearly frictionless electric motor or generator.

internetconnect

SCLINKS
NSTA

TOPIC: Superconductors
GO TO: www.scilinks.org
KEYWORD: HW046

CAREER APPLICATION

What would it be like to . . .

- develop high-strength, ultralight ceramics for interplanetary travel?
- discover the first room-temperature superconductor?
- formulate a material that can replace human bones and tendons?

Science/Math Career Preparation	
High School	**College**
Biology	Physics
Chemistry	Chemistry
Physics	Mathematics
Mathematics	Biology

Materials Scientist

A materials scientist is interested in discovering materials that will withstand harsh conditions, have unusual properties, or perform unique functions. These materials might include the following: a lightweight plastic that conducts electricity; a ceramic that will superconduct; extremely light but strong materials to construct a space platform; a plastic that can replace iron and aluminum in building automobile engines; a new building material that expands and contracts very little, even when temperatures vary as much as 500 K; or a strong, flexible, but extremely tough material that can replace bone or connective tissue in surgery. Materials engineers develop such materials and discover ways to mold or shape them into usable forms. Many materials scientists work in the aerospace industry, developing new materials to reduce the mass of aircraft, rockets, and space vehicles.

What trends are found in the periodic table?

OBJECTIVES

▶ **Describe** periodic trends in atomic radius, ionization energy, electron affinity, melting points, and boiling points.

▶ **Relate** trends in the periodic table to the atomic structures of the elements.

Periodic trends

You have read that elements are arranged in the periodic table in order of increasing atomic number. The elements are further organized into groups and periods. The arrangement of the periodic table reveals trends, or general tendencies, in the physical and chemical properties of elements. In this section you will look at some of these trends and learn how they can be explained in terms of electron configuration.

What is a trend? A trend is a predictable change in a particular direction. For example, as you move down Group 1, reactivity increases for each element. In other words, there is a trend toward greater reactivity among the alkali metals. This trend is illustrated in **Figure 4-21.** Knowing the various trends for elements in the periodic table enables you to make logical predictions about chemical behavior.

Periodic trends in atomic radii

The exact size of an atom is difficult to determine. It is determined by the volume occupied by the electrons surrounding the nucleus. The electrons in an atom are modeled as clouds, with no clear-cut boundary. The probability of encountering electrons decreases with distance from the nucleus, but the outer boundaries are fuzzy and actually depend on

▶ **FIGURE 4-21**

Chemical reactivity increases somewhat from top to bottom for Group 1 elements. Reactions of lithium, sodium, and potassium with water are shown.

Lithium

Sodium

Potassium

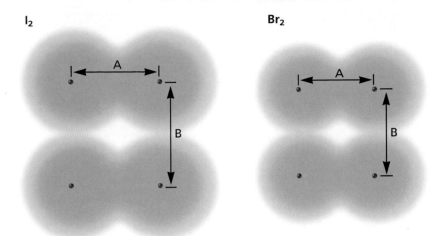

I₂   Br₂

FIGURE 4-22 ◄

Lines A and B represent the distances between centers of like atoms that are in contact. Two ways of measuring atomic radii are shown: bond radius and van der Waals radius.

the physical and chemical condition of the atoms. Radii are usually determined for atoms that are chemically bonded or close together in the solid state, such as Br_2 and I_2. Half the distance between the nuclei of the atoms in each molecule is called the **bond radius.** Line segment A in **Figure 4-22** represents twice the bond radius of the halogen atom in question.

Line segment B represents the distance between the nuclei in adjacent nonbonded molecules, which is equal to twice the distance called the **van der Waals radius.** The van der Waals radius is sometimes used to state the size of atoms, but data are available for only a few of the main-group elements. Because of the "fuzziness" of atoms, van der Waals radii are generally not very precise. In this book, bond radius will be used to denote the size of atoms because there are more data available.

The bond radius is about two-thirds of the van der Waals radius and is known with great precision. The problem is that the bond types, even for the same atom, may be quite different. For example, the bonds between tin atoms in metallic tin are very different from the bonds between tin atoms and chlorine atoms in $SnCl_4$. Therefore, the bond radius of a tin atom in metallic tin is different from the bond radius of a tin atom in $SnCl_4$. Even with this limitation, measuring the bond radius is a useful way to compare the sizes of atoms.

bond radius

one-half the distance from center to center of two like atoms bonded together

van der Waals radius

half the distance between the nuclei in adjacent non-bonded molecules

Atomic radius increases as you move down a group

There is a general trend toward larger radii as you proceed down a group, as shown in **Figure 4-23** on page 136. This is caused by the addition of another principal energy level from one period to the next. The electrons in the inner energy levels are between the nucleus and the outermost electrons and therefore shield the outer electrons

STUDY SKILLS

ORGANIZING WHAT YOU'VE LEARNED

Organizing the information you have learned will help you both in understanding the information and in memorizing it. There are several strategies you can use to organize both your class notes and important ideas from the text. These strategies can also help you to develop and structure paragraphs for research papers and essay exams. Two of these are concept mapping and power notes, which are explained in detail in Appendix B.

Periodic Table of Atomic Radii (pm)

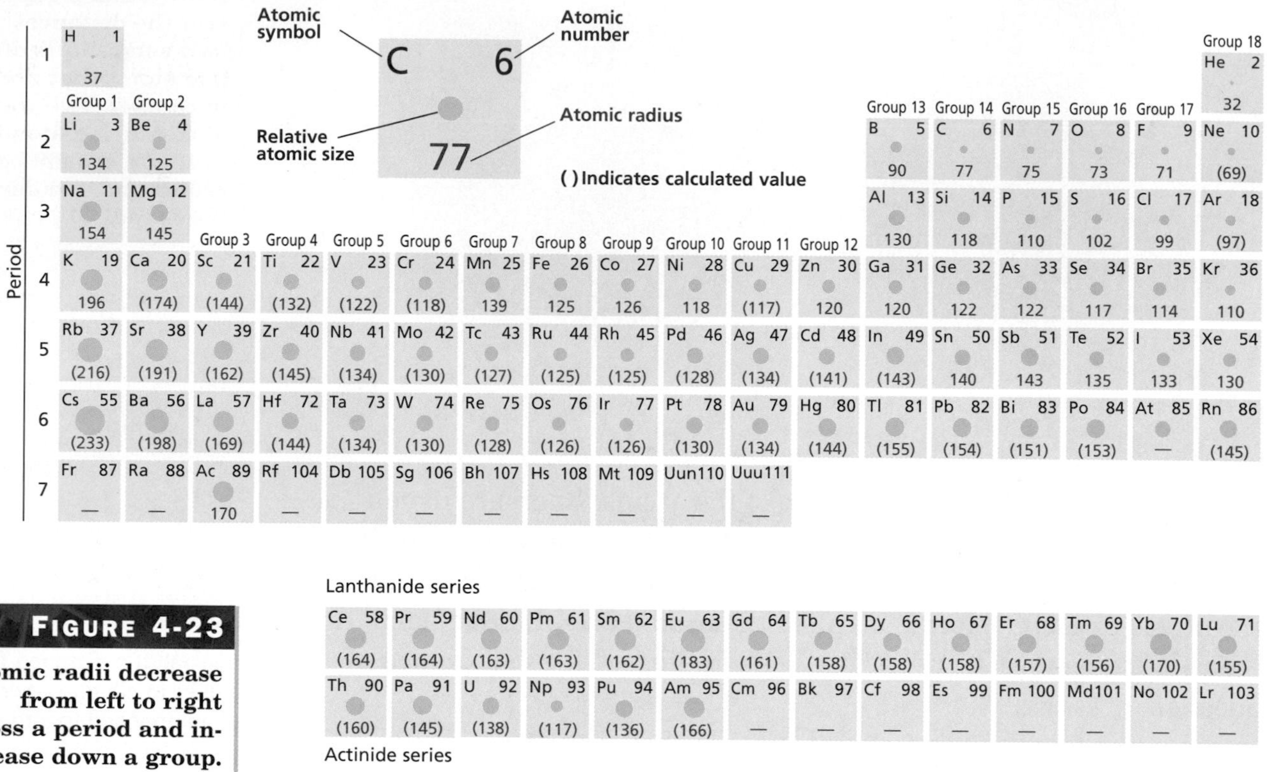

Atomic symbol

Atomic number

C   6

Relative atomic size

Atomic radius

77

( ) Indicates calculated value

H 1																	He 2
37																	32

Figure 4-23 table values (as read):

Period 1: H 1 — 37; He 2 — 32
Group 1 / Group 2 ... Group 13–18
Period 2: Li 3 — 134; Be 4 — 125; B 5 — 90; C 6 — 77; N 7 — 75; O 8 — 73; F 9 — 71; Ne 10 — (69)
Period 3: Na 11 — 154; Mg 12 — 145; Al 13 — 130; Si 14 — 118; P 15 — 110; S 16 — 102; Cl 17 — 99; Ar 18 — (97)
Period 4: K 19 — 196; Ca 20 — (174); Sc 21 — (144); Ti 22 — (132); V 23 — (122); Cr 24 — (118); Mn 25 — 139; Fe 26 — 125; Co 27 — 126; Ni 28 — 118; Cu 29 — (117); Zn 30 — 120; Ga 31 — 120; Ge 32 — 122; As 33 — 122; Se 34 — 117; Br 35 — 114; Kr 36 — 110
Period 5: Rb 37 — (216); Sr 38 — (191); Y 39 — (162); Zr 40 — (145); Nb 41 — (134); Mo 42 — (130); Tc 43 — (127); Ru 44 — (125); Rh 45 — (125); Pd 46 — (128); Ag 47 — (134); Cd 48 — (141); In 49 — (143); Sn 50 — 140; Sb 51 — 143; Te 52 — 135; I 53 — 133; Xe 54 — 130
Period 6: Cs 55 — (233); Ba 56 — (198); La 57 — (169); Hf 72 — (144); Ta 73 — (134); W 74 — (130); Re 75 — (128); Os 76 — (126); Ir 77 — (126); Pt 78 — (130); Au 79 — (134); Hg 80 — (144); Tl 81 — (155); Pb 82 — (154); Bi 83 — (151); Po 84 — (153); At 85 — —; Rn 86 — (145)
Period 7: Fr 87 — —; Ra 88 — —; Ac 89 — 170; Rf 104 — —; Db 105 — —; Sg 106 — —; Bh 107 — —; Hs 108 — —; Mt 109 — —; Uun 110; Uuu 111

Lanthanide series

Ce 58 — (164); Pr 59 — (164); Nd 60 — (163); Pm 61 — (163); Sm 62 — (162); Eu 63 — (183); Gd 64 — (161); Tb 65 — (158); Dy 66 — (158); Ho 67 — (158); Er 68 — (157); Tm 69 — (156); Yb 70 — (170); Lu 71 — (155)

Actinide series

Th 90 — (160); Pa 91 — (145); U 92 — (138); Np 93 — (117); Pu 94 — (136); Am 95 — (166); Cm 96 — —; Bk 97 — —; Cf 98 — —; Es 99 — —; Fm 100 — —; Md 101 — —; No 102 — —; Lr 103 — —

▲ **FIGURE 4-23**

Atomic radii decrease from left to right across a period and increase down a group.

electron shielding

the reduction of the attractive force between a positively charged nucleus and its outermost electrons due to the cancellation of some of the positive charge by the negative charge of the other electrons

from the full charge of the nucleus. This phenomenon is called **electron shielding.** Because the outermost electrons are not subject to the full charge of the nucleus, they are not held as close to the nucleus.

As you move down a group, the nuclear charge increases. At the same time, the screening of the inner electrons also increases. The net result is that the effective nuclear charge acting on the outer electrons is almost constant, regardless of the energy level in which the outer electrons are located. For example, the effective nuclear charge acting on the outermost electron in a cesium atom is about the same as it is in a sodium atom.

Atomic radius decreases as you move across a period

The trend to smaller atoms across a period is caused by the increasing positive charge of the nucleus. From left to right within a period, each atom has one more proton and one more electron than the element before it. However, the additional electrons are going into the same energy levels. Electrons in an outer energy level do not screen the other electrons in that energy level very effectively. Consequently, as the nuclear charge increases across a period, the effective nuclear charge also increases, pulling the electrons closer to the nucleus and reducing the size of the atom. The addition of electrons to *d* orbitals, as in the interval Ca to Ga, has little effect on atomic radius.

Atomic Radii of Main-Block Elements

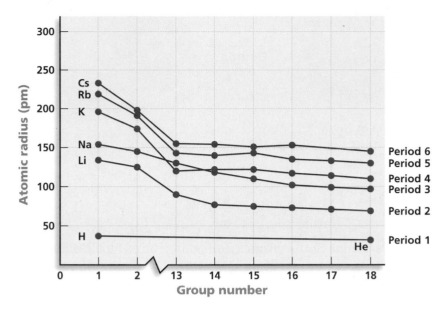

FIGURE 4-24 ◀

As you move across a period, the radii of atoms tend to decrease due to an increase in effective nuclear charge. As you move to the next highest period, the effective nuclear charge remains about the same, but there are more main energy levels, so the sizes of the atoms are greater.

As you can see in **Figure 4-24,** this trend is less pronounced in periods where there are many electrons between the nucleus and the outermost energy level. As you move from left to right in a period, one proton is added to the nucleus and one electron is added to the outer energy level. As you proceed from left to right in the period, the effective positive charge increases gradually, pulling the electrons closer to the nucleus. As the electrons are pulled closer to the nucleus, they get closer to one another and repulsions occur. Finally, the stage is reached when the electrons will not come much closer and the size of the atom tends to level off.

CONCEPT CHECK

1. What is a trend?
2. What trend is found in the reactivity of the alkali metals?
3. What trend is there among atomic radii as you move across a period? down a group?
4. What is electron shielding? How does it affect atomic radius?

Ionization energy, electron affinity, and melting points

Recall that atoms are electrically neutral. However, if enough energy is added, an atom may lose an electron to become a positive ion. Imagine that you can reach into an atom and remove one of the outermost electrons, creating an ion. The energy you use to remove the electron is the **ionization energy** of the atom. **Figure 4-25,** on the next page, illustrates this process. The lithium ion is smaller than the lithium atom because the single electron has been removed from the outer energy level. The process of removing an electron can be expressed as an equation.

ionization energy

the amount of energy needed to remove an outer electron from a specific atom or ion in its ground state and in the gas phase

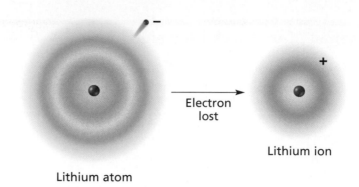

Electron lost

Lithium ion

Lithium atom

$$A + \text{energy} \longrightarrow A^+ + e^-$$
$$\text{atom} \qquad \text{ion}$$

Figure 4-26 shows ionization energies for some main-block elements. Examine Figure 4-26, and determine which group of elements has the lowest ionization energy.

Ionization energies increase across a period and decrease down a group

Periodic trends in ionization energies are opposite those for atomic size. Ionization energy tends to increase across a period and decrease down a group. As mentioned above, as more protons are added to the nucleus, the effective nuclear charge acting on the outermost electrons increases, holding the electrons more tightly to the nucleus. Hence ionization energy increases across a period.

Ionization Energies of Main-Block Elements

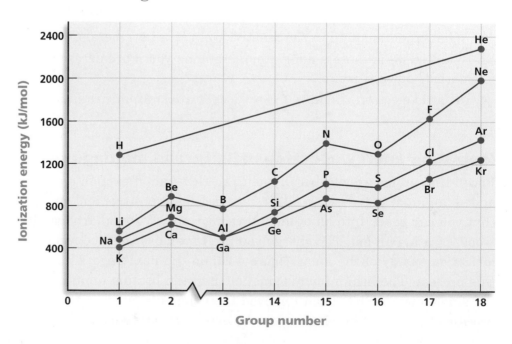

► **FIGURE 4-26**

Ionization energies are shown for the main-block elements of the first four periods. The periodic trend in ionization energy is the opposite of that for atomic size.

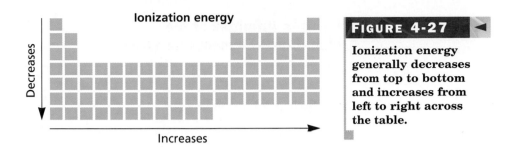

Ionization energy

Decreases

Increases

FIGURE 4-27 ◄

Ionization energy generally decreases from top to bottom and increases from left to right across the table.

Similarly, as you move down a group, the number of energy levels between the nucleus and the outermost electrons increases and the outermost electrons are farther from the nucleus. The effective nuclear charge is about the same, so the outer electrons are held less tightly to the nucleus, and less energy is required to remove one of them.

Moreover, as you move down a group, the outermost electrons are farther from the nucleus. According to Coulomb's law, which you read about in Chapter 3, the force between two charged particles decreases as the distance between the particles increases. Thus, as you move down a group, attractive forces between the nucleus and the outermost electrons decrease and the energy necessary to remove an electron from the atom decreases. The general trends are shown in **Figure 4-27.**

Periodic trends in electron affinity

The ability of an atom to attract and hold an electron is called **electron affinity.** You may wonder why a neutral atom would attract electrons in the first place. The answer is that the electrons in the orbitals generally do not shield the nuclear charge to a full 100%. An approaching electron therefore may experience a net pull because the effective nuclear charge is greater than zero. The electron enters a vacant orbital. This is illustrated in **Figure 4-28.**

When an atom gains an extra electron, it becomes a negative ion. In most cases energy is given off in the process. This process can be represented by the following equation.

$$A + e^- \longrightarrow A^- + \text{energy}$$
$$\text{atom} \longrightarrow \text{ion}$$

electron affinity

the energy emitted upon the addition of an electron to an atom or group of atoms in the gas phase

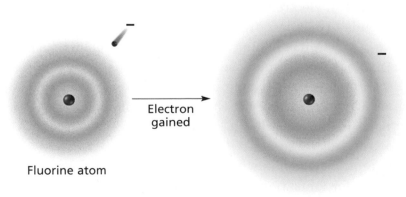

Electron gained

Fluorine atom

Fluoride ion

FIGURE 4-28 ◄

A fluorine atom gains an electron to become a negatively charged ion. Energy is emitted in the process, so the electron affinity of fluorine is assigned a negative value.

TABLE 4-3 Electron Affinities of the Main-Block Elements (in kJ/mol)

1							2
H −72.77							**He** (7)
3 **Li** −59.6	4 **Be** (17)*	5 **B** −26.7	6 **C** −121.9	7 **N** −7	8 **O** −141.0	9 **F** −328.2	10 **Ne** (8)
11 **Na** −52.9	12 **Mg** (14)	13 **Al** −42.6	14 **Si** −133.6	15 **P** −72.0	16 **S** −200.4	17 **Cl** −348.6	18 **Ar** (9)
19 **K** −48.4	20 **Ca** (−4)	31 **Ga** −30	32 **Ge** −119.0	33 **As** −78	34 **Se** −195.0	35 **Br** −324.5	36 **Kr** (10)
37 **Rb** −46.9	38 **Sr** (−11)	49 **In** −29	50 **Sn** −107.3	51 **Sb** −103	52 **Te** −190.2	53 **I** −295.2	54 **Xe** (11)
55 **Cs** −45.5	56 **Ba** (−14)	81 **Tl** −20	82 **Pb** −35.1	83 **Bi** −91.3	84 **Po** (−180)	85 **At** (−270)	86 **Rn** (11)

*Numbers in parentheses were calculated.

In this text, a negative electron affinity indicates that energy is released when the atom gains an electron. A positive value indicates that energy is needed to add the electron to an atom.

Electron affinity is much more difficult to measure, or calculate, than ionization energy. This is especially true for the noble gas and alkaline-earth elements. Many previous texts gave these elements very large positive values. Only recently have values become available for many elements. Electron affinities for the main block elements are given in **Table 4-3.**

Electron affinity becomes more negative across a period

In a general way, electron affinity becomes more negative across a period and tends to decrease from top to bottom in a group. Think about the effects of electron shielding: across a period, shielding remains constant as nuclear charge increases. Therefore, the atom's attraction for extra electrons increases. Going down a group, both shielding and nuclear charge increase. However, the effect of shielding more than offsets the increase in nuclear charge. Therefore, the atom's attraction for extra electrons decreases.

Electron affinity trends within groups of elements are not as regular as trends for ionization energy. As you can see in Table 4-3, there are exceptions to this general trend. The alkaline-earth metals are one of these exceptions. An electron added to an alkaline-earth metal must go into a *p* orbital and is shielded to a greater extent by *s* electrons. The reason the effect is so large is not clear.

Periodic trends in melting and boiling points

Melting points and boiling points for elements in the sixth period are shown in **Figure 4-29.** At first, as the number of electrons increases, the melting and boiling points increase. This indicates stronger bonding. However, at about the stage where the *d* orbitals become half-filled, the melting and boiling points begin to decrease. This indicates that the added electrons become less involved in bonding. Finally, at the element mercury, a deep minimum is reached where the *d* orbitals are completely filled. The filled *d* orbitals result in low chemical bond strength and a low boiling point for mercury. For the same reason, zinc

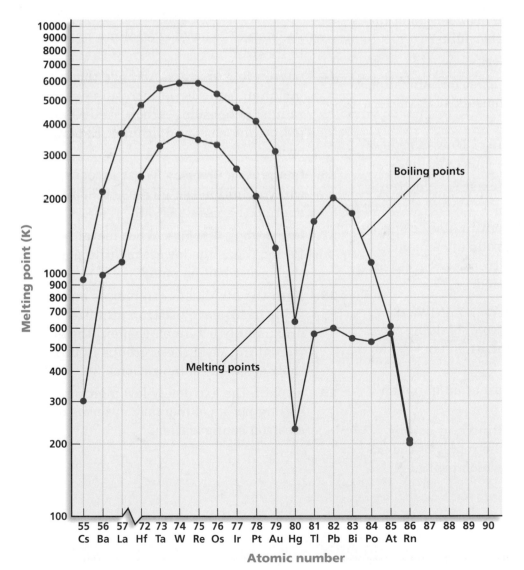

Melting Points and Boiling Points of Period-6 Elements

FIGURE 4-29 ◄

Melting points and boiling points of Period 6 elements in solid and liquid phases show a periodic trend.

and cadmium exhibit low melting and boiling points in their respective periods.

As p electrons are added, we see a similar rise and fall, with the maximum near the stage where the p orbitals are half filled. A minimum is reached when the p orbitals are filled and the atoms no longer bond. The noble gases are monatomic and have no chemical bonding forces between atoms. Therefore, their melting and boiling points are unusually low.

SECTION REVIEW

Total recall

1. Why is it difficult to measure the size of an atom?

2. What does the term *atomic radius* mean?

3. What is the difference between bond radius and van der Waals radius?

4. What is ionization energy?

5. What periodic trends exist for ionization energy? What exceptions exist in these trends?

6. What is electron affinity? How is it different from ionization energy?

7. What periodic trends exist for electron affinity?

8. What trends are evident in atomic size as you proceed down a group of elements? How do each of these trends progress as you move across a period?

9. Define the term *electron shielding*.

10. What effect does electron shielding have on atomic size? on ionization energy? on electron affinity?

11. What happens when an atom gains an extra electron?

12. The periodicity of melting and boiling points in Period 6 is the result of the addition of electrons to which orbitals?

Critical thinking

13. When an atom loses an electron, what is its charge? What do you think happens to the size of the atom?

14. When an atom gains an electron, what is its charge? What do you think happens to its size?

15. **Interpreting Graphics** Arrange the following atoms in order of increasing atomic radius: potassium, carbon, rubidium, iodine, fluorine, and lithium. Explain the order.

16. **Interpreting Graphics** What exceptions can you find in the increase of ionization energies across a period?

17. **Interpreting Graphics** What metal in Period 6 has the lowest melting point? the lowest boiling point?

18. Both the alkaline-earth metals and the noble gases have electron affinities of approximately 0 kJ/mol. Explain the electron affinities of these groups in terms of their electron configurations.

19. Explain the extremely low melting and boiling points of mercury in terms of electron configuration.

Where did the elements come from?

OBJECTIVES

▶ **Distinguish** between naturally occurring and synthetic elements.

▶ **Describe** how the naturally occurring elements are formed.

▶ **Describe** how particle accelerators are used to create synthetic elements.

Natural and synthetic elements

Chemists have identified 93 naturally occurring elements. Three of these elements, technetium, promethium, and neptunium, are not found on Earth but have been detected in the spectra of stars. The nebula shown in **Figure 4-30** is a region in the galaxy where new stars are formed.

Chemists have created, or *synthesized,* more elements than the 93 that occur naturally. These are the *synthetic elements.* Most of the transuranium elements are synthetic. Those naturally occurring elements that are found on Earth in minute amounts, like francium and astatine, or not at all are usually categorized as synthetic elements.

Naturally occurring elements are created in the center of stars

According to current theory, some time between 12 billion and 16 billion years ago the entire universe could fit on a pinhead. Then with unbelievable violence the universe exploded, an event scientists named the big bang. Immediately after the big bang, temperatures were in the millions of kelvins, so high that matter could not exist, only energy. As the universe expanded, it cooled. When the universe cooled to a few thousand kelvins, some of its energy was converted to matter in the form of electrons, protons, and neutrons. As the universe continued to cool, these particles formed the first atoms, almost all hydrogen but also some helium.

Over time, huge clouds of hydrogen accumulated. Gravitational attraction pulled the clumps of hydrogen closer and closer together. As the clouds became denser, pressures and temperatures at the centers of the hydrogen clouds increased, and stars

FIGURE 4-30 ▼

Technetium, promethium, and neptunium have been detected in the spectra of stars.

FIGURE 4-31

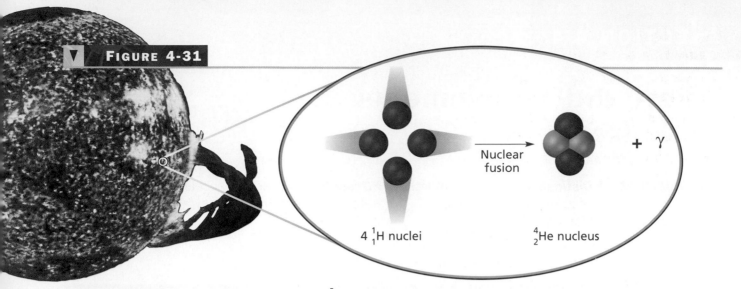

a Nuclear fusion in the nearest star, our sun, has provided the Earth with energy for billions of years. Fusion reactions also create elements heavier than hydrogen.

b The single helium nucleus has less mass than the four hydrogen nuclei from which it is formed. The small amount of mass "lost" during fusion is converted to energy. The symbol γ, the Greek letter gamma, indicates that energy is released in the form of gamma radiation.

nuclear reaction

a reaction that involves a change in the composition of the nucleus of an atom

were born. In the high-temperature centers of stars, nuclear reactions took place. A **nuclear reaction** is a reaction involving protons and neutrons in the nuclei of atoms. In the nuclear reactions in the centers of the first stars, hydrogen nuclei fused with one another to form helium nuclei. This *nuclear fusion* reaction is modeled in **Figure 4-31.** Nuclear fusion reactions can take place only under conditions of extreme heat, such as the conditions found in stars. There the kinetic energy of the nuclei is great enough to overcome the repulsion between positively charged protons. For example, our sun converts about 3.6×10^{11} kg (4×10^8 tons) of hydrogen into helium every second.

Notice in Figure 4-31b the mass of a helium nucleus compared with the mass of the hydrogen nuclei that fuse to form it. The mass "lost" in a fusion reaction is actually converted to energy. Einstein's equation $E = mc^2$ describes this mass-to-energy conversion quantitatively. The constant, c, is the speed of light. The energy produced by fusion reactions is enough to maintain the extremely high temperatures in the centers of the stars. As the hydrogen is used up, the star shrinks and the temperature in the star's center increases. As the temperature increases, helium nuclei fuse with one another to form elements of higher atomic number. As the temperature continues to rise, elements of still higher atomic number are formed. **Figure 4-32** shows an example of this process. The most massive atoms formed by this process are iron and nickel. Geologists believe that the core of the Earth is composed of a mixture of iron and nickel.

When a star the size of the sun uses up all of the hydrogen and helium in its center, it collapses and then expands as a red giant. As this red giant forms, some atoms are torn apart, producing free protons and neutrons. These particles are absorbed by the nuclei of other atoms, creating elements with atomic numbers greater than that of iron and that

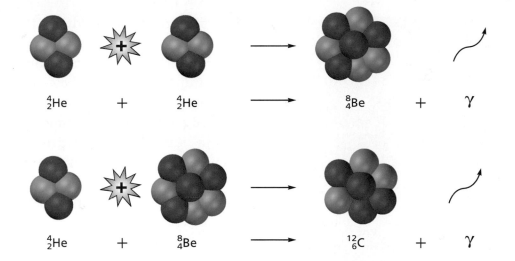

$$^4_2He + ^4_2He \longrightarrow ^8_4Be + \gamma$$

$$^4_2He + ^8_4Be \longrightarrow ^{12}_6C + \gamma$$

of nickel. The super-hot red giant expels some of its matter into space, including the elements it has produced. If the star is considerably larger than the sun, the star will eventually explode as a supernova and matter will spread across space for millions of kilometers. This matter includes, of course, all the elements previously formed in the star, including those with atomic numbers greater than iron and nickel.

Some of the matter from the supernova eventually condensed into new stars. Like earlier stars, these stars were mostly hydrogen, but they also contained heavier elements formed in the previous generation of stars. In turn, these new stars evolved, giving rise to a third generation, that was further enriched with heavy elements. The current theory indicates that the sun is a fourth- or fifth-generation star. When the sun first formed, it contained all the naturally occurring elements.

CONCEPT CHECK

1. Where were all the naturally occurring elements formed?
2. What is the most common element in the universe?

Artificial elements

Transmutations are a type of nuclear reaction

Many of the activities of the alchemists were directed toward changing, or *transmuting,* ordinary metals into gold. Although alchemists made many discoveries that contributed to the development of modern chemistry, their attempts to transmute metals were doomed from the start. What the alchemists didn't know was that a **transmutation** is a nuclear reaction that cannot be achieved by ordinary chemical means.

While studying the passage of high-speed alpha particles through water vapor in a cloud chamber, Ernest Rutherford noted some long, thin tracks. These tracks turned out to be caused by protons, the nuclei

transmutation

the process of changing one nucleus into another by radioactive disintegration or bombardment with other particles

FIGURE 4-33

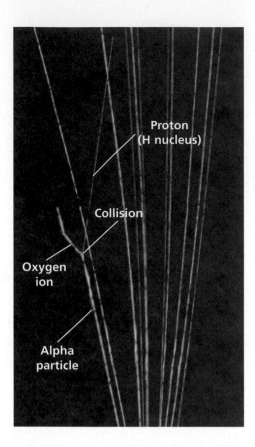

Proton
(H nucleus)

Collision

Oxygen
ion

Alpha
particle

of hydrogen. While studying the passage of alpha particles through air, Rutherford noted the same long, thin tracks. Somehow protons were being produced. He guessed correctly that atomic nuclei in air were disintegrating upon being struck by helium nuclei into hydrogen nuclei (protons) plus the nuclei of some other atom.

The American W. D. Harkins and the Englishman P.M.S. Blackett studied this strange phenomenon further. Blackett took photos of 400,000 alpha particle tracks in the cloud chamber and found that eight of them forked to form a Y, as shown in **Figure 4-33.** Harkins and Blackett determined that the long, thin track was made by a proton. What produced the short, thick track? A transmutation had occurred—an isotope of oxygen was formed. In modern notation, the transmutation reaction is as follows.

$$\ce{^4_2He + ^{14}_7N -> ^{17}_8O + ^1_1H}$$

This remarkable discovery started a flood of research. Before long, other transmutation reactions were discovered by bombarding various elements with alpha particles.

The cyclotron accelerates charged particles

It occurred to several scientists that charged particles, such as electrons or ions, could be accelerated by devices of the proper design. One of the best known of these devices is the *cyclotron,* invented in 1930 by the American E. O. Lawrence. In a cyclotron, charged particles are given successive pulses of energy, which accelerate the particles to very high energies. These extremely energetic ions are then made to collide with atomic nuclei. The accelerated ions fuse with the target nuclei to produce nuclei of much higher atomic number.

Using cyclotrons, scientists were able to prepare many new elements, including the transuranium elements.

The synchrotron is used to create superheavy elements

There is a limit to the energies that can be attained with the cyclotron. As the velocity of an accelerated particle increases, its kinetic energy

Synthetic Element Trivia

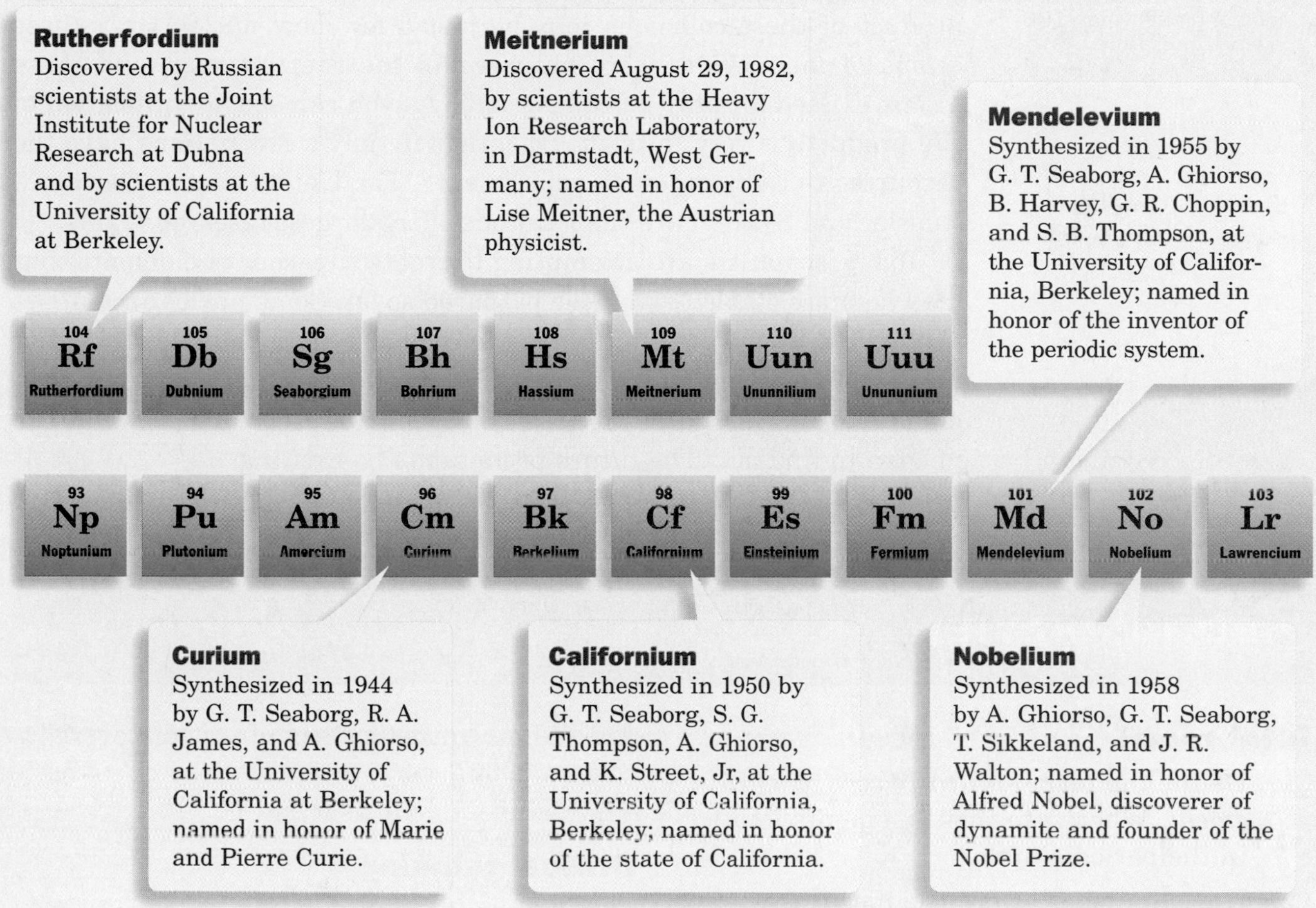

Rutherfordium
Discovered by Russian scientists at the Joint Institute for Nuclear Research at Dubna and by scientists at the University of California at Berkeley.

Meitnerium
Discovered August 29, 1982, by scientists at the Heavy Ion Research Laboratory, in Darmstadt, West Germany; named in honor of Lise Meitner, the Austrian physicist.

Mendelevium
Synthesized in 1955 by G. T. Seaborg, A. Ghiorso, B. Harvey, G. R. Choppin, and S. B. Thompson, at the University of California, Berkeley; named in honor of the inventor of the periodic system.

104	105	106	107	108	109	110	111
Rf	**Db**	**Sg**	**Bh**	**Hs**	**Mt**	**Uun**	**Uuu**
Rutherfordium	Dubnium	Seaborgium	Bohrium	Hassium	Meitnerium	Ununnilium	Unununium

93	94	95	96	97	98	99	100	101	102	103
Np	**Pu**	**Am**	**Cm**	**Bk**	**Cf**	**Es**	**Fm**	**Md**	**No**	**Lr**
Neptunium	Plutonium	Amercium	Curium	Berkelium	Californium	Einsteinium	Fermium	Mendelevium	Nobelium	Lawrencium

Curium
Synthesized in 1944 by G. T. Seaborg, R. A. James, and A. Ghiorso, at the University of California at Berkeley; named in honor of Marie and Pierre Curie.

Californium
Synthesized in 1950 by G. T. Seaborg, S. G. Thompson, A. Ghiorso, and K. Street, Jr, at the University of California, Berkeley; named in honor of the state of California.

Nobelium
Synthesized in 1958 by A. Ghiorso, G. T. Seaborg, T. Sikkeland, and J. R. Walton; named in honor of Alfred Nobel, discoverer of dynamite and founder of the Nobel Prize.

increases as well. As the particle reaches a velocity of about one-tenth the speed of light, the particle acquires enough energy that the equation $E = mc^2$ becomes a problem. According to $E = mc^2$, the increase in the particle's energy must be balanced by an increase in its mass. Due to its increased mass, the particle accelerates more slowly, causing it to arrive too late for the next pulse.

The solution to the delayed arrival of the particle is the *synchrotron*, which times the impulses to match the acceleration of the particles. A synchrotron can accelerate fewer types of particles than a cyclotron can, but enormous energies can be attained.

Once they have been accelerated in the synchrotron, the particles are made to collide head on with one another. See **Figure 4-34** for synthetic elements created with such collisions. The energy of collision is equal to the sum of the individual kinetic energies. These high energies of

FIGURE 4-34 ▲

All the highlighted elements are synthetic. Those shown in red were created by colliding moving particles with stationary targets. The elements shown in blue were created by colliding nuclei.

superheavy element

an element with an atomic number greater than 106

collision enable massive nuclei to interact. In this way, elements more massive than the actinides, **superheavy elements,** can be prepared. Because only an extremely small number of nuclei actually collide, the product of these collisions may be just a few new nuclei. Only three atoms of meitnerium were prepared in the first attempt, and these atoms existed for only 0.0034 seconds! As you can see, identification of the products is very difficult. Scientists in only a few nations have the resources to carry out such experiments. The United States, Germany, Russia, and Sweden are the locations of the largest research teams.

Today, scientists are attempting to create superheavy elements that may be more stable than those prepared so far. Some nuclear scientists predict an "island of stability" in the region of atomic number 114, and perhaps these elements, if they can be prepared, will be stable. But can element 114 be prepared? No one knows for sure. More experiments are needed to find out. The future promises to be exciting.

$\mathcal{S}$ECTION REVIEW

Total recall

1. Define the term *naturally occurring element*. Where are these elements located in the periodic table?

2. How and where were the naturally occurring elements created?

3. What element is the building block for all other natural elements?

4. What is a synthetic element?

5. What is a nuclear reaction?

6. What is transmutation?

7. In the first observed transmutation, nitrogen was bombarded with alpha particles to produce a hydrogen nucleus. The other product was an ion of which element?

8. How do scientists use cyclotrons to create synthetic elements?

9. How are superheavy elements prepared?

10. What do scientists mean by the term *island of stability* with respect to superheavy synthetic elements?

11. What synthetic element was discovered in 1982?

Critical thinking

12. Why is the mass of a helium atom slightly less than the mass of hydrogen atoms from which it was formed?

13. Why are the elements with atomic numbers greater than 92 referred to as transuranium elements?

14. Describe two processes that scientists use to create synthetic elements.

15. Which transuranium elements are not actinides?

16. Why is the following word equation not an example of a transmutation?
zinc + copper sulfate $\longrightarrow$
copper + zinc sulfate

17. **Story Clue** Where are the elements used in dental fillings created?

Now that you have completed the chapter, you should be able to answer the questions about the mysterious death of George Decker.

LOOKING BACK

Which metal melts first in gold fillings? in silver fillings?

Gold fillings contain gold, with added silver, platinum, and palladium, and trace amounts of zinc, iron, and copper. According to Figure 4-30, the metal in gold fillings with the lowest melting point is zinc, which has a melting point of 420°C. Silver fillings contain equal amounts of silver and mercury, with trace amounts of copper. The metal in silver fillings with the lowest melting point is mercury, which has a melting point of −39°C and a boiling point of 357°C.

Why did Decker's process work for gold fillings but prove fatal with silver fillings?

As the periodic trend in melting points predicts, all metals in gold fillings melt and boil at relatively high temperatures. To separate the metals, Decker heated the mixture until it melted. The liquid zinc, copper, and iron reacted with oxygen in the air and were easily skimmed off the top, leaving the gold and silver behind. Decker tried the same technique with silver fillings. However, the melting point of the silver-filling mixture is actually higher than the boiling point of mercury. When Decker melted silver fillings, the mercury evaporated before the copper and silver in the fillings could be separated. Decker produced toxic mercury vapors.

What element was most likely responsible for George Decker's death?

Mercury was the most likely cause of the tissue damage and inflammation that brought on Decker's pneumonia.

80
Hg
Mercury
200.59
$[Xe]4f^{14}5d^{10}6s^2$

Silver-white metal that is slightly volatile at room temperature. Poisonous! Readily absorbed through the respiratory tract, through the skin, and through the gastrointestinal tract. Spilled and heated elemental mercury is especially hazardous.

HIGHLIGHTS

KEY TERMS

4-1

actinide
alkali metal
alkaline-earth metal
group
halogen
lanthanide
main-group element

metal
noble gas
nonmetal
period
periodic law
plasma
salt
semiconductor
transition metals

4-2

alloy
conduction band
crystal

4-3

bond radius
electron affinity

electron shielding
ionization energy
van der Waals radius

4-4

nuclear reaction
superheavy element
transmutation

KEY CONCEPTS

4-1 What makes a group of elements?

▶ According to the periodic law, properties of elements are periodic functions of their atomic numbers.

▶ In the periodic table, elements are ordered by increasing atomic number. Rows are called periods; columns are called groups.

▶ Two major families include the lanthanides and the actinides.

▶ Groups include the alkali metals, the alkaline-earth metals, the halogens, and the noble gases.

▶ Elements of the same group have similar characteristic properties even though their electron configurations may differ in some cases.

4-2 What gives metals their distinctive properties?

▶ Metals are excellent conductors of electricity and heat.

▶ In a solid metal the outer electrons bind a metal atom to its neighboring atoms to hold them together.

▶ In metals, very little or no energy is required to move electrons from their orbitals to the conduction band where they can conduct electricity.

▶ Some metals are ductile and malleable.

▶ The atoms in a metal assume an orderly arrangement to form a crystal.

4-3 What trends are found in the periodic table?

▶ Periodic trends are related to the atomic structure of the elements.

▶ The atomic radius of the elements usually decreases as you move left to right across a period and tends to increase down a periodic table group.

▶ Ionization energy and electron affinity generally increase as you move left to right across a period and decrease as you move down a group.

▶ Melting points and boiling points vary in a periodic way across a period.

4-4 Where did the elements come from?

▶ Naturally occurring elements (atomic numbers 1–93) were formed in the interior of stars. Synthetic elements (atomic numbers above 93) are made by research scientists.

▶ All elements larger than helium are formed by nuclear reactions in which nuclei are merged.

▶ Synthetic elements are made in particle accelerators, which launch particles with high enough kinetic energies to cause nuclear reactions.

KEY SKILLS

Examine the periodic table before your exam.

Be sure you understand the information it contains and how trends for atomic radius, ionization energy, electron affinity, and melting and boiling points progress across a period and down a group.

REVIEW & ASSESS

TERM REVIEW

1. The halogen elements represent a ——. (group, period)

2. Ca, Be, and Mg are ——. (alkali metals, alkaline-earth metals)

3. A mixture of two or more metals is known as a(n) ——. (alloy, superheavy element)

4. Half the distance between the nuclei in adjacent nonbonded molecules is known as the —— radius. (bond, van der Waals)

5. The element californium is classified as a(n) ——. (actinide, lanthanide)

6. Every period on the table ends with a(n) ——. (main-group element, noble gas)

7. Electron shielding most affects ——. (ionization energy, electron affinity, radius)

8. Only a metal has a(n) —— that is close to the energy levels of the electrons in their outermost orbitals. (conduction band, ionization energy)

9. The energy emitted when an atom gains an electron is known as ——. (ionization energy, electron affinity)

10. Most synthetic elements fall into the —— group of the periodic table. (lanthanide, actinide, transition metal)

11. Nuclear reactions produce ——. (superheavy elements, salts)

CONCEPT & SKILLS REVIEW

ORGANIZATION OF THE PERIODIC TABLE

1. How do chemists use the periodic law to classify elements?

2. Yttrium, which follows strontium in the periodic table, has an atomic number one greater than strontium. Barium is 18 atomic numbers after strontium, but it falls directly beneath it in the periodic table. Does strontium share more properties with yttrium or barium? Explain your answer.

3. What determines the vertical arrangement of the periodic table?

4. What determines the horizontal arrangement of the periodic table?

5. All halogens are highly reactive. What causes this similarity among the halogens?

6. What property do the noble gases share? How does this property relate to the electron configuration of the noble gases?

7. Why is beryllium placed in Group 2?

8. Use the periodic table to describe the properties of the following elements.
   a. bromine, Br   e. rubidium, Rb
   b. barium, Ba   f. neptunium, Np
   c. xenon, Xe   g. promethium, Pm
   d. tungsten, W

9. Argon differs from both chlorine and potassium by one proton each. Compare the reactivity and electron configurations of these three elements.

10. How do the electron configurations of the transition metals differ from the electron configurations of the metals in Groups 1 and 2?

11. How do the electron configurations of the actinide and lanthanide series differ from the electron configurations of the other transition metals?

12. What groups make up the main-block elements?

13. Why is hydrogen in a family by itself?

14. Compare the modern periodic table to Mendeleev's periodic table in **Figure 4-2.** List the differences between Mendeleev's periodic table and the modern table.

15. Identify the discrepancies in Mendeleev's table that were rectified in Moseley's table.

16. While at an amusement park, you inhale helium from a balloon to make your voice higher pitched. A friend says this practice is dangerous because the helium will react with your blood and produce toxic compounds. Is your friend correct? Explain.

17. a. What is happening to the sodium atom shown in the diagram below?
 b. How will the electron configuration of the atom change when the atom becomes an ion?
 c. Could a potassium atom behave in a similar way? Explain.

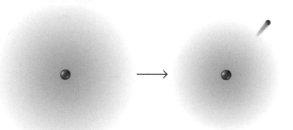

18. In Mendeleev's periodic table, he placed Be, Mg, Zn, and Cd in one group and Ca, Sr, Ba, and Pb in another group. Use the electron configurations of these elements as evidence to support this order.

19. Why would you never expect a Ca^+ or Na^{2+} ion to exist?

20. Calcium ions, Ca^{2+}, play an important role in muscle relaxation. Potassium ion, K^+, is also found in your body. Why is there no danger of K^+ and Ca^{2+} reacting with each other?

21. You read a science fiction story about an alien race of silicon-based life-forms. Use information from the periodic table to hypothesize why the author chose silicon over other elements. **(Hint: Life on Earth is carbon-based.)**

PROPERTIES OF METALS

22. Explain why metals are good conductors of electricity.

23. Why is a nonmetal, carbon, added to iron to make nails?

24. Describe how atoms are arranged in a metal.

25. As more shells are added to atoms, the energies of the outer orbitals get closer and closer. Use this to explain why C is nonmetal, but Pb is a metal.

26. Use Figure 4-27 to explain why the reactivity of alkali metals increases down the group.

27. Compare the energy gaps between the conduction band and the outermost electrons in metals and nonmetals.

28. Why is metallic nature not considered an innate property of metals?

29. What evidence do we have that atoms are spherical in shape?

30. Describe the similarities and differences between a face-centered cubic metal crystal and a hexagonal close-packed metal crystal.

31. How will a room-temperature superconductor affect our lives?

PERIODIC TRENDS

32. Why don't scientists define atomic radius as the radius of a single electron cloud?

33. What periodic trends occur for atomic radius?

34. Use an analogy of a football team's offensive line protecting the quarterback to explain the shielding effect of electrons.

35. How does the periodic trend in atomic radius relate to the addition of electrons?

36. Define ionization energy and electron affinity.

37. a. What periodic trends exist for ionization energy?
   b. How does this trend relate to different energy levels?

38. What happens to electron affinity values as you move left to right across a period? Explain why these values change as they do.

39. Identify which trends in the diagrams below describe atomic radius and ionization energy.

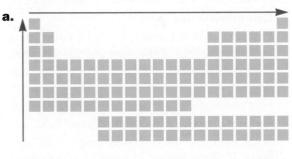

a.

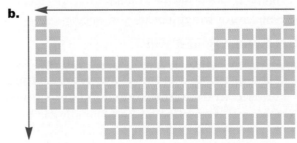

b.

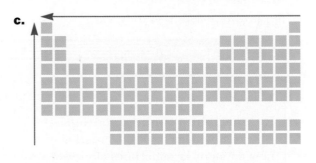

c.

40. How do the trends in atomic radius compare with the trends in ionization energy?

41. Name three periodic trends you encounter in your life.

42. A scientist may measure the radius of an atom five different times and get five different re-sults. His method is correct, and his instrumentation is working properly. Explain the results.

CREATING THE ELEMENTS

43. When two elements are involved in a nuclear reaction, a different element is created. How does this happen?

44. How does the nuclear fusion process create energy?

45. Cite two reasons why hydrogen is involved in the most common nuclear fusion reaction.

46. Compare the two charts below. Why are the most abundant elements in Earth's crust not the most abundant in the universe? Explain how the elements in stars formed the elements in Earth's crust.

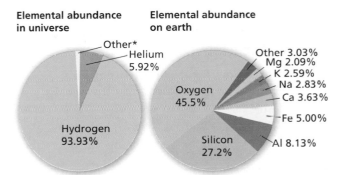

Elemental abundance in universe

Elemental abundance on earth

Other*
Helium 5.92%
Hydrogen 93.93%

Other 3.03%
Mg 2.09%
K 2.59%
Na 2.83%
Ca 3.63%
Oxygen 45.5%
Fe 5.00%
Silicon 27.2%
Al 8.13%

*Oxygen 0.075%, carbon 0.047%, nitrogen 0.0094%, neon 0.0087%, magnesium 0.0042%, silicon 0.0030%, other 0.0027%

47. Irene Joliot Curie created the first artificial radioactive isotope, phosphorus-30, in 1934 when she bombarded aluminum-27, a shiny metal with conductive properties, with helium nuclei. The resulting product was a nonmetal with completely different properties. What caused the change in properties?

48. Years ago, many people dreamed of transforming lead, an abundant metal, into gold, a rare and highly prized metal. Could gold be made from lead using the nuclear processes described in this chapter?

49. Why are technetium, promethium, and neptunium considered naturally occurring elements even though they are not found on Earth?

50. Why must a synchrotron be used to create a superheavy element?

51. How could the transmutation of copper-65 to zinc-65 be performed?

LINKING CHAPTERS

1. Theme: Classification and trends
Explain the nature of the observations that Dmitri Mendeleev used to construct his periodic table.

2. Electron configuration and quantum numbers
a. How does the electron configuration of alkali metals differ from that of the halogens?
b. What quantum numbers are the same for the last electron in the alkaline-earth metals?
c. What quantum numbers are the same for the last electron in all noble gases?

3. Theme: Classification and trends
a. What trends were first used to classify the elements?
b. What trends were discovered after the elements were classified in the periodic table?

4. Mixtures and compounds
How would you prove that an alloy is a mixture and not a compound?

ALTERNATIVE ASSESSMENTS

Performance assessment

1. Your teacher will give you an index card that identifies the ionization energy and electron affinity of an element. Identify the element by analyzing these periodic trends.

2. You are given a sample of an unknown element. Design a set of procedures that you could use to determine if the unknown is a metal, a nonmetal, or a metalloid. Organize your procedures in the form of a flow chart like the one for classifying matter that is found in Chapter 2.

3. Design an experiment to show that the conductivity of a metal increases as the temperature decreases and decreases as the temperature increases. Test various metals to compare their conductivities at different temperatures.

Portfolio projects

1. Cooperative group project
Construct your own periodic table, or obtain one of the posters available that show related objects in a periodic arrangement, like vegetables or fruits. Describe the organization of the table and the trends it exemplifies. Use this table to make predictions about your subject matter.

2. Chemistry and you
In many labeled foods, the mineral content is stated in terms of the mass of the element, in a stated quantity of food. Minerals are essential to your health. Examine the product labels of the foods you eat. Determine which elements are represented in your food and what function each element serves in the body. Make a poster of foods that are good sources of the minerals you need.

3. Chemistry and you
Select an alloy. You can choose one that has been mentioned in this chapter, or use the library or the Internet to find a different one. Obtain information on how the alloy is made. Is this process different from the one that was first used to make the alloy? What practical applications does the alloy have?

4.

internet**connect**

SCI**LINKS** NSTA

TOPIC: Synthetic elements
GO TO: www.scilinks.org
KEYWORD: HW047

Research and communication
The announcement of the creation of a new element is sometimes claimed by two groups of scientists working in different parts of the world. Research the history of one such element. What methods were used to create the element? How are disputes as to which group was actually the first to create the element settled in the scientific community?

TEST PREP

1. As you move down the periodic table from carbon through lead, bond radii ———.
   a. generally increase
   b. generally decrease
   c. do not change
   d. vary unpredictably

2. The only element that has some of the properties of both alkali metals and halogens and is considered to be a chemical family by itself is ———.
   a. hydrogen   c. uranium
   b. carbon   d. helium

3. As electrons are added to the outer shells of atoms within a period, the atoms generally have ———.
   a. increasing radii, increasing ionization energies, and increasing electron affinity values
   b. decreasing radii, decreasing ionization energies, and decreasing electron affinity values
   c. decreasing radii, increasing ionization energies, and decreasing electron affinity values
   d. decreasing radii, increasing ionization energies, and increasing electron affinity values

4. The periodic law states that ———.
   a. no two electrons with the same spin can be found in the same place in an atom
   b. the physical and chemical properties of the elements are functions of their atomic number
   c. electrons exhibit properties of both particles and waves
   d. the chemical properties of elements can be grouped according to periodicity

5. In the modern periodic table, elements are ordered according to ———.
   a. decreasing atomic mass
   b. Mendeleev's original design
   c. increasing atomic number
   d. when they were discovered

6. The energy it takes to remove an electron from an atom ——— as you move left to right across the period, from gold through bismuth.
   a. generally increases
   b. generally decreases
   c. does not change
   d. varies unpredictably

7. Group 17 elements, the halogens, are the most reactive of the nonmetals because they ———.
   a. are the farthest to the right of the periodic table
   b. require only one electron to form the stable configurations of the noble gases
   c. have the largest atomic radii
   d. have the greatest ionization energies

8. If oxygen is more abundant than carbon throughout the universe, then ———.
   a. carbon is more abundant than oxygen in the stars
   b. oxygen is more abundant than carbon in the stars
   c. carbon is not found in the stars
   d. oxygen is not found in the stars

9. Superconductivity of a metal refers to the ———.
   a. increase in electrical conductivity at higher temperatures
   b. decrease in the strength of bonds between metal atoms at lower temperatures
   c. increase in the energy level of the conduction band
   d. loss of all resistance to conductivity at low temperatures

10. ——— is created in the center of stars.
    a. Curium   c. Einsteinium
    b. Gold   d. Americium

Ionic Compounds

IONS IN THE YEARBOOK

Click. The photography schedule is almost impossible: shooting 25 different clubs and teams in just two days. Students are everywhere, dressed in robes and uniforms. It's time for yearbook photos! One of the student photographers takes charge. She has assorted gadgets hanging from her neck and shoulder: a camera loaded with black-and-white film, a camera loaded with color film, light meters, and a bag of special lenses. "Move in just a little, please . . . that's better, thanks. You in the back, . . . yes, you in the cowboy hat . . . dark glasses off, please. Are you all ready?. . . smile." *Click.* "One more, just in case, please." *Click.* "That's good."

The student photographers capture the year on film, but film-processing technicians make those photos come alive. Film processing requires quite a bit of knowledge about chemistry.

Photographic film is a sheet of clear plastic coated with a very thin layer of *emulsion*. Spread throughout the emulsion are many tiny crystals of light-sensitive silver salts. Silver iodide, AgI, is more light sensitive than silver bromide, $AgBr$, which in turn is more sensitive than silver chloride, $AgCl$. Most photographic film contains $AgBr$ and a small amount of AgI. These silver salts are ionic compounds consisting of silver ions, Ag^+, and a halogen ion, either I^-, Br^-, or Cl^-.

With the click of the shutter, light falls for a very brief instant of time on the photographic film. When this happens, the film is said to be *exposed.* The changes brought about by exposure are subtle indeed—because you can't see any change at all. However, some of the salt crystals now have silver atoms, Ag, on their edges. There are many such atom-edged crystals where the light was strongest. There are few where the light was dim, and there are none where no light fell. At this stage, the film has what is called a *latent image.*

The film is developed using several steps that all involve reactions with ions. Working in a room dimly lit by red light, film technicians add chemicals called *stoppers* and *fixers* to control the reactions started by light. In this chapter you will learn some of the basic concepts that underlie the photographic process and will find out how ions make their way into the yearbook.

CHAPTER LINKS

How do the properties of silver atoms differ from those of silver ions?

How can exposure to light change the chemical structure of a compound?

Although light falls on the entire salt crystal, why do silver atoms form only at the edges of the crystal?

How are ions different from atoms?

OBJECTIVES

▶ **Identify** ions that are isoelectronic with the noble gases.

▶ **Explain** why the properties of ions differ from the properties of their parent atoms.

▶ **Relate** an atom's tendency to form an ion to the element's position in the periodic table and to the octet rule.

▶ **Describe** the consequences of the electroneutrality principle.

▶ **Name** cations, anions, and salts.

▶ **Write** formulas for binary compounds.

Simple ions

ion

an atom or group of atoms that has an electric charge because it has lost or gained electrons

Think of an **ion** as an atom that has gained or lost one or more electrons. An ion is like an atom, but the number of electrons does not equal the number of protons, so it has a net electric charge. When a sodium atom loses its outermost electron, it becomes a positively charged ion that we call a *sodium ion*.

$$[\text{Na}] = 1s^2 2s^2 2p^6 3s^1$$
$$[\text{Na}^+] = 1s^2 2s^2 2p^6$$

The following equation shows the formation of a sodium ion from a sodium atom.

$$\text{Na} \longrightarrow \text{Na}^+ + e^-$$

▼ **FIGURE 5-1**

The sodium ion has a net +1 charge and is written as Na⁺.

Look at **Figure 5-1.** How does a sodium ion compare with a sodium atom? Are the properties the same? Even though the name of the element, sodium, is the same, a sodium atom behaves very differently from a

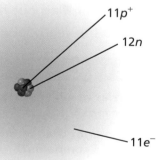

Sodium atom, Na

a The sodium ion has 10 electrons instead of 11.

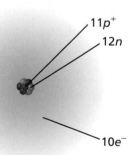

Sodium ion, Na⁺

b The electron configuration of the sodium ion is the same . . .

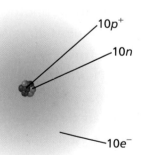

Neon atom, Ne

c . . . as that of a neon atom.

sodium ion. Using the same name for both the atom and ion signifies that the nucleus is unchanged. The ion still has 11 protons and 12 neutrons, like the atom. But chemical properties depend on the number of electrons and their configuration. A sodium ion has only 10 electrons, and they are configured just like the electrons in a neon atom.

$$[Ne] = 1s^2 2s^2 2p^6$$

Does that mean that a sodium ion is a neon atom? Certainly not. Does it mean that the sodium ion has properties similar to those of the neon atom? Well, not quite; but the chemical properties of a sodium ion are certainly closer to those of a neon atom than they are to a sodium atom. The differences arise because the sodium ion has a positive charge.

Changes in electron arrangements change chemical properties

Recall that neon is one of the noble gases and, as such, is virtually inert. It is therefore not surprising that the sodium ion, Na^+, with the same electron structure is very stable and has no chemical properties other than those resulting from its positive charge and its ability to fill space.

Ions with a positive charge are known as **cations;** they have more protons than electrons. Negatively charged ions, such as the Cl^- ion, are called **anions,** and they have more electrons than protons, as shown in **Figure 5-2.** The Cl^- ion also has a noble-gas configuration. It matches that of the argon atom, but it carries a net negative charge acquired by the addition of a single electron to the chlorine atom.

$$[Cl^-] = 1s^2 2s^2 2p^6 3s^2 3p^6 = [Ar]$$
$$[Cl] = 1s^2 2s^2 2p^6 3s^2 3p^5$$

The following equation shows the formation of the chloride ion from the chlorine atom.

$$Cl + e^- \longrightarrow Cl^-$$

Collections of cations are never found without a similar number of anions (or electrons) nearby to effectively neutralize the charges. The concept of having equal numbers of opposite charges is called **electroneutrality.**

cation

an ion that has a positive charge

anion

an ion that has a negative charge

electroneutrality

the condition of having equal numbers of positive and negative charges

FIGURE 5-2 ▼

Contrast this model for a chloride ion with the model for a sodium ion in Figure 5-1.

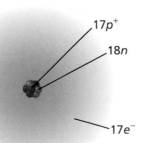

Chlorine atom, Cl

a The chlorine atom forms a stable ion by gaining an electron.

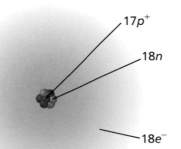

Chloride ion, Cl⁻

b The chloride ion, Cl⁻, . . .

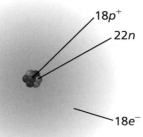

Argon atom, Ar

c . . . has the same electron configuration as an argon atom.

Many simple ions have a noble-gas configuration

Sodium and chlorine are not the only atoms that form ions with an electron configuration identical to that of a noble gas. The sulfur atom can acquire two extra electrons and become an anion with the same configuration as an argon atom.

$$[S] = 1s^2 2s^2 2p^6 3s^2 3p^4 \quad (16e^-, 16p^+)$$
$$[S^{2-}] = 1s^2 2s^2 2p^6 3s^2 3p^6 \quad (18e^-, 16p^+)$$
$$[Ar] = 1s^2 2s^2 2p^6 3s^2 3p^6 \quad (18e^-, 18p^+)$$

In fact, most of the elements that are near the noble gases in the periodic table have atoms that gain electrons and thereby come to share the stable electron configuration of a noble gas. **Table 5-1** lists the electron configurations of some ions that match the configurations of noble gases. Atoms and ions with the same configuration are said to be **isoelectronic** with each other. The ions of elements in Groups 15–17 have configurations that are isoelectronic with noble gases in the same period. Ions of elements in Groups 1, 2, 3, and Al^{3+} have configurations that are isoelectronic with noble gases in the previous period. Like the

isoelectronic

having the same electron configuration as another atom

TABLE 5-1 Some Ions with Noble-Gas Configurations							Group 18 Noble Gases
Group 1	**Group 2**	**Group 3**	**Group 13**	**Group 15**	**Group 16**	**Group 17**	Helium **He** $1s^2$
Li$^+$ $1s^2$	**Be^{2+}** $1s^2$			**N^{3-}** [He]$2s^2 2p^6$	**O^{2-}** [He]$2s^2 2p^6$	**F$^-$** [He]$2s^2 2p^6$	Neon **Ne** [He]$2s^2 2p^6$
Na$^+$ [He]$2s^2 2p^6$	**Mg^{2+}** [He]$2s^2 2p^6$		**Al^{3+}** [He]$2s^2 2p^6$	**P^{3-}** [Ne]$3s^2 3p^6$	**S^{2-}** [Ne]$3s^2 3p^6$	**Cl$^-$** [Ne]$3s^2 3p^6$	Argon **Ar** [Ne]$3s^2 3p^6$
K$^+$ [Ne]$3s^2 3p^6$	**Ca^{2+}** [Ne]$3s^2 3p^6$	**Sc^{3+}** [Ne]$3s^2 3p^6$		**As^{3-}** [Ar]$3d^{10} 4s^2 4p^6$	**Se^{2-}** [Ar]$3d^{10} 4s^2 4p^6$	**Br$^-$** [Ar]$3d^{10} 4s^2 4p^6$	Krypton **Kr** [Ar]$3d^{10} 4s^2 4p^6$
Rb$^+$ [Ar]$3d^{10} 4s^2 4p^6$	**Sr^{2+}** [Ar]$3d^{10} 4s^2 4p^6$	**Y^{3+}** [Ar]$3d^{10} 4s^2 4p^6$			**Te^{2-}** [Kr]$4d^{10} 5s^2 5p^6$	**I$^-$** [Kr]$4d^{10} 5s^2 5p^6$	Xenon **Xe** [Kr]$4d^{10} 5s^2 5p^6$
Cs$^+$ [Kr]$4d^{10} 5s^2 5p^6$	**Ba^{2+}** [Kr]$4d^{10} 5s^2 5p^6$	**La^{3+}** [Kr]$4d^{10} 5s^2 5p^6$					

Ions that are isoelectronic with a noble gas are denoted by the same color. The small table at right shows the periodic table positions of the ions listed in Table 5-1.

sodium ion, most of the ions in Table 5-1 are inert, and all of them are colorless.

Perhaps you have noticed that in Table 5-1 the elements that form simple cations are metals and the elements that form simple anions are nonmetals. This conclusion is a general rule that can be understood in terms of the principles discussed in Chapter 4. Atoms of nonmetals can achieve the stable noble-gas configuration by gaining electrons. Losing electrons enables the atoms of some metals to match the electron number of the noble gas in the previous period. The tendency of atoms to match the electron configuration of the s and p orbitals of a noble gas is called the **octet rule.** You will learn more about the octet rule in Chapter 6.

Transition metals form stable Ions too

Not all simple ions are isoelectronic with noble-gas atoms. The ions listed in **Table 5-2** do not fit this pattern. They are mostly transition metals from Periods 4, 5, and 6. Notice that apart from Re^-, these ions are all cations. In addition, the lanthanide and actinide elements form cations, mostly with +3 charges, that are not isoelectronic with the noble gases. Notice that some elements form more than one cation.

octet rule

the tendency of atoms of elements to gain or lose electrons so that their outer s and p orbitals are full with eight electrons

| TABLE 5-2 | Stable Ions Formed by the Transition Elements and Some Other Metals |

Group 4	Group 5	Group 6	Group 7	Group 8	Group 9	Group 10	Group 11	Group 12	Group 13	Group 14
Ti^{2+} Ti^{3+}	V^{2+} V^{3+}	Cr^{2+} Cr^{3+}	Mn^{2+} Mn^{3+}	Fe^{2+} Fe^{3+}	Co^{2+} Co^{3+}	Ni^{2+}	Cu^+ Cu^{2+}	Zn^{2+}	Ga^{2+} Ga^{3+}	Ge^{2+}
		Mo^{3+}	Tc^{2+}			Pd^{2+}	Ag^+ Ag^{2+}	Cd^{2+}	In^+ In^{2+} In^{3+}	Sn^{2+}
Hf^{4+}			Re^-			Pt^{2+} Pt^{4+}	Au^+ Au^{3+}	Hg_2^{2+} Hg^{2+}	Tl^+ Tl^{3+}	Pb^{2+}

The small table at left shows the periodic-table positions of the ions listed in Table 5-2.

internet connect

SC*LINKS*
NSTA

TOPIC: Salt formation
GO TO: www.scilinks.org
KEYWORD: HW051

Names and formulas for ions and salts

Simple cations borrow their names from the names of the elements. K^+ is the potassium ion, and Zn^{2+} is the zinc ion. When an element forms two or more ions, the ions are distinguished by roman numerals to indicate charge. In the case of copper, Cu, the two ions are denoted as follows.

$$Cu^+ \text{ copper(I) ion} \qquad Cu^{2+} \text{ copper(II) ion}$$

When we speak about such ions, we say "copper one ion" or "copper two ion." **Figure 5-3** shows compounds formed between copper and chlorine.

Binary ionic compounds are easy to name

The name of a simple anion is also formed from the name of the element, but it ends in *-ide*. Thus, Cl^- is the *chloride* ion, O^{2-} is the *oxide* ion, and P^{3-} is the *phosphide* ion.

The electroneutrality principle means that the total negative charge on the anions equals the total positive charge on the cations. The whole system has no net charge and is therefore neutral. Any chemical compound composed of oppositely charged ions is called an **ionic compound.**

An ionic compound composed of a simple cation and a simple anion is called a **binary ionic compound.** The adjective *binary* indicates that the compound is composed of two elements. Common table salt, NaCl, is composed of equal numbers of sodium ions, Na^+, and chloride ions, Cl^-.

Naming binary ionic compounds is simple. The name consists of two words: the name of the cation followed by the name of the anion.

NaCl sodium chloride $CuCl_2$ copper(II) chloride
ZnS zinc sulfide Mg_3N_2 magnesium nitride

ionic compound

any chemical compound that is composed of oppositely charged ions

binary ionic compound

an ionic compound that consists of cations of one element and the anions of another element

FIGURE 5-3 ▼

Melting point	430°C	498°C
Density (at 25°C)	4.14 g/cm^3	3.39 g/cm^3
Percentage composition	64.19% Cu 35.81% Cl	47.26% Cu 52.74% Cl
Other physical properties	white crystalline powder; sparingly soluble in water, practically insoluble in alcohol and acetone	yellow to brown powder that readily absorbs moisture; soluble in water, alcohol, and acetone
Other chemical properties	turns green when exposed to moist air	forms a blue-green dihydrate, $CuCl_2 \cdot 2H_2O$, in moist air

Formulas must indicate the relative numbers of cations and anions. Because both ions carry a single charge, sodium chloride is composed of equal numbers of the ions Na^+ and Cl^-. The formula for sodium chloride is usually written as NaCl, which looks as if it is a molecule of bonded sodium and chlorine atoms. But, because it is composed of ions, a more appropriate formula would be

$$Na^+Cl^-$$

Remember, though, that the formula is not usually written this way. Rather the formula is written simply as NaCl.

The cation in zinc sulfide has a +2 charge and the anion has a −2 charge. Again there is a one-to-one ratio in the salt. Zinc sulfide has the formula ZnS.

Magnesium nitride is another story. The magnesium ion, Mg^{2+}, has two positive charges, and the nitride ion, N^{3-}, has three negative charges. We must combine cations and anions in such a way that there are as many negative charges as there are positive charges. Three Mg^{2+} cations are needed for every two N^{3-} anions to produce an electrically neutral compound. That way, there are six positive charges and six negative charges. **Subscripts** are used to denote the three magnesium ions and two nitride ions. Therefore, the formula for magnesium nitride is Mg_3N_2. The reason for the subscripts becomes clear by writing magnesium nitride as follows, though this is not the standard way of writing this salt's formula.

$$[Mg^{2+}]_3[N^{3-}]_2$$

subscript

a whole number written below and to the right of an element's symbol that is used to denote the number of atoms in a formula

Write formulas for binary ionic compounds

What is the formula for aluminum oxide?

1 Write the symbol and charges for the cation and anion
Use Tables 5-1 and 5-2 as guides. Remember that the name of the anion has an *-ide* ending.

▶ symbol for aluminum cation: Al^{3+} ▶ symbol for oxide anion: O^{2-}

2 Write the symbols for the ions side by side, beginning with the cation

$$Al^{3+}O^{2-}$$

3 Find the least common multiple of the ions' charges
▶ The least common multiple of 3 and 2 is 6. To get a neutral compound, you would need a total of six positive charges and six negative charges.

▶ To get six positive charges, you need two Al^{3+} ions because

$$2 \times 3+ = 6+.$$

▶ To get six negative charges, you need three O^{2-} ions because

$$3 \times 2- = 6-.$$

Therefore, the ratio of Al^{3+} to O^{2-} is 2Al:3O, and the formula is

$$Al_2O_3$$

SECTION REVIEW

Total recall

1. How could each of the following atoms react to achieve a stable octet?
   a. iodine   **c.** sulfur
   b. barium   **d.** krypton

2. Write formulas for the following binary compounds:
   a. calcium chloride
   b. magnesium oxide
   c. sodium iodide
   d. magnesium fluoride
   e. calcium sulfide
   f. potassium nitride
   g. copper(I) bromide
   h. aluminum nitride

3. Write formulas for the following binary compounds:
   a. iron(II) oxide   **e.** iron(III) chloride
   b. iron(III) oxide   **f.** niobium(V) chloride
   c. lead(IV) oxide   **g.** manganese(II) iodide
   d. tin(II) oxide   **h.** silver(I) sulfide

4. Name the following binary ionic compounds. If the metal forms more than one cation, be sure to denote the charge.
   a. Rb_2O **c.** FeF_3
   b. $BaCl_2$ **d.** $CrCl_3$

Critical thinking

5. In terms of electron configurations, explain why potassium bromide has the formula KBr instead of K_2Br or KBr_2.

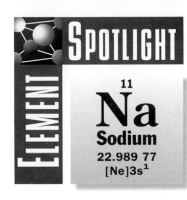

11
Na
Sodium
22.989 77
[Ne]3s¹

For most people, the daily intake of sodium should not exceed 2400 mg.

WHERE IS IT?

Earth's Crust
2.36% by mass

Seventh most abundant element

Fifth most abundant metal

Sea Water
30.61% of all dissolved materials

1.03% by mass taking the water into account

internet connect

SC*LINKS*
NSTA

TOPIC: Sodium
GO TO: www.scilinks.org
KEYWORD: HW052

A BRIEF HISTORY

A major nutritional mineral

Sodium plays a major role in the regulation of fluid balance within the body. Most sodium in the diet comes from the use of table salt, NaCl, to season and preserve foods. Sodium is also supplied by a variety of compounds, including sodium carbonate and sodium hydrogen carbonate in baked goods. Sodium benzoate is a preservative in carbonated beverages. Sodium citrate and sodium glutamate are used in packaged foods as flavor additives.

In ancient Rome, salt was so scarce and highly prized that it was used as a form of payment. Today, however, salt is plentiful in the diet, and many people must limit their intake of sodium as a precaution against high blood pressure, heart attacks, and strokes.

Industrial Uses

▶ Common table salt is the most important commercial sodium compound. It is used in ceramic glazes, metallurgy, soap manufacture, home water softeners, highway de-icing, herbicides, fire extinguishers, and resins.

▶ The United States produces about 42.1 million metric tons of sodium chloride per year.

▶ Other important sodium compounds include sodium hydroxide, sodium carbonate, and sodium silicate.

▶ Sodium is used in sodium vapor lamps for lighting highways, stadiums, and industrial complexes.

▶ Liquid sodium is used as a coolant in liquid-metal fast-breeder nuclear reactors.

Nutrition Facts
Serving Size ¾ cup (30g)
Servings Per Container About 14

Amount Per Serving	Corn Crunch	with ½ cup skim milk
Calories	120	160
Calories from Fat	15	20
	% Daily Value**	
Total Fat 2g*	3%	3%
Saturated Fat 0g	2%	0%
Cholesterol 0mg	0%	1%
Sodium 160mg	7%	9%
Potassium 65mg	2%	6%
Total Carbohydrate 25g	8%	10%
Dietary Fiber 3g		
Sugars 3g		
Other Carbohydrate 11g		
Protein 2g		

*Amount in Cereal. A serving of cereal plus skim milk provides 2g fat, less 5mg cholesterol, 220mg sodium, 270mg potassium, 31g carbohydrate (19g sugars) and 6g protein.

**Percent Daily Values are based on a 2,000 calorie diet. Your daily values may be higher or lower depending on your calorie needs:

	Calories	2,000	2,500
Total Fat	Less than	65g	80g
Sat Fat	Less than	20g	25g
Cholesterol	Less than	300mg	300mg
Sodium	Less than	2,400mg	2,400mg
Potassium		3,500mg	3,500mg
Total Carbohydrate		300g	375g
Dietary Fiber		25g	30g

● **1807:** Sir Humphry Davy isolates sodium by the electrolysis of caustic soda (NaOH) and names the metal.

● **1940:** The Food and Nutrition Board of the National Research Council develops the first Recommended Dietary Allowances

1200   1800   1900   2000

● **1251:** The Wieliczka Salt Mine, located in Krakow, Poland, is started. The mine is still in use today.

● **1930:** Sodium vapor lamp is introduced for street lighting.

● **1990:** Nutrition Labeling and Education Act defines a Daily Reference Value for sodium to be listed in the Nutrition Facts portion of a food label.

What holds a salt together?

OBJECTIVES

▶ **Describe** the nature of ionic bonding.

▶ **Explain** what is meant by a crystal structure, and distinguish between the structures of NaCl and CsCl.

▶ **Explain** the energy changes that occur in the formation of a salt.

▶ **Summarize** the properties of binary ionic compounds.

Ionic bonding

In the previous section it was explained that simple cations are atoms of metallic elements from which one or more electrons have been removed. Likewise, simple anions are formed by adding one or more electrons to the atoms of nonmetallic elements. You also learned that ionic compounds are cations and anions combined in small whole-number proportions to produce a state of electroneutrality. But why do elements lose or gain electrons and then come together to form a compound? Let's explore this process using a familiar example.

Sodium is a reactive Group 1 metal. Chlorine, a reactive Group 17 nonmetal, is a poisonous yellowish green gas that consists of molecules with two chlorine atoms bonded together. When the two elements are placed together, a violent exothermic reaction occurs, as shown in **Figure 5-4.** The white residue, a compound formed from two dangerous el-

FIGURE 5-4

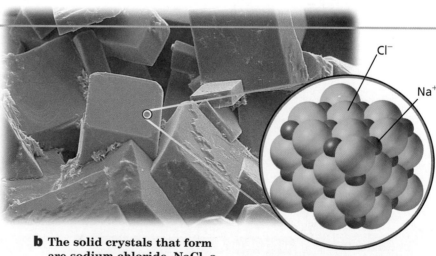

Cl⁻

Na⁺

a When a small piece of sodium, a very reactive metal, is lowered into a flask filled with the poisonous gas chlorine, a violent reaction occurs, forming a white solid.

b The solid crystals that form are sodium chloride, NaCl, a common compound used as a flavor enhancer.

c Using a technique called X-ray diffraction, chemists have collected data that can be used to build a model of a sodium chloride crystal.

ements, is something you probably eat every day—table salt. Chemists call it *sodium chloride* instead of salt because the word *salt* can be used to describe any one of thousands of different compounds. Yet all binary salts have something in common; they consist of ions and therefore share certain properties.

All ionic compounds are electrically neutral. They are made of cations and anions combined in a simple whole-number ratio. Sodium chloride consists of white cube-shaped crystals that are hard and brittle. Figure 5-4b is a photograph of sodium chloride taken with a high-powered microscope. Because the crystal is strong and rigid, sodium chloride must be heated to a high temperature of 801°C (1074 K) before it melts. Some force is holding the ions tightly together. Chemists use the word *bond* to describe a force that holds atoms or ions together. There are several kinds of bonds. You studied the metallic bond in Chapter 4 and will learn about the covalent bond in Chapter 6. The **ionic bond** holds salts and other ionic compounds together.

The crystal structures of salts depend on the sizes of the ions

All salts are held together by ionic bonds. The force of attraction between the +1 charge on a sodium ion and the −1 charge on a chloride ion creates the ionic bond in sodium chloride. The structure of salts shows that the attraction between ions extends beyond a single cation and a single anion. This attraction is so far-reaching that many sodium and chloride ions are pulled together into a tightly packed structure. The tight packing of the ions causes common salt to have a distinctive crystal arrangement—the one shown in **Figure 5-5.**

ionic bond

the coulombic force of attraction between ions of opposite charge

---

FIGURE 5-5 ▼

This diagram models the arrangement of ions in a sodium chloride crystal.

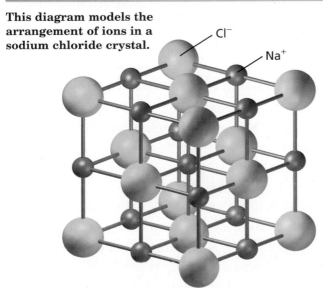

Cl⁻

Na⁺

a The ions are actually in contact with each other, as in Figure 5-4; here they are shown separated so that you can see their relative positions.

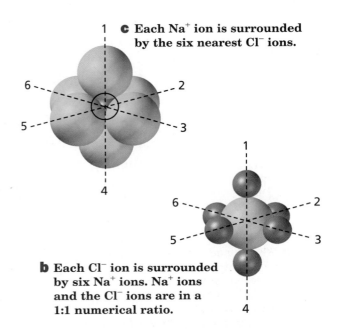

c Each Na⁺ ion is surrounded by the six nearest Cl⁻ ions.

b Each Cl⁻ ion is surrounded by six Na⁺ ions. Na⁺ ions and the Cl⁻ ions are in a 1:1 numerical ratio.

QUICKLAB

Can You Tell a Crystal by Its Shape?

Materials
samples of two different white crystalline solids, microscope

Problem
No tasting is allowed. One of the solids is table salt. Use the microscope or magnifying lens to predict which substance is salt based on its crystal shape.

Analysis
1. Descibe the geometric shape for the crystals in both samples.
2. Could you identify the salt?
3. Why do you think so?

coulombic force

the attraction or repulsion between two objects that have electric charges

halide

a salt that is composed of cations combined with anions of one of the halogen elements

crystal lattice

a repetitive geometric arrangement of points in space about which atoms, ions, or molecules are arranged to form a crystal structure

How many chloride anions surround each sodium cation? How does this number compare with the number of sodium cations that, in turn, surround each chloride anion? In the sodium chloride structure, notice that each ion is closest to six oppositely charged ions. The next closest are 12 similarly charged ions, then 8 more oppositely charged ions, and so on. The net effect is that the **coulombic force** of attraction of the oppositely charged ions is significantly greater than the coulombic force of repulsion from the ions of like charge. In fact, the net effect turns out to be 1.748 times as great as for just a pair of Na^+ and Cl^- ions. This attractive force is what holds clusters of ions together. Figure 5-5 could apply equally as well to any halide of sodium. The **halides** (the name is derived from *halogen*) comprise all the simple anions, namely F^-, Cl^-, Br^-, I^-, and At^-, formed from the Group 17 elements.

The smallest crystal of table salt that you could see would still contain more than a billion billion (10^{18} in scientific notation) Na^+ and Cl^- ions, all in one gigantic lattice. A particular packing arrangement of points in space is called a **crystal lattice.** Each sodium cation is surrounded by six anions, which in turn are surrounded by six cations— *except at the edges.* The ions are less uniformly arranged at the edges of a crystal, creating weak points. Disruptions start at these weak points. When a salt dissolves in water, the ions must be stripped off one layer at a time. Dissolving therefore can be a slow process.

Ionic compounds do not consist of molecules

A crystal of NaCl is composed of Na^+ ions and Cl^- ions held together by coulombic forces resulting from their opposite charges. There are no NaCl molecules. Therefore, the formula NaCl simply indicates that there is a 1:1 ratio of ions in the salt. In fact, the formulas of all ionic compounds represent the simplest numerical ratio between cations and anions. The simplest ratio of ions is called the formula unit for the compound. Because a formula is written as the simplest ratio or formula unit, we do not see formulas like $Na_{10}Cl_{10}$ or $Sr_{10}Cl_{20}$ for ionic salts.

You cannot be absolutely sure that something is made of ions or molecules just by looking at its formula. That determination must be made in the laboratory. But elements in Groups 1 and 2 and in Groups 16 and 17 will almost always form ionic compounds.

Salts have ordered packing arrangements

The ions in a salt form repeating patterns, with each ion held in place by an excess of attractive coulombic forces over repulsive coulombic forces. The way the ions are arranged is common to many different salts. For example, silver bromide, lead(II) sulfide, vanadium(III) nitride, and all the halides of lithium, potassium, and rubidium match the way the sodium halides are packed. Not all one-cation-to-one-anion salts, however, have the same crystal lattice as sodium chloride. The cesium chloride structure consists of one Cs^+ cation surrounded by *eight* Cl^- anions. Models for the NaCl and CsCl crystal structures are shown in **Figure 5-6.** Despite their differences, the crystals of both of these salts are made of simple repeating units that are cubic in shape. The smallest repeating unit in a crystal lattice is called a **unit cell.**

The sodium chloride and cesium chloride structures differ in the number of nearest neighbors that each ion possesses—six for the ions in NaCl, eight for those in CsCl. What determines the crystal pattern for a salt? Cesium ions are larger than sodium ions. The larger cesium ion can be surrounded by more chloride ions, causing cesium chloride to pack in an arrangement with eight, rather than six, nearest neighbors.

The structures shown in Figure 5-6 apply only to crystals containing an equal number of cations and anions. One structure that occurs in many salts with ions in a two-to-one ratio is shown in **Figure 5-7.** It is known as the calcium fluoride lattice because CaF_2 was the first one-cation-to-two-anion salt whose structure was discovered by X-ray crystallography. You can see that the lattice has twice as many anion sites as cation sites. Sodium sulfide, Na_2S, also crystallizes this lattice, but the sites are reversed to accommodate its two-cations-to-one-anion ratio.

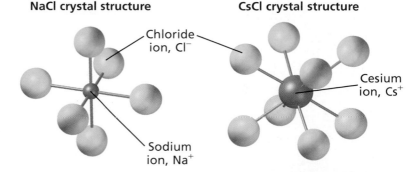

NaCl crystal structure

Chloride ion, Cl^-

Sodium ion, Na^+

CsCl crystal structure

Cesium ion, Cs^+

FIGURE 5-6 ▲

The crystal structure of cesium chloride, CsCl, differs from that of NaCl because the Cs^+ cation is significantly larger than the Na^+ cation.

unit cell

the simplest repeating unit of a crystal lattice

FIGURE 5-7 ▼

Calcium ion, Ca^{2+}

Flouride ion, F^-

a The mineral *fluorite* contains calcium fluoride.

b Each calcium ion is surrounded by eight fluoride ions.

CONCEPT CHECK

1. What force holds ionic crystals together?
2. Crystals of the ionic compounds CaF_2 and $CaCl_2$ have different structures. Suggest a reason for this difference.

Energy aspects of salt formation

As **Figure 5-8** illustrates, the elements sodium and chlorine spontaneously combine in a flash of yellow light when they are brought together. The reaction is evidently exothermic, but where does the energy come from?

Electron transfer between atoms is usually an endothermic process

Recall that ionization energy is the energy that must be supplied to remove the outermost electron from an atom. Atoms always resist having their electrons removed, so ionization energies are always positive. In the case of sodium, the energy needed to remove the outermost electron is 495 kJ/mol. The ionization process could be written as follows.

$$Na(g) + 495 \text{ kJ/mol} \longrightarrow Na^+(g) + e^-$$

Notice that this equation describes the removal of an electron from a gaseous sodium atom.

Electron affinity is the energy needed to put an extra electron onto a neutral atom. Most electron affinities are negative, indicating that the recipient atom easily accepts another electron. Chlorine atoms are willing acceptors of extra electrons; they have an electron affinity that is equal to –349 kJ/mol. As an equation, this process can be expressed as follows.

$$Cl(g) + e^- - 349 \text{ kJ/mol} \longrightarrow Cl^-(g)$$

or

$$Cl(g) + e^- \longrightarrow Cl^-(g) + 349 \text{ kJ/mol}$$

By adding the above equation to the equation for the removal of an electron from an Na atom, we find that the electron transfer from a sodium atom to a chlorine atom is an endothermic reaction absorbing 146 kJ/mol overall. *Energy is needed for this reaction to occur.*

$$Na(g) + Cl(g) + 146 \text{ kJ/mol} \longrightarrow Na^+(g) + Cl^-(g)$$

The energy we just calculated was for transferring an electron between *isolated* atoms to create gaseous ions that are *separated* from each other. This is a very different situation from what happens in the flask shown in Figure 5-8.

The formation of ions is only one part of bonding

If adding an electron to a chlorine atom cannot supply enough energy to remove an electron from a sodium atom, why does an ionic bond form? The chemistry of the following salt-forming reaction can be thought of as five steps, which are shown in **Figure 5-9.** The steps do not represent the actual reactions for the formation of NaCl. Keep in mind that the starting materials are sodium metal and chlorine gas. Chlorine gas consists of pairs of bonded atoms. The final product is crystalline sodium chloride. From Figure 5-9, notice that the chief driving force for the reaction is the last step, in which the separated ions come together to form the crystal lattice.

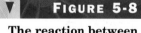

▼ **FIGURE 5-8**

The reaction between sodium metal and chlorine gas is a spontaneous exothermic reaction.

3. No energy is required to convert chlorine into the gaseous state because it is already a gas. However, energy must be added to break up 0.5 mol of Cl_2 molecules to produce 1 mol of chlorine atoms.

$$\tfrac{1}{2}Cl_2(g) + energy \longrightarrow Cl(g)$$

Electron lost

2. More energy must be added to remove one electron from each sodium atom.

$$Na(g) + energy \longrightarrow Na^+(g) + e^-$$

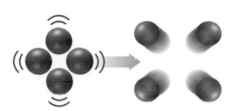

1. Energy must be added to convert 1 mol of sodium from a solid to a gas.

$$Na(s) + energy \longrightarrow Na(g)$$

At the Initial Energy State: The reactants, solid sodium and chlorine gas, start at an initial energy state that is assigned a value of zero at 25°C and 1 atm of pressure.

$$Na(s) \text{ and } Cl_2(g)$$

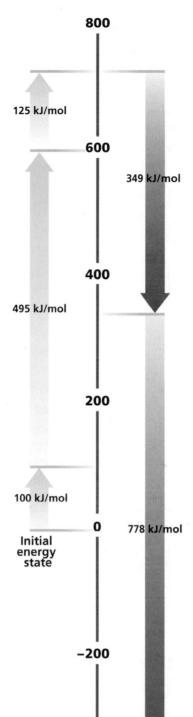

800

125 kJ/mol

600

349 kJ/mol

400

495 kJ/mol

200

100 kJ/mol

0
Initial
energy
state

778 kJ/mol

−200

−400

Electron gained

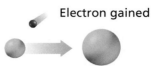

4. Some energy is given off when an electron is added to each chlorine atom to form a Cl^- ion. This is an exothermic process.

$$Cl(g) + e^- \longrightarrow Cl^-(g) + energy$$

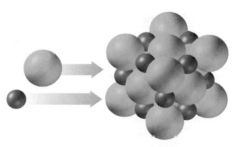

Lattice forms

5. Much more energy is given off when Na^+ and Cl^- ions come together to form an ionic crystal of NaCl.

$$Na^+(g) + Cl^-(g) \longrightarrow NaCl(s) + energy$$

Note that the energy state of crystalline NaCl is more than 400 kJ/mol below the initial energy state of the reactants, Na(s) and $Cl_2(g)$.

FIGURE 5-9 ▲

The reaction between Na(s) and $Cl_2(g)$ to form sodium chloride can be broken down into steps. More energy is released during the exothermic steps than is absorbed during the endothermic steps, so the overall reaction is exothermic.

Forming bonds in a lattice releases energy

The energy released in the fifth step in the sequence illustrated in Figure 5-9 is called the **lattice energy.** This is the energy released when the crystal structure is formed from well-separated ions. In the case of sodium chloride, the lattice energy is 778 kJ/mol, which is greater than the total energy input needed for steps 1, 2, and 3 of Figure 5-9. Without the lattice energy, there would not be enough energy from step 4 to make the overall process spontaneous. *Lattice energy is the key to ionic bond formation.*

Lattice energy is calculated by measuring the energy of all the subreactions as well as the energy released in the overall reaction. Lattice energies of some ionic compounds are given in **Table 5-3.** Generally those compounds with smaller ions, or greater charge, will have higher lattice energies. Notice in Table 5-3 that the lattice energy of lithium chloride is greater than that of lithium iodide. The chloride ion is much smaller than the iodide ion.

TABLE 5-3   Lattice Energies for Some Ionic Compounds

Compound name	Formula	kJ/mol
Lithium chloride	LiCl	861
Lithium bromide	LiBr	818
Lithium iodide	LiI	759
Sodium chloride	NaCl	778
Sodium bromide	NaBr	751
Sodium iodide	NaI	700
Magnesium oxide	MgO	3760
Magnesium sulfide	MgS	3160
Calcium oxide	CaO	3385
Calcium sulfide	CaS	2775

lattice energy

the energy released when well separated atoms, ions, or molecules come together to form a crystal

CONCEPT CHECK

1. **Interpreting Tables**   Using the trends in Table 5-3, predict whether the lattice energy of CsCl is larger or smaller than that of KCl.
2. **Interpreting Graphics**   What steps in Figure 5-9 are endothermic processes? What step involves bond formation?
3. What steps in Figure 5-9 show change-of-state processes?

Properties of binary ionic compounds

A binary ionic compound consists of a simple cation paired with a simple anion in a combination that results in electroneutrality. All the salts that we have discussed so far in this chapter are binary ionic compounds. Metallic oxides (which are not classified as salts) are also binary ionic compounds.

Like most other binary ionic compounds, table salt is fairly hard and brittle. *Hard* means the crystal is able to resist a large force applied to it. *Brittle* means that when the applied force becomes too strong to resist, the crystal develops a widespread fracture rather than a localized dent. Both of these properties can be attributed to the regular planes of ionic charges that all crystal lattices possess.

The ions in a crystal are arranged in a repeating pattern, forming layers. As long as the layers stay in a fixed position relative to one an-

FIGURE 5-10 ▼

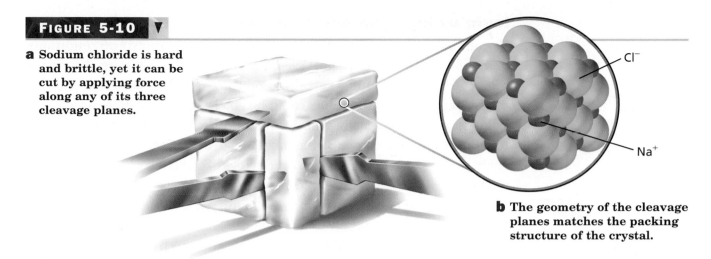

a Sodium chloride is hard and brittle, yet it can be cut by applying force along any of its three cleavage planes.

Cl⁻

Na⁺

b The geometry of the cleavage planes matches the packing structure of the crystal.

other, the ionic compound will be hard and it will take a lot of energy to break all the bonds between the ions. However, if a force causes one layer to move slightly, ions of the same sign will be next to each other. When a force is large enough to reposition a layer of ions, the repulsive force between the layers will cause the layers to break apart. **Figure 5-10** shows cleavage planes for NaCl.

internetconnect

SCLINKS.
NSTA
TOPIC: Salt properties
GO TO: www.scilinks.org
KEYWORD: HW053

Salts melt and boil at high temperatures

All ionic compounds share certain properties because of the strong attraction between their ions. Compare the boiling point of sodium chloride with that of water, a molecular compound—1413°C compared with 100°C. Similarly, most other binary ionic compounds have high melting and boiling points, as you can see in **Table 5-4.** Because each ion in these compounds forms strong bonds to neighboring ions, considerable energy is required to free them from their fixed locations, which must occur for the compound to melt. Still more energy is needed to move ions out of the liquid state and cause boiling.

TABLE 5-4 **Melting and Boiling Points of Compounds**

Compound name	Formula	Type of compound	Melting point		Boiling point	
			°C	K	°C	K
Calcium iodide	CaI_2	ionic	784	1057	1100	1373
Carbon tetrachloride	CCl_4	covalent	−23	250	77	350
Hydrogen fluoride	HF	covalent	−83	190	20	293
Hydrogen sulfide	H_2S	covalent	−86	188	−61	212
Iodine monochloride	ICl	covalent	27	300	97	370
Magnesium fluoride	MgF_2	ionic	1261	1534	2239	2512
Methane	CH_4	covalent	−182	91	−164	109
Sodium chloride	NaCl	ionic	801	1074	1413	1686

Ionic solids *generally* do not conduct electricity

To conduct an electric current, a substance must satisfy two conditions: it must contain charged particles, and those particles must be free to move. Ionic compounds certainly contain charged particles. So one might expect that ionic solids could be good conductors. Recall that particles in a solid have some vibrational motion; however, they remain in fixed locations, as shown by the model in **Figure 5-11a.** Thus, ionic solids, such as salts, generally are not conductors of electricity because the ions cannot move through the crystal.

However, when the ions can move about, salts are excellent electrical conductors. This situation occurs when a salt melts or dissolves. When a salt melts, the ions that make up the crystal can freely move past each other, as **Figure 5-11b** illustrates. Molten salts are good conductors of electricity, though they do not conduct as well as metals. Similarly, if a salt dissolves in water, its ions are no longer held tightly in the crystal; they are free to move, as shown by the model in **Figure 5-11c,** and the solution becomes an electrical conductor.

As often happens in chemistry, there are exceptions to the rule. There is a small class of compounds called *solid ionic conductors* that allow electricity to pass through their crystals. The lattices of these compounds have an unusually open structure, so certain ions can move past others, jumping from one lattice site to another. In the *mixed salt*

internet connect

SC**LINKS**
NSTA

TOPIC: Nonconductors
GO TO: www.scilinks.org
KEYWORD: HW054

▼ FIGURE 5-11

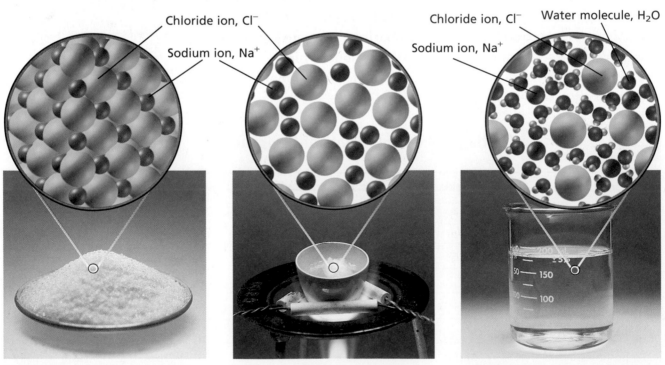

a Charged particles in an ionic solid are rigidly held in fixed positions.

b When ionic solids melt, the ions are able to move about more freely.

c When ionic solids are dissolved in water, the ions are able to move about in a mixture with water molecules.

TABLE 5-5 **Some Characteristics of Ionic Compounds**

• Are solids at room temperature
• Are hard and brittle
• Generally have high melting points and boiling points
• Generally do not conduct electricity when in solid form
• Are good conductors of electricity in the liquid state and when dissolved in water

silver rubidium iodide, $RbAg_4I_5$, the Ag^+ cations are mobile, even at room temperature. More compounds join the class of solid ionic conductors as the temperature rises.

Zirconium oxide, ZrO_2, does not conduct electricity at ordinary temperatures, but it does conduct at high temperatures. At temperatures well below its melting point, about 3000 K, the O^{2-} ions can move through the crystal lattice. This behavior is the basis of a device that controls emissions from the exhaust of automobiles. An electrochemical cell containing ZrO_2 as a separator measures the percentage of oxygen in the exhaust gases. The car's computer then adjusts the fuel-to-air ratio to obtain the best performance of the engine with the least emission of polluting gases.

SECTION REVIEW

Total recall

1. In the formation of most ionic crystals from free atoms, which step gives off the largest amount of energy, thereby driving the reaction?

2. Explain why the dissolution of a salt can be a slow process.

3. Explain why ionic compounds do not conduct electric current in the solid phase but do conduct in the liquid phase or when dissolved in water.

Critical thinking

4. **Interpreting Tables** Look at Table 5-3, on page 172. How is the size of an anion related to the lattice energy for compounds of Group 1 cations? Does this trend hold for compounds of Group 2 cations?

5. **Interpreting Tables** Table 5-4, on page 173, shows the melting and boiling points of ionic compounds and covalent compounds. What conclusions can you draw about the forces holding ionic crystals together as compared with the forces holding molecular crystals together?

6. **Interpreting Graphics** Use Figure 5-9, on page 171, to describe how the formation of $CaCl_2$ would differ from that of NaCl.

7. **Story Clue** What part of the silver halide crystal is most affected by light when film is exposed?

What are polyatomic ions?

OBJECTIVES

▶ **Explain** how polyatomic ions and their salts are named and how their formulas relate to their names.

▶ **Describe** the pattern used in naming oxyanions.

▶ **Assign** oxidation numbers to atoms in polyatomic ions and their compounds.

▶ **Discuss** differences between silicate minerals, hydrates, and conventional salts.

Many atoms can form one ion

polyatomic ion

an electrically charged group of two or more chemically bonded atoms that functions as a single ion

In Section 5-1, the adjective *simple* was used to describe an ion formed from a single atom. A simple ion could also be called *monatomic,* meaning "one-atom." Just as the prefixes *mono-* and *mon-* mean "one," so *poly-* means "many." The term **polyatomic ion** means a charged group of two or more bonded atoms that functions as a single ion. Atoms in a polyatomic ion are covalently bonded, but the ion as a whole forms ionic bonds with other ions in the same way that simple ions do. The peroxide ion, O_2^{2-}, the mercury(I) ion, Hg_2^{2+}, the azide ion, N_3^-, and the polysulfide ion, S_5^{2-}, each consists of atoms of a single element. Most polyatomic ions consist of atoms of several elements.

Fertilizers contain compounds with polyatomic ions

The purpose of the fertilizers shown in **Figure 5-12** is to supply potassium, nitrogen, and phosphorus in a form that plants can readily use.

◀ FIGURE 5-12

Compounds containing polyatomic ions supply soil with nitrogen, phosphorus, and potassium in ratios to meet the needs of specific plants.

N-P-K
15-30-15

N-P-K
15-10-7

N-P-K
36-6-6

Some potassium in fertilizers is in the form of K_2CO_3. The formulas for two compounds that can supply nitrogen are NH_4NO_3 and $(NH_4)_2SO_4$. The phosphorus often comes from $Ca(H_2PO_4)_2$. All these ionic compounds contain polyatomic ions. Most ionic compounds are called **salts,** whether their ions are simple or polyatomic (the exceptions are when oxide or hydroxide anions are present.) In K_2CO_3 or $Ca(H_2PO_4)_2$, the anion is polyatomic and the cation is a simple metal ion. In NH_4NO_3, both the anion and the cation are polyatomic.

salt

an ionic compound that is composed of cations bonded to anions, other than oxide or hydroxide anions

The names of polyatomic ions can be complicated

You'll find that the nomenclature of polyatomic ions is not completely logical. Nevertheless there are rules you can count on to help you remember how to name some compounds.

Many polyatomic ions contain oxygen. The endings *-ite* and *-ate* show the presence of oxygen. Such ions are called **oxyanions.** If they are negatively charged, these oxyanion names do *not* specify exactly how many oxygen atoms are present. Sulf**ate** has four, nitr**ate** has three, acet**ate** has two. Often there are several oxyanions that differ only in the number of oxygen atoms present. For example, sulfur forms the SO_3^{2-} and SO_4^{2-} oxyanions. In such cases, the ion with more oxygen takes the *-ate* ending, sulfate in this case; the ion with less oxygen takes the *-ite* ending, sulfite. **Table 5-6** shows the names given to common oxyanions. Notice the pattern in the naming of these ions.

oxyanion

a negative polyatomic ion containing oxygen

The presence of hydrogen in a polyatomic anion is often indicated by the ion's name starting with *hydrogen*. The prefixes *mono-* and *di-* are also used. Thus, HPO_4^{2-} and $H_2PO_4^-$ are monohydrogen phosphate and dihydrogen phosphate ions, respectively. The prefix *thio-* means "replace an oxygen by a sulfur" in the formula, as in potassium thiosulfate, $K_2S_2O_3$, compared with potassium sulfate, K_2SO_4. **Table 5-7,** on the next page, is a complete listing of the names and formulas for common polyatomic ions.

| TABLE 5-6 | Naming Conventions for Some Oxyanions |

	Oxyanion formula	Number of oxygen atoms	Oxyanion name
With chlorine	ClO^-	1	*hypo*chlor*ite*
(other halogens	ClO_2^-	2	chlor*ite*
form similarly	ClO_3^-	3	chlor*ate*
named oxyanions)	ClO_4^-	4	*per*chlor*ate*
With sulfur	SO_3^{2-}	3	sulf*ite*
	SO_4^{2-}	4	sulf*ate*
With nitrogen	NO_2^-	2	nitr*ite*
	NO_3^-	3	nitr*ate*

HOW TO Write the name of a compound containing a polyatomic ion

What is the name of the compound with the formula K_2CO_3?

1 Name the cation

You already know that K is potassium and that it forms a singly charged cation, K^+, of the same name. The subscript *2* indicates that there are two potassium ions, as shown below. Recall that salts are electrically neutral overall, so the two positive charges of the two potassium ions must be balanced by two negative charges associated with the carbonate anion, CO_3^{2-}.

2 Name the anion

The anion component of the salt is CO_3^{2-}. It helps to think of the formula as follows, though it is not written that way.

$$[K^+]_2[CO_3^{2-}]$$

If you consult **Table 5-7,** you will see that the CO_3^{2-} ion is called the *carbonate ion.*

K_2CO_3 is made of two potassium cations, each with one positive charge... K^+ K^+ ← K_2CO_3 → CO_3^{2-} ...and a single doubly charged anion, a carbonate ion.

3 Name the salt

Remember that the name of a salt is just the names of its ions. K_2CO_3 is potassium carbonate.

TABLE 5-7 Some Polyatomic Ions

Ion name	Formula	Ion name	Formula	Ion name	Formula
Acetate	CH_3COO^-	Dihydrogen phosphate	$H_2PO_4^-$	Oxalate	$C_2O_4^{2-}$
Ammonium	NH_4^+	Dimercury(I) or mercury(I)	Hg_2^{2+}	Perchlorate	ClO_4^-
Arsenate	AsO_4^{3-}	Hydrogen carbonate (bicarbonate)	HCO_3^-	Permanganate	MnO_4^-
Azide	N_3^-			Peroxide	O_2^{2-}
Bromate	BrO_3^-	Hydrogen sulfate	HSO_4^-	Phosphate	PO_4^{3-}
Carbonate	CO_3^{2-}	Hydroxide	OH^-	Sulfate	SO_4^{2-}
Chlorate	ClO_3^-	Hypochlorite	ClO^-	Sulfite	SO_3^{2-}
Chlorite	ClO_2^-	Methylammonium	$CH_3NH_3^+$	Thiocyanate	SCN^-
Chromate	CrO_4^{2-}	Monohydrogen phosphate	HPO_4^{2-}	Thiosulfate	$S_2O_3^{2-}$
Cyanide	CN^-	Nitrate	NO_3^-	Uranyl	UO_2^{2+}
Dichromate	$Cr_2O_7^{2-}$	Nitrite	NO_2^-		

Write the formula for a compound containing a polyatomic ion

A fertilizer shown in Figure 5-12 has calcium dihydrogen phosphate as an ingredient. What is the formula for this salt?

1 **Use Table 5-7 to determine the formula and charge for the polyatomic ion**

Dihydrogen phosphate is $H_2PO_4^-$. Notice that dihydrogen phosphate has seven atoms from three different elements, plus one extra electron.

2 **Determine the formula and charge for the cation**

Because the calcium ion is Ca^{2+}, we clearly need two dihydrogen phosphate anions for each calcium cation. The diagram below shows how we can assemble this information to create the formula $Ca(H_2PO_4)_2$.

Notice the use of parentheses to show that *everything* inside the parentheses is doubled by the subscript 2 outside. The formula written without the parentheses, CaH_2PO_{42}, would imply 42 oxygen atoms. Sometimes we need two sets of parentheses, such as in the case of mercury(I) phosphate, $(Hg_2)_3(PO_4)_2$.

For every calcium cation in calcium dihydrogen phosphate... Ca^{2+} $H_2PO_4^-$ $H_2PO_4^-$ ...there must be two dihydrogen phosphate anions.

$$Ca(H_2PO_4)_2$$

The two anions are shown in parentheses and designated by the subscript 2.

1. In what ways are polyatomic ions like simple ions? In what ways are they different?

2. Identify and name the cations and anions that make up the following ionic compounds and indicate the charge on each ion:
   a. $NaClO_3$
   b. K_2SO_3
   c. $(NH_4)_2CrO_4$
   d. $Al_2(SO_4)_3$

3. Name the compounds represented by the following formulas:
   a. Na_3AsO_4
   b. NH_4ClO_4
   c. $Ca(NO_2)_2$
   d. $Fe(OH)_3$

4. Write formulas for the following compounds:
   a. mercury(II) sulfate
   b. calcium cyanide
   c. rubidium oxalate
   d. lithium thiosulfate
   e. potassium dichromate
   f. potassium chromate
   g. sodium azide
   h. methylammonium sulfide

Oxidation numbers
Polyatomic ions and the oxidation number concept

The charges listed for ions are used to denote a transfer of electrons in the formation of an ionic bond. Atoms within polyatomic ions are bonded covalently. In the next chapter you will learn that in covalent bonds electrons are shared between atoms. Unlike transferred electrons in ionic bonds, shared electrons in covalent bonds are not considered part of either of the atoms that share them. For example, the bonds between sulfur and oxygen atoms in the sulfate ion, SO_4^{2-}, contain shared electrons. Neither sulfur nor oxygen is an ion in SO_4^{2-}. Chemists have devised a scheme for polyatomic ions and molecular compounds to describe the distribution of electrons among bonded atoms. This convention is called **oxidation number.** Unlike the charge on an ion, an oxidation number does not have a real physical meaning. Even though we assign a charge to an atom in a polyatomic ion or molecular compound, that atom is not an ion and does not possess a real charge. Because each oxygen atom is assigned an oxidation number of –2, the sulfur atom in SO_4^{2-} is assigned an oxidation number of +6. **Figure 5-13** is a list of guidelines that can be used in assigning oxidation numbers. The model on the next page takes you through the process of assigning oxidation numbers.

oxidation number

a number assigned to an atom in a polyatomic ion or molecular compound based on an assumption of complete transfer of electrons

► **FIGURE 5-13**

Use these guidelines when determining the oxidation state of any atom in a formula.

Some Guidelines for Assigning Oxidation Numbers

1. The oxidation number of any free (uncombined) element is zero.

2. The oxidation number of a monatomic ion is equal to the charge on the ion.

3. The more electronegative element in a binary compound is assigned the number equal to the charge it would have if it were an ion.

4. The oxidation number of each hydrogen atom is + 1 unless it is combined with a metal, then it has a state of – 1.

5. The oxidation number of fluorine is always – 1 because it is the most electronegative atom.

6. The oxidation number of each oxygen atom in most of its compounds is – 2. When combined with F, oxygen has a number of + 2. In peroxides, such as H_2O_2, oxygen has an oxidation number of – 1.

7. In compounds, the elements of Group 1 and Group 2, and aluminum have positive oxidation numbers of + 1, + 2, and + 3, respectively.

8. The algebraic sum of the oxidation numbers for all the atoms in a compound is zero.

9. The algebraic sum of the oxidation numbers for all the atoms in a polyatomic ion is equal to the charge on that ion.

HOW TO Assign oxidation numbers to atoms in a polyatomic ion

Assign oxidation numbers to all atoms in $S_2O_7^{2-}$.

1 If you know an element's oxidation number, start by placing those oxidation numbers above the elements

From rule 6, you know that oxygen has an oxidation number of –2.

$$S_2\overset{-2}{O}{}_7^{2-}$$

2 If more than one atom of an element is present in the formula, calculate the total charge contributed by those atoms by multiplying the charge on the individual atom by its subscript in the formula

For oxygen the total charge is calculated as follows:

$$O: (-2)7 = -14$$

$$S_2\underset{-14}{\overset{-2}{O}}{}_7^{2-}$$

3 Determine the charge needed to reach a net –2 for the ion

$$2S + (-14) = -2$$

$$2S = +12$$

4 Divide that charge by the number of atoms to determine the oxidation number for each atom

$$S = \frac{12}{2}$$

$$S = +6$$

In $S_2O_7^{2-}$ the oxidation state assigned to S is +6 and to O is –2.

CONCEPT CHECK

1. Determine the oxidation number assigned to Mn in MnO_4^-.
2. Determine the oxidation number assigned to each atom in NH_4^+.
3. Determine the oxidation number assigned to P in H_3PO_4.
4. Determine the oxidation number for each atom in BF_3.
5. Determine the oxidation number for each atom in the following compounds:
   a. $KMnO_4$
   b. $PbSO_4$
   c. iron(III) carbonate
   d. cobalt(II) nitrite

Silicates and hydrates
Even rocks consist of salts

All the rocks on Earth began as igneous rock, such as granite, which forms when molten magma solidifies. Weathering leads to sedimentary rock, such as sandstone. The action of heat and pressure converts other rocks into metamorphic rock, such as slate. Rocks contain inorganic crystalline materials called **minerals.** Some minerals are, in effect, salts of metal cations and oxyanions of silicon. They differ from the salts that you have studied so far in that some of them have large anions.

The **silicates** are one class of minerals whose anions are composed of long chains, sheets, or networks of alternating silicon and oxygen atoms with periodic negative charges. A simple example is the $Si_4O_{12}^{10-}$ anion shown in **Figure 5-14a.** The negative charges of these anions are balanced by the presence of metal cations such as Mg^{2+} in $Mg_3(Si_2O_6H)_2$. The silicate ions are arranged in layers in the mineral talc. This structure gives talc a slippery feel because the layers slide past each other.

Feldspars, the most abundant rocks in Earth's crust, are aluminosilicates that have some of the silicon atoms replaced by aluminum atoms. Feldspars can consist of large aluminosilicate anions with sodium, potassium, or calcium cations. As the rock slowly weathers, the cations are washed out and the rock eventually crumbles into clay. The semiprecious gem garnet, shown in **Figure 5-14b,** is an aluminosilicate that includes iron and has the formula $Fe_3Al_2(SiO_4)_3$.

mineral

a naturally occurring inorganic substance that has a definite composition and ordered structure

silicate

any of the compounds containing silicon, oxygen, one or more metals, and possibly hydrogen

▼ **FIGURE 5-14**

a Silicates are composed of long chains of anions arranged as shown in the model.

b Garnet is an aluminosilicate with an iron cation.

c Feldspars are the most abundant rocks on Earth. Half Dome, in Yosemite National Park, is composed of feldspars.

FIGURE 5-15 ▼

a Anhydrous copper(II) sulfate, $CuSO_4$, is a white powder . . .

b . . . but when it is stirred in water, a blue solution forms.

c After the water evaporates, blue crystals form that are copper(II) sulfate pentahydrate, $CuSO_4 \cdot 5H_2O$.

Some salts form hydrates

If you dissolve a soluble salt in water and then allow the water to evaporate, you don't always recover the same material you started with. **Figure 5-15** shows stages in such an experiment. When water is added to the white salt in the beaker, the salt dissolves, but the resulting solution becomes blue. If the water evaporates, blue crystals form. The white salt is copper(II) sulfate, $CuSO_4$. The blue salt that was recovered after the evaporation process is called copper(II) sulfate *pentahydrate.* The blue product still contains the Cu^{2+} cation and the SO_4^{2-} anion in a one-to-one ratio, but in addition, it has five water molecules for each pair of ions. The formula for the blue salt is written as follows.

hydrate

an ionic compound that contains precise numbers of water molecules in its crystal lattice

anhydrous

without water

$$CuSO_4 \cdot 5H_2O$$

Ionic compounds, like $CuSO_4$, with water molecules incorporated into their crystal lattices are called **hydrates.** The water molecules are referred as *water of hydration.* When a hydrated ionic compound is heated to drive off all the water, the remaining salt is **anhydrous,** which means "without water." The specific number of water molecules per formula unit of the ionic compound is indicated by the Greek prefixes *mono-, di-, tri-, tetra-, penta-,* and so on. **Table 5-8** shows examples of the use of prefixes in naming hydrates.

Not all hydrates have another color in their anhydrous form. Sodium carbonate, Na_2CO_3, forms the hydrate $Na_2CO_3 \cdot 10H_2O$, which is called sodium

TABLE 5-8

Names and Formulas for Some Common Hydrates

Name	Formula
Barium chloride dihydrate	$BaCl_2 \cdot 2H_2O$
Barium hydroxide octahydrate	$Ba(OH)_2 \cdot 8H_2O$
Calcium nitrate tetrahydrate	$Ca(NO_3)_2 \cdot 4H_2O$
Calcium sulfate dihydrate	$CaSO_4 \cdot 2H_2O$
Calcium sulfate hemihydrate	$CaSO_4 \cdot 1/2H_2O$
Cobalt(II) nitrate hexahydrate	$Co(NO_3)_2 \cdot 6H_2O$
Cobalt(II) sulfate heptahydrate	$CoSO_4 \cdot 7H_2O$
Iron(III) chloride hexahydrate	$FeCl_3 \cdot 6H_2O$
Iron(III) nitrate nonahydrate	$Fe(NO_3)_3 \cdot 9H_2O$
Magnesium sulfate heptahydrate	$MgSO_4 \cdot 7H_2O$

carbonate *decahydrate*. *Deca-* is the prefix that denotes 10. This compound is also known as washing soda. Both the anhydrous salt and the hydrate are white, though they have different crystal lattices.

The ratio of water molecules in a hydrate is determined experimentally. You cannot predict the number of water molecules in the formula for a hydrate by looking at the formula for its anhydrous form. There are even hydrates called hemihydrates (meaning "half hydrate"). For example, potassium perborate hemihydrate has the formula $KBO_3 \cdot 1/2H_2O$.

Some anhydrous salts absorb moisture so readily that they can be used as drying agents to remove moisture from air or to remove water from liquids and gases other than those in air.

SECTION REVIEW

Total recall

1. How are minerals related to salts?

2. Describe the structure of a silicate.

3. Write formulas for the following compounds:
   a. ammonium monohydrogen phosphate
   b. zinc carbonate
   c. cobalt(II) acetate
   d. lead(II) azide
   e. copper(I) carbonate
   f. copper(II) chromate
   g. ammonium acetate
   h. ammonium dichromate
   i. calcium peroxide
   j. cobalt(II) phosphate

4. Write formulas for the following compounds:
   a. iron(II) bromide hexahydrate
   b. nickel(II) hydroxide dihydrate
   c. copper(II) phosphate trihydrate
   d. aluminum nitrate nonahydrate
   e. barium perchlorate tetrahydrate
   f. barium oxalate monohydrate

5. Name the following compounds:
   a. $CoSO_4$ e. $CoSO_4 \cdot 7H_2O$
   b. $Fe_2(C_2O_4)_3$ f. $Fe_3(PO_4)_2 \cdot 8H_2O$
   c. $Mn(NO_3)_2$ g. $Mn(NO_3)_2 \cdot 6H_2O$
   d. $NaClO$ h. $NaClO \cdot 5H_2O$

6. Describe a method that you could use to obtain $MgSO_4$ from $MgSO_4 \cdot 7H_2O$.

7. **Interpreting Tables** Using Table 5-8, write the prefixes used to denote 2, 4, 6, 7, and 9 water molecules in a hydrate formula.

8. **Story Clue** In photography, solid AgBr is dissolved in a solution of sodium thiosulfate. Write the formula for sodium thiosulfate.

9. Determine the oxidation number of bromine in the following polyatomic ions:
   a. bromate   c. hypobromite
   b. bromite   d. perbromate

10. Determine the oxidation number for each element in the following formulas:
    a. $HClO_4$ c. $Fe(NO_3)_3$
    b. $Al_2(SO_4)_3$ d. $(NH_4)_2Cr_2O_7$

Critical thinking

11. Suppose that a new nonmetal element is discovered and named *loftium*. How would the loftate and loftite ions compare in charge and composition? How would the hypoloftite and perloftate ions compare with the loftite and loftate ions?

12. How does oxidation number differ from the charge on an ion? In what case are the oxidation number and charge the same?

The technician *develops* the film by placing it in a special developer solution that is mildly alkaline. The developer must be at just the right temperature and concentration and must remain in contact with the film for just the right length of time if the photograph is to be picture perfect. During the development stage, silver halide crystals that have silver atoms around their edges are converted to silver metal.

To stop further development, a *stopper* is added, followed by a *fixer*, which removes all the remaining silver halide crystals. When the film has been through these two solutions (they are sometimes combined) and has been thoroughly washed with pure water, it is safe to bring the film out of the darkroom. After it dries, the film has islands of silver metal distributed throughout the emulsion. There is a lot of silver where the light fell the strongest, and none where no light fell. At this stage, the film is called a *negative.* The negative is dark where the scene was lightest and light where the scene was darkest.

Next comes the printing process. Using an enlarger, the technician projects light through the negative and onto a sheet of photographic paper. The paper contains silver chloride, AgCl. The entire photographic process—exposure, development, stopping, fixing, washing, and drying—is carried out again on the print. This process causes a second reversal, so that ultimately the dark areas on the print correspond to the dark areas on the original scene to form a positive image.

Color-film processing is similar to the black-and-white process just described. However, color-film emulsions consist of three distinct silver halide-impregnated layers, each incorporating a different-colored dye to make the final three-color print.

LOOKING BACK

How do the properties of silver atoms differ from those of silver ions?

A silver ion contains one less electron than a silver atom, which gives the ion an overall 1+ charge.

How can exposure to light change the chemical structure of a compound?

Light provides the energy needed to drive the reaction that changes silver ions to silver atoms.

Although light falls on the entire salt crystal, why do silver atoms form only at the edges of the crystal?

Recall that the silver bromide and silver iodide crystals are distributed throughout a gelatin matrix and exposed to light. The energy of the light is sufficient to knock one electron off a bromide ion, leaving an unstable bromine atom in the salt lattice.

$$Br^-(s) + light\ energy \longrightarrow e^- + Br(s)$$

Attracted to the positive charges of the Ag^+ ions, the free electron moves through the lattice. The Ag^+ ions at the crystal's edge are not surrounded by six bromide ions, and they *are* susceptible to a reaction with the wandering electron.

$$Ag^+(edge) + e^- \longrightarrow Ag(edge)$$

So it is the instability of ions at the surface of the ionic crystal that leads to the formation of latent images.

$\mathcal{H}$IGHLIGHTS

KEY TERMS

5-1
anion
binary ionic compound
cation
electroneutrality
ion
ionic compound

isoelectronic
octet rule
subscript

5-2
coulombic force
crystal lattice
halide

ionic bond
lattice energy
unit cell

5-3
anhydrous
hydrate
mineral

oxidation number
oxyanion
polyatomic ion
salt
silicate

KEY CONCEPTS

5-1 How are ions different from atoms?

▶ Some atoms may gain or lose electrons to achieve electron configurations that are isoelectronic with a noble gas.

▶ Ions are electrically charged particles that have different chemical properties than their parent atoms.

▶ Metals tend to form cations, while nonmetals tend to form anions.

▶ Ionic compounds are named by joining the cation and anion names.

▶ The subscripts in the formula for an ionic compound indicate the lowest electrically neutral whole-number ratio of cations to anions.

5-2 What holds a salt together?

▶ The opposite charges of anions and cations attract, forming a tightly packed substance of bonded ions called a crystal structure.

▶ Salts have high melting and boiling points and usually do not conduct electricity in the solid state.

▶ Salts conduct electricity when melted or dissolved in water.

▶ An input of energy is needed to break chemical bonds between atoms. Energy is released when bonds form between atoms.

▶ An ionic compound will form if the energy released to create anions and form the crystal structure is greater than the energy absorbed to create cations.

5-3 What are polyatomic ions?

▶ A polyatomic ion is a group of two or more atoms bonded together that functions as a single unit.

▶ Parentheses are used to group polyatomic ions in a chemical formula with a subscript.

▶ Oxidation numbers are a convention for assigning a relative charge to atoms that share electrons.

▶ Polyatomic ions are found in silicates.

▶ Hydrates are compounds that contain water molecules within the crystal lattice.

KEY SKILLS

Review the following models before your exam. Be sure you can write formulas and name compounds.

How To Write formulas for binary ionic compounds (p. 164)

How To Write the name of a compound containing a polyatomic ion (p. 178)

How To Write the formula for a compound containing a polyatomic ion (p. 179)

How To Assign oxidation numbers to atoms in a polyatomic ion (p. 181)

REVIEW & ASSESS

TERM REVIEW

1. By losing an electron, a metal atom becomes a(n) ———.
   (cation, anion)

2. CaO is an example of a ———.
   (binary compound, cation)

3. The driving force in the formation of a salt is the ———.
   (lattice energy, nuclear force)

4. The simplest repeating unit that makes up a crystal is the ———.
   (unit cell, crystal lattice)

5. A(n) ——— is a negatively charged polyatomic ion containing oxygen.
   (oxyanion, oxycation)

CONCEPT & SKILLS REVIEW

FORMATION OF IONS

1. Propose a reason why magnesium forms Mg^{2+} ions and not Mg^{6-} ions.

2. Complete the table below.

Atom	Ion	Noble-gas configuration of ion
S		
Be		
I		
Rb		
O		
Sr		
F		

3. Why are most metals found in nature as ores and not as pure metals?

4. A classmate insists that sodium gains a positive charge when it becomes an ion because it gains a proton. Explain this student's error.

5. Which of the following diagrams illustrates the electron diagram for a potassium ion found in the nerve cells of your body? (Hint: potassium's atomic number is 19.)

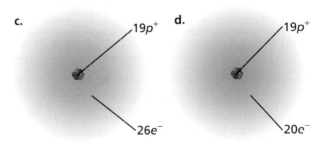

6. Write a chemical symbol for each of the following particles. If the particle is an ion, indicate its charge and identify it as a cation or an anion.

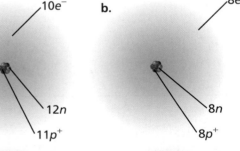

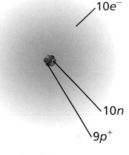

7. The electron configuration for a lithium atom is $1s^22s^1$. The configuration for an iodine atom is $1s^22s^22p^63s^23p^64s^23d^{10}4p^65s^24d^{10}5p^5$. Write the electron configurations for the ions that form lithium iodide, a salt used in photography.

BINARY COMPOUNDS AND NOMENCLATURE

8. Complete the table below, and then use it to answer the questions that follow.

Element	Ion	Name of ion
Barium	Ba^{2+}	
Chlorine		chloride
Chromium	Cr^{3+}	
Fluorine	F^-	
Manganese		manganese(II)
Oxygen		oxide

a. Write the formula for a salt found in electrical batteries containing manganese and chlorine.

b. Write the formula for a compound containing chromium and fluorine used to treat silk.

c. Write the formula for a compound containing barium and oxygen used to manufacture lubricating-oil detergents.

9. Why are there no rules for naming Group 18 ions?

10. Write formulas for the following compounds.
   a. aluminum fluoride, used in ceramics
   b. magnesium oxide, an antacid
   c. calcium sulfide, used in luminous paints
   d. strontium bromide, an anticonvulsant

11. Write formulas for the following compounds.
   a. cadmium(II) bromide, used in process engraving
   b. palladium(II) chloride, used in some photographic toning solutions
   c. vanadium(V) oxide, an ingredient in yellow glass
   d. cobalt(II) sulfide, used as a catalyst

12. Use **Table 5-2** to write all possible formulas for the ionic compounds listed.
   a. iron chloride
   b. copper oxide
   c. tin fluoride
   d. mercury chloride
   e. manganese oxide
   f. chromium chloride

13. Explain what is wrong with each of the following chemical formulas:
   a. $RbCl_2$ **c.** $NaCs$
   b. $Ge_{12}S_{24}$ **d.** $NaNe$

14. Explain the error contained in each of the following formulas for barium chloride:
   a. Ba_2Cl **c.** Ba_2Cl_4
   b. $BaCl_3$

IONIC COMPOUNDS

15. Use the table below to identify the chemicals listed as ionic or molecular. State reasons for your answers.

Substance	State at room temperature	Conducts electricity at room temperature	Melting point (°C)	Conducts electricity as a liquid
KI	solid	no	680	yes
Fe	solid	yes	1535	yes
$AlPO_4$	solid	no	1460	yes
CH_4	gas	no	−182.6	no
NaBr	solid	no	755	yes
$C_6H_{12}O_6$	solid	no	150	no

16. Determine the ratio of cations to anions for the following compounds:
  a. strontium chloride, an ingredient in fireworks
  b. rubidium chloride, an ingredient in drugs
  c. aluminum chloride, an ingredient in wood preservatives
  d. barium oxide, a substance used in making detergents for lubricating oils
  e. aluminum oxide, an ingredient in some dental cements
  f. aluminum nitride, a substance used in making semiconductors

17. Why do most ionic compounds have such high melting and boiling points?

18. Under the right conditions, ionic substances can conduct electricity very well. Describe these conditions, and explain why an ionic substance would be a poor choice as a conductor for a computer circuit board.

19. Does a cube of salt have a different unit cell than powdered salt has? Explain your answer.

20. Label the drawings below as representing a solid, a liquid, or an aqueous solution. State whether the substance pictured will or will not conduct electricity.

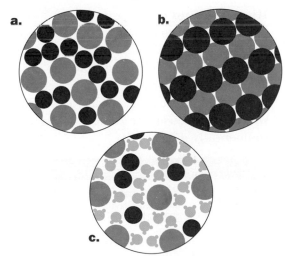

21. Sodium chloride can be prepared by reacting sodium metal with chlorine gas. Another way to prepare it is to combine sodium hydroxide and hydrochloric acid and allow any water present to evaporate. Will the method of preparation affect the type of unit cell and crystalline structure of NaCl? Explain.

22. The equations below show the energy changes that are necessary for calcium bromide, $CaBr_2$, to form from the elements calcium and bromine. Is formation of $CaBr_2$, from its elements, an exothermic or an endothermic process? Explain.

$$Ca(s) + 8.5 \text{ kJ} \longrightarrow Ca(g)$$
$$Ca(g) + 1735 \text{ kJ} \longrightarrow Ca^{2+}(g) + 2e^-$$
$$Br_2(g) + 193 \text{ kJ} \longrightarrow 2Br(g)$$
$$2Br(g) + 2e^- \longrightarrow 2Br^-(g) + 650 \text{ kJ}$$
$$Ca^{2+}(g) + 2Br^-(g) \longrightarrow CaBr_2(s) + 2176 \text{ kJ}$$

POLYATOMIC IONS

23. Why is the strontium nitrate found in roadside emergency flares represented as $Sr(NO_3)_2$ rather than SrN_2O_6?

24. What is the difference between the chlorite ion and the chlorate ion? **(Hint: Refer to Table 5-7.)**

25. Write the symbol and charge for each ion found in the following compounds:
  a. NaClO
  b $(NH_4)_2CO_3$
  c. K_2HPO_4
  d. CuCN
  e. FeC_2O_4
  f. $Mn(CH_3COO)_2$
  g. Hg_2SO_4

26. Write formulas for the following compounds:
  a. potassium hydrogen phosphate, an ingredient in nondairy creamers
  b. strontium nitrate, an ingredient in red safety flares
  c. lithium sulfate, an antidepressant
  d. magnesium dihydrogen phosphate, used to make wood fireproof.

27. Write formulas for the following compounds:
  a. ammonium acetate, a meat preservative
  b. mercury(I) nitrate, used to blacken brass
  c. titanium(III) sulfate, used as a stain remover
  d. chromium(III) phosphate, a green pigment

28. Determine the subscripts that are most likely in the formulas for ionic substances of the following elements:
  a. an alkali metal and a halogen
  b. an alkaline-earth metal and a halogen
  c. an alkali metal and a member of Group 16
  d. an alkaline-earth metal and a member of Group 16

29. How many atoms of each element are contained in a single formula unit of iron(III) formate, $Fe(HCOO)_3 \cdot H_2O$, a compound used as a preservative?

OXIDATION NUMBERS

30. Assign oxidation numbers to the atoms in the chlorate ion, ClO_3^-, which is used in explosives.

31. Assign oxidation numbers to the atoms in a bicarbonate ion, HCO_3^-.

32. Assign oxidation numbers to the atoms in the following ions: $AuCl_4^-$, $Zn(OH)_4^{2-}$, VO_2^+, $S_2O_3^{2-}$, $H_2BO_3^-$, BH_4^-.

33. Assign oxidation numbers to the atoms in lead chloride, $PbCl_2$.

34. Assign oxidation numbers to the atoms in magnesium hydroxide, $Mg(OH)_2$, an antacid.

35. Assign oxidation numbers to the atoms in the following compounds: PbS, MnO_2, $LiAlH_4$, Na_2O_2, HgO, NiO(OH), $PbSO_4$.

LINKING CHAPTERS

1. Electron configurations

Scientists have been able to create fluoride compounds with krypton and xenon. However, fluorine will not form compounds with helium or neon. Use the different electron configurations of the noble gases to explain why fluorine can form compounds with certain noble gases.

2. Metals

Although metals and salts have similar lattice structures, metals are used for electrical wiring. Why aren't salts used?

ALTERNATIVE ASSESSMENTS

Performance assessment

1. Devise a set of criteria that will allow you to classify the following substances as ionic or nonionic: $CaCO_3$, Cu, H_2O, NaBr, and C (graphite). Show your criteria to your instructor, and obtain some of the substances. Are these substances ionic or nonionic?

Portfolio projects

1. Research and communication

Use an analogy, a picture, a mechanical model, or a computer program to create your own model of an ionic bond. Present your model to the class, and explain the ways your model does or does not match experimental observations.

2. Chemistry and you

Ions play an important physiological role in your body. Select one such ion, and write a report detailing its function. Be sure to include recent medical information.

3. Cooperative activity/Group project

Keep the ingredients labels from all of the food products you eat in one day. Make a list of all the salts contained in each product. As a class, compile a master list identifying which salts were eaten by the most people. Research the properties and uses of the salts that were most frequently eaten; then, as a class, create an information poster describing the functions of these compounds.

4. Research and communication

Free radicals are atoms with electrons that are not in pairs; thus, they do not have an octet. Some people believe that free radicals are responsible for cancer, the effects of aging, and the depletion of the ozone layer. Find out what would cause free radicals to be so environmentally dangerous.

5. internetconnect

SC/LINKS
NSTA

TOPIC: Salt subtitutes
GO TO: www.scilinks.org
KEYWORD: HW056

Research and communication

Many people follow low-sodium diets. However, they still desire a flavor enhancer like common table salt. Research the different types of salt substitutes and the physiological effects of each. Determine which is the safest salt substitute, and organize your information in a report.

1. The correct formula for a copper atom that has lost two electrons is ———.
   a. Co^+ c. Cu^{2-}
   b. Co^{2+} d. Cu^{2+}

2. The electroneutrality principle ———.
   a. states that the number of cations equals the number of anions
   b. is demonstrated in any polyatomic ion
   c. states that the net charge on a binary ionic compound is zero
   d. All of the above

3. Which of the following atoms can become iso-electronic with a noble gas when the atom forms an ion?
   a. argon   c. nickel
   b. potassium   d. iron

4. In forming NaCl, energy is required to ———.
   a. change chlorine to a gas
   b. add an electron to a chlorine atom
   c. remove an electron from a sodium atom
   d. bring together the sodium ions and chloride ions

5. Which of the following is not a characteristic of a salt?
   a. hardness
   b. a high melting point
   c. an ability to conduct electricity in the molten state
   d. an ability to conduct electricity in the solid state

6. Which elements on the periodic table are most likely to form two or more ions?
   a. halides   c. transition metals
   b. alkali metals d. noble gases

7. The factor that changes the unit cell structure for NaCl from that of CsCl is ———.
   a. lattice energy   c. crystal structure
   b. ion size   d. ion charge

8. Which of the following compounds does not contain a polyatomic ion?
   a. sodium azide   c. sodium sulfite
   b. sodium sulfate d. sodium sulfide

9. The correct formula for ammonium azide is ———.
   a. NH_4N_3 c. N_4H_4
   b. $(NH_4)_2NH_3$ d. $NH_4(N_3)_2$

10. When writing the formula for a compound that contains a polyatomic ion, ———.
    a. the anion's formula is written first
    b. superscripts are used to show the number of polyatomic ions present
    c. parentheses must be used if the number of polyatomic ions is greater than 1.
    d. the polyatomic ion must always be placed in parentheses

11. The concept of electroneutrality involves equal numbers of ———.
    a. anions and cations
    b. positive and negative charges
    c. molecules
    d. ionic bonds

12. The prefix used to denote six water molecules in a hydrate formula is ———.
    a. *hemi-*   c. *hepta-*
    b. *penta-*   d. *hexa-*

13. The correct name for NH_4CH_3COO is ———.
    a. ammonium carbonate
    b. ammonium hydroxide
    c. ammonium acetate
    d. ammonium nitrate

14. Which of the following is the correct formula for iron(III) sulfate?
    a. Fe_3SO_4 c. $Fe_2(SO_4)_3$
    b. $Fe_3(SO_4)_2$ d. $3FeSO_4$

15. The oxidation number of N in NO_3^- is ———.
    a. +5   c. −2
    b. −5   d. +2

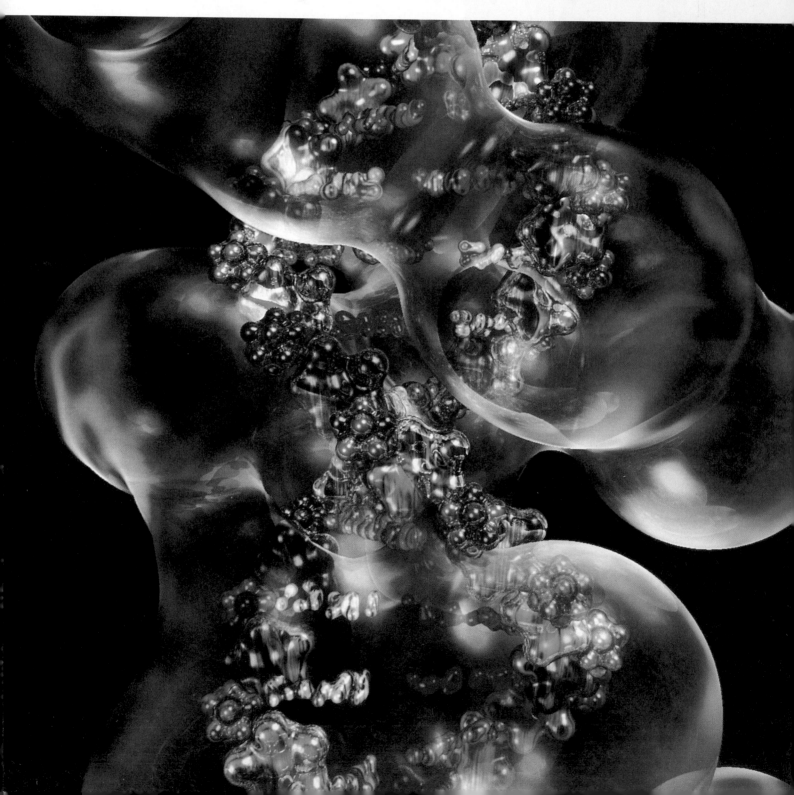

CHAPTER 6

Covalent Bonds and Molecular Forces

LIFE, WATER, AND MARS

On December 19, 1997, four people set a record for the longest stay in a closed chamber in the United States. The crew spent 91 days in a two-chamber complex as part of the Lunar-Mars Life Support Test Project sponsored by the National Aeronautics and Space Administration (NASA).

Plans are under way for four crew members to spend 425 days in a five-chamber complex starting in the year 2006. This project is a major component in NASA's plans to send a manned mission to Mars.

Interest in Mars has recently been rekindled by evidence that life may have once existed there. In 1996, chemical examination of a meteorite from Mars revealed the presence of organic molecules. In July 1997, photographs taken by the *Pathfinder* spacecraft revealed crusty soil and numerous rocks with smooth, rounded surfaces. Photographs taken by the *Mars Global Surveyor* spacecraft in January 1998 revealed a canyon about 2.5 km wide.

The smooth rocks, crusty soil, and canyons suggest to scientists that water was once abundant on Mars, perhaps as much as 4 billion years ago. Today, Mars is bone dry.

But the presence of water on Mars in the past means that life could have once existed on the planet.

Life as we know it is not possible without water. Living organisms are 70% to 90% water by mass. Most of the chemical reactions required for life take place in water. Water also has many interesting physical properties that help make it a very important compound. Mars may not be the only celestial body that once supported life. In 1979, the *Voyager* spacecraft sent back to Earth images of a lunar surface that appeared to be covered by a shell of ice. Europa, one of Jupiter's moons, appears to be nearly covered with ice. Some scientists believe that beneath that ice may be an ocean and thus water that might harbor life.

In this chapter you will explore covalent compounds. Based on your study of these compounds, you should be able to answer the following questions about water.

CHAPTER LINKS

Why don't the two hydrogen atoms in water give up their sole electrons to the oxygen atom to form an ionic bond?

Based on its composition, what is the actual chemical name for water?

What is the three-dimensional structure of water?

Why do some atoms form covalent bonds?

OBJECTIVES

▶ **Explain** how a covalent bond forms between two atoms.

▶ **Describe** the change in energy and stability as a covalent bond forms.

▶ **Describe** the differences between covalent and ionic bonds and between polar and nonpolar covalent bonds.

▶ **Describe** the influence of electronegativity difference on bonding.

▶ **Classify** the types of bonds between atoms using electronegativity values.

Sharing electrons

Chemical reactions involve changes in the distribution of electrons as the reactants combine to form products. In one kind of chemical change, the type discussed in the previous chapter, electrons transfer from one atom to another to form ions. Sodium metal reacting with chlorine gas to form the ionic compound sodium chloride, NaCl, is an example of this type of reaction. The reaction of hydrogen and oxygen to form water involves another kind of rearrangement—the sharing of electrons between atoms. When hydrogen and oxygen are combined, electrons rearrange to produce a new, more stable compound—water—and energy is released as heat and light. The hot flame shown in **Figure 6-1** was produced by this reaction.

internetconnect

SCLINKS.
NSTA
TOPIC: Covalent bonds
GO TO: www.scilinks.org
KEYWORD: HW061

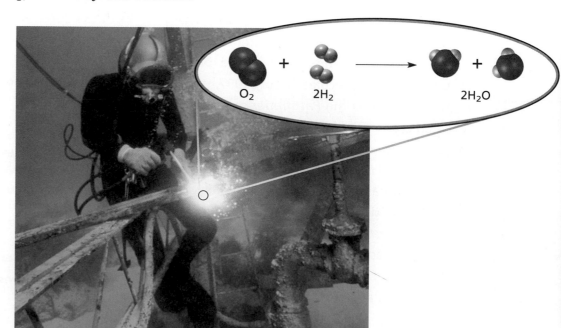

O_2 + $2H_2$ ⟶ $2H_2O$

▶ **FIGURE 6-1**

This diver is using an oxyhydrogen torch to cut metal. It works even underwater because of the intense heat given off by the reaction between hydrogen and oxygen.

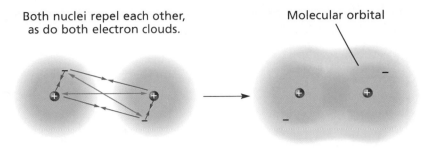

Both nuclei repel each other, as do both electron clouds.

Molecular orbital

The nucleus of each atom attracts both electron clouds.

FIGURE 6-2 ◄

When the forces of attraction and repulsion between atoms balance, a covalent bond is formed, and the two electrons move about the nuclei in a single molecular orbital.

Molecular orbitals are formed from overlapping atomic orbitals

The simplest example of sharing electrons occurs in diatomic molecules, such as hydrogen, H_2, and oxygen, O_2. When two hydrogen atoms approach each other, the positive nucleus of each atom attracts its own electron and the electron of the other atom. At the same time, the positive nuclei of the two atoms repel each other. Likewise, the electron clouds of the atoms repel. Because the two atoms are of the same element, neither has enough attraction to take an electron from the other. Instead of forming ions, the two hydrogen atoms *share* electrons. The two shared electrons form a single electron cloud around both hydrogen nuclei. The result is a diatomic molecule that is more stable than either hydrogen atom alone. **Figure 6-2** illustrates the balancing of forces to form an H_2 molecule.

The H_2 molecule is stable because each hydrogen atom now has a *shared pair* of electrons. This gives both atoms a stability similar to that of a helium configuration. This bond in which electrons are shared between two atoms is a **covalent bond.**

A bond in which two atoms share one pair of electrons between them is called a *single bond*. A single bond can be represented by a single line, so H_2 can also be written as H—H. The shared electrons moving about in the space surrounding the two nuclei are in a **molecular orbital.** A molecular orbital results from the overlap of two atomic orbitals.

covalent bond

a bond formed when two or more valence electrons are attracted by the positively charged nuclei of two atoms and are thus shared between both atoms

molecular orbital

a region where an electron pair is most likely to exist as it travels in the three-dimensional space around two nuclei

FIGURE 6-3 ◄

The sugar (sucrose, $C_{12}H_{22}O_{11}$) and water in this cup of tea are examples of covalent, or molecular, compounds.

As a covalent bond forms between two atoms, they reach a distance from each other at which attractive and repulsive forces are balanced and the energy is at a minimum.

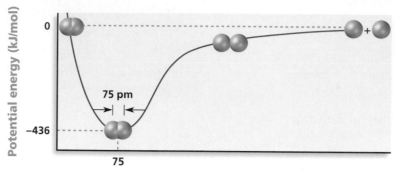

Potential Energy Curve for H_2

Covalent bonds occur at a potential energy minimum

The energy change that takes place as two atoms approach each other is depicted in **Figure 6-4.** Moving from right to left along the curve, you see the two H atoms approaching each other. As they come nearer, the potential energy of the combination becomes lower and lower until it reaches the minimum value of -436 kJ/mol at a distance of 75 pm. At the lowest energy, the H–H combination is most stable because lower energy means greater stability. At the distance of 75 pm, the repulsion between the like charges equals the attraction of the opposite charges. This is considered the length of the H–H bond. If the atoms come closer than 75 pm, the two nuclei and the electrons repel strongly, and the energy rises sharply.

Bonded atoms vibrate, and bonds vary in strength

bond length

the distance between two bonded atoms at their minimum potential energy; the average distance between two bonded atoms

Although models often show bonds as rigid "sticks," the nuclei are not at a fixed distance from each other. Instead, the two nuclei vibrate back and forth like a spring, coming closer and then stretching farther apart, as shown in **Figure 6-5.** The distance of minimum energy is the average distance between the nuclei. This is known as the **bond length.**

► **FIGURE 6-5**

The two atoms involved in a covalent bond vibrate back and forth about an average distance.

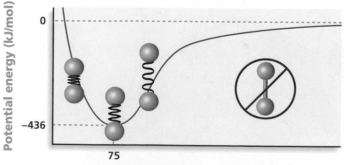

The Bond/Spring Analogy

TABLE 6-1   Bond Energies and Bond Lengths for Bonds in Diatomic Molecules

	Bond energy (kJ/mol)	Bond length (pm)
H–F	570	92
C–F	552	138
O–O	498	121
H–H	436	75
H–Cl	432	127
C–Cl	397	177
H–Br	366	141
H–I	299	161
C–Br	280	194
Cl–Cl	243	199
C–I	209	214
Br–Br	193	229
F–F	159	142
I–I	151	266

Because the potential energy minimum of the H–H bond is –436 kJ/mol, 436 kJ/mol of energy must be supplied to a hydrogen molecule in order to break the bond and separate the two hydrogen atoms. The energy required to break a bond between two atoms and separate them is the **bond energy.**

Table 6-1 lists the energies and lengths of some common bonds. Note that the bonds with the highest bond energy (those with the "strongest" bonds) usually involve the elements H or F. Note also that, with a few exceptions, there is a general trend for stronger bonds to have shorter bond lengths.

bond energy

the energy required to break a chemical bond between two atoms and separate them

CONCEPT CHECK

1. Why is the hydrogen molecule, H_2, more stable than the individual hydrogen atoms that bond to form it?
2. What is created when two atomic orbitals overlap?
3. What happens to the potential energy as two atoms approach each other to form a covalent bond?
4. What is the distance of minimum potential energy between two atoms in a covalent bond?
5. List four examples of covalent compounds.

Electronegativity and bonding

electronegativity

the tendency of an atom to attract bonding electrons to itself when it bonds with another atom

nonpolar covalent bond

an attraction between two atoms in which bonding electrons are shared equally between the atoms

You learned in Chapter 5 that when sodium and chlorine combine, an electron is removed from sodium and transferred to chlorine to form Na^+ and Cl^- ions. However, when H_2 and O_2 react, they bond by sharing electrons to form water. What factors cause some combinations of atoms to form ions and other combinations of atoms to form covalent bonds?

Atoms share electrons equally or unequally

To help explain why some combinations of atoms form ionic bonds and some form covalent bonds, the concept of **electronegativity** was developed. Linus Pauling, a Nobel Prize–winning chemist, assigned electronegativity values to the elements. He assigned fluorine—the element most likely to form ionic bonds—an electronegativity of 4.0. **Table 6-2** gives the electronegativity for each element. You can see in **Figure 6-6** that electronegativity values generally increase as you go from left to right across a period. In going down a group, electronegativity values generally decrease.

In a molecule such as H_2, the atoms are identical, so they pull on the bonding electrons with the same force. The electrons are shared equally. Such a covalent bond, in which the bonding electrons are shared equally, is called a **nonpolar covalent bond,** or a *pure covalent bond.*

If the electronegativities of two atoms are equal, they form a nonpolar covalent bond. If

▼ **FIGURE 6-6**

Electronegativity tends to decrease down a group and increase across a period.

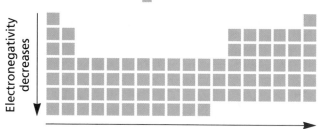

Electronegativity decreases

Electronegativity increases

TABLE 6-2 Electronegativities

H 2.2																	
Li 1.0	Be 1.6											B 2.0	C 2.6	N 3.0	O 3.4	F 4.0
Na 0.9	Mg 1.3											Al 1.6	Si 1.9	P 2.2	S 2.6	Cl 3.2
K 0.8	Ca 1.0	Sc 1.4	Ti 1.5	V 1.6	Cr 1.7	Mn 1.6	Fe 1.9	Co 1.9	Ni 1.9	Cu 2.0	Zn 1.7	Ga 1.8	Ge 2.0	As 2.2	Se 2.5	Br 3.0
Rb 0.8	Sr 1.0	Y 1.2	Zr 1.3	Nb 1.6	Mo 2.2	Tc 1.9	Ru 2.2	Rh 2.3	Pd 2.2	Ag 1.9	Cd 1.7	In 1.8	Sn 1.9	Sb 2.0	Te 2.1	I 2.7
Cs 0.8	Ba 0.9	La 1.1	Hf 1.3	Ta 1.5	W 2.4	Re 1.9	Os 2.2	Ir 2.2	Pt 2.3	Au 2.5	Hg 2.0	Tl 1.8	Pb 2.1	Bi 2.0	Po 2.0	At 2.2
Fr 0.7	Ra 0.9	Ac 1.1														

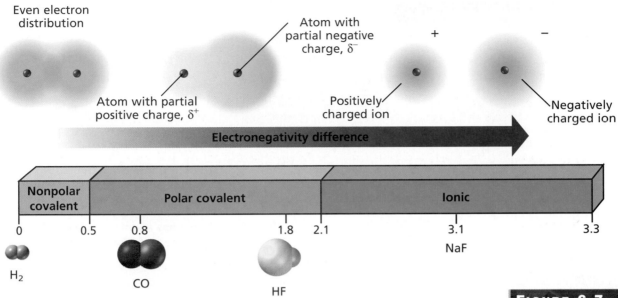

FIGURE 6-7 ▲

Electronegativity differences can be used to predict the properties of a bond. Keep in mind that a whole range of bond polarity is possible and that there are no strict lines dividing bond types.

the electronegativities are greatly different, an ionic bond is formed. Between these two extremes is a range of bonding in which electrons are shared, but not equally. These bonds are called **polar covalent bonds.** A polar covalent bond occurs when two atoms form a covalent bond but one atom attracts electrons more strongly than the other atom. The attraction is not strong enough to transfer an electron from one atom to the other. The more electronegative atom, which attracts electrons more strongly, has a higher *electron density* than the less electronegative atom. **Figure 6-7** shows a model of the molecular orbital around a polar covalent molecule. Note that electrons are much more likely to be found around the more electronegative atom.

Bonds are more appropriately classified by bond character

The actual electronegativity value of an atom is not as important as electronegativity differences between bonding atoms. For any bond between two atoms, the electronegativity difference can be easily calculated. The larger this value is, the more polar the bond is. Bonds between atoms with very large electronegativity differences are considered to have more ionic character than covalent character. Eventually, the electronegativity difference is so great that one of the atoms has essentially removed an electron permanently from the other atom. At an electronegativity difference larger than 2.1, the bond is usually ionic.

There is a general rule that can be used to predict the type of bond that forms between two atoms. If the *difference* in electronegativity is between zero and 0.5, the bond is nonpolar covalent. If the difference in electronegativity is between 0.5 to 2.1, the bond is polar covalent. If the difference is larger than 2.1, the bond is usually ionic.

polar covalent bond

an attraction between two atoms in which bonding electrons are localized on the more electronegative atom

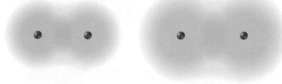

H₂
F₂
HF

a Both H₂ and F₂ have nonpolar bonds. The bonding electrons are shared equally between the two atoms.

b When H and F combine, they form a highly polarized bond in which electrons are pulled more toward the F atom. As a result, the molecule has a somewhat negative end and a somewhat positive end.

For example, the compound AlF_3 is predicted to be ionic because the electronegativity difference between Al and F is 2.4. All three of the Al—F bonds are predicted to be ionic. On the other hand, the compound $AlCl_3$ is predicted to be polar covalent because the electronegativity difference between Al and Cl is 1.6. So each of the three Al—Cl bonds is polar covalent. Physical properties differ significantly between nonpolar covalent compounds, polar covalent compounds, and ionic compounds.

dipole

a molecule in which one end has a partial positive charge and the other end has a partial negative charge

Polar molecules have positive and negative ends

The word *polar* suggests that these bonds have ends that are somehow opposite one another, like the two poles of a magnet or a battery. Hydrogen fluoride, H—F, is an example of a molecule with a polar bond. The electronegativity of fluorine is much higher than the electronegativity of hydrogen. Therefore, the fluorine atom attracts electrons much more strongly than the hydrogen atom does. With a greater electron density, the fluorine atom in the HF molecule has a partial negative charge. The hydrogen atom, having its electron pulled away, has a partial positive charge, as you can see in **Figure 6-8.** Note that this is not an ionic bond; the electron is not completely transferred from hydrogen to fluorine. A molecule in which one end has a partial positive charge and the other end has a partial negative charge is called a **dipole.**

▼ FIGURE 6-9

HF(*aq*), or hydrofluoric acid, is used to etch glass.

To emphasize the dipole nature of the HF molecule, the formula can be written as $H^{\delta+}-F^{\delta-}$. The symbol δ is a lowercase Greek *delta,* which is used in science and mathematics to indicate *partial.* In the case of $H^{\delta+}-F^{\delta-}$ and other polar molecules, it is used to indicate a partial positive charge, δ^+, on one end of a bond and a partial negative charge, δ^-, on the other end. A molecule may have polar bonds but not be a dipole, as you will see later. This occurs when a molecule contains more than one polar bond, and the polar bonds cancel each other out.

Dipole Moment and Bond Energy for Hydrogen Halides

Molecule	Dipole moment	Bond energy
H–F	1.8	570 kJ/mol
H–Cl	1.0	432 kJ/mol
H–Br	0.8	366 kJ/mol
H–I	0.5	298 kJ/mol

Electronegativity is related to the dipole moment

While Pauling was assigning electronegativities, he noted a connection between the polarity of a bond and the strength of that bond. The polarity of a molecule is measured by the *dipole moment*. A larger dipole moment indicates a higher degree of polarity.

Of the compounds in **Table 6-3,** hydrogen fluoride has the greatest polarity, as indicated by its largest dipole moment. It also has the strongest bond. Hydrogen iodide has the least polarity. Consequently, it has the weakest bond. As the polarity of the molecule increases, its bond strength increases.

SECTION REVIEW

Total recall

1. Describe the attractive forces and repulsive forces that occur as two atoms move closer together.

2. Compare the motion of a bond between two atoms to that of a spring.

Critical thinking

3. What is bond energy? How does bond energy (or the strength of a bond) relate to the length of a covalent bond?

4. How does an element's electronegativity relate to its position on the periodic table.

5. Compare the degree of polarity in HF, HCl, HBr, and HI.

Practice problems

6. Use Figure 6-7 and Table 6-2 to classify the bond between the following as nonpolar covalent, polar covalent, or ionic.
   a. Cs and Br
   b. H and S
   c. Ca and O
   d. Si and Cl
   e. As and P
   f. Se and Br

7. In the previous question, which atom in each pair has the higher electron density?

8. **Story Clue** Is the covalent bond between hydrogen and oxygen in water polar or nonpolar? Explain your choice.

How are molecules depicted?

▶ **Draw** Lewis structures to show the arrangement of valence electrons among atoms in molecules and polyatomic ions.

▶ **Explain** the differences between single, double, and triple covalent bonds.

▶ **Draw** resonance structures for simple molecules and polyatomic ions, and recognize when resonance structures are required.

▶ **Name** binary inorganic compounds using prefixes, roots, and suffixes.

Lewis electron-dot structures

valence electron

an electron in the outermost energy level of an atom, where it can participate in bonding

As you know, the electrons in the outermost energy level of an atom are involved in bonding, both ionic and covalent. These outer-level electrons are referred to as **valence electrons.** G. N. Lewis, the American chemist, is responsible for important theories of bonding and valency. In 1920 Lewis developed a system to represent bonding in compounds. This system uses electron-dot diagrams in which dots represent valence electrons.

While Lewis dot structures are valuable tools for understanding bonding, they are merely diagrams and in no way represent the actual location of the valence electrons. In an atom, valence electrons are in atomic orbitals of specific shape and orientation. Once valence electrons become part of a bond, they are in molecular orbitals surrounding the two nuclei involved in the bond. The exact location of an electron at any particular time is impossible to determine.

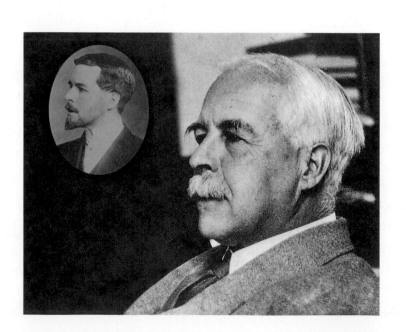

▶ **FIGURE 6-10**

G. N. Lewis (1875–1946) not only developed important theories of bonding, but also gave a new definition to acids and bases.

TABLE 6-4	Lewis Dot Structures of the Second Period Elements

Element	Electron configuration	Lewis dot structure
Li	$1s^2 2s^1$	Li·
Be	$1s^2 2s^2$	Ḃe·
B	$1s^2 2s^2 2p^1$	Ḃ·
C	$1s^2 2s^2 2p^2$	·Ċ·
N	$1s^2 2s^2 2p^3$	:Ṅ·
O	$1s^2 2s^2 2p^4$	:Ö·
F	$1s^2 2s^2 2p^5$	:Ḟ·
Ne	$1s^2 2s^2 2p^6$	:N̈e:

Covalent bonds can be modeled with Lewis structures

A **Lewis structure** represents the valence electrons in a molecule. The nuclei and the electrons of the inner energy levels, the inner shells, are represented by the symbol of the element. A hydrogen atom has the electron configuration $1s^1$; it has only one valence electron. When drawing its Lewis structure, hydrogen's nucleus and lone valence electron are represented by the hydrogen symbol with a dot, H·.

When two hydrogen atoms form a covalent bond, they share two electrons, which are represented by a pair of dots written between the symbols. Hydrogen can never share more than two electrons, so this represents a stable hydrogen molecule in which both atoms share a pair of electrons.

H:H

Next consider a chlorine atom, which has the electron configuration $1s^2 2s^2 2p^6 3s^2 3p^5$. Only the electrons in the outermost energy level are involved in bonding, so in the Lewis structure only the seven valence electrons of chlorine, $3s^2 3p^5$, are represented by dots. As you know, electrons usually occur in pairs with opposite spins, so you write three pairs and one unpaired electron around the chlorine symbol as follows.

·C̈l:

Recall that noble gases, with eight valence electrons, are the most stable elements. An octet of electrons is a stable configuration. So when two chlorine atoms bond, they each share one electron, giving both atoms a stable octet and forming a covalent bond.

:C̈l:C̈l:

Each chlorine atom in Cl_2 has three pairs of electrons that are not involved in the bond. These are called the **unshared pairs,** or lone pairs. Notice that each atom is surrounded by four pairs of electrons, showing that each atom has a stable octet of electrons.

Lewis structure

a structure in which atomic symbols represent nuclei and inner-shell electrons, and dots are used to represent valence electrons

FIGURE 6-11 ▲

To write an element's Lewis structure, determine the number of valence electrons for the atom. Then place a corresponding number of dots around the element's symbol, as shown.

unshared pair

a pair of valence electrons not involved in bonding to another atom

single bond

a covalent bond in which one pair of electrons is shared between two atoms

When drawing electron-dot diagrams, the pair of dots representing a shared pair, or a **single bond,** can also be shown by a long dash.

$$H:H \quad \text{or} \quad H-H$$

$$:\overset{..}{\underset{..}{Cl}}:\overset{..}{\underset{..}{Cl}}: \text{ or } :\overset{..}{\underset{..}{Cl}}-\overset{..}{\underset{..}{Cl}}:$$

When deciding how to arrange the valence electrons around the symbol, keep in mind that all locations must contain an unpaired electron before any location can contain a pair of electrons. The Lewis structure for carbon, with four valence electrons, is as follows.

$$\cdot\overset{\cdot}{\underset{\cdot}{C}}\cdot$$

Pairing the electrons can be done in any order, but it is often done so that any unpaired electrons are oriented conveniently for bonding. Examine the following model of a chemical reaction; the unpaired electrons on the hydrogen and chlorine atoms are oriented toward each other.

$$H\cdot + \cdot\overset{..}{\underset{..}{Cl}}: \longrightarrow H-\overset{..}{\underset{..}{Cl}}:$$

HOW TO   Draw Lewis structures

Until now, you have examined only very simple Lewis structures. But how do you represent the Lewis structures of more-complicated molecules, such as CH_3I?

1 Determine the total number of valence electrons in the compound

▸ First draw the Lewis structures of the separate atoms. Carbon has four valence electrons. Hydrogen has only one electron. Iodine has seven valence electrons. Remember that each side of the element's symbol should be given one electron before any electrons are paired.

$$\cdot\overset{\cdot}{\underset{\cdot}{C}}\cdot \quad H\cdot \quad H\cdot \quad H\cdot \quad \cdot\overset{..}{\underset{..}{I}}:$$

Now add the valence electrons of each atom.

$$1 \text{ C atom with 4 electrons} = 1 \times 4 = 4$$
$$3 \text{ H atoms with 1 electron} = 3 \times 1 = 3$$
$$1 \text{ I atom with 7 electrons} = 1 \times 7 = 7$$

Total number of valence electrons = 14

2 **Arrange the atoms' symbols to show how the atoms bond**

▸ Be sure to distribute the paired dots so that there are eight electrons around each atom (so that the octet rule is followed). Hydrogen is an exception; it is stable with only a duet of electrons. Hydrogen and iodine, lacking one electron each, will form only one bond.

$$\begin{array}{c} \text{H} \\ \text{H:C:I:} \\ \text{H} \end{array}$$

3 **Compare the number of valence electrons used in the structure with the number available from step 1**

▸ There are two electrons in each covalent bond and three unshared pairs around the iodine atom.

$$4 \text{ covalent bonds with 2 electrons each} = 4 \times 2 = 8$$
$$3 \text{ lone pairs of electrons around I} = 3 \times 2 = 6$$

Total number of electrons shown = 14

4 **Change each pair of dots that represents a shared pair of electrons to a single dash**

$$\begin{array}{c} \text{H} \\ | \\ \text{H–C–I:} \\ | \\ \text{H} \end{array}$$

5 **Be sure that all atoms, with the exception of hydrogen, follow the octet rule**

Both carbon and iodine have stable octets. Each hydrogen atom has a duet. Note that H forms only one bond. It will always be "outside" on Lewis structures.

CONCEPT CHECK

1. Draw Lewis structures for iodine monochloride, ICl, and hydrogen bromide, HBr.

2. Using iodomethane, CH_3I, as a model, draw the Lewis structure for dichloromethane, CH_2Cl_2.

3. Draw the Lewis structure for methanol, CH_3OH. Draw the CH_3 part first, then add O and H.

4. Draw the Lewis structure for ethane, C_2H_6.

Multiple bonds

Atoms can share more than one pair of electrons in a bond

Consider the bond between two oxygen atoms forming an O_2 molecule. Oxygen is in Group 16. Therefore, it has six valence electrons.

$$:\ddot{O}\cdot \quad \cdot\ddot{O}:$$

In order to achieve an octet, each atom needs two more electrons. Therefore, each atom shares two electrons with the other atom. The covalent bond formed by the sharing of two pairs of electrons is a double bond, represented as follows.

$$:\ddot{O}::\ddot{O}: \quad \text{or} \quad :\ddot{O}=\ddot{O}:$$

Oxygen can form double bonds, as in O_2 above, or it can form single bonds with two other atoms, as in methanol, CH_3OH.

Another example of a molecule containing a double bond is the plant pheromone ethene, C_2H_4, also called ethylene, shown in **Figure 6-12.** The four hydrogen atoms each form a single bond with carbon.

$$\begin{array}{cc} H & H \\ H:\ddot{C}\cdot & \cdot\ddot{C}:H \end{array}$$

Each carbon atom has two nonbonded electrons and needs two more electrons to complete an octet. The only possibility is that they bond to each other with a double bond, as oxygen does in the oxygen molecule.

$$\begin{array}{cc} H\ H & H\ H \\ H:\ddot{C}::\ddot{C}:H & \text{or} \quad H-C=C-H \end{array}$$

The elements carbon, nitrogen, and oxygen commonly form double bonds. Hydrogen and the halogens usually share one pair of electrons, so they do not form multiple bonds. Sulfur rarely forms a true double bond; the only common example of a double-bonded sulfur compound is carbon disulfide, CS_2.

Nitrogen and carbon atoms can share three pairs of electrons to form a triple bond. Consider the molecule N_2. Each nitrogen atom has five valence electrons, and each needs three more for a stable octet. Each nitrogen atom contributes three electrons to form a triple bond. Six electrons constitute three electron-pair bonds.

$$:N::N: \quad \text{or} \quad :N\equiv N:$$

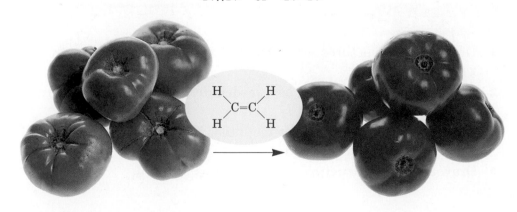

► **FIGURE 6-12**

Ethene, C_2H_4, is a pheromone found in most plants. Tomatoes release ethene as they ripen.

The compound ethyne, C_2H_2, commonly called acetylene, also contains a triple bond.

$$H{:}C{::}C{:}H \quad \text{or} \quad H-C{\equiv}C-H$$

Nitrogen can form three single bonds, a combination of a double and single bond, or one triple bond. Carbon can form four single bonds or a combination of single, double, and triple bonds. Carbon almost always forms a total of four bonds.

HOW TO Draw Lewis structures with multiple bonds

If no arrangement of single bonds provides an appropriate Lewis structure, the molecule could contain multiple bonds. Keep this in mind as you draw the Lewis structure for formaldehyde, CH_2O.

1 Determine the total number of valence electrons

▸ Draw the Lewis structures of the separate atoms.

$$\cdot\dot{C}\cdot \quad H\cdot \quad H\cdot \quad {:}\dot{\ddot{O}}\cdot$$

$$\begin{aligned}
\text{1 C atom with 4 electrons} &= 1 \times 4 = & 4 \\
\text{2 H atoms with 1 electron} &= 2 \times 1 = & 2 \\
\text{1 O atom with 6 electrons} &= 1 \times 6 = & 6 \\
\hline
\text{Total number of valence electrons} &= & 12 \text{ valence electrons}
\end{aligned}$$

2 Arrange the atoms' symbols to show how the atoms are bonded

▸ The carbon atom is in the center. Carbon forms four bonds; two hydrogen atoms and one oxygen atom form a total of four bonds. Therefore, these atoms must be bonded directly to carbon.

$$\begin{array}{c}
{:}\text{O}{:} \\
{::} \\
H{:}C{:}H
\end{array}$$

3 Compare the number of valence electrons used in the structure with the number available from step 1

▸ All 12 valence electrons are accounted for.

$$\begin{aligned}
\text{4 covalent bonds with 2 electrons each} &= 4 \times 2 = & 8 \\
\text{2 lone pairs of electrons around O} &= 2 \times 2 = & 4 \\
\hline
\text{Total number of electrons shown} &= & 12
\end{aligned}$$

4 Change each pair of dots that represent shared pairs of electrons to a single dash

$$\begin{array}{c}
{:}\text{O}{:} \\
\| \\
H-C-H
\end{array}$$

5 Be sure that all atoms, with the exception of hydrogen, follow the octet rule

▸ Both carbon and oxygen atoms have stable octets.

Some molecules are represented by more than one Lewis structure

If you wanted to draw the structure for sulfur dioxide, SO_2, you would start with the sulfur atom in the middle. Sulfur and oxygen have six electrons each, so you might expect a double bond between sulfur and one of the oxygen atoms.

If the second oxygen atom is placed so that it uses one of the sulfur atom's unshared pairs of electrons to complete its octet, the following Lewis structure results. In this structure, each atom has an octet of electrons, although one shared pair of electrons comes entirely from the sulfur atom. When a shared pair of electrons originates from one atom, the bond is called a *coordinate-covalent bond.*

$$\ddot{O}=\ddot{S}-\ddot{O}\!: \quad \text{or} \quad \ddot{O}\!::\!\ddot{S}\!:\!\ddot{O}\!:$$

Experimental evidence shows that this structure is not correct. Data show that both of the S—O bonds in SO_2 are the same length—shorter than a single S—O bond, but longer than a double S—O bond. In addition, SO_2 is chemically more stable than it would be if it contained a single bond on one end and a double bond on the other.

You can draw two possible Lewis structures for SO_2. These two structures are called **resonance structures.**

$$\ddot{O}=\ddot{S}-\ddot{O}\!: \quad \longleftrightarrow \quad :\ddot{O}-\ddot{S}=\ddot{O}$$

Experimental evidence indicates that the actual structure is a sort of average or *resonance hybrid,* of the two possible structures drawn. This structure is sometimes represented as follows.

$$:\ddot{O}\!-\!-\!\ddot{S}\!-\!-\!\ddot{O}\!:$$

The dotted lines represent two bonding pairs of electrons that are shared by all three atoms at the same time. When electrons are shared between more than two atoms at the same time, the electrons are said to be *delocalized.*

resonance structure

a possible Lewis dot structure of a molecule for which more than one Lewis structure can be written

▶ **FIGURE 6-13**

Sulfur dioxide, SO_2, is a byproduct of coal-burning power plants. It is one of the leading contributors to acid rain.

FIGURE 6-14 ◄

Brown nitrogen dioxide gas is extremely poisonous and is produced in the series of reactions leading to smog.

The resonance model explains why the bonds between S and O are identical in both length and strength. It also shows that the molecule is more stable than either of the Lewis structures indicates. Resonance can explain the existence of molecules that have odd numbers of electrons and do not follow the octet rule, such as NO_2. The resonance structures of NO_2 are illustrated below. The presence of the odd number of electrons indicates that NO_2 will readily react with other substances.

$$:\ddot{O}-N-\ddot{O} \longleftrightarrow \ddot{O}-N\ \ddot{O}:$$

Although it may seem easy to draw a Lewis structure for nitrogen dioxide, no single structure satisfies the octet rule. Nitrogen dioxide is a resonance hybrid of the structures shown.

Lewis structures can represent bonding in polyatomic ions

The ammonium ion, NH_4^+, is a common polyatomic ion. It is found in items such as the smelling salts shown in **Figure 6-15.** To draw the Lewis structure of the ammonium ion, first consider the structure of the ammonia molecule, NH_3, from which the ammonium ion is derived. Nitrogen is a Group 15 element. That tells you that nitrogen has five valence electrons. Therefore, nitrogen can achieve a stable octet by forming three covalent bonds, one with each hydrogen atom.

$$\begin{array}{c} H \\ H:\ddot{N}: \\ \ddot{H} \end{array}$$

$$\left[\begin{array}{c} H \\ H:\ddot{N}:H \\ H \end{array}\right]^+$$

Ammonium ion

FIGURE 6-15 ◄

An ammonium cation forms when a hydrogen ion combines with an ammonia molecule. Smelling salts often contain an unstable ionic compound composed of ammonium ions, NH_4^+, and carbonate ions, CO_3^{2-}.

Ammonium ions form when ammonia is combined with a substance that easily gives up hydrogen ions, H^+. Hydrogen chloride, HCl, is one such substance. A hydrogen ion is simply the nucleus of the hydrogen atom, a proton. It has no electrons to share. The formation of an ammonium ion from ammonia and a proton is as follows.

$$
\begin{array}{ccccc}
\overset{\displaystyle H}{\underset{\displaystyle H}{H\!:\!\overset{..}{\underset{..}{N}}\!:}} & + & H^+ & \longrightarrow & \left[\overset{\displaystyle H}{\underset{\displaystyle H}{H\!:\!\overset{..}{\underset{..}{N}}\!:\!H}}\right]^+
\end{array}
$$

Ammonia molecule   Proton   Ammonium ion

Notice that the nitrogen atom in ammonia has an unshared pair of electrons. The hydrogen ion can bond to nitrogen's unshared pair of electrons, forming a coordinate-covalent bond. The nitrogen atom retains its stable octet, and all four hydrogen atoms have a stable duet of electrons. After the hydrogen ion has bonded to nitrogen, all four hydrogen atoms are equivalent. The structure is enclosed in brackets to indicate that the positive charge is distributed over the entire ammonium ion.

HOW TO   Draw Lewis structures of polyatomic ions

When drawing a Lewis structure of a polyatomic ion, take the ionic charge into account and add or subtract electrons when determining the total number of valence electrons. How would you draw the Lewis structure of the NH_4^+ ion if you did not know how it formed?

1   **Determine the total number of valence electrons in the ion**

▶ First draw the Lewis structures of the separate atoms. Nitrogen has five valence electrons. Hydrogen has one valence electron.

$$:\!\overset{..}{N}\!\cdot \quad H\cdot \quad H\cdot \quad H\cdot \quad H\cdot$$

▶ Now add the valence electrons of each atom. The polyatomic ion has a charge of 1+, meaning that it has one less electron than it would have if it were a neutral molecule. Subtract one electron for the positive charge on the ion.

$$
\begin{array}{lr}
\text{1 N atom with 5 valence electrons} = 1 \times 5 = & 5 \\
\text{4 H atoms with 1 valence electron} = 4 \times 1 = & 4 \\
\text{charge on ammonium ion} \quad +1 & -1 \\
\hline
\text{Total number of valence electrons} = & 8
\end{array}
$$

2   **Arrange the atoms' symbols to show how the atoms are bonded**

$$\overset{\displaystyle H}{\underset{\displaystyle H}{H\!:\!\overset{..}{N}\!:\!H}}$$

3 Compare the number of valence electrons used in the structure with the number available from step 1

▸ There are two electrons in each covalent bond.

$$\frac{\text{4 covalent bonds with 2 electrons each} = 4 \times 2 = 8}{\text{Total number of electrons shown} = 8}$$

▸ This matches the number of electrons determined in step 1.

4 Change each pair of dots that represents a shared pair of electrons to a single dash

▸ There are four pairs of bonding electrons in the ammonium ion. Therefore, there are four single covalent bonds in the Lewis structure.

$$\begin{array}{c} \text{H} \\ | \\ \text{H--N--H} \\ | \\ \text{H} \end{array}$$

5 Indicate the delocalized charge

▸ Place brackets around the ion, and place a 1+ charge outside the bracket to indicate that the charge is spread over the entire ion.

$$\left[\begin{array}{c} \text{H} \\ | \\ \text{H--N--H} \\ | \\ \text{H} \end{array}\right]^{+}$$

6 Be sure that all atoms, with the exception of hydrogen, follow the octet rule

▸ The N atom has a stable octet. Each H atom has a stable duet.

CONCEPT CHECK

1. Draw resonance structures for the NO_2 molecule and the SO_3 molecule.

2. Draw a Lewis dot structure for the methylammonium ion, $CH_3NH_3^+$. (Hint: Carbon and nitrogen are bonded together by a single covalent bond.)

3. Draw Lewis structures for the NO_3^- ion and the SO_3^{2-} ion. Remember that resonance structures may be necessary to adequately describe an ion.

4. Draw Lewis structures for the following molecules.

   a. carbon dioxide, CO_2

   b. hypochlorous acid, HOCl

   c. chloroethene, C_2H_3Cl, also called vinyl chloride

   d. hydrogen cyanide, HCN

5. A benzene molecule, C_6H_6, is a ring of six carbon atoms. Each carbon atom is bonded to two other carbon atoms as well as to one hydrogen atom. Draw the two resonance structures of benzene.

Naming covalent compounds

Naming conventions for most covalent, or molecular, compounds are relatively straightforward, especially for binary compounds that are inorganic. Organic compounds have their own special naming scheme, as you will see in Chapter 7. As shown below, inorganic molecular compounds are generally named in a way similar to the methods used to name the salts that were described in Chapter 5. Chemists distinguish two compounds composed of the same elements by specifying the number of each type of atom in the compound's name.

$$P_4O_6 \qquad\qquad P_4O_{10}$$

tetraphosphorus hexoxide   tetraphosphorus decoxide

The most common naming system uses prefixes, roots, and suffixes

The system of prefixes shown in **Table 6-5** is used in naming most inorganic binary compounds. Prefixes and suffixes are usually attached to root words. In the case of a binary molecular compound, the root word is the name of the element. The first element named is usually the one first written in the formula—the least electronegative element. If the molecule contains only one atom of the first element given in the formula, the prefix *mono-* is omitted in the name of the compound. For example, to distinguish between the two oxides of carbon, the prefixes *mono-* and *di-* are used.

$$CO \qquad\qquad CO_2$$

carbon monoxide   carbon dioxide

Each compound contains only one carbon atom, so no prefix for carbon is used in naming either compound.

TABLE 6-5 **Prefixes for Naming Covalent Compounds**

Prefix	Number of Atoms	Example	Name
mono-	1	NO	nitrogen monoxide
di-	2	SiO_2	silicon dioxide
tri-	3	SO_3	sulfur trioxide
tetra-	4	SCl_4	sulfur tetrachloride
penta-	5	$SbCl_5$	antimony pentachloride
hexa-	6	CeB_6	cerium hexaboride
hepta-	7	IF_7	iodine heptafluoride
octa-	8	Np_3O_8	trineptunium octoxide
nona-	9	I_4O_9	tetraiodine nonoxide
deca-	10	S_2F_{10}	disulfur decafluoride

The element with the higher electronegativity value is usually written last and has the ending *-ide,* just as anions in an ionic compound do. The compound CO has one oxygen atom and is named carbon *mono*oxide. The compound CO_2 has two oxygen atoms, and so it is named carbon *di*oxide. Notice that the vowels *o* and *a* are dropped from a prefix before a root that begins with a vowel. For example, you have sulfur hexafluoride, SF_6, but dinitrogen tetroxide, N_2O_4. Several compounds have common names that are widely used in place of the technical name. For example, H_2O is always called *water,* not *dihydrogen monoxide.*

SECTION REVIEW

Total recall

1. Which electrons in an atom are involved in bonding?

2. List three rules for drawing Lewis structures with many atoms.

3. What do you call electrons that are shared among several atoms at the same time?

Critical thinking

4. Use the electronic structure of a noble gas to explain why atoms are most stable when they have an octet of valence electrons.

5. Why does the five-atom grouping NH_4^+ exist only as a cation?

6. Draw a Lewis structure to show where the unshared pairs of electrons exist in carbon dioxide, CO_2.

Practice problems

7. Write the number of valence electrons for atoms with each of the following electron configurations.
   a. $1s^2 2s^2$
   b. $1s^2 2s^2 2p^3$
   c. $1s^2 2s^2 2p^6 3s^2 3p^2$
   d. $1s^2 2s^2 2p^6 3s^2 3p^6 4s^1$

8. Identify each element in item 7, and write its Lewis dot structure.

9. Draw Lewis structures for each of the following molecules and ions.
   a. bromine, Br_2
   b. trimethyl amine, $N(CH_3)_3$
   c. ozone, O_3 (Hint: form O_2 first)
   d. hydronium ion, H_3O^+
   e. bromine monofluoride, BrF
   f. hydrazine, N_2H_4
   g. nitrite ion, NO_2^-

10. **Interpreting Tables** Use the system of prefixes and suffixes in Table 6-5 to name the following compounds.
    a. SiO_2 c. SnI_4
    b. PBr_3 d. N_2O_3

11. Write the formula of each of the following compounds.
    a. phosphorus pentabromide
    b. pentaboron nonahydride
    c. diphosphorus trioxide
    d. dinitrogen tetroxide

12. **Story Clue** Draw the Lewis structure for water.

How are molecular shapes determined?

OBJECTIVES

▶ *Predict* the shape of a molecule from its Lewis structure using VSEPR theory.

▶ *Associate* the polarity of molecules with their shapes.

▶ *Relate* the boiling point of a molecular substance to the shape and polarity of its molecules.

Molecular shapes

The three-dimensional shape of a molecule is an important factor in determining its physical and chemical properties. For example, the protein hemoglobin transports oxygen through your bloodstream to all parts of your body. Its structure is shown in **Figure 6-16.** One type of genetic mutation causes the shape of hemoglobin to change, resulting in a life-threatening condition called sickle cell anemia.

▼ **FIGURE 6-16**

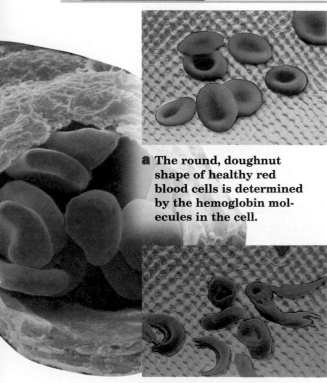

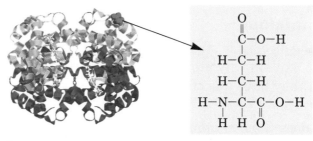

a The round, doughnut shape of healthy red blood cells is determined by the hemoglobin molecules in the cell.

b Hemoglobin consists of four polypeptide chains; a fragment of one chain is shown in green.

c Each of the chains is a polymer of 141–146 amino acid subunits, such as the glutamic acid monomer shown here.

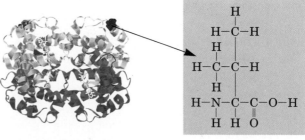

d Because of their shape, sickle cells clog small blood vessels.

e A genetic mutation causes glutamic acid to be replaced by valine, shown in red.

f The sickle shape results from the valine substitution.

A Lewis structure can help you predict the shape of a molecule

A molecule with a relatively simple molecular formula also has a simple shape. In a molecule of only two atoms, such as HF, shown in **Figure 6-17,** or H_2, only a linear shape is possible. But for molecules of more than two atoms, molecular shapes become more complicated.

There is frequently no obvious relationship between the molecular formula of a compound and its shape. Look at the models of carbon dioxide, CO_2, and sulfur dioxide, SO_2, shown in **Figure 6-18.** Their formulas are similar, so why is CO_2 linear, while SO_2 is bent?

There is a simple model that can be used to determine the three-dimensional arrangement of the atoms in a molecule. This model is based on the **valence shell electron pair repulsion (VSEPR) theory.** According to this theory, you can predict the shape of a molecule by knowing the number of electron pairs around a central atom. The pairs can be bonding or nonbonding. Because like-charges repel each other, the electron pairs position themselves as far apart as possible.

Determine molecular geometry based on the number of electron pairs

The first step in determining the geometry of a molecule or polyatomic ion is to count the number of electron clouds surrounding the central atom. Each single or multiple bond counts as one electron group. Each nonbonding electron pair counts. Look at the Lewis structure for carbon dioxide below.

$$\ddot{O}=C=\ddot{O}$$

There are two double bonds around the central carbon atom. Therefore, there are two electron groups around this atom.

Electron clouds have a negative charge, and like charges repel each other. That means that the electron groups around an atom will repel one another and will remain as far apart as possible. If a central atom has only two electron groups, the molecule will be linear. These two electron groups are as far apart as they can get when they are on opposite sides of the carbon atom.

FIGURE 6-17 ▲

Molecules with only two atoms, such as HF, have a linear shape.

VSEPR (valence shell electron pair repulsion) theory

a simple model that predicts the general shape of a molecule based on the repulsion between both bonding and nonbonding electron clouds

internet**connect**

SCI*LINKS*
NSTA

TOPIC: Molecular shapes
GO TO: www.scilinks.org
KEYWORD: HW062

FIGURE 6-18 ▼

Even though carbon dioxide and sulfur dioxide have the same number of atoms, they have different shapes.

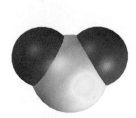

Sulfur dioxide

Carbon dioxide

FIGURE 6-19

When a molecule consists of a central atom bonded to three other atoms, its shape will be trigonal planar as long as there are only three electron groups determining its geometry.

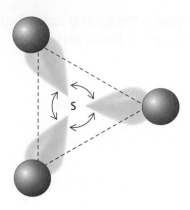

What happens if there are three electron groups? Look at the resonance structures for sulfur trioxide, SO_3.

$$\ddot{O}=\overset{\displaystyle :\ddot{O}:}{\underset{}{S}}-\ddot{O}: \longleftrightarrow :\ddot{O}-\overset{\displaystyle :\ddot{O}:}{\underset{}{S}}-\ddot{O}: \longleftrightarrow :\ddot{O}-\overset{\displaystyle :\ddot{O}:}{\underset{}{S}}=\ddot{O}$$

Because of resonance, the three electron clouds surrounding the sulfur atom in SO_3 are identical, as shown in **Figure 6-19.** In order to be as far apart as possible, the groups arrange like three spokes of a wheel, extending out from the sulfur atom. This geometry of electron clouds is called *trigonal planar.* Because the atoms and bonds are equivalent, the angle between the bonds is 120°.

What happens if one of the electron pairs is a lone pair? This was the case with sulfur dioxide, shown in Figure 6-18. The nonbonding electrons repel the bonding electrons, causing the three electron pairs to orient in a trigonal planar geometry, but the shape of the triatomic molecule is angular, or bent.

Examine **Figure 6-20.** Four electron pairs are farthest apart when they orient themselves toward the corners of a tetrahedron, as shown in the methane, CH_4, molecule. This geometry is more difficult to view on a page because the atoms are now spread in three dimensions. If the pairs are all equivalent (if there are four identical bonds on the central atom), all four of the angles between the bonds are 109.5°.

FIGURE 6-20 ▼

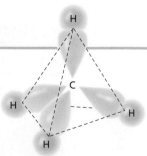

a A tetrahedral shape cannot be shown accurately with a flat structural formula.

b The true shape can be shown only by a three-dimensional model or . . .

c . . . with wedge-shaped bonds that seem to recede or protrude from the plane of the page.

d Another way to portray the tetrahedral shape is to show the location of the atoms' bonding orbitals within the molecule.

Predicting molecular shapes

Determine the shapes of NH_3 and H_2O molecules.

1 **Draw Lewis structures**

$$H-\overset{\cdot\cdot}{N}-H \qquad H-\overset{\cdot\cdot}{\underset{\cdot\cdot}{O}}:$$
$$\vert \qquad\qquad \vert$$
$$H \qquad\qquad H$$

2 **Count the electron clouds around the central atoms**

▶ NH_3 has three bonds to H atoms and one nonbonding pair: four electron clouds.

▶ H_2O has two bonds to H atoms and two nonbonding pairs: four electron clouds.

3 **Apply the proper VSEPR geometry**

▶ Both atoms have a tetrahedral arrangement of electron clouds.

4 **Account for unbonded pairs**

▶ If the unshared electron pair on nitrogen is placed in one of the positions of the tetrahedron, the shape of the molecule is actually trigonal pyramidal.

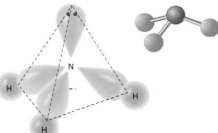

Ammonia, NH_3

▶ The water molecule will have an angular, or bent, shape.

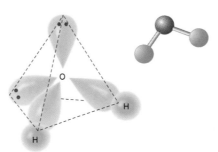

Water, H_2O

PRACTICE PROBLEMS

1. Draw a Lewis structure for each of the following molecules, and then use the VSEPR theory to predict the shape of each.

 a. NH_2Cl **b.** $ONCl$

2. Draw Lewis structures and then use the VSEPR theory to determine the shape of each of the following polyatomic ions.

 a. NO_3^- **b.** NH_4^+

How does shape affect properties?

Earlier you learned that the shape of a molecule such as hemoglobin affects its physical and chemical properties. Many of these properties depend on the polarity of the molecule. For molecules containing more than two atoms, molecular polarity depends on both the polarity of each bond and its orientation. For example, contrast CO_2, whose two electron clouds give it a linear shape, with H_2O, whose four electron clouds give it a bent shape.

The double bonds between C and O in CO_2 are polar because oxygen attracts electrons more strongly than does carbon. However, the linear shape of the molecule causes the two bond dipoles to act in opposite directions, canceling each other and causing the molecular polarity to be zero. In the water molecule, the polar H—O bonds are oriented at a 105° angle to each other, which creates a dipole for the molecule. The symbol $\longleftrightarrow$ is used to indicate a dipole. The arrow points to the region of greater electron density. **Figure 6-21** illustrates this concept for H_2O and CO_2.

Positive ends of polar molecules attract negative ends of other molecules. So more energy is required to separate these polar molecules than nonpolar molecules. Section 6-4 will further explain this phenomena by examining the boiling points of many polar molecules compared with nonpolar molecules.

▼ **FIGURE 6-21**

The bond polarities in a water molecule add together, causing a molecular dipole. In carbon dioxide, bond polarities extend in opposite directions, canceling each other.

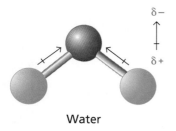

$\delta-$

$\delta+$

Water

Carbon dioxide, CO_2
(no molecular dipole)

$\mathcal{S}$ECTION REVIEW

Total recall

1. In VSEPR theory, what information about a central atom do you need in order to predict the shape of a molecule?

Critical thinking

2. What is the general relationship between the polarity of the molecules of different substances and the boiling points of those substances? Explain why this relationship exists.

3. Why does the presence of an unshared pair of electrons in the NH_3 molecule cause the molecule to have a trigonal pyramidal shape rather than a trigonal planar shape?

4. **Story Clue** Assume that the water molecule is linear like CO_2. How would water's physical properties be different, if at all, from the properties it has as a bent molecule?

Practice problems

5. Determine the shape of Br_2 and HBr molecules. Which is more polar and why?

6. Use VSEPR to determine the shapes of SCl_2, PF_3, and NCl_3 molecules. Which of these will be the most polar? Consider both shape and electronegativity differences.

What forces exist between molecules?

OBJECTIVES

▶ *Contrast* ionic solids and co-valent solids.

▶ *Describe* the types of forces that exist between molecules.

▶ *Explain* how a hydrogen bond differs from other polar-polar forces.

Physical characteristics of covalent compounds

Most covalent compounds melt at lower temperatures than ionic compounds do. You can see in **Table 6-6** that ionic substances tend to be solids with high melting points, and molecular substances are more likely to be gases, liquids, or solids with low melting points.

These differences between ionic and covalent substances result from differences in attractions between particles. Recall that ionic substances consist of separate ions, each of which is attracted to all ions of opposite charge. These attractions tend to hold the ions tightly in a crystal lattice that can be disrupted only by heating to very high temperatures.

TABLE 6-6 | **Comparing Ionic and Molecular Substances**

Type of substance	Common use	State at room temperature	Melting point (°C)	Boiling point (°C)
Ionic substances				
Potassium chloride, KCl	salt substitute	solid	770	sublimes at 1500
Sodium chloride, NaCl	table salt	solid	801	1413
Calcium fluoride, CaF_2	fluoridation of water	solid	1423	2500
Covalent molecular substances				
Oxygen, O_2	respiration	gas	−218	−183
Methane, CH_4	natural gas	gas	−182	−164
Ethyl acetate, $CH_3CH_2OOCCH_3$	fingernail polish	liquid	−84	77
Water, H_2O	many	liquid	0	100
Naphthalene, $C_{10}H_8$	mothballs	solid	80	218

Intermolecular forces hold molecules together

Covalent substances consist of molecules. If there are no attractive forces between molecules, the substance will exist as a gas because an attractive force is required to hold molecules together as liquids and solids. Because covalent solids have lower melting points than ionic solids have, the forces between molecules must be weaker than attractive forces between ions of opposite charge. Forces that exist between molecules are called **intermolecular forces.**

intermolecular force

an attraction that exists between molecules

You can see how the strength of intermolecular forces varies by comparing the molecular compounds listed in Table 6-6. Oxygen must have very weak intermolecular forces because oxygen must be cooled to a very low temperature to form liquid oxygen. In contrast, naphthalene must have much stronger intermolecular forces because it is a solid at room temperature. Why do we see such differences?

Dipole forces affect melting points and boiling points

Recall that one end of a polar molecule has a partial positive charge and the opposite end has a partial negative charge. Because opposite charges attract, the positive end of one molecule can attract the negative end of another molecule, holding the two molecules together. The force that exists between the positive and negative ends of polar molecules is called a *dipole force.* Dipole forces allow molecular substances to exist as solids and liquids.

The more polar the molecules are, the stronger the dipole force between molecules. Look again at the molecular compounds listed in Table 6-6. Oxygen and methane are nonpolar molecules, but molecules of ethyl acetate and water are polar. Because of dipole forces attracting the molecules to each other, ethyl acetate and water melt and boil at much higher temperatures than oxygen and methane, which have no dipole forces.

QUICKLAB

CONSUMER ACTIVITY

Watery Attraction

When hair and a nylon comb are rubbed together, electrons are transferred to the comb, which acquires a negative charge. When the charged comb comes close a stream of water, the positive end of the water dipoles are attracted to the negatively charged comb, causing the stream to move toward the comb.

Materials   nylon hair comb, faucet with cold running water

Problem   Turn on a cold water faucet. Adjust the stream to a width of 1.5 mm. Make sure the stream is a steady flow. Pull a comb through your hair several times. Holding the comb about 10 cm below the faucet, slowly bring the teeth of the comb closer to the water. Observe what happens. Repeat these steps. Note any changes in your initial observations. Adjust the faucet to produce a larger stream of water, and repeat the experiment.

Analysis

1. How does distance between the comb and the water stream affect your observations?
2. How does a second "charging" of the comb affect the bending of the water stream?
3. When the size of the water stream is increased, does it bend more or less than it originally bent?

TABLE 6-7   Boiling Points of the Hydrogen Halides

Substance	HF	HCl	HBr	HI
Boiling point (°C)	20	−85	−67	−35
Electronegativity difference	1.8	1.0	0.8	0.5

Hydrogen bonds are stronger dipole forces

Figure 6-8, on page 200, shows a model of a dipole in which a hydrogen atom is bonded to an atom that is much more electronegative. Some compounds that fit this model are listed in **Table 6-7.** Compare the boiling points and electronegativity differences of these hydrogen halides.

The boiling points increase moderately from HCl to HBr to HI, but notice the jump in the boiling point of HF. One reason the boiling point of HF is so high is that strong dipole forces exist between HF molecules due to the large electronegativity difference between H and F.

Another factor pertains to the nature of the hydrogen atom, which is small and has only one electron. When that electron is pulled away strongly by a highly electronegative atom, there are no underlying electrons as there would be in all elements other than helium. The attraction leaves the single proton of the hydrogen nucleus partially exposed. As a result, hydrogen's proton is strongly attracted to the electron-rich fluorine end of another HF molecule. This especially strong form of dipole attraction is called a **hydrogen bond.** It can be a rather strong intermolecular force, but it is not as strong as a full covalent bond.

hydrogen bond

a form of dipole attraction in which a hydrogen atom bonded to a strongly electronegative atom is attracted to another electron-rich atom

Hydrogen bonds form with highly electronegative atoms

Strong hydrogen bonds usually form between molecules in which hydrogen is bonded to a small atom with a high electronegativity, particularly fluorine, oxygen, or nitrogen. The HCl, HBr, and HI molecules are somewhat polar, but they are much larger than HF, so the distance between molecules is greater. Consequently, the hydrogen bonds are much weaker in these substances. **Figure 6-22** shows an example of hydrogen bonding with oxygen.

Water is one of the more unusual covalent compounds because of the great extent to which it can participate

FIGURE 6-22 ◄

Many of water's unique properties are a result of hydrogen bonding in three dimensions. This bonding causes water molecules to stick together.

in strong hydrogen bonding. In water, two hydrogen atoms are bonded to oxygen by polar covalent bonds. With its angular shape, each molecule can form two hydrogen bonds with neighboring molecules. As a result, the intermolecular forces in water are strong.

Hydrogen bonding explains water's unique properties

Because molecules of water are held together by hydrogen bonds, water's boiling point is higher than nearly all other covalent compounds of similar molecular size and mass. Compare the boiling points of water, 100°C, and hydrogen sulfide, −60.3°C. Water is more polar than hydrogen sulfide because oxygen is much more electronegative than sulfur. The electronegativity difference in the H—S bond is only 0.4, which means that the bond is essentially nonpolar. However, the electronegativity difference in the H—O bond is 1.2, so the bond is polar. As a result, H_2O molecules hydrogen-bond strongly but H_2S molecules do not. Water has a much higher boiling point than hydrogen sulfide because of this difference in intermolecular forces. Hydrogen bonding is an important factor in many of the chemical reactions that make life possible. DNA strands in your cells are held together by hydrogen bonds. Hydrogen bonding also attracts enzymes to the molecules they cause to react to build essential materials and release energy in your body.

internet**connect**

SC*LINKS*
NSTA

TOPIC: Hydrogen bonding
GO TO: www.scilinks.org
KEYWORD: HW063

CONCEPT CHECK

1. What causes the differences in melting points and boiling points between ionic and molecular substances?
2. In which phase will a substance with no intermolecular forces most likely be found?
3. Hydrogen bonds form between what atoms?
4. Explain why the hydrogen bonds between HF molecules are much stronger than those between HBr, HI, and HCl molecules.

▶ **FIGURE 6-23**

Dry ice is used to keep food products cold during shipping.

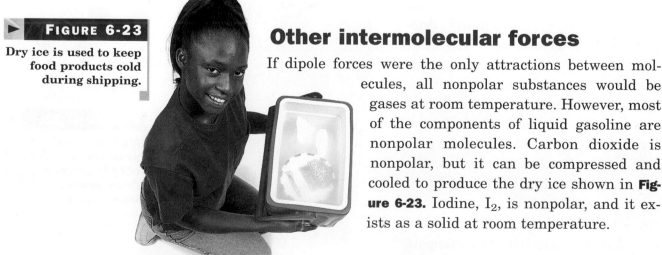

Other intermolecular forces

If dipole forces were the only attractions between molecules, all nonpolar substances would be gases at room temperature. However, most of the components of liquid gasoline are nonpolar molecules. Carbon dioxide is nonpolar, but it can be compressed and cooled to produce the dry ice shown in **Figure 6-23.** Iodine, I_2, is nonpolar, and it exists as a solid at room temperature.

Intermolecular forces exist between nonpolar molecules

As the temperature of a liquid is raised, the random motion of molecules increases. Eventually, the kinetic energy is high enough that molecules overcome the intermolecular forces and separate from each other. This is the point at which the liquid boils. Therefore, the boiling temperature of a substance is a good measure of the force of attraction between molecules or between atoms. Consider the fact that the boiling points of the noble gases He, Ar, and Rn are −269°C, −186°C, and −62°C, respectively.

Higher boiling points of the noble gases indicate increased forces of attraction between the atoms. This was explained by the German physicist Fritz W. London in 1930. He found that boiling point increases roughly as the number of electrons in the molecule or atom increases. These forces of attraction are called **London forces,** or *dispersion forces.* They exist between all molecules but are usually overshadowed by dipole forces in polar substances.

London forces result from temporary dipoles

London forces of attraction exist because any atom or molecule becomes a dipole at any instant when its electrons are unequally distributed around the nucleus or nuclei. This *instantaneous dipole* polarizes a nearby molecule, causing that molecule to also become an instantaneous dipole. The momentary dipoles attract each other momentarily. This attraction brings the molecules together until the repulsion of the outer electrons equals the London force of attraction. This balance of forces determines the spacing of the molecules in the liquid or solid state. **Figure 6-24** illustrates how London forces arise. The attractive force increases as the number of electrons in the molecules increases.

London force

an attraction between atoms and molecules caused by the formation of instantaneous dipoles in the atoms and molecules

FIGURE 6-24 ▼

FIGURE 6-24 ▼

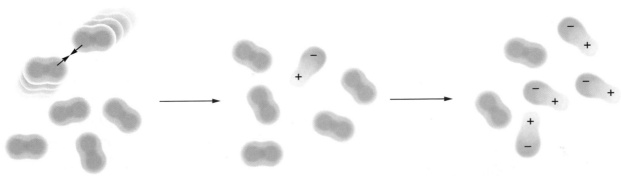

a Random motions of electrons can create momentary dipoles . . .

b . . . causing the formation of dipoles in adjacent molecules.

c These instantaneous dipoles attract each other.

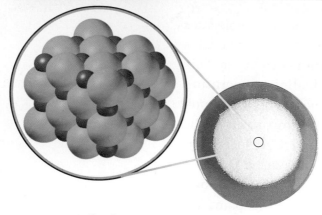

a In the sodium chloride crystal, each ion is strongly attracted to six oppositely charged ions. NaCl has a melting point of 801°C . . .

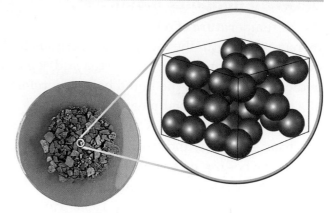

b . . . but in iodine crystals, the particles are neutral molecules that are not as strongly attracted to each other. I_2 has a melting point of 114°C.

London and dipole forces between molecules are usually much weaker than ionic forces in crystals. The very strong forces of ionic bonds lead to much higher melting points and boiling points for ionic compounds than for molecular compounds. Compare the properties of an ionic compound with those of a molecular compound in **Figure 6-25**.

ⓈECTION REVIEW

Total recall

1. If there are no attractive forces between molecules in a substance, should the substance exist as a gas, a liquid, or a solid?

2. Describe the relationship between electronegativity and hydrogen bonding.

3. What type of intermolecular force holds together the DNA strands in your body?

4. How are London forces between molecules produced?

Critical thinking

5. Compare the melting and boiling points of molecular and ionic substances. How do these differences relate to bond types?

6. How does a hydrogen bond differ from ordinary dipole attraction?

7. Compare and contrast ordinary dipole attraction and London forces.

8. The molecular mass of methane, CH_4, is 16.05 g/mol, and its boiling point is −164°C. The molecular mass of water, H_2O, is 18.02 g/mol, only slightly more than that of methane. However, water's boiling point is 100°C, which is 264°C higher than that of methane. How can you account for this large difference?

9. Explain how the formation of instantaneous dipoles causes attractive forces between nonpolar molecules.

Now that you have finished your study of co-valent bonds, you should be able to answer the questions that were posed in the opening story.

LOOKING BACK

One of Jupiter's moons, Europa, appears to be nearly covered by ice. Scientists speculate that life could exist in oceans below this ice shell.

Why don't the two hydrogen atoms in water give up their sole electrons to the oxygen atom to form an ionic bond?

With its six valence electrons, an oxygen atom needs two more electrons to achieve a stable octet. The two hydrogen atoms, each with one electron, seem to be perfect candidates to give up their two electrons and form two ionic bonds. But the electronegativity difference is small, and oxygen cannot "steal" hydrogen's electrons. Consequently, they share electrons. By sharing electrons and forming a covalent bond, the oxygen atom in a water molecule can have a stable octet and each hydrogen atom can have a stable duet of electrons.

The electronegativity of oxygen is 3.4, and the electronegativity of hydrogen is 2.2. Therefore, a bond between hydrogen and oxygen has an electronegativity difference of 1.2, making the bond a polar covalent bond.

Based on its composition, what is the actual chemical name for water?

The full chemical name for water is dihydrogen monoxide, reflecting that a water molecule contains two hydrogen atoms and one oxygen atom.

What is the three-dimensional structure of water?

The Lewis structure for water is as follows.

H_2O has two bonds to H atoms and two nonbonding pairs for a total of four electron clouds. A water molecule thus has the geometry of a tetrahedron, with two hydrogen atoms occupying two legs and two nonbonding pairs occupying the other two legs. As a result, a water molecule has a bent shape. This bent shape means that water is a polar molecule, a physical feature that has important chemical applications. You will learn more about the special properties of water in Chapter 13.

This Mars rock, named Yogi, has a smooth, rounded surface. This surface indicates that the rock may have been worn down by water.

KEY TERMS

6-1
bond energy
bond length
covalent bond
dipole
electronegativity
molecular orbital
nonpolar covalent bond
polar covalent bond

6-2
Lewis structure
resonance structure
single bond
unshared pair
valence electron

6-3
VSEPR (valence shell electron pair repulsion) theory

6-4
hydrogen bond
intermolecular force
London force

KEY CONCEPTS

6-1 Why do some atoms form covalent bonds?

▶ Covalent bonds form when atoms share pairs of electrons.

▶ The greater the electronegativity difference is, the more polar the bond is.

6-2 How are molecules depicted?

▶ A Lewis structure represents an atom's nucleus and inner-shell electrons with the element's symbol and its valence electrons with dots.

▶ Some molecules have more than one valid Lewis structure. This is called resonance, and it makes the molecules more stable and affects geometry.

▶ Molecular compounds are named using the elements' names and a system of prefixes and suffixes.

6-3 How are molecular shapes determined?

▶ VSEPR theory states that electron pairs in the valence shell stay as far apart as possible.

▶ This model can be used to qualitatively predict the shapes of molecules, including linear, planar, trigonal pyramidal, and tetrahedral.

6-4 What forces exist between molecules?

▶ Ionic substances have much stronger forces of attraction between particles than do covalent substances.

▶ If the molecules are polar, then added electrical attractions exists between the dipoles.

▶ If one of the atoms in a strong dipole is a hydrogen atom, the polar-polar force is stronger. This force is called a hydrogen bond.

▶ Intermolecular forces of attraction, such as London forces, dipole forces, and hydrogen bonds, pull molecules together.

KEY SKILLS

Review the following models before your exam. Be sure you can solve these types of problems.

How To Draw Lewis structures (p. 204)

How To Draw Lewis structures with multiple bonds (p. 207)

How To Draw Lewis structures of polyatomic ions (p. 210)

Sample Problem 6A: Predicting molecular shapes (p. 217)

REVIEW & ASSESS

1. Two atoms of differing electronegativity form a(n) ——.
(London force, intermolecular force, polar covalent bond)

2. In a ——, atomic symbols represent nuclei and inner-shell electrons.
(London force, Lewis electron dot structure, double bond)

3. A molecule with a positive end and a negative end is called a ——.
(dipole, molecular compound, covalent bond)

4. Pulling two bonded atoms apart requires putting in energy equal to the ——.
(covalent bond, bond energy, intermolecular force)

5. —— helps explain molecular shape.
(bond energy, VSEPR theory, electronegativity)

6. The force between a hydrogen atom bonded to a highly electronegative atom and another electron-rich atom is called a ——.
(hydrogen bond, polar covalent bond, London force)

7. Some molecules are represented by two or more Lewis structures called ——.
(resonance hybrids, resonance structures, molecular orbitals)

8. A —— is the region where an electron is most likely to exist as it travels around two nuclei in a covalent bond.
(atomic orbital, molecular orbital, resonance structure)

9. Atoms share electrons equally in a(n) ——.
(nonpolar covalent bond, ionic bond, polar covalent bond)

10. Molecules are attracted to each other by ——.
(electronegativity, bond energy, intermolecular forces)

CHEMICAL BONDS

1. a. How does a covalent bond differ from an ionic bond?
   b. How do molecular compounds differ from ionic compounds?

2. What is the general trend relating bond energy and bond length?

3. a. Draw and label the forces that affect atoms in a covalent bond.
   b. Explain why bonding electrons are able to come relatively close to each other.
   c. Why is a spring a better model than a stick for a covalent bond?

4. Contrast the distribution of electrons in a covalent bond and an ionic bond.

5. What is the periodic trend in electronegativity?

6. What determines the electron distribution of a bond?

7. Describe the energy changes involved when two atoms come together and form a covalent bond.

8. Do atoms actually remain at the distance stated as the bond length?

9. Describe the electron distribution in a polar covalent bond, and compare it with the electron distribution in a nonpolar covalent bond.

10. Use Table 6-2 and electronegativity differences to predict whether the bonds between the following pairs of elements are ionic, polar covalent, or nonpolar covalent.
    a. Na–F
    b. K–Cl
    c. N–O
    d. H–I
    e. Al–O
    f. S–O
    g. Cl–Br

11. Arrange the following diatomic molecules in order of increasing bond polarity. You may need to refer to Table 6-2 and Figure 6-7.
a. I—Cl
b. H—F
c. H—Br

LEWIS STRUCTURES

12. In a Lewis structure, what does a chemical symbol, such as C, represent?

13. What kind of bond is formed between two atoms that share two electron pairs? three electron pairs?

14. Determine the number of valence electrons in boron, nitrogen, and fluorine. Draw the electron-dot diagram for each.

15. a. What term is used when molecules have more than one valid Lewis structure?
b. How does this affect the stability of a molecule?

16. Explain what is wrong with the following structures, then correct each one.
a. H—H—$\ddot{\underset{\cdot\cdot}{S}}$:

b. H—$\overset{\displaystyle :O:}{\underset{\displaystyle \|}{C}}$=$\ddot{O}$—H

c. $\underset{\displaystyle :\ddot{C}l \quad \ddot{C}l:}{\overset{\displaystyle :\ddot{C}l:}{\underset{\displaystyle \|}{N}}}$

17. Unlike other elements, noble gases are relatively inert. When they do react, they sometimes do not follow the octet rule. Examine the following Lewis structure for the molecule XeO_2F_2.

$$:\ddot{O}—\overset{\displaystyle :\ddot{F}:}{\underset{\displaystyle :\ddot{F}: \quad \ddot{O}:}{Xe\cdot}}$$

a. Do the valence electrons of the Xe atom follow the octet rule? Explain.
b. How many unshared pairs of electrons are present in this molecule?
c. Can this molecule form a hydrogen bond? Explain.

18. Boron trifluoride, BF_3, reacts violently with various compounds, including water and ammonia.
a. Draw the Lewis structure for BF_3, showing a single covalent bond between the central B atom and each F atom.
b. Draw the Lewis structures for water and ammonia. Explain why they react so readily with BF_3.
Hint: what might their unshared pairs do?

Practice Problems

19. Draw Lewis structures for the following molecules. (Remember, hydrogen can form only one covalent bond.)
a. NF_3
c. CH_3OH
b. $SiCl_4$

20. Draw Lewis structures for the following molecules:
a. ClF
c. HOCl
b. CCl_2F_2

21. Draw Lewis structures for the following molecules:
a. O_2
c. HCN
b. CS_2

22. Draw Lewis structures for the following molecules exhibiting resonance:
a. SO_2
c. O_3
b. N_2O (Hint: the order of the atoms is NNO.)

23. Draw Lewis structures for the following molecules:
a. a refrigerant with one C atom, one H atom, and three F atoms
b. a natural-gas ingredient with two C atoms and six H atoms

24. Draw Lewis structures for the following polyatomic ions.
a. OH^-
c. NO^{2+}
b. NO^{2-}

25. NO_3^- has three resonance structures. Draw two of them.

NAMES AND FORMULAS FOR MOLECULAR COMPOUNDS

26. Using the system of prefixes and suffixes, name the following compounds:
 a. SF_4
 b. BCl_3
 c. PBr_5
 d. N_2O_5
 e. S_2Cl_2
 f. SO_3

27. Give formulas for the following compounds:
 a. carbon disulfide
 b sulfur hexafluoride
 c. dinitrogen tetroxide
 d. chlorine trifluoride

Practice Problems

28. Name the following compounds whose Lewis structures are shown:
 a.

$$:\!\overset{\displaystyle ..}{\underset{\displaystyle ..}{F}}\!:$$
$$:\!\overset{\displaystyle ..}{F}\!-\!\overset{\displaystyle |}{C}\!-\!\overset{\displaystyle ..}{F}\!:$$
$$:\!\overset{\displaystyle ..}{\underset{\displaystyle ..}{F}}\!:$$

 c. $H\!-\!\overset{..}{\underset{..}{O}}\!-\!\overset{..}{\underset{..}{O}}\!-\!H$

 b.

$$:\!\overset{\displaystyle ..}{\underset{\displaystyle ..}{O}}\!:$$
$$:\!\overset{\displaystyle ..}{O}\!-\!\overset{\displaystyle |}{Xe}\!-\!\overset{\displaystyle ..}{O}\!:$$

29. Draw the Lewis structure for each of the following compounds:
 a. carbon tetrachloride
 b nitrogen tribromide
 c. dichlorine oxide

MOLECULAR SHAPES

30. Why do the electron clouds around a central atom stay as far apart as possible?

31. Name the following molecular shapes:

 a. **b.** **c.**

Practice Problems

32. Determine the shape of the following compounds:
 a. ClF
 b. OF_2
 c. NF_3
 d. CF_4
 e. BF_3

33. Draw the shapes of the following ions:
 a. NH_4^+
 b. OCl^-
 c. CO_3^{2-}

34. Use these Lewis structures to deduce the shape of the molecules.
 a. $H\!-\!C\!\equiv\!C\!-\!H$
 b. $:\!\overset{..}{\underset{..}{Cl}}\!-\!\overset{..}{\underset{..}{O}}\!-\!\overset{..}{\underset{..}{Cl}}\!:$
 c. $:\!\overset{..}{\underset{..}{Br}}\!-\!\overset{..}{\underset{\displaystyle |}{P}}\!-\!\overset{..}{\underset{..}{Br}}\!:$
 $\quad\quad:\!\overset{}{\underset{..}{Br}}\!:$

35. Draw the Lewis structures of BF_3 and NF_3, and determine their shapes.

FORCES BETWEEN MOLECULES

36. List two intermolecular forces of attraction.

37. What is a hydrogen bond?

38. Why do compounds exhibiting hydrogen bonds boil at a higher temperature than similar polar compounds without hydrogen bonds?

39. Describe London forces and compare them to dipole forces.

40. How does size affect the force of attraction between noble gas atoms?

41. a. What affects the strength of London forces in molecular compounds?
 b. Why are the London forces between H_2 molecules very weak?

42. Describe dipole forces, London forces, and hydrogen bonds in terms of water molecules.

43. a. Describe what attractive force(s) must be overcome to melt ice.
 b. Describe what attractive force(s) must be overcome to produce hydrogen gas and oxygen gas from the water that forms from the melted ice.

44. Explain why CH_3OH can form a hydrogen bond with water but CH_4 cannot. (Hint: Draw the Lewis structure for both compounds.)

45. Why does SO_2 have a higher boiling point than CO_2? (Hint: Determine the shape of each molecule, and then compare the intermolecular force that would be present between their respective molecules.)

46. Explain why melting and boiling points of molecular compounds are usually lower than those of ionic compounds.

47. Which compound in each pair has the higher boiling point? Explain.
   a. NaF and F_2
   b. Cl_2 and F_2
   c. CO_2 and SO_2
   d. H_2O and H_2S

48. Arrange the following pairs according to the strength of the intermolecular force that exists between the two molecules or ions in the pair:
   a. polar molecule and polar molecule
   b. nonpolar molecule and nonpolar molecule
   c. ion and ion

LINKING CHAPTERS

	Carbon and carbon	Oxygen and oxygen	Carbon and nitrogen
Single	376 kJ/mol	214 kJ/mol	331 kJ/mol
Double	720 kJ/mol	498 kJ/mol	644 kJ/mol
Triple	962 kJ/mol	N/A	937 kJ/mol

1. Theme: Classification and trends
   The table above shows different bond energies for single, double, and triple bonds.
   a. Which is the shortest type of bond?
   b. Predict how the N—O bond would compare to the N=O bond in terms of bond energy.

2. Ionic compounds
   a. What kind of attractive force is responsible for the binding of water in hydrated salts such as $CuSO_4 \cdot 5H_2O$?
   b. Describe the attractive forces involved in the dissolving of NaCl in water.

3. Molar mass
   Find the molar mass of each of the following polyatomic ions:

   a. $\left[\begin{array}{c} :\ddot{O}: \\ | \\ :\ddot{O}-S-\ddot{O}: \\ | \\ :\ddot{O}: \end{array}\right]^{2-}$

   c. $\left[\begin{array}{c} :\ddot{O}: \\ | \\ :\ddot{O}-\ddot{C}l-\ddot{O}: \\ | \\ :\ddot{O}: \end{array}\right]^{-}$

   b. $\left[\begin{array}{c} :O: \\ \| \\ :\ddot{O}-N-\ddot{O}: \end{array}\right]^{-}$

   d. $[:C\equiv N:]^{-}$

ALTERNATIVE ASSESSMENTS

Performance assessment

1. Molecular structure plays a large part in function. Design an experiment that demonstrates this relationship between molecular structure and function. If your plan gets your teacher's approval, test your design.

Portfolio projects

1. Chemistry and you
   Searching for the perfect artificial sweetener—great taste with no calories—has been the focus of chemical research for some time. Molecules such as aspartame and saccharin owe their sweetness to their size and shape. One theory holds that any sweetener must have three sites that fit into the proper taste buds on the tongue. This theory is appropriately known as the "triangle theory." Research artificial sweeteners to develop a model to show how the triangle theory operates.

2. Cooperative activity
   Some central atoms achieve an expanded valence when they form a covalent bond. This means that the atom has more than an octet of valence electrons. One example is phosphorus pentachloride, PCl_5. Draw the Lewis structure for this compound. Each group should find as many examples as possible of molecules that contain an atom with an expanded valence. Draw their Lewis structures. If possible, determine the shape of each of these molecules.

3. internet**connect**

SC**LINKS**
NSTA

TOPIC: Silicon
GO TO: www.scilinks.org
KEYWORD: HW064

Research and communication
Covalently bonded solids, such as silicon, used in computer components, are harder than pure metals. Research theories that explain the hardness of covalently bonded solids and their usefulness in the computer industry. Present your findings to the class.

1. A chemical bond results from the mutual attraction of the nuclei for ——.
   a. electrons   c. protons
   b. neutrons   d. dipoles

2. A nonpolar covalent bond is unlikely to form between two atoms that differ in ——.
   a. electronegativity   c. density
   b. state of matter   d. polarity

3. To draw a Lewis structure, it is not necessary to know ——.
   a. bond energies
   b. the number of valence electrons for each atom
   c. the types of atoms in the molecule
   d. the number of atoms in the molecule

4. Multiple covalent bonds may occur in atoms that contain carbon, nitrogen, or ——.
   a. chlorine   c. hydrogen
   b. oxygen   d. helium

5. The Lewis structure of methane, CH_4, contains —— covalent bonds.
   a. 3   c. 4
   b. 5   d. 8

6. VSEPR states that the electrostatic repulsion between electron pairs surrounding an atom causes ——.
   a. an electron sea to form
   b. these pairs to be oriented as far apart as possible
   c. positive ions to form
   d. a bond to break

7. In a polar covalent bond, the electronegativity of the two atoms is ——.
   a. approximately the same
   b. so different that one atom takes an electron away from the other atom
   c. different, but the electrons are still shared by both atoms
   d. zero

8. According to VSEPR theory, the shape of an AB_4 molecule with no unshared electrons would be ——.
   a. linear   c. octahedral
   b. bent   d. tetrahedral

9. Compared with covalent bonds, the strength of intermolecular forces is generally ——.
   a. weaker
   b. about the same
   c. stronger
   d. too variable to compare

10. In writing a Lewis structure for a polyatomic ion, one electron must be added for each unit of ——.
    a. moles
    b. positive charge
    c. mass
    d. negative charge

11. In Lewis electron-dot structures, the atomic symbol represents ——.
    a. valence electrons
    b. the nucleus and inner-shell electrons
    c. atomic number
    d. a stable octet of electrons

12. Due to the presence of an unshared pair of electrons, the shape of ammonia, NH_3, is ——.
    a. tetrahedral
    b. linear
    c. trigonal pyramidal
    d. octahedral

13. The energy released in the formation of a covalent bond is the difference between zero and the ——.
    a. maximum potential energy
    b. kinetic energy of the atom
    c. minimum potential energy
    d. bond length expressed in picometers

Carbon and Organic Compounds

COVALENT BONDING AND TRASH BAGS

What is the largest structure ever made by humans? It's not the Great Wall of China that extends across northern China for 6300 km. It is the Fresh Kills landfill on Staten Island, New York. If the amount of trash the landfill holds were spread over 1000 football fields, the mound would be as tall as a 21-story building. Begun in 1948 atop a swamp, the Fresh Kills landfill currently receives up to 18 000 metric tons of garbage every day, but plans have been made to close the landfill by 2002.

The average person in the United States produces 1.8 kg (4 lb) of trash each day, about 55% of which will end up in a landfill. With landfills such as Fresh Kills filling up or closing, the challenge of getting rid of so much trash is overwhelming.

The best solution is to reduce the amount of trash produced. In addition, trash should be separated into biodegradable and non-biodegradable material. Bacteria in the soil can readily decompose biodegradable material. Because biodegradable waste makes up a large part of total household waste, we can drastically reduce the amount of garbage going into landfills by sending this material to a compost facility. At a compost facility, materials such as food and yard trimmings are converted into fertile soil. A few communities have already set up composting programs.

Trash bags have been a target in the search for biodegradable materials because people often put biodegradable material into nonbiodegradable trash bags. The trash bag acts as a barrier, preventing bacteria in the soil from breaking down the material inside the bag. Most plastic trash bags are made of polyethylene, a nonbiodegradable plastic. In the 1980s, corn starch was combined with polyethylene to create trash bags that were considered to be biodegradable. While the cornstarch did degrade, plastics were left in the soil. Since then, bags have been developed that are nearly 100% biodegradable. Because truly biodegradable products are more expensive, the market for them remains small.

Carbon is the major element in a wide range of biodegradable and nonbiodegradable compounds, from a banana peel to a polyethylene trash bag. In this chapter, you will learn about the nature of carbon and its many compounds.

CHAPTER LINKS

What determines whether something is biodegradable?

What is the structure of polyethylene?

Why is polyethylene so stable?

What kinds of covalent compounds can carbon form?

OBJECTIVES

▶ **Differentiate** between two allotropes of carbon.

▶ **Relate** the structures of diamond and graphite to their properties.

▶ **Describe** the bonding in alkanes, alkenes, and alkynes.

▶ **Classify** organic molecules by their functional groups.

Carbon and the covalent bond

Carbon is unique among the elements in that it forms long-chain and ring compounds by forming strong bonds with other carbon atoms. Also, carbon compounds have low chemical reactivity compared with compounds of other nonmetals. As a result, an enormous variety of stable carbon compounds with very diverse properties exist.

There must be something special about the bonding properties of carbon that makes so many compounds possible. Carbon nearly always forms covalent bonds. Three factors make the bonding of carbon unique. The first factor is the strong bonds between carbon atoms. This property is in contrast to other second-period nonmetals. Oxygen-oxygen single bonds, as in $HO-OH$, hydrogen peroxide, are so weak that this compound decomposes at room temperature.

The second factor is the low reactivity of carbon compounds compared with compounds of other elements. Butane, C_4H_{10}, is stable in air and catches fire only when a spark hits it. In contrast, the corresponding silicon compound, tetrasilane, Si_4H_{10}, catches fire spontaneously in air. Carbon tetrachloride, CCl_4, does not react with water at room temperature, whereas silicon tetrachloride, $SiCl_4$, reacts very rapidly.

The third factor is the geometry of carbon compounds. With four outer electrons, carbon can form four single covalent bonds. The most stable arrangement of these bonds has them pointing to the corners of a tetrahedron with angles near 109°.

▼ **FIGURE 7-1**

The great strength of carbon-carbon bonds makes long-chain molecules, such as the polyethylene used to make milk jugs, possible.

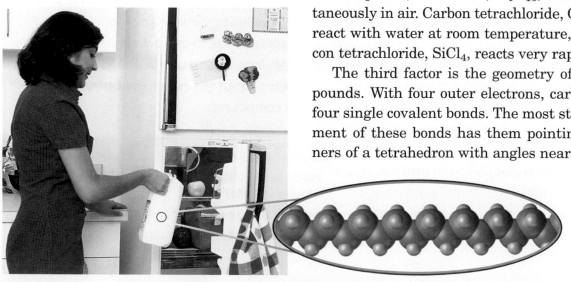

FIGURE 7-2 ▼

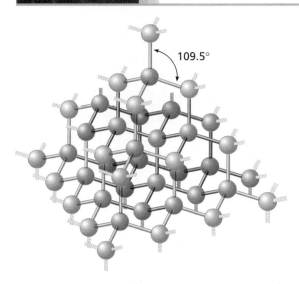

109.5°

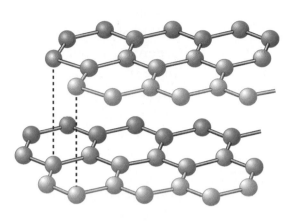

a Because the tetrahedral network of carbon atoms is very strong, diamond is the hardest substance known.

b Electrons can pass freely along the planes, so graphite is a conductor of electricity even though carbon is a nonmetal.

Diamond and graphite are covalent network solids

The crystal structure of diamond, an **allotrope** of carbon, involves many carbon atoms, each bonded at an angle of 109.5°. Diamond is a **covalent network solid.** Any crystal of a covalent network solid is an enormous single molecule containing trillions of atoms. The structure of diamond can be seen in **Figure 7-2a.** Gemstones are not the only use for diamond. The hardness of this solid makes it suitable for many industrial uses, such as grinding and polishing tools like dental drills.

Graphite is another allotrope of carbon. The carbon atoms in graphite are bonded in a hexagonal pattern and lie in planes. The bonds within each plane are very strong, and each plane can be considered a giant molecule, as shown in **Figure 7-2b.** Weaker London forces hold the planes together so that the planes can slip past each other. This makes graphite a good lubricant. The sliding layers also allow graphite to be used in the application with which you are probably most familiar, pencil lead. You can write with a pencil because the graphite layers that make up the pencil point slide apart, leaving a trail of graphite on the paper.

allotropes

forms of an element differing in either bonding or structure

covalent network solid

solid composed of atoms covalently bonded in a network in two or three dimensions

CONCEPT CHECK

1. List the three special factors involved in the bonding of carbon atoms.
2. What are allotropes?
3. Draw a Lewis dot structure of C_2H_6 to show how each carbon forms four covalent bonds.

internet**connect**

SC*LINKS*
NSTA

TOPIC: Diamond/Graphite
GO TO: www.scilinks.org
KEYWORD: HW071

Organic compounds

Most compounds of carbon are referred to as organic compounds. Organic compounds contain carbon, of course, and most also contain hydrogen. In addition, many other elements, including oxygen, nitrogen, sulfur, phosphorus, and the halogens, can bond to the carbon atoms. Organic compounds include proteins, carbohydrates, nucleic acids, lipids (fats), and plastics. A few of the organic compounds around you can be seen in **Figure 7-3.** More than 12 000 000 organic compounds are known, and thousands of new ones are discovered or synthesized each year. There are more known compounds of carbon than compounds of all the other 111 elements combined.

hydrocarbon

the simplest class of organic compounds, consisting of only hydrogen and carbon atoms

alkane

a hydrocarbon that contains only single bonds

Hydrocarbons are the simplest organic molecular compounds

Just as the name suggests, **hydrocarbons** are compounds that consist only of hydrogen and carbon atoms. Hydrocarbons are grouped into three categories based on the type of bonding that exists between the carbon atoms. The simplest hydrocarbons are called **alkanes.** They are

▼ **FIGURE 7-3**

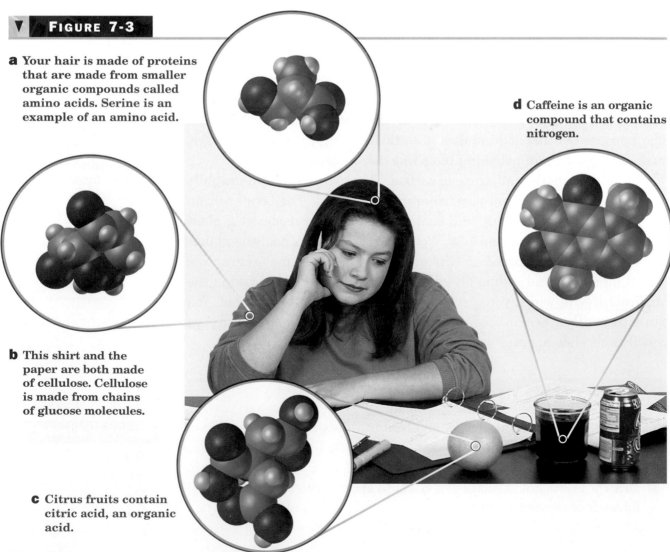

a Your hair is made of proteins that are made from smaller organic compounds called amino acids. Serine is an example of an amino acid.

d Caffeine is an organic compound that contains nitrogen.

b This shirt and the paper are both made of cellulose. Cellulose is made from chains of glucose molecules.

c Citrus fruits contain citric acid, an organic acid.

FIGURE 7-4 ◄

Butane is a hydrocarbon that is frequently used as a fuel for outdoor cooking stoves.

the major components in petroleum. The carbon atoms in alkanes are connected only by single bonds. Butane is a simple example of an alkane.

$$\begin{array}{ccccc} & H & H & H & H \\ & | & | & | & | \\ H - & C - & C - & C - & C - H \\ & | & | & | & | \\ & H & H & H & H \end{array}$$

Butane

Butane has four C atoms and 10 H atoms. These same atoms, shown in the structural formula for butane above, can also be arranged in the structure of 2-methylpropane, shown below and in **Figure 7-5.**

$$\begin{array}{ccccc} & H & & H & & H \\ & | & & | & & | \\ H - & C & - & C & - & C - H \\ & | & & | & & | \\ & H & & H - C - H & & H \\ & & & | \\ & & & H \end{array}$$

2-methylpropane

When the same number and type of atoms can be arranged in different structures, the different molecules are called **isomers.** Isomers are different compounds that have somewhat different physical and chemical properties. For the formula C_4H_{10}, there are two isomers: butane and 2-methylpropane. The number of isomers grows as the number of carbon atoms increases. $C_{10}H_{22}$ has 75 possible isomers, and $C_{20}H_{42}$ has more than 100 000 possible isomers.

The second class of hydrocarbons comprises the **alkenes.** Alkenes are hydrocarbons that contain at least one double bond between two carbon atoms. You have already learned that hydrocarbons are fairly unreactive due to the strong bonds between carbon atoms. The bond energy for a C–C single bond in ethane is 376 kJ/mol. The bond energy for a C=C double bond in ethene is 720 kJ/mol. If each component of the double bond were as strong as a single bond (376 kJ/mol), the bond energy of the double bond would be twice that of a single bond, or 752 kJ/mol.

isomers

compounds with the same number and types of atoms but differing geometric arrangements

alkene

a hydrocarbon that contains one or more double bonds

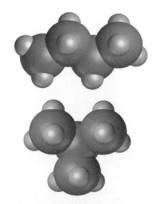

FIGURE 7-5 ▲

These two isomers show that hydrocarbons can be either linear, also called straight-chain, like butane, or branched, like 2-methylpropane.

► **FIGURE 7-6**

Limonene, also called oil of lemon, is an alkene.

The actual bond energy for the double bond is less than this value. Each of the two components of the double bond is weaker than a single bond. Therefore, alkenes are much more reactive than alkanes.

Oxyacetylene torches are used to weld and cut metal. In these torches, the fuel gas ethyne, commonly called acetylene, burns in pure oxygen to produce a very hot flame. Ethyne, $H-C\equiv C-H$, is the simplest member of the third class of hydrocarbons, known as **alkynes.** The triple bond is even more reactive than the double bond of an alkene. Therefore, the triple bond of alkynes is the least stable of the three types of bonds. Alkynes are the most reactive of all hydrocarbons.

alkyne

a hydrocarbon with one or more triple bonds

benzene

a six-membered ring of carbon atoms pictured with alternating double and single bonds, indicating delocalized electrons

Carbon atoms can form rings

Carbon atoms that bond covalently to one another can also form ring structures. Recall the structure of butane from page 237. Four carbon atoms can also form a ring structure. Cyclobutane is the name of the ring compound with four carbon atoms. Its structure is shown below. Cyclobutane is an example of a *cycloalkane,* a hydrocarbon with a ring structure that contains only single bonds.

Benzene, C_6H_6, is one of the most important organic ring compounds. The following structures depict a benzene ring with alternating single and double bonds. All of these bonds are equivalent.

▼ **FIGURE 7-7**

Electron orbitals in benzene overlap to form continuous orbitals, or delocalized clouds.

Benzene exhibits resonance as described in Chapter 6. The delocalized clouds of electrons are depicted in **Figure 7-7.** These delocalized electrons

FIGURE 7-8 ◄

Naphthalene, used as a
moth repellent, is made
from two benzene rings
fused together.

lead to extra stability of the compound. Consequently, in most of its reactions, benzene does not react the way an alkene would. It behaves
more like an alkane. To designate the presence of delocalized electrons,
benzene is commonly represented by a hexagon with a ring inside it. Notice that the hydrogen atoms attached to each corner of the hexagon are
not shown in this simplified representation.

Benzene is the basis of a class of organic compounds called **aromatic
compounds.** Included in this class are naphthalene, which is found in
mothballs, and benzaldehyde, which is used in synthetic flavorings.

internet**connect**

SC
INKS.
NSTA

TOPIC: Aromatic compounds
GO TO: www.scilinks.org
KEYWORD: HW073

aromatic compound

a compound containing a
ring of carbon atoms pic-
tured with alternating single and double bonds with
delocalized electrons that
provide great stability

functional group

a group of atoms that give
characteristic properties to
organic compounds

CONCEPT CHECK

1. Draw a structural formula for the straight-chain hydrocarbon with
   the molecular formula C_3H_6. Is this an alkane, alkene, or alkyne?
2. Can molecules with the molecular formulas C_4H_{10} and $C_4H_{10}O$
   be isomers of one another? Why or why not?
3. Give the structural formulas for an alkane, an alkene, and an
   alkyne, each containing seven carbon atoms.
4. What are cycloalkanes?

Other organic compounds

Many organic compounds, including those in living things, contain at
least one carbon atom that is covalently bonded not to hydrogen but to
atoms of elements other than hydrogen, especially oxygen and nitrogen,
but also sulfur and the halogens. These groups of atoms that include elements other than carbon and hydrogen constitute **functional groups.**
Each functional group has unique chemical properties. For example,

ethers are polar, but not as polar as water. They have low boiling points, and they do not form hydrogen bonds with themselves but form weak ones with water.

Many common organic functional groups can be seen in **Figure 7-9.** Organic compounds are commonly classified by the functional groups they contain. **Table 7-1** gives an overview of some common classes of organic compounds and their functional groups; Table 7-1 includes the molecules shown in Figure 7-9.

▼ **FIGURE 7-9**

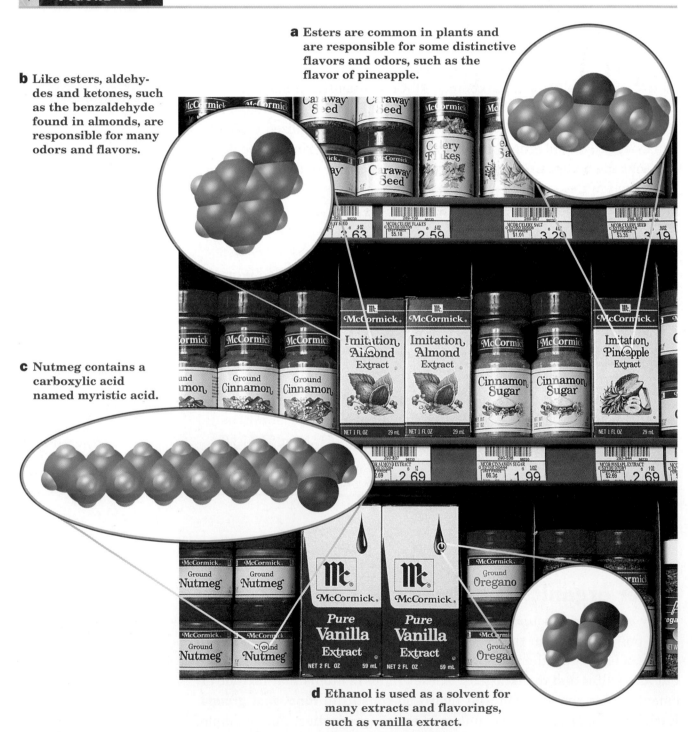

a Esters are common in plants and are responsible for some distinctive flavors and odors, such as the flavor of pineapple.

b Like esters, aldehydes and ketones, such as the benzaldehyde found in almonds, are responsible for many odors and flavors.

c Nutmeg contains a carboxylic acid named myristic acid.

d Ethanol is used as a solvent for many extracts and flavorings, such as vanilla extract.

TABLE 7-1 **Classes of Organic Compounds**

Class	Functional group	Example
Alcohol	$-OH$	H H | | H$-$C$-$C$-$OH | | H H ethanol
Aldehyde	O || $-$C$-$H	benzaldehyde
Halide	$-$F, Cl, Br, I	Cl | F$-$C$-$Cl | Cl trichlorofluoromethane (Freon 11)
Amine	| $-$N |	H₃C and CH₃ arrangement caffeine
Carboxylic acid	O || $-$C$-$OH	H H H H H H H H H H H H H O O | | | | | | | | | | | | | || H$-$C$-$C$-$C$-$C$-$C$-$C$-$C$-$C$-$C$-$C$-$C$-$C$-$C$-$C$-$OH | | | | | | | | | | | | | H H H H H H H H H H H H H tetradecanoic acid (myristic acid)
Ester	O || $-$C$-$O$-$	H H H O H H | | | || | | H$-$C$-$C$-$C$-$C$-$O$-$C$-$C$-$H | | | | | H H H H H ethyl butanoate
Ether	$-$O$-$	O$-$CH₃ (on benzene ring) methyl phenyl ether (anisole)
Ketone	O || $-$C$-$	H O H | || | H$-$C$-$C$-$C$-$H | | H H propanone (acetone)

Functional groups determine properties

The presence of a functional group in an organic compound causes the compound to have chemical and physical properties that differ greatly from those of the corresponding hydrocarbon. Compare the structural formulas of the molecules shown in **Table 7-2.** Each of these compounds has four carbon atoms, but each compound has very different properties.

Compare the boiling point of butane with that of the other compounds in Table 7-2. Butane is a gas at room temperature. Butane contains only C—C single bonds and C—H bonds. The molecule is nonpolar. Butane has no strong intermolecular forces, so it has a very low boiling point and a lower density than all of the other 4-carbon molecules.

Now compare 1-butanol with diethyl ether. Both compounds have the same molecular formula, $C_4H_{10}O$. The only difference is the way the atoms are arranged; they are isomers. Yet this small structural difference makes a huge difference in the physical and chemical properties of the compounds. The compound 1-butanol boils at a higher temperature than water, at 117.2°C, and can be used to dissolve varnish. On the other hand, diethyl ether boils just below body temperature, at 34.5°C, and was once used as an anesthetic. The 1-butanol has the higher boiling point because the alcohol molecules form hydrogen bonds, which cause greater attraction between molecules. Butanoic acid also forms strong hydrogen bonds.

TABLE 7-2 Comparing Different Classes of Organic Compounds

Name	Structural formula	Melting point (°C)	Boiling point (°C)	Density (g/mL)
Butane		−138.4	−0.5	0.5788
1-butanol		−89.5	117.2	0.8098
Butanoic acid		−4.5	165.5	0.9577
2-butanone		−86.3	79.6	0.8054
Diethyl ether		−116.2	34.5	0.7138

2-methyl-1-propanol
(isobutyl alcohol)

1-butanol

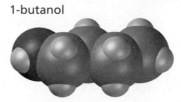

FIGURE 7-10 ◄

Both of these molecules are alcohols. They are isomers because they both have the molecular formula $C_4H_{10}O$.

The compounds within each class have similar physical and chemical properties. For example, many alcohols, aldehydes, and ketones are soluble in water because they are very polar and can form hydrogen bonds with water molecules. Examine the two molecules in **Figure 7-10.** Isobutyl alcohol boils at 108°C and has a density of 0.8018 g/mL. 1-butanol is the molecule shown in Table 7-2. It boils at 117°C and has a density of 0.8098 g/mL. These two alcohols are isomers, just as 1-butanol and diethyl ether are isomers. However, because they are both alcohols, they are more similar in their properties, even though their atoms are arranged differently.

SECTION REVIEW

Total recall

1. What is an alkane? an alkene? an alkyne?

2. Draw the resonance structures for benzene.

3. In addition to carbon and hydrogen atoms, list four elements that can bond to carbon in organic compounds.

4. How are organic compounds classified?

5. Give two examples of covalent network solids.

Critical thinking

6. Explain why some alcohols and organic acids can be soluble in water, whereas hydrocarbons are virtually insoluble.

7. Compare and contrast the structures of an alcohol, an aldehyde, and an organic acid, all of which contain oxygen and hydrogen in their functional groups.

8. **Story Clue** Polyethylene is a long alkane chain. Why is the polyethylene in trash bags so unreactive?

Practice problems

9. Identify all of the functional groups in the following molecules:
   a. cinnamaldehyde   **b.** salicylic acid

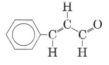

10. State the class of organic compound for each of the following structural formulas:

   a.
   $$H-\overset{\overset{\displaystyle O}{\|}}{C}-OH$$

   b.
   $$H-\overset{\overset{\displaystyle H}{|}}{\underset{\underset{\displaystyle H}{|}}{C}}-\overset{\overset{\displaystyle H}{|}}{\underset{\underset{\displaystyle H}{|}}{C}}-O-\overset{\overset{\displaystyle H}{|}}{\underset{\underset{\displaystyle H}{|}}{C}}-\overset{\overset{\displaystyle H}{|}}{\underset{\underset{\displaystyle H}{|}}{C}}-H$$

   c.
   $$H-\overset{\overset{\displaystyle H}{|}}{\underset{\underset{\displaystyle H}{|}}{C}}-\overset{\overset{\displaystyle O}{\|}}{C}-\overset{\overset{\displaystyle H}{|}}{\underset{\underset{\displaystyle H}{|}}{C}}-\overset{\overset{\displaystyle O}{\|}}{C}-\overset{\overset{\displaystyle H}{|}}{\underset{\underset{\displaystyle H}{|}}{C}}-H$$

   d.
   $$H-\overset{\overset{\displaystyle H}{|}}{\underset{\underset{\displaystyle H}{|}}{C}}-\overset{\overset{\displaystyle H}{}}{\underset{\underset{\displaystyle H}{}}{N}}$$

   e.
   $$H-\overset{\overset{\displaystyle H}{|}}{\underset{\underset{\displaystyle Cl}{|}}{C}}-H$$

11. **Interpreting Tables** State the class of each molecule in Table 7-2.

How are carbon compounds named and drawn?

OBJECTIVES

▶ **Name** a simple hydrocarbon, given its structural formula.

▶ **Draw** the structural formula for a simple organic compound, given the compound's name.

▶ **Decipher** different models for organic structures to identify functional groups, and determine molecular formulas.

Naming straight-chain hydrocarbons

Inorganic carbon compounds, such as carbon *di*oxide, CO_2, are named using the system of prefixes and suffixes introduced in Chapter 6. Organic compounds have their own systematic naming scheme. This naming scheme includes suffixes and prefixes that denote the class of organic compound.

The names of all alkanes end with the suffix *-ane*. The simplest alkane is methane, which is the main component of natural gas. The names and formulas for the first 10 straight-chain alkanes are given in **Table 7-3.** Notice that the first four do not have prefixes that denote the number of carbon atoms in the chain. For molecules of five or more carbon atoms, the prefix makes clear the number of carbon atoms in the chain. The names of the straight-chain alkanes are the basis for naming most other organic compounds.

TABLE 7-3 **Straight-Chain Alkane Nomenclature**

Number of carbon atoms	Name	Formula
1	methane	CH_4
2	ethane	CH_3-CH_3
3	propane	$CH_3-CH_2-CH_3$
4	butane	$CH_3-CH_2-CH_2-CH_3$
5	pentane	$CH_3-CH_2-CH_2-CH_2-CH_3$
6	hexane	$CH_3-CH_2-CH_2-CH_2-CH_2-CH_3$
7	heptane	$CH_3-CH_2-CH_2-CH_2-CH_2-CH_2-CH_3$
8	octane	$CH_3-CH_2-CH_2-CH_2-CH_2-CH_2-CH_2-CH_3$
9	nonane	$CH_3-CH_2-CH_2-CH_2-CH_2-CH_2-CH_2-CH_2-CH_3$
10	decane	$CH_3-CH_2-CH_2-CH_2-CH_2-CH_2-CH_2-CH_2-CH_2-CH_3$

The names of alkenes and alkynes are based on the names of alkanes

Hydrocarbons that contain double or triple bonds are called **unsaturated hydrocarbons.** Unsaturated hydrocarbons with at least one double bond are alkenes. The names of alkenes end in the suffix *-ene*. The simplest alkene is *ethene*, C_2H_4, commonly called ethylene. The next simplest alkene has three carbon atoms. Note that the alk*ane* with three carbon atoms is called prop*ane*. Likewise, the alk*ene* with three carbon atoms is called prop*ene*. The naming of all simple alkenes works this same way; the *-ane* suffix from the name of the alkane with the same number of carbon atoms is replaced by *-ene*.

Unsaturated hydrocarbons with triple bonds, alkynes, are named using the same system of prefixes and suffixes. The names of alkynes end in *-yne,* so the proper chemical name of acetylene, which has two carbon atoms, is *ethyne*. Besides being used in welding and cutting metals, ethyne is used in the manufacture of some plastics.

Ethene and ethyne have only one position in the molecule that can contain the multiple bond. It may appear that the double bond of propene can be at either of two locations, but these two locations are equivalent. The position of a double or triple bond must be specified for a longer hydrocarbon chain. To do this, you first number the carbon atoms in the chain. You can begin numbering from either end of the chain. The multiple bond must have the lowest possible number. Look at the following ways of numbering butene. Which numbering system do you think is correct?

The correct name of the above alkene is 1-butene; 1 is a lower number than 3, so the molecule is correctly numbered from right to left.

unsaturated hydrocarbon

a hydrocarbon that has at least one double or triple bond between carbon atoms

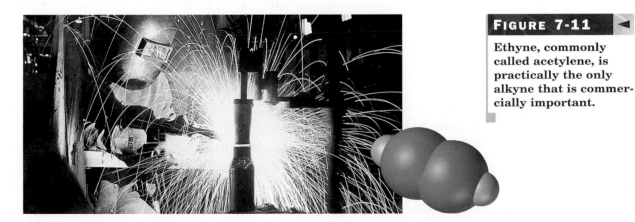

FIGURE 7-11 ◄

Ethyne, commonly called acetylene, is practically the only alkyne that is commercially important.

If there is more than one multiple bond in a molecule, *di-, tri-*, etc. are used to denote the number of multiple bonds. For example, the following molecule is called 1,3-pentadiene.

$$\begin{array}{c} H \quad\; H\; H\; H \\ \backslash \quad\; |\;\; |\;\; | \\ C{=}C{-}C{=}C{-}C{-}H \\ / \quad\;\; |\quad\quad\; | \\ H \quad\; H \quad\quad H \end{array}$$

CONCEPT CHECK

1. Name the following compounds.

   a.
   $$\begin{array}{c} H \quad\; H\; H \quad\;\; H \\ \backslash \quad\; |\;\; | \quad\;\; / \\ C{=}C{-}C{=}C \\ / \quad\quad\quad\quad\; \backslash \\ H \quad\quad\quad\quad\; H \end{array}$$

   b.
   $$\begin{array}{c} \quad\quad H\; H\; H \\ \quad\quad |\;\; |\;\; | \\ H{-}C{\equiv}C{-}C{-}C{-}C{-}H \\ \quad\quad |\;\; |\;\; | \\ \quad\quad H\; H\; H \end{array}$$

   c.
   $$\begin{array}{c} H \quad\quad\quad\; H \\ |\quad\quad\quad\;\; | \\ H{-}C{-}C{\equiv}C{-}C{-}H \\ |\quad\quad\quad\;\; | \\ H \quad\quad\quad\; H \end{array}$$

2. Draw the structural formulas for the following hydrocarbons.

   a. propyne   **b.** 2-hexene   **c.** 1, 6-heptadiyne

3. Correctly number the carbon atoms in the following compound.

$$\begin{array}{c} H\; H \quad\quad\quad H\; H\; H\; H \\ |\;\; | \quad\quad\quad |\;\; |\;\; |\;\; | \\ H{-}C{-}C{-}C{\equiv}C{-}C{-}C{-}C{-}C{-}H \\ |\;\; | \quad\quad\quad |\;\; |\;\; |\;\; | \\ H\; H \quad\quad\quad H\; H\; H\; H \end{array}$$

Naming nonlinear hydrocarbons

Nonlinear hydrocarbons include cyclic hydrocarbons and branched hydrocarbons. The cyclic alkanes are named according to the number of carbon atoms in the largest ring, as if they were straight chains, but the name is preceded by the prefix *cyclo-*, as in cyclobutane.

When you are faced with trying to name a hydrocarbon that is not a simple straight chain or ring, you should first determine the number of carbon atoms in the longest carbon chain. This is the *parent* compound, and this chain takes its name from the corresponding alkane in Table 7-3. Keep in mind that this chain may not appear straight in a structural formula. For example, consider the following alkane.

$$\begin{array}{c} H \quad\;\; H \quad\;\; H\; H\; H\; H \\ |\quad\quad |^{3} \quad\; |^{4}\; |^{5}\; |^{6}\; |^{7} \\ H{-}C{-\!-\!-}C{-\!-\!-}C{-}C{-}C{-}C{-}H \\ |\quad\quad |^{2} \quad |\;\; |\;\; |\;\; | \\ H \;\; H{-}C{-}H\; H\; H\; H\; H \\ \quad\quad\;\; |^{1} \\ \quad\quad H{-}C{-}H \\ \quad\quad\quad | \\ \quad\quad\quad H \end{array}$$

The longest chain contains seven carbon atoms. You must now assign numbers to the carbon atoms along the chain. Number the carbon atoms in the chain so that the branch or branches attached to the chain have the lowest numbers possible. There is a —CH_3 *alkyl* group attached to the third carbon from the left side of the chain in this example. This branch has one carbon atom. Alkyl groups are named using the same prefixes used to name alkanes. It is called a *methyl* group. The name of this compound is *3-methylheptane*.

If there is more than one group attached to the chain, the position of attachment of *each* group is given. The prefixes *di-, tri-, tetra-*, etc., are used if the same group is attached more than once.

With alkenes that have alkyl groups attached to the chain, the longest chain containing the double bond is the parent compound. This chain is numbered just as it would be if the branches were not there.

FIGURE 7-12 ▲

The haze that settles over the Blue Ridge Mountains of Virginia and North Carolina contains 2-methyl-1, 3-butadiene, also called *isoprene*.

To correctly name the above compound, number the chain from left to right. The correct name is *2-ethyl-1-pentene*.

HOW TO   Name branched hydrocarbons

Many organic structural formulas look quite confusing, but keep in mind that the name will be based on one of the simple alkane names in Table 7-3. By following the steps below, you can correctly name many complicated molecules.

1   Identify and name the parent hydrocarbon chain

▸ Because there are no multiple bonds and the longest continuous chain has five carbon atoms, the parent chain is *pentane*.

2 Number the longest chain so that the branches are attached to the lowest possible numbers

▶ The chain should be numbered from the left to the right so that the locations of the branches are at carbon atoms 2, 2, and 4.

3 Name the groups that make up the branches

▶ There are three alkyl groups with one carbon atom each. These are methyl groups.

4 Name the molecule

▶ The molecule has three methyl groups at locations 2, 2, and 4 on a pentane chain. Use prefixes to denote the number of alkyl groups. Therefore, the name of the molecule is 2,2,4-trimethylpentane.

The names of most organic compounds with functional groups are based on their parent hydrocarbon

Compounds with functional groups are named using the same system used for hydrocarbons with branched chains. The parent, or longest, chain is named first; then a suffix or prefix indicating the functional group is added to the hydrocarbon name. **Table 7-4** lists the suffixes and prefixes for some of the functional groups you have learned about.

When necessary, the location of the functional group is noted in the same way that the location of hydrocarbon branches is noted. Aldehyde and acid groups are always on the end of a molecule, so a number is not usually given in the name. Following are a few typical compounds and their proper names. The system for determining the proper names of organic compounds was developed by the International Union of Pure and Applied Chemistry (IUPAC). Keep in mind that chemists still use common names for many compounds, such as acetylene for ethyne. Common names are given below the proper ones in these examples.

| TABLE 7-4 | Naming Functional Groups |

Class of compound	Suffix or prefix
Alcohol	-ol
Aldehyde	-al
Amine	amino-
Carboxylic acid	-oic acid
Ketone	-one

2-propanol
isopropyl alcohol

Propanone
acetone

Ethanoic acid
acetic acid

Fats can be *saturated* or *unsaturated*

A fat is an ester made from glycerol, correctly named 1,2,3-propanetriol, and a carboxylic acid called a *fatty acid*. Fatty acids are long straight chains of carbon and hydrogen with a carboxylic acid group on the end of the molecule. A saturated fatty acid is a fatty acid that contains only single bonds between the carbon atoms. Hexadecanoic acid, commonly called palmitic acid, shown below, is one such fatty acid.

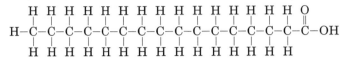

Some people eat foods containing too much **saturated fat.** The animal fats found in butter, milk, and meat are significant sources of saturated fats, but animal fats are not the only source of saturated fats. Tropical oils, such as coconut oil and palm-kernel oil, have even larger proportions of saturated fats. Consumption of saturated fats can cause health problems because these fats can be stored by the body and lead to weight and cholesterol problems.

saturated fat

a fat primarily containing saturated fatty acids

An unsaturated fatty acid is a fatty acid that contains one or more double bonds. Oleic acid, shown below, is an unsaturated fatty acid.

H—C—C—C—C—C—C—C—C—C=C—C—C—C—C—C—C—C—C—OH

Nutritionists usually recommend that people try to eat foods that contain **unsaturated fats.** A general rule of thumb for good nutrition is to try to use fats that contain a high proportion of unsaturated fatty acids, such as canola oil and olive oil. Fats are a necessary part of the diet. For example, linoleic acid is a vital raw material for the construction of cell membranes. It is an essential fatty acid in the human diet because the body cannot make linoleic acid on its own.

unsaturated fat

a fat primarily containing unsaturated fatty acids

CONCEPT CHECK

1. Name the following compound.

2. Draw the structural formula for 2,3,4-trimethylnonane.
3. Draw the structural formulas for the following organic compounds.
   a. 1,2,3-propanetriol, or glycerol
   b. hexanal
   c. 2-octanone

| TABLE 7-5 | Advantages and Disadvantages of Molecular Models |
| | |

Type of model	Example	Advantages	Disadvantages
Chemical formula	C_6H_{12}	shows numbers of atoms in a molecule	does not show bonds, atom sizes, or shape
Structural formula		shows arrangement of all atoms and bonds in a molecule	does not show actual shape of molecule or atom sizes; larger molecules can be too complicated to easily draw
Skeletal structure		shows arrangements of carbon chains; is simple	does not show actual shape or atom sizes; does not show all atoms or bonds
Space-filling model		shows three-dimensional shape of molecule; shows most of the space taken by electrons	uses false colors to differentiate between elements; bonds are not clearly indicated; parts of large molecules may be hidden

Representing organic molecules

Table 7-5 shows four ways of representing an organic molecule, in this case cyclohexane.

Each type of model used to represent a molecule has both advantages and disadvantages. Each type highlights a different feature of a molecule, from the number and kind of atoms in the simple chemical formula to the three-dimensional shape in the space-filling model.

One disadvantage shared by all of these models is that they portray a three-dimensional object on a flat surface. Another disadvantage of the models is that they cannot show the internal motion within molecules. The atoms within each molecule are constantly vibrating—stretching, compressing, bending, and twisting. Today, molecular modeling is often done on computers so that chemists can look at a molecule from a variety of angles and examine its internal motion.

Organic structural formulas can be drawn in a simplified form

Throughout most of this text you have seen structural formulas used to represent organic molecules. Organic structures are sometimes represented by what are called *skeletal structures,* which leave out some of the carbon and hydrogen atoms. This style shows the carbon framework of a molecule only as lines representing bonds. Carbon atoms are

FIGURE 7-13 ▼

a The chemical name for aspirin is acetylsalicylic acid.

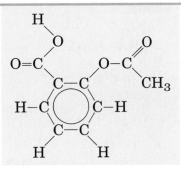

b Because the complete structural formula of acetylsalicylic acid is complex, . . .

c . . . chemists usually draw its skeletal structure instead. The presence of a benzene ring indicates that it is an aromatic compound.

understood to be at the intersection of these lines together with enough hydrogen atoms to satisfy carbon's need to form four bonds. You are already familiar with the skeletal structure for benzene. **Figure 7-13** uses both a structural formula and a skeletal structure to represent aspirin. Notice that the skeletal structure is simpler and quicker to draw than the complete structural formula.

Atoms other than carbon and hydrogen are always shown; this emphasizes the presence of any functional groups. Carbon atom chains are shown in a zigzag pattern to indicate the tetrahedral arrangement of bonds between a carbon atom and other atoms.

HOW TO   Decipher skeletal structures

Unlike most other amino acids, tryptophan, shown below, cannot be manufactured by the human body, so it must be available in the diet. For this reason, tryptophan is called an essential amino acid. What is the molecular formula for tryptophan?

1 Place carbon atoms at all unmarked bond junctions.

2 Place enough hydrogen atoms on carbon atoms so that each carbon atom has four bonds.

$$C_{11}H_{12}N_2O_2$$

3 To determine the molecular formula, count the number of atoms of each element. List carbon first, followed by hydrogen. Other atoms are listed alphabetically.

$$C_{11}H_{12}N_2O_2$$

SECTION REVIEW

Total recall

1. What is the primary disadvantage of the four models that are used to represent a molecule?

2. What is the common name for ethyne?

3. How does an unsaturated fatty acid differ from a saturated fatty acid?

4. What is the suffix used to identify an aldehyde?

5. How many carbon atoms are present in heptene?

6. Which class of organic compounds forms the basis for naming most other carbon compounds?

Critical thinking

7. Why do the names of aldehydes and organic acids not always contain numbers indicating the position of the aldehyde and acid groups?

8. What are the rules for assigning numbers to carbon atoms when naming branched hydrocarbons?

9. Why must your diet contain some fats?

10. Why are unsaturated fatty acids a better dietary choice than saturated fatty acids?

Practice problems

11. Draw the structural formula for each of the following compounds.
    a. 1,4-dichlorohexane
    b. 2-pentanone
    c. 2-bromo-4-chloroheptane
    d. 1-chloro-3-octyne

12. Name each of the following compounds.
    a.

    b.

What is a polymer?

OBJECTIVES

▶ **Describe** the formation of a polymer from monomers.

▶ **Distinguish** between addition polymers and condensation polymers.

▶ **Name** at least two natural polymers and two synthetic polymers.

▶ **Describe** the properties of elastomers, fibers, and plastics, and give an example of each.

Polymer basics

In Chapter 2 you learned how accidental discoveries can have an effect on the progress of science and technology. The development of a field of science known as polymer chemistry was the result of several accidental discoveries that took place over a number of years. The discovery of Teflon in 1938, which you read about in Chapter 2, was one such discovery. But the first accidental discovery that helped to develop the field of polymer chemistry was made in 1839, almost 100 years before the discovery of Teflon. That year, an American inventor named Charles Goodyear found a way to make rubber, a natural polymer, stronger and more durable.

Rubber is a natural product obtained from trees, such as the one shown in **Figure 7-14.** But because it is soft and weak, natural rubber is of little practical use. Goodyear was working with natural rubber mixed with sulfur when he accidentally dropped some of his mixture onto a hot stove. He noticed that the rubber did not melt but instead got much

internet**connect**

SC*L*INKS.
NSTA

TOPIC: Polymers
GO TO: www.scilinks.org
KEYWORD: HW075

FIGURE 7-14 ◀

The fluid flowing from this *Hevea brasiliensis,* or rubber tree, is a suspension of rubber particles in water. This suspension is called a latex.

The vulcanization of rubber by Charles Goodyear made automobile tires possible. Goodyear's name has now become an emblem of the tire industry.

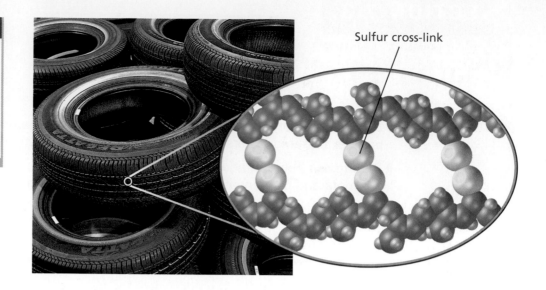

Sulfur cross-link

▲ FIGURE 7-16

Nylon 66, shown here being wound onto a stirring rod, is made from the reaction of hexanedioic acid, also called adipic acid, and 1,6-diaminohexane.

polymer

a large organic molecule composed of smaller units bonded together

stronger. What Goodyear accidentally discovered is known today as *vulcanized* rubber, shown in **Figure 7-15.** The vulcanization process makes rubber stronger by joining the polymer chains together with sulfur links. Vulcanized rubber is a compound used today to make tires, rain gear, and rubber bands.

Polymers move into the 20th century

In 1907, a Belgian-born American chemist named Leo Baekeland was experimenting with reactions between certain organic compounds. In the past, chemists had thrown away what they considered to be the waste byproducts of these reactions. Baekeland, however, decided to investigate a byproduct that was formed by a reaction between two organic compounds, phenol and formaldehyde. He exposed the byproduct to high pressure and high temperature. He found that he could not soften or dissolve the substance after it had been exposed to these conditions. What Baekeland had accidentally discovered became known as Bakelite®, a compound used today to make billiard balls, telephones, and electrical insulators. Bakelite was also used to form the handles of pots and pans because it is a good heat insulator.

In the late 1930s, Wallace Carothers, a chemist working for the Dupont company, mixed two organic compounds to produce a substance that was sticky and that easily fell apart. Because of these physical properties, Carothers thought the substance was of little practical use. But one of his co-workers, Julian Hill, put a small ball of this sticky substance on the end of a glass rod. He then slowly pulled the rod away from the sticky mass and observed how easily the material could be stretched into long, silky fibers, as you can see in **Figure 7-16.** What Carothers and Hill discovered was nylon 66, a compound woven into sheer hosiery for women.

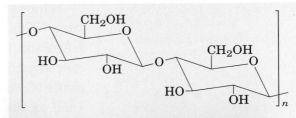

Vulcanized rubber, Bakelite, and nylon 66 are only a few of the polymers that have become an integral part of our daily lives. A **polymer** is a large chainlike molecule that is built from smaller units. Because of their large size, polymers are also known as *macromolecules*. To appreciate their size, consider the molecular masses of polymers; some are in the range of 50 000 amu. Compare this with the molecular mass of water, which is 18 amu.

Polymers are made up of subunits called monomers

Many macromolecules are found in living things. These include proteins, carbohydrates, and nucleic acids. Because they are present in living things, these macromolecules are known as *natural polymers*. The rubber that Goodyear worked with was a natural polymer. In Figure 7-3, on page 236, you saw that paper and cotton clothing are made of cellulose, a natural polymer. In fact, cellulose is the most abundant natural polymer in the world. **Figure 7-17** better illustrates the cellulose polymer.

Baekeland and Carothers were among the first to make *synthetic polymers*. Today, synthetic polymers are an important part of our economy. Nearly half the industrial chemists employed in the United States work in some area of polymer chemistry. In 1996, more than 120 kg, or 270 lb, of plastic, one type of synthetic polymer, was produced per person in the United States. **Figure 7-18** shows just some of the many consumer products that contain plastic.

FIGURE 7-17 ▲

Cellulose is the polymer found in cotton. Hydrogen bonds hold the long chains of glucose monomers together in a large network.

FIGURE 7-18 ◄

How many different plastic items can you spot in this photo? There are at least 10.

Whether natural or synthetic, polymers have similar basic structures. This structure was first proposed in 1920 by the German chemist Hermann Staudinger. Before Staudinger proposed his theory of polymer structure, most chemists believed that these large molecules were made of smaller molecules that were held together by weak attractions, such as the London forces you studied in Chapter 6. Staudinger, however, suggested that polymers were built from smaller units, known as **monomers,** held together by strong chemical bonds. At the time, his idea did not receive much support from other chemists. Gradually, however, experimental evidence was obtained that supported Staudinger's position. In 1953, he was awarded the Nobel Prize in chemistry for his work on polymer structure, something he had proposed more than 30 years earlier.

monomer

the small unit from which polymers form

Some polymers form by addition

Although all polymers are formed from monomers bonded to one another, there are two ways in which this process can occur. One leads to the formation of an addition polymer. An **addition polymer** forms when monomers combine end to end. Two monomers simply join to form a dimer. Next a third monomer is added, then a fourth, a fifth, and so on. This process continues until the polymer is complete.

addition polymer

a polymer formed by chain addition reactions between monomers that contain a double bond

Consider how polyethylene is made. The monomer from which polyethylene is made is ethene, C_2H_4. Recall from Section 7-2 that ethene is commonly called ethylene, hence the name polyethylene for the polymer it forms. In forming a polymer, ethene molecules join together. As you can see in the following equation, each time two ethene molecules are joined together, the double bond present in each molecule changes to two single bonds. The equation below is written using condensed structures. The atoms are all shown, but the bonds between the carbon and hydrogen atoms are not shown.

$$CH_2{=}CH_2 + CH_2{=}CH_2 \longrightarrow -CH_2{-}CH_2{-}CH_2{-}CH_2{-}$$

Notice the open single bonds at each end of the product where additional ethene molecules can connect. The process of adding an ethene molecule continues until polyethylene is eventually produced. Polyethylene is a very long alkane polymer chain.

Because thousands of ethene molecules are joined to form polyethylene, the formula for the polymer is written using a shorthand form of notation. The formula for polyethylene is written as $+CH_2{-}CH_2)_n$. This formula shows n units of the polymer chain. The subscript n represents the number of ethene monomers

Polyvinyl acetate, an addition polymer, is used in latex paints.

that were joined to form the polymer. In the case of polyethylene, n is a number in the thousands.

The process of joining monomers to form an addition polymer is not perfect. Occasionally, a monomer may be added so that the chain branches. For example, an ethene monomer is sometimes added to form a side chain, as you can see in the following structural formula.

$$-CH_2-CH_2-CH-CH_2-$$
$$\begin{array}{c} | \\ CH_2 \\ | \\ CH_3 \end{array}$$

A polymer with many side chains cannot pack tightly. This type of polyethylene is known as a low-density polyethylene, LDPE. LDPE is used primarily to manufacture tough, transparent film for wrapping a wide variety of consumer products, such as the one shown in **Figure 7-20.**

Polymers with very few side chains can pack tightly together. This type of polyethylene is known as high-density polyethylene, HDPE. Because of its higher density, HDPE has greater strength and rigidity than LDPE. The major use of HDPE is in the manufacture of plastic bottles for juices, milk, shampoos, bleaches, and other liquids. Unlike LDPE, HDPE is recycled in most communities.

QUICKLAB

Properties of Polymers

How can you differentiate between HDPE and LDPE? Think about the properties of these two types of plastics.

Materials
2 plastic pieces (2 × 2 in.) labeled A and B

Problem
You know the basic structures of the two types of polyethylene. How do these structural differences translate into differences in physical properties? Use the following three tests to determine which piece is LDPE and which is HDPE. To test the rigidity of A and B, try to bend both pieces. To test hardness, press into the plastic squares with your fingernail and try to make a permanent indentation. Finally, test strength by attempting to tear each plastic piece. If the pieces do not tear, try cutting each piece with a pair of scissors.

Analysis
1. Which piece of plastic is more rigid?
2. Which piece is harder?
3. Can you tear either piece? Is one piece easier to cut than the other?
4. Using your observations in items 1, 2, and 3, which piece of plastic is LDPE and which is HDPE?

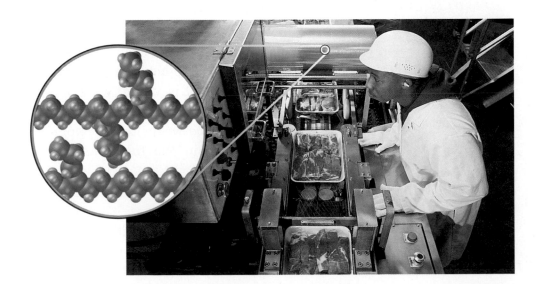

FIGURE 7-20 ◀

LDPE plastic wrap protects meat from spoiling. It also prevents food-borne illness by keeping harmful bacteria away from the meat.

Some polymers form through condensation

You saw in Figure 7-3, on page 236, that proteins are made of small molecules called amino acids. When proteins are formed, water is released as two amino acids bond together. These natural macromolecules are known as **condensation polymers.** A condensation polymer is made when monomers are joined, and water or another small molecule, such as HCl, is produced as a byproduct. The synthesis of proteins generally occurs in the cell where amino acids are linked into long chains. The bonds linking the amino acids are called **peptide bonds.** When a small number of amino acids condense, the product is a *polypeptide.* The following chemical equation illustrates a condensation reaction between the amino acids alanine and serine. Notice that a molecule of water is split off in the reaction, as shown in red.

condensation polymer

a polymer formed by reactions in which water or another small molecule is a byproduct

peptide bond

the bond formed between the carboxylic acid group of one amino acid and the amine group of another amino acid

$$HO-\overset{\overset{O}{\|}}{C}-\overset{\overset{H}{|}}{\underset{\underset{CH_3}{|}}{C}}-\overset{\overset{H}{|}}{N}-H \;+\; HO-\overset{\overset{O}{\|}}{C}-\overset{\overset{H}{|}}{\underset{\underset{H_2C-OH}{|}}{C}}-NH_2 \longrightarrow HO-\overset{\overset{O}{\|}}{C}-\overset{\overset{H}{|}}{\underset{\underset{CH_3}{|}}{C}}-\overset{\overset{H}{|}}{N}-\overset{\overset{O}{\|}}{C}-\overset{\overset{H}{|}}{\underset{\underset{H_2C-OH}{|}}{C}}-NH_2 \;+\; H_2O$$

Alanine   Serine   Peptide bond

Many synthetic polymers also are condensation polymers. Consider how a common type of polyester named polyethylene terephthalate, PET, is synthesized. PET is frequently used to make permanent-press clothing and soda bottles. The monomers used to make polyester are ethylene glycol (1,2-ethanediol) and terephthalic acid, as shown below.

$$n\,HO-CH_2-CH_2-OH \;+\; n\,HO-\overset{\overset{O}{\|}}{C}-\!\!\underset{}{\bigcirc}\!\!-\overset{\overset{O}{\|}}{C}-OH \longrightarrow$$

Ethylene glycol   Terephthalic acid

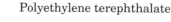

$$+O-CH_2-CH_2-O-\overset{\overset{O}{\|}}{C}-\!\!\underset{}{\bigcirc}\!\!-\overset{\overset{O}{\|}}{C}\,\rangle_n \;+\; 2n\,H_2O$$

Polyethylene terephthalate

▼ **FIGURE 7-21**

This thread is made from polyester. The thread can be woven into polyester fabrics that are used to make many types of clothing.

How is a condensation polymer similar to the addition polymer polyethylene? How is it different? Both polymers are made by joining small molecules together into a long chain. When polyethylene is made from ethene molecules, a double bond breaks and new single bonds form between the molecules. When PET is made, water splits out from between the acid and the alcohol, forming an ester linkage between the monomers. Recall that esters contain the functional group

$$-O-\overset{\overset{O}{\|}}{C}-.$$

Therefore, PET is a polyester.

Another synthetic polymer that is synthesized through a condensation reaction is nylon 66. You read earlier that Carothers and Hill discovered this polymer in the late 1930s. They combined two compounds, 1,6-diaminohexane and hexanedioic acid, or adipic acid, whose condensed structures are shown in the reaction below. Again, the —H and —OH to form water are shown in red.

$$n\text{H}-\overset{\overset{\text{H}}{|}}{\text{N}}-\text{CH}_2-\text{CH}_2-\text{CH}_2-\text{CH}_2-\text{CH}_2-\text{CH}_2-\overset{\overset{\text{H}}{|}}{\text{N}}-\text{H} + n\text{HO}-\overset{\overset{\text{O}}{\|}}{\text{C}}-\text{CH}_2-\text{CH}_2-\text{CH}_2-\text{CH}_2-\overset{\overset{\text{O}}{\|}}{\text{C}}-\text{OH} \longrightarrow$$

1,6-diaminohexane   Adipic acid

$$\left(\text{N}-\text{CH}_2-\text{CH}_2-\text{CH}_2-\text{CH}_2-\text{CH}_2-\text{CH}_2-\overset{\overset{\text{H}}{|}}{\text{N}}-\overset{\overset{\text{O}}{\|}}{\text{C}}-\text{CH}_2-\text{CH}_2-\text{CH}_2-\text{CH}_2-\overset{\overset{\text{O}}{\|}}{\text{C}}\right)_n + 2n\text{H}_2\text{O}$$

Nylon 66

Look at the structure of the nylon 66 polymer molecule. There are six carbon atoms on each side of the monomer. This accounts for the 66 label following the nylon name.

CONCEPT CHECK

1. What do the letters LDPE represent?
2. Would it be possible to have an addition reaction between two different monomers? Why or why not?
3. Why can a molecule with only one functional group *not* undergo a condensation reaction to form a polymer?
4. What two functional groups are in an amino acid?

Types of Polymers

Synthetic polymers are classified on the basis of their elasticity, or ability to stretch and snap back to their original shape. Those that can be highly stretched and return to their original shape are known as **elastomers.** Some elastomers can be stretched to more than 10 times their normal length and still snap back to their original shape. The vulcanized rubber that Goodyear made is an example of an elastomer. Polymers that exhibit little or no elasticity are classified as **fibers.** Cellulose is an example of a fiber. Those synthetic polymers that are more elastic than fibers but less elastic than elastomers are classified as **plastics.** Bakelite is an example of a plastic.

elastomer

a polymer that has elastic properties similar to rubber

fiber

a polymer that has a threadlike structure and is highly resistant to being stretched

plastic

a polymer that is able to be shaped or molded without destroying the macromolecule

Elastomers mimic a natural polymer

Rubber is a good example of an elastomer. You read earlier that rubber is a natural polymer. Natural rubber is an addition polymer made from the monomer 2-methyl-1,3-butadiene, commonly called isoprene.

$$2n\text{H}_2\text{C}=\overset{\overset{\text{CH}_3}{|}}{\text{C}}-\text{CH}=\text{CH}_2 \longrightarrow \left[\begin{array}{c}\text{H}_3\text{C} \quad\quad \text{H} \;\; \text{H}_3\text{C} \quad\quad \text{H} \\ \text{C}=\text{C} \quad\quad\quad \text{C}=\text{C} \\ \text{H}_2\text{C} \quad\quad \text{CH}_2-\text{CH}_2 \quad \text{CH}_2\end{array}\right]_n$$

Isoprene   Polyisoprene

During World War II, the Japanese army occupied much of the Far East, where rubber plantations were commonly found. As a result, the United States launched a massive effort to develop synthetic rubber that could be used to make the tires needed for military vehicles. One type of synthetic rubber is made from an addition polymerization reaction between two monomers—styrene and 1,3-butadiene, shown below.

$$n\,CH{=}CH_2 + n\,CH_2{=}CH{-}CH{=}CH_2 \longrightarrow +CH_2{-}CH{=}CH{-}CH_2{-}CH{-}CH_2\overset{}{\underset{}{)}}_n$$

Styrene   1,3-butadiene   Polystyrene butadiene (SBR)

Today synthetic rubber, also known as SBR, styrene butadiene rubber, accounts for approximately 50% of the world's total rubber production.

Fibers are used in clothing

Each year, billions of kilograms of fibers are produced in the United States, most of it for the clothing we wear. Some of these macromolecules are derived from cellulose, a natural fiber, and are known as semisynthetic fibers because they are made by modifying cellulose in some way.

Most of the fibers made today are truly synthetic. You are probably wearing some article of clothing that contains a synthetic fiber. It may be the nylon in the blouse you are wearing, the acrylic fibers in the sweater you got for your birthday, or the polyester in your pants.

Nylon was the first fiber to result from a deliberate effort to create a synthetic polymer. As women's dresses became shorter during the early 1900s, stockings became more fashionable. However, silk, the main material used to make stockings, was expensive. You read earlier how Carothers and Hill succeeded in making nylon 66. This synthetic polymer was in such high demand that nylon stockings had to be rationed when they were first sold to the public in 1939. **Figure 7-22** illustrates some of the modern uses for nylon.

Other common synthetic fibers include acrylic and polyester. Acrylic, which is sold under the trade name Orlon®, is a synthetic fiber that feels like wool but is less expensive and can be machine-washed with-

FIGURE 7-22

Today nylon is used to make ropes, fishing line, nets, and even clothing such as waterproof jackets and vests.

FIGURE 7-23

Acrylic sweaters have a texture similar to wool, but they are machine-washable.

out shrinking. As a result, Orlon has become a useful fabric for winter clothing. Polyester has now become a more popular synthetic fiber than nylon. The best known polyester is Dacron®, a fiber used extensively in clothing and to make sails for boats.

All three of these synthetic fibers have raised concerns about flammability when they are used to make clothing, especially children's clothing. The heat energy from a fire breaks the bonds that hold the monomers together. The fragments that are produced then react with oxygen in the air to continue the combustion reaction, or burning, often adhering to the skin of the person wearing the clothing. To safeguard against this danger, these fibers are often made flame retardant. One way to reduce flammability is to change the fibers that are at the surface of the material. In flame-retardant clothing, the surface fibers are extensively cross-linked to one another, making it harder to break the bonds that hold them together. As a result, the fibers char as a group rather than burn as fragments. The charred fibers on the surface serve to insulate the fibers that are underneath.

FIGURE 7-24 ▼

a Polyamide fibers similar to nylon can be linked to form a material that can protect firefighters from flames. This material is called Nomex®.

b Polyamide fibers can also be linked together to form a material that is so strong it can be used to make bulletproof vests. This material is called Kevlar®.

Plastics are made from petroleum

Also known as crude oil, petroleum originally came from marine life, both plant and animal. Over millions of years, intense pressure and high temperature transform the decaying matter into petroleum. The time it takes for crude oil to be formed is important because if we exhaust our supply of this natural resource, it will be impossible to replace. Petroleum is the source of a number of compounds that we have come to rely on, including the gasoline that drives our cars and the plastics that can be found in nearly every consumer product. **Table 7-6** lists a few of the compounds obtained from petroleum and their uses.

In 1912, Fritz Klatte, a German chemist, made an accidental polymer discovery. Before the advent of electric lighting, many houses were lit using acetylene, or ethyne, gas. After electricity took the place of acetylene, researchers tried to find new uses for the leftover fuel. Klatte mixed acetylene with hydrochloric acid and found that he had made vinyl chloride (the third entry in Table 7-6). He left the product sitting on a shelf, and after a short while it polymerized. The pure polyvinyl chloride, PVC, that Klatte had made was a hard, brittle solid that decomposed easily. There were no practical applications for this polymer. Fourteen years

TABLE 7-6   Organic Chemicals from Petroleum

Compound	Formula	Common name	Major uses	Production (in metric tons per year)
Benzene		benzene	plastics, dyes	7.77×10^6
1,4-benzene-dicarboxylic acid	$HO-\overset{O}{\underset{\|}{C}}\!\!-\!\!\bigcirc\!\!-\!\!\overset{O}{\underset{\|}{C}}\!\!-OH$	terephthalic acid	plastics	3.61×10^6
Chloroethene	$CH_2{=}CH-Cl$	vinyl chloride	plastics	7.54×10^6
1,2-dichloroethane	$Cl-CH_2-CH_2-Cl$	ethylene dichloride	plastics, solvents	1.19×10^7
1,2-ethanediol	$HO-CH_2-CH_2-OH$	ethylene glycol	plastics, antifreeze	3.53×10^6
Ethene	$CH_2{=}CH_2$	ethylene	plastics, solvents	2.32×10^7
Ethenyl-benzene	$CH{=}CH_2$	styrene	plastics	5.16×10^6
Methanol	CH_3-OH	methyl alcohol	plastics, solvents	9.69×10^6
Propene	$CH_2{=}CH-CH_3$	propylene	plastics	1.25×10^7

FIGURE 7-25 ◄

In many parts of the United States, old water pipes are being replaced by PVC pipes. These new pipes can safely deliver water without the danger of corrosion and breakage that characterizes old metal pipes.

later, in 1926, Waldo Semon, an American chemist, discovered that the addition of certain compounds, now called *plasticizers,* made PVC flexible and heat-resistant.

Because the amount of petroleum available is limited, a conscious effort should be made to recycle plastics whenever possible. If we do not reduce our use of petroleum, there will eventually be no petroleum resources left. Products that require petroleum as a raw material, including most synthetic plastics and many pharmaceuticals, will become difficult to make. Recycling not only will help protect our environment and save our natural resources but also will save many non-natural resources on which our society has become dependent.

internet**connect**

SC*LINKS*

NSTA

TOPIC: Recycling codes
GO TO: www.scilinks.org
KEYWORD: HW076

SECTION REVIEW

Total recall

1. Name the three types of synthetic polymers.

2. In addition to the polymer, what other product is formed when a condensation polymer forms?

3. What raw material is used to synthesize most plastics?

4. Write the structural formula for the monomer used to synthesize polyethylene.

Critical thinking

5. How would polymers be different if their monomers were held together by weak attractions, as scientists first suggested?

6. Why is petroleum a nonrenewable raw material?

7. How do the physical properties of polyethylene depend on the side chains that form when its monomers are joined?

8. Copolymers are made from two different monomers. For example, some plastic food wrap is an addition polymer made from 1,1-dichloroethene and chloroethene. Draw a possible structure for this copolymer showing a structure that is four monomers in length.

9. **Story Clue** Draw the skeletal structure of part of a polyethylene molecule. The molecule should be eight monomers long.

RECYCLING CODES FOR PLASTIC PRODUCTS

Sorting your plastics

More than half the states in the United States have enacted laws that require plastic products to be labeled with numerical codes that identify the type of plastic used in them. These codes are shown in the following table. Used plastic products can be sorted by these codes and properly recycled or processed. Only Codes 1 and 2 are widely accepted for recycling. Codes 3 and 6 are rarely recycled. Find out what types of plastics are recycled in your area. Knowing what the numerical codes mean will give you an idea of how successfully a given plastic product can be recycled. This may affect your decision to buy or not buy particular items.

Recycling Codes for Plastic Products

Recycling code	Type of plastic	Physical properties	Examples	Uses for recycled products
1	polyethylene terephthalate (PET)	tough, rigid; can be a fiber or a plastic; solvent resistant; sinks in water	soda bottles, clothing, electrical insulation, automobile parts	backpacks, sleeping bags, carpet, new bottles, clothing
2	high density polyethylene (HDPE)	rough surface; stiff plastic; resistant to cracking	milk containers, bleach bottles, toys, grocery bags	furniture, toys, trash cans, picnic tables, park benches, fences
3	polyvinyl chloride (PVC)	elastomer or flexible plastic; tough; poor crystallization; unstable to light or heat; sinks in water	pipe, vinyl siding, automobile parts, clear bottles for cooking oil, blister packaging	toys, playground equipment
4	low density polyethylene (LDPE)	moderately crystalline, flexible plastic; solvent resistant; floats on water	shrink wrapping, trash bags, dry-cleaning bags, frozen-food packaging, meat packaging	trash cans, trash bags, compost containers
5	polypropylene (PP)	rigid, very strong; fiber or flexible plastic; light-weight; heat- and stress-resistant	heatproof containers, rope, appliance parts, outdoor carpet, luggage, diapers, automobile parts	brooms, brushes, ice scrapers, battery cable, insulation, rope
6	polystyrene (P/S, PS)	somewhat brittle, rigid plastic; resistant to acids and bases but not organic solvents; sinks in water, unless it is a foam	fast-food containers, toys, videotape reels, electrical insulation, plastic utensils, disposable drinking cups, CD jewel cases	insulated clothing, egg cartons, thermal insulation

LOOKING BACK

What determines whether something is biodegradable?

To be broken down in the soil, organic substances must have bonds that can be broken by microorganisms. Food and lawn trimmings contain such bonds.

Over the past few years, some biodegradable plastics have been developed. One of these materials is polycaprolactone, a polyester. The $-\overset{\overset{\displaystyle O}{\|}}{C}-O-$ groups are attacked by microorganisms much more rapidly than the C–C or C–H bonds in polyethylene. Some biodegradable bags available today are made from nearly 100% cornstarch, a naturally biodegradable substance.

What is the structure of polyethylene?

Polyethylene contains chains of thousands of single carbon-carbon bonds. In polyethylene, each carbon atom is also bonded to at least two hydrogen atoms. Polyethylene is a giant alkane chain.

Why is polyethylene so stable?

Alkanes are very unreactive. The long chains of unreactive bonds make the decomposition of polyethylene extremely difficult. Consequently, most plastics will remain in the environment for a long time. In the pie chart below, you can see that plastics make up about 12% of the contents of landfills.

If biodegradable material is inside plastic bags, it is essentially nonbiodegradable. The need for environmentally friendly plastic bags has become even greater now that several states require communities to cut down on the amount of waste going into landfills. The price of biodegradable trash bags is slightly higher than the traditional polyethylene bags, but composting is much cheaper than maintaining a landfill or incinerator. Furthermore, the environmental cost of growing landfills is very high.

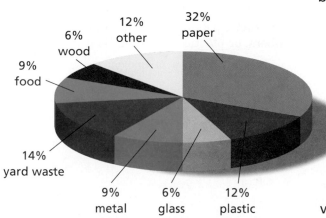

12% other
6% wood
9% food
32% paper
14% yard waste
9% metal
6% glass
12% plastic

KEY TERMS

7-1
alkane
alkene
alkyne
allotropes
aromatic compound
benzene
covalent network solid

functional group
hydrocarbon
isomers

7-2
saturated fat
unsaturated fat
unsaturated hydrocarbon

7-3
addition polymer
condensation polymer
elastomer
fiber

monomer
peptide bond
plastic
polymer

KEY CONCEPTS

7-1 What kinds of covalent compounds can carbon form?

▸ Carbon, with its ability to form four covalent bonds, can form molecules and network solids in a variety of shapes.

▸ Hydrocarbons, the simplest organic compounds, contain just carbon and hydrogen atoms.

▸ The alkanes, alkenes, and alkynes are hydrocarbons. Organic compounds containing rings with delocalized electrons are aromatic hydrocarbons.

▸ Organic compounds are named and identified by functional groups, which are groups of atoms responsible for a molecule's distinctive chemical and physical properties.

▸ Classes of organic compounds include alcohols, ethers, aldehydes, organic acids, esters, ketones, and amines.

7-2 How are carbon compounds named and drawn?

▸ The names of the alkanes form the basis for naming most other organic compounds.

▸ In naming an organic compound, the carbon atoms are numbered so that any multiple bonds or branches have the lowest possible numbers.

▸ Unsaturated fats, with at least one double bond between the carbon atoms, are a better choice for diets than saturated fats, which contain only single bonds between the carbon atoms.

▸ Organic molecules can be represented in various ways, and each model has advantages and disadvantages.

7-3 What is a polymer?

▸ A polymer is a large chainlike macromolecule made by bonding thousands of monomers together.

▸ Addition polymers form by combining monomers end to end.

▸ Condensation polymers form when monomers are joined, and a small molecule is also produced.

▸ Natural polymers include proteins, nucleic acids, cellulose, and rubber.

▸ Synthetic polymers are classified as elastomers, fibers, or plastics, based on their elasticity.

KEY SKILLS

Review the following models before your exam. Be sure you can solve these types of problems.

How To Name branched hydrocarbons (p. 247)

How To Decipher skeletal structures (p. 251)

REVIEW & ASSESS

TERM REVIEW

1. An organic compound that contains a benzene ring is known as an ——.
(aromatic compound, alkane)

2. When a(n) —— forms, a small molecule such as water is also produced.
(addition polymer, condensation polymer)

3. If a triple bond is present between two carbon atoms, then the hydrocarbon is classified as an ——.
(alkene, alkyne, alkane)

4. Diamond and graphite are examples of ——.
(hydrocarbons, covalent network solids)

5. A fat formed from fatty acids that have carbon-carbon double bonds is known as a(n) ——.
(unsaturated fat, saturated fat)

6. The unit that forms a polymer is known as a(n) ——.
(monomer, elastomer)

7. A(n) —— is a polymer that is highly resistant to being stretched.
(plastic, fiber, elastomer)

8. Some elements exist in more than one physical form. Each of these forms is known as an ——.
(isomer, allotrope)

CONCEPT & SKILLS REVIEW

CARBON COMPOUNDS

1. **a.** Draw two isomers that have the molecular formula C_3H_6O.
   b. Classify each isomer based on the functional group it contains.

2. Explain why triple bonds are easier to break than single bonds.

3. **a.** Why does carbon form more compounds than chlorine?
   b. Why is diamond hard and strong?
   c. Why is graphite slippery?

4. Silicon, like diamond, can form covalent network solids. What property do these two elements share that gives them this common chemical property?

5. Aldehydes and ketones contain the $-\overset{\overset{O}{\|}}{C}-$ functional group. What makes them different?

6. Suggest a reason why diamond is less reactive chemically than graphite.

7. When ethene is mixed with Br_2, the double bond in the hydrocarbon is broken and the two bromine atoms are added to the molecule. Draw the structure that forms.

8. Explain why ethane does not react like ethene when it is mixed with Br_2 under the same conditions.

9. Br_2 reacts with benzene by replacing one of its hydrogen atoms.
   a. Draw the structural formula of the compound that forms in this chemical reaction.
   b. Explain why this is known as a substitution reaction.

10. When propyne reacts with H_2 under the proper conditions, the triple bond is broken and hydrogen atoms are added to the alkyne. An alkane is formed.
    a. Draw the structural formula for the alkane that forms.
    b. What is the name of this alkane?

Practice Problems

11. Draw two structural formulas for an alcohol with the molecular formula C_3H_8O.

12. Draw the structure of a straight-chain hydrocarbon with the formula C_5H_{10}. Is it classified as an alkene or an alkyne? Explain your choice.

13. Classify the organic compounds shown below by their functional groups.

a.

$$H-\underset{\underset{H}{|}}{\overset{\overset{H}{|}}{C}}-\underset{\underset{H}{|}}{\overset{\overset{H}{|}}{C}}-\underset{\underset{H}{|}}{\overset{\overset{H}{|}}{C}}-\overset{\overset{O}{\|}}{C}-OH$$

b.

c.

14. What functional groups are present in a molecule of adrenaline, whose structural formula is shown below?

ORGANIC NOMENCLATURE

15. Draw structural formulas that show the difference between 1-pentanol and 2-pentanol.

16. Use Table 7-4 to identify the functional group from the name for each of the following organic compounds:
   a. propanol   **c.** propanal
   b. ethanoic acid **d.** hexanone

17. When propene reacts with water, the double bond is broken and an $-OH$ group is added to the middle carbon atom, and $-H$ is added to an end carbon.
   a. Draw the structural formula of the organic compound that forms.
   b. Name the molecule that is the product of this reaction.

18. When 2-methylpropene is mixed with HI, 2-iodo-2-methylpropane is produced.
   a. Draw the structural formula of the organic reactant.
   b. Draw the structural formula of the product.

19. Use Table 7-3 to name the following straight-chain alkanes:
   a. C_7H_{16} **c.** $C_{10}H_{22}$
   b. C_4H_{10} **d.** C_3H_8

20. Name the following organic compounds:
   a.

   b.

   c.

   d. Write molecular formulas for the compounds shown in (a), (b), and (c).

21. Name the following organic compounds:
   a.

   b.

   c. Write molecular formulas for the compounds shown in (a) and (b).

22. Name the following compounds:
   a.

$$CH_3-\overset{}{C}=CH-\underset{\underset{CH_3}{|}}{\overset{\overset{CH_3}{|}}{C}}-CH_3$$

   b.

$$CH_3-CH_2-\underset{\underset{CH_3}{|}}{\overset{\overset{CH_3}{|}}{C}}-C\equiv C-CH_3$$

   c. $CH_3-CH_2-\underset{\underset{CH_2-CH_3}{|}}{C}=CH-CH_2-CH_3$

   d. $CH_3-CH=\underset{\underset{CH_2-CH_2-CH_3}{|}}{C}-CH_2-CH_2-CH_2-CH_3$

23. Draw the structural formula for each of the following compounds:
   a. 1,4-dichlorohexane
   b. 2-bromo-4-chloroheptane

REPRESENTATIONS OF ORGANIC MOLECULES

24. a. Draw a structural formula for an alkene with 15 carbon atoms. What is the chemical formula of this compound?
   b. Draw a structural formula for an alkyne with 19 carbon atoms. What is the chemical formula of this compound?

25. Compare the advantages of structural formulas with those of chemical formulas.

Practice Problems

26. Convert the following structural formula to its simplified version:

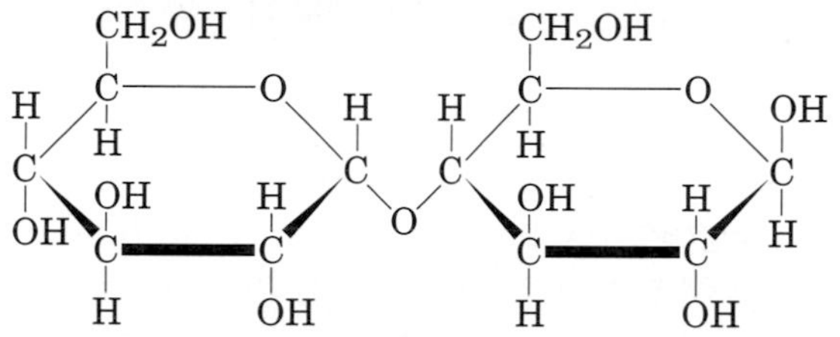

Maltose

27. Draw structural formulas for the following:
a. butanoic acid, a component of butter
b. 1-nonanol, used in making artificial lemon oil
c. 2-pentanone, a solvent
d. Write molecular formulas for the compounds in (a), (b), and (c).

28. The skeletal structure for vitamin A is shown below. Draw its structural formula.

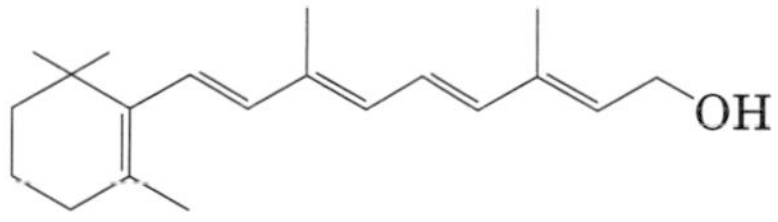

29. The skeletal structure for proline, an amino acid, is shown below. Draw its structural formula.

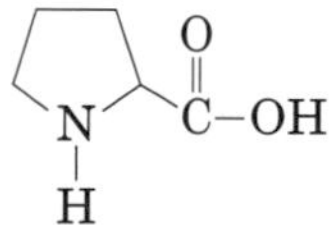

POLYMERS

30. What are two types of reactions by which polymers can be formed?

31. What is the structural requirement for a molecule to be a monomer in an addition polymer?

32. Explain the molecular difference between HDPE and LDPE.

33. Could ethanoic acid be used as a monomer in a condensation polymer? Why or why not?

34. A process that adds strength to polymers is known as cross-linking. This process involves the creation of covalent bonds between adjacent linear polymer chains. For example, the sulfur added in the vulcanization of rubber forms covalent bridges between adjacent chains. Predict how cross-linking would affect the elasticity of a polymer.

35. Cross-linking a polymer will also decrease a polymer's flammability. Suggest a reason for this change in a polymer's chemical property.

36. The following is the structural formula for vinyl acetate.

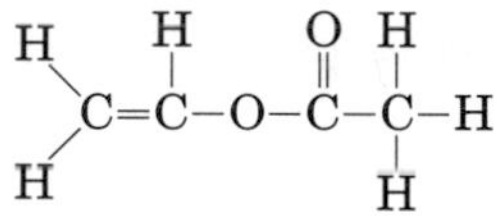

a. Predict how this monomer polymerizes to form polyvinylacetate, a polymer used in latex paints. Will the polymer be an addition polymer or a condensation polymer? (Hint: Only the ethene group forms the polymer chain.)
b. Draw a structural formula of two vinyl acetate monomers in the polymer.

Practice Problems

37. Ethylene glycol, $HO-CH_2-CH_2-OH$, is a monomer that forms a condensation polymer used as a car wax. Draw a portion of this wax polymer showing four molecules of the monomer that have combined.

38. Polymethyl methacrylate, sold under the trade names Plexiglass® and Lucite®, is an addition polymer made from the monomer methyl methacrylate, whose structural formula is shown below.

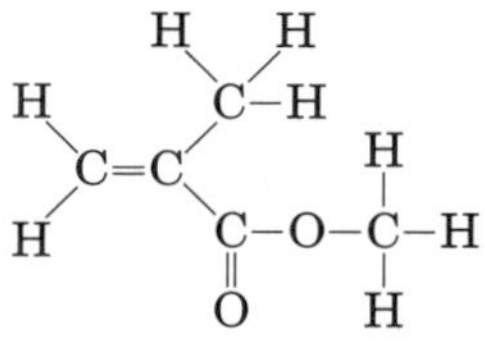

Draw a portion of a Plexiglass polymer showing four monomers that have combined.

39. The Kevlar that is used in bulletproof vests is a condensation polymer that could be made from the following monomer:

$$\text{H}_2\text{N} - \bigcirc - \overset{\overset{\displaystyle O}{\|}}{\text{C}} - \text{OH}$$

Draw a portion of a Kevlar polymer showing four molecules of a monomer that have combined.

40. Draw the structural formula showing how three molecules of the following monomer would combine to form a condensation polymer:

$$\text{HO} - \overset{\overset{\displaystyle H}{|}}{\underset{\underset{\displaystyle H}{|}}{\text{C}}} - \overset{\overset{\displaystyle H}{|}}{\underset{\underset{\displaystyle H}{|}}{\text{C}}} - \overset{\overset{\displaystyle O}{\|}}{\text{C}} - \text{OH}$$

41. An organic acid, lactic acid, is used as a monomer to form a polyester that is used to make surgical sutures that will dissolve in the body. The formula for lactic acid is shown below.

$$\text{H} - \overset{\overset{\displaystyle H}{|}}{\underset{\underset{\displaystyle H}{|}}{\text{C}}} - \overset{\overset{\displaystyle H}{|}}{\underset{\underset{\displaystyle OH}{|}}{\text{C}}} - \overset{\overset{\displaystyle O}{\|}}{\text{C}} - \text{OH}$$

Draw the structure that forms when two molecules of a lactic acid monomer combine to begin forming a condensation polymer.

LINKING CHAPTERS

1. Theme: Classification and trends
Polymers are also classified on the basis of their response to heat. Those that soften upon heating but remain chemically unchanged are known as thermoplastic polymers. Those that change chemically on heating are classified as thermosetting polymers. Suggest how a thermoplastic polymer might differ structurally from a thermosetting polymer to account for their differences in response to heating.

2. Lewis structures
Draw the Lewis structures for ethane, ethene, and ethyne.

3. Hydrogen and the halogens
Explain why replacing hydrogen atoms with halogen atoms will reduce the flammability of a polymer.

ALTERNATIVE ASSESSMENTS

Performance assessment

1. Devise an experiment to study how well biodegradable plastics break down. If your teacher approves your plan, conduct a class experiment to test the procedure on products labeled "biodegradable."

Portfolio projects

1. Chemistry and you
Make a record of the foods you consume in a single day. Compare the content labels from the foods, and list the chemicals in them. With the aid of your teacher and some reference books, try to classify the organic chemicals by their functional groups.

2. Research and communication
Covalently bonded solids, such as silicon, an element used in computer components, are harder than some pure metals. Research theories that explain the hardness of covalently bonded solids and their usefulness in the computer industry. Present your findings to the class.

3.

internetconnect	
SCI*LINKS*™ NSTA	TOPIC: Recycling plans GO TO: www.scilinks.org KEYWORD: HW077

Research and communication
Many everyday materials can be reused or recycled. However, recyclable products are continually deposited into landfills like Fresh Kills. Research the waste-management methods of your community. Write local waste-management officials to find out what has been done to reduce the amount of landfill space needed for your community's refuse. With your class, organize a plan to publicize the recycling programs available in your area.

$\mathcal{T}$EST $\mathcal{P}$REP

1. Which of the following hydrocarbons must be an alkane?
   a. CH_4
   b. C_5H_{10}
   c. C_7H_{12}
   d. $C_{14}H_{26}$

2. The functional group that classifies an organic compound as an organic acid is _____.
   a. $\underset{\text{—C—OH}}{\overset{\overset{\textstyle O}{\|}}{}}$
   b. —OH
   c. $-CH_3$
   d. $\underset{\text{—C—H}}{\overset{\overset{\textstyle O}{\|}}{}}$

3. An alkane with the formula C_8H_{18} is called _____.
   a. octene
   b. octyne
   c. octane
   d. propane

4. During a condensation polymerization, _____.
   a. single bonds replace all double bonds that are present in the monomer
   b. water is often produced
   c. alcohol groups are formed
   d. an aldehyde group is changed to a ketone group

5. In naming an organic compound, _____.
   a. the locations of all functional groups are omitted
   b. the number of carbon atoms in the molecule is not a factor to consider
   c. begin by identifying and naming the longest hydrocarbon chain
   d. use side chains as the basis for naming the molecule

6. Which of the following would have the greatest number of isomers?
   a. C_2H_6
   b. C_3H_8
   c. C_6H_6
   d. $C_{20}H_{42}$

7. Which of the following could *not* exist as isomers?
   a. C_7H_{16}
   b. C_5H_{10}
   c. C_3H_8
   d. $C_6H_{12}O_6$

8. Examine the following structural formula:

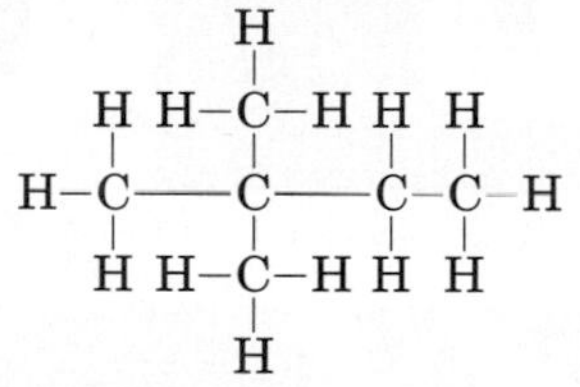

$$\begin{array}{c}\text{H}\\\text{H H--C--H H H}\\\text{H--C}\!-\!\!-\!\!-\!\text{C}\!-\!\!-\!\!-\!\text{C--C--H}\\\text{H H--C--H H H}\\\text{H}\end{array}$$

The correct name for this organic compound is _____.
   a. 2,2-dimethylbutane
   b. 2,2-dimethylpropane
   c. 2,2-dimethylnonane
   d. 3,3-dimethylbutane

9. Examine the following skeletal structure:

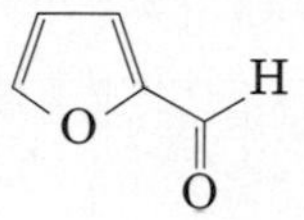

The correct chemical formula for this compound is _____.
   a. $C_2H_4O_2$
   b. $C_5H_4O_2$
   c. $C_5H_8O_2$
   d. CHO

10. Which of the following is an aromatic compound?
   a. 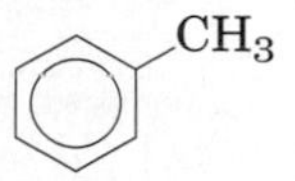 CH_3
   b. 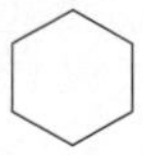
   c. 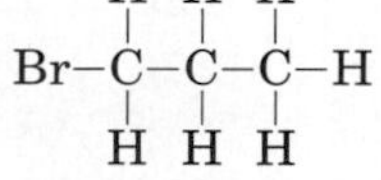 $\begin{array}{c}\text{H H H}\\\text{Br--C--C--C--H}\\\text{H H H}\end{array}$
   d. 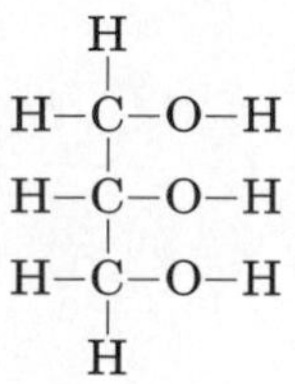 $\begin{array}{c}\text{H}\\\text{H--C--O--H}\\\text{H--C--O--H}\\\text{H--C--O--H}\\\text{H}\end{array}$

CHAPTER

8

The Mole

SIR HUGH'S BOOK

In 1951, Sir Hugh Beaver of Ireland had a disagreement with his friends over which bird flew the fastest. Sir Hugh searched many reference books but could find nothing to resolve the argument. As a result, he created a book that would be an official list of the largest, the tallest, the smallest, the most, the hottest, and so on—the extremes of everything that could be measured.

Beaver was also the managing director of the Guinness Brewing Company, so with the backing of his company, the first *Guinness Book of World Records* was published in 1955 and has been updated every year since then. Today you can learn the following from this book:

▶ The largest pumpkin on record weighed 481 kg.

▶ The longest model train to run under its own power has 650 cars, four engines, and a length of 70 m.

▶ The heaviest mammal ever found was a blue whale that weighed 172 000 kg.

▶ A man in California did 46 001 push-ups in 24 hours.

▶ The United States gold reserve in 1996 was over 8 000 000 kg in mass.

▶ The largest diamond ever found weighed 3106 carats, or 621.2 g.

▶ The distance from Earth to the farthest known galaxy is 13.1 billion light-years, or 1.24×10^{23} km.

▶ The rarest element in Earth's crust is astatine, with an estimated mass of 0.16 g in the entire crust.

Quantities such as 1.24×10^{23} km are truly astronomical; the word *astronomic* is applied to numbers so huge that it is hard to imagine what they mean.

Extremely small quantities are also difficult to imagine. A common soil bacterium might be 1/1 000 000 m (1×10^{-6} m) in length, with a volume close to $(1 \times 10^{-6}$ m$)^3$, or 1×10^{-18} m^3. One of these bacteria is much too small to see with the unaided eye, but 84 billion copper atoms or about 30 billion water molecules would fit into the same space.

Because atoms, ions, and molecules are so small, an invisible quantity of matter may contain many billions of these particles. Chemists must have a way to count particles that are too small to be seen. Using a balance to find the mass is the most practical way to measure a small quantity of matter. In this chapter, you will learn how chemists use the simple relationship between the enormous number of atoms in a mole and the mass of those atoms to describe elements and compounds quantitatively.

CHAPTER LINKS

How can chemists count atoms by using a balance?

How many astatine atoms exist in Earth's crust?

If you traveled to the farthest galaxy, how many atoms of carbon would you have to drop per kilometer to use up all of the atoms in the largest diamond?

How are atoms counted and measured?

OBJECTIVES

▸ **Explain** the relationship between atomic mass and atomic mass units.

▸ **Use** a periodic table to determine the relative atomic masses of elements.

▸ **Solve** problems involving moles, atoms, and molar mass.

▸ **Calculate** the mass of individual atoms.

Avogadro's constant and the mole

As you read in Chapter 3, atoms are extremely small. Macroscopic samples of elements contain an enormous number of individual atoms. For convenience, chemists created a quantity to represent the number of particles in a sample of a given substance. The quantity is the *amount of substance* or simply *amount*. A new unit was created to express the amount of substance. This unit, called the *mole* (mol), is defined as the number of atoms in exactly 12 g of carbon-12.

The number of particles in a mole is called Avogadro's constant or number. The most recent measurement of Avogadro's constant gave 6.0221367×10^{23} per mole. Avogadro's constant may be used to measure any kind of particle, such as the atoms, ions, or molecules shown in **Figure 8-1** as well as electrons and even bonds. For the calculations in this text, Avogadro's constant will be rounded to 6.022×10^{23}/mol.

▼ **FIGURE 8-1**

One mole represents 6.022×10^{23} particles. The particles can be atoms in elements, molecules in molecular compounds, or ions in ionic compounds. Examples of a variety of molar quantities are shown.

AVOGADRO'S CONSTANT 6.022×10^{23}

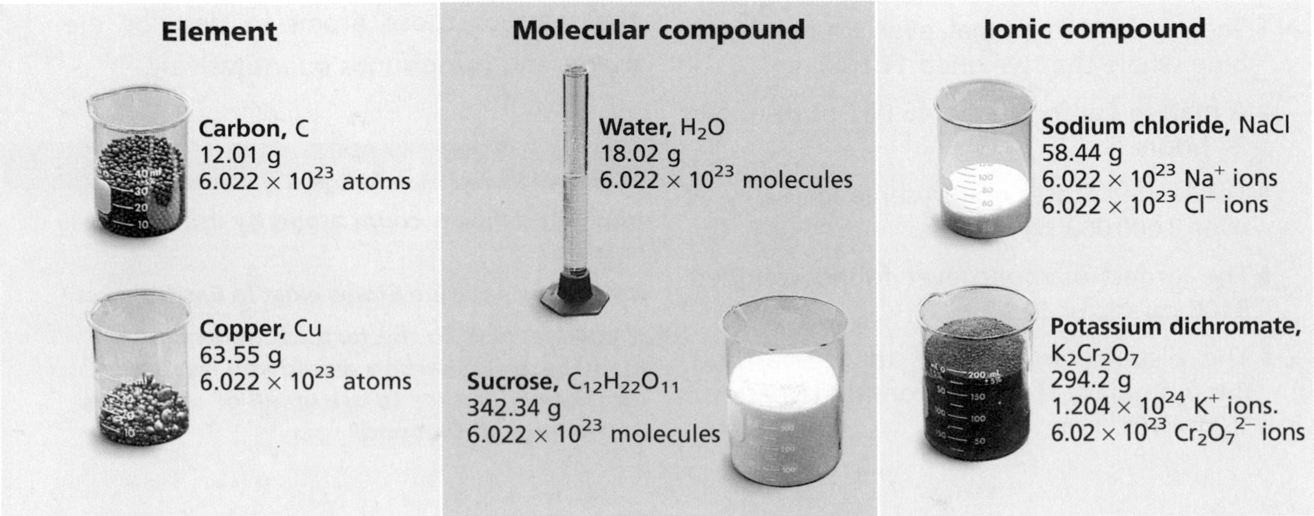

Element	Molecular compound	Ionic compound

Element

Carbon, C
12.01 g
6.022×10^{23} atoms

Copper, Cu
63.55 g
6.022×10^{23} atoms

Molecular compound

Water, H_2O
18.02 g
6.022×10^{23} molecules

Sucrose, $C_{12}H_{22}O_{11}$
342.34 g
6.022×10^{23} molecules

Ionic compound

Sodium chloride, NaCl
58.44 g
6.022×10^{23} Na^+ ions
6.022×10^{23} Cl^- ions

Potassium dichromate, $K_2Cr_2O_7$
294.2 g
1.204×10^{24} K^+ ions.
6.02×10^{23} $Cr_2O_7^{2-}$ ions

TABLE 8-1 Counting Units

Unit	Example	Unit	Example
1 dozen	12 objects	1 ream	500 sheets of paper
1 score	20 objects	1 hour	60 seconds
1 gross	144 objects	1 mole	6.022×10^{23} particles

Keep in mind that the mole is a counting unit used for measuring an amount of a substance in the same way that a dozen represents 12 of something. **Table 8-1** shows you examples of other familiar counting units.

Amount in moles can be converted to number of atoms

Avogadro's constant can be used to convert an amount in moles to an equivalent number of atoms. The conversion is similar to changing 20 dozen eggs into the equivalent number of individual eggs. The conversion factor is the number of eggs per dozen.

$$20 \text{ dozen} \times \frac{12 \text{ eggs}}{1 \text{ dozen}} = 240 \text{ eggs}$$

The same logic process is used to convert 2.66 mol of an element to the equivalent number of atoms. The conversion factor, Avogadro's constant, is the number of objects, in this case atoms, per 1 mol.

$$2.66 \text{ mol} \times \frac{6.022 \times 10^{23} \text{ atoms}}{1 \text{ mol}} = 1.60 \times 10^{24} \text{ atoms}$$

This answer makes sense because when you start with more than 1 mol, you should end up with more than 6.022×10^{23} atoms.

The reverse calculation is similar, only the conversion factor is inverted. Suppose you have a sample of iron that contains 2.54×10^{24} atoms. How many moles is that? The setup is as follows.

$$2.54 \times 10^{24} \text{ atoms} \times \frac{1 \text{ mol Fe}}{6.022 \times 10^{23} \text{ atoms}} = 4.22 \text{ mol Fe}$$

This answer makes sense because there are more than 6.022×10^{23} atoms, so there will be more than 1 mol.

You can use **Figure 8-2** to help you remember how to convert the number of atoms to an amount in moles, or an amount in moles to the number of atoms.

internet**connect**

SC*L*INKS
NSTA
TOPIC: Avogadro's constant
GO TO: www.scilinks.org
KEYWORD: HW081

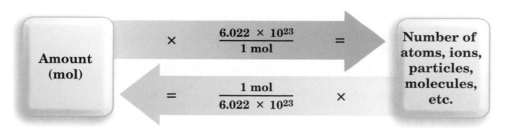

FIGURE 8-2 ◄

By using Avogadro's constant, 6.022×10^{23} mol, you can convert from amounts to numbers, or vice versa.

The sample problems throughout this book are set up to help you learn to solve problems efficiently. Most sample problems are divided into three steps. Each step emphasizes a specific set of activities that will help you develop your problem-solving skills.

1 List what you know

Don't start using your calculator yet.

A big mistake that beginning chemistry students make is to take the numbers from a problem statement and begin using the calculator before they know what the problem means. First, you must find out what information is given in the problem statement.

▶ Read the problem twice.

▶ List the quantities given in the statement of the problem. Always include the units with each value.

▶ Determine what is being asked for, including units.

2 Set up the problem

▶ First analyze what needs to be done to get the answer. Use the values and units given in the problem as your starting point. Then determine the relationships needed to get from the given values to the answer.

▶ Determine and list any other information that is needed, such as conversion factors or atomic masses obtained from the periodic table.

▶ Write down your setup with all the conversion factors. Check to see how the units cancel. If they cancel to give the units needed for your answer, the setup is most likely correct.

3 Calculate and verify

▶ Make a quick estimate of the answer by rounding the numbers in the setup and making a quick calculation.

▶ Do the calculation. Do not round off between steps—round off the answer at the end of the calculation.

▶ Check the size of the answer. Should it be larger or smaller than the value given? Ask yourself, Is this answer reasonable? For example, if the number of atoms is less than 1, the answer cannot possibly be correct.

CONCEPT CHECK

1. What quantity is represented by the mole?

2. What value should you use for Avogadro's constant in your calculations?

3. **Critical Thinking** In Figure 8-1, why is the number of potassium ions greater than 6.022×10^{23}?

Converting amount in moles to number of atoms

Determine the number of atoms present in 2.5 mol of silicon.

1 **List what you know**
- amount of Si = 2.5 mol
- number of Si atoms = ? atoms

2 **Set up the problem**
- Use Figure 8-2 to determine which factor will take you from moles to the number of atoms.

$$\text{Avogadro's constant} = \frac{6.022 \times 10^{23} \text{ atoms}}{1 \text{ mol}}$$

- Multiply the number of moles by this factor.

3 **Calculate and verify**

$$2.5 \text{ mol Si} \times \frac{6.022 \times 10^{23} \text{ atoms Si}}{1 \text{ mol Si}} = 1.5 \times 10^{24} \text{ atoms Si}$$

The answer has the correct units and is greater than Avogadro's constant, which makes sense because you started with more than 1 mol.

Converting number of atoms to an amount in moles

Convert 3.01×10^{23} atoms of silicon to moles of silicon.

1 **List what you know**
- number of Si atoms = 3.01×10^{23}
- amount of Si = ? mol

2 **Set up the problem**

Use Figure 8-2 to determine which factor will take you from the number of atoms to moles. The following factor will give you the correct unit.

$$\frac{1 \text{ mol}}{6.022 \times 10^{23} \text{ atoms}}$$

Multiply this factor by the number of silicon atoms to get moles of silicon.

$$3.01 \times 10^{23} \text{ atoms Si} \times \frac{1 \text{ mol Si}}{6.022 \times 10^{23} \text{ atoms Si}} = ? \text{ mol Si}$$

3 **Calculate and verify**

Solve and cancel like units in the numerator and denominator.

$$3.01 \times 10^{23} \text{ atoms Si} \times \frac{1 \text{ mol Si}}{6.022 \times 10^{23} \text{ atoms Si}} = 0.500 \text{ mol Si}$$

The answer has the correct units and is less than 1 mol, which makes sense because you started with less than Avogadro's constant of atoms.

1. How many atoms are present in 3.7 mol of sodium?

2. How many atoms are present in 155 mol of arsenic?

3. How many moles of xenon is 5.66×10^{26} atoms?

4. How many moles of silver is 2.888×10^{15} atoms?

Relative atomic mass and the periodic table

At the time of Mendeleev, chemists knew the relative masses of atoms for most of the known elements. Unfortunately, chemists had no idea what the actual masses of atoms were; they knew only that they were very small and that even a microgram of an element contained an enormous number of atoms.

Why are relative atomic masses not exact whole numbers? In other words, why isn't the relative atomic mass of sodium exactly 23? One reason is that the sum of the masses of an appropriate number of neutrons, protons, and electrons is not a whole number. The constituent particles of atoms have the following relative masses.

Proton	1.007276 amu
Neutron	1.008665 amu
Electron	0.0005488 amu

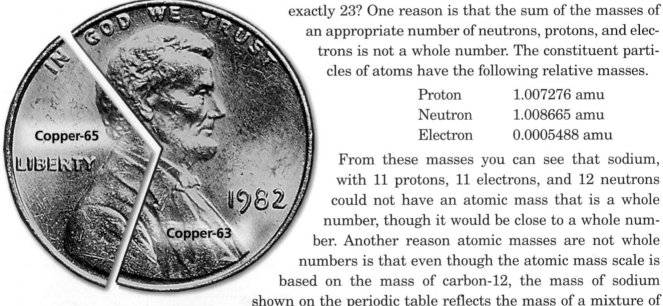

From these masses you can see that sodium, with 11 protons, 11 electrons, and 12 neutrons could not have an atomic mass that is a whole number, though it would be close to a whole number. Another reason atomic masses are not whole numbers is that even though the atomic mass scale is based on the mass of carbon-12, the mass of sodium shown on the periodic table reflects the mass of a mixture of sodium isotopes. Most elements are mixtures of isotopes. Let's look at how the presence of several isotopes for an element affects its atomic mass.

Copper has a relative atomic mass of 63.54 amu. In nature, copper consists of a mixture of two isotopes, copper-63 and copper-65. The abundance of the copper-63 atom is 69.17% and that of copper-65 atom is 30.83%. The relative atomic mass of copper is a weighted average of these two isotopes. The following sample problem shows how the average atomic mass of an element is calculated from data for each of its isotopes.

The mass of a copper-63 atom is 62.94 amu and that of a copper-65 atom is 64.93 amu. Using this data and the abundance of these two isotopes, determine the average atomic mass of native copper. The abundance of copper-63 is 69.17%. The abundance of copper-65 is 30.83%.

1 **List what you know**

- mass of a copper-63 atom = 62.94 amu
- abundance of copper-63 = 69.17%
- mass of copper-65 = 64.93 amu
- abundance of copper-65 = 30.83%
- average atomic mass of Cu = ? g

2 **Calculate and verify**

The average atomic mass of copper is the sum of the contribution of the masses of each isotope to the total mass. This type of average is called a *weighted average*. Each isotope contributes a mass equal to its mass multiplied by its fraction (or decimal equivalent) of all naturally occurring copper atoms. The fraction or decimal equivalent of each isotope is the percentage of that isotope divided by 100. Therefore, the decimal fraction is found by moving the decimal point of the percentage two places to the left.

Isotope	Percentage		Decimal equivalent
copper-63	69.17%	=	0.6917
copper-65	30.83%	=	0.3083

The decimal equivalents of the isotopes are multiplied by the mass of the isotope then added together to determine the average atomic mass.

$$\underset{\text{copper-63}}{(62.94 \text{ amu})(0.6917)} + \underset{\text{copper-65}}{(64.93 \text{ amu})(0.3083)} = 63.55 \text{ amu}$$

Verify your answer by comparing the result with the average atomic mass of copper given on the periodic table. Both are 63.55, so the result is correct.

PRACTICE PROBLEMS

1. Calculate the average atomic mass for silicon if 92.21% of its atoms have a mass of 27.98 amu, 4.70% have a mass of 28.98 amu, and 3.09% have a mass of 29.97 amu.

2. Calculate the average atomic mass of oxygen. Oxygen has three naturally occurring isotopes: oxygen-16, with a mass of 15.99 amu; oxygen-17, with a mass of 17.00 amu; and oxygen-18, with a mass of 18.00 amu. The relative abundances are 99.76%, 0.038%, and 0.20%, respectively.

3. Calculate the average atomic mass for iron. Iron has four naturally occurring isotopes. Iron-54 has a relative abundance of 5.90% and a mass of 53.94 amu. Iron-56 has a relative abundance of 91.72% and a mass of 55.93 amu. Iron-57 has a relative abundance of 2.10% and a mass of 56.94 amu. Iron-58 has a relative abundance of 0.280% and a mass of 57.93 amu.

FIGURE 8-4

By using the molar mass of a substance, you can convert between the amount in moles and the mass in grams of the substance.

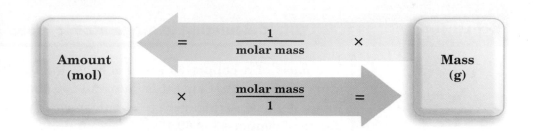

Molar mass relates moles to grams

During your study of chemistry, there will be many situations when you will need to know either the mass in grams of a given number of moles of a substance or the number of moles in a given mass of a substance. Fortunately, the mole is defined in a way that makes these conversions easy.

Suppose you need to find the mass in grams of 1 mol of helium atoms. You know that there are 6.022×10^{23} helium atoms in 1 mol. Using the periodic table, you round off the atomic mass of helium to 4.00 amu. Recall from Chapter 3 that 1 amu is approximately 1.66×10^{-24} g. You can use this information in the following calculation to find the mass of 1 mol of helium atoms.

$$1 \text{ mol He} \times \frac{6.022 \times 10^{23} \text{ atoms He}}{1 \text{ mol He}} \times \frac{4.00 \text{ amu}}{1 \text{ atom He}} \times \frac{1.66 \times 10^{-24} \text{ g He}}{1 \text{ amu}} = 4.00 \text{ g He}$$

The mass in grams of 1 mol of an element or compound is numerically equal to the atomic or formula mass. This relationship holds true for all elements. The **molar mass** of an element is numerically equal to the element's atomic mass and has the unit grams per mole (g/mol). Note: For calculations throughout this text, atomic masses are rounded to two places to the right of the decimal point. Thus, the molar mass of carbon is 12.01 g/mol, and the molar mass of iron is 55.85 g/mol.

These molar masses are used as conversion factors. **Figure 8-4** shows the relationship between moles and the mass in grams of a substance. Suppose you must determine the mass in grams of 3.50 mol of the element copper. By checking the periodic table, you find the atomic mass of copper. This mass, 63.546, is rounded to 63.55 amu. Therefore, the molar mass of copper will be given as 63.55 g/mol in your calculations.

molar mass

the mass in grams equal to the sum of all the atomic masses of the component atoms of a substance

FIGURE 8-5

For consistency, molar masses from the periodic table in this text are rounded to two places to the right of the decimal point.

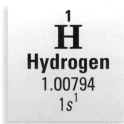

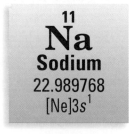

1.00794 rounds to 1.01

22.989768 rounds to 22.99

35.4527 rounds to 35.45

Determine the mass in grams of 3.50 mol of copper.

1 List what you know

▸ amount of Cu = 3.50 mol   ▸ mass of Cu = ? g

2 Set up the problem

▸ Use Figure 8-4 to determine which factor will take you from the number of moles to the number of grams. That factor is the molar mass of copper.

$$\frac{63.55 \text{ g Cu}}{1 \text{ mol Cu}}$$

Multiply the number of moles by this factor.

$$3.50 \text{ mol Cu} \times \frac{63.55 \text{ g Cu}}{1 \text{ mol Cu}} = ? \text{ g Cu}$$

3 Calculate and verify

▸ Solve and cancel like units in the numerator and denominator.

$$3.50 \text{ mol Cu} \times \frac{63.55 \text{ g Cu}}{1 \text{ mol Cu}} = 222 \text{ g Cu}$$

▸ The answer has the units requested in the problem. An answer of more than 63.55 g (the molar mass) makes sense because you started with more than 1 mol. The answer is rounded to three places to conform to the least precise measurement in the problem.

Determine the number of moles represented by 237 g of copper.

1 List what you know

▸ mass of Cu = 237 g   ▸ amount of Cu = ? mol

2 Set up the problem

▸ Use Figure 8-4 to determine which factor will take you from the number of grams to moles. That factor is the molar mass of copper.

$$\frac{1 \text{ mol Cu}}{63.55 \text{ g Cu}}$$

▸ Multiply the number of grams by this factor.

$$237 \text{ g Cu} \times \frac{1 \text{ mol Cu}}{63.55 \text{ g Cu}} = ? \text{ mol Cu}$$

3 Calculate and verify

▸ Solve and cancel like units in the numerator and denominator.

$$237 \text{ g Cu} \times \frac{1 \text{ mol Cu}}{63.55 \text{ g Cu}} = 3.73 \text{ mol Cu}$$

The average mass of atoms can be calculated from molar mass

Now that you know how to convert between moles, Avogadro's constant, and molar mass, you can calculate the average mass of an atom of any element. The process is no different from finding the mass of a single egg when you know the mass of a dozen eggs. For example, the mass shown on a package of a dozen eggs is 720.6 g. How do you find the mass of one egg? The answer is simple. Divide 720.6 g by 12 eggs to get the mass per egg.

$$\frac{720.6 \text{ g}}{12 \text{ eggs}} = 60.05 \text{ g/egg}$$

Using factor-label analysis, the problem would be set up as follows.

$$\frac{720.6 \text{ g}}{\text{doz}} \times \frac{1 \text{ doz}}{12 \text{ eggs}} = 60.05 \text{ g/egg}$$

The same process is applied to finding the mass of a single atom in Sample Problem 8F. In this case, instead of a dozen, you will work with Avogadro's constant for the number of atoms.

SAMPLE PROBLEM 8F   **Finding the mass of an atom**

Find the mass of a single silicon atom.

1 List what you know

- molar mass of silicon = 28.09 g/mol
- Avogadro's constant = 6.022×10^{23}/mol
- mass of one silicon atom = ?

2 Set up the problem

- You know the number of atoms in 28.09 g. You can divide the mass by the number of atoms to get the mass per atom. Or you can express the relationships above as factors that will give g/atom as an answer.

$$\frac{28.09 \text{ g Si}}{\text{mol Si}} \quad \text{and} \quad \frac{1 \text{ mol Si}}{6.022 \times 10^{23} \text{ atoms Si}}$$

3 Calculate and verify

- Solve and cancel like units in the numerator and denominator.

$$\frac{28.09 \text{ g Si}}{\text{mol Si}} \times \frac{1 \text{ mol Si}}{6.022 \times 10^{23} \text{ atoms Si}} = 4.665 \times 10^{-23} \text{ g/atom Si}$$

- The answer has the units specified by the problem. A very small value for mass makes sense because you are calculating the mass of a single atom. More than 99% of the mass of a silicon atom is due to the protons and neutrons in its nucleus. The electrons that occupy most of the volume of the atom contribute very little to the atom's mass.

Section Review

Total recall

1. What is a weighted average? How is a weighted average calculated? How is a percentage converted to its decimal equivalent?

2. Why does the atomic mass of an element as given on the periodic table often differ from the mass of any of the element's known isotopes?

3. How is a mole defined?

4. Why is it incorrect to say that a mole is a quantity?

Critical thinking

5. **Interpreting Graphics** Use Figure 8-2 to explain how amount in moles can be converted to a number of atoms and how a number of atoms can be converted to an amount in moles.

6. **Interpreting Graphics** Use Figure 8-4 to explain how amount in moles can be converted to mass in grams and how mass in grams can be converted to amount in moles.

7. What is the relationship between atomic mass and atomic mass units?

8. **Interpreting Graphics** Use the models shown in Figure 8-2 and Figure 8-4 to develop your own graphic model for finding the mass of an atom. Your model should also include how to find the molar mass of an element, given the mass of a single atom.

Practice problems

9. Find the mass in grams of 8.6 mol of bromine atoms.

10. Find the mass in grams of 7.55 mol of silicon atoms.

11. How many moles are in 38 g of carbon atoms?

12. How many moles are in 2.0 g of hydrogen atoms?

13. Determine the number of moles represented by each of the following masses:
    a. 0.3545 g chlorine
    b. 184.2 g sodium
    c. 0.320 g copper
    d. 282.4 g iron

14. Element X has two naturally occurring isotopes. The isotope with a mass number of 10 has a relative abundance of 20.%. The isotope with a mass number of 11 has a relative abundance of 80.%. Use these figures to estimate the average atomic mass for element X. Identify element X and state its atomic number.

15. Calculate the mass in grams of each of the following:
    a. 1.38 mol N
    b. 6.022×10^{23} atoms of Ag
    c. 2.57×10^8 mol S
    d. 1.20×10^{15} atoms O

16. Calculate the number of atoms present in each of the following:
    a. 2 mol Fe
    b. 40.1 g Ca
    c. 4.5 mol boron-11
    d. 184.2 g Na

17. **Interpreting Graphics** Determine the following:
    a. the average mass of a hydrogen atom in grams
    b. the average mass of a europium atom in grams
    c. the average mass of a platinum atom in grams

How is the mole concept related to chemical formulas?

OBJECTIVES

▶ **List** the information you can derive about a compound from its chemical formula.

▶ **Determine** the molar mass and percentage composition of a compound from its formula.

▶ **Derive** a compound's empirical formula from its percentage composition.

▶ **Calculate** the molecular formula of a compound from its empirical formula and its formula mass.

Chemical formulas and moles

After studying Section 8-1, you may think that moles are useful for counting only the number of atoms in a sample of an element, but that is not so! Moles can be used to count molecules and ions as well. In fact, moles are especially useful when dealing with compounds. They allow us to look at the composition of a compound in a quantitative way.

Formulas reveal composition

A chemical formula tells you what elements are present in a compound. The formula for KBr, shown in **Figure 8-6,** reveals that the compound contains the elements potassium and bromine.

A formula also tells you the ratio of atoms or ions in the compound. The formula KBr indicates that potassium bromide is made of ions in the ratio of one potassium cation, K^+, for each bromide anion, Br^-. Just as the formula H_2O indicates that water contains hydrogen and oxygen atoms in a 2:1 ratio, so the formula for strontium chloride, $SrCl_2$, indicates that there is one Sr^{2+} cation for every two Cl^- anions, a 1:2 ratio.

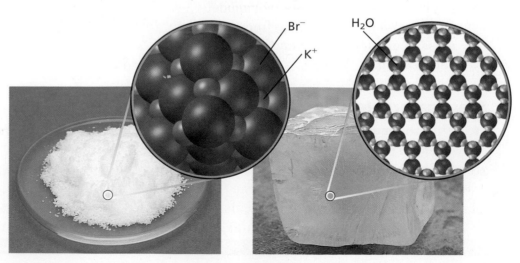

▶ **FIGURE 8-6**

Though any sample of a compound contains many atoms and ions, the chemical formula gives the simplest ratio of those atoms or ions.

Br^-

K^+

H_2O

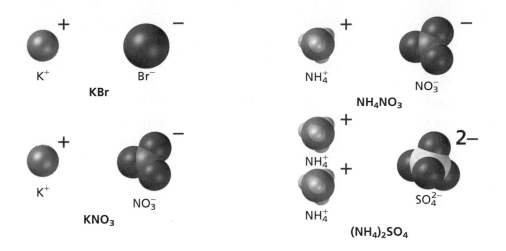

FIGURE 8-7 ◄

When you read a chemical formula, think about how the atoms are organized. Notice that polyatomic ions are distinct groups of atoms bound together. Each is treated as a unit.

The meaning of a formula does not change when polyatomic ions are involved. Potassium nitrate has the formula KNO_3. Just as the formula for the binary salt, KBr, indicates a 1:1 ratio of K^+ cations to Br^- anions, the formula KNO_3 indicates a ratio of one K^+ cation to one NO_3^- anion. This formula also illustrates why it is important to be able to recognize polyatomic ions at a glance. If you realize immediately that NO_3 in a formula is a nitrate ion, NO_3^-, you won't have to wonder whether KNO_3 consists of a KN^+ and an O_3^- ion. Similarly, if you recognize that NH_4 in a formula represents the ammonium ion NH_4^+ and that NO_3 represents the nitrate ion, you can see why the formula of ammonium nitrate is written NH_4NO_3 instead of, say, $H_4N_2O_3$. The formula NH_4NO_3 shows immediately that ammonium nitrate consists of ammonium and nitrate ions in a 1:1 ratio. When a compound contains polyatomic ions, you should think of it as cations and anions, like those compounds shown in **Figure 8-7.**

Each polyatomic ion consists of a specific number of atoms with an overall electric charge. Except for coulombic attraction, ions are independent of one another. For these reasons, the formula of ammonium sulfate is written as $(NH_4)_2SO_4$. This formula clearly indicates that ammonium sulfate consists of two ammonium ions for each sulfate ion. If the formula were written as $N_2H_8SO_4$, the number of atoms would be correct but the formula would no longer clearly show the identity of the ions in the substance.

internet connect

SC*LINKS*
NSTA

TOPIC: Chemical formulas
GO TO: www.scilinks.org
KEYWORD: HW082

Formulas are used to calculate molar masses

Because a formula tells you what atoms (or ions) are present in a compound, you are able to determine the mass of a mole of the compound. The simplest formula for most elements is denoted by the element's symbol, for example, the symbol for silver, is Ag. A mole of the elements Ag, Na, Mg, or Ne contains 6.022×10^{23} atoms of that element. The molar mass of most elements equals the atomic mass of the element expressed in grams. Molecular forms of elements, such as H_2, O_3, and P_4 have molar masses equal to the sum of the masses of the number of atoms in the formula.

We also use the simplest formula to represent a mole of a compound. Chemists often use the term *formula unit* when referring to ionic compounds because ionic compounds do not have a molecular composition. A **formula unit** of an ionic compound is the unit that represents the simplest ratio of cations to anions. A formula unit of NaCl consists of one Na^+ and one Cl^- ion. One mole of an ionic compound consists of 6.022×10^{23} of these formula units. One mole of a molecular compound, like H_2O, consists of 6.022×10^{23} molecules. The molar mass of an ionic compound or molecular compound is the sum of the masses of all the atoms in the formula expressed in grams. For example, the molar mass of KNO_3 is found by adding the atomic masses of one potassium atom, one nitrogen atom, and three oxygen atoms and then expressing the numerical sum in grams. The molar mass of H_2O is found by adding the atomic masses of two hydrogen atoms and one oxygen atom and then expressing the numerical sum in grams. **Table 8-2** compares the formula units and molar masses of three ionic compounds. Sample Problem 8G shows you how to calculate the molar mass.

| **TABLE 8-2** | **Calculating Molar Mass for Ionic Compounds** |

Formula	Formula unit	Calculation of molar mass
$ZnCl_2$	Zn^{2+} Cl^- Cl^-	1 Zn = 1×65.39 g/mol 2 Cl = 2×35.45 g/mol —————————— $ZnCl_2$ = 136.29 g/mol
$ZnSO_4$	Zn^{2+} SO_4^{2-}	1 Zn = 1×65.39 g/mol 1 S = 1×32.07 g/mol 4 O = 4×16.00 g/mol —————————— $ZnSO_4$ = 161.46 g/mol
$(NH_4)_2SO_4$	NH_4^+ NH_4^+ SO_4^{2-}	2 N = 2×14.01 g/mol 8 H = $8 \times$ 1.01 g/mol 1 S = 1×32.07 g/mol 4 O = 4×16.00 g/mol —————————— $(NH_4)_2SO_4$ = 132.17 g/mol

SAMPLE PROBLEM 8G Calculating molar mass

Calculate the molar mass of barium nitrate, $Ba(NO_3)_2$.

1 List what you know

- formula of barium nitrate: $Ba(NO_3)_2$
- formula mass of $Ba(NO_3)_2$ = ? g

2 Set up the problem

- Determine the amount in moles for each element in 1 mol of barium nitrate. Each mole of $Ba(NO_3)_2$ contains:

$$\begin{gathered}1 \text{ mol Ba}\\ 2 \text{ mol N}\\ 6 \text{ mol O}\end{gathered}$$

- Use the periodic table to find the molar mass of each element in the formula.

$$\begin{aligned}\text{molar mass of Ba} &= 137.33 \text{ g/mol (rounded masses)}\\ \text{molar mass of N} &= 14.01 \text{ g/mol}\\ \text{molar mass of O} &= 16.00 \text{ g/mol}\end{aligned}$$

3 Calculate and verify

- Multiply each mass by the correct number of moles for each atom. Add the masses to determine the molar mass of $Ba(NO_3)_2$.

$$\begin{aligned}\text{mass of 1 mol Ba} &= 137.33 \text{ g/mol}\\ \text{mass of 2 mol N} &= 28.02 \text{ g/mol}\\ \text{mass of 6 mol O} &= 96.00 \text{ g/mol}\\ \hline \text{molar mass of } Ba(NO_3)_2 &= 261.35 \text{ g/mol}\end{aligned}$$

- The answer has the correct units. The sum of the molar masses can be approximated as 140 + 30 + 100 = 270, which is very near the calculated value.

SAMPLE PROBLEM 8H Calculating molar mass of compounds

Glycerol, a common ingredient in cosmetics, has the structural formula shown below. Calculate the molar mass of glycerol.

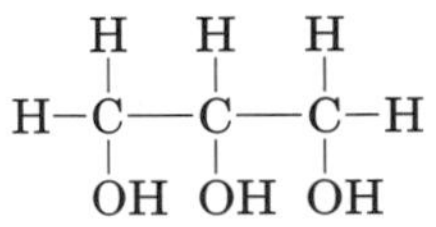

H H H
H–C—C—C–H
OH OH OH

1 List what you know

- Analyze the structural formula to determine the numbers of each atom.

$$\begin{gathered}3 \text{ atoms of carbon}\\ 3 \text{ atoms of oxygen}\\ 8 \text{ atoms of hydrogen}\end{gathered}$$

Thus, the formula of glycerol can be written as $C_3H_8O_3$.

- molar mass of $C_3H_8O_3$ = ? g/mol

2 **Set up the problem**

Determine the molar masses for all atoms involved.

▶ molar mass of carbon = 12.01 g/mol
▶ molar mass of oxygen = 16.00 g/mol
▶ molar mass of hydrogen = 1.01 g/mol

3 **Calculate and verify**

▶ Multiply each mass by the correct number of moles for each atom. Add the masses to determine the molar mass of $C_3H_8O_3$.

$$
\begin{array}{r}
\text{mass of 3 mol C} = 36.03 \text{ g/mol} \\
\text{mass of 8 mol H} = \;\;8.08 \text{ g/mol} \\
\text{mass of 3 mol O} = 48.00 \text{ g/mol} \\
\hline
\text{molar mass of } C_3H_8O_3 = 92.11 \text{ g/mol}
\end{array}
$$

▶ The answer has the correct units. The sum of the molar masses can be approximated as 40 + 10 + 50 = 100, which is very near the calculated value.

PRACTICE PROBLEMS

1. Calculate the molar mass of each of the following compounds:

a. $KClO_3$

b. $Ca(H_2PO_4)_2$

c. $KMnO_4$

d. $CH_3CH_2CH_2CH_2CH_3$

e.

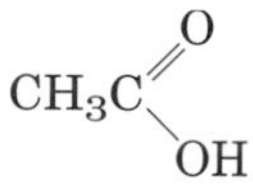

CH_3C with =O and OH
Acetic acid

f.

$H-C-C-C-C-OH$ with H's
(four carbons, H H H H above and H H H H below)

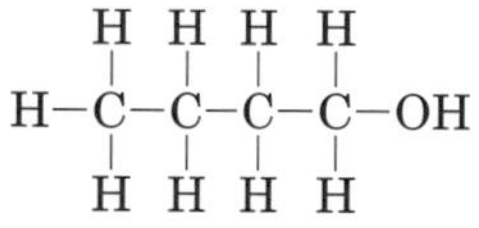

g.

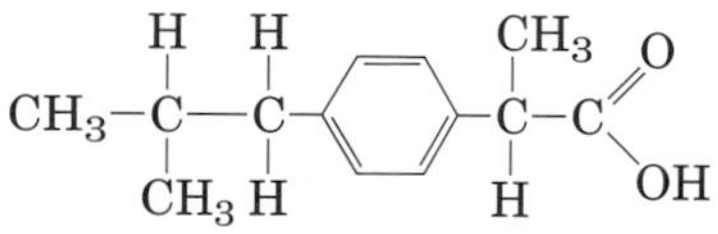

Ibuprofen

h. $Mg(OH)_2$

i. $(NH_4)_2PO_4$

j.

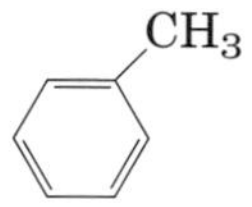

CH_3
Toluene

k.

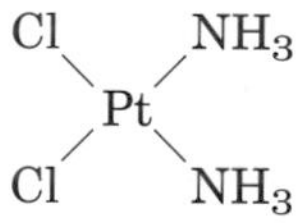

Cl   NH$_3$
  Pt
Cl   NH$_3$
Cisplatin

2. Write the formula and then calculate the molar mass of each of the following compounds:

a. sodium hydrogen carbonate

b. potassium dichromate

c. magnesium perchlorate

d. aluminum sulfate

e. iron(III) hydroxide

f. tin(II) chloride

g. perchloric acid

h. nickel(II) chloride hexahydrate

Fe$_2$O$_3$ FeO

FIGURE 8-8 ▲

Iron forms two different compounds with oxygen. The ratios of atoms in the formulas differ, so the two compounds have different percentage compositions.

Using analytical data

Some chemists carry out chemical reactions called *syntheses* (singular: *synthesis*) to produce new compounds for many different uses. Chemists must be able to determine the identities of the substances they have synthesized. One procedure that chemists use to identify an unknown substance is *elemental analysis*. This technique tells chemists what elements are present in the compound and their percent by mass. The information gained from this analysis is the **percentage composition** of the substance. For example, a compound that is 88.7% oxygen and 11.3% hydrogen has a percentage composition that matches that of water, H$_2$O. A compound that is 60.7% chlorine and 39.3% sodium has a percentage composition that matches that of sodium chloride, NaCl. These data along with further tests are used to identify an unknown compound. **Figure 8-8** shows a percentage composition comparison for two iron oxide compounds.

percentage composition

the percentage by mass of each element in a compound

Empirical formulas can be determined from elemental analysis data

Percentage composition data allow you to calculate the *simplest* ratio among the elements of a compound. A formula that represents this simplest ratio is called an **empirical formula.** For example, ammonium nitrite has the true formula NH$_4$NO$_2$ and consists of ammonium, NH$_4^+$, and nitrite, NO$_2^-$, ions in a 1:1 ratio. Using data from an elemental analysis, a chemist would calculate the empirical formula to be NH$_2$O because this formula represents the *simplest* ratio of elements.

For many compounds, the empirical formula and the true formula are the same. To calculate an empirical formula from the percentage composition, convert the mass percent of each element to grams and then to moles. Then, as is done in Sample Problem 8I, compare the amounts to find the simplest whole-number ratio among the elements in the compound. The method is to divide each amount by the smallest of all the amounts. This process will give a coefficient of 1 for the atoms present in the smallest amount. After this step, additional multiplication may be necessary to convert all the coefficients to the smallest whole numbers. These numbers are the subscripts in the empirical formula.

empirical formula

a formula that represents the simplest ratio among the elements of a compound

One of the substances in a new alkaline battery is composed of 63.0% manganese and 37.0% oxygen by mass. Determine the empirical formula of the compound in the battery.

1 List what you know

- percentage Mn = 63.0%
- percentage O = 37.0%
- empirical formula = $Mn_?O_?$

2 Set up the problem

- Convert the given percentages to grams by assuming that you have exactly 100 g of the unknown substance.

$$63.0\% \text{ Mn} \times 100 \text{ g} = 63.0 \text{ g Mn}$$
$$37.0\% \text{ O} \times 100 \text{ g} = 37.0 \text{ g O}$$

- To convert the mass of each element into amount in moles, determine the molar masses of Mn and O from the periodic table.

$$\text{molar mass Mn} = 54.94 \text{ g/mol}$$
$$\text{molar mass O} = 16.00 \text{ g/mol}$$

3 Calculate

- Calculate the amounts of Mn and O in moles. Round your answers to the correct number of significant figures.

$$63.0 \text{ g Mn} \times \frac{1 \text{ mol Mn}}{54.94 \text{ g Mn}} = 1.146705497 \text{ mol Mn (calculator answer)}$$

$$= 1.15 \text{ mol Mn}$$

$$37.0 \text{ g O} \times \frac{1 \text{ mol O}}{16.00 \text{ g O}} = 2.3125 \text{ in mol O (calculator answer)}$$

$$= 2.31 \text{ mol O}$$

- To determine the simplest ratio of moles in the compound, divide the amount of each element by the smallest amount. The smallest amount in this case is 1.15.

$$\frac{1.15 \text{ mol Mn}}{1.15} = 1.00 \text{ mol Mn}$$

$$\frac{2.31 \text{ mol O}}{1.15} = 2.01 \text{ mol O}$$

- Slight deviations from exact whole numbers should be expected because you are working with analytical data.

$$\text{mol ratio} = \frac{1.00 \text{ mol Mn}}{2.01 \text{ mol O}} = \frac{1 \text{ mol Mn}}{2 \text{ mol O}}$$

- Write the empirical formula of the compound by using the smallest whole number ratio of manganese to oxygen.

$$MnO_2$$

Chemical analysis of a clear liquid shows that it is 60.0% C, 13.4% H, and 26.6% O. Calculate the empirical formula of this substance.

1 List what you know

▸ percentage C = 60.0%   ▸ percentage O = 26.6%
▸ percentage H = 13.4%   ▸ empirical formula = $C_?H_?O_?$

2 Set up the problem

▸ Assume that you have a 100.0 g sample of the liquid, and convert the percentages to grams.

$$60.0\% \text{ C} \times 100.0 \text{ g} = 60.0 \text{ g C}$$
$$13.4\% \text{ H} \times 100.0 \text{ g} = 13.4 \text{ g H}$$
$$26.6\% \text{ O} \times 100.0 \text{ g} = 26.6 \text{ g O}$$

▸ To convert the mass of each element into amount in moles, determine the molar masses of C, H, and O from the periodic table.

molar mass of C: 12.01 g/mol
molar mass of H: 1.01 g/mol
molar mass of O: 16.00 g/mol

3 Calculate and verify

▸ Calculate the amounts of C, H, and O in moles. Round your answers to the correct number of significant figures.

$$60.0 \text{ g C} \times \frac{1 \text{ mol C}}{12.00 \text{ g C}} = 5.00 \text{ mol C}$$

$$13.4 \text{ g H} \times \frac{1 \text{ mol H}}{1.01 \text{ g H}} = 13.3 \text{ mol H}$$

$$26.6 \text{ g O} \times \frac{1 \text{ mol O}}{16.00 \text{ g O}} = 1.66 \text{ mol O}$$

▸ At this point you could write the formula as $C_5H_{13.3}O_{1.66}$, but you know that subscripts in chemical formulas are always whole numbers.
▸ The empirical formula is the simplest whole-number ratio of the atoms. To find the simplest ratio, divide the amount of each element by the amount of the least-abundant element, in this case 1.66.

$$\frac{1.66 \text{ mol O}}{1.66} = 1.00 \text{ mol O}$$

$$\frac{5.00 \text{ mol C}}{1.66} = 3.012048193 \text{ mol C} = 3.01 \text{ mol C}$$

$$\frac{13.3 \text{ mol H}}{1.66} = 8.012048193 \text{ mol H} = 8.01 \text{ mol H}$$

▸ The calculation shows that the ratio of atoms in the compound is 3C : 8H : 1O. Therefore, the empirical formula for the clear liquid is C_3H_8O. To verify, use the empirical formula and relative molar masses to calculate the percent composition of this compound. The results should be very near the values given in the problem.

1. A dead alkaline battery is found to contain a compound of manganese and oxygen. Its percentage composition is 70.0% Mn and 30.0% O. What is the empirical formula of this substance?

2. What is the empirical formula for a compound that contains 38.77% Cl and 61.23% O?

Molecular formulas are multiples of empirical formulas

For some compounds, the empirical formula is the same as the molecular formula. Such is the case with water, H_2O, and nitric acid, HNO_3. But for most compounds, the **molecular formula** is a whole-number multiple of the empirical formula.

Consider the three molecular compounds in **Table 8-3.** The first compound, formaldehyde, is toxic and can cause cancer. The second, acetic acid, gives vinegar its sour taste. The third, glucose, is a type of sugar found in sports drinks and other foods.

Molecular formulas are calculated using the empirical formulas and molar mass data. The empirical formula is a multiple of the molecular formula as shown by the following relationship.

$$n(\text{empirical formula}) = \text{molecular formula}$$

Note that n is always a whole number, and it is occasionally a very large number. With formaldehyde, $n = 1$; for acetic acid, $n = 2$; and for glucose, $n = 6$. Likewise, the true molar mass of the compound must be a whole-number multiple of the molar mass of the empirical formula.

molecular formula

type and actual number of atoms in a compound

TABLE 8-3 **Comparing Empirical and Molecular Formulas**

Compound	Empirical formula	Molecular formula	Molar mass (g)	Space-filling model
Formaldehyde	CH_2O	CH_2O (same as empirical formula)	30.03	
Acetic acid	CH_2O	$C_2H_4O_2$ ($2 \times$ empirical formula)	60.06	
Glucose	CH_2O	$C_6H_{12}O_6$ ($6 \times$ empirical formula)	180.18	

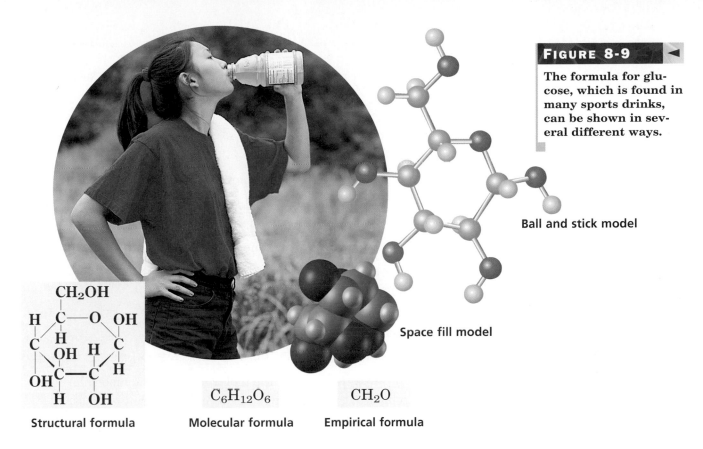

FIGURE 8-9 ◄

The formula for glucose, which is found in many sports drinks, can be shown in several different ways.

Ball and stick model

Space fill model

$C_6H_{12}O_6$

Molecular formula

CH_2O

Empirical formula

Structural formula

Different representations for the formula of glucose are shown in **Figure 8-9.** It has the same empirical formula, CH_2O, but a different molecular formula than the other compounds listed in Table 8-3. Because their structures and molecular formulas are entirely different, these compounds have quite different chemical and physical properties.

If you know both the empirical formula and the molar mass of a compound, you can determine its molecular formula. Fortunately, there are experimental methods for determining molar mass, even though the formula of the compound is not known.

SAMPLE PROBLEM 8K

Determining a molecular formula from an empirical formula

The empirical formula of a compound is found to be P_2O_5. The molar mass of the compound is 284 g/mol. Determine the molecular formula of the compound.

1 List what you know

▶ empirical formula = P_2O_5
▶ molar mass = 284 g/mol
▶ molecular formula = ?

2 Set up the problem

▶ Look up the molar masses of the elements on the periodic table. You will need these values to determine the molar mass of the empirical formula.

molar mass of P = 30.97 g P

molar mass of O = 16.00 g O

3 **Calculate**

▶ Calculate the molar mass of a compound with the empirical formula P_2O_5.

$$
\begin{aligned}
\text{mass of 2 mol P} &= \ \ 61.94 \text{ g/mol} \\
\text{mass of 5 mol O} &= \ \ 80.00 \text{ g/mol} \\
\hline
\text{molar mass of } P_2O_5 &= 141.94 \text{ g/mol}
\end{aligned}
$$

▶ Solve for n, the factor relating the empirical and molecular formulas.

$$
n = \frac{\text{molar mass of compound}}{\text{molar mass of empirical formula}}
$$

▶ Substitute the molar masses into the equation above, and solve for n.

$$
n = \frac{\text{molar mass of compound}}{\text{molar mass of empirical formula}} = \frac{284 \text{ g/mol}}{141.94 \text{ g/mol}} = 2.001 \cong 2
$$

▶ Once the value of n has been calculated, multiply the empirical formula by that value to get the molecular formula.

$$
n \text{ (empirical formula)} = 2(P_2O_5) = P_4O_{10}
$$

▶ To verify your answer, calculate the molar mass for the molecular formula, and compare it with the given experimental formula mass.

PRACTICE PROBLEMS

1. Determine the molecular formula of a compound having an empirical formula of CH and an experimental molar mass of 78 g/mol.

2. The empirical formula of the anticancer drug altretamine is $C_3H_6N_2$. A chemist experimentally determines its molar mass to be 214. What is the molecular formula for this drug?

Percentage composition can be calculated from a chemical formula

If you want to know the percentage composition of a compound, calculate the composition from the chemical formula of the compound. Remember that the percentage of a component part is found using the following equation.

$$
\% = \frac{\text{mass of component}}{\text{mass of whole}} \times 100
$$

Look back at the iron examples in Figure 8-8. The percentages shown were calculated as follows.

$$
\begin{aligned}
\text{mass of 2 mol Fe atoms} &= 2 \text{ mol} \times 55.85 \text{ g/mol} = 111.7 \text{ g} \\
\text{mass of 3 mol O atoms} &= 3 \text{ mol} \times 16.00 \text{ g/mol} = \ \ 48.00 \text{ g} \\
\hline
\text{total mass of } Fe_2O_3 &= 159.7 \text{ g}
\end{aligned}
$$

$$
\% \text{ Fe} = \frac{111.7 \text{ g Fe}}{159.7 \text{ g } Fe_2O_3} \times 100 = 69.9\%
$$

$$
\% \text{ O} = \frac{48.00 \text{ g O}}{159.7 \text{ g } Fe_2O_3} \times 100 = 30.1\%
$$

Sample Problem 8L shows this process for another compound.

Calculate the percentage composition of copper(I) sulfide, a copper ore called chalcocite.

1 List what you know

▶ the name of the compound and its formula: copper(I) sulfide, Cu_2S

▶ percentage composition = ?% Cu, ?% S

2 Set up the problem

▶ To determine the molar mass of Cu_2S, find the molar mass of each element on the periodic table.

$$\text{molar mass of Cu} = 63.55 \text{ g/mol}$$
$$\text{molar mass of S} = 32.07 \text{ g/mol}$$

▶ Determine the molar mass of the compound Cu_2S.

$$\text{mass of 2 mol Cu} = 2 \text{ mol Cu} \times 63.55 \text{ g/mol Cu} = 127.10 \text{ g}$$
$$\underline{\text{mass of 1 mol S} = \quad 32.07 \text{ g}}$$
$$\text{molar mass of } Cu_2S = 159.17 \text{ g/mol}$$

▶ To find the fraction that each element contributes to the molar mass, divide the total mass of that element by the total mass of the compound. Change to percent by multiplying by 100.

$$\text{mass \% Cu} = \frac{\text{mass of 2 mol Cu}}{\text{molar mass of } Cu_2S} \times 100$$

$$\text{mass \% S} = \frac{\text{mass of 1 mol S}}{\text{molar mass of } Cu_2S} \times 100$$

3 Calculate and verify

▶ Substitute the masses into the equations shown above. Round the calculator result to the correct number of significant figures.

$$\text{mass \% Cu} = \frac{127.10 \text{ g Cu}}{159.17 \text{ g } Cu_2S} \times 100 = 79.8517308\% \text{ (calculator answer)}$$
$$= 79.852\%$$

$$\text{mass \% S} = \frac{32.07 \text{ g S}}{159.17 \text{ g } Cu_2S} \times 100 = 20.14826915\% \text{ (calculator answer)}$$
$$= 20.15\%$$

▶ Verify by adding the percentages. They should total 100.00% ± 0.02%.

$$79.852\% + 20.15\% = 100.00\%$$

▶ The answers are correct. Percentage composition values of more-complex compounds sometimes do not add to exactly 100.00% because of rounding errors.

PRACTICE PROBLEMS

1. Calculate the percentage composition of glucose, $C_6H_{12}O_6$.

2. Calculate the percentage composition of sucrose, $C_{12}H_{22}O_{11}$.

Determine the percentage of water by mass in sodium carbonate decahydrate, $Na_2CO_3 \cdot 10H_2O$.

1   **List what you know**

▶ hydrate formula = $Na_2CO_3 \cdot 10H_2O$
▶ percentage water = ?% H_2O

2   **Set up the problem**

▶ Start by determining the molar mass of Na_2CO_3 alone. Obtain the molar masses of the elements from the periodic table.

$$
\begin{aligned}
2 \text{ mol Na} &= 2 \times 22.99 \text{ g/mol} = &45.98 \text{ g Na} \\
1 \text{ mol C} &= &12.01 \text{ g C} \\
3 \text{ mol O} &= 3 \times 16.00 \text{ g/mol} = &48.00 \text{ g O} \\
\hline
\text{molar mass of } Na_2CO_3 &= &105.99 \text{ g/mol}
\end{aligned}
$$

▶ Determine the mass of 10 mol H_2O.

$$
\begin{aligned}
20 \text{ mol H} &= 20 \times 1.01 \text{ g/mol} = &20.2 \text{ g H} \\
10 \text{ mol O} &= 10 \times 16.00 \text{ g/mol} = &160.0 \text{ g O} \\
\hline
\text{mass of 10 mol } H_2O &= &180.2 \text{ g}
\end{aligned}
$$

▶ Determine the molar mass of $Na_2CO_3 \cdot 10H_2O$.

$$
\begin{aligned}
1 \text{ mol } Na_2CO_3 &= 105.99 \text{ g} \\
10 \text{ mol } H_2O &= 180.2 \text{ g} \\
\hline
\text{molar mass } Na_2CO_3 \cdot 10H_2O &= 286.2 \text{ g/mol}
\end{aligned}
$$

▶ Write the equation for the percentage of water in $Na_2CO_3 \cdot 10H_2O$.

$$
\text{mass \% } H_2O = \frac{\text{mass of 10 mol } H_2O}{\text{molar mass of } Na_2CO_3 \cdot 10H_2O} \times 100
$$

3   **Calculate and verify**

▶ Substitute your values, and calculate the answer.

$$
\begin{aligned}
\text{mass \% } H_2O &= \frac{180.2 \text{ g } H_2O}{286.2 \text{ g } Na_2CO_3 \cdot 10H_2O} \times 100 \\
&= 62.9629629\% \text{ (calculator answer)} \\
&= 62.96\% \ H_2O
\end{aligned}
$$

▶ The calculation can be approximated as $200/300 \times 100 = 66.7$, which is near the answer obtained.

SECTION REVIEW

Total recall

1. What is a formula unit?

2. Explain how an empirical formula differs from a molecular formula.

3. In addition to the empirical formula, what other information is needed to determine the molecular formula of a compound?

Critical thinking

4. Write the empirical formula for each of the following:
   a. $C_6H_8O_6$
   b. S_2O_4
   c. $C_2H_5O_2N$
   d. $(CH_2)_2(OH)_2$
   e. $CH_3(CH_2)_2COOH$

5. Why does a laboratory analysis not yield exact whole numbers when you are determining the empirical formula of a compound from its percentage composition?

6. Identify the ions that make up one formula unit of each of the following:
   a. $MgCO_3$
   b. ammonium sulfite
   c. chromium(III) nitrate

Practice problems

7. Calculate the molar mass of each of the following:
   a. calcium acetate
   b. iron(II) phosphate
   c. $C_7H_5NO_3S$, saccharin, an artificial sweetener
   d. $C_9H_8O_4$, acetylsalicylic acid
   e. 2,2-dimethylbutane

8. Calculate the empirical formula for each of the following compounds, whose percentage compositions are given.
   a. 87.42% N, 12.58% H
   b. 13.2% B, 86.8% Cl
   c. 14.6% C, 39.0% O, 46.3% F

   d. 21.56% Zn, 36.23% Mn, 42.21% O
   e. 58.77% C, 13.81% H, and 27.42% N

9. Determine the molecular formula for each of the following:
   a. a compound with the empirical formula CHO and a molar mass of 116.1 g/mol
   b. a compound with the empirical formula BCl_2 and a molar mass of 163 g/mol
   c. a compound with the empirical formula $NPCl_2$ and a molar mass of 347.66 g/mol

10. Calculate the percentage composition of each of the following compounds:
    a. $SrBr_2$
    b. $CaSO_4$
    c. $Mg(CN)_2$
    d. $Pb(CH_3COO)_2$

11. Determine the formula and then calculate the molar mass of each of the following compounds:
    a. strontium sulfide
    b. ammonium fluoride
    c. zinc acetate
    d. mercury(II) bromate

12. Determine the percentage composition of each of the following compounds:
    a. lead(II) chlorate
    b. dinitrogen pentoxide
    c. $Fe_2(SO_4)_3$
    d. $CuSO_4 \cdot 5H_2O$
    e. COOH

13. Anhydrous $CaCl_2$ is used as a drying agent because it forms hydrates such as $CaCl_2 \cdot 6H_2O$. How many grams of $CaCl_2$ would it take to absorb 33.5 g of water if all of the $CaCl_2$ were converted to $CaCl_2 \cdot 6H_2O$?

Silicon and semiconductors

14
Si
Silicon
28.0855
$[Ne]3s^23p^2$

Silicon's most familiar use is in the production of microprocessor chips.

WHERE IS IT?

Earth's Crust
27.72% by mass

internetconnect

SCILINKS
NSTA
TOPIC: Silicon
GO TO: www.scilinks.org
KEYWORD: HW083

Computer microprocessor chips are made from thin slices, or wafers, of a pure silicon crystal. The wafers are doped with elements such as boron, phosphorus, and arsenic in order to confer semiconducting properties on the silicon. A photographic process places patterns for several chips onto one wafer. Gaseous compounds of metals are allowed to diffuse into the open spots in the pattern, and then the pattern is removed. This process is repeated several times to build up complex microdevices on the surface of the wafer. When the wafer is finished and tested, it is cut into individual chips.

Industrial Uses

▶ Silicon and its compounds are used to add strength to alloys of aluminum, magnesium, copper, and other metals.

▶ When doped with elements of Group 13 or Group 15, silicon becomes a semiconductor. This property is important in the manufacture of computer chips and photovoltaic cells.

▶ Silicon dioxide (quartz) crystals are used for piezoelectric crystals for radio-frequency control oscillators and digital watches and clocks.

▶ Organic compounds containing silicon, carbon, chlorine, and hydrogen are used to make silicone polymers, which are used in water repellents, electrical insulation, hydraulic fluids, lubricants, and caulks.

A large number of integrated circuit chips can be produced on the same silicon wafer. The wafer will be cut up into individual chips.

A BRIEF HISTORY

1811: Joseph Louis Gay-Lussac and Louis Thenard prepare impure amorphous silicon from silicon tetrafluoride.

1854: Henri S. C. Deville prepares crystalline silicon.

1958: Jack Kilby and Robert Noyce produce the first integrated circuit on a silicon chip.

1800

1900

1824: Jöns Jacob Berzelius prepares pure amorphous silicon and is credited with the discovery of the element.

1904: F. S. Kipping produces the first silicone compound.

1943: Commercial production of silicone rubber, oils, and greases begins in the United States.

Some events or objects designated in the *Guinness Book of World Records* are the largest and the smallest. You have learned in this chapter that chemists work with large numbers of very small things. They have learned that it is possible to "count" atoms by using the mass of a substance. The relationship between mass and the number of atoms is based on Avogadro's constant. Now that you have completed the chapter, you should be able to answer questions about numbers of atoms.

LOOKING BACK

How can chemists count atoms by using a balance?

Chemists have created the periodic table which lists the average atomic masses of all elements. One interpretation of the atomic mass is that it is the mass in grams of one mole of the element, consisting of 6.022×10^{23} atoms. Therefore, the number of atoms in a sample of a substance is given by

$$\text{number of atoms} = \frac{(\text{mass of sample, in g})(6.022 \times 10^{23}/\text{mol})}{(\text{atomic mass, in g/mol})}$$

How many astatine atoms exist in Earth's crust?

The molar mass of astatine is 210 g/mol, but only 0.16 g is present in Earth's crust, which is $0.16/210$ mol $= 0.000\,76$ mol. The relationship above, therefore, gives the number of astatine atoms on Earth as

$$\frac{(0.16\ \text{g})(6.022 \times 10^{23}\ \text{At atoms/mol})}{210\ \text{g/mol}} =$$
$$4.6 \times 10^{20}\ \text{At atoms}$$

This value is the same as 460 billion billion.

If you traveled to the farthest galaxy, how many atoms of carbon would you have to drop per kilometer to use up all of the atoms in the largest diamond?

The mass of the largest diamond is 621.2 g and because the diamond is pure carbon, the number of carbon atoms it contains is

$$\frac{621.2\ \text{g C}}{12.01\ \text{g/mol C}} \times \frac{6.022 \times 10^{23}\ \text{C atoms}}{\text{mol}}$$
$$= 3.115 \times 10^{25}\ \text{C atoms}$$

The farthest galaxy is 1.24×10^{23} km away, so for every kilometer you travel, you have to drop the following.

$$\frac{3.115 \times 10^{25}\ \text{C atoms}}{1.24 \times 10^{23}\ \text{km}} = 251\ \text{atoms/km}$$

$\mathscr{H}$IGHLIGHTS

KEY TERMS

8-1
molar mass

8-2
empirical formula
formula unit
molecular formula
percentage composition

KEY CONCEPTS

8-1 How are atoms counted and measured?

▶ Amounts of substances are measured in moles. Amount is the quantity; mole is the unit used to express that quantity.

▶ Avogadro's constant 6.022×10^{23}/mol, expresses a number of things—atoms, molecules, ions, particles, formula units, etc.—in one mole.

▶ Conversions made between the amount in moles and the number of atoms require the use of Avogadro's constant.

▶ The average atomic mass of an element is the weighted average of the masses of the element's isotopes.

▶ Conversions made between moles and mass in grams require the use of molar mass.

8-2 How is the mole concept related to chemical formulas?

▶ An empirical formula shows the elements and the ratio of atoms or ions that are present in a compound.

▶ The molar mass of a compound can be calculated from its chemical formula.

▶ If the percent composition of a compound is known, then its empirical formula can be determined; if its molecular or empirical formula is known, then its percentage composition can be calculated.

▶ The molecular formula of a compound can be determined from its empirical formula and molar mass.

▶ The molar mass of a hydrate includes the mass of the water of hydration.

KEY SKILLS

Review the following models before your exam. Be sure you can solve these types of problems.

Sample Problem 8A: Converting amount in moles to number of atoms (p. 277)

Sample Problem 8B: Converting number of atoms to amount in moles (p. 277)

Sample Problem 8C: Calculating average atomic mass (p. 279)

Sample Problem 8D: Converting amount in moles to mass (p. 281)

Sample Problem 8E: Converting mass to amount in moles (p. 281)

Sample Problem 8F: Finding the mass of an atom (p. 282)

Sample Problem 8G: Calculating molar mass (p. 287)

Sample Problem 8H: Calculating molar mass of compounds (p. 287)

Sample Problem 8I: Determining an empirical formula from composition data (p. 290)

Sample Problem 8J: Calculating empirical formulas from percentage composition (p. 291)

Sample Problem 8K: Determining a molecular formula from an empirical formula (p. 293)

Sample Problem 8L: Using a chemical formula to determine percentage composition (p. 295)

Sample Problem 8M: Determining the percentage composition of hydrates (p. 296)

REVIEW & ASSESS

TERM REVIEW

1. A formula expressing the simplest ratio of cations to anions in an ionic compound is known as a(n) ——.
(empirical formula, formula unit)

2. The number of particles in 1 mol of a substance is known as ——.
(Avogadro's constant, molar mass)

3. —— is the mass in grams of 1 mol of a substance. (Average atomic mass, Molar mass)

4. The simplest ratio among the elements represents the compound's ——.
(empirical formula, percentage composition)

5. —— represents the number of atoms in exactly 12 g of carbon-12.
(One mole, Avogadro's constant)

CONCEPT & SKILLS REVIEW

RELATING MOLES TO NUMBER OF ATOMS

1. Relate the mole to two other counting units.

2. How would you determine the number of atoms in 2 mol of gallium?

3. How is Avogadro's constant related to moles?

4. Why are moles used to represent the number of atoms in a sample of a given substance?

Practice Problems

5. How many atoms of oxygen enter your lungs when you inhale 5.00×10^{-2} mol of oxygen atoms? (Hint: See Sample Problem 8A.)

6. How many atoms are in the 6.75×10^{-2} mol of mercury within the bulb of a thermometer? (Hint: See Sample Problem 8A.)

7. Assume that you have 2.59 mol of aluminum foil. How many atoms of aluminum do you have? (Hint: See Sample Problem 8A.)

8. How many moles of gold are in 1.00 L of sea water if there are 1.50×10^{17} atoms in the sample? (Hint: See Sample Problem 8B.)

9. How many moles are in a copper penny containing 1.80×10^{21} atoms? (Hint: See Sample Problem 8B.)

AVERAGE ATOMIC MASS

10. How is the carbon-12 atom used to define atomic mass units?

11. Why is the atomic mass of nitrogen 14.0067 and not 14.?

12. If you examine a periodic table, you will see that several elements have atomic masses very close to whole numbers. What is the likely cause?

Practice Problems

13. The lithium found in a hearing-aid battery has two naturally occurring isotopes. Lithium-6 has a mass of 6.015121 amu and an abundance of 7.42%. Lithium-7 has a mass of 7.016003 amu and an abundance of 92.58%. Calculate the average atomic mass of lithium. (Hint: See Sample Problem 8C.)

14. Silver found in most jewelry has two naturally occurring isotopes. Silver-107 has a mass of 106.905092 amu and an abundance of 51.35%. Silver-109 has a mass of 108.904757 amu and an abundance of 48.65%. Calculate the average atomic mass of silver. (Hint: See Sample Problem 8C.)

RELATING AMOUNT TO MASS

15. How are moles related to atomic mass?

16. How is molar mass related to average atomic mass?

17. Describe how you would determine the number of moles present in a given mass of a known substance.

18. A neon sign contains 4.50×10^{-2} mol of neon. How many grams of Ne gas are in this sign? **(Hint: See Sample Problem 8D.)**

19. How many grams are in the 2.00 mol of phosphorus used to coat your television screen? **(Hint: See Sample Problem 8D.)**

20. How many grams are present in 7.2 mol of table salt, NaCl? **(Hint: See Sample Problem 8D.)**

21. A cup of hot chocolate contains 35.0 mg of sodium. How many moles of sodium are in the hot chocolate? **(Hint: See Sample Problem 8E.)**

22. One cup of whole milk contains 290. mg of calcium. How many moles of calcium are in the milk? **(Hint: See Sample Problem 8E.)**

23. An aspirin tablet contains 325 mg of acetylsalicylic acid, $C_9H_8O_4$. How many moles of acetylsalicylic acid are in each tablet? **(Hint: See Sample Problem 8E.)**

24. Calculate the mass of the following atoms by using Avogadro's constant and the atomic masses from the periodic table.
a. Au
b. Ag
c. Hg
d. argon
e. astatine
f. aluminum
(Hint: See Sample Problem 8F.)

25. What is the molar mass of barium carbonate? **(Hint: see Sample Problem 8G.)**

26. Calculate the molar mass of TNT. The chemical formula for TNT is $C_6H_2CH_3(NO_2)_3$. **(Hint: See Sample Problem 8G.)**

27. Calculate the molar masses of each of the following organic molecules. **(Hint: See Sample Problem 8H.)**

a.
Alanine

b.
Pentanoic acid

c.
2-ethyl-3-methyl-1-butene

d.
Cyclopropane

DERIVING FORMULAS FROM PERCENTAGE COMPOSITION

28. When purifying metals from mined ores, why is it important to know the percentage composition of the ore?

29. During winter vacation, you work at a ski resort covering icy sidewalks with a substance containing 26.2% N, 7.5% H, and 66.3% Cl. What is the formula for this compound? **(Hint: See Sample Problem 8I.)**

30. Magnetite is an iron ore with natural magnetic properties. It contains 72.4% Fe and 27.6% O. What is the formula for magnetite? **(Hint: See Sample Problem 8I.)**

31. Phosphorus forms two oxides. One has 56.34% P and 43.66% O. The other has 43.64% P and 56.36% O. What are the empirical formulas for these compounds? **(Hint: See Sample Problem 8I.)**

32. A 175.0 g sample of the flavor enhancer monosodium glutamate, MSG, contains 56.15 g C, 9.43 g H, 74.81 g O, 13.11 g N, and 21.49 g Na. What is its empirical formula? **(Hint: See Sample Problem 8I.)**

33. Vanillin is a common flavoring agent used in foods. This compound consists of 63.15% C, 5.30% H, and 31.55% O. Its molar mass is 152 g/mol. Determine both its empirical formula and its molecular formula. **(Hint: See Sample Problem 8J.)**

34. Acetylene is a colorless gas used as a fuel in welding torches. Its empirical formula is CH, and its molar mass is 26.04 g/mol. What is its molecular formula? **(Hint: See Sample Problem 8K.)**

35. *Para*-dichlorobenzene is an ingredient in mothballs that has a molar mass of 147.00 g/mol and an empirical formula of C_3ClH_2. What is its molecular formula? **(Hint: See Sample Problem 8K.)**

EMPIRICAL AND MOLECULAR FORMULAS

36. What does an empirical formula represent?

37. Write both the empirical formula and the molecular formula for ascorbic acid, commonly known as vitamin C. A molecule of ascorbic acid contains six carbon atoms, eight hydrogen atoms, and six oxygen atoms.

38. The full name for the active ingredient in a bleaching compound used on hair is dihydrogen dioxide. What is the molecular formula for this compound? What is its empirical formula?

39. Determine the molecular formula for each of the following:
   a. a compound with the empirical formula CoC_4O_4 and a molar mass of 341.94 g/mol
   b. a compound with the percent composition 74.03% C, 8.70% H, and 17.27% N, and a molar mass of 162 g/mol

Practice Problems

40. Oleic acid has the following composition: 76.54% C, 12.13% H, 11.33% O. If the experimental molar mass is 282 g/mol, what is the molecular formula of oleic acid?

DETERMINING PERCENTAGE COMPOSITION

41. What information can be determined about a compound from its percentage composition?

42. What information is needed to calculate the percentage composition of a compound?

Practice Problems

43. What is the percentage composition of ammonium nitrate, NH_4NO_3, a common fertilizer? **(Hint: See Sample Problem 8L.)**

44. Tin(IV) oxide, SnO_2, is the ingredient that gives fingernail polish its characteristic luster. What is the percentage composition of SnO_2? **(Hint: See Sample Problem 8L.)**

45. Some antacids use compounds of calcium, a mineral that is often lacking in the diet. What is the percentage composition of calcium carbonate, a common antacid ingredient? **(Hint: See Sample Problem 8L.)**

46. A superconductor has the formula $YBa_2Cu_3O_7$. What is the percentage composition of the substance? **(Hint: See Sample Problem 8L.)**

47. Which iron ore has more pure iron per kilogram of ore, Fe_2O_3 or Fe_3O_4? **(Hint: See Sample Problem 8L.)**

48. What percentage of ammonium carbonate, $(NH_4)_2CO_3$, an ingredient in smelling salts, is the ammonium ion, NH_4^+? **(Hint: See Sample Problem 8L.)**

49. Which yields a higher percentage of pure aluminum per gram, aluminum phosphate or aluminum chloride? **(Hint: See Sample Problem 8L.)**

WATER OF HYDRATION

50. How does the formula mass of a hydrate differ from that of the anhydrous form of the same compound?

Practice Problems

51. What percentage of $CoCl_2 \cdot 6H_2O$, which is used as a humidity indicator, is $CoCl_2$? **(Hint: See Sample Problem 8M.)**

52. What percentage of the paint pigment blue-violet hydrated chromium(III) sulfate, $Cr_2(SO_4)_3 \cdot 18H_2O$, is $Cr_2(SO_4)_3$? **(Hint: See Sample Problem 8M.)**

53. Soil in several regions has a reddish tinge due to the presence of iron in the form of limonite, $Fe_2O_3 \cdot \frac{3}{2}H_2O$. What percentage of limonite is water? **(Hint: See Sample Problem 8M.)**

54. Which substance, anhydrous cobalt(II) chloride, $CoCl_2$, or anhydrous magnesium chloride, $MgCl_2$, will absorb the most water per gram if both form a hexahydrate with 6 mol of water per mole of salt?

55. Aluminum chlorohydrate is an ingredient used in some antiperspirants. In its anhydrous form, it has 30.93% Al, 45.86% O, 20.32% Cl, and 2.89% H.

a. What is the empirical formula for aluminum chlorohydrate?

b. Aluminum chlorohydrate forms a hydrated compound with 2.00 mol H_2O/1.00 mol compound. What is the percentage composition of the hydrate?

LINKING CHAPTERS

1. Isotopes
Table 3-3, on page 90, lists the stable isotopes of lead and their atomic masses. Calculate the average atomic mass for lead.

2. Theme: Classification and trends
Mendeleev organized his periodic table by arranging the elements according to their atomic masses. This resulted in some elements being misplaced. For example, locate the elements K and Ar on a periodic table. If these two elements were arranged according to their atomic masses, what impact would this have?

3. Chemical bonds
Describe the bond types that are present in a hydrated salt, such as $Na_2CO_3 \cdot 10H_2O$.

4. Atomic theory
Explain how empirical and molecular formulas support the law of multiple proportions.

ALTERNATIVE ASSESSMENTS

Performance assessment

1. Your teacher will give you a note card with one of the following formulas on it:

$NaCH_3COO \cdot 3H_2O$
$MgCl_2 \cdot 6H_2O$
$MgSO_4 \cdot 7H_2O$
$LiC_2H_3O_2 \cdot 2H_2O$

Design an experiment to determine the percentage of water by mass in the hydrated salt described by the formula. Be sure to explain

what steps you will take to ensure that the salt is completely dry. If your teacher approves your design, obtain the salt. What percentage of water does it contain?

2. Using a hydrated salt, design an experimental procedure that supports the law of conservation of mass. If your teacher approves your design, carry out the experiment.

Portfolio projects

1. Research and communication
Research some methods chemists initially used to arrive at Avogadro's constant. Then compare these methods with modern methods.

2. Chemistry and you
Sulfuric acid has a great affinity for water. Because of this property, sulfuric acid is used as a drying, or dehydrating, agent in the manufacture of a number of consumer products. Search the Internet for information on the use of sulfuric acid as a dehydrating agent. Present your findings to the class.

3.

SCiLINKS.	TOPIC: Mass spectrometry
NSTA	GO TO: www.scilinks.org
	KEYWORD: HW084

Research and communication
The most accurate method for determining the mass of an element involves the use of a device known as a mass spectrometer. This instrument is also used to determine the isotopic composition of a natural element. Check the library and the Internet for information on how a mass spectrometer operates. Draw a model that illustrates its operation, and present the model to the class.

1. Which of the following molar masses should be used in a problem with hydrated copper(II) sulfate pentahydrate, $CuSO_4 \cdot 5H_2O$?
   a. 159.62 g/mol
   c. 249.72 g/mol
   b. 177.64 g/mol
   d. 339.82 g/mol

2. One mole of NaCl contains 6.022×10^{23} ____.
   a. atoms
   c. formula units
   b. molecules
   d. ions

3. The molecular formula for acetylene is C_2H_2; the molecular formula for benzene is C_6H_6. The empirical formula for both these compounds is ____.
   a. CH
   c. C_6H_6
   b. C_2H_2
   d. $(CH)_2$

4. If the empirical formula of a compound is known, then ____.
   a. its true formula is also known
   b. its percentage composition can be calculated
   c. the arrangements of its atoms is also known
   d. the percentage water in the compound can be determined

5. To calculate the average atomic mass of an element, which of the following must be known?
   a. the atomic number and the atomic mass of each isotope
   b. the atomic mass and the symbol of each isotope
   c. the number of atoms present in each isotope
   d. the atomic mass and relative abundance of each isotope

6. The units for molar mass are ____.
   a. g/mol
   c. g/atoms
   b. atoms/mol
   d. mol/g

7. Which of the following compounds has the highest percentage composition of oxygen?
   a. CH_4O
   c. H_2O
   b. CO_2
   d. Na_2CO_3

8. The molar mass of a compound is calculated by ____.
   a. adding the number of atoms present in the compound
   b. adding the atomic masses of all the atoms in the compound and expressing that value in grams
   c. multiplying Avogadro's constant times the number of atoms present in the compound
   d. dividing the number of grams of the sample by Avogadro's constant

9. The formula for a compound that consists of 1.2% H, 42.0% Cl, and 56.8% O is ____.
   a. HClO
   c. $HClO_3$
   b. $HClO_2$
   d. $HClO_4$

10. The percentage composition of H_2SO_4 is ____.
    a. 2.5% H, 39.1% S, 58.5% O
    b. 2.1% H, 32.7% S, 65.2% O
    c. 28.6% H, 14.3% S, 57.1% O
    d. 33.3% H, 16.7% S, 50% O

11. To calculate the mass of an atom, which of the following must be known?
    a. the atomic mass and the symbol of each isotope
    b. the atomic number of the symbol of each isotope
    c. the molar mass and Avogadro's constant
    d. the atomic mass and the number of isotopes for the element

12. To calculate the amount of a compound in moles, which of the following must be known?
    a. the atomic mass and the symbol of each isotope
    b. the mass of the compound and its molar mass
    c. the atomic mass and Avogadro's constant
    d. the formula and Avogadro's constant

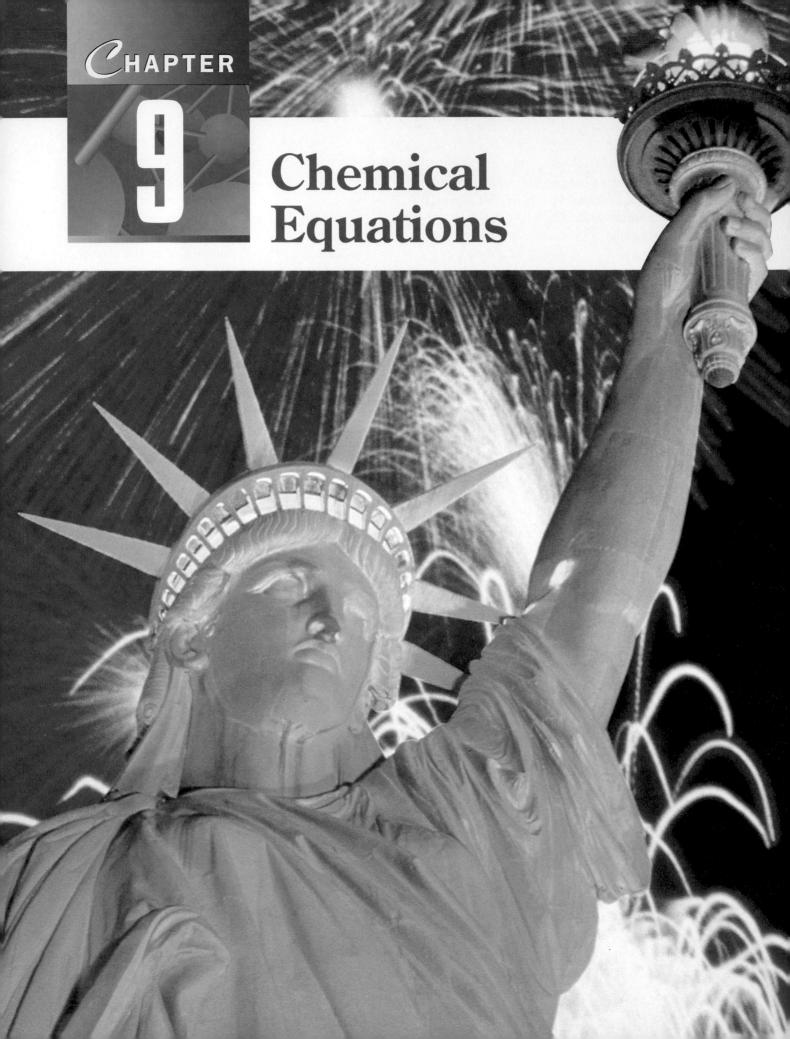

CHAPTER 9

Chemical Equations

REACTIVITY AND THE STATUE OF LIBERTY

One day in 1985, several people climbed inside the Statue of Liberty even though it was closed to visitors. A man scoured the inside of the statue with white powder. What was he doing? Why?

The man was part of a team working with the National Park Service on an $85 million project to restore the 100-year-old statue which had become damaged by corrosion.

He sprayed sodium hydrogen carbonate, $NaHCO_3$, from a combination pressure sprayer/vacuum cleaner to remove a layer of tar from inside the statue. The tar had prevented salt water from leaking into the statue. Over time, the tar had deteriorated and the statue leaked.

A team of workers searched for something rough enough to remove the tar but gentle enough to avoid damaging the statue's thin copper coating. The team tried ground walnut shells, corncobs, glass beads, rice, and sugar. $NaHCO_3$ was chosen because it is a mildly corrosive substance that effectively removed tar without damaging the underlying copper layer. Forty tons of $NaHCO_3$ was used to scour all 300 sheets of copper in the statue.

The French sculptor Frederic Bartholdi chose copper for the statue's exterior because of the metal's softness and malleability, the same properties that make the statue difficult to clean. Copper sheets were shaped and hung on a framework of 1800 iron bars. Iron was used to build the statue's framework because it was the strongest and most flexible material available at a reasonable cost.

Copper and iron, like most other metals, can react to form ionic compounds. The copper shell reacted with moisture and oxygen in the air to produce several green compounds, including $CuCO_3 \cdot Cu(OH)_2$, $CuSO_4 \cdot 3Cu(OH)_2$, and $CuSO_4 \cdot 2Cu(OH)_2$. These compounds constitute the green coating, or *patina*, on the outside of the statue.

By 1985, the iron supports had also reacted with moisture and air to form rust, which consists of hydrated oxides, such as $Fe_2O_3 \cdot 3H_2O$. Some of the iron bars had rusted to half their original thickness.

In this chapter, you will study chemical reactions. This information will enable you to appreciate the solution to the corrosion of the Statue of Liberty.

CHAPTER LINKS

Why did the iron support beams corrode much more than the thin copper coating?

What types of chemical reactions had taken place?

How could corrosion be prevented in the future?

What is a chemical reaction?

▶ **List** evidence that suggests a chemical reaction might have occurred and evidence that proves a chemical reaction has occurred.

▶ **Describe** a chemical reaction using a word equation.

▶ **Describe** endothermic and exothermic reactions in terms of bond energies.

▶ **Relate** conservation of mass to the rearrangement of atoms in a chemical reaction.

▶ **Explain** how a nonspontaneous reaction can occur.

▶ **Explain** why reactants must be brought into contact for a reaction to occur.

Chemical change

You see chemical changes taking place all the time—in iron that rusts, in leaves that change color, in milk that sours, and in a car engine that converts gasoline and air into energy and exhaust fumes. Chemical changes also happen inside you. Both digestion and respiration involve chemical changes.

A *chemical reaction* describes a change in composition—the process by which one or more substances are changed into one or more different substances. Recall from Chapter 1 that in any chemical reaction the original substances, which can be elements or compounds, are known as *reactants*. The substances created are called *products*. One chemical reaction that you probably see quite often is shown in **Figure 9-1.**

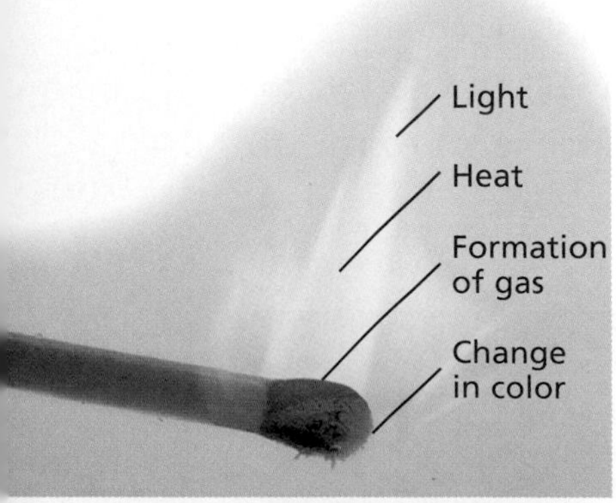

Evidence of a chemical change

To understand what is involved in a chemical reaction, consider the safety match. When a match is struck against the matchbook cover, several observations can be made. Heat and light are released as a flame, and the match head changes color. In addition, a puff of smoke rises from the match and a hissing sound is heard.

How do you know what has happened to the match? It appears to have undergone a chemical change because the materials left after it has burned appear very different from those present at the beginning.

Observations that suggest a chemical reaction is taking place are the evolution of energy as heat, light, or sound; the production of a gas; the formation of a precipitate; or a change in color.

Though this kind of evidence suggests that a chemical change has taken place, it is not conclusive. For real proof, you need to analyze the

Light

Heat

Formation of gas

Change in color

FIGURE 9-1

Chemical changes occur as a match burns.

FIGURE 9-2 ◀

When two solutions are mixed, a color change and the formation of a solid precipitate are indications that a chemical reaction has probably occurred.

products and demonstrate that at least one new substance is present. **Figure 9-2** shows another example of noticeable changes that indicate a chemical reaction may have occurred—the formation of a precipitate.

Sometimes changes occur that appear to be chemical but are not. If analysis of the product reveals that it has the same chemical composition and molecular structure as the reactant, then the process is classified as a *physical change* rather than a *chemical reaction*. Condensation, melting, and crystallization are physical changes that at first glance can appear to be chemical reactions.

Reactions involve rearrangements of atoms

In chemical reactions, reactants are converted into products. The law of conservation of mass states that mass cannot be created or destroyed. This means that *the products of a reaction are made up of the same number and kinds of atoms as were present in the reactants*. A chemical reaction is the following process.

internetconnect
SCILINKS
NSTA
TOPIC: Chemical reactions
GO TO: www.scilinks.org
KEYWORD: HW091

$$\text{Set of atoms in a particular arrangement} \rightarrow \text{Same set of atoms in a different arrangement}$$

In chemical reactions, atoms do not become other kinds of atoms, nor do they appear or disappear. *The bonding patterns among the atoms are merely rearranged.* Sometimes few atoms are involved, but even when thousands of atoms are involved in a reaction, there are always the same number and kinds of atoms after the reaction as there were before the reaction.

CONCEPT CHECK

1. List four observations that signify a chemical change.
2. Describe what happens to atoms during a chemical reaction.
3. What *proves* that a chemical reaction has taken place?

Chemical reactions release or absorb energy

Why are heat, light, and sound considered strong indicators that a chemical change has occurred? Each is evidence that energy has been liberated. Most chemical reactions occurring at mild temperatures release energy in some form. For example, when iron reacts with oxygen to produce 1 mol of iron(III) oxide, 824.8 kJ of energy is released, usually as heat. This exothermic reaction is represented by the word equation shown below.

iron + oxygen $\longrightarrow$ 1 mol of iron(III) oxide + 824.8 kJ

Unlike exothermic reactions, endothermic reactions rarely occur at room temperature. Only mildly endothermic reactions occur spontaneously at room temperature because the energy needed can be continuously supplied by the surroundings. One that does occur is the decomposition of dinitrogen pentoxide to nitrogen dioxide and oxygen gas.

1 mol of dinitrogen pentoxide + 52.3 kJ $\longrightarrow$

dinitrogen tetroxide + oxygen gas

When a reaction is said to occur naturally, it is implied that the process happens unaided. At times something, such as a spark, is required to initiate a reaction, but once the reaction is in progress it continues to generate products *as long as reactants are supplied*. The scientific term for a process like this is *spontaneous reaction*. A forest fire is an example of a spontaneous exothermic reaction, whereas the decomposition reaction above is an example of a spontaneous endothermic reaction.

A nonspontaneous reaction can occur when it is linked to an energy source

Hydrogen and oxygen react to produce water in a spontaneous exothermic reaction. In the electrolysis experiment illustrated in **Figure 9-3,** the reverse reaction occurs.

water + 572 kJ $\longrightarrow$ hydrogen + 1 mol oxygen

At mild temperatures the breakdown of water will never occur spontaneously. Energy must be supplied to drive the endothermic reaction. In the experiment, a battery supplies this energy in the form of an electric current.

Exothermic reactions yield stronger bonds

In Chapter 1, you read that the energy changes in a chemical reaction involve breaking and forming bonds. For exothermic reactions, such as the synthesis of water from hydrogen and oxygen, energy is released because the bonds holding the products together are *stronger* than those in the reactants. The stronger a bond is, the

▼ **FIGURE 9-3**

Breaking down water by electrolysis requires an input of energy because the reaction is endothermic.

more energy released when the bond forms. The energy released is then available to break additional bonds in the reactants, driving the reaction toward more product formation.

Particles must collide for a chemical reaction to occur

When a safety match is lit, one reactant, potassium chlorate, $KClO_3$, is on the match head, and the other reactant, phosphorus, P_4, is on the matchbook's striking surface. The reaction begins when the two substances are brought together by striking the match head across the striking surface, as shown in **Figure 9-4.**

When reactants are brought together, collisions occur between the reactant particles. If these collisions happen with enough energy, the bonds in the reactants are broken, allowing new bonds to form. If the collisions are too gentle, the particles may bounce off one another unchanged. In the match example, friction from sliding the match across the striking surface produces the energy needed to induce the forceful collisions that start the reaction. Increasing the temperature of a system can also provide the energy needed to induce forceful collisions.

FIGURE 9-4

The chemical reactants for igniting safety matches are $KClO_3$, on the match head, and P_4, on the striking surface.

SECTION REVIEW

Total recall

1. What is a chemical reaction?

2. What is the only way to prove that a chemical reaction has occurred?

3. In an exothermic reaction, are the bonds in the products stronger or weaker than the bonds in the reactants?

4. In an exothermic reaction, are the bonds in the products higher or lower in energy than those in the reactants?

Critical thinking

5. At what point will a spontaneous reaction stop?

6. What drives the decomposition of water in an electrolysis experiment?

7. What is the role of collisions in chemical reactions?

8. Decide whether the reactions that occur in each of the following situations are exothermic or endothermic. Explain your choice.
   a. the burning of gasoline in a car's engine
   b. fireworks exploding in the sky

9. When an orange compound is heated, it reacts by giving off nitrogen gas, green crystals of chromium(III) oxide, and water vapor. What elements were contained in the original compound?

10. In item 9, was the change chemical or physical? How do you know?

11. **Story Clue** What evidence indicated that chemical reactions had taken place inside the Statue of Liberty?

How are chemical equations for reactions written?

OBJECTIVES

▶ **Translate** word equations into formula equations.

▶ **Relate** conservation of mass to a balanced equation.

▶ **Write** a balanced chemical equation for a reaction.

▶ **Distinguish** between coefficients in a chemical equation and subscripts in a chemical formula.

Constructing a chemical equation

You know that symbols represent elements and formulas represent compounds. In the same way, equations are used to represent chemical reactions. A correctly written **chemical equation** describes the type and number of atoms that are rearranged during a reaction.

chemical equation

an expression showing the formulas and the relative amounts of the reactants and products in a chemical reaction

A word equation describes a reaction

In Section 9-4 you will learn about five types of chemical reactions. One of these is called combustion, and it occurs when oxygen reacts with another substance. **Figure 9-5** shows ethanol reacting with oxygen in a combustion reaction. Water and carbon dioxide are produced. This chemical reaction can be represented by a *word equation.*

$$\text{ethanol} + \text{oxygen} \longrightarrow \text{carbon dioxide} + \text{water}$$

In word equations, the arrow means "react to form" and the plus sign means "and."

▼ **FIGURE 9-5**

The combustion of ethanol is part of a cooking process known as flambé.

A word equation translates into a formula equation

The formulas for ethanol, oxygen gas, carbon dioxide, and water can replace the words in the word equation to make a *formula equation.* The word *ethanol* carries no quantitative meaning, but the formula CH_3CH_2OH does—it means one molecule of ethanol. The word *ethanol* can be replaced by CH_3CH_2OH. Question marks are used in the equation below to signify that the number of ethanol molecules is not yet known. The other three words in the word equation are also replaced by the corresponding formula preceded by a question mark. This gives the following *unbalanced formula equation.*

$$?CH_3CH_2OH + ?O_2 \longrightarrow ?CO_2 + ?H_2O$$

TABLE 9-1   Testing an Equation for Balance

	Reactants	Products	Balance?
Unbalanced formula equation	$CH_3CH_2OH + O_2$	$CO_2 + H_2O$	
Carbon atoms	2	1	no
Hydrogen atoms	6	2	no
Oxygen atoms	3	3	yes

Balancing requires patience

The number of atoms of each element is conserved during a chemical reaction. A correctly written chemical equation reflects this observation. To satisfy the law of conservation of mass, you should insert **coefficients** into a chemical equation. This process is referred to as *balancing* an equation. *There are equal numbers of atoms for each element on each side of the equation when an equation is balanced.* The procedure shown in **Table 9-1** can be used to test whether an equation is balanced or not. Count the atoms of each element on both sides of the equation.

There are two carbon atoms in the reactant column and only one in the product column of Table 9-1. How can the carbon atoms be balanced? To balance the number of carbon atoms, you need to double the number of carbon dioxide molecules in the products.

$$CH_3CH_2OH + ?O_2 \longrightarrow 2CO_2 + ?H_2O$$

The 2 is called a coefficient and indicates that there are two carbon dioxide molecules. Coefficients are normally integers. When a coefficient is equal to 1, the 1 is omitted for simplicity.

$$CH_3CH_2OH \; \textbf{\textit{not}} \; 1CH_3CH_2OH$$

Coefficients are written in front of a formula and multiply the entire formula. Now count the atoms of the trial equation, as in **Table 9-2.**

The carbon atoms now balance, but the hydrogen atoms do not. In addition, the oxygen atoms have been thrown out of balance. It is easiest

coefficient

numeral used in a chemical equation to indicate relative amounts of reactants or products

TABLE 9-2   Testing a Trial Equation

	Reactants	Products	Balance?
Trial equation	$CH_3CH_2OH + O_2$	$2CO_2 + H_2O$	
Carbon atoms	2	2	yes
Hydrogen atoms	6	2	no
Oxygen atoms	3	5	no

TABLE 9-3 **Second Trial Equation**

	Reactants	Products	Balance?
Trial equation	$CH_3CH_2OH + O_2$	$2CO_2 + 3H_2O$	
Carbon atoms	2	2	yes
Hydrogen atoms	6	6	yes
Oxygen atoms	3	7	no

to begin by balancing elements that occur in only one reactant and one product. Therefore, hydrogen should be balanced before oxygen.

There are six hydrogen atoms in the reactants and two in the products. An easy way to balance these atoms is to find the lowest common multiple of the numbers, which in this case is 6. To have six hydrogen atoms on each side of the equation, multiply the water molecule by 3. Test out the new equation, as in **Table 9-3.**

The oxygen atoms still are not balanced. Multiplying the number of oxygen molecules by three results in an equal number of oxygen atoms on both sides of the equation. Test it out as in **Table 9-4.**

TABLE 9-4 **Third Trial Equation**

	Reactants	Products	Balance?
Trial equation	$CH_3CH_2OH + 3O_2$	$2CO_2 + 3H_2O$	
Carbon atoms	2	2	yes
Hydrogen atoms	6	6	yes
Oxygen atoms	7	7	yes

There are equal numbers of carbon, hydrogen, and oxygen atoms on both sides of the equation; the equation is balanced. Replacing the question marks in the formula equation with the appropriate coefficients now gives the correct chemical equation.

$$CH_3CH_2OH + 3O_2 \longrightarrow 2CO_2 + 3H_2O$$

► **FIGURE 9-6**

When there are equal numbers of each type of atom on both sides of an equation, the equation is balanced.

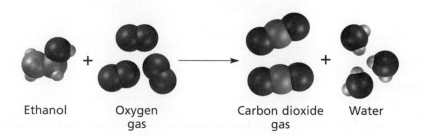

Ethanol   Oxygen gas   Carbon dioxide gas   Water

This balanced equation is represented by models in **Figure 9-6.** Count the number of atoms for each element on each side of the arrow. Are they equal?

Tips on balancing chemical equations are summarized in **Figure 9-7.**

Tips for Balancing Equations

1. Delay the balancing of elements (often hydrogen and oxygen) that occur in several reactants or products.

2. If the same polyatomic ions appear on both sides of the equation, treat them as single units, like monatomic ions.

3. After considering tips 1 and 2, balance the elements left to right.

4. Remember, balancing one element may unbalance others.

5. For ionic equations, be sure charges are balanced.

FIGURE 9-7 ◄

Use these tips to organize your approach to balancing equations.

SAMPLE PROBLEM 9A   **Balancing chemical equations**

The **first step in the commercial production of nitric acid is the combustion of ammonia in the presence of a catalyst. The exothermic reaction produces nitrogen monoxide and water vapor. Write and balance the equation for this reaction.**

1 **Write the word equation**

ammonia + oxygen $\longrightarrow$ nitrogen monoxide + water + heat

2 **Write the unbalanced formula equation**

$$?NH_3 + ?O_2 \longrightarrow ?NO + ?H_2O$$

3 **Count the number of atoms for each element**

	Reactants	Products	Balance?
Trial equation	$NH_3 + O_2$	$NO + H_2O$	
Nitrogen atoms	1	1	yes
Oxygen atoms	2	2	yes
Hydrogen atoms	3	2	no

Insert coefficients for atoms one element at a time

Note that hydrogen occurs in only one substance in the products and reactants, but it occurs in the reactants' side in odd numbers and on the products' side in even numbers. To get an even number on the reactants' side, use a trial coefficient of 2 in front of NH_3. Then balance the nitrogen and hydrogen on the products' side.

	Reactants	Products	Balance?
Trial equation	$2NH_3 + O_2$	$2NO + 3H_2O$	
Nitrogen atoms	2	2	yes
Oxygen atoms	2	5	no
Hydrogen atoms	6	6	yes

We now have the same odd-even problem with oxygen. There are an even number of oxygen atoms on the reactants' side and an odd number on the products' side. By doubling all coefficients, you will have an even number of oxygen atoms on both sides.

	Reactants	Products	Balance?
Trial equation	$4NH_3 + 2O_2$	$4NO + 6H_2O$	
Nitrogen atoms	4	4	yes
Oxygen atoms	4	10	no
Hydrogen atoms	12	12	yes

As a final step, change the coefficient for oxygen gas to 5 so that the oxygen atoms balance.

	Reactants	Products	Balance?
Trial equation	$4NH_3 + 5O_2$	$4NO + 6H_2O$	
Nitrogen atoms	4	4	yes
Oxygen atoms	10	10	yes
Hydrogen atoms	12	12	yes

5

Check to be sure that the number of atoms of each element is equal on both sides of the equation.

$$4NH_3 + 5O_2 \longrightarrow 4NO + 6H_2O$$

PRACTICE PROBLEMS

1. Balance the following equations:

   a. $? ZnS + ? O_2 \longrightarrow ? ZnO + ? SO_2$

   b. $? C_2H_2 + ? O_2 \longrightarrow ? CO_2 + ? H_2O$

   c. $CS_2 + O_2 \longrightarrow CO_2 + SO_2$

   d. $N_2O_5 + NO \longrightarrow NO_2$

Balancing ionic equations

In addition to mass and number of atoms, electric charge is conserved in a chemical reaction. Equal positive and negative charges are produced when a cat is stroked, generating static electricity. A similar reaction occurs when hydrogen chloride gas dissolves in water.

$$HCl + H_2O \longrightarrow Cl^- + H_3O^+$$

It is important to realize that while positive and negative charges are produced, the total charge on the reactant side must equal the total charge on the product side. In this example, the sum of electric charges on each side is zero. There is no charge on the left side of the equation, and on the right side 1+ plus 1− equals zero.

SECTION REVIEW

Total recall

1. Explain the differences between a word equation, an unbalanced formula equation, and a chemical equation.

2. When balancing an equation, should the coefficients or the subscripts be adjusted to balance the equation?

3. List the steps in balancing a chemical equation.

4. In an ionic equation, what must be balanced in addition to the number and type of atoms?

Critical thinking

5. Use diagrams of particles to explain why four atoms of silver can produce only two molecules of silver sulfide, even when there is an excess of sulfur atoms.

6. Indicate which of the numbers in the following equation are coefficients and which are subscripts.

$$3H_2SO_4 + 2Al \rightarrow Al_2(SO_4)_3 + 3H_2$$

Practice problems

7. Write the following reactions as word equations and then as formula equations.

   a. Hydrogen reacts with chlorine to produce hydrogen chloride.

   b. Aluminum and iron(III) oxide react to produce aluminum oxide and iron.

   c. Potassium chlorate decomposes to yield potassium chloride and oxygen.

   d. Calcium hydroxide and hydrochloric acid react to produce calcium chloride and water.

8. Balance all of the equations you wrote for item 7.

9. Balance the following equations.

   a. $CaSi_2 + SbCl_3 \longrightarrow Si + Sb + CaCl_2$
   b. $Al + CH_3OH \longrightarrow (CH_3O)_3Al + H_2$
   c. $P_4 + O_2 \longrightarrow P_2O_5$
   d. $Fe + O_2 \longrightarrow Fe_2O_3$

10. **Story Clue** Write balanced equations for the following reactions.

    a. Copper and oxygen form copper(II) oxide.

    b. Iron and oxygen form iron(II) oxide.

What does a chemical equation tell you?

OBJECTIVES

▶ **Describe** how the conditions for a chemical reaction can be specified in the chemical equation.

▶ **Include** information about the states of reactants and products in a chemical equation.

▶ **Interpret** a chemical equation in terms of the relative numbers of molecules involved.

▶ **Determine** whether a reaction is endothermic or exothermic using information from a chemical equation.

▶ **Derive** mole ratios from a balanced chemical equation.

▶ **Calculate** energy changes in reactions using mole ratios and ΔH values.

Equations and recipes

Equations describe a system that rearranges atoms and bonds to make new substances. Formulas are used to represent the products and reactants in a reaction. Equations can also contain much more information.

Figure 9-9 shows the ingredients in store-bought bread. This listing differs from a recipe. The ingredients list does not tell you that the bread needs to bake in the oven at a specific temperature. The order in which the ingredients should be mixed is not specified, and the amount of each ingredient is missing.

The recipe shown in Figure 9-9 contains the information needed to produce a loaf of bread and tells the number of loaves the recipe will yield. Like a recipe, many chemical equations contain more than just the identities of reactants and products.

▼ **FIGURE 9-9**

To make bread, you need a recipe. Like a recipe, a chemical equation can contain instructions and can show the conditions under which a reaction will occur.

Sandwich Bread

- 5 cups warm water
- 2 packages dry yeast
- 8 tablespoons sugar
- 6 cups flour
- 8 tablespoons shortening
- 8 teaspoons salt

In large bowl, combine 5 cups warm water with 2 packages dry yeast. When yeast is dissolved add sugar, flour, salt and shortening. Stir and blend with a spoon. Let rise until double in size. Spoon into large bread pans. Let rise again. Bake at 350° for 45 minutes or until golden brown. Cool on racks. Makes 4 large loaves.

MADE FROM: UNBROMATED UNBLEACHED ENRICHED WHEAT FLOUR (FLOUR, MALTED BARLEY FLOUR, NIACIN, REDUCED IRON, THIAMIN MONONITRATE (VITAMIN B1), RIBOFLAVIN (VITAMIN B2), FOLIC ACID), WATER, UNBROMATED STONE GROUND 100% WHOLE WHEAT FLOUR, YEAST, HIGH FRUCTOSE CORN SYRUP, NONFAT MILK*, WHEAT GLUTEN, SOY FIBER, WHOLE WHEAT FLAKES, SPENT WHEAT (WHEAT BRAN, WHEAT PROTEIN, MALTODEXTRIN), SALT, HONEY, UNSULPHURED MOLASSES, VEGETABLE MONO AND DIGLYCERIDES, POTATO FLOUR, DATEM (DOUGH CONDITIONER), CALCIUM PROPIONATE TO RETARD SPOILAGE, DEGERMINATED WHITE CORN FLOUR, GUAR GUM, SOY FLOUR, SOY LECITHIN, ENZYMES AND PARTIALLY HYDROGENATED VEGETABLE SHORTENING (SOYBEAN AND COTTONSEED OILS).
*ADDS A TRIVIAL AMOUNT OF CHOLESTEROL

TABLE 9-5 | Arrow Labels That Show Reaction Conditions

Symbol	Meaning
$\longrightarrow$	"produces" or "yields," indicating result of reaction
$\overset{\longrightarrow}{\longleftarrow}$	reaction in which products can reform into reactants; final result is a mixture of products and reactants
$\overset{\Delta}{\longrightarrow}$ or $\overset{heat}{\longrightarrow}$	reactants are heated; temperature is not specified
$\overset{0°C}{\longrightarrow}$	specific temperature at which reaction is carried out
$\overset{1.0 \times 10^8 \text{ kPa}}{\longrightarrow}$	pressure at which reaction is carried out
$\overset{Pd}{\longrightarrow}$	chemical formula of a catalyst, a substance added to speed up a reaction

Reaction conditions and physical states are shown in equations

Information about *the conditions under which a reaction occurs* is often found above or below the arrow. Examples of reaction conditions depicted in equations are shown in **Table 9-5.**

An equation can show the physical state of the reactants and products, as in **Table 9-6.** If an element or compound exists in more than one form but retains the same formula, the form is often indicated in parentheses. For example, C(*graph*) indicates carbon in the form of graphite, while C(*diamond*) indicates carbon in the form of diamond.

An example of the use of state symbols in an equation is the conversion of ethane to ethene and hydrogen.

$$C_2H_6(g) \xrightarrow[Cr_2O_3]{800 \text{ K}} C_2H_4(g) + H_2(g)$$

This equation tells you that the reaction proceeds at 800 K and in the presence of chromium(III) oxide, a catalyst. In addition, you are told that the reactant and products are in the gaseous state.

TABLE 9-6 | State Symbols

Symbol	Meaning
(*s*) or (*cr*)	solid or crystal
(*l*)	liquid
(*g*)	gas
(*aq*)	in aqueous solution (dissolved in water)
$\downarrow$	solid precipitate product
$\uparrow$	gaseous product

TABLE 9-7 Interpreting a Balanced Chemical Equation

Equation	$C_6H_{12}O_6$	+	$6O_2$	→	$6CO_2$	+	$6H_2O$
Moles	1		6	→	6		6
Molecules	$(6.02 \times 10^{23}) \times 1$		$(6.02 \times 10^{23}) \times 6$	→	$(6.02 \times 10^{23}) \times 6$		$(6.02 \times 10^{23}) \times 6$
Molar mass (g/mol)	180.18		32.00		44.01		18.02
Mass (g)	180.18		192.00	→	264.06		108.12
Total mass (g)		372.18		→		372.18	

Quantitative relationships

Equations reveal the number of formula units involved

Using coefficients from a balanced equation, you can predict how much of each reactant is needed to make a certain amount of product. Consider the equation for cellular respiration.

$$C_6H_{12}O_6(aq) + 6O_2(g) \longrightarrow 6CO_2(g) + 6H_2O(l) + \text{energy}$$

This equation can be read in terms of formula units or molecules as well as in terms of moles, as you can see in **Table 9-7.**

For this reaction, you know that mass is conserved and that atoms are conserved. But the total number of moles and molecules do not necessarily remain the same on both sides of an equation because molecules are created and destroyed as atoms are rearranged.

Balanced equations show proportions

What would happen if you had 3 moles of glucose instead of one? How many moles of CO_2 and H_2O would form? One mole of glucose would require 6 moles of O_2 molecules and would produce 6 moles of CO_2 molecules and 6 moles of H_2O molecules. Two moles of glucose would require 12 moles of O_2 molecules and would produce 12 moles of CO_2 molecules and 12 moles of H_2O molecules. The reaction of 3 moles of glucose molecules would require 18 moles of O_2 and would produce 18 moles each of CO_2 and H_2O.

Rather than counting all of the reactants and products or running the reaction one mole at a time, imagine that the entire equation has been multiplied by three. If an entire equation is multiplied by a number, it is basically the same equation, but proportionately larger. Notice that the mole ratio stays constant.

$$C_6H_{12}O_6 + 6O_2 \longrightarrow 6CO_2 + 6H_2O$$

1 mol	6 mol	6 mol	6 mol
3 mol	18 mol	18 mol	18 mol

Relative amounts in equations can be expressed in moles

The molar interpretation of the cellular respiration reaction, shown in Table 9-7, can be expressed as ratios of reactants and products.

$$1 \text{ mol } C_6H_{12}O_6 : 6 \text{ mol } O_2 : 6 \text{ mol } CO_2 : 6 \text{ mol } H_2O$$

For any pair of molecules or formula units, a *mole ratio* can be determined by comparing the coefficients from the balanced chemical equation. Mole ratios should be expressed as the lowest whole number ratios. For example, the mole ratio of glucose to carbon dioxide would be 1:6.

$$1 \text{ mol } C_6H_{12}O_6 : 6 \text{ mol } CO_2$$

Mole ratios can be used like conversion factors to compare amounts of substances. In this way, you can determine exactly how much of a reactant is needed for the reaction or how much of a product can be expected. For example, 3 mol of $C_6H_{12}O_6$ would create 18 mol of CO_2.

$$3 \text{ mol } C_6H_{12}O_6 \times \frac{6 \text{ mol } CO_2}{1 \text{ mol } C_6H_{12}O_6} = 18 \text{ mol } CO_2$$

CONCEPT CHECK

1. Calculate the number of moles of H_2O produced by 4 mol of O_2 in the cellular respiration reaction.
2. How many moles of glucose would it take to produce 24 moles of CO_2 in the cellular respiration reaction?
3. What quantities are represented by coefficients in a chemical equation?

Energy changes in equations

The decomposition reaction of ethane to produce ethene and hydrogen is an endothermic reaction, which means that energy is absorbed. The quantity of energy involved can be written as part of the equation for the reaction.

$$C_2H_6(g) + 137 \text{ kJ} \longrightarrow C_2H_4(g) + H_2(g)$$

This equation tells you that 137 kJ of energy is required to convert all the molecules in 1 mol of ethane to form 1 mol of ethene and 1 mol of hydrogen gas. Because energy must be added to ethane for the endothermic reaction to occur, the energy is written on the reactant side of the equation. Because energy is released in an exothermic reaction, like the one in **Figure 9-10,** it is considered a product and is written on the right side of the equation, as shown for the following reaction.

$$2Al(s) + 3Br_2(l) \longrightarrow 2AlBr_3(s) + 1055 \text{ kJ}$$

FIGURE 9-10 ▲

The reaction of aluminum and bromine is exothermic.

enthalpy

the total energy content of
a system

The amount of energy released or absorbed in a chemical reaction is often expressed as ΔH, where Δ stands for "change in," and H represents **enthalpy,** the total energy content of a system. In Chapter 11 you will study how ΔH values are determined. For now you need to know that in exothermic reactions, ΔH values are negative because energy is released when the stronger bonds of the products are created. In endothermic reactions, energy is added to the system and ΔH values are positive because the energy needed to break the bonds increases the total energy of the system. For the $AlBr_3$ exothermic reaction, $\Delta H = -1055$ kJ, and for the endothermic decomposition of ethane, $\Delta H = +137$ kJ.

Energy depends on the states of the reactants and products; the states must be specified, as the following examples demonstrate.

$$2H_2(g) + O_2(g) \longrightarrow 2H_2O(g) + 484 \text{ kJ}$$

$$2H_2(g) + O_2(g) \longrightarrow 2H_2O(l) + 572 \text{ kJ}$$

The second reaction, which shows product formation in the liquid state, is more exothermic because energy is released as water vapor condenses.

Consider the following reaction, which essentially represents what happens when iron rusts.

$$4Fe(s) + 3O_2(g) + 6H_2O(g) \longrightarrow 2(Fe_2O_3 \cdot 3H_2O)(s) + 1842 \text{ kJ}$$

Here 1842 kJ means that 1842 kilojoules are released when 4 mol of Fe and 3 mol of O_2 are converted into 2 mol of Fe_2O_3. If you want to know the amount of energy released *per mole of iron,* then divide the energy released in the reaction by 4, because the equation involves 4 mol of Fe.

$$\frac{1842 \text{ kJ}}{4 \text{ mol Fe}} = \frac{460 \text{ kJ}}{\text{mol Fe}}$$

internetconnect

SC*LINKS*

NSTA

TOPIC: Endothermic/Exothermic reactions
GO TO: www.scilinks.org
KEYWORD: HW092

▼ **FIGURE 9-11**

The energy potential contained in a 57 g (2.0 oz) candy bar is the same as the energy used during 24 minutes of basketball.

Getting a "feel" for energies

Perhaps you don't have much of an idea what a joule, kilojoule, or megajoule is. In Chapter 2, a joule was stated as the amount of energy needed to bring a cheeseburger to one's mouth. A joule is also roughly the energy expended in one beat of your heart. A kilojoule is the energy that a 45 kg (100 lb) person expends climbing a flight of stairs.

The energy that your body receives when you eat a 57 g (2.0 oz) candy bar, which is made mainly of sucrose, $C_{12}H_{22}O_{11}$, is the energy needed to sustain you in the activity shown in **Figure 9-11.** That energy can be calculated from the following chemical equation.

$$C_{12}H_{22}O_{11}(s) + 12O_2(g) \longrightarrow 12CO_2(g) + 11H_2O(l) + 5645 \text{ kJ}$$

The recommended energy intake is 9 MJ per day for an average 18-year-old female and 12 MJ per day for an average male. Because 1 food Calorie is equal to 4.184 J, the recommended energy intake in calories is approximately 2100 Cal for a female and 2800 Cal for a male.

Energy can be expressed as part of a mole ratio

Let's return to the reaction of glucose and oxygen to form carbon dioxide and water. How much energy does this reaction release? The ΔH value for this reaction is given along with the balanced equation.

$$C_6H_{12}O_6(aq) + 6O_2(g) \longrightarrow 6CO_2(g) + 6H_2O(l)$$

$$\Delta H = -2870 \text{ kJ/mol glucose}$$

Notice that this ΔH value is expressed in kilojoules per *mole of glucose*. This ΔH value is for the combustion of glucose. For every mole of glucose combusted, 2870 kJ of heat energy is released. This can be shown by the following ratios:

2870 kJ : 1 mol $C_6H_{12}O_6$: 6 mol O_2 : 6 mol CO_2 : 6 mol H_2O

Thus, you can calculate the energy released by the reaction that produces 24 mol of H_2O.

$$24 \text{ mol } H_2O \times \frac{2870 \text{ kJ}}{6 \text{ mol } H_2O} = 11\,500 \text{ kJ}$$

In a similar way, the energy produced or consumed for any amount of reactant or product can be calculated for any chemical reaction. All that is needed is the chemical equation for the reaction and the corresponding ΔH.

SAMPLE PROBLEM 9B   Calculating energy for a specific reaction

Calculate the energy liberated when 100. g of glucose undergoes cellular respiration.

1 List what you know

▸ Mass of $C_6H_{12}O_6$ = 100. g
▸ Energy liberated = ?

2 Set up the problem

Start with a balanced equation. The respiration equation follows:

$$C_6H_{12}O_6(aq) + 6O_2(g) \longrightarrow 6CO_2(g) + 6H_2O(l) + 2870 \text{ kJ}$$

To calculate the amount of reactant, you'll need to find the molar mass of $C_6H_{12}O_6$ by using the atomic masses from the periodic table.

$$6 \times 12.01 \text{ g/mol} = 72.06 \text{ g/mol}$$
$$12 \times 1.01 \text{ g/mol} = 12.12 \text{ g/mol}$$
$$\underline{6 \times 16.00 \text{ g/mol} = 96.00 \text{ g/mol}}$$
$$= 180.18 \text{ g/mol}$$

To calculate the amount of glucose, divide the given mass of $C_6H_{12}O_6$ by the molar mass of $C_6H_{12}O_6$.

$$\text{Amount of } C_6H_{12}O_6 = \frac{100. \text{ g } C_6H_{12}O_6}{180.18 \text{ g/mol } C_6H_{12}O_6} = 0.555 \text{ mol } C_6H_{12}O_6$$

The respiration equation lists the energy output as 2870 kJ/mol. Because the coefficient of $C_6H_{12}O_6$ in the equation is 1, the value is 2870 kJ/mol of $C_6H_{12}O_6$.

For 0.555 mol:

$$\text{energy liberated} = 0.555 \text{ mol } C_6H_{12}O_6 \times \frac{2870 \text{ kJ}}{1 \text{ mol } C_6H_{12}O_6} = 1590 \text{ kJ}$$

100. g is a little more than half the mass of 1 mol of glucose, so the value 0.555 mol is reasonable. We expect the energy output to be a little more than half of 2870 kJ, which is close to 1590 kJ.

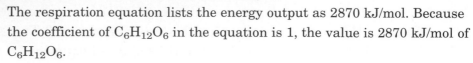

SECTION REVIEW

Total recall

1. What does the bread recipe tell you that the ingredients label on the bread package does not?

2. What symbols are used in a chemical equation to indicate the formation of a solid precipitate?

3. Given a chemical equation, how do you determine a mole ratio?

4. In a chemical equation describing an exothermic reaction, is the energy written to the right or to the left of the arrow?

Critical thinking

5. Which of the following equations represent exothermic reactions?
   a. $H_2(g) + Cl_2(g) \longrightarrow 2HCl(g) + 185 \text{ kJ}$
   b. $2Al_2O_3(s) + 3351.4 \text{ kJ} \longrightarrow$
   $$4Al(s) + 3O_2(g)$$
   c. $C(s) + H_2O(g) \longrightarrow CO(g) + H_2(g)$
   $\Delta H = +131.3 \text{ kJ}$
   d. $SnCl_2(s) + Cl_2(g) \longrightarrow SnCl_4(l)$
   $\Delta H = -186.2 \text{ kJ}$

6. Describe the states of the reactants and products in each of the following equations.
   a. $2KClO_3(s) \longrightarrow 2KCl(s) + 3O_2(g) + 78 \text{ kJ}$
   b. $CaCO_3(s) + 178 \text{ kJ} \longrightarrow CaO(s) + CO_2(g)$
   c. $NH_4NO_3(s) \longrightarrow$
   $$N_2O(g) + 2H_2O(g) + 36 \text{ kJ}$$
   d. $N_2(g) + 3H_2(g) \longrightarrow 2NH_3(g) + 92.0 \text{ kJ}$

7. Write the mole ratios for each of the reactions in item 6.

Practice problems

8. Using the mole ratios in item 7, determine the number of moles of each product could be formed given the following reactant amounts.
   a. reaction 6a with 16.0 mol $KClO_3$
   b. reaction 6b with 6.00 mol $CaCO_3$
   c. reaction 6c with 7.00 mol NH_4NO_3
   d. reaction 6d with 9.00 mol H_2 and an excess of N_2

9. For each of the equations in item 6 and amounts in item 8, calculate the energy for each reaction. Also indicate whether the reaction is exothermic or endothermic.

How are chemical reactions classified?

OBJECTIVES

▶ **Classify** a given reaction as a combustion, decomposition, double-displacement, displacement, or synthesis reaction.

▶ **Write** chemical equations representing each type of chemical reaction.

▶ **Use** the activity series to predict whether a given reaction will occur and what its products will be.

▶ **Write** total and net ionic equations for double-displacement reactions.

Reaction types

The number of different chemical reactions is astronomical. When many reactions are similar, it is convenient to give a name to that type of reaction. You should be acquainted with five general types of reactions. Not every reaction can be classified under one of these headings because some reactions fit into more than one category.

Oxygen combines with other elements in combustion

Many substances, including almost all organic compounds, will react with oxygen, often producing oxide compounds. These reactions are usually highly exothermic, releasing a large amount of energy as light, heat, or sound. Such reactions are known as **combustion** reactions. Like the pressure needed to create friction between a match and a matchbook, an initial "push" is often required to start combustion. **Figure 9-12** shows a familiar example of combustion—a Bunsen burner flame consuming natural gas (methane, CH_4) and oxygen and producing carbon dioxide and water vapor.

$$CH_4(g) + 2O_2(g) \longrightarrow CO_2(g) + 2H_2O(g) + 803 \text{ kJ}$$

combustion

a violently exothermic reaction, usually with oxygen, to form oxide(s)

Oxygen participates in oxidation reactions

Not all reactions with oxygen are as dramatic as combustion. One such reaction is called *oxidation*. The rusting of iron, which you read about earlier, is an oxidation reaction.

$$4Fe(s) + 3O_2(g) + 6H_2O(g) \longrightarrow 2(Fe_2O_3 \cdot 3H_2O)(s)$$

FIGURE 9-12 ◄

The complete combustion of any hydrocarbon, such as methane, yields only carbon dioxide and water. Incomplete combustion can yield carbon monoxide, CO.

Another example of an oxidation reaction is the souring of alcohol in wines by the formation of acetic acid.

$$C_2H_5OH(aq) + O_2(aq) \longrightarrow CH_3COOH(aq) + H_2O(l)$$

The word *oxidation* has a more general meaning that will be addressed in Chapter 17.

Compounds are made in synthesis reactions

synthesis

chemical reaction in which atoms or simple molecules combine to form a compound that is more complex

In **synthesis** reactions, complex molecules are made from simpler substances, as shown by the following example.

$$6CO_2(g) + 6H_2O(l) \longrightarrow C_6H_{12}O_6(aq) + 6O_2(g)$$

Plants can synthesize complex molecules, such as starch, caffeine, and chlorophyll, starting from the simple molecules CO_2 and H_2O and a few common ions. The reaction shown above is the synthesis of glucose from carbon dioxide and water.

Polymerization reactions are a form of synthesis

In *polymerization,* a series of synthesis reactions takes place to produce a very large molecule. Recall from Chapter 7 that the trick to making these big molecules is to take special small molecules called monomers and connect them to make a *polymer.* The simplest polymer is polyethylene, which is made by combining thousands of ethene molecules.

$$nC_2H_4(g) \longrightarrow (C_2H_4)_n(s)$$

The petrochemical industry manufactures large quantities of polyethylene ("polythene") and other related polymers. Some of these are itemized in **Figure 9-13.**

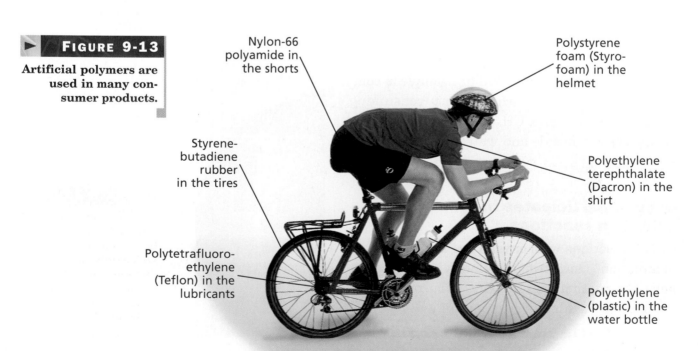

▶ **FIGURE 9-13**

Artificial polymers are used in many consumer products.

Nylon-66 polyamide in the shorts

Polystyrene foam (Styrofoam) in the helmet

Styrene-butadiene rubber in the tires

Polyethylene terephthalate (Dacron) in the shirt

Polytetrafluoroethylene (Teflon) in the lubricants

Polyethylene (plastic) in the water bottle

Compounds are broken down during decomposition

A reaction in which a compound is broken down into smaller substances is known as **decomposition.** The following reactions are decomposition reactions.

$$CH_3OH(g) \longrightarrow CO(g) + 2H_2(g)$$

$$Al_2(SO_4)_3(s) \longrightarrow Al_2O_3(s) + 3SO_3(g)$$

CONCEPT CHECK

1. Cite two examples of oxidation reactions.
2. Polymerization reactions are a subclass of what type of chemical reaction?
3. Contrast synthesis and decomposition reactions.

Displacement reactions
Elements trade places in displacement reactions

When a piece of aluminum foil is added to a solution of copper(II) chloride, reddish copper metal starts to form on the aluminum foil, and some of it falls to the bottom of the container. Aluminum is *displacing* copper in the solution to form copper metal.

$$2Al(s) + 3CuCl_2(aq) \longrightarrow 2AlCl_3(aq) + 3Cu(s)$$

One way to think of this reaction is as a **displacement reaction.** Before the reaction begins, aluminum atoms are in the elemental form, and copper(II) ions are in solution. After the reaction, the copper atoms are in elemental form and aluminum ions are with chloride ions in solution. In effect, the aluminum atoms and copper ions switch places.

The activity series ranks reactivity

Experiments involving displacement reactions have been summarized in the **activity series,** shown in **Table 9-8.** The activity series is a list of elements organized according to their tendency to react (their "activity"). The more readily an element reacts with other substances, the greater its activity.

The more-active elements tend to be more stable as cations in aqueous solution than in elemental form. If a more-active element, such as potassium, and a compound containing a less-active element, such as H_2O (which contains hydrogen), are brought together, the more-active element will replace the less-active element in the compound, as shown below.

$$2K(s) + 2HOH(l) \longrightarrow 2KOH(s) + H_2(g)$$

---

decomposition

chemical reaction in which a single compound is broken down to produce two or more simpler substances

displacement reaction

chemical reaction in which one element replaces another element in a compound that is in solution

activity series

arrangement of elements in the order of their tendency to react with water and acids

---

TABLE 9-8

Activity Series

Element	Reactivity
Li Rb K Ba Sr Ca Na	react with cold water and acids, replacing hydrogen; react with oxygen, forming oxides
Mg Al Mn Zn Cr Fe Cd	react with steam (but not cold water) and acids, replacing hydrogen; react with oxygen, forming oxides
Co Ni Sn Pb	do not react with water; react with acids, replacing hydrogen; react with oxygen, forming oxides
H₂ Sb Bi Cu Hg	react with oxygen, forming oxides
Ag Pt Au	fairly unreactive; form oxides only indirectly

In the activity series elements are arranged in order of activity, with the most active element at the top. *In general, an element can displace those below it from compounds in solution but not those above it.*

In addition to predicting displacement reactions, the activity series can help predict some synthesis and decomposition reactions. In general, compounds of active metals are readily synthesized, but such compounds do not easily decompose to re-form the metal. On the other hand, compounds of less active metals decompose readily but are difficult to make. For example, the synthesis of potassium compounds from their elements can be carried out more easily than the synthesis of compounds of nickel or tin.

Along with predicting whether a reaction will occur, the activity series provides indications of how easily and quickly the reaction will proceed. *In general, the farther apart two elements are on the activity series, the more likely it is that the higher one will quickly displace the lower one in compounds.*

internet**connect**

SCI**LINKS**
NSTA

TOPIC: Activity series
GO TO: www.scilinks.org
KEYWORD: HW094

SAMPLE PROBLEM 9C   Using the activity series to write equations

Write a balanced chemical equation for the reaction that will occur if the metals copper and zinc are placed in a solution containing copper (II) and zinc cations. $Cu(s)$, $Zn(s)$, $Cu^{2+}(aq)$, and $Zn^{2+}(aq)$ are present.

1 **Check the activity series for the more reactive metal**

Zinc is higher on Table 9-8 than copper. This means that zinc metal will form a zinc cation as the product, displacing the copper ion from the solution. So the zinc metal and copper(II) ion will be the reactants.

$$Zn(s) + Cu^{2+}(aq) \longrightarrow Cu(s) + Zn^{2+}(aq)$$

2 **Check other combinations of reactants for reactions**

The reaction of Cu with Cu^{2+} and the reaction of Zn with Zn^{2+} will not produce any new compounds. Furthermore, because Cu is lower than Zn on the activity series, it will not replace Zn ions. Thus, no other combination of reactants will result in a reaction.

PRACTICE PROBLEMS

1. Rank the following in order of increasing activity: aluminum, barium, copper, iron, and zinc.

2. Using Table 9-8, arrange the following reactions in order of decreasing tendency to occur. Indicate which would not occur at all. For those reactions that would occur, predict the products that would be formed.
    a. $Zn(s) + Cu^{2+}(aq) \longrightarrow$
    b. $Mg(s) + Pb^{2+}(aq) \longrightarrow$
    c. $Ni(s) + Al^{3+}(aq) \longrightarrow$
    d. $Cu(s) + Ag^{+}(aq) \longrightarrow$

In double-displacement reactions, atoms appear to be exchanged between compounds

The reaction shown in **Figure 9-14** is the product of two colorless solutions being mixed. Where they react, a bright yellow solid forms. A reaction commonly described as a **double-displacement reaction** is occurring. The colorless solutions were prepared by dissolving potassium iodide, KI, in water and dissolving lead(II) nitrate, $Pb(NO_3)_2$, in water. The product of the reaction that forms the yellow precipitate is the salt lead(II) iodide, PbI_2, which is an insoluble yellow ionic compound. The reaction that formed this precipitate resulted from the interaction of lead(II) cations and iodide anions.

$$Pb^{2+}(aq) + 2I^-(aq) \longrightarrow PbI_2(s)$$

Nitrate anions and the potassium cations play no role in the reaction and remain dissolved in the solution, so they are not shown in the equation above.

A century ago, it was not realized that when salts dissolve in water, their ions become completely separated. Chemists at the time wrote the equation for the reaction shown in Figure 9-14 as follows.

$$2KI(aq) + Pb(NO_3)_2(aq) \longrightarrow PbI_2(s) + 2KNO_3(aq)$$

When written this way, it looks like the two cations have changed partners and for that reason, such a precipitation reaction was called a double-displacement reaction. The products' side of the equation shows that lead(II) ions bond with iodide ions, and potassium ions bond with nitrate ions. The two cations have *displaced* each other in the reaction. But the formula $KNO_3(aq)$ really represents separated K^+ ions and NO_3^- ions that are dispersed throughout the solution. It is important to remember what the symbol (aq) means when it follows the formula for an ionic compound. Though it is no longer accepted that an equation written in this way best describes the reaction, the term double-displacement is still used.

Double-displacement reactions are more accurately written as net ionic equations

When ionic compounds such as KI and $Pb(NO_3)_2$ dissolve in water, the solutions are mixtures of ions and water molecules.

$$KI(aq) = K^+(aq) + I^-(aq)$$

$$Pb(NO_3)_2(aq) = Pb^{2+}(aq) + 2NO_3^-(aq)$$

The reaction is better represented by listing all of the ions in the reactants and products as a total ionic equation.

$$2K^+(aq) + 2I^-(aq) + Pb^{2+}(aq) + 2NO_3^-(aq) \longrightarrow PbI_2(s) + 2K^+(aq) + 2NO_3^-(aq)$$

double-displacement reaction

chemical reaction in which ions from two compounds interact in solution to form a product

FIGURE 9-14 ▲

The yellow cloud of lead(II) iodide precipitate is formed as a product of the double-displacement reaction.

When these four ions are mixed, two of them, Pb^{2+} and I^-, bond to form a solid, PbI_2. The other two ions, K^+ and NO_3^- appear on both sides of the total ionic equation. Because they remain unchanged in the reaction, they are called **spectator ions.** Double-displacement reactions are often written using **net ionic equations,** which only show the ions involved in the reaction. Spectator ions, such as K^+ and NO_3^-, are omitted from net ionic equations. That is why the ionic equation is written as the following net ionic equation.

$$2K^+(aq) + 2I^-(aq) + Pb^{2+}(aq) + 2NO_3^-(aq) \longrightarrow PbI_2(s) + 2K^+(aq) + 2NO_3^-(aq)$$

$$Pb^{2+}(aq) + 2I^-(aq) \longrightarrow PbI_2(s)$$

SECTION REVIEW

Total recall

1. What two compounds are generally produced when organic compounds burn?

2. Name three complex molecules synthesized by plants.

3. Explain how to use the activity series to predict chemical behavior.

4. What are the spectator ions in the reaction that precipitates PbI_2?

Critical thinking

5. Assume that a displacement reaction occurs between H_2O and the following metals, and write a balanced chemical equation for the reaction. Remember that H_2O can be written as HOH.
   a. Ba   **b.** Rb   **c.** Zn

6. Assume that a synthesis reaction occurs between $O_2(g)$ and the following metals, and write a balanced chemical equation for the reaction.
   a. Cu   **b.** Mn   **c.** Pb

7. Balance each of the following equations, and indicate the class of reaction each belongs in.

   a. $?Cl_2(g) + ?Br^-(aq) \longrightarrow ?Cl^-(aq) + ?Br_2(l)$
   b. $?CaO(s) + ?H_2O(l) \longrightarrow ?Ca(OH)_2(aq)$
   c. $?Ag^+(aq) + ?SO_4^{2-}(aq) \longrightarrow ?Ag_2SO_4(s)$
   d. $?Zn(s) + ?Cu^{2+}(aq) \longrightarrow ?Zn^{2+}(aq) + ?Cu(s)$

Practice problems

8. Write balanced chemical equations for the following reactions:
   a. synthesis of sulfuric acid, H_2SO_4, from water and sulfur trioxide
   b. combustion of butane, C_4H_{10}
   c. decomposition of potassium chlorate to form potassium chloride and oxygen
   d. displacement reaction for zinc and copper(II) sulfate in aqueous solution
   e. double-displacement reaction for silver nitrate and sodium chloride in aqueous solution

9. Predict whether a reaction would occur when the materials indicated are brought together. For each reaction that would occur, complete and balance the equation, omitting any spectator ions.
   a. $?Ni(s) + ?H_2O(l) \longrightarrow$
   b. $?Mg(s) + ?Cu(NO_3)_2(aq) \longrightarrow$
   c. $?Ba(s) + ?O_2(g) \longrightarrow$
   d. $?H_2SO_4(aq) + ?KOH(aq) \longrightarrow$

FIRE EXTINGUISHERS

internet**connect**

SCI LINKS
NSTA

TOPIC: Fire extinguishers
GO TO: www.scilinks.org
KEYWORD: HW095

A fire is a combustion reaction in progress. Three things are needed for a combustion reaction to occur: a fuel, an oxidizer, and an ignition source. If any one of these three is absent, combustion cannot occur. Hence, to fight a fire, the goal is to remove one or more of these parts. To prevent air from reaching the combustible material, a layer of some nonflammable substance, often a gas, can be applied. Because fires are accelerated by high temperatures, another tactic would be to cool the burning material to reduce the fire's severity.

Types of fires

Different types of fuels require different firefighting methods. Fire extinguishers display codes indicating which types of fires they can put out. Water is used on Class A fires involving solid fuels, such as wood. The water cools the fuel so that it does not react as readily. The steam that is produced helps to displace the air around the fire. A Class B fire, in which the fuel is a liquid or gas, is best put out by carbon dioxide, CO_2. Because carbon dioxide is more dense than air, it forms a layer underneath the air, cutting off the O_2 supply for the combustion reaction. While the CO_2 in the fire extinguisher is in the liquid state, it is delivered as a cloud in which grains of solid CO_2 are mixed with the cold gas.

Dry chemical extinguishers

Class C fires involving a "live" electric circuit can also be extinguished by CO_2. Liquid water cannot be used, or there will be a danger of electric shock. Some Class C fire extinguishers contain a dry chemical that smothers the fire by interrupting the chain reaction that is occurring. For example, a competing reaction may take place with the con-

tents of the fire extinguisher and the intermediates of the reaction. Class C fire extinguishers usually contain compounds such as ammonium dihydrogen phosphate, $NH_4H_2PO_4$, or sodium hydrogen carbonate, $NaHCO_3$.

Finally, Class D fires involve burning metals. These fires cannot be extinguished with CO_2 or water because these compounds may react with some hot metals. For these fires, nonreactive dry powders are used to cover the metal and keep it separate from oxygen. One kind of powder contains finely ground sodium chloride crystals mixed with a special polymer that allows the crystals to adhere to any surface, even a vertical one. Another is finely ground graphite powder, which not only cuts off the oxygen supply but also absorbs heat. Most fire extinguishers can be used with more than one type of fire. Check the fire extinguishers in your home and school to find out the kinds of fires they are designed to put out.

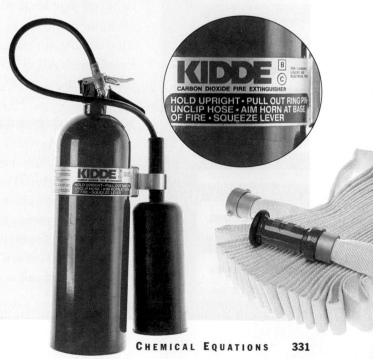

PROTEASE INHIBITORS: CONTROLLING REACTIONS

Viruses

HIV, or human immunodeficiency virus, is the virus that causes AIDS by severely weakening the human immune system. Since the discovery of HIV in 1983, scientists have searched for drugs that will combat the growth of the virus in human cells. Protease inhibitors are one of the newest classes of drugs to be developed in this fight.

Viruses are not living cells, but they are bits of genetic material (RNA or DNA) combined with protein molecules, including enzymes. Viruses enter (infect) cells and release their genetic material. The host cell uses this genetic material as a code to produce more viruses.

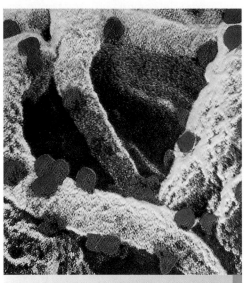

HIV are shown here as red spheres on T-cells.

HIV and the Immune System   HIV has a particular affinity for a type of white blood cell called a *helper T-cell.* Each of these helper T-cells is vital in regulating the activity of many other blood cells that destroy invading pathogens. This response to pathogens is called the immune response; it enables humans to fight off bacterial and viral diseases. Destruction of many T-cells weakens immune defenses so much that the body fails to ward off common infections. This condition results in active acquired immunodeficiency syndrome, or AIDS. People with AIDS usually die from infections that would cause little problem in people without AIDS.

HIV: A Retrovirus   The HIV virus is classified as a *retrovirus,* a virus that contains RNA, which it carries into the cell along with an enzyme called *reverse transcriptase.* You may recall from your biology class that a cell's master copy of its genetic material is DNA that remains in the nucleus. The HIV virus uses the reverse transcriptase enzyme to make a DNA copy of the RNA genetic pattern. The DNA segment enters the cell's nucleus, where it becomes a part of the cell's genetic code. There, it causes the cell to produce all of the parts needed to make new viruses. The new viruses are assembled and leave the host cell to infect new cells. The host cell is usually destroyed in the process.

Drugs for HIV Infection

Inhibiting Viral Reproduction   Most of the drugs that have been used to treat HIV infections are compounds that inhibit the reverse transcriptase enzyme, in turn preventing the RNA segment from forming a DNA copy. The new protease inhibitors do their work after the parts of the virus have been produced. The proteins that are needed to assemble new viruses are made in long chains that must be cut apart into the individual proteins. Protease is an enzyme that breaks the chains in the right places. Inhibiting protease keeps many of the new viruses from assembling.

Treatment But Not a Cure   Not even these new protease inhibitors can completely rid a person of HIV infection. However, combinations of drugs that inhibit the HIV reproduction process have proven successful in maintaining high T-cell levels and very low virus levels. With such treatment, many patients are able to lead essentially normal, productive lives.

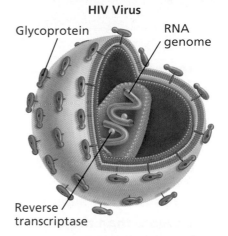

HIV Virus

Glycoprotein

RNA genome

Reverse transcriptase

HIV contains RNA in its core.

internet**connect**

SCI*LINKS*
NSTA

TOPIC: Protease inhibitors
GO TO: www.scilinks.org
KEYWORD: HW096

CAREER APPLICATION

What would it be like to ...

‣ diagnose diseases and provide individualized care for patients?

‣ treat patients and prescribe medications?

‣ counsel families who have members with severe illnesses?

Science/Math Career Preparation	
High School	**College**
Biology	Biology
Chemistry	Chemistry
Mathematics	Mathematics
Physics	Physics

Nurse Practitioner

A nurse practitioner does all of the things that registered nurses in hospitals or physicians' offices do. In fact, most nurse practitioners (NPs) begin as nurses and after a few years of experience study to become a nurse practitioner. Nurse practitioners have some of the same responsibilities as physicians. NPs can perform extensive diagnoses of disease, carry out medical tests, counsel families, and in some cases, prescribe medicine. They often have specialties, such as pediatrics, mental health, and geriatrics. For some families, the NP is the primary health care provider.

People who choose this profession generally study biology, chemistry, physics, and mathematics. In college, the nursing candidates study analytical and organic chemistry, physics, and biology courses. After graduating, a person gains experience in the profession, takes advanced courses, and works under the supervision of a physician or other NP. Finally, an NP must pass a certification exam.

Nurse practitioners can provide very personalized care.

At the beginning of this chapter you read about problems associated with the restoration of the Statue of Liberty.

LOOKING BACK

Why did the iron support beams corrode much more than the thin copper coating?

When the tar coating wore away, salt water acted as an electrical conductor between the copper and iron. Because copper is below iron in the activity series, iron corroded preferentially. The rust that formed crumbled easily. The patina, which consists of ionic copper compounds, is insoluble in water and therefore protected the remaining copper from reacting with substances in the air and rain.

What types of chemical reactions had taken place?

The iron and copper had been oxidized by oxygen and rainwater. Rainwater is slightly acidic, and its acidity increases from pollutants in the atmosphere. The acidity may have aided the oxidation of iron, as you can see from the activity series.

How could corrosion be prevented in the future?

When considering replacement materials, the restoration team had to choose materials that resist oxidation more effectively. Two alloys, or mixtures of metals, were used to replace the rusted iron bars. One of them, *ferallium,* is a very strong iron-aluminum alloy that resists corrosion. It was used to connect the framework to the statue's structural tower. The twisting framework required a more flexible,

corrosion-resistant alloy. In those cases, *316L stainless steel,* an alloy of metals such as Cr, Fe, and Ni was used.

In addition, the bars of the structure were painted with sealants to prevent corrosion. To make the top coat resistant to graffiti, an undercoat containing potassium silicate and zinc dust was applied. An epoxy polyamide polymer was used on top of that.

To keep the copper shell from touching the new frame, a layer of solid polytetrafluoroethylene (Teflon) was inserted between the shell and the frame. Finally, the cracks between the copper sheets were sealed to keep out sea spray. A silicone sealant was used for this because silicone withstands changes in temperature, and doesn't corrode or discolor the statue's copper coating.

$\mathscr{H}$IGHLIGHTS

KEY TERMS

9-2
chemical equation
coefficient

9-3
enthalpy

9-4
activity series

combustion
decomposition
displacement reaction
double-displacement
   reaction

net ionic equation
spectator ion
synthesis

KEY CONCEPTS

9-1 What is a chemical reaction?

▶ A chemical reaction involves the rearrangement of atoms from the reactants into new substances, also called the products.

▶ The only way to prove that a change is a chemical change is to demonstrate that the new substances produced have chemical properties different from those of the reactants.

▶ A nonspontaneous reaction can be made to occur by linking it to an energy source.

▶ Reactants must collide with sufficient energy and the correct orientation for a reaction to occur.

9-2 How are chemical equations for reactions written?

▶ A formula equation uses atomic symbols to describe the rearrangement of atoms of the reactants to form the products in a chemical reaction.

▶ The mass, number, and types of atoms remain the same on both sides of a balanced equation.

▶ Coefficients indicating amounts of reactants and products can be adjusted to balance a chemical equation. Subscripts within a chemical formula cannot be changed.

▶ The charge must also balance in an ionic equation.

9-3 What does a chemical equation tell you?

▶ Notations in a chemical equation can indicate conditions required for a reaction to occur as well as the states of matter for the substances in the reaction.

▶ The coefficients in a balanced equation can be interpreted in terms of formula units, number of molecules, atoms, or ions, or as a mole ratio.

▶ Chemical equations may describe energy changes in a reaction. ΔH indicates the energy absorbed as heat for the overall reaction.

9-4 How are chemical reactions classified?

▶ Five basic types of chemical reactions include combustion, synthesis, decomposition, displacement, and double displacement.

▶ An activity series predicts displacement reactions. Any element on the list will displace elements below it from compounds that are in solution.

▶ Double-displacement reactions can be represented by net ionic equations indicating only the ions that are changed by the reaction.

KEY SKILLS

Review the following models before your exam. Be sure you can solve these types of problems.

Sample Problem 9A: Balancing chemical equations (p. 315).

Sample Problem 9B: Calculating energy for a specific reaction (p. 323).

Sample Problem 9C: Using the activity series to write equations (p. 328).

REVIEW & ASSESS

TERM REVIEW

1. When written correctly, a _____ describes which and how many atoms are rearranged in a reaction.
   (coefficient, double-displacement reaction, chemical equation)

2. Simple molecules combine to make more-complex ones in a _____ reaction.
   (decomposition, synthesis, transfer)

3. In a _____ reaction, one element replaces another in a compound that is in solution.
   (displacement, double-displacement, polymerization)

4. A _____ does not appear in a net ionic equation because it remains unchanged in the chemical reaction.
   (coefficient, monomer, spectator ion)

5. In a chemical equation, _____ indicate the relative amount of reactants and products in a chemical reaction.
   (coefficients, spectator ions, monomers)

6. Oxygen participates in _____ reactions, which produce oxides.
   (decomposition, combustion, transfer)

7. Ions that remain unchanged in a reaction in aqueous solution do not appear in a _____.
   (chemical equation, net ionic equation, coefficient)

8. A single compound is broken down into simpler substances in a _____ reaction.
   (double-displacement, combustion, decomposition)

9. If you want to predict whether a displacement reaction will occur, you can look at the _____.
   (coefficient, formula, activity series)

10. A polymer is made up of many _____.
    (coefficients, monomers, spectator ions)

11. Ions from two compounds in solution interact to form at least one new product in a _____ reaction.
    (displacement, double-displacement, synthesis)

12. The total energy content of a system is called the _____.
    (chemical equation, enthalpy, coefficient)

CONCEPT & SKILLS REVIEW

CHEMICAL REACTIONS

1. Calcium oxide, CaO, is an ingredient in cement mixes. When water is added, CaO reacts in an exothermic reaction to form calcium hydroxide, $Ca(OH)_2$. The properties of CaO are different from those of $Ca(OH)_2$.
   a. Are the bonds stronger in the reactants or in the products? Explain your answer.
   b. What evidence is there that this is a chemical reaction?

2. Use the concepts of bond energy and stability to explain why most naturally occurring chemical reactions are exothermic.

3. A student writes the following statement in a lab report: The atoms of the reactants are destroyed, and the atoms of the products are created; energy is also created.
   a. Explain the scientific inaccuracies in the student's statement.
   b. How could the student correct the inaccurate statement?

4. Considering that reactants must collide for a reaction to occur, answer the following:
   a. Why do liquids generally react faster than solids, and why do gases generally react faster than liquids?
   b. Why do gasoline pumps display labels warning against smoking while pumping gas?

c. Why is this precaution not a major concern around a solid flammable substance, such as a block of candle wax or wood?

5. What evidence can you provide that chemical reactions are responsible for the growth process that a human body undergoes?

6. If you allow a sample of ocean water to evaporate, all that is left is a mixture of salts. Why is this process not a chemical reaction even though a visible change has occurred?

BALANCING CHEMICAL EQUATIONS

7. Differentiate between formula equations and balanced chemical equations.

8. Why can coefficients, but not subscripts, be changed to balance a chemical equation?

9. The white paste that lifeguards rub on their nose to prevent sunburn contains zinc oxide, $ZnO(s)$, as an active ingredient. Zinc oxide is produced by burning zinc sulfide.

$$2ZnS(s) + 3O_2(g) \longrightarrow 2ZnO(s) + 2SO_2(g)$$

a. What is the coefficient for sulfur dioxide?
b. What is the subscript for oxygen gas?
c. How many atoms of oxygen react?
d. How many atoms of oxygen appear in the total number of sulfur dioxide molecules?

10. The following equations are balanced for mass, but they are still not written correctly. Explain why.

$$Cd(s) + 2OH^- \longrightarrow Cd(OH)_2$$

$$2NH_4^+(aq) \longrightarrow 2NH_3(g) + H_2(g)$$

INFORMATION IN CHEMICAL EQUATIONS

11. What is the significance of the positive or negative sign before the ΔH value in a chemical reaction?

12. Describe the information provided in the following equation.

$$Si(s) + 2CH_3Cl(g) \xrightarrow[\text{300°C}]{\text{Cu powder}} (H_3C)_2SiCl_2(l)$$

13. Dinitrogen monoxide, commonly known as laughing gas, is made by heating a solution of the salt ammonium nitrate. Water is also produced in this reaction. Write a balanced equation for this reaction, including all the appropriate notations.

14. Methyl alcohol, CH_3OH, is a clean-burning fuel. The alcohol can be made by reacting carbon monoxide and hydrogen gas.
a. What is the mole ratio of substances in this reaction?
b. How many moles of methanol can be made from 500 mol of hydrogen gas and more than enough carbon monoxide?
c. How many moles of carbon monoxide would actually react in item (b)?

15. To obtain pure silicon for use in semiconductors, silicon tetrachloride gas is reacted with magnesium metal. The products are magnesium chloride salt and solid silicon.
a. Write a balanced equation for this reaction, including all the appropriate notations.
b. The reaction releases 625.6 kJ of heat energy. How many kilojoules of heat energy are released per mole of magnesium metal in this reaction?

CLASSIFYING CHEMICAL REACTIONS

16. Explain the difference between displacement and double-displacement reactions.

17. Use Table 9-8 to predict which of the following metals would be the best to plate metal components of a boat to prevent corrosion.
a. Rb   b. Cr   c. Ba

18. Use Table 9-8 to predict which of the following metals would be the best choice as a container for concentrated sulfuric acid, H_2SO_4.
a. Sn   b. Mn   c. Pt

19. How do total and net ionic equations differ?

20. Which ions in a total ionic equation are called spectator ions? Why?

21. What other reaction type(s) are also combustion reactions? Explain why combustion reactions are linked to these categories.

22. What are some of the characteristics of each of these five common chemical reactions?
  a. combustion
  b. synthesis
  c. decomposition
  d. displacement
  e. double-displacement

23. The saline solution used to soak contact lenses is primarily NaCl dissolved in water. Which of the following ways to designate the solution is incorrect?
  a. $NaCl(aq)$ **b.** $NaCl(s)$
  c. $Na^+(aq) + Cl^-(aq)$

24. Use Table 9-8 to predict whether the following reactions are possible. Explain your answers.
  a. $Ni(s) + MgSO_4(aq) \longrightarrow NiSO_4(aq) + Mg(s)$
  b. $3Mg(s) + Cr_2(SO_4)_3(aq) \longrightarrow$
  $3MgSO_4(aq) + 2Cr(s)$
  c. $Ba(s) + 2H_2O(l) \longrightarrow Ba(OH)_2(aq) + H_2(g)$

25. When heated, tungsten metal usually forms an oxide compound in a synthesis reaction. Light bulb filaments are made of tungsten. Use the information in the diagram to explain why the light bulb filament does not form an oxide compound.

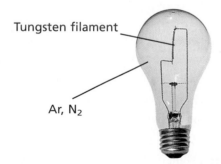

Tungsten filament

Ar, N_2

Practice Problems

26. Balance the following equations.
  a. $CaH_2(s) + H_2O(l) \longrightarrow Ca(OH)_2(aq) + H_2(g)$
  b. $CH_3CH_2CCH(g) + Br_2(l) \longrightarrow$
  $CH_3CH_2CBr_2CHBr_2(l)$
  c. $Pb^{2+}(aq) + OH^-(aq) \longrightarrow Pb(OH)_2(s)$
  d. $NO_2(g) + H_2O(l) \longrightarrow HNO_3(aq) + NO(g)$

27. Translate the following word equations into balanced chemical equations.
  a. silver nitrate + potassium iodide $\longrightarrow$
  silver iodide + potassium nitrate

b. nitrogen dioxide + water $\longrightarrow$
  nitric acid + nitrogen monoxide
  c. silicon tetrachloride + water $\longrightarrow$
  silicon dioxide + hydrochloric acid
  d. ammonium dichromate $\longrightarrow$
  nitrogen + chromium(III) oxide + water
  e. iron(III) oxide + magnesium $\longrightarrow$
  magnesium oxide + iron

28. Molecular models of unbalanced chemical equations are pictured below. On your own sheet of paper, draw molecular diagrams corrected to reflect the balanced equations.
  a. $CH_4 + O_2 \longrightarrow CO_2 + H_2O$

CH₄   O₂   CO₂   H₂O

  b. $Sb + I_2 \longrightarrow SbI_3$

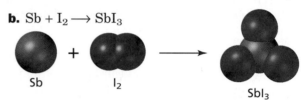

Sb   I₂   SbI₃

  c. $H_2 + N_2 \longrightarrow NH_3$

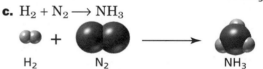

H₂   N₂   NH₃

29. Balance the following ionic equations for mass and charge.
  a. $Ag^+(aq) + Cu(s) \longrightarrow Cu^{2+}(aq) + Ag(s)$
  b. $Sn^{+2}(aq) + Ag^+(aq) \longrightarrow Sn^{4+}(aq) + Ag(s)$
  c. $Al(s) + Fe^{2+}(aq) \longrightarrow Al^{3+}(aq) + Fe(s)$

30. Carbon tetrachloride is used as an intermediate chemical in the manufacture of other chemicals. It is prepared by allowing chlorine gas to react with methane. Hydrogen chloride is also formed in this reaction. Write the balanced chemical equation for the production of carbon tetrachloride. **(Hint: See Sample Problem 9A.)**

31. Sodium hydroxide is produced commercially by the electrolysis of aqueous sodium chloride. Hydrogen and chlorine gases are also produced. Write the balanced chemical equation for the production of sodium hydroxide. **(Hint: See Sample Problem 9A.)**

32. List the product that is missing in each of the following equations.
  a. $MgO + 2HCl \longrightarrow MgCl_2 + ?$
  b. $NH_4NO_3 \longrightarrow 2H_2O + ?$

33. Iron(III) chloride, $FeCl_3$, is a chemical used in photography. It can be produced by reacting iron and chlorine. Identify the chemical equation that is balanced, and explain what is wrong with the two that are not.
  a. $Fe(s) + Cl_3(g) \longrightarrow FeCl_3(s)$
  b. $2Fe(s) + 3Cl_2(g) \longrightarrow 2FeCl_3(s)$
  c. $Fe(s) + 3Cl_2(g) \longrightarrow Fe_2Cl_3(s)$

34. List the reactant that is missing in the following equations.
  a. $Na_2SO_4(aq) + ? \longrightarrow BaSO_4(s) + 2NaCl(aq)$
  b. $? \longrightarrow 2H_2O(l) + O_2(g)$

35. How many moles of HCl can be made from 6.15 mol of H_2 and an excess of Cl_2?

36. Aluminum sulfate, $Al_2(SO_4)_3$, is used to fireproof fabrics. It can be formed from a reaction with H_2SO_4.

$$Al_2O_3(s) + 3H_2SO_4(aq) \longrightarrow$$
$$Al_2(SO_4)_3(aq) + 3H_2O(l)$$

  a. How many moles of $Al_2(SO_4)_3$ would be produced if 6 mol of H_2SO_4 reacted with an excess of Al_2O_3?
  b. How many moles of Al_2O_3 are required to make 2 mol of H_2O?
  c. If 588.0 mol of Al_2O_3 react with excess H_2SO_4, how many moles of each of the products would be produced?

37. Copper(II) nitrate, $Cu(NO_3)_2$, is used to give a dark finish to items made of copper metal, making them appear antique. Copper(II) nitrate can be produced by reacting copper metal with nitric acid. Complete the following table for this reaction.

$$3Cu(s) + 8HNO_3(aq) \longrightarrow$$
$$3Cu(NO_3)_2(aq) + 4H_2O(l) + 2NO(g)$$

Equation	Cu	HNO₃	Cu(NO₃)₂	H₂O	NO
State					
Moles					
Molar mass					
Total mass					

38. 1,3-butadiene gas is an intermediate in the production of synthetic rubber, which is widely used in many products, from electrical insulation to car tires. This gas can be obtained by putting butane gas under high pressure and heat. Refer to the word equation below to answer the following questions.

heat energy + butane $\xrightarrow{\text{Catalyst}}$
1,3-butadiene + hydrogen

  a. Is this reaction exothermic or endothermic?
  b. If 236.5 kJ of heat are absorbed, what would be ΔH for the reaction?
  c. Write the full equation for the reaction, along with the ΔH value.

39. Write the balanced chemical equation for the synthesis of the antacid magnesium oxide from magnesium metal and oxygen gas. **(Hint: See Sample Problem 9A.)**

40. Write the balanced chemical equation for the synthesis of the pollutant nitrogen dioxide from nitrogen monoxide and oxygen gas. **(Hint: See Sample Problem 9A.)**

41. Sucrose, $C_{12}H_{22}O_{11}$, is the sugar used to sweeten many foods. Inside the body, it is broken down to produce H_2O and CO_2.

$$C_{12}H_{22}O_{11} + 12O_2 \longrightarrow 12CO_2 + 11H_2O$$
$$\Delta H = -5.65 \times 10^3 \text{ kJ/mol } C_{12}H_{22}O_{11}$$

  a. List all of the ratios that can be derived from this equation.
  b. Three teaspoons (0.0695 mol) of table sugar are mixed in a glass of iced tea. How much energy will the person drinking this iced tea gain from the sugar? **(Hint: See Sample Problem 9B.)**

42. Write a balanced chemical equation for the reaction that will occur if the following ingredients are mixed together. **(Hint: See Sample Problem 9C.)**

$$Pb(s), Pb^{2+}(aq), Zn(s), \text{ and } Zn^{2+}(aq)$$

43. Write the balanced equation for each of the following reactions:
  a. the combustion of propane gas, C_3H_8, to produce water and carbon dioxide
  b. the decomposition of magnesium carbonate to produce magnesium oxide and carbon dioxide

c. the double-displacement reaction between copper(II) nitrate and ammonium sulfide

d. the transfer of a proton in a water solution from HCl to NH_3

e. the synthesis of platinum(IV) fluoride from platinum and fluorine gas

44. Terephthalic acid and ethylene glycol, shown below, can combine to synthesize a dimer molecule of the polyethylene terephthalate polymer used in film production. During the reaction, a molecule of water is formed. Write the balanced equation for this reaction.

Terephthalic acid   Ethylene glycol

45. Write the total and net ionic equations for the reaction in which the antacid $Al(OH)_3$ neutralizes the stomach acid HCl. This reaction is a double-displacement reaction.

a. Identify the spectator ions in this reaction.

b. What would be the advantages of using $Al(OH)_3$ as an antacid rather than $NaHCO_3$, which undergoes the following reaction with stomach acid?

$$NaHCO_3(aq) + HCl(aq) \longrightarrow$$
$$NaCl(aq) + H_2O(aq) + CO_2(g)$$

LINKING CHAPTERS

1. Theme: Conservation of energy
When wood is burned, energy is released in the form of heat and light. Explain why this change does not violate the law of conservation of energy.

2. Theme: Structural formulas
Neoprene is a polymer used to make shoes and gloves.

a. Identify the monomer in a neoprene molecule by drawing its Lewis structure.

b. What is the empirical formula of neoprene?

3. Theme: Classifications and trends
Although cesium is not included in the activity series in Table 9-8, where would you expect it to appear based on its position in the periodic table?

ALTERNATIVE ASSESSMENTS

Performance assessment

1. Design an experiment to test different antacids on the market. Include $NaHCO_3$, $Mg(OH)_2$, $CaCO_3$, and $Al(OH)_3$ in your data. Discover which one neutralizes the most acid and what byproducts are formed. Show your experiment to your teacher for approval. If your experiment is approved, obtain the necessary chemicals from your teacher and test your procedure.

Portfolio projects

1. Chemistry and you
For one day, record situations that show evidence of a chemical change. Identify the reactants and the products, and determine whether there is proof of a chemical reaction. Classify each of the chemical reactions according to the five common reaction types in the chapter.

2. Chemistry and you
Research safety tips for dealing with fires. Create a poster or brochure about fire safety that explains both these tips and their basis in science.

3. Research and communication
Many products are labeled biodegradable. Choose several biodegradable items on the market, and research the decomposition reactions involved. Be sure to take into account any special conditions that must occur for the substance to biodegrade. Present your information to the class to help inform the students about what products are best for the environment.

1. According to the law of conservation of matter, the total mass of the reacting substances is ———.
   a. always more that the total mass of the products
   b. always less than the total mass of the products
   c. sometimes more and sometimes less than the total mass of the products
   d. always equal to the total mass of the products

2. In a chemical equation, the symbol (*aq*) indicates that the substance is ———.
   a. water   c. an acid
   b. dissolved in water   d. insoluble

3. The ratio of chlorine to hydrogen chloride in the reaction $H_2(g) + Cl_2(g) \longrightarrow 2HCl(g)$ is ———.
   a. 1:1   c. 2:1
   b. 1:2   d. 2:2

4. The tendency for a displacement reaction to occur increases as the ———.
   a. interval between any two elements in the activity series decreases
   b. temperature decreases
   c. valence electrons are used up
   d. interval between any two atoms in the activity series increases

5. The coefficients in a chemical equation ———.
   a. show the number of grams of each substance that would react
   b. indicate the number of moles of each substance
   c. are the molar masses of the substances
   d. show the valence electrons for each atom

6. A reaction in which the ions of two compounds exchange places in aqueous solution to form two new compounds is called a(n) ———.
   a. synthesis reaction
   b. double-displacement reaction
   c. decomposition reaction
   d. combustion reaction

7. To balance a chemical equation, it is permissible to adjust the ———.
   a. coefficients
   b. subscripts
   c. formulas of the products
   d. number of products

8. The use of a double arrow in a chemical equation indicates that the reaction ———.
   a. is reversible
   b. requires heat
   c. is written backwards
   d. has not been confirmed in the laboratory

9. When reading a word equation, the plus sign, +, represents the word ———.
   a. *and*   c. *react*
   b. *heat*   d. *yield*

10. Negative changes in enthalpy indicate that a reaction is ———.
    a. endothermic   c. nonspontaneous
    b. exothermic   d. a synthesis reaction

11. The formation of polymers is a type of reaction called ———.
    a. decomposition   c. synthesis
    b. displacement   d. oxidation

12. Net ionic equations accurately represent ——— involving ionic compounds in solution.
    a. double displacement reactions
    b. oxidation reactions
    c. synthesis reactions
    d. all of the above

13. Elements in the activity series are arranged by ———.
    a. atomic number
    b. position in the family
    c. ionization energy
    d. experimentally determined order

reactants

products

MASS RELATIONSHIPS AND FEEDING THE ARMY

At dinnertime, the soldiers were miles from a field kitchen. They each pulled out a meal pouch, inserted it into a small bag, and added water. Within 15 minutes, the soldiers were eating hot meals.

The dinner is one of the U.S. Army's "Meal, Ready-to-Eat," or MRE, rations. Each MRE is a main dish within a pouch made of aluminum foil and plastic. In 1985, researchers at the Army's Natick Research, Development, and Engineering Center invented a way to heat MREs using a special "Flameless Ration Heater," or FRH.

Each FRH is a plastic sleeve that holds a pad containing metal particles embedded in a polymeric matrix. The metal is an alloy of 90% magnesium and 10% iron. The entire package has a mass of 20.0 g, of which about 8.1 g is magnesium.

In the FRH, the water reacts with magnesium in an exothermic reaction.

$$Mg(s) + 2H_2O(l) \longrightarrow$$
$$Mg(OH)_2(s) + H_2(g) + 353 \text{ kJ}$$

The energy released by this reaction warms the meal to 60°C. To speed the reaction, iron was added to the FRH. Both iron and magnesium react readily with warm water but since iron is a less active metal than magnesium,

the magnesium first reacts. Earlier models of the FRH used more than 60 mL of water, but the latest version requires only 45 mL.

Before the FRH was developed, the Army issued bars of trioxane, $C_3H_6O_3$, to warm meals. The bars came in 15 g and 30 g sizes and were burned in a combustion reaction, releasing about 500 kJ of energy for a 30 g bar.

The necessity of heating meals with equipment that is lightweight and easy to use is one shared by the Army and by people involved in outdoor activities such as camping. A heater similar to the FRH is available for campers. It uses the energy released when water reacts with calcium oxide.

$$CaO(s) + H_2O(l) \longrightarrow Ca(OH)_2(s) + 65.2 \text{ kJ}$$

How do the amounts and masses of substances in a reaction compare? In this chapter, you will learn how to determine the amount of reactant needed for a reaction and how to predict the amount of product that is made. You can apply these same principles to determine the most effective way to heat an MRE.

CHAPTER LINKS

Why was the magnesium-water reaction of the FRH chosen over trioxane and calcium oxide?

Why is there a difference between the amount of water that is added and the amount of water that the reaction requires?

How much can a reaction produce?

OBJECTIVES

▶ **Distinguish** between composition stoichiometry and reaction stoichiometry.

▶ **Apply** a three-step method to solve stoichiometry problems.

▶ **Use** mole ratios and molar masses to create conversion factors for solving stoichiometry problems.

Stoichiometry

In Chapter 9, you learned that reactions can be used to make new products, to break down reactants, and to provide a source of energy. But the predictions you made in Chapter 9 relate only to the *identities* and *relative amounts* of the products and reactants. It is also very useful to predict exactly *how much mass* of a substance will be involved in a reaction. Such predictions are a part of chemistry known as **stoichiometry**.

stoichiometry

mass and amount relationships between reactants and products in a chemical reaction

Moles: the language of equations

When calculating masses of reactants or products, keep in mind that *balanced* equations give the relative numbers of moles of substances involved in the reaction and not the actual amounts of substances present. *When solving stoichiometry problems, you must start from a balanced equation.* Consider the reaction between ammonia and oxygen, as shown by the following equation.

$$4NH_3(g) + 5O_2(g) \longrightarrow 4NO(g) + 6H_2O(g)$$

The equation states that 4 mol NH_3 react with 5 mol O_2 to produce 4 mol NO and 6 mol H_2O. See the space-filled model in **Figure 10-1.**

▼ **FIGURE 10-1**

Equations show the relative, not actual, quantities of substances present.

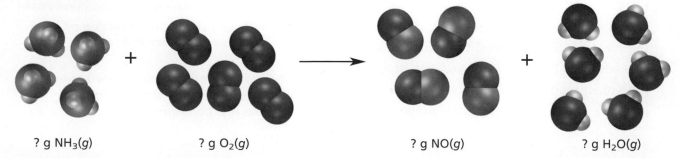

? g $NH_3(g)$? g $O_2(g)$? g $NO(g)$? g $H_2O(g)$

Suppose you have only 2.4 mol NH_3. How many mol O_2 are needed? You need to carry out a mole-to-mole conversion.

$$mol\ NH_3 \longrightarrow mol\ O_2$$

Recall from Chapter 9 that coefficients in chemical equations provide mole ratios that can be used as conversion factors. Because the amount of O_2 is asked for, the conversion factor you set up should have moles of O_2 in the numerator. You are given the amount of NH_3, so the denominator of your conversion factor should include the amount of NH_3 relative to moles of O_2, as shown in the balanced chemical equation on page 344.

$$\frac{5\ mol\ O_2}{4\ mol\ NH_3}$$

Use this information to carry out the conversion.

$$2.4\ mol\ NH_3 \times \frac{5\ mol\ O_2}{4\ mol\ NH_3} = 3.0\ mol\ O_2$$

All stoichiometric calculations involving equations use mole ratios at some point.

Making chemicals in large amounts

The makers of artificial flavors for products, such as banana ice cream and banana-flavored bubble gum, use stoichiometry in synthesizing the flavors. The substance providing most of the taste and smell of bananas is 3-methylbutyl acetate, or isoamyl acetate. Isoamyl acetate belongs to the group of organic compounds known as esters. **Esters** are among the organic chemicals responsible for the aromas and flavors of fruits. The ester functional group is indicated in red on the structure of isoamyl acetate in **Figure 10-2.**

Because there are so many compounds in a banana, it is difficult to isolate and purify natural flavoring. It is more cost-effective to

ester

an organic compound often responsible for the aromas and flavors of fruits

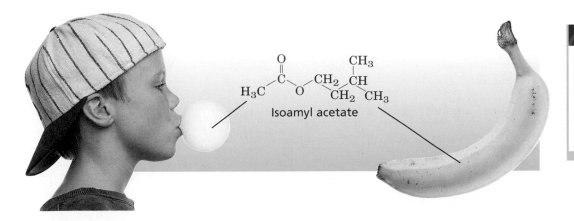

Acetic acid   Isoamyl alcohol   Isoamyl acetate   Water

Isoamyl acetate

FIGURE 10-2 ◄

Isoamyl acetate is the compound primarily responsible for a banana's fruity flavor. It is used in a variety of artificially flavored products.

Ethyl butyrate

Ethyl acetate

Benzaldehyde

4-(4-hydroxyphenyl) 2-butanone
or raspberry ketone

▲ **FIGURE 10-3**

Many flavors and aromas are attributed to organic chemicals such as esters, aldehydes, alcohols, and ketones.

synthesize isoamyl acetate in the lab using the reaction shown on page 345. The other flavor chemicals shown in **Figure 10-3** are also often synthesized as artificial flavorings.

Consider the following question: *If a flavoring manufacturer has 450. g isoamyl alcohol and more than enough acetic acid to react with all of it, what is the maximum mass of banana flavoring that can be made?* Questions that deal with masses involved in reactions are examples of *reaction stoichiometry.*

Organize what you already know

When faced with a problem like this one, a good way to start is to make a table or list of all of the information given in the problem as well as the answer you are trying to find. *Remember to include units for all quantities.* The sections of **Table 10-1** include this initial information. The question mark in the table indicates the answer that is sought. Problems like this are often called *mass-mass problems* because the data given and the answer sought are mass amounts.

Start by figuring out more than just what the problem tells you. Determine the molecular formulas from the structural formulas for isoamyl alcohol and acetic acid shown on page 345.

In Chapter 5, you learned how to use the periodic table to calculate molar masses of reactants and products. Such calculations are called *composition stoichiometry* because they describe the mathematical relationships among the elements that make up a substance. The values for molar mass are shown in Table 10-1. *For almost all chemistry problems of this type, you will need the molar masses of the substances involved.*

The most important piece of information that you need now is the balanced chemical equation for the reaction. Because a balanced chemical equation provides mole ratios for the substances in the reaction, you

| **TABLE 10-1** | Some Data for the Banana-Flavoring Problem |

Reactants and products	Amount	Molecular formula	Molar mass
Isoamyl alcohol	450. g	$C_5H_{11}OH$	88.17 g/mol
Acetic acid	excess	$C_2H_4O_2$	60.06 g/mol
Isoamyl acetate	? g	$CH_3COOC_5H_{11}$	130.21 g/mol
Water	not given	H_2O	18.02 g/mol

can compare relative amounts of the reactants and products. In the balanced equation for isoamyl acetate synthesis, all of the coefficients are 1, so all of the mole ratios are 1:1.

$$C_5H_{11}OH(l) + CH_3COOH(l) \xrightarrow{HCl} CH_3COOC_5H_{11}(l) + H_2O(l)$$

In the equation, hydrochloric acid, HCl, is added to speed up the reaction and therefore is written above the arrow. The equation shows that 1 mol isoamyl alcohol and 1 mol acetic acid react to make 1 mol isoamyl acetate and 1 mol water. *For almost all chemistry problems, you need a balanced chemical equation so that you can find the mole ratios.* Because the problem gives and asks for mass, you must first convert the given mass to amount, use the mole ratio to get moles of the unknown, then convert from amount to mass of the unknown. Remember that mole ratios can only be used to convert amount. Mass, volume, and other quantities must be converted to moles before a mole ratio can be used.

$$g \text{ of } A \longrightarrow mol \text{ of } A \longrightarrow mol \text{ of } B \longrightarrow g \text{ of } B$$

Divide the calculation into steps.

1. Calculate moles of isoamyl alcohol

You are given 450. g of isoamyl alcohol, shown in **Figure 10-4,** and you need to convert from grams of alcohol to moles of alcohol. This requires multiplication by a conversion factor as yet unknown.

$$450. \text{ g } C_5H_{11}OH \times ? \longrightarrow mol \text{ } C_5H_{11}OH$$

The units on both sides must match, so moles of alcohol must be introduced in the numerator on the left, and grams of alcohol must be in the denominator to cancel the unit grams of alcohol.

$$450. \text{ g } C_5H_{11}OH \times \frac{1 \text{ mol } C_5H_{11}OH}{? \text{ g } C_5H_{11}OH} = ? \text{ mol } C_5H_{11}OH$$

This step makes the units equal on both sides of the equation. Now you need to figure out the actual conversion factor needed. It is the inverse of the molar mass, which you calculated for Table 10-1.

$$450. \text{ g } C_5H_{11}OH \times \frac{1 \text{ mol } C_5H_{11}OH}{88.17 \text{ g } C_5H_{11}OH} = 5.10 \text{ mol } C_5H_{11}OH$$

CH_3
|
CH   CH_2
H_3C   CH_2   OH
Isoamyl alcohol

FIGURE 10-4

The molar mass of isoamyl alcohol, one of the reactants in the banana-flavoring synthesis reaction, is 88.17 g/mol.

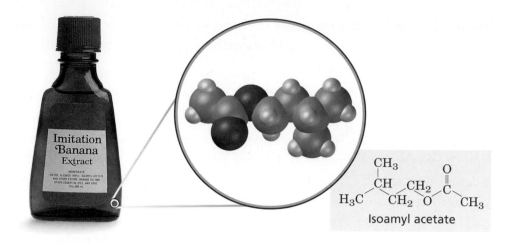

Besides being used as a flavoring agent, isoamyl acetate is also used as an ingredient in air fresheners, as a solvent, and as an ingredient in the manufacture of artificial leather, artificial pearls, and waterproof varnishes.

Isoamyl acetate

2. Use the mole ratio to calculate amount of isoamyl acetate

You know from the equation that 1 mol of isoamyl alcohol produces 1 mol of isoamyl acetate, shown in **Figure 10-5.** So, just as before, use the mole ratio in the equation to convert from the amount of one substance to the amount of another.

$$5.10 \text{ mol } C_5H_{11}OH \times \frac{1 \text{ mol } CH_3COOC_5H_{11}}{1 \text{ mol } C_5H_{11}OH} = 5.10 \text{ mol } CH_3COOC_5H_{11}$$

3. Use molar mass to calculate mass of isoamyl acetate

You now know the amount of isoamyl acetate, but you were asked to find the mass of this product. Just as before, you need a conversion factor. Use units to determine it. The unit *g CH₃COOC₅H₁₁* needs to be in the numerator, and *mol CH₃COOC₅H₁₁* must be in the denominator in order to produce the correct units for the answer. The molar mass of the isoamyl acetate can then be calculated.

$$5.10 \text{ mol } CH_3COOC_5H_{11} \times \frac{130.21 \text{ g } CH_3COOC_5H_{11}}{1 \text{ mol } CH_3COOC_5H_{11}} =$$

$$664 \text{ g } CH_3COOC_5H_{11}$$

Verify your answer. The units are correct, and there are three significant figures. Because the molar mass of the acetate is larger than that of the alcohol, the product mass should be larger. 664 g is larger than the 450. g alcohol used, so the answer is probably correct.

4. Combine all the steps

All of these calculations can be combined rather than done separately. If you keep steps separate, make sure to round only the final answer, not the intermediate steps, to the correct number of significant digits.

$$450. \text{ g } C_5H_{11}OH \times \frac{1 \text{ mol } C_5H_{11}OH}{88.17 \text{ g } C_5H_{11}OH} \times \frac{1 \text{ mol } CH_3COOC_5H_{11}}{1 \text{ mol } C_5H_{11}OH} \times$$

$$\frac{130.21 \text{ g } CH_3COOC_5H_{11}}{1 \text{ mol } CH_3COOC_5H_{11}} = 664 \text{ g } CH_3COOC_5H_{11}$$

Three-step method

In solving stoichiometry problems, it is important to think about what the problem means, rather than just multiplying and dividing the given values with your calculator. In Chapter 8 you learned about the three-step method used in solving the Sample Problems. Because the ability to solve stoichiometry problems is crucial to your success in chemistry, the method is repeated here for you to review before working with the Sample Problems that follow. As you work through your homework problems, it may be useful to refer to this page for suggestions. The Sample Problems that follow can also provide helpful hints.

Remember that *the way to convert from one substance to another is to relate the reaction stoichiometry **in moles**.* For this you need to start with a balanced equation. Use the mole ratios from the balanced equation to convert substances. If your data from the problem are in grams, convert them to moles first. If they are in kilograms, convert to grams before proceeding.

HOW TO   Solve stoichiometry problems

1   List what you know

- Read the problem carefully.
- Organize the information from the problem statement in a list or table.
- Identify what you are asked to find, and write down the units for the answer.
- If there is a reaction, write an equation for it, making sure that it is balanced so that you'll have the correct mole ratios.
- List any conversion factors that you might need, such as molar masses, mole ratios, and unit conversions.

2   Set up the problem

- First analyze what needs to be done to get to the answer. See if there is any information not given in the problem that you need for the answer.
- Write the formulas for all substances you will be working with, and determine their molar masses. Use a periodic table where necessary.
- Identify which value given in the problem can be used as a starting point. Write it on a sheet of paper. Write an equals sign to the right of the starting point and then a question mark with the units of the answer. Fill in the units of the conversion factors and the actual numerical values necessary to convert from what is given in the problem to what is sought in the answer.
- Many chemistry problems (and virtually all stoichiometry problems) require the quantities of substances to be in moles, so use the molar masses from step (1) to convert the mass into moles, if necessary.

- If you need to change from the amount of one substance to the amount of another substance, use mole ratios derived from the coefficients of the balanced chemical equation. Remember that the mole ratio is not always 1:1.

- Be sure to convert the data into appropriate units, such as *grams* instead of *kilograms,* or vice versa, depending on what units you are given and want to find.

- When you have finished writing down your plan with all of the conversion factors, as shown in **Figure 10-6,** check to see how the units cancel each other. If they all cancel to give you the units you need for the answer, the setup is probably correct.

3 Calculate and verify

- Begin your calculations by working through the setup in step (2). In the examples in this book, numbers are not rounded off between steps in calculations.

- When you have finished your calculations, remember to round off and make sure that the answer has the correct number of significant figures.

- Always report the answer with the correct units. Do not write the answer as just a number.

- Verify your answer by estimating. One way to do this is to round off the numbers in the problem setup and make a quick calculation. Another excellent aid is to compare conversion factors in the setup and decide whether the answer should be bigger or smaller than the initial value.

- Make sure your answer is reasonable. For example, if you began with 5.3 mg of one reactant and your answer is that it will make 725 g of a product, you know that you need to double-check all of your work.

▼ FIGURE 10-6

Most stoichiometry problems can be solved using this flowchart.

Mass-Mass Stoichiometry

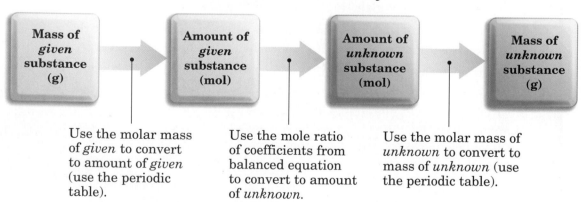

Mass of *given* substance (g) → Amount of *given* substance (mol) → Amount of *unknown* substance (mol) → Mass of *unknown* substance (g)

Use the molar mass of *given* to convert to amount of *given* (use the periodic table).

Use the mole ratio of coefficients from balanced equation to convert to amount of *unknown.*

Use the molar mass of *unknown* to convert to mass of *unknown* (use the periodic table).

A hungry soldier is ready to prepare one of his MREs. How many grams of water must he add to ensure that all of the 8.1 g magnesium used in an FRH react to produce heat?

$$Mg(s) + 2H_2O(l) \longrightarrow Mg(OH)_2(s) + H_2(g) + 353 \text{ kJ}$$

1 List what you know

- Mass of magnesium used: 8.1 g
  Mass of water needed: ? g

2 Set up the problem

- To solve the problem, you will need the molar masses and mole ratio of magnesium and water.
  molar mass of magnesium: Mg, 24.30 g/mol
  molar mass of water: H_2O, 18.02 g/mol
- To convert from the mass of Mg given to the mass of H_2O needed, first convert to moles and use the mole ratio to link the two amounts. This is a problem of the type already considered.

  g of Mg $\longrightarrow$ mol of Mg $\longrightarrow$ mol of H_2O $\longrightarrow$ g of H_2O

  Therefore, you use the procedure in Figure 10-6. First convert the grams of magnesium into moles, then convert moles of magnesium to moles of water, and finally convert moles of water into grams of water.

  $$8.1 \text{ g Mg} \times \frac{1 \text{ mol Mg}}{24.30 \text{ g Mg}} \times \frac{2 \text{ mol H}_2\text{O}}{1 \text{ mol Mg}} \times \frac{18.02 \text{ g H}_2\text{O}}{1 \text{ mol H}_2\text{O}} = ? \text{ g H}_2\text{O}$$

3 Calculate and verify

- Use your calculator to work through the setup. Be sure to round to the correct number of significant figures, which is two.
  Calculator answer: 12.01333 g H_2O
  Answer to two significant figures: 12 g H_2O
- Verify your answer by rounding the numbers in the setup and estimating.
  If the units are correct and the number is close to the estimate, the answer is probably correct.

PRACTICE PROBLEMS

1. Tin(II) fluoride, also known as stannous fluoride, is added to some dental products to help prevent cavities. What mass of tin(II) fluoride can be made from 55.0 g of hydrofluoric acid, HF, if there is more than enough tin?

$$Sn(s) + 2HF(aq) \longrightarrow SnF_2(aq) + H_2(g)$$

2. Chlorobenzene, C_6H_5Cl, is used in the production of many important chemicals, such as aspirin, dyes, and disinfectants. What mass in grams of chlorobenzene can be made from 40.0 g of benzene if more than enough chlorine is present?

$$C_6H_6(l) + Cl_2(g) \longrightarrow C_6H_5Cl(s) + HCl(g)$$

3. What mass of fluorescein can be made from 25.00 kg resorcinol?

Two resorcinol   One phthalic   One fluorescein   Two water
                       anhydride

Other stoichiometric calculations
Problems with amounts in moles

Some stoichiometry problems involve data or answers in mole quantities instead of mass quantities. These problems can be solved with an approach similar to that used to solve the problems having both data and answers in grams. But there are fewer steps with this approach because one or both molar mass conversions are unnecessary, as shown in **Figure 10-7,** which has some of the same steps as **Figure 10-6.** If both the answer and the given data are in moles, the only conversion factor necessary to solve the problem is the mole ratio.

▶ **FIGURE 10-7**

If a stoichiometry problem involves quantities in moles, it can be solved in fewer steps than are required to solve problems with quantities in grams.

Mass of given	Amount of given	Amount of unknown	Mass of unknown

Mass-to-Mass Problem-Solving Plan

1. Always begin with a balanced chemical equation.
2. Use the molar mass of the given substance to convert from mass of given to amount of given.
3. Use the mole ratio of coefficients from the balanced chemical equation to change from amount of given to amount of unknown.
4. Use the molar mass of unknown to convert from amount of unknown to mass of unknown.

Mole-to-Mass Problem-Solving Plan

1. Always begin with a balanced chemical equation.
2. Use the mole ratio of coefficients from the balanced chemical equation to change from amount of given to amount of unknown.
3. Use the molar mass of the unknown substance to convert from amount of unknown to mass of unknown.

The human body needs at least 1.03×10^{-2} mol O_2 every minute. If all of this oxygen is used for the cellular respiration reaction that oxidizes glucose to carbon dioxide and water, what mass of glucose does the human body consume each minute?

$$C_6H_{12}O_6(aq) + 6O_2(aq) \longrightarrow 6CO_2(aq) + 6H_2O(l)$$

1 **List what you know**

▶ Amount of O_2 used each minute: 1.03×10^{-2} mol O_2
▶ Mole ratio: 1 mol $C_6H_{12}O_6$:6 mol O_2
▶ Mass of glucose needed each minute: ? g

Because oxygen is already given in a mole amount, the molar mass of O_2 is unnecessary.

2 **Set up the problem**

▶ Calculate molar mass from the periodic table.
 molar mass of $C_6H_{12}O_6$: 180.18 g/mol
▶ Analyze what needs to be done to get the answer. You are given moles of oxygen, so you can immediately convert to moles of glucose using the mole ratio from the balanced equation. Then you can use the molar mass to determine the mass in grams of the glucose.

$$1.03 \times 10^{-2} \text{ mol } O_2 = ? \text{ g } C_6H_{12}O_6$$

You need to go from moles of O_2 to moles of glucose to grams of glucose using two conversions.

$$1.03 \times 10^{-2} \text{ mol } O_2 \times \frac{1 \text{ mol } C_6H_{12}O_6}{6 \text{ mol } O_2} \times \frac{180.18 \text{ g } C_6H_{12}O_6}{1 \text{ mol } C_6H_{12}O_6} = ? \text{ g } C_6H_{12}O_6$$

3 **Calculate and verify**

▶ Use your calculator to work through the setup. Be sure to round to the correct number of significant figures, which is three.
 Calculator answer: 0.3093090 g of glucose
 Answer to three significant figures: 0.309 g of glucose
▶ Verify your answer by rounding off the numbers in the setup and estimating.

PRACTICE PROBLEMS

1. Use the information in Sample Problem 10B to determine the mass of carbon dioxide that would be produced each minute.

2. Use the information in Sample Problem 10B to determine the mass of water that would be produced each minute.

3. Calculate the mass of isoamyl acetate which can be produced when 6 mol of isoamyl alcohol are reacted with 6 mol of acetic acid.

$$C_5H_{11}OH(l) + CH_3COOH(l) \xrightarrow{\text{HCl}} CH_3COOC_5H_{11}(l) + H_2O(l)$$

Use this flow chart to solve stoichiometric calculations involving density.

Volume-Molecule Stoichiometry

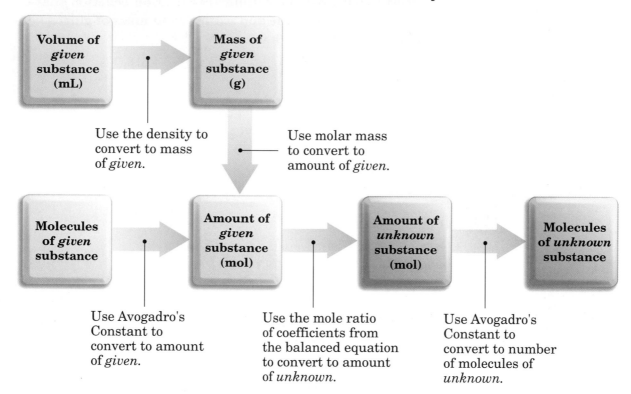

Using density with stoichiometry

Remember that the key to solving any reaction stoichiometry problem is to convert to amount and to use the balanced equation to change from the amount of one substance to the amount of another. Once the amount is determined, conversion factors such as molar mass can be used to convert to the mass in grams. Similarly, once the volume is known, the density can be used to convert to mass, and if mass is known, the density of a substance can be used to convert from mass to volume. Converting between mass and volume adds one or more steps to stoichiometric calculations. Look at the flow diagram shown in **Figure 10-8.** This solution scheme can be used as a guide for solving most stoichiometry problems involving density or to calculate the number of molecules. If the units for the given quantity is in mL, start with the volume box from the diagram. If the units for the given quantity is molecules, formula units, or atoms, start with the molecule box from the diagram. Follow the arrows and operations to the box in the diagram that yields the answer.

Recall from Chapter 2 that density is defined as the mass of a substance per unit volume expressed mathematically as $D = m / V$. Use the density value to set up a conversion factor that will cancel the units in the measurement you have and leave the units of the measurement for the answer, as shown in Sample Problem 10C on page 355.

In space shuttles, the CO_2 that the crew exhales is removed from the air by a reaction within canisters of lithium hydroxide, LiOH. On average, each astronaut exhales about 20.0 mol of CO_2 daily. What volume of water will be produced from 20.0 mol of CO_2 if an excess of LiOH is present? (Hint: the density of water is about 1.00 g/mL.)

$$CO_2(g) + 2LiOH(s) \longrightarrow Li_2CO_3(aq) + H_2O(l)$$

1 List what you know

- Amount of CO_2: 20.0 mol CO_2
- Density of H_2O: 1.00 g/mL
- Mole ratio: 1 mol CO_2:1 mol H_2O
- Volume of H_2O produced: ? mL

2 Set up the problem

- Calculate molar mass using the periodic table.
  molar mass of H_2O: 18.02 g/mol
- Analyze what needs to be done to get the answer. You are given moles of CO_2, so you first convert to moles of water using the mole ratio. Then use the molar mass to find out the mass of water.

$$20.0 \text{ mol } CO_2 \times \frac{1 \text{ mol } H_2O}{1 \text{ mol } CO_2} \times \frac{18.02 \text{ g } H_2O}{1 \text{ mol } H_2O} \times \underline{\qquad} = ? \text{ mL } H_2O$$

- Next convert from the mass of H_2O to the volume of H_2O using the inverse of the density as the conversion factor. The correct conversion factor will have g H_2O in the denominator and mL H_2O in the numerator.

$$20.0 \text{ mol } CO_2 \times \frac{1 \text{ mol } H_2O}{1 \text{ mol } CO_2} \times \frac{18.02 \text{ g } H_2O}{1 \text{ mol } H_2O} \times \frac{1 \text{mL } H_2O}{1.00 \text{ g } H_2O} = ? \text{ mL } H_2O$$

3 Calculate and verify

- Use your calculator to work through the setup. Be sure to round to the correct number of significant figures, which is three.
  Calculator gives: 360.3 mL H_2O
  Answer to three significant figures: 360. mL H_2O
- Verify your answer by rounding off the numbers in the setup and estimating.

PRACTICE PROBLEMS

1. Calculate the mass of lithium hydroxide used to obtain 1.5 L of water.

2. The reaction that causes cake batter to rise involves the production of CO_2 from $NaHCO_3$ when the $NaHCO_3$ reacts with an acid, such as acetic acid, CH_3COOH (vinegar.) What volume of CO_2 gas will be created when 15.0 g $NaHCO_3$ are used? (Note: at baking temperature, the density of CO_2 is about 1.10 g/L.)

$$NaHCO_3(s) + CH_3COOH(aq) \longrightarrow CH_3COONa(aq) + H_2O(l) + CO_2(g)$$

Calculating the number of atoms or formula units

Just as molar mass, density, and mole ratios can be used as conversion factors in problems, Avogadro's constant, 6.022×10^{23}, can be used to calculate the number of atoms or formula units involved in a reaction. This approach was shown in Figure 10-8. The two points to remember are the same as with other stoichiometry problems.

▶ Be certain that you work with moles.

▶ Make sure that you set up the conversion factors so that the quantity sought is in the numerator and the quantity given is in the denominator.

SECTION REVIEW

Total recall

1. Write the chemical equation describing the synthesis of artificial banana flavoring.

2. What conversion factor is used to determine the number of atoms participating in a reaction?

Critical thinking

3. Why do you need to use amount to solve stoichiometry problems? Why can't you just convert from mass to mass?

4. Use the three-step method to solve the following problems. The equation below shows the use of the reactants hydrazine, N_2H_4, and dimethylhydrazine, $(CH_3)_2N_2H_2$, as rocket propellants. For each problem, assume that you start with 1200. kg of N_2H_4 and that it is completely used up by the reaction.

$$2N_2H_4(l) + (CH_3)_2N_2H_2(l) + 3N_2O_4(l) \longrightarrow$$
$$6N_2(g) + 2CO_2(g) + 8H_2O(g)$$

a. Calculate how many moles of N_2O_4 are needed.

b. Calculate how many grams of $(CH_3)_2N_2H_2$ are needed.

c. Calculate how many molecules of N_2 are produced.

5. Aspirin is made by allowing salicylic acid to react with acetic anhydride.

$$C_7H_6O_3 + C_4H_6O_3 \xrightarrow{HCl} C_9H_8O_4 + C_2H_4O_2$$

| Salicylic acid | Acetic anhydride | Aspirin | Acetic acid |

What mass of salicylic acid is needed to make one aspirin tablet, which is 0.35 g?

6. **Story Clue** At the temperature within an FRH, 60°C, the density of hydrogen gas is 0.073 g/L. How many liters of H_2 gas are produced by an FRH?

7. **Story Clue** Take a look at the amount of heat energy produced per gram of reactants for each of the magnesium and calcium oxide reactions on page 343. If the mass of the reactants were the deciding factor, which reaction would be most effective? (Hint: Remember to include the mass of water necessary for the two reactions.)

SECTION 10-2

How much does a reaction really produce?

OBJECTIVES

- ***Distinguish*** between a limiting reactant and an excess reactant.
- ***Identify*** the limiting reactant in a problem, and calculate the theoretical yield.
- ***Distinguish*** between theoretical yield and actual yield.
- ***Calculate*** the percentage yield, given the actual yield and the quantity of the limiting reactant.
- ***Use*** percentage yield to calculate actual yield.

Leftover reactants

You now know how to use mole ratios and other conversion factors to figure out how much of a product is produced by a chemical reaction. All previous reactions and calculations described an *ideal situation.* Some assumptions were made: there were always enough reactants so that none were left over, and all reactions went to completion, producing only the products indicated in the equation. The reactions proceeded exactly as written; no unwanted or unexpected products were formed.

These assumptions are useful when learning how reactions and equations work and how to make predictions from them. But to treat real reactions accurately, you must take additional factors into account, such as the amounts of all reactants, the completeness of the reaction, and the product lost in the process.

Reactants combine in specific whole-number ratios

Have you ever tried to assemble a bicycle only to discover that you didn't have enough nuts for the bolts that were supplied, as shown in **Figure 10-9**? For every bolt, you needed a nut, so the shortage of nuts limited what you could do. Or have you ever been in a car that ran out of gas? The car needed both gas and oxygen from the air to run. Once the gas was gone, it wouldn't run, no matter how much oxygen was present.

A similar limitation occurs in all chemical reactions. When a chemical reaction occurs, the reactants are seldom present in ratios of amounts equal to their mole ratios. There may be too much of one reactant or too little of another. For example, reconsider the reaction used to make the banana-flavored ester, isoamyl acetate.

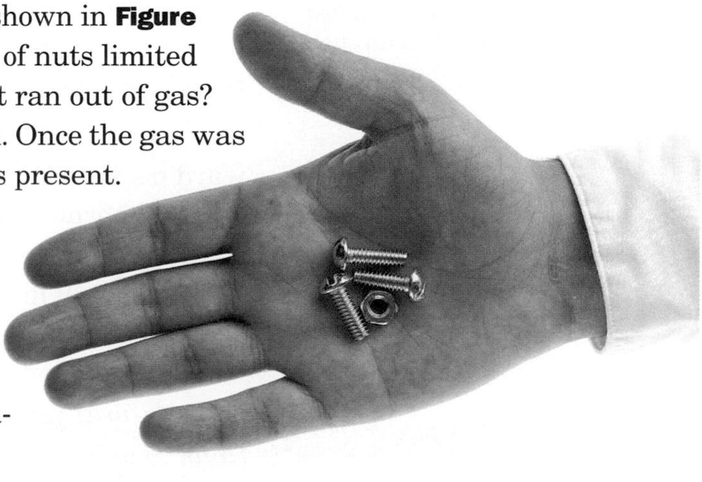

FIGURE 10-9

With only one nut, you can make only a single nut-bolt pair, no matter how many bolts you have. Similarly, when one reactant in a chemical reaction is used up, the reaction can no longer proceed.

The reactants

The products

Excess reactants

+

▲ **FIGURE 10-10**

Making a cheese-burger can be an analogy for a reaction with limiting reactants. The number of cheese-burgers you can make is limited by the one critical ingredient.

excess reactant

reactant that will not be completely used up in a reaction that goes to completion

limiting reactant

reactant that is consumed completely in a reaction that goes to completion

According to the following equation, for every mole of acetic acid, a mole of isoamyl alcohol is needed. What mass of isoamyl acetate could be made if there were 20 mol of acetic acid and only 1 mol of isoamyl alcohol?

$$H_3C-\overset{\displaystyle O}{\underset{\displaystyle }{C}}-OH \;+\; HO-CH_2-\overset{\displaystyle CH_3}{\underset{\displaystyle CH_2-CH_3}{CH}} \longrightarrow H_3C-\overset{\displaystyle O}{\underset{\displaystyle }{C}}-O-CH_2-\overset{\displaystyle CH_3}{\underset{\displaystyle CH_2-CH_3}{CH}} \;+\; H_2O$$

Acetic acid   Isoamyl alcohol   Isoamyl acetate   Water

One mole of acetic acid reacts with 1 mol of isoamyl alcohol. After that, the isoamyl alcohol reactant is used up, and none is available to react with the other 19 mol of acetic acid. Obviously, the reaction would stop after forming only 1 mol of each product even though there were 20 mol of one reactant at the start. An excess of this reactant would be left over, as in the analogy illustrated in **Figure 10-10.**

An **excess reactant** is not completely used up in a chemical reaction. In the preceding example, acetic acid is the excess reactant. Some of this reactant will be left over when the reaction is complete. On the other hand, isoamyl alcohol is known as the **limiting reactant.** A limiting reactant is used up first and thus limits the amount of other reactants that can participate in a chemical reaction. The limiting reactant also limits the amount of product that can be formed.

Determining the limiting reactant

Determining the limiting reactant in this case was fairly straightforward because the mole ratio in the balanced equation was 1:1. You could easily determine which reactant would be totally used up after the reaction was complete. For more complicated problems, first determine the number of moles of each reactant, as shown in Sample Problem 10D. Then use the mole ratios to determine how much of the other reactants would be needed by each reactant. *Whichever reactant runs out first will be the limiting reactant and should be used in stoichiometric calculations to determine the maximum amount of product possible.*

SAMPLE PROBLEM 10D Determining the limiting reactant

Carbon monoxide can be combined with hydrogen to produce methanol, CH_3OH. Methanol is used as an industrial solvent, as a reactant in synthesis, and as a clean-burning fuel for some race cars. If you had 152.5 g CO and 24.50 g H_2. What mass of CH_3OH could be produced?

1 List what you know

- Mass of CO: 152.5 g CO
- Mass of H_2: 24.50 g H_2
- Mass of CH_3OH produced: ? g CH_3OH

2 Set up the problem

- Balance the chemical equation for the reaction:

$$CO(g) + 2H_2\,(g) \longrightarrow CH_3OH(l)$$

- Calculate molar masses using the periodic table.
  molar mass of CO: 28.01 g/mol
  molar mass of H_2: 2.02 g/mol
  molar mass of CH_3OH: 32.05 g/mol

3 Calculate and verify

- To determine which reactant is the limiting reactant, first figure out how many moles of each reactant are present.

$$152.5\ \cancel{g\ CO} \times \frac{1\ mol\ CO}{28.01\ \cancel{g\ CO}} = 5.444\ mol\ CO\ present$$

$$24.50\ \cancel{g\ H_2} \times \frac{1\ mol\ H_2}{2.02\ \cancel{g\ H_2}} = 12.1\ mol\ H_2\ present$$

- Then figure out how much of the first reactant would be needed to use up all of the second reactant. Compare this with the amount actually present.

$$12.1\ \cancel{mol\ H_2} \times \frac{1\ mol\ CO}{2\ \cancel{mol\ H_2}} = 6.06\ mol\ CO\ needed$$

Because the amount of CO present is not enough to react with all the H_2, CO is the limiting reactant.

- Use the limiting reactant to set up the stoichiometric calculation.

$$5.444\ \cancel{mol\ CO} \times \frac{1\ \cancel{mol\ CH_3OH}}{1\ \cancel{mol\ CO}} \times \frac{32.05\ g\ CH_3OH}{1\ \cancel{mol\ CH_3OH}} = ?\ g\ CH_3OH$$

- Calculate, and round to the correct number of significant digits.
  Calculator answer: 174.4802 g CH_3OH
  Answer to four significant figures: 174.5 g CH_3OH
- Verify your answer by rounding off the numbers in the setup and estimating.

$$5.5 \times \frac{1}{1} \times \frac{30}{1} \approx 150$$

1. Hydrochloric acid, HCl(*aq*), secreted in your stomach can be neutralized in a double-displacement reaction by taking an antacid such as aluminum hydroxide, $Al(OH)_3$. If 34.0 g HCl are secreted and 12.0 g $Al(OH)_3$ are taken, is there enough $Al(OH)_3$ to react with all of the HCl?

2. Ammonia, NH_3, is used throughout the world as a fertilizer. To manufacture ammonia, nitrogen, N_2, is combined with hydrogen, H_2, in a synthesis reaction. If 92.7 kg N_2 and 265.8 kg H_2 are used, which is the limiting reactant?

Cost is a factor in selecting the limiting reactant

In industry, the least expensive reactant is usually used as the excess reactant. In this way, the expensive reactant is more completely used up, while some of the cheaper reactant is left over.

In addition to being cost-effective, this practice can be used to control which reactions happen. One example is the production of cider vinegar, shown in **Figure 10-11,** from apple juice. At first, the original apple juice is kept where there is no oxygen. When no oxygen is present, the microorganisms in the apple juice cannot use the cellular respiration reaction as a source of energy. Instead, they use an alternative pathway in which the glucose is fermented, or broken down, into molecules of ethanol. The resulting solution is hard cider.

Excess oxygen is used in the next step in the production of cider vinegar. Once the ethanol in hard cider is exposed to air, the organisms use atmospheric oxygen to produce acetic acid, resulting in cider vinegar. Because the oxygen in the air costs nothing and is abundant, the makers of cider vinegar pump air through hard cider as they make it into vinegar. In this way, oxygen is not the limiting reactant. Ethanol is the limiting reactant, so it is entirely consumed in the reaction.

Similarly, the manufacturers of the banana flavoring discussed at the beginning of the chapter use acetic acid as the excess reactant because it costs much less than isoamyl alcohol. For example, acetic acid costs about $11 for 500 mL (525 g), while 500 mL (406 g) of isoamyl alcohol costs about $16. When compared mole for mole, isoamyl alcohol is almost three times as expensive as acetic acid. With an excess of acetic acid, none of the more expensive isoamyl alcohol is wasted.

▼ **FIGURE 10-11**

Makers of cider vinegar use special tanks and equipment to pump air through hard cider so that oxygen, O_2, is the excess reactant.

A chemical equation tells what could happen

Although equations tell you what *should* happen, they can't always tell you what *will* happen. For example, a reaction will stop once the limiting reactant has been used up, regardless of how much of the other reactants is present.

| **TABLE 10-2** | Predictions and Measurements for Isoamyl Acetate Synthesis | | | |

Reactants	Formula	Mass	Amount present	Amount needed for reaction
Isoamyl alcohol	$C_5H_{11}OH$	500.0 g	5.67 mol (limiting reactant)	5.67 mol
Acetic acid	CH_3COOH	1.25×10^3 g	20.8 mol	5.67 mol

Products	Formula	Amount expected	Theoretical yield (mass expected)	Actual yield (mass produced)
Isoamyl acetate	$CH_3COOC_5H_{11}$	5.67 mol	738 g	590 g
Water	H_2O	5.67 mol	102 g	81.6 g

Sometimes reactions don't match the proportions of reactants consumed and products generated defined by equations. The mass of product expected from stoichiometric calculations is called the **theoretical yield.** But in most cases, the **actual yield,** the mass of product actually obtained, is less than expected. An actual yield can be much less than the theoretical yield. How can this be? Reconsider the banana-flavoring problem.

When a worker at the flavoring factory mixes 500.0 g isoamyl alcohol with 1.25×10^3 g acetic acid, the stoichiometric calculations that account for isoamyl alcohol being a limiting reactant give the results summarized in the second half of **Table 10-2.** But when the actual yield is measured, it is less than was expected. What went wrong?

As mentioned, some reactions do not go to completion. As reactants form products, some of the products react to re-form the original reactants. Because this reverse reaction is occurring, some of the reactants are always present. When the forward reaction occurs at the same rate as the reverse reaction, the system is said to be in **chemical equilibrium.** In a chemical equation, chemical equilibrium is indicated by double arrows, as shown below. You will study chemical equilibrium in more detail in Chapters 12 and 14.

theoretical yield

calculated maximum amount of product possible from a given amount of reactant

actual yield

measured amount of product experimentally produced from a given amount of reactant

chemical equilibrium

condition where the forward reaction occurs at the same speed as the reverse reaction, and all reactants and products are present

$$
\text{Acetic acid} \quad + \quad \text{Isoamyl alcohol} \quad \underset{\text{Decomposition}}{\overset{\text{Synthesis}}{\rightleftharpoons}} \quad \text{Isoamyl acetate} \quad + \quad \text{H}_2\text{O}
$$

Acetic acid   Isoamyl alcohol   Isoamyl acetate   Water

Percentage yield is a way to describe reaction efficiency

There is a way of relating the theoretical yield of a reaction to its actual yield. This ratio describes reaction efficiency. For example, a worker in the flavoring factory kept track of the results of several attempts to make isoamyl acetate, as shown in **Table 10-3.**

TABLE 10-3 — Data from Several Trials of Isoamyl Acetate Synthesis

Mass of isoamyl alcohol used (g)	Theoretical yield of isoamyl acetate (g)	Actual yield of isoamyl acetate (g)
500.	738	590
500.	738	599
500.	738	579
500.	738	582
500.	738	603

percentage yield

ratio of actual yield to the theoretical yield multiplied by 100

As you can see, the actual yields are close. The **percentage yield** describes how close actual yield is to the theoretical yield.

$$\text{percentage yield} = \frac{\text{actual yield}}{\text{theoretical yield}} \times 100$$

The percentage yield figures for the values shown in Table 10-3 are 79.9%, 81.2%, 78.5%, 78.9%, and 81.7%. These values are all close, but why aren't they equal? Competing side reactions and purification techniques are two ways in which products can be lost. In addition, products that form as gases are often hard to collect, thus lowering percentage yields. While these factors all result in product loss, they are not exact processes, and the mass of product lost almost always varies from day to day. So to determine a general figure for predicting reaction yields, the percentage yield figures are usually averaged over several different trials. For this set of values, the average is 80.0%.

Describing yields in this way is similar to using statistics to describe how frequently a player scores in sports. For example, if you try 20 layups during a basketball game, your theoretical score is 40 points. However, if you make only 10 of those shots, your actual score is 20 points. Your shooting percentage is 50%.

Actual percentage yields must be measured experimentally. However, after closely observing many different reactions, experienced chemists can recognize patterns and reaction types that allow them to make pretty good *estimates* of percentage yield.

The batting average shown on the back of baseball cards, like the one in **Figure 10-12,** is similar to percentage yield because it is a ratio of the number of hits to the number of times at bat.

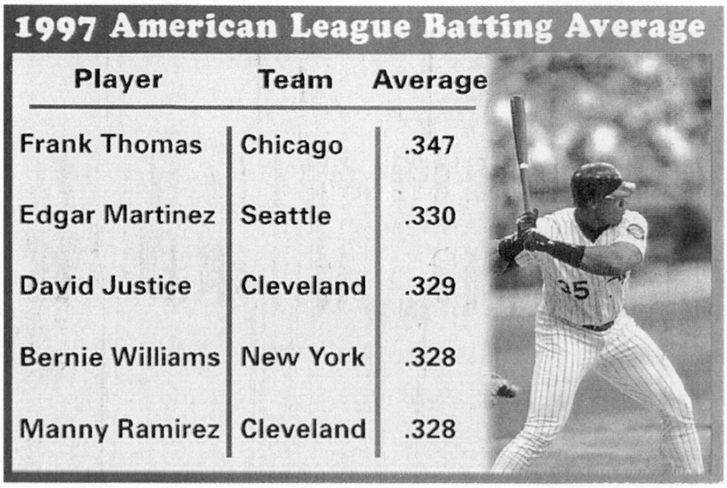

▼ **FIGURE 10-12**

A baseball player's batting average is similar to percentage yield because it is a ratio of the number of hits achieved and the number of hits possible.

1997 American League Batting Average

Player	Team	Average
Frank Thomas	Chicago	.347
Edgar Martinez	Seattle	.330
David Justice	Cleveland	.329
Bernie Williams	New York	.328
Manny Ramirez	Cleveland	.328

SAMPLE PROBLEM 10E Calculating percentage yield

A student is synthesizing aspirin by adding 200.0 g of salicylic acid to an excess of acetic anhydride. Calculate the percentage yield if 231 g of aspirin is produced. (Hint: Before you can determine the percentage yield, you must first calculate the theoretical yield of aspirin based on the amount of the limiting reactant supplied.)

1 List what you know

- Mass of limiting reactant: 200.0 g $C_7H_6O_3$
- Mole ratio: 1 mol $C_7H_6O_3$: 1 mol $C_9H_8O_4$
- Actual yield: 231 g $C_9H_8O_4$
- Theoretical yield: ? g $C_9H_8O_4$
- Percentage yield: ? %

2 Set up the problem

- Write and balance the chemical equation:

$$C_7H_6O_3 + C_4H_6O_3 \longrightarrow C_9H_8O_4 + C_2H_4O_2$$

- Calculate molar masses using the periodic table.
  molar mass of limiting reactant: 138.12 g/mol $C_7H_6O_3$
  molar mass of product: 180.18 g/mol $C_9H_8O_4$

3 Calculate and verify

- Before you can calculate percentage yield, you must calculate theoretical yield by using the molar masses and mole ratios in a mass-mass conversion.

$$200.0\ \cancel{g\ C_7H_6O_3} \times \frac{1\ \cancel{mol\ C_7H_6O_3}}{138.12\ \cancel{g\ C_7H_6O_3}} \times \frac{1\ \cancel{mol\ C_9H_8O_4}}{1\ \cancel{mol\ C_7H_6O_3}} \times \frac{180.18\ g\ C_9H_8O_4}{1\ \cancel{mol\ C_9H_8O_4}} = ?\ g\ C_9H_8O_4$$

  Calculator answer: 260.9035621 g $C_9H_{10}O_4$
  Rounded answer: 260.9 g $C_9H_{10}O_4$

- Calculate percentage yield from the actual and theoretical yields.

$$\frac{231\ \text{g actual}}{260.9\ \text{g theoretical}} \times 100 = ?\ \%\ \text{yield}$$

  Calculate, and round to the correct number of significant digits, which is three.
  Calculator answer: 88.539670% yield
  Rounded answer: 88.5% yield

- Verify your answer by rounding the numbers in the setup and estimating.

$$200 \times \frac{1}{150} \times \frac{1}{1} \times \frac{200}{1} = \frac{4}{3} \times 200 \approx 250$$

$$\frac{230}{250} \times 100 \approx 90\%$$

1. One step in making *para*-aminobenzoic acid, PABA, an ingredient in some suntan lotions, involves replacing one of the hydrogen atoms in a toluene molecule with an —NO$_2$ group directly opposite the —CH$_3$ group. Calculate the percentage yield if 550.0 g of toluene added to an excess of nitric acid provides 305 g of the ρ-nitrotoluene product.

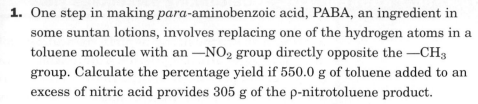

| Toluene C$_7$H$_8$ | Nitric acid | ρ-Nitrotoluene C$_7$H$_7$NO$_2$ | Water |

2. One reason for the low yield in the reaction shown above is a competing side reaction that produces a nitrotoluene product that cannot be used to make PABA. After 550.0 g of toluene reactant was used with an excess of nitric acid, 468 g of this other product remained. Calculate its percentage yield.

CH$_3$ + HNO$_3$ $\xrightarrow{H_2SO_4}$ CH$_3$ NO$_2$ + H$_2$O

| Toluene C$_7$H$_8$ | Nitric acid | o-Nitrotoluene C$_7$H$_7$NO$_2$ | Water |

Percentage yield figures can be used to predict actual yield

Take another look at the banana-flavoring reaction. The worker in the flavoring factory is concerned with the efficiency of the reaction. Recall from pages 362-363 that the ratio of the theoretical yield of the reaction to the actual yield can be used to calculate efficiency of a reaction.

After calculating the theoretical yield of the reaction in the usual way, you can use the percentage yield as a conversion factor. The easiest way to do this is to rewrite the percentage as the number of grams of actual yield per 100 g of theoretical yield. Suppose the reaction for synthesizing artificial banana flavoring gives the product, isoamyl acetate, in 61.7% yield.

$$61.7\% \text{ yield} = \frac{61.7 \text{ g actual yield}}{100 \text{ g theoretical yield}} \times 100$$

Theoretically, 150.0 g of isoamyl alcohol should provide 221.4 g of isoamyl acetate. But you know from the equation with the percentage yield to expect only about 61.7% of that isoamyl acetate to actually be formed. What does this tell the worker about the efficiency of the reaction? That 150.0 g of isoamyl alcohol actually provides 136.6 g of isoamyl acetate.

$$61.7\% = \frac{? \text{ g actual yield}}{221.4 \text{ g theoretical yield}} \times 100$$

Using percentage yield

A more-efficient way to synthesize the compound that was used to produce PABA for suntan lotion involves a slightly different starting material known as isopropylbenzene. This reaction usually has a 91% yield because the bulky isopropyl group hinders the nitro group from entering the ring next to it. What mass of the product, *para*-nitro-isopropylbenzene, can you expect if 775 g of isopropylbenzene reacts with an excess of nitric acid?

H₃C CH₃ CH ⬡ Isopropylbenzene	+ HNO₃ Nitric acid	$\xrightarrow{H_2SO_4}$	H₃C CH₃ CH ⬡ NO₂ p-Nitro-isopropylbenzene	+ H₂O Water

1 List what you know

▶ This is a case in which a table for organizing data is useful.

Substance	Formula	Molar mass	Mass	Mole ratio
Isopropylbenzene	C_9H_{12}	? g/mol	775 g	1
***para*-nitro-isopropylbenzene**	$C_9H_{11}NO_2$	? g/mol	? g	1

Percentage yield: 91%

2 Set up the problem

▶ Calculate molar masses using the periodic table.
molar mass of isopropylbenzene: 120.21 g/mol
molar mass of *para*-nitro-isopropylbenzene: 165.21 g/mol
First set up the calculation for theoretical yield. Then use the percentage yield as a conversion factor to calculate actual yield.

$$775 \text{ g } C_9H_{12} \times \frac{1 \text{ mol } C_9H_{12}}{120.21 \text{ g } C_9H_{12}} \times \frac{1 \text{ mol } C_9H_{11}NO_2}{1 \text{ mol } C_9H_{12}} \times$$

$$\frac{165.21 \text{ g } C_9H_{11}NO_2}{1 \text{ mol } C_9H_{11}NO_2} \times \frac{91 \text{ g actual}}{100 \text{ g theoretical}} = ? \text{ g } C_9H_{11}NO_2$$

3 Calculate and verify

▶ Calculate, and round to the correct number of significant figures, which is two.
Calculator answer: 969.25673 g $C_9H_{11}NO_2$
Rounded answer: 970 g $C_9H_{11}NO_2$
▶ Verify your answer by rounding off the numbers in the setup and estimating.

$$800 \times \frac{1}{120} \times \frac{1}{1} \times \frac{160}{1} \times 0.9 \approx 960$$

Total recall

1. Distinguish between the limiting reactant and the excess reactant in a chemical reaction. How do chemists decide which reactant to use as the limiting reactant in a chemical reaction?

2. What is chemical equilibrium, and how is it indicated in a chemical equation?

3. What number describes a reaction's efficiency?

Practice problems

4. Titanium(IV) oxide, TiO_2, is used as a pigment in paints and as a whitening and coating agent for paper. It can be made by reacting O_2 with $TiCl_4$.

$$TiCl_4(g) + O_2(g) \longrightarrow TiO_2(s) + 2Cl_2(g)$$

   a. If 3.5 mol of $TiCl_4$ reacts with 4.5 mol of O_2, identify both the limiting and excess reactants.
   b. What amount of excess reactant will remain if the reaction goes to completion?
   c. What amount of each product should be formed if the reaction goes to completion?

5. When phosphorus burns in the presence of oxygen, P_4O_{10} is produced. In turn, P_4O_{10} reacts with water to produce phosphoric acid, H_3PO_4.

$$P_4O_{10}(g) + H_2O(l) \longrightarrow H_3PO_4(aq)$$

   a. Write a balanced chemical equation for the reaction shown above.
   b. When 100.0 g of P_4O_{10} reacts with 200.0 g of H_2O, what is the theoretical yield of phosphoric acid?
   c. If the actual yield is 126.2 g of H_3PO_4, what is the percentage yield for this reaction?

6. Quicklime, CaO, can be prepared by roasting limestone, $CaCO_3$, according to the chemical equation below. When 2.00×10^3 g of $CaCO_3$ are heated, the actual yield of CaO is 1.05×10^3 g. What is the percentage yield?

$$CaCO_3(s) \longrightarrow CaO(s) + CO_2(g)$$

7. Aluminum reacts with an aqueous solution containing excess copper(II) sulfate. If 1.85 g of Al reacts and the percentage yield of Cu is 56.6%, what mass of Cu is produced? (Hint: Remember to balance the equation.)

$$Al(s) + CuSO_4(aq) \longrightarrow Cu(s) + Al_2(SO_4)_3$$

8. If 50.0 g of benzaldehyde reacts with acetaldehyde, which is in excess, to make cinnamaldehyde and the percentage yield is 94.5%, how many grams of cinnamaldehyde will be produced?

Benzaldehyde + Acetaldehyde →

Cinnamaldehyde + Water

9. **Story Clue** When using an FRH, soldiers add 45 mL of water. What volume of water is theoretically necessary for the reaction of the 10.1 g of magnesium in the FRH? (Hint: the density of water is 1.0 g/mL.)

10. **Story Clue** Using your answer to Practice Problem 9, state whether water or magnesium is the limiting reactant.

How can stoichiometry be used?

OBJECTIVES

▶ *Relate* volume calculations in stoichiometry to the inflation of automobile safety air bags.

▶ *Use* the concept of limiting reactants to explain why fuel-air ratios affect engine performance.

▶ *Compare* the efficiency of pollution-control mechanisms in cars using percentage yield.

Stoichiometry and cars

So far in your study of stoichiometry, you have examined a number of chemical reactions with practical applications—from banana flavoring to cosmetics to aspirin. Here's one more application that you might not know about. During the 1960s, automobile manufacturers introduced driver safety air bags for protection. Air bags have saved the lives of thousands of drivers and passengers involved in accidents. The functioning of an air bag depends on stoichiometry.

Air-bag design depends on stoichiometric precision

Air bags are designed to protect occupants in a car from injuries during a high-speed front-end collision, as shown in **Figure 10-13.** When inflated, air bags slow the motion of the occupants so that they do not strike the steering wheel, windshield, or instrument panel as hard as they would without the air bag.

Stoichiometry is used by air-bag designers to ensure that air bags do not underinflate or overinflate. Bags that underinflate do not provide enough protection for the occupants, and bags that overinflate can cause injury and can even rupture, making them useless. To protect occupants adequately, air bags must fully inflate within one-tenth of a second after impact. The systems that make an air bag work this quickly are shown in **Figure 10-14.** A front-end collision transfers energy to a crash sensor that signals the firing of an igniter, which is similar to a small blasting cap. The igniter provides heat energy to start a reaction in a mixture called the *gas generant,* which forms a gaseous product. The igniter also raises the temperature and

FIGURE 10-13 ▼

When used in combination with seat belts, air bags can lessen the severity of injuries in a front-end collision.

► **FIGURE 10-14**

A series of events takes place, eventually producing the nitrogen gas that inflates the air bag.

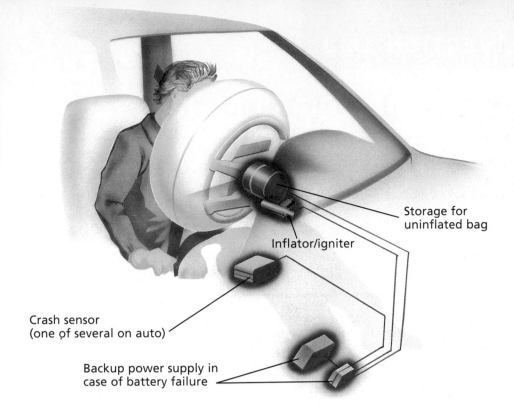

Storage for uninflated bag

Inflator/igniter

Crash sensor (one of several on auto)

Backup power supply in case of battery failure

pressure within the inflator, a metal vessel, so that the reaction occurs at a rate fast enough to fill the bag before the occupant strikes it. The inflator releases the gas into the bag while a high-efficiency filter keeps the reactants and the solid products away from the occupant.

For most current systems, the gas generant is a solid mixture of sodium azide, NaN_3, and an oxidizer. The gas that inflates the bag is almost pure nitrogen gas, N_2, which is produced in the following decomposition reaction.

$$2NaN_3(s) \longrightarrow 2Na(s) + 3N_2(g)$$

However, this reaction alone cannot inflate the bag fast enough, and the sodium metal produced is a dangerously reactive substance. Oxidizers such as ferric oxide, Fe_2O_3, are included in the gas generant so that they can react immediately with the sodium metal. This exothermic reaction raises the temperature more than a hundred degrees so that the gas fills the bag faster.

$$6Na(s) + Fe_2O_3(s) \longrightarrow 3Na_2O(s) + 2Fe(s) + 418 \text{ kJ}$$

But even sodium oxide is unsafe because it is an extremely corrosive substance. Eventually, it reacts with carbon dioxide, CO_2, and moisture from the air to form sodium hydrogen carbonate, or baking soda.

$$Na_2O(s) + 2CO_2(g) + H_2O(g) \longrightarrow 2NaHCO_3(s)$$

The amount of gas needed to fill an air bag of a certain volume depends on the volume of gas available and the density of the gas. Gas density, in turn, depends on temperature. To calculate the amount of gas generant necessary, air-bag designers must know the stoichiometry of the reactions and account for energy changes in the reactions, which may change the temperature and thus the density of the gas.

Assume that 65.1 L of N_2 gas is needed to inflate an air bag to the proper size. What mass of NaN_3 must be included in the gas generant to generate this volume of N_2? (Hint: The density of N_2 gas at this temperature is about 0.916 g/L.)

1 List what you know

▶ Volume of N_2: 65.1 L N_2
▶ Density of N_2: 0.916 g/L
▶ Mass of reactant: ? g NaN_3

2 Set up the problem

▶ Write and balance the chemical equation.
   balanced chemical equation: $2NaN_3(s) \longrightarrow 2Na(s) + 3N_2(g)$
▶ Calculate molar masses using the periodic table.
   molar mass of NaN_3: 65.02 g/mol
   molar mass of N_2: 28.02 g/mol
▶ First the product amount must be converted from a volume to a mass using density. Then it must be converted from a mass to an amount in moles using molar mass. Next the mole ratio is used to determine moles of reactant needed. Then the mass of reactant is calculated using molar mass as a conversion factor.

$$mL\ N_2 \longrightarrow g\ N_2 \longrightarrow mol\ N_2 \longrightarrow mol\ NaN_3 \longrightarrow g\ NaN_3$$

$$65.1\ L\ N_2 \times \frac{0.916\ g\ N_2}{1\ L\ N_2} \times \frac{1\ mol\ N_2}{28.02\ g\ N_2} \times \frac{2\ mol\ NaN_3}{3\ mol\ N_2} \times \frac{65.02\ g\ NaN_3}{1\ mol\ NaN_3} = ?\ g\ NaN_3$$

3 Calculate and verify

▶ Calculate, and round to the correct number of significant digits.
   Calculator answer: 92.2495035 g NaN_3
   Answer to three significant figures: 92.2 g NaN_3
▶ Verify your answer by rounding the numbers in the setup and estimating.

PRACTICE PROBLEMS

1. Calculate the number of grams of Fe_2O_3 that must be added to the gas generant for this mass of NaN_3.

2. Calculate the mass of sodium hydrogen carbonate produced in the air-bag reaction.

3. The density of $NaHCO_3$ is 2.20 g/mL. What volume of $NaHCO_3$ is produced by the reaction?

4. What mass of water and of sodium acetate would be produced by the reaction of $NaHCO_3$ and CH_3COOH to fill the above air bag with CO_2? Recall the volume of the air bag is 65.1 L. (Hint: The density of CO_2 at room temperature is 2.68 g/L.)

▲ FIGURE 10-15

Isooctane, one of the components found in gasoline, has properties that are similar to those of gasoline, which is a mixture.

Engine efficiency depends on reactant proportions

The gasoline used for automobiles can be treated as if it were pure isooctane, (2,2,4-trimethylpentane), whose structure is shown in **Figure 10-15.** This molecule has a molar mass that is about the same as the weighted average of the molecules within the gasoline. The other reactant in gasoline combustion is oxygen, which is only 20.9% of air by volume. The reaction for gasoline combustion can be written as follows.

$$2C_8H_{18}(l) + 25O_2(g) \longrightarrow 16CO_2(g) + 18H_2O(g) + 10\ 900\ kJ$$

For efficient combustion, the two reactants must be mixed in a mole ratio that is close to the one shown in the balanced chemical equation. If either reactant is restricted too much, the engine might stall. If you pump the gas pedal too much before starting, the mixture will contain almost entirely gasoline, and the lack of oxygen may prevent the mixture from burning. This is referred to as "flooding the engine." On the other hand, if there is too much oxygen and not enough gasoline, the engine will stall just as if the car were out of gas. These situations are illustrated in the model carburetor in **Figure 10-16.**

▼ FIGURE 10-16

Engine running at normal speeds

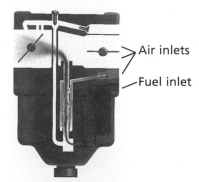
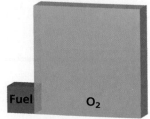

1:16 fuel-oxygen ratio by mass

Engine starting

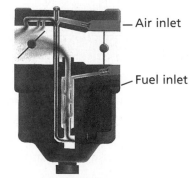

1:12 fuel-oxygen ratio by mass

Engine idling

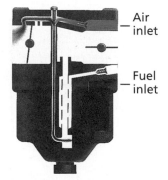

1:9 fuel-oxygen ratio by mass

a Under ordinary running conditions, an engine's fuel-oxygen ratio is maintained by the carburetor at 1:16, instead of the 1:12.5 (2:25) stoichiometric mole ratio. The mixture is slightly "lean," meaning that gasoline is the limiting reactant. Oxygen is in excess.

b When an engine is starting, the mixture is very "rich," with a 1:12 mole ratio of fuel to oxygen. Oxygen is the limiting reactant, and gasoline is in excess.

c When an engine is idling, the reaction mixture is kept rich at a 1:9 fuel-oxygen mole ratio. Oxygen is the limiting reactant. This ensures that there will always be plenty of fuel for the combustion reaction.

What volume of air must react with 1.00 L of isooctane for combustion to occur completely? At 20°C, the density of isooctane is 0.692 g/mL and the density of oxygen is 1.33 g/L. (Hint: Air is 21% O_2, so use the conversion factor 21 L O_2 / 100 L air.)

1 **List what you know**

▶ Make a table to organize the data.

Reactant	Formula	Molar mass	Density	Volume
Isooctane	C_8H_{18}	? g/mol	0.692 g/mL	1.00 L
Oxygen	O_2	? g/mol	1.33 g/L	? L

Percentage of oxygen in air: 21% oxygen
Volume of air needed: ? L

2 **Set up the problem**

▶ Write and balance the chemical equation:

$$2C_8H_{18} + 25O_2 \longrightarrow 16CO_2 + 18H_2O$$

▶ Calculate molar masses.
molar mass of isooctane: 114.26 g/mol
molar mass of oxygen: 32.00 g/mol

▶ The volume of isooctane must be converted to mass and then to moles. Then the mole ratio is used to convert to moles of oxygen. The moles of oxygen must be converted to mass and then to volume of oxygen. Then the percentage of oxygen in air is used to convert to volume of air.

$$1.00 \text{ L } C_8H_{18} \times \frac{1000 \text{ mL}}{1 \text{ L}} \times \frac{0.692 \text{ g } C_8H_{10}}{1 \text{ mL } C_8H_{18}} \times \frac{1 \text{ mol } C_8H_{18}}{114.26 \text{ g } C_8H_{18}} \times$$

$$\frac{25 \text{ mol } O_2}{2 \text{ mol } C_8H_{18}} \times \frac{32.00 \text{ g } O_2}{1 \text{ mol } O_2} \times \frac{1 \text{ L } O_2}{1.33 \text{ g } O_2} \times \frac{100 \text{ L air}}{21 \text{ L } O_2} = ? \text{ L air}$$

3 **Calculate and verify**

▶ Calculate, and round off correctly.
Calculator answer: 8.6736307×10^3 L air
Rounded answer: 8.7×10^3 L air

1. Figure 10-16a describes the fuel-air *mole* ratio necessary for ordinary running conditions. Indicate what volume of the limiting reactant would need to be added to bring the following fuel volume ratios to the proper stoichiometric ratio.
   a. 3.00 L of isooctane: 35 000.0 L of air
   b. 24.75 L of isooctane: 2.00×10^5 L of air
   c. 57.3 mL of isooctane: 400.0 L of air

2. What volume of liquid water is produced from the combustion of 1.0 L of 2,2,4-trimethylpentane, C_8H_{18}?

TABLE 10-4 — Clean Air Act Standards for 1996 Air Pollution*

Pollutant	Cars	Light trucks	Motorcycles
Hydrocarbons	0.25 g/km	0.50 g/km	5.0 g/km
Carbon monoxide	2.1 g/km	2.1–3.1 g/km, depending on truck size	12 g/km
Oxides of nitrogen (NO, NO_2)	0.25 g/km	0.25–0.68 g/km, depending on truck size	not regulated

*Note: Excludes standards for diesel-powered vehicles. EPA standards for cars and light trucks are actually expressed in grams per mile at 75°F.

Car designers use stoichiometry to control pollution

Automobiles are the primary source of air pollution in many parts of the world. The Clean Air Act was enacted in 1968 to address the issue of the amount of photochemical smog, as shown in **Figure 10-17,** and other pollution caused by automobile exhaust. This act was amended in 1990 to set new, more-restrictive emission control standards for automobiles driven in the United States. **Table 10-4** lists the latest standards for automobile exhaust. The standards are issued by the U.S. Environmental Protection Agency. The maximum allowable amount of pollutant the vehicle can produce per kilometer driven is shown in Table 10-4.

The equation for the combustion of isooctane shows most of what happens when gasoline burns but it does not tell the whole story. For example, if the fuel-air mixture is improperly balanced and there is not enough oxygen, as when a car is started, some carbon monoxide will be produced instead of carbon dioxide. In cold weather, cars need even more fuel to start than usual, so unburned hydrocarbons come out as exhaust and more carbon monoxide is formed. In addition, the high-temperature environment of the engine promotes the formation of nitrogen oxides from the nitrogen and oxygen in air.

One of the Clean Air Act standards limits the amount of nitrogen oxides, NO and NO_2, that a car can emit. Such compounds can combine with oxygen and water in the atmosphere to produce nitric acid, a constituent of acid rain. In addition, these compounds can react with oxygen to produce another harmful chemical, ozone. Because these chemicals are produced in reactions that are catalyzed by energy from the sun's ultraviolet light, they form what is referred to as photochemical smog. Although photochemical smog is easy to detect around many cities, it is caused by very small amounts of pollutants.

▼ **FIGURE 10-17**

Smog is a problem for many cities in the world. It not only is unpleasant to look at but also can make breathing difficult for many people.

FIGURE 10-18 ◄

The catalytic converters used in automobiles effectively decrease nitrogen oxides, carbon monoxide, and hydrocarbons in exhaust, unless the converter is exposed to leaded gasoline or conditions of extreme heat.

Catalytic converter containing ceramic pellets coated with platinum, palladium, or rhodium catalysts

Formation of photochemical smog begins when NO_2 molecules absorb light. The NO_2 decomposes as it absorbs this energy and produces oxygen *atoms* and nitrogen(II) oxide molecules. In turn, the oxygen atoms produced by the NO_2 decomposition react with oxygen molecules in the air to produce ozone.

$$NO_2(g) \xrightarrow{\text{ultraviolet light}} NO(g) + O(g)$$

$$O_2(g) + O(g) \longrightarrow O_3(g)$$

You may already know that ozone in the upper atmosphere serves as a protective shield against the sun's ultraviolet rays. But closer to Earth, ozone is a very reactive molecule that can crack rubber, corrode metals, and damage living tissues. In addition, ozone can undergo a complex series of reactions with any hydrocarbons that are not completely burned by a car's engine. The products of these reactions also contribute to photochemical smog.

Automobile manufacturers use stoichiometry to predict when adjustments will be necessary to keep exhaust emissions within legal limits. Because the units in Table 10-4 are *grams per kilometer,* auto manufacturers must consider how much fuel the vehicle will burn to move a certain distance. Automobiles with better gas mileage will use less fuel per kilometer. Cars that are more fuel efficient should also have slightly lower emissions per kilometer.

Most cars have catalytic converters, like the one shown in **Figure 10-18,** to treat the exhaust before it is released into the air. The platinum, palladium, or rhodium found in these converters assists in the decomposition of NO_2 into N_2 and O_2, harmless gases already found in the air. Catalytic converters also decrease emissions of CO and hydrocarbons. But catalytic converters perform at their best in warm weather and when the ratio of fuel to air in the engine is very close to the proper stoichiometric ratio. Newer cars include on-board computers and oxygen sensors to make sure the proper ratio is maintained so that the engine and the catalytic converter work at top efficiency.

internetconnect

SC*LINKS*

NSTA

TOPIC: Catalytic converters
GO TO: www.scilinks.org
KEYWORD: HW103

SAMPLE PROBLEM 10I Calculating yields: pollution

What mass of ozone, O_3, could be produced from 3.50 g of NO_2 contained in a car's exhaust? The net equation for this reaction is shown.

$$NO_2(g) + O_2(g) \longrightarrow NO(g) + O_3(g)$$

1 List what you know

- Balanced equation: $NO_2(g) + O_2(g) \longrightarrow NO(g) + O_3(g)$
- Mass of reactant: 3.50 g NO_2
- Mass of product: ? g O_3

2 Set up the problem

- Calculate molar masses.
  molar mass for NO_2: 46.01 g/mol
  molar mass for O_3: 48.00 g/mol
- First the mass of NO_2 must be converted to moles. Then the mole ratio is used to convert to moles of ozone. The moles of ozone are then converted to mass of ozone.

$$3.50 \text{ g } \cancel{NO_2} \times \frac{1 \text{ } \cancel{\text{mol } NO_2}}{46.01 \text{ g } \cancel{NO_2}} \times \frac{1 \text{ } \cancel{\text{mol } O_3}}{1 \text{ } \cancel{\text{mol } NO_2}} \times \frac{48.00 \text{ g } O_3}{1 \text{ } \cancel{\text{mol } O_3}} = ? \text{ g } O_3$$

3 Calculate

- Calculate, and round off correctly.

Calculator answer: 3.651380135 g O_3

Correct answer: 3.65 g O_3

SECTION REVIEW

Total recall

1. What type of reaction is used to produce the nitrogen gas used in air bags?
2. How is photochemical smog produced?
3. What substances are used in catalytic converters to eliminate CO and hydrocarbons?

Practice problems

4. What volume of N_2 gas is produced if 22.4 g of NaN_3 were placed inside an air-bag igniter.
5. What mass of O_2 could react with 18.3 g of O produced from the NO_2 emitted in a car's exhaust.
6. What mass of O_3 would be produced by the O_2 and O in item 5?
7. Assume that 74.0 g of isooctane must be combusted to drive a car for 1.0 km. Assume that all of the carbon atoms in the isooctane form CO. What mass of CO is produced?

At the beginning of this chapter, you learned about how the Army invented a way to make sure soldiers get hot meals without the use of combustion.

LOOKING BACK

Why was the magnesium-water reaction of the FRH chosen over trioxane and calcium oxide?

Soldiers have a great deal of equipment to carry. The less mass devoted to warming equipment, the better. Soldiers also operate under hectic conditions. The simpler the process used for meal preparation, the better. From the story, you know that the reaction of 1 mol of Mg produces more than five times as much energy as the reaction of 1 mol of CaO. When equal masses are compared, the advantage is even greater. But mole for mole and gram for gram, trioxane releases far more energy than does the Mg reaction. Why was this method discarded?

Trioxane must be used outside, it must be lit with matches or a lighter, and it takes longer to heat a meal. Conversely, an FRH can be used safely in vehicles, tents, ships, planes, and buildings. Furthermore, the energy released in the combustion of trioxane cannot be directly used to heat MREs. Instead, the burning trioxane has to heat a metal cup of water containing the MRE pouch.

Why is there a difference between the volume of water that is added and the volume of water the reaction requires?

To warm a meal in the FRH, 45 mL of water is added, even though the balanced chemical equation requires only 12 mL. Because it is inexpensive and readily available, water is used in excess. Thus, the more expensive magnesium is the limiting reactant and is completely consumed in the reaction. The extra water also provides efficient heat transfer over a larger area and makes up for any water absorbed by the porous pad.

The designers of this system had to consider how varying quantities of water would affect the reaction. If too little water was added, the reaction would not go to completion, some magnesium would be wasted, and not as much energy would be generated. On the other hand, excess water would absorb heat that could be warming the meal. A balance between these competing concerns provided the most efficient FRH.

CHAPTER 10

HIGHLIGHTS

KEY TERMS

10-1
ester
stoichiometry

10-2
actual yield
chemical equilibrium

excess reactant
limiting reactant

percentage yield
theoretical yield

KEY CONCEPTS

10-1 How much can a reaction produce?

▶ Reaction stoichiometry compares the mass and amount of substances in a chemical reaction.

▶ Composition stoichiometry describes the relationship among the elements within a substance.

▶ Stoichiometry problems can be solved with conversion factors created from mole ratios, molar masses, density, and Avogadro's constant.

10-2 How much does a reaction really produce?

▶ Once the limiting reactant has been used up, no more product can be formed, no matter how much of the other reactant(s) remains.

▶ The theoretical yield is the calculated maximum mass of product possible from a given mass of reactants.

▶ The actual yield is the mass of product experimentally measured after the reaction of a given mass of reactants.

▶ Percentage yield is 100 times the ratio of actual yield to theoretical yield. Percentage yield describes reaction efficiency.

10-3 How can stoichiometry be used?

▶ Stoichiometry is used by automobile designers to maximize a car's safety and performance while minimizing its environmental impact.

▶ Engineers apply stoichiometry to automobile air bags, fuel delivery systems, and pollution control devices.

KEY SKILLS

Review the following models before your exam. Be sure you can solve these types of problems.

How To Solve stoichiometry problems (p. 349)

Sample Problem 10A: Mass-mass stoichiometry (p. 351)

Sample Problem 10B: Mole-mass stoichiometry (p. 353)

Sample Problem 10C: Stoichiometric calculations with density (p. 355)

Sample Problem 10D: Determining the limiting reactant (p. 359)

Sample Problem 10E: Calculating percentage yield (p. 363)

Sample Problem 10F: Using percentage yield (p. 365)

Sample Problem 10G: Air-bag stoichiometry and density (p. 369)

Sample Problem 10H: Stoichiometric calculations: air-fuel ratio (p. 371)

Sample Problem 10I: Calculating yields: pollution (p. 374)

REVIEW & ASSESS

1. If the forward reaction is occurring at the same speed as the reverse reaction, a chemical reaction is said to be in ——.
(stoichiometry, limiting reactant, chemical equilibrium)

2. A(n)—— is often responsible for the flavor of a fruit.
(organic acid, ester, limiting reactant)

3. When a reaction goes to completion, the —— is not totally consumed.
(limiting reactant, excess reactant, actual yield)

4. You can determine the maximum amount of product expected from a reaction by calculating the ——.
(actual yield, percentage yield, theoretical yield)

5. If you want to know how much mass of a substance will be involved in a reaction, you should look at the reaction's ——.
(stoichiometry, actual yield, chemical equilibrium)

6. The relationship between actual yield and theoretical yield is expressed as the ——.
(differential yield, stoichiometry, percentage yield)

7. In a chemical reaction, the —— is consumed when the reaction goes to completion.
(excess reactant, limiting reactant, actual yield)

8. The —— is what chemists observe in a laboratory.
(actual yield, stoichiometry, theoretical yield)

CONCEPT & SKILLS REVIEW

STOICHIOMETRY

1. Explain the difference between reaction stoichiometry and composition stoichiometry.

2. Why is a balanced chemical equation required to solve stoichiometry problems?

3. A reaction between hydrazine, N_2H_4, and dinitrogen tetroxide, N_2O_4, has been used to launch rockets into space. The reaction produces nitrogen gas and water vapor, as shown in the unbalanced equation below.

$$N_2H_4(l) + N_2O_4(l) \longrightarrow N_2(g) + H_2O(g)$$

a. Write the balanced chemical equation for the reaction.
b. What is the mole ratio of N_2H_4 to N_2?
c What is the mole ratio of N_2O_4 to H_2O?
d. What amount of water will be produced from 14 000 mol of hydrazine used by a rocket?

Practice Problems

4. Various processes, including gasoline combustion in automobiles and industrial burning of fossil fuels, can result in the production of sulfur dioxide, SO_2. The SO_2 can undergo a series of reactions with oxygen and water in the air to form sulfuric acid eventually, as shown in the equation below. This acid mixes with moisture to form acid precipitation. If 0.500 g of sulfur dioxide from pollutants reacts with excess water and oxygen found in the air, what mass of sulfuric acid can be produced? **(Hint: See Sample Problem 10A.)**

$$2H_2O(l) + O_2(g) + 2SO_2(g) \longrightarrow 2H_2SO_4(aq)$$

5. Oxygen gas can be produced by decomposing potassium chlorate using the reaction below. If 125 g of $KClO_3$ is heated and decomposes completely. What amount of oxygen gas is produced? **(Hint: See Sample Problem 10B.)**

$$2KClO_3(s) \longrightarrow 2KCl(s) + 3O_2(g)$$

6. Oxygen gas and water are produced by the decomposition of hydrogen peroxide. If 10.0 mol of H_2O_2 decomposes, what volume of oxygen will be produced? Assume the density of oxygen is 1.429 g/L. **(Hint: See Sample Problem 10C.)**

$$2H_2O_2(aq) \longrightarrow 2H_2O(l) + O_2(g)$$

7. One of the intermediate steps in the production of nitric acid is the reaction between ammonia and oxygen. If 25 mol of ammonia gas react with excess oxygen, how many liters of NO will be produced? Assume the density of NO is 1.340 g/L. **(Hint: See Sample Problem 10C.)**

$$4NH_3(g) + 5O_2(g) \longrightarrow 4NO(g) + 6H_2O(g)$$

LIMITING REACTANTS

8. Differentiate a limiting reactant from an excess reactant.

9. Do all reactions have a limiting reactant? Explain.

10. When copper metal is added to a silver nitrate solution, silver metal and copper(II) nitrate are produced. If 100.0 g of copper metal is added to a solution containing 100.0 g of silver nitrate, what mass of silver metal will be produced? **(Hint: See Sample Problem 10D.)**

11. A fruit-scented air freshener can be made by reacting butanoic acid with methanol to produce methyl butanoate and water. How many grams of methyl butanoate can be produced if 50.0 g of butanoic acid reacts with 40.0 g of methanol? **(Hint: See Sample Problem 10D.)**

Butanoic acid   Methanol

Methyl butanoate   Water

12. Identify the limiting reactant and the excess reactant in the following situations:
  a. firewood burning in a campfire
  b. stomach acid reacting with a tablet of $Mg(OH)_2$
  c. sulfur compounds from the air tarnishing silver
  d. NO_2 gas reacting with oxygen and water vapor in air to produce acid rain

PERCENTAGE YIELD

13. a. Differentiate theoretical yield from actual yield.
  b. How is actual yield determined?
  c. How is theoretical yield determined?

14. Why do many chemical reactions produce less than the amount of product predicted by stoichiometry?

15. Magnesium metal is usually obtained from dissolved magnesium ions in sea water. A series of reactions produces magnesium chloride. Electrolysis is then used to decompose the magnesium chloride salt into magnesium metal and chlorine gas, as shown by the equation below. If 185 g of magnesium is recovered from 1000.0 g of magnesium chloride, what is the percentage yield for this reaction? **(Hint: See Sample Problem 10E.)**

$$MgCl_2(l) \longrightarrow Mg(s) + Cl_2(g)$$

16. The combustion of methane produces carbon dioxide and water. Assume that 2.0 mol of CH_4 burned in the presence of excess air. What is the percentage yield if the reaction produces 87.0 g CO_2? **(Hint: See Sample Problem 10E.)**

$$CH_4(g) + 2O_2(g) \longrightarrow CO_2(g) + 2H_2O(g)$$

17. Coal gasification is a process that converts coal into methane gas. If this reaction has a percentage yield of 85%, how much methane can be obtained from 1.255 g of coal? (Assume coal to be 100% carbon.)

$$2C(s) + 2H_2O(l) \longrightarrow CH_4(g) + CO_2(g)$$

18. If the percentage yield for the coal gasification process in item 17 is increased to 95.0%, how much methane can be obtained from 2.75 g of carbon?

19. A sandpaper company uses silicon carbide, SiC, to make its product. Reacting silicon dioxide with graphite yielded 30.0 kg of SiC. The theoretical yield is 991 mol. What is the percentage yield?

20. a. Can actual yield ever exceed theoretical yield? Explain.
  b. In the lab, you run an experiment that appears to have a percentage yield of 115%. Propose possible reasons for this result.

PRACTICAL USES OF STOICHIOMETRY

21. Use stoichiometry to explain the following problems that a lawn mower may have:
   a. A lawn mower fails to start because the engine floods.
   b. A lawn mower stalls after starting cold and idling.

22. Use stoichiometry to explain why a 4.00 kg firework would produce more light than a 2.00 kg firework containing the same proportion of reactants.

Practice Problems

23. Phosphate baking powder is a mixture of starch, sodium hydrogen carbonate, and calcium dihydrogen phosphate. When mixed with water, phosphate baking powder releases carbon dioxide gas, causing a dough or batter to bubble and rise.

$$2NaHCO_3(aq) + Ca(H_2PO_4)_2(aq) \longrightarrow 2Na^+(aq) + Ca^{2+}(aq) + 2HPO_4^{2-}(aq) + 2CO_2(g) + 2H_2O(l)$$

If 0.750 L of CO_2 is needed for a cake and each kilogram of baking powder contains 168 g of $NaHCO_3$, what mass of baking powder must be used to generate this amount of CO_2? The density of CO_2 at baking temperature is about 1.25 g/L. **(Hint: See Sample Problem 10G.)**

24. The addition of yeast can make bread rise because the yeast produces CO_2 from glucose, $C_6H_{12}O_6$, according to the equation below. Assume that 0.50 L of carbon dioxide is required for a loaf of bread. What mass of $C_6H_{12}O_6$ must be broken down by yeast to produce this amount of CO_2? The density of CO_2 at baking temperature is about 1.25 g/L. **(Hint: See Sample Problem 10G, and balance the equation.)**

$$C_6H_{12}O_6(s) \longrightarrow C_2H_5OH(l) + CO_2(g)$$

25. Plaster of Paris, $CaSO_4 \cdot \frac{1}{2}H_2O$, has many uses, including castings and dental cement. It can be obtained by heating gypsum, $CaSO_4 \cdot 2H_2O$. How many liters of water vapor evolve when 5.00 L of gypsum is heated at 110°C to produce plaster of Paris? At 110°C the density of $CaSO_4 \cdot 2H_2O$ is 2.32 g/mL, and

the density of water vapor is 0.581 g/L. **(Hint: See Sample Problem 10H.)**

$$2CaSO_4 \cdot 2H_2O(s) \longrightarrow$$
$$2CaSO_4 \cdot \tfrac{1}{2}H_2O(s) + 3H_2O(g)$$

26. Builders and dentists must store plaster of Paris, $CaSO_4 \cdot \frac{1}{2}H_2O$, in airtight containers to prevent it from absorbing water vapor and changing back into gypsum, $CaSO_4 \cdot 2H_2O$. If 7.50 kg of plaster of Paris absorbed excess water vapor, what volume of gypsum would form? The density of $CaSO_4 \cdot 2H_2O$ is 2.32 g/mL. **(Hint: See Sample Problem 10H.)**

$$2CaSO_4 \cdot \tfrac{1}{2}H_2O(s) + 3H_2O(g) \longrightarrow$$
$$2CaSO_4 \cdot 2H_2O(s)$$

27. Gold can be recovered from sea water by reacting the water with an active metal such as zinc, which is refined from zinc oxide. The zinc displaces the gold in the water. What mass of gold can be recovered if 2.00 g of ZnO and an excess of sea water are available? **(Hint: See Sample Problem 10I.)**

$$2ZnO(s) + C(s) \longrightarrow 2Zn(s) + CO_2(g)$$
$$2Au^{3+}(aq) + 3Zn(s) \longrightarrow 3Zn^{2+}(aq) + 2Au(s)$$

28. Explain the stoichiometry involved in blowing air on the base of a dwindling campfire to keep the coals burning.

29. Why would it be unreasonable for an amendment to the Clean Air Act to call for 0% pollution emissions from cars with combustion engines?

LINKING CHAPTERS

1. Recognizing reaction types
   Determine the conversion factors needed for the following problems. Be sure to write a balanced equation first.
   a. What mass of oxygen gas is evolved from the decomposition of a known amount of water?
   b. What amount of hydrochloric acid is needed to completely react with a known mass of zinc in a single-displacement reaction?

c. What amount of calcium carbonate is produced in a double-displacement reaction between a known mass of calcium nitrate and potassium carbonate?

2. Theme: Equilibrium and change
In some reactions the products react to reform the reactants. How is this reversal of a reaction similar to the dissolution and recrystallization of sugar from a saturated solution of sugar in iced tea?

ALTERNATIVE ASSESSMENTS

Performance assessment

1. Design an experiment to measure the percentage yields for the reactions listed below. If your teacher approves your design, acquire the necessary materials, and carry out your plan to obtain percentage yield data.
a. $Zn(s) + 2HCl(aq) \longrightarrow ZnCl_2(aq) + H_2(g)$
b. $2NaHCO_3(s) \longrightarrow Na_2CO_3 + H_2O(g) + CO_2(g)$
c. $CaCl_2(aq) + Na_2CO_3(aq) \longrightarrow$
$$CaCO_3(s) + 2NaCl(aq)$$
d. $NaOH(aq) + HCl(aq) \longrightarrow NaCl(aq) + H_2O(l)$
(Note: use only dilute NaOH and HCl, less concentrated than 1.0 mol/L.)

2. Your teacher will give you an index card specifying a volume of a gas. Reactants to make the gas will also be listed. Describe exactly how you would make the gas from the reactants. Include a method of collecting the gas without allowing it to mix with the air. Then specify how much of each reactant you need.

Choose a limiting reactant and explain your choice. If your teacher approves your plan, obtain the necessary materials and make the gas. (Hint: Look up the density of the gas in a chemical handbook.)

Portfolio projects

1. Research and communication
Research the composition of gasoline sold in your area. Contact a gasoline company to discover what formulations are used. Investigate whether the mixtures change by season or by geographic area. Find out if your area has any guidelines regarding gasoline additives that reduce air pollution. Present your findings in the class.

2. Cooperative activity
Investigate corporate, governmental, or private use of alternative fuel sources for vehicles. Hold a class debate to compare the costs and environmental effects of these alternative fuels.

3. Chemistry and you
Visit a car maintenance shop to find out how you can help reduce air pollution by increasing your car's efficiency. Make a checklist of tasks to perform regularly to help meet this goal.

4. Research and communication
Research the production of the following pollutants: methane, CH_4; mercury, Hg; lead, Pb; chlorine, Cl_2; and sulfur oxides, SO_X. Determine the stoichiometry involved in the production of each of these chemicals. Contact the EPA, and gather information on what you can do to help reduce pollution by these chemicals.

1. Stoichiometry problems require the use of a _____.
   a. table of bond energies
   b. Lewis structure
   c. chart of electron configurations
   d. mole ratio

2. In the chemical equation $A + B \longrightarrow C + D$, if you know the mass of A, you can determine _____.
   a. the mass of any of the other reactants and products
   b. only the mass of C and D combined
   c. only the mass of B
   d. only the mass of A and B combined

3. In order to solve a mass-mass stoichiometry problem it is necessary to know the _____.
   a. coefficients of the balanced equation
   b. phases of the reactants and products
   c. rate at which the reaction occurs
   d. chemical names of the reactants and products

4. For the reaction $N_2 + 3H_2 \longrightarrow 2NH_3$, _____ mol of N_2 is required to produce 18 mol of NH_3.
   a. 9   c. 18
   b. 27   d. 36

5. If a chemical reaction involving substances A and B stops when B is completely used, then B is referred to as the _____.
   a. excess reactant
   b. primary reactant
   c. limiting reactant
   d. primary product

6. The measured amount of a product obtained from a chemical reaction is called the _____.
   a. mole ratio
   b. theoretical yield
   c. percentage yield
   d. actual yield

7. If a chemist calculates the maximum amount of product that might be obtained in a chemical reaction, he or she is calculating the _____.
   a. theoretical yield   c. percentage yield
   b. mole ratio   d. actual yield

8. Knowing the mole ratio of a reactant and product in a chemical reaction would allow one to determine _____.
   a. the energy released in the reaction
   b. the mass of the product produced from a known mass of reactant
   c. the speed of the reaction
   d. whether the reaction was reversible

9. In stoichiometry, chemists are mainly concerned with _____.
   a. the types of bonds found in compounds
   b. energy changes occurring in chemical reactions
   c. mass relationships in chemical reactions
   d. speed with which chemical reactions occur

10. In the reaction $6CO_2 + 6H_2O \longrightarrow C_6H_{12}O_6 + 6O_2$, the mole ratio of CO_2 to $C_6H_{12}O_6$ is _____.
    a. 1:2   c. 6:1
    b. 1:1   d. 1:4

11. In a chemical reaction, the reactant remaining after all of the limiting reactant is completely used is referred to as the _____.
    a. product
    b. controlling reactant
    c. excess reactant
    d. catalyst

Causes of Change

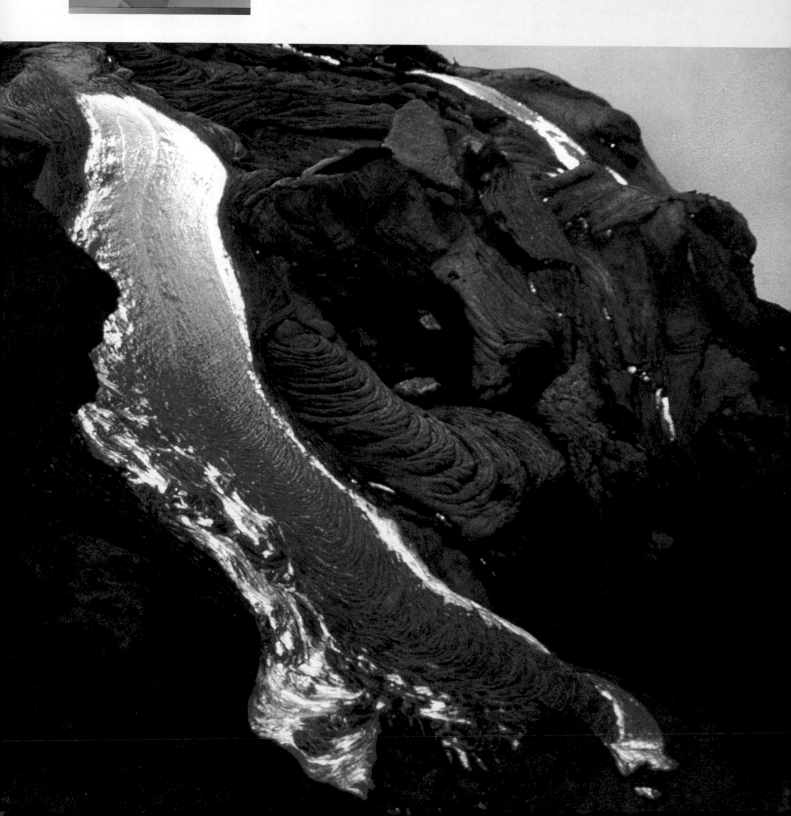

ENERGY AND LOW-EMISSION CARS

Engineers have long been searching for alternative energy sources to replace petroleum products in automobiles. Petroleum-based fuels produce toxic emissions, and petroleum reserves will eventually be exhausted.

Engineers have investigated solar-powered and battery-powered vehicles as well as internal-combustion engines that burn substances not made from fossil fuels. Hydrogen is one of the most promising alternative energy sources examined so far.

Hydrogen gas has two big advantages as a fuel. When compared to gasoline it produces few toxic emissions. The combustion of gasoline produces hydrocarbons and nitrogen and carbon oxides. These compounds contribute to acid rain, photochemical smog, and the greenhouse effect. When hydrogen is burned, no hydrocarbons or carbon oxides are emitted, and only small quantities of nitrogen oxides are produced. Second, the energy available from 1 g of hydrogen gas far exceeds that given off by other fuels, as shown in the table. Hydrogen gas has three times the energy content of gasoline.

So why aren't hydrogen-powered cars on the roads? One reason is the high cost of making such a car. Another reason is the expense of producing and distributing huge supplies of hydrogen gas.

Some people worry about the danger of storing hydrogen gas because it is highly reactive. But it is no more dangerous than storing gasoline or natural gas, which also react with oxygen. A serious obstacle to using hydrogen gas as a fuel is that it *cannot easily be liquefied.* There is no economical way to cool the gas to its boiling point of 20 K ($-253°C$). As a gas at ordinary pressure, nearly 3000 L of H_2 is needed to match the energy equivalent of 1 L of gasoline. Vehicles could carry compressed H_2, but that would require using unacceptably heavy cylinders.

Fuel (1 g)	Energy (kJ/g)
Methanol, $CH_3OH(l)$	23
Ethanol, $C_2H_5OH(l)$	30
Gasoline (octane), $C_8H_{18}(l)$	48
Propane, $C_3H_8(g)$	50
Natural gas (methane), $CH_4(g)$	56
Hydrogen, $H_2(g)$	142

CHAPTER LINKS

What drives the H_2 combustion reaction?

Is there a safe and economical way to carry H_2 in a car?

Would the use of hydrogen-powered cars lead to less pollution?

How does heat differ from other forms of energy?

OBJECTIVES

▶ *Cite* the two principles that govern most natural events.

▶ *Distinguish* between heat and temperature.

▶ *Propose* a qualitative explanation of entropy.

▶ *Define* molar heat capacity, and **calculate** its value from temperature measurements taken during heating experiments.

Governing principles

This chapter explores the driving forces behind chemical reactions and explains why reactions occur. Because chemical reactions are natural events, their driving forces may be found by examining other events in nature. Natural events are often accompanied by a decrease in energy, an increase in disorder, or both. For example, think about the water flow in a waterfall. Water that has fallen to the foot of a waterfall has a lower potential energy than it had at the top. Another example is a spinning wheel, which loses kinetic energy as it gradually slows down and stops. Of course the energy lost in these examples does not disappear. It becomes another form of energy, usually heat.

A natural event that is accompanied by an increase in disorder is the release of gas into the atmosphere. When gases are discharged into the atmosphere, they mix with the air and disperse. Another example of a natural event accompanied by increased disorder is seen in autumn, when leaves change color, fall, and scatter. This entropy increase is illustrated in **Figure 11-1**. In both of these examples the

▶ **FIGURE 11-1**

Falling leaves are an example of a natural event accompanied by an increase in disorder.

natural event results in a decrease in order. Later in the chapter, you will see that a decrease in energy and an increase in disorder govern chemical reactions. Energy and disorder in simpler processes, such as cooling and boiling, will also be examined. First you will learn the difference between heat and temperature.

Heat and temperature are different

Heat is thermal energy. Like other forms of energy, heat is measured in *joules*. A hot object has more heat than an otherwise similar cold object. When the two objects are placed in contact, energy spontaneously flows into the cooler object until the objects are the same temperature. This phenomenon is illustrated in **Figure 11-2a.** The total heat content of the two blocks shown in the diagram remains constant because the gain in thermal energy by the cool block exactly equals the loss in thermal energy by the warm block.

Certainly you have a natural sense of what is hot and what is cold. But what is *temperature*? In **Figure 11-2b,** the beaker on the left has a higher heat content than the beaker on the right, but its temperature is lower. That is because temperature represents the *intensity* of thermal energy, whereas heat indicates the *quantity* of thermal energy.

The SI temperature unit is the *kelvin,* although scientific thermometers are usually graduated in *degrees Celsius*. The interval in the two scales is the same, so a temperature *difference* has the same numerical value in kelvins and in degrees Celsius. For example, consider the temperature difference between the two blocks in Figure 11-2a.

$$\Delta T = T_{left} - T_{right} = 40°C = 40 \text{ K}$$

On the other hand, because 0.00°C is equal to 273.15 K, *individual temperatures are different* on the two scales.

$$T_{left} = 65°C = 338 \text{ K}$$
$$T_{right} = 25°C = 298 \text{ K}$$

FIGURE 11-2 ▼

a Heat always flows from a warmer object to a cooler object.

b The liquid on the left has a higher heat content than the liquid on the right. The large volume of the liquid on the left disperses the heat, so the liquid has a lower temperature.

QUICKLAB

A Randomness Model

In this activity, you will model the random positions of molecules by using individual playing cards to represent molecules.

Materials 3 different playing cards

Problem Obtain a set of three different playing cards from your instructor. Put the cards in as many different arrangements as you can. Record the number of possible arrangements. Next select one card to always be in the first (or leftmost) position. Record the number of possible arrangements. Repeat, this time keeping two cards in a constant position. Record the number of possible arrangements.

Analysis

1. What is the relationship between the possible number of arrangements and the number of cards that can be arranged? How does restricting the position of one card affect the number of arrangements?
2. If randomness is the number of distinguishable arrangements, which set is most random? the least random?
3. Entropy is a measure of disorder in systems. Using this definition, which set models the greatest entropy? the least entropy?

Both temperature and heat reflect kinetic energy

The atoms in a gas, liquid, or solid are in constant motion, which means they have kinetic energy. The heat, or thermal energy, of a body is the *total random kinetic energy of its atoms*. The temperature of a substance, on the other hand, reflects the *average random kinetic energy of its atoms*. Remember that kinetic energy is related to velocity. Atoms move faster at high temperatures and slower at lower temperatures. Imagine a piece of gold metal being cooled. As heat is removed, the temperature falls, and the kinetic energy of the gold atoms decreases. As the kinetic energy decreases, the velocity of the atoms decreases. In solids, atoms move by vibrating in their crystal lattice. Some of the atoms vibrate faster than others, but the average speed of the atomic vibrations falls as the temperature decreases. By the time the temperature reaches absolute zero (0.00 K), the atoms have practically stopped moving.

Can you now appreciate the importance of the Kelvin temperature scale? Its zero corresponds to the absence of motion. There are no negative temperatures on the Kelvin scale because you can't have negative motion. Always convert temperatures to the Kelvin scale before carrying out heat and temperature calculations.

Water shows a steady increase in temperature when heated

Think about how the temperature of a beaker of water changes as energy is supplied to the system by a 100 W heater. If the beaker contains 360.3 g of H_2O (20.00 mol) initially at 15°C and the heater is switched on, the water temperature starts to rise. If the temperature is recorded every 15 seconds until it reaches 30°C, you get the data in **Figure 11-3.** The recorded temperatures are converted to kelvins and graphed against time.

After an initial lag, the temperature rises steadily with time. A straight line has been drawn through some of the data points, and its slope can be measured using the following formula.

$$\text{slope} = \frac{y_2 - y_1}{x_2 - x_1}$$

$$= \frac{T_2 - T_1}{t_2 - t_1} = \frac{\Delta T}{\Delta t}$$

You may remember the slope formula as the following.

$$\text{slope} = \frac{\text{rise}}{\text{run}}$$

Scientists use the symbol Δ as a shorthand way of writing "change in." So $\Delta T/\Delta t$ means the change in temperature, ΔT, that occurs while time is changing by an interval, Δt.

If you choose any two points on the line that are not data points and substitute them in the equation for determining slope, you can determine the rate at which the temperature increases. For example, during a time interval of 150 seconds the temperature rose 9.9 K. The rate is calculated as follows.

$$\text{slope} = \frac{\Delta T}{\Delta t} = \frac{9.9\ \text{K}}{150\ \text{s}} = 0.066\ \text{K/s}$$

The temperature increases by 0.066 kelvins per second during most of the experiment.

What energy changes occur in this experiment? The temperature increase is evidence that the thermal energy of the water increases. How much heat is required to produce a temperature rise of 1 K? That quantity depends on the substance being heated and is called a substance's *heat capacity*. You may recall that heat capacity was introduced in Chapter 2 as a property of matter. The heat capacity of an object is the thermal energy needed to raise its temperature by 1 K. Chemists are most interested in energies per mole, so they measure the **molar heat capacity** of substances. Molar heat capacity is given the symbol C and is the *heat required to increase the temperature of 1 mol of a substance by 1 K. C* is just the specific heat capacity for a substance that you learned about in Chapter 2. In the following equation, q is the heat needed to increase the temperature of n moles of a substance by ΔT.

$$q = nC\Delta T$$

You can now determine the molar heat capacity of water by using the data from the experiment and the equation for q. This process is demonstrated in Sample Problem 11A.

Change in Water Temperature on Heating

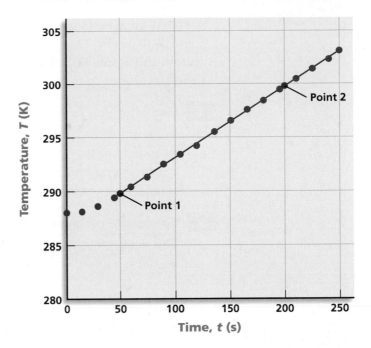

FIGURE 11-3

Experimental data points cluster around a straight line when temperature is plotted against time.

molar heat capacity

the heat required to increase the temperature of 1 mol of a substance by 1 K

A 100 W heater is used to heat 20.00 mol of water. The temperature is recorded every 15 s and the data are plotted to produce the graph shown in Figure 11-3. The slope of the graph is calculated to be 0.066 K/s. Use these data to calculate the molar heat capacity for water.

1   List what you know

▶ amount of water = 20.00 mol
▶ capacity of the heater = 100. W
▶ rate of temperature increase $(\Delta T / \Delta t)$ = 0.066 K/s
▶ molar heat capacity of water = ?J/K•mol

2   Set up the problem

The molar heat capacity for water, C, is defined as the amount of heat required to raise the temperature of 1 mol of H_2O by 1 K.

$$C = \frac{q}{n\Delta T}$$

First calculate how much heat was input. One watt equals one joule per second (1 J/s). The total heat supplied by a 100 W heater over a time interval, Δt, can be found by the following equation.

$$q = (100. \text{ J/s})\Delta t$$

There are 20.00 mol of water in the beaker, n = 20.00 mol. Substitute the known values to calculate C.

$$C = \frac{q}{n\Delta T} = \frac{(100. \text{ J/s})\Delta t}{n\Delta T}$$

In the above expression you see $\dfrac{\Delta t}{\Delta T}$. This fraction is the inverse of the slope, so 1/slope is substituted into the equation.

3   Calculate and verify

$$C = \frac{q}{n\Delta T} = \frac{(100. \text{ J/s})\Delta t}{n\Delta T} = \frac{100. \text{ J/s}}{n(slope)}$$

$$= \frac{100. \text{ J/\cancel{s}}}{(20.00 \text{ mol})(0.066 \text{ K/\cancel{s}})} = 76 \text{ J/K•mol}$$

Solving the expression gives an answer in J/K•mol. The unit of molar heat capacity is *joules per kelvin per mole,* so the units are correct.

PRACTICE PROBLEMS

1. Use the molar heat capacity for water from Sample Problem 11A to calculate the amount of heat energy needed to raise the temperature of 90.0 g of H_2O from 35°C to 45°C.

2. Use the molar heat capacity for water from Sample Problem 11A to calculate the amount of heat energy needed to raise the temperature of 1.8 g of H_2O from 10.0°C to 80.0°C.

Molar heat capacity depends on the number of atoms

The experimental C value just calculated for water is close to the molar heat capacity value listed in **Table 11-1.** Notice the uniform heat capacities of metals and the *identical* molar heat capacities of the noble gases.

A mole of tungsten has a mass of 184 g, whereas a mole of aluminum has a mass of only about 27 g. So you might predict that more heat would be needed to increase the temperature of 1 mol of tungsten by 1 K than to increase the temperature of 1 mol aluminum by 1 K. But Table 11-1 shows that mole for mole, the same heat input is needed to raise 1 mol of either metal by 1 K. Aluminum and tungsten have the same molar heat capacity. The reason is that heat energy is taken up by increasing the kinetic energies of the atoms, and there are exactly the same number of atoms in 1 mol of each metal. The type of metal atom is largely irrelevant. It's the number of atoms that affects the molar heat capacity of a substance.

Notice that the C values in Table 11-1 for the metal chlorides are close to a 2:3:4 ratio. This is the ratio of the total numbers of ions in the formula. For example, there are 1.5 times as many ions in 1 mol of $BaCl_2$ in 1 mol of NaCl, so you would predict a 50% larger molar heat capacity for $BaCl_2$. There are twice as many ions per mole in Hg_2Cl_2 as in NaCl, so you would predict twice the molar heat capacity of Hg_2Cl_2 compared with NaCl.

TABLE 11-1 Molar Heat Capacities

Substance	C (J/K•mol)
Iron, Fe(s)	25.1
Silver, Ag(s)	25.3
Tungsten, W(s)	24.2
Aluminum, Al(s)	24.2
Sodium chloride, NaCl(s)	50.5
Barium chloride, $BaCl_2$(s)	75.1
Mercury(I) chloride, Hg_2Cl_2(s)	102.0
Water, H_2O(s)	37.4
Water, H_2O(l)	75.3
Water, H_2O(g)	36.8
Octane, C_8H_{18}(l)	254.0
Helium, He(g)	20.8
Neon, Ne(g)	20.8
Argon, Ar(g)	20.8
Hydrogen, H_2(g)	28.8
Nitrogen, N_2(g)	29.1
Chlorine, Cl_2(g)	33.9

CONCEPT CHECK

1. What two tendencies drive natural events?
2. What kind of energy is heat, and what unit is it measured in?
3. Distinguish between heat and temperature in terms of the kinetic energy of atoms.
4. **Interpreting Graphics** Which of the two blocks shown in Figure 11-2a gained energy?
5. **Interpreting Graphics** If the beakers in Figure 11-2b held the *same* volume of liquid but their temperatures were still as shown, which flask would contain more thermal energy?
6. **Interpreting Graphics** What are the temperatures of the liquid samples in Figure 11-2b in kelvins? What is the temperature *difference* between the liquid on the right and the liquid on the left in degrees Celsius? in kelvins?

Thermodynamics

The invention of the steam engine 200 years ago and the Industrial Revolution brought urbanization and other exciting changes to the world. These technological advances led to a new branch of science called **thermodynamics.**

Thermo- means "heat," and *dynamics* means "motion." Thermodynamics originally referred to the study of the conversion of heat into mechanical energy. Thermodynamics has since been expanded to include all energy changes that accompany physical and chemical processes.

thermodynamics

the branch of science concerned with the energy changes accompanying physical and chemical processes

Heat energy is disorderly atomic motion

Why is heat different from other kinds of energy? Scientists picture the thermal energy of an iron wheel, for example, as the kinetic energy of the Fe atoms randomly vibrating in their metallic lattice. When 45 kJ of heat is applied to a 10 kg wheel, the wheel gets 10 K hotter. Each atom receives about 7.5×10^{-20} J of the supplied thermal energy. The additional energy makes each Fe atom vibrate a little faster. The vibrations are random in that the direction one atom moves is not related to the directions its neighbors move. The atoms behave independently.

Consider a wheel that is rotated to produce 45 kJ of mechanical energy. As in the previous example, the energy supplied is distributed among the kinetic energies of the Fe atoms. Each atom receives approximately 7.5×10^{-20} J. This is the same amount of energy that is received when the wheel is heated. However, this time the extra kinetic energy is *concerted;* all atoms move in the same direction.

Thus, heat energy is described as energy of disorderly atomic motion, while other forms of energy are seen as orderly motion or orderly arrangements of particles. Recall that nature favors changes that proceed toward lower energy and greater disorder. The tendency toward greater disorder explains why it is easier to convert other forms of energy to heat energy and why the reverse process is inefficient.

entropy

a measure of the randomness or disorder of a system

▼ **FIGURE 11-4**

Ice has a lower entropy than liquid water because it has more order.

Entropy measures disorder

Disorder is quantified as a property called **entropy.** Entropy is a measure of the total disorder in a substance or system. Chemists are mainly concerned with *molar entropy,* which is the quantity of entropy possessed by 1 mol of a substance. It is expressed in the same units used for molar heat capacity, J/K•mol, and is represented by the symbol S. **Figure 11-4** shows water in two of its three states. The molar entropies of water in its three states are very different. Molar entropies are always positive, except at 0.0 K, where they are generally zero. The entropy of a substance increases with temperature. The molar entropy of $H_2O(l)$ is 69.9 J/mol•K at 298 K. The molar entropy of $H_2O(g)$ is 188.7 J/mol•K.

The gaseous form of water has a much greater entropy than the liquid form. The liquid form has a greater entropy than ice. Atoms in the crystal lattice of a solid are highly ordered, so it makes sense that they have a low entropy. Atoms or molecules in liquids can move more freely than those in solids. Thus, liquids have greater molar entropies than solids. Atoms and molecules in the gaseous state have the most freedom to move, so their molar entropies are the greatest.

The entropy of a substance increases with temperature. With few exceptions, the entropy of a pure substance is zero at absolute zero (0 K). That is because all substances are solids, and most have perfectly ordered crystal lattices at 0 K. No disorder means no entropy.

SECTION REVIEW

Total recall

1. **a.** Define *entropy*.
   b. Define *molar entropy*.
2. What is the SI unit for temperature?
3. Describe what happens to all atoms at 0.00 K.
4. **a.** What is the symbol for molar heat capacity?
   b. What is the symbol for molar entropy?
5. Define *thermodynamics*.
6. What is the common term used for thermal energy?

Critical thinking

7. What natural driving force causes ice to melt spontaneously at room temperature?
8. **Interpreting Tables** Examine Table 11-1. Explain why the molar heat capacity of octane is the highest value listed on this table.
9. Why is the molar entropy of water vapor higher than that of ice?

10. How is it possible that the temperature *difference* has the same numerical value in kelvins and in degrees Celsius?
11. **a.** What is the relationship between heat and kinetic energy?
    b. What is the relationship between temperature and kinetic energy?

Practice problems

12. Use Table 11-1 to predict the molar heat capacity of $AlCl_3(s)$.
13. **Story Clue** Use the table on page 383 to calculate the quantity of energy liberated when 1 mol of $H_2(g)$ is combusted.
14. Use the molar heat capacity for aluminum from Table 11-1 to calculate the amount of heat energy needed to raise the temperature of 260 g of aluminum from 0°C to 125°C.
15. Use the molar heat capacity for iron from Table 11-1 to calculate the amount of heat energy needed to raise the temperature of 260 g of iron from 0°C to 125°C.

How does temperature affect enthalpy and entropy?

OBJECTIVES

▶ *Classify* properties of matter as extensive or intensive.

▶ *Describe* the temperature, enthalpy, and entropy changes in a substance when it is heated.

▶ *Calculate* the molar enthalpy change for a substance on heating.

Thermodynamic properties

Thermodynamics is concerned with much more than the conversion of heat into mechanical energy. Thermodynamics deals with energy transformations of all kinds. To study the relationship between energy and matter, we shall look at three properties. One of these properties is entropy. Another property is enthalpy. Enthalpy was introduced in Section 9-3. The third property used in discussing thermodynamics is called *Gibbs energy*. Gibbs energy is described in Section 11-3.

Enthalpy is the energy of an atom or molecule

You may think of enthalpy as the heat, or thermal energy, of a substance. When something is heated at constant pressure, its enthalpy increase equals the thermal energy it receives. The symbol for molar enthalpy is H because enthalpy was once called "heat content." A change in enthalpy can be measured when a substance is heated or cooled, but scientists have no way to measure the enthalpy itself. Scientists have, therefore, agreed to assign *all elements under standard conditions a molar enthalpy of zero*. Writing a small superscript zero, as in H^0, means "under standard conditions."

extensive property

a property that depends on the amount of material present

Enthalpy and entropy are extensive properties

These properties of matter—enthalpy and entropy—may be new to you, and they are easy to confuse. Think of enthalpy as the *energy* that is "inside" an object or substance. Entropy, on the other hand, measures the *amount of disorder* "inside" a body or substance and is not a form of energy.

In your study of chemistry you have come across many properties of matter. Some are listed in **Table 11-2.** The properties are divided into two groups. **Extensive properties** depend on how much of the material you're dealing

TABLE 11-2 Properties of Matter

Extensive	Intensive
Mass, m	Density, D
Volume, V	Pressure, P
Heat capacity, C	Temperature, T
Enthalpy, H	Concentration, c
Entropy, S	

with, so the quantity of substance must be specified. **Intensive properties** are specific to the particular substance and do not depend on how much material is present. For example, you can say that the density of copper is 8.960 g/cm^3 because density is an intensive property. But you must specify a particular sample size when discussing the mass or volume of copper. Enthalpy and entropy are extensive properties because they depend on the amount of substance. **Table A-13** in the Appendix lists the molar enthalpies and molar entropies, which are intensive properties, for many elements and compounds.

Temperature affects molar enthalpy

Revisit the experiment described in Figure 11-3. Over a 150 second interval, 20.00 mol of water received 15.0 kJ of thermal energy. How much did the water's molar enthalpy increase? The total enthalpy increase was equal to the heat input, q. So the *molar* enthalpy increase, ΔH, can be found by dividing by n, the moles of water.

$$\Delta H = \frac{q}{n} = \frac{15.0 \text{ kJ}}{20 \text{ mol}} = 0.750 \text{ kJ/mol}$$

You saw in Section 11-1 that the amount of heat, q, delivered to n mol of a substance to raise the substance's temperature by ΔT is represented by the following equation.

$$q = nC\Delta T$$

Thus, the molar enthalpy change of a substance is related to its molar heat capacity, C, using the following equation.

$$\Delta H = \frac{q}{n} = \frac{nC\Delta T}{n} = C\Delta T$$

So the molar enthalpy change of a substance upon heating is simply the molar heat capacity multiplied by the temperature change. Use this formula to check the calculation from the experiment. In Figure 11-3, the temperature increase between Point 1 and Point 2 is 9.9 K, and the measured molar heat capacity of water is 76 J/K•mol.

$$\Delta H = (76 \text{ J/K•mol})(9.9 \text{ K}) = 750 \text{ J/mol} = 0.750 \text{ kJ/mol}$$

Both equations for ΔH produce the same result.

SAMPLE PROBLEM 11B **Calculating molar enthalpy change**

How much does the molar enthalpy change when a 92.3 g block of ice is cooled from –0.2°C to –5.4°C?

1 **List what you know**

▶ Mass of H$_2$O(s) = 92.3 g
▶ Initial temperature = –0.2°C
▶ Final temperature = –5.4°C
▶ Molar enthalpy change, ΔH = ?

2 **Set up the problem**

- You will need the molar heat capacity of ice from Table 11-1. The unit for molar heat capacity includes kelvins, so you will have to convert the Celsius temperatures in the problem to kelvins.

$$C = 37.4 \text{ J/K} \cdot \text{mol from Table 11-1}$$

$$(-0.2 + 273.15) \text{ K} = 273.0 \text{ K}$$

$$(-5.4 + 273.15) \text{ K} = 267.8 \text{ K}$$

- Calculate the temperature change.

$$\Delta T = T_{final} - T_{initial} = 267.8 \text{ K} - 273.0 \text{ K} = -5.2 \text{ K}$$

- The appropriate equation to calculate the molar enthalpy change is the following.

$$\Delta H = C\Delta T$$

3 **Calculate and verify**

- Substitute the values into the equation.

$$\Delta H = (37.4 \text{ J/K} \cdot \text{mol})(-5.2 \text{ K})$$

- Solve, and cancel like units in the numerator and the denominator.

$$\Delta H = \frac{37.4 \text{ J}}{\text{K} \cdot \text{mol}} \times (-5.2 \text{ K}) = -1.9 \times 10^2 \text{ J/mol} = -0.19 \text{ kJ/mol}$$

- The enthalpy change is negative, which is expected for a cooling process.
- The temperature change is about –5 K, and the molar heat capacity is about 40 J/K•mol. Multiplying these numbers gives about –200 J/mol, which is close to the calculated answer.

PRACTICE PROBLEMS

1. Calculate ΔH when 100. mL of $H_2O(l)$ is heated from 41.7°C to 76.2°C.

2. The molar heat capacity of $Al(s)$ is 24.2 J/K•mol. Calculate ΔH when 1 mol of $Al(s)$ is cooled from 128.5°C to 22.6°C.

3. The molar heat capacity of $C_2H_5OH(g)$ is 420. J/K•mol. What was the temperature change if $\Delta H = 618.5$ J/mol?

Notes on Sample Problem 11B

Notice in Sample Problem 11B that the mass of the ice, though given, was not needed to solve the problem. It is common for a scientist to have more information than is needed to solve a problem. Never feel that you have to use all the data given. Second, recall that the Δ notation always means the final value minus the initial value and never the other way around, even if $T_{initial}$ is larger than T_{final}.

$$\Delta T = T_{final} - T_{initial}$$

Third, notice that because temperature differences are the same on the Kelvin and Celsius scales, you will still get the correct answer if you work in degrees Celsius rather than kelvins. However, this is not generally true in thermodynamic calculations, and you are strongly advised to adopt the good habit of *always* converting Celsius data to kelvins. Finally, note that molar heat capacities are always tabulated in units that include joules, whereas enthalpies are usually reported in terms of *kilo*joules. An easy mistake is to forget about the factor of 1000 needed to convert from one to the other.

Temperature also affects entropy

Unlike enthalpy, entropy can be measured directly. At absolute zero all substances are solids and most have perfectly ordered crystal lattices. No disorder means no entropy.

The reason entropy increases with temperature is that atoms do not share energy evenly, even in an element. At any instant, some atoms have more than the average energy while others have less. This uneven distribution of energy is an example of disorder. The more energy there is to distribute, the more opportunity there is for uneven distribution. A system with more energy has more disorder.

$\mathcal{S}$ECTION REVIEW

Total recall

1. Name three state properties studied in thermodynamics.

2. Classify each of the following as an extensive or intensive property of matter:
   a. melting point   d. ductility
   b. color   e. molar mass
   c. texture

3. How are enthalpy and entropy affected by an increase in temperature?

4. Should ΔH be positive or negative for an exothermic process?

5. What is the unit used to express entropy? enthalpy?

Critical thinking

6. Why are all elements under standard conditions assigned a molar enthalpy of zero?

7. Why is the molar entropy of water vapor higher than that of ice?

Practice problems

8. A block of ice is cooled from $-0.5°C$ to $-10.1°C$. Calculate the temperature change, ΔT, in degrees Celsius and in kelvins.

9. Calculate ΔH when an 80.2 g block of ice is heated from $-8.4°C$ to $-5.2°C$.

10. Calculate ΔH when 22.5 g of $H_2O(l)$ is cooled from $48.3°C$ to $25.2°C$.

11. The molar heat capacity of benzene, $C_6H_6(l)$, is 136 J/K•mol. Calculate ΔH when the temperature of 15.4 g of $C_6H_6(l)$ changes from $19.7°C$ to $46.8°C$.

12. The molar heat capacity of diethyl ether, $(C_2H_5)_2O(l)$, is 172. J/K•mol. What is the temperature change if $\Delta H = -186.9$ J/mol?

13. **Story Clue** Calculate ΔH when the temperature of 1 mol of $H_2(g)$ is increased by $25°C$. Use Table 11-1 for data.

What happens during a change of state?

OBJECTIVES

▶ **List** the different changes of state.

▶ **Describe** how the enthalpy and entropy of a substance are affected by melting and boiling.

▶ **Define** the quantities represented by the following symbols: ΔH_{vap}, ΔS_{fus}, and ΔG.

▶ **Calculate** T_{mp}, ΔH_{fus}, or ΔS_{fus} given the other two quantities.

▶ **Use** ΔG to predict whether a change of state will occur.

Changing states for water

You are probably most familiar with changes of state for water. The common state of water is as a liquid. The solid form is ice. The gaseous form is steam. A diagram relating *changes of state* is shown in **Figure 11-5.** You see from the diagram that most change-of-state processes have names; however, the direct conversion of a gas to a solid is not denoted by a specific term. Other changes of state, not shown on the diagram, include transitions between two different solid forms, such as the change between the gray and white varieties of tin. Though a change of state is a lot like a chemical reaction, it is considered a physical process.

▶ **FIGURE 11-5**

This map shows how change of state processes are related.

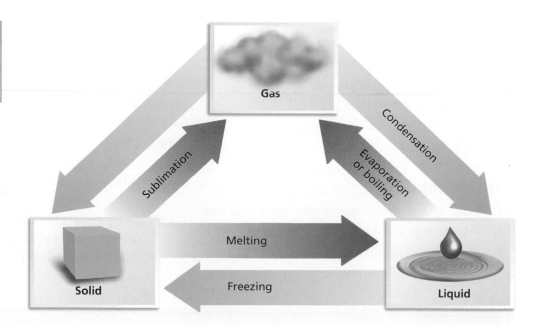

Enthalpy and entropy change dramatically during a change of state

Thermal energy is needed to melt ice and to boil water. Thermal energy increases the kinetic energy of molecules, allowing them to break free of intermolecular forces. With enough added thermal energy, molecules in a solid enter the liquid phase and molecules in a liquid enter the gas phase. The added thermal energy not only causes a change of state but also increases the molar enthalpy of water.

Figure 11-6 shows enthalpy changes with temperature over a range that includes the melting and boiling points of water. Notice the sudden enthalpy increases that occur at the melting point, 273.15 K, and the boiling point, 372.78 K. The enthalpy increase for a change of state is much larger than that which occurs during the rise in temperature for the substance at each state. The slopes of the slowly rising lines in the graph are the molar heat capacities of $H_2O(s)$, $H_2O(l)$, and $H_2O(g)$. The large heat capacity of liquid water is probably due to breaking hydrogen bonds.

Entropy also changes dramatically during melting and boiling processes. A graph of the molar entropy changes for water as it changes state looks similar to Figure 11-6.

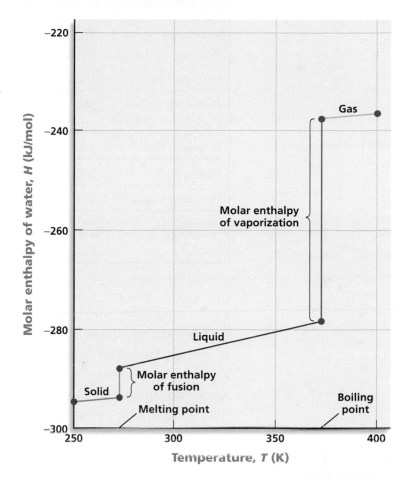

FIGURE 11-6 ▲

The molar enthalpy of water rises gently with temperature in the solid, liquid, and gaseous ranges. Sudden leaps occur at the melting and boiling temperatures.

Change of state

The molar enthalpy change that occurs during melting is called the **molar enthalpy of fusion,** or *heat of fusion* (ΔH_{fus}). It is the difference between the enthalpy of 1 mol of a substance in its liquid and solid states.

$$\Delta H_{fus} = H(\text{liquid at mp}) - H(\text{solid at mp})$$

In this expression, *mp* refers to the melting point of the substance.

Similarly, the **molar enthalpy of vaporization,** or *heat of vaporization,* is the difference between the molar enthalpies of 1 mol of a substance in its gaseous and its liquid states.

$$\Delta H_{vap} = H(\text{gas at bp}) - H(\text{liquid at bp})$$

In the equation, *bp* refers to the boiling point of the substance. The molar entropies of fusion and vaporization, ΔS_{fus} and ΔS_{vap}, are defined similarly.

molar enthalpy of fusion

the heat absorbed when 1 mol of a substance melts

molar enthalpy of vaporization

the heat absorbed when 1 mol of a liquid vaporizes

Substance	T_{mp} (K)	ΔH_{fus} (kJ/mol)	ΔS_{fus} (J/K·mol)	T_{bp} (K)	ΔH^0_{vap} (kJ/mol)	ΔS^0_{vap} (J/K·mol)
Nitrogen, N_2	63	0.719	11.4	77	5.59	72.2
Hydrogen sulfide, H_2S	188	2.38	12.6	213	18.7	87.8
Bromine, Br_2	270	10.57	39.8	332	29.5	88.6
Water, H_2O	273	6.01	22.0	373	40.7	108.8
Benzene, C_6H_6	279	10.59	38.0	353	30.8	87.2
Sodium, Na	371	2.60	7.0	1156	98.0	84.8
Lead, Pb	601	4.77	7.9	2023	177.8	87.9

TABLE 11-3 Molar Enthalpies and Entropies of Fusion and Vaporization

Like water, almost all substances can exist in the three common states of matter. **Table 11-3** lists the molar enthalpies and entropies of fusion and vaporization for some elements and compounds. Because intermolecular forces are not significant in the gaseous state, a similar extent of disordering occurs for almost all substances when 1 mol of liquid is converted to 1 mol of gas. This similarity in disorder explains the similar values for ΔS_{vap}.

Enthalpy and entropy determine state

Liquid H_2O at 273.3 K will never freeze, and ice maintained at 273.0 K will never melt. Only at 273.15 K (0.00°C) can liquid and solid H_2O permanently coexist. Why is H_2O a liquid at one temperature and a solid at another?

Nature's tendency to lower energy corresponds thermodynamically to ΔH being negative. Likewise, nature's drive toward disorder corresponds to ΔS being positive. During changes of state, changes in enthalpy and entropy oppose each other. The relative values of ΔH and $T\Delta S$ determine which state is preferred. At 273.3 K, the enthalpy and entropy values for water are as follows.

$$\Delta H_{fus} = 6.009 \text{ kJ/mol} = 6009 \text{ J/mol}$$

$$T\Delta S_{fus} = (273.3 \text{ K})(22.00 \text{ J/K·mol}) = 6013 \text{ J/mol}$$

Though the values are close, the more-disordered liquid state is favored over the lower energy state of ice. Therefore, H_2O is a liquid at 273.3 K. At 273.0 K, however, the drive to decrease energy dominates, and water freezes.

$$\Delta H_{fus} = 6.009 \text{ kJ/mol} = 6009 \text{ J/mol}$$

$$T\Delta S_{fus} = (273.0 \text{ K})(22.00 \text{ J/K·mol}) = 6006 \text{ J/mol}$$

FIGURE 11-7 ▼

a Water condenses on the wings of the dragonfly when $\Delta H_{vap} > T\Delta S_{vap}$.

b Water freezes on the flower when $\Delta H_{fus} > T\Delta S_{fus}$.

At high enough temperatures, $T\Delta S_{fus}$ exceeds ΔH_{fus}, so all solids eventually melt unless they decompose or sublime. The melting point is the temperature at which ΔH_{fus} equals $T\Delta S_{fus}$. In other words, the melting point of a solid equals the molar enthalpy of fusion divided by the molar entropy of fusion.

$$T_{mp} = \frac{\Delta H_{fus}}{\Delta S_{fus}}$$

Boiling occurs when the drive toward disorder overcomes the tendency to lose energy. Condensation, shown in **Figure 11-7,** occurs when the tendency to lose energy overcomes the drive to increase disorder. In other words, when $\Delta H_{vap} > T\Delta S_{vap}$, the liquid state is favored. The gas state is preferred when $\Delta H_{vap} < T\Delta S_{vap}$. The ΔH_{vap} and $T\Delta S_{vap}$ *terms* are equal at the boiling point of a substance and therefore:

$$T_{bp} = \frac{\Delta H_{vap}}{\Delta S_{vap}}$$

Pressure can affect change-of-state processes

Water left in an uncovered vessel slowly disappears, or *evaporates*. During **evaporation,** a liquid becomes a gas at a temperature well below its boiling point. A similar phenomenon is not seen with the solid/liquid phase transition. Ice cubes in a freezer do not melt at temperatures below water's freezing point.

The boiling point of a liquid is affected greatly by atmospheric pressure, whereas the change in freezing point is very small. In Denver,

evaporation

the process by which molecules in a nonboiling liquid escape the liquid surface and enter the gas phase

Colorado, where the atmospheric pressure is typically 0.84 atm, water boils at 369 K (96°C), but ice still melts at exactly 273.15 K (0.00°C).

Boiling points are pressure-dependent because pressure has a large effect on the entropy of a gas. There is always some water vapor pressure in the air. When this vapor pressure is less than the standard pressure, water's entropy of vaporization is higher than the standard value listed in Table 11-3. So the liquid-gas transition can occur at temperatures below the normal boiling point. Chapter 12 discusses vapor pressure in detail.

Evaporation is rather slow despite being a spontaneous process. There are two reasons for this. The first reason is that vaporization is an endothermic process. Evaporation removes thermal energy and produces cooling. People sweat when they are hot and when they exercise, as in **Figure 11-8.** The evaporation of sweat cools the body. At lower temperatures, evaporation is slower and less likely to occur because the average energy of random motion is lower. The second reason evaporation is slow is that the water vapor formed by evaporation can remain close to the surface and increase the local humidity. When laundry is hung out to dry, the breeze accelerates evaporation by dispersing the water vapor.

Gibbs energy determines spontaneity

The relative values of H and S determine whether a phase transition will occur. Josiah Willard Gibbs, a professor at Yale University, described a new thermodynamic property that incorporates H and S. This is called the **Gibbs energy.** For 1 mol of a substance, G is the *molar Gibbs energy,* defined by the following equation.

$$G = H - TS$$

An older name for Gibbs energy is *molar free energy.* Gibbs energy values are based on a convention similar to that used for enthalpies. Elements are assigned a Gibbs energy of zero under standard conditions.

Scientists use the word *spontaneous* to describe a process that actually occurs or is likely to occur without continuous outside assistance. For example, the melting of ice at 300 K (27°C) is a spontaneous process. The avalanche shown in **Figure 11-9** is also spontaneous. The combustion

▲ **FIGURE 11-8**

A runner sweats when the body overheats as a result of exertion. As sweat evaporates, the body is cooled.

Gibbs energy

a thermodynamic property incorporating both enthalpy and entropy

▶ **FIGURE 11-9**

An avalanche is a spontaneous process driven by an increase in disorder and a decrease in energy.

of gasoline is a spontaneous process, even though a spark must initiate the reaction.

You can use the change in Gibbs energy to compare the change in enthalpy and the change in entropy using the following relationship.

$$\Delta G = \Delta H - T\Delta S$$

A *process is spontaneous if ΔG is negative. All spontaneous processes occur with a decrease in Gibbs energy. When ΔG is exactly zero, the system is in a state of equilibrium.*

The Gibbs energy equation applies to change-of-state processes as well as to chemical reactions. A change of state occurs spontaneously when there is a decrease in Gibbs energy.

SECTION REVIEW

Total recall

1. List the six changes of state.

2. What is ΔS_{fus} for 1 mol of benzene?

3. Write the equations that define ΔS_{fus} and ΔS_{vap}.

4. Name two properties that change dramatically during a change of state.

5. Select any example from Table 11-3 other than water, and show that the following relationship holds.

$$T_{mp} = \frac{\Delta H_{fus}}{\Delta S_{fus}}$$

6. **Interpreting Tables** Select any example from Table 11-3, and show that the following relationship holds:

$$T_{bp} = \frac{\Delta H_{vap}}{\Delta S_{vap}}$$

7. How does atmospheric pressure affect the boiling point of a substance?

8. What equation defines molar Gibbs energy?

9. For a process to be spontaneous, what must be true of the ΔG value?

10. What do the symbols ΔH_{vap} and ΔS_{fus} represent?

11. What causes a change of state?

Critical thinking

12. In terms of enthalpy and entropy, when does melting occur?

13. Explain why liquid H_2O at 273.3 K will never freeze.

14. Why is the gas state favored when $T > \dfrac{H_{vap}}{\Delta S_{vap}}$?

15. What must be true of a process if the ΔH value is positive and the $T\Delta S$ value is negative?

16. Determine the change-of-state process described by each of the following.
    a. $\Delta H_{vap} > T\Delta S_{vap}$
    b. $\Delta H_{fus} < T\Delta S_{fus}$
    c. $\Delta H_{vap} < T\Delta S_{vap}$
    d. $\Delta H_{fus} > T\Delta S_{fus}$

Practice problem

17. Consider the following change of state.

$$Br_2(l) \longrightarrow Br_2(g)$$

$\Delta H_{vap} = 29.5$ kJ/mol
$\Delta S_{vap} = 88.6$ J/mol
Calculate the boiling point of $Br_2(l)$.

How does thermodynamics apply to reactions and nutrition?

OBJECTIVES	
▶ **Explain** the principles of calorimetry.	▶ **Classify** reactions as exothermic or endothermic, disordering or ordering, and spontaneous or nonspontaneous on the basis of thermodynamic data.
▶ **Use** data tables to calculate ΔH, ΔS, and ΔG for any reaction under standard conditions.	
▶ **Predict** the spontaneity of any reaction for which you know ΔH and ΔS.	▶ **Use** Nutrition Facts data to determine the energy content of food.

Chemical calorimetry

calorimeter

a device used to measure the heat absorbed or released in a chemical or physical change

You already know that a negative ΔH accompanies an exothermic reaction and a positive ΔH accompanies an endothermic reaction. How are ΔH values determined? Sometimes ΔH values are calculated by using data tables that have been built over many years. ΔH values can also be measured using a device called a **calorimeter,** which is shown in **Figure 11-10.** This type of calorimeter is used to measure energy changes when substances undergo combustion. The data you get from calorimetry experiments are changes in temperature. Heat cannot be measured directly, so the change in temperature is used in an equation to determine ΔH for a reaction.

▶ **FIGURE 11-10**

A bomb calorimeter is used to measure enthalpies of combustion.

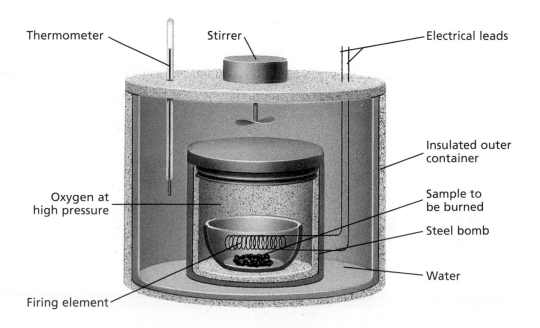

Thermometer · Stirrer · Electrical leads · Insulated outer container · Sample to be burned · Steel bomb · Water · Oxygen at high pressure · Firing element

Calorimetry provides measurements used in determining ΔH

One method for measuring the ΔH of a reaction is known as **adiabatic calorimetry.** The word *adiabatic* means "not allowing heat to pass through" and refers to the fact that no energy leaves the system. In an adiabatic system, the reaction occurs in a vessel that is surrounded by a vacuum jacket similar to a thermos bottle. When the reaction occurs, the heat evolved or consumed by the reaction changes the temperature. The amount of reactant, the temperature change, and the heat capacity are used in an equation to calculate ΔH for the reaction.

The bomb calorimeter, shown in Figure 11-10, is used to measure energy transfers that result from a combustion reaction. This type of calorimeter is a useful tool for helping nutritionists determine the energy equivalent of food, as in **Figure 11-11.** In a bomb calorimeter, most organic matter, including foodstuffs, fabrics, and plastics, will ignite easily, will burn rapidly, and may even explode. The size of the sample to be burned is selected so that oxygen will be in excess during combustion. Under these conditions the combustion of organic matter is a complete reaction that yields carbon dioxide and water.

The whole "bomb" is immersed in a stirred-water bath. The water bath absorbs heat from the reaction of combustion for the substance. The energy released by the combustion equals the energy absorbed by the water and the calorimeter. The absorption of energy causes the temperature of the calorimeter and water to increase.

The temperature rise, ΔT, of the water bath in the calorimeter is used to determine the molar enthalpy.

adiabatic calorimetry

method of measuring the heat absorbed or released in a chemical or physical change in which no heat is allowed to enter or leave the system

Hess's law

law stating that the overall enthalpy change in a reaction is equal to the sum of the enthalpy changes of the individual steps in the process

Hess's law allows you to combine enthalpy changes

Any two processes that start with the reactants in the same condition and finish with the products in the same condition will involve the same enthalpy change. This statement is the basis of **Hess's law,** which states that the overall enthalpy change in a reaction is equal to the sum of the enthalpy changes for the individual steps in the process. If the heats of reaction for the partial reactions are known, then they can be combined to give the heat change for the overall reaction. For example, you can use Hess's law to find ΔH for the reaction that fuels the hydrogen-powered car.

$$2H_2(g) + O_2(g) \longrightarrow 2H_2O(g)$$

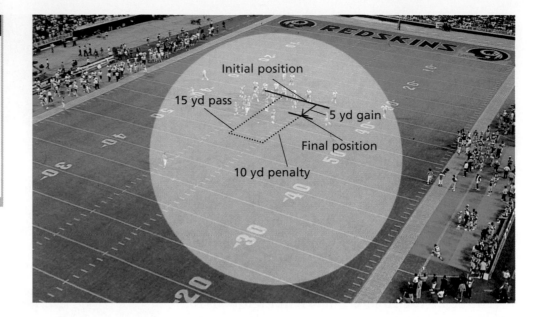

To find ΔH for the combustion of 2 mol of H_2, start with data for the enthalpy of the reaction of hydrogen and oxygen to produce water in the *liquid* state.

$$2H_2(g) + O_2(g) \longrightarrow 2H_2O(l) \ \Delta H = -571.66 \text{ kJ}$$

You can also use data for the enthalpy of vaporization of water.

$$2H_2O(l) \longrightarrow 2H_2O(g) \ \Delta H = 88.02 \text{ kJ}$$

The principle of Hess's law allows you to add the last two equations, canceling $H_2O(l)$, which is common to both sides. The enthalpies are also added because they are part of the expressions.

$$2H_2(g) + O_2(g) \longrightarrow 2H_2O(l) \qquad \Delta H = -571.66 \text{ kJ}$$

$$2H_2O(l) \longrightarrow 2H_2O(g) \qquad \Delta H = \quad\ 88.02 \text{ kJ}$$

$$\overline{2H_2(g) + O_2(g) + 2H_2O(l) \longrightarrow 2H_2O(l) + 2H_2O(g) \ \Delta H = -483.64 \text{ kJ}}$$

Thermodynamic data are compiled through experiments and the application of Hess's law

Enthalpies listed in Table A-13 of the Appendix are based on the convention that the enthalpy of all the elements at standard temperature, 298.15 K (25.00°C), is zero. The enthalpy of a compound is called the **standard enthalpy of formation,** symbolized by ΔH_f^0, because such enthalpy changes accompany the formation reaction represented below.

elements (at 298.15 K) $\longrightarrow$ one mole of compound (at 298.15 K)

For simplicity, you can think of the entries in the table as being just molar enthalpies, H^0, under standard conditions.

It is possible to use thermodynamic data to calculate the enthalpy change for any reaction that involves compounds listed in the table. Using the data in Table A-13, you can determine if certain reactions are exothermic or endothermic. An example of this procedure is shown in Sample Problem 11C.

standard enthalpy of formation

the amount of heat released or absorbed when 1 mol of compound is made from its elements under standard conditions

Calculate the change in enthalpy, ΔH^0, for the following reaction using data from Table A-13.

$$H_2(g) + CO_2(g) \longrightarrow H_2O(g) + CO(g)$$

Is the reaction exothermic or endothermic?

1 **List what you know**

▶ Products: $H_2O(g) + CO(g)$
▶ Reactants: $H_2(g) + CO_2(g)$

2 **Set up the problem**

▶ The change in enthalpy for any reaction is found by subtracting the sum of the enthalpies of the reactants from the sum of the enthalpies of the products.

$$\Delta H^0 = \text{sum of } H^0_{\text{(products)}} - \text{sum of } H^0_{\text{(reactants)}}$$

▶ Find the values from Table A-13 of the Appendix.

$$H^0_{H_2O} = -241.8 \text{ kJ/mol} \qquad H^0_{H_2} = 0$$

$$H^0_{CO} = -110.5 \text{ kJ/mol} \qquad H^0_{CO_2} = -393.5 \text{ kJ/mol}$$

▶ The coefficients in the equation are all 1's in this case. Therefore,

$$\text{sum of } H^0_{products} = [(1 \text{ mol})(-214.8 \text{ kJ/mol}) + (1 \text{ mol})(-110.5 \text{ kJ/mol})]$$

$$\text{sum of } H^0_{reactants} = [(1 \text{ mol})(-393.5 \text{ kJ/mol}) + (1 \text{ mol})(0)]$$

▶ Substitute these values in the equation.

$$\Delta H^0 = [(-241.8 \text{ kJ}) + (-110.5 \text{ kJ})] - (-393.5 \text{ kJ})$$

3 **Calculate**

$$\Delta H^0 = (-352.3 \text{ kJ}) - (-393.5 \text{ kJ}) = 41.2 \text{ kJ}$$

The reaction is endothermic because ΔH^0 is positive.

PRACTICE PROBLEMS

1. The Romans used CaO as a building material similar to mortar. CaO was mixed with water to produce $Ca(OH)_2$, which reacted slowly with CO_2 in the air to form limestone, $CaCO_3$. This reaction is represented as follows.

$$Ca(OH)_2(s) + CO_2(g) \longrightarrow H_2O(g) + CaCO_3(s)$$

Determine the ΔH value for this reaction using the data given below.

Substance	ΔH^0_f(kJ/mol)	Substance	ΔH^0_f(kJ/mol)
$Ca(OH)_2(s)$	−986.1	$H_2O(g)$	−241.8
$CO_2(g)$	−393.5	$CaCO_3(s)$	−1206.9

Hess's law can also be applied to entropy calculations

Table A-13 also lists molar entropy values. Entropies can be determined, so the entropy values are not based on assigning a zero entropy to the elements. The values for S^0 are given at standard temperature, 298.15 K. The data for gases are at a standard pressure of 1 atm, and the data for dissolved substances are at a standard concentration near 1 mol/L.

Hess's law can be applied to S values to calculate the overall entropy of a reaction, ΔS^0. The procedure is shown in Sample Problem 11D.

SAMPLE PROBLEM 11D   **Calculating change in entropy**

Calculate the entropy change for the following reaction using data from Table A-13.

$$H_2(g) + CO_2(g) \longrightarrow H_2O(g) + CO(g)$$

Does the reaction proceed toward a more ordered or more disordered state?

1 **List what you know**
- Products: $H_2O(g) + CO(g)$
- Reactants: $H_2(g) + CO_2(g)$

2 **Set up the problem**
- The change in entropy for any reaction is found by subtracting the sum of the entropies of the reactants from the sum of the entropies of the products.

$$\Delta S^0 = \text{sum of } S^0_{(products)} - \text{sum of } S^0_{(reactants)}$$

- Find the molar entropies from Table A-13.

$S^0_{H_2O} = 188.7$ J/K•mol $S^0_{H_2} = 130.7$ J/K•mol

$S^0_{CO} = 197.6$ J/K•mol $S^0_{CO_2} = 213.8$ J/K•mol

- Substitute the values into the equation for ΔS^0.

$\Delta S^0 = [(1 \text{ mol})(188.7 \text{ J/K•mol}) + (1 \text{ mol})(197.6 \text{ J/K•mol})] -$
$$[(1 \text{ mol})(130.7 \text{ J/K•mol}) + (1 \text{ mol})(213.8 \text{ J/K•mol})]$$

3 **Calculate and verify**

$$\Delta S^0 = 386.3 \text{ J/K} - 344.5 \text{ J/K} = 41.8 \text{ J/K}$$

- The reaction has a positive entropy; it produces a net disordering.

PRACTICE PROBLEMS

1. Using Table A-13, calculate the entropy change for the following fuel-generating reaction.

$$2Fe(s) + 3H_2O(g) \longrightarrow Fe_2O_3(s) + 3H_2(g)$$

Remember to account for coefficients in the equation when calculating. Does the reaction produce more disorder or less?

2. Calcium carbonate, $CaCO_3$, decomposes into calcium oxide and carbon dioxide. What is the entropy change for this reaction?

$$CaCO_3(s) \longrightarrow CO_2(g) + CaO(s)$$

Substance	S^0(J/K•mol)
$CaCO_3(s)$	+92.9
$CO_2(g)$	+213.8
$CaO(s)$	+38.2

3. What is the entropy change for converting graphite to diamond? Is this entropy change favorable to the conversion?

graphite:	$S^0 = +5.7$ J/K•mol
diamond:	$S^0 = +2.4$ J/K•mol

Gibbs energy calculations are used to determine if a reaction is spontaneous

There are two ways of using thermodynamic data tables to find the change in Gibbs energy, ΔG^0, that accompanies a chemical reaction. One way is to calculate ΔH^0 and ΔS^0 and use the following equation.

$$\Delta G^0 = \Delta H^0 - T\Delta S^0$$

This method can be used when a specific temperature is given in the problem.

The second equation for calculating ΔG^0 is similar to the equation you used to calculate ΔH^0 and ΔS^0 in Sample Problems 11C and 11D. The following equation is based on the fact that ΔG^0 is a state property.

$$\Delta G^0 = \text{sum of } G^0_{(products)} - \text{sum of } G^0_{(reactants)}$$

If the calculation of ΔG^0 results in a value that is positive, the reaction is not spontaneous. If the calculation of ΔG^0 results in a value that is negative, the reaction is spontaneous. If ΔG^0 is zero, then neither the forward nor the reverse reaction is favored and the reaction system is at equilibrium. Both methods for calculating ΔG^0 are shown in Sample Problem 11E.

SAMPLE PROBLEM 11E | **Calculating change in molar Gibbs energy**

Calculate the change in Gibbs energy, ΔG^0, for the following reaction using data from Sample Problems 11C and 11D.

$$H_2(g) + CO_2(g) \longrightarrow H_2O(g) + CO(g)$$

Is the reaction spontaneous at 25°C?

1 **List what you know**
- Values of ΔH^0 and ΔS^0 have already been calculated
- $\Delta H^0 = 41.2$ kJ/mol
- $\Delta S^0 = 0.0418$ kJ/K (this value was converted from J/K)

2 Set up the problem and calculate

▶ Substitute ΔH^0 and ΔS^0 into the equation for ΔG^0.

$$\Delta G^0 = \Delta H^0 - T\Delta S^0$$

$$\Delta G^0 = (41.2 \text{ kJ}) - [(298.15 \text{ K})(0.0418 \text{ kJ/K})] = 28.7 \text{ kJ}$$

▶ **Alternative method:** A second method of calculating ΔG^0 uses G^0 values from Table A-13 and the following equation.

$$\Delta G^0 = G^0_{(products)} - G^0_{(reactants)}$$

▶ Now use this method to determine ΔG^0 for the reaction.

$$\Delta G^0 = G^0_{(products)} - G^0_{(reactants)}$$

$$= [(1 \text{ mol})(-228.6 \text{ kJ/mol}) + (1 \text{ mol})(-137.2 \text{ kJ/mol})] -$$

$$[0 + (1 \text{ mol})(-394.4 \text{ kJ/mol})]$$

$$= 28.6 \text{ kJ}$$

▶ Both methods give practically the same answer. For this reaction, a positive value of ΔG^0 means the reaction is *not* spontaneous. Hydrogen does not react with carbon dioxide at room temperature.

PRACTICE PROBLEMS

1. Use either of the methods shown in Sample Problem 11E to calculate the Gibbs energy change for the following reaction.

$$2\text{Fe}(s) + 3\text{H}_2\text{O}(g) \longrightarrow \text{Fe}_2\text{O}_3(s) + 3\text{H}_2(g)$$

Is this reaction spontaneous at 25°C?

2. Graphite and steam can react to produce water gas. This fuel is a mixture of several gases, but contains mostly carbon monoxide gas and hydrogen gas. When water gas is made industrially, the reaction is carried out at temperatures near 900°C. Are the products or reactants favored at this temperature? (Hint: Assume that ΔH and ΔS are constant at all temperatures.)

$$\text{H}_2\text{O}(g) + \text{C}(graphite) \longrightarrow \text{CO}(g) + \text{H}_2(g) \quad \Delta H = +135.5 \text{ kJ} \quad \Delta S = +148.8 \text{ J/K}$$

3. Holding the temperature of the reactants in the water-gas reaction, shown in item 2, at 900°C is expensive. What is the lowest temperature that could be used to produce a spontaneous reaction? (Hint: Assume that ΔS and ΔH do not change and that $\Delta G = -0.1$ kJ.)

Enthalpy and entropy together determine reaction spontaneity

Recall that Gibbs energy combines changes in enthalpy and entropy for a chemical reaction according to the following equation.

$$\Delta G = \Delta H - T\Delta S$$

The net effect of these changes determines whether the reaction is spontaneous ($-\Delta G$) or nonspontaneous ($+\Delta G$.)

Sometimes nature's tendency toward lower enthalpy and higher entropy act together to favor or disfavor a particular chemical reaction. The reaction of potassium with water, shown in **Figure 11-13,** occurs instantaneously due to the resulting large decrease in energy for the products. Sometimes the effects of entropy and enthalpy are in opposition. **Table 11-4** summarizes the four possible combinations of enthalpy and entropy changes for any chemical reaction. Remember how the chemist defines *spontaneous*—a reaction that is not spontaneous will *not* occur, and a reaction that is spontaneous *may* occur.

FIGURE 11-13 ◄

The spontaneous reaction between potassium metal and water is driven by a large decrease in energy.

TABLE 11-4	**Relating Enthalpy and Entropy Changes to Spontaneity**

ΔH	ΔS	ΔG	Is the reaction spontaneous?
Negative (exothermic)	positive (disordering)	negative	yes, at all temperatures
Negative (exothermic)	negative (ordering)	either sign + or −	only at $T < \dfrac{\Delta H}{\Delta S}$
Positive (endothermic)	positive (disordering)	either sign + or −	only at $T > \dfrac{\Delta H}{\Delta S}$
Positive (endothermic)	negative (ordering)	positive	never

CONCEPT CHECK

1. What thermodynamic properties does the Gibbs energy equation include?
2. What does the calculation of a negative ΔG allow you to predict for a reaction?
3. What does the calculation of a positive ΔG allow you to predict for a reaction?
4. Under what conditions can an endothermic reaction be spontaneous?

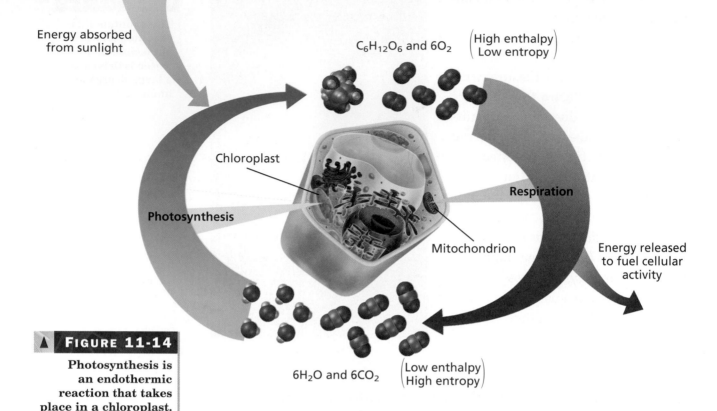

Energy absorbed from sunlight

$C_6H_{12}O_6$ and $6O_2$ (High enthalpy / Low entropy)

Chloroplast

Respiration

Photosynthesis

Mitochondrion

Energy released to fuel cellular activity

$6H_2O$ and $6CO_2$ (Low enthalpy / High entropy)

▲ **FIGURE 11-14**

Photosynthesis is an endothermic reaction that takes place in a chloroplast. Respiration is an exothermic reaction that takes place in a mitochondrion.

Nutrition and thermodynamics
Food energy is just another reaction enthalpy

Essentially, the food you eat is oxidized to reclaim the energy that was stored in the food molecules by the plant or animal. The simplest illustration is provided by the food molecule *glucose*.

Green plants make glucose from carbon dioxide and water by the process of photosynthesis, which is shown in the following equation.

$$2870 \text{ kJ/mol} + 6CO_2(g) + 6H_2O(l) \longrightarrow C_6H_{12}O_6(s) + 6O_2(g)$$

$$\Delta H^0 = 2870 \text{ kJ}$$

$$\Delta S^0 = -259 \text{ J/K}$$

$$\Delta G^0 = 2947 \text{ kJ}$$

This reaction is endothermic, is ordering, and has a large positive Gibbs energy change; nothing favors this reaction. How does a plant make such a nonspontaneous reaction occur? The secret is the energy of sunlight, which is used to bring about a series of complicated biochemical reactions whose overall result is summarized by the equation above. A *chloroplast* is the organelle where a plant carries out photosynthesis. Of course, the plant is not making glucose for our benefit, but to power its own biochemistry. **Figure 11-14** shows a chloroplast as well as a *mitochondrion,* the organelle where the cell reoxidizes glucose for its own energy needs.

Humans use the energy in glucose and other carbohydrates for their own needs. But the reaction that goes on in your body is the same one that the glucose is destined to undergo in the mitochondria. It's an oxidation reaction that is the exact reverse of photosynthesis.

$$C_6H_{12}O_6(s) + 6O_2(g) \longrightarrow 6CO_2(g) + 6H_2O(l)$$

$$\Delta H^0 = -2870 \text{ kJ}$$

$$\Delta S^0 = 259 \text{ J/K}$$

$$\Delta G^0 = -2947 \text{ kJ}$$

Notice that this reaction is spontaneous and is strongly favored not only because it is exothermic but also because the products are at a higher state of disorder. The food energy that you get from eating glucose is exactly what the equation reports: 2870 kJ per mole of glucose, or 15.9 kJ/g.

Recall from Chapter 8 that combustion and oxidation can refer to the same chemical reaction. The distinction is solely in the burning that accompanies a combustion. The same energy is released in either case. Thus, one way to determine ΔH for glucose is to burn it in a bomb calorimeter. Glucose is a pure substance, whereas most foodstuffs are not. If a calorimeter is used to combust a peanut, the enthalpy of combustion corresponds accurately to the food energy that you would obtain from eating that peanut.

Some components of some foods are not nutritious. For example, you cannot digest cellulose, although it will combust in a bomb calorimeter. Food scientists have to make corrections to calorimetric data to allow for these situations.

Metabolic rate is a measure of your energy consumption

Your body needs energy to carry out all the tasks your daily life demands—not only to power your muscles but also to digest food, to respire, to keep you warm, and to carry out all the other biochemical processes needed to sustain your health and growth.

If you eat more food than your body needs, excess energy intake is often stored either as glycogen in the liver or as fat. To some degree, the extent of this energy storage depends on the food you eat. Fat is a more efficient storage medium than carbohydrates and protein. It has a much higher energy content per gram than other nutrients, as **Table 11-5** shows.

Of course, your energy needs depend on your activity; an athlete needs more energy than a hospital patient, for example. The digestion of food itself requires considerable energy, so a person's resting metabolic rate, or RMR, is defined as the energy he or she expends when resting or sleeping *with an empty stomach*. You expend more energy than your RMR when you carry out other activities.

A metabolic rate is a rate of energy consumption, so its SI unit is *joules per*

internetconnect

SC*i*LINKS

NSTA

TOPIC: Nutrition/Thermodynamics
GO TO: www.scilinks.org
KEYWORD: HW114

TABLE 11-5	Energy Content of Carbohydrates, Proteins, and Fats	
Nutrient	**kJ/g**	**Cal/g**
Carbohydrate	17	4
Protein	17	4
Fat	38	9

► **FIGURE 11-15**

The FDA's standard-
ization of nutritional
labeling has made it
possible to compare
nutritional composi-
tions of similar foods.

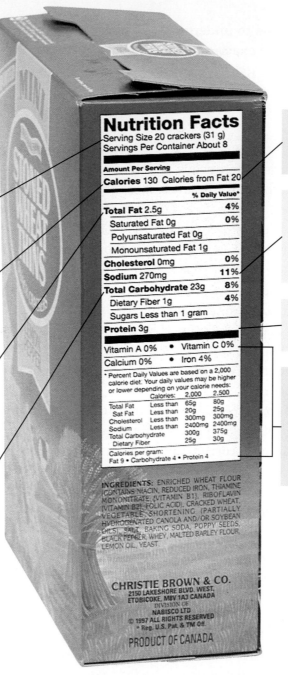

Serving size
Volume and mass of a
standard portion

Calories
Fuel value of the food
for the serving size listed

Total fat
Mass of the fat in the
serving size listed with a
breakdown of the mass
of saturated fat

Total carbohydrate
Mass of complex carbo-
hydrates, fiber, and sug-
ars in the serving size
listed

Calories from fat
Energy equivalent of the
fat grams for the serving
size listed

Sodium and potassium
Mass of each mineral in
the serving size listed.
One teaspoon of table
salt has a mass of about
2 g.

Protein
Mass of protein in the
serving size listed

**Vitamins and other
minerals**
Values listed are the percentage of total daily
requirement for that
vitamin or mineral that
is provided in the serving
size listed.

second or *watts*. The usual metric unit, *kilojoules per day,* is more convenient and is used in most of the world. Instead of the kilojoule, an
older unit is still used primarily in the United States. This energy unit
goes by two names. It is called either a *kilocalorie* (kcal) or a *Calorie*
(Cal). The Calorie is the unit used on the "Nutrition Facts" label required by law on all packaged foods. A Nutrition Facts label is shown
in **Figure 11-15.** The conversions are as follows.

$$1 \text{ kcal} = 1 \text{ Cal} = 4.184 \text{ kJ}$$

You can easily find data on the energy content of most of the foods you
eat. Most of the packaged food you get from the grocery store provides
a lot of nutritional information. The labels in Figure 11-15 are in the
style now mandated by the Food and Drug Administration (FDA).

TABLE 11-6 — Energy and Nutrient Breakdown of Some Foods*

Food and measure	Calories	Kilojoules	Carbohydrate (g)	Protein (g)	Fat (g)
Apple, 1 medium	81	339	21.1	0.3	0.5
Cheeseburger, 4.1 oz	310	1297	31.2	15.0	13.8
Cola soft drink, 6 oz	72	301	19.0	0	0
French fries, 3.4 oz	320	1339	36.3	4.4	17.1
Potato, baked, 7.1 oz	220	920	51.0	4.7	0.2
Potato chips, 1 oz	150	628	15.0	1.0	10.0
Pretzels, 1 oz	110	460	22.0	2.0	2.0
Yogurt with fruit, 8 oz	240	1004	43.0	9.0	3.0
Yogurt, low-fat frozen, 3 oz	100	418	22.0	4.0	0.8

*These figures have been rounded and represent average values.

SECTION REVIEW

Total recall

1. How is Hess's law used to determine the ΔH of a reaction?

2. Predict what conditions, if any, are needed to make the following changes spontaneous.
   a. exothermic reaction with an increase in entropy
   b. reaction with an increase in both enthalpy and entropy

Practice problems

3. Using the following values, compute the ΔG value for each reaction and predict whether it will occur spontaneously.

Reaction	ΔH (kJ)	Temperature	ΔS (J/K)
1	+125	293 K	+35
2	−85.2	127 K	+125
3	−275	500°C	+450

4. **Story Clue** Hydrogen gas can be prepared for use in cars in several ways, such as by the decomposition of water or hydrogen chloride.

$$2H_2O(l) \longrightarrow 2H_2(g) + O_2(g)$$
$$2HCl(g) \longrightarrow H_2(g) + Cl_2(g)$$

Use the following data to determine whether these reactions can occur spontaneously at 25°C. Assume that ΔH and ΔS are constant.

	H^0 (kJ/mol)	S^0 (J/K·mol)
$H_2O(l)$	−285.8	+70.0
$H_2(g)$	0	+130.7
$O_2(g)$	0	+205.1
$HCl(g)$	−92	+187
$Cl_2(g)$	0	+223.1

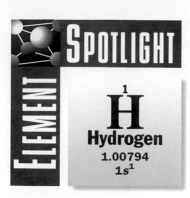

| 1 |
| H |
| **Hydrogen** |
| 1.00794 |
| $1s^1$ |

Hydrogen an element unto itself

Hydrogen is a unique element in many respects. Its scarcity on Earth is partially due to the low density of hydrogen gas. The low density permits hydrogen molecules to escape the Earth's gravitational pull and drift into space.

Hydrogen does not fit comfortably anywhere in the periodic table. However, it could be placed in Group 1 because it has a single valence electron. It can also be placed with the halogens in Group 17 because it can accept an electron to produce a hydride ion, H^-, and easily forms covalent bonds with carbon.

Industrial Uses

▶ Hydrogen gas is prepared industrially by the thermal decomposition of hydrocarbons. Natural gas, oil-refinery gas, gasoline, fuel oil, and crude oil are the principal raw materials.

▶ Most of the hydrogen gas produced is used for synthesizing ammonia.

▶ Hydrogen is used in the hydrogenation of unsaturated vegetable oils to make solid fats.

▶ Liquid hydrogen is a clear, colorless liquid with a boiling point of $-252.87°C$, the lowest boiling point of any known liquid other than liquid helium. Because of its low temperature, liquid hydrogen is used to cool superconducting materials.

▶ Liquid hydrogen is used to fuel rockets that explore space, launch satellites, and power spacecrafts.

While the H atom is the most abundant atom in the universe, only 3% of the atoms in the Earth's crust are hydrogen.

WHERE IS IT?

Universe
approximately 93% of all atoms

Earth's Crust
0.9% by mass

internetconnect

SCI*LINKS*
NSTA
TOPIC: Hydrogen
GO TO: www.scilinks.org
KEYWORD: HW115

A BRIEF HISTORY

1766: Henry Cavendish prepares a pure sample of hydrogen and distinguishes it from other gases. He names it "inflammable air."

1937: The *Hindenburg*, a hydrogen-filled dirigible, explodes during a landing in Lakehurst, New Jersey.

1783: Jacques Charles fills a balloon with hydrogen and flies in a basket over the French countryside.

1931: Harold Urey discoveres deuterium, an isotope of hydrogen, in water.

1600   1700   1800   1900

1660: Robert Boyle prepares hydrogen from a reaction between iron and sulfuric acid.

1783: Antoine Lavoisier names hydrogen. It means "water former."

1898: James Dewar produces liquid hydrogen and develops a glass vacuum flask to hold it.

1934: Ernest Rutherford, Marcus Oliphant, and Paul Harteck discover tritium.

1996: Scientists at Lawrence Livermore National Laboratory succeed in making solid metallic hydrogen.

At the beginning of this chapter, you explored hydrogen-powered cars. Let's revisit the three questions posed at that time considering what you now know about the forces that drive chemical reactions and changes of state.

LOOKING BACK

What drives the H_2 combustion reaction?

Natural processes are driven by a decrease in enthalpy, an increase in entropy, or both. Hydrogen combustion is accompanied by a decrease in both entropy and enthalpy. Entropy decreases as three molecules become two molecules—an ordering process. As often happens the enthalpy effect far outweighs the entropy effect.

Is there a safe and economical way to carry H_2 in a car?

Yes. Hydrogen can form interstitial hydrides in which the hydrogen enters the lattice of a metallic element without forming bonds. Through simple temperature and pressure adjustments, hydrogen absorbed on the metal can be easily recovered. Unfortunately, the best metal for this purpose, palladium, is too scarce and costly to use in mass-produced automobiles. Titanium and manganese alloys with similar properties to palladium are inexpensive alternatives.

In fact, the experimental car is equipped with tanks that contain plates of a manganese/titanium alloy. The exothermic absorption of hydrogen on the metal plates in fueling and the endothermic reverse process require complex cooling and heating equipment.

Because of the complicated fuel-handling system, a hydrogen-powered car could cost 50% more to mass-produce than its gasoline-powered counterpart.

Would the use of hydrogen-powered cars lead to less pollution?

Unfortunately, one tank of absorbed hydrogen provides only as much mileage as about half a full tank of gas. As a gasoline replacement, massive quantities of H_2 would need to be produced. H_2 can easily be made by the electrolysis of water, but that requires electrical energy. An increased demand for electrical energy requires more power stations. Because most of the present-day power stations burn fossil fuels, pollution will be about the same.

There is concern that hydrogen-powered cars may merely move the pollution from the highways to the neighborhoods of electricity-generating power plants, but battery-powered cars present the same concern.

Despite obstacles, engineers at several car firms believe that use of hydrogen-powered cars will be common one day.

HIGHLIGHTS

KEY TERMS

11-1
entropy
molar heat capacity
thermodynamics

11-2
extensive property
intensive property

11-3
molar enthalpy of fusion
molar enthalpy of
vaporization
Gibbs energy

11-4
adiabatic calorimetry
calorimeter
Hess's law
standard enthalpy of
formation

KEY CONCEPTS

11-1 How does heat differ from other forms of energy?

▶ The two natural driving forces are a decrease in energy and an increase in disorder.

▶ Heat represents the quantity of thermal energy; temperature represents the intensity of thermal energy.

▶ An increase in the heat and temperature of a substance reflects an increase in the random kinetic energy of its atoms.

▶ The molar heat capacity of a substance is the quantity of heat required to increase the temperature of 1 mol of a substance by 1 K.

▶ The molar heat capacity depends on the number of atoms a substance contains.

▶ Entropy is the measure of the total disorder of a system.

11-2 How does temperature affect enthalpy and entropy?

▶ Enthalpy is the total energy of a substance.

▶ Absolute enthalpy, represented by H, cannot be measured; changes in enthalpy, represented by ΔH, can be measured.

▶ Absolute entropy, represented by S, and change in entropy, represented by ΔS, can be measured.

11-3 What happens during a change of state?

▶ Both enthalpy and entropy change dramatically during changes of state.

▶ The relative values of ΔH and $T\Delta S$ determine physical state.

▶ Gibbs energy combines the ΔH and $T\Delta S$ of a process and is used to predict spontaneity.

11-4 How does thermodynamics apply to reactions and nutrition?

▶ Calorimetry can be used to determine the ΔH of a reaction.

▶ Hess's law can be used to determine the ΔH for an overall reaction by adding the ΔH values for the individual steps in the overall process.

▶ Thermodynamic data can be used to determine if a reaction is endothermic ($\Delta H > 0$) or exothermic ($\Delta H < 0$), ordering ($\Delta S < 0$) or disordering ($\Delta S > 0$), and spontaneous ($\Delta G < 0$) or not ($\Delta G > 0$).

▶ Metabolic rate is the rate of energy consumption by the body.

KEY SKILLS

Sample Problem 11A: Calculating the molar heat capacity of a substance (p. 388)

Sample Problem 11B: Calculating molar enthalpy change (p. 393)

Sample Problem 11C: Calculating change in enthalpy (p. 405)

Sample Problem 11D: Calculating change in entropy (p. 406)

Sample Problem 11E: Calculating change in molar Gibbs energy (p. 407)

REVIEW & ASSESS

TERM REVIEW

1. The disorder possessed by 1 mol of a substance is quantified in its _____.
(molar entropy, molar heat capacity)

2. A(n) _____ is a property of matter that is independent of the quantity of matter that is present.
(extensive property, intensive property)

3. The difference between the molar enthalpy of 1 mol of a substance in its gaseous state and 1 mol in its liquid state is known as the substance's _____.
(molar enthalpy of fusion, molar enthalpy of vaporization)

4. The quantity involving both enthalpy and entropy is _____.
(the molar Gibbs energy, molar heat capacity)

5. The symbol H_f^0 represents the _____ of a compound.
(entropy, standard enthalpy of formation)

6. The ΔH of a reaction can be calculated with the help of _____.
(adiabatic calorimetry, the resting metabolic rate)

CONCEPT & SKILLS REVIEW

HEAT ENERGY AND MOLAR HEAT CAPACITY

1. Explain why the liquid in a thermometer rises when it gets hotter outdoors and drops when it gets cooler in terms of the kinetic energy of atoms in the liquid.

2. What compound unit is represented by the watt?

3. Flask A contains 500 mL of water at 25°C, and flask B contains 250 mL of water at 50°C. Which flask has a higher heat content? Explain your choice.

4. How does the number of atoms in a molecule of a substance affect its molar heat capacity?

5. Explain what happens in terms of thermal energy when ice is used to freeze a liquid.

Practice Problems

6. A student performs an experiment to determine the molar heat capacity of a sample of silica, SiO_2, with a mass of 4.0 g. The silica absorbs 121 J of heat, and its temperature increases from 0.0°C to 41.0°C. What is the molar heat capacity of the glass? **(Hint: See Sample Problem 11A.)**

7. Calculate the amount of heat energy transferred in the following situations:
   a. the temperature of 1.0 g of water rises from 22.5°C to 24.5°C
   b. the temperature of 3.0 g of silver rises from 46.0°C to 47.0°C
   c. the temperature of 7.0 g of tungsten rises from 0°C to 5°C
   d. the temperature of 11.0 g of iron rises from 240°C to 244°C

ENTROPY AND ENTHALPY

8. Why do molar entropies always have positive values?

9. Predict how the molar entropy of $CO_2(g)$ would compare with the molar entropy of $CO_2(s)$. Explain your answer.

10. The molar entropy of $C(g)$ at 298 K is 158.096 J/K•mol. The molar entropy of $CO_2(g)$ at 298 K is 213.74 J/K•mol. What does this data indicate about the relative motion of the atoms in these two gases?

11. Why are entropy and enthalpy considered extensive properties?

12. What does ΔT represent?

13. What does a positive ΔH value indicate about the temperature change in a substance?

14. What does a negative ΔS value indicate about the temperature change in a substance?

15. Explain why $AlCl_3$ has a molar heat capacity that is approximately four times that of a metallic crystal.

16. If the molar heat capacity and the temperature change are known, why is the mass of a substance not needed to calculate its molar enthalpy change?

Practice Problems

17. The molar heat capacity of $BaCl_2(s)$ is 75.1 J/K•mol. Calculate ΔH when the temperature of one mole is raised from 50°C to 66°C. **(Hint: See Sample Problem 11B.)**

18. The molar heat capacity of $(C_2H_5)_2O(g)$ is 108 75.1 J/K•mol. Calculate ΔH when the temperature of one mole drops from 68.5°C to 42.7°C. **(Hint: See Sample Problem 11B.)**

CHANGE OF STATE

19. Explain why changes of state are considered physical transitions and not chemical processes.

20. How does an enthalpy change that accompanies a change of state compare with an enthalpy change that accompanies the heating of an individual phase? Explain the difference.

21. What makes the molar entropy of vaporization for water higher than most other substances?

22. During melting, heat is added, the temperature does not change, yet enthalpy increases. How can this be?

23. How are entropy and enthalpy involved in the boiling process?

24. Why is the gas phase favored when $T\Delta S_{vap} > \Delta H_{vap}$?

25. Describe what happens in terms of entropy and enthalpy when $O_2(g)$ becomes $O_2(l)$.

26. a. What is the relation between the enthalpy change and the entropy change during a change of state?
b. What determines the direction of the change of state?

MOLAR GIBBS ENERGY

27. Draw a graph with ΔH on the x-axis and ΔS on the y-axis. In each quadrant of the graph, indicate what conditions, if any, are necessary to make a reaction spontaneous for each combination of positive and negative ΔH and ΔS values.

28. The entropy change for the spontaneous reaction to make NOCl from its elements at a low temperature is negative. Is the enthalpy change positive or negative?

29. What drives photosynthesis, a chemical reaction with a large positive ΔH value?

30. At high temperatures, does enthalpy or entropy have a greater effect on a reaction's molar Gibbs energy? Explain your answer.

31. Nitrogen dioxide, $NO_2(g)$, has a standard enthalpy of formation of 33.1 kJ/mol. Dinitrogen tetroxide, $N_2O_4(g)$, has a standard enthalpy of formation of 9.1 kJ/mol. What is the enthalpy change for synthesizing N_2O_4 from NO_2?

Practice Problems

32. Use Hess's law to calculate the change in enthalpy for the combustion of 1 mol of carbon monoxide to form carbon dioxide. Oxygen is in elemental form. **(Hint: See Sample Problem 11C.)**

33. The diagram below represents an interpretation of Hess's law for the following reaction.

$$Sn(s) + 2Cl_2(g) \longrightarrow SnCl_4(l)$$

Use the diagram to determine ΔH for each step and the net reaction.

$$Sn(s) + Cl_2(g) \longrightarrow SnCl_2(l) \qquad \Delta H = ?$$
$$SnCl_2(s) + Cl_2(g) \longrightarrow SnCl_4(l) \qquad \Delta H = ?$$
$$Sn(s) + 2Cl_2(g) \longrightarrow SnCl_4(l) \qquad \Delta H = ?$$

(Hint: See Sample Problem 11C.)

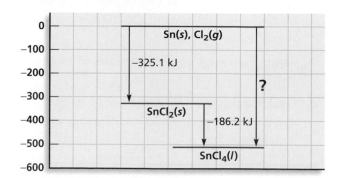

34. Solid iron will slowly oxidize into iron oxide, Fe_2O_3, if it is left untreated in the open air. What is the entropy change for this reaction?

$$4Fe(s) + 3O_2(g) \longrightarrow 2Fe_2O_3(s)$$

(Hint: See Sample Problem 11D.)

Substance	S (J/K•mol)
$Fe(s)$	27.3
$O_2(g)$	205.0
$Fe_2O_3(s)$	87.4

35. Ammonium nitrate is a common fertilizer that can become a powerful explosive when it undergoes rapid decomposition. What is the entropy change for this reaction?

$$2NH_4NO_3(s) \longrightarrow 2N_2(g) + 4H_2O(g) + O_2(g)$$

(Hint: See Sample Problem 11D.)

Substance	S (J/K•mol)
$NH_4NO_3(s)$	151.1
$N_2(g)$	191.6
$H_2O(g)$	188.7
$O_2(g)$	205.0

36. Titanium chloride, $TiCl_4$, is an intermediate chemical formed in the production of titanium metal, a substance used extensively in aerospace technology. Will the reaction for the production of $TiCl_4$ be spontaneous if it is carried out at 100.0°C? Show your work.

$$TiO_2(s) + 2Cl_2(g) \longrightarrow TiCl_4(l) + O_2(g)$$
$$\Delta H = +140.5 \text{ kJ}$$
$$\Delta S = -38.9 \text{ J/K}$$

(Hint: See Sample Problem 11E.)

37. Will the combustion of benzene be spontaneous if the temperature is 25°C? Show your work.

$$2C_6H_6(l) + 15O_2(g) \longrightarrow 12CO_2(g) + 6H_2O(l)$$
$$\Delta H = -6535 \text{ kJ}$$
$$\Delta S = -439.1 \text{ J/K}$$

(Hint: See Sample Problem 11E.)

1. Molar mass
Specific heat capacity is the thermal energy needed to raise the temperature of 1 g of a substance by 1 K, and it has the unit J/K•g. For example, the specific heat capacity of $(CH_2OH)_2(l)$, ethylene glycol or antifreeze, is 2.42 J/K•g. Calculate the molar heat capacity of $(CH_2OH)_2(l)$.

2. Theme: Systems and interactions
The block of ice in Sample Problem 11B on page 393 constitutes a system. The negative ΔH value indicates that the system lost thermal energy. As you learned, energy cannot be created or destroyed. Where did the energy go?

3. Theme: Equilibrium and change
At 1109.15 K the reaction of oxygen gas (O_2) to form ozone (O_3) has a ΔG value of zero. What does this tell you about the reaction involving these two gases?

4. Theme: Systems and interactions
Inside a calorimeter, two systems interact. What are these two systems, and how do they interact?

Performance assessment

1. Design an experiment to measure the molar heat capacities of zinc and copper. If your teacher approves the design, obtain the materials needed and conduct the experiment. When finished, compare your experimental values with those from a chemical handbook or other reference source.

2. Develop a procedure to measure the ΔH of a reaction. If your teacher approves, test your procedure by measuring the ΔH value of the following reaction. Determine the accuracy of your method by comparing your ΔH with the accepted ΔH value.

$$CH_3COONa(s) \longrightarrow Na^+(aq) + CH_3COO^-(aq)$$

3. Design an experiment to determine the ΔH_{fus} for $H_2O(s)$. If your teacher approves the design, obtain the materials needed and carry out the experiment. Compare your experimental value with that listed on Table 11-3.

Portfolio projects

1. Chemistry and you

Hand warmers depend on chemical reactions that have a negative ΔH value. Research these hand warmers to find out what reactions they use. Prepare a report that includes the advantages and disadvantages of each type. Experiment to see if you can prepare a more efficient or less expensive hand warmer.

2. Chemistry and you

Evaluate your own diet after researching diet issues such as starchy carbohydrates versus sugary carbohydrates, complete versus incomplete proteins, and saturated versus unsaturated fats. Write a report on some of the controversies that exist regarding food choices.

3. Cooperative activity

Conduct research on different mechanisms that lower the entropy of a system. Decide which are most effective. Present your findings to the class.

4. internet**connect**

SC*L*INKS
NSTA

TOPIC: Alternative fuels
GO TO: www.scilinks.org
KEYWORD: HW116

Research and communication

The chapter story examines one alternative fuel for cars. Conduct research on the public and private uses of alternative fuels in automobiles and other combustion engines. Determine which ones can be used and produced with the least environmental impact. Present your findings to the class.

1. An adiabatic calorimeter can be used to determine the ——— of a reaction.
   a. ΔG c. ΔH
   b. ΔS d. molar Gibbs energy

2. The temperature of a substance is a measurement of the ———.
   a. total kinetic energy of its atoms
   b. entropy of the substance
   c. average kinetic energy of its atoms
   d. molar heat capacity of the substance

3. Which of the following energy conversions would be least efficient?
   a. heat energy $\longrightarrow$ mechanical energy
   b. mechanical energy $\longrightarrow$ potential energy
   c. electrical energy $\longrightarrow$ mechanical energy
   d. chemical energy $\longrightarrow$ light energy

4. An example of an intensive property in matter would be its ———.
   a. mass   c. entropy
   b. volume   d. temperature

5. Which of the following physical properties do all the noble gases share?
   a. molar heat capacity
   b. entropy
   c. boiling point
   d. electron configuration

6. When carrying out thermodynamic calculations, always ———.
   a. convert joules to kilojoules
   b. convert Celsius data to kelvins
   c. determine the ΔH value first
   d. convert moles to grams

7. The melting point of a solid can be defined as the ———.
   a. molar enthalpy of vaporization
   b. molar enthalpy of fusion divided by the molar entropy of fusion
   c. point at which enthalpy and entropy are equal
   d. condensation point of the gas

8. Which of the following two conditions will favor a spontaneous reaction?
   a. increase in entropy and decrease in enthalpy
   b. increase in entropy and increase in enthalpy
   c. decrease in entropy and decrease in enthalpy
   d. decrease in entropy and increase in enthalpy

9. Respiration is a spontaneous reaction as reflected by ———.
   a. $\Delta H > 0$ c. $\Delta G < 0$
   b. $\Delta S < 0$ d. $\Delta G > 0$

10. The gasification of coal is a method of producing methane. The overall reaction has three separate steps, with the following heats of reaction.

    Step 1: $C(s) + O_2(g) \longrightarrow CO_2(g)$
    $\Delta H_c^0 = -393.5$ kJ
    Step 2: $2H_2(g) + O_2(g) \longrightarrow 2H_2O(l)$
    $\Delta H_c^0 = -571.6$ kJ
    Step 3: $CH_4(g) + 2O_2(g) \longrightarrow CO_2(g) + 2H_2O(l)$
    $\Delta H_c^0 = -890.8$ kJ

    What is the ΔH for the following overall reaction for the gasification of coal?

    $$C(s) + 2H_2(g) \longrightarrow CH_4(g)$$
    a. -393.5 kJ   c. 0 kJ
    b. -74.3 kJ   d. $+890.8$ kJ

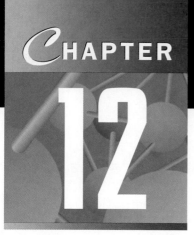

CHAPTER 12

Gases and Liquids

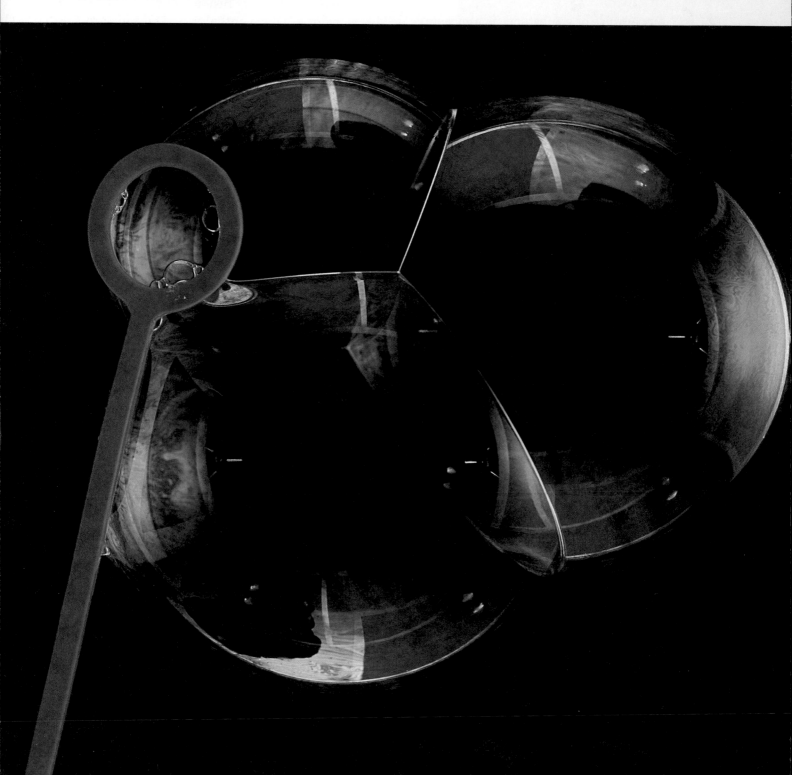

ASCENT INTO THE OZONE

In the still air, the sun begins to rise above the horizon. The busy team of scientists, awake for hours, monitors atmospheric conditions to be sure they are right. Today looks like a great day for the research team—today, there will be a launch.

As the sun rises, a growing silver form appears in the distance. A strange hissing sound fills the air. The shape, now recognizable as a huge balloon, takes form as it inflates with helium.

The ground crew continues to monitor atmospheric conditions as other scientists turn their attention to the expanding balloon. When the top of the partially inflated balloon extends about 250 m into the air, it is ready for launch. Though the balloon is only a fraction of the size it will be when it is completely inflated, it is still capable of lifting a cargo of telescopes, cameras, and recording equipment with a total mass of more than 700 kg. With the data provided by these instruments, scientists can derive a clearer picture of what is happening in the upper atmosphere.

When the restraining lines are removed, the balloon ascends to about 38 000 m above Earth's surface. This mission, like many others before it, involves collecting data on the ever-changing ozone layer in the atmosphere. After collecting data for several days, the payload falls back to Earth, and the instruments are retrieved by scientists. The data collected will become part of the monthly log scientists use to determine conditions in the atmosphere and make predictions about the ozone layer.

With the advent of satellites, you might expect the use of balloons to be obsolete, but balloons offer several advantages over satellites. Balloons are much cheaper to build and launch, and a balloon can collect data from within the ozone layer, while a satellite can merely provide data from an aerial perspective above the layer.

The principles used in launching balloons were discovered nearly 150 years ago. In studying these ideas, you will find information to help you answer the following questions.

CHAPTER LINKS

Why is the balloon only partially inflated at launch?

How do scientists know how much to inflate the balloon?

Why do scientists monitor the ozone layer?

What gases are thought to be responsible for changes in the ozone layer?

What is being done to protect the ozone layer?

What are the characteristics of gases?

OBJECTIVES

▶ **Describe** the general properties of gases.

▶ **Relate** the kinetic-molecular theory to the properties of an ideal gas.

▶ **Define** pressure, and give the SI unit for pressure.

▶ **Describe** the events that are believed to be responsible for global warming.

▶ **Explain** the depletion of ozone in the stratosphere.

Properties of gases

kinetic-molecular theory

the theory that explains the behavior of gases at the molecular level

ideal gas

a model that effectively describes the behavior of gases under most conditions

Each state of matter has its own characteristic properties. The properties of gases can be explained by a model called the **kinetic-molecular theory.** Models are used in science to make predictions. Models explain the facts available and often lead to correct predictions. The kinetic-molecular theory was developed in the mid-1800s, and it is still extremely useful as a model for predicting gas behavior. This theory makes some major assumptions about a theoretical gas often called an **ideal gas.**

Gases are fluids

Gases are fluids, which means that they flow just as liquids do. Gases also transmit and exert pressure equally in all directions. Gas molecules are in constant motion and frequently collide with one another and with the walls of their container, as illustrated in **Figure 12-1.** The kinetic-molecular theory assumes that collisions between ideal gas molecules are elastic. Normally, collisions between everyday objects are not elastic. A collision is said to be elastic when there is no loss in the total amount of kinetic energy involved in the collision. According to the kinetic-molecular theory, there are no net attractive or repulsive forces between ideal gas molecules, allowing collisions between these molecules to be elastic.

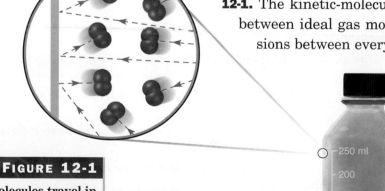

▶ **FIGURE 12-1**

Gas molecules travel in a straight-line motion until they collide with each other or the walls of their container.

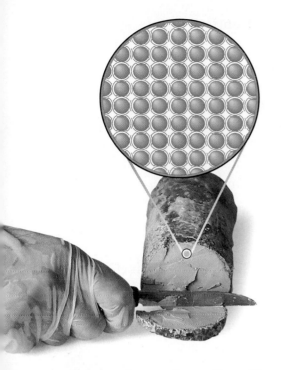
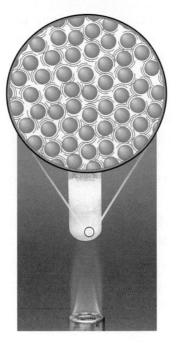
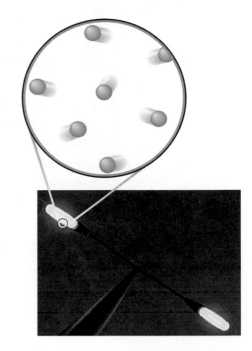

Gases have low density

Compared with liquids and solids, gases have a very low density. To explain the low density of gases, the kinetic-molecular theory states that molecules of an ideal gas are so small that the volume of the individual molecules can almost be ignored when compared with the total volume of the gas. Gases are mostly empty space, while particles in solids and liquids are in contact with each other, as shown in **Figure 12-2.** This distance between particles illustrates why a substance in the liquid or solid state always has a greater density than the same substance in the gaseous state.

FIGURE 12-2 ▲

Particles of sodium metal in three different states are shown. Sodium exists in a gaseous state in a sodium-vapor lamp.

Gases are highly compressible

Suppose you fill a syringe with liquid and try to push the plunger in when the opening is plugged. Nothing happens. It takes enormous pressure to reduce the volume of a liquid or solid. However, if there is a gas or mixture of gases, such as air, in the syringe, it does not take much pressure to move the plunger down and compress the gases, as shown in **Figure 12-3.**

FIGURE 12-3 ▼

The volume of gas in the syringe is reduced when the plunger is pushed inward.

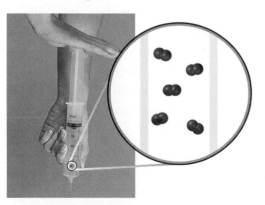
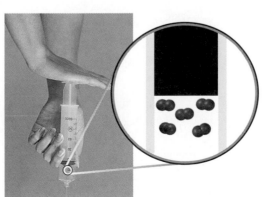

The volume occupied by a gas is almost entirely empty space because the volume filled by the gas molecules is very small. You know that gases are made up of tiny particles that are far apart from each other relative to their size; therefore, it is easy to understand that applying a small pressure will move the gas molecules closer together, decreasing the volume of the gas. Steel cylinders containing gases under pressure are widely used in industry. When they are full, these cylinders may contain 100 times as many gas molecules as would be contained in nonpressurized containers of the same size.

Gases completely fill a container and exert pressure equally in all directions

A solid has a distinctive shape and volume. A liquid has a distinctive volume but assumes the shape of its container. In contrast, a gas fills the entire container and exerts pressure on the container in all directions. The pressure exerted on a container by a gas is the result of gas molecules colliding against it, as illustrated in Figure 12-1.

The temperature of a gas determines the average kinetic energy of its particles

The kinetic energy of a gas molecule can be expressed using the kinetic-energy equation that relates kinetic energy to one-half the mass, m, multiplied by the square of the speed, v.

$$KE = \frac{1}{2}mv^2$$

▼ **FIGURE 12-4**

Increasing the temperature of a sample of gas shifts the energy distribution in the direction of greater average kinetic energy.

According to the kinetic-molecular theory, the average kinetic energy of gas particles depends on the temperature of the gas. Remember that the collisions of ideal gas particles are elastic and therefore do not affect the kinetic energy of the system. **Figure 12-4** shows how energy is distributed in a sample of gas molecules. Most of the gas molecules are traveling near the average speed, a few are traveling at lower speeds, and a few are traveling at very high speeds. The blue curve shows the speed of gas molecules at 25°C (298 K). The red curve shows gas molecules at a temperature 10°C higher. Notice that the shape of the curve changes when the temperature increases. As the temperature increases, the average speed increases slightly. But, as shown on the graph, the number of very high energy molecules, indicated by the shaded area, has increased greatly, perhaps doubling.

Energy Distribution of Gas Molecules
at Different Temperatures

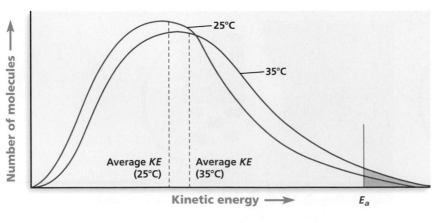

1. Why are gases considered fluids?
2. What is an elastic collision?
3. According to the kinetic-molecular theory, what does the average kinetic energy of gas particles depend on?

The atmosphere is a sea of gases

The atmosphere exerts pressure on the surface of Earth

Every day you are surrounded by gases. Earth's atmosphere is a gaseous mixture of elements and compounds. The atmosphere is composed of gas molecules that have mass. As these molecules move and collide with Earth's surface, they exert pressure. You already have an idea of what pressure is, but now it must be defined more precisely.

Pressure is the force on a surface divided by the area of that surface.

$$\text{pressure} = \frac{\text{force}}{\text{area}}$$

In SI, force is measured in **newtons** (N), and the unit of area is meters squared (m^2). Therefore, the SI unit for pressure is the **pascal** (Pa) and is derived from the units of force and area.

$$1 \text{ pascal (Pa)} = 1 \text{ N/m}^2$$

There are other ways to express pressure. For example, as shown in **Figure 12-5,** the atmosphere exerts pressure on the surface of Earth. This same pressure causes a sealed column of mercury to rise in a barometer. How does this barometer measure the pressure exerted by the atmosphere? Due to its weight, the column of mercury exerts a pressure downward. The atmosphere exerts a pressure that is transmitted

pressure

the force exerted per unit area

newton

the force that will increase the speed of a 1 kg mass by 1 m/s each second that force is applied

pascal

a unit of pressure equal to the force of 1 N on 1 m^2

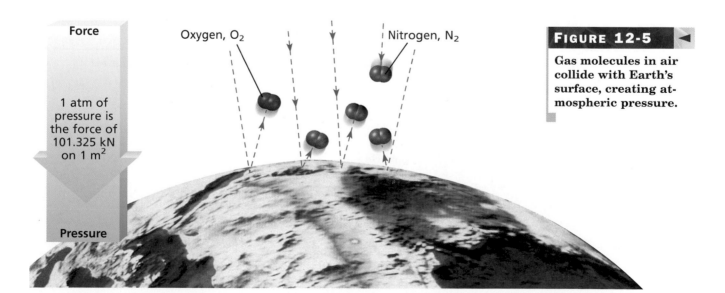

Force

1 atm of pressure is the force of 101.325 kN on 1 m^2

Pressure

Oxygen, O_2

Nitrogen, N_2

FIGURE 12-5

Gas molecules in air collide with Earth's surface, creating atmospheric pressure.

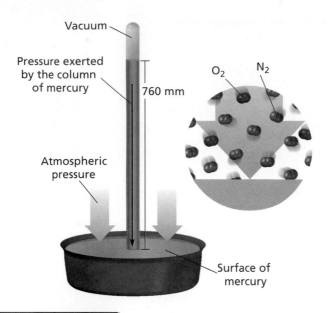

Vacuum

Pressure exerted
by the column
of mercury

760 mm

O₂   N₂

Atmospheric
pressure

Surface of
mercury

▲ **FIGURE 12-6**

In the sealed column of a mercury barometer, the mercury falls until the pressure exerted by its weight equals the atmospheric pressure.

standard temperature and pressure (STP)

standard conditions for a gas at 0°C and 1 atm

upward through the fluid mercury to the mercury in the column. The mercury in the column falls only until the pressure exerted downward by its weight is equal to the pressure exerted upward by the atmosphere. The force per unit area exerted by the atmosphere on the mercury column is called atmospheric pressure. An illustration of a mercury barometer is shown in **Figure 12-6.**

Although water could be used in a barometer, it is an impractical choice because the atmosphere would support a column of water more than 10 m high. The density of mercury is 13.7 times greater than the density of water. Because of its very high density, mercury provides a practical column height of less than 1 m. At sea level, the atmosphere maintains the mercury at an average height of 760 mm. One millimeter of mercury is called a torr, in honor of Evangelista Torricelli, the Italian physicist who invented the barometer. The pressure of one standard atmosphere is equal to 101 325 pascals, or 101.325 kilopascals. Other units of pressure include the bar and pound per square inch (psi). One goal of the scientific community is to eventually have only one unit of pressure in common use—the pascal. The units of pressure are summarized in **Table 12-1.**

To study the effects of changing temperature and pressure on a gas, it is useful to have a standard for comparison. Scientists have specified a set of standard conditions called **standard temperature and pressure,** or **STP.** This text will use the following conditions for STP.

$$STP = 0°C \text{ and } 1 \text{ atm}$$

TABLE 12-1 **Pressure Units**

Unit	Abbreviation	Equivalent number of pascals
Atmosphere	atm	1 atm = 101 325 Pa
Bar	bar	1 bar = 100 025 Pa
Millimeter of mercury	mm Hg	1 mm Hg = 133.322 Pa
Pascal	Pa	
Pound per square inch	psi	1 psi = 6.892 86 × 10³ Pa
Torr	torr	1 torr = 133.322 Pa

Earth's changing climate

If not for the sun, Earth would be a completely frozen globe. Earth receives electromagnetic radiation from the sun. The fate of this radiant energy is shown in **Figure 12-7.** Most of the visible radiation is reflected back into space by clouds, dust in the atmosphere, and the surface of Earth. About one-third of the electromagnetic radiation from the sun reaches Earth's surface and is absorbed. This absorbed radiant energy warms the surface of Earth and in turn warms the atmosphere.

Greenhouse gases trap radiant energy

All objects with a temperature above 0 K radiate energy, and this is true of Earth. The radiant energy from Earth that goes out into space is heat radiation in the infrared region of the spectrum, as shown in Figure 3-20, on page 92. Certain gases in the atmosphere, called greenhouse gases, absorb much of this infrared radiation and emit it back toward Earth's surface, causing Earth to be warmer than it otherwise might be.

internet**connect**

SC*LINKS*.

NSTA

TOPIC: Greenhouse gases
GO TO: www.scilinks.org
KEYWORD: HW121

FIGURE 12·7

Greenhouse gases in the atmosphere can trap radiant energy by reflecting it back to Earth.

greenhouse effect

an increase in the temperature of Earth caused by reflected solar radiation that is trapped in the atmosphere

This warming mechanism, referred to as the **greenhouse effect,** is illustrated in Figure 12-7. Natural greenhouse warming keeps Earth at a habitable temperature. Greenhouse gases include water vapor, H_2O, carbon dioxide, CO_2, methane, CH_4, dinitrogen monoxide, N_2O, and chlorofluorocarbons, CFCs.

Earth is becoming warmer

Over the past century, Earth has become warmer. In the past 100 years, the average increase in global air temperature has been about 0.6°C. This seems to be a small amount, but if you consider that the last ice age was caused by an average decrease in global temperature of about 5°C, you can begin to understand the effects this increase might have.

Many scientists who study the atmosphere believe that a primary cause of the warming is the increase in the concentration of greenhouse gases. Levels of CO_2 in the atmosphere have increased and have contributed to the warming. Some scientists believe that most of the increase in CO_2 levels is caused by combustion of fossil fuels: coal, petroleum, and natural gas. Many everyday activities involve the combustion of fossil fuels. Driving a car, cooking on an outdoor grill, and using electricity produced by coal-fired generators all involve combustion processes. Another source of CO_2 in our atmosphere comes from the burning of forests, most of them tropical rain forests.

There has also been an increase in artificial greenhouse gases. These are mostly chlorofluorocarbons once used in refrigeration and air-conditioning but now banned in the United States. The structures of two typical chlorofluorocarbons are depicted in **Figure 12-8.**

Ozone depletion allows more ultraviolet radiation to reach Earth

About 9% of the radiant energy emitted by the sun is ultraviolet radiation. Ultraviolet radiation is a mutagen because it can cause a mutation, including various forms of skin cancer, some of which can be fatal. Ozone, O_3, is an extremely good absorber of ultraviolet light, and it

internet**connect**

SC*LINKS*

NSTA

TOPIC: Ozone depletion
GO TO: www.scilinks.org
KEYWORD: HW122

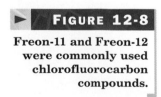

▶ **FIGURE 12-8**

Freon-11 and Freon-12 were commonly used chlorofluorocarbon compounds.

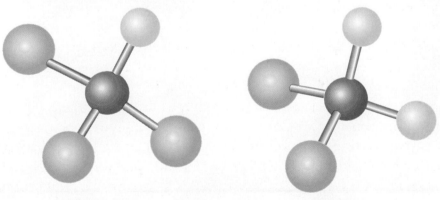

Freon-11   Freon-12

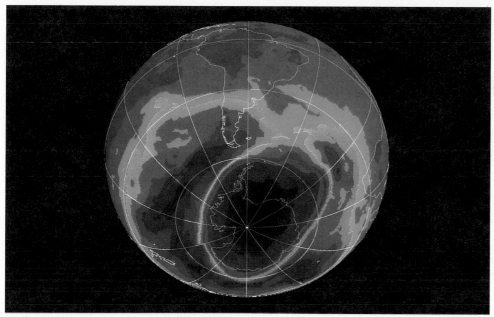

FIGURE 12-9 ◄

The black region over Antarctica shows the area of greatest ozone depletion, called the ozone hole.

blocks most of the ultraviolet light from reaching Earth. Upon absorbing ultraviolet light, ozone breaks apart into an oxygen molecule and an oxygen atom.

The ozone layer is thin and extremely fragile. Unfortunately, chlorofluorocarbons are destroying the ozone layer. The CFC molecules diffuse into the atmosphere over many years. There, the energetic ultraviolet radiation breaks them apart, liberating Cl atoms. The resulting atom is a chlorine **free radical,** Cl•, that reacts rapidly with an ozone molecule to form molecular oxygen and chlorine monoxide, ClO, as shown by the following equation.

$$Cl•(g) + O_3(g) \longrightarrow ClO(g) + O_2(g)$$

The resulting chlorine monoxide is very reactive. It reacts with O atoms formed by the decomposition of O_3 to form the more stable O_2 molecule.

$$ClO(g) + O(g) \longrightarrow Cl•(g) + O_2(g)$$

The first reaction destroys the ozone. The second reaction consumes reactive O atoms needed to form ozone. The Cl• formed in the second reaction then becomes available to repeat the sequence. In this **chain reaction,** one Cl• may destroy thousands of ozone molecules before it diffuses down to the troposphere.

There has always been an annual decrease in the ozone concentration around the South Pole during September and October. But since 1977, the decrease has been so great that it is referred to as an ozone hole. This decrease in ozone level is shown in **Figure 12-9.** In recent years, the size of the ozone hole has averaged approximately 21 million square kilometers.

To halt the destruction of the ozone layer, 163 nations became parties to the Montreal Protocol, which called for ending the production of all CFCs by industrialized nations by 1996 and for banning their use in developing countries by 2010. However, CFCs already in the atmosphere continue to damage the ozone layer.

free radical

an atom or molecule that has one or more unpaired electrons and is therefore very reactive

chain reaction

a self-sustaining nuclear or chemical reaction in which the product from one step acts as a reactant for the next step

CONSUMER FOCUS

NON-CFC AIR CONDITIONING

A less toxic alternative

In keeping with the limits set for CFCs by the Montreal Protocol, car manufacturers have developed new air-conditioning systems that use a hydrofluorocarbon, 1,1,1,2-tetrafluoroethane, called HFC-134a, as the **refrigerant** instead of the traditional dichlorodifluoromethane, CFC-12.

HFC-134a is believed to have low toxicity and appears to have little effect on the ozone layer. However, the chemical differences between CFC-12 and HFC-134a result in some major problems for consumers.

New air-conditioning systems required

HFC-134a *cannot* be used in an air-conditioning system that was built specifically for CFC-12.

internet**connect**

SC**LINKS**
NSTA

TOPIC: Non-CFCs
GO TO: www.scilinks.org
KEYWORD: HW123

Conversion to HFC-134a requires a complete redesign of the existing air-conditioning system. Because non-CFC air conditioning is a new technology, consumers should have work performed only at reputable service stations by knowledgeable mechanics.

SECTION REVIEW

Total recall

1. What causes the pressure exerted by gas molecules on their container?

2. **Interpreting Tables** What is the conversion factor to change atmospheres to pascals?

Critical thinking

3. Describe the relationship between average molecular kinetic energy of gases and temperature.

4. Why are scientists concerned about burning fossil fuels?

5. **Interpreting Graphics** Notice that more molecules have a certain kinetic energy at 25° C than at 35° C at points on the graph in Figure 12-4, on page 426. Explain.

What behaviors are described by the gas laws?

OBJECTIVES

▶ **Relate** the ideal gas model to the observed behavior of real gases.

▶ **State** the following laws describing the behavior of gases: Boyle's law, Dalton's law, Charles's law, Avogadro's

law, Gay-Lussac's law, and Graham's law.

▶ **Use** these laws to solve problems.

▶ **Describe** the relationship between gas behavior and chemical formulas.

The gas laws

In Section 12-1 you learned how gases exert pressure. In this section you will study the mathematical relationships that relate the variables used to describe a gas under specific conditions. Each variable is represented by a symbol.

P – pressure exerted by the particles

T = temperature in kelvins of the particles

V = volume occupied by the particles

n = number of moles of the particles

The pressure and the volume of a gas are related

Recall from Section 12-1 that gases are highly compressible and exert pressure. The English scientist Robert Boyle studied the relationship between the volume and the pressure of a gas and published his results in 1662. He found that at constant temperature, all gases behave the same when compressed; that is, as increasing pressure is applied to a gas in a closed container, the volume of the gas decreases. Recall the diagram of the syringe in Figure 12-3. The volume of the syringe decreased as pressure was applied. **Table 12-2** shows pressure-volume data for an experiment similar to those performed by Boyle.

The data in Table 12-2 show that the volume is inversely proportional to the pressure. Graphing these data produces

TABLE 12-2 **Pressure-Volume Data for a Gas at Constant Temperature**

Pressure (kPa)	Volume (L)	PV (kPa•L)
100	0.500	50.0
150	0.334	50.1
200	0.250	50.0
250	0.200	50.0
300	0.167	50.1
350	0.142	49.7
400	0.125	50.0
450	0.111	50.0

► **FIGURE 12-10**

The volume versus pressure graph represents an inverse relationship: as pressure increases, volume decreases.

Volume vs. Pressure for a Fixed Amount of Gas at Constant Temperature

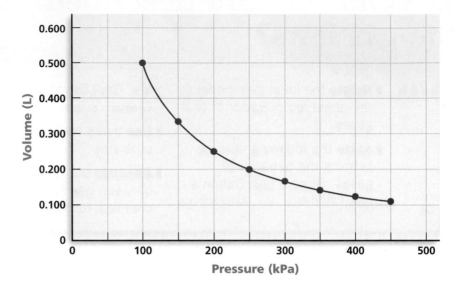

the curve shown in **Figure 12-10.** By examining the points along this curve, you can see that as the pressure of a gas increases, its volume decreases while keeping the temperature of the system constant. As the pressure of the gas decreases, its volume increases. Another way to consider the information in Table 12-2 is to plot the data in the product column, *PV,* against *P,* as in **Figure 12-11.** The horizontal line produced by the data points shows that the product of the pressure and the volume of a given sample of gas at constant temperature is a constant.

$$PV = k$$

► **FIGURE 12-11**

The product of the pressure and volume of a gas at constant temperature is a constant value.

PV vs. Pressure for a Fixed Amount of Gas at Constant Temperature

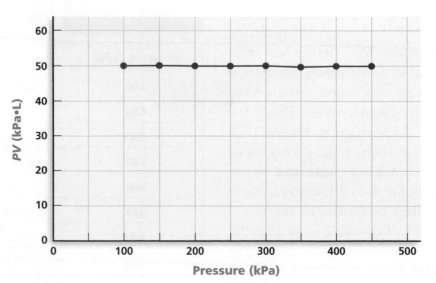

FIGURE 12-12 ▼

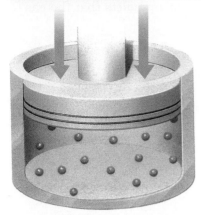

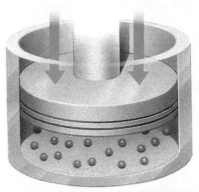

a Gas molecules in a car-engine cylinder expand to fill the cylinder.

b As the container volume decreases, the gas molecules move closer together, increasing their concentration and their pressure.

The relationship expressed by these data is known as **Boyle's law,** one of the oldest valid scientific laws in existence today. If the product, *PV,* is measured for a given amount of gas under one set of conditions, P_1V_1, and then under another set of conditions, P_2V_2, both products are found to be equal to the constant, *k*. Therefore, they are equal to each other. Using this information, Boyle's law can also be expressed as follows.

$$P_1V_1 = k$$
$$P_2V_2 = k$$
$$P_1V_1 = P_2V_2$$

How is this relationship explained by the kinetic-molecular theory? As mentioned in Section 12-1, gas pressure is caused by the collision of gas molecules with the walls of their container. If the volume is reduced by half, the gas concentration is doubled, and the number of collisions with the walls of the container is doubled, as shown in **Figure 12-12.** Therefore, the pressure is also doubled.

Boyle's law

the volume of a given amount of gas at constant temperature is inversely proportional to the pressure

SAMPLE PROBLEM 12A Solving pressure-volume problems

The gas in a balloon has a volume of 7.5 L at 100 kPa. The balloon is released into the atmosphere, and the gas in it expands to a volume of 11 L. Assuming a constant temperature, what is the pressure on the balloon at the new volume?

1 **List what you know**

▶ $V_1 = 7.5$ L
▶ $P_1 = 100$ kPa
▶ $V_2 = 11$ L
▶ $P_2 = ?$ kPa

2 Set up the problem

▶ The volume of the gas has increased. Boyle's law predicts that the gas pressure will decrease.

$$P_1V_1 = P_2V_2$$
$$P_2 = \frac{P_1V_1}{V_2}$$

▶ Multiply the known pressure by the ratio of volumes that will result in a decrease in pressure.

$$P_2 = 100 \text{ kPa} \times \frac{7.5 \text{ L}}{11 \text{ L}}$$

3 Calculate and verify

$$P_2 = 100 \text{ kPa} \times \frac{7.5 \cancel{L}}{11 \cancel{L}} = 68 = 70 \text{ kPa (rounded to 1 significant figure)}$$

▶ The final pressure has decreased as predicted.

PRACTICE PROBLEMS

1. A flask contains 155 cm^3 of hydrogen collected at a pressure of 22.5 kPa. Under what pressure would the gas have a volume of 90.0 cm^3 at the same temperature? (Recall that 1 cm^3 = 1 mL.)

2. If the pressure exerted on a 300.0 mL sample of hydrogen gas at constant temperature is increased from 0.500 atm to 0.750 atm, what will be the final volume of the sample?

3. A helium balloon has a volume of 5.0 L at a pressure of 101.3 kPa. The balloon is released and reaches an altitude of 6.5 km at a pressure of 50.7 kPa. If the gas temperature remains the same, what is the new volume of the balloon? Assume that pressures are the same inside and outside the balloon.

4. A sample of oxygen gas has a volume of 150. mL at a pressure of 0.947 atm. What will the volume of the gas be at a pressure of 1.000 atm if the temperature remains constant?

The total pressure of a mixture of gases can be calculated

partial pressure

the pressure of an individual gas in a gas mixture that contributes to the total pressure of the mixture

Dalton's law of partial pressures

the total pressure in a gas mixture is the sum of the partial pressures of the individual components, each behaving as if the other gases were absent

Suppose you want to calculate the pressure of a mixture of gases rather than that of a single gas. An English chemist named John Dalton investigated the pressure exerted by a mixture of various gases on its container, and he presented his results in 1805. He found that in a mixture of gases, each gas exerts a pressure as if it were alone in the container. The pressure of a gas in a mixture is called the **partial pressure** of that gas. The total pressure of a mixture of gases is equal to the sum of the partial pressures of the individual gases. This statement is known as **Dalton's law of partial pressures.** Dalton's law is written as follows.

$$P_{total} = P_A + P_B + P_C$$

P_{total} is the total pressure of the mixture. P_A, P_B, and P_C are the partial pressures of the mixture's component gases, A, B, and C.

How is Dalton's law of partial pressures explained by the kinetic-molecular theory? All the gas molecules are moving about at random, and they have an equal chance to collide with the container wall. Each gas exerts a pressure on the container wall proportional to its number of molecules in the container. The presence of other gas molecules does not change this fact.

Another way to determine partial pressures

Dalton was not aware of the concept of moles. But because we are, we can use the **mole fraction** of a gas in a mixture to calculate the partial pressure of that gas. The mole fraction is the number of moles of a particular substance divided by the total number of moles in a mixture. If A, B, and C are the components of a gas mixture, then the mole fraction of gas A is represented mathematically as follows.

$$\text{mol fraction} = \frac{\text{mol A}}{\text{mol A} + \text{B} + \text{C}}$$

The air we breathe is a mixture of gases that contains 0.78 mole fraction of N_2, 0.21 mole fraction of O_2, and 0.01 mole fraction of argon, Ar. The mixture has a total pressure of 0.97 atm. What is the partial pressure of each gas in the mixture? The following equation shows that the partial pressure of a gas can be calculated by multiplying the total pressure of the system by the mole fraction of the specific gas. Accordingly, the partial pressure of nitrogen in this mixture of gases is 0.76 atm, and the partial pressures of oxygen and argon in the mixture are 0.20 atm and 0.01 atm, respectively.

$P_{total} = P_{nitrogen} + P_{oxygen} + P_{argon}$

$P_{total} = (0.97 \text{ atm} \times 0.78) + (0.97 \text{ atm} \times 0.21) + (0.97 \text{ atm} \times 0.01)$

$P_{total} = 0.76 \text{ atm} + 0.20 \text{ atm} + 0.01 \text{ atm} = 0.97 \text{ kPa}$

QUICKLAB

Pressure Relief

Pressure builds up in closed systems such as boiler tanks and pressure cookers. Relief valves allow the pressure to be released when it gets too high. In this activity, you will use pressure-volume relations to modify the balloon-in-a-bottle apparatus.

Materials round latex balloon, PET bottle, rubber band

Problem

1. Blow up the balloon and let the air out.
2. Put the round part of the balloon inside the bottle. Roll the neck of the balloon over the mouth of the bottle and secure the balloon with a rubber band.
3. Try to blow up the balloon. Record the results.
4. Answer items 1 and 2 below.
5. Design a modification to the balloon-in-a-bottle apparatus that will allow the balloon to inflate. Answer item 3 below.
6. If your teacher approves your design, try it out.

Analysis

1. What happens to air that is trapped in the bottle when you blow into the balloon?
2. What causes the balloon to expand? Why can you not blow up the balloon?
3. Describe your design modification, and include a sketch, if applicable. Explain, in terms of pressure, why your design works.

mole fraction

the number of moles of one component compared with the total number of moles in the mixture expressed as a ratio

Atmospheric pressure changes with altitude

The mole fraction of oxygen in dry air at sea level is 0.21. Therefore, the oxygen partial pressure is close to 21 kPa. As the altitude increases, pressure decreases, but the composition of the air changes very little. This means that the partial pressure of oxygen also decreases with an increase in altitude. Consequently, as altitude increases, a person takes in less and less oxygen with each breath.

Gases expand greatly when heated and contract greatly when cooled

Heating a gas will make it expand. Gas molecules move faster when heat energy is added to them, causing them to strike with more force against the walls of their container. The more frequent and more forceful collisions make the volume of a yielding container, such as a balloon, increase. Likewise, gas volumes decrease greatly when the gas is cooled.

Charles's law

the volume of a sample of gas at constant pressure is directly proportional to the absolute temperature

The volume change of a gas caused by a change of temperature at constant pressure is expressed by **Charles's law.** Jacques Charles discovered that the volume is directly proportional to the temperature on the Kelvin scale at constant pressure. In **Table 12-3,** each gas volume is divided by its corresponding temperature. At constant pressure, the volume of a given sample of gas divided by its absolute temperature is a constant, k. This relationship can be stated as the mathematical representation of Charles's law.

$$\frac{V}{T} = k$$

The ratio, V/T, for the same gas sample at any set of volume-temperature conditions (at constant pressure) will always equal the same constant, k. Therefore, Charles's law can also be expressed as follows.

$$\frac{V_1}{T_1} = \frac{V_2}{T_2}$$

TABLE 12-3 **Volume-Temperature Data for a Gas at a Constant Pressure**

Volume (mL)	Temperature (K)	V/T (mL/K)
748	373	2.01
567	283	2.00
545	274	1.99
545	273	2.00
546	272	2.01
402	200	2.01
199	100	1.99

Volume vs. Temperature for a Fixed Amount of Gas at Constant Pressure

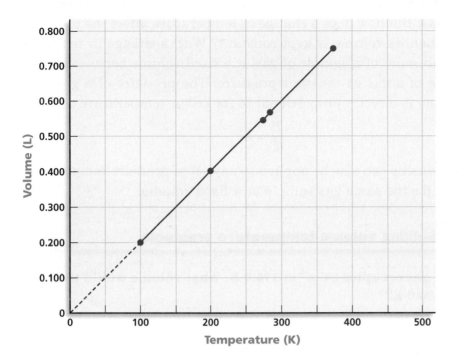

FIGURE 12-13 ◄

When kelvins are used on the temperature scale of the graph, the relationship between volume and temperature can be expressed as a direct proportion.

The volume-temperature data is graphed using the Kelvin scale in **Figure 12-13.** When the line produced in Figure 12-13 is extended to 0 K, the gas's volume becomes zero. Does a gas volume become zero at absolute zero? No. Before this temperature is reached, the gas condenses to a liquid and then freezes to a solid, which has a finite volume. Charles's law is illustrated in **Figure 12-14.**

FIGURE 12-14 ▼

a Air-filled balloons are dipped into liquid nitrogen.

b The extremely low temperature of the nitrogen causes them to shrink in volume.

c When the balloons are removed from the liquid nitrogen, the air inside them quickly warms, and the balloons expand to their original volume.

Gas pressure increases with an increase in temperature

You have seen that changes in temperature and pressure affect the volume of a gas. But how does a change in temperature affect the pressure of a gas when its volume is kept constant? With a change in temperature, the pressure of a sample of gas at a fixed volume behaves just as the volume of a gas at constant pressure. The pressure of a gas in a fixed volume is directly proportional to its kelvin temperature.

$$\frac{P}{T} = k$$

This relationship can also be applied to any set of pressure-temperature conditions for the same gas sample at a fixed volume.

SAMPLE PROBLEM 12B **Solving volume-temperature problems**

A sample of gas occupies 24 m³ at 175.0 K. What volume would the gas occupy at 400.0 K?

1 **List what you know**

- $V_1 = 24 \text{ m}^3$
- $T_1 = 175.0 \text{ K}$
- $T_2 = 400.0 \text{ K}$
- $V_2 = ? \text{ m}^3$

2 **Set up the problem**

- The temperature of the gas is increased. Charles's law predicts that the gas volume will also increase.

$$\frac{V_1}{T_1} = \frac{V_2}{T_2}; \text{ therefore } V_2 = \frac{V_1 T_2}{T_1}$$

- Multiply the known volume by the ratio of temperatures that will result in an increase in volume.

$$V_2 = 24 \text{ m}^3 \times \frac{400.0 \text{ K}}{175.0 \text{ K}}$$

3 **Calculate and verify**

$$V_2 - 24 \text{ m}^3 \times \frac{400.0 \text{ K}}{175.0 \text{ K}} = 55 \text{ m}^3$$

- The ratio of temperatures is greater than 1, which means the volume increases, as predicted.

PRACTICE PROBLEMS

1. Gas in a balloon occupies 2.5 L at 300.0 K. The balloon is dipped into liquid nitrogen that is at a temperature of 80.0 K. What volume will the gas in the balloon occupy at this temperature?

2. The gas in a sealed can is at a pressure of 3.00 atm at 25°C. A warning on the can tells the user not to store the can in a place where the temperature will exceed 52°C. What would the gas pressure in the can be at 52°C?

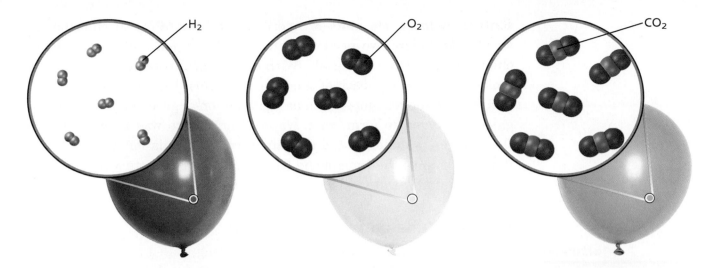

FIGURE 12-15

At the same tempera-
ture and pressure,
balloons of equal vol-
ume contain equal
numbers of molecules,
regardless of which
gas they contain.

Gas behavior and chemical formulas

Gases with equal volumes under the same conditions have an equal number of molecules

In 1811, the Italian physicist Amadeo Avogadro made a bold proposition. He proposed that equal volumes of different gases under the
same conditions have the same number of molecules. This proposal is
respresented in **Figure 12-15** and is known as **Avogadro's law.** Unfortunately, Avogadro's valuable insight was not recognized immediately,
mainly because scientists at the time did not realize that there is a difference between atoms and molecules. In 1875, the Italian chemist
Stanislao Cannizzaro made use of Avogadro's law to determine the
true formulas of a number of gaseous chemical compounds.

Gases at constant temperature and pressure form compounds with each other in definite proportions

In 1808, the French scientist Joseph Gay-Lussac made an interesting
discovery. If the pressure and temperature are kept constant, gases
react in volume proportions that are whole numbers. This is called **Gay-
Lussac's law of combining volumes.** For example, consider the formation
of gaseous hydrogen chloride from the reaction of hydrogen gas and
chlorine gas. One volume of hydrogen reacts with one volume of chlorine
to form two volumes of hydrogen chloride. Let us use Avogadro's law and
assume that two molecules of hydrogen chloride are formed, one in each
of the two boxes on the right in **Figure 12-16.** Each HCl molecule must

Avogadro's law

equal volumes of different
gases under the same con-
ditions of temperature and
pressure have the same
number of molecules

**Gay-Lussac's law of
combining volumes**

at constant temperature
and pressure, gases react
in volume proportions that
are whole numbers (equivalent to the coefficients in
the balanced chemical
equation)

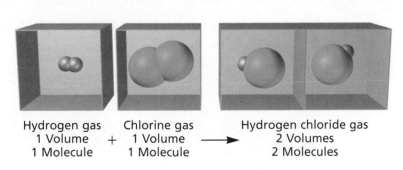

Hydrogen gas   Chlorine gas   Hydrogen chloride gas
  1 Volume   +   1 Volume   →   2 Volumes
  1 Molecule   1 Molecule   2 Molecules

FIGURE 12-16

Hydrogen molecules
combine with chlorine
molecules in a 1:1 vol-
ume ratio to produce
twice the volume of
hydrogen chloride.

contain at least one atom of hydrogen and one atom of chlorine, as shown. Therefore, we need two atoms of hydrogen and two atoms of chlorine as starting materials. With one molecule of hydrogen and one molecule of chlorine, each of the molecules must be diatomic.

Using other reactions, such as the reaction of gaseous hydrogen and gaseous oxygen to form water vapor, Cannizarro was able to deduce that oxygen is diatomic and that the correct formula for water is H_2O. It was not until the time of the Civil War that chemists knew the correct formula for water.

Gases effuse and diffuse rapidly

The passage of a gas through a small opening, called **effusion,** is illustrated in **Figure 12-17.** Effusion occurs, for example, when there is a small leak in a tire: the air in the tire effuses through the hole. The Scottish scientist Thomas Graham studied this gas behavior in detail. He found that at constant temperature and pressure, the rate of effusion of a gas is inversely proportional to the square root of its density; in other words, it is inversely proportional to the square root of its molar mass, M. This is stated mathematically when comparing the speed of effusion, v, of two gases, A and B.

$$\frac{v_A}{v_B} = \sqrt{\frac{M_B}{M_A}}$$

For example, compare the speed of effusion of H_2 with that of O_2.

$$\frac{v_{H_2}}{v_{O_2}} = \sqrt{\frac{M_{O_2}}{M_{H_2}}} = \sqrt{\frac{32 \text{ g/mol}}{2 \text{ g/mol}}} = \sqrt{16} = 4$$

The answer of 4 means that hydrogen gas effuses through a small opening four times as fast as oxygen. Molecules of low molar mass travel

O_2

N_2

▶ **FIGURE 12-17**

Molecules of nitrogen and oxygen from the air inside the bicycle tire effuse out through a small nail hole.

faster on average than heavy molecules. Hydrogen, with the lowest molar mass, travels the fastest of any atom or molecule.

Graham's law of effusion is explained by the kinetic-molecular theory. At the same temperature, the average kinetic energy of all gases is the same. We can write the following relationship to compare the kinetic energies for molar quantities of two gases, A and B.

$$\tfrac{1}{2}M_A v_A{}^2 = \tfrac{1}{2}M_B v_B{}^2$$

The rate of effusion is proportional to the speed of the molecules because their speed determines the rate at which they hit the opening. Solving the equation on the previous page for the ratio of speeds gives the ratios of the rates of effusion.

$$\frac{v_A}{v_B} = \sqrt{\frac{M_B}{M_A}}$$

When you open a bottle of household ammonia, it doesn't take long for the odor of ammonia gas, NH_3, to fill the room. Gaseous molecules of the compounds responsible for the smell are traveling at high speeds in all directions and are mixing quickly with molecules of other gases in the air in a process called **diffusion.** Gases diffuse through each other at a very rapid rate. During diffusion a substance moves from a region of high concentration to a region of low concentration. Eventually, the mixture becomes homogeneous, as seen in the bottle of bromine gas in **Figure 12-18.**

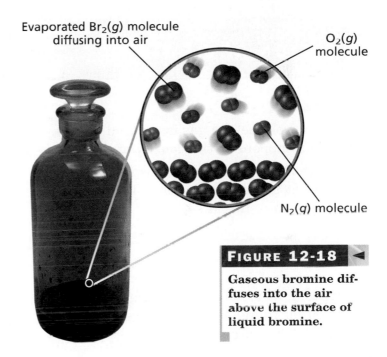

Evaporated $Br_2(g)$ molecule diffusing into air

$O_2(g)$ molecule

$N_2(g)$ molecule

FIGURE 12-18 ◄

Gaseous bromine diffuses into the air above the surface of liquid bromine.

SAMPLE PROBLEM 12C   Comparing molecular speeds

Oxygen molecules have an average speed of about 480 m/s at room temperature. On average, how fast are molecules of sulfur trioxide, SO_3, traveling at the same temperature?

1 List what you know

▶ $v_{O_2} = 480$ m/s
▶ $v_{SO_3} = ?$ m/s

2 Set up the problem

▶ To use the equation for Graham's law, you need the molar masses of O_2 and SO_3. Calculate the molar mass of O_2 and SO_3.

mass of 2 mol O = 2(16.00 g)	mass of 1 mol S = 32.07 g
$M_{O_2} = 32.00$ g/mol	mass of 3 mol O = 3(16.00 g)
	$M_{SO_3} = 80.07$ g/mol

▶ Use the equation for Graham's law, and solve for v_{SO_3}.

$$\frac{v_{SO_3}}{v_{O_2}} = \sqrt{\frac{M_{O_2}}{M_{SO_3}}} \qquad\qquad v_{SO_3} = v_{O_2}\sqrt{\frac{M_{O_2}}{M_{SO_3}}}$$

3 **Calculate and verify**

$$v_{SO_3} = 480 \text{ m/s}\sqrt{\frac{32.00 \text{ g/mol}}{80.07 \text{ g/mol}}} = 3.0 \times 10^2 \text{ m/s}$$

▶ SO_3 is heavier, so its speed is slower than that of oxygen.

SECTION REVIEW

Total recall

1. If the volume of a gas is reduced by half, what happens to the density of the gas?

2. In Denver, would the atmospheric pressure be greater or less than the atmospheric pressure at sea level?

Critical thinking

3. Using the ideas of the kinetic-molecular theory, which of the following gases is best for filling automobile tires: CO_2, N_2, or He? Explain your choice.

4. Inexpensive balloons filled with air deflate within a few days because the pores in the walls of these balloons are larger than most of the molecules that are found in air. Explain why helium-filled balloons collapse faster than those filled with air.

Practice problems

5. **Story Clue** At 40 km above Earth, the pressure is about 2.87×10^2 Pa. A helium balloon launched from Earth's surface at 1.000 atm of pressure has a volume of 30.0 m³. What will be the volume of the balloon at 40 km? Assume that the temperature of the He stays constant.

6. At a certain temperature, molecules of chlorine gas travel at 0.380 km/s. What is the speed of sulfur dioxide gas molecules under the same conditions?

7. Given that atoms of neon gas effuse at 800. m/s at a given temperature, calculate the rate of effusion for molecules of butane gas, C_4H_{10}, at the same temperature.

8. The average speed of helium atoms is 1.20×10^3 m/s at a certain temperature. What is the average speed of HCl molecules at the same temperature?

9. Compare the rate of effusion of molecules of water vapor with that of molecules of carbon dioxide gas at the same pressure and temperature.

10. Hydrogen sulfide, H_2S, has a very strong rotten-egg odor. Methyl salicylate, $C_8H_{10}O_3$, has a wintergreen odor. Benzaldehyde, C_7H_6O, has an almond odor. If vapors for these three substances were released at the same time from across the room, which would you smell first? Why?

Nitrogen cycle

Nitrogen gas is the most abundant gas in the atmosphere. Nitrogen is important for photosynthesis and for making the proteins, nucleic acids, vitamins, enzymes, and hormones needed by plants and animals to live. Unfortunately, plants and animals cannot directly use nitrogen gas. The nitrogen must be converted into forms they can use.

Nitrogen-fixing bacteria convert atmospheric nitrogen into substances that green plants absorb from the soil. Animals then eat these plants or eat other animals that feed on these plants. When the animals and plants die and decay, the nitrogen in the decomposed organic matter returns to the atmosphere and the soil. With the return of nitrogen to the soil as ammonium salts, the nitrogen cycle starts all over again.

Nitrogen-fixing bacteria can convert atmospheric nitrogen into chemical compounds, such as ammonia, that can be used by green plants in the formation of proteins.

Industrial Uses

▶ Nitrogen is used in the synthesis of ammonia.

▶ Ammonia is used to produce fertilizer, explosives, nitric acid, urea, hydrazine, and amines.

▶ Liquid nitrogen is used in superconductor research and as a cryogenic supercoolant for storing biological tissues.

▶ Nitrogen gas is used as an inert atmosphere for storing and processing reactive substances.

▶ Nitrogen gas, usually mixed with argon, is used for filling incandescent light bulbs.

A BRIEF HISTORY

1774–1777: Antoine Lavoisier determines that nitrogen is an element.

1200   1700   1800   1900

1772: Nitrogen is discovered by Daniel Rutherford in Scotland, Joseph Priestley and Henry Cavendish in England, and Carl Scheele in Sweden.

1909: Fritz Haber, a German chemist, discovers a method for synthesizing ammonia from hydrogen gas and nitrogen gas. The method is still used today and is called the Haber-Bosch process.

How do the gas laws fit together?

OBJECTIVES

▶ *Use* the ideal gas law and combined gas law to solve mathematical problems.

▶ *Apply* your knowledge of reaction stoichiometry to solve gas stoichiometry problems.

Putting it together: the ideal gas law
The ideal gas law relates all four gas variables

ideal gas law

the equation of state for an ideal gas in which the product of the pressure and volume is proportional to the product of the absolute temperature and the amount of gas expressed in moles

Boyle's law, Charles's law, and Avogadro's law can be combined into one equation that gives the relationships between P, V, T, and n for any sample of gas. This relationship is called the **ideal gas law.** When any three variables are given, the fourth can be calculated. The ideal gas law is frequently used when the pressure, volume, and temperature do not change. The ideal gas law is represented mathematically as follows.

$$PV = nRT$$

R is a proportionality constant, and the value used depends on the units for pressure and volume. The amount n is always expressed in moles, and the temperature is always in kelvins. A temperature in degrees Celsius must be converted to the Kelvin scale before the ideal gas law can be used. In this text we will almost always use kilopascals and liters, so the value you will use for R is as follows.

$$R = \frac{8.314 \ \text{L} \cdot \text{kPa}}{\text{mol} \cdot \text{K}}$$

If the gas law problem gives pressure data in atmospheres, R can also be expressed as follows.

$$R = \frac{0.0821 \ \text{L} \cdot \text{atm}}{\text{mol} \cdot \text{K}}$$

When using the ideal gas law, pay close attention to the units of pressure and volume so that you choose the correct value for R. Use the ideal gas law when you know three of the variables describing the gaseous state (P, V, n, T) and you wish to calculate the fourth. Sample Problem 12D shows this type of problem.

▼ **FIGURE 12-19**

Balloonists use the gas laws to predict the conditions of their flight.

A sample of carbon dioxide with a mass of 0.250 g is placed in a 350.0 mL container at 400.0 K. What is the pressure exerted by the gas?

1 List what you know

- There is no change of conditions for the gas, so this is a straightforward ideal gas law problem.
- mass of CO_2 = 0.250 g
- P = ? kPa
- V = 350.0 mL
- T = 400.0 K
- n = ? mol
- R = 8.314 L•kPa/mol•K

2 Set up the problem

- The molar mass of CO_2 must be calculated.

$$\text{molar mass of } CO_2 = 44.01 \text{ g/mol}$$

- The mass of CO_2 in grams must be converted into moles.

$$\text{mol } CO_2 = \frac{0.250 \text{ g } CO_2}{44.01 \text{ g/mol } CO_2} = 5.68 \times 10^{-3} \text{ mol } CO_2$$

- The volume unit must be compatible with the value of R used; therefore, the volume must be converted from milliliters to liters.

$$\frac{1 \text{ L}}{1000 \text{ mL}} \times 350.0 \text{ mL} = 0.3500 \text{ L}$$

- Use the ideal gas law to find the fourth variable, pressure.

$$PV = nRT$$
$$P = \frac{nRT}{V}$$

3 Calculate

- Substitute the values given in the problem into the equation.

$$P = \frac{(5.68 \times 10^{-3} \text{ mol})(8.314 \text{ L•kPa/mol•K})(400.0 \text{ K})}{(0.3500 \text{ L})}$$

$$P = 54.0 \text{ kPa}$$

PRACTICE PROBLEMS

1. A 500. g block of dry ice (solid CO_2) becomes a gas at room temperature. Calculate the volume of gas produced at 25°C and 975 kPa.

2. Calculate the volume of 1.00 mol of CO_2 gas at STP.

3. The average lung capacity of humans is about 4.0 L. Assuming you are breathing pure oxygen, how many moles of oxygen gas can your lungs hold at 37°C (body temperature) and 110 kPa?

4. What mass in grams of chlorine gas, Cl_2, is contained in a 10.0 L tank at 27°C and 3.50 atm of pressure? (Assume that all Cl_2 in the tank is in gaseous form.)

The combined gas law is derived from the ideal gas law

In many problems the quantity of gas does not change; that is, the number of moles remains constant. We merely change a given quantity of gas from one set of pressure, volume, and temperature conditions to another set. We can easily derive a general gas law for this circumstance by rearranging the ideal gas law.

$$R = \frac{P_1 V_1}{n_1 T_1} = \frac{P_2 V_2}{n_2 T_2}$$

If the amount of gas, n, does not change, n can be canceled out of both expressions. The remaining two expressions are equal to each other because they are both equal to the product nR. The following relationship is often referred to as the **combined gas law,** or *general gas law*. In calculations you must make sure that the units for each variable are the same on each side of the equation.

$$\frac{P_1 V_1}{T_1} = \frac{P_2 V_2}{T_2} \quad \text{or} \quad \frac{PV}{T} = k$$

combined gas law

the gas law for a given quantity of gas that is changed from one set of *P, V,* or *T* conditions to another

---

SAMPLE PROBLEM 12E   Using the combined gas law

A weather balloon containing helium with a volume of 410.0 L rises in the atmosphere and is cooled from 27°C to –27°C. The pressure on the gas is reduced from 110.0 kPa to 25.0 kPa. What is the volume of the gas at the lower temperature and pressure?

1 List what you know

- $P_1 = 110.0$ kPa
- $V_1 = 410.0$ L
- $T_1 = 27°C + 273 = 300.$ K

- $P_2 = 25.0$ kPa
- $V_2 = ?$ L
- $T_2 = -27°C + 273 = 246$ K

2 Set up the problem

- Because conditions change but the amount of gas does not change, use the combined gas law equation and solve for the new volume.
- In this problem the temperature change will cause the volume to decrease, and the pressure change will cause the volume to increase. Keep this in mind as you set up the problem and calculate your answer.

$$\frac{P_1 V_1}{T_1} = \frac{P_2 V_2}{T_2} \qquad V_2 = \frac{V_1 T_2 P_1}{T_1 P_2}$$

3 Calculate and verify

- Substitute the values given into the equation.

$$V_2 = 410.0 \text{ L} \times \frac{246 \text{ K}}{300. \text{ K}} \times \frac{110.0 \text{ kPa}}{25.0 \text{ kPa}}$$

$$V_2 = 1.48 \times 10^3 \text{ L}$$

- The pressure ratio is much larger than the temperature ratio, so the pressure reduction will have a greater effect on the volume than the decrease in temperature. The new volume will be larger than 410 L.

1. A gas occupies 2.0 m³ at 100.0 K, exerting a pressure of 100.0 kPa. What volume will the gas occupy at 400.0 K if the pressure is increased to 200.0 kPa?

2. An 8.00 L sample of neon gas at a temperature of 23°C exerts a pressure of 900.0 kPa. If the gas is compressed to 2.00 L and the temperature is raised to 225°C, what will the new pressure be?

3. A sample of methane gas that initially occupies 850.0 mL at 500.0 Pa and 500.0 K is compressed to a volume of 700.0 mL. To what temperature will the gas need to be cooled to lower the pressure of the gas to 200.0 Pa?

4. A sample of carbon dioxide gas occupies 45 m³ at 750 K and 500. kPa. What is the volume of this gas at STP?

Gas stoichiometry

Gas volumes can be determined from mole ratios in balanced equations

Avogadro's law allows us to interpret equations representing reactions of gases in terms of volumes as well as moles. His work showed us that the mole ratio of two gases at the same temperature and pressure is the same as the volume ratio. This relationship greatly simplifies the calculation of the volume of product or reactant in a chemical reaction involving gaseous reactants and products. For example, consider the following equation for the production of ammonia.

$$3H_2(g) + N_2(g) \longrightarrow 2NH_3(g)$$

Equal volumes of gases contain equal numbers of molecules at the same temperature and pressure. Therefore, 3 L of hydrogen will contain three times as many molecules as 1 L of nitrogen, and 2 L of ammonia will contain twice as many molecules as 1 L. Consequently, 3 L of H_2 will react with 1 L of N_2 to form 2 L of NH_3, and no H_2 or N_2 will be left over. Equations give ratios of moles; they also give ratios of volumes of gases.

We can ask the following question: How many liters of H_2 are needed to react completely with 22 L of N_2? By using the coefficients from the balanced equation, we arrive at the following conversion factor.

$$\frac{3 \text{ L } H_2}{1 \text{ L } N_2}$$

Therefore, the solution to the problem is as follows.

$$22 \text{ L } N_2 \times \frac{3 \text{ L } H_2}{1 \text{ L } N_2} = 66 \text{ L } H_2$$

The ideal gas law can also be used to solve gas stoichiometry problems.

STUDY SKILLS

ORGANIZING THE GAS LAWS

It may help to organize all of the gas laws introduced in this chapter into a table. For each gas law, you may want to include an explanation of the law's use, an example, and its mathematical representation. You can then use the table as a reference when working problems in the chapter and when studying for the test.

How many liters of hydrogen gas will be produced at 280.0 K and 96.0 kPa if 40.0 g of sodium react with excess water according to the following equation?

$$2Na(s) + 2H_2O(l) \longrightarrow 2NaOH(aq) + H_2(g)$$

1 List what you know

- $V = ?$ L
- $P = 96.0$ kPa
- $n = ?$ mol
- $R = 8.314$ L·kPa/mol·K
- $T = 280.0$ K

2 Set up the problem

- Use the mole ratio in the balanced chemical equation to determine the number of moles of hydrogen that can be produced. The mole ratio between Na and H_2 is

$$\frac{2 \text{ mol Na}}{1 \text{ mol } H_2}$$

- Look up the molar mass of sodium.

$$Na = 22.99 \text{ g/mol}$$

- Convert 40.0 g Na to moles using the molar mass.

$$\frac{40.0 \text{ g Na}}{22.99 \text{ g/mol}} = 1.74 \text{ mol Na}$$

- Use the correct form of the mole ratio from the balanced chemical equation to calculate the number of moles of H_2 produced.

$$1.74 \text{ mol Na} \times \frac{1 \text{ mol } H_2}{2 \text{ mol Na}} = 0.870 \text{ mol } H_2$$

- Use the ideal gas law to calculate the volume of hydrogen produced under the temperature and pressure conditions given.

$$PV = nRT$$

- Rearrange the ideal gas law by dividing both sides of the equation by P in order to solve for the volume of hydrogen gas.

$$V = \frac{nRT}{P}$$

3 Calculate

- Substitute the values given into the equation shown above. Solve for volume.

$$V = \frac{(0.870 \text{ mol } H_2)(8.314 \text{ L·kPa/mol·K})(280.0 \text{ K})}{(96.0 \text{ kPa})}$$

$$V = 21.1 \text{ L of } H_2$$

Total recall

1. What three gas laws can be combined into the ideal gas law?

2. **a.** In this text, in what units is R usually expressed?
   b. Why must the units of P, V, T, and n match up to those of R in solving problems?
   c. What would be the units for R if P is in pascals, T is in kelvins, V is in liters, and n is in moles?

3. How is the combined gas law derived, and under what circumstance is it used to solve problems?

4. How does Avogadro's law help to determine gas volumes from balanced chemical equations?

Practice problems

5. A sample of carbon dioxide has a mass of 35.0 g and occupies 2.5 L at 400 K. What pressure does the gas exert?

6. What volume is occupied by 0.45 g of nitrogen gas measured at 100. kPa and a room temperature of 20°C?

7. A 1.0 L sample of nitrogen gas exerts 2.5 atm of pressure at 250 K.
   a. What is the density of the gas expressed in g/L?
   b. What is the density of the gas in g/L at STP?

8. How many moles of sulfur dioxide gas, SO_2, are contained in a 4.0 L container at 450 K and 5.0 kPa?

9. A 10.0 L tank of helium gas is filled to a pressure of 400 psi. Assuming no loss of gas, how many balloons, each containing 4.0 L of helium at 100 kPa, could you fill?

10. When heated, solid iron(III) hydroxide decomposes to produce iron(III) oxide and water vapor. If 0.75 L of water vapor is produced at 227°C and 1.0 atm.
    a. How many grams of $Fe(OH)_3$ were used?
    b. How many grams of Fe_2O_3 are produced?

11. The synthesis of hydrogen chloride occurs according to the following equation.

    $$H_2(g) + Cl_2(g) \longrightarrow 2HCl(g)$$

    If 3.0 L of H_2 are used, how many liters of HCl can be produced? What do you have to assume to answer this question?

12. In the presence of a Pt catalyst, ammonia and oxygen react to form nitrogen monoxide and water, as shown by the following equation.

    $$4NH_3(g) + 5O_2(g) \xrightarrow{Pt} 4NO(g) + 6H_2O(g)$$

    Assume that the temperature and pressure stay constant at 350.0 K and 100.0 kPa. What volume of O_2 is needed to burn 15 L of ammonia?

13. Solid LiOH has been used in spacecraft to remove exhaled CO_2 from the environment, as shown by the following equation.

    $$2LiOH(s) + CO_2(g) \longrightarrow Li_2CO_3(s) + H_2O(l)$$

    What mass of LiOH must be used to absorb the carbon dioxide that exerts a partial pressure of 5.0 kPa at 15°C in a space laboratory with dimensions of 4.0 m × 2.5 m × 8.0 m?

SUPERCRITICAL FLUIDS

New Uses for Carbon Dioxide

If the temperature and pressure of a substance are above their critical values, that substance is referred to as a supercritical fluid. In recent years, many supercritical fluids have been used for their very effective and selective ability to dissolve other substances. This is especially true of carbon dioxide. Carbon dioxide can be made into a supercritical fluid at a relatively low temperature and pressure, so little energy is used in preparing it. Supercritical CO_2 can also be used just above room temperature. It is cheap, nontoxic, nonflammable, and easily removed.

$C_8H_{10}N_4O_2$

Caffeine gives coffee its bitter taste; it also gives some people who drink coffee a feeling of restlessness.

Getting a Good Night's Sleep   Supercritical CO_2 is used to remove caffeine from coffee beans. First the green coffee beans are soaked in water. The absorbed water increases the size of the bean and also dissolves the caffeine inside the bean. The beans are then placed in the top of a 70 ft high column. Supercritical CO_2 fluid at approximately 93°C and 250 atm enters at the bottom of the

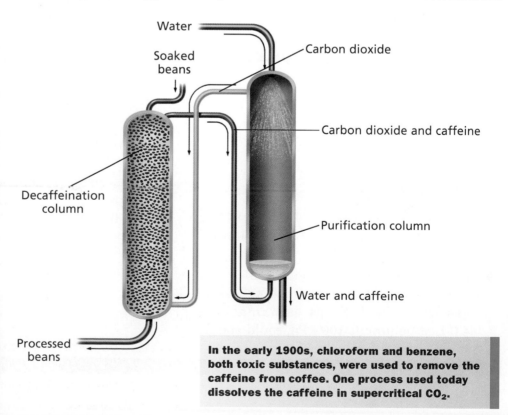

Water

Soaked beans

Carbon dioxide

Carbon dioxide and caffeine

Decaffeination column

Purification column

Water and caffeine

Processed beans

In the early 1900s, chloroform and benzene, both toxic substances, were used to remove the caffeine from coffee. One process used today dissolves the caffeine in supercritical CO_2.

column. The caffeine diffuses out of the beans and into the CO_2. The beans near the bottom of the column are in contact with the freshest supercritical CO_2. This ensures that the concentration of caffeine inside the beans is always greater than the caffeine concentration of the CO_2, forcing the dissolved caffeine within the beans to diffuse out into the CO_2. It takes about five hours for fresh beans to move down and out of the column.

The decaffeinated beans are removed from the bottom of the column, dried, and roasted as usual. The caffeine-rich CO_2 is removed at the top and passed upward through another column. Droplets of water fall through the supercritical CO_2 fluid and dissolve out the caffeine. The water solution of caffeine is then sold to soft-drink manufacturers. The CO_2, now purified, is recirculated to be used again.

internet**connect**

SC*LINKS*
NSTA

TOPIC: Supercritical fluids
GO TO: www.scilinks.org
KEYWORD: HW125

Other Uses Supercritical CO_2 is also used for other purposes. Some of these applications are extracting flavoring oils from various vegetable products, such as ginger oil from ginger root and spearmint oil from mint leaves; determining pesticide and PCB levels in water; and determining organic compounds in soil.

CAREER APPLICATION

What would it be like to . . .
▶ have a part in developing new foods?
▶ determine the safety of foods we eat?

Science/Math Career Preparation	
High School	**College**
Chemistry	Chemistry
Biology	Biochemistry
Mathematics	Microbiology
	Mathematics

Food Scientist

Important and rewarding professions include those of food technologists and food scientists. Food science is the study of the chemistry, microbiology, and processing of foods. Food technicians are responsible for testing foods for their quality and acceptability in carefully controlled taste tests. Microbiologists employed by the food industry monitor the safety of food products. Food analysts work in laboratories to monitor the composition of foods and the presence of pesticides. Some food scientists are involved in the creation of new food products or food ingredients, such as artificial sweeteners.

During their course of study, college students in the field of food science can gain valuable experience working for food manu-

facturers and government agencies, such as the U.S. Food and Drug Administration. This extra experience can help students find a job after graduation.

What conditions will cause a gas to condense?

OBJECTIVES

▶ **List** the conditions under which gases deviate from ideal behavior.

▶ **Relate** attractive forces to boiling point.

▶ **Interpret** a phase diagram.

▶ **Relate** vapor pressure to temperature.

▶ **Define** boiling point in terms of vapor pressure.

Forces of attraction

The gas laws described in this chapter were discovered long ago. They produced correct results, considering the methods of measurement available at the time. Later, more-careful measurements showed that real gases deviate from these ideal gas laws. **Figure 12-20** compares the behavior of an ideal gas with some real gases at different pressures. Real gases deviate particularly when the pressure is high because the molecules spend a larger fraction of time in close proximity to one another. The molecules are so close together that attractive forces become significant. Similar deviations between predicted and actual gas volumes occur at low temperatures. At low temperatures, gas molecules slow down, again making the attractive forces between them more significant.

▶ **FIGURE 12-20**

The ratio of *PV/nRT* for any ideal gas is one, which is represented by the dashed line. Using actual measurements for real gases, you can see that they deviate from the ideal.

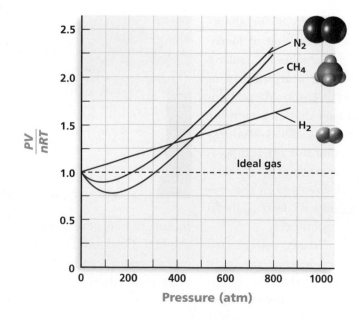

Behavior of Real Gases vs. an Ideal Gas

At extremely high pressures, gas volumes are actually higher than calculated. The gases are more difficult to compress because the volume of molecules is now significant compared with the total volume. There is less space to compress the gas into. In both cases, the conditions allow particle size and the attractive forces between molecules to significantly affect the actual volume. Thus, low temperatures and high pressures favor deviations from the ideal gas law. In contrast, high temperatures and low pressures favor a gas's behaving more like the kinetic-molecular theory predicts it should. If the temperature is low enough and the pressure is high enough, the attractive forces between particles will be so strong that the gas will condense to form a liquid or solid. There are two assumptions made by the kinetic-molecular theory that do not represent the behavior of real gases.

▶ The volume of the gas molecules is negligible.

▶ There are no attractive forces between gas molecules.

Vapor pressure increases with temperature

A common gas that condenses easily is water vapor. This is due to the fairly strong hydrogen bonds formed between water molecules. You can see water vapor condense in clouds or on any cold surface, such as a glass with ice in it.

Though water exists mostly as a liquid at room temperature and pressure, water in an open container evaporates over a period of time until it all finally "disappears." The water vapor formed during **evaporation** is like any other gas in that it exerts pressure and it expands and contracts with temperature changes. You may have noticed that in a closed system, such as in a sealed bottle of water, water does not *appear* to evaporate.

When placed in a closed container, such as the one in **Figure 12-21,** water does evaporate until the air in the container is *saturated* with water vapor. When the air is saturated with vapor, the molecules in the vapor condense to a liquid as fast as the liquid evaporates, and the two processes of evaporation and **condensation** continue at equal rates.

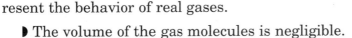

The two opposing arrows in the equation above represent a system in dynamic equilibrium. Recall from Chapter 8 that equilibrium describes reversible processes occurring at the same rate. The evaporation and condensation are proceeding at the same rate, so there is no net change. In a closed container, the pressure due to the water vapor reaches a maximum value (at a given temperature) called the equilibrium vapor pressure, or simply the **vapor pressure.**

evaporation

the process by which particles escape from the surface of a nonboiling liquid and enter the gas state

condensation

the process by which a gas changes to a liquid

vapor pressure

the pressure exerted by a vapor in equilibrium with its liquid state at a given temperature

Vapor Pressures of Diethyl Ether, Ethanol, and Water at Various Temperatures

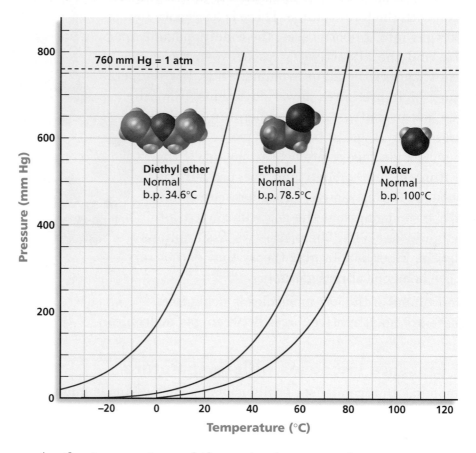

As the temperature of the water increases, its vapor pressure increases. **Figure 12-22** shows how the vapor pressure of three liquids increases with temperature. When the vapor pressure equals the external pressure on the liquid, the liquid begins to boil. The temperature at which boiling occurs is called the boiling point. At high altitudes, the boiling point of liquids is lower than at sea level. In Denver, Colorado, water will boil at about 94°C. Do not confuse boiling with cooking. Cooking vegetables in Denver, where water usually boils near 94°C, is a slower process because the water is at a lower temperature, even though it is boiling. Also, remember that water boiling rapidly is no hotter than water at a slow boil. The temperature of the water remains constant during the boiling process.

There are fundamental differences between evaporation and boiling. Evaporation occurs at temperatures lower than the boiling point of the liquid. Also, evaporation occurs at the *surface* of the liquid, whereas in boiling, bubbles of vapor arise *inside* the body of the liquid. For a bubble to form, the pressure of the atmosphere on the surface of the liquid must be overcome. This pressure is the total pressure of all the gases in the atmosphere, not just that of the water vapor. Whereas the vapor pressure of the liquid alone is important in evaporation, the total atmospheric pressure is what controls the boiling process.

Phase diagrams relate physical state to temperature and pressure

Think of a closed container with steam, water, ice, and air as a system. Within this system, H_2O can exist in the solid **phase,** the liquid phase, and the gas phase. A **phase diagram** is a graph that shows the temperatures and pressures at which a substance exists in different phases. The phases are at equilibrium with each other along the lines of the diagram. Look at **Figure 12-23,** the phase diagram for water. Segment AD is the vapor pressure–temperature curve for liquid water and its vapor. On segment $AD,$ liquid and vapor coexist. Any point along segment AD represents the change of state from a liquid to a vapor and from a vapor to a liquid where the two distinct phases of liquid and vapor are in equilibrium with each other. Notice that point E, the **normal boiling point** of water, falls on segment AD. At the boiling point of water, the liquid and vapor phases are in equilibrium with each other. You can now see why boiling point can also be defined as the temperature at which the vapor pressure equals the external, or atmospheric, pressure. If the external pressure is greater than 101.325 kPa, water boils at a higher temperature. If the pressure is less than 101.325 kPa, water boils at a lower temperature.

As you increase the temperature of a liquid, its vapor pressure increases. As a result, the density of the vapor increases. At the same time, the density of the liquid decreases. Eventually, at some temperature and pressure, liquid and vapor have the same density, and vapor,

phase

any part of a system that has uniform composition and properties

phase diagram

a graphic representation of the relationships between the physical states (phases) of a substance at different pressures and temperatures

normal boiling point

the temperature at which a substance boils at 1.0000 atm of pressure

Phase Diagram for H₂O

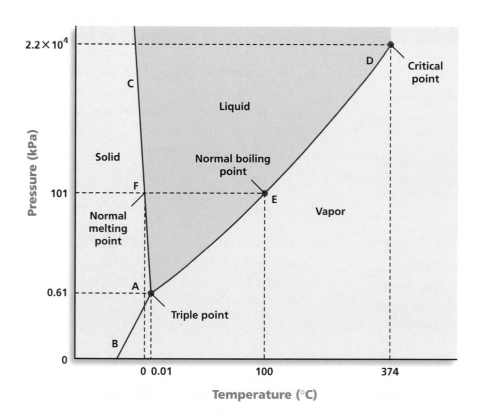

FIGURE 12-23 ◄

The phase diagram for water can be used to predict the physical state of water at different temperatures and pressures. Note that the diagram is not drawn to scale.

as such, ceases to exist. This is the **critical point** of the substance, point D. For water the critical conditions are 374°C and 22.1 MPa (218 atm). If the pressure is high enough, it is possible to heat substances beyond the critical point to produce supercritical fluids. Among the very interesting properties of supercritical fluids is their ability to dissolve other substances.

Segment *BA* is the vapor pressure–temperature curve for the vapor phase. On segment *BA,* solid and vapor coexist. Segment *BA* represents the temperatures and pressures at which water vapor and ice are in equilibrium. Ice undergoes **sublimation** along this curve, and water vapor solidifies. Point *A* on the graph denotes coordinates of special significance. Point *A* is the **triple point** of water, that is, the point at which three phases of water exist in equilibrium. The triple point of water is 0.010°C and 0.612 kPa. The sublimation region of the graph always lies below the triple point.

Segment *CA* represents temperatures and pressures at which the liquid is in equilibrium with the solid and no vapor is present. On segment *CA,* solid and liquid coexist. For water, this line has a negative slope, meaning an increase in pressure decreases the melting point. This behavior, which differs from almost all other substances, occurs because the density of solid ice is less than the density of liquid water. Point *F* corresponds to the normal freezing/melting point, 0.000°C, for water at 1 atm (101.325 kPa).

$\mathscr{S}$ECTION REVIEW

Total recall

1. What common gas condenses easily?

2. What is the difference between evaporation and boiling?

3. As the temperature of water increases, what happens to its vapor pressure?

Critical thinking

4. Under what conditions do real gases behave differently from ideal gases?

5. Will turning up the heat on the stove under a pot of boiling water and pasta make the pasta cook faster? Explain your answer.

6. **Interpreting Graphics** Use the phase diagram for water to estimate the physical state of water under the following conditions.
   a. 75 kPa and 50°C
   b. 101 kPa and 80°C
   c. 25 kPa and 100°C

7. When heated slowly at standard pressure, I_2 sublimes. What does this mean? Look up the melting points of the halogens in a handbook. Explain the differences in melting point in terms of attractive forces.

In addition to collecting data on the ozone layer, balloons have been used to chart the Milky Way galaxy, collect dust from comets and meteorites, and photograph the sun. New balloons are being designed to lift a 100 cm telescope into the atmosphere to explore the center of our galaxy. These new balloons have a volume of over 1 million cubic meters and are able to lift cargos of over 3500 kg.

LOOKING BACK

Why is the balloon only partially inflated at launch?

The volume of the balloon increases as the balloon ascends into the atmosphere, and the pressure on the balloon decreases. If the balloon were completely inflated at the launch site, there would be no room for the expanding helium as the balloon ascended, and the larger volume of gas inside would burst the balloon.

How do scientists know how much to inflate the balloon?

Based on the volume they want the balloon to have at its cruising altitude, they use gas laws to calculate the mass and volume of gas needed at launch.

Why are scientists monitoring the ozone layer?

Destruction of the ozone layer increases the amount of UV radiation that reaches Earth's surface, which can result in an increased incidence of mutations and skin cancers.

How are chlorofluorocarbons responsible for changes in the ozone layer?

Chlorofluorocarbons, or CFCs, are broken apart by UV radiation in the stratosphere to form chlorine atoms that react with ozone in a chain reaction to form oxygen gas. One chlorine atom is capable of reacting with as many as 10 000 ozone molecules.

What is being done to protect the ozone layer?

The Montreal Protocol stipulates the following provisions for developed countries. Developing countries have an additional 10 years to comply.

- 100% phaseout of CCl_4 and CH_3CCl_3 in 1996
- production freeze of CFCs in 1996; 100% phaseout by 2010
- production freeze of methyl chloride in 1995

$\mathcal{H}$IGHLIGHTS

KEY TERMS

12-1

chain reaction
free radical
greenhouse effect
ideal gas
kinetic-molecular theory
newton
pascal
pressure
STP

12-2

Avogadro's law
Boyle's law
Charles's law
Dalton's law of partial
   pressures
diffusion
effusion
Gay-Lussac's law of com-
   bining volumes
Graham's law of effusion

mole fraction
partial pressure

12-3

combined gas law
ideal gas law

12-4

condensation
critical point

vapor pressure
evaporation
normal boiling point
phase
phase diagram
sublimation
triple point

KEY CONCEPTS

12-1 **What are characteristics of gases?**

▶ Gases are fluids that have very low, variable densities.

▶ The kinetic-molecular theory is a model of gas behavior based on assumptions about a theoretical gas known as an ideal gas.

▶ When released into the atmosphere, some gases lead to environmental problems.

12-2 **What behaviors are described by the gas laws?**

▶ Boyle's law describes the indirect proportionality between the volume and pressure of a gas.

▶ Dalton's law relates the partial pressures of the individual gases in a gas mixture to the total pressure of the mixture.

▶ Charles's law describes the direct proportionality between the volume of a gas and its temperature.

▶ Avogadro's law states that equal volumes of gases at equal temperatures and pressures contain equal numbers of molecules.

▶ Gay-Lussac's law of combining volumes states that at the same temperature and pressure, gases react in volume ratios that are whole numbers.

▶ Graham's law states that, at the same temperature and pressure, the effusion rates for two gases are inversely proportional to the square roots of their molar masses.

12-3 **How do the gas laws fit together?**

▶ The ideal gas law relates pressure, volume, temperature, and amount of any gas.

▶ The combined gas law relates pressure, volume, amount, and temperature of a gas sample under two sets of conditions.

12-4 **What conditions will cause a gas to condense?**

▶ The behavior of real gases deviates from ideal at high pressures and low temperatures.

▶ A phase diagram is a graph depicting the phases of a substance as determined by pressure and temperature.

KEY SKILLS

Sample Problem 12A: Solving pressure-volume problems (p. 435)

Sample Problem 12B: Solving volume-temperature problems (p. 440)

Sample Problem 12C: Comparing molecular speeds (p. 443)

Sample Problem 12D: Using the ideal gas law (p. 447)

Sample Problem 12E: Using the combined gas law (p. 448)

Sample Problem 12F: Using the ideal gas law to solve stoichiometry problems (p. 450)

REVIEW & ASSESS

TERM REVIEW

1. A collision is said to be ——— when there is no loss in the total kinetic energy involved in the collision.
(elastic, inelastic)

2. ——— gas molecules exert no attractive or repulsive forces on each other.
(Real, Ideal)

3. The number of moles of a particular substance divided by the total number of moles in a mixture is the ———.
(triple point, mole fraction)

4. A free radical is a very reactive substance with ——— electrons.
(paired, unpaired)

5. ——— law relates the pressure and volume of a gas at constant temperature.
(Charles's, Boyle's)

6. ——— law relates the volume and temperature of a gas at constant pressure.
(Charles's, Boyle's)

7. The passage of a gas through a small opening is called ———.
(diffusion, effusion)

8. Evaporation occurs ——— a liquid.
(inside, at the surface of)

CONCEPT & SKILLS REVIEW

DESCRIBING A GAS

9. **a.** What assumption does the kinetic-molecular theory make about the volume of an ideal gas particle?
b. Describe the motion of an ideal gas particle.

10. How does the combustion of a fossil fuel contribute to the greenhouse effect?

11. How would the shape of a curve showing the kinetic-energy distribution of gas mol-

12. **a.** List the four variables in the ideal gas law equation that are used to describe a gas.
b. Why must a specific temperature be stated when working with gas data?

13. **a.** Briefly describe how a barometer works.
b. Why is mercury used instead of water to measure atmospheric pressure?

14. What technologies have been affected by the Montreal Protocol?

15. A ball is dropped from a distance of 2.0 m above the floor.
a. If the collision is elastic, how high will the ball bounce?
b. If the collision is inelastic, will the ball bounce higher or lower than 2.0 m?

16. Gas companies often store their fuel supplies in liquid form in large storage tanks. Liquid nitrogen is used to keep the temperature low enough for the fuel to remain condensed in liquid form. Although continuous cooling is expensive, storing a condensed fuel as a liquid is still more economical than storing it as a gas. Give one reason why storing a liquid is more economical than storing a gas.

17. Below is a diagram showing the effects of pressure on a column of mercury and on a column of water. Which system is under a higher pressure? Explain your choice.

Mercury   **Water**

BOYLE'S LAW AND CHARLES'S LAW

18. a. Describe the relationship between the volume and temperature of the gas in Table 12-3.

b. List possible reasons why the values in the V/T column of Table 12-3 are not exactly the same.

c. Which gas law is verified by the data in Table 12-3?

19. What type of relationship between pressure and volume does Boyle's law express?

20. Above 100°C and at constant pressure, two volumes of hydrogen react with one volume of oxygen to form two volumes of gaseous water. Set up a diagram similar to the one on page 441 for this reaction, and determine the molecular formulas for oxygen and water.

21. A gas bubble forms in the bloodstream of a diver at 50 m below the surface. What happens to the volume of the bubble as the diver ascends to the surface and the pressure is reduced?

22. Why do your ears sometimes pop when you drive down a steep incline or descend in an airplane?

23. Use the kinetic-molecular theory to explain Charles's law.

24. Use Charles's law to explain the danger of throwing a sealed can filled with a volatile gas into a fire.

25. In a science fiction story, the main character visits a planet where the temperature is −15 K. Use Charles's law to explain why this temperature is unrealistic.

26. Use Boyle's law to explain why "bubble wrap" pops when you squeeze it.

Practice Problems

27. A flexible container with 2.00 L of methyl bromide has an internal pressure of 506.6 kPa at 25°C. What is the volume of methyl bromide at standard pressure if the temperature remains constant? (Hint: See Sample Problem 12A.)

28. At a deep-sea station 200. m below the surface of the Pacific Ocean, workers live in a pressurized environment. How many liters of gas at STP on the surface must be compressed to fill the underwater environment with 2.00×10^7 L of gas at 20.0 atm? Assume that temperature remains constant. (Hint: See Sample Problem 12A.)

29. A child receives a balloon filled with 2.30 L of helium from a vendor at an amusement park, where the temperature is 311 K. What will the volume of the balloon be when the child brings the balloon home to an air-conditioned house at 295 K? (Hint: See Sample Problem 12B.)

30. A sample of hydrogen exerts a pressure of 0.329 atm at 47°C. The gas is heated to 77°C at constant volume. What will its new pressure be? (Hint: See Sample Problem 12B.)

DALTON'S LAW AND GRAHAM'S LAW

31. How are mole fractions used to find partial pressures of gas mixtures?

32. Use the diffusion process to explain how a perfume travels through the air.

33. Differentiate between diffusion and effusion.

34. What ratios are compared in Graham's law?

Practice Problems

35. The average speed of nitrogen molecules is 500.0 m/s at room temperature. What is the average speed of helium molecules at the same temperature? (Hint: See Sample Problem 12C.)

36. Carbon dioxide molecules travel at an average speed of 450. m/s at a certain temperature. How fast would oxygen molecules travel at the same temperature? (Hint: See Sample Problem 12C.)

37. How do the average velocities of neon molecules and krypton molecules compare when both gases are at the same temperature?

38. The refrigerant released when a typical automobile air-conditioning system is being repaired contains CCl_2F_2. If 365 g of CCl_2F_2 is released into the atmosphere from one air-conditioning unit, calculate the number of moles of chlorine atoms made available to react with ozone.

39. If one chlorine atom can destroy up to 10 000 ozone molecules, calculate the amount of ozone destroyed by the chlorine atoms from item 38.

40. A mixture of gases is under a pressure of 0.95 atm. The mixture contains 0.037 mole fraction of helium and 0.009 mole fraction of xenon. What are the partial pressures of these two gases?

IDEAL GAS LAW, COMBINED GAS LAW, AND STOICHIOMETRY

41. What determines the value for the constant R?

42. Which gas variable is held constant when the combined gas law is being used to analyze gas behavior?

43. How can a balanced chemical equation be used to determine the volume of a gas that will be produced from the represented reaction?

Practice Problems

44. Suppose you have a 500.0 mL container that holds 0.0500 mol of oxygen gas at a room temperature of 32°C. What is the pressure inside the container? **(Hint: See Sample Problem 12D.)**

45. How many grams of oxygen gas must be in a 10.0 L container to exert a pressure of 97.0 kPa at a temperature of 25°C? **(Hint: See Sample Problem 12D.)**

46. A sample of helium has a volume of 500. mL at STP. What will be its new volume if the temperature is increased to 325 K and its pressure is increased to 125 kPa? **(Hint: See Sample Problem 12E.)**

47. A 3.00 L sample of air exerts a pressure of 101 kPa at 300.0 K. What pressure will the air exert if the temperature is increased to 400.0 K and the air is allowed to expand to 15.0 L? **(Hint: See Sample Problem 12E.)**

48. How many liters of hydrogen gas can be produced at 300.0 K and 104 kPa pressure if 20.0 g of sodium metal is reacted with water according to the following equation? **(Hint: See Sample Problem 12F.)**

$$2Na(s) + 2H_2O(l) \longrightarrow 2NaOH(aq) + H_2(g)$$

49. Magnesium will burn in oxygen to form magnesium oxide as represented by the following equation.

$$2Mg(s) + O_2(g) \longrightarrow 2MgO(s)$$

What mass of magnesium will react with 500.0 mL of oxygen at 150°C and 70.0 kPa? **(Hint: See Sample Problem 12F.)**

50. A plastic weather balloon is filled with 90.0 L of hydrogen gas at ground level, where the pressure is 99.0 kPa and the temperature is 20.0°C. The balloon will burst if its volume exceeds 300.0 L. Can the balloon rise above the altitude of Mount Everest, where the pressure drops to 32.1 kPa and the temperature decreases by 64.4°C?

51. Calculate the density of helium at STP using the ideal gas law equation. Check your answer with a reference source that lists gas densities.

52. Suppose a certain automobile engine has a cylinder with a volume of 500.0 mL that is filled with air (21% oxygen) at a temperature of 55°C and a pressure of 101.0 kPa. What mass of octane must be injected to react with all of the oxygen in the cylinder?

$$2C_8H_{18}(l) + 25O_2(g) \longrightarrow 16CO_2(g) + 18H_2O(g)$$

53. Air is 20.9% oxygen by volume.
  a. How many liters of air are needed for the combustion of 25.0 L of octane vapor, $C_8H_{18}(g)$?
  b. What volume of each product is produced?

54. Methanol, CH_3OH, is made by using a catalyst to react carbon monoxide with hydrogen at high temperature and pressure. If 450.0 mL of CO and 825 mL of H_2 are allowed to react, answer the following. (Hint: First write the balanced chemical equation for this reaction.)
  a. Which reactant is in excess?
  b. How much of that reactant remains when the reaction is complete?
  c. What volume of $CH_3OH(g)$ is produced?

CONDENSATION AND LIQUIDS

55. Why do real gases deviate from ideal gas behavior?

56. Use the following graph of the vapor pressure of water versus temperature to answer these questions:

   a. At what point(s) does water boil at standard atmospheric pressure?

   b. At what point(s) is water only in the liquid phase?

   c. At what point(s) is water only in the vapor phase?

   d. At what point(s) is liquid water in equilibrium with water vapor?

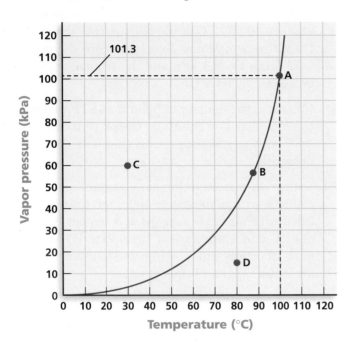

57. Use the phase diagram for water on page 457 to determine the physical state of water under the following conditions:

   a. 200 kPa and 0°C

   b. 0.61 kPa and 0.01°C

   c. 50 kPa and 200°C

   d. 50 kPa and 10°C

LINKING CHAPTERS

1. Empirical formula

   An unknown gas was analyzed and found to contain 80% carbon and 20% hydrogen. Determine the empirical formula for the gas.

2. Properties related to electron configuration

   In Period 2 of the periodic table, nitrogen, oxygen, fluorine, and neon are gases at STP. Neon is the only one of these elements that is not diatomic in the gaseous state. How do you explain this observation?

ALTERNATIVE ASSESSMENTS

Performance assessment

1. Design and perform an experiment to measure the molar mass of the gas found inside a disposable butane lighter. Measure the mass and volume of the gas at a known temperature and pressure. Use the ideal gas law equation, $PV = nRT$, to find molar mass. Compare your answer with the known molar mass of butane. Try different brands of lighters, and compare the results.

Portfolio projects

1. Research and writing

   Hydrochlorofluorocarbons, HCFCs, are being used as alternatives to CFCs. HCFCs, which have hydrogen atoms in the molecules, decompose more readily in the atmosphere. Use library resources to find out why these compounds will also be phased out by the Montreal Protocol.

2. Chemistry and you

   Locate a hot-air-balloon group, and discuss with group members how they use the gas laws to fly their balloons. The group may be willing to give a demonstration. Report your experience to your class.

1. The kinetic-molecular theory states that ideal gas molecules ——.
   a. have weight and take up space
   b. are in constant, rapid, random motion
   c. exert attractive and repulsive forces on each other
   d. have high densities compared with liquids and solids

2. Pressure can be measured in ——.
   a. grams   c. pascals
   b. meters   d. liters

3. It is thought that CFCs are harmful to the atmosphere because ——.
   a. they block the ozone in the lower atmosphere from diffusing to higher regions
   b. they do not readily decompose when exposed to sunlight
   c. they produce free radicals that break down molecules of ozone
   d. they form a layer within the atmosphere that reflects radiant energy back into space

4. A sample of oxygen gas has a volume of 150 mL when its pressure is 0.947 atm. If the pressure is increased to 0.987 atm and the temperature remains constant, the new gas volume will be ——.
   a. 140 mL   c. 200 mL
   b. 160 mL   d. 240 mL

5. A sample of neon gas occupies a volume of 752 mL at 25°C. What volume will the gas occupy at 50°C if the pressure remains constant?
   a. 694 mL
   b. 752 mL
   c. 815 mL
   d. 955 mL

6. A sample of gas in a closed container at a temperature of 100.0°C and a pressure of 3.0 atm is heated to 300.0°C. What pressure does the gas exert at the higher temperature?
   a. 2.7 atm   c. 4.6 atm
   b. 3.5 atm   d. 5.9 atm

7. Predict which gas will effuse through a small opening fastest.
   a. the gas with the greatest molecular mass
   b. the gas with the least molecular mass
   c. the most-polar gas molecules
   d. All of the gases will effuse at equal rates.

8. What is the pressure exerted by a 0.500 mol sample of nitrogen gas in a 10.0 L container at 298 K?
   a. 1.80×10^4 atm   c. 490 atm
   b. 4.90×10^2 atm   d. 1.22 atm

9. A helium-filled balloon has a volume of 50.0 L at 25°C and 1.08 atm. What volume will it have at 0.855 atm and 10.0°C?
   a. 37.6 L   c. 60.0 L
   b. 41.7 L   d. 66.5 L

10. What volume of chlorine gas at 38°C and 1.63 atm is needed to react completely with 10.4 g of sodium to form NaCl?
    a. 3.54 L   c. 7.90 L
    b. 4.45 L   d. 10.2 L

11. Potatoes will cook faster at sea level than at higher altitudes because the water used to cook them will ——.
    a. be boiling more rapidly
    b. boil at a lower temperature
    c. increase in temperature while boiling
    d. boil at a higher temperature

12. The phase diagram for water shows that ——.
    a. water can exist as a solid, liquid, and gas at the same temperature and pressure
    b. water cannot exist as a solid, liquid, and gas at the same conditions of temperature and pressure
    c. water's normal boiling point and normal melting point exist at the same temperature
    d. solid water cannot sublime to form water vapor

CHAPTER 13

Solutions

SOLUBILITY AND THE ARCTIC BEAR HUNT

In northern Canada, a helicopter hovers over the snow. Dr. Malcolm Ramsay, an ecologist at the University of Saskatchewan and an expert on polar bears, leans out of the doorway to keep a polar bear in sight. As Ramsay aims his rifle, the bear lumbers through the snow to escape. Ramsay fires, and the bear runs faster.

Ramsay signals the pilot to land in a clearing. He unloads his equipment, and the helicopter departs. By the time Ramsay reaches the bear, the tranquilizer filled dart has done its job, and the animal lies quietly in the snow.

Ramsay begins a physical examination that will take hours. The bear is hoisted into the air to be weighed. Large syringes are filled with blood samples. A tooth is extracted; its growth rings will tell the animal's age. A sample of fat tissue is taken. As the bear begins to stir, Ramsay packs his gear and waves to the returning helicopter. The polar bear will now resume its migration to Hudson Bay.

The tissue samples are sent to a laboratory for analysis. The results Ramsay gets from the lab are worrisome. The bear's fat tissue contains polychlorinated biphenyls, better known as PCBs. Ramsay has found that the concentration of PCBs in the bear's fat tissue is 8 ppm (parts per million). Polar bears are not the only ones affected. Tissue from fish, seals, and other animals has also been found to contain PCBs. This family of synthetic nonpolar organic compounds has been used industrially in electrical and mechanical equipment for decades. Originally, scientists believed that PCBs were biologically inert, but in the 1970s they discovered that laboratory animals exposed to PCBs had higher than normal rates of birth defects and liver cancer.

With a knowledge of how oily chemicals mix and dissolve, Ramsay and other scientists believe they have found answers to some puzzling questions through their research. In this chapter, you will explore the principles of solubility, and then you will apply those principles to answer some of the questions that environmental scientists have about PCBs.

CHAPTER LINKS

Why would you not expect to find PCBs dissolved in Hudson Bay or any other body of water?

Why were the PCBs not removed from the polar bear's system by the kidneys?

How did PCBs end up in the bear's fat?

What is a solution?

OBJECTIVES

▶ **Distinguish** between solutions, suspensions, and colloids.

▶ **Explain** the role of a solute and a solvent in a solution.

▶ **Describe** some techniques chemists use to separate mixtures.

▶ **Relate** various ways that concentrations may be expressed.

▶ **Use** units of molarity in stoichiometric calculations.

▶ **Describe** the procedure for making a solution of prescribed molarity.

Mixtures

You learned in Chapter 1 about the distinction between pure substances and mixtures. Mixtures can by classified into *homogeneous* mixtures, all parts of which have the same composition, and *heterogeneous* mixtures, which are not uniform in composition, though they may appear to be. This chapter is mainly about homogeneous mixtures, or *solutions*.

The potter shown in **Figure 13-1** uses water to help sculpt the sides of a clay pot. As she dips her clay-covered fingers into a container of water, the water turns gray-brown. The clay-water mixture appears uniform. However, if the container sits overnight, the next day the potter will see a muddy layer at the bottom with clear water above. The ingredients of this type of mixture, called a **suspension,** have separated. In a suspension, the particles remain thoroughly mixed while the liquid is being stirred, but later they settle to the bottom. The clay does not dissolve in water; it merely breaks up into small pieces that are so light that, for a time, they remain buoyed up by the surrounding water.

suspension

a mixture that appears uniform while being stirred but separates into different phases when agitation ceases

▼ **FIGURE 13-1**

Before settling

After settling

a Initially, the clay-water mixture seems homogeneous, like a solution.

b Over time, however, the mixture separates into two distinct layers.

FIGURE 13-2 ▼

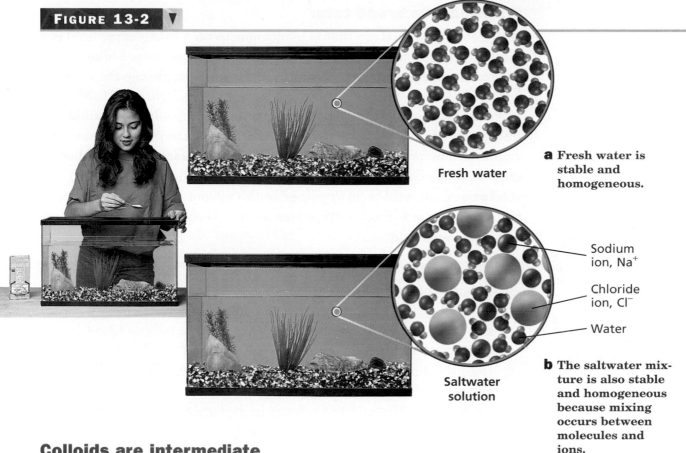

Fresh water

a Fresh water is stable and homogeneous.

Sodium ion, Na$^+$

Chloride ion, Cl$^-$

Water

Saltwater solution

b The saltwater mixture is also stable and homogeneous because mixing occurs between molecules and ions.

Colloids are intermediate between suspensions and solutions

Milk, on the other hand, does not settle. You might be tempted to think that milk is a homogeneous mixture or even a pure substance. Under a high-powered microscope, however, you would see that milk contains globules of fat and small lumps of casein, a protein, in a clear liquid called whey. Milk is what scientists call a **colloid,** a mixture in which very small isolated regions of one component (the lumps of fat and casein) are dispersed throughout the major component (the whey). Though small, the isolated regions contain millions of molecules.

Solutions are stable, homogeneous mixtures

A student working in a pet shop is asked to prepare some water for a saltwater aquarium. She fills an aquarium with fresh water. Then she adds a carefully measured quantity of salt crystals to the aquarium, as shown in **Figure 13-2,** and stirs. These crystals are a mixture of salts formulated to produce the same composition as sea water. After stirring, the student can no longer see grains of salt that are distinct from the water. No matter how long she waits, the salt will not spontaneously separate from the water. The salt has dissolved to form a stable homogeneous mixture. The particles of each substance are dispersed throughout the mixture, making it a true solution. The dissolved particles, ions in this case, are individually in contact with the water molecules, not clustered together as they are in colloids or suspensions.

colloid

a mixture in which small particles are suspended throughout a solvent

internet**connect**

SC*i*LINKS$_{sm}$
NSTA

TOPIC: Colloids
GO TO: www.scilinks.org
KEYWORD: HW131

Solution is a broad term

Technically, any mixture that is homogeneous on a microscopic level is a solution. According to that definition, air is a solution, as are alloys, such as brass, bronze, and steel. However, when most people use the word *solution,* they are usually referring to a homogeneous *liquid* mixture. A homogeneous liquid mixture has one primary component—a liquid—as well as one or more additional ingredients that are present in smaller amounts. The primary ingredient is called the **solvent,** and the other ingredients, which may be solid, liquid, or gas in their pure state(s), are **solutes** and are said to be *dissolved* in the solvent. By far the most common solutions are those with water as the solvent. Such solutions are called **aqueous** solutions.

solvent

the substance in which the solute dissolves to make the solution

solute

the substance dissolved in a solution

aqueous

describing a solution in which the solvent is water

> ### CONCEPT CHECK
>
> **1.** Classify the following mixtures as homogeneous or heterogeneous:
> - **a.** freshly squeezed orange juice   **c.** human blood
> - **b.** tap water   **d.** sand
>
> **2.** Does a solution have to be a liquid mixture? Explain why or why not.
>
> **3.** Name the solute and the solvent in an aqueous sodium chloride solution.

Expressing concentration
Molarity is the ratio of solute amount (in moles) to solution volume (in liters)

A method is needed to express how much solute is present in a solution, either in relation to a quantity of solvent or to a quantity of solution. Such a ratio is a measure of the **concentration.** You learned in Chapter 3 that the mole is the SI unit for amounts of substances, such as the amount of reactants and products in chemical reactions. The mole is also a basis of the concentration unit called **molarity,** M.

concentration

the quantity of solute in a specific quantity of solvent or solution

molarity

a concentration unit, expressed as moles of solute per liter of solution

$$\text{molarity (M)} = \frac{\text{moles of solute}}{\text{liters of solution}} = \frac{\text{mol}}{\text{L}}$$

Though determined and used as a ratio, molarity is always regarded as a quotient, as shown in the following example.

$$\frac{0.036 \text{ mol LiCl}}{0.040 \text{ L solution}} = \frac{0.90 \text{ mol LiCl}}{\text{L solution}} = 0.90 \text{ M LiCl}$$

It is easy to calculate molarity when the volume of solution is exactly 1 L. In the real world, however, most situations will involve more or less than 1 L of solution. Keep in mind that molarity is a ratio—the amount of solute divided by the volume of solution. Once you make a 0.90 M solution, the ratio of the amount of solute to the volume of solution is *constant,* regardless of how much of the solution you sample.

A concentration can be expressed in many forms. Certain concentration measures are used in medicine, others in pollution control, and still others in biological research, as described in **Table 13-1.** It is possible to convert among all the ways of expressing concentration, but you may need to know molar masses and densities.

If you simply mixed a liter of solvent with the proper amount of solute to prepare a liter of solution of a specific concentration, the final solution would generally have a volume slightly greater or smaller than 1 L, depending on the relative densities of the solvent and the solution. The definition of *molarity* is based on the amount of solute in the final volume of the solution. To make a solution that has a volume of exactly 1.000 L when finished, you must follow the very specific procedure shown on the next page.

TABLE 13-1   Measures of Concentration

Name	Abbreviation or symbol	Units	Areas of application
Grams of solute per hundred grams of solvent	g/100 g	$\dfrac{\text{g solute}}{\text{100 g solvent}}$	to determine solubilities; in medical products
Mass percent or weight percent	% or %w/w	$\dfrac{\text{g solute}}{\text{g solution}} \times 100$	in biological research
Parts per million	ppm*	$\dfrac{\text{g solute}}{\text{1 000 000 g solution}}$	to express small concentrations
Parts per billion	ppb*	$\dfrac{\text{g solute}}{\text{1 000 000 000 g solution}}$	to express very small concentrations, as in pollutants or contaminants
Parts per trillion	ppt*	$\dfrac{\text{g solute}}{\text{1 000 000 000 000 g solution}}$	to express extremely small concentrations, as with isotopes used as tracers in medicine
Molarity	M	$\dfrac{\text{mol solute}}{\text{L solution}}$	in solution stoichiometry reactions
Molality	m	$\dfrac{\text{mol solute}}{\text{kg solvent}}$	with calculation of properties such as boiling-point elevation and freezing-point depression
Mole fraction	*x*	$\dfrac{\text{mol solute}}{\text{total mol solution}}$	in solution thermodynamics
Volume percent	% V/V	$\dfrac{\textit{volume} \text{ solute}}{\textit{volume} \text{ solution}} \times 100$	with liquid-liquid mixtures
Mass-volume percent	% w/v	$\dfrac{\text{g solute}}{\text{mL solution}} \times 100$	in many commercial products

*When applied to gases, ppm means mL of the solute per million mL (1 m^3) of solution, and similarly for ppb and ppt.

$CuSO_4 \cdot 5H_2O$ is one of the compounds used to produce the chemiluminescence in light sticks. To make this solution, each liter will require 0.5000 mol of $CuSO_4 \cdot 5H_2O$. Start by calculating the mass of copper(II) sulfate pentahydrate, $CuSO_4 \cdot 5H_2O$, needed. To convert this amount to a mass, multiply by the molar mass of $CuSO_4 \cdot 5H_2O$ (mass of $CuSO_4 \cdot 5H_2O$ = 0.5000 mol × 249.68 g/mol = 124.8 g).

Add some solvent (water) to the calculated mass of $CuSO_4 \cdot 5H_2O$ in the beaker to dissolve it, and then pour the solution into a 1.000 L volumetric flask.

Rinse the beaker with more water several times, and each time pour the rinse water into the flask until the solution almost reaches the neck of the flask.

Stopper the flask, and swirl thoroughly until all of the solid is dissolved.

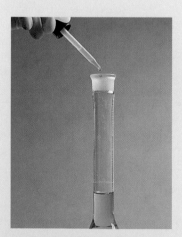

Carefully fill the flask exactly to the 1.000 L mark with more water.

Restopper, and invert the flask at least 10 times to ensure complete mixing.

The resulting solution has 0.5000 mol of solute dissolved in 1.000 L of solution—a 0.5000 M concentration.

Calculating molarity

What is the molarity of a potassium chloride solution that has a volume of 400.0 mL and contains 85.0 g of KCl?

1 List what you know

▶ solution volume = 400.0 mL

▶ solute mass = 85.0 g KCl

▶ molarity of KCl solution = ? M

2 Set up the problem

▶ Calculate the molar mass of the solute, KCl.

$$\text{molar mass of KCl} = 74.55 \text{ g/mol}$$

▶ Because the units of molarity are mol/L, the mass must be converted to an amount in moles and the volume of solution must be converted to liters. Place the solute quantity over the solution volume, even though they are not yet in the correct units. Use the conversion factor that will change milliliters to liters. Then use the conversion factor from the molar mass that will give the amount of solute in moles.

$$\frac{\text{g KCl}}{\text{mL solution}} \times \frac{1000 \text{ mL}}{1 \text{ L}} \times \frac{1 \text{ mol KCl}}{\text{g KCl}} = \frac{\text{mol KCl}}{\text{L}}$$

3 Calculate

▶ Substitute the values given.

$$\frac{85.0 \text{ g KCl}}{400.0 \text{ mL}} \times \frac{1000 \text{ mL}}{1 \text{ L}} \times \frac{1 \text{ mol KCl}}{74.55 \text{ g KCl}} = \frac{2.85 \text{ mol KCl}}{\text{L}} = 2.85 \text{ M}$$

▶ This result can be expressed as 2.85 M, 2.85 mol/L, or 2.85 molar. They all mean the same thing.

$$\text{molar} = \text{mol/L} = \text{M}$$

Determining the mass of solute

Sodium thiosulfate, $Na_2S_2O_3$, is used as a fixer when developing photographic film. What is the mass in grams of $Na_2S_2O_3$ needed to make 100.0 mL of a 0.250 M solution?

1 List what you know

▶ solution volume = 100.0 mL

▶ solution molarity = 0.250 M $Na_2S_2O_3$

▶ mass of $Na_2S_2O_3$ = ? g

2 Set up the problem

▶ Calculate the molar mass of the solute, $Na_2S_2O_3$.

$$\text{molar mass of } Na_2S_2O_3 = 158.12 \text{ g/mol}$$

▶ Remember what you are asked for and what you are given. You are try-ing to find out the mass in grams, given a solution volume and molarity.

▶ Set up your calculation, using the conversion factors correctly to achieve the answer. Convert the solution volume to the amount in moles using the solution molarity given. The amount in moles can then be converted to mass using the molar mass of the solute. (This problem can be done in one or several steps.)

$$\text{mL solution} \times \frac{1\ \text{L}}{1000\ \text{mL}} \times \frac{\text{mol Na}_2\text{S}_2\text{O}_3}{1\ \text{L}} \times \frac{\text{g Na}_2\text{S}_2\text{O}_3}{1\ \text{mol Na}_2\text{S}_2\text{O}_3} = \text{g Na}_2\text{S}_2\text{O}_3$$

3 Calculate

▶ Substitute the values given.

$$100.0\ \cancel{\text{mL}} \times \frac{1\ \cancel{\text{L}}}{1000\ \cancel{\text{mL}}} \times \frac{0.250\ \cancel{\text{mol Na}_2\text{S}_2\text{O}_3}}{1\ \cancel{\text{L}}} \times \frac{158.12\ \text{g Na}_2\text{S}_2\text{O}_3}{1\ \cancel{\text{mol Na}_2\text{S}_2\text{O}_3}} =$$

$$3.95\ \text{g Na}_2\text{S}_2\text{O}_3$$

SAMPLE PROBLEM 13C   Using solution stoichiometry

What volume in milliliters of a 0.500 M solution of copper(II) sulfate, $CuSO_4$, is needed to react with an excess of aluminum to provide 11.0 g of copper?

1 List what you know

▶ molarity of reactant = 0.500 M $CuSO_4$
▶ mass of product = 11.0 g Cu
▶ solution volume = ? mL

2 Set up the problem

▶ Write the balanced chemical equation for the reaction.

$$3CuSO_4(aq) + 2Al(s) \longrightarrow 3Cu(s) + Al_2(SO_4)_3(aq)$$

▶ Look up the molar mass of Cu.

$$\text{molar mass of Cu} = 63.55\ \text{g/mol}$$

▶ As in all these types of problems, remember what you are asked for and what you are given. You are trying to find the solution volume. You are given the molarity of the solution and the mass of one of the products.

▶ Set up your calculation, using the conversion factors correctly to achieve the answer. Convert the mass of Cu to moles, then use the mole ratio of $CuSO_4$: Cu from the balanced chemical equation to determine the number of moles of $CuSO_4$. The moles of $CuSO_4$ solution can be con-verted to volume using the reciprocal of molarity. This calculation can be done in two steps, as follows.

$$\text{g Cu} \times \frac{1\ \text{mol Cu}}{\text{g Cu}} \times \frac{\text{mol CuSO}_4}{\text{mol Cu}} = \text{mol CuSO}_4$$

$$\text{mol CuSO}_4 \times \frac{\text{L solution}}{\text{mol CuSO}_4} \times \frac{1000\ \text{mL}}{1\ \text{L solution}} = \text{mL CuSO}_4\ \text{solution}$$

Or the calculation can be combined into one step, as follows.

$$\text{g Cu} \times \frac{1 \text{ mol Cu}}{\text{g Cu}} \times \frac{\text{mol CuSO}_4}{\text{mol Cu}} \times \frac{\text{L solution}}{\text{mol CuSO}_4} \times \frac{1000 \text{ mL}}{1 \text{ L solution}} =$$

$$\text{mL CuSO}_4 \text{ solution}$$

3 Calculate

▶ Substitute the values given.

$$11.0 \text{ g Cu} \times \frac{1 \text{ mol Cu}}{63.55 \text{ g Cu}} \times \frac{3 \text{ mol CuSO}_4}{3 \text{ mol Cu}} \times \frac{1 \text{ L solution}}{0.500 \text{ mol CuSO}_4} \times$$

$$\frac{1000 \text{ mL solution}}{1 \text{ L solution}} = 346 \text{ mL CuSO}_4 \text{ solution}$$

PRACTICE PROBLEMS

1. What is the molarity of a sodium hypochlorite household bleach made from the equivalent of 125 g of NaClO in 2.0 L of solution?

2. What volume in milliliters of a 0.375 M solution of sodium hydrogen carbonate, $NaHCO_3$, is needed to provide 15.3 g of $NaHCO_3$?

3. What volume in liters of a 2.5 M solution of acetic acid, CH_3COOH, is needed to provide 256 g of acetic acid?

4. What mass in grams of copper sulfate pentahydrate, $CuSO_4 \cdot 5H_2O$, is needed to make 75.0 mL of a 0.2500 M solution?

5. What mass in kilograms of table sugar (sucrose, $C_{12}H_{22}O_{11}$) is needed to make 3.50 L of a 1.15 M solution?

6. The calcium phosphate used in fertilizers can be made according to the following unbalanced chemical equation.

$$H_3PO_4(aq) + Ca(OH)_2(s) \longrightarrow Ca_3(PO_4)_2 (aq) + H_2O(l)$$

What mass in grams of each product would be formed if 7.5 L of 5.00 M phosphoric acid reacted with an excess of calcium hydroxide? (Hint: First balance the chemical equation.)

7. What is the molarity of a solution composed of 6.25 g of HCl in 0.300 L of solution?

8. The compound $C_4H_4Au_2CaO_4S_2$ is used in the treatment of rheumatoid arthritis. What mass in milligrams of this compound is needed to make 10.0 mL of a 0.0100 M solution?

9. What is the molarity of a solution composed of 5.8 g of potassium iodide, KI, dissolved in enough water to make 0.125 L of solution?

10. **a.** How many moles of NaOH are contained in 65.0 mL of a 2.2 M solution of NaOH in water?
    b. How many grams of NaOH does this represent?

11. What volume in liters of a 1.50 M solution of NaCl is needed for a reaction that requires 146.3 g of NaCl?

12. What is the molar concentration of a solution composed of 8.210 g of potassium chromate, K_2CrO_4, dissolved in enough water to make 0.500 L of solution?

Separating mixtures

There are many ways to separate mixtures into their components. The best method to use in a particular case depends on the properties and quanities of the ingredients. The methods illustrated in **Figure 13-3a** through **Figure 13-3d** rely on the physical properties of the ingredients to effect a separation. Notice that these methods can be done outside a chemistry lab. In fact, you may use one or more of these methods right in your home. For example, you may use filtration to make coffee, and you may use evaporation when you cook.

▼ FIGURE 13-3

a Decanting gently separates a liquid from solids that have settled. To decant a mixture, simply pour the liquids off and leave the solids behind. First, however, the solid content of the suspension must be well settled.

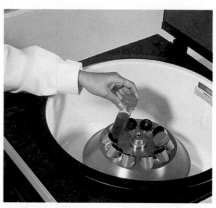

b A centrifuge is a tool used to separate mixtures, the components of which have different densities. The centrifuge spins rapidly; the resulting force pushes dense matter outward.

c Ground coffee is separated from liquid coffee by filration. The filtrate—the liquid and any particles smaller than the holes in the filter—collect in the coffeepot. The solid grounds are retained in the filter.

d In saltwater ponds such as this one, sea water evaporates, and salts, mainly sodium chloride, are left behind. This simple method of salt production is still widely used.

Chromatography is widely used in industry and research

Chromatography may be used to separate the components of a liquid or gaseous mixture so that they may be isolated or identified. The method works because different dissolved substances are attracted differently to solvents and other media, such as solid surfaces.

Paper chromatography is a powerful separation technique. It can be used to separate the dyes in ink. Water or some other solvent dissolves the ink. The solvent containing the ink travels up the paper by *capillary action,* the attraction of the surface of a liquid to the surface of a solid. The dissolved dyes from the ink travel at different rates according to the attraction that they have for the solvent or the paper, as shown in **Figure 13-4.** Those most attracted to the paper travel the slowest. They remain in a rather low position on the paper. The dyes that have the least attraction for the paper travel fastest and farthest. The resulting chromatogram displays bands of different colors.

Laboratories use chromatography to isolate and identify the agents that give foods their flavor and give perfumes their aroma. Law enforcement officers use chromatography to determine the blood alcohol level of motorists suspected of drunk driving.

INQUIRYLAB

The Color of M&M® Candies

In this activity you will investigate whether the colors of candies are single dyes or whether these candies are colored with a mixture of different dyes.

Materials

M&M candies, chromatography paper, developing solution (0.1% NaCl)

Problem

Design an experiment that will determine whether M&M candies contain mixtures of dyes or whether they are single dyes. For example, is the orange color a result of mixing two primary colors? What about the other colors?

Analysis

1. Summarize your results in a report that includes your experimental procedure, a data table that summarizes your results, and the experimental evidence.
2. Be sure to answer the questions posed in the problem statement.

chromatography

a technique for separating components of a mixture by placing the mixture in a mobile phase that is passed over a stationary phase

---

FIGURE 13-4 ▼

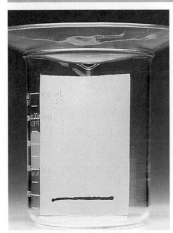

a In chromatography, ink marks are made on absorbent paper, which is then suspended in contact with a solvent.

b The finished chromatogram, shown at right, displays different dyes found in the ink sample.

Distillation can be used to separate components of a solution

distillation

a separation process in which a liquid component is evaporated from a solution and the vapor is condensed to liquid, usually for the purpose of purification

If you have ever left a pot of boiling salted water on a stove until all the liquid boils away, you have performed a **distillation.** Distillation separates components of a mixture based on their boiling points. As one component reaches its boiling point, its vapor is removed and allowed to cool and condense. This process continues until all the desired components have been separated from the mixture.

In a few locations throughout the world, distillation is used to obtain drinking water from sea water. However, because the process requires a lot of energy, it is expensive. Distillation is used on a wide scale in the petroleum industry to separate crude petroleum into its component fractions. These fractions have many uses. Gasoline, heating oil, lubricants, and raw materials used in the plastics industry are all separated from the crude-oil mixture by distillation.

$\mathcal{S}$ECTION REVIEW

Total recall

1. Explain why a suspension is classified as a heterogeneous mixture.

2. How is distillation used to prepare pure water from tap water?

3. Give two examples of the practical uses of chromatography.

Critical thinking

4. Identify the following as solutions or suspensions:
   a. muddy river water
   b. orange juice
   c. chlorinated water in a swimming pool
   d. diet soda

5. Name the solute(s) and solvents in the following solutions:
   a. carbonated water
   b. sugar water
   c. black coffee with sugar
   d. diet iced tea with lemon

Practice problems

6. What is the molar concentration of these solutions?
   a. 0.0750 mol of $NaHCO_3$ in 115 mL of solution
   b. 0.750 mol of $NaCH_3COO$ in 115 mL of solution

7. **a.** What is the molar concentration of a solution composed of 3.0 mol of solute in 2.0 L of solution?
   b. How many moles would there be in 350 mL of this solution?

8. What is the molar concentration of a solution composed of 5.85 g of potassium iodide, KI, dissolved in enough water to make 0.1250 L of solution?

9. Describe in your own words exactly how you would prepare 1.00 L of a 0.85 M solution of sodium chloride, NaCl.

10. **Story Clue** On page 467 you read that Dr. Ramsay's test on bear fat revealed a PCB concentration of 8 ppm. How many milligrams of PCB would there be in 35 g of bear fat?

Does substance A dissolve in substance B?

OBJECTIVES

▶ *Explain* why predicting solubility is difficult.

▶ *Describe* the effects of temperature on solubility.

▶ *Discuss* the features that influence whether pairs of compounds will dissolve in each other.

▶ *Relate* how molecular polarity affects solubility.

▶ *Examine* practical applications of solubility principles.

Solubility

The student pictured in **Figure 13-5** is exploring **solubility.** He has three pure compounds—water, H_2O, lithium chloride, LiCl, and toluene, $C_6H_5CH_3$—and is combining them in pairs. In two cases, nothing appears to happen. After these mixtures are shaken, two layers form, with the denser ingredient on the bottom of the test tube. In the case of

solubility

the maximum amount of a chemical that will dissolve in a given quantity of a solvent at a specified temperature while the solution is in contact with undissolved solute

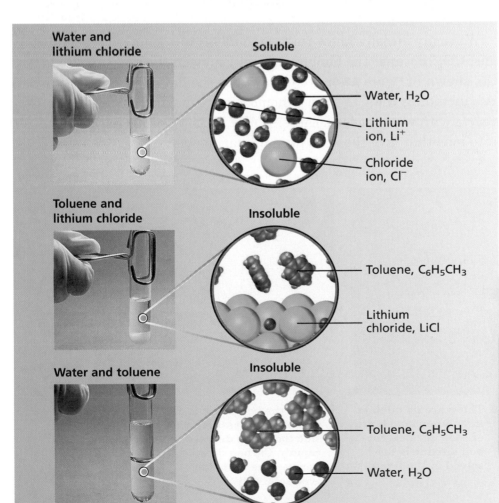

Water and lithium chloride

Soluble

Water, H_2O

Lithium ion, Li^+

Chloride ion, Cl^-

Toluene and lithium chloride

Insoluble

Toluene, $C_6H_5CH_3$

Lithium chloride, LiCl

Water and toluene

Insoluble

Toluene, $C_6H_5CH_3$

Water, H_2O

FIGURE 13-5 ◀

When H_2O and LiCl are mixed, a solution forms. However, $C_6H_5CH_3$ does not form a solution with either LiCl or H_2O.

lithium chloride and water, a single phase is formed—a clear aqueous solution containing lithium ions, Li$^+$, and chloride ions, Cl$^-$. From the preliminary experimental results, we might say that lithium chloride is **soluble** in water but **insoluble** in toluene and that water and toluene are insoluble in each other.

But appearances can be deceptive, and you have to be cautious when discussing solubility. If you were to carefully analyze the two layers from the water-toluene mixture, you would find a very small amount of toluene in the aqueous layer and a similarly small concentration of water in the toluene layer. And if the student had chosen a slightly larger sample of lithium chloride, he would have gotten a different result in the first experiment. Not all the salt would have dissolved. Solubility is not a matter of yes or no. It is a matter of how much.

Gases can dissolve in liquids

If you look at an unopened soda bottle, the liquid inside has no bubbles. But what happens once you open an ice-cold bottle of soda? First there is a hissing sound of gas escaping. Then you can see bubbles rising in the liquid. When you first taste the soda, it is tart and there is plenty of fizz. If the soda is allowed to stand, it tastes flat. Why does this happen? Where did the bubbles come from? What can you do to keep soda from going flat? If you apply what you already know about gases and solutions, you may be able answer some of these questions.

You may already know that the bubbles in soda are carbon dioxide gas, CO_2. Because the bubbles are not visible in the unopened soda bottle, shown in **Figure 13-6a,** you know that the liquid contents of the bottle, including the CO_2, are a homogeneous solution. Part of the CO_2 reacts with water to form carbonic acid, H_2CO_3, which partially ionizes into ions that give the soda its tangy, acidic taste.

soluble

can be dissolved in a particular solvent

insoluble

does not dissolve appreciably in a particular solvent

▼ **FIGURE 13-6**

CO$_2$ under high pressure above solvent

Dissolved CO$_2$ molecules

a There are no bubbles in an unopened bottle of soda because carbon dioxide is dissolved in the liquid.

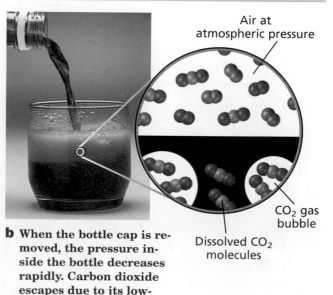

Air at atmospheric pressure

CO$_2$ gas bubble

Dissolved CO$_2$ molecules

b When the bottle cap is removed, the pressure inside the bottle decreases rapidly. Carbon dioxide escapes due to its lowered solubility.

Gas solubility depends on pressure

In an unopened bottle of soda, some carbon dioxide is in the gas above the liquid level and some is in the liquid itself. We say that the solution in the bottle is **saturated.** This means that, even though there is more CO_2 available, the liquid is holding as much carbon dioxide solute as it can under the present conditions. The concentration of the solute in the saturated solution is the solubility of the solute under the prevailing conditions of temperature and pressure.

Chemists now understand the details of the relationship between pressure and gas solubility. **Henry's law** sums up their findings. In an unopened soda bottle, there is a much higher partial pressure of carbon dioxide in the neck of the bottle, above the liquid, than there is in the air outside the bottle. This greater partial pressure causes more CO_2 to dissolve in the soda than would be possible standing in air. When the bottle is opened, much of the dissolved CO_2 escapes into the air and the partial pressure of carbon dioxide in the bottle's neck soon equals that of the CO_2 in the air. The decrease in the partial pressure of CO_2 inside the bottle causes several things to happen. The solubility of the CO_2 in the soda is reduced, and the excess CO_2 bubbles out of solution, as shown in **Figure 13-6b,** on page 480. The dissolved gas given off as foam from a **supersaturated** solution is called *effervescence.*

A special case: gas solubility and diving

The principles of gas solubility are used in a variety of situations other than soda bottling. Knowledge of these principles is a life-or-death matter for the underwater diver shown in **Figure 13-7.**

When divers are underwater, their bodies are subject to more pressure than at the surface. As a result, the pressure of the air that they breathe must be increased to force the air out of the air tank and into their lungs. Blood is a water-based mixture. Oxygen is carried by hemoglobin molecules within the blood cells in this mixture. But some of the oxygen and other gases, such as nitrogen, which makes up most of air, dissolve in the blood just as carbon dioxide dissolves in soda.

If a diver breathing pressurized air rises to the surface too quickly, decompression sickness, also called the bends, can result. What causes the bends? The sudden decrease from high pressure underwater to normal atmospheric pressure at the surface is similar to the pressure decrease that takes place when you open a soda bottle. Gases, such as nitrogen, that dissolve in blood and body fluids bubble out of solution. Such bubbles in the blood can block blood flow in smaller blood vessels, press on tissues, and affect nerve impulses, causing the intense pain that incautious divers may experience.

saturated

containing the amount of solute specified by the solubility

Henry's law

the solubility of a gas in a liquid is directly proportional to the partial pressure of that gas on the surface of the liquid

supersaturated

containing more than the amount of solute specified by the solubility at a given set of conditions

FIGURE 13-7 ▼

Underwater divers breathing pressurized air must return to the surface gradually to prevent the bends.

When oil and water are mixed, they do not form a solution. Instead, the less dense oil forms a layer on top of the water.

One solution is to rise to the surface slowly, but today most deep-sea divers prevent the bends by breathing an oxygen-helium mixture instead of compressed air that contains nitrogen. Because helium is less soluble than nitrogen, less of it dissolves in the body tissues, so if a diver has to return to the surface rapidly, there is less gas bubbling out of the diver's blood.

Gas solubility decreases with increasing temperature

After your soda bottle is open and the soda is allowed to warm, the soda forms fewer bubbles and tastes flat. Even if you compare the taste of a newly opened warm soda with that of a newly opened cold soda, you will find that the warm soda will taste somewhat flat. Warm soda tastes flat because there is less CO_2 dissolved in it. Chemists have found that other gases behave similarly; their solubility in liquids decreases with increasing temperature.

Liquids and miscibility

Certain pairs of liquids form a single phase—a solution—when they are mixed, no matter what the relative amounts of the liquids are. These liquids are **miscible.** A mixture of ethylene glycol and water is an example. Ethylene glycol, which is commonly called glycol, is the most common antifreeze, a substance added to radiator water to prevent it from freezing in cold climates or overheating in warm climates.

Certain other pairs of liquids, such as the oil and water shown in **Figure 13-8,** scarcely mix at all. They are **immiscible.** Each liquid is almost insoluble in the other; instead they form two layers, with the denser liquid on the bottom.

miscible

indicates liquids that will dissolve in each other

immiscible

indicates liquids that will not dissolve appreciably in each other

Polarity of the solvent and solute is important

When treating solubilities, a rule of thumb is "like dissolves like." You learned in Chapter 6 that molecules can be polar or nonpolar. Generally speaking, polar solvents dissolve polar compounds, and nonpolar solvents dissolve nonpolar compounds. **Figure 13-9** shows a sugar cube, which is made of polar sucrose molecules, dissolving in water, a polar solvent.

In the dissolving process, attractive forces between solute particles are disrupted and replaced by new attractions between solute and solvent. If the new solvent-solute attractions are similar to the attractive forces in the solute, the energy needed to form the solution is low. The enthalpy factor is usually favorable for one substance to dissolve in another. This means that the dipole forces between polar solvent molecules easily replace the similar forces between polar solute molecules and form a solution. Also, the London forces between nonpolar solvent molecules require little energy to replace similar forces between nonpolar solute molecules.

To understand the dissolving process, you must also consider entropy. There is a natural tendency for substances to mix. Imagine a container with gas A on one side of a partition and gas B on the other side. If you were to remove the partition, molecules of A and of B eventually would be thoroughly mixed because of this natural tendency for disorder. The dissolution of one substance in another requires a negative free energy change. This usually, but not always, results from a negative enthalpy change and a positive entropy change.

Hydrogen bonding also plays a role

You encountered hydrogen bonding in Chapter 6. High solubility is expected when hydrogen bonds form between solute and solvent molecules. If molecule A forms hydrogen bonds with other A molecules but not with molecules of B, it is very probable that substance A will not mix with substance B.

In summary, there are two guidelines that can be used to predict the mutual solubility of pairs of compounds.

1. Two compounds that are both polar or both nonpolar are likely to be miscible.
2. Two compounds that can form hydrogen bonds with each other are likely to be miscible.

However, the most reliable way to tell if two compounds are mutually soluble is to follow the example of the student in Figure 13-5 on page 479, that is, to mix the compounds and observe the result.

FIGURE 13-9 ▲

You can see the sucrose in the sugar cube going into solution with the surrounding water solvent.

CONCEPT CHECK

1. Why are gas bubbles not visible in an unopened bottle of soda?
2. Explain what happens to gases dissolved in the blood when a diver rises to the water's surface very quickly.
3. Identify the following pairs of compounds as miscible or immiscible:
   a. antifreeze and water   c. toluene and water
   b. ethanol and water   d. acetic acid and water
4. How does rising temperature affect the solubility of gases in water?

Solubility principles at work
Dry cleaners use solubility principles to remove stains

Why do some clothes need to be dry-cleaned, while others do not? Washing with water and detergents cleans most clothes. But there are three situations in which dry cleaning may be necessary—if your clothes have a stubborn stain, such as ink or rust; if you have spilled something greasy on your clothes; or if the label on the clothing recommends dry cleaning.

In spite of its name, dry cleaning does involve liquids. The process uses a nonpolar liquid solvent—tetrachloroethylene, C_2Cl_4 (also known as perchloroethylene, shown in **Figure 13-10**). As you now know, nonpolar solvents will dissolve nonpolar materials. Fats, greases, and oils fall into that category and are notoriously difficult to remove from fabrics by water-based washing.

▲ **FIGURE 13-10**

The most commonly used dry-cleaning solvent is tetrachloroethylene, C_2Cl_4.

Vitamin C dissolves in water

The human body needs vitamins. Vitamins control chemical reactions within the body. Not getting enough of a vitamin can make you sick, but so can getting too much. The reasons relate to solubility.

People who have poor diets have suffered from scurvy since at least the time of the Crusades, nearly 1000 years ago. Soldiers and sailors were especially susceptible to scurvy, which causes fatigue and bleeding of the gums and prevents wounds from healing.

The first controlled study of the effects of diet on scurvy was in 1747 when James Lind, a doctor in the British Royal Navy, compared the reactions of sailors suffering from scurvy when given cider, garlic, mustard, vinegar, ocean water, oranges, or lemons. The sailors who received citrus fruits recovered. We now know that citrus fruits are rich in vitamin C. **Figure 13-11** illustrates important information about vitamin C.

▼ **FIGURE 13-11**

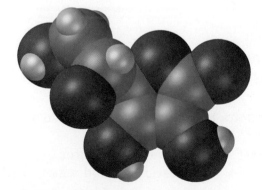

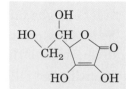

a Lemons, oranges, grapefruits, and limes are rich sources of vitamin C.

b The most common form of vitamin C is ascorbic acid, shown here.

c Because ascorbic acid is highly polar, it is very soluble in water but insoluble in fat and oil.

Researchers have found that vitamin C has several vital functions, the most important being its role in the synthesis of collagen. Collagen is the protein that makes up tendons, gives strength to teeth and bones, and most importantly, knits endothelial cells together to make blood vessels.

To synthesize collagen where it is needed, vitamin C must be distributed throughout the body. Vitamin C is easily transported by the blood because it is water-soluble.

In the belief that vitamin C combats the common cold, some people prefer to take it in large doses. Is it possible to take too much? Probably not. When intake increases, the vitamin C level rises, but then the kidneys begin excreting the vitamin faster. Your kidneys are so good at regulating water-soluble vitamins that overdosing on vitamin C is very unlikely.

Vitamin A dissolves in oils and fats

For decades, children have been told, "Eat your carrots so you will have good vision." There is some truth to the saying because carrots, and some other vegetables, contain carotenes that your body easily converts into vitamin A. If you do not get enough vitamin A, you may lose your ability to see at night due to a disorder called night blindness.

Vitamin A affects vision because the human body uses it to make a pigment called visual purple, one of the vital light-sensitive molecules in the retina. Vitamin A is also needed for normal growth of the skin, respiratory tract, cornea, and other epithelial tissues, as well as for bone growth and tooth development. Fortunately, most people get enough vitamin A from the variety of foods that they eat. Some sources of vitamin A and its structure are shown in **Figure 13-12.**

FIGURE 13-12 ▼

a Sources of vitamin A include dark green leafy vegetables, carrots, broccoli, tomatoes, and egg yolks.

b Vitamin A is also known as retinol because it plays a vital role in helping the retina of your eye detect light.

c The vitamin A molecule is mainly composed of carbon and hydrogen, making it nonpolar.

The body's use of vitamins follows solubility principles

Vitamin A is nonpolar and is therefore soluble in fat. Excess vitamin A is stored in the fat of the liver. It can be released to your tissues when you are not getting enough from your diet. However, this vitamin's excellent solubility in fat means that it is not soluble in water or in the watery blood serum. Other fat-soluble vitamins are vitamin D and vitamin E.

When vitamin A is secreted from the liver, it is packaged with a molecule of retinol-binding protein. The retinol-binding protein makes a nonpolar substance mix with water. This large, globular, water-soluble molecule carries the water-insoluble vitamin A molecule through the blood to the tissues where it is needed.

Because vitamin A is present in food only in small amounts, it is usually impossible to consume too much. But sometimes people become enthusiastic about improving their diet and start taking large quantities of vitamin supplements. Large doses of vitamin A, taken for many weeks, can overload the storage capacity of the liver and raise the concentration of the vitamin throughout the body to toxic levels. Toxicity symptoms include dry, rough skin, cracked lips, hair loss, headaches, muscle and joint pain. Among pregnant women, vitamin A toxicity can lead to babies with birth defects.

Why is it possible to overdose on vitamin A but not on vitamin C? Vitamin A is fat-soluble; vitamin C is water-soluble. The kidneys remove chemicals that are toxic or too concentrated from the blood. You would expect, therefore, that the kidneys would remove excesses of both vitamin A and vitamin C. But while the kidneys do a thorough job of regulating small water-soluble molecules, they are far less effective in processing large molecules, including many proteins. This means that vitamin A is only gradually metabolized, or broken down by chemical reactions within the cells.

SECTION REVIEW

Total recall

1. Why do bubbles escape from a soda that has just been opened?

2. Name two factors that affect solubility.

3. Describe one practical example of solubility principles.

4. Why does cold soda taste less flat than warm soda?

5. Why is an oxygen-helium mixture favored over compressed air in a diver's air tanks?

Critical thinking

6. Explain why CO_2 is a nonpolar molecule even though it possesses two dipolar bonds.

7. **Story Clue** Based on the fact that PCBs have been found in the fat tissue of polar bears, what can you predict about the solubility of PCBs?

What causes conductivity in solutions?

OBJECTIVES

▶ **Identify** substances that are good, intermediate, and poor conductors of electricity.

▶ **Discuss** nonelectrolytes, weak electrolytes, and strong electrolytes.

▶ **Describe** the enthalpy and entropy changes that accompany the dissolution of an ionic solid.

Electrical conduction

In Chapter 5 you learned that some substances can conduct electricity and some cannot. Two requirements must be satisfied for a substance to behave as an electrical conductor. First, the substance must contain particles with positive charges and others with negative charges. Second, the charged particles must be able to move about within the substance. Solid sodium chloride, NaCl, meets the first requirement but not the second one. NaCl is made of nothing but Na^+ and Cl^- ions, but they cannot move. Conversely, pure water meets the second requirement but not the first. Ions are able to move about in water, but there are virtually none present in pure water.

Separately, neither NaCl nor H_2O can conduct electricity, but when combined in an aqueous solution, they form a conductor. The ions are provided by the solute; the opportunity to move is provided by the fluidity of the solvent.

conductivity

the ability to conduct an electric current

FIGURE 13-13 ▼

The presence of ions in a solution being tested provides the conductivity to light the bulb.

Electrical conductivities span a wide range

A material's ability to conduct electricity is referred to as its **conductivity.** Conductivity can be measured by suitable electrical equipment. Generally speaking, aqueous ionic solutions are much better conductors than water and much worse conductors than metals.

The apparatus shown in **Figure 13-13** assesses the conductivity of aqueous solutions. The device uses electricity to power a light bulb, except that there is a gap in the circuit between the two electrode rods. These rods dip into the beaker containing the test solution. If the solution has a high conductivity, there is electrical continuity between the rods and the bulb lights up. The brightness of the light is a measure of the solution's conductivity. The brighter the light is, the greater the conductivity.

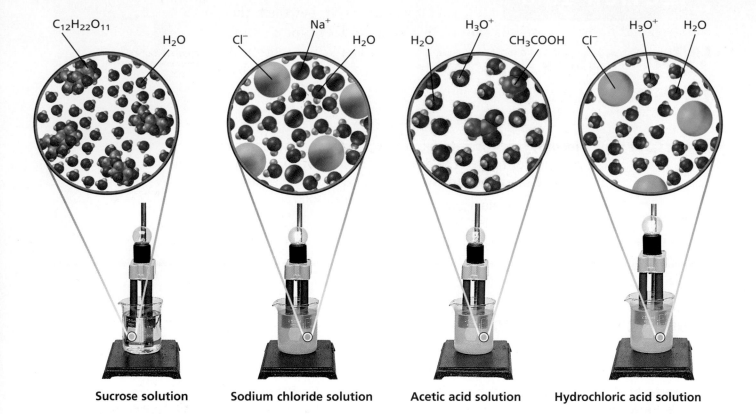

| Sucrose solution | Sodium chloride solution | Acetic acid solution | Hydrochloric acid solution |

▲ **FIGURE 13-14**

For solutions at the same concentration, the brightness of the bulb is an indication of the conductivity.

Figure 13-14 shows four different aqueous solutions being tested. The brightest light occurs when hydrogen chloride, HCl, is the solute. The light from the aqueous NaCl solution is also bright, whereas the acetic acid solution, CH_3COOH, barely allows the bulb to glow. No light at all comes from the bulb when sucrose (table sugar), $C_{12}H_{22}O_{11}$, is the solute. Three of the solutions conduct electricity, although one does so poorly. The fourth has no greater conductivity than pure water has.

Electrolytes provide a liquid with ions

electrolyte

a substance that, when dissolved in a solvent, increases the solvent's conductivity

Any substance that, when dissolved in a liquid solvent, increases that solvent's conductivity is called an **electrolyte.** This classification is based not on any feature of the substance itself but on how the substance behaves when dissolved in water or some other liquid. Thus, an electrolyte may be a solid, a liquid, or a gas, and it may be ionically or covalently bonded. Electrolytes are further classified as *strong electrolytes* or *weak electrolytes*. As you might expect, strong electrolytes provide a high conductivity, whereas weak electrolytes dissolve to produce a solution that is only mildly conducting.

Acetic acid is considered a weak electrolyte because its solutions exhibit low conductivity, lighting the bulb only dimly in Figure 13-14. Sodium chloride and hydrogen chloride are classified as strong electrolytes because their aqueous solutions have high conductivities, lighting the bulb brightly. When a solution does not contain charged particles, there is nothing to transport the electricity between the electrodes, and the bulb will not light. Any solute in this type of solution is called a **nonelectrolyte.** An example is sucrose. When dissolved in water, sucrose, $C_{12}H_{22}O_{11}$, produces no measurable conductivity change even in an apparatus much more sensitive than the one shown in Figure 13-13 on page 487.

Strong electrolytes confer conductivity because they introduce a large quantity of ions into the solution. Sodium chloride is already wholly ionic as a solute. Dissolving it merely separates the ions from each other.

$$NaCl(s) \xrightarrow{H_2O} Na^+(aq) + Cl^-(aq)$$

In the case of hydrogen chloride, which is a gaseous covalent solute, a chemical reaction occurs in addition to a dissolution.

$$HCl(g) + H_2O(l) \longrightarrow H_3O^+(aq) + Cl^-(aq)$$

One mole of solute produces 1 mol of chloride ions and 1 mol of cations. You would expect the conductivity of these solutions to increase proportionally to their concentration, and this is exactly what happens.

Acetic acid is a weak electrolyte. Dissolving acetic acid in water forms a solution that contains acetic acid molecules, water molecules, acetate ions, and **hydronium ions.** The reaction that takes place is shown as a chemical equation with models in **Figure 13-15.** The double arrows are used to show that both reactants and products exist in the solution because the conversion to ions is not complete. In fact, as much as 99% of the acetic acid may remain as molecules. Because of its low percentage of ionization, a weak electrolyte solution's conductivity is not directly proportional to its concentration. Acids and bases are discussed further in Chapter 15.

Keep in mind that the use of the term *strong* as related to electrolytes has nothing to do with their concentration in a solution. Likewise the term *weak* has nothing to do with dilute solutions. For example, HCl is a strong electrolyte in solution, whether the solution is very concentrated (10 M) or very dilute (0.000 001 M). A very dilute solution, however, has low conductivity. Similarly, CH_3COOH is a weak electrolyte in solution is, no matter how concentrated or dilute the solution is.

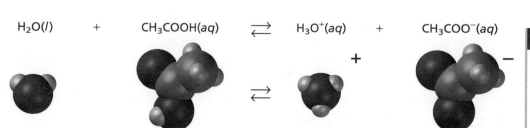

$H_2O(l)$ + $CH_3COOH(aq)$ $\rightleftharpoons$ $H_3O^+(aq)$ + $CH_3COO^-(aq)$

Water   Acetic acid   Hydronium ion   Acetate ion

FIGURE 13-15 ◄

When acetic acid dissolves in water, most of the acid remains as un-ionized molecules in equilibrium with ions.

Places never to set your electric eel

▲ **FIGURE 13-16**

A person can suffer severe electric shock when electricity comes in contact with water.

Tap water conducts electricity

The instructions included with a hair dryer warn of the danger of dropping it into a tub or sink full of water. When using extension cords outdoors, you are cautioned to keep them away from water. Electricity and water are a hazardous combination that, at times, can prove fatal. **Figure 13-16** provides a reminder of this danger.

Have you ever wondered why you should avoid water when you are using electricity? The contents of the water, rather than the water itself, create the danger. You have already learned that water is a good solvent. Unlike distilled water, which does not conduct enough electricity to light the bulb in the conductivity apparatus, tap water contains various ions from dissolved minerals. Depending on where your water supply comes from, your tap water may contain various dissolved salts and other solutes. Because ground water, such as well water, comes in contact with so many mineral deposits, it may have a greater concentration of salts than does surface water, such as lakes and rivers. These salts generally do not give tap water high conductivity, but the dilute solution may nevertheless conduct the small quantity of electricity needed to cause a painful or lethal electric shock. That is why you have to be careful when using electricity near water. If you are swiming in a pool, a lake, or the ocean and a thunderstorm comes into the area, keep in mind that chlorinated water, ground water, and salt water are conductors of electricity. Get out of the water during a thunderstorm. Also remember not to seek shelter under a tree. Electrolytes in the sap of trees make them conductors, so lightning frequently finds a path to the ground through the trunk of a tree.

CONCEPT CHECK

1. Identify the following as conductors or nonconductors of electricity.
   a. solid NaCl   **c.** copper wire
   b. pure water   **d.** oxygen gas
2. Arrange the following substances according to their performance as an electrolyte, listing the strongest electrolyte first:
   a. sucrose   **b.** hydrogen chloride   **c.** acetic acid
3. Explain why swimming in a pool during a thunderstorm is dangerous.

The dissolving process

What happens when table salt, sodium chloride, dissolves in a polar solvent, such as water? And why does it dissolve? You know that NaCl has an ionic lattice and that strong bonds hold it together as a solid. Energy needs to be provided to overcome the powerful attraction between the neighboring ions in the **dissociation** process shown in the equation below.

$$NaCl(s) \xrightarrow{\text{H}_2\text{O}} Na^+(aq) + Cl^-(aq)$$

Though dissociation is energetically disfavored, the entropy factor favors the creation of separated ions. It is clear that without the water the enthalpy factor wins out in the solid state— otherwise sodium chloride would spontaneously vaporize. What is different when the dissociation occurs in an aqueous solution?

There are several factors involved. One is that the force of attraction between two ions is diminished when the space between them is filled by a liquid. Another very important factor is **hydration.** Remember from Chapter 6 that water is a dipole; its molecule has a positive end and a negative end. The positive end of a water molecule is attracted to an anion, while its negative end is similarly attracted to a cation. Accordingly, water molecules like to cluster around ions of either charge, as depicted in **Figure 13-17.**

Enthalpy and entropy affect the solubility of salts

You would expect the hydration process to be exothermic, and indeed it is. Moreover, you would expect the energy release to be greater the smaller the ion and the larger its charge. These predictions are confirmed in practice. On the other hand, small ionic size and large ionic charge are precisely the factors that contribute to making the lattice energy of the crystal large. So the two energy terms shown in Figure 13-17 are both large, and either may dominate.

The situation is similar with entropy. The drive toward increasing entropy favors the dissociation process, but hydration decreases the solution's entropy because the water molecules become more ordered

dissociation

a process in which a compound separates into fragments, such as simpler molecules, atoms, radicals, or ions

hydration

the process by which water molecules surround each ion as it moves into solution

FIGURE 13-17 ▼

Individual ions are separated from the solid lattice by absorbed energy before they are hydrated by water molecules. Energy is released when hydrated ions are released from the lattice.

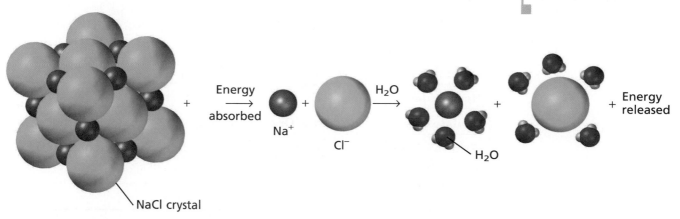

NaCl crystal

Energy absorbed → Na⁺ + Cl⁻ → H₂O → H₂O + Energy released

when they become localized around an ion. The result is that it is no easier to predict the solubility of salts in water than it is to predict other solubilities.

Solubilities of ionic compounds

Though difficult to predict, the solubilities of ionically bonded electrolytes, mostly solid salts, are quite easy to measure. A qualitative classification into *soluble* and *insoluble* is sometimes useful, and **Table 13-2** provides a classification that is helpful in predicting the solubility of many ionic compounds.

Technically, all salts dissolve to some, possibly minute, extent and most have a solubility limit beyond which no more will dissolve. Solubilities of ionic compounds, too, depend on temperature. Unlike the solubility of gases, the solubility of most ionic compounds increases as the temperature increases.

TABLE 13-2	**Solubility of Common Ionic Compounds**

Compounds containing these ions are soluble in water:
Acetates, $CH_3CO_2^-$, *except* that of Fe^{3+}
Alkali metal (Group 1) compounds *except* LiF
Ammonium, NH_4^+, compounds
Bromides, Br^-, *except* those of Ag^+, Hg_2^{2+}, and Pb^{2+}
Chlorates, ClO_3^-
Chlorides, Cl^-, *except* those of Ag^+ and Hg_2^{2+}
Iodides, I^-, *except* those of Ag^+, Hg_2^{2+}, and Pb^{2+}
Nitrates, NO_3^-
Perchlorates, ClO_4^-
Sulfates, SO_4^{2-}, *except* those of Ca^{2+}, Ba^{2+}, Pb^{2+}, Sr^{2+}, and Hg_2^{2+}
Compounds containing these ions are insoluble in water:
Carbonates, CO_3^{2-}, *except* those of Group 1 and NH_4^+
Chromates, CrO_4^{2-}, *except* those of Group 1 and NH_4^+
Hydroxides, OH^-, *except* those of Group 1, Ca^{2+}, Sr^{2+}, and Ba^{2+}
Oxalates, $C_2O_4^{2-}$, *except* those of Group 1 and NH_4^+
Oxides, O^{2-}, *except* those of Group 1, Ca^{2+}, Sr^{2+}, and Ba^{2+} (which form hydroxides)
Phosphates, PO_4^{3-}, *except* those of Group 1 and NH_4^+
Sulfides, S^{2-}, *except* those of Group 1, Group 2, and NH_4^+

Solubility can be exceeded

In a saturated solution, some excess solute remains, and the mass that dissolves is equal to the solubility value for that temperature. Supersaturated liquid-solid solutions also exist, and some show very interesting behavior. Supersaturated solutions are able to contain more than the solubility as long as there is no excess undissolved solute remaining. Refer to the photos of the hand warmer Heat Solution™ shown in **Figure 13-18** as you read the following description. Inside the plastic pack, 60 g of sodium acetate, $NaCH_3COO$, has been combined with 100 mL of water. When the $NaCH_3COO$ solution is heated to 100°C, all of the $NaCH_3COO$ completely dissolves. **Figure 13-18a** confirms that the solution is unsaturated, and no undissolved salt remains. When the solution is allowed to cool to 20°C, crystals of solute *should* start to form. **Figure 13-18b** shows that they do not. Instead, the solution becomes increasingly supersaturated. However, if you disturb the cooled solution by clicking the disk in the center of the pack, crystallization immediately occurs, as shown in **Figure 13-18c**. Sodium acetate is an electrolyte with a highly endothermic enthalpy of solution. The heat required to dissolve the crystals is regenerated when recrystallization of the cold solution occurs.

FIGURE 13-18 ▼

On a cold day it can be comforting to use a hand warmer.

Cooling

Unsaturated

a At 100°C, 60 g of $NaCH_3COO$ will dissolve completely in the 100 mL of water contained in a Heat Solution pack.

Supersaturated

b When the solution is cooled to 20°C, $NaCH_3COO$ does not crystallize unless the solution is disturbed.

Crystallization

Heat to re-use

Saturated

c Clicking the disk in the center of the pack triggers rapid exothermic crystallization. The hand warmer can be reused if it is heated above the saturation point again.

CONSUMER FOCUS

SPORTS DRINKS

Replacing lost electrolytes

Whenever you perform hard physical labor or participate in sports activities, you sweat. When you sweat, you need to drink water to replace the lost fluids containing electrolytes.

The next time you shop for sports drinks, look at labels. Check the labels for electrolytes, such as **potassium** ions, K^+; **sodium** ions, Na^+; and **calcium** ions, Ca^{2+}. The electrolytes serve important roles in various physiological functions, including nerve-impulse conduction and muscle contraction.

Ion pumps

At rest, a nerve cell uses "ion pumps" to maintain a high concentration of Na^+ ions outside the cell and of K^+ ions inside the cell. These ions do not diffuse through the membrane when the nerve cell is at rest. However, when the cell is stimulated, ions pass through the cell membrane, moving Na^+ ions inside the nerve cell and K^+ ions outside the nerve cell. When the cell re-

TOPIC: Sports drinks
GO TO: www.scilinks.org
KEYWORD: HW133

turns to its resting state, Na^+ ions are again pumped out and the K^+ ions diffuse in to compensate, readying the cell for the next stimulus.

Muscle contractions also depend on the movement of ions. When muscle cells are stimulated, Ca^{2+} ions go into the cells and cause protein fibers to slide together, resulting in a muscle contraction. When Ca^{2+} ions move back outside the cells, the muscle relaxes.

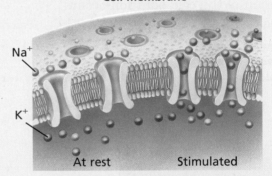

Cell membrane

Na^+

K^+

At rest   Stimulated

SECTION REVIEW

Total recall

1. What two conditions must a substance meet in order to behave as an electrical conductor?

2. Why does tap water conduct electricity?

3. What usually happens to the entropy of a system as a salt dissolves? What usually happens to the enthalpy?

4. Does the solubility of most ionic compounds increase or decrease with temperature?

Critical thinking

5. Explain how a soluble salt with a highly exothermic enthalpy of solution could also be used in a hand warmer. Would this hand warmer be reusable?

6. Identify the ions that are produced when the following compounds dissociate in water:
   a. HNO_3
   b. NH_4CH_3COO
   c. KOH
   d. CH_3COOH

How are a liquid's properties changed by solutes?

OBJECTIVES

▶ **Define** colligative properties.

▶ **Explain** why a liquid's boiling point is elevated but its freezing point is depressed when a solute dissolves.

▶ **Describe** how the magnitude of a colligative property depends on the amount of solute and on the chemistry of the dissolution process.

▶ **Compare** and contrast the roles of emulsifiers and surfactants.

▶ **Explain** what hard water is and why its occurrence makes detergents superior to soaps.

Colligative properties

Dissolving a solute in a liquid can produce new chemical properties in the resulting solution. Adding sodium hydroxide to water, for example, creates a solution with many chemical properties that the water did not previously possess. But the *physical* properties of water are also changed when substances dissolve in it. So too are its *solvent* properties, such as how well the water mixes with other compounds.

When you cook pasta or vegetables in boiling water, you may find that the recipe calls for the addition of salt to the water. Though its purpose is to enhance the food's flavor, the salt has a slight effect on the boiling process. Adding salt to the water *elevates* its boiling point. Salted water boils at a slightly higher temperature. The **boiling-point elevation** is 0.51 K for every mole of solute particles added to 1 kg of water.

The converse effect is found during freezing; a solute *depresses* the freezing point. This change is called **freezing-point depression.** Dilute aqueous solutions invariably freeze at lower temperatures. When homemade ice cream is being prepared, as in **Figure 13-20** on the next page, salt is mixed into the water-ice bath to reduce the temperature of the ice-salt mixture. Preparation temperatures below 0°C make better ice cream.

boiling-point elevation

the difference between the boiling point of a solution and that of the pure solvent

freezing-point depression

the difference between the freezing point of a pure solvent and that of a solution

FIGURE 13-19 ◀

If you add 58.44 g (1 mol) of NaCl to 1000 g of water, the boiling point increases by 1 K.

▲ **FIGURE 13-20**

An ice cream maker uses an ice-salt-water mixture to provide a temperature that is colder than that of ice and water alone.

colligative property

a physical property that is dependent on the number of solute particles present rather than on the identity of those particles

The identity of the solute is unimportant

Each of these properties of solutions—boiling-point elevation and freezing-point depression—is an example of a **colligative property.** Colligative properties depend only on the concentration of the solute particles rather than on the solute's identity. If there are several solutes present, the effect is additive; the total number of solute moles in a given quantity of solvent determines the magnitude of the effect.

Both of these colligative properties arise because the vapor pressure of an aqueous solution is less than that of pure water at the same temperature. Vapor-pressure lowering is also a colligative property. The vapor pressure decreases because the presence of solute particles lowers the concentration of solvent molecules at the liquid's surface. How does this lowering of vapor pressure affect the solvent's boiling and freezing points?

Figure 13-21 illustrates the difference between water's boiling point and freezing point and those of an aqueous solution. Recall that the boiling point of a liquid is the temperature at which the liquid's vapor pressure reaches atmospheric pressure. Because the vapor pressure of water is lowered by the addition of a nonvolatile solute, the solution must be heated to a higher temperature in order for its vapor pressure to reach atmospheric pressure, at which point the solution boils. Figure 13–21 illustrates how the boiling point is increased by the lowering of the vapor pressure curve. On the other hand, the freezing point of a substance is the temperature at which the liquid and solid phases are

► **FIGURE 13-21**

This is a modified phase diagram for pure water (red lines) and for an aqueous solution (blue lines). The addition of a solute has the effect of extending the range of the liquid phase.

Solute Effects on the Vapor Pressure of a Pure Solvent

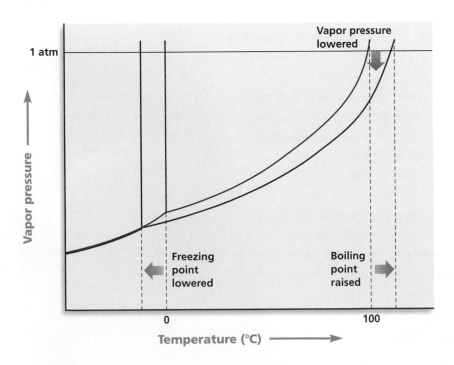

in equilibrium, which means that their vapor pressures must be equal. Because the addition of a solute to water lowers the vapor pressure of water, the vapor pressures of water and ice can only be equal at a temperature lower than the freezing point of pure water. Therefore, the addition of a solute lowers the freezing point of water.

The concentration of the solute affects freezing- and boiling-point changes

Any solute, whether an electrolyte or a nonelectrolyte, contributes to the colligative property of the solution. The intensity of the effect depends on the number of solute particles (molecules and ions) in a certain mass of solvent. The more particles there are, the greater the freezing-point depression and the boiling-point elevation are. Based on the number of moles of solute particles produced, 1 mol of sodium chloride is expected to be twice as effective dissolved in water as 1 mol of sucrose, $C_{12}H_{22}O_{11}$. In practice, however, due to interionic attractions, the effect is slightly less than twofold. Likewise, 1 mol of calcium chloride, $CaCl_2$, is predicted to be three times as effective, for reasons that **Figure 13-22** illustrates. The following equations show how 1 mol, 2 mol, and 3 mol of solute particles arise when 1 mol each of sucrose, sodium chloride, and calcium chloride are dissolved in water.

$$C_{12}H_{22}O_{11}(s) \xrightarrow{H_2O} C_{12}H_{22}O_{11}(aq)$$

$$NaCl(s) \xrightarrow{H_2O} Na^+(aq) + Cl^-(aq)$$

$$CaCl_2(s) \xrightarrow{H_2O} Ca^{2+}(aq) + 2Cl^-(aq)$$

FIGURE 13-22 ▼

Colligative properties depend on the number of particles formed by the solute in the solution. Sugar, table salt, and calcium chloride form aqueous solutions with differing colligative properties.

Sucrose solution

Sodium chloride solution

Calcium chloride solution

internet**connect**

SC*I*LINKS.
NSTA

TOPIC: Emulsions
GO TO: www.scilinks.org
KEYWORD: HW134

emulsion

colloidal-sized droplets (about 100 nm in diameter) of one liquid suspended in another liquid

▼ **FIGURE 13-23**

Oil and vinegar will mix if shaken vigorously. However, the particles of oil and vinegar do not make a homogeneous solution.

Emulsions

You have probably heard the saying that oil and water do not mix. It is true. They are immiscible liquids. You can demonstrate it the next time you prepare an oil-and-vinegar salad dressing.

Place about 60 mL of olive oil in a small bottle or carafe. Add about half as much vinegar, which is a solution of acetic acid and water. You will see the vinegar sink through the oil and collect at the bottom, as shown in **Figure 13-23.** This observation indicates two things—that vinegar is denser than olive oil, and that the two liquids are immiscible. If you cap the container and shake it well, you will see a turbulent mixture of oil and vinegar. What you cannot see are millions of microscopic droplets of vinegar surrounded by oil. This mixture is called an **emulsion.** The droplets formed in an emulsion are colloidal particles, discussed in Section 13-1. They are smaller than the particles in a suspension but larger than the particles in a solution.

This salad-dressing emulsion is temporary. As soon as you stop shaking the container, the droplets of vinegar begin to come together and sink, the oil rises, and the layers of each eventually reappear. Clearly, the olive oil and vinegar are immiscible. This is expected because olive oil is almost nonpolar, while the aqueous vinegar solution is polar.

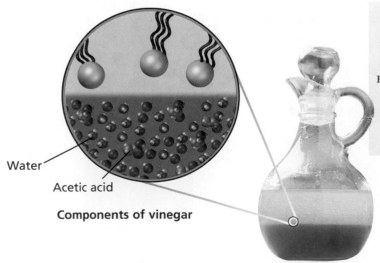

Water

Acetic acid

Components of vinegar

Typical oil molecule
Oleic acid triglyceride

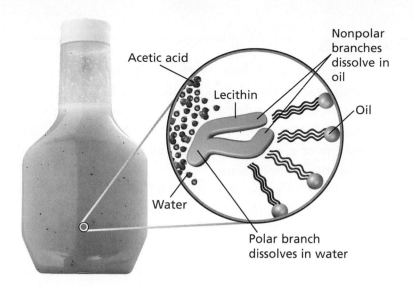

Acetic acid

Lecithin

Nonpolar branches dissolve in oil

Oil

Water

Polar branch dissolves in water

FIGURE 13-24 ◄

An oil-and-vinegar emulsion can be stabilized by adding an emulsifier, such as lecithin. The emulsifier acts as a bridge between the oil and the aqueous vinegar, preventing the droplets within each component from coming together.

Emulsions can be stabilized

The next time you are at the grocery store, look at the commercial oil-and-vinegar salad dressings. You will see two types. The traditional type has distinct layers, just like the dressing shown in Figure 13-23. The newer type, shown in **Figure 13-24,** has no layers because the oil and vinegar have been mixed with another ingredient, an **emulsifier,** that ensures the layers stay mixed.

Lecithins, found in all living organisms, are a family of several similar molecules that stabilize emulsions. Lecithins are obtained commercially by extraction from soybeans. Eggs are also rich in lecithins. You may decide to convert your oil-and-vinegar dressing into mayonnaise, which you can do by beating in an egg yolk. The egg yolk serves as an emulsifier. As you can see in Figure 13-24, lecithin molecules have three major branches. The two longer branches are nonpolar, but the shorter third branch is polar.

The role of lecithins is to dissolve in both oil and water when these solvents are present together. Each molecule of lecithin dissolves partly in the oil and partly in the water, linking two immiscible liquids. Lecithins stabilize emulsions, preventing separation. They modify the properties of water and aqueous solutions, making them accommodate nonpolar molecules.

It is often said that emulsifiers make oil and water mix. A better description is to say that they coat the tiny globules of oil and stabilize the emulsion, keeping the oil and water mixed. The next time you eat a candy bar, read its label. You will often find lecithin listed.

emulsifier

a substance that stabilizes an emulsion by forming a layer between two immiscible liquids

CONCEPT CHECK

1. Explain how you can get oil and water to "mix."

2. Are emulsions temporary mixtures or stable mixtures?

3. What is the role of a lecithin in forming a mixture?

Surfactants

Have you ever gotten dirty from working outside and tried to clean your hands with water alone? You would have been only partly successful because much of the dirt would have remained on your hands. To get your hands really clean, plain water is not enough. You have to use small amounts of a surfactant, such as **soap,** with the water. The reason again relates to emulsions.

Perspiration is a mixture of water and oils. Oils keep your skin soft. Over a period of time, the oils accumulate and coat your skin with an oily layer in which flakes of old skin, dirt, and bacteria become embedded. To remove all of the dirt, you must first emulsify the oil by scrubbing, then stabilize it with an emulsifier such as soap. Only then can the soap-and-oily-dirt emulsion be rinsed away from your skin by more water.

Though chemically dissimilar in some ways, a soap anion and a lecithin molecule both have a nonpolar hydrocarbon chain that is oil soluble. The lecithin molecule has a polar end, the soap ion has an ionic end, both of which are water soluble. When you wash your hands with soap, as shown in **Figure 13-25,** one end of the soap ion dissolves in the oil, forming a tiny sphere called a **micelle,** while the other end—on the outside of the micelle—dissolves in the surrounding water. The oil droplet stays suspended in the water and can be easily washed away.

The characteristic property of a **surfactant** is its ability to form a layer between two dissimilar phases. Soap shows this property in forming micelles and in its ability to form bubbles. In a soap bubble, a thin film of water is coated on both surfaces by soap molecules. The nonpolar end of these micelles is able to be next not only to oils but also to another nonpolar fluid, air.

soap

a sodium or potassium salt of a long-chain fatty acid

micelle

a spherical arrangement formed by molecules of fat or fatlike substances in an aqueous environment

surfactant

a class of salts, valued for their cleansing properties, whose anions possess a negatively charged "head" and a long nonpolar "tail"

► **FIGURE 13-25**

When you wash with soap, you create an emulsion of oil droplets dispersed in water and stabilized by soap.

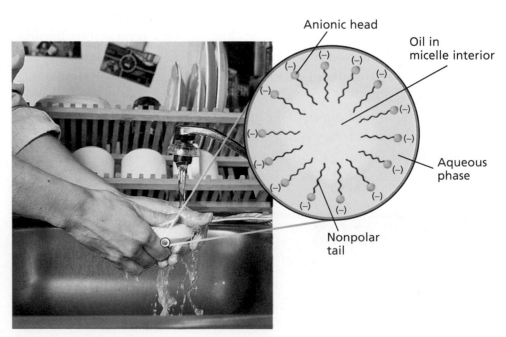

Anionic head

Oil in micelle interior

Aqueous phase

Nonpolar tail

Hard water destroys soap's surfactant abilities

Though soap's texture is very different from most other salts, soap is a salt. Potassium palmitate is a typical soap; it dissolves in water to form the potassium ion, $K^+(aq)$, and the palmitate anion, $C_{15}H_{31}COO^-(aq)$. It is the $C_{15}H_{31}$ part of the anion that forms a long zigzag "tail," shown in Figure 13-25, which constitutes the nonpolar section of the surfactant. The COO^- part is polar and has a strong affinity for water.

Soaps are not ideal cleaning agents because some palmitate salts are insoluble in water. If the water in your home comes from an underground source, it may be hard water, which contains calcium or magnesium ions. These cations combine with the palmitate anion to form insoluble salts, such as the one shown in the following equation.

$$Ca^{2+}(aq) + 2C_{15}H_{31}COO^-(aq) \longrightarrow Ca(C_{15}H_{31}COO)_2(s)$$

You may have seen this salt in the form of a scum or bathtub ring. If you use soap and hard water in the washing machine, this salt forms a scum that clings to fabric and makes the clothes look dingy.

detergent

a surfactant other than a soap

Detergents outperform soaps in hard water

In the 1930s, chemists developed soap substitutes called **detergents.** Detergents can be used in hard water without forming insoluble salts. Today, almost all laundry products are detergents.

To replace soap, synthetic chemists kept the long zigzag hydrocarbon tail of the soap but substituted a different anionic head group, such as that shown in **Figure 13-26.** Like soaps, these ions are surfactants; they have one end that is charged and soluble in water and another end that is nonpolar. Unlike soaps, however, their calcium and magnesium salts are soluble.

FIGURE 13-26 ▼

Sodium dodecylbenzene sulfonate is an anionic surfactant. This ionic compound does not make an insoluble scum with calcium or magnesium ions.

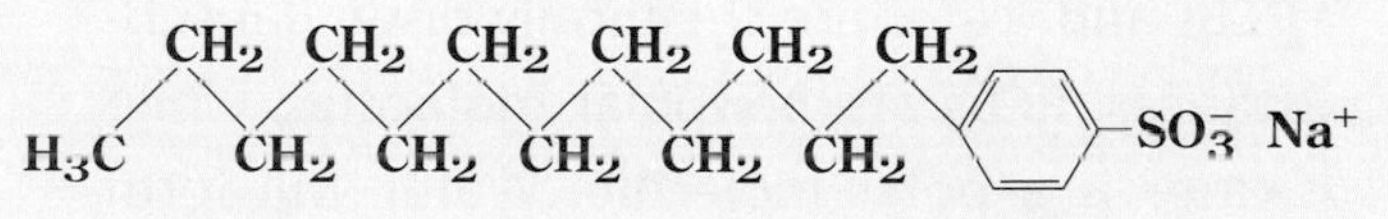

SECTION REVIEW

Total recall

1. What is the only aspect of a solute that is important in conferring a colligative property to a solution?

2. How are the behaviors of emulsifiers and surfactants in solution similar?

3. How are soaps and detergents different?

4. What is the purpose of adding salt to cooking water?

Critical thinking

5. Why does 1 mol of table salt lower water's freezing point to a greater extent than does 1 mol of table sugar added to an equal mass of water?

6. Why is a substance that contains only ionic bonds not a good emulsifier?

7. How does an emulsion differ from a homogeneous mixture?

At the beginning of this chapter you followed Dr. Malcolm Ramsay as he examined a polar bear and took samples of its fat tissue to determine the PCB content. So far, the concentration of PCBs found in the bear has caused it no apparent harm, but scientists are still concerned about the polar bears. The way PCBs dissolve in fat makes it possible for the concentration of PCBs to increase in the bears even if the amount of PCBs in the environment does not change. Now that you have completed the chapter, you should be able to answer the questions about PCBs and polar bears.

LOOKING BACK

Why would you not expect to find PCBs dissolved in Hudson Bay or any other body of water?

PCBs and water are chemically dissimilar substances. PCBs are nonpolar molecules, while water is a polar molecule. Water will form hydrogen bonds with itself but not with PCB molecules. All these things would lead you to expect not to find PCBs dissolved in any body of water to an appreciable extent.

In fact, the concentration of PCBs in Hudson Bay's water is very small, about 5×10^{-14} mol/L, or one PCB molecule for every 1×10^{15} water molecules. However, this is enough to worry Professor Ramsay. He and his colleagues know that this concentration will become magnified enormously as the PCB molecules make their way up the food chain.

Why were the PCBs not removed from the polar bear's system by the kidneys?

The kidneys are good at regulating the amount of water-soluble substances in the body by excreting them as waste. However, PCBs are not water-soluble and therefore would not be removed from the animal's body by the kidneys.

How did PCBs end up in the bear's fat?

When a seal eats a fish, the oil-soluble PCBs end up in the seal's oily blubber in concentrations that are even higher than those in fish. Because polar bears prey on seals, PCBs become concentrated in polar bears' fat. The animals that are the most likely to have PCBs concentrated in their fatty tissues are polar bears. They are at the top of the food chain and live for a long time.

KEY TERMS

13-1

aqueous
chromatography
colloid
concentration
distillation
molarity
solute
solvent
suspension

13-2

Henry's law
immiscible
insoluble
miscible
saturated
solubility
soluble
supersaturated

13-3

conductivity
dissociation
electrolyte
hydration
hydronium ion
nonelectrolyte

13-4

boiling-point elevation
colligative property
detergent
emulsifier
emulsion
freezing-point depression
micelle
soap
surfactant

KEY CONCEPTS

13-1 **What is a solution?**

▶ A solution is a homogeneous mixture in which the particles remain dissolved.

▶ A solution is made by dissolving a solute in a solvent; water is the solvent in aqueous solutions.

▶ Many methods can be used to separate the components in a mixture.

▶ Concentration can be expressed in various ways; a common concentration measure in chemistry is molarity.

13-2 **Does A dissolve in B?**

▶ The solubility of a substance can depend on the chemical nature of the solute and solvent, the pressure, the temperature, hydrogen bonding, enthalpy, and entropy.

▶ Because of the many factors that can affect solubility, predicting solubilities is very difficult.

▶ Solubility principles have many applications, including dry-cleaning and vitamin storage in the body.

13-3 **What causes conductivity in solutions?**

▶ Substances that do not dissociate in solution are nonelectrolytes; those that dissociate to a slight extent are weak electrolytes; those that dissociate completely are strong electrolytes.

▶ The ions provided by dissolved electrolytes give electrical conductivity to solutions.

▶ The solubility of salts in water depends on enthalpy and entropy.

▶ A solution is supersaturated when it contains more than the amount of solute specified by the solubility at a given temperature.

13-4 **How are a liquid's properties changed by solutes?**

▶ Colligative properties depend solely on the concentration of the solute in solution.

▶ Colligative properties include freezing-point depression and boiling-point elevation.

▶ Emulsifiers and surfactants enable two immiscible substances to mix.

▶ Detergents are more effective than soaps in hard water.

KEY SKILLS

How To Prepare 1.000 L of a 0.5000 M solution (p. 472)

Sample Problem 13A Calculating molarity (p. 473)

Sample Problem 13B Determining the mass of solute (p. 473)

Sample Problem 13C Using solution stoichiometry (p. 474)

REVIEW & ASSESS

1. A mixture in which the particles are uniformly dispersed but later settle at the bottom of the container is called a ——.
   (suspension, colloid, solution)

2. A substance that, when added to a liquid, allows the fluid to conduct an electric current is a(n) ——.
   (electrolyte, surfactant, micelle)

3. The number of moles of solute dissolved per liter of solution is known as the ——.
   (solubility, molarity)

4. The spherical arrangement formed by a group of lipid molecules in an aqueous environment is known as a(n) ——.
   (micelle, emulsion)

5. A molecule that has an uneven distribution of charge is said to be ——.
   (immiscible, polar)

6. —— is the term that is used to describe NaCl when it dissolves in water.
   (Emulsifier, Strong electrolyte)

7. A solution that contains more than the amount of solute specified by the solubility at a given temperature is said to be ——.
   (supersaturated, immiscible, aqueous)

8. The material dissolved in a solution is the ——.
   (solvent, solute)

9. The process by which water molecules surround ions in solution is called ——.
   (hydration, dissociation, conductivity)

10. A compound that experiences only a small degree of dissociation in an aqueous solution is said to be a ——.
    (nonelectrolyte, weak electrolyte, strong electrolyte)

SOLUTIONS, SUSPENSIONS, COLLOIDS

1. **a.** What is a solution?
   b. Identify and define the two components of a solution.
   c. Give two examples of common solutions.

2. **a.** How does a suspension differ from a colloid?
   b. Give two examples of common suspensions.
   c. Give two examples of common colloids.

3. Explain how distillation can be used to obtain drinking water from sea water.

4. Explain how chromatography separates the components in a solution.

5. List these mixtures in order of increasing particle size: muddy water (settles after a few hours), sugar water, ketchup (settles after an extended period of time), sand in water (settles rapidly), salt water.

CONCENTRATION AND MOLARITY

6. Describe in detail how you would make 250.0 mL of a 0.500 M solution of NaCl with equipment found in your chemistry lab.

7. You have 500 mL of a 0.5 M NaOH solution. For an experiment, you need 0.1 M NaOH. Describe how you would make 100 mL of a 0.1 M NaOH solution from the 0.5 M NaOH.

Practice Problems

8. Determine the molarity of each of the following solutions. **(Hint: See Sample Problem 13A.)**
   a. 0.250 mol of $FeCl_3$ in 2.00 L of solution
   b. 0.015 mol of $KMnO_4$ in 350 mL of solution
   c. 3.5×10^{-4} mol of $NaCH_3COO$ in 25.0 mL of solution

9. Determine the molarity of each of the following solutions. **(Hint: See Sample Problem 13A.)**
   a. 20.0 g of NaOH in enough H_2O to make 2.00 L of solution
   b. 14.0 g of NH_4Br in enough H_2O to make 150.0 mL of solution
   c. 65.0 g of $CuCl_2$ in enough H_2O to make 300.0 mL of solution

10. How many moles of each solute would be required to prepare each of the following solutions? **(Hint: See Sample Problem 13B.)**
    a. 1.0 L of a 4.0 M $AgNO_3$ solution
    b. 2.50 L of a 0.500 M HCl solution
    c. 400.0 mL of a 0.250 M HNO_3 solution

11. How many moles of each solute would be required to prepare each of the following solutions? **(Hint: See Sample Problem 13B.)**
    a. 30.0 mL of a 0.0100 M H_3PO_4 solution
    b. 5 mL of an 18 M H_2SO_4 solution
    c. 250.0 mL of a 1.00×10^{-4} M CH_3OH solution

12. What mass of solid $Ca_3(PO_4)_2$ results if 750.0 mL of 6.00 M H_3PO_4 react with an excess of $Ca(OH)_2$ according to the following equation? **(Hint: See Sample Problem 13C.)**

    $2H_3PO_4(aq) + 3Ca(OH)_2(aq) \longrightarrow$
    $$Ca_3(PO_4)_2(s) + 6H_2O(l)$$

13. A yellow pigment in some artists' oil paints is cadmium sulfide. What mass of cadmium sulfide would be made if 350.0 mL of 2.00 M $(NH_4)_2S$ reacted with 400.0 mL of 1.50 M $Cd(NO_3)_2$ according to the following equation? **(Hint: See Sample Problem 13C.)**

    $(NH_4)_2S(aq) + Cd(NO_3)_2(aq) \longrightarrow$
    $$2NH_4NO_3(aq) + CdS(s)$$

14. You are determining the concentration of a solution of salt water by evaporating different samples and measuring the mass of salt that remains. Your data are shown below. Calculate the molar concentration of the original solution.

Sample volume (mL)	Mass of NaCl (g)
25	2.9
50.0	5.6
75	8.5
100.0	11.3

15. The actual molarity of the solution in item 14 is determined to be 2.00 M. Calculate the percent error in the calculated concentration of the salt water.

16. The owner's manual for an outboard motor gives the proportion for mixing gasoline and oil as 100:1. You have 2.5 L of gasoline. According to the manual, how much oil do you need to mix with this much gasoline?

17. A shipment of shark meat was destroyed after it was found to contain 1.76 ppm methyl mercury, $[HgCH_3]^+$, which is higher than the legal limit of 1.00 ppm.
    a. If the shark meat had a mass of 12.5 kg, what mass of methyl mercury was present in the shark meat?
    b. What is the maximum number of grams of methyl mercury the shark meat could contain and still be considered safe according to the legal limit?

18. Prolonged exposure to lead or lead salts is toxic. To prevent lead poisoning, the current standard for lead in paint is 600.0 ppm, though some older paints had a concentration of 5.00×10^4 ppm. On average, a bucket of paint has a mass of 900.0 g.
    a. Calculate the maximum mass of lead in a bucket of new paint of average mass.
    b. Calculate the mass of lead in a bucket of old paint, based on the concentration and mass given.

SOLUBILITY AND POLARITY

19. Use **Table 13-2** to determine whether the following compounds are soluble in water:
    a. copper(II) sulfate
    b. copper(II) sulfide
    c. iron(III) chloride
    d. aluminum acetate

20. Explain what is meant by the chemist's expression, "like dissolves like."

21. If you mix silver nitrate with water, will it dissolve? If you mix potassium chloride with water, will it dissolve? If you mix the contents of these two combinations, will anything settle to the bottom? If so, what will settle?

22. Plot a solubility graph for $AgNO_3$ with the data below. Plot grams of solute (in increments of 50 g) per 100 g of H_2O on the vertical axis and the temperature in degrees Celsius on the horizontal axis.

  a. Estimate the solubility of $AgNO_3$ at 30°C, 55°C, and 75°C.

  b. At what temperature would the solubility of $AgNO_3$ be 275 g per 100 g of H_2O?

  c. If 98.5 g of $AgNO_3$ were added to 100 g of H_2O at 10°C, would the resulting solution be saturated or unsaturated?

Grams of solute per 100 g of H_2O	Temperature (°C)
122	0.0
216	20.0
311	40.0
440	60.0
585	80.0
733	100.0

AQUEOUS SOLUTIONS

23. In each of the diagrams shown below, 5.0 g of sodium acetate has been added to different concentrations of sodium acetate solutions, leading to the results noted. Indicate whether each of the original solutions was unsaturated, saturated, or supersaturated.

  a.

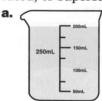

  Rapid recrystallization of more than the added amount

  b.

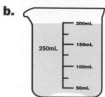

  Added amount remains undissolved

  c.

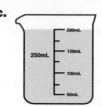

  Most of the added amount dissolves

24. a. What property is common to all electrolytes?

  b. How could you safely determine whether or not an unknown aqueous solution contains ions?

25. Rate the solutions below from most conductive to least conductive.

  a. 1.0 M KOH solution

  b. 10.0 M ammonia solution

  c. 2.0 M glucose solution

26. When you touch an appliance that has a short circuit, an electric current travels through your body, giving you a shock. What feature of the human body allows the electric current to travel through it?

APPLICATIONS OF SOLUBILITY

27. Foods and beverages are often fortified with vitamins. For instance, many fruit juices contain vitamin C. Why do fruit juices not contain vitamin A?

28. Explain why it is inaccurate to say that emulsifiers actually make insoluble chemicals dissolve. What really happens to the insoluble chemicals?

29. Explain why detergents are better emulsifiers than soaps in hard water, which contains calcium and magnesium ions.

30. Butter is an emulsion containing about 80% oily butterfat and 16% water. During the process of making butter, it is churned, or stirred very quickly, for a long period of time. Explain why the churning step is necessary in converting cream to butter.

31. What are the chemical characteristics of a good dry-cleaning solvent? How do they differ from the chemical characteristics of a good emulsifier?

32. The table below lists the solubility of three gases in grams of solute per 100 g of water at various temperatures. Use the data to plot a solubility versus temperature graph for each gas listed, with grams of solute per 100 g of H_2O on the vertical axis and temperature in degrees Celsius on the horizontal axis. Then answer the questions that follow.

Gas	20°C	30°C	40°C	50°C	60°C
CO_2	0.169	0.126	0.097	0.076	0.058
H_2S	0.38	0.30	0.24	0.19	0.15
Cl_2	0.73	0.57	0.46	0.39	0.33

a. Estimate the solubility of each gas at 45°C.
b. At what temperature would the solubility of Cl_2 be 0.50 g per 100 g of H_2O?
c. If a solution contains 0.100 g of CO_2 in 100 g of H_2O at 35°C, is it unsaturated, saturated, or supersaturated?
d. Assuming that other gases follow the pattern of these three gases, should you heat or cool water if you are trying to dissolve a gas in it?

33. Explain the role of solubility in accounting for the fact that you are more likely to overdose on vitamin A than on vitamin C.

34. Crayon companies recommend treating wax stains on clothes by spraying them with WD-40 lubricant, applying dishwashing liquid, and then washing them. Explain why.

35. To produce ice cubes that are clear instead of cloudy, should hot or cold water be used? Explain your answer.

Practice Problems

36. Ascorbic acid, vitamin C, has the formula $C_6H_8O_6$. What is the molarity of a solution of ascorbic acid if the concentration is 5.0 mg/L? **(Hint: See Sample Problem 13A.)**

37. A cup (250 mL) of whole milk contains about 0.4 mg of riboflavin, $C_{17}H_{20}N_4O_6$. What is the molarity of riboflavin in the milk? **(Hint: See Sample Problem 13A.)**

LINKING CHAPTERS

1. Precipitation reactions
Use **Table 13-2** to predict whether any precipitate will form when the following solutions are mixed. If a precipitate does form, what would you expect it to be?
a. $KOH(aq)$ and $NaNO_3(aq)$
b. $CaCl_2(aq)$ and $H_2CO_3(aq)$
c. $Na_2S(aq)$ and $FeBr_3(aq)$

2. Endothermic and exothermic processes
Enthalpy of solution refers to the total enthalpy change that accompanies the addition of 1 mol of solute to a large volume of solvent. The table below shows the enthalpy of solution for various solutes dissolved in water. Use it to answer the following questions:
a. Which solutes have endothermic enthalpies of solution?
b. Which solutes would increase the temperature of the solution?
c. Which solutes would dissolve better in hot water? Cite reasons for your answer.

Solute	Enthalpy of solution (kJ/mol)
Hydrogen chloride, $HCl(g)$	−74.84
Potassium chloride, $KCl(s)$	+17.22
Potassium hydroxide, $KOH(s)$	−57.61
Potassium nitrate, $KNO_3(s)$	+34.89
Silver nitrate, $AgNO_3(s)$	+22.59
Sodium chloride, $NaCl(s)$	+3.88
Sodium hydroxide, $NaOH(s)$	−44.51
Sodium nitrate, $NaNO_3(s)$	+20.50

3. Classification and trends

Use the table from item 2 for these questions.

a. The enthalpy of solution for rubidium chloride, RbCl, is not given in the table. Predict how its enthalpy of solution compares with that of potassium chloride, KCl. (Hint: Examine the chart closely, looking for patterns, and examine a periodic table.)

b. Arrange the following compounds in order of their enthalpies of solution, beginning with the most exothermic: NaBr, LiBr, RbBr, KBr.

ALTERNATIVE ASSESSMENTS

Performance assessment

1. Design a solubility experiment to identify an unknown substance that is CsCl, RbCl, LiCl, NH_4Cl, KCl, or NaCl. (Hint: You will need a solubility versus temperature graph for each of the salts.) If your instructor approves your design, get a sample from the instructor, and perform your experiment.

2. The more concentrated an aqueous solution of ethylene glycol is, the more dense it is. Mechanics keep this in mind when they check the antifreeze in a car's radiator. Using the data for ethylene glycol solutions shown below, graph the density versus the concentration. Then determine the concentration of a solution with a density of 1.030 g/mL. What density would you predict for a 2.50 M solution?

Concentration (M)	Density (g/mL)
0.65	1.003
1.30	1.008
3.30	1.024
7.50	1.057

3. Computer spreadsheet

Many reagent chemicals used in the lab are sold in the form of concentrated aqueous solutions, as shown in the table below. Different volumes are diluted to 1.00 L to make less-concentrated solutions. Create a spreadsheet that will calculate the volume of concentrated reagent needed to make 1.00 L solutions of any molar concentration that you enter.

Reagent	Concentration (M)
H_2SO_4	18
HCl	12.1
HNO_3	16
H_3PO_4	14.8
CH_3COOH	17.4
NH_3	15

Portfolio projects

1. Chemistry and you

For 1 week, record instances in which you use a mixture of some type. Identify whether each mixture is a solution, a suspension, an emulsion, or a heterogeneous mixture. If possible, identify the different components of each mixture.

2. Research and communication

Emergency-response teams working with oil spills use chemical and physical properties of oil and water along with solubility principles to control and clean up spills. Research the techniques used, and explain why they work. Present your findings to the class.

3. Chemistry and you

Read the labels of three different over-the-counter vitamin supplements. Write down the amount of vitamin A supplied in one tablet of each supplement. What dosage of each supplement could cause vitamin A toxicity (which is determined to be >15 000 µg/day)? (Hint: To convert IUs to µg, multiply by 0.025.)

4.

internet**connect**

SC*LINKS*
NSTA

TOPIC: Vitamin supplements
GO TO: www.scilinks.org
KEYWORD: HW135

Research and communication

Research the many arguments for and against the use of vitamin supplements. What is the role of the U.S. Food and Drug Administration in the regulation of vitamin supplements? Prepare an argument for or against the increased regulation of vitamin supplements, and debate the issue in class.

1. Two immiscible liquids can be mixed by the addition of a(n) ——.
   a. weak electrolyte
   c. colloid
   b. emulsifier
   d. hydronium ion

2. —— of NaOH must be used to prepare 2.5 L of a 0.010 M solution.
   a. 0.01 g
   c. 2.5 g
   b. 1.0 g
   d. 0.4 g

3. The molarity of 300.0 mL of a sodium carbonate solution that contains 22.5 g of Na_2CO_3 is ——.
   a. 0.700 M
   c. 0.100 M
   b. 0.210 M
   d. 1.210 M

4. Water is an excellent solvent because ——.
   a. it is a covalent compound
   b. of its polarity
   c. it does not form any electrolytes in aqueous solution
   d. of its colligative properties

5. Two liquids are likely to be immiscible if ——.
   a. both have nonpolar molecules
   b. both have polar molecules
   c. one has nonpolar molecules and the other has polar molecules
   d. one is water and the other is another polar solvent

6. A(n) —— would increase the solubility of a gas in a liquid.
   a. decrease in temperature
   b. decrease in atmospheric pressure
   c. increase in temperature
   d. agitation of the solution

7. Acetic acid is considered a weak electrolyte because it ——.
   a. is immiscible in water
   b. forms both hydronium ions and hydroxide ions in aqueous solution
   c. lowers the boiling point of water
   d. does not fully ionize in aqueous solution

8. Which of the following molecules is a dipole?
   a.

   b.

   c.

   d.

9. The boiling-point elevation is ——.
   a. 0.51 K for every mole of solute particles present in 1 kg of water
   b. 0.51 K for every mole of solute particles present in 1 mol of water
   c. 1 K for every mole of solute particles present in 1 mol of water
   d. 1 K for every mole of solute particles present in 1 kg of water

10. Because vitamin A is fat-soluble, it ——.
    a. does not mix well with nonpolar substances
    b. is stored in the liver
    c. passes out of the body in the urine
    d. cannot accumulate in the body

CHAPTER

14 Chemical Equilibrium

FERTILIZERS, EXPLOSIVES, AND WORLD WAR I

On July 28, 1914, Austria-Hungary declared war on Serbia. Six days later, Germany, an ally of Austria-Hungary, declared war on France. German troops stormed through Belgium and a short time later invaded France. The German army expected a quick victory, but the French and British forces resisted, and the battle escalated into World War I, four years of grueling trench warfare.

The Allies quickly set up a blockade in the Atlantic Ocean to prevent supplies from reaching Germany. The Germans especially needed sodium nitrate imported from Chile. They needed this mineral to make nitric acid, some of which was used to make fertilizers that were needed to increase food production in the relatively small country. But the bulk of the nitric acid was used to make explosives, such as trinitrotoluene (TNT) and nitroglycerin. If access to Chilean sodium nitrate had been cut off, the German armies would have run out of explosives in a fairly short time and the war would have ground to a halt.

In a remarkable coincidence, in 1913 the German chemist Carl Bosch commercialized a chemical procedure for synthesizing ammonia. Ammonia could be used as the basis for the production of nitric acid. He started with a process developed by Fritz Haber in 1904 that combined nitrogen and hydrogen according to the following equation.

$$N_2(g) + 3H_2(g) \longrightarrow 2NH_3(g)$$

Even before World War I, chemists realized that they needed to discover a process similar to the one used by nitrogen-fixing bacteria to fix atmospheric nitrogen into other useful chemical compounds. As early as the 1890s, chemists had shown that small amounts of ammonia could be synthesized at high temperatures and at atmospheric pressure from elemental hydrogen and nitrogen.

Bosch improved the yield of ammonia by properly choosing the pressure and temperature of the reaction system. By 1913, Germany was producing ammonia in industrial quantities. The German army had a continuous supply of explosives, and the war dragged on until November 1918.

CHAPTER LINKS

How would increasing the pressure of the reaction to produce ammonia affect the ammonia yield?

How would increasing the reaction temperature affect the amount of ammonia produced in this exothermic reaction?

What is an equilibrium system?

OBJECTIVES

▶ **Distinguish** between reactions that go to completion and those that do not.

▶ **Determine** whether the forward or reverse reaction is favored when a stress is applied to an equilibrium system using Le Châtelier's principle.

▶ **Describe** complex-ion behavior in aqueous equilibrium.

▶ **Discuss** examples of equilibrium systems.

Reversible and completion reactions

When you look at the components of a chemical reaction, you are looking at how compounds and elements react to form products. In studying reactions, you may have observed changes such as the formation of a precipitate or the evolution of a gas. Reactions that produce these types of changes often proceed very nearly to completion. **Figure 14-1** shows a reaction that produces a precipitate. Two examples of reactions that go to completion or very nearly to completion are shown in the following equations.

$$NaHCO_3(aq) + CH_3COOH(aq) \longrightarrow NaCH_3COO(aq) + CO_2(g) + H_2O(l)$$
Formation of a gas

$$NaCl(aq) + AgNO_3(aq) \longrightarrow AgCl(s) + Na^+(aq) + NO_3^-(aq)$$
Formation of a precipitate

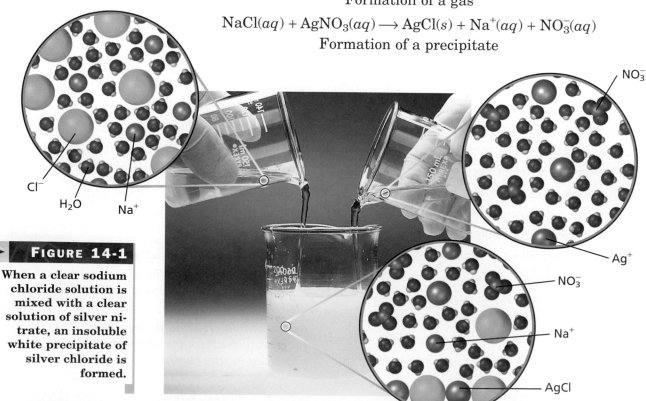

▶ **FIGURE 14-1**

When a clear sodium chloride solution is mixed with a clear solution of silver nitrate, an insoluble white precipitate of silver chloride is formed.

Reversible reactions reach equilibrium

Some reactions do not proceed to completion. Instead, the reaction ceases before the reactants are fully consumed. If the reactants and products of such a reaction are kept in a closed system, where nothing can escape, the reaction may proceed in either direction. Recall that a system consists of all the components that are being studied at a given time.

A reversible reaction that you might encounter is the recharging of an automobile battery. The interior of the battery has lead plates, lead(IV) oxide plates, and a sulfuric acid solution, H_2SO_4. The reversible reaction that takes place within a car battery is represented by the following equation. Notice that the arrows in the equation point in both directions, indicating a reversible reaction.

FIGURE 14-2 ▲

The spots on this leopard cub are the result of chemical reactions that were not able to reach equilibrium. The concentration of the chemicals involved in the formation of the cub's pelt varied in different regions, causing the distinctive patterns.

$$Pb(s) + PbO_2(s) + 2H_2SO_4(aq) \rightleftarrows 2PbSO_4(s) + 2H_2O(l) + energy$$

When the battery is used for power, the forward reaction occurs, releasing energy in the form of electricity. If you leave your car lights on, the forward reaction (discharge) will continue until most of the PbO_2 is used up, and the battery "dies." The reverse reaction occurs when electricity from an outside source is fed into the circuit. You must force the reverse reaction (charge) by passing a direct current through the battery in the opposite direction, as happens when the alternator charges your battery.

Reversible reactions lead to an equilibrium system when the forward and reverse reactions occur at equal rates and the conditions remain the same. At equilibrium, the total amount of particles remains constant. Because our model of a system at equilibrium has constant concentrations, we can use this information to determine the completeness of the reaction and to make predictions.

Consider the following equation, which represents the reaction of acetic acid with 3-methyl-1-butanol, $C_5H_{11}OH$, to form the ester 3-methylbutyl acetate, $C_7H_{14}O_2$, and water. Recall from Chapter 7 that esters are organic compounds that can be used as flavoring agents. The ester formed in this reaction is commonly known as banana oil or pear oil. It is often used to add flavor to syrups and mineral waters.

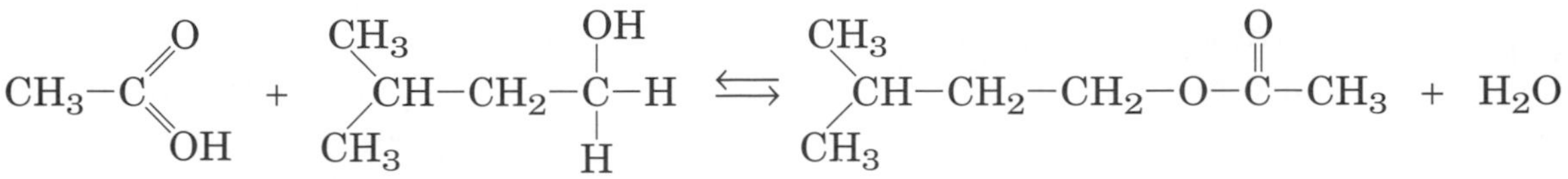

acetic acid + 3-methyl-1-butanol ⇌ 3-methylbutyl acetate (banana oil) + water

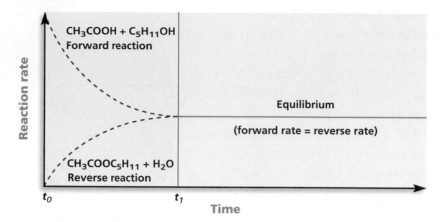

FIGURE 14-3

The rate of the forward and reverse reactions for the equilibrium system of the banana-oil reaction can be shown graphically.

Rate Comparison for the Equilibrium System
$$CH_3COOH + C_5H_{11}OH \rightleftharpoons CH_3COOC_5H_{11} + H_2O$$

Reaction rate

$CH_3COOH + C_5H_{11}OH$
Forward reaction

Equilibrium

(forward rate = reverse rate)

$CH_3COOC_5H_{11} + H_2O$
Reverse reaction

t_0 t_1

Time

Opposing reaction rates are equal at equilibrium

Figure 14-3 shows a graph of what happens as the reaction that produces banana oil attains equilibrium. Initially, the concentration of each product, water and 3-methylbutyl acetate, is zero, and the rate of the reverse reaction is zero. At the same time, the concentration of each reactant, acetic acid and 3-methyl-1-butanol, is at a maximum, and the rate of the forward reaction is the maximum rate. The rate of the forward reaction decreases as reactants are used up, and the rate of the reverse reaction increases until finally, at time t_1, the rates become equal and the equilibrium condition begins.

At equilibrium, the individual concentrations of the reactants and the products undergo no further changes as long as conditions remain the same. However, chemical reactions continue to occur even after equilibrium is reached. Although the macroscopic properties no longer change (the system appears unchanging), the forward and reverse reactions are still occurring. In other words, the reactions do not stop at equilibrium but maintain constant concentrations of reactants and products. The reactants continue forming products, and the reverse reaction continues at the same rate, with the products re-forming reactants. That is why any chemical equilibrium system is really a dynamic situation, not a static one.

To understand the difference between a dynamic situation and a static situation, imagine that you and a friend are each standing on a treadmill, similar to those shown in **Figure 14-4.** If you stand still on the treadmill and do not move at all, your situation can be described as static; there is no change in your position, and you and the equipment are at rest. If your friend runs at a steady pace on the treadmill, the situation is described as being in dynamic equilibrium because your friend and the treadmill are moving at a constant rate but your friend's position does not change.

FIGURE 14-4

Two people on different treadmills, one standing still and one running, illustrate static and dynamic situations.

Equilibrium systems and stress

Equilibrium is established in a reversible reaction when the forward and reverse reactions occur at the same rate and when the amounts of the reactants and products are constant. One example of a reversible reaction involves oxides of nitrogen, as represented by the following equation.

$$2NO_2(g) \rightleftharpoons N_2O_4(g)$$
Brown   Colorless

internet**connect**

SC*LINKS*
NSTA
TOPIC: Factors affecting equilibrium
GO TO: www.scilinks.org
KEYWORD: HW141

Pressure changes may alter gaseous equilibrium systems

According to the balanced equation above, 2 mol of nitrogen dioxide, NO_2, reacts to produce 1 mol of dinitrogen tetroxide, N_2O_4. When the system reaches equilibrium, there will be no change in the amounts of reactants and products until something alters the system. The factors that can alter an equilibrium system are called stresses. Suppose the NO_2/N_2O_4 equilibrium mixture is subjected to an increase in pressure caused by decreasing the volume of the container, as shown in **Figure 14-5.** Let us explore the system's response to an increase in pressure. Remember that the pressure of a gas in a container is caused by collisions of molecules against the walls of the container. The system can

a Low pressure

b Higher pressure

c New equilibrium

FIGURE 14-5 ◄

A decrease in volume increases the pressure and the concentrations of both NO_2 and N_2O_4, disturbing the equilibrium and temporarily making the mixture darker. The color fades as more N_2O_4 is formed to reduce the pressure and restore equilibrium.

relieve the stress by favoring the reaction that produces fewer gas molecules. Fewer gas molecules will exert less pressure. If the forward reaction is favored, two molecules of NO_2 will form one molecule of N_2O_4, decreasing the total number of molecules in the system and therefore moderating the increase in pressure. Observations show that an increase in pressure caused by a decrease in volume actually does favor the forward reaction, forming more N_2O_4 molecules.

You can follow the changes in concentrations of the two gases by observing the changes in the color of the gas mixture. In Figure 14-5a, a medium brown equilibrium mixture of NO_2 and N_2O_4 is contained in the syringe. When pressure is applied to the gas inside the syringe, the equilibrium is disturbed, as shown in Figure 14-5b. The volume decreases, altering the concentrations of the two gases and temporarily changing the color to dark brown. To restore the equilibrium position, the forward reaction is favored, as shown in Figure 14-5c, forming more colorless N_2O_4 molecules and giving the gas mixture a lighter color.

Temperature affects equilibrium systems

You have seen how changing the pressure affected the equilibrium between $NO_2(g)$ and $N_2O_4(g)$. Now consider what happens when the temperature is changed. The NO_2/N_2O_4 equilibrium system is shown at three different temperatures in **Figure 14-6.** At 25°C, the system at equilibrium is a medium shade of brown. When cooled to 0°C, the color of the mixture of gases in the flask is lighter. We can see that some of the dark brown NO_2 is no longer present and that more of the colorless N_2O_4 has formed. At 100°C, the contents of the flask are darker. We observe that more of the brown NO_2 has formed at the higher temperature.

The NO_2/N_2O_4 system discussed exemplifies an important principle developed by the French chemist Henri Louis Le Châtelier. This principle enables us to predict how changes imposed on a system at equilibrium will affect the status of the system. **Le Châtelier's principle** tells us how a system at equilibrium reacts to an applied stress. Le Châtelier defined *stress* as a change in the temperature or pressure of the system or a change in the concentration of a component.

Le Châtelier's principle

if a system at equilibrium is disturbed by applying stress, the system attains a new equilibrium position to accommodate the change and tends to relieve the stress

▶ **FIGURE 14-6**

Temperature changes put stress on equilibrium systems, causing either the forward or reverse reaction to be favored.

0°C
Very light brown

25°C
Medium brown

100°C
Dark brown

Consider the following exothermic reaction.

$$2NO_2(g) \overset{25°C}{\rightleftarrows} N_2O_4(g) + 57.2 \text{ kJ}$$

Le Châtelier's principle states that a system at equilibrium will react to relieve any stress placed on it. In the preceding reaction, heat energy is one of the products. Therefore, by lowering the reaction temperature, one of the products (heat) is being removed. As the temperature drops, the system reacts in a way that relieves this stress. To accomplish this, more NO_2 is converted to N_2O_4, causing the gas to become lighter in color. When the rate of the forward reaction is greater than the rate of the reverse reaction, the forward arrow can be shown as longer than the reverse arrow, and the equation is written as follows.

$$\underset{\text{Brown}}{2NO_2(g)} \xrightleftharpoons[\longleftarrow]{\overset{\text{during}}{\text{cooling}}} \underset{\text{Colorless}}{N_2O_4(g)} + 57.2 \text{ kJ}$$

Forward reaction favored

The system reaches a new equilibrium state with constant macroscopic properties at the new temperature of 0°C. As long as this temperature is maintained, the gas in the flask will remain a light brown. The rates of the forward and reverse reactions are again equal.

On the other hand, by increasing the temperature to 100°C, more heat energy is added to the system. The system reacts to relieve the stress and absorbs some of the heat. The reverse reaction is favored, so more brown NO_2 is formed as equilibrium is reestablished.

$$\underset{\text{Brown}}{2NO_2(g)} \xleftarrow[\longleftarrow]{\overset{\text{during}}{\text{heating}}} \underset{\text{Colorless}}{N_2O_4(g)} + 57.2 \text{ kJ}$$

Reverse reaction favored

Another example of the effect of temperature on a system at equilibrium is shown in **Figure 14-8.** A solution of cobalt(II) chloride at room temperature is pink. The forward reaction, forming the blue solution, is an endothermic reaction. The reversible reaction is shown in the following equation.

$$\underset{\text{Pink}}{Co(H_2O)_6^{2+}(aq)} + 4Cl^-(aq) \xrightleftharpoons{\text{heat}} \underset{\text{Blue}}{CoCl_4^{2-}(aq)} + 6H_2O(l)$$

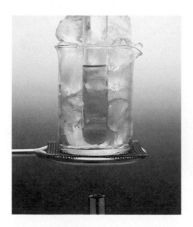

FIGURE 14-8 ◄

Depending on whether heat energy is removed or added, the reverse or forward reaction will be favored, forming a pink solution or a blue solution, respectively.

Removing heat from the equilibrium system favors the reverse reaction and the formation of more of the pink ion. If the cold solution is allowed to warm, adding heat back into the system, the forward reaction will be favored and more of the blue ion will be produced.

Changes in concentration alter equilibrium systems

One way to affect which reaction will be favored in an equilibrium system is to change a concentration in a reaction mixture. This can be done by removing a product or adding a reactant. Suppose you remove a product from an equilibrium reaction system. The system will react to the stress of removing a product by favoring the reaction that will produce more of that product. On the other hand, if you were to add a reactant to an equilibrium reaction system, the system would react to the stress by favoring the reaction that would consume the additional reactant. Consider the following example and its illustration in **Figure 14-9.**

Aspirin can cause damage to the walls of the stomach. Aspirin, acetylsalicylic acid, can exist in both its ionized form and nonpolar molecular form in the stomach. When aspirin combines with water, as when you swallow a tablet, some of the aspirin forms ions, shown by the forward reaction represented in the following equation.

$$\text{Acetylsalicylic acid} + H_2O \rightleftharpoons \text{Acetylsalicylate ion} + H_3O^+$$

Acetylsalicylic acid   Acetylsalicylate ion

$$H_2O + \text{Aspirin} \rightleftharpoons \text{Aspirin}^- + H_3O^+$$

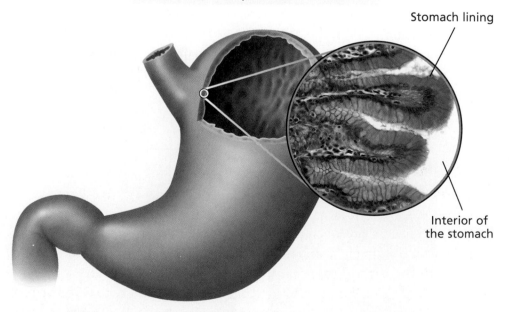

Stomach lining

Interior of the stomach

▶ **FIGURE 14-9**

Aspirin molecules re-form in the reverse reaction of the equilibrium system inside a human stomach. Once the molecules pass through the stomach lining to the cells of the stomach, they are converted back to ions by the forward reaction.

In the ionized (acetylsalicylate) form, aspirin cannot pass through the stomach's protective lining. When acetylsalicylate ions remain in the stomach, they come into contact with a high concentration of H_3O^+ ions. The large number of H_3O^+ ions puts a stress on the equilibrium system, increasing the rate of the reverse reaction represented in the equation on the previous page. In the reverse reaction, nonpolar aspirin molecules are formed. These molecules then pass through the protective lining of the stomach and into the cells of the stomach itself. Once in the stomach cells, the H_3O^+ ion concentration is low, causing the forward reaction that produces the acetylsalicylate ions to be favored. These ions cannot pass back into the interior of the stomach, so they are trapped in the stomach cells, where they can cause damage.

One way to reduce the irritating effect of aspirin is to take buffered aspirin, in which aspirin is combined with an added ingredient, such as calcium carbonate. The carbonate ion reduces the amount of H_3O^+ ions within the contents of the stomach by reacting with them to form the bicarbonate ion, HCO_3^-, which reacts with additional H_3O^+ ions to form carbonic acid, H_2CO_3. These reactions are shown by the following equations.

$$H_3O^+(aq) + CO_3^{2-}(aq) \rightleftarrows HCO_3^-(aq) + H_2O(l)$$

$$H_3O^+(aq) + HCO_3^-(aq) \rightleftarrows H_2CO_3(aq) + H_2O(l)$$

Lowering the H_3O^+ ion concentration in the stomach favors the formation of acetylsalicylate ions, which cannot pass through the lining of the stomach. These acetylsalicylate ions pass into the intestines. They are then absorbed through the intestinal walls, limiting their irritating effect on the stomach.

CONCEPT CHECK

1. Name two factors that can disturb an equilibrium system.
2. Why does a pressure increase on a gaseous system at equilibrium favor the reaction that produces fewer gas molecules?
3. Why is removing a product from an equilibrium system as it forms a way to help produce maximum yield of that product?

Complex ion equilibria

Complex ions are composed of a central metal ion bonded to a specific number of other ions or polar molecules. For example, $[Cu(NH_3)_4]^{2+}$, shown in **Figure 14-10,** is a complex ion. Each ammonia molecule, NH_3, furnishes a pair of electrons to form what is called a *coordinate covalent bond* with the central copper ion. The formation of a complex ion generally involves a reversible reaction that reaches equilibrium. Many complex ions have color, and their reactions can be tracked by color changes.

complex ion

an ion having a structure in which a central atom or ion is bonded by coordinate covalent bonds to other ions or molecules

FIGURE 14-10 ▼

In this complex ion, $[Cu(NH_3)_4]^{2+}$, the ammonia molecules are bonded to the central copper ion.

TABLE 14-1 Examples of Complex Ions

Complex ion	Color
$[Co(NH_3)_5Cl]^{2+}$	violet
$[Co(NH_3)_5H_2O]^{3+}$	red
$[Co(NH_3)_6]^{3+}$	yellow-orange
$[Co(CN)_6]^{3-}$	pale yellow
$[Ni(NH_3)_6]^{2+}$	blue-violet
$[Cu(NH_3)_4]^{2+}$	blue-purple
$[Cu(H_2O)_4]^{2+}$	light blue
$[Fe(CN)_6]^{4-}$	yellow
$[Fe(CN)_6]^{3-}$	red
$[Fe(SCN)(H_2O)_5]^{2+}$	deep red
$[Zn(NH_3)_4]^{2+}$	colorless

ligand

a molecule or ion that is bonded to the central atom of a complex ion

In this section, you will see how changing a concentration in a complex-ion equilibrium system also illustrates Le Châtelier's principle.

Complex ion behavior is affected by stresses

In our example, copper is the central metal ion that is bonded to four ammonia molecules. The molecules (or ions) that are bonded to the central metal atom are often referred to as **ligands.** Some common ligands are ions such as Cl^-, F^-, and CN^- and polar molecules such as NH_3 and H_2O. Examples of complex ions are listed in **Table 14-1.**

Figure 14-11 shows two solutions containing complex ions of copper. As the equation beneath the figure shows, the complex ion in the beaker on the left consists of a Cu^{2+} ion bonded to four water molecules. This complex ion produces a light blue color in the solution. When an excess of ammonia solution is added to this light-blue solution, a deep blue-purple color forms, as shown in the beaker on the right. This blue-purple color is characteristic of the $[Cu(NH_3)_4]^{2+}$ complex ion. Ammonia molecules have replaced the water molecules bonded to the copper ion, as shown by the equation.

Complex ions containing transition metals usually have a distinct color that helps to identify which ion is present in higher concentration in the solution. Exceptions are complex ions containing Ag^+, Zn^{2+}, Cd^{2+}, and Hg^{2+}, which are usually colorless. Table 14-1 lists the characteristic colors of some transition metal-complex ions. The reaction that forms complex ions is reversible and eventually reaches equilibrium. However, either the forward or the reverse reaction can be favored, depending on the stress applied. For example, if more NH_3 is added to the light blue solution, the stress causes the forward reaction, which consumes NH_3, to be favored. Thus, the color of the system will change to blue-purple.

$$[Cu(H_2O)_4]^{2+} + 4NH_3 \rightleftarrows [Cu(NH_3)_4]^{2+} + 4H_2O$$

Some other chemical equations representing aqueous equilibrium reactions involving complex ions are shown below.

$$[Zn(H_2O)_4]^{2+} + 4NH_3 \rightleftarrows [Zn(NH_3)_4]^{2+} + 4H_2O$$
Colorless   Colorless

$$[Ni(H_2O)_6]^{2+}(aq) + 6NH_3(aq) \rightleftarrows [Ni(NH_3)_6]^{2+}(aq) + 6H_2O(l)$$
Green   Blue-violet

Practical use of Le Châtelier's principle and complex ions

Have you ever seen a weather indicator that appears blue when the weather is supposed to stay dry and turns pink when it is supposed to rain? This simple little item involves some interesting chemistry. The color changes are shown in **Figure 14-12**. The weather indicator contains a piece of fabric or paper that has absorbed a solution of cobalt(II) chloride, $CoCl_2$. The equation for the reaction involved follows.

$$[CoCl_4]^{2-} + 6H_2O \rightleftarrows [Co(H_2O)_6]^{2+} + 4Cl^-$$
Blue   Pink

Le Châtelier's principle explains these color changes. When the humidity is high, the $[CoCl_4]^{2-}$ reacts with water vapor in the air and forms the pink complex ion that has six water molecules bonded to cobalt, $[Co(H_2O)_6]^{2+}$. When the moisture in the air is low, the reverse reaction is favored, and the blue $[CoCl_4]^{2-}$ forms.

SECTION REVIEW

Total recall

1. Name one reversible reaction you may encounter in your everyday life.

2. In a complex ion, what type of chemical bond is formed between the ligands and the central metal atom?

3. Name one characteristic of complex-ion chemistry that makes some reactions easy to monitor.

Critical thinking

4. When antacid tablets are added to water, a chemical reaction occurs, as evidenced by the production of bubbles. Is this a reaction that goes to completion or one that reaches an equilibrium? Explain your answer.

5. Using the equations for complex ions found on pages 520 and 521, develop a hypothesis about how each system would change under the following conditions.
   a. NH_3 is added to the copper complex-ion system.
   b. $[CoCl_4]^{2-}$ is removed from the cobalt complex-ion system.
   c. Water is added to the zinc complex-ion system.

6. **Story Clue** How would the removal of ammonia as it is made in the Haber process affect the equilibrium?

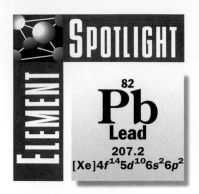
Get the lead out

Humans have known for many centuries that lead is toxic, but lead is still used in many common materials. High levels of lead were used in paints until the 1940s. Since then, the lead compounds in paints have gradually been replaced with less toxic titanium compounds. However, many older buildings still have significant amounts of lead paint, and many also have lead solder in their water pipes.

Lead poisoning is caused by the absorption of lead through the digestive tract, lungs, or skin. Children living in older homes are especially susceptible to lead poisoning. Paint chips that contain lead have a sweet taste that young children like to chew on.

The hazards of lead poisoning can be greatly reduced through programs that increase public awareness, the removal of lead-containing paint from old buildings, and the screening of children for lead exposure.

Lead inside the human body interferes with the production of red blood cells and can cause damage to the kidneys, liver, brain, and other organs.

WHERE IS IT?

Earth's Crust
<0.01% by mass

GET THE LEAD OUT

KEEP YOUR CHILD SAFE FROM LEAD!

Posters such as this one are part of public-awareness programs to reduce the hazards of lead poisoning.

Industrial Uses

▶ The largest industrial use of lead is in the manufacture of storage batteries.

▶ Solder used for joining metals is often an alloy of lead and tin.

▶ Other lead alloys are used to make bearings for gasoline and diesel engines, type metal for printing, corrosion-resistant cable coverings, and ammunition.

▶ Lead sheets and lead bricks are used to shield workers and sensitive objects from X rays.

A BRIEF HISTORY

1977: U.S. government restricts lead content in paint.

3000 B.C.	1000 B.C.	A.D. 1	A.D. 1000

3000 B.C.: Egyptians refine and use lead to make art figurines.

600 B.C.: Lead ore deposits are discovered near Athens; they are mined until the second century A.D.

60 B.C.: Romans begin making lead pipes, lead sheets for waterproofing roofs, and lead crystal.

How is equilibrium measured?

OBJECTIVES
▶ **Write** K_{eq} expressions for reactions in equilibrium.

▶ **Calculate** concentrations of reactants or products in an equilibrium system using K_{eq} values.

▶ **Write** K_{sp} expressions for the solubility of slightly soluble salts.

▶ **Determine** concentrations using K_{sp} expressions.

The equilibrium constant, K_{eq}

Consider the following reaction again.

$$2NO_2(g) \rightleftarrows N_2O_4(g)$$

When the NO_2 is first placed in a container, no N_2O_4 is present. The rate of the reverse reaction is zero. After this first instant, the NO_2 will immediately begin to form N_2O_4. As this reaction proceeds, there is less NO_2 present, and therefore the rate of the forward reaction gradually decreases. As more N_2O_4 is formed, the collisions between these molecules increase. These collisions can cause NO_2 to re-form. The rate of the reverse reaction increases. Eventually the rates of the forward and reverse reactions are equal, and equilibrium is reached.

In systems at equilibrium, the reactants continue to form the products, and the products react to re-form the reactants at the same rate. Consequently, the equilibrium concentrations of reactants and products remain constant.

FIGURE 14-13 ◀

The creation of stalactites and stalagmites is a result of a reversible chemical reaction.

K_{eq} quantitatively describes the equilibrium state

When working with equilibrium systems, you can make calculations involving the concentrations of the products and the reactants. When a system has reached equilibrium, the relationship between the concentrations of reactants and products can be expressed mathematically. The mathematical product of the concentrations of the products, raised to an appropriate power, divided by the mathematical product of the concentrations of the reactants, raised to an appropriate power, is a constant called the **equilibrium constant, K_{eq}.** For the NO_2/N_2O_4 equilibrium system, the equilibrium-constant expression is written as follows.

equilibrium constant

for a reversible reaction in equilibrium, an expression that relates the concentrations of the reactants and products at a specific temperature to a constant

$$K_{eq} = \frac{[N_2O_4]}{[NO_2]^2}$$

Each formula in brackets represents the concentration of that substance in mol/L at equilibrium. Each concentration is raised to a power equal to its coefficient in the balanced chemical equation for that reaction. In the example shown, the concentration of NO_2 is squared because the coefficient of NO_2 is 2 in the balanced equation.

Now consider the following equilibrium expressions for the condensation of water vapor and the decomposition of calcium carbonate.

$$H_2O(g) \rightleftarrows H_2O(l)$$
$$CaCO_3(s) \rightleftarrows CaO(s) + CO_2(g)$$

The first equation contains a pure liquid, $H_2O(l)$, and the second contains two pure solids, $CaCO_3(s)$ and $CaO(s)$. Because the concentrations of pure liquids and solids do not change to any measurable extent, they can be considered constant. As constants, the concentrations of pure liquids and solids are not included in equilibrium-constant expressions. The K_{eq} expressions for the two equations shown above are written as follows.

$$K_{eq} = 1/[H_2O(g)]$$
$$K_{eq} = [CO_2(g)]$$

QUICKLAB

CONSUMER ACTIVITY

Finding Equilibrium

Equilibrium reactions do not start out at equilibrium. Instead, they begin with more reactants than products and eventually reach a state of equilibrium, where the amount of products and reactants remains constant. In this activity, you will see firsthand how a process reaches equilibrium and how changing conditions will affect the forward and reverse reactions.

Materials 2 (5 gal) aquariums, water, 2 sets of measuring cups

Procedure Label one aquarium "Products" and the other one "Reactants." Fill the reactants aquarium full of water, but leave the products aquarium empty for now. One student should be in charge of reactants and one in charge of products. Give each student a 1-cup measuring cup. They should begin to dip into their aquarium and pour the contents into the other's aquarium. Make sure they dip and pour at the same rate. What happens to the amount of reactants? What happens to the amount of products? Revise the procedure to favor the forward reaction.

Analysis 1. Does the system reach a state of equilibrium?
2. Which variables could you change to favor the reverse reaction?

Determining K_{eq} for reactions at equilibrium

The actual value for a particular K_{eq} must be determined experimentally. Once the system has reached equilibrium, the chemist must sample the reactants and products, analyze them, and calculate the concentrations of all substances involved in the reaction. When determining the K_{eq} value for a particular reaction, the temperature under which the concentrations are measured must be specified. The value of the equilibrium constant for a specific reaction is dependent on the temperature of that system. **Table 14-2** lists values for equilibrium constants for some representative reactions. You can see that the same reaction has different K_{eq} values at different temperatures. As temperature increases, K_{eq} increases for endothermic reactions and decreases for exothermic reactions.

The equilibrium constant can be calculated when all the concentrations of reactants and products are known. Just as with all mathematical expressions, the equilibrium-constant expression can be used to solve for an unknown quantity. Specifically, an unknown concentration can be calculated if the K_{eq} and all but one of the concentration values are known. Do not assume that pure solids and pure liquids are not important to equilibrium systems because they do not appear in the equilibrium expression. These substances are just as essential to establishing equilibrium as the other substances in the reaction, but you do not need to know their concentrations when calculating K_{eq}.

TABLE 14-2	**Equilibrium Constants**

Equation	K_{eq} value	Temperature (°C)
$2NO_2(g) \rightleftharpoons N_2O_4(g)$	1250	0
	165	25
	22.6	55
	2.0	100
$CO_2(g) + H_2(g) \rightleftharpoons CO(g) + H_2O(g)$	2.2	1400
	4.6	2000
$N_2(g) + O_2(g) \rightleftharpoons 2NO(g)$	4.5×10^{-31}	25
	6.7×10^{-10}	627
	1.65×10^{-3}	2027
$H_2(g) + I_2(g) \rightleftharpoons 2HI(g)$	113	250
	57	427
	18	1127
$N_2(g) + 3H_2(g) \rightleftharpoons 2NH_3(g)$	3.3×10^8	25
	1.7×10^2	227
	4.2	327
	0.29	427
	3.8×10^{-2}	527

At a temperature of 25°C, the following concentrations (in mol/L) of the reactants and products for the reaction involving carbonic acid and water are present.

$[H_2CO_3] = 3.3 \times 10^{-2}$ M, $[H_3O^+] = 1.19 \times 10^{-4}$ M, and $[HCO_3^-] = 1.19 \times 10^{-4}$ M

What is the K_{eq} value for the following reaction at equilibrium in a dilute aqueous solution?

$$H_2CO_3(aq) + H_2O(l) \rightleftarrows H_3O^+(aq) + HCO_3^-(aq)$$

1 **List what you know**
- $[H_2CO_3] = 3.3 \times 10^{-2}$ M
- $[H_3O^+] = 1.19 \times 10^{-4}$ M
- $[HCO_3^-] = 1.19 \times 10^{-4}$ M
- The $[H_2O]$ will not be included in the calculation because it is considered to be constant in this dilute solution.
- $K_{eq} = ?$

2 **Set up the problem**
- Write the K_{eq} expression for this reaction.

$$K_{eq} = \frac{[H_3O^+][HCO_3^-]}{[H_2CO_3]}$$

- Substitute the given values into the expression.

$$K_{eq} = \frac{(1.19 \times 10^{-4})^2}{(3.3 \times 10^{-2})}$$

3 **Calculate**

$$K_{eq} = \frac{(1.19 \times 10^{-4})^2}{(3.3 \times 10^{-2})} = 4.3 \times 10^{-7}$$

PRACTICE PROBLEMS

1. For the following reaction, equilibrium is established at a certain temperature when the following concentrations (in mol/L) are present: $[CO_2] = 0.012$ M, $[H_2] = 0.014$ M, $[CO] = 0.019$ M, and $[H_2O] = 0.019$ M. Calculate the K_{eq} value for this reaction. Note that the $[H_2O]$ must be included because it is a gas in this reaction.

$$CO_2(g) + H_2(g) \rightleftarrows CO(g) + H_2O(g)$$

2. For the system involving N_2O_4 and NO_2 at equilibrium at a temperature of 100°C, the concentration of N_2O_4 is 4.0×10^{-2} mol/L, and the concentration of NO_2 is 1.4×10^{-1} mol/L. What is the K_{eq} value for the reaction to form N_2O_4?

3. An equilibrium mixture at 852 K is found to contain 3.61×10^{-3} mol/L of SO_2, 6.11×10^{-4} mol/L of O_2, and 1.01×10^{-2} mol/L of SO_3. Calculate the equilibrium constant, K_{eq}, for the following reaction.

$$2SO_2(g) + O_2(g) \rightleftarrows 2SO_3(g)$$

SAMPLE PROBLEM 14B Calculating concentrations using the equilibrium constant

Ammonia gas is soluble in water. An aqueous solution of ammonia is known as ammonium hydroxide. The equilibrium existing in this solution can be represented by the following equation.

$$NH_3(aq) + H_2O(l) \rightleftharpoons NH_4^+(aq) + OH^-(aq)$$

K_{eq} for this reaction equals 1.8×10^{-5} at a temperature of 298 K. The equilibrium concentration of NH_3 is 6.82×10^{-3} M, and the equation shows that the equilibrium concentration of NH_4^+ equals the equilibrium concentration of OH^-. Calculate the concentration of the ammonium ion at equilibrium.

1 List what you know

- $K_{eq} = 1.8 \times 10^{-5}$
- $[NH_3] = 6.82 \times 10^{-3}$ M
- The $[H_2O]$ is not included in the K_{eq} expression because as a pure liquid, it is considered to be constant.
- $[NH_4^+] = [OH^-] = ?$ M

2 Set up the problem

- Write the K_{eq} expression for this reaction.

$$K_{eq} = \frac{[NH_4^+][OH^-]}{[NH_3]}$$

- Substitute the known values into the expression.

$$1.8 \times 10^{-5} = \frac{[NH_4^+][OH^-]}{(6.82 \times 10^{-3})}$$

- Solve for $[NH_4^+][OH^-]$.

$$[NH_4^+][OH^-] = (1.8 \times 10^{-5})(6.82 \times 10^{-3})$$

3 Calculate

$$[NH_4^+][OH^-] = (1.8 \times 10^{-5})(6.82 \times 10^{-3}) = 1.2 \times 10^{-7}\ M^2$$

- Because $[NH_4^+] = [OH^-]$, you can think of this calculation as $(x)(x) = x^2$.
- The concentration of the ammonium ion, $[NH_4^+]$, is found by taking the square root of $1.2 \times 10^{-7}\ M^2$.

$$[NH_4^+]^2 = 1.2 \times 10^{-7}\ M$$

$$[NH_4^+] = 3.5 \times 10^{-4}\ M$$

PRACTICE PROBLEMS

1. In the presence of a catalyst, methanol, CH_3OH, can be prepared by the reaction of H_2 and CO at high temperatures according to the following equation.

$$CO(g) + 2H_2(g) \rightleftharpoons CH_3OH(g)$$

What is the concentration of $CH_3OH(g)$ in mol/L if $[H_2] = 0.080$ M, $[CO] = 0.025$ M, and $K_{eq} = 290$ at 700 K?

2. Using a K_{eq} value of 1.65×10^{-3} at 2027°C for the reaction below, what is the equilibrium concentration of nitrogen monoxide, NO, when the concentrations of nitrogen and oxygen at equilibrium are 1.8×10^{-3} mol/L and 4.2×10^{-4} mol/L, respectively?

$$N_2(g) + O_2(g) \rightleftarrows 2NO(g)$$

3. The following equation shows the equilibrium reaction between sulfur dioxide and oxygen.

$$2SO_2(g) + O_2(g) \rightleftarrows 2SO_3(g)$$

At 600°C, the K_{eq} for this reaction is 4.32 when $[SO_3] = 0.260$ mol/L and $[O_2] = 0.045$ mol/L. Calculate the equilibrium concentration for SO_2.

The value of K_{eq} can be used to make predictions about equilibrium systems

Now that you know how to calculate K_{eq}, what kind of information does that value provide? If K_{eq} has a value close to 1, the products of the concentrations (raised to the appropriate power) in the numerator and the denominator are approximately equal. Therefore, if K_{eq} is approximately equal to 1, there are roughly equal concentrations of reactants and products at equilibrium.

In reactions that have a K_{eq} value much larger than 1, the original reactants are largely converted to products, and the concentration at equilibrium of products will be greater than the concentration of reactants. For reactions that have a K_{eq} value much smaller than 1, the forward reaction occurs only to a very small extent before equilibrium is established. The reverse reaction is favored, resulting in a larger concentration of reactants than products at equilibrium. By knowing the value of K_{eq} for a specific reaction, you can estimate whether reactants or products will be more abundant at equilibrium. In addition, by using known values of K_{eq}, you can make calculations and predictions about equilibrium systems, as you saw in the previous practice problems.

CONCEPT CHECK

1. What does K_{eq}, the equilibrium constant, tell you about a system at equilibrium?

2. Is the value of K_{eq} dependent on the temperature or the pressure of the system at equilibrium?

3. Can the same reaction have different K_{eq} values? Why or why not?

4. Why is the value of K_{eq} for a particular reaction calculated using concentrations from experimental data?

5. What does a chemical formula in brackets, such as $[N_2O_4]$, represent?

The solubility product constant, K_{sp}

K_{sp} is a special equilibrium constant for very slightly soluble ionic substances

Recall from Chapter 13 that solubility refers to the maximum amount of a solute that will dissolve per unit volume of a solvent to produce a saturated solution. In Chapter 13, solubility was expressed in units of grams of solute per 100 g of water. Solubility can also be expressed as concentration in moles of solute per liter of solution (mol/L). As you will see in this section, solubility is related to the equilibrium-constant expression for the process of dissolution.

In Section 14-1 you learned about reactions going to completion. There are two ways of looking at these reactions. Consider the following reaction, also shown in Figure 14-1, on page 512.

$$Na^+(aq) + Cl^-(aq) + Ag^+(aq) + NO_3^-(aq) \longrightarrow AgCl(s) + Na^+(aq) + NO_3^-(aq)$$

The precipitation of AgCl goes nearly to completion, but virtually no reaction goes entirely to completion. In the reaction represented above, a very low concentration of Ag^+ and Cl^- ions still exists in the solution. This concentration of ions in solution represents the solubility of AgCl at the given temperature. AgCl is considered an insoluble salt. Actually, most salts described as insoluble will dissolve to some extent in water and are more accurately described as being *very slightly soluble*. In such cases, an extremely small concentration of the salt saturates the solution, usually less than 0.01 M.

An example of a slightly soluble salt is barium sulfate, $BaSO_4$. The equation representing the dissociation of this salt in aqueous equilibrium follows.

$$BaSO_4(s) \rightleftharpoons Ba^{2+}(aq) + SO_4^{2-}(aq)$$

The concentration of $BaSO_4$ in the solid state is a constant and does not need to be included in the equilibrium expression. The K_{eq} expression for this reaction is written as follows.

$$K_{eq} = [Ba^{2+}][SO_4^{2-}]$$

The equilibrium expression above can also be thought of as governing the solubility of $BaSO_4(s)$ in water. When dealing with solubilities of slightly soluble salts, a new constant called the **solubility product constant, K_{sp},** is used. The K_{sp} expression for the dissociation of $BaSO_4$ follows.

$$K_{sp} = [Ba^{2+}][SO_4^{2-}]$$

The solubility product constant of a salt is the product of the equilibrium concentrations of its ions, each raised to a power equal to its coefficient in the balanced chemical equation.

Recall that the concentration of any pure solid or liquid substance is a constant.

solubility product constant

the equilibrium constant for a slightly soluble ionic solid in equilibrium with its ions in a saturated solution

FIGURE 14-14 ▼

Seashells are made mostly of calcium carbonate, which is considered to be insoluble in sea water. The shells' composition keeps them from dissolving noticeably in water.

Therefore, a solubility-product-constant expression contains only concentrations of ions formed during the solution process. Only substances that can change concentration, such as gases or substances in solution (solutes), are included in equilibrium expressions.

Each ion concentration is raised to the power equal to its coefficient in the balanced chemical equation

Just as in writing equilibrium constants, the concentration of each ion in a K_{sp} expression is raised to the power corresponding to its coefficient in the balanced chemical equation. Here are some examples.

$$Fe(OH)_3(s) \rightleftarrows Fe^{3+}(aq) + 3OH^-(aq)$$

$$K_{sp} = [Fe^{3+}] [OH^-]^3$$

$$Ca_3(PO_4)_2(s) \rightleftarrows 3Ca^{2+}(aq) + 2PO_4^{3-}(aq)$$

$$K_{sp} = [Ca^{2+}]^3 [PO_4^{3-}]^2$$

Table 14-3 gives K_{sp} values for several slightly soluble salts at 25°C. These K_{sp} values apply only in dilute solutions. When the concentration of any ion (whether involved in the equilibrium reaction or not) is greater than about 0.1 M, the electrical attractions between positive and negative ions disturb the equilibrium, and the K_{sp} values for these systems do not apply. That is one reason why K_{sp} values are seldom given to more than two significant figures.

TABLE 14-3 Solubility Product Constants at 25°C

Salt	K_{sp}	Salt	K_{sp}
Ag_2CO_3	8.4×10^{-12}	CuS	1.3×10^{-36}
Ag_2CrO_4	1.1×10^{-12}	$Fe(OH)_3$	2.6×10^{-39}
Ag_2S	1.1×10^{-49}	FeS	1.6×10^{-19}
AgBr	5.4×10^{-13}	$MgCO_3$	6.8×10^{-6}
AgCl	1.8×10^{-10}	$MnCO_3$	2.2×10^{-11}
AgI	8.5×10^{-17}	PbS	9.0×10^{-29}
$Al(OH)_3$	2.0×10^{-31}	$PbSO_4$	1.8×10^{-8}
$BaSO_4$	1.1×10^{-10}	$SrSO_4$	3.4×10^{-7}
$Ca_3(PO_4)_2$	2.1×10^{-33}	$ZnCO_3$	1.2×10^{-10}
$CaSO_4$	7.1×10^{-5}	ZnS	2.9×10^{-25}

SAMPLE PROBLEM 14C   Calculating K_{sp} from solubility

Consider the dissociation of the salt CaF_2 in water.

$$CaF_2(s) \rightleftarrows Ca^{2+}(aq) + 2F^-(aq)$$

Most parts of the oceans are nearly saturated with CaF_2. In a region where evaporation raises the concentration of dissolved materials, the mineral fluorite, CaF_2, may precipitate. A saturated solution of CaF_2 at 25°C is 3.4×10^{-4} M. Calculate the solubility product constant for CaF_2.

1 **List what you know**
- Saturated CaF_2 is 3.4×10^{-4} M.
- The balanced chemical equation is $CaF_2(s) \rightleftarrows Ca^{2+}(aq) + 2F^-(aq)$
- $K_{sp} = ?$

2 **Set up the problem**

▶ Write the K_{sp} expression for the reaction.

$$K_{sp} = [Ca^{2+}][F^-]^2$$

▶ 3.4×10^{-4} mol of CaF_2 dissolves in each liter of solution. Using the mole ratio from the balanced chemical equation, you know that each liter of the solution contains 3.4×10^{-4} mol of Ca^{2+} and $2(3.4 \times 10^{-4})$, or 6.8×10^{-4}, mol of F^-.

▶ Substitute these concentration values raised to the correct power in the K_{sp} expression.

$$K_{sp} = (3.4 \times 10^{-4})(6.8 \times 10^{-4})^2$$

3 **Calculate**

▶ Solve the expression for K_{sp}.

$$K_{sp} = (3.4 \times 10^{-4})(6.8 \times 10^{-4})^2 = 1.57216 \times 10^{-10}$$

▶ Round to two significant figures.

$$K_{sp} = 1.6 \times 10^{-10}$$

SAMPLE PROBLEM 14D   **Calculating concentrations using K_{sp}**

At a temperature of 298 K, the concentration of Ca^{2+} in a given saturated solution of CaF_2 is 2.2×10^{-4} M and the K_{sp} for CaF_2 is 1.6×10^{-10}. Calculate the concentration of F^- in the solution.

1 **List what you know**

▶ $[Ca^{2+}] = 2.2 \times 10^{-4}$ M
▶ $K_{sp} = 1.6 \times 10^{-10}$
▶ $[F^-] = ?$ M

2 **Set up the problem**

▶ Write the K_{sp} expression for the dissociation process.

$$K_{sp} = [Ca^{2+}][F^-]^2$$

▶ Substitute the known values into this expression.

$$1.6 \times 10^{-10} = (2.2 \times 10^{-4})[F^-]^2$$

▶ Rearrange to solve for $[F^-]^2$.

$$[F^-]^2 = \frac{1.6 \times 10^{-10}}{(2.2 \times 10^{-4})} = 7.27 \times 10^{-7} \ M^2$$

3 **Calculate**

▶ Solve for $[F^-]$ by determining the square root of the above result on your calculator.

$$[F^-] = \sqrt{7.27 \times 10^{-7} \ M^2} = 8.5264295 \times 10^{-4} \ M \ \text{(calculator answer)}$$

▶ Round the final calculator answer to two significant figures.

$$[F^-] = 8.5 \times 10^{-4} \ M$$

1. What is the K_{sp} value for $Ca_3(PO_4)_2$ at 298 K if the concentrations in an aqueous solution at equilibrium with excess solid are determined to be 3.42×10^{-7} M for Ca^{2+} ions and 2.28×10^{-7} M for PO_4^{3-} ions?

2. The K_{sp} value for silver carbonate is 8.4×10^{-12} at 298 K. The concentration of carbonate ions in a saturated solution is 1.28×10^{-4} M. What is the concentration of silver ions?

3. Copper(I) bromide is dissolved in water to saturation at 25°C. The concentration of Cu^+ ions in solution is 7.9×10^{-5} mol/L. Calculate the K_{sp} for copper(I) bromide at this temperature.

4. Calculate the concentration of Pb^{2+} ions in solution when $PbCl_2$ is dissolved in water. The concentration of Cl^- ions in this solution is found to be 2.86×10^{-2} mol/L. At 25°C, the K_{sp} of $PbCl_2$ is 1.17×10^{-5}.

5. What mass of Ag^+ ions will be present in 2.0 L of a saturated solution of AgCl at 25°C? (Hint: Using Table 14-3 on page 530, first calculate the concentration of Ag^+ ions that will be present in this solution.)

6. What is the concentration of Cu^+ ions in a saturated solution of copper(I) chloride, given that the K_{sp} of CuCl is 1.72×10^{-7} at 25°C?

internet**connect**

*SCi*LINKS.

NSTA

TOPIC: Common ion effect
GO TO: www.scilinks.org
KEYWORD: HW143

▼ **FIGURE 14-15**

The light areas on this X ray of the digestive tract show the insoluble barium sulfate.

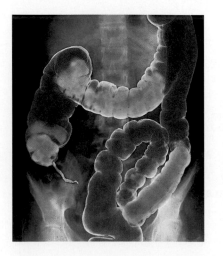

Common ion effect
Practical uses of equilibrium constants and the common ion effect

Barium sulfate, $BaSO_4$, is usually called an insoluble salt, which means that only an extremely small portion of it will dissolve in water. Doctors use $BaSO_4$ as an X-ray contrast medium. (The heavy barium atom absorbs X rays more readily than other atoms present.) The patient ingests solid $BaSO_4$ powder that is suspended in water. The $BaSO_4$ will appear as light areas on the X-ray film. By studying these light areas, like those shown in **Figure 14-15**, doctors can diagnose problems in the patient's digestive tract. Doctors must make sure that almost no Ba^{2+} ions are present to dissolve in the patient's body fluids because Ba^{2+} ions are poisonous. To ensure that the concentration of Ba^{2+} ions will not exceed the safety level, a soluble salt, such as Na_2SO_4, which also contributes SO_4^{2-} ions in solution, is added to increase the SO_4^{2-} ion concentration and to reduce the Ba^{2+} ion concentration.

Na_2SO_4 dissociates, as shown by the following equation.

$$Na_2SO_4(s) \longrightarrow 2Na^+(aq) + SO_4^{2-}(aq)$$

Dissolving the Na_2SO_4 increases the concentration of SO_4^{2-} ions in the solution. These SO_4^{2-} ions affect the chemical reaction involving the dissociation of $BaSO_4$. Consider the following equation.

$$BaSO_4(s) \rightleftharpoons Ba^{2+}(aq) + SO_4^{2-}(aq)$$

As $[SO_4^{2-}]$ increases, $[Ba^{2+}]$ must decrease in order to keep the K_{sp} constant. Some Ba^{2+} reacts with some of the added SO_4^{2-}, re-forming solid $BaSO_4$. This precipitation of some $BaSO_4$ causes a lower concentration of Ba^{2+} ions in the solution. Adding the Na_2SO_4 has the effect of reducing the concentration of Ba^{2+} ions in the solution. Because SO_4^{2-} ions are present in both $BaSO_4$ and Na_2SO_4, sulfate is referred to as the **common ion.**

The displacement of an ionic equilibrium caused by the presence of more than one source for a reactant or product ion is called the **common ion effect.** Remember from Le Châtelier's principle that changing the concentration of any of the ions involved in the reaction can have an effect on the equilibrium of the system. When Na_2SO_4 is added to the saturated solution of $BaSO_4$, a stress is put on the system. The increase in the concentration of SO_4^{2-} ions in the solution disturbs the equilibrium and favors the reverse reaction. Less $BaSO_4$ dissolves in the presence of the common ion, thereby causing a decrease in the Ba^{2+} ion concentration in the solution.

common ion

an ion that is present in two or more substances involved in an ionic chemical equilibrium

common ion effect

the reduction in the solubility of an ionic compound by the addition of a soluble compound that provides an ion in common with it

$\mathcal{S}$ECTION REVIEW

Total recall

1. What information does the K_{eq} value for a reaction provide?

2. Why are pure liquids and pure solids not included in equilibrium-constant expressions?

Critical thinking

3. Write the K_{eq} expression for each of the following reactions:
   a. silver chloride in an aqueous solution
   b. silver chromate in an aqueous solution
   c. calcium phosphate in an aqueous solution

4. Write the solubility product expression for the slightly soluble compound aluminum hydroxide, $Al(OH)_3$.

5. The K_{sp} of PbS is 9.0×10^{-29}; that of $Ca_3(PO_4)_2$ is smaller, 2.1×10^{-33}. Yet PbS is much less soluble. Explain why this is not a contradiction.

Practice problems

6. Given that the K_{sp} value of CuS is 1.3×10^{-36}, what is the concentration of Cu^{2+} ions in a saturated solution?

7. For the reaction $H_2(g) + I_2(g) \rightleftharpoons 2HI(g)$ at 425°C, calculate [HI], given $[H_2] = [I_2] = 4.79 \times 10^{-4}$ M and $K_{eq} = 54.3$.

8. Carbon reacts with carbon dioxide to produce carbon monoxide and reaches equilibrium, as shown by the following equation.

$$C(s) + CO_2(g) \rightleftharpoons 2\,CO(g)$$

At equilibrium, a 2.0 L reaction vessel is found to contain 0.40 mol C, 0.20 mol CO_2, and 0.10 mol CO. Determine the K_{eq} for this reaction. Be sure to express the concentrations as mol/L.

At the beginning of this chapter you learned that before World War I, nitric acid was made by a reaction involving sodium nitrate. Nitric acid was the principal ingredient in the reaction that produces explosives. By 1913, the work of Fritz Haber and Carl Bosch made it possible to produce ammonia on an industrial scale. The ammonia could then be used in the production of nitric acid for use in fertilizer and explosives.

Today ammonia is produced on an industrial scale in plants like this one.

LOOKING BACK

How would increasing the pressure of the reaction to produce ammonia affect the ammonia yield?

Before Germany could produce enough nitric acid to fulfill its needs, much research had to be done. First, Haber learned that the mixing of nitrogen and hydrogen to yield ammonia had to be done under high pressure. An increase in pressure would favor the reaction that produces the fewest number of gas molecules, in this case the forward reaction and the product ammonia. For commercial production today, the reaction is carried out at pressures ranging from 200 to 400 atm.

$$N_2(g) + 3H_2(g) \longrightarrow 2NH_3(g)$$

How would increasing the reaction temperature affect the amount of ammonia produced in this exothermic reaction?

Haber discovered that the reaction temperature had to be high in order for the reaction to progress at a reasonable speed. However, the production of ammonia is exothermic, so raising the temperature favors the reverse reaction, decreasing the ammonia yield. More experiments were needed to find the minimum temperature that would give a speedy reaction and produce sufficient amounts of ammonia.

Bosch discovered that a catalyst containing a mixture of iron(II) and iron(III) oxide called magnetic iron oxide, Fe_3O_4, enabled the reaction to be carried out at a lower temperature than would otherwise be practical, at temperatures ranging from 400°C to 650°C. Removing the ammonia from the batch as soon as it is formed is another way of manipulating the equilibrium system to favor the forward reaction.

In 1918, Fritz Haber received a Nobel Prize in chemistry for his invention of the process for synthesizing ammonia, a discovery that increased food production but also prolonged the war. The Nobel Prizes were established through a will set up by Alfred Nobel, a Swedish chemist who had become wealthy from his discovery of dynamite. Nobel later developed strong misgivings about the possible uses of his discovery, and the Nobel Prizes were his contribution to the welfare of mankind.

KEY TERMS

14-1

complex ion
Le Châtelier's principle
ligand

14-2

common ion
common ion effect
equilibrium constant
solubility product
    constant

KEY CONCEPTS

14-1 What is an equilibrium system?

▶ Reactions that go to completion or nearly to completion include those whose products include such substances as a precipitate or a gas.

▶ Reactions that are reversible can re-form the reactants. When the forward and reverse reactions occur at equal rates, the reaction is at equilibrium.

▶ A system stays at equilibrium until conditions change. Le Châtelier's principle describes how stress—changes in temperature, pressure, and concentration—can favor the forward or reverse reaction of the equilibrium system.

▶ At equilibrium, the individual concentrations of the reactants and products undergo no further changes as long as all reaction conditions remain the same.

▶ A chemical equilibrium system is a dynamic system, not a static one.

▶ The formation of a complex ion generally involves a reversible reaction. Many complex ions containing transition metals form colorful compounds.

14-2 How is equilibrium measured?

▶ The equilibrium constant, K_{eq}, is a value that expresses the relationship between the concentrations of substances present at equilibrium in a reversible reaction at a given temperature.

▶ The solubility product constant, K_{sp}, is the equilibrium constant for a slightly soluble solid in equilibrium with its ions in a saturated solution.

▶ Adding a common ion to a solution displaces the ionic equilibrium of the system and can cause the forward or reverse reaction to be favored.

▶ The concentrations of pure liquids and solids do not change and therefore can be considered constant. As constants, these concentrations are not included in equilibrium constant expressions.

▶ The value of K_{eq} for a given equilibrium system can be used to determine whether the formation of products or reactants will be favored.

▶ K_{sp} values apply only in dilute solutions. When the concentration of any ion is greater than approximately 0.1 M, the attraction between positive and negative ions disturbs the equilibrium.

KEY SKILLS

Review the following models before your exam. Be sure you can solve these types of problems.

Sample Problem 14A: Calculating K_{eq} from equilibrium concentrations (p. 526)

Sample Problem 14B: Calculating concentrations using the equilibrium constant (p. 527)

Sample Problem 14C: Calculating K_{sp} from solubility (p. 530)

Sample Problem 14D: Calculating concentrations using K_{sp} (p. 531)

REVIEW & ASSESS

TERM REVIEW

1. At equilibrium, when there are roughly equal concentrations of reactants and products, K_{eq} will be close to ——.
   (one, zero)

2. Ions or molecules that are bonded to a central metal atom are referred to as ——.
   (ligands, common ions)

3. The sulfate ion, SO_4^{2-}, present in a solution of $BaSO_4$ and Na_2SO_4 is called the ——.
   (complex ion, common ion)

4. The mathematical representation of the solubility of a compound in solution is the ——.
   (solubility product constant, equilibrium constant)

5. One example of a stress on an equilibrium system as defined by Le Châtelier is ——.
   (an increase in pressure, an increase in solubility)

6. The cruise control on a car is an example of a —— process.
   (dynamic, static)

CONCEPT & SKILLS REVIEW

SOLUTIONS IN EQUILIBRIUM

1. Use **Figure 14-3** to answer the following questions:
   a. What is happening to the rate of formation of H_2O before the system reaches equilibrium?
   b. When is the rate of the forward reaction the greatest?

2. Draw two diagrams that depict the difference between the microscopic and macroscopic events that occur when a reaction is at equilibrium.

3. Identify the ligands in the following complex ions:

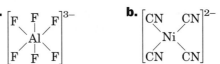

4. A home economics teacher instructs students to add several teaspoons of sugar to their homemade lemonade and then stir until the sugar stops dissolving. Is this instruction chemically correct? Explain.

5. Ethyl acetate, $CH_3COOC_2H_5(l)$, is used to make artificial silk and is prepared by reacting acetic acid, $CH_3COOH(l)$, and ethanol, $C_2H_5OH(l)$. Water is also produced in this reaction.
   a. Write the balanced equation for this reaction.
   b. If the production of ethyl acetate is not sufficient, what would increase the yield?
   c. Why is it a good idea to remove ethyl acetate as it forms?

6. Carbonated beverages contain carbonic acid in solution. The reaction that occurs upon opening the bottle is represented by the following equation:

$$H_2CO_3(aq) \rightleftharpoons H_2O(l) + CO_2(g)$$

What changes in conditions would cause the forward reaction to be favored?

EQUILIBRIUM CONSTANTS

7. Although the K_{eq} value is known as the equilibrium constant, **Table 14-2** shows that one reaction can have several different K_{eq} values. Why is it still called a constant?

8. Predict the approximate relative concentration(s) of the reactant and the products in the decomposition reaction of phosphorus pentachloride if K_{eq} is ——.
   a. much larger than 1   c. equal to 1
   b. much smaller than 1

$$PCl_5(g) \rightleftharpoons PCl_3(g) + Cl_2(g)$$

9. Use **Table 14-2** to determine whether the following equations favor the forward or the reverse reaction at the given temperature:
   a. $2HI(g) \rightleftarrows H_2(g) + I_2(g)$ at 250°C
   b. $N_2(g) + O_2(g) \rightleftarrows 2NO(g)$ at 25°C
   c. $N_2(g) + 3H_2(g) \rightleftarrows 2NH_3(g)$ at 25°C
   d. $N_2(g) + 3H_2(g) \rightleftarrows 2NH_3(g)$ at 527°C
   e. $N_2O_4(g) \rightleftarrows 2NO_2(g)$ at 55°C

10. Write equilibrium constant expressions for the following reactions:
    a. $2NO_2(g) \rightleftarrows N_2O_4(g)$
    b. $CO(g) + Cl_2(g) \rightleftarrows COCl_2(g)$
    c. $AgCl(s) \rightleftarrows Ag^+(aq) + Cl^-(aq)$
    d. $CH_3COOH(aq) + H_2O(l) \rightleftarrows H_3O^+(aq) + CH_3COO^-(aq)$

11. Relate Le Châtelier's principle to the common ion effect.

Practice Problems

12. Vinegar—a solution of acetic acid, CH_3COOH, and water—is used in varying concentrations for different household tasks.

    $CH_3COOH(aq) + H_2O(l) \rightleftarrows$
    $\qquad\qquad H_3O^+(aq) + CH_3COO^-(aq)$

    If the concentration of the acetic acid solution at equilibrium is 3.00 M and the $[H_3O^+] = [CH_3COO^-] = 7.22 \times 10^{-3}$ M, what is the K_{eq} value for acetic acid? **(Hint: See Sample Problem 14A.)**

13. Aniline, $C_6H_5NH_2$, is a weak base. If the concentration of aniline is 0.0600 M at equilibrium and the $[C_6H_5NH_3^+] = [OH^-] = 5.08 \times 10^{-6}$ M, what is the K_{eq} value for aniline? **(Hint: See Sample Problem 14A.)**

    $C_6H_5NH_2(l) + H_2O(l) \rightleftarrows$
    $\qquad\qquad C_6H_5NH_3^+(aq) + OH^-(aq)$

14. Phenol, C_6H_5OH, is used as a disinfectant in many household cleaning solutions. If the equilibrium concentration of phenol is 1.61×10^{-3} M, what are the concentrations of H_3O^+ and $C_6H_5O^-$? K_{eq} for phenol is 1.60×10^{-10} at 25°C. **(Hint: See Sample Problem 14B.)**

15. Benzoic acid, C_6H_5COOH, is a slightly soluble acid used in food preservation. K_{eq} for benzoic acid is 6.30×10^{-5} at 25°C. For a solution of benzoic acid that has an equilibrium concentration of 0.0200 M, what are the concentrations of H_3O^+ and $C_6H_5COO^-$? **(Hint: See Sample Problem 14B.)**

16. The solubility of cobalt(II) sulfide, CoS, is 1.7×10^{-13} M. Calculate the solubility product constant for CoS. **(Hint: See Sample Problem 14C.)**

17. What is the solubility product constant for copper(I) sulfide, Cu_2S, given that its solubility is 8.5×10^{-17} M? **(Hint: See Sample Problem 14C.)**

18. Aluminum hydroxide, $Al(OH)_3$, is used to waterproof fabrics. If the OH^- concentration is 2.8×10^{-8} M, what is the concentration of Al^{3+}? See Table 14-3 for the K_{sp} of $Al(OH)_3$. **(Hint: See Sample Problem 14D.)**

19. Silver sulfide, Ag_2S, is an ingredient used to make ceramics. If the Ag_2S in your dog's ceramic water dish dissolves in the water, giving an Ag^+ concentration of 4.93×10^{-17} M, what concentration of S^{2-} will be in your dog's water? See Table 14-3 for the K_{sp} of Ag_2S. **(Hint: See Sample Problem 14D.)**

20. What is the concentration of F^- ions in a saturated solution that is 0.10 M in Ca^{2+}? The K_{sp} of CaF_2 is 1.6×10^{-10}.

21. Silver bromide, AgBr, is used to make photographic black-and-white film. Calculate the concentration of Ag^+ and Br^- ions in a saturated solution at 25°C.

22. Write K_{eq} expressions for the following reactions:
    a. $4H_3O^+(aq) + 2Cl^-(aq) + MnO_2(s) \rightleftarrows$
    $\qquad\qquad Mn^{2+}(aq) + 6H_2O(l) + Cl_2(g)$
    b. $As_4O_6(s) + 6H_2O(l) \rightleftarrows 4H_3AsO_3(aq)$

23. The following equation shows an equilibrium reaction between hydrogen and carbon dioxide.

$$H_2(g) + CO_2(g) \rightleftharpoons H_2O(g) + CO(g)$$

At 986°C, the following data were obtained at equilibrium in a 2.0 L reaction vessel.

Substance	Number of moles
H_2	0.4693
CO_2	0.0715
H_2O	0.2296
CO	0.2296

Calculate the K_{eq} for this reaction.

24. Write an equilibrium-constant expression for each reaction listed in **Table 14-2.**

25. The figure below shows the results of adding three different chemicals to distilled water and stirring well.

a. Which substance(s) is completely soluble in water?

b. Is it correct to say that AgCl is completely insoluble? Explain your answer. Is $Ba(OH)_2$ completely insoluble?

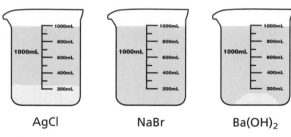

AgCl   NaBr $Ba(OH)_2$

26. A solution has $[Ca^{2+}] = 0.10$ M. As F^- ion is added, a precipitate of $CaF_2(s)$ will eventually form. What is the concentration of F^- ions when the precipitate just begins to form? (Hint: The solution will be saturated, and $K_{sp} = 1.6 \times 10^{-10}$ will apply.)

LINKING CHAPTERS

1. Percent yield

Using Le Châtelier's principle, devise one way to increase the percent yield of product from a reversible chemical reaction.

2. Theme: Equilibrium and change

a. If a process is in equilibrium, does that mean nothing is changing?

b. If a reversible reaction favors the formation of the products, are any reactants still present?

3. Electron configuration

Complex ions of Ag^+, Zn^{2+}, Cd^{2+}, and Hg^{2+} are usually colorless. What electron configuration do these ions have in common?

ALTERNATIVE ASSESSMENTS

Performance assessment

1. Your instructor will give you an index card with a specific equilibrium reaction on it. Describe how you would alter the reaction to produce either more of the products or more of the reactants. Show your method to your instructor. If your method is approved, obtain the necessary materials from your instructor and perform the experiment.

Portfolio projects

1. Models in science

Develop a model that demonstrates the concept of a chemical equilibrium. Be sure that your model includes the impact of Le Châtelier's principle on equilibrium and the common ion effect.

2. internet**connect**

SCI**LINKS**
NSTA

TOPIC: Separating ions
GO TO: www.scilinks.org
KEYWORD: HW144

Research and communication

Many different pollutants are in the form of ions dissolved in water. Industries must remove these ions from their waste water to avoid exposing the environment to harmful chemicals. Research the use of solubility principles and equilibrium to remove the ions listed below. Write a report about the effect that these chemicals have on our environment.

a. Pb^{2+} **c.** Cl^- **e.** PO_4^{3-}

b. Ba^{2+} **d.** SO_4^{2-}

1. —— will *not* affect the equilibrium of a reaction.
   a. A change in temperature
   b. The addition of a catalyst
   c. Increasing the concentration of the reactants
   d. Decreasing the concentration of the products

2. Examine the following equation for an equilibrium system.

   $$NaF(s) + 0.90 \text{ kJ} \rightleftharpoons Na^+(aq) + F^-(aq)$$

   The reverse reaction would be favored by ——.
   a. increasing the temperature
   b. increasing the pressure
   c. adding KF(s) to the reaction
   d. adding more NaF(s)

3. If the K_{eq} value is larger than one, then ——.
   a. the concentrations of the products equal those of the reactants
   b. a catalyst must have been added to the reaction
   c. the reaction must be endothermic
   d. the forward reaction is favored

4. NaCl does not have a K_{sp} value because this salt ——.
   a. cannot participate in an equilibrium reaction
   b. does not form aqueous solutions
   c. is very soluble in water
   d. retains its crystal lattice structure in aqueous solution

5. Consider the following equation for an equilibrium system:

   $$2PbS(s) + 3O_2(g) + C(s) \rightleftharpoons$$
   $$2Pb(l) + CO_2(g) + 2SO_2(g)$$

   The concentration(s) that would be included in the denominator of the equilibrium-constant expression are ——.
   a. $Pb(l)$, $CO_2(g)$, $SO_2(g)$
   b. $PbS(s)$, $O_2(g)$, $C(s)$
   c. $O_2(g)$, $Pb(l)$, $CO_2(g)$, $SO_2(g)$
   d. $O_2(g)$

6. A reaction that has reached equilibrium is a reaction in which ——.
   a. the concentration of the reactants equals the concentration of the products
   b. the rate of the reverse reaction equals the rate of the forward reaction
   c. all conditions are static
   d. products are no longer being formed

7. If an exothermic reaction has reached equilibrium, then increasing the temperature will ——.
   a. favor the forward reaction
   b. favor the reverse reaction
   c. favor both the forward and reverse reaction
   d. have no effect on the equilibrium

8. The K_{eq} value for a reaction must specify the temperature at which the concentrations are measured because the K_{eq} value ——
   a. is a constant
   b. does not have any units
   c. will change if the temperature changes
   d. may or may not be larger than 1

9. Consider the following reaction:

   $$COBr_2(g) \rightleftharpoons CO(g) + Br_2(g)$$

   At 73°C, the K_{eq} value for this reaction is 0.190. This K_{eq} value indicates that ——.
   a. the reverse reaction is favored
   b. the forward reaction is favored
   c. the reaction has reached equilibrium
   d. the concentrations of $CO(g)$ and $Br_2(g)$ are greater than the concentration of $Br_2(g)$

CHAPTER 15

Acids and Bases

CHEMICAL FOES DO BATTLE

Nestled in the New England uplands, the lake is a beautiful sight. Glacier-smoothed rocks fringe its southern shore, while to the north stately pines and leafless maples cloak the hills that crowd the Canadian border. Now, in the cold light of an early February evening, the lake is covered by a thick layer of ice. But the tranquillity is suddenly shattered by a noisy convoy of dump trucks driving onto the frozen surface. They disperse and unload piles of gray rock over the ice. What is going on? Why is this mechanical invasion taking place?

Formerly, the lake was a favorite haunt of fishers, both human and feathered. But as the fish population has declined in recent years, the anglers have departed and the ospreys have died or gone elsewhere in search of food. What is responsible for the death of this lake? Acid precipitation is to blame. Prevailing wind patterns carry polluting gases from the Midwest to Canada and the Northeast. The gases originate in the power plants, refineries, and smelters of America's industrial heartland, a region whose commercial products are consumed throughout the country. Some factories, such as steel-producing plants, burn fossil fuels, as do automobiles. The fuels contain sulfur, nitrogen, and other contaminants that become gaseous pollutants when the fuel is burned. These gases dissolve in atmospheric water to form acids, which are then washed from the air by summer rains and winter snows. Regions such as this one, where there is a large snowpack in winter, are especially vulnerable because the spring melt releases a sudden rush of acidic water. Acids have accumulated in the lake, killing much of the plant and animal life that once flourished in it.

A group of environmentalists have chartered the fleet of trucks to deposit limestone from a quarry hundreds of miles away onto the frozen lake. They plan to combat the polluting, not to mention deadly, acidity by introducing a base into the lake. They hope to rehabilitate the lake's ecology and restore the lake to its former state. In this chapter, you will learn that bases counteract the effects of acids. As you read through the chapter, consider the following questions.

CHAPTER LINKS

How are the industrial gases responsible for acid rain?

Why did environmentalists transport limestone into the region instead of using local rock?

Why was the operation carried out during the winter?

What are acids and bases?

OBJECTIVES

▶ **Describe** the distinctive properties of acids and bases.

▶ **Distinguish** between the terms *strong* and *weak* as they apply to acids and bases.

▶ **Explain** the unusually high electrical conductivities of acidic solutions.

▶ **Use** K_w to calculate a solution's hydronium ion or hydroxide ion concentration.

▶ **Name** and describe the functional groups that characterize organic acids and bases.

Acids

strong acid

an acid that ionizes completely in aqueous solution

weak acid

an acid that is a weak electrolyte

How would you describe the tastes of the beverages and fruits shown in **Figure 15-1**? Some are sweet, but all have a quality to their taste that people describe as sour, tart, or acidic. Is there anything that these sour-tasting substances have in common? Indeed there is. They all contain chemicals known as acids.

Acids are hydronium ion generators

When the term *acid* is used, chemists usually think of the definition proposed by Swedish chemist Svante Arrhenius. In a modern version of this definition, an acid is a substance that, when dissolved in water, increases the hydronium ion, H_3O^+, concentration of the water.

Both **strong acids** and **weak acids** exist. These adjectives, *strong* and *weak*, have the same meanings that they did in Chapter 13, where

▼ **FIGURE 15-1**

Fruits and fruit juices contain citric and ascorbic acids, carbonated beverages contain carbonic acid, and vinegar contains acetic acid.

Carbonic acid

Acetic acid

Citric acid

Ascorbic acid

TABLE 15-1 Some Strong and Weak Acids

Strong acids	Weak acids
Chloric acid, $HClO_3$	Acetic acid, CH_3COOH
Hydrobromic acid, HBr	Boric acid, H_3BO_3
Hydrochloric acid, HCl	Hydrocyanic acid, HCN
Hydriodic acid, HI	Hydrofluoric acid, HF
Nitric acid, HNO_3	Hydrosulfuric acid, H_2S
Perchloric acid, $HClO_4$	Hypochlorous acid, HClO
Periodic acid, HIO_4	Nitrous acid, HNO_2
Permanganic acid, $HMnO_4$	Phosphoric acid, H_3PO_4
Sulfuric acid, H_2SO_4	Sulfurous acid, H_2SO_3

internet**connect**

SC*LINKS*
NSTA

TOPIC: Acids
GO TO: www.scilinks.org
KEYWORD: HW151

strong and weak electrolytes were discussed. A *strong acid* is an acid that ionizes completely in aqueous solution to form ions, one of which is the hydronium ion. Nitric acid, HNO_3, is an example of a strong acid. The following equation represents its reaction with water.

$$HNO_3(l) + H_2O(l) \longrightarrow H_3O^+(aq) + NO_3^-(aq)$$

When a *weak acid* dissolves in water, only a small fraction of its molecules ionize. An example of a weak acid is hypochlorous acid, HClO. Its reaction with water is represented by the following equation.

$$HClO(aq) + H_2O(l) \rightleftharpoons H_3O^+(aq) + ClO^-(aq)$$

Recall from Chapter 14 that the double arrows in this equation indicate equilibrium. Hypochlorite ions, ClO^-, are reacting with hydronium ions to form HClO at the same rate that HClO molecules are reacting with water to form ions. **Table 15-1** lists the names and formulas of several strong and weak acids.

Acid solutions are good conductors of electricity

In addition to their sour taste, aqueous acid solutions share the ability to conduct electricity, as illustrated in **Figure 15-2.** This is because acids, like other electrolytes, produce ions when dissolved in solution. Strong acids are particularly good conductors of electricity because the hydronium ion can move faster than other ions, and electricity is conducted by this ion movement. Why is that?

When an ion—for example, a sodium ion, Na^+—moves through water, it has to push the water molecules out of its way. The H_3O^+ ion, however, does not. Instead of pushing the water molecule aside, like other ions do, the hydronium ion transfers a proton to the impeding H_2O molecule. This proton transfer converts the water molecule to a hydronium ion, and the former hydronium ion reverts to a water

FIGURE 15-2 ▼

Hydrochloric acid solution is a good conductor of electricity. It ionizes completely in water, causing the bulb to be brightly lit.

a Successive transfers of protons from H_3O^+ to H_2O make the hydronium ion appear to move through a solution much faster than an ion can actually move.

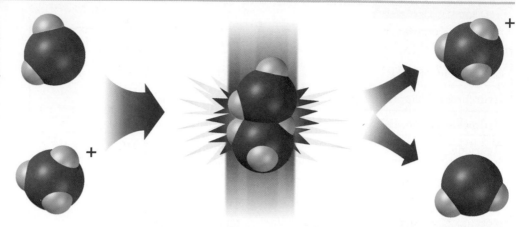

b The movement of a proton through an acid solution resembles the movement of a pail of water along a bucket brigade.

▲ **FIGURE 15-4**

The hydronium ions formed by hydrochloric acid in aqueous solution react with zinc to produce hydrogen gas.

molecule. In turn, the new hydronium ion passes a proton to a third water molecule. The process of proton transfer in an acid solution is illustrated in **Figure 15-3.**

Hydronium ions react with some metals

Another property shared by many acids is the ability to react with metals above hydrogen in the activity series to produce hydrogen gas. This reaction is actually a property of the hydronium ion and not of the acid itself. An example is the reaction of hydrochloric acid and zinc, which is illustrated in **Figure 15-4** and represented by the following net ionic equation. Notice that even though hydrochloric acid has the formula HCl, only the H_3O^+ ions produced by the acid appear in the equation.

$$2H_3O^+(aq) + Zn(s) \longrightarrow 2H_2O(l) + Zn^{2+}(aq) + H_2(g)$$

Not all acids react with zinc as readily as hydrochloric acid does. Reactions involving acids and metals depend on the amount of hydronium ion present, which in turn depends on the strength and concentration of the acid. The *strength* of an acid is a measure of how much it ionizes in solution. The strength of an acid has nothing to do with its *concentration,* which is the amount of dissolved acid per liter of solution.

Organic acids are carboxylic acids

You learned in Chapter 7 that molecules of most organic acids have the characteristic carboxyl group, —COOH. These compounds are called **carboxylic acids.** When a carboxylic acid ionizes in aqueous solution, the result is a hydronium ion and an anion with the following group.

$$\underset{\underset{-C-O^-}{\overset{\|}{}}}{\overset{O}{}}$$

Although the negative charge is shown as being located on one oxygen atom of the carboxyl group, experiments show that the oxygen atoms share the negative charge equally.

carboxylic acid

an organic compound that contains the carboxyl functional group

---

CONCEPT CHECK

1. Why is nitric acid classified as a strong acid whereas hypochlorous acid is considered a weak acid?
2. Describe the movement of the hydronium ion through an aqueous solution.
3. What products are formed when a metal reacts with a strong acid?
4. Why is the carboxyl group considered to be acidic?

Bases

According to Arrhenius, a base is a substance that increases the concentration of hydroxide ions, OH^-, when dissolved in water. Unlike acids, which are usually liquids or gases, many bases are solids. Solutions of bases are slippery to the touch. **Figure 15-5** shows some bases with which you may be familiar. A base that dissolves easily in water is called an *alkali,* and the resulting solution is said to be *alkaline.* Many cleaning agents are classified as alkaline because of their high concentration of hydroxide ions. These ions interact with oil and grease by a process that you learned about in Section 13-4.

Even though acids taste sour and bases feel slippery, *it is not safe* to use these properties to identify substances. Solutions of acids or bases can cause serious burns to living tissue.

Bases are hydroxide ion generators

Sodium hydroxide, NaOH, is an example of a *strong base.* It is an ionic compound, and it is very soluble in water. Sodium hydroxide is classified as a strong base because it fully dissociates in solution, as shown by the following equation.

$$NaOH(s) \xrightarrow{H_2O} Na^+(aq) + OH^-(aq)$$

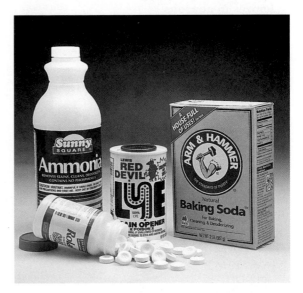

FIGURE 15-5 ▼

Many household products contain bases, such as sodium hydroxide, NaOH(s), and ammonia, NH₃(aq).

| TABLE 15-2 | Some Strong and Weak Bases |

Strong bases	Weak bases
Barium hydroxide, $Ba(OH)_2$	Ammonia, NH_3
Calcium hydroxide, $Ca(OH)_2$	Aniline, $C_6H_5NH_2$
Potassium hydroxide, KOH	Potassium carbonate, K_2CO_3
Sodium hydroxide, NaOH	Sodium carbonate, Na_2CO_3
Sodium phosphate, Na_3PO_4	Trimethylamine, $(CH_3)_3N$

internetconnect

SC*LINKS*
NSTA

TOPIC: Bases
GO TO: www.scilinks.org
KEYWORD: HW152

Some examples of strong and weak bases are listed in **Table 15-2,** and one of each is shown in **Figure 15-6.**

As you can see from Table 15-2, several of the strong bases are the hydroxides of metals in Groups 1 and 2 of the periodic table. This is why Group 1 elements are called alkali metals and Group 2 elements are called alkaline earth metals. It is easy to see how these compounds produce OH^- ions in solution because the solid bases already contain hydroxide ions. However, some strong bases and most weak bases are not hydroxide compounds. How, then, can these substances produce hydroxide ions in solution? To find out, look at what happens when ammonia, a typical weak base, dissolves in water.

Ammonia, a gas at room temperature, dissolves readily in water. Most of the ammonia molecules do not react with water to form ions, so ammonia is classified as a *weak base.*

$$NH_3(aq) + H_2O(l) \rightleftarrows NH_4^+(aq) + OH^-(aq)$$

▼ FIGURE 15-6

a Ammonia only slightly ionizes in aqueous solution. Therefore, most of the ammonia remains as neutral molecules in solution.

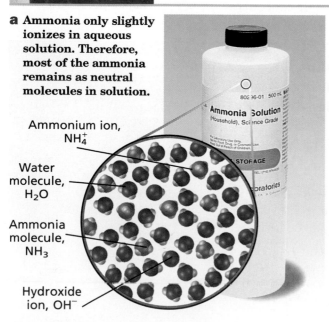

Ammonium ion, NH_4^+

Water molecule, H_2O

Ammonia molecule, NH_3

Hydroxide ion, OH^-

b Sodium hydroxide is a strong base. There are no sodium hydroxide molecules left in solution.

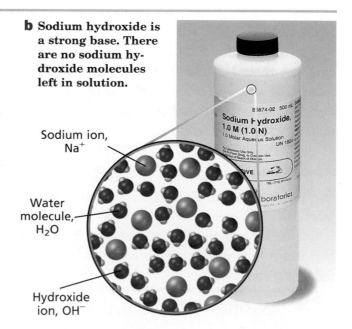

Sodium ion, Na^+

Water molecule, H_2O

Hydroxide ion, OH^-

Because bases produce ions in solution, solutions of bases, like solutions of acids, are electrical conductors.

Organic bases contain nitrogen

All important organic bases can be viewed as derivatives of ammonia, NH_3. Recall from Chapter 6 that ammonia is not a flat molecule. Instead, the three hydrogen atoms and the unshared pair of electrons form the four corners of a tetrahedron, as shown in **Figure 15-7.** This unshared pair of electrons gives ammonia the character of a base.

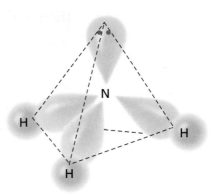

FIGURE 15-7 ▲

Ammonia and organic amines are classified as bases because the nitrogen atom has an unshared pair of electrons that can accept a hydrogen ion from an acid.

Organic compounds in which one or more organic groups replace the hydrogen atoms in ammonia are called **amines.** Amines, like ammonia, are weak bases that ionize slightly in water. The replacement of one hydrogen atom in ammonia by an organic group does not eliminate ammonia's ability to accept a proton. In fact, an amine can still act as a base even if two (or all three) of ammonia's hydrogen atoms are replaced by organic groups.

Just as ammonia forms the ammonium cation, methylamine forms the methylammonium ion, $CH_3NH_3^+$, and pyridine forms the pyridinium ion, $C_5H_5NH^+$.

$$CH_3NH_2(aq) + H_2O(l) \rightleftharpoons CH_3NH_3^+(aq) + OH^-(aq)$$

Compounds such as pyridine, C_5H_5N, in which the nitrogen atom is incorporated into a ring structure, also act as bases, as indicated by the equation below.

amine

an organic compound that contains a nitrogen atom and that can be considered a derivative of ammonia

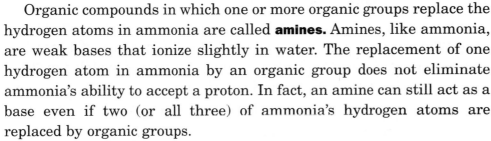

Amines that have only one organic group, such as CH_3NH_2, are called *primary amines*. Similarly, amines that have two hydrogen atoms replaced by two organic groups are called *secondary* amines. Finally, *tertiary* amines contain a nitrogen atom that is bonded to three organic groups. Pyridine is an example of a tertiary amine.

CONCEPT CHECK

1. Write an equation for the dissociation of the strong base $Ca(OH)_2$.

2. Write an equation showing how aniline, $C_6H_5NH_2$, acts as a weak base when dissolved in water.

3. Does ammonia still act like a weak base even when its hydrogen atoms are replaced by organic groups? Explain.

When acids and bases meet

Dissolving a base in water increases the OH^- ion concentration; dissolving an acid in water increases the H_3O^+ ion concentration. But what happens if a base *and* an acid are added to water? The hydronium ions and hydroxide ions react with each other to form water, as shown by the following equation.

$$H_3O^+(aq) + OH^-(aq) \longrightarrow 2H_2O(l)$$

This reaction is called a **neutralization reaction.**

neutralization reaction

a reaction in which hydronium ions from an acid and hydroxide ions from a base react to produce water molecules

The self-ionization of water

Recall from Chapter 14 that even pure water has a small concentration of hydronium ions. This is a result of the *self-ionization* of water. The self-ionization of water is an equilibrium system; it is modeled in **Figure 15-8** and in the following chemical equation.

$$2H_2O(l) \rightleftharpoons H_3O^+(aq) + OH^-(aq)$$

You can see from the reaction equation that the self-ionization of pure water produces equal amounts of H_3O^+ ions and OH^- ions. Therefore, the concentrations of these ions in pure water must be equal.

$$[OH^-] = [H_3O^+]$$

Experiments show that in pure water at 25°C, the concentrations of H_3O^+ ions and OH^- ions are equal to 1.00×10^{-7} mol/L.

Recall from Chapter 14 that an equilibrium constant, K_{eq}, can be calculated for a reaction that reaches equilibrium. Because the self-ionization of water is an equilibrium reaction, the equilibrium constant for this reaction, called K_w, can be calculated as follows.

$$K_w = [H_3O^+][OH^-] = (1.00 \times 10^{-7})(1.00 \times 10^{-7})$$

$$K_w = 1.00 \times 10^{-14}$$

This new constant, K_w, is called the ionic product constant of water or the *autoionization constant* for water. Note that K_w has no unit.

In dilute solutions of acids and bases at 25°C, the product of $[H_3O^+]$ and $[OH^-]$ must equal 1.00×10^{-14}. Because K_w is a constant, once you know the concentration of either the H_3O^+ ions or the OH^- ions in a solution, you can easily find the concentration of the other.

▼ **FIGURE 15-8**

Two water molecules can react to produce a hydronium ion and a hydroxide ion.

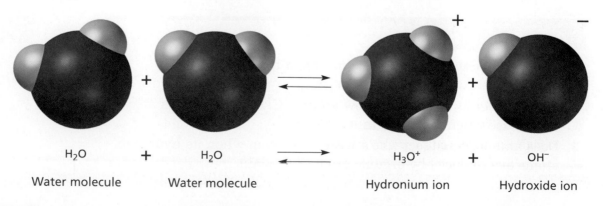

| H_2O | + | H_2O | $\rightleftharpoons$ | H_3O^+ | + | OH^- |
| Water molecule | | Water molecule | | Hydronium ion | | Hydroxide ion |

SAMPLE PROBLEM 15A Determining $[OH^-]$ using K_w

What is $[OH^-]$ in a 3.00×10^{-5} M solution of HCl?

1 List what you know

- Concentration of HCl solution = 3.00×10^{-5} M
- $[OH^-]$ = ? M

2 Set up the problem

- Because HCl is a strong acid, 1 mol of HCl produces 1 mol of H_3O^+.

$$[H_3O^+] = 3.00 \times 10^{-5}\ M$$

- Use the ion product of water to calculate the concentration of OH^- ions.

$$K_w = [H_3O^+][OH^-] = 1.00 \times 10^{-14}$$

3 Calculate

- Rearrange the K_w expression and calculate $[OH^-]$.

$$[OH^-] = \frac{K_w}{[H_3O^+]} = \frac{1.00 \times 10^{-14}}{3.00 \times 10^{-5}} = 3.33 \times 10^{-10}\ M$$

SECTION REVIEW

Total recall

1. **Interpreting Tables** Classify the following as either a strong acid, a strong base, a weak acid, or a weak base.
   a. sodium carbonate
   b. potassium hydroxide
   c. hydrobromic acid
   d. hydrofluoric acid
2. Why does the hydronium ion concentration of an aqueous solution decrease when the hydroxide ion concentration increases?
3. Describe the self-ionization of water.

Critical thinking

4. Explain how an acid can be considered weak, even in a concentrated solution.
5. How does $[OH^-]$ in an aqueous solution of sodium carbonate compare with $[OH^-]$ in a sodium hydroxide solution of similar concentration?
6. Can you neutralize a strong acid solution by adding an equal volume of a weak base having the same molarity as the acid? Support your position.

Practice problems

7. An aqueous solution is prepared by dissolving 86.5 g of the strong acid HNO_3 in water to make 2.3 L of solution at 298 K. What is $[OH^-]$ in this solution?
8. At normal body temperature (310 K, 37°C), the ion product of water is 2.50×10^{-14}. What are the concentrations of hydronium ions and hydroxide ions in water at this temperature?

Can the strengths of acids and bases be quantified?

OBJECTIVES

▶ *State* the Brønsted-Lowry definitions of an acid and a base.

▶ *Differentiate* between monoprotic, diprotic, and triprotic acids.

▶ *Write* chemical equations showing how an amphoteric

species can behave as both an acid and a base.

▶ *Identify* conjugate acid-base pairs.

▶ *Calculate* K_a from the hydronium ion concentration of a weak acid solution.

Brønsted-Lowry classification

The definition of an acid that was given on page 542 is a modern version of the one proposed by Arrhenius in the late nineteenth century. The Arrhenius definition of acids has several drawbacks, one of which is that it applies only to aqueous solutions. HCl is an acid whether it is in the form of a pure gas or in a water solution. Another drawback is that the Arrhenius definition cannot clearly classify species that can increase or decrease $[H_3O^+]$, depending on the conditions.

Acids donate protons

Brønsted-Lowry acid

any ion or molecule that can donate a proton to another species

In 1923, a broader definition of *acid* was independently proposed by the Danish chemist Johannes Brønsted and the British scientist Thomas Lowry. A **Brønsted-Lowry acid** is any molecule or ion that can transfer a *proton*—a hydrogen atom nucleus—to another species. The transfer of a proton from an acid to water is shown in **Figure 15-9.**

Because all of the Arrhenius acids you have studied so far donate a proton (hydrogen ion) to a water molecule to form a hydronium ion, they are included in the Brønsted-Lowry definition of an acid. Sulfuric acid, H_2SO_4, is one example.

$$H_2SO_4(l) + H_2O(l) \longrightarrow H_3O^+(aq) + HSO_4^-(aq)$$

▶ **FIGURE 15-9**

The ionization of an HCl molecule in water illustrates the transfer of a proton from HCl to H₂O to form a hydronium ion, H₃O⁺.

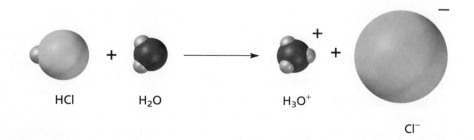

HCl   H₂O   H₃O⁺   Cl⁻

The hydrogen sulfate ion, HSO_4^-, is also a Brønsted-Lowry acid because it too can donate a proton to a water molecule.

$$HSO_4^-(aq) + H_2O(l) \rightleftharpoons H_3O^+(aq) + SO_4^{2-}(aq)$$

Note that a Brønsted-Lowry acid is simply a proton donor. Nothing requires that the proton be transferred to water. The following reaction between HSO_4^- and CO_3^{2-} equally establishes hydrogen sulfate's role as a proton donor and therefore an acid.

$$HSO_4^-(aq) + CO_3^{2-}(aq) \rightleftharpoons HCO_3^-(aq) + SO_4^{2-}(aq)$$

Some acids can donate more than one proton

Many common acids donate only *one* proton per molecule. For this reason, such acids are called **monoprotic acids.** Nitric acid, shown in **Figure 15-10a,** is a typical monoprotic acid; it reacts with water according to the following equation.

$$HNO_3(l) + H_2O(l) \longrightarrow H_3O^+(aq) + NO_3^-(aq)$$

Acids that donate more than one proton per molecule are called *polyprotic acids*. For example, each molecule of sulfuric acid, H_2SO_4, shown in **Figure 15-10b,** has two ionizable hydrogen atoms and can donate *two* protons. Therefore, H_2SO_4 is a **diprotic acid.** In the reaction between H_2SO_4 and water, the two hydronium ions produced are formed in two distinct steps. The first step generates one hydronium ion and a hydrogen sulfate ion, HSO_4^-.

$$H_2SO_4(l) + H_2O(l) \longrightarrow H_3O^+(aq) + HSO_4^-(aq)$$

In the second step, the hydrogen sulfate anion donates a proton to form a second hydronium ion and a sulfate ion, SO_4^{2-}.

$$HSO_4^-(aq) + H_2O(l) \rightleftharpoons H_3O^+(aq) + SO_4^{2-}(aq)$$

Similarly, phosphoric acid, H_3PO_4, shown in **Figure 15-10c,** is a **triprotic acid,** an acid molecule that can donate *three* protons.

monoprotic acid

an acid that can donate one hydrogen ion per molecule

diprotic acid

an acid that can donate two hydrogen ions per molecule

triprotic acid

an acid that can donate three hydrogen ions per molecule

FIGURE 15-10 ▼

a Nitric acid is a monoprotic acid. It has only one ionizable hydrogen atom per molecule.

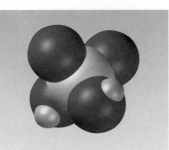

b Sulfuric acid is a diprotic acid. Each of its molecules can form two hydronium ions when dissolved in water.

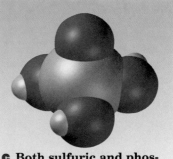

c Both sulfuric and phosphoric acids are polyprotic. Phosphoric acid is triprotic. It has three ionizable hydrogen atoms.

$$\begin{array}{ccc} \text{H} & \text{O} \\ | & \| \\ \text{H}-\text{C}-\text{C}-\text{OH} \\ | \\ \text{H} \end{array}$$

▲ **FIGURE 15-11**

Although acetic acid
has four hydrogen
atoms, only the one
shown in red ionizes
in water.

Brønsted-Lowry base

any atom, ion, or molecule
that can accept a proton
from another species

It would be easy to assume that the number of protons an acid molecule can donate equals the number of hydrogen atoms that it contains. However, this is not always the case. For example, acetic acid has four hydrogen atoms, but it is monoprotic. Only the hydrogen atom that is part of the carboxyl group is ionized in water.

Bases accept protons

As you might expect, a **Brønsted-Lowry base** is any atom, ion, or molecule that receives a proton from another species. Chemists say that acids *donate* protons and bases *accept* them. Ammonia is a typical base. It ionizes in aqueous solution by accepting a proton from water, as shown by the following equation.

$$NH_3(aq) + H_2O(l) \rightleftharpoons NH_4^+(aq) + OH^-(aq)$$

Again, notice that the Brønsted-Lowry definition of a base, unlike that of Arrhenius, does not mention water. For example, ammonia does not have to react in aqueous solution to qualify as a Brønsted-Lowry base. Even in the gas phase ammonia accepts a proton from hydrogen chloride, as shown in **Figure 15-12.** This reaction produces the ionic compound NH_4Cl, which is composed of NH_4^+ and Cl^- ions.

$$HCl(g) + NH_3(g) \longrightarrow NH_4Cl(s)$$

► **FIGURE 15-12**

$HCl(g)$ and $NH_3(g)$
that have each es-
caped from aqueous
solution combine to
form a cloud of solid
ammonium chloride.

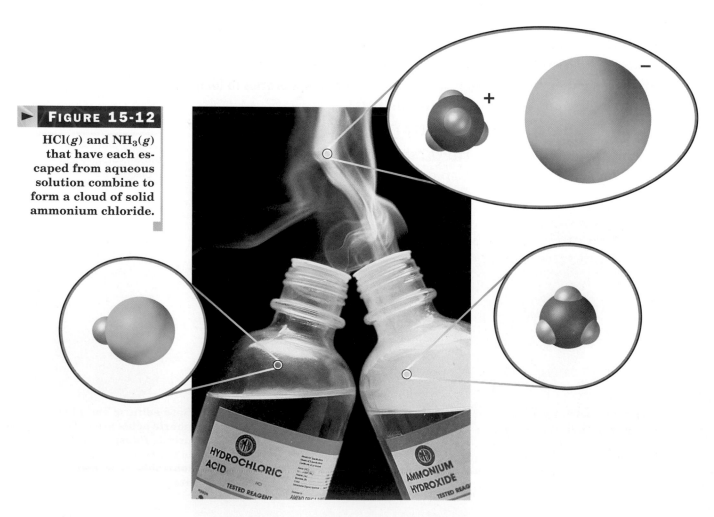

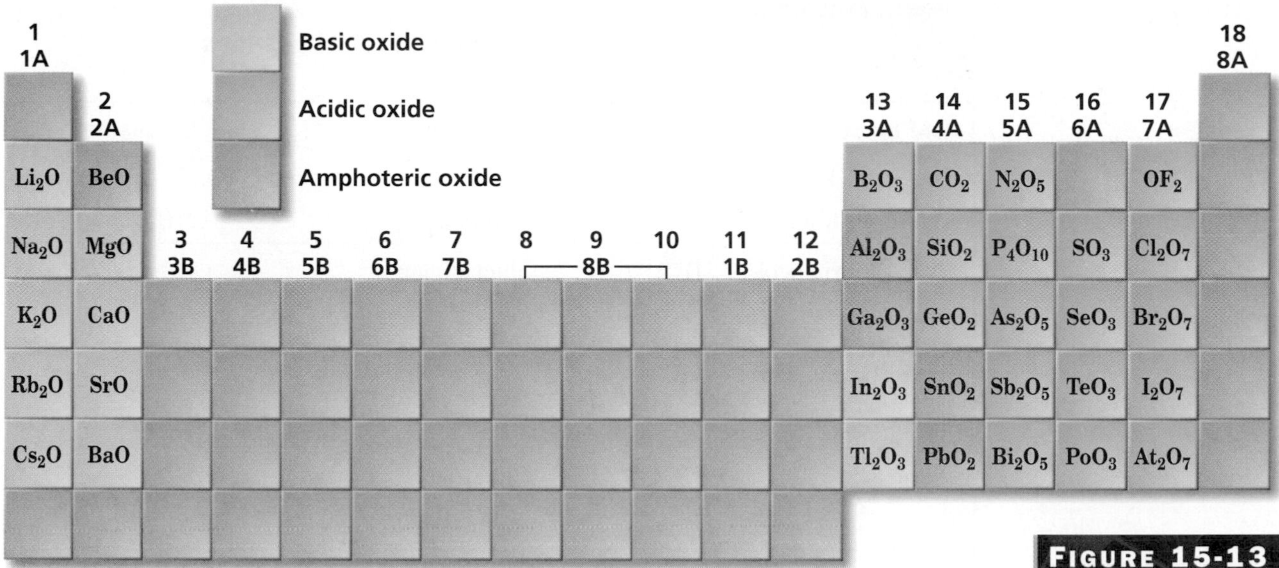

| 1 1A | | Basic oxide | | | | | | | | | | | | | | | 18 8A |

Basic oxide

Acidic oxide

Amphoteric oxide

| | | 13 3A | 14 4A | 15 5A | 16 6A | 17 7A |

Li_2O BeO

| 3 3B | 4 4B | 5 5B | 6 6B | 7 7B | 8 | 9 —8B— | 10 | 11 1B | 12 2B |

B_2O_3 CO_2 N_2O_5 OF_2

Na_2O MgO Al_2O_3 SiO_2 P_4O_{10} SO_3 Cl_2O_7

K_2O CaO Ga_2O_3 GeO_2 As_2O_5 SeO_3 Br_2O_7

Rb_2O SrO In_2O_3 SnO_2 Sb_2O_5 TeO_3 I_2O_7

Cs_2O BaO Tl_2O_3 PbO_2 Bi_2O_5 PoO_3 At_2O_7

FIGURE 15-13 ▲

Periodic trends determine whether an element will form a basic, acidic, or amphoteric oxide.

Some species are both acids and bases

Is water an acid or a base? Water can act as an acid by donating a proton, and it can act as a base by accepting a proton.

$$H_2O(l) + H_2O(l) \rightleftharpoons OH^-(aq) + H_3O^+(aq)$$

Therefore, water is both an acid and a base.

A species that can act as either an acid or a base is described as **amphoteric.** The hydrogen carbonate ion is an example of an amphoteric species. It behaves as an acid when it reacts with a hydroxide ion, as shown by the following equation.

$$HCO_3^-(aq) + OH^-(aq) \rightleftharpoons CO_3^{2-}(aq) + H_2O(l)$$

But it behaves as a base in the presence of an acid such as formic acid, HCOOH.

$$HCOOH(aq) + HCO_3^-(aq) \rightleftharpoons HCOO^-(aq) + H_2CO_3(aq)$$

amphoteric

any molecule or ion that can act as either an acid or a base

Each base has a conjugate acid, and each acid has a conjugate base

Look again at the equation for the reversible reaction of ammonia, NH_3, with water.

$$NH_3(aq) + H_2O(l) \rightleftharpoons NH_4^+(aq) + OH^-(aq)$$
$$\text{base} \qquad \text{acid}$$

Water donates a proton to ammonia; it is an acid. Ammonia accepts a proton from water; it is a base. The ammonium ion is what forms when NH_3 has accepted a proton, and the hydroxide ion is what forms when water has lost a proton. Note that this reaction is reversible. It can be written as follows.

$$NH_4^+(aq) + OH^-(aq) \rightleftharpoons NH_3(aq) + H_2O(l)$$
$$\text{acid} \qquad \text{base}$$

TABLE 15-3 Acids and Their Conjugate Bases

Acid name	Acid formula	Conjugate base name	Conjugate base formula
Ammonium ion	NH_4^+	ammonia	NH_3
Hydrochloric acid	HCl	chloride ion	Cl^-
Hydrocyanic acid	HCN	cyanide ion	CN^-
Hydrofluoric acid	HF	fluoride ion	F^-
Hydronium ion	H_3O^+	water	H_2O
Nitric acid	HNO_3	nitrate ion	NO_3^-
Nitrous acid	HNO_2	nitrite ion	NO_2^-
Phosphoric acid	H_3PO_4	dihydrogen phosphate ion	$H_2PO_4^-$
Sulfuric acid	H_2SO_4	hydrogen sulfate ion	HSO_4^-

conjugate acid

the acid formed when a base accepts a proton

conjugate base

the base formed when an acid donates a proton

In this reaction, the ammonium ion donates a proton to the hydroxide ion. NH_4^+ is an acid, and OH^- is a base. The ammonium ion is called the **conjugate acid** of the base, ammonia. The hydroxide ion is called the **conjugate base** of the acid, water.

$$NH_3(aq) + H_2O(l) \rightleftharpoons \quad NH_4^+(aq) \quad + \quad OH^-(aq)$$
$$\text{base} \qquad \text{acid} \qquad \text{conjugate acid} \quad \text{conjugate base}$$

By convention, the term *conjugate* is used for the acid and base on the right side of the equation. Every Brønsted-Lowry acid has a conjugate base. **Table 15-3** gives you more examples of acids and their conjugate bases.

CONCEPT CHECK

1. In the following equations, identify which reactant is the Brønsted acid and which reactant is the Brønsted base.
   a. $CH_3NH_2(aq) + H_2O(l) \rightleftharpoons CH_3NH_3^+(aq) + OH^-(aq)$
   b. $HSO_4^-(aq) + H_2O(l) \rightleftharpoons H_3O^+(aq) + SO_4^{2-}(aq)$

2. In the following reactions, identify whether H_2O behaves as a Brønsted acid or a Brønsted base.
   a. $HClO_4(aq) + H_2O(l) \longrightarrow H_3O^+(aq) + ClO_4^-(aq)$
   b. $H_2O(l) + SO_3^{2-}(aq) \rightleftharpoons HSO_3^-(aq) + OH^-(aq)$

3. Phosphoric acid, H_3PO_4, can donate three hydrogen ions in three distinct steps. Write an equation for each of these three ionization steps.

4. Acetic acid, CH_3COOH, is a weak monoprotic acid. Why is it classified as a monoprotic acid even though it contains four hydrogen atoms?

Weak acids and bases

Consider the reaction represented by the following equation, in which one arrow is longer than the other.

$$A(aq) + B(aq) \rightleftharpoons C(aq) + D(aq)$$

Recall from Chapter 14 that chemists say the forward reaction in this example is *favored*. When the reaction reaches equilibrium, the products C and D will be abundant and at least one reactant will be scarce.

Some acids are better proton donors than others

Reconsider the reaction of formic acid, HCOOH, with the hydrogen carbonate ion. The forward reaction is favored.

$$\underset{\text{acid}}{HCOOH(aq)} + HCO_3^-(aq) \rightleftharpoons HCOO^-(aq) + \underset{\text{acid}}{H_2CO_3(aq)}$$

If you mix equal amounts of all four of the species in this equation—formic acid, hydrogen carbonate ion, formate ion, and carbonic acid—you will find that after mixing, the concentrations of $HCOO^-$ and H_2CO_3 will increase at the expense of $HCOOH$ and HCO_3^-. Because $HCOOH$ is more likely to lose a hydrogen ion than H_2CO_3 is, $HCOOH$, shown in **Figure 15-14,** is the stronger acid.

Some bases accept protons more readily than others

Now look at the same reaction from the standpoint of the bases.

$$\underset{\text{base}}{HCOOH(aq)} + HCO_3^-(aq) \rightleftharpoons \underset{\text{base}}{HCOO^-(aq)} + H_2CO_3(aq)$$

Both HCO_3^- and $HCOO^-$ are weak bases; therefore, both can accept a proton. But when all four species are mixed in equal concentrations, it

---

FIGURE 15-14 ▼

a The name *formic acid* comes from *formica,* the Latin word for "ant." Some species of ants produce this acid and inject it into their victims when they bite.

b Formic acid was first isolated by distillation from ants in 1670.

c If you are bitten by ants, your body will eventually neutralize the acidity of the formic acid with bases, mainly the hydrogen carbonate ion, HCO_3^-, in your blood. A model of formic acid is shown.

Vinegar consists of about a 5% solution of acetic acid. This gives vinegar its sour taste.

Water, H₂O

Acetate ion, CH₃COO⁻

Acetic acid, CH₃COOH

Hydronium ion, H₃O⁺

is the hydrogen carbonate ion, HCO_3^-, that accepts the proton more readily. The formate ion, $HCOO^-$, is a weaker base and therefore cannot compete with HCO_3^-.

The formate ion, $HCOO^-$, is the conjugate base of formic acid, and carbonic acid, H_2CO_3, is the conjugate acid of the hydrogen carbonate ion. You know that of the two acids, formic acid is the stronger acid. You also know that the hydrogen carbonate ion is the stronger of the two bases. This leads to a very important conclusion. *In an acid/base reaction, the conjugate base of the stronger acid is the weaker base, and the conjugate acid of the stronger base is the weaker acid.*

K_a is the acid-ionization constant

acid-ionization constant

the equilibrium constant for a reaction in which an acid donates a proton to water

It is possible not only to compare the strengths of acids and bases qualitatively, as you have seen, but also to express these strengths quantitatively. The equilibrium constant of the ionization of a weak acid in water is known as the **acid-ionization constant** and is symbolized by K_a. The acid-ionization constant is really just an equilibrium constant, K_{eq}, applied to the ionization of an acid in water. Consider the equilibrium established when acetic acid is dissolved in water, as in the vinegar shown in **Figure 15-15.**

$$CH_3COOH(aq) + H_2O(l) \rightleftharpoons H_3O^+(aq) + CH_3COO^-(aq)$$

The equilibrium expression for this reaction is written as follows.

$$K_a = \frac{[H_3O^+][CH_3COO^-]}{[CH_3COOH]} = 1.75 \times 10^{-5}$$

Recall that only solutes appear in equilibrium expressions; solvents, such as water, are omitted. Also remember that K_a is a unitless quantity.

Physical chemists have carefully measured the acid-ionization constants of hundreds of acids. Values for a few of these are reproduced in **Table 15-4.** The arrows on this table illustrate that the conjugate of a stronger acid or base is a weaker base or acid, respectively.

TABLE 15-4 Relative Strengths of Acids and Bases

Conjugate acid	Formula	K_a	Conjugate base	Formula
Hydronium ion	H_3O^+	5.53×10^1	water	H_2O
Sulfurous acid	H_2SO_3	1.23×10^{-2}	hydrogen sulfite ion	HSO_3^-
Hydrogen sulfate ion	HSO_4^-	1.02×10^{-2}	sulfate ion	SO_4^{2-}
Phosphoric acid	H_3PO_4	7.52×10^{-3}	dihydrogen phosphate ion	$H_2PO_4^-$
Nitrous acid	HNO_2	6.76×10^{-4}	nitrite ion	NO_2^-
Formic acid	$HCOOH$	1.82×10^{-4}	formate ion	$HCOO^-$
Benzoic acid	C_6H_5COOH	6.46×10^{-5}	benzoate ion	$C_6H_5COO^-$
Acetic acid	CH_3COOH	1.76×10^{-5}	acetate ion	CH_3COO^-
Carbonic acid	H_2CO_3	4.30×10^{-7}	hydrogen carbonate ion	HCO_3^-
Hydrogen sulfite ion	HSO_3^-	6.61×10^{-8}	sulfite ion	SO_3^{2-}
Dihydrogen phosphate ion	$H_2PO_4^-$	6.31×10^{-8}	monohydrogen phosphate ion	HPO_4^{2-}
Hypochlorous acid	$HClO$	2.95×10^{-9}	hypochlorite ion	ClO^-
Ammonium ion	NH_4^+	5.75×10^{-10}	ammonia	NH_3
Hydrogen carbonate ion	HCO_3^-	4.68×10^{-11}	carbonate ion	CO_3^{2-}
Monohydrogen phosphate ion	HPO_4^{2-}	4.47×10^{-13}	phosphate ion	PO_4^{3-}
Water	H_2O	1.81×10^{-16}	hydroxide ion	OH^-

Increasing acid strength (left margin, upward arrow)

Increasing base strength (right margin, downward arrow)

SAMPLE PROBLEM 15B   Calculating K_a of a weak acid

A vinegar sample is found to be 0.837 M acetic acid. Its hydronium ion concentration is measured as 3.86×10^{-3} mol/L. Calculate K_a for CH_3COOH.

1 List what you know
- $[CH_3COOH] = 0.837$ M
- $[H_3O^+] = 3.86 \times 10^{-3}$ mol/L
- $K_a = ?$

2 Set up the problem

▸ CH_3COOH is monoprotic, so one H_3O^+ is formed for every CH_3COOH that ionizes, and $[CH_3COO^-] = [H_3O^+]$.

▸ Also, $[CH_3COOH]_{final} = [CH_3COOH]_{initial} - [CH_3COO^-]$.

▸ Write the equilibrium expression for K_a.

$$K_a = \frac{[H_3O^+][CH_3COO^-]}{[CH_3COOH]_{final}}$$

3 Calculate and verify

▸ Substitute the concentration of each component into the equilibrium expression, and compute K_a.

$$[CH_3COO^-] = [H_3O^+] = 3.86 \times 10^{-3}$$

$$[CH_3COOH]_{final} = 0.837 - 0.00386 = 0.833$$

$$K_a = \frac{[H_3O^+][CH_3COO^-]}{[CH_3COOH]_{final}} = \frac{(3.86 \times 10^{-3})^2}{0.833} = 1.79 \times 10^{-5}$$

▸ The calculated value, $K_a = 1.79 \times 10^{-5}$, is very near the literature value of 1.75×10^{-5} found in Table 15-4. Therefore, the answer is reasonable.

$\mathcal{S}$ECTION REVIEW

Total recall

1. In the following reactions, identify and label the conjugate acid-base pairs.
   a. $H_3PO_4(aq) + NO_2^-(aq) \rightleftarrows$
   $\qquad\qquad HNO_2(aq) + H_2PO_4^-(aq)$
   b. $CN^-(aq) + HCO_3^-(aq) \rightleftarrows$
   $\qquad\qquad HCN(aq) + CO_3^{2-}(aq)$
   c. $HCN(aq) + SO_3^{2-}(aq) \rightleftarrows$
   $\qquad\qquad HSO_3^-(aq) + CN^-(aq)$

2. What is meant by *polyprotic acid*?

3. Why is water considered amphoteric?

4. How does Arrhenius's definition fail to classify $HCl(g)$ as an acid?

Critical thinking

5. **Interpreting Tables** Use Table 15-4 to determine which direction is favored in the following reaction.
   $$H_2CO_3 + H_2O \rightleftarrows HCO_3^- + H_3O^+$$

6. Write all three K_a expressions for H_3PO_4. Which will have the smallest value?

7. **a.** What is the relationship between the strength of an acid and the strength of its conjugate base?
   b. What is the relationship between the strength of a base and the strength of its conjugate acid?

8. Benzoic acid ionizes to form benzoate ions and hydronium ions. The K_a of benzoic acid is 6.30×10^{-5}. Use the following equation to calculate $[H_3O^+]$ in a 0.200 M solution of benzoic acid.
   $$H_2O(l) + C_6H_5COOH(aq) \rightleftarrows$$
   $$C_6H_5COO^-(aq) + H_3O^+(aq)$$

9. Butanoic acid, C_3H_7COOH, ionizes in water to form $C_3H_7COO^-$ ions and H_3O^+ ions. When 0.20 mol of the acid is dissolved in 500.0 mL of water, $[H_3O^+]$ of this solution is 2.50×10^{-3} M. Calculate K_a for butanoic acid.

How are acidity and pH related?

OBJECTIVES

▶ **State** the definition of pH, and explain the relationship between pH and H_3O^+ ion concentration.

▶ **Perform** calculations using pH, $[H_3O^+]$, $[OH^-]$, and quanti-

tative descriptions of aqueous solutions.

▶ **Describe** two methods of measuring pH.

▶ **Describe** how a buffer solution is able to resist changes in pH.

Determining pH

You have probably seen commercials in which products such as cosmetics, soaps, or shampoos are described as "pH balanced." In fact, you probably use one of these products every day, just like the student seen in **Figure 15-16.** Maybe you even know that pH has something to do with how acidic or basic a material is and that the pH of pure water is 7.

What do pH values mean?

You know from Sections 15-1 and 15-2 that a solution's hydronium ion concentration measures how acidic or basic the solution is. To better

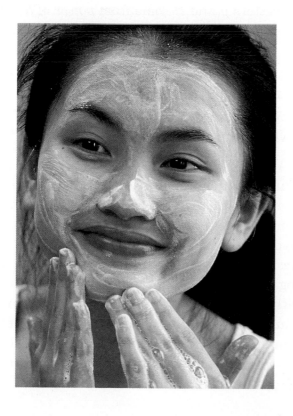

FIGURE 15-16 ◀

Soap manufacturers sometimes make claims about the pH of their products. The pH value is a measure of how acidic or basic a material is.

TABLE 15-5 pH Values at Specified [H_3O^+]

Sample	Solution	[H_3O^+](M)	pH
1	0.100 mol HCl in 1.00 L of H_2O	1.00×10^{-1}	1.00
2	0.100 mol NaCl in 1.00 L of H_2O	1.00×10^{-7}	7.00
3	0.100 mol NaOH in 1.00 L of H_2O	1.00×10^{-13}	13.00

understand this relationship between acidity and hydronium ion concentration, consider the three solutions found in **Table 15-5.**

Solution 2 is described as **neutral** because it has equal concentrations of hydronium ions and hydroxide ions. Solution 3 is *basic* because it has a lower concentration of H_3O^+ ions than OH^- ions. Solution 1 is *acidic* because it has a higher concentration of H_3O^+ ions than OH^- ions.

neutral

describes a solution that contains equal concentrations of hydronium ions and hydroxide ions

Notice that these three solutions span an immense range of hydronium ion concentrations: the concentration in Solution 1 is a million times more than the concentration in Solution 2 and a trillion times more than that in Solution 3. As you can see, working with hydronium ion concentrations can involve negative exponents or long chains of zeros. To simplify these expressions, chemists have adopted a system devised in 1909 by the Danish chemist Søren Peter Sørensen. Sørensen focused his attention on the magnitude of the power of 10 that results when hydronium ion concentration is expressed in scientific notation. He proposed using the negative of the power of 10 (the negative logarithm) and calling it the **pH** (the letters *p* and *H* come from *power of hydrogen*) of the solution. Using Sørensen's definition for the three solutions previously discussed results in the pH values listed in Table 15-5.

pH

the negative logarithm of the hydronium ion concentration in a solution

How can you calculate pH from [H_3O^+]?

Based on Sørensen's definition, the relationship between [H_3O^+] and pH is given by the following mathematical equation.

$$pH = -\log[H_3O^+] = \log(1/[H_3O^+])$$

This equation can be used to determine either the pH or the [H_3O^+], depending on the information given. You can see in Table 15-5 that as the hydronium ion concentration *increases,* the pH *decreases.* The pH decreases because the negative logarithm of a number is the same as the logarithm of the reciprocal of the number, and as a number increases, its reciprocal decreases. For example, a tenfold increase in [H_3O^+] decreases the pH by 1.00, and a thousandfold decrease in [H_3O^+] increases the pH by 3.00.

STUDY SKILLS

USING MNEMONICS

Mnemonic devices are effective tools to aid you in learning chemical concepts. To help you remember which end of the pH range is acidic and which is basic, use the following mnemonic device: the first letter of the alphabet, A (for acid), corresponds to the first number, 0.

It is easy to find the pH or the $[H_3O^+]$ of a solution by using a scientific calculator. Because calculators differ, check your manual to find out exactly which keys are used for log and antilog functions.

1 **Calculate pH from $[H_3O^+]$**

▶ **Key in the value of $[H_3O^+]$.**

You can but do not have to use scientific notation. To enter the value in scientific notation, key in the first part of the number, then press the exponent key and key in the exponent. If your exponent is negative, you will need to press the sign-change key before you key in the value of the exponent.

▶ **Press** $\boxed{\text{LOG}}$ **(the base-10 logarithm key).**

▶ **Press the sign-change key, which is usually labeled** $\boxed{+/-}$ **.**

2 **Calculate $[H_3O^+]$ from pH**

▶ **Key in the pH value.**

▶ **Change its sign by pressing** $\boxed{+/-}$ **.**

▶ **Press** $\boxed{10^x}$ **.**

This key raises 10 to the power of the number displayed on your calculator. With –pH displayed, it gives 10^{-pH}, which equals $[H_3O^+]$.

SAMPLE PROBLEM 15C   Calculating the pH of an acidic solution

What is the pH of a 0.00010 M solution of HCl, a strong acid?

1 **List what you know**

▶ Concentration of HCl = 0.00010 M

▶ pH = ?

2 **Set up the problem**

▶ Because HCl is a strong acid, the hydronium ion concentration equals the concentration of the solution.

$$[H_3O^+] = 0.00010 \text{ M} = 1.0 \times 10^{-4} \text{ M}$$

▶ Write the equation for pH.

$$pH = -\log(1.0 \times 10^{-4})$$

3 **Calculate**

▶ Use your calculator to determine the log of 1.0×10^{-4}. A special rule is applied for reporting the log using the correct number of significant figures. Only digits to the right of the decimal count as significant figures. Here, your given value has two significant figures. Therefore, your answer should have two digits to the right of the decimal.

$$pH = -(-4.00) = 4.00$$

1. Calculate the pH of each of the following solutions.
   a. 0.010 M HNO_3
   b. 4.7×10^{-2} M HBr
   c. 3.85×10^{-3} M HI
   d. 5.5×10^{-4} M HCl

2. What is the concentration of a nitric acid solution with a pH of 2.50?

3. What is the pH of a solution made by diluting 10.0 mL of 2.00 M HCl to 500.0 mL with water?

How does pH relate to K_a and K_w?

You have now calculated the pH of strong acid solutions, but what about the pH of solutions of weak acids? In order to calculate pH information for weak acids, you must find the hydronium ion concentration using the equilibrium expression and the acid-ionization constant. Examine the following example, which uses the weak acid benzoic acid.

$$C_6H_5COOH(aq) + H_2O(l) \rightleftharpoons C_6H_5COO^-(aq) + H_3O^+(aq)$$

$$K_a = \frac{[C_6H_5COO^-][H_3O^+]}{[C_6H_5COOH]} = 6.31 \times 10^{-5}$$

By rearranging the above equation, and given the appropriate concentration data, you can solve for $[H_3O^+]$ and determine the pH of the solution.

To find the pH of basic solutions, first think of the relationship between the hydronium ion concentration and the hydroxide ion concentration in any solution.

$$K_w = [H_3O^+][OH^-] = 1.00 \times 10^{-14}$$

By rearranging the above expression, you can use the ionic product constant of water to relate pH to $[OH^-]$.

SAMPLE PROBLEM 15D Calculating the pH of a basic solution

What is the pH of a 0.0136 M solution of $Ba(OH)_2$, a strong base?

1 List what you know
  ▸ Concentration of $Ba(OH)_2$ = 0.0136 M
  ▸ pH = ?

2 Set up the problem
  ▸ Use the given data to determine the concentration of hydroxide ions. Recognize that 1 mol of $Ba(OH)_2$ produces 2 mol of OH^- ions.

   concentration of OH^- = 2 × concentration of $Ba(OH)_2$

  ▸ Use the ionic product of water to calculate $[H_3O^+]$.

   $$K_w = [H_3O^+][OH^-] = 1.00 \times 10^{-14}$$

  ▸ Use the definition of pH to calculate its value.

   $$pH = -\log[H_3O^+]$$

> Calculate [OH⁻].

$$[OH^-] = 2 \times (0.0136) = 0.0272 \text{ M}$$

> Solve the K_w equation for $[H_3O^+]$, substitute data into the equation, and calculate $[H_3O^+]$.

$$[H_3O^+] = \frac{K_w}{[OH^-]} = \frac{1.00 \times 10^{-14}}{0.0272} = 3.68 \times 10^{-13} \text{ M}$$

> Determine pH, and round your answer to the correct number of significant figures.

$$pH = -\log(3.68 \times 10^{-13})$$

$$pH = -(-12.435) = 12.435$$

PRACTICE PROBLEMS

1. What is the pH of a 0.00256 M KOH solution?

2. Calculate the pH of a 1.00 L solution made by dissolving 1.40 g of NaOH in water.

3. Determine the pH of human blood in which [OH⁻] is 2.60×10^{-7} M.

How is pH measured?

There are two ways to measure pH. The first method is quick and convenient but not particularly accurate. The second is accurate but more complicated and more expensive than the first.

The first method relies on the fact that certain dyes, called **indicators,** have different colors in solutions of different pH. Thymol blue is an example of an indicator. It is yellow in solutions with a pH between 3 and 8 and blue in solutions with a pH of 10 and above. In solutions with a pH between 8 and 10, thymol blue exhibits shades of green. **Figure 15-17** shows the structures of the yellow and blue forms of this dye. The yellow form is a weak acid with an acid-ionization constant around 1.0×10^{-9}, and the blue form is its conjugate base.

indicator

dye that changes to different colors in solutions of different pH

FIGURE 15-17 ▼

The indicator thymol blue is yellow in neutral and acidic solutions. As the OH⁻ concentration of the solution increases, the indicator turns blue.

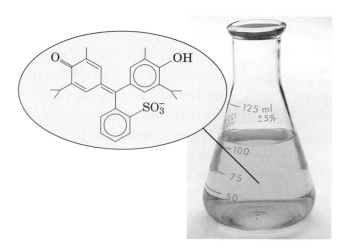
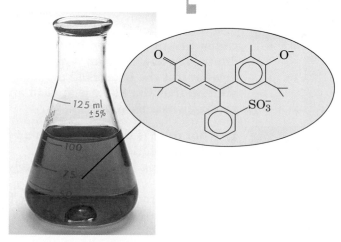

► **FIGURE 15-18**

The pH of these substances is easily determined by comparing the color the substance turns a strip of pH paper with the color scale on the pH-paper dispenser.

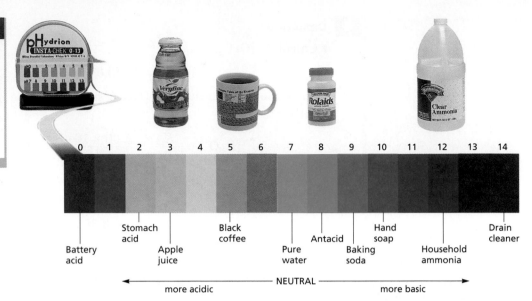

| 0 | 1 | 2 | 3 | 4 | 5 | 6 | 7 | 8 | 9 | 10 | 11 | 12 | 13 | 14 |

Battery acid · Stomach acid · Apple juice · Black coffee · Pure water · Antacid · Baking soda · Hand soap · Household ammonia · Drain cleaner

←——— more acidic ——— NEUTRAL ——— more basic ———→

pH meter

an electronic device that measures pH

In addition to thymol blue, many other indicators exist. Every indicator changes color over a certain pH range. Some change at acidic (low) pH values, while others change at basic pH values even greater than 10. Because many different indicators exist, it is possible to prepare mixtures that can give a continuous gradation of color through a wide pH range. The color of a strip of pH paper, as depicted in **Figure 15-18,** can be matched against a standard color chart to easily measure the pH of a solution.

pH meters are more accurate than indicators

The second way to measure pH is to use a **pH meter,** which measures pH by determining the voltage between two electrodes. A pH meter provides a direct digital reading of the pH of the solution into which the electrodes are dipped. Careful experiments using a pH meter can yield accurate pH readings with a precision of ±0.01. This is a much more exact result than can be obtained by judging the color change of an indicator in solution.

QUICKLAB

CONSUMER ACTIVITY

An Acid Among Us

You know that taste and feel are not safe ways to determine whether a substance is an acid or a base, so how can you figure out which household products are acids and which are bases?

Materials red cabbage (cut up), blender, strainer, 500 mL beaker, water, assorted household cleaners and food products, small beakers, spatula

Procedure Use the blender to grind the red cabbage with water. Strain the liquid into the large beaker, and dilute. You now have an indicator. Using your indicator, test the household products. Start with an item that you know is an acid and one that you know is a base.

Analysis
1. What color is the indicator in acidic solution? in basic solution?
2. Are cleaning products more likely to be acidic or basic?
3. Are food products more likely to be acidic or basic?

internet**connect**

SCI*LINKS*™
NSTA

TOPIC: Buffers
GO TO: www.scilinks.org
KEYWORD: HW155

CONCEPT CHECK

1. Explain why pH meters provide a more accurate reading of pH values than do indicators.

2. How can pH paper indicate such a wide range of pH values?

3. What color would a solution of thymol blue be if it had a high concentration of hydroxide ions?

Buffer solutions

You can see in **Table 15-6** that the pH of blood is 7.4. Keeping your blood pH within the very narrow range of 7.35 to 7.45 is crucial to your health. If your pH gets outside the range of 7.35 to 7.45, you will become ill. At a blood pH lower than 7.35, you suffer acidosis. At a blood pH higher than 7.45, you suffer alkalosis. How does your body control the pH of blood within such narrow bounds? It relies on the properties of **buffer solutions**—solutions that resist changes in pH due to the addition of acids or bases. These solutions are said to be *buffered* against changes in pH.

buffer solution

a solution that resists changes in pH

A buffer has two ingredients

A buffer solution, often simply called a *buffer,* is a solution of a weak acid and its conjugate base in approximately equal amounts. For example, consider a solution made by dissolving 1 mol each of acetic acid, CH_3COOH, and sodium acetate, $NaCH_3COO$, in water. Sodium acetate is a strong electrolyte that ionizes completely in aqueous solution, as shown by the following equation.

$$NaCH_3COO(s) \xrightarrow{\text{H}_2\text{O}} Na^+(aq) + CH_3COO^-(aq)$$

On the other hand, acetic acid is a weak acid that is scarcely ionized at all in water. The ionization of acetic acid, shown by the following equation, reaches equilibrium by forming only very small amounts of H_3O^+ ions and CH_3COO^- ions.

$$CH_3COOH(aq) + H_2O(l) \rightleftarrows H_3O^+(aq) + CH_3COO^-(aq)$$

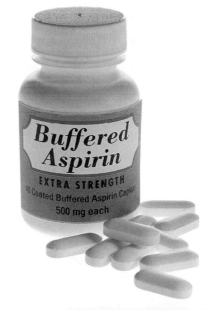

FIGURE 15-19 ▲

Many medications are buffered to protect your body from changes in pH that can be harmful.

TABLE 15-6	Typical pH Values of Human Body Fluids		
Solution	**pH**	**Solution**	**pH**
Gastric juice	1.5	Blood	7.4
Urine	6.0	Tears	7.4
Saliva	6.5	Pancreatic juice	7.9
Milk	6.6	Bile	8.2

FIGURE 15-20

The left-hand beaker in each photo contains a neutral solution. The right-hand beaker contains a solution to which hydrochloric acid has been added.

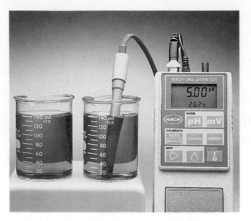

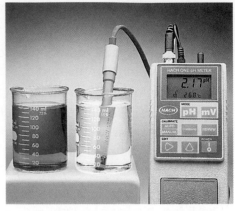

a When a small amount of HCl is added to a buffered solution, the pH of the solution does not change dramatically.

b When HCl is added to an unbuffered solution, the solution's pH drops significantly. This drop can be seen on the pH meter or in the color change of an indicator.

When additional acetate ions from $NaCH_3COO$ appear in this weak acid solution, the reverse reaction is favored even more strongly, and more acetic acid forms.

$$CH_3COOH(aq) + H_2O(l) \rightleftharpoons H_3O^+(aq) + CH_3COO^-(aq)$$

This change in equilibrium is in accordance with Le Châtelier's principle, which was discussed in Chapter 14. In that chapter you also learned about the *common-ion effect,* of which this is also an example. The acetate ion is the common ion in this case, and almost all of the acetate ions in the solution are supplied by the sodium acetate because sodium acetate ionizes much more completely than acetic acid does. As a result of the change in equilibrium, the concentration of $CH_3COO^-(aq)$ is practically equal to the concentration of dissolved $NaCH_3COO$. Likewise, the amount of $CH_3COOH(aq)$ will be very close to the amount of CH_3COOH that was originally dissolved.

How does a buffer control pH?

Why is it that a buffered solution resists changes in pH? Look at what happens to the acetic acid–sodium acetate solution when a small amount of strong acid is added. Remember that H_3O^+ ions and CH_3COO^- ions can combine to form CH_3COOH, shifting the equilibrium further to the left.

$$CH_3COOH(aq) + H_2O(l) \rightleftharpoons H_3O^+(aq) + CH_3COO^-(aq)$$

As a result, the added H_3O^+ ions are "used up," and the pH changes very little.

Conversely, when a small amount of a strong base is added to the buffer solution, the OH^- ions react with CH_3COOH to produce more acetate ions, shifting the equilibrium to the right. Consequently, the added OH^- ions raise the pH very little.

$$OH^-(aq) + CH_3COOH(aq) \rightleftharpoons H_2O(l) + CH_3COO^-(aq)$$

A solution containing a weak acid and its conjugate base in nearly equal concentrations can absorb added H_3O^+ ions and OH^- ions, thus minimizing pH changes. Now you can understand that when manufacturers of shampoos and antacids boast that their products are buffered, they mean that the products contain substances in solution that can absorb small amounts of acids or bases with a result of little or no change in pH.

The liquid portion of blood is an example of a buffer solution. This buffering system helps keep the pH of blood between 7.35 and 7.45. The buffering system in blood is the weak acid H_2CO_3 (carbon dioxide combined with water) and its conjugate base, the hydrogen carbonate ion, HCO_3^-.

$$H_2CO_3(aq) + H_2O(l) \rightleftarrows H_3O^+(aq) + HCO_3^-(aq)$$

The equilibrium of the buffering system in blood is important to maintaining good health. Many medical conditions can disrupt the equilibrium of this system, resulting in either acidosis or alkalosis, both of which can be serious and even fatal. Uncontrolled diabetes and intoxication are common causes of acidosis and alkalosis, respectively.

$\mathcal{S}$ECTION REVIEW

Total recall

1. Explain what is meant by the pH of a solution.

2. Name the two methods of measuring pH.

Critical thinking

3. Explain the relationship between the self-ionization of water and the pH of a neutral solution.

4. Explain what a buffer does. What two ingredients does a buffer contain?

5. The phosphate buffer system consists of the dihydrogen phosphate ion, $H_2PO_4^-$, and the monohydrogen phosphate ion, HPO_4^{2-}. Describe how this system reacts to maintain a constant pH when OH^- ions are added.

6. **Interpreting Graphics** Describe how a benzoic acid–sodium benzoate buffer reacts with both H_3O^+ and OH^- ions. (Hint: See the formula for benzoic acid on page 562.)

Practice problems

7. One aqueous solution of a base has a pH of 8. A second has a pH of 11. Which solution has the larger concentration of OH^- ions? How many times larger? Which solution has the larger concentration of H_3O^+ ions? How many times larger?

8. An aqueous solution has a pH of 3.10. Determine $[H_3O^+]$ and $[OH^-]$ of this solution.

9. **Interpreting Tables** Refer to Table 15-6 on page 565. Calculate $[H_3O^+]$ and $[OH^-]$ in human saliva.

10. The $[OH^-]$ of apple juice is 3.2×10^{-11} M. Determine its pH.

ANTACIDS

Stomach acids and antacids

According to Table 15-6, the pH of gastric juice in the human stomach is 1.5. This strongly acidic environment is essential to activate digestive enzymes that work in the stomach, such as pepsin. Acidity is provided by approximately 0.03 M concentration of hydrochloric acid, HCl(*aq*). Sometimes a person's stomach generates too much acid. This causes the discomfort known as heartburn that results when the acid solution is forced into the esophagus. Heartburn can be temporarily relieved by taking an **antacid** to neutralize the excess stomach acid.

Although antacids contain a variety of ingredients, they all contain a base that counteracts stomach acid. The base is either sodium hydrogen carbonate, $NaHCO_3$, calcium carbonate, $CaCO_3$, aluminum hydroxide, $Al(OH)_3$, or magnesium hydroxide, $Mg(OH)_2$.

Dangers of excess metals from antacids

In any antacid, the carbonate, hydrogen carbonate, or hydroxide ion is the base that neutralizes the excess stomach acid. However, the metal in the antacid is also important. Antacids containing $NaHCO_3$ work fastest because $NaHCO_3$ is much more soluble than other antacid substances. Overuse of these antacids, however, can raise the level of sodium ions in the body, just as salt does. Overuse can also seriously disrupt the acid-base balance in your blood.

Because of the risks associated with an excess of sodium, some antacid manufacturers have substituted calcium carbonate, $CaCO_3$, for $NaHCO_3$. But if taken in large amounts, calcium can promote kidney stones. Too much aluminum

internet**connect**

SC/LINKS™
NSTA

TOPIC: Antacids
GO TO: www.scilinks.org
KEYWORD: HW153

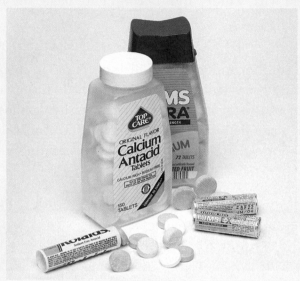

ingested from antacid products, such as $Al(OH)_3$, can interfere with the body's absorption of important minerals, such as phosphorus, which is needed to maintain healthy bones. Also, some people believe there is a connection between the ingestion of aluminum ions and Alzheimer's disease. This belief may be misguided because it is not yet known whether aluminum plays a role in the onset of Alzheimer's disease. Excess magnesium from antacids with $Mg(OH)_2$ may pose problems for people with kidney trouble.

You should know the active ingredient in any antacid product before you ingest it, and you should never use an antacid product for more than a few days without consulting a doctor. It is best to avoid the need for an antacid in the first place. You can minimize the production of excess stomach acid by following a healthy diet, avoiding stress, and limiting your consumption of coffee, fatty foods, and chocolate.

What is a titration?

OBJECTIVES

▶ **Write** an ionic equation for a neutralization reaction, and identify its reactants and products.

▶ **Describe** the conditions at the equivalence point in a titration.

▶ **Tell** how a buret is used in a titration.

▶ **Discuss** two methods used to detect the equivalence point in a titration.

▶ **Calculate** the unknown concentration of an acid or base using titration data.

▶ **Explain** how you would select an indicator for an acid-base titration.

Neutralization

The solution of a strong acid, shown in the beaker on the left in **Figure 15-21,** contains a high concentration of hydronium ions—high enough to react with metals such as zinc. The solution of a strong base, shown in the beaker on the right, contains a high concentration of hydroxide ions—high enough to free a grease-clogged drain. But if you mix these two solutions in the correct proportions, you get an aqueous solution that has neither of these properties—it will not react with metals and it cannot unclog a drain. How can you account for this significant change in properties?

The change occurs because large concentrations of $H_3O^+(aq)$ ions and $OH^-(aq)$ ions cannot exist together in the same solution. Upon mixing of

internet**connect**

SC*LINKS*
NSTA

TOPIC: Titration/Indicators
GO TO: www.scilinks.org
KEYWORD: IIW154

FIGURE 15-21 ▼

The neutralization reaction between solutions of nitric acid and sodium hydroxide produces a solution of sodium nitrate.

a This beaker contains a solution of nitric acid, a strong acid. It turns pH paper red.

c The reaction produces a sodium nitrate solution, which has a neutral pH of 7.

b This beaker contains a solution of sodium hydroxide, a strong base. It turns pH paper blue.

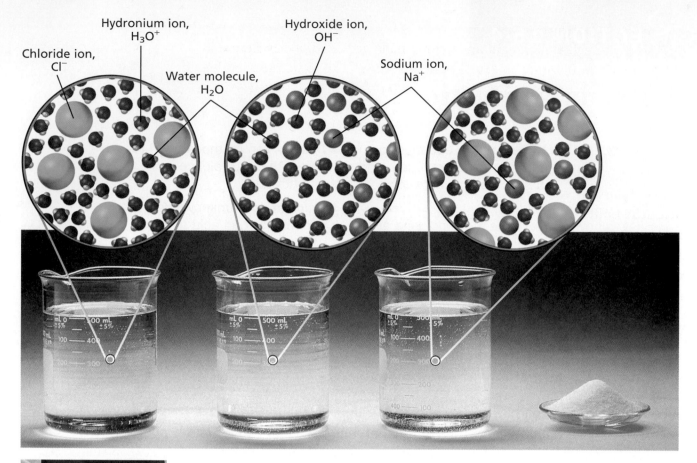

Chloride ion, Cl⁻

Hydronium ion, H₃O⁺

Water molecule, H₂O

Hydroxide ion, OH⁻

Sodium ion, Na⁺

▲ **FIGURE 15-22**

When HCl(*aq*) reacts with NaOH(*aq*), the reaction produces NaCl(*aq*). When the water is evaporated, pure sodium chloride salt is left.

the solutions, most of the hydronium ions from the acid solution and most of the hydroxide ions present in the base solution combine to form water in a neutralization reaction.

$$H_3O^+(aq) + OH^-(aq) \longrightarrow 2H_2O(l)$$

All strong acid–strong base neutralizations are the same reaction

When strong acid and strong base solutions having equal amounts of H_3O^+ and OH^- ions are mixed, as in the third beaker in **Figure 15-22,** virtually all of the hydronium and hydroxide ions react to form water. The H_3O^+ and OH^- ions remaining have concentrations of 1×10^{-7} M each, as they do in pure water. The pH of the solution will be 7.

The resulting solution contains only spectator ions. For example, suppose that the strong acid is nitric acid, HNO_3, which in aqueous solution consists of hydronium ions and nitrate ions, NO_3^-, and that the base is sodium hydroxide, which in aqueous solution consists of hydroxide ions and sodium ions, Na^+. After the contents of the two beakers are combined, the resulting solution will contain water, NO_3^- ions, and Na^+ ions. This is just an aqueous solution of sodium nitrate. You can prepare the same solution by dissolving the *salt* sodium nitrate, $NaNO_3$, in water. As you can see, the neutralization of an Arrhenius acid by an Arrhenius base in aqueous solution produces a salt and water.

$$acid + base \longrightarrow salt + water$$

No matter which strong acid and strong base are used, every neutralization reaction in aqueous solution is the same—the ionic reaction between H_3O^+ ions and OH^- ions to form water. Only the spectator ions differ.

Principles of titrations

The point at which a neutralization reaction is complete is known as the **equivalence point.** When a strong base is used to neutralize a strong acid, the equivalence point is the point at which the amount of added hydroxide ions exactly equals the amount of hydronium ions originally in solution. At a temperature of 25°C, H_3O^+ and OH^- ions have concentrations of 1.00×10^{-7} M each at the equivalence point, the same concentrations that they have in pure water.

The operation of gradually adding one solution to another to reach an equivalence point is known as a **titration.** The How To feature on pages 574–575 of this section will show you how to use burets to carry out a titration. If an acid is to be titrated with a base, one buret may be used to measure the volume of the acid into the titration flask, and a second buret may be used to deliver and measure the volume of **titrant** needed as shown in **Figure 15-23.** In this case, the titrant is the base solution. Titrations can just as well be carried out the other way around, delivering an acid into a base solution. However, you cannot determine the concentration of one solution unless the concentration of the other is known accurately. A **standard solution** is one whose concentration is accurately known, normally because it has previously been used to titrate a precisely weighed mass of a solid acid or base. A standard solution is usually used as the titrant.

equivalence point

the point in a titration when the amount of added base or acid exactly equals the amount of acid or base originally in solution

titration

the operation of gradually adding one solution to another to reach an equivalence point

titrant

the solution added to another solution in a titration

standard solution

a solution whose concentration is accurately known

FIGURE 15-23 ▼

a The How To feature on pages 574–575 of this section will show you how to use burets like those shown here to carry out a titration.

b When reading the liquid level in a buret, you must read the level at the bottom of the meniscus.

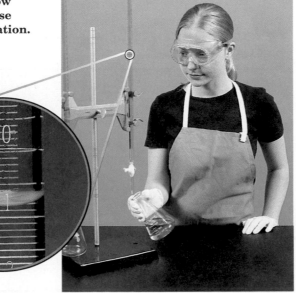
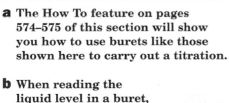

Strong Acid Titrated with Strong Base

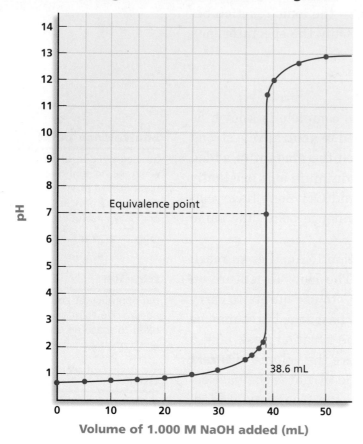

Volume of 1.000 M NaOH added (mL)

transition range

the pH range through which an indicator changes color

Detecting the equivalence point

A titration is accurate only if it ends at the equivalence point, but how will you know when that point arrives? Several methods are available for detecting the equivalence point. As the two most common techniques are explained, assume that a strong acid is being titrated with a strong base, which means that the acid is in the flask and the base is the titrant being added from the buret.

One method of detecting the equivalence point is to use a pH meter, which you read about in Section 15-3. A pH meter can be used to monitor changes in H_3O^+ concentration. The pH values obtained during a titration can be used to generate a titration curve such as the one shown in **Figure 15-24.** Notice in the graph that the equivalence point, the place of most rapid change, corresponds to pH 7, the point of neutralization for a strong acid–strong base reaction.

The oldest method of detecting the equivalence point is to use an indicator. An indicator exhibits one color at low pH values and another color at high pH values. You read about indicators in Section 15-3.

Table 15-7 lists a few of the indicators that chemists have evaluated. All indicators have a **transition range,** often about 2 pH units wide. At pH values within its transition range, an indicator exists partially in its acid form and partially in its base form. As a result, its color is intermediate

TABLE 15-7 Transition Ranges of Some Indicators

Indicator name	Acid color	Transition range (pH)	Base color
Thymol blue	red	1.2–2.8	yellow
Methyl orange	red	3.1–4.4	orange
Litmus	red	5.0–8.0	blue
Bromthymol blue	yellow	6.0–7.6	blue
Thymol blue	yellow	8.0–9.6	blue
Phenolphthalein	colorless	8.0–9.6	red
Alizarin yellow	yellow	10.1–12.0	red

pH 5   pH 7   pH 9
          Bromthymol blue

pH 7   pH 9   pH 11
          Phenolphthalein

FIGURE 15-25 ▲

Bromthymol blue
changes color between
a pH of 6.0 and 7.6. It
is ideal for a titration
involving a strong acid
and a strong base. Phe-
nolphthalein changes
color between a pH of
8.0 and 9.6. It is suit-
able for the titration
of a weak acid with
a strong base.

between the acid and base colors. Notice that thymol blue can exist in three different colored forms; therefore, it has two transition ranges.

Which indicator do I choose?

Choosing an indicator for a titration of a strong acid with a strong base is easy. Because the equivalence point occurs at pH 7, you would choose an indicator that has a transition range around this value. The point at which the indicator changes color is the **end point** of a titration. If you choose the right indicator, the end point and the equivalence point will be the same.

Not all titrations have equivalence points at pH = 7.0. When a weak acid is titrated with a strong base, the equivalence point is at a pH greater than 7.0. If a strong acid is titrated with a weak base, the equivalence point is at a pH lower than 7.0. **Figure 15-25** shows how different indicators are effective for different types of titrations.

end point

the point in a titration at which the indicator changes color

CONCEPT CHECK

1. What indicators could you use if a solution of HCl, a strong acid, is titrated with a solution of Na_2CO_3, a weak base?

2. Why should an indicator be chosen so that the equivalence point and the end point coincide during a titration?

3. How is the concentration of a standard solution of an acid or a base usually determined?

4. Write the ionic equations for the neutralization reaction that occurs between the following.
   a. HNO_3 and $Ca(OH)_2$
   b. KOH and H_2SO_4

5. If a titration between a weak acid and a strong base has an equivalence point at a pH of 9.5, which indicators could be used to detect the equivalence point of the titration?

This procedure would be used to determine the unknown concentration of an acid by titrating it with a standardized base solution. Decide which of the burets will be used for the acid and which will be used for the base. Label each buret to avoid confusion. Rinse the acid buret three times with the acid to be used in the titration. Use the base solution to rinse the other buret in the same manner.

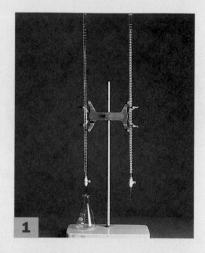

Fill the acid buret with the acid solution to a point above the 0 mL mark.

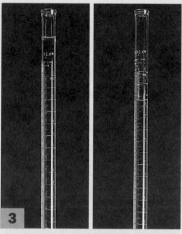

Release some acid to remove any air bubbles and to lower the volume into the calibrated portion of the buret.

Record the exact volume of the acid in the buret to the nearest 0.01 mL as your starting point.

Release a volume of acid (determined by your lab procedure) into a clean, dry Erlenmeyer flask.

Record the new volume reading, and subtract the starting volume from it to find the volume of acid added.

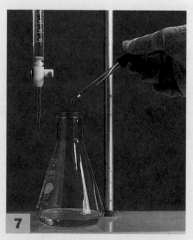

Add three drops of an appropriate indicator (phenolphthalein in this case) to the flask.

Fill the other buret with standardized base solution to a point above the 0 mL mark. The concentration of the standardized base solution is known because it was previously used to titrate a precisely weighed mass of a solid acid.

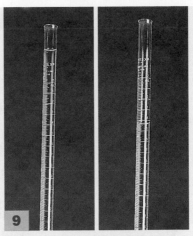

8

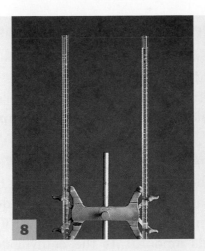

9

Release some base from the buret so that the volume is in the calibrated portion of the buret.

10

Record the exact volume of the base to the nearest 0.01 mL as your starting point.

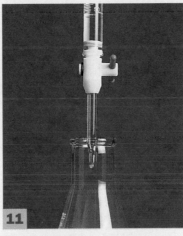

11

Place the flask containing the acid under the base buret. Notice that the tip of the buret extends into the mouth of the flask.

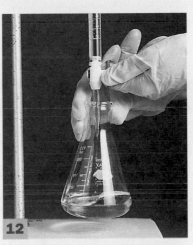

12

Slowly release base from the buret into the flask while *constantly* swirling the flask. The pink color should fade with swirling.

13

Near the end point, add base drop by drop.

14

The end point is reached when a very light pink color remains after 30 seconds of swirling.

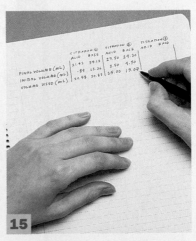

15

Record the new volume, and determine the volume of base added.

Titration calculations

No matter what method you use to detect the equivalence point in a titration, the next step is always the same. Remember that the goal of a titration is to determine the amount of a substance, such as the amount of nitric acid in the sample being titrated.

Volumes of solution are measured

At the equivalence point in a titration of a strong acid with a strong base, the amount of hydroxide ions added equals the initial amount of hydronium ions. Recall from Chapter 13 that molarity multiplied by volume yields amount. At the equivalence point, the amount of added base equals the amount of acid originally present in solution. This relationship is often expressed symbolically by the following equation, where c_{OH^-} and $c_{H_3O^+}$ are concentrations of OH^- and H_3O^+, respectively, and V_{OH^-} and $V_{H_3O^+}$ are volumes of OH^- and H_3O^+, respectively.

$$c_{OH^-} \times V_{OH^-} = c_{H_3O^+} \times V_{H_3O^+}$$

SAMPLE PROBLEM 15E   **Calculating concentration from titration data**

A student titrates 40.00 mL of an HCl solution of unknown concentration with a 0.5500 M NaOH solution. The volume of base solution needed to reach the equivalence point is 24.64 mL. What is the molarity of the HCl solution?

1 List what you know

▶ Volume of HCl solution titrated = 40.00 mL
▶ Concentration of NaOH titrant = 0.5500 M
▶ Volume of NaOH titrant = 24.64 mL
▶ Concentration of HCl solution = ? M

2 Set up the problem

▶ Write out the titration reaction.

$$HCl(aq) + NaOH(aq) \longrightarrow NaCl(aq) + H_2O(l)$$

▶ Use the net ionic equation for a strong acid–strong base titration.

$$H_3O^+(aq) + OH^-(aq) \longrightarrow 2H_2O(l)$$

▶ Relate the concentrations of acid and base to the concentrations of H_3O^+ and OH^- ions, respectively. NaOH is a strong base that ionizes to produce 1 mol of OH^- ions per 1 mol of NaOH dissolved. HCl is a monoprotic strong acid that ionizes to give 1 mol of H_3O^+ ions per 1 mol of HCl dissolved.

$$c_{OH^-} = 0.5500 \text{ M}$$

$$c_{H_3O^+} = ?$$

▶ Use the concentration-volume relationship to calculate $c_{H_3O^+}$.

$$c_{OH^-} \times V_{OH^-} = c_{H_3O^+} \times V_{H_3O^+}$$

3 Calculate and verify

▶ Solve the concentration-volume equation for $c_{H_3O^+}$, substitute data values, and calculate.

$$c_{H_3O^+} = \frac{c_{OH^-} \times V_{OH^-}}{V_{H_3O^+}} = \frac{0.5500 \text{ mol/L} \times 0.02464 \text{ L}}{0.04000 \text{ L}} = 0.3388 \text{ mol/L}$$

Concentration of HCl = 0.3388 M

▶ The NaOH concentration was 0.5500 M. The volume of NaOH solution required (≈ 25 mL) was a bit more than half the volume (≈ 40 mL) of HCl titrated. Therefore, the concentration of the acid must be a bit more than half the concentration of the base, so ≈ 0.34 M is a reasonable result.

$\mathcal{S}$ECTION REVIEW

Total recall

1. What two products are formed in a neutralization reaction?

2. What is the determining factor in selecting an indicator to use in a titration?

3. What is the equivalence point of a titration? Describe the two methods that are used to detect the equivalence point in a titration.

Critical thinking

4. Why is a buret rather than a graduated cylinder used in a titration?

5. **Interpreting Tables** Refer to Table 15-7 on page 572. Explain why methyl orange is not a good choice when titrating a strong acid with a strong base.

6. Explain the difference between end point and equivalence point. Why is it important that both occur at approximately the same pH in a titration?

7. Assume that the equivalence point is reached when 0.0103 M CH_3COOH is titrated with 0.0117 M KOH. Predict what the pH of the resulting solution will be. What pH will result by titrating 0.00203 M HNO_3 with 0.00404 NaOH until the equivalence point is reached?

8. Explain why the titration of a strong acid with a weak base ends at a pH lower than 7. Use chemical equations to explain what happens.

Practice problems

9. If 20.6 mL of 0.010 M aqueous HCl are required to titrate 30.0 mL of an aqueous solution of NaOH to the equivalence point, what is the molarity of the NaOH solution?

10. In the titration of 35.0 mL of liquid drain cleaner containing NaOH, 50.08 mL of 0.409 M HCl must be added to reach the equivalence point. What is the concentration of the base in the cleaner?

11. Calculate the volume of 0.256 M $Ba(OH)_2$ that must be added to titrate 46.0 mL of 0.407 M $HClO_4$. (Hint: Write the equation for the reaction and note the mole ratios.)

12. Potassium hydrogen phthalate is a monoprotic acid with a molar mass of 204.23 g/mol that is often used to standardize basic solutions. If a 2.00 g sample of potassium hydrogen phthalate is titrated with 34.7 mL of an NaOH solution, what is the molarity of the NaOH solution?

At the beginning of this chapter, you read about the acidification of a New England lake and the efforts to restore the lake's ecological health. Now that you know more about acids and bases, let us reconsider the questions that were posed.

LOOKING BACK

How are the industrial gases responsible for acid rain?

The industrial gases responsible for acid rain are oxides of nitrogen and sulfur, such as $NO_2(g)$ and $SO_2(g)$. These gases dissolve in rainwater and in snow by reactions such as the following.

$$2NO_2(g) + 3H_2O(l) \longrightarrow$$
$$2H_3O^+(aq) + NO_2^-(aq) + NO_3^-(aq)$$

The hydronium ions produced by such reactions are evidenced by a lowering of the rain's pH. Rain-fed streams convey the acidity to the lake, and the accumulation of H_3O^+ ions leads to detrimental biological effects.

Why did environmentalists transport limestone into the region instead of using local rock?

Not all rock exhibits basic properties, and evidently the rock basin in which the lake is nestled is made of an inactive mineral, such as granite. If the rock basin were made of limestone, the lake would have been naturally protected against acidification.

Limestone consists mainly of the base calcium carbonate, which reacts with hydronium ions by the following reaction.

$$CaCO_3(s) + H_3O^+(aq) \longrightarrow$$
$$Ca^{2+}(aq) + HCO_3^-(aq) + H_2O(l)$$

As the acidity is neutralized, the lake's ecological health is restored. Because limestone is insoluble in acid-free water, there is no fear of dangerously high pH levels that could occur if bases such as NaOH(s) were used to combat lake acidity.

Why was this operation carried out during the winter?

The most convenient way to distribute the limestone evenly is to spread the rock on the ice and allow the rock to drop to the lake bed during the spring thaw. Other methods can be expensive and may destroy the fragile shoreline.

$\mathcal{H}$IGHLIGHTS

KEY TERMS

15-1
amine
carboxylic acid
neutralization reaction
strong acid
weak acid

15-2
acid-ionization constant
amphoteric
Brønsted-Lowry acid
Brønsted-Lowry base
conjugate acid
conjugate base
diprotic acid
monoprotic acid
triprotic acid

15-3
buffer solution
indicator
neutral
pH
pH meter

15-4
end point
equivalence point
standard solution
titrant
titration
transition range

KEY CONCEPTS

15-1 What are acids and bases?

▶ Acids generate hydronium ions in aqueous solution; bases generate hydroxide ions in aqueous solution.

▶ Strong acids and strong bases ionize completely in aqueous solution and are good electrical conductors. Weak acids and bases ionize only partially.

▶ Given either the hydronium ion or hydroxide ion concentration, the K_w can be used to calculate the concentration of the other ion in aqueous solution.

15-2 Can the strengths of acids and bases be quantified?

▶ A Brønsted-Lowry acid is a proton donor, and a Brønsted-Lowry base is a proton acceptor. Some compounds, such as water, can function as both and are considered amphoteric.

▶ A conjugate acid forms when a Brønsted-Lowry base accepts a proton. A conjugate base forms when a Brønsted-Lowry acid releases a proton.

▶ Acids and bases are ranked according to their strengths on the basis of their ionization constants, K_a, or on those of their conjugate acids.

15-3 How are acidity and pH related?

▶ The pH is the negative logarithm of the hydronium ion concentration in a solution.

▶ The pH can be measured with the use of an indicator or a pH meter.

▶ A buffer consists of a weak acid and its conjugate base and resists changes in the pH of a solution.

15-4 What is a titration?

▶ When mixed in the proper stoichiometric ratios, acids and bases neutralize each other.

▶ The concentration of an acidic or basic solution can be determined through a titration.

▶ The equivalence point of a strong acid–strong base titration occurs when the amount of H_3O^+ or OH^- added equals the amount of OH^- or H_3O^+ that was originally present.

KEY SKILLS

Review the following models before your exam. Be sure you can solve these types of problems.

How To Use logarithms in pH calculations (p. 561)

How To Carry out a titration (p. 574)

Sample Problem 15A Determining $[OH^-]$ using K_w (p. 549)

Sample Problem 15B Calculating K_a of a weak acid (p. 557)

Sample Problem 15C Calculating the pH of an acidic solution (p. 561)

Sample Problem 15D Calculating the pH of a basic solution (p. 562)

Sample Problem 15E Calculating concentration from titration data (p. 576)

REVIEW & ASSESS

TERM REVIEW

1. The process by which hydronium ions react with hydroxide ions to produce water is known as ——.
(titration, neutralization)

2. Ammonia is an example of a ——.
(weak base, weak acid)

3. The substance formed when an acid donates a proton to another species is known as a ——.
(conjugate acid, conjugate base)

4. A substance that can act as either an acid or a base is said to be ——.
(amphoteric, diprotic)

5. Because of its small ——, the hydrogen carbonate ion, HCO_3^-, is considered a weak conjugate acid.
(K_a, K_w)

6. A basic material that can be used to neutralize excess stomach acidity is a(n) ——.
(buffer solution, antacid)

7. The pH of a solution is directly related to its —— concentration.
(hydronium ion, hydroxide ion)

8. To measure the pH of a solution as accurately as possible, a(n) —— is used.
(pH meter, indicator)

9. The two ingredients in a buffer include a —— and its conjugate base.
(weak acid, diprotic acid)

10. The solution in a titration whose concentration is accurately known is the ——.
(titrant, standard solution)

11. When the H_3O^+ concentration equals the OH^- concentration in a strong acid–strong base titration, then the —— has been reached.
(end point, equivalence point)

12. A carboxylic acid contains the functional group ——.
(—COOH, —COO)

CONCEPT & SKILLS REVIEW

ACIDS AND BASES

1. Compare the properties of an acid with those of a base.

2. Write the equation that shows the reaction between magnesium metal and hydrochloric acid.

3. Explain the relationship between the self-ionization of water and K_w.

4. Why are weak acids and weak bases poor conductors of electricity?

5. What is the difference between the strength of an acid and its concentration?

6. Water is not included in the equilibrium expression to show what happens in the self-ionization of water. Why not?

7. What unit is implied by brackets placed around the formula of an acid or a base?

8. Explain how the bulb in **Figure 15-2** on page 543 will glow if the solution is replaced with boric acid ($K_a = 5.8 \times 10^{-10}$).

9. Explain what the hydronium ion can do in solution that no other cation can do.

10. Why is rainwater normally slightly acidic?

11. What is neutralization?

12. Write an equation for the reaction between hydrocyanic acid, HCN, and water. Label the acid, base, conjugate acid, and conjugate base in the reaction.

13. Explain how the hydrogen carbonate ion, HCO_3^-, acts as an amphoteric ion.

14. Explain how the acetate ion formed as a product in the following forward reaction acts as a base in the reverse reaction.

$$CH_3COOH(aq) + H_2O(l) \rightleftharpoons$$
$$CH_3COO^-(aq) + H_3O^+(aq)$$

Acid	Formula	Value of K_a
Arsenic	H_3AsO_4	5.62×10^{-3}
Acetic	CH_3COOH	1.76×10^{-5}
Benzoic	C_6H_5COOH	6.5×10^{-5}
Cyanic	$HCNO$	7.4×10^{-4}
Phosphoric	H_3PO_4	7.5×10^{-3}
Hydrofluoric	HF	6.8×10^{-4}
Carbonic	H_2CO_3	4.3×10^{-7}

15. Use the table above to answer the following questions:
    a. Which is the strongest acid? Why?
    b. Which acid ionizes the least? Why?

16. Write an equilibrium expression for the ionization of phenol, a weak monoprotic acid whose formula is C_6H_5OH.

17. Place the following acids in order of increasing strength:
    a. valeric acid $K_a = 1.5 \times 10^{-5}$
    b. glutaric acid $K_a = 3.4 \times 10^{-4}$
    c. hypobromous acid $K_a = 2.5 \times 10^{-9}$
    d. acetylsalicylic acid $K_a = 3.3 \times 10^{-4}$

18. Classify sulfurous acid, H_2SO_3, based on what it does in an aqueous solution.

19. Explain why sodium hydroxide, NaOH, is used in oil refining to remove acids.

20. Identify each of the following as an acid or a base according to the Brønsted-Lowry classification. For each species, write the formula and the name of its conjugate.
    a. CH_3COO^-
    b. HCN
    c. $H_2C_2O_4$
    d. $C_6H_5NH_3^+$

Practice Problems

21. Calculate the hydroxide ion concentration in a 0.010 M HCl solution at 298 K. **(Hint: See Sample Problem 15A.)**

22. At 60°C, the value of K_w is 1.0×10^{-13}. Calculate the concentrations of hydronium ions and hydroxide ions in water at this temperature.

23. The value of K_w at 0°C is 1.14×10^{-15}. Calculate the concentrations of hydronium ions and hydroxide ions in pure water at 0°C. How do these concentrations compare with the concentrations of hydronium and hydroxide ions in pure water at 25°C?

24. Propanoic acid is used in the production of plastics. K_a for propanoic acid is 1.4×10^{-5}. If 0.600 g of this acid is dissolved in water to make 250.0 mL of solution, what would be the hydronium ion concentration of the solution? The following equation shows the ionization of propanoic acid in water:

$$H_2O(l) + C_2H_5COOH(aq) \rightleftharpoons$$
$$C_2H_5COO^-(aq) + H_3O^+(aq)$$

25. An alkaline solution is prepared by dissolving 12 g of NaOH in 2.5 L of water. What is the hydroxide ion concentration in this solution? the hydronium ion concentration?

26. Aqueous hypoiodous acid, HIO, exists in the following equilibrium:

$$HIO(aq) + H_2O(l) \rightleftharpoons H_3O^+(aq) + IO^-(aq)$$

The hypoiodite ion, IO^-, has a concentration of 2.14×10^{-6} M in a 0.200 M aqueous solution of HIO. What is the acid-ionization constant of hypoiodous acid?

27. If the hydronium ion concentration of sea water at 298 K is 5.0×10^{-9} M, what is the hydroxide ion concentration in this sea water? **(Hint: See Sample Problem 15A.)**

28. Lactic acid gives sour milk its taste. Lactic acid is a weak acid that dissociates as shown in the following equation:

$$CH_3CHOHCOOH(aq) \rightleftharpoons$$
$$CH_3CHOHCOO^-(aq) + H_3O^+(aq)$$

Assume that the concentration of lactic acid in sour milk is 0.100 M and that the concentration of hydronium ions is 3.72×10^{-3} M. Calculate the K_a for lactic acid. **(Hint: See Sample Problem 15B.)**

29. The hydroxide ion concentration of human blood at 25°C is 2.6×10^{-7} M. What is the hydronium ion concentration of human blood?

30. A solution is prepared by dissolving 0.56 g of benzoic acid in enough water to make 1.0 L of solution. Benzoic acid ionizes in aqueous solution, as shown in the following equation:

$$C_6H_5COOH(aq) \rightleftharpoons C_6H_5COO^-(aq) + H_3O^+(aq)$$

The K_a of benzoic acid is 6.5×10^{-5}. Calculate the hydronium ion concentration in this solution, assuming that a negligible amount of benzoic acid ionizes.

PH

31. A solution of HCl has a pH of 1.00. You add NaOH to the solution, and the pH rises to 1.18. What happened? What does this have to do with the relationship of acids to bases along the pH scale? Can you estimate what amounts of HCl and NaOH might have been used?

32. Use two arbitrary pH values to show mathematically how the concentration of H_3O^+ increases as pH decreases.

33. How does the pH of human blood remain extremely constant?

34. Explain why a 1.00 M acetic acid solution does not have a low pH.

35. Explain why a 0.10 M hydrochloric acid solution has a low pH.

36. How can a pH be negative?

37. Why is the pH of a polyprotic acid primarily determined by its first dissociation?

38. What would be the pH of a 2.0 M NaCl solution? Explain your answer.

39. How does the strength of an acid relate to the pH of its solutions?

40. How does the K_a value of an acid relate to the pH of its solutions?

Practice Problems

41. What is the pH of a 0.025 M NaOH solution?

42. Determine the pH of a 8.75×10^{-4} M HCl solution. **(Hint: See Sample Problem 15C.)**

43. The pH of the precipitation in an area near a power plant is 3.45. What is the OH^- ion concentration in this precipitation?

44. The pH of a glass of soda water is 4.3. What is the $[H_3O^+]$?

45. What is the pH of a 2.5×10^{-5} M KOH solution?

46. What is the pH of an ammonia solution that has a hydroxide ion concentration of 10^{-3} M? **(Hint: See Sample Problem 15D.)**

47. A solution of 5% acetic acid has a concentration of 0.83 M and a K_a of 1.8×10^{-5}. What is the pH of the solution?

48. What are the concentrations of all of the components of a benzoic acid solution if K_a is 6.5×10^{-5}, pH is 2.96, and C_6H_5COOH is 0.020 M?

49. The pH of a solution is 3.9. Calculate the hydroxide ion concentration of this solution.

50. What is the OH^- concentration of a solution of HNO_3 with a pH value of 2.89?

51. The pH of one sample of fruit juice is 2.80. Determine both the hydronium and hydroxide ion concentrations in this juice sample.

TITRATION

52. Write the complete molecular and net ionic equations for the neutralization of sulfuric acid with potassium hydroxide.

53. Describe the role of an indicator in the titration of an unknown acid against a standardized base.

54. Why is the transition range of an indicator critically important when performing different titrations?

55. How is the color change of an indicator related to pH?

56. For the following titrations, select the best indicator from these choices: bromphenol blue, bromthymol blue, phenol red.
   a. formic acid, HCOOH, with NaOH
   b. perchloric acid with LiOH
   c. sulfuric acid with potassium hydroxide
   d. ammonia with hydrochloric acid

Indicator	Acid color	pH range of color	Base color
Thymol blue	red	1.2–2.8	yellow
Bromphenol blue	yellow	3.0–4.6	blue
Bromcresol green	yellow	2.0–5.6	blue
Bromthymol blue	yellow	6.0–7.6	blue
Phenol red	yellow	6.6–8.0	red
Alizarin yellow	yellow	10.1–12.0	red

57. Refer to the table above to answer the following questions:

    a. Which indicator would be the best choice for a titration with an end point at a pH of 4.0?

    b. Which indicators would work best for a titration of a weak base with a strong acid?

58. Why is a different indicator used for a strong acid–strong base titration than for a weak acid–strong base titration?

59. Why does an indicator need to be a weak acid or a weak base?

60. How is the transition range of an indicator related to the end point of a titration?

61. A 50 mL solution of CH_3COOH is titrated with a 1.000 M NaOH solution. Describe what species (molecules and ions) are present in the titration flask at the following points in the titration:

    a. pH 6

    b. pH 9

    c. pH 11

62. In the titration of a weak acid with a strong base, the pH of the equivalence point is higher than 7. Use the concept of conjugate acids and bases to explain why the pH is in the basic range.

63. A student passes an end point in a titration. Is it possible to add an additional measured amount of the unknown and continue the titration? Explain how this process might work. How would the answer for the calculation of the molarity of the unknown differ from the answer the student would have gotten if the titration had been run properly?

Practice Problems

64. You wish to determine the molarity of a lactic acid solution. A 150.0 mL sample of lactic acid, $CH_3CHOHCOOH$, is titrated with 125 mL of 0.750 M NaOH. What is the molarity of the acid sample? **(Hint: See Sample Problem 15E.)**

65. Formic acid is used in the production of leather. Residue from leather production is tested to determine the concentration of formic acid. A 50.0 mL sample of formic acid, $HCOOH$, is neutralized by 35.0 mL of 0.250 M NaOH. What is the molarity of the formic acid solution?

66. If 35.40 mL of 1.000 M HCl is neutralized by 67.3 mL of NaOH, what is the molarity of the NaOH solution?

67. If 50.00 mL of 1.000 M H_2SO_4 is neutralized by 35.4 mL of KOH, what is the molarity of the KOH solution?

68. If 18.5 mL of a 0.350 M H_2SO_4 solution neutralizes 12.5 mL of aqueous LiOH, how many grams of LiOH was used to make 1.00 L of the LiOH solution?

69. An HCl solution has a pH of 2.40. Calculate the amount of hydronium ions in 125.5 mL of this solution.

70. An NaOH solution has a pH of 10.50. What volume of this solution would contain 8.0×10^{-5} mol of OH^- ions? What volume of 0.010 M HCl would be required to titrate this solution to the equivalence point?

71. An HNO_3 solution has a pH of 3.06. What amount of 0.015 M NaOH will be required to titrate 65.0 mL of the HNO_3 solution to reach the equivalence point?

72. Explain how weak acids in the body can help maintain the buffering capacity of a living system.

LINKING CHAPTERS

1. Applying scientific laws

How do nitrous acid, HNO_2, and nitric acid, HNO_3, demonstrate the law of multiple proportions?

2. Stoichiometry

An excess of zinc reacts with 250.0 mL of 6.00 M sulfuric acid.
a. What mass of $ZnSO_4$ is produced?
b. What volume of $H_2(g)$ is produced at STP?

3. Stoichiometry

A seashell (mostly $CaCO_3$) is placed in a solution of HCl. From the reaction, 1.50 L of CO_2 is produced at 25°C and 100 kPa.
a. What mass of $CaCO_3$ was consumed in the reaction?
b. If the HCl solution was 2.00 M, what volume was used in this reaction?

4. Balancing equations

Write balanced equations for each of the following reactions between acids and metal oxides:
a. $MgO(s) + H_2SO_4(aq) \longrightarrow$
b. $CaO(s) + HCl(aq) \longrightarrow$
c. $Al_2O_3(s) + HNO_3(aq) \longrightarrow$
d. $ZnO(s) + H_3PO_4(aq) \longrightarrow$

5. Balancing equations

Write balanced equations for each of the following reactions between acids and carbonates:
a. $BaCO_3(s) + HCl(aq) \longrightarrow$
b. $MgCO_3(s) + HNO_3(aq) \longrightarrow$
c. $Na_2CO_3(s) + H_2SO_4(aq) \longrightarrow$
d. $CaCO_3(s) + H_3PO_4(aq) \longrightarrow$

ALTERNATIVE ASSESSMENTS

Performance assessment

1. Design an experiment to measure the pH of four types of hair shampoo: baby shampoo, shampoo for extra body, shampoo for oily hair, and shampoo with conditioner. Chart any patterns you detect. Also compare and contrast two brands of "pH balanced" shampoo.

2. Your teacher will give you a solution to test for pH. Describe exactly how you would test the solution. If your teacher approves your plan, complete the test.

3. Design an experiment to test the neutralization effectiveness of various brands of antacid. Show your procedure, including all safety procedures and cautions, to your teacher for approval. Write an advertisement for the antacid you judge to be the most effective. Cite data from your experiments as part of your advertising claims.

Portfolio projects

1. Chemistry and you

Collect data on the acidity of rain in your area over the last 10 years. Graph the data, and make a prediction concerning acid-rain damage in your area by the year 2010. Provide evidence to support your prediction.

2.

Research and communication

A reaction between baking soda, $NaHCO_3$, and a baking batter that contains acidic ingredients produces carbon dioxide gas. The reaction results in a fluffier cake. Some recipes rely on baking powder instead of baking soda. Research the ingredients of regular baking powder and double-acting baking powder to discover how they differ from baking soda. Which is more likely to be used in creating a light, fluffy cake? How does the pH affect the final product?

1. Which of the following aqueous solutions would have the highest concentration of hydronium ions?
   a. nitrous acid
   b. acetic acid
   c. potassium carbonate
   d. periodic acid

2. When an acid reacts with a metal, _____.
   a. the hydronium ion concentration increases
   b. the metal forms anions
   c. water is produced
   d. the K_w value is changed

3. The K_w value can be affected by _____.
   a. dissolving a salt in the solution
   b. changes in temperature
   c. changes in the hydroxide ion concentration
   d. the presence of a strong acid

4. Which of the following is a strong diprotic acid?
   a. H_2O
   b. H_3PO_4
   c. H_2SO_4
   d. H_2O_2

5. The stronger an acid is, _____.
   a. the smaller its K_a value
   b. the stronger its conjugate base
   c. the more hydronium ions produced in aqueous solution
   d. the more hydroxide ions produced in aqueous solution

6. Identify the species that is considered a base according to Brønsted-Lowry but not according to Arrhenius.
   a. H_2SO_4
   b. $NH_3(g)$
   c. KOH
   d. $Ca(OH)_2$

7. Which of the following solutions would have a pH value greater than 7?
   a. $[OH^-] = 2.4 \times 10^{-2}$ M
   b. $[H_3O^+] = 1.53 \times 10^{-2}$ M
   c. 0.0001 M HCl
   d. $[OH^-] = 4.4 \times 10^{-9}$ M

8. If the pH of a solution of a strong base is known, the _____ of the solution can be calculated.
   a. molarity
   b. $[OH^-]$
   c. $[H_3O^+]$
   d. All of the above

9. A neutral aqueous solution _____.
   a. has a 7 M H_3O^+ concentration
   b. contains neither hydronium ions nor hydroxide ions
   c. has an equal number of hydronium ions and hydroxide ions
   d. contains buffers that resist changes in pH

10. Which of the following indicators is the best choice to use when titrating a strong base with a weak acid?
    a. thymol blue
    b. alizarin yellow
    c. methyl orange
    d. bromthymol blue

11. Identify the salt that is produced when a solution of H_2SO_4 is titrated with a solution of $Ca(OH)_2$.
    a. calcium sulfate
    b. calcium hydroxide
    c. calcium oxide
    d. calcium phosphate

12. In functioning as a base, an amine molecule with its unshared pair of electrons can accept a(n) _____.
    a. hydroxide ion
    b. carboxyl group
    c. proton
    d. amino group

Reaction Rates

MORE RED TIDES IN OUR FUTURE?

In 1987, large numbers of fish along the North Carolina and Maryland coasts began to die. Scientists soon discovered that a hidden algae was to blame.

The variety of algae that caused these fish to die is called *Pfiesteria piscicida* (derived from the Latin term for "fish killer"). A short-term warming of the water in that area of the Atlantic Ocean caused a huge increase in the algae population. This warming was caused by the Gulf Stream, a warm-water current that flows up the eastern coast of North America and across the ocean to Europe. In 1987, the Gulf Stream swept in closer to shore than usual.

The algae produce chemicals that are toxic not only to marine life but also to humans. The algae give off a neurotoxin called domoic acid, which paralyzes fish so that they cannot breath. Shellfish, such as oysters and clams, are not themselves harmed by the domoic acid, but they store it in their bodies. Humans who consume these shellfish can become seriously ill. Domoic acid has been found to cause irritation of the eyes and throat, severe headaches, and short-term memory loss.

Gymnodinium breve is another algae that produces toxins. In addition to poisons, they produce red pigments that can be seen in the water where the algae grow. When the pigment is visible, it is called a *red tide.* Red tides occur when these algae *bloom.* An algal bloom is a rapid increase in population.

Algal blooms occur seasonally and are an important part of marine life cycles. The Red Sea probably got its name from seasonal red tides. In the central Pacific Ocean, an event called El Niño triggers a warming of water every few years. During El Niño periods, such as the one that occurred in 1997 and 1998, unusually large red tides can be observed around Pacific islands. These algal blooms, like the bloom off the North Carolina and Maryland coasts, can cause large numbers of fish to die.

Domoic acid

CHAPTER LINKS

How does temperature affect reaction rate?

How does the warming of coastal waters disturb the ecological balance of an area?

Why might eating oysters and other shellfish harvested in the summer months be more of a risk than eating shellfish harvested in the winter months?

What is a reaction rate?

OBJECTIVES ▶ *Calculate* the rate of a reaction in terms of the disappearance of a reactant or appearance of a product.

▶ *Determine* the effects of changing concentrations on a rate given a rate law expression.

Rate is a ratio

How could you make the following statements more informative? *The level on the gas gauge went down. The car sped down the highway. Hydrogen gas bubbled from the solution.* Although these statements identify the changes taking place, they would be more informative if they were expressed in terms of numbers: *The level on the gas gauge fell at a rate of one-fourth of a tank per 35 minutes. The car was traveling 88 km/h (55 mi/h). One-half liter of hydrogen gas was generated in 14 minutes.* Each of the measurable changes is expressed as a function of time. These values are called rates. The car travels at a rate of 88 km/h. Hydrogen gas was evolved at a rate of 0.5 L per 14 minutes.

Rates usually change over the period of time they are measured. For example, suppose you're traveling on an interstate highway. At 2:15 P.M. you pass mile marker 92. At 4:30 P.M. you pass mile marker 227. Your travel speed (rate) is the distance you traveled divided by the elapsed time. But this reflects your average speed. You may have been slowed down by a car in front of you, or you may have sped up to pass another car. You also may have stopped to get gas. Your speed changed. As you

FIGURE 16-1

The winner of the race is the car that travels at the highest average rate.

were slowing down to pull up to the gas pump, your speed decreased steadily. By looking at your speedometer, you can determine your rate of travel at any given time. This instantaneous rate of travel is equal to a very short distance traveled divided by a very small time interval.

Just as you can determine average and instantaneous rates for a car traveling on a highway, you can determine average and instantaneous rates for any change. When the change under consideration is a chemical reaction, the rate is called a **reaction rate. Chemical kinetics** is the study of reaction rates and the factors that affect them.

Reaction rate is an experimental quantity

A reaction rate tells how fast a chemical change takes place. It is an experimental quantity found by measuring the disappearance of a reactant or the appearance of a product over a period of time. Expressing a rate requires the ability to accurately measure a change in some variable, such as volume, temperature, color, mass, concentration, or acidity. Study **Figure 16-2.** Magnesium metal has been added to hydrochloric acid. The ionic equation for this reaction is written as follows.

$$\text{Mg}(s) + 2\text{H}_3\text{O}^+(aq) + 2\text{Cl}^-(aq) \longrightarrow \text{Mg}^{2+}(aq) + 2\text{Cl}^-(aq) + \text{H}_2(g) + 2\text{H}_2\text{O}(l)$$

reaction rate

the decrease in reactant concentration or increase in product concentration per unit of time as a reaction proceeds

chemical kinetics

the branch of chemistry concerned with reaction rates and how reactions occur

▼ **FIGURE 16-2**

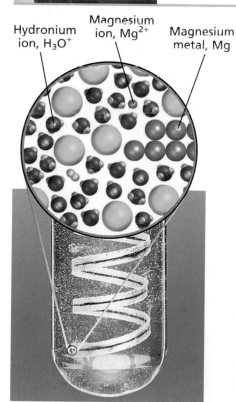

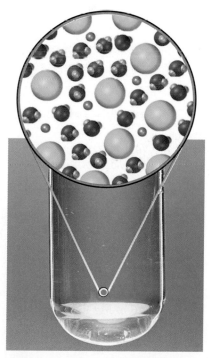

Hydronium ion, H_3O^+ Magnesium ion, Mg^{2+} Magnesium metal, Mg   Chloride ion, Cl^- Water molecule, H_2O

a When Mg is added to aqueous HCl, H_2 and H_2O are formed as two H_3O^+ ions react. The decrease in $[\text{H}_3\text{O}^+]$ means an increase in pH.

b The Mg piece becomes smaller as its atoms become Mg^{2+} ions. The rate at which H_2 is made decreases as the Mg is used up.

c The reaction continues until the Mg piece disappears, because it is the limiting reagent.

QUICKLAB

CONSUMER ACTIVITY

Measuring Reaction Rate

The reaction rate involved in the dissolution of an effervescent tablet in water is easy to measure. You can determine the average rate of reaction in terms of the disappearance of the tablet.

Materials cup, water, effervescent tablet, balance, stopwatch

Problem How can you determine the rate of reaction when an effervescent tablet dissolves in water? Use the balance to measure the mass of the tablet. Use the stopwatch to measure the time elapsed as the tablet dissolves.

Analysis
1. Determine the average rate of the reaction in terms of the disappearance of the effervescent tablet. What units do you use?

2. Can you think of another method for determining the rate of this reaction? What other change in the materials do you observe?

3. Repeat the procedure using warm water. How does the rate change with the temperature of the water?

What observations indicate that a reaction is taking place? Bubbles are coming off the piece of metal because H_2 gas is being produced. The metal piece is getting smaller and finally disappears. A pH meter can be used to tell that the concentration of H_3O^+ ions is decreasing during the reaction.

How can rate be measured? The rate of this reaction can be expressed as the rate of disappearance of Mg or H_3O^+ or by the rate of appearance of H_2 or Mg^{2+}. In practice, the rate of appearance of Mg^{2+} is difficult to determine because the ions remain in aqueous solution, making their concentrations difficult to measure. Therefore, the appearance of Mg^{2+} will almost never be used to determine the rate of this reaction.

You can determine the rate using one of the measurable properties of this reaction: the decrease in mass of Mg, the decrease in hydronium ion concentration (or acidity), or the volume of hydrogen gas formed. Any one of the three observable properties permits you to express the change from initial to final conditions that occurs over the course of the reaction. Dividing the change in each of the measured properties by the total time elapsed during the reaction gives the **average rate** for the reaction.

average rate

the change in a measured property (usually concentration) divided by the total time elapsed

▶ **FIGURE 16-3**

Average rate can be determined by monitoring a reaction and measuring the total time elapsed. For the reaction of Mg and HCl, you can monitor the disappearance of Mg.

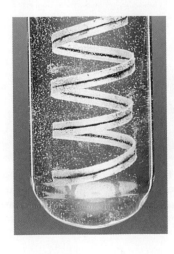

TABLE 16-1 **Reaction Rate Data and Calculations for the Reaction of Mg in Aqueous HCl**

Property	Initial quantity	Final quantity	Change in quantity	Change in quantity (mol)	Time elapsed (s)	Average rate = $\dfrac{\text{change}}{\text{time elapsed}}$
Mass of Mg	0.376 g	0.000 g	−0.376 g	−0.0155	32	rate = $\dfrac{0.0155 \text{ mol Mg}}{32 \text{ s}}$ = 0.00048 mol/s
Volume of H₂	0.0 mL	418 mL	418 mL	0.0154*	32	rate = $\dfrac{0.0154 \text{ mol H}_2}{32 \text{ s}}$ = 0.00048 mol/s
[H₃O⁺]**	0.500 M	0.293 M	−0.207 M	−0.0310	32	rate = $\dfrac{0.0310 \text{ mol H}_3\text{O}^+}{32 \text{ s}}$ = 0.00097 mol/s

* determined using the ideal gas law equation at 40°C and 0.947 atm
** determined from the pH of the 150 mL solution

Rate can be noted from the disappearance of a reactant or the appearance of a product

Table 16-1 summarizes the calculation of the average reaction rate using data obtained by each of the methods for measuring change in the reaction between magnesium and hydrochloric acid. At the end of the reaction, you have no magnesium left; consequently, subtracting the initial mass of magnesium from the final mass of magnesium yields a negative number. By convention, reaction rates are always written as positive values. Therefore, when rate is determined in terms of the disappearance of a reactant, the change is multiplied by −1 to give a positive value for the rate.

How do the three values in the rate column of Table 16-1 compare? The reaction rate calculated in terms of the mass of magnesium is equal to that calculated in terms of the hydrogen gas. The reaction rate calculated in terms of the hydronium ion concentration, however, is twice as large as that determined in terms of either Mg or H_2. This difference suggests that hydronium ions are disappearing twice as fast as magnesium atoms are and that hydronium ions are also disappearing twice as fast as hydrogen gas is appearing. How can you account for this difference? Look again at the balanced equation for the overall reaction.

$$Mg(s) + 2H_3O^+(aq) \longrightarrow Mg^{2+}(aq) + H_2(g) + 2H_2O(l)$$

Consider the coefficients for Mg, H_3O^+, and H_2. Both Mg and H_2 have coefficients of 1. So H_2 is formed as rapidly as Mg disappears. The mole ratio between H_3O^+ and Mg, however, is 2:1. This means that 2 mol of H_3O^+ must be used for every 1 mol of Mg consumed. The ratio indicates that the rate for the disappearance of H_3O^+ is twice as fast as that for the disappearance of Mg. The mole ratio between H_3O^+ and H_2 is also 2:1. To compensate for this effect of stoichiometry on reaction rate, chemists divide the rate of change for each reactant or product by its coefficient in the balanced chemical equation. Thus, for the reaction between Mg and aqueous HCl, the reaction rate is expressed as follows.

$$\text{rate} = \frac{-1}{1} \times \frac{\Delta(\text{mol Mg})}{\Delta t} = \frac{1}{1} \times \frac{\Delta(\text{mol H}_2)}{\Delta t} = \frac{-1}{2} \times \frac{\Delta(\text{mol H}_3\text{O}^+)}{\Delta t}$$

The units for a reaction rate must always be expressed. The units for the rate in the above equation are moles per second. However, reaction rates are usually stated as $\frac{\text{concentration}}{\text{time}}$. When concentration units are moles of a substance per liter of solution (M), the general equation for rate is written as follows.

$$\text{rate} = \frac{-1}{a} \times \frac{\Delta[\text{reactant}]}{\Delta t} = \frac{1}{b} \times \frac{\Delta[\text{product}]}{\Delta t}$$

The minus sign makes the decrease in reactant concentration a positive number. The a is the coefficient of the reactant in the balanced chemical equation; b is the coefficient of the product. For example, sodium hypochlorite is prepared according to the following equation.

$$\text{Cl}_2(aq) + 2\text{NaOH}(aq) \longrightarrow \text{NaOCl}(aq) + \text{NaCl}(aq) + \text{H}_2\text{O}(l)$$

The rate can be expressed as follows. The change in H_2O is ignored because a slight addition to the solvent is difficult to measure.

$$\text{rate} = \frac{-1}{1} \times \frac{\Delta[\text{Cl}_2]}{\Delta t} = \frac{-1}{2} \times \frac{\Delta[\text{NaOH}]}{\Delta t} = \frac{1}{1} \times \frac{\Delta[\text{NaOCl}]}{\Delta t} = \frac{1}{1} \times \frac{\Delta[\text{NaCl}]}{\Delta t}$$

Very few chemical reactions proceed at a constant rate throughout the entire process. Most reactions are fast at the beginning, when all of the reactant concentrations are high, and slow down as the reactants are consumed. In some reactions, the rate becomes constant when the reaction reaches equilibrium. In other reactions, the rate decreases to zero when the reaction nears completion.

CONCEPT CHECK

1. The concentration of a substance involved in a reaction changes from 4.0 M to 2.0 M in 40 minutes. Is the substance a reactant or a product? Explain how you know. Express the average rate of this reaction in M/min.

2. Ammonia is formed from its elements according to the equation below.

$$\text{N}_2(g) + 3\text{H}_2(g) \longrightarrow 2\text{NH}_3(g)$$

One mole of N_2 is mixed with 1 mol of H_2 in a 1 L container. After 5 seconds, the reaction is stopped and the gases are remeasured. There are 0.9 mol of N_2, and 0.7 mol of H_2. Calculate the average reaction rate in terms of each reactant.

3. Given the following chemical equation, write expressions for the rate in terms of each reactant and product.

$$\text{KClO}_3(aq) + 6\text{HCl}(aq) \longrightarrow 3\text{Cl}_2(g) + 3\text{H}_2\text{O}(l) + \text{KCl}(aq)$$

Magnesium, an unlimited resource

Extracting magnesium from sea water is an efficient and economical process. Sea water is mixed with lime, CaO, from oyster shells to form insoluble magnesium hydroxide, Mg(OH)₂, which can be easily filtered out. Hydrochloric acid is added to the solid to form magnesium chloride, which undergoes electrolysis to produce pure magnesium metal.

If 90 million metric tons of Mg were extracted per year for 1 million years, the Mg content of the oceans would drop by 0.01%.

WHERE IS IT?

Earth's Crust
2.5% by mass

eighth most abundant element

Sea Water
0.13% by mass

internet connect

SC**LINKS**
NSTA

TOPIC: Magnesium
GO TO: www.scilinks.org
KEYWORD: HW161

Industrial Uses

◗ Magnesium oxide, MgO, is used in paper manufacturing, as well as in fertilizers, pharmaceuticals, and household cleaners.

◗ Magnesium hydroxide, Mg(OH)₂, suspended in aqueous solution is known as *milk of magnesia* and is used as an antacid.

◗ Magnesium is used in fireworks, and as a heat-resistant material in the form of MgO.

◗ Magnesium is the lightest metal used in industrial construction; its density is less than two-thirds that of aluminum.

◗ Magnesium alloys are used in aircraft fuselages, engine parts, missiles, luggage, optical and photo equipment, lawn mowers, and portable tools.

Spinach is a good source of dietary magnesium. Magnesium is the central atom in the green plant pigment chlorophyll.

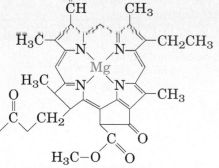

Chlorophyll-a

A BRIEF HISTORY

● **1833:** Michael Faraday makes magnesium metal through the electrolysis of molten magnesium chloride.

● **1852:** Robert Bunsen designs an electrolytic cell that allows molten Mg to be collected without burning when it makes contact with the air.

1800   **1900**

● **1828:** A.A.B. Bussy obtains the first pure magnesium metal.

● **1808:** Humphry Davy discovers that the compound *magnesia alba* is the oxide of a new metal.

● **1944:** L. M. Pidgeon discovers how to extract magnesium from its ore, dolomite.

FIGURE 16-4

Pieces of magnesium ribbon react more rapidly with HCl in the beaker at right because it is more concentrated than the HCl in the beaker at left.

FIGURE 16-5

The colorless gas HI decomposes at an observable rate, as can be seen by the production of violet iodine gas.

rate law

an expression for the rate of a reaction as a function of the concentration of one or more reactants

order

the exponent on the concentration for a specified reactant in a rate law expression

The effect of concentration on rate

Examine the two photographs in **Figure 16-4.** The reaction on the right is more vigorous than the reaction on the left. Both beakers contain aqueous hydrochloric acid and magnesium, but the solution on the right has a higher concentration of HCl than the solution on the left.

With some reactions, doubling the concentration doubles the rate. But with other reactions, doubling the concentration causes a fourfold increase in the reaction rate. This is true for the decomposition of HI to form H_2 and I_2, shown in **Figure 16-5.** In this type of reaction, the rate is proportional to the square of the reactant concentration. There are even reactions for which increasing the concentration has no effect on the reaction rate. How can that be true? It was all a mystery until chemists began to look at reaction *mechanisms* and *rate laws*.

Determining a general rate law equation

Experiments show that reaction rate is directly proportional to reactant concentration raised to some power, *n*. This proportionality is made an equality by the inclusion of *k,* the experimentally determined rate constant.

$$\text{rate} = k[A]^n$$

This equation is a general **rate law.** The exponent, *n,* is called the **order** with respect to substance A and *must be determined from experimental data.*

It is possible for a reaction to have a rate that is independent of a particular reactant concentration. In this case, the reaction is of zero order with respect to that reactant. Look again at the rate law equation. A reaction that is first order with respect to A has a value of 1 for *n.* With an exponent of 1, the reaction rate will be proportional to the concentration of A. If the data show that doubling the concentration of reactant A causes the rate to double, you know the rate law must be first order. Sample Problem 16A gives an example of a reaction that is not first order. It is still possible to determine the rate law equation.

SAMPLE PROBLEM 16A Determining a rate law

Determine the rate law equation for the following reaction, given the experimental data shown.

$$3A \longrightarrow C$$

Concentration of A	Reaction rate
0.2 M	1.0 M/s
0.4 M	4.0 M/s

1 List what you know

- When the concentration of A is 0.2 M, the reaction rate is 1.0 M/s.
- When the concentration of A is 0.4 M, the reaction rate is 4.0 M/s.
- When the concentration of A doubles, the rate quadruples.

2 Set up the problem

- Write rate law equations for the data given using rate = $k[A]^n$.

$$\text{rate}_1 = 1.0 \text{ M/s} = k[0.2 \text{ M}]^n$$

$$\text{rate}_2 = 4.0 \text{ M/s} = k[0.4 \text{ M}]^n$$

3 Calculate

- Divide the two rate equations and solve for n.

$$\frac{4.0 \text{ M/s}}{1.0 \text{ M/s}} = \frac{k[0.4 \text{ M}]^n}{k[0.2 \text{ M}]^n}$$

$$4.0 = 2^n$$

For this simple problem, you can see that $n = 2$.

$$4 = 2^2$$

Logarithmic solution

- For more complex equations, logarithms can be used to solve for n. Take the logarithm of both sides of the equation.

$$\log(4.0) = \log(2)^n$$

You have an equation in which the variable you want to solve for is an exponent. To rearrange the equation so that the variable is no longer an exponent, use the following law of logarithms.

$$\log(2)^n = n\log(2)$$

Substitute and solve.

$$\log(4.0) = n\log(2)$$
$$0.602 = n(0.301)$$
$$n = 2$$

- Write the rate law for the chemical equation.

$$\text{rate} = k[\text{A}]^2$$

1. Look again at the reaction for the decomposition of hydrogen iodide.

$$2HI(g) \longrightarrow H_2(g) + I_2(g)$$

The rate of this reaction changes with the concentration of HI according to the following experimental data.

[HI]	0.010	0.020	0.040
Rate	8.2×10^{-3} M/s	3.3×10^{-2} M/s	0.13 M/s

Determine the rate law equation for this reaction.

2. By what factor will the rate of a reaction increase if a reactant's concentration is doubled? Use the following values as the order with respect to that reactant.
   a. 0   **b.** 3   **c.** 4

Rate laws for reactions with more than one reactant

The rate law equations you have looked at so far have been for reactions involving only one reactant. But what about cases in which there are two or more reactants?

If more than one reactant is found to contribute to the rate of the reaction, then all contributing reactants must appear in the rate law. The general rate law equation for a reaction in which two components, A and B, affect the rate is written as follows.

$$\text{rate} = k[A]^n[B]^m$$

overall reaction order

the sum of all the exponents in a rate law expression

The value of n is the order with respect to reactant A. The value of m is the order with respect to reactant B. The **overall reaction order** is equal to the sum of m and n. Again, these exponents can be determined only by experimentation.

If you double the concentration of A and find that the rate doubles, you know that the reaction is first order with respect to A. This would be the same as it would be if A were the only reactant. To find the reaction order with respect to B, you must run the reaction again, this time holding [A] constant but changing the concentration of B. If [B] is doubled and the reaction rate quadruples, the reaction is second order with respect to B. This is the same result as in Sample Problem 16A. For the reaction of A and B in this example, the rate law would be written as follows.

$$\text{rate} = k[A][B]^2$$

The overall order of this reaction is third order.

Rate laws cannot be derived from a chemical equation

Do not confuse the exponents in the rate law with those in an equilibrium expression. Exponents in equilibrium expressions are coefficients in the balanced chemical equation; *exponents in the rate law must be derived from experimental data.* The equilibrium expression for the decomposition of N_2O_5 is derived from its balanced chemical equation.

$$2N_2O_5 \rightleftharpoons 4NO_2 + O_2$$

$$K_{eq} = \frac{[NO_2]^4[O_2]}{[N_2O_5]^2}$$

N_2O_5 has an exponent of 2 because its coefficient in the balanced chemical equation is 2. However, the experimentally determined rate law expression for this same reaction is the following.

$$\text{rate} = k[N_2O_5]^1$$

The difference between the exponents in a rate law and those in an equilibrium equation comes from the difference between a balanced chemical equation and a reaction *mechanism.*

A cartoonist named Rube Goldberg drew images of imaginary machines that performed a seemingly simple task using many steps. An example of one of his machines is shown in **Figure 16-6.** Like this machine, most chemical reactions proceed through a series of steps called a pathway, or **mechanism.** The slowest step in the pathway determines the reaction rate and is called the **rate-determining step.**

Each reaction step is called an **elementary step.** The rate law is determined by the rate-determining step, so there may be substances in the elementary steps that do not appear in the rate law. Also, many substances may be made and used during the course of the reaction. These **intermediates** do not appear in the rate law expression.

It is very important to keep in mind that a balanced chemical equation and a reaction mechanism are two different expressions. A rate law can be written from a mechanism, never from a balanced chemical equation. Because many reaction pathways occur very rapidly, it can be difficult to determine mechanisms. In fact, mechanisms are commonly disproved and newer ones are proposed.

mechanism

a proposed sequence of steps that describes how reactants are changed into products

rate-determining step

the slowest elementary step in a reaction mechanism

elementary step

a single step in the mechanism of a reaction

intermediate

a structure formed in one elementary step but consumed in a later step of a mechanism

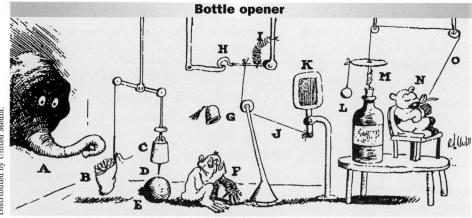

RUBE GOLDBERG™ and © of Rube Goldberg, Inc. Distributed by United Media.

Bottle opener

Elephant (A) eats peanuts (B)—as bag gets lighter weight (C) drops and spike (D) punctures balloon (E)—explosion scares monkey (F)—his hat (G) flies off and releases hook (H), causing spring (I) to pull string (J) which tilts tennis racket (K)—racket hits ball (L), making it spin around on attached string, thereby screwing corkscrew into cork (M)—ball hits sleeping dog (N) who jumps and pulls cork out of bottle with string (O)—my how simple!

FIGURE 16-6 ◀

Some mechanisms are easier to figure out than others. Try to determine the rate-determining step in this mechanism.

Rates can be manipulated

For most chemical reactions, the reaction rate is highest at the beginning, when reactant concentrations are highest, and decreases as reactants are used up and products are formed. Other than concentration, what affects the rate of a chemical reaction? The next section identifies four of the five factors that affect reaction rates and explains why or how the rate is affected. The fifth factor will be discussed in Section 16-3.

SECTION REVIEW

Total recall

1. Explain why the rate of a simple reaction is likely to be fastest at the beginning of the reaction.

Critical thinking

2. What is meant by a rate law for a chemical reaction? Why can a rate law not be written from a balanced chemical equation?

3. For each of the following reactions, write one expression for the reaction rate that uses a reactant and one expression that uses a product.
   a. $2H_2O_2(aq) \longrightarrow 2H_2O(l) + O_2(g)$
   b. $Cl_2(aq) + 2OH^-(aq) \longrightarrow$
   $\qquad OCl^-(aq) + Cl^-(aq) + H_2O(l)$
   c. $2NH_3(aq) + 6OCl^-(aq) \longrightarrow$
   $\qquad 3Cl_2(g) + N_2(g) + 6OH^-(aq)$
   d. $NH_4NO_3(aq) \longrightarrow N_2O(g) + 2H_2O(l)$

4. How does a reactant with an order of zero in the rate law affect the reaction rate?

5. Dinitrogen pentoxide decomposes into nitrogen dioxide and oxygen according to the following equation.

$$2N_2O_5(g) \longrightarrow 4NO_2(g) + O_2(g)$$

   If the change in O_2 concentration was found to be 2.5 M/s, what is the reaction rate in terms of N_2O_5?

6. **Story Clue** Compare the limiting of algae growth by a shortage of nutrients with the limiting reagent in a chemical reaction.

Practice problems

7. Express the reaction rate in terms of the rate of change of each reactant and each product in the following reactions:
   a. $4PH_3(g) \longrightarrow P_4(s) + 6H_2(g)$
   b. $S^{2-}(aq) + I_3^-(aq) \longrightarrow S(s) + 3I^-(aq)$
   c. $C_2H_4(g) + Br_2(g) \longrightarrow C_2H_4Br_2(g)$

8. Ammonia, NH_3, reacts with O_2 to form NO and H_2O as follows:

$$4NH_3(g) + 5O_2(g) \longrightarrow 4NO(g) + 6H_2O(g)$$

   a. At the instant when NH_3 is reacting at a rate of 0.80 M/min, what is the rate at which O_2 is disappearing?
   b. At what rate is each product being formed?

9. The observed rate law for the reaction of NO with Cl_2 is written as follows:

$$\text{rate} = k[NO]^2[Cl_2]$$

   What is the order of reaction with respect to NO? with respect to Cl_2? for the overall reaction?

10. If the rate of a reaction is expressed by $k[B]^2$, how would the rate change if the concentration of B were increased by a factor of 1.41? if it were decreased by a factor of 0.5?

How can reaction rates be explained?

OBJECTIVES

▶ *List* four major factors that affect the rate of a reaction, and describe how changes in each factor affect the rate.

▶ *Discuss* how collision theory explains reaction rates.

The factors that influence rate of reaction

You are already familiar with one of the factors that influence rates of chemical reactions. You learned in Section 16-1 that concentration can have an effect on reaction rates.

The identity of the substances involved in a reaction is even more important to the rate than the reactant concentrations, as shown in **Figure 16-7.** When you build a campfire, you do not use rocks; you use wood. If the tiniest spark is introduced into a mixture of H_2 and O_2, a violent explosion can occur as the reaction proceeds very quickly. If the same spark is introduced into a mixture of H_2 and N_2, nothing happens.

If you have ever tried to start a campfire, you also know that you do not start with logs. You start with small twigs or crumpled newspapers. The more finely divided a solid is, the easier it is to cause it to react. This illustrates the third factor in determining reaction rates—surface area.

The fourth factor is temperature. Sugar dissolves faster in hot tea than it does in iced tea. An increase in temperature speeds up a reaction. The remainder of this section will discuss the factors that influence the rates of chemical reactions in more detail.

▨ internet**connect** ≣

SC/INKS.

◀ NSTA ▶

TOPIC: Factors affecting rate
GO TO: www.scilinks.org
KEYWORD: HW162

FIGURE 16-7 ◀

Potassium reacts very rapidly with water. Iron also reacts with water, but the reaction is much slower.

The nature of the reactants affects reaction rate

Reactions involve the making and breaking of bonds. The rate at which bonds break and re-form depends on the type of bond and the nature of the molecules in which the bonds are found. Some processes, like the potassium and water reaction, take place very rapidly, while others, like the oxidation of lead by oxygen dissolved in water, take place very slowly if at all. The nature of a reactant is not a variable that can be adjusted to improve reaction rate.

Surface area affects rate of reaction

If you have ever tried to sweeten tea with sugar cubes, you know that it is much easier to dissolve the sugar if the cubes are crushed. Crushing the cube increases its surface area. The larger surface area allows more sugar molecules to contact the solution. Sugar dissolving in tea is a physical process, not a chemical one, but the explanation for this observation also applies to chemical reactions.

Reactions in which the reactants are all gases or liquids can happen quickly because the fluid particles are free to mix and collide. Particles in a solid, however, are in relatively fixed positions; only particles at the surface of the solid come into contact with other reactants. Therefore, if the surface area of the solid is increased, the number of particles available for reaction increases as well, and the reaction rate increases.

When wood burns, a reaction occurs between the wood and the oxygen in the air. The larger the area where oxygen can contact the wood, the more rapidly the wood will burn. **Figure 16-8** illustrates this point by showing that it is easier to ignite tiny twigs than it is to ignite a large piece of wood.

▼ **FIGURE 16-8**

a Division of a solid makes the exposed surface of the solid larger.

b More divisions mean more exposed surface.

c Hence, more surface is available for other reactant molecules to come together.

Temperature influences reaction rate

What do you do if you have a group of people coming for dinner and your food is not cooking fast enough? The best way to speed up the cooking process is to raise the temperature of your stove or oven. The cooking of food, like any chemical reaction, will generally occur faster at higher temperatures. Likewise, wood can lie around for centuries and not oxidize very much. But put a hot flame to it, and it oxidizes rapidly.

CONCEPT CHECK

1. For each of the following pairs, choose the substance or process that you would expect to react more rapidly.
   a. 5 cm of thick copper wire or 5 cm of thin copper wire
   b. dissolving granulated sugar or sugar cubes
   c. zinc in HCl(*aq*) at 20°C or zinc in HCl(*aq*) at 35°C
   d. hydrogen reacting with iodine at 300°C or at 500°C
2. Identify the factor that affects a reaction rate but cannot itself be adjusted.
3. A reaction occurs in 30 seconds as evidenced by a color change. The same color change occurs when the reaction is run at a lower temperature, but this time it takes 60 seconds. Is the rate of the second trial greater or less than the first?

FIGURE 16-9 ▲

A lizard gathers radiant energy from sunlight to warm its body. This increase in body temperature allows the lizard to move faster by increasing the rate of its metabolic reactions.

Modeling how reactions proceed

If two molecules approach each other, the outer electrons on each molecule repel the electrons on the other molecule. Ordinarily the molecules just bounce off each other. If these molecules are going to react chemically, they must collide with enough energy to cause the outer electrons to merge with each other to some extent. This merging of electrons leads to the formation of new bonds. Only the very high energy molecules have enough energy to bump and merge electrons.

The activation-energy diagram models a reaction's progress

Many reactions double or triple in rate when the temperature increases by as little as 10°C. This is an enormous effect. How can this rate increase be explained?

As you have already learned, molecules are in constant motion and have kinetic energy. At higher temperatures, molecules move faster and have greater kinetic energies. In Chapter 12 you learned that the average molar kinetic energy of a molecule is proportional to the absolute temperature, R, the ideal gas constant being the proportionality factor.

$$\text{average molar kinetic energy} = \tfrac{3}{2}RT$$

For any chemical reaction to occur, the reactant molecules must have a certain energy. This energy is called the **activation energy,** E_a. The activation energy is much greater than the average energy of reactant molecules. The shaded region of Figure 12-4 page, 426, shows that a temperature increase of 10° roughly doubles or triples the number of molecules with energies equal to or greater than the activation energy. This explains the drastic effect of temperature changes on reaction rates. The activation energy is like a hill the reactants must climb in order to reach the products. At higher temperatures, more molecules have sufficient energy to climb the hill.

When molecules collide successfully, they form an **activated complex.** **Figure 16-10** shows how the activated complex is formed when the molecules collide with enough energy to equal the activation energy. The left side of each curve represents the energy of the reactant molecules. The right side of each curve represents the energy of the products. Note that the energy of the products in each reaction is less than the energy of the reactants. Both of the reactions shown in Figure 16-10 are exothermic processes.

The activation energy in Figure 16-10b is lower than that in 16-10a. A lower activation energy means that the molecules do not need as much energy to react. Reactions with lower activation energies occur at greater rates than reactions with higher activation energies.

Colliding particles need the right orientation to react

If molecules have enough energy to equal E_a, will they react? They may or may not. As shown in Figure 16-10, a possible activated complex for the decomposition of HI has the two H atoms together and the two I

▼ **FIGURE 16-10**

The peak of each curve represents the energy of an activated complex.

Activation Energies for the Decomposition of HI and HBr

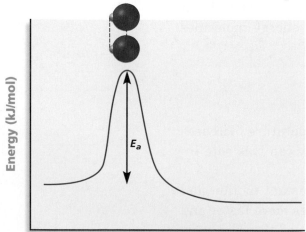

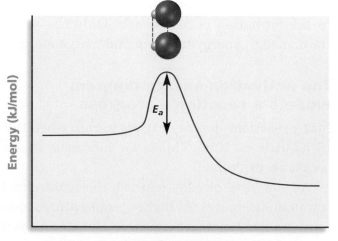

a The difference in energy between the bottom of this curve and the peak is the energy of activation for the decomposition of HI.

b The decomposition of HBr occurs at a faster rate than the decomposition of HI because this reaction has a lower activation energy.

FIGURE 16-11 ◄

Ethanol and acetic acid can collide in many orientations but will seldom be oriented suitably for a reaction.

Ethanol   Acetic acid

atoms together. The molecules must collide in this orientation to react. The chance of randomly moving particles colliding with the correct orientation is fairly low, especially among complicated molecules.

Figure 16-11 illustrates how unlikely it is for complex molecules such as ethanol and acetic acid to collide with the one orientation that will allow them to react. Can you imagine how seldom these molecules meet so that they are positioned in the orientation necessary for them to react?

$\mathcal{S}$ECTION REVIEW

Total recall

1. When will a collision lead to chemical reaction?

2. Compare and contrast activation energy and activated complex.

Critical thinking

3. **Interpreting Graphics** Arrange the three energy curves below in order of increasing E_a values. If each curve represents a separate reaction, which reaction would you predict to be the slowest?

4. Using what you know about the kinetic energy of molecules, explain why reaction rates vary greatly when temperature changes.

5. Compare the potential energies of the following stages of an endothermic reaction: reactants, activated complex, and products.

6. **Story Clue** Predict how the concentration of domoic acid along the North Carolina and Maryland coasts might change over the course of a year.

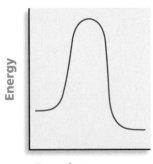

Energy

Reaction progress

a

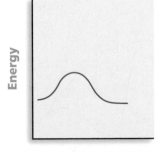

Energy

Reaction progress

b

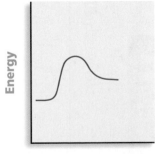

Energy

Reaction progress

c

How do catalysts change the rates of chemical reactions?

OBJECTIVES

▶ **Describe** how catalysts affect E_a and the rate of a reaction.

▶ **Explain** the mechanism of enzyme action in terms of chemical bonds and energy.

▶ **Give** an example of an inhibitor used to prevent chain reactions from occurring.

Pathways are modified by catalysts

catalyst

a substance added to a chemical reaction to increase the rate that is not itself changed in the reaction

catalysis

the process by which reaction rates are increased by the addition of a catalyst

The energy diagram for a reaction indicates that if the height of the energy hill—or activation energy—is increased, the rate decreases. If the height of the hill is reduced, the rate increases. Lowering the activation energy means changing to a new reaction mechanism. A **catalyst** lowers the energy barrier by forming an activated complex of lower energy. In short, it provides the reactant molecules with a more favorable, lower energy pathway to the products. This process is called **catalysis.**

Hydrogen peroxide, H_2O_2, decomposes slowly over time, as represented by the following reaction.

$$2H_2O_2(aq) \longrightarrow 2H_2O(l) + O_2(g)$$

Comparison of Pathways for the Decomposition of H_2O_2

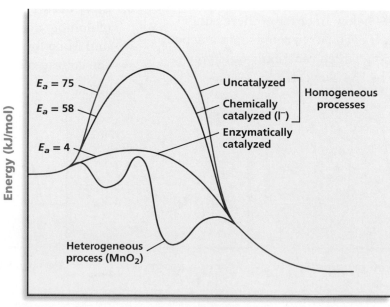

▶ **FIGURE 16-12**

Activation energy for a reaction can be reduced by adding a catalyst to the system. Some catalysts work better than others. For example, MnO_2 is a better catalyst for the decomposition of H_2O_2 than I⁻.

$E_a = 75$ — Uncatalyzed ⎤ Homogeneous
$E_a = 58$ — Chemically catalyzed (I⁻) ⎦ processes
— Enzymatically catalyzed
$E_a = 4$

Heterogeneous process (MnO_2)

Energy (kJ/mol)

Reaction progress

A 30% solution of H_2O_2 will decompose at a rate of about 0.5% per year at room temperature. This rate corresponds to the uncatalyzed curve in the energy diagram for the decomposition of H_2O_2 shown in **Figure 16-12.** If iodide ions, I^-, from potassium iodide, KI, are added to the peroxide solution, the activation energy is lowered from 75 kJ/mol to 58 kJ/mol. The I^- ions form a reaction intermediate, IO^-, when they react with H_2O_2 molecules. The IO^- ions then react with other H_2O_2 molecules to regenerate iodide ions as products are formed. The I^- ions are a catalyst for the decomposition of H_2O_2 because they are added to the reaction to increase the reaction rate but are not actually used up in the overall reaction. The iodide ion is an example of a **homogeneous catalyst** for the decomposition of hydrogen peroxide because KI and H_2O_2 are both in aqueous solution. Catalysts sometimes appear above the arrow in chemical equations.

$$2H_2O_2(aq) \xrightarrow{\text{KI}} 2H_2O(l) + O_2(g)$$

Catalase and manganese dioxide also catalyze the decomposition of H_2O_2 by lowering the E_a for the reaction to 4 kJ/mol or less. Note that although a catalyst changes the value for E_a of a reaction, the value of ΔH for the reaction is left unchanged. If a reaction is exothermic without a catalyst, the same amount of energy is released when the reaction is carried out with a catalyst. Likewise, an endothermic reaction absorbs the same quantity of energy with or without a catalyst.

The lowest energy pathway shown on Figure 16-12 is an example of a **heterogeneous catalyst.** The catalyst, manganese dioxide, is a solid, whereas the hydrogen peroxide is in solution. Catalysts in heterogeneous systems have the advantage of being more easily separated from the reaction products. A comparison of the catalyzed and uncatalyzed decomposition of H_2O_2 appears in **Figure 16-13.** Note that no observable changes are taking place in the uncatalyzed reaction, but the hydrogen peroxide decomposes rather vigorously in the presence of MnO_2.

homogeneous catalyst

a catalyst that is in the same phase as all of the reactants and products in a system

heterogeneous catalyst

a catalyst whose phase is different from the reactants'

FIGURE 16-13 ▼

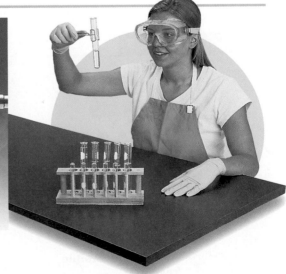

a The decomposition of H_2O_2 is such a slow process without a catalyst that no reaction is observed.

b In contrast, a very rapid decomposition of H_2O_2 occurs in the presence of MnO_2.

An enzyme speeds up the reaction that produces the dark pigment in this cat's fur at cooler temperatures. That is why the cooler regions of the cat's body have the darker fur.

enzyme

a large protein molecule that catalyzes chemical reactions in living things

substrate

the molecule or molecules with which an enzyme interacts

Enzymes are nature's catalysts

Reactions of organic compounds are generally slow. If living things had to depend on uncatalyzed reactions, life as we know it could not exist. Catalysts found in biological systems are called **enzymes.** Most enzymes are large protein molecules. Like all catalysts, enzymes are not used up in a reaction, so only small amounts are needed. However, unlike most catalysts, enzymes catalyze a particular type of reaction because the enzyme molecule has a specific three-dimensional conformation. That is, a specific location on the enzyme is shaped to receive a specific reactant, just as a specific lock is shaped to accept a specific key. Look at the interaction between the enzyme and **substrate** shown in **Figure 16-15.**

The substrate must have the correct structure to bind to the enzyme's active site. The active site of the enzyme molecule is where catalysis takes place. During the catalytic process, the enzyme's active site distorts the bonds in the substrate. This distortion strains the substrate's bonds and weakens them. The reaction progresses more rapidly because the already weakened bonds need less energy to get to the activated complex, making the E_a value lower than that for the uncatalyzed reaction. When the substrate is positioned within the active site, the activated complex at the top of the energy hill is formed. After this point, the product is made and it leaves the active site. The overall ΔH for the reaction does not change, but the activation energy is lowered.

Enzyme supplements reduce the effects of lactose intolerance

The human body has hundreds of highly specialized enzymes that control growth, reproduction, and other processes. Enzymes in the body speed up the chemical processes that sustain life. Most reactions in the body are so complex that if they were not catalyzed, they would require extremely high temperatures to occur at rates fast enough for life to exist. Fortunately, enzymes alter reaction pathways so that the

▼ **FIGURE 16-15**

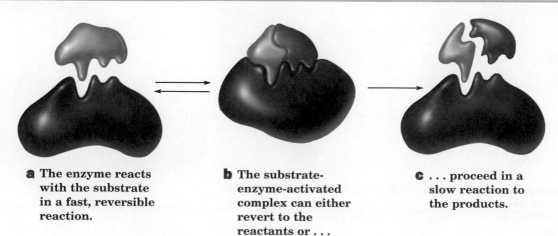

a The enzyme reacts with the substrate in a fast, reversible reaction.

b The substrate-enzyme-activated complex can either revert to the reactants or . . .

c . . . proceed in a slow reaction to the products.

FIGURE 16-16 ▲

The complex sugar lactose causes problems for some people in digesting milk, ice cream, cheese, and other dairy products.

complex reactions of metabolism occur at 37.0°C (98.6°F) at a rate several million times faster than they would without a catalyst.

Lactose is a sugar found in many dairy products. Lactase is a digestive enzyme that breaks down lactose into its constituent sugars, glucose and galactose. Some people lack the ability to produce lactase. These people have what is known as lactose intolerance. Undigested lactose molecules collect in the intestine and attract water. As a result, a person with lactose intolerance can experience painful cramps or diarrhea after ingesting foods with lactose. Enzyme supplements can be added to or taken with dairy products to break down the lactose.

Enzymatic cleaners reduce protein buildup on contact lenses

Modern contact lenses are made of plastics that absorb a great deal of water. Most lenses are gas permeable to enable sensitive corneas to receive the oxygen they require. However, the protein matter in tears can clog the pores in contact lenses, making both lenses and eyes susceptible to bacterial growth and potentially serious damage. Protein buildup is removed from the lenses by special enzymatic cleaners. These enzymes are known as proteases because they break down proteins into amino acids, which can be easily washed away, leaving the contact lenses clear and clean.

internet connect

SC*L*INKS

NSTA

TOPIC: Enzymes
GO TO: www.scilinks.org
KEYWORD: HW163

CONCEPT CHECK

1. What effect does a catalyst have on ΔH for a reaction?

2. A reaction occurs without the addition of a catalyst. A chemist determines its rate law. The rate law for the same reaction is determined after a catalyst has been added. Will the two rate laws be the same? Explain your answer.

3. What is a catalyst? Explain the effect of a catalyst on the rate of chemical reactions. How does a catalyst influence the activation energy required by a particular reaction?

Chain reactions and inhibitors

internet**connect**

sci**LINKS**

NSTA

TOPIC: Inhibitors
GO TO: www.scilinks.org
KEYWORD: HW164

Many reactions occur by mechanisms consisting of repeated elementary steps in which one reaction initiates the next reaction. These are called chain reactions. In Chapter 10 you encountered one that is involved in the destruction of the ozone layer. Chlorofluorocarbons diffuse into the stratosphere, where ultraviolet light disintegrates them, forming chlorine atoms with an unpaired electron. These atoms then initiate the destructive chain reaction shown below.

$$Cl\cdot + O_3 \longrightarrow ClO\cdot + O_2$$

$$ClO\cdot + O\cdot \longrightarrow Cl\cdot + O_2$$

The Cl atom, with its unpaired electron, is a free radical. One Cl radical can destroy thousands of O_3 molecules and O radicals (which are the precursors of ozone). This continues until the Cl atoms diffuse down into the troposphere.

The decomposition of hydrogen peroxide solution involves free radicals in the mechanism. Hydrogen peroxide solutions usually contain an **antioxidant.** The antioxidant preserves the hydrogen peroxide by destroying free radicals. It acts as an **inhibitor,** interrupting chain reactions. Many reactions of O_2 and O_3 involve free radicals. Ordinary rubber is attacked by atmospheric oxygen and even by traces of ozone, and it degrades rather rapidly. Most rubber products, especially tires, contain antioxidants that remove free radicals and slow down the reaction. Reactions of oxygen in the body form free radicals. Many people believe that free radicals are harmful in the body. Some dietary supplements contain antioxidants, such as vitamin C and selenium. The effectiveness of these supplements has not been proven.

antioxidant

a substance that can prevent chain reactions involving O_2 and O_3

inhibitor

a substance added to a chemical reaction to slow the reaction down

Inhibitors and catalysts work together

If combustion in an automobile engine were 100% efficient, the engine would convert gasoline into only carbon dioxide and water. Unfortunately, significant amounts of nitrogen oxides, carbon monoxide, and unburned hydrocarbons are discharged out of the car's tailpipe and into the air. For this reason, modern cars are equipped with catalytic converters to reduce pollution. Catalytic converters consist mainly of active platinum and

▼ **FIGURE 16-17**

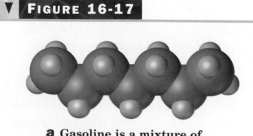

a Gasoline is a mixture of hydrocarbons. Some are straight, like heptane, . . .

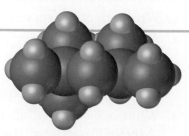

b and others are branched, like 2, 2, 4-trimethylpentane (isooctane).

palladium metals that catalyze the conversion of carbon monoxide, hydrocarbons, and nitrogen oxides to carbon dioxide, water, and nitrogen.

Gasoline is a mixture of hydrocarbons obtained from the fractional distillation of petroleum. Two of the many components of gasoline are shown in **Figure 16-17.** Some of the hydrocarbon chains in gasoline are straight, and some are branched. The branched chains burn more slowly and smoothly than the straight chains do. Therefore, the higher the percentage of branched chains in the gasoline mixture, the more efficiently it burns. If the gas burns too quickly inside the cylinder, it causes engine knock.

To inhibit the fast combustion that causes knocking, tetraethyl lead was once added to gasoline. At the time, tetraethyl lead was an attractive choice because it mixed readily with gasoline, was inexpensive, and did its job well. However, scientists did not realize how much lead would be dumped into the atmosphere or how serious the effects of lead poisoning would be. Lead itself is a relatively inert metal, but its compounds are toxic to most biological systems because they inhibit the actions of enzymes.

Cars equipped with catalytic converters must use unleaded gasoline. Lead ruins the platinum catalyst in the catalytic converters by covering it with a layer of lead that renders the active sites useless. Other antiknock agents, such as ethanol, *t*-butyl methyl ether, and aromatic compounds, are now used.

$\mathcal{S}$ECTION REVIEW

Total recall

1. **Interpreting Graphics** Sketch an energy diagram for a simple reaction, and label E_a. On the same plot, sketch how the diagram might look if the reaction went through catalysis.

2. How does catalysis speed up a chemical reaction?

Critical thinking

3. A particular reaction is found to have the following rate law.

$$\text{rate} = k[\text{A}][\text{B}]^2$$

How is the rate affected by each of the following changes?

a. the concentration of A is cut in half

b. the concentration of B is tripled

c. a catalyst is added

d. the temperature is increased

e. the concentration of A is doubled, and the concentration of B is cut in half

4. For enzyme-catalyzed reactions, the rate of reaction no longer increases after the substrate concentration reaches a certain level. Suggest a reason for this observation.

5. Predict how a catalyst would affect a reaction that reaches equilibrium.

6. Explain why there must be many different enzymes to catalyze all of the reactions in the body.

LOOKING BACK

How does temperature affect reaction rate?

Reactant molecules are more likely to have higher kinetic energies at higher temperatures. This translates into a greater number of molecules with energies above the activation energy. These molecules are then capable of colliding with adequate energy to cause a reaction. With more molecules able to react, the rate of a reaction increases. Metabolic reactions involved in growth and reproduction also experience an increased rate at increased temperature. This is why the rate of algae growth increases with the warming of their environment.

How does the warming of coastal waters disturb the ecological balance of an area?

As long as environmental conditions remain fairly constant, an ecological system in any region will reach a steady state. However, when a change is made in the environment, the balance shifts. This shift functions just as a shift in the equilibrium of a chemical reaction does. Any change disrupts the balance of the entire system.

Pfiesteria piscicida are naturally occurring organisms in the ocean that normally feed off fish. However, the increase in water temperature shifts the balance between the fish and the algae in favor of *Pfiesteria piscicida.* As you have learned, an increase in temperature increases the rate of chemical reactions, including those involved in the growth of organisms such as algae. But all reactions are

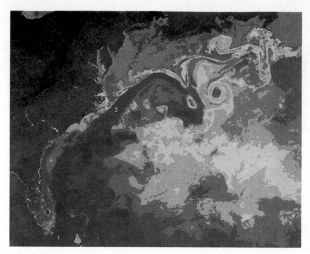

The Gulf Stream is a warm water current that flows up the eastern coast of the United States.

not equally accelerated, which means that some organisms will be favored by an increase in temperature. *Pfiesteria piscicida* is one such organism. For this reason, large algal blooms are more likely to occur in warmer water, killing unusually large numbers of fish.

Why might eating oysters and other shellfish harvested in the summer months be more of a risk than eating shellfish harvested in the winter months?

During the colder months, the rate of growth of algae such as *Pfiesteria piscicida* and *Gymnodinium breve* slows as the rates of their metabolic reactions slow. The organisms can remain fairly dormant; they do not emit toxins into coastal waters. In warmer months, the toxic algae populations develop faster due to the increased water temperatures. Shellfish harvested during these warmer periods have a higher likelihood of being contaminated with domoic acid. For this reason the oyster harvest season has traditionally occurred in the fall and winter.

KEY TERMS

16-1
average rate
chemical kinetics
elementary step
intermediate
mechanism
order
overall reaction order

rate-determining step
rate law
reaction rate

16-2
activated complex
activation energy

16-3
antioxidant
catalysis
catalyst
enzyme

heterogeneous catalyst
homogeneous catalyst
inhibitor
substrate

KEY CONCEPTS

16-1 What is a reaction rate?

▶ The average reaction rate is expressed as the ratio of a measured change, usually with concentration units, to the time interval during which the change takes place.

▶ Reaction rates generally decrease as the reaction progresses.

▶ The reaction rate is proportional to the concentration of each reactant raised to some power. This exponent must be determined experimentally for each reaction.

▶ The mechanism of a reaction usually involves a step-by-step sequence. The slowest step determines the overall rate and is called the rate-determining step.

16-2 How can reaction rates be explained?

▶ Factors affecting the reaction rate include the nature of the reactants as well as their concentration, temperature, and surface area.

▶ Increasing the concentration, temperature, or surface area of the reactants increases the reaction rate because the number of effective collisions between reactants increases.

▶ Not all molecular collisions result in a reaction. Molecules must have the proper orientation and sufficient kinetic energy to bring reactants together in such a way that new bonds can form.

16-3 How do catalysts change the rates of chemical reactions?

▶ Catalysts increase the reaction rate by lowering the energy barrier for the reaction. Catalysts can be recovered unchanged after the reaction is complete.

▶ Enzymes are catalysts found in biological systems. They bind substrates in their active site to form an activated complex. The shape of the substrate is altered, weakening its bonds until it decomposes and the reaction products are released from the enzyme.

▶ Inhibitors, such as antioxidants, can decrease the rate of a chain reaction.

KEY SKILLS

Review the following model before your exam. Be sure you can solve this type of problem.

Sample Problem 16A: Determining a rate law (p. 595)

REVIEW & ASSESS

TERM REVIEW

1. During a chemical reaction a(n) ——— may be formed but disappears.
(catalyst, intermediate, substrate)

2. Summing the exponents in a rate law expression yields the ———.
(elementary step, overall reaction order)

3. Antioxidants serve as ——— to prevent some harmful reactions in the body.
(catalysts, inhibitors, free radicals)

4. If a reaction is too slow to be practical, you could try ——— to speed it up.
(catalysis, activation energy, average rate)

5. A reaction mechanism may have one ——— or many.
(rate-determining step, elementary step)

6. If a reaction has a very high ———, it will likely be a slow reaction.
(order, activation energy, reaction rate)

7. For a reaction mechanism that has three steps, if the first two steps are fast, then the third step must be the ———.
(rate-determining step, elementary step)

8. The ——— of a reaction can be determined from the reaction's mechanism. It cannot be determined from a balanced chemical equation.
(reaction rate, rate law, average rate)

CONCEPT & SKILLS REVIEW

CLOCKING CHEMICAL REACTIONS

1. Give the appropriate units for expressing the rates of the following processes:
a. water dripping from a leaky faucet
b. a person's walking speed on an exercise path
c. a fan blade rotating
d. water evaporating from a 1 L container

2. a. List four physical properties or observations that can be measured during a chemical reaction to determine the reaction rate.
b. For each of the four variables that you listed in (a), what equipment would be necessary for making measurements?

3. Why does a minus sign appear in some reaction rate expressions?

4. Why might measuring the rate of the following reaction be difficult?

$$H_2(g) + CO_2(g) \longrightarrow H_2O(g) + CO(g)$$

Practice Problems

5. Write an expression for the rate of the decomposition of acetoacetic acid into acetone and CO_2.

$$H_3C-\overset{\overset{\displaystyle O}{\|}}{C}-CH_2\overset{\overset{\displaystyle O}{\|}}{C}OH(l) \longrightarrow$$

$$H_3C-\overset{\overset{\displaystyle O}{\|}}{C}-CH_3(l) + CO_2(g)$$

6. The reaction between methanol and hydrochloric acid to form methyl chloride and water is written as follows:

$$CH_3OH(aq) + H_3O^+(aq) + Cl^-(aq) \longrightarrow$$
$$CH_3Cl(aq) + H_2O(l)$$

The concentration of H_3O^+ was measured at various times, as shown in the following table:

Time	$[H_3O^+]$
0 min	1.83 M
79 min	1.67 M
158 min	1.52 M
316 min	1.30 M
632 min	1.00 M

a. Prepare a graph of H_3O^+ concentration versus time. Determine the average rate of the reaction for each of the four time intervals.
b. Is the rate constant throughout the reaction? Explain your answer.

7. Ethene, also called ethylene, reacts with chlorine gas to form 1,2-dichloroethane, as shown in the following equation:

$$CH_2{=}CH_2(g) + Cl_2(g) \longrightarrow Cl{-}CH_2{-}CH_2{-}Cl(l)$$

Two moles of chlorine gas are mixed with 3.3 mol of ethene in a 500 mL flask. After 10 minutes, the reaction is stopped and the amounts of the gases are measured again. There are 1.3 mol of Cl_2 and 2.6 mol of $CH_2{=}CH_2$. Calculate the average reaction rate.

8. Calculate the average rate of the following reaction:

$$H_2S(aq) + Cl_2(g) \longrightarrow S(s) + 2HCl(aq)$$

Time (min:s)	Concentration of H₂S (mol/L)
1:30	2.30
1:42	0.57

9. Many solutions to environmental problems involve changing a soluble toxic substance into a solid that can be filtered out. If mercury(II) chloride, a highly toxic substance in aqueous solution, is treated with sodium oxalate, mercury precipitates from the solution as mercury(I) chloride, and carbon dioxide is released as a gas.

$$2HgCl_2(aq) + Na_2C_2O_4(aq) \longrightarrow$$
$$2NaCl(aq) + 2CO_2(g) + Hg_2Cl_2(s)$$

a. Write a rate expression with respect to $HgCl_2$.
b. Would it be easier to monitor the formation of Hg_2Cl_2 than the formation of the other two products?
c. Examine the data in the table below. Is 30 minutes sufficient time to treat 0.050 M $HgCl_2$ with 0.40 M $Na_2C_2O_4$? Would 1 hour suffice? Why or why not?

10. A mixture of nitric acid and hydrochloric acid, called aqua regia, is used to dissolve gold and platinum. Nitrosyl chloride, NOCl, is present in the solution. A 0.95 M NOCl solution slowly decomposes into nitrogen monoxide and chlorine, causing the color of the aqua regia to change from reddish brown to light green.

$$2NOCl(soln) \longrightarrow 2NO(g) + Cl_2(g)$$

a. Use the following graph to determine the average rate of decrease in NOCl concentration during the first 90 days and between days 360 and 450.
b. Propose a reason why the rates for days 1–90 and days 360–450 differ.

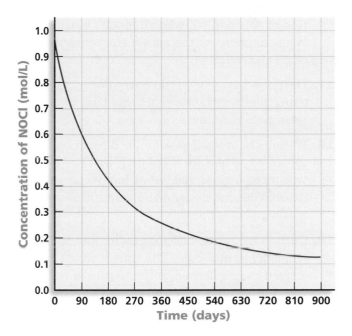

REPRESENTING REACTION RATES

11. How is the order of reaction with respect to a reactant determined from experimental data?

Trial	Initial concentration of HgCl₂ (M)	Initial concentration of Na₂C₂O₄ (M)	Initial concentration of NaCl (M)	Δt (min)	Final concentration of NaCl (M)
1	0.050	0.10	0.00	30	0.0010
2	0.050	0.20	0.00	30	0.0042
3	0.050	0.40	0.00	30	0.0168

12. Why aren't the coefficients in a balanced equation used to write the rate law expression?

13. Determine the overall reaction order for each of the following rate law expressions:
a. rate = $k[N_2O_5]$
b. rate = $k[CH_3OH]^2[(C_6H_5)_3CCl]$
c. rate = $k[O_3][NO]$

14. How does the energy of the activated complex compare with the energies of reactants and products?

15. Compare an intermediate with an activated complex.

16. If the rate law expression for a reaction is determined to be rate = $k[A]^2$ and the concentration of A is tripled, what happens to the rate? What happens to the rate if the concentration of A is halved?

17. Describe how you would carry out a typical experiment with two reactants that would determine a rate law expression.

18. If the rate law expression for a reaction is determined to be rate = $k[A][B]^2$ and the concentration of A is halved, what happens to the rate? What happens to the rate if the concentration of B is halved?

19. Carbon monoxide and oxygen bind to the hemoglobin molecule. The time it takes for the oxygen to be released to the tissues is measured in seconds. The release of CO from hemoglobin takes from five to eight hours. Both reactions are first order with respect to the oxygen and carbon monoxide complexes with hemoglobin. Compare the kinetics of these reactions, and explain why carbon monoxide poisoning occurs.

20. The hydrolysis of thioacetamide is described by the following chemical equation:

$$CH_3CSNH_2(aq) + H_2O(l) \longrightarrow$$
$$H_2S(aq) + CH_3CONH_2(aq)$$

The rate law is determined to be rate = $k[H_3O^+][CH_3CSNH_2]$. How does adding some 0.1 M NaOH to a solution that is 0.10 M in both hydronium ion and thioacetamide affect the rate?

21. If you were told that the rate law expression for the following reaction is second order with respect to H_2O because the coefficient is 2, how would you respond?

$$CaC_2(s) + 2H_2O(l) \longrightarrow C_2H_2(g) + Ca(OH)_2(s)$$

Practice Problems

22. Given the following data, write a rate law expression for the decomposition of manganese oxide. **(Hint: See Sample Problem 16A.)**

$$2Mn_2O_7(aq) \longrightarrow 4Mn(s) + 7O_2(g)$$

Mn₂O₇ (M)	Rate (M/s)
7.5×10^{-5}	1.2×10^{-4}
1.5×10^{-4}	4.8×10^{-4}

23. The rate law for a reaction is found to be rate = $k[X]^3$. By what factor does the rate increase if [X] is tripled?

24. Given the following reaction:

$$NO_2(g) + CO(g) \longrightarrow CO_2(g) + NO(g)$$

If the CO concentration is held constant and the NO_2 concentration is doubled, the rate of formation of CO_2 quadruples. However, doubling the concentration of CO has no effect on the rate of CO_2 being formed.
a. Write a rate law expression for this reaction.
b. Determine the order of the reaction with respect to NO_2 and with respect to CO.

25. Determine the factor by which the rate changes for the reaction with the rate law rate = $k[A]^n[B]^m$ if both [A] and [B] are doubled, given the following values of n and m:
a. $n = 0, m = 2$
b. $n = 2, m = 2$
c. $n = 1, m = 3$

CAUSES FOR VARIOUS REACTION RATES

26. If the temperature of the reactants is raised, are all of the reactant particles likely to have enough energy to form products? Why?

27. Why does grinding a solid cause an increase in the reaction rate of the material?

28. The conversion of cyclopropane to propene is shown below. The first-order rate constant, k, is $6.1 \times 10^{-2} \, s^{-1}$ at 500°C.

$$H_2C\!-\!\!\!\overset{\displaystyle CH_2}{\triangle}\!\!\!-\!CH_2 \longrightarrow H_3C\!-\!CH\!=\!CH_2$$

a. Write the rate law expression for this reaction.

b. Determine the actual rate if the concentration of cyclopropane is 0.015 M.

c. The rate constant is $5.70 \times 10^{-4} \, s^{-1}$ at 25°C. How do you account for the difference in rate at the two temperatures?

29. Why is the basic chemical nature of a substance important when studying chemical kinetics?

30. Why does a change in the concentration of reactants usually change the reaction rate?

31. Use graphs to illustrate the following situations:
a. an exothermic reaction with a relatively large E_a value
b. an exothermic reaction with a relatively small E_a value

32. At normal body temperature (37°C), the body can survive for only 5 minutes without oxygen. When the body temperature is lowered to a state of hypothermia (28–30°C), the body can survive almost 30 minutes without damage to tissues. Why?

33. Iron nails will corrode slowly when placed in sulfuric acid. If iron filings are substituted, the corrosion will occur more rapidly. Why?

34. White phosphorus will ignite and burn spontaneously around 34°C according to the following equation:

$$P_4(s) + 5O_2(g) \longrightarrow P_4O_{10}(s)$$

a. Do you think that E_a is large or small? Explain.
b. Draw an energy diagram for this reaction.
c. On the graph, label the following: x and y axes, reactants, products, activated complex, and E_a.
d. Propose two ways that white phosphorus could be stored to prevent a reaction with oxygen.

35. Explosions sometimes occur in factories where wheat is ground into flour. Would a factory containing processed flour be more likely to sustain an explosion than a factory containing whole grains of wheat? Why? What is the difference?

ACTIVITY OF ENZYMES AND INHIBITORS

36. In the diagram below, the energy pathway for a reaction is represented by the curved line. Draw another line representing the possible energy pathway that might result if an enzyme were present. Is the reaction exothermic or endothermic? Does ΔH change when the catalyst is present?

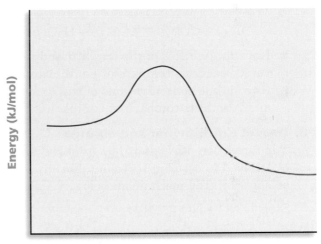

Reaction progress

37. Briefly describe the process involved in the enzyme-catalyzed conversion of a substrate to a product.

38. What is the difference between a homogeneous catalyst and a heterogeneous catalyst?

39. Explain the effect of an inhibitor on the rate of a free-radical reaction.

40. A certain nerve gas, soman, inhibits the enzyme cholinesterase. Antidotes to poisoning by this nerve gas are cholinesterase reactivators. Suggest what can happen to a body's nervous system when it is inhibited by this nerve gas.

41. Look up the formula for t-butyl methyl ether. Compare its formula with that of 2,2,4-trimethylpentane. Why do you think they are good antiknock agents?

1. Molarity

H_2O_2 is stored in dark bottles because light increases the rate of decomposition.

$$2H_2O_2(l) \longrightarrow 2H_2O(l) + O_2(g)$$

A 500 mL bottle of 1.50 M H_2O_2 decomposes at an average rate of 0.25 M/h in a clear bottle and at a rate of 0.013 M/y in a dark bottle. What is the difference in H_2O_2 concentration in the two bottles after three hours?

2. Theme: Equilibrium and change

The following reaction has an equilibrium constant of 0.771 at 750°C.

$$H_2(g) + CO_2(g) \rightleftharpoons CO(g) + H_2O(g)$$

a. How do the rates of the forward and reverse reactions compare at equilibrium?

b. How do the concentrations of the products and reactants compare at equilibrium?

3. Theme: Equilibrium and change

The formation of N_2 and H_2O from NO and H_2 is believed to occur in three equilibrium steps, as shown in the mechanism below.

Step 1: $NO + NO \rightleftharpoons N_2O_2$

Step 2: $N_2O_2 + H_2 \rightleftharpoons N_2O + H_2O$

Step 3: $N_2O + H_2 \rightleftharpoons N_2 + H_2O$

When the elementary steps are added together, the K_{eq} of the overall reaction is equal to the product of K_{eq} for all the steps.

a. Write K_{eq} expressions for each step and for the overall reaction.

b. Why do concentration terms for the intermediates not appear in the K_{eq} expressions for the overall equation?

4. Theme: Systems and interactions

Iodine monochloride, ICl, a substance used to determine the degree of unsaturation of fats and oils, is a gas above 97°C. ICl reacts with hydrogen gas to form I_2 gas and HCl gas.

$$2\ ICl(g) + H_2(g) \longrightarrow I_2(g) + 2HCl(g)$$

The rate law for this reaction is rate = $k[ICl][H_2]$. At 230°C, k has a value of 0.163 $M^{-1}s^{-1}$. At 240°C k increases to 0.348 $M^{-1}s^{-1}$.

a. If [ICl] and [H_2] are both 0.020 M, compare the rates at 230°C and 240°C.

b. Compare the rates at 230°C for reactant concentrations of 0.010 M and 0.020 M, respectively.

c. Which has a greater effect on the reaction rate, a 10°C increase in temperature or a doubling of a concentration?

5. Stoichiometry

Given the following reaction, write expressions for the rate of the reaction in terms of each product and reactant.

$$5Sb^{3+}(aq) + 2MnO_4^-(aq) + 36H_2O(l) \longrightarrow$$
$$5SbO_4^{3-}(aq) + 2Mn^{2+}(aq) + 24H_3O^+(aq)$$

Performance assessment

1. Boilers are used to heat large buildings. Deposits of $CaCO_3$, $MgCO_3$, and $FeCO_3$ can hinder the boiler operation. Aqueous solutions of hydrochloric acid are commonly used to remove these deposits. The general equation for the reaction is written as follows:

$$MCO_3(s) + 2H_3O^+(aq) \longrightarrow$$
$$M^{2+}(aq) + 3H_2O(l) + CO_2(g)$$

M stands for Ca, Mg, or Fe. Design an experiment to determine the effect of various HCl concentrations on the rates of this reaction. Present your design to a panel group.

Portfolio project

1. internet**connect**

SC**LINKS**
NSTA

TOPIC: Biochemical processes
GO TO: www.scilinks.org
KEYWORD: HW165

Research and communication

Many of the chemical reactions that take place in living organisms are catalyzed by specific enzymes. Choose a biochemical process, such as respiration, photosynthesis, vision, or muscular contraction. Prepare a diagram of this process, and detail all of the chemical reactions that occur, noting the enzymes associated with each reaction.

1. The sequence of steps that occurs in a reaction process is called the _____.
   a. heterogeneous reaction
   b. rate law
   c. overall reaction
   d. reaction mechanism

2. In order to be effective, a collision requires _____.
   a. enough energy only
   b. favorable orientation only
   c. enough energy and a favorable orientation
   d. a reaction mechanism

3. In an endothermic reaction, _____.
   a. energy of products < activation energy < energy of reactants
   b. energy of reactants < activation energy < energy of products
   c. energy of products < energy of reactants < activation energy
   d. energy of reactants < energy of products < activation energy

4. How does the energy of the activated complex compare with the energies of the reactants and products?
   a. It is lower than the energy of the reactants and the energy of the products.
   b. It is lower than the energy of the reactants but higher than the energy of the products.
   c. It is higher than the energy of the reactants but lower than the energy of the products.
   d. It is higher than the energy of the reactants and the energy of the products.

5. If a collision between molecules is very gentle, the molecules are _____.
   a. more likely to be orientated favorably
   b. less likely to be orientated favorably
   c. likely to react
   d. likely to rebound without reacting

6. Reaction rate is proportional to the change in _____.
   a. reactant concentration per degree Celsius
   b. reactant concentration per unit time
   c. temperature per unit time
   d. time per reactant concentration

7. Which of the following may affect reaction rate?
   a. nature of reactants
   b. surface area
   c. temperature
   d. all of the above

8. A substance that slows down a reaction process is called a(n) _____.
   a. inhibitor   c. catalyst
   b. reactant   d. activated complex

9. A rate law relates _____.
   a. reaction rate and temperature
   b. reaction rate and concentration
   c. temperature and concentration
   d. energy and concentration

10. The human body uses _____ to speed up reactions that are necessary for life.
    a. reactants   c. collisions
    b. enzymes   d. temperature

11. In an energy-profile graph, the activated complex is represented at the _____.
    a. left end of the curve
    b. right end of the curve
    c. bottom of the curve
    d. peak of the curve

12. Raising temperature _____.
    a. increases average molecular motion
    b. decreases average molecular motion
    c. has no effect on average molecular motion
    d. does not allow collision theory to operate

CHAPTER 17

Electrochemistry

FARADAY'S FISH

Michael Faraday was an outstanding physicist and chemist who lived from 1791 to 1867. He was one of the world's most versatile experimentalists. Although Faraday was both a brilliant chemist and a brilliant physicist, he never performed experiments in the field of biology. So why would this scientist keep a fish in his laboratory?

Faraday made many important chemical discoveries in his laboratory in London's Royal Institution. He was the first to make benzene and liquid chlorine. He made breakthroughs in many fields of physics, but he is perhaps best remembered for his invention of the electric motor, which converts electrical energy into mechanical energy. He also invented the *dynamo,* which converts mechanical energy into electrical energy. His passion for chemistry and electricity led him to found the field of electrochemistry, the branch of science that is the subject of this chapter.

The fish in Faraday's lab was a *torpedo ray.* You are probably familiar with the word *torpedo* in the context of a naval weapon. It is from this fish that the weapon derives its name. Faraday's interest in the torpedo ray arose because, like his dynamo, it could gen-erate electricity. In fact, many fish produce pulses of electricity. Most electric fish use the reflection of these pulses as a navigation and hunting aid in much the same way that bats use sonar. This ability allows electric fish to navigate and find food in very murky water. A few species, notably the electric eel, the torpedo ray, and the electric catfish, use their ability to generate electricity as a weapon. These fish can produce enough voltage to stun or even kill their prey. Large electric eels have even been known to produce enough electricity to kill adult humans.

As you read this chapter, you will learn about electrochemical cells that generate electricity. Electricity is a movement of charge. You have already learned about two types of charged particles, electrons and ions. Electric current is generated by the movement of one or both of these two types of charged particles. Electrochemical cells, such as batteries, generate electricity as a flow of electrons and ions. Electric fish, such as the torpedo ray, generate electricity as a flow of ions.

CHAPTER LINKS

How does the torpedo ray generate electricity in its electric-organ cells?

Would you expect electric organs to be more useful to fish that swim in salt water or fresh water? in clear water or murky water?

How is it possible for large voltages, as great as 600 V in some electric eels, to be produced?

What is electrochemistry all about?

OBJECTIVES

▶ **Convert** voltage and charge to electrical energy.

▶ **Explain** the significance of Faraday's constant.

▶ **Distinguish** between anodic and cathodic reactions.

▶ **Define,** with examples, the terms *electrode, cathode,* and *anode.*

▶ **Explain** the distinctions between electrolytic, galvanic, and equilibrium cells.

Introduction to electricity

Electrochemistry is the union of electricity and chemistry. You probably know more about chemistry than you do about electricity, so this chapter will start with some of the fundamentals of electricity.

Figure 17-1 shows the components of a typical flashlight. There are two *cells,* or *batteries.* Each cell has a metal *terminal* at each end. Near the top terminal you will find a *positive* symbol, either + or $\oplus$. The *negative* terminal, at the bottom of the cell, might have a – or $\ominus$. Both terminals are made of metal, and both contain electrons, but there is a greater electron density at the negative terminal. Think of the greater density as being caused by "electrical pressure" inside the battery pushing electrons away from the positive terminal and into the negative terminal.

voltage

an electric potential difference

volt

the SI unit of voltage

Volts measure "electrical pressure"

This "electrical pressure" is called **voltage,** or *electric potential,* and is measured in **volts** (V). The cells that power your flashlight are likely labeled "1.5 V." When the batteries are placed *in series,* as in Figure 17-1, the voltages add up, giving a total potential of 3.0 V.

▶ **FIGURE 17-1**

When the switch of a flashlight is closed, electrons driven by the "pressure" of the battery are forced through the thin tungsten filament of the bulb. This flow of electrons makes the filament so hot that light is emitted.

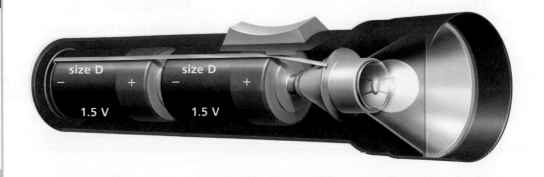

When you turn on the flashlight, you create a continuous path for the electrons to flow through. The electrons at the negative terminal respond to their higher "pressure" and flow through the metal circuit to the positive terminal. While they are flowing from negative to positive, the electrons pass through the tungsten filament in the light bulb, heating the filament and causing it to glow. When you turn off the flashlight, you break the metallic path, and electron flow is prevented.

internet connect

SC**LINKS**

NSTA

TOPIC: Electrical energy
GO TO: www.scilinks.org
KEYWORD: HW171

Electrical energy is easy to calculate

A **coulomb** is the unit used to measure electric charge. You already encountered it in Chapter 3, where you learned that the charge on a single electron is negative, with a magnitude of $1.602\,177 \times 10^{-19}$ C. Therefore, –1 C is to the charge on $6.241\,508 \times 10^{18}$ electrons.

If you examine the bulb in an ordinary flashlight, you might find that it has "0.5 A" inscribed on the base. What does this mean? The letter A is the abbreviation for **ampere,** the unit of electric current. Current is the flow of charge per unit of time. One ampere is defined as 1 C/s. Every second, 0.5 C, or about 3×10^{18} electrons, pass through the flashlight bulb. It's no wonder the filament gets hot! The units have been defined so that it is easy to relate electricity to energy. One joule of energy is used when 1 C moves across a potential of 1 V.

$$\text{energy (J)} = \text{potential (V)} \times \text{charge (C)}$$

coulomb

the SI unit of electric charge

ampere

the SI unit of electric current; equal to 1 C/s

Electricity can be measured by the mole

Chemists generally measure amounts in terms of mole units. You know how much electric charge there is in one electron, so how much electric charge is there in 1 mol of electrons? Avogadro's constant tells you that there are $6.022\,137 \times 10^{23}$ electrons in 1 mol of electrons. As mentioned above, the charge on one electron has the magnitude of $1.602\,177 \times 10^{-19}$ C. Multiplying these constants together gives $96\,485.309$ C/mol, which is represented by the symbol F. This is called Faraday's constant in honor of Michael Faraday, the father of electrochemistry.

FIGURE 17-2 ▲

The words *electrode, anode, cathode, ion, anion,* and *cation* were all introduced by Michael Faraday.

CONCEPT CHECK

1. A typical lightning bolt has about 10.0 C of charge. How many electrons are in a typical lightning bolt?

2. A charge of 9.0 mC passes through a length of thin wire in 3.5 seconds.

   a. What is the current in the wire?

   b. How many electrons would pass through the section of wire in 10.0 seconds?

   c. If a voltage of 4.5 V is applied to the wire, how much energy is dissipated in 5.0 minutes using the current from item (a)?

Electrodes

In Chapter 4 you learned that metals are good conductors of electricity. They conduct by electron motion. In Chapter 13 you found that electrolyte solutions conduct electricity by the motion of ions, not electrons. All conductors can be classified into two groups: those that conduct by *electron* motion and those that conduct by *ion* motion.

What happens when a substance that conducts by electron motion is placed in contact with a material that conducts by the motion of ions? This junction between an electronic conductor and an ionic conductor is called an **electrode.** Electronic conduction can transfer electricity through the metal and up to the junction. Likewise, ionic conduction can transfer electricity through the solution and up to the junction. But without something special happening, the electricity cannot cross the junction itself. The "something special" that must occur is called an *electrode reaction.*

If electrons are consumed, the reaction is cathodic

Electrode reactions involve the transfer of electrons. If the electronic conductor gives up electrons to the ionic conductor in the electrode reaction, then the electrode is said to be a **cathode** and the reaction is *cathodic.* The flow of electrons and ions at a cathode is shown in **Figure 17-3.** The copper strip is the electronic conductor that gives up electrons to the ionic conductor, the copper(II) sulfate solution.

The chemistry that occurs at a cathode is described as **reduction.** The conversion of copper(II) ions to copper metal shown in Figure 17-3 is a reduction reaction.

$$Cu^{2+}(aq) + 2e^- \longrightarrow Cu(s)$$

You can see in Figure 17-3 that during reduction, copper is deposited on the metal strip. Solid metal appears as the product. This process of depositing a metal on a conductive surface is used in the **electroplating** of silver onto jewelry and flatware.

Neutral species can also undergo reduction at a cathode. For example, chlorine is reduced to chloride ions according to the following equation.

$$Cl_2(aq) + 2e^- \longrightarrow 2Cl^-(aq)$$

Another example of a cathodic reaction is one in which the solvent itself is reduced. This reaction occurs at the cathode during the *electrolysis* of water.

$$2H_2O(l) + 2e^- \longrightarrow H_2(g) + 2OH^-(aq)$$

electrode

the junction between a metallic conductor and an ionic conductor, often an electrolyte solution

cathode

the electrode at which reduction takes place

reduction

a chemical reaction in which the reactant gains electrons

electroplating

an electrochemical process in which a metal ion is reduced and solid metal is deposited on a surface

▼ **FIGURE 17-3**

Copper(II) ions are reduced as they gain electrons at the cathode.

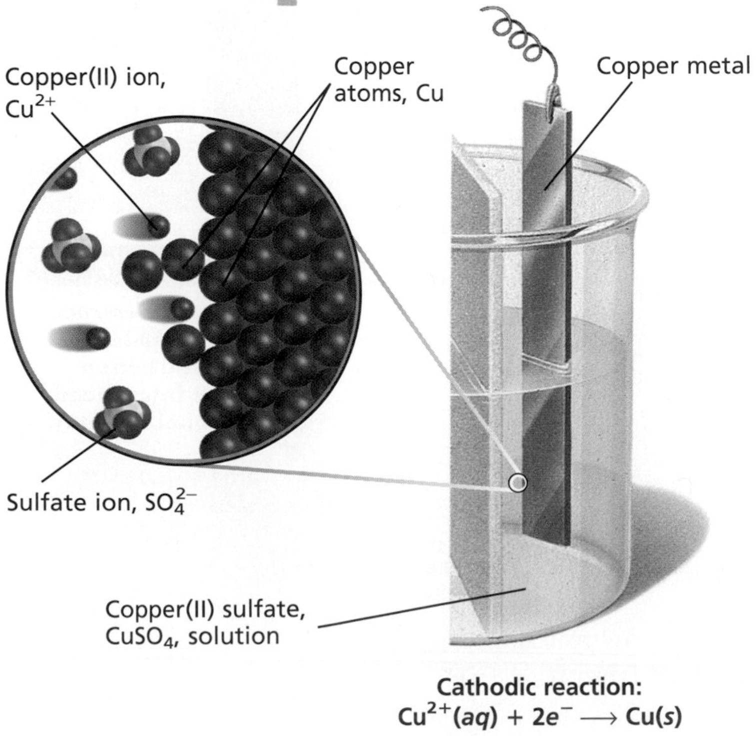

Copper(II) ion, Cu^{2+}

Copper atoms, Cu

Copper metal

Sulfate ion, SO_4^{2-}

Copper(II) sulfate, $CuSO_4$, solution

Cathodic reaction:
$Cu^{2+}(aq) + 2e^- \longrightarrow Cu(s)$

If electrons are released, an anodic reaction has occurred

An **anode** is an electrode at which electrons are generated, as shown in **Figure 17-4.** The anode shown in the figure involves the reaction of zinc atoms to form zinc ions according to the following equation.

$$Zn(s) \longrightarrow Zn^{2+}(aq) + 2e^-$$

A reaction occurring at an anode is an *anodic* reaction, and the resulting chemical change is called **oxidation.** Electrons are evolved at the anode during the electrolysis of water.

$$6H_2O(l) \longrightarrow 4e^- + O_2(g) + 4H_3O^+(aq)$$

The rusting of iron is another example of an oxidation reaction. Iron metal in the presence of water forms iron(III) oxide, also known as rust.

$$2Fe(s) + 11H_2O(l) \longrightarrow$$
$$Fe_2O_3 \cdot 2H_2O(s) + 6H_3O^+(aq) + 6e^-$$

Notice that the beakers in Figures 17-3 and 17-4 appear to be cut in half. Each beaker shows only part of a complete picture. These electrode reactions appear to occur on their own, but that never actually happens. Reduction reactions always occur with oxidation reactions. The electrons used in reduction must come from an oxidation reaction. The overall reaction is an oxidation-reduction reaction, or **redox reaction.** Although electrons cancel out of redox equations, when the reaction occurs electrochemically, the electrons are often indicated above the arrow, as shown in the following equation that combines the cathodic and anodic reactions from Figures 17-3 and 17-4.

$$Zn(s) + Cu^{2+}(aq) \xrightarrow{2e^-} Zn^{2+}(aq) + Cu(s)$$

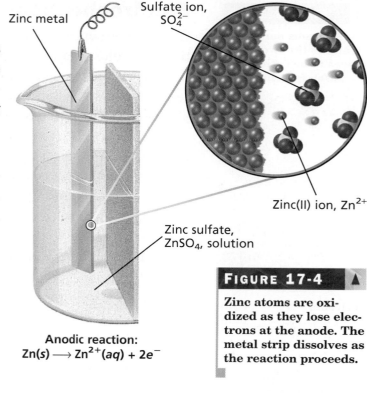

Zinc sulfate, ZnSO$_4$, solution

Anodic reaction:
$$Zn(s) \longrightarrow Zn^{2+}(aq) + 2e^-$$

FIGURE 17-4 ▲

Zinc atoms are oxidized as they lose electrons at the anode. The metal strip dissolves as the reaction proceeds.

📶 internet**connect** ≡

SC*i*LINKS™

NSTA

TOPIC: Electroplating
GO TO: www.scilinks.org
KEYWORD: HW172

anode

the electrode at which oxidation takes place

oxidation

a chemical reaction in which the reactant loses electrons

redox reaction

any chemical process in which both oxidation and reduction occur

CONCEPT CHECK

1. Identify the following reactions as oxidation or reduction reactions.
   a. $Na \longrightarrow Na^+ + e^-$
   b. $Cr_2O_7^{2-} + 14H^+ + 6e^- \longrightarrow 2Cr^{3+} + 7H_2O$
   c. $2Cl^- \longrightarrow Cl_2 + 2e^-$
   d. $Br_2 + 2e^- \longrightarrow 2Br^-$

2. Identify which of the following reactions is an anodic reaction and which is a cathodic reaction. Write the balanced overall ionic equation for the redox reaction between these two.

$$Cd(s) \longrightarrow Cd^{2+}(aq) + 2e^-$$
$$I_3^-(aq) + 2e^- \longrightarrow 3I^-(aq)$$

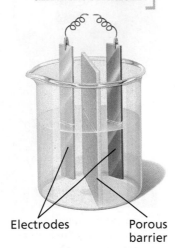

Electrodes   Porous barrier

electrochemical cell

an apparatus through which electricity can flow that includes at least two electrodes and at least one electrolyte solution

▼ **FIGURE 17-6**

Copper is refined in an electrolytic cell.

Electrochemical cells

Electrons produced by an anode must be consumed by a cathodic reaction. Therefore, an anode must be paired with a cathode. The two electrodes combine in an **electrochemical cell.** The simplest electrochemical cell consists of two pieces of metal in an electrolyte solution. **Figure 17-5** shows a common type of electrochemical cell in which a porous barrier divides the cell into two compartments. Ions are allowed to pass through this barrier so that electricity can flow between the compartments.

An *electrode* was defined as a surface: the junction between an electronic conductor and an ionic conductor. That definition is technically correct, but be aware that the words *electrode, anode,* and *cathode* are also used to refer to the pieces of metal. The words *anode* and *cathode* are often incorrectly interchanged with *positive* and *negative* electrodes. An anode may be the positive *or* the negative electrode of a cell; the anode is wherever oxidation occurs. The cathode may be the positive *or* negative electrode; it is wherever reduction occurs.

There are three kinds of electrochemical cells. The cell depicted in Figure 17-5 has wires that are not attached to anything. What those wires are attached to determines whether the cell is an electrolytic cell, a galvanic cell, or an equilibrium cell.

Electrolytic cells are used to refine metals

The cell shown in **Figure 17-6** illustrates a copper-refining plant. A power source drives electricity through the cell. The anode is impure copper containing zinc, gold, and silver. The electrolyte is an acidified $CuSO_4$ solution. The following chemical equation shows that copper metal is oxidized to copper(II) ions that go into solution at the anode.

$$Cu(s) \longrightarrow 2e^- + Cu^{2+}(aq)$$

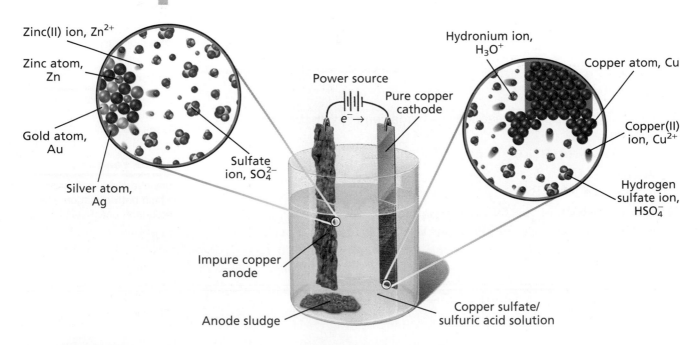

Zinc(II) ion, Zn^{2+}

Zinc atom, Zn

Gold atom, Au

Silver atom, Ag

Sulfate ion, SO_4^{2-}

Power source

Pure copper cathode

$e^- \rightarrow$

Impure copper anode

Anode sludge

Copper sulfate/ sulfuric acid solution

Hydronium ion, H_3O^+

Copper atom, Cu

Copper(II) ion, Cu^{2+}

Hydrogen sulfate ion, HSO_4^-

Exactly the opposite reaction occurs at the cathode, which is a strip of pure copper.

$$Cu^{2+}(aq) + 2e^- \longrightarrow Cu(s)$$

The solid copper dissolves from the impure anode. The copper ions then move through the solution toward the cathode, where they are deposited as pure metal. The impurities include active metals, such as zinc, which also oxidize and dissolve from the anode.

$$Zn(s) \longrightarrow 2e^- + Zn^{2+}(aq)$$

Unlike the copper ions, these impurities are not reduced at the cathode, so they remain in solution. Inactive impurities, such as platinum, silver, and gold, fall to the bottom of the vessel as *anode sludge*. The sludge is such a valuable source of these expensive elements that their recovery more than justifies the cost of the copper-refining process.

The cell used to refine impure copper uses an external power source to drive a chemical reaction. It is an example of an **electrolytic cell.** Electrolytic cells convert electrical energy into chemical energy. **Galvanic cells** do the opposite; they convert chemical energy into electrical energy.

TOPIC: Electrochemical cells
GO TO: www.scilinks.org
KEYWORD: HW173

electrolytic cell

an electrochemical cell in which electrical energy is used to drive two electrode reactions and bring about desired chemical changes

galvanic cell

an electrochemical cell in which two electrode reactions occur spontaneously and produce electrical energy

---

SAMPLE PROBLEM 17A   Calculating electric charge used in an electrolytic cell

How much electric charge is used in refining 1.0000 kg of copper?

1 List what you know

▶ Mass of Cu = 1.0000 kg = 1000.0 g
▶ Charge = ? C

2 Set up the problem

▶ Write the chemical equation for the reaction involved in refining copper.

$$Cu^{2+}(aq) + 2e^- \longrightarrow Cu(s)$$

From this equation you see that 2 mol of electrons is required to reduce 1 mol of Cu^{2+} to 1 mol of Cu.

▶ In order to calculate the amount of electricity required for the process, you must convert the mass of copper to the amount of copper in moles. To do this, you need to know the molar mass of copper.

$$1 \text{ mol Cu} = 63.55 \text{ g}$$

▶ Set up your equation. Remember that you must first convert the 1000.0 g Cu to the amount of Cu in moles. Because 1 mol of Cu is produced by 2 mol of electrons, you must next include a factor to determine the amount of electrons involved in refining the given mass of copper. Then you must use Faraday's constant to determine the amount of electricity needed.

$$1000.0 \text{ g Cu} \times \frac{1 \text{ mol Cu}}{63.55 \text{ g Cu}} \times \frac{2 \text{ mol } e^-}{1 \text{ mol Cu}} \times \frac{96\,485 \text{ C}}{\text{mol } e^-} = ? \text{ C}$$

Calculate and verify

▶ Calculate and round off correctly.

$$1000.0 \text{ g Cu} \times \frac{1 \text{ mol Cu}}{63.55 \text{ g Cu}} \times \frac{2 \text{ mol } e^-}{1 \text{ mol Cu}} \times \frac{96\,485 \text{ C}}{\text{mol } e^-} = 3.037 \times 10^6 \text{ C}$$

▶ Check your answer by estimating with round figures.

$$\frac{(10^3)(2)(1 \times 10^5)}{60} \approx 3 \times 10^6$$

PRACTICE PROBLEMS

1. The copper refining cell requires only a small voltage, typically 0.25 V. How much energy is required to refine 1.0 kg of copper? (Hint: Use the result from Sample Problem 17A.)

2. Ag^+ ions are reduced at a cathode to produce silver metal. Calculate how much silver metal is produced at the cathode in 30.0 minutes if a current of 1.50 A flows through a solution containing Ag^+.

Galvanic cells produce electrical energy

▼ FIGURE 17-7

A Daniell cell produces the electrical energy used to illuminate the light bulb as electrons move through the filament from the anode to the cathode.

A Daniell cell is illustrated in **Figure 17-7.** Galvanic cells like this one were used as power sources in the early days of electrical research. The zinc anode is dissolving as zinc ions enter the solution. The cathodic and anodic reactions are as follows. Note that the same number of elec-

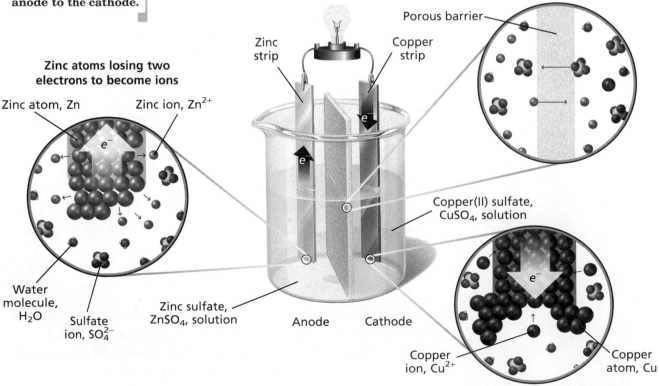

Zinc atoms losing two electrons to become ions

Zinc atom, Zn   Zinc ion, Zn^{2+}

e^-

Water molecule, H_2O

Sulfate ion, SO_4^{2-}

Zinc sulfate, $ZnSO_4$, solution

Zinc strip   Copper strip

e^-

e^-

Porous barrier

Copper(II) sulfate, $CuSO_4$, solution

Anode   Cathode

e^-

Copper ion, Cu^{2+} Copper atom, Cu

Copper(II) ions gaining two electrons to become atoms

trons are given up in oxidation at the anode as are used in reduction at
the cathode.

$$\text{oxidation: } Zn(s) \longrightarrow 2e^- + Zn^{2+}(aq)$$
$$\text{reduction: } Cu^{2+}(aq) + 2e^- \longrightarrow Cu(s)$$

Figure 17-7 also shows the movement of ions through the porous barrier. Solid copper is depositing at the cathode. In which direction are
the electrons moving through the light bulb of this Daniell cell?

Equilibrium cells are cells without reactions

Look at the cell in Figure 17-5, on page 624. The electrodes in this cell
are not joined to complete a circuit, so no electricity flows and no reactions occur. This cell is still an electrochemical cell. Cells through which
no electricity flows are called **equilibrium cells.** Equilibrium cells are
used to determine thermodynamic data and other useful information.
For example, the pH meter in Chapter 15 contains a probe that is an
equilibrium cell. Notice that because there are no electrode reactions
taking place, an equilibrium cell does not have an anode or a cathode.
Those labels apply only to electrolytic and galvanic cells.

equilibrium cell

an electrochemical cell
in which no electric
current flows

SECTION REVIEW

Total recall

1. Explain how the flow of electrons in a
   flashlight produces light.

2. How does an equilibrium cell differ from
   an electrolytic cell and a galvanic cell?
   How is it similar to the two?

Critical thinking

3. Why must reduction always be accompanied by oxidation, and vice versa?

4. Correct the following statement: Oxidation is a reaction in which a chemical
   species gains electrons at the cathode.

Practice problems

5. Calculate how much electric charge is
   present in 2.5 mol of electrons.

6. A car battery operates at 12.0 V and is
   rated at 100 ampere-hours, which means
   that the battery can deliver 5.0 A of current for 20.0 hours. How much energy
   can this battery generate in 1.0 minute
   when operating at these conditions?

7. Write balanced equations to represent
   the following electrode reactions.
   a. reduction of Pt^{2+} to Pt
   b. oxidation of Fe^{2+} to Fe^{3+}
   c. reduction of S to S^{2-}
   d. reduction of Br_2 to Br^-
   e. oxidation of Au to Au^{3+}

8. **Story Clue** An electric fish can produce
   exactly 300 discharges per second. Each
   discharge has a potential of 100.0 mV
   and a current of 1.00 A. How much energy is released with each discharge?

9. **Story Clue** An electric eel can produce a
   discharge of 600.0 V. It does this by combining the voltages of individual *electro-
   plates*. If each electroplate produces
   150.0 mV, how many plates are required
   to give off the total discharge?

How are electrolytic cells used?

OBJECTIVES

▶ **Explain** how nonspontaneous chemical reactions can be driven by electrolytic cells.

▶ **Describe** briefly the following electrolytic processes: sodium production, water electrolysis, and electrowinning of Al.

▶ **Calculate** the electricity and energy requirements of an electrolytic cell.

Electrosynthesis of sodium

Pure sodium metal does not occur in nature. By mass, about 2.7% of sea water can be considered to be sodium chloride, NaCl. Sodium is also found in nature as nitrate, carbonate, and sulfate salts, and in more complex minerals. A lot of sodium exists in the form of the cation, Na^+, but getting it into the form of the element $Na(s)$ is not easy.

You learned in Chapter 4 that sodium metal is very reactive. This means that the synthesis of Na is very endothermic.

$$NaCl(s) \longrightarrow Na(s) + 1/2Cl_2(g) \; \Delta H = 411 \text{ kJ}$$

Such reactions are almost always nonspontaneous.

In Chapter 11 you learned about one trick to get an endothermic reaction to occur. If the process has a positive entropy change, it will be spontaneous at a sufficiently high temperature. The decomposition of sodium chloride changes a solid into a solid and a gas; the entropy of this system increases.

$$NaCl(s) \longrightarrow Na(s) + 1/2Cl_2(g) \; \Delta S = 90.6 \text{ J/K}$$

▶ **FIGURE 17-8**

Most of the salt in the oceans is the product of rain rinsing salts from rocks and minerals into the sea.

How high must the temperature be to make the decomposition of NaCl spontaneous? This temperature can be determined by the following calculation.

$$\Delta G = \Delta H - T\Delta S < 0$$

$$T > \frac{\Delta H}{\Delta S} = \frac{411 \text{ kJ}}{0.0906 \text{ kJ/K}} = 4540 \text{ K}$$

Such a high temperature (which is only a little less than the temperature at the sun's surface) is not practical in manufacturing.

Electrochemistry makes sodium production possible

Sodium is manufactured by the electrolysis of molten sodium chloride. This method is named the Downs process and is carried out industrially in a **Downs cell,** as shown in **Figure 17-9.** The cell reaction is given by the following equation.

$$Na^+(l) + Cl^-(l) \xrightarrow{\ e^-\ } Na(l) + 1/2Cl_2(g)$$

Notice that this is virtually the same equation for a nonspontaneous decomposition on the previous page; this is because NaCl is ionic.

This redox reaction can be divided into two reactions. Cl^- is oxidized at the anode, and Na^+ is reduced at the cathode.

anode: $Cl^-(l) \longrightarrow e^- + 1/2Cl_2(g)$
cathode: $Na^+(l) + e^- \longrightarrow Na(l)$

How is it possible for each of these half-reactions to occur when the overall process is nonspontaneous? Remember that voltage is analogous to electron pressure. The cathode in a Downs cell is at a negative voltage, which means it has a high pressure of electrons. The high pressure

Downs cell

an electrolytic cell that uses a graphite anode and an iron cathode to produce sodium metal

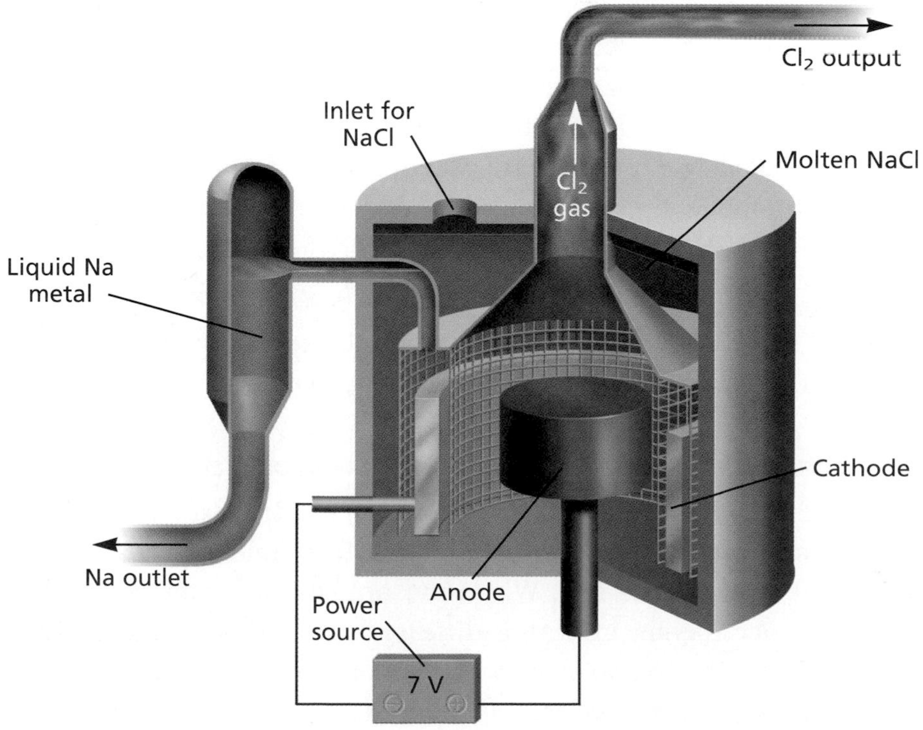

Inlet for NaCl

Cl₂ output

Cl₂ gas

Molten NaCl

Liquid Na metal

Na outlet

Power source

7 V

Anode

Cathode

FIGURE 17-9

In a Downs cell the electrolysis of molten NaCl produces elemental sodium and chlorine.

forces electrons onto the sodium ions. Think of the anode as an electron vacuum. It has a voltage that is positive enough to pull electrons away from the chloride ions.

Pure NaCl melts at 1074 K, but some $CaCl_2$ is added to lower the melting point. (Remember from Chapter 13 the colligative property of freezing point depression.) This allows the cell to operate at about 860 K.

The Downs process demonstrates a typical electrolytic cell. Electrical energy drives a nonspontaneous process. In many respects, the operation of electrolytic cells is similar to photosynthesis; nonchemical energy is used to cause a nonspontaneous chemical process. Photosynthesis uses light energy, and **electrosynthesis** uses electrical energy.

electrosynthesis

a synthesis reaction that is carried out in an electrochemical cell using an electric current

CONCEPT CHECK

1. Use the concept of electron pressure to explain how electrochemistry makes sodium production possible.
2. Calculate the temperature at which the following reaction would become spontaneous. Is this a practical way to produce hydrogen industrially?

$$Cu(s) + H_2O(l) \rightarrow CuO(s) + H_2(g)$$

$$\Delta H = 128.6 \text{ kJ}$$

$$\Delta S = 70.2 \text{ J/K}$$

electrolysis

the decomposition of a substance by an electric current

Electrolysis of water

If cars like the hydrogen car described in Chapter 11 ever become practical, a reliable supply of low-cost hydrogen will be needed to fuel them. Some hydrogen is currently available as a byproduct of petroleum refining. Hydrogen can also be made by passing steam over hot iron, but any large demand for H_2 will more likely be met by the **electrolysis** of water.

Figure 17-10 shows the laboratory equipment used in the electrolysis of water. The following reactions occur at the anode and cathode.

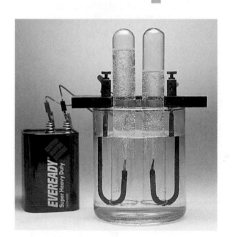

anode: $6H_2O(l) \longrightarrow 4e^- + O_2(g) + 4H_3O^+(aq)$
cathode: $4H_2O(l) + 4e^- \longrightarrow 2H_2(g) + 4OH^-(aq)$

The overall reaction occurs when the applied voltage is at least 1.23 V, but for the cell to be practical, about 2.0 V is required.

What if two different cell reactions are possible?

Sodium chloride is often used as the electrolyte in the electrolysis of water. The solution contains the same ions that are present in a Downs cell. Why then are the electrode reactions in the electrolysis of water different from those in the Downs process? When two electrode reactions are possible, the one that occurs at a lower voltage is favored.

Calculating energy needed for electrolysis

How much electrical energy is required to generate 1.000 L of H_2 at 25°C and 1.00 atm pressure by the electrolysis of water?

1 **List what you know**

▶ V = 1.000 L
▶ T = 25°C = 298 K
▶ P = 1.00 atm = 101 kPa
▶ Electrical energy = ? J

2 **Set up the problem**

▶ You are given the volume of hydrogen, so you must use the ideal gas law to determine the amount of H_2.

$$PV = nRT$$

$$n = \frac{PV}{RT} = \frac{101 \text{ kPa} \times 1.000 \text{ L}}{8.314 \text{ kPa} \cdot \text{L/K} \cdot \text{mol} \times 298 \text{ K}}$$

▶ Write the chemical equation involved in the electrolysis of water.

$$4H_2O(l) + 4e^- \longrightarrow 2H_2(g) + 4OH^-(aq)$$

For every 2 mol of H_2 made, 4 mol of e^- are used.

▶ Use Faraday's law to calculate the charge. First determine the amount of electrons required to produce the amount of H_2 calculated above.

$$\text{charge} = n \times \frac{4 \text{ mol } e}{2 \text{ mol } H_2} \times \frac{96\,485 \text{ C}}{\text{mol } e^-}$$

▶ You have learned that the cell used in the electrolysis of water operates at a voltage of 2.0 V. Use this voltage and the charge calculated above to calculate the electrical energy.

$$\text{electrical energy} - \text{voltage} \times \text{charge} = 2.0 \text{ V} \times ? \text{ C}$$

3 **Calculate**

▶ Calculate and round off correctly.

$$n = \frac{PV}{RT} = \frac{101 \text{ kPa} \times 1.000 \text{ L}}{8.314 \text{ kPa} \cdot \text{L/K} \cdot \text{mol} \times 298 \text{ K}} = 0.0408 \text{ mol}$$

$$\text{charge} = 0.0408 \text{ mol } H_2 \times \frac{4 \text{ mol } e}{2 \text{ mol } H_2} \times \frac{96\,485 \text{ C}}{\text{mol } e} = 7.87 \times 10^3 \text{ C}$$

$$\text{electrical energy} = 2.0 \text{ V} \times 7.87 \times 10^3 \text{ C} = 1.6 \times 10^4 \text{ J} = 16 \text{ kJ}$$

PRACTICE PROBLEMS

1. Calculate how much electrical energy is required to generate 1.000 L of oxygen by the electrolysis of water under the same conditions.

2. How many moles of chlorine gas would be produced in 1.0 hour in a Downs cell that is operated at a current of 3.0×10^4 A?

The electrowinning of aluminum

Metallurgists describe getting a metal from its ore as *winning* the metal. Aluminum is won from its ore, bauxite, by the electrochemical Hall-Héroult process, illustrated in **Figure 17-11.** This process is the largest single user of electricity in the United States, consuming nearly 5% of the total electrical power generated. This electrical energy consumption makes the electrowinning of aluminum a very expensive process.

Bauxite is impure alumina, Al_2O_3. The alumina is first purified from the ore and then dissolved in molten cryolite, Na_3AlF_6, at a temperature of about 970°C. Huge carbon-lined iron tanks hold this molten mixture. At the high temperature at which the cell is operated, the aluminum metal is a liquid and is more dense than the molten mixture, so it falls to the floor of the tank. The liquid aluminum on the tank floor is in contact with the carbon-lined tank, and it serves as the cathode. Reduction occurs at the cathode to produce more molten aluminum metal.

Carbon rods dip into the molten cryolite solution and function as anodes. Carbon is the species oxidized at the anode to produce gaseous carbon dioxide. Therefore, the carbon rods are eaten away by this reaction and must be replaced periodically.

The process has been used for more than a century, but the chemistry that goes on during the dissolution and the electrochemical reactions are not well understood. Although scientists still debate exactly how the Hall-Héroult process works, they do agree that 12 electrons are transferred in the overall reaction shown below.

$$2Al_2O_3(s) + 3C(s) \xrightarrow{\;12e^-\;} 4Al(l) + 3CO_2(g)$$

▼ **FIGURE 17-11**

The Hall-Héroult process is used to manufacture aluminum by the electrolysis of dissolved alumina, Al_2O_3.

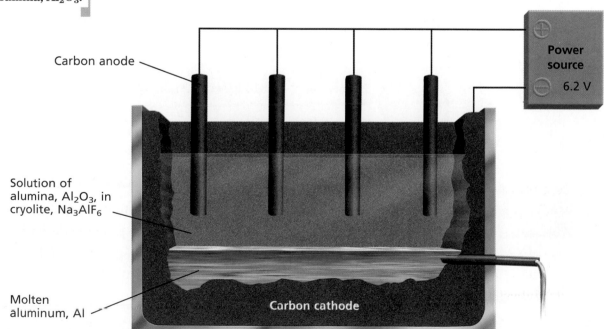

Carbon anode

Power source

6.2 V

Solution of alumina, Al_2O_3, in cryolite, Na_3AlF_6

Molten aluminum, Al

Carbon cathode

Electrical energy is an expensive raw material

Why does aluminum production use so much electricity? Look at the last equation. Twelve electrons produce four aluminum atoms. So each mole of Al needs the following amount of electricity.

$$\frac{12 \ \text{mol } e^-}{4 \ \text{mol Al}} \times \frac{96\,485 \ \text{C}}{\text{mol } e^-} = \frac{2.8946 \times 10^5 \ \text{C}}{\text{mol Al}}$$

The Hall-Héroult cell operates at an average voltage of 6.2 V. The amount of energy needed to produce 1 mol (27 g) of aluminum can be calculated as follows.

$$6.2 \ \text{V} \times 2.8946 \times 10^5 \ \text{C} = 1.8 \times 10^6 \ \text{J}$$

This much energy is needed to drive the electrochemical reactions. Additional energy is needed to keep the cell at a temperature that is high enough to melt the cryolyte.

A standard aluminum soft-drink can has a mass of about 27 g. The next time you open a can of soda, consider this: The beverage contains only about 600 J of *food* energy, but 3000 times that amount of energy was required to produce the can. Recycling aluminum metal is very important because it takes so much energy to manufacture it. Without recycling, we remove aluminum from the ground as bauxite, spend a lot of energy and money to process it, and then return it to the ground as landfill. What a waste!

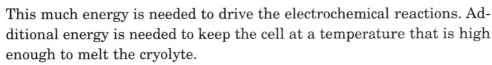

SECTION REVIEW

Total recall

1. What form of energy is used to drive an electrolytic cell?

2. List three commercial products made by using electrolytic cells.

3. Write the equation for the cathodic reaction that occurs in an electrolytic cell that is used to make sodium.

Critical thinking

4. Explain why raising the temperature to decompose sodium chloride into sodium metal is not a good way to extract the sodium from the salt.

5. Why is it so important to recycle aluminum products rather than to simply discard them?

Practice problems

6. Calculate the energy needed to produce 100.0 g of aluminum in the Hall-Héroult cell.

17
Cl
Chlorine
35.4527
$[Ne]3s^2 2p^5$

Chlorine gives us clean drinking water

The practice of chlorinating drinking water to disinfect it began in the early twentieth century. Chlorinating water greatly reduced the number of infectious diseases. No other method of disinfecting drinking water is as inexpensive and reliable as chlorination. Today, chlorine is used as a disinfectant in almost every drinking-water treatment plant in the United States and Canada. This method will probably continue to be used well into the twenty-first century.

Many Third World regions have outbreaks of deadly diseases, such as cholera and typhoid fever, that could easily be prevented by disinfecting water supplies with chlorine.

WHERE IS IT?

Earth's Crust
0.045% by mass

Oceans
30.61% of dissolved materials; 1.9% by mass

internet**connect**

SCi**LINKS**
NSTA
TOPIC: Chlorine
GO TO: www.scilinks.org
KEYWORD: HW174

Industrial Uses

- ▶ Chlorine is a strong oxidizing agent. It is used as a bleaching agent for paper, pulp, and textiles.
- ▶ Chlorine gas is used as a germicide for drinking water.
- ▶ Chlorine gas is used in the production of bromine compounds for use as a fire retardant.
- ▶ Sodium chloride, which is table salt, is one of the most important chlorine-containing compounds.
- ▶ Plastics, such as the vinyl used in automobile upholstery and sporting goods, contain chlorine.
- ▶ Many pharmaceuticals, including antibiotics and allergy medications, require chlorine for their manufacture.

Chlorine gas and chlorine compounds are used to purify swimming pools.

A BRIEF HISTORY

1774: C. W. Scheele isolates chlorine gas, then called dephlogisticated marine acid air.

1810: Henry Davy proves that chlorine is a new element and names it.

1908: P. Sommerfeld shows that HCl is present in the gastric juices of animals.

1600   **1700**   **1800**   **1900**

1648: J. R. Glauber prepares concentrated hydrochloric acid.

1801: W. Cruickshank recommends the use of Cl_2 as a disinfectant.

1902: J. C. Downs patents the Downs cell for the production of $Cl_2(g)$ and $Na(s)$.

How do batteries work?

OBJECTIVES

▶ **Explain** the difference between primary and secondary galvanic cells.

▶ **Describe** briefly the electrochemistry used in fuel cells, Leclanché cells, and lead-acid batteries.

▶ **Calculate** the electricity output of a galvanic cell and the changes in the amounts of reactants in the cell.

▶ **Describe** conditions that lead to corrosion and things that can be done to prevent it.

Galvanic cells

The last section described electrolytic cells. Galvanic cells work in the opposite direction as electrolytic cells. Galvanic cells convert chemical energy into electrical energy.

Electrochemical power sources can be divided into **primary cells** and **secondary cells.** Primary cells function only as galvanic cells. A primary cell can be either a *fuel cell* or a *battery*. A primary battery is thrown away when its active materials are used up. Primary fuel cells are never used up because the reactants are supplied from outside the cell. Secondary cells can operate electrolytically as well as galvanically. Secondary cells include *storage cells, accumulators,* or *rechargeable batteries*.

primary cell

a galvanic cell converting chemical energy to electrical energy; it cannot be recharged

secondary cell

an electrochemical cell that can act as a galvanic cell or, on recharge, as an electrolytic cell

fuel cell

a galvanic cell in which electricity is produced using reactants supplied from outside the cell

Fuel cells could revolutionize power production

In concept, **fuel cells** are very simple. **Figure 17-13** shows that the fuel and oxidizer are supplied to the two electrodes from outside the cell. The two electrodes are separated by a thin layer of electrolyte.

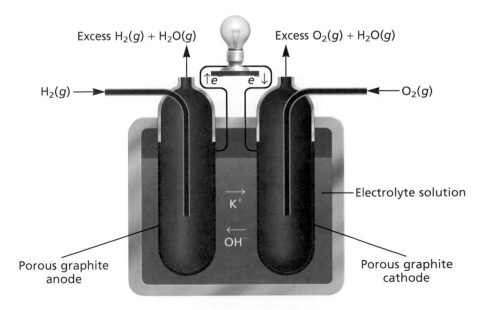

Excess $H_2(g)$ + $H_2O(g)$ Excess $O_2(g)$ + $H_2O(g)$

$H_2(g)$ →

← $O_2(g)$

↑e   e↓

K^+

OH^-

Electrolyte solution

Porous graphite anode

Porous graphite cathode

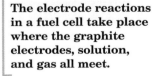

FIGURE 17-13 ◀

The electrode reactions in a fuel cell take place where the graphite electrodes, solution, and gas all meet.

In conventional power plants, the chemical energy in the fuel is turned first into heat then into mechanical energy and finally into electricity. This is an inefficient process. The fuel cell *directly* converts chemical energy into electrical energy. This direct conversion is simpler, and it avoids the problem that only a fraction of heat energy can ever be converted into another energy form. Perfectly efficient energy conversion is theoretically possible with fuel cells. Fuel-cell design is an active area of electrochemical research, and a few experimental power plants using fuel cells are already in operation.

> ### CONCEPT CHECK
>
> 1. Explain the difference between primary and secondary cells.
> 2. Explain why fuel cells theoretically could produce electrical energy in a perfectly efficient way.
> 3. List two other names for secondary cells.

battery

self-contained galvanic cells that convert chemical energy into electrical energy

Portable energy—the battery

Batteries supply energy to a variety of devices, from small wristwatches to the starters on diesel-truck engines. There are many types of batteries, and each has its own chemistry. Most batteries use a metal as the active material of the negative electrode. The battery *positive* is usually made up of metal oxides in higher-than-normal valence states, as shown in **Table 17-1.** These oxides are usually poor conductors of electricity, so their conductivity must be improved by mixing the oxide with graphite or by putting the oxide on a metal grid. A porous barrier is included so that the electrodes do not touch each other. The electrolyte solutions are concentrated to improve conductivity and to decrease the amount of liquid inside the battery.

▲ **FIGURE 17-14**

How many different types of batteries can you find around your home?

| **TABLE 17-1** | **Common batteries** |

Battery type	Negative	Positive	Voltage
Leclanché	Zn $\longrightarrow$ Zn(II)	Mn(IV) $\longrightarrow$ Mn(III)	1.5 V
Silver oxide	Zn $\longrightarrow$ Zn(II)	Ag(I) $\longrightarrow$ Ag	1.5 V
Lithium	Li $\longrightarrow$ Li(I)	various	up to 4 V
NiCad	Cd $\rightleftarrows$ Cd(II)	Ni(III) $\rightleftarrows$ Ni(II)	1.4 V
Lead-acid	Pb $\rightleftarrows$ Pb(II)	Pb(IV) $\rightleftarrows$ Pb(II)	12.00 V

Dry cells aren't dry

The common zinc-carbon battery was invented over a century ago by the French chemist Georges Leclanché. **Figure 17-15a** shows a model of a Leclanché cell. A carbon rod, the battery's positive terminal, contacts a wet paste of carbon; ammonium chloride, NH_4Cl; manganese(IV) oxide, MnO_2; starch; and water. The reaction in this paste is as follows.

$$2MnO_2(s) + 2NH_4^+(aq) + 2e^- \longrightarrow$$
$$Mn_2O_3(s) + 2NH_3(aq) + H_2O(l)$$

The zinc case constitutes the negative of the cell. It dissolves in the following oxidation reaction.

$$Zn(s) \longrightarrow 2e^- + Zn^{2+}(aq)$$

The zinc ions combine with the ammonia made at the positive to form $Zn(NH_3)_4^{2+}$, the chloride salt of which is the white material you see on old corroded batteries.

The $NH_4^+(aq)$ ions cause the electrolytic paste to be acidic. That is why this cell is called *acidic*. The *alkaline cell*, shown in **Figure 17-15b,** is a newer, better version of the Leclanché cell. It is gradually replacing the acidic version. If you look at the batteries in electronic devices around your home, you will probably find many alkaline cells. They are similar to the acidic version, but the ammonium chloride is replaced by

QUICK**LAB**

Listen Up

In 1786, Luigi Galvani believed that he had discovered "animal electricity" because his experiments showed that dead frogs convulsed when they were part of electric circuits that contained dissimilar metals. In the 1800s, Volta proved the current was due to the metals rather than the frogs. In this activity, you will construct a potato cell and collect evidence of current flow.

Materials

raw potato, Cu strip, Zn strip, earphone, 2 alligator clips or electrical tape

Problem

1. Press the Cu and Zn strips into the potato about 0.5 cm apart. Do not allow the metals to touch one another.
2. Touch the wires from the earphone to both metals at the same time. What do you hear?
3. Touch the wires from the earphone to one metal only. What do you hear?

Analysis

1. Compare the results from step 2 with the results from step 3. Suggest an explanation for any similarities or differences.
2. Suggest an explanation for the sound.

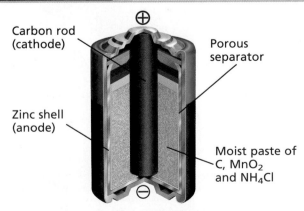

Carbon rod (cathode)
Porous separator
Zinc shell (anode)
Moist paste of C, MnO_2 and NH_4Cl

a The familiar flashlight battery has two versions. The *acidic* version is illustrated here.

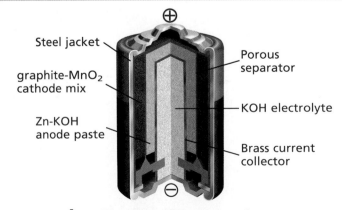

Steel jacket
graphite-MnO_2 cathode mix
Zn-KOH anode paste
Porous separator
KOH electrolyte
Brass current collector

b Unlike the acidic version, the *alkaline* Leclanché cell does not have a central carbon rod.

potassium hydroxide. The presence of a strong base gives the alkaline cell its name. The electrode reactions are shown below.

$$\text{positive: } 2MnO_2(s) + H_2O(aq) + 2e^- \longrightarrow Mn_2O_3(s) + 2OH^-(aq)$$
$$\text{negative: } Zn(s) + 2OH^-(aq) \longrightarrow 2e^- + Zn(OH)_2(s)$$

A steel outer shell is needed to prevent the caustic contents from leaking out of the battery. Because of this extra packaging cost, alkaline cells are slightly more expensive than their acidic counterpart.

The automobile battery

The standard automobile battery is a lead-acid storage battery. The lead-acid battery has six cells mounted side by side in a single case, as illustrated in **Figure 17-16.** The cells are coupled together so that each 2.0 V cell adds to the 12.0 V overall battery. Lead-acid batteries are very heavy, but lighter alternatives have never become popular because the lead-acid battery is able to deliver the large surges of electricity needed to start cold automobile engines.

A fully charged lead-acid cell is made up of a stack of alternating lead, Pb, and lead(IV) oxide, PbO_2, plates isolated from each other by layers of porous separators. All of these parts sit in a concentrated solution of sulfuric acid. Intercell connectors link the positive of one cell to the negative of the next cell, so the six cells are in series. When the cell discharges, it acts as a galvanic cell. The following reactions occur.

$$\text{negative: } Pb(s) + HSO_4^-(aq) + H_2O(l) \longrightarrow 2e^- + PbSO_4(s) + H_3O^+(aq)$$
$$\text{positive: } PbO_2(s) + HSO_4^-(aq) + 3H_3O^+(aq) + 2e^- \longrightarrow PbSO_4(s) + 5H_2O(l)$$

Notice that lead sulfate, $PbSO_4$, is produced at *both* electrodes. Also note that two electrons are transferred in the overall cell reaction.

These reactions are reversed during the recharging cycle. During this cycle, the automobile battery functions as an electrolytic cell. The energy to drive the recharging of the cell comes from an external source, such as the alternator of a car's engine.

▼ **FIGURE 17-16**

A lead-acid battery is housed in a thick plastic or rubber case. This prevents leakage of the corrosive sulfuric acid.

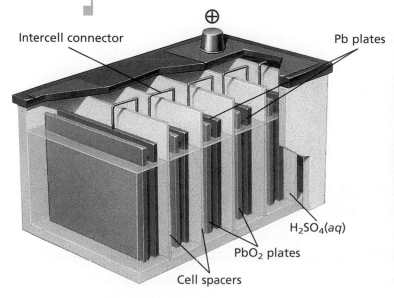

Intercell connector

Pb plates

$H_2SO_4(aq)$

PbO_2 plates

Cell spacers

If you allow a 12 V car battery to completely run down so that its 1.6 MJ of energy is spent, what mass of lead sulfate is created?

1 List what you know

▸ Electrical energy = 1.6 MJ = 1.6×10^6 J
▸ Battery voltage = 12 V
▸ Mass of $PbSO_4$ = ? g

2 Set up the problem

▸ Use the energy and voltage to determine the charge.

$$\text{energy} = \text{voltage} \times \text{charge}$$

$$\text{charge} = \frac{\text{energy}}{\text{voltage}} = \frac{1.6 \times 10^6 \text{ J}}{12 \text{ V}} = ? \text{ C}$$

Recall the chemical equations on page 638; 2 mol of electrons flows when 2 mol of $PbSO_4$ is produced. That is a mole ratio of 1:1. Use the charge calculated above along with Faraday's constant to determine the amount of lead(II) sulfate produced per cell. Remember that the battery consists of six cells.

$$\text{amount of } PbSO_4/\text{cell} = \text{charge} \times \frac{\text{mol } e^-}{96\,485 \text{ C}} \times \frac{1 \text{ mol } PbSO_4}{1 \text{ mol } e^-} = ? \text{ mol/cell}$$

▸ Convert amount to mass by using the molar mass of $PbSO_4$.

$$\text{molar mass of } PbSO_4 = 303.3 \text{ g/mol}$$

3 Calculate and verify

▸ Calculate the answer, and round correctly.

$$\text{charge} = \frac{1.6 \times 10^6 \text{ J}}{12 \text{ V}} = 1.33 \times 10^5 \text{ C}$$

$$\text{amount of } PbSO_4 = 1.33 \times 10^5 \text{ C} \times \frac{\text{mol } e^-}{96\,485 \text{ C}} \times \frac{1 \text{ mol } PbSO_4}{1 \text{ mol } e^-} = 1.38 \text{ mol } PbSO_4$$

$$\text{mass of } PbSO_4/\text{cell} = 1.38 \text{ mol} \times 303.3 \text{ g/mol} = 420 \text{ g } PbSO_4/\text{cell}$$

▸ The total mass for the battery is
$$420 \text{ g/cell} \times 6 \text{ cells} = 2520 \text{ g} = 2.5 \text{ kg } PbSO_4$$

▸ Verify your answer by working the problem backward.

$$\frac{(420 \text{ g})(96\,485 \text{ C/mol})(2 \text{ V/cell})}{303.3 \text{ g/mol}} = 2.7 \times 10^5 \text{ J/cell}$$

$$2.7 \times 10^5 \text{ J/cell} \times 6 \text{ cells} = 1.6 \times 10^6 \text{ J}$$

PRACTICE PROBLEMS

1. Calculate the mass of lead that was used up as the 12 V car battery in Sample Problem 17C ran down.

2. An alkaline Leclanché cell has a voltage of 1.54 V. The anodic reaction involves the oxidation of zinc as shown in the following equation.

$$Zn(s) + 2OH^- (aq) \longrightarrow Zn(OH)_2(s) + H_2O(l) + 2e^-$$

What mass of $Zn(OH)_2$ is produced after the battery has delivered 1.3 kJ of energy?

Corrosion cells

Oxygen is so reactive that any metal except gold can spontaneously oxidize in air. Fortunately for our civilization, many of these metal oxidation reactions are very slow. The disintegration of metals through oxidation is called **corrosion.** The general equation for the corrosion of metal, M, by oxygen is as follows.

$$2M(s) + (n/2)O_2(g) \longrightarrow M_2O_n(s)$$

Agents other than O_2 can cause corrosion. Some metals can also corrode when placed in contact with water or an acidic aqueous solution. Take iron, for example, which can be oxidized to iron(III) ions according to the following equation.

$$2Fe(s) + 11H_2O(l) \longrightarrow Fe_2O_3 \cdot 2H_2O(s) + 6H_3O^+(aq) + 6e^-$$

You know that oxidation reactions must always be accompanied by reduction reactions. If a metal corrodes, or oxidizes, then the oxygen, water, or hydronium ion must be reduced. As you have seen with other galvanic cells, oxidation and reduction do not have to occur at the same site. **Figure 17-17** illustrates how oxidation can occur at an *anodic site,* while reduction occurs simultaneously at a *cathodic site.* This system looks very similar to the galvanic cells you have already studied.

Corrosive conditions are all around us

The corrosion of metals generally requires three ingredients: oxygen, water, and ions. These three ingredients are very easy to find together. Even pure rainwater contains a few H_3O^+ and HCO_3^- ions from dissolved carbon dioxide. This means that all exposed metalwork is a potential target for corrosion. Corrosion problems are even worse in areas where ion concentrations are high, such as in marine environments and where salts are spread on icy roads.

corrosion

the deterioration of metals due to oxidation reactions with their environment

▼ **FIGURE 17-17**

This cathodic reaction occurs where the O_2 concentration is relatively high. The anodic reaction occurs in a region where the O_2 concentration is rather low, such as in a pit in the metal.

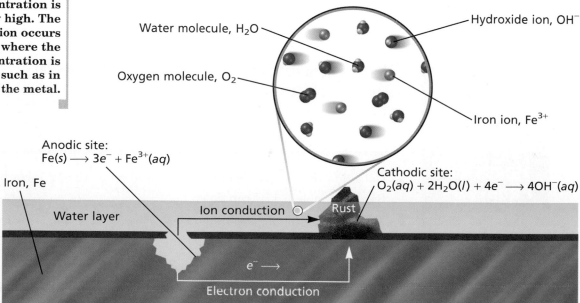

Water molecule, H_2O

Hydroxide ion, OH^-

Oxygen molecule, O_2

Iron ion, Fe^{3+}

Anodic site:
$Fe(s) \longrightarrow 3e^- + Fe^{3+}(aq)$

Iron, Fe

Cathodic site:
$O_2(aq) + 2H_2O(l) + 4e^- \longrightarrow 4OH^-(aq)$

Water layer

Ion conduction

Rust

$e^- \longrightarrow$

Electron conduction

Where two different metals are in contact with one another, corrosion is more likely. This is because the more-active metal provides the anodic region and the less-active metal provides the cathodic region. Corrosion is often the cause of plumbing leaks where steel and copper water pipes are joined.

How to curb corrosion

Corrosion is a major economic problem. Approximately 20% of all iron and steel produced replaces corroded structures. That is why corrosion prevention is a major focus of electrochemical research. An obvious response to corrosion is to paint the metal or to coat it with some other material that will not corrode. However, once a crack occurs in the coating, a corrosion cell forms.

Ironically, it is better to coat steel with another metal, one that *does* corrode. Trash cans, for example, are made of zinc-coated steel. The coating does not stop corrosion; in fact, it promotes it. But, it is the zinc that corrodes first, making the steel underneath last much longer than it would without the protective zinc layer. This is the principle behind equipping ships and pipelines with **sacrificial anodes.** The sacrificial anode makes use of the fact that when two different metals are in contact with one another, corrosion is likely. The sacrificial anode, which is not necessary to the structure, dissolves anodically, but in doing so it protects the ship or pipeline from corrosion. Therefore, it protects the more important structural metal. This process is called *cathodic protection*.

FIGURE 17-18 ▲

The Alaskan oil pipeline is *cathodically protected* by a parallel zinc cable.

sacrificial anode

metal attached to a metallic structure that serves as an anode, preventing the corrosion of the structural metal

SECTION REVIEW

Total recall

1. What advantages do fuel cells have over standard power plants?

2. Explain what is meant by the term *secondary cell.*

3. List three conditions that foster corrosion.

Critical thinking

4. How is a fuel cell similar to a battery? How is it different?

5. Why is the name *dry cell* a misnomer?

6. Why does a car rust quickly at a place where the paint has been chipped?

7. Explain why a small piece of zinc is usually attached to a boat's propeller shaft.

FUEL CELLS

internet**connect**

SCI**LINKS**
NSTA

TOPIC: Fuel cells
GO TO: www.scilinks.org
KEYWORD: HW175

Historical Perspective

In 1839, Sir William Robert Grove, a British lawyer and physicist, built the first fuel cell. More than 100 years later, this fuel cell finally found a practical application.

The United States Space Program Finds Uses for Fuel Cells

During the middle part of the twentieth century, the space race was on. The United States was rushing to turn a lunar landing from science fiction into reality. Space capsules required electrical energy to keep the astronauts warm and to power electrical systems. During

During the 1960s and 1970s, fuel cells provided on-board electricity and drinking water for the Apollo and Gemini space capsules.

the Mercury project—the first six missions into space—the flights were very short. Batteries were sufficient to power the capsules. But later programs needed electrical power for much longer periods of time; fuel cells became the best solution for the problem. Today, fuel cells are critical to the space shuttle missions and to future missions on the international space station.

In 1970, fuel cells played a critical role in the *Apollo 13* mission. A short circuit in a fuel cell caused an explosion in an oxygen tank. This damaged the spacecraft and caused a loss of oxygen needed for breathing and for generating electricity. For this reason, *Apollo 13* never made it to the moon as planned.

Fuel Cells Have Many Uses

Electrical Power Systems   There are many problems with conventional power stations that burn fossil fuels to generate electricity. These stations first produce heat energy, which is converted to mechanical energy, which is then converted to electrical energy. They are only about 40% efficient. Standard power plants give off pollutants that lead to acid rain and other environmental problems. Fuel-cell power stations currently being tested can operate at up to 80% efficiency. They also give off 80% less pollution than fossil-fuel-burning stations. The maximum theoretical efficiency of fuel cells is 100%.

Blood Alcohol Testing   Blood alcohol testing is very important to traffic-law enforcement. Police officers need quick and simple ways to determine a suspect's blood alcohol level in the field. If the suspect is carried back to the station or to a medical facility for a blood or urine test, so much time may elapse that their blood alcohol content (BAC) will no longer indicate impairment. Fuel cells, such as the one shown on the right, provide a quick and accurate way to measure BAC from a breath sample. The alcohol and oxygen in a person's breath are the two reactants in this electrochemical cell.

Ethanol is oxidized to acetic acid at the anode. At the cathode, gaseous oxygen is reduced and combined with hydrogen ions (released from the anode) to form water. The reactions generate an electric current. The magnitude of the current generated is related to the BAC.

A small pump ensures that a precise sample size is delivered into the fuel cell inside this device.

CAREER APPLICATION

What would it be like to . . .
▸ design ways to reduce pollution?
▸ work with high-tech materials?
▸ develop renewable fuel sources?

Science/Math Career Preparation	
High School	**College**
Mathematics	Mathematics
Chemistry	Chemistry
Physics	Physics
	Engineering

Chemical Engineer

Chemical engineers do much of the ongoing fuel-cell research. These scientists combine knowledge of chemistry, physics, and mathematics to link laboratory chemistry with its industrial applications. As with any scientist, they must be good problem solvers as well.

There are many types of careers open to chemical engineers. They can find alternative, renewable fuel sources, such as fuel cells and diesel fuels made from sewage sludge. They design new recyclable materials and devise new ways of recycling materials that are already in existence. Chemical engineers clean up and prevent much of the pollution in the environment.

Chemical engineers use lab techniques that you may be familiar with from your own chemistry laboratory. These include distillation, evaporation, absorption, separation, and mixing. A chemical engineer can move these techniques from the laboratory to the large scale required by industry. Many of the synthetic fibers in your clothing were developed by chemical engineers. Although you may have seen nylon made in your chemistry laboratory, it would be difficult to make enough nylon using this method to satisfy the demand for nylon clothing and other items. Chemical engineers find ways to optimize chemical processes, as with the production of nylon, and make them industrially practical.

What can be learned from an equilibrium cell?

OBJECTIVES

▶ *Explain* the meaning of the voltage produced by an equilibrium cell.

▶ *Predict* the direction of cell reactions, and *explain* the reactions in terms of electron transfers using a table of standard electrode potentials.

Equilibrium cell voltages

equilibrium voltage

the voltage of a cell as measured by a voltmeter when no current is flowing

A voltmeter can measure cell voltage without allowing any appreciable current to flow through the electrochemical cell. The cell is neither producing nor using electrical energy. It is neither an electrolytic cell nor a galvanic cell. It is an equilibrium cell, and the voltage measured by the voltmeter is the **equilibrium voltage**, ΔE.

Electrochemical equilibrium will become clearer after you study **Figure 17-19.** This figure shows three cells, each attached to an adjustable power source. If the applied voltage differs from the equilibrium voltage even a little bit, current flows in one direction or the other. No cur-

▼ **FIGURE 17-19**

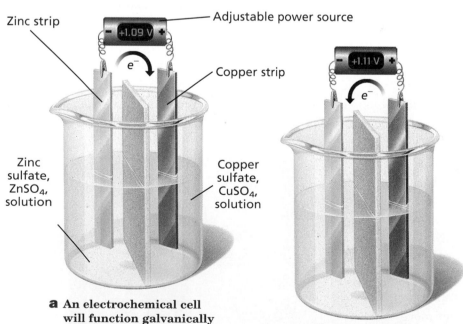

Zinc strip

Adjustable power source

+1.09 V

e^-

Copper strip

Zinc sulfate, ZnSO₄, solution

Copper sulfate, CuSO₄, solution

+1.11 V

e^-

+1.10 V

a An electrochemical cell will function galvanically if the voltage applied is less than the equilibrium voltage, . . .

b . . . electrolytically if the voltage applied is greater than the equilibrium voltage, . . .

c . . . and as an equilibrium cell if the applied voltage equals the equilibrium voltage.

rent flows when the applied voltage exactly matches the equilibrium voltage. The state of the cell shown in Figure 17-19c is exactly the same as that in Figure 17-5 on page 624—both are equilibrium cells.

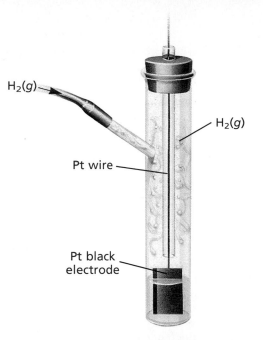

Cell potentials are measured using the standard hydrogen electrode

There are so many combinations of electrode reactions that it would be nearly impossible to measure the cell voltages for all of them. It is much easier to choose one electrode as a standard and to pair it with all the others. The one that has been chosen for this purpose is the **standard hydrogen electrode** (SHE).

The SHE is made up of an aqueous solution of a strong acid in which the effective H_3O^+ concentration is 1.000 M. A platinum electrode is dipped into this solution, and a stream of hydrogen gas at a pressure of 1.0 atm bubbles in, as shown in **Figure 17-20.**

Of course, the voltage of a single electrode cannot be measured because voltage is a difference in "electron pressure." The SHE is conventionally assigned an electrode potential of 0.00 V. Therefore, if you connect a copper electrode to a SHE with a voltmeter, the reading on the voltmeter indicates only the voltage coming from the copper electrode. This means that the **standard electrode potential** of any electrode is defined as the voltmeter reading when the electrode is coupled to a SHE in the way shown in **Figure 17-21.** The standard electrode potential is sometimes called the *standard reduction potential* because the electrode reactions are usually written as reduction reactions.

FIGURE 17-21 ▼

When an electrode is paired with a SHE, its *standard electrode potential* is given by the voltmeter reading.

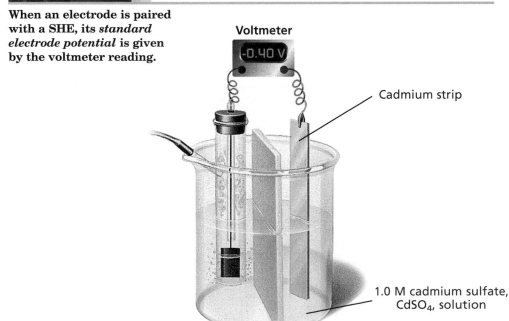

Voltmeter

-0.40 V

Cadmium strip

1.0 M cadmium sulfate, $CdSO_4$, solution

For example, the measurement shown in Figure 17-21 indicates that -0.40 V is the standard electrode potential for the following reaction.

$$Cd^{2+} + 2e^- \longrightarrow Cd$$

Remember, this value is not the *actual* voltage of a single electrode. True electrode potentials cannot be measured; electrodes must always be paired. **Table 17-2** includes a number of standard electrode potentials that have been determined by pairing each electrode with a standard hydrogen electrode. In each case, ion concenrations are 1.00 M and gases are at 1.0 atm.

This table is the **electrochemical series** of the elements. Notice that the elements are in the same order as they are in the activity series, which was introduced in Chapter 9. The higher the element is in the electrochemical series, the more likely it is to be oxidized.

You have already seen that a chemical reaction such as the following can be thought of as two electrode reactions occurring together.

$$Cu^{2+}(aq) + Zn(s) \longrightarrow Cu(s) + Zn^{2+}(aq)$$

You can use the electrochemical series to determine the direction of an electron-transfer reaction. The above reaction occurs in the direction shown by the arrow because zinc is higher in the series than copper is, thus zinc is more likely to be oxidized than copper.

Table 17-3 gives even more electrode potentials. Tables 17-2 and 17-3 may be used

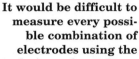

▼ **FIGURE 17-22**

It would be difficult to measure every possible combination of electrodes using the technique shown here. This is why the SHE is used as a reference for all other electrodes.

TABLE 17-2	**Standard electrode potentials for some elements**

Electrode reaction	E^0(V)	Electrode reaction	E^0(V)
$Li^+(aq) + e^- \longrightarrow Li(s)$	-3.0401	$Pb^{2+}(aq) + 2e^- \longrightarrow Pb(s)$	-0.1262
$K^+(aq) + e^- \longrightarrow K(s)$	-2.931	$Fe^{3+}(aq) + 3e^- \longrightarrow Fe(s)$	-0.037
$Ca^{2+}(aq) + 2e^- \longrightarrow Ca(s)$	-2.868	$Cu^{2+}(aq) + 2e^- \longrightarrow Cu(s)$	$+0.3419$
$Na^+(aq) + e^- \longrightarrow Na(s)$	-2.71	$I_2(s) + 2e^- \longrightarrow 2I^-(aq)$	$+0.5355$
$Mg^{2+}(aq) + 2e^- \longrightarrow Mg(s)$	-2.372	$Hg_2^{2+}(aq) + 2e^- \longrightarrow 2Hg(l)$	$+0.7973$
$Al^{3+}(aq) + 3e^- \longrightarrow Al(s)$	-1.662	$Ag^+(aq) + e^- \longrightarrow Ag(s)$	$+0.7996$
$Zn^{2+}(aq) + 2e^- \longrightarrow Zn(s)$	-0.7618	$Br_2(l) + 2e^- \longrightarrow 2Br^-(aq)$	$+1.066$
$Fe^{2+}(aq) + 2e^- \longrightarrow Fe(s)$	-0.447	$Cl_2(g) + 2e^- \longrightarrow 2Cl^-(aq)$	$+1.358$
$Cd^{2+}(aq) + 2e^- \longrightarrow Cd(s)$	-0.4030	$F_2(g) + 2e^- \longrightarrow 2F^-(aq)$	$+2.866$

TABLE 17-3 More standard electrode potentials

Electrode reaction	E^0 (V)
$Zn(OH)_2(s) + 2e^- \longrightarrow Zn(s) + 2OH^-(aq)$	−1.249
$2H_2O(l) + 2e^- \longrightarrow H_2(g) + 2OH^-(aq)$	−0.828
$PbSO_4(s) + H_3O^+(aq) + 2e^- \longrightarrow Pb(s) + HSO_4^-(aq) + H_2O(l)$	−0.42
$2H_3O^+(aq) + 2e^- \longrightarrow H_2(g) + 2H_2O(l)$	0.000
$AgCl(s) + e^- \longrightarrow Ag(s) + Cl^-(aq)$	+0.222
$O_2(g) + 2H_2O(l) + 4e^- \longrightarrow 4OH^-(aq)$	+0.401
$I_3^-(aq) + 2e^- \longrightarrow 3I^-(aq)$	+0.536
$Fe^{3+}(aq) + e^- \longrightarrow Fe^{2+}(aq)$	+0.771
$MnO_2(s) + 4H_3O^+(aq) + 2e^- \longrightarrow Mn^{2+}(aq) + 6H_2O(l)$	+1.224
$O_2(g) + 4H_3O^+(aq) + 4e^- \longrightarrow 6H_2O$	+1.229
$Cr_2O_7^{2-}(aq) + 14H_3O^+(aq) + 6e^- \longrightarrow 2Cr^{3+}(aq) + 21H_2O(l)$	+1.232
$PbO_2(s) + 4H_3O^+(aq) + 2e^- \longrightarrow Pb^{2+}(aq) + 6H_2O(l)$	+1.455
$MnO_4^-(aq) + 8H_3O^+(aq) + 5e^- \longrightarrow Mn^{2+}(aq) + 12H_2O(l)$	+1.507
$PbO_2(s) + HSO_4^-(aq) + 3H_3O^+(aq) + 2e^- \longrightarrow PbSO_4(s) + 5H_2O(l)$	+1.691
$Ce^{4+}(aq) + e^- \longrightarrow Ce^{3+}(aq)$	+1.72
$Ag_2O_2(s) + 4H^+(aq) + e^- \longrightarrow 2Ag(s) + 2H_2O(l)$	+1.802

to predict the direction of cell reactions and redox reactions. Think of E^0 as a measure of the tendency of the electrode to consume electrons. In other words, a more positive standard electrode potential means the electrode is more likely to be a cathode and the reaction is more likely to proceed in the direction shown in the tables. For example, Ce^{4+}/Ce^{3+}, with an E^0 of +1.72 V, can overpower Fe^{3+}/Fe^{2+}, with an E^0 of only +0.771 V, so that the following reaction occurs spontaneously.

$$Ce^{4+}(aq) + Fe^{2+}(aq) \xrightarrow{e^-} Ce^{3+}(aq) + Fe^{3+}(aq)$$

SAMPLE PROBLEM 17D Predicting the direction of electrochemical reactions

Write the equation for the cell reaction that will occur spontaneously in a cell that contains a mercury, Hg_2^{2+}/Hg, electrode and a cadmium, Cd^{2+}/Cd, electrode.

1 List what you know
 ▸ Electrodes: Hg_2^{2+}/Hg and Cd^{2+}/Cd

2 Set up the problem

▶ Find the two electrode reactions in the tables of standard electrode potentials. Compare the values of their standard electrode potentials.

$$Hg_2^{2+}(aq) + 2e^- \longrightarrow 2Hg(l) \ E^0 = +0.7973 \ V$$
$$Cd^{2+}(aq) + 2e^- \longrightarrow Cd(s) \ E^0 = -0.4030 \ V$$

3 Calculate

▶ The standard electrode potential for mercury is greater than that for cadmium. Therefore, mercury has a greater tendency to be reduced. Cadmium will be oxidized, so the cadmium reaction shown above will be reversed. Note that two electrons are transferred in each reaction. If the number of electrons transferred were not the same, coefficients would have to be added to one or both reactions to balance the electrons.

$$Hg_2^{2+}(aq) + Cd(s) \xrightarrow{\ 2e^-\ } 2Hg(l) + Cd^{2+}(aq)$$

$\mathcal{S}$ECTION REVIEW

Total recall

1. A voltage source is attached to an electrochemical cell. The cell has an equilibrium voltage of 0.57 V. The voltage source is set at 0.44 V. Is the electrochemical cell acting as a galvanic or an electrolytic cell?

2. What does SHE represent? What electrode potential value is assigned to SHE?

3. What is a voltmeter?

Critical thinking

4. The standard electrode potential for the reduction of $Zn^{2+}(aq)$ to $Zn(s)$ is –0.762 V. What does this value indicate?

5. How is an equilibrium cell different from both a galvanic cell and an electrolytic cell?

Practice problems

6. Explain why the following reaction will not occur spontaneously.

$$Mg^{2+}(aq) + Pb(s) \longrightarrow Mg(s) + Pb^{2+}(aq)$$

7. Write an equation for the electrochemical reaction that occurs spontaneously between the following two electrodes.

$$AgCl(s) + e^- \longrightarrow Ag(s) + Cl^-(aq)$$
$$Ce^{4+}(aq) + e^- \longrightarrow Ce^{3+}(aq)$$

8. Would the following electrochemical reaction be spontaneous as written?

$$PbSO_4(s) + H_3O^+(aq) + Ca(s) \longrightarrow$$
$$Pb(s) + HSO_4^-(aq) + Ca^{2+}(aq) + H_2O(l)$$

9. Write the equation for the reaction that occurs between the following two electrodes.

$$I_2(s) + 2e^- \longrightarrow 2I^-(aq)$$
$$Pb^{2+}(aq) + 2e^- \longrightarrow Pb(s)$$

10. Write the equation for the reaction that occurs between the following two electrodes.

$$Fe^{3+}(aq) + 3e^- \longrightarrow Fe(s)$$
$$2H_2O(l) + 2e^- \longrightarrow H_2(g) + 2OH^-(aq)$$

At the beginning of this chapter, you read about Michael Faraday's interest in electric fish. You were asked to consider several questions.

LOOKING BACK

How does the torpedo ray generate electricity in its electric-organ cells?

The method used by the electric fish is similar to that used by nerve cells, from which the electric organs of fish have probably evolved. The electric-organ cells have a semipermeable membrane that allows potassium ions, K^+, to enter the cell but does not allow sodium ions, Na^+, to enter the cell. A pump system removes sodium ions from the interior of the cell, causing potassium ions to diffuse from outside the cell into the cell's interior. This *sodium ion pump* creates a concentration difference between the exterior and interior of the cell. This concentration gradient produces a potential difference of about 0.08 V. When the fish needs to create an electric pulse, a sodium ion *gate* on the outside of the cell wall opens, allowing Na^+ ions to flood out of the cell's interior. This sets up the potential difference between the interior and exterior of the cell.

Would you expect electric organs to be more useful to fish that swim in salt water or fresh water? in clear water or murky water?

Pure, or fresh, water is a very poor conductor of electricity. Sea water is a much better conductor of electricity because of its high concentration of dissolved salts. This means that you might expect ocean, but not freshwater, fish to use electric organs. Many freshwater rivers, however, also contain enough ions to allow fish to use electric organs. The electric catfish found in the Nile River is one example.

In fairly clear water, fish can easily navigate and hunt without the use of electric organs. In murky water, their sense of sight is of limited value. Fish need another method of finding their way. It is under these conditions that the electric organ finds use as a "sixth sense" for navigation and prey detection.

How is it possible for large voltages, as great as 600 V in some electric eels, to be produced?

Most small flashlights require a voltage of 3.0 V. A standard flashlight battery has a voltage of only 1.5 V. In order to generate the necessary voltage, two batteries are placed *in series*, one behind the other. Using the same principle, a large torpedo ray can have up to a half-million electric plates in a stack, or *in series*, producing a lethal voltage.

KEY TERMS

17-1
ampere
anode
cathode
coulomb
electrochemical cell
electrode
electrolytic cell
electroplating
equilibrium cell

galvanic cell
oxidation
redox reaction
reduction
volt
voltage

17-2
Downs cell
electrolysis
electrosynthesis

17-3
battery
corrosion
fuel cell
primary cell
sacrificial anode
secondary cell

17-4
electrochemical series
equilibrium voltage
standard electrode
  potential
standard hydrogen
  electrode

KEY CONCEPTS

17-1 What is electrochemistry all about?

▸ The relationship between electricity and chemistry is known as electrochemistry.

▸ Electric potential is measured in volts (V), electric current is measured in amperes (A), and electric charge is measured in coulombs (C).

▸ Electrical energy equals electric potential multiplied by electric charge (J = V × C).

▸ Cathodic reactions involve reduction in which electrons are consumed, while anodic reactions involve oxidation in which electrons are created.

▸ Electrode reactions occur in electrochemical cells.

17-2 How are electrolytic cells used?

▸ An electrolytic cell uses electrical energy to drive a nonspontaneous redox reaction.

▸ A Downs cell is an electrolytic cell used to produce sodium metal and chlorine gas.

▸ An electrolytic cell can be used to decompose water into hydrogen gas and oxygen gas.

▸ Aluminum is commercially prepared by the electrolysis of Al_2O_3 obtained from bauxite ore.

17-3 How do batteries work?

▸ Galvanic cells, which include batteries and fuel cells, use cell reactions to convert chemical energy into electrical energy.

▸ Corrosion occurs because of electrode reactions usually involving metals and oxygen.

▸ Corrosion can be curbed by coating a metal with paint or another metal, or by attaching a sacrificial anode.

17-4 What can be learned from an equilibrium cell?

▸ An equilibrium cell can be used to measure the equilibrium voltage.

▸ The standard electrode potential of an electrode is determined by coupling it with a standard hydrogen electrode (SHE), which is assigned an electrode potential of 0.00 V.

▸ An element with a positive electrode potential is likely to be reduced, while an element with a negative electrode potential is likely to be oxidized.

KEY SKILLS

Review the following models before your exam. Be sure you can solve these types of problems.

Sample Problem 17A: Calculating electric charge used in an electrolytic cell (p. 625)

Sample Problem 17B: Calculating energy needed for electrolysis (p. 631)

Sample Problem 17C: Calculating the mass of products of galvanic cell reactions (p. 639)

Sample Problem 17D: Predicting the direction of electrochemical reactions (p. 647)

REVIEW & ASSESS

TERM REVIEW

1. Oxidation takes place at the ——.
   (cathode, anode)

2. A —— could be used to produce electricity with nearly perfect efficiency.
   (Downs cell, standard hydrogen electrode, fuel cell)

3. The outcome of oxidation-reduction reactions can be determined using the ——.
   (electrochemical series, fuel cell)

4. The rusting of iron is an example of ——.
   (sacrificial anodes, corrosion)

5. No current flows in a(n) ——.
   (Downs cell, primary cell, equilibrium cell)

6. —— corrode faster than the structural metal they protect.
   (Electrodes, Sacrificial anodes)

7. —— can be used to produce sodium metal.
   (Electroplating, Electrosynthesis)

8. A(n) —— converts electrical energy into chemical energy.
   (galvanic cell, electrolytic cell)

CONCEPT & SKILLS REVIEW

ELECTROCHEMISTRY

1. What is an electrochemical cell?

2. What is a redox reaction?

3. Use Figure 17-7, on page 626, to answer the following questions:
   a. Explain what will happen to the zinc and copper strips over time.
   b. Explain what would happen if the porous barrier were removed.
   c. In what direction do electrons flow through the wire?

4. Identify the following reactions as either reduction or oxidation. Indicate whether they occur at the cathode or anode.
   a. $Ra(s) \longrightarrow Ra^{2+}(aq) + 2e^-$
   b. $Hg_2^{2+}(aq) + 2e^- \longrightarrow 2Hg(l)$
   c. $Pb(s) + SO_4^{2-}(aq) \longrightarrow PbSO_4(s) + 2e^-$
   d. $O_2(g) + 2H_2O(l) + 4e^- \longrightarrow 4OH^-(aq)$

5. The process of oxidation may or may not involve oxygen. Explain this statement.

6. What is the Faraday constant? How is this constant used?

7. Complete the following table.

	Oxidation/ reduction	Loss or gain of electrons	Change in charge of reactant
Cathode			
Anode			

8. Describe the difference between an electrolytic cell and a galvanic cell.

9. Explain how a metallic object is electroplated.

10. Refer to the diagram below to answer the following questions:

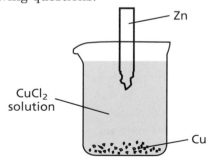

a. What macroscopic observations suggest that a chemical reaction has taken place?
b. Write an equation to show what happened to the Zn metal.
c. Explain where the Cu metal came from that collected at the bottom of the beaker.
d. Write an equation to show how the Cu metal was formed.

11. What voltage is needed to generate 9.6 kJ of electrical energy that carries a charge of 80.0 C?

12. Label the cathode and anode in the diagram below. Write the equations for the redox reactions that are taking place in this electrochemical cell.

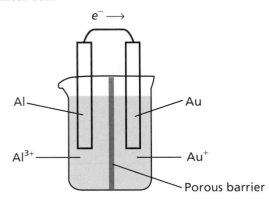

$e^- \longrightarrow$

Al — Au
Al^{3+} — Au^+
Porous barrier

13. An ordinary 60 W light bulb (120 V) is designed for a current of 0.50 A. If your utility company sells electricity at 2.2¢/MJ, how much money do you waste by leaving a light on during an 8 hour night?

14. Batteries are sometimes listed with their "cranking power." This is the amount of current the battery can produce for a period of 30 seconds. If a battery has a cranking power of 1300 A at a voltage of 7.2 V, how much energy is supplied by the battery in 30.0 seconds?

15. Remote controls for TVs and VCRs usually require two AAA batteries. Each battery generates 1.5 V and a total electric current of 60.0 mA. Calculate how much electrical energy is expended each time a button on the remote control is pressed. Assume that each use takes 1.0 second.

ELECTROLYTIC CELLS

16. What does an electrolytic cell do?

17. Why is a battery or some other energy source connected to an electrolytic cell?

18. Tap water contains salts, such as NaCl. Why doesn't sodium metal form during the electrolysis of tap water?

19. What products would be made if a Downs cell operated with NaBr(l) instead of NaCl(l)?

20. What is the oxidation reaction that occurs during the electrolysis of water?

21. Write equations to show what happens at the anode and cathode when molten NaI is placed in an electrolytic cell.

22. How is photosynthesis different from electrosynthesis? How is it similar?

23. How much electric charge is needed to produce 1.000 kg of Na metal from the Na^+ ions in NaCl? **(Hint: See Sample Problem 17A.)**

24. A current of 2.50 A is passed through a solution containing Cu^{2+} ions for 4.00 hours. Calculate the mass of Cu atoms that form at the cathode. **(Hint: See Sample Problem 17A.)**

25. The Hall-Héroult process requires 5.4×10^4 kJ to produce 1.0 kg of aluminum. The enthalpy of fusion for aluminum is 10.7 kJ/mol. Prove mathematically that recycling aluminum saves energy.

26. What volume of F_2 gas is produced when molten KF is electrolyzed by a current of 20.0 A for 2.00 hours? Assume that the gas is collected at 1.00 atm and 298 K. **(Hint: See Sample Problem 17B.)**

27. Hydrogen is being tested as a possible fuel. Hydrogen gas can be produced at the cathode during the electrolysis of sulfuric acid. The cathodic reaction is written as follows.

$$2H_3O^+(aq) + 2e^- \longrightarrow H_2(g) + 2H_2O(l)$$

Calculate how much electrical energy must be supplied to produce 1.00 L of hydrogen at 1.00 atm and 298 K if the electrolytic cell operates at 1.23 V. **(Hint: See Sample Problem 17B.)**

GALVANIC CELLS

28. What are the differences between an alkaline dry cell and a zinc-carbon dry cell?

29. Explain how cathodic protection works to prevent corrosion.

30. Stainless steel contains chromium, which reacts with oxygen. Why might this metal be added to iron to make the stainless steel? The standard electrode potential of Cr^{3+}/Cr is -0.744.

31. Write the oxidation reaction showing what happens to iron ship hulls when they corrode in ocean water.

32. Explain why the terms *cathode* and *anode* cause confusion when they are used to refer to a rechargeable battery.

33. Identify the reactants that are supplied to a fuel cell aboard the space shuttle.

34. Explain why a rechargeable battery is considered a combination galvanic/electrolytic cell.

35. How does painting a metal protect it against corrosion?

Practice Problems

36. The cathodic reaction that occurs in an alkaline battery is shown by the following equation.

$$2MnO_2(s) + H_2O(l) + 2e^- \longrightarrow$$
$$Mn_2O_3(s) + 2OH^-(aq)$$

Calculate the mass of $MnO_2(s)$ that must be added to this 1.54 V battery to produce a total of 22.8 kJ of energy. **(Hint: See Sample Problem 17C.)**

37. What mass of water will be produced after a 12 V car battery has completely run down and delivered its 1.6 MJ of energy? **(Hint: See Sample Problem 17C.)**

EQUILIBRIUM CELLS

38. How can you tell from Table 17-2, on page 646, that $Cl_2(g)$ is likely to be reduced?

39. Explain why the voltage of a single electrode cannot be determined.

40. Explain how the voltages in Table 17-3 were determined.

41. Examine the following reaction.

$$Cu(s) + Fe^{2+}(aq) \rightarrow Cu^{2+}(aq) + Fe(s)$$

Predict whether this reaction will take place spontaneously in a galvanic cell. Explain your answer.

42. Compare the standard reduction potential for a metal with the reactivity of that metal.

Practice Problems

43. Write an equation for the electrochemical reaction that would occur in a galvanic cell in which one electrode is made of zinc metal in an aqueous solution of zinc ions and the other electrode contains liquid bromine. **(Hint: See Sample Problem 17D.)**

44. Write an equation for the electrochemical reaction that would spontaneously occur between potassium metal in aqueous potassium ions and solid zinc hydroxide with zinc metal in a hydroxide solution.

45. If a galvanic cell were made with a magnesium electrode and a cadmium electrode in which each electrode is bathed by a solution of its ions, which metal would be the cathode and which would be the anode?

46. Predict whether each of the following reactions will occur spontaneously as written. Write a balanced overall equation for each reaction that does occur.
 a. $K + Al^{3+} \longrightarrow$
 b. $Li^+ + Zn \longrightarrow$
 c. $Cu + Cl_2 \longrightarrow$
 d. $AgCl + Ca^{2+} \longrightarrow$
 e. $Ce^{3+} + I_3^- \longrightarrow$

LINKING CHAPTERS

1. **Theme: Conservation**
   In a balanced redox reaction, what is being conserved?

2. **Energy and ions**
   In Chapter 5, you learned that iron can form either of two ions, Fe^{3+} or Fe^{2+}. Use the reactions and E^0 values in Table 17-2 to determine which oxidation state is preferred. Explain your reasoning.

3. **Gibbs Free energy**
   a. What would you expect the ΔG value to be for a galvanic cell?
   b. What is the ΔG value of the cell reaction in an electrolytic cell?
   c. What is the ΔG value of a dead dry cell?
   d. Electrical energy is Gibbs free energy, ΔG, and in theory, it is all available for work. Use the following equation to calculate the amount of electrical work generated per gram of water produced in a fuel cell that operates at 60% efficiency.

   $$2H_2(g) + O_2(g) \longrightarrow 2H_2O(l)$$

ALTERNATIVE ASSESSMENTS

Performance assessment

1. Your teacher will assign you a known metal with an unknown reduction potential. Devise a method to determine the E^0 value of the metal from a list of metals with known E^0 values. Present your method to your teacher.

2. Investigate the development and operation of the sodium-sulfur battery being proposed to run electric cars. Choose a stand for or against its use, and present your findings in a persuasive speech to your classmates.

Portfolio projects

1. **Chemistry and you**
   For one week, keep a record of how many times you use devices powered by batteries. Record what kind of device you used and the number and type of batteries it contained. Your teacher will provide you with various batteries and a balance. Record the mass of each type of battery you used during the week. Assuming that your battery usage is typical of everyone in the country, estimate the mass of waste material produced by battery usage in one year. Write a short report offering ways to reduce the amount of waste.

2. **Cooperative group project**
   In small groups, research the environmental effects of different types of batteries. Analyze both the production and waste costs. Share your research with the other groups in the class.

3. **Chemistry and you**
   Consumer use of rechargeable batteries is growing. Many people either own devices using rechargeable batteries or have access to them. Nickel-cadmium batteries, a common type of rechargeable battery, are used in cellular phones, electric shavers, and portable video-game systems. Make a list of the items that you come into contact with that use nickel-cadmium batteries or other rechargeable batteries. Write a short essay about technology that was not and could not have been available before the development of the nickel-cadmium battery.

4. internet**connect**

   SC*LINKS*™
   NSTA

   TOPIC: Redox reactions
   GO TO: www.scilinks.org
   KEYWORD: HW176

   Research and communication
   Redox reactions are not limited to electrochemical cells and batteries. Research common occurrences of redox reactions, and identify the chemical that is oxidized and the chemical that is reduced.

1. In the following reaction, which species is being reduced?

$$2K + Br_2 \longrightarrow 2K^+ + 2Br^-$$

   a. K only
   c. both K and Br_2
   b. Br_2 only
   d. neither K nor Br_2

2. The electrode at which reduction occurs is ——.
   a. always the anode
   b. always the cathode
   c. either the anode or the cathode
   d. always the half-cell

3. In an galvanic cell, the anode ——.
   a. can be either positive or negative
   b. is positive
   c. is not charged
   d. is negative

4. In a cell with Zn/Zn^{2+} and Cu/Cu^{2+} electrodes, ——.
   a. Cu is oxidized and Zn^{2+} is reduced
   b. Cu is reduced and Zn^{2+} is oxidized
   c. Cu^{2+} is oxidized and Zn is reduced
   d. Cu^{2+} is reduced and Zn is oxidized

5. When water is electrolyzed, oxygen gas is formed at ——.
   a. the anode only
   b. the cathode only
   c. the midpoint between the anode and cathode
   d. both the anode and the cathode

6. Sulfuric acid, H_2SO_4, or a similar substance is added to water that is to be electrolyzed in order to ——.
   a. react with the water
   b. keep the electrode clean
   c. provide adequate conductivity
   d. supply energy

7. In a Downs cell, which of the following is produced at the anode?
   a. H_2
   c. Cl_2
   b. Na
   d. O_2

8. When a rechargeable cell is being recharged, the cell acts as a(n) ——.
   a. fuel cell
   b. electrolytic cell
   c. galvanic cell
   d. equilibrium cell

9. When silver is electroplated onto an object, Ag^+ is ——.
   a. oxidized at the anode
   b. reduced at the anode
   c. oxidized at the cathode
   d. reduced at the cathode

10. The standard automobile battery consists of six ——.
   a. lead(IV) oxide-lead-sulfuric acid cells
   b. copper(II) oxide-copper-sulfuric acid cells
   c. zinc oxide-zinc-sulfuric acid cells
   d. iron(III) oxide-iron-sulfuric acid cells

11. A battery that can be recharged is an example of a(n) ——.
   a. primary cell
   b. equilibrium cell
   c. secondary cell
   d. Downs cell

12. The equilibrium voltage of a cell is measured when ——.
   a. the cell is operating as a galvanic cell
   b. the cell is operating as an electrolytic cell
   c. the temperature of the cell is 25°C
   d. no current is flowing through the cell

THE ICEMAN MEETS NUCLEAR CHEMISTRY

While hiking through the Alps near the border between Austria and Italy, in September 1991, Helmut and Erika Simon noticed something protruding from the ice. At first the Simons thought they had stumbled across a discarded doll covered with ice.

But on closer inspection, the Simons realized they were looking at the frozen body of a man. Sticking out of the ice were the head and shoulders of a prehistoric man, now known throughout the world as the Iceman.

For four days following the discovery, workers struggled to free the Iceman's body. They hacked away at the ice using axes and ski poles, unaware of the importance of what they were uncovering. The Iceman's left hip was broken with a jackhammer, and much of his clothing was destroyed. But when the figure was finally freed, the workers were astonished by what they saw.

The body was amazingly well preserved. The Iceman stood 5 ft 2 in. tall and appeared to be somewhere between 25 and 40. He had wavy, medium-length, dark hair and a beard. He wore clothes made of animal skins and boots stuffed with grass to keep his feet warm. His skin bore markings in various spots, including stripes on his right ankle and a cross behind his left knee.

The Iceman had been carrying a stone knife, a wooden backpack, a small bag containing a flint lighter and some kindling, a bow and a quiver containing 14 arrows, and a copper ax. Shortly after the Iceman's body was freed from the ice, an archaeologist examined the ax. The age of the ax indicated that the Iceman lived about 4000 years ago.

If the Iceman is indeed that old, then his body is the oldest ever retrieved from an Alpine glacier. And at over 10 000 feet, the site where the Iceman was found is the highest point at which any prehistoric human has ever been found in Europe. Moreover, the Iceman is one of the best-preserved early humans ever found.

Scientists immediately arranged to have the body placed in a freezer, where the temperature would be maintained at a constant −6°C and the humidity at a constant 98%. These conditions would replicate those of the ice in which the body was preserved for so long.

CHAPTER LINKS

Exactly when did the Iceman die?

How did scientists determine what the Iceman looked like when he was alive?

How did the Iceman die?

Which atomic nuclei are stable?

OBJECTIVES

▶ **Describe** how the strong nuclear force acts among nucleons.

▶ **Discuss** the nature and origin of binding energy.

▶ **Account** for the increase in nuclear stability of the smaller nuclei followed by the decrease in stability of the larger nuclei as atomic number increases.

Nuclear stability

You learned in Chapter 3 of Ernest Rutherford's famous gold-foil experiment, which solved a basic riddle about the distribution of charge and mass in an atom. Rutherford's results showed that all of the atom's positive charge and almost all of its mass are contained in an extremely small nucleus. This discovery led to another mystery about the nucleus. Protons are positively charged, and when packed together in a nucleus they exert a tremendous force of electrostatic repulsion on each other. So why doesn't the nucleus fly apart?

Nuclei are composed of both protons and neutrons. The number of protons is the *atomic number, Z,* and the total number of protons and neutrons is the *mass number, A.* The symbol for the nucleus of an atom of element X is shown in **Figure 18-1.**

The protons and neutrons in a nucleus are collectively known as **nucleons. A nuclide** is any combination of these protons and neutrons. You already know that *isotopes* are atoms that have the same atomic number but different mass numbers. In other words, isotopes are nuclides that have the same number of protons but different numbers of neutrons. The following nuclei are stable isotopes of tellurium.

$$^{122}_{52}\text{Te} \qquad ^{124}_{52}\text{Te} \qquad ^{128}_{52}\text{Te}$$

A related term is *isobar,* which refers to atoms that have the same mass number but different atomic numbers. The following stable nuclei are isobars.

$$^{124}_{54}\text{Xe} \qquad ^{124}_{52}\text{Te} \qquad ^{124}_{50}\text{Sn}$$

Notice they have different numbers of protons, Z, but the same mass number, A.

nucleons

the protons and neutrons that make up the nucleus of an atom

nuclide

any combination of protons and neutrons in a nucleus

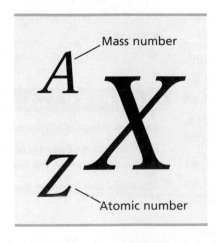

▶ **FIGURE 18-1**

X represents the element, *Z* is the element's atomic number, and *A* is the element's mass number.

Mass number

Atomic number

FIGURE 18-2 ▼

In this nucleus, the strong nuclear force acts only over a distance of only a few nucleon diameters. Attractions occur between protons A and B, neutrons D and E and the more distant proton C and neutron F, but not as strongly.

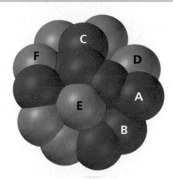

The strong force holds the nucleus together

Electrostatic repulsion occurs between the protons of a nucleus. In 1935, the Japanese physicist Hideki Yukawa proposed the theory that some other force overwhelms the electrostatic repulsion among protons. This force is called the **strong nuclear force** and is exerted by nucleons on one another when they are very close to each other. Forces that hold nucleons together are generally called *binding forces.*

Although the strong nuclear binding force is much stronger than the electrical force, it acts only over very *short* distances. Look at the nucleus illustrated in **Figure 18-2.** The nucleons are close enough together for each nucleon to attract all of the other nucleons by the strong nuclear force. In larger nuclei the strong nuclear force does not reach far enough to allow each nucleon to attract all others. However, the much weaker electrostatic repulsion between protons does act over large distances. When there is an imbalance between the strong nuclear force and electrostatic repulsion, the nucleus decays. You will learn more about nuclear decay in section 18-2.

strong nuclear force

the force of attraction among the particles of a nucleus that overcomes electrostatic repulsion and holds the nucleus together

Binding energy comes from loss of mass

Because the strong nuclear force of attraction holds the nuclear particles together, the nucleus is at a lower energy state than are its separated nucleons. A system becomes more stable when it moves to a lower energy state. When protons and neutrons that are far apart come together to form a nucleus, energy is given off because of the increased stability of the nucleus. This stabilization reaction can be written as follows.

separated nucleons ⟶ nucleus + energy

The energy produced in the above reaction is enormous compared with the energy changes that take place in ordinary chemical reactions. Nuclear energy is produced at the expense of mass, implying that the mass of the nucleus is less than the combined masses of the separated nucleons. This difference in mass is known as the **mass defect.** For helium, $_2^4\text{He}$, the mass of the nucleus is about 0.75% less than the total mass of two protons and two neutrons. This energy released, *E,* and decrease in mass, *m,* are related according to Einstein's mass-energy equation.

$$E = mc^2$$

mass defect

the mass lost by conversion to energy when a nucleus forms from separated nucleons

The constant c, 3.00×10^8 m/s, is the speed of light. Notice that if mass, m, is expressed in kilograms, and c^2 in m²/s², the product mc^2 will have the units kg•m²/s² so that E will be calculated directly in joules, the *SI* unit of energy.

The energy emitted when nucleons come together is the **nuclear binding energy.** You could also say that the nuclear binding energy is the energy required to separate a nucleus into its components.

nuclear binding energy

the energy emitted when nucleons come together to form a nucleus; also the energy needed to break a nucleus into individual, separated nucleons

Binding energy is easily calculated

Consider the stable oxygen isotope, $^{16}_{8}O$, with a mass number of 16. One atom of this isotope contains eight protons and eight neutrons, as well as eight electrons in two energy levels. The total mass of all its separate particles is equivalent to eight hydrogen atoms, each with a mass of 1.007 825 amu, combined with eight neutrons, each with a mass of 1.008 665 amu. In **Figure 18-3,** you can see how the total mass of these particles compares with the actual mass of a $^{16}_{8}O$ atom. The mass defect for one atom of $^{16}_{8}O$ is 0.137 005 amu, as shown in Figure 18-3. Einstein's mass-energy equation can be used to calculate the binding energy. Remember to convert amu per atom to grams per mole when calculating binding energy.

Binding energy is one indicator of nuclear stability

The binding energy, 1.23×10^{13} J, results from the formation of a mere 16 g of oxygen nuclei. That is roughly the amount of energy required to heat 4.6 million liters of liquid water from 0°C to 100°C and boil it away completely.

As you know, the more energy released in a process, the more stable are the products of that process. The binding energy of a selenium, $^{80}_{34}Se$, nucleus is much greater than that of a $^{16}_{8}O$ nucleus. Does this difference

► **FIGURE 18-3**

The mass defect is the difference between the mass of the nucleus and the sum of the masses of its protons, neutrons and electrons.

Mass defect

Oxygen nucleus

$^{16}_{8}O$ isotope = 8(1.007 825 amu) + 8(1.008 665 amu)

$\phantom{^{16}_{8}O \text{ isotope }}$ = 8.062 600 amu + 8.069 320 amu

$\phantom{^{16}_{8}O \text{ isotope }}$ = 16.131 920 amu

m = (total mass of separate nucleons) − (mass of nucleus)

 = 16.131 920 − 15.994 915

 = 0.137 005 amu per isotope of $^{16}_{8}O$

Relative Stability of Nuclei

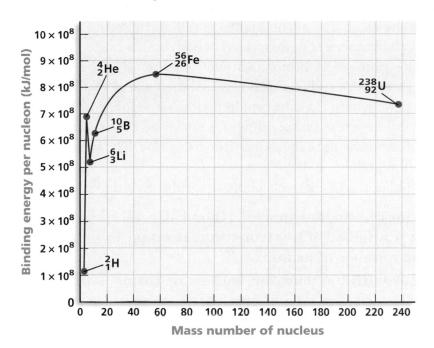

FIGURE 18-4 ◀

The plot of average binding energy per nucleon versus mass number indicates the relative stability of nuclei. Isotopes that have a high binding energy per nucleon are more stable. $^{56}_{26}Fe$ is the most stable nucleus.

in energy mean that the $^{80}_{34}Se$ nucleus is more stable than the $^{16}_{8}O$ nucleus? Not necessarily. After all, $^{80}_{34}Se$ contains many more nucleons than $^{16}_{8}O$ does. To make a fair comparison you must look at the binding energy *per nucleon*. Look at the graph of these energies versus mass number in **Figure 18-4**. Notice that the binding energy per nucleon rises rapidly among the lighter nuclei. The higher the binding energy per nucleon, the more tightly the nucleons are held together.

Moving farther to the right, the binding energy per nucleon begins to level off. It reaches a maximum when the atomic mass number, *A,* is around 55, as seen with iron, cobalt, and nickel. The most stable nuclei are $^{56}_{26}Fe$ and $^{58}_{28}Ni$. These isotopes are relatively abundant in the universe, and they are the major components of the Earth's core.

Beyond these elements, the nucleus is too large for added nucleons to increase the overall attraction among the particles. As you move even farther to the right, repulsions become more significant, and the binding energy per nucleon decreases gradually. Beyond mass number 209, no stable nuclide exists.

CONCEPT CHECK

1. How do the nuclides $^{16}_{8}O$, $^{15}_{8}O$, and $^{15}_{7}N$ differ?
2. Why do nuclei not fly apart as a result of electrostatic repulsion?
3. How do stable nuclides with very low mass numbers differ from those with high mass numbers?

Predicting nuclear stability

What other factors affect nuclear stability? Look at the graph in **Figure 18-5**. It shows all 256 of the known stable nuclei represented by red dots. Here the number of neutrons, *N*, of each stable nucleus is plotted against the number of protons (atomic number *Z*). The pattern formed by plotting these stable nuclei is called the **band of stability.** The maroon line shows where the data would lie for *N/Z* = 1. For lighter nuclei, the data fall near the maroon line. As nuclei become heavier, *N/Z* approaches 1.5, and the data lie nearer the green line. The band of stability is shown in yellow.

The graph in Figure 18-5 reveals additional rules for nuclear stability.

1. **Except for the smallest nuclei, $_1^1$H and $_2^3$He, all stable nuclei contain a number of neutrons that is equal to or greater than the number of protons.**

2. **A nucleus with too many or too few neutrons is unstable.** For small atoms, the ratio of neutrons, *N*, to protons, *Z*, is very close to one. As the nuclei get larger, this ratio increases gradually until it is near 1.5 for the largest atoms.

The following rules are not obvious at first on the graph, but they become clear when Figure 18-5 is viewed carefully.

3. **Nuclei with even numbers of nucleons are more stable.** Almost 60% of all stable nuclei have even numbers of both protons and neutrons. From this fact, it is safe to assume that an even-even combination is particularly stable. Of the four odd-odd nuclei, all are small, with a *N/Z* ratio equal to one. Of the 50 odd-even nuclei, 20 are nuclei of elements that have only one stable nuclide.

4. **Nuclei with so-called *magic numbers* of protrons and *magic numbers* of neutrons tend to be more stable than others.** These numbers—2, 8, 20, 28, 50, 82, and 126—apply to the number of protons or the number of neutrons. Notice in Figure 18-4 the large binding energy of $_2^4$He. This is a very small even-even nucleus with two protons and two neutrons. This extra stability also shows up in the element calcium, which has six stable isotopes ranging from $_{20}^{40}$Ca to $_{20}^{48}$Ca. All have 20 protons, and the two shown have 20 and 28 neutrons, respectively. Tin, with the magic number of

▼ **FIGURE 18-5**

The graph below shows the number of protons and neutrons for all 256 of the known stable nuclei.

Neutron-Proton Ratios of Stable Nuclei

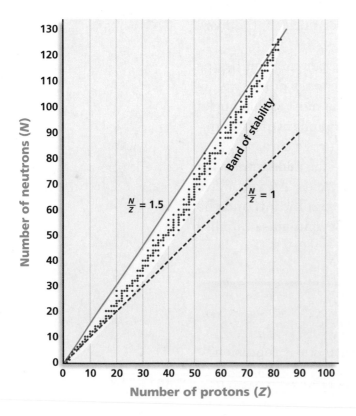

50 protons, has 10 stable isotopes, the greatest number of any element. The heaviest stable element, bismuth, with only one stable isotope, has the magic number of 126 neutrons in $^{209}_{83}$Bi.

5. **Of two neighboring isobars, at least one is unstable.** Refer to the three examples of isobars at the beginning of this section. Notice that the nuclei of atomic numbers 51 and 53 are missing. These two missing isobars are nuclei, $^{124}_{51}$Sb and $^{124}_{53}$I. They are the neighboring isobars of the stable nuclides; therefore, they are unstable.

SECTION REVIEW

Total recall

1. What are the nucleons of an atom?
2. What role does the strong nuclear force play in the structure of an atom?
3. What is the band of stability?
4. Explain the difference between isotopes and isobars.
5. What is mass defect?
6. What is the nuclear binding energy?
7. Why is bismuth, $^{209}_{83}$Bi, stable?
8. Which is more stable, nuclei with an even number of nucleons or nuclei with an odd number of nucleons?

Critical thinking

9. Which is generally more stable, a small nucleus or a large nucleus? Explain.
10. How does nuclear binding energy relate to the stability of an atom?
11. Which is expected to be more stable, $^{6}_{3}$Li or $^{9}_{3}$Li?
12. **a.** What creates the electrostatic repulsion in the nucleus of an atom?
    b. How is the repulsive force overcome?
    c. What would happen if this force were not overcome?

13. **Interpreting Graphics** Use Figure 18-5 and the rules for predicting nuclear stability to determine whether the following isotopes are stable or unstable.
    a. $^{32}_{15}$P   **d.** $^{24}_{12}$Mg
    b. $^{14}_{6}$C   **e.** $^{97}_{43}$Tc
    c. $^{51}_{23}$V

14. Why are certain numbers referred to as magic numbers in terms of atomic nuclei?

15. **Story Clue** What element is the basis of all of the organic substances found in living things?

16. **Interpreting Graphics** Use Figure 18-4 to answer the following:
    a. For the elements shown, what happens to the binding energy as the mass number for the nucleus increases?
    b. Which is more stable, the hydrogen isotope or the helium isotope?

17. Which elements have no stable isotopes? (Examine Figure 18-5 carefully)

What kinds of nuclear change occur?

OBJECTIVES

▶ **Describe** the particles and electromagnetic waves that make up radioactive emissions.

▶ **Distinguish** between radioactive decay, fission, fusion, and transmutation.

▶ **Balance** nuclear equations.

▶ **Classify** nuclear reactions from their equations.

▶ **Describe** the characteristics of a chain reaction.

Radioactive processes

You could say that nuclear changes are easier to understand than chemical changes because only four classes of nuclear changes occur. The first class is the spontaneous change of an unstable nucleus to form a more stable one. This change involves the emission of particles or electromagnetic rays, or both, and is generally called radioactivity. We now know that **radioactivity** is the breakdown (decay) of unstable nuclei to produce alpha particles, beta particles, and, almost always, gamma rays. Before examining the four classes of nuclear changes, look at the properties of the particles summarized in **Table 18-1.**

radioactivity

the process during which unstable nuclei undergo spontaneous nuclear decay and emit particles and electromagnetic waves

| **TABLE 18-1** | **Characteristics of Nuclear Particles and Rays** |

Particle	Mass (amu)	Charge	Symbol	Stopped by
proton	1.007 276 47	+1	$p, p^+, {}^1_1\text{H}$	a few sheets of paper
neutron	1.008 664 90	0	$n, n^0, {}^1_0 n$	a few centimeters of Pb
β particle (electron)	0.000 548 580	−1	$\beta, \beta^-, {}^{\ 0}_{-1}e^*$	a few sheets of aluminum foil
positron†	0.000 548 580	+1	$\beta^+, {}^{\ 0}_{+1}e^*$	same as electron
alpha particle (He-4 nucleus)	4.001 506 17	+2	$\alpha, \alpha^{2+}, {}^4_2\text{He}$	skin or one sheet of paper
gamma ray	0	0	γ	several centimeters of Pb

*The superscript zero in the symbols for electron and positron does not mean that they have zero mass. It means their *mass number* is zero.

†The positron is the *antiparticle* of the electron. Each particle has an antiparticle, but only the positron is important here.

internetconnect

SCI**LINKS**
NSTA

TOPIC: Radioactive emissions
GO TO: www.scilinks.org
KEYWORD: HW181

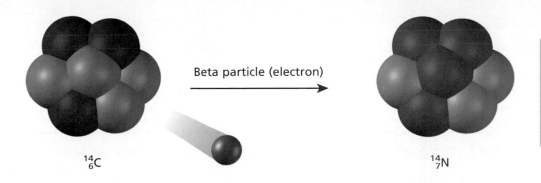

FIGURE 18-6 ◄

When the unstable carbon-14 nucleus emits a beta particle, it changes into a nitrogen-14 nucleus.

$^{14}_{6}C$

$^{14}_{7}N$

Stabilizing nuclei by converting neutrons into protons

Recall from Section 18-1 that the stability of a nucleus depends on the ratio of neutrons to protons, the N/Z ratio. If the number of neutrons is too great for a particular atomic number, the nucleus will decay and emit radiation.

It is possible for a neutron in an unstable nucleus to emit a high-energy electron, called a **beta particle** (β particle), and change to a proton. This process is called *beta decay* and is the usual process by which nuclei with too many neutrons become more stable.

$$^{1}_{0}n \xrightarrow{\text{beta decay}} {}^{1}_{+1}p + {}^{0}_{-1}e$$

Because this process changes a neutron to a proton, the atomic number of the nucleus increases by one, as you can see in **Figure 18-6.** In other words, through beta decay, carbon can become a different element, nitrogen. However, the mass number does not change because the total number of nucleons does not change.

$$^{14}_{6}C \longrightarrow {}^{14}_{7}N + {}^{0}_{-1}e$$

beta particle

a high-energy electron emitted from the nucleus when a neutron changes to a proton

Stabilizing nuclei by converting protons into neutrons

A second reason for nuclear instability is that a nucleus has too few neutrons. There are two ways that a nucleus with too few neutrons can become more stable.

1. Electron capture In this process, the nucleus merely absorbs one of the atom's electrons, usually from the 1s orbital. This changes a proton into a neutron, thereby decreasing the atomic number by one but keeping the mass number the same.

$$^{1}_{+1}p + {}^{0}_{-1}e \xrightarrow{\text{electron capture}} {}^{1}_{0}n$$
$$\text{orbital}$$
$$\text{electron}$$

A typical nucleus that decays by this process is chromium-51. This unstable nuclide has a neutron-to-proton ratio that is too low; therefore, it needs a larger number of neutrons. The change that occurs as it converts a proton into a neutron is shown in the following equation.

$$^{51}_{24}Cr + {}^{0}_{-1}e \xrightarrow{\text{electron capture}} {}^{51}_{23}V + \gamma$$

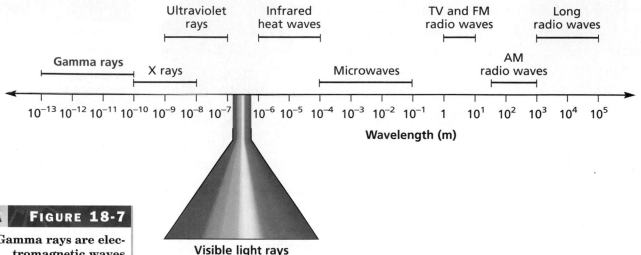

Ultraviolet rays   Infrared heat waves   TV and FM radio waves   Long radio waves

Gamma rays   X rays   Microwaves   AM radio waves

10^{-13} 10^{-12} 10^{-11} 10^{-10} 10^{-9} 10^{-8} 10^{-7} 10^{-6} 10^{-5} 10^{-4} 10^{-3} 10^{-2} 10^{-1} 1 10^1 10^2 10^3 10^4 10^5

Wavelength (m)

Visible light rays

▲ **FIGURE 18-7**

Gamma rays are electromagnetic waves emitted by decaying nuclei. Gamma rays are at the high-energy, short-wavelength end of the electromagnetic spectrum.

gamma ray

high-energy electromagnetic radiation produced by decaying nuclei

The final symbol in the equation, γ, indicates the emission of gamma radiation. Many nuclear changes leave the nucleus in an energetic, or excited, state. When the nucleus stabilizes, this energy is given off in the form of **gamma rays.** This electromagnetic radiation has high energy and a short wavelength, as shown by **Figure 18-7.** Gamma rays are emitted in almost every radioactive disintegration.

2. **Positron emission** Nuclei that are further out of balance in favor of protons can become stable by emitting positrons, the *antiparticles* of electrons. The process is similar to *beta* emission, but in this case, a positron is emitted by a proton instead of an electron being emitted by a neutron. As in electron capture, the proton is also changed into a neutron.

$$^{1}_{+1}p \xrightarrow{\text{positron emission}} {}^{1}_{0}n + {}^{0}_{+1}e$$

Note that the mass number stays the same but the atomic number decreases by one. The isotope chromium-49 decays by this process, as shown below.

$$^{49}_{24}\text{Cr} \longrightarrow {}^{49}_{23}\text{V} + {}^{0}_{+1}e$$

The positron is a beta antiparticle, but unlike a beta particle, a positron seldom makes it into the surroundings. Instead, the positron usually collides with its antiparticle, the electron. Any time a particle collides with its antiparticle, all of the mass of the two particles is converted entirely into electromagnetic energy—two gamma rays going in opposite directions. This process is called **annihilation of matter.**

$$^{0}_{-1}e + {}^{0}_{+1}e \xrightarrow{\text{annihilation}} 2\gamma$$

annihilation of matter

the event that occurs when a particle collides with its antiparticle and both are changed into electromagnetic energy

The gamma rays from electron-positron annihilation have a characteristic wavelength and identify decay by positron emission. Such gamma rays have been detected coming from the center of the Milky Way galaxy.

Stabilizing nuclei by losing alpha particles

If a nucleus is very large and has too few neutrons, it can decay in another way—by emitting alpha particles. None of the elements above atomic number 83 and mass number 126 have stable isotopes, and many decay by emitting alpha particles as well as by electron capture. Look at the following example.

$$\ce{^{238}_{92}U} \xrightarrow{\text{alpha decay}} \ce{^{234}_{90}Th} + \ce{^{4}_{2}He}$$

The atomic number decreases by two, and the mass number decreases by four. Alpha particles have very low penetrating ability, as shown in Table 18-1, because they are large and soon collide with other matter. Exposure to external sources of alpha radiation is usually of little consequence. However, if substances that undergo alpha decay are ingested or inhaled, the radiation can be quite damaging.

Many heavy nuclei go through a series of reactions called a *decay series* before they reach a stable state. The decay series for uranium-238 is shown in **Figure 18-8.** After the $\ce{^{238}_{92}U}$ nucleus decays to $\ce{^{234}_{90}Th}$, the nucleus is still unstable because it has too many neutrons. This nucleus undergoes beta decay to produce an isotope of protactinium.

By another beta decay, $\ce{^{234}_{91}Pa}$ changes to $\ce{^{234}_{92}U}$. These nuclides, which have too few neutrons, undergo a sequence of five alpha decays. You

Uranium-238 Decay Series

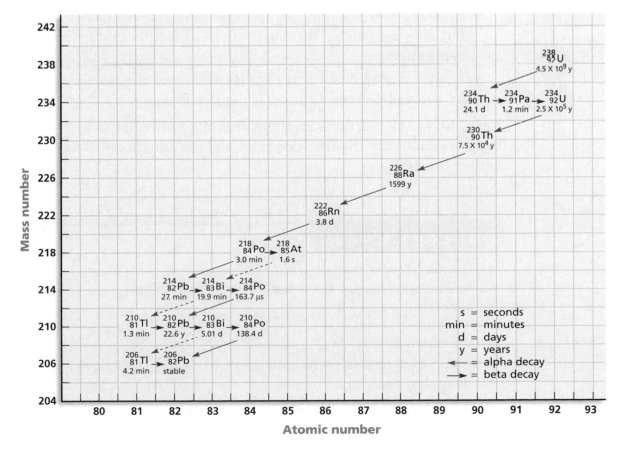

will learn more about the concept of nuclear decay as it relates to half-life in section 18-3. After several more decays (and after perhaps millions of years), the nucleus finally becomes a stable isotope, $^{206}_{82}Pb$. Figure 18-8, on page 667, shows the complete sequence of reactions.

Nuclear equations are also balanced

Look back at all of the nuclear equations that have appeared so far in this chapter. Notice that the total of the mass numbers (superscripts) on one side of the equation always equals the total of the mass numbers on the other side of the equation. Likewise, the totals of the atomic numbers (subscripts) on each side of the equation are equal. Look at the following nuclear equations, and notice that they balance in terms of both mass and charge.

$$^{234}_{90}Th \longrightarrow {}^{234}_{91}Pa + {}^{0}_{-1}e \quad \begin{array}{l} [234 = 234 + 0 \text{ mass balance}] \\ [90 = 91 + (-1) \text{ charge balance}] \end{array}$$

$$^{238}_{92}U \longrightarrow {}^{234}_{90}Th + {}^{4}_{2}He \quad \begin{array}{l} [238 = 234 + 4 \text{ mass balance}] \\ [92 = 90 + 2 \text{ charge balance}] \end{array}$$

When you write and balance a nuclear equation, keep the following rules in mind.

1. The total of the mass numbers is the same on both sides of the equation.
2. The total nuclear charge is the same on both sides of the equation.
3. Emission of a beta particle, $^{0}_{-1}e$, increases the atomic number by one but does not change the mass number.
4. Emission of a positron, $^{0}_{+1}e$, decreases the atomic number by one but does not change the mass number. Electron capture has the same effect.
5. Emission of an alpha particle, $^{4}_{2}He$, decreases the atomic number by two and decreases the mass number by four.

If you know the reactants and products of a particular nuclear reaction, you can apply the first two rules and the equation will work out automatically.

CONCEPT CHECK

1. How do each of the following radioactive emissions change the atomic number and the mass number of a nucleus?
   a. positron emission
   b. alpha emission
   c. beta emission
2. Which type of emission would result in each of the following nuclear changes?
   a. $^{15}_{6}C \longrightarrow {}^{15}_{7}N$ b. $^{147}_{62}Sm \longrightarrow {}^{143}_{60}Nd$

Artificial transmutations

At the beginning of this section you read that there are four classes of nuclear changes. So far you have learned about one class in which a nucleus decays by adding or losing particles. Two other types of nuclear changes are fission and fusion. These are classified as artificial transmutations because they usually do not occur naturally on Earth. In recent years, however, scientists have discovered natural deposits of uranium that show signs of having undergone fission reactions in the geological past.

Large unstable nuclei can split in two

Observe what is happening to the single-celled organism shown in **Figure 18-9.** The organism is dividing in two by a process called cell division, or fission. Large, unstable atomic nuclei can also undergo fission. **Nuclear fission** refers to a nuclear reaction in which a very heavy nucleus splits into two smaller nuclei, each having a higher binding energy per nucleon than the original nucleus. There are two kinds of fission: spontaneous and induced. A very small fraction of naturally occurring uranium atoms are of the isotope $^{235}_{92}U$, which undergoes spontaneous fission. However, most fission reactions are induced artificially by bombarding nuclei with neutrons.

The energy yield of fission reactions is very high. For example, the fission of 1 g of uranium-235 generates as much energy as the combustion of 2700 kg of coal. Fission reactions are the source of energy used to generate electricity in nuclear power plants. Uranium-235 and plutonium-239 are the main radioactive isotopes used in these reactors. In one possible fission reaction, the uranium-235 nucleus absorbs a neutron. Then the uranium-236 nucleus splits in two, forming two smaller nuclides. In the process a few neutrons are ejected. The product nuclei have far too many neutrons, and are intensely radioactive, emitting

nuclear fission

a nuclear reaction in which a very heavy nucleus splits into two smaller nuclei of approximately equal mass

internet**connect**

SC*LINKS*
NSTA

TOPIC: Fission
GO TO: www.scilinks.org
KEYWORD: HW182

FIGURE 18-9 ▼

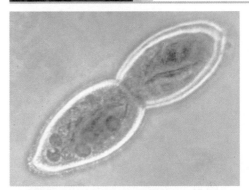

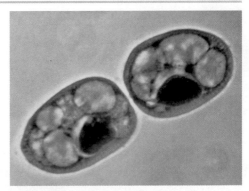

a The single-celled paramecium is about to undergo fission, a process of reproduction. The term *fission* has nearly the same meaning in biology as it does in chemistry.

b The paramecium has fissioned, or divided, into two smaller organisms, just as a nucleus divides into smaller nuclei during nuclear fission.

beta particles. This is the "nuclear waste". The following equation represents the first reaction shown in **Figure 18-10,** in which three neutrons are emitted.

$$^{235}_{92}U + ^{1}_{0}n \longrightarrow [^{236}_{92}U] \xrightarrow{\text{nuclear fission}} ^{93}_{36}Kr + ^{140}_{56}Ba + 3\,^{1}_{0}n$$

temporary
nuclide

chain reaction

a nuclear reaction that sustains itself because the particles produced in the reaction, which go on to initiate the same reaction in other nuclei, are the same as the particles that started the reaction

critical mass

the smallest mass of radioactive material needed to sustain a chain reaction

As you can see in Figure 18-10, each of the three neutrons emitted by the fission of one nucleus can cause the fission of another uranium-235 nucleus. Again some neutrons are emitted. These reactions continue one after another as long as a sufficient concentration of uranium-235 remains. This process is called a **chain reaction.** One characteristic of a chain reaction is that the particle (neutron) that starts the reaction is also produced in the reaction. A minimum quantity of radioactive material is needed to sustain a chain reaction. The amount must be sufficient for most neutrons to be captured by other nuclei before they leave the material. The smallest mass of radioactive material needed to sustain a chain reaction is known as the **critical mass.**

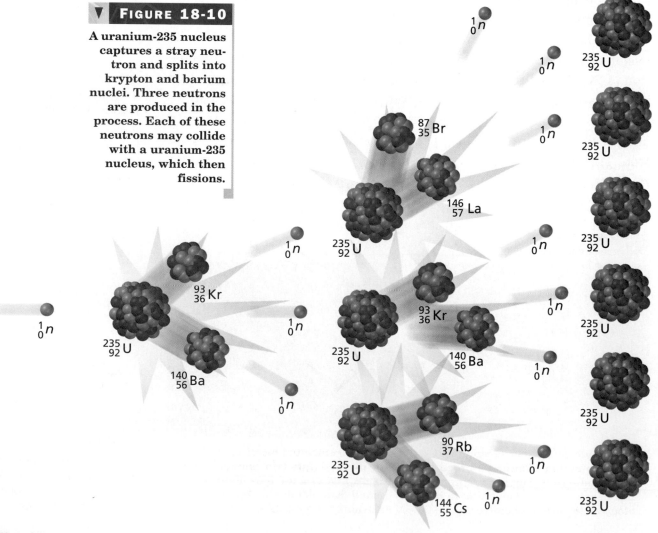

▼ **FIGURE 18-10**

A uranium-235 nucleus captures a stray neutron and splits into krypton and barium nuclei. Three neutrons are produced in the process. Each of these neutrons may collide with a uranium-235 nucleus, which then fissions.

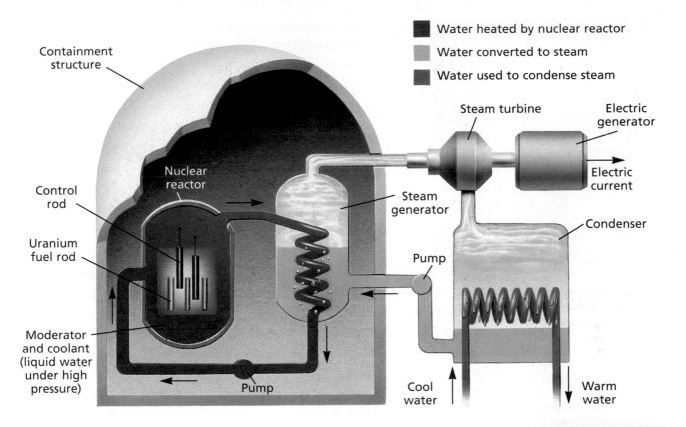

Water heated by nuclear reactor

Water converted to steam

Water used to condense steam

Containment structure

Nuclear reactor

Control rod

Uranium fuel rod

Moderator and coolant (liquid water under high pressure)

Pump

Steam generator

Steam turbine

Electric generator

Electric current

Condenser

Pump

Cool water

Warm water

FIGURE 18-11 ▲

This model of a nuclear power plant shows a pressurized light-water reactor, the type most often used to generate electricity in the United States. The rate of the chain reaction is controlled by moving the control rods in and out. Note that each of the three water systems is isolated from the others for safety reasons.

In a nuclear reactor, represented in **Figure 18-11,** the fuel rods are surrounded by a *moderator,* a substance that slows down neutrons. Graphite and ordinary water are effective moderators. Heavy water, deuterium oxide, $^2_1H_2O$, is a more efficient moderator.

Control rods are used to adjust the rate of the chain reactions. These rods absorb some of the free neutrons produced by fission. Moving these rods into and out of the reactor controls the number of neutrons that are available to continue the chain reaction. If these control rods were removed, an uncontrolled chain reaction would occur. The heat from an uncontrolled reaction, in the worst case, could cause a *meltdown* of the reactor. A failure of control systems followed by fire, explosion, and meltdown occurred at Chernobyl, Ukraine, in 1986, killing many people and poisoning the environment for many years with radioactive elements.

Some small nuclei can join to form heavier nuclei

Fusion is the third class of nuclear change. As the term suggests, **nuclear fusion** occurs when two small nuclei combine, or fuse, to form a larger, more stable nucleus. The new nucleus has a higher binding energy, and energy is released as it forms. This results in a more stable nucleus. In fact, fusion releases tremendous amounts of energy. It is the process by which the sun produces energy and the process that occurs in the explosion of a hydrogen bomb, shown in **Figure 18-12.**

internet**connect**

SC/LINKS
NSTA

TOPIC: Fusion
GO TO: www.scilinks.org
KEYWORD: HW183

nuclear fusion

the combining of two small nuclei to form a larger, more stable nucleus with the release of energy

The hydrogen bomb uses nuclear fusion. As a result, an exploding hydrogen bomb has even greater destructive power than the first nuclear bombs, which were fission bombs.

In the sun, fusion combines four hydrogen nuclei to form a single $_2^4\text{He}$ nucleus. The temperature of the sun's core, where some of the fusion reactions occur, is about $1.5 \times 10^7 \,^\circ\text{C}$. Very high pressures and very high temperatures are required to bring the nuclei together. When the hydrogen nuclei are fused to form a larger nucleus, some mass is lost and converted to energy. Even more energy is released per gram of reactant in fusion than in fission.

Fusion reactions are hard to contain

Currently, scientists are investigating ways to control fusion reactions so that they may be used for both energy generation and research. If fusion reactions are ever to become a practical source of energy, the energy given off must be greater than the energy required to start them. At the moment, scientists are near the break-even point.

In fusion reactions, the reactants are in the form of a *plasma,* a random mixture of positive nuclei and electrons. The biggest problem scientists must overcome is containing this plasma at the tremendous temperatures required for fusion to occur. No form of solid matter can withstand such conditions. Scientists currently use extremely strong magnetic fields to suspend the charged plasma particles in space. In this way, the plasma can be kept from contacting the container walls. Scientists have also experimented with high-powered laser light to start the fusion process.

The following is a typical fusion reaction.

$$_1^3\text{H} + {}_1^2\text{H} \longrightarrow {}_2^4\text{He} + {}_0^1 n + 1.7 \times 10^{12} \text{ J/mol of He}$$

Sea water is the source for the deuterium, $_1^2\text{H}$. Tritium, $_1^3\text{H}$, must be produced in a nuclear reactor, often by bombarding lithium-6 atoms with neutrons from the fission reaction in progress.

$$_3^6\text{Li} + {}_0^1 n \longrightarrow {}_1^3\text{H} + {}_2^4\text{He} + 4.3 \times 10^{11} \text{ J/mol of } _1^3\text{H}$$

New nuclides can be produced by nuclear bombardment

The three types of nuclear change that you have read about so far are spontaneous processes in which unstable nuclides move toward stability. It is also possible to create new nuclides by bombarding a nucleus with other particle nuclei. This process is called **transmutation** and is the modern-day equivalent of the early alchemists' attempts to turn lead into gold. In 1919, Rutherford became the first to recognize a transmutation while experimenting with how far alpha particles travel in various gases. When he used air or nitrogen, a reaction occurred that yielded two products. Careful study identified these products as hydrogen and an isotope of oxygen. The alpha particle is absorbed into the nitrogen nucleus, and then the energetic *compound nucleus* emits a proton to stabilize itself.

transmutation

creating new nuclei by bombarding a nucleus with energetic particles

$$^{14}_{7}\text{N} + ^{4}_{2}\text{He} \longrightarrow [^{18}_{9}\text{F}] \longrightarrow ^{17}_{8}\text{O} + ^{1}_{1}\text{H}$$

└── Unstable compound nucleus

When the discovery of transmutation became known, scientists began to bombard almost every known element with alpha particles, producing hundreds of new radioactive nuclides. The yields were very low because the nucleus of a target atom strongly repels the positively charged alpha particle. Therefore, very few alpha particles have enough kinetic energy to overcome this repulsion. Refer to Chapter 4 for information on particle acceleration.

SECTION REVIEW

Total recall

1. What is the name given to a high-energy electron that is emitted from an unstable nucleus?

2. Write the nuclear equation that shows how electron capture by a nucleus changes a proton into a neutron.

3. How is critical mass related to a chain reaction?

4. What is transmutation?

5. What was the first artificial transmutation carried out by scientists?

6. Describe what happens when a positron and electron collide.

7. **a.** What is nuclear fission?
   b. How does it differ from nuclear fusion?

Critical thinking

8. Write the balanced equations for the following nuclear reactions:
   a. Uranium-233 undergoes alpha decay.
   b. Copper-66 undergoes beta decay.
   c. Beryllium-9 and an alpha particle combine to form carbon-13. The carbon-13 nucleus then emits a neutron.
   d. Uranium-238 absorbs a neutron. The product then undergoes successive beta emissions to become plutonium-239.

9. **Interpreting Graphics** Write a possible fission reaction for uranium-235 producing isotopes of Sr and Xe. The equation should show that two neutrons are emitted. Divide the remaining neutrons between Sr and Xe roughly in proportion to their atomic numbers.

10. A fusion reaction that takes place in the sun is the combination of two helium-3 nuclei to form two hydrogen atoms and one other atom. Write the balanced nuclear equation for this fusion reaction. Be sure to include both products that are formed.

11. What happens to a nucleus that is very large and has too few neutrons?

12. **Story Clue** Assume that some of the carbon atoms in the Iceman's body are $^{14}_{6}\text{C}$ atoms. What will happen to these atoms as time passes?

RADIOACTIVITY

Historical Perspective

In 1903, Marie Curie, her husband, Pierre, and Henri Becquerel were jointly awarded a Nobel Prize for their study of radioactivity. They had observed that compounds of the elements uranium and thorium gave off an unusual energy, causing the surrounding air to become slightly warmer. This energy also exposed photographic paper and killed small organisms in the vicinity. Marie Curie called these energy-producing elements *radioactive,* which describes a substance that has undergone nuclear decay and emits radiation.

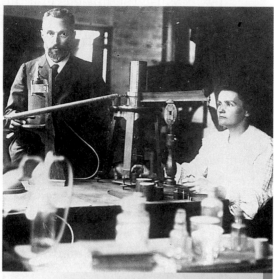

Marie Curie and her husband, Pierre

Unfortunately, the harmful effects of radiation were not realized until much later, after both Marie and Pierre suffered permanent physical damage as a result of their scientific research.

Radiology: A New Medical Field   World War I marked the first medical use of radiation. During that war, Marie Curie took charge of the Military Radiological Service, where she taught military doctors about *radiology,* the branch of medicine that uses ionizing radiation for diagnosis and treatment. During the war, X rays were used mostly to locate fractures and to detect the position of bullets. Early radiology relied heavily on the use of X rays.

Advances in Radiological Technology

CAT Scan   During a computerized axial tomography (CAT) scan, a computer monitors the body's reaction to X rays directed at the body from a number of different angles. The computer then assembles images of many different cross sections of the body. CAT scans enable doctors to see the features of organs with similar densities. It is especially helpful in the diagnosis of problems with the brain and spinal cord.

MRI and NMR   Magnetic resonance imaging (MRI) relies on the body's absorption of radio waves in a magnetic field. Nuclear magnetic resonance (NMR) is a process in which a computer depicts an image from inside the body by reading the body's absorption of radio waves. NMR aids doctors in the early detection of heart disease, multiple sclerosis, and cancer.

PET Scan Positron emission tomography (PET) scans detects gamma rays from positron-electron annihilation. For example, a patient is given glucose, some of whose molecules contain carbon-11, a positron emitter. A gamma-ray detector measures the gamma rays from various regions of the brain, determing the rate of glucose metabolism. Doctors have found this procedure helpful in diagnosing brain disorders. For example, schizophrenics metabolize much less glucose in the brain than normal.

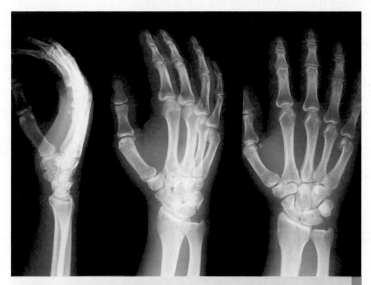

The bones in the right hand and wrist of this patient are visible in this Xray.

CAREER APPLICATION

What would it be like to . . .
- operate technologically advanced computer equipment?
- perform radiological procedures?
- help to diagnose patients?

Science/Math Career Preparation	
High School	**College**
Mathematics	Mathematics
Biology	Biology
Chemistry	Chemistry
Physics	Physics

Radiological Technician

An important career in the radiology industry is that of a radiological, or X-ray, technician. A radiological technician makes sure that patients are ready for the imaging process. Technicians administer substances, such as barium sulfate, that make internal body parts visible to X rays. They also provide patients with safety equipment to protect them from high doses of radiation, and they operate the radiological equipment. The equipment ranges from X-ray machines to computer-aided imaging equipment necessary for CAT scans or PET scans.

People who choose the career of a radiological technician generally study mathematics, biology, chemistry, and physics in high school. These courses prepare them for American Medical Association (AMA)–approved professional or academic programs that range in duration from 1 to 4 years. These programs are available at vocational schools, hospitals, colleges and universities, and in the armed forces. Radiological technicians must usually be licensed in the state where they work.

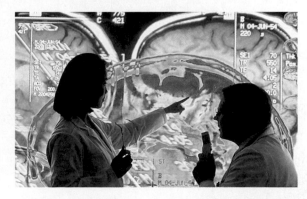

How is nuclear chemistry used?

OBJECTIVES

▶ **Define** the half-life of a radioactive nuclide.

▶ **Describe** how the half-life of a radioactive isotope is used to determine the age of an object.

▶ **Describe** how the process of neutron activation is used to analyze objects.

▶ **Identify** possible health hazards of radiation exposure.

Half-life

At the beginning of this chapter, you read that an archaeologist estimated the Iceman died about 4000 years ago. From the shape and composition of the Iceman's ax, the archaeologist reasoned that the Iceman lived during the early Bronze Age, which began around 2200 B.C. However, the ax blade was found to be made of pure copper and not bronze. This indicates that the Iceman must have been older, because the Age of Copper began around 4000 B.C. and lasted until the start of the Bronze Age. But rather than determining the Iceman's age solely on the basis of objects found with him, scientists also calculated his age by analyzing radioactive isotopes in his body.

half-life

the time required for half of a sample of radioactive atoms to decay

Radioactive isotopes decay at definite rates

The rate of nuclear decay is usually given in terms of the half-life. One **half-life** is the time that it takes for half a sample of a particular radioactive isotope to decay. This half-life is a constant value and is not influenced by any external conditions, such as temperature and pressure.

The use of radioactive isotopes to determine the age of an object is called *radioactive dating*. It is based on the fact that each radioactive nuclide has a characteristic half-life. Radioactive dating can be used to establish the age of ancient objects, as shown in **Figure 18-13.**

Although this rule does not always hold true, in general, the more unstable a nuclide is, the shorter its

▶ **FIGURE 18-13**

Using radioactive dating techniques, scientists determined this Incan vessel to be about 550 years old.

TABLE 18-2	Half-Lives of Some Radioactive Isotopes	
Isotope	**Half-life**	**Radiation emitted**
Carbon-14	5.715×10^3 years	β^-
Potassium-40	1.28×10^9 years	β^-, electron capture, γ
Radon-222	3.82 days	α, γ
Radium-226	1.60×10^3 years	α, γ
Thorium-230	7.54×10^4 years	α, γ
Thorium-234	24.10 days	β^-, γ
Uranium-235	7.04×10^8 years	α, γ
Uranium-238	4.47×10^9 years	α, γ
Plutonium-239	2.41×10^4 years	α, γ

half-life is and the faster it decays. Protium and deuterium are examples of unstable nuclei that have infinite half-lives. **Figure 18-14** shows another example of a radioactive isotope with a short half-life, iodine-131. **Table 18-2** lists the half-lives for a few radioactive isotopes. For example, the half-life of the radioactive isotope carbon-14 provides the key to the age of the Iceman. Nearly all of the carbon on Earth is present as the stable isotope carbon-12; less than one-millionth of one percent of the carbon in Earth's atmosphere is the radioactive isotope carbon-14. This minute amount of carbon-14 is continuously formed by cosmic rays in the Earth's atmosphere striking nitrogen-14 atoms. Because carbon-12 and carbon-14 have the same electron configuration, they react chemically in an identical fashion. Both of these carbon isotopes combine with oxygen to form carbon dioxide, which is taken in by plants and used in photosynthesis. Therefore, all plants on Earth contain carbon compounds with a small amount of carbon-14.

Photosynthetic organisms, such as plants, are the basis of Earth's food chain. As a result, all animals that eat plants contain the same

FIGURE 18-14 ▼

The radioactive isotope $^{131}_{53}I$ has a half-life of 8.07 days. In each successive 8.07-day period, half the atoms of $^{131}_{53}I$ in the original sample decay to $^{131}_{54}Xe$.

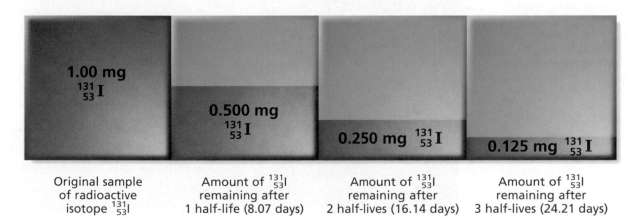

| Original sample of radioactive isotope $^{131}_{53}I$ | Amount of $^{131}_{53}I$ remaining after 1 half-life (8.07 days) | Amount of $^{131}_{53}I$ remaining after 2 half-lives (16.14 days) | Amount of $^{131}_{53}I$ remaining after 3 half-lives (24.21 days) |

1.00 mg $^{131}_{53}I$ — 0.500 mg $^{131}_{53}I$ — 0.250 mg $^{131}_{53}I$ — 0.125 mg $^{131}_{53}I$

ratio of carbon-14 to carbon-12 as the plants. Other animals eat those animals, and so on up the food chain, so all animals contain radioactive carbon-14. These atoms of carbon-14 undergo radioactive decay to become N-14, emitting beta particles in the process.

$$^{14}_{6}C \longrightarrow {}^{14}_{7}N + {}^{0}_{-1}e$$

Plants take in carbon dioxide throughout their lives. Therefore, they constantly replenish lost carbon-14. Animals also maintain a constant level of carbon-14. But when a plant or animal dies, it stops taking in fresh supplies of carbon-containing substances, so replenishment of carbon-14 stops. The half-life of carbon-14 is 5715 years. So from the time an organism dies, the amount of carbon-14 in its body decays by half every 5715 years. In other words, half of the carbon-14 atoms now present in a living plant or animal will have decayed 5715 years after its death. In another 5715 years, half of the remaining carbon-14 atoms will have decayed, leaving one-fourth of the original amount.

Once an archaeologist has measured the amounts of carbon-12 and carbon-14 in a fossil or other object, the ratio of carbon-14 to carbon-12 is compared with the ratio of these isotopes in a sample of similar material whose age is known. Using this technique of radioactive dating with carbon-14, scientists have concluded that the Iceman lived about 5000 years ago, between 3500 and 3000 B.C.

Radioactive dating is used to measure geologic time

Scientists' ability to date objects using carbon-14, as shown in Figure 18-15, is limited by two factors. The first limitation is that C-14 cannot be used to date objects composed of material that was never alive, such as clay or rocks. The second limitation is that after four half-lives, the amount of radioactive C-14 remaining in an object is too small to give

▶ **FIGURE 18-15**

Scientists determined the age of this cave painting, from the Cosquer cave, in France, to be approximately 16 500 years old. Carbon-14 was used to date the painting because organic materials were used in the paint.

Rate of Decay

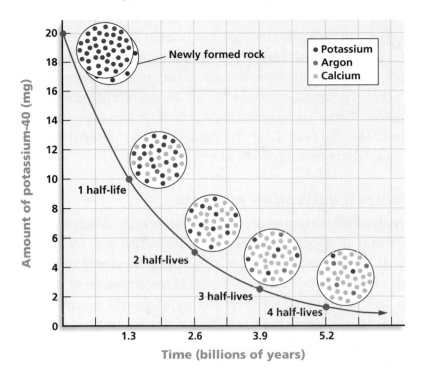

FIGURE 18-16 ◄

Potassium-40 decays to argon-40 and calcium-40, but scientists monitor only the ratio of potassium-40 to argon-40 to determine the age of the object.

reliable data. Consequently, C-14 is not useful for dating specimens that are more than about 25 000 years old. Anything older must be dated on the basis of a radioactive isotope that has a half-life longer than that of carbon-14.

Potassium-40, with a half-life of 1.28 billion years, represents only about 0.012% of the potassium present in the earth today. Potassium-40 is useful in dating ancient rocks and minerals. Potassium-40 produces two different isotopes in its radioactive decay. About 11% of the potassium-40 in a mineral decays to argon-40, which may remain in the sample. The remaining 89% of potassium-40 decays to calcium-40, which is not useful for radioactive dating because it cannot be distinguished from other calcium in the rock. The argon-40, however, can be measured. **Figure 18-16** shows the decay of potassium-40 through four half-lives. The amount of argon detected, relative to the potassium-40, shows the age of a mineral.

Other isotopes with even longer half-lives than potassium-40 have been used to determine the age of the Earth. By measuring these isotopes, scientists have estimated Earth to be an impressive 4.5 billion years old.

Smoke detectors contain sources of alpha particles

How does a smoke detector, like the one shown in **Figure 18-7,** work? Alpha particles travel only short

FIGURE 18-17 ▼

This smoke detector contains a minute amount of $^{241}_{95}Am$, an alpha emitter. These ionized alpha particles allow a steady current to flow between two electrodes. When smoke particles interrupt the current, an alarm sounds.

distances, even in gases. When alpha particles travel through a gas, they attract electrons from molecules of the gas, changing the gas molecules to ions. The ionized gas is then able to conduct an electrical current. This principle is the basis of smoke detectors, shown in Figure 18-17, which contain a small amount of an alpha emitter such as $^{241}_{95}Am$. When smoke particles mix with the gas, they reduce the current flow. In response, the circuits of the smoke detector set off an alarm.

Neutron activation analysis

Neutron activation analysis has been used to determine the composition of objects such as meteorites. Also, the identification of elements by neutron activation has been put to use in forensic science. It can be used to reveal the presence of certain elements and yield a rough analysis of an element's composition. Firing a gun leaves very small residues of antimony, barium, and copper on a person's hand. Neutron activation analysis can reveal the presence of these elements on residues taken from a suspect's hand.

Exposure to radiation must be monitored

The effects of nuclear radiation on the body are cumulative. Repeated exposure to small doses of radiation over a long period of time can be as dangerous as a single large dose if the total amount of radiation received is equal. People working with radioactivity, whether in medicine or industry, must therefore monitor the amount of radiation to which they are exposed. The woman in **Figure 18-18** is wearing a simple device to monitor her exposure to radiation—a film badge. Remember that Becquerel discovered radioactivity when it fogged his sealed photographic plates. This film badge works on exactly the same principle. Every week or so, the film from the badge is developed. Any darkening

▲ **FIGURE 18-18**

This worker wears a radiation detector to monitor the level of nuclear radiation to which she is exposed.

TABLE 18-3	Effect of Whole-Body Exposure to a Single Dose of Radiation
Dose (rems)	**Probable effect**
0–25	no observable effect
25–50	slight decrease in white blood cell count
50–100	marked decrease in white blood cell count
100–200	nausea, loss of hair
200–500	ulcers, internal bleeding
>500	death

of the film indicates that the badge wearer was exposed to radiation, and the degree of darkening indicates the total amount of exposure.

The biological effect of exposure to nuclear radiation is expressed in a unit known as a *rem*. **Table 18-3** on page 680, lists the effects of exposure to various doses of radiation. People who work with radioactive isotopes are advised to limit their exposure to 5 rems per year. This exposure is 1000 times higher than the recommended exposure level for most people, including you.

$\mathcal{S}$ECTION REVIEW

Total recall

1. What does neutron activation analysis reveal about a sample?
2. Identify three practical applications of nuclear chemistry.
3. What is a rem?
4. Identify the radioactive nuclide used to date ancient rocks and minerals.
5. What does PET stand for?
6. Why do workers exposed to radiation wear film badges?
7. What is meant by "the half-life of a radioactive nuclide"?

Critical thinking

8. Explain how carbon-14 is used to determine the age of an object.
9. Airline crews are exposed to between 0.5 and 0.7 rems of radiation per year, which is a higher exposure than most people receive. What do you think causes this higher exposure?
10. **Interpreting Tables** A practical rule is that a radioactive nuclide is essentially gone after 10 half-lives. What percentage of the original radioactive nuclide is left after 10 half-lives? How long will it take for 10 half-lives to pass for plutonium-239? Refer to Table 18-2 on page 677.
11. **Interpreting Tables** Give two reasons why uranium-235 is considered a greater health threat than radon-222. Refer to Table 18-2 on page 677.
12. Why would carbon-14 not be a good choice to use in smoke detectors?
13. No observable effects are noted in a person exposed to a single dose of 0–25 rems. So why are people who work with radioactive isotopes advised to limit their exposure to only 5 rems per year?
14. **Story Clue** If the Iceman's body has a carbon-14 to carbon-12 ratio of one-half times that found in a living organism, how old is the Iceman? How old would he be if the carbon-14 to carbon-12 ratio were one-quarter times that found in a living organism?
15. What fraction of an original sample of a radioactive isotope remains after three half-lives?
16. How many half-lives of radon-222 have passed in 11.46 days? If 5.2×10^{-8} g of radon-222 remain in a sealed box after 11.46 days, how much was present in the box initially? Refer to Table 18-2 on page 677.
17. Would an emitter of alpha particles be useful in measuring the thickness of a sheet of steel? Explain your answer.

You began your study of nuclear reactions by reading about the Iceman. Now that you have completed your study of nuclear chemistry, reconsider the questions that were asked at the beginning of the chapter.

LOOKING BACK

Exactly when did the Iceman die?

By radioactive dating with carbon-14 scientists have determined that the Iceman lived sometime between 3500 and 3000 B.C., during the Age of Copper. The Age of Copper lasted from about 4000 to 2200 B.C. It was the Iceman's ax blade of copper that helped scientists focus on that time period. The blade was originally thought to be bronze, which looks similar to copper. Analysis revealed its true chemical identity.

How did scientists determine what the Iceman looked like when he was alive?

To reconstruct the Iceman's face, scientists used nuclear imaging techniques on the Iceman's skull to generate three-dimensional computer images. Based on these images, and tables of anatomical data scientists built a three-dimensional model of the Iceman's skull. They then used clay to duplicate his muscles and soft polyurethane to reconstruct his skin. The completed model showed that the Iceman had distinctive features—a broad nose, a protruding lower lip, and a prominent chin.

How did the Iceman die?

Nuclear imaging techniques provided the key to answering this question. Scientists believe that the Iceman died from exhaustion, perhaps from being exposed too long to adverse weather conditions. In this state of exhaustion, the Iceman lay down on his left side in a small depression in the mountain, where he froze to death. His body was gradually covered with snow, which eventually turned into the hard ice coffin in which the Iceman lay buried for the next 5000 years.

A sculpted model of the Iceman's skull was reconstructed using measurements, three-dimensional computer images, x-rays, and CT scans.

Soft urethane was used to reconstruct the facial features of the Iceman.

KEY TERMS

18-1
band of stability
mass defect
nuclear binding energy
nucleon

nuclide
strong nuclear force
18-2
annihilation of matter
beta particle

chain reaction
critical mass
gamma ray
nuclear fission
nuclear fusion

radioactivity
transmutation
18-3

half-life

KEY CONCEPTS

18-1 Why are some atomic nuclei stable?

▶ The strong nuclear force overcomes the repulsive force between protons to keep a nucleus intact.

▶ The energy released when nucleons form a nucleus is known as the nuclear binding energy.

▶ The mass that is converted to energy when nucleons form a nucleus is known as the mass defect.

▶ If the mass defect is known, the nuclear binding energy can be calculated by using the equation $E = mc^2$.

▶ The ratio of neutrons to protons in stable nuclei defines a band of stability that includes the stable nuclei.

18-2 What kinds of nuclear change occur?

▶ Unstable nuclei are radioactive and can emit radiation in the form of alpha particles, beta particles, and gamma rays.

▶ Unstable nuclei with too many neutrons usually emit beta particles.

▶ Unstable nuclei with too few neutrons can undergo either electron capture or positron emission, emitting gamma rays in the process.

▶ Large nuclei with too few neutrons frequently emit alpha particles.

▶ Nuclear equations are balanced in terms of mass and charge.

▶ In nuclear fission, a heavy nucleus splits into two smaller nuclei; in nuclear fusion, two smaller nuclei combine to form one larger nucleus.

▶ Nuclear fission reactions that cause other fissions are chain reactions. Sustained chain reactions must be controlled to avoid a nuclear explosion.

▶ Nuclear reactions result in a transmutation.

18-3 How is nuclear chemistry used?

▶ Half-life is the time required for one half of the mass of a radioactive isotope to decay.

▶ The half-life of the carbon-14 isotope can be used to date organic material that is up to 20 000 years old. Other radioactive isotopes are used to date older rock and mineral formations.

▶ Radioactive isotopes have a number of practical applications in industry, medicine, and chemical analysis.

▶ The biological effects of radiation are measured in units called rems.

KEY SKILLS

Before your exam be sure you understand the concept of a half-life. Also be sure you understand the rules for predicting nuclear stability and for balancing nuclear equations.

REVIEW & ASSESS

TERM REVIEW

1. The energy emitted when a nucleus forms is known as the ———.
(strong nuclear force, nuclear binding energy)

2. A ——— can be either a proton or a neutron.
(beta particle, nucleon, gamma ray)

3. The high-energy electromagnetic radiation produced by decaying nuclei is known as a(n) ———.
(gamma ray, alpha particle)

4. When two smaller nuclei have combined, ——— has occurred.
(nuclear fission, nuclear fusion)

5. The creation of a new nuclei as a result of bombarding the nucleus with other nuclei is called a ———.
(chain reaction, transmutation)

6. When an unstable nucleus decays, emitting particles and energy, the process is called ———.

(annihilation of matter, radioactivity)

7. ——— is the smallest mass of radioactive material needed to sustain a chain reaction.
(mass defect, critical mass)

8. The time required for 50% of a sample of a radioactive isotope to decay is known as its ———.

(half-life, radioactivity)

CONCEPT & SKILLS REVIEW

NUCLEAR STABILITY

1. Explain how the strong nuclear force holds a nucleus together despite the repulsive forces between protons.

2. Describe what happens to unstable nuclei.

3. a. What is the relationship among number of protons, number of neutrons, and the stability of the nucleus for small atoms?
b. What is the relationship among number of protons, number of neutrons, and the stability of the nucleus for large atoms?

4. What is the relationship between binding energy and the formation of a nucleus from protons and neutrons?

5. What is the relationship between mass defect and binding energy?

6. Why is nuclear stability better indicated by binding energy per nucleon than by total binding energy per nucleus?

7. Medium-mass nuclei have larger binding energies per nucleon than heavier nuclei. What can you conclude from this fact?

NUCLEAR CHANGES

8. What is the relationship between an alpha particle and a helium nucleus?

9. The decay of uranium-238 results in the spontaneous ejection of an alpha particle. Write the nuclear equation that describes this process.

10. Compare the penetrating powers of alpha particles, beta particles, and gamma rays.

11. What type of radiation is emitted in the decay described by the following equation?

$$^{43}_{19}\text{K} \longrightarrow {}^{43}_{20}\text{Ca} + \text{?}$$

12. Is the decay of an unstable isotope into a stable isotope always a one-step process? Explain.

13. How does artificial transmutation differ from natural radioactive decay?

14. a. What role does the neutron serve in starting a nuclear chain reaction and in keeping it going?

b. Why must neutrons in a chain reaction be controlled?

c. Why must there be a minimum mass of material in order to sustain a chain reaction?

15. a. Describe the similarities and differences between fusion and fission.

b. Under what conditions does fusion occur?

16. What difficulties must be overcome before fusion can be used as a practical source of energy?

17. The plutonium isotope $^{239}_{94}Pu$ is sometimes detected in nuclear reactors. Consider that nuclear fuel contains a large portion of the common uranium isotope $^{238}_{92}U$ in addition to fissionable $^{235}_{92}U$. Describe a process by which $^{239}_{94}Pu$ might form in a nuclear reactor.

18. What is the difference between a moderator and a control rod in a nuclear reactor?

19. Why are elevated temperatures necessary to initiate fusion reactions but not fission reactions?

20. Why do lighter elements undergo fusion more readily than heavier elements?

21. The release of radioactive strontium into the atmosphere was once a major concern, especially for infants whose main food source was milk. Why were scientists concerned about radioactive strontium? **(Hint: Check a periodic table for the members of the group that include strontium.)**

22. Plutonium is one of the most toxic substances known to humans. Once inside the body, plutonium ions are easily oxidized to form Pu^{4+} ions. These Pu^{4+} ions behave chemically much like Fe^{3+} ions. What effect would these Pu^{4+} ions have on the body? **(Hint: What role does Fe play in the body?)**

23. Concerns have recently been raised about the levels of radon gas in homes. Although radon is a noble gas and is therefore chemically inert, it is unstable and radioactive. When a radon-222 nucleus decays, an alpha particle is emitted. Write the nuclear equation to show what happens when a radon-222 nucleus decays. What is the other product that forms?

24. Why do positron emission and electron capture have the same effect on a nucleus?

USING NUCLEAR REACTIONS

25. The radiation given off by iodine-131 in the form of beta particles is used to treat cancer of the thyroid gland. Write the nuclear equation to show what happens when an iodine-131 nucleus decays.

26. Why is the constant rate of decay of radioactive nuclei so important in radioactive dating?

27. The Environmental Protection Agency has been concerned about the levels of radon gas in homes. The half-life of one radon isotope is 3.8 days. If a sample of gas taken from a basement contains 4.38 µg of radon-222, how much radon will remain in the sample after 15.2 days?

28. A pathologist working in a police laboratory wants to analyze a small sample of blood from a crime scene. He cannot damage the blood sample because it will be used in court as evidence. What kind of radioactive analysis should he use? Why?

29. Many cancer patients lose their hair during radiation therapy. How is this hair loss related to rem exposure?

30. Describe a situation outside of chemistry that illustrates the concept of half-life.

31. Why would someone working around radioactive waste in a landfill use a radiation monitor instead of a watch to determine when the workday is over? At what point would that person decide to stop working?

32. Radioactive isotopes are often used as "tracers" to follow the path of an element through a chemical reaction. For example, the oxygen atoms in O_2 produced by a plant during photosynthesis come from the oxygen in H_2O and not the oxygen in carbon dioxide, CO_2. Explain how you could use a radioactive isotope of oxygen to identify the source of the oxygen atoms in the O_2 produced during photosynthesis.

33. Phosphorus-32 is used to treat a certain form of leukemia. Starting with 10.0 mg of phosphorus-32, how many milligrams would be left after 57 days? The half-life of phosphorus-32 is 14.3 days.

34. Copper-64 is used to study brain tumors. Assume that the original mass of a sample of copper-64 is 26.00 g. After 64 hours, all that remains is 0.8125 g of copper-64. What is the half-life of this radioactive isotope?

LINKING CHAPTERS

1. Structure of the nucleus
Compare the behavior of nucleons in a nuclear reaction with the behavior of nucleons in a chemical reaction.

2. Theme: Classification and trends
Explain the relationship among atomic number, size of the nucleus, and stability.

3. Density
Calculate the density in g/cm^3 of uranium-235 if 8.0 m^3 has a mass of 1.5×10^5 kg.

4. Writing equations
One radioactive decay series that begins with uranium-235 and ends with lead-207 shows the following sequence of emissions: alpha, beta, alpha, beta, alpha, alpha, alpha, alpha, beta, beta, and alpha. Write an equation for each reaction in the series.

ALTERNATIVE ASSESSMENTS

Performance assessment

1. Your teacher will give you an index card listing the name of a radioactive isotope. Predict what type of emission this isotope will give off when it decays. Write a balanced nuclear equation that shows the decay process.

2. Design an experiment that uses 128 pennies to illustrate the concept of half-life.

Portfolio projects

1. Chemistry and you
Your local grocery store may sell perishable foods that have been irradiated. Find out what stores in your area sell irradiated foods, and determine the shelf life of these foods. What are the shelf lives of the same foods without irradiation? Do research to identify foods that are routinely irradiated even though their label may not indicate. Report your findings to the class.

2. Research and communication

a. Research some important historical findings that have been validated through radioactive dating. Report your findings to the class.

b. You have made an important archaeological or geological find. Describe how you will determine which method of radioactive dating to use.

3.

	TOPIC: Radiation effects on humans
SC*L*INKS. NSTA	GO TO: www.scilinks.org
	KEYWORD: HW185

Research and communication
Compare the physiological effects on humans of the different kinds of radiation. Find out if any adults you know are exposed to radiation at work. Ask about the kind of radiation involved and what precautions they take to avoid the harmful effects of radiation. Report your findings to the class.

4.

	TOPIC: Nuclear power
SC*L*INKS. NSTA	GO TO: www.scilinks.org
	KEYWORD: HW186

Research and communication
Find out about the use of nuclear power in this country. How many plants are currently supplying power? How many are in the construction stage? How does the use of nuclear power in the United States compare with that in Europe?

1. Atoms with the same mass number but different atomic numbers are known as ———.

   a. isotopes   c. nucleons
   b. alpha particles   d. isobars

2. When protons and neutrons form a nucleus,
   a. some mass is gained.
   b. energy is absorbed.
   c. some mass is converted to energy.
   d. electrons are captured by the nucleus that forms.

3. Which of the following combinations of proton number and neutron number yields a nucleus that is least stable?
   a. even/even   c. odd/even
   b. even/odd   d. odd/odd

4. When smaller nuclei contain too few neutrons, they ———.
   a. tend to emit beta particles
   b. emit positrons or capture electrons
   c. undergo a chain reaction
   d. cannot undergo a transmutation

5. Which of the following nuclear equations is correctly balanced?
   a. $^{37}_{18}\text{Ar} + ^{0}_{-1}e \longrightarrow ^{37}_{17}\text{Cl}$
   b. $^{6}_{3}\text{Li} + 2^{1}_{0}n \longrightarrow ^{4}_{2}\text{He} + ^{3}_{1}\text{H}$
   c. $^{254}_{99}\text{Es} + ^{4}_{2}\text{He} \longrightarrow ^{258}_{101}\text{Md} + 2^{1}_{0}n$
   d. $^{14}_{7}\text{N} + ^{4}_{2}\text{He} \longrightarrow ^{17}_{8}\text{O} + ^{2}_{1}\text{H}$

6. Gamma rays ———.
   a. have the same energy as beta particles
   b. are not produced during a transmutation
   c. have no charge and no mass
   d. are not a form of electromagnetic radiation

7. Combining a nucleus of curium-246 with a nucleus of carbon-12 will produce a nucleus of ———.
   a. einsteinium-254
   b. nobelium-258
   c. fermium-254
   d. mendelevium-256

8. The half-life of thorium-234 is 24 days. If you start with a 42.0 g sample of thorium-24, how much will remain after 72 days?
   a. 42.0 g   c. 10.5 g
   b. 21.0 g   d. 5.25 g

9. Alpha particles can safely be used in smoke detectors because they ———.
   a. are not a form of radiation
   b. cannot even penetrate paper
   c. are harmless even if swallowed
   d. combine with beta particles to produce a neutron

10. Every radioactive isotope ———.
   a. emits an alpha particle
   b. has a characteristic half-life
   c. exists as an isobar
   d. has an atomic number greater than 92

LABORATORY PROGRAM

EXPLORATION
TECHNIQUE BUILDER

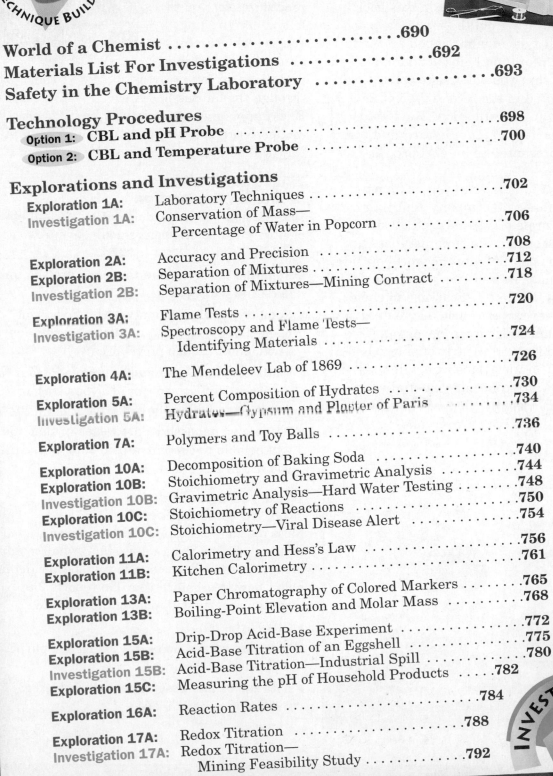

INVESTIGATION

PROBLEM SOLVING

Meeting today's challenges

Even though you have already taken science classes with lab work, you will find the two types of laboratory experiments in this book organized differently from those you have done before. The first type of lab is called an Exploration. Each *Exploration* helps you gain skills in lab techniques that you will use to solve a real problem presented in the second type of lab, which is called an Investigation. The *Exploration* serves as a *Technique Builder,* and the *Investigation* is presented as an exercise in *Problem Solving.*

Both types of labs refer to you as an employee of a professional company, and your teacher has the role of supervisor. Lab situations are given for real-life circumstances to show how chemistry fits into the world outside of the classroom. This will give you valuable practice with skills that you can use in chemistry and in other careers, such as creating a plan with available resources, developing and following a budget, and writing business letters.

As you work in these labs, you will better understand how the concepts you studied in the chapters are used by chemists to solve problems that affect life for everyone.

Explorations

The Explorations provide step-by-step procedures for you to follow, encouraging you to make careful observations and interpretations as you progress through the lab session. Each Exploration gives you an opportunity to practice and perfect a specific lab technique or concept that will be needed later in an Investigation.

What you should do before an Exploration

Preparation will help you work safely and efficiently. The evening before a lab, be sure to do the following:

▶ **Read the lab procedure** to make sure you understand what you will do.

▶ **Read the safety information** that begins on page 693, as well as any safety information provided in the lab procedure itself.

▶ **Write down any questions** you have in your lab notebook so that you can ask your teacher about them before the lab begins.

▶ **Prepare all necessary data tables** so that you will be able to concentrate on your work when you are in the lab.

What you should do after an Exploration

Most teachers require a lab report as a way of making sure that you understand what you are doing. Your teacher will give you specific details about how to organize your lab reports, but most lab reports will include the following:

▶ **title** of the lab

▶ **summary paragraph(s)** describing the purpose and procedure

▶ **data tables and observations** that are organized and comprehensive

- ▶ **worked-out calculations** with proper units
- ▶ **answers that are,** boxed, circled, or highlighted for items in the *Analysis and Interpretation, Conclusions,* and *Extensions* sections

Investigations

The Investigations differ from Explorations because they do not provide step-by-step instructions. In each Investigation, you are required to develop your own procedure to solve a problem presented to your company by a client. You must decide how much money to spend on the project and what equipment to use. Although this may seem difficult, the Investigations contain a number of clues about how to successfully solve the problem.

What you should do before an Investigation

Before you will be allowed to work on the lab, you must turn in a preliminary report. Usually, you must describe in detail the procedure you plan to use, provide complete data tables for the data and observations you will collect, and list exactly what equipment you will need and the costs. Only after your teacher, acting as your supervisor, approves your plans are you allowed to proceed. Before you begin writing a preliminary report, follow these steps.

- ▶ **Read the Investigation thoroughly,** and search for clues.
- ▶ **Jot down notes** in your lab notebook as you find clues.
- ▶ **Consider what you must measure** or observe to solve the problem.

- ▶ **Think about Explorations** you have done that used a similar technique or reaction.
- ▶ **Imagine working through a procedure,** keeping track of each step, and determining what equipment you need.
- ▶ **Carefully consider** whether your approach is the best, most efficient one.

What you should do after an Investigation

After you finish, organize a report of your data as described in the Memorandum. This is usually in the form of a one- or two-page letter to the client. Your teacher may have additional requirements for your report. Carefully consider how to convey the information the client needs to know. In some cases, a graph or diagram can communicate information better than words can. As a part of your report, you must include an invoice for the client that explains how much the client owes and how much you charged for each part of the procedure. Remember to include the cost of your work in the analysis.

If you need help with graphing or with using significant figures, ask your teacher.

Materials list for Investigations

Refer to the Equipment and Chemical lists below when planning your procedure for the Investigation labs. Include in your budget only the items you will need to solve the problem presented to your company by the client. Remember, you must always include the cost of lab space and the standard disposal fee in your budget.

Equipment	Cost per item/unit
Aluminum foil	$1000/cm^2$
Balance	5000
Beaker, 250 mL	1000
Beaker, 400 mL	2000
Beaker tongs	1000
Büchner funnel	2000
Bunsen burner/related equipment	10 000
Buret	5000
Cobalt glass plate	2000
Crucible and cover	5000
Crucible tongs	2000
Desiccator	3000
Drying oven	5000
Erlenmeyer flask, 250 mL	1000
Evaporating dish	1000
Filter flask with sink attachment	2000
Filter paper	500/piece
Flame-test wire	2000
Glass funnel	1000
Glass plate	1000
Glass stirring rod	1000
Graduated cylinder, 100 mL	1000
Hot plate	8000
Index card (3 × 5 in.)	1000
Lab space/fume hood/utilities	15 000/day
Litmus paper	1000/piece
Magnetic stirrer	5000
Mortar and pestle	2000
Paper clips	500/box
pH meter	3000
pH paper	2000/piece
pH probe	5000
Plastic bags	500/each
Ring stand/ring/wire gauze or pipe-stem triangle	2000

Equipment	Cost per item/unit
Ring stand with buret clamp	2000
Rubber policeman	500
Spatula	500
Spectroscope	15 000
Standard disposal fee	2000/g of product
Stopwatch	5000
6 test tubes/holder/rack	2000
Thermistor probe	2000
Thermometer	2000
Wash bottle	500
Watch glass	1000
Weighing paper	500/piece

FINES

OSHA safety violation	2000/incident

REAGENTS and ADDITIONAL MATERIALS

Chemical	Cost per item/unit
0.02 M $KMnO_4$	1000/mL
1.0 M H_2SO_4	1000/mL
0.5 M HCl for titration	500/mL
0.5 M NaOH for titration	500/mL
0.5 M Na_2CO_3 solution	1000/mL
1.0 M $CuCl_2$	1000/mL
1 M HCl	500/mL
Gypsum sample	500/g
Ice	500
$MgCl_2$	500/g
Mossy zinc, Zn	500/g
NaCl	500/g
Phenolphthalein	2000
Plaster of Paris sample	500/g
Rock salt	2000
$Zn(NO_3)_2$	500/g

No refunds on returned chemicals or unused equipment.

SAFETY IN THE CHEMISTRY LABORATORY

Any chemical can be dangerous if it is misused. Always follow the instructions for the experiment. Pay close attention to the safety notes. Do not do anything differently unless you are instructed to do so by your teacher.

Chemicals, even water, can cause harm. The challenge is to know how to use chemicals correctly. If you follow the rules stated below, pay attention to your teacher's directions, and follow the precautions on chemical labels and in the experiments, then you will be using chemicals correctly.

◆ THESE SAFETY RULES ALWAYS APPLY IN THE LAB

1. Always wear a lab apron and safety goggles.
Laboratories contain chemicals that can damage your clothing even if you aren't working on an experiment at the time. Keep the apron strings tied.

Some chemicals can cause eye damage and even blindness. If your safety goggles are uncomfortable or if they cloud up, ask your teacher for help. Try lengthening the strap, washing the goggles with soap and warm water, or using an anti-fog spray.

2. Do not wear contact lenses in the lab.
Even if you wear safety goggles, chemicals can get between contact lenses and your eyes and cause irreparable eye damage. If your doctor requires you to wear contact lenses instead of glasses, then you should wear eye-cup safety goggles in the lab. Ask your doctor or your teacher how to use this very important and special eye protection.

3. NEVER WORK ALONE IN THE LABORATORY.
Do lab work only under the supervision of your teacher.

4. Wear the right clothing for lab work.
Necklaces, neckties, dangling jewelry, long hair, and loose clothing can knock things over or catch on fire. Tuck in neckties, or take them off. Do not wear a necklace or other dangling jewelry, including hanging earrings. It also might be a good idea to remove your wristwatch so that it is not damaged by a chemical splash.

Pull back long hair, and tie it in place. Wear cotton clothing if you can. Nylon and polyester fabrics burn and melt more readily than cotton does. It's best to wear fitted garments, but if your clothing is loose or baggy, tuck it in or tie it back so that it does not get in the way or catch on fire. It is also important to wear pants, not shorts or skirts.

Wear shoes that will protect your feet from chemical spills. Do not wear open-toed shoes or sandals or shoes with woven leather straps. Shoes made of solid leather or polymer are preferred over shoes made of cloth.

5. Only books and notebooks needed for the experiment should be in the lab.
Do not bring textbooks, purses, bookbags, backpacks, or other items into the lab; keep these things in your desk or locker.

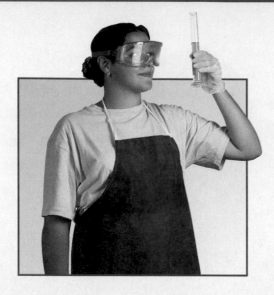

6. Read the entire experiment before entering the lab.

Memorize the safety precautions. Be familiar with the instructions for the experiment. Only materials and equipment authorized by your teacher should be used. When you do your lab work, follow the instructions and safety precautions described in the experiment.

7. Read chemical labels.

Follow the instructions and safety precautions stated on the labels.

8. Walk with care in the lab.

Sometimes you will have to carry chemicals from the supply station to your lab station. Avoid bumping into other students and spilling the chemicals. Stay at your lab station at other times.

9. Food, beverages, chewing gum, cosmetics, and smoking are NEVER allowed in the lab.

(You should already know this.)

10. NEVER taste chemicals or touch them with your bare hands.

Keep your hands away from your face and mouth while working, even if you are wearing gloves.

11. Use a sparker to light a Bunsen burner.

Do not use matches. Be sure that all gas valves are turned off and that all hot plates are turned off and unplugged when you leave the lab.

12. Be careful with hot plates, Bunsen burners, and other heat sources.

Keep your body and clothing away from flames. Do not touch a hot plate after it has just been turned off because it is probably still hot. The same is true of glassware, crucibles, and other things that have been removed from the flame of a Bunsen burner or from a drying oven.

13. Do not use electrical equipment with frayed or twisted wires.

14. Be sure your hands are dry before you use electrical equipment.

Before plugging an electrical cord into a socket, be sure the equipment is turned off. When you are finished with the equipment, turn it off. Before you leave the lab, unplug the equipment, but be sure to turn it off FIRST.

15. Do not let electrical cords dangle from work stations.

Dangling cords can cause tripping or electrical shocks. The area under and around electrical equipment should be dry, and cords should not lie in puddles of spilled liquid.

16. Know fire-drill procedures and the locations of exits.

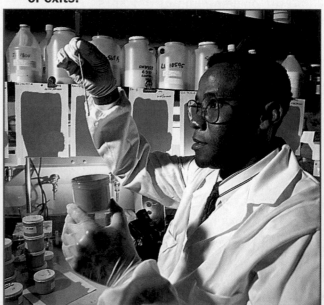

17. **Know the location and operation of safety showers and eyewash stations.**

18. **If your clothes catch on fire, walk to the safety shower, stand under it, and turn it on.**

19. **If you get a chemical in your eyes, walk immediately to the eyewash station, turn it on, and lower your head so that your eyes are in the running water.**

    Hold your eyelids open with your thumbs and fingers, and roll your eyeballs around. Flush your eyes continuously for at least 15 minutes. Call out to your teacher as you do this.

20. **If you spill anything on the floor or lab bench, call your teacher rather than trying to clean it up by yourself.**

    Your teacher will tell you if it is OK for you to do the cleanup; if not, your teacher will know how the spill should be cleaned up safely.

21. **If you spill a chemical on your skin, wash the chemical off at the sink and call your teacher.**

    If you spill a solid chemical on your clothing, brush it off carefully without scattering it onto somebody else, and call your teacher. If you get liquid on your clothing, wash it off right away using the faucet at the sink, and call your teacher. If the spill is on your pants or somewhere else that will not fit under the sink faucet, use the safety shower. Remove the pants or other affected clothing while you are under the shower, and call your teacher. (It may be temporarily embarrassing to remove pants or other clothing in front of your class, but failing to flush that chemical off your skin could cause permanent damage.)

22. **The best way to prevent an accident is to stop it before it happens.**

    If you have a close call, tell your teacher so that you and your teacher can find a way to prevent it from happening again. Otherwise, the next time, it could be a harmful accident instead of just a close call. If you get a head-

ache, feel sick to your stomach, or feel dizzy, tell your teacher immediately.

23. **All accidents, no matter how minor, should be reported to your teacher.**

24. **For all chemicals, take only what you need.**

    If you take too much and have some left over, DO NOT put it back in the bottle. If a chemical is accidently put into the wrong bottle, the next person to use it will have a contaminated sample. Ask your teacher what to do with leftover chemicals.

25. **NEVER take any chemicals out of the lab.**

26. **Horseplay and fooling around in the lab are very dangerous.**

    NEVER be a clown in the laboratory.

27. **Keep your work area clean and tidy.**

    After your work is done, clean your work area and all equipment.

28. **Always wash your hands with soap and water before you leave the lab.**

29. **All of these rules apply all of the time you are in the lab.**

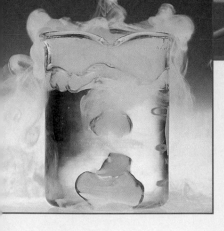

SAFETY SYMBOLS

To highlight specific types of precautions, the following symbols are used throughout the lab program. Remember that no matter what safety symbols you see in the lab instructions, all 29 of the safety rules previously described should be followed at all times.

CLOTHING PROTECTION

▶ Wear laboratory aprons in the laboratory. Keep the apron strings tied so that they do not dangle.

EYE SAFETY

▶ Wear safety goggles in the laboratory at all times. Know how to use the eyewash station.

CLEAN UP

▶ Keep your hands away from your face and mouth.

▶ Always wash your hands before leaving the laboratory.

CHEMICAL SAFETY

▶ Never taste, eat, or swallow any chemicals in the laboratory. Do not eat or drink any food from laboratory containers. Beakers are not cups, and evaporating dishes are not bowls.

▶ Never return unused chemicals to their original containers.

▶ It helps to label the beakers and test tubes containing chemicals. (This is not a new rule, just a good idea.)

▶ Never transfer substances by sucking on a pipet or straw; use a suction bulb.

WASTE DISPOSAL

▶ Some chemicals are harmful to our environment. You can help protect the environment by following the instructions for proper disposal.

GLASSWARE SAFETY

▶ Never place glassware, containers of chemicals, or anything else near the edges of a lab bench or table.

HAND SAFETY

▶ If a chemical gets on your skin or clothing or in your eyes, rinse it immediately, and alert your teacher.

CAUSTIC SAFETY

▶ If a chemical is spilled on the floor or lab bench, tell your teacher, but do not clean it up yourself unless your teacher says it is OK to do so.

HEATING SAFETY

▶ When heating a chemical in a test tube, always point the open end of the test tube away from yourself and other people.

Refer to the list of rules on pages 693–695, and identify whether a specific rule applies or whether the rule presented is a new rule.

1. Tie back long hair, and confine loose clothing.
(Rule ? applies.)

2. Never reach across an open flame.
(Rule ? applies.)

3. Use proper procedures when lighting Bunsen burners. Turn off hot plates, Bunsen burners, and other heat sources when they are not in use.
(Rule ? applies.)

4. Heat flasks or beakers on a ring stand with wire gauze between the glass and the flame.
(Rule ? applies.)

5. Use tongs when heating containers. Never hold or touch containers while heating them. Always allow heated materials to cool before handling them.
(Rule ? applies.)

6. Turn off gas valves when they are not in use.
(Rule ? applies.)

7. Use flammable liquids only in small amounts.
(Rule ? applies.)

8. When working with flammable liquids, be sure that no one else is using a lit Bunsen burner or plans to use one.
(Rule ? applies.)

9. What additional rules apply to every lab?
(Rule ? applies.)

10. Check the condition of glassware before and after using it. Inform your teacher of any broken, chipped, or cracked glassware because it should not be used.
(Rule ? applies.)

11. Do not pick up broken glass with your bare hands. Place broken glass in a specially designated disposal container.
(Rule ? applies.)

12. Never force glass tubing into rubber tubing, rubber stoppers, or wooden corks. To protect your hands, wear heavy cloth gloves or wrap toweling around the glass and the tubing, stopper, or cork, and gently push in the glass.
(Rule ? applies.)

13. Do not inhale fumes directly. When instructed to smell a substance, use your hand to wave the fumes toward your nose, and inhale gently.
(Rule ? applies.)

14. Keep your hands away from your face and mouth.
(Rule ? applies.)

15. Always wash your hands before leaving the laboratory.

Finally, if you are wondering how to answer the question that asks what additional rules apply to every lab, here is the correct answer.

Any time you see any of the safety symbols, you should remember that all 29 of the numbered laboratory rules always apply.

CBL and pH Probe Setup

MATERIALS

▶ **CBL**

▶ **graphing calculator with link cable**

▶ **Vernier pH amplifier and pH electrode**

▶ **Vernier adapter cable**

SETUP

1. Connect the CBL to the graphing calculator. Use the unit-to-unit link cable and the input/output ports located at the base of each unit.

2. Plug the pH amplifier into the Vernier adapter cable. The adapter cable should be connected to CH1 of the CBL system. *(Note: the pH electrode should be connected to the pH amplifier.)*

3. Firmly press in all cable ends.

4. Turn on the CBL unit and the graphing calculator.

5. **To start the CHEMBIO program:**

   ▶ Press the PRGM key on the graphing calculator.

   ▶ Select the CHEMBIO option from the list.

   ▶ Press ENTER after PrgmCHEMBIO appears on the screen.

   ▶ When the Vernier Software introduction screen appears, press enter to continue.

6. **To set up the graphing calculator and CBL unit for pH measurement:**

   ▶ Select the SET UP PROBES option from the MAIN MENU.

   ▶ Enter the number of probes.

   ▶ Select the pH option from the SELECT PROBES menu.

   ▶ Enter the channel number.

   ▶ Select the USE STORED option from the CALIBRATION menu.

7. **To set up the graphing calculator and CBL unit for data collection:**

   ▶ Select the COLLECT DATA option from the MAIN MENU.

   ▶ Select the MONITOR INPUT option from the DATA COLLECTION menu.

8. Allow the system to warm up for 30 seconds before continuing. Refer to the Exploration for lab setup. When you are ready to measure the pH, press ENTER on the graphing calculator. The pH reading is displayed on the screens of the CBL unit and the graphing calculator.

(Note: No readings are stored when the INPUT mode is in use.)

9. When you are finished with the lab, rinse the pH probe with distilled water. Press the + key on the graphing calculator to quit MONITOR INPUT.

10. If you are setting up the CBL unit and graphing-calculator system to take pH readings over a specific interval of time, replace steps 5–6 with steps 11–12.

11. To set up the calculator and CBL unit for timed data collection:

▶ Select COLLECT DATA from the MAIN MENU.

▶ Select TIME GRAPH from the DATA COLLECTION menu. Follow the directions on the calculator screen to allow the system to warm up, then press enter.

▶ Enter the time interval between samples in seconds.

▶ Enter the number of samples and press ENTER.

▶ Select USE TIME SETUP to continue. If you want to change the sample time or sample number, select MODIFY SETUP.

▶ Enter the minimum pH on the (Y min) line.

▶ Enter the maximum pH on the (Y max) line.

▶ Enter the number of pH increments on the (Y scl) line.

12. Refer to the Exploration for lab setup. When you are ready to begin monitoring data, press ENTER on the graphing calculator. After data collection stops, press ENTER to display a graph of pH-versus-time. Examine the data points along the curve. As you move the cursor to the right or left, the time (X) and pH (Y) values of each data point are displayed below the graph. Determine the initial pH and final pH, and record these values in your data table.

13. To print a copy of the graph use the TI-Graph Link cable and program to transfer the graph of pH-versus-time from the graphing calculator to a Macintosh or IBM-compatible computer.

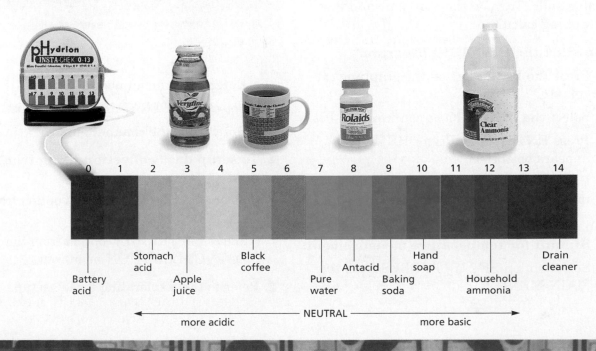

| 0 | 1 | 2 | 3 | 4 | 5 | 6 | 7 | 8 | 9 | 10 | 11 | 12 | 13 | 14 |

Battery acid
Stomach acid
Apple juice
Black coffee
Pure water
Antacid
Baking soda
Hand soap
Household ammonia
Drain cleaner

← more acidic — NEUTRAL — more basic →

CBL and Temperature Probe Setup

MATERIALS

▶ **CBL**

▶ **graphing calculator with link cable**

▶ **temperature probe**

SETUP

1. Connect the CBL to the graphing calculator. Use the unit-to-unit link cable and the input/output ports located at the base of each unit.

2. Connect the temperature probe to the CH1 port of the CBL system. Firmly press in all cable ends. Turn on the CBL unit and the graphing calculator.

3. To start the CHEMBIO program:

▶ Press the PRGM key on the graphing calculator.

▶ Select the CHEMBIO option from the list.

▶ Press ENTER after PrgmCHEMBIO appears on the screen.

▶ Press ENTER after the Vernier Software introduction screen appears.

4. To set up the graphing calculator and CBL unit for temperature measurement:

▶ Select option SET UP PROBES from the MAIN MENU.

Trigger Mode

The Trigger mode on the graphing calculator and CBL unit may be used in laboratory exercises that require recording measurements until a constant temperature is reached or that require recording untimed temperature measurements. A stopwatch will be necessary to record the time interval in lab exercises using this method.

▶ Enter 1 for the number of probes.

▶ Select TEMPERATURE from the list.

▶ Enter 1 for the channel number.

1. To setup data collection using trigger mode:

▶ Select the COLLECT DATA option from the MAIN MENU.

▶ Select the TRIGGER option from the DATA COLLECTION menu.

2. Refer to the Exploration for lab setup.

3. **To collect a temperature reading:**

 ▶ Press TRIGGER on the CBL.

 ▶ Select the MORE DATA option from the TRIGGER menu to take another temperature reading.

4. When constant temperature is reached or you are through recording, select STOP from the TRIGGER menu. Press ENTER to continue. *(Note: make sure to record all temperature readings in your data table.)*

Timed Graph Mode

1. **To setup data collection using the timed graph mode:**

 ▶ Select the COLLECT DATA option from the MAIN MENU.

 ▶ Select the option TIME GRAPH from the DATA COLLECTION menu.

 ▶ Enter the time interval between each temperature reading. If this number is not outlined in the Exploration, ask your teacher what time interval is appropriate for the lab.

 ▶ Enter the number of samples the CBL should record. (If this number is not given, it can be calculated by multiplying the total time in minutes by 60 seconds, then dividing by the time interval). Press ENTER.

 ▶ Select the USE TIME SETUP to continue.

 ▶ Enter the minimum temperature on the (Y min) line. If the value is a negative number, remember to use the (−), and not the − option.

 ▶ Enter the maximum temperature on the (Y max) line. Enter the temperature increment on the (Y scl) line.

2. The CBL and graphing calculator are now set up for data collection. Refer to the Exploration before you begin collecting data.

3. Press ENTER on the graphing calculator when you are ready to begin temperature readings.

4. **To view a graph of temperature versus time:**

 ▶ Select the COLLECT DATA option from the MAIN MENU.

 ▶ Select the option TIME GRAPH from the DATA COLLECTION menu.

 ▶ Enter the time interval between each temperature reading.

 ▶ Enter the number of samples taken. Press ENTER to continue.

 ▶ Select the USE TIME SETUP option to continue.

 ▶ Enter the minimum temperature on the (Y min) line. If the value is a negative number, remember to use the (−), and not the − option.

 ▶ Enter the maximum temperature on the (Y max) line. Enter the temperature increment on the (Y scl) line.

 ▶ Press ENTER. The calculator should plot your data. Press ENTER again to see the line graph. Use the arrow keys to trace the graph. Time in seconds is graphed on the x-axis, and the temperature readings are graphed on the y-axis.

5. If your teacher allows, you may print a copy of the temperature-versus-time graph by transferring the graph from the calculator to a Macintosh or IBM-compatible computer using the TI-Graph Link cable and program.

1A | Laboratory Techniques

OBJECTIVES

▶ Demonstrate proficiency in using a Bunsen burner, a triple-beam balance, and a graduated cylinder.

▶ Demonstrate proficiency in handling solid and liquid chemicals.

▶ Develop proper safety techniques for all lab work.

▶ Apply data-collecting techniques.

▶ Use graphing techniques to plot data.

MATERIALS

▶ 100 mL graduated cylinder

▶ 250 mL beakers, 2

▶ Bunsen burner and related equipment

▶ copper wire

▶ crucible tongs

▶ evaporating dish

▶ heat-resistant mat

▶ NaCl

▶ spatula

▶ test tube

▶ triple-beam balance

▶ wax paper or weighing paper

Situation

You have applied to work at a company that does research, development, and analysis work. Although the company does not require employees to have extensive chemical experience, all applicants are tested for their ability to follow directions, heed safety precautions, perform simple laboratory procedures, clearly and concisely communicate results, and make logical inferences.

The company will consider your performance on the test in deciding whether to hire you and what your initial salary will be.

Always wear safety goggles and a lab apron to protect your eyes and clothing. If you get a chemical in your eyes, immediately flush the chemical out at the eyewash station while calling to your teacher. Know the location of the emergency lab shower and eyewash station and the procedures for using them.

Do not touch any chemicals. If you get a chemical on your skin or clothing, wash the chemical off at the sink while calling to your teacher. Make sure you carefully read the labels and follow the precautions on all containers of chemicals that you use. If no precautions are stated on the label, ask your teacher what precautions to follow. Do not taste any chemicals or items used in the laboratory. Never return leftover chemicals to their original containers; take only small amounts to avoid wasting supplies.

When using a Bunsen burner, confine long hair and loose clothing. If your clothing catches fire, WALK to the emergency lab shower and use it to put out the fire. Do not heat glassware that is broken, chipped, or cracked. Use tongs or a hot mitt to handle heated glassware and other equipment; heated glassware does not always look hot.

Background

Pay close attention to the procedures and safety precautions because you will continue to use them throughout your work if you are hired by this company. In addition, you will need to pay attention to what is happening around you, make careful observations, and keep a clear and legible record of these observations in your lab notebook.

Problem

This laboratory orientation session will teach you some of the following techniques:

▶ how to use a Bunsen burner
▶ how to handle solids and liquids
▶ how to use a triple-beam balance
▶ how to practice basic safety techniques in lab work

Preparation

1. Organizing Data

Copy the data tables in your lab notebook.

2. Record in your lab notebook where the following items are located and how each item is used: emergency lab shower, eyewash station, and emergency telephone numbers.

3. Check to be certain that the gas valve at your lab station and at the nearest lab station are turned off. Notify your teacher immediately if a valve is on because the fumes must be cleared before any work continues.

Data Table 1

Material	Mass (g)
Weighing paper	
Weighing paper + NaCl	

Data Table 2

Material	Mass (g) — step 11	Mass (g) — step 12
Empty beaker		
Beaker + 50 mL of water		
50 mL of water		
Beaker + 100 mL of water		
100 mL of water		
Beaker + 150 mL of water		
150 mL of water		

Figure A

Technique

4. Compare the Bunsen burner in **Figure A** with your burner. Construction may vary, but the air and methane gas, CH_4, always mix in the barrel, the vertical tube in the center of the burner.

5. Partially close the air ports at the base of the barrel, turn the gas on full, hold the sparker about 5 cm above the top of the barrel, and proceed to light. Adjust the gas valve until the flame extends about 8 cm above the barrel. Adjust the air supply until you have a quiet, steady flame with a sharply defined, light-blue inner cone. **If an internal flame develops, turn off the gas valve and let the burner cool down. Otherwise, the metal of the burner can get hot enough to set fire to anything nearby that is flammable. Before you relight the burner, partially close the air ports.**

6. Using crucible tongs, hold a 10 cm piece of copper wire for 2–3 seconds in the part of the flame labeled a in **Figure B**. Repeat for the parts of the flame labeled b and c. Record your observations in your lab notebook.

7. Experiment with the flame by completely closing the air ports at the base of the burner. Observe and record the color of the flame and the sounds made by the burner. Using crucible tongs, hold an evaporating dish in the tip of the flame for about 3 minutes. Place

the dish on a heat-resistant mat, and shut off the burner. After the dish cools, examine its underside, and record your observations.

8. Before using the triple-beam balance, make sure that it is level and that the pointer rests at zero. If all slider masses are set at zero but the pointer is not at zero, adjust the calibration knob. To avoid discrepancies, use the same balance for all measurements during a lab activity. **Never put chemicals directly on the balance pan.**

9. Place a piece of weighing paper on the balance pan. Determine the mass of the paper by adjusting the masses on the various sliding scales. Record this mass to the nearest 0.01 g in your data table. Then move the 10 g slide to the 10 g position, and move the 1 g slide to the 3.00 g position. Put a small quantity of NaCl on a separate piece of weighing paper. Then transfer some of the NaCl to the weighing paper on the balance pan until you nearly balance the pointer. Slide the masses until the pointer is exactly balanced, and record the exact mass to the nearest 0.01 g in your data table.

10. Remove the weighing paper and NaCl from the balance pan. Lay the test tube flat on the table, and transfer the NaCl into the tube by rolling the weighing paper and sliding it into the test tube. As you lift the test tube to a vertical position, tap the

Figure B

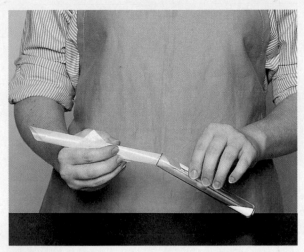

Figure C

paper gently, and the solid will slip into the test tube, as shown in **Figure C.**

11. Measure the mass of a dry 250 mL beaker, and record it in your data table. Add water up to the 50 mL mark, determine the new mass, and record it in your data table. Repeat the procedure by filling the beaker to the 100 mL mark and then to the 150 mL mark, and record the mass each time. Subtract the mass of the empty beaker from the other measurements to determine the masses of the water.

12. Repeat step 11 with a second dry 250 mL beaker, but use a graduated cylinder to measure the volumes of water to the nearest 0.1 mL before pouring the water into the beaker. Read the volumes using the bottom of the meniscus, the curve formed by the water's surface.

Cleanup and Disposal

13. Clean all apparatus and your lab station. Put the wire, NaCl, and weighing paper in the containers designated by your teacher. Pour the water from the beakers into the sink. Scrub the cooled evaporating dish with soap, water, and a scrub brush. Be certain that the gas valves at your lab station and the nearest lab station are turned off. Be sure lab equipment is completely cool before storing it. Always wash your hands thoroughly after all lab work is finished and before you leave the lab.

Analysis and Interpretation

1. Organizing Ideas
Based on your observations, which type of flame is hotter: the flame formed when the air ports are open or the flame formed when they are closed? What is the hottest part of the flame? (Hint: The melting point of copper is 1083°C.)

2. Analyzing Information
Which of the following measurements could have been made by your balance: 3.42 g of glass, 5.666 72 g of aspirin, or 0.000 017 g of paper?

3. Organizing Data
Make a graph of mass versus volume for data from steps 11 and 12. The mass of water (g) should be graphed along the y-axis as the dependent variable, and the volume of water (mL) should be graphed along the x-axis as the independent variable.

Conclusions

4. Relating Ideas
When methane is burned, it usually produces carbon dioxide and water. If there is a shortage of oxygen, the flame is not as hot, and black carbon solid is formed. Which steps in the lab demonstrate these flames?

5. Inferring Conclusions
Which is the most accurate method for measuring volumes of liquids, a beaker or a graduated cylinder? Explain why.

Extensions

1. Resolving Discrepancies
In Mandeville High School, Jarrold got only partway through step 7 of this experiment when he had to put everything away. Soon after Jarrold left, his lab drawer caught on fire. How did this happen?

2. Relating Ideas
The density of water is equal to its mass divided by its volume. Calculate the density of water using your data from step 11. Then calculate the density of water using your data from step 12.

1A | Conservation of Mass
Percentage of Water in Popcorn

THE PROBLEM

Juliette Brand Foods

January 9, 1999

Director of Research
CheMystery Labs, Inc.
52 Fulton Street
Springfield, VA 22150

Dear Director of Research:

Juliette Brand Foods is preparing to enter the rapidly expanding popcorn market with a new popcorn product. As you may know, the key to making popcorn pop is the amount of water contained within the kernel.

Thus far, the product development division has created three different production techniques for the popcorn, each of which creates popcorn with differing amounts of water. We need an independent lab such as yours to measure the percentage of water contained in each sample and to determine which technique produces the best-popping popcorn.

I've enclosed samples from each of the three techniques, labeled "technique beta," "technique gamma," and "technique delta." Please bill us when the work is complete.

Sincerely,

Mary Biedenbecker

Mary Biedenbecker
Director
Product Development Division

References

Popcorn "pops" because of the natural moisture inside each kernel. When the internal water is heated above 100°C, the kernel expands rapidly and the liquid water changes to a gas, which takes up much more room than the liquid.

The percentage of water in popcorn can be determined by the following equation.

$$\frac{\text{mass}_{\text{before}} - \text{mass}_{\text{after}}}{\text{mass}_{\text{before}}} \times 100$$

$$= \% \text{ H}_2\text{O in unpopped popcorn}$$

The popping process works best when the kernels are first coated with a small amount of vegetable oil. Be certain you account for the presence of this oil when measuring masses.

CheMystery Labs, Inc.
52 Fulton Street
Springfield, VA 22150

MEMORANDUM

Date: January 11, 1999

To: Leon Fuller
From: Martha Li-Hsien

We have a budget of $250,000 for this project to take care of equipment, lab space, and labor costs. It is important that we use these funds conservatively and obtain quality results.

Your team needs to design a procedure for determining the percentage of water in three samples of popcorn. Some of the popcorn was damaged in mailing, so each team will have only 80 kernels of popcorn per technique. Be sure to use your samples carefully!

Before you begin the lab work, I must approve your procedure. Give me the following items as soon as possible:
- detailed one-page plan for your procedure, including any necessary data tables
- detailed list of the equipment and materials you will need with itemized and total costs for the accounting department. (Remember, coming in under the $250,000 budget increases our profits, so don't order all the equipment available; order just what you need to get the job done right!)

When finished, prepare a report in the form of a two-page letter to Mary Biedenbecker that includes the following:
- paragraph summarizing how you analyzed the samples
- your findings about the percentage of water in each sample, including calculations and a discussion of the multiple trials
- detailed and organized data table
- graph comparing your findings with those of the other teams
- detailed invoice showing all costs, services, and employee hours spent on this project
- suggestions for reducing costs and improving the analysis procedure

For prices of materials, see page 692.

Required Precautions

Safety goggles and a lab apron must be worn at all times.

Confine long hair and loose clothing.

Do not eat the popcorn; it is for testing purposes only.

Remember, hot glass does not look hot. Be sure to use beaker tongs when handling glassware.

Spill Procedures/ Waste-Disposal Methods

- The popped popcorn should be disposed of in the designated waste container.
- Clean the area and all equipment after use.

2A | Accuracy and Precision

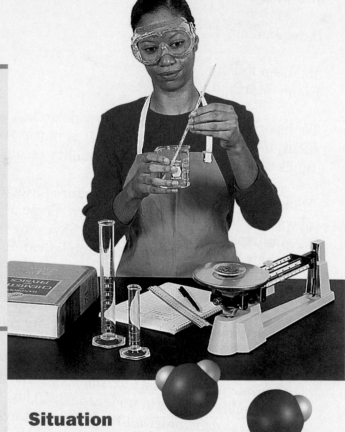

OBJECTIVES

▶ Use experimental measurements in calculations.

▶ Demonstrate proficiency in measuring masses and volumes.

▶ Organize data by compiling it in tables.

▶ Calculate an average value from class data.

▶ Relate absolute deviation, average deviation, uncertainty, and percentage error, and use them as methods for gauging accuracy and precision.

MATERIALS

▶ 15 cm plastic ruler

▶ 25 mL graduated cylinder

▶ 100 mL graduated cylinder

▶ 250 mL beaker

▶ balance

▶ chemical handbook or other source of density values for water and metals

▶ distilled water

▶ metal shot

▶ nonmercury thermometer

▶ stopwatch or clock with a second hand

OPTIONAL EQUIPMENT

▶ CBL unit

▶ graphing calculator with link cable

▶ Vernier temperature probe

Situation

As part of your orientation as a new employee at a chemical firm, you must participate in an assessment of your lab skills. This survey will help you evaluate the accuracy of your equipment and the precision of your lab technique.

Background

Accuracy is how close to the actual value a measurement is; *precision* is how close each measurement is to others in the set.

The accuracy of a measurement can be determined only if you have some way of knowing what the measurement should be. One indicator of accuracy is the percentage error, which can be calculated using the following equation.

$$\frac{value_{accepted} - value_{measured}}{value_{accepted}} \times 100 = \text{percentage error}$$

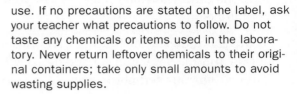

Precision indicates whether the experimental data are consistent. Three common statistical tools used to check precision are *absolute deviation, average deviation,* and *uncertainty in measurement.* Absolute deviation is the difference between a single experimental value and the average of all values. Average deviation is the sum of the absolute deviations for an entire data set divided by the total number of measurements. The uncertainty of a measurement is expressed as plus or minus one unit of the last significant digit, indicating the last digit is an estimate. The percentage uncertainty is determined by dividing the uncertainty by the measurement and multiplying this value by 100, as shown.

$$\frac{\pm\, 0.01\ cm}{24.65\ cm} \times 100 = \pm\, 0.04\%$$

Problem

You will use measurement and analysis skills to evaluate measurements of length, volume, mass, and temperature. You will also determine the identity of a metal sample by calculating its density and comparing the result to density values for various metals found in chemical handbooks.

Data Table 1

Measuring tool	Smallest division
Ruler	
100 mL graduated cylinder	
25 mL graduated cylinder	
Balance	

Data Table 2

Inside diameter of 100 mL cylinder		Mass of 25 mL cylinder with water and metal	
Height of 50 mL mark on 100 mL cylinder		Temperature of water (after 2 min)	
Mass of dry 25 mL cylinder		(after 4 minutes)	
Volume of water added to 25 mL cylinder		(after 6 minutes)	
Mass of 25 mL cylinder with water		(after 8 minutes)	
Volume of metal shot and water		Density of water at above temperature from handbook	

Preparation

1. Organizing Data

Copy the data tables on page 709 in your lab notebook.

2.

Locate a handbook for finding densities of metals and for determining the density of water at various temperatures.

3.

If you are using the Vernier temperature probe and CBL units, refer to pages 700–701 for equipment setup.

Technique

4.

Record in your data table the smallest division on the ruler and the smallest division on the 100 mL graduated cylinder.

5.

Measure the inside diameter of the 100 mL graduated cylinder using the ruler. Measure the height of the cylinder's 50 mL mark. Record these measurements in your data table.

6.

Examine the 25 mL graduated cylinder. What is the smallest division? Examine the scale on the balance. What is the smallest division? Record the answers with units in your data table.

7.

Using the balance, determine the mass of the dry 25 mL cylinder to the nearest 0.1 g. Record this mass in your data table.

8.

Fill the 250 mL beaker half-full with water. Using a thermometer or a Vernier temperature probe, determine the temperature of the water to the nearest 0.1°C. To do this, gently put the thermometer or probe in the water, being careful not to break it. Wait 2 minutes before recording the temperature of the water in your lab notebook. After another 2 minutes, record the temperature again. Repeat this process every 2 minutes until two consecutive temperature measurements are the same. In a handbook, look up the density of water at that temperature, and record it in your data table. **Never use a thermometer to stir anything. It will break easily. The glass wall surrounding the bulb must be very thin to**

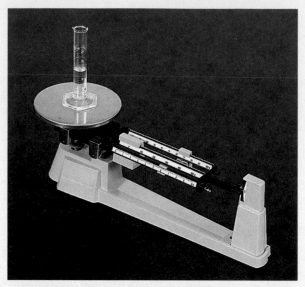

Figure A

provide quick and accurate temperature readings.

9.

Pour between 10 mL and 15 mL of water from the beaker into the 25 mL graduated cylinder. Read the volume to the nearest 0.1 mL, and record it in your data table. Determine the combined mass of the water and the cylinder to the nearest 0.1 g, as shown in **Figure A.** Record this value in your data table. Keep the water in the cylinder for the next step.

10.

Add enough of the sample of metal shot to the cylinder to increase the volume by at least 5 mL. Determine the volume and the mass of the water and shot together in the graduated cylinder, and record your measurements.

Cleanup and Disposal

11.

Clean all apparatus and your lab station. Remove the metal shot from the cylinder, and place it in the container designated by your teacher. Pour the water down the sink. Wash your hands thoroughly after cleaning up the lab area and equipment.

Analysis and Interpretation

1. Organizing Data

What is the uncertainty in a measurement made by each of these devices: the ruler, the

100 mL graduated cylinder, the 25 mL graduated cylinder, and the balance?

2. Organizing Data
Calculate the volume of the 100 mL graduated cylinder up to its 50 mL mark. (Hint: $V = \pi r^2 h$ for a cylinder.)

3. Analyzing Data
Assume the accepted value for the volume of a graduated cylinder up to the 50 mL mark is 50.00 mL. Calculate the percentage error in your calculations from item 2.

4. Organizing Data
Calculate the mass of water as determined by the balance. Calculate the mass of water from its measured volume and its known density. Using the mass obtained by the balance as the accepted value and the value calculated from the density as the experimental value, calculate the percentage error. Be sure to follow significant-figure rules in your calculations.

5. Organizing Data
Subtract the volume of the water from the combined volume of the metal and the water to calculate the volume of the metal alone. Subtract the mass of the water and cylinder from the mass of the metal, water, and cylinder to determine the mass of the metal; then calculate its density. Show all your work.

6. Evaluating Data
Record the metal-density calculations made by the other teams, and calculate the average density of the unknown metal. Calculate the average deviation for the measurements.

Conclusions

7. Inferring Conclusions
Compare your value and the class average of the unknown metal's density with the densities for metals given in the handbook. Determine the identity of the metal.

8. Evaluating Methods
Calculate the percentage error by comparing your experimental value with the value you found in the handbook. Then calculate percentage error for the class average. Which is more accurate, the class average or your value?

Extensions

1. Evaluating Conclusions
Marie and Jason determined the density of a liquid three times. The values they obtained were 2.84 g/mL, 2.85 g/mL, and 2.80 g/mL. The accepted value is 2.40 g/mL. Are the values that Marie and Jason determined precise? Are the values accurate? Explain your answers. Calculate the percentage error and uncertainty of each measurement.

2. Applying Ideas
When you are cutting the legs of a table to make them shorter, precision is more important than accuracy. Explain why.

3. Applying Ideas
A store has a balance with a scale marked in gram units, and each unit is divided in half by a smaller mark. A student working in the store after school measured a sample mass as 5.367 g using this balance. What is wrong with this measurement?

4. Applying Ideas
It is said that the ancient Greek mathematician and scientist Archimedes used density to determine that a goldsmith had cheated when making a crown for the king. Explain what steps you would take to alter this lab procedure to check a metal's purity.

2B | Separation of Mixtures

OBJECTIVES

▶ Recognize how the solubility of a salt varies with temperature.

▶ Demonstrate proficiency in fractional crystallization and in vacuum filtration or gravity filtration.

▶ Determine the percentage of two salts recovered by fractional crystallization.

MATERIALS

▶ 50 mL NaCl–KNO₃ solution

▶ 100 mL graduated cylinder

▶ 150 mL beakers, 4

▶ balance

▶ beaker tongs or hot mitt

▶ Bunsen burner and related equipment or hot plate

▶ distilled water

▶ filter paper

▶ glass stirring rod

▶ ice

▶ nonmercury thermometer

▶ ring and wire gauze

▶ ring stand

▶ rock salt

▶ rubber policeman

▶ spatula

▶ tray, tub, or pneumatic trough

▶ vacuum filtration setup with Büchner funnel, one-hole rubber stopper, filter flask, and tubing; or gravity-filtration setup with glass funnel, ring, and ring stand

OPTIONAL EQUIPMENT

▶ CBL unit

▶ graphing calculator with link cable

▶ Vernier temperature probe

Situation

Your company has been contacted by a firework factory. A mislabeled container of sodium chloride, NaCl, was accidentally mixed with potassium nitrate, KNO₃. KNO₃ is used as an oxidizer in fireworks to ensure that the fireworks burn thoroughly. The fireworks company wants your company to investigate ways they could separate the two compounds. They have provided an aqueous solution of the mixture for you to work with.

Always wear safety goggles and a lab apron to protect your eyes and clothing. If you get a chemical in your eyes, immediately flush the chemical out at the eyewash station while calling to your teacher. Know the location of the emergency lab shower and eyewash station and the procedures for using them.

Do not touch any chemicals. If you get a chemical on your skin or clothing, wash the chemical off at the sink while calling to your teacher. Make sure you carefully read the labels and follow the precautions on all containers of chemicals that you use. If no precautions are stated on the label, ask your teacher what precautions to follow. Do not taste any chemicals or items used in the laboratory. Never return leftover chemicals to their original containers; take only small amounts to avoid wasting supplies.

When using a Bunsen burner, confine long hair and loose clothing. If your clothing catches on fire, WALK to the emergency lab shower and use it to put out the fire. Do not heat glassware that is broken, chipped, or cracked. Use tongs or a hot mitt to handle heated glassware and other equipment; heated glassware does not always look hot.

Background

The substances in a mixture can be separated by physical means. For example, if one substance dissolves in a liquid solvent but another does not, the mixture can be filtered. The substance that dissolved will be carried through the filter by the solvent, but the other substance will not. Because both $NaCl$ and KNO_3 dissolve in water, filtering alone cannot separate them. However, there are differences in the way they dissolve. The graph in Figure A shows the same amount of sodium chloride dissolving in water regardless of the temperature of the water. On the other hand, potassium nitrate is very soluble in warm water but much less soluble at $0°C$.

Problem

You will make use of the differences in solubility to separate the two salts. This technique is known as fractional crystallization. If the water solution of $NaCl$ and KNO_3 is cooled from room temperature to a temperature near $0°C$, some KNO_3 will crystallize. This KNO_3 residue can then be separated from the $NaCl$ solution by filtration. The $NaCl$ can be isolated from the filtrate by evaporation of the water. To determine whether this method is efficient, you will measure the mass of each of the recovered substances. Then your client can decide whether this method is cost-effective.

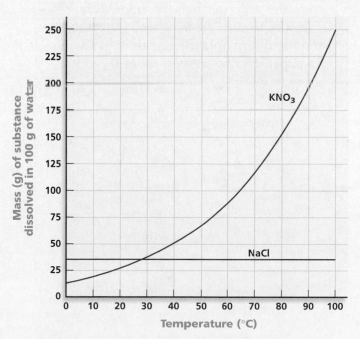

Figure A This graph shows the relationship between temperature and the solubility of $NaCl$ and KNO_3.

FILTRATION-TECHNIQUE OPTION

Figure B   Vacuum filtration

Figure C   Gravity filtration

Vacuum-Filtration Setup

1. To set up a vacuum filtration, screw an aspirator nozzle onto the faucet. Attach the other end of the plastic tubing to the side arm of the filter flask.

2. Place a one-hole rubber stopper on the stem of the funnel, and fit the stopper snugly in the neck of the filter flask, as shown in **Figure B.**

3. Place a piece of filter paper on the bottom of the funnel so that it is flat and covers all of the holes in the funnel.

4. When you are ready, turn on the water at the faucet that has the aspirator nozzle attached. This creates a vacuum, which helps the filtering process go much faster. If the suction is working properly, the filter paper should be pulled against the bottom of the funnel, covering all of the holes. If the filter paper appears to have bubbles of air under it or is not centered well, turn the water off, reposition the filter paper, and begin again.

Gravity-Filtration Setup

1. Set up a ring stand with a ring. Gently rest a glass funnel inside the ring, and place a beaker under the glass funnel, as shown in **Figure C.**

2. Fold a piece of filter paper in half along its diameter, and then fold it again to form a quadrant, as shown in **Figure D.** Separate the folds of the filter paper so that three thicknesses are on one side and one thickness is on the other.

3. Fit the filter paper in the funnel, and wet it with a little water so that it will adhere to the sides of the funnel. Gently but firmly press the paper against the sides of the funnel so that no air is between the funnel and the filter paper. Be certain that the filter paper does not extend above the sides of the funnel.

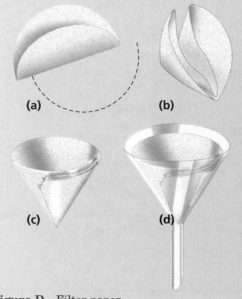

(a)   (b)

(c)   (d)

Figure D   Filter paper

Preparation

1. Organizing Data

Copy the data table below in your lab notebook.

2. Obtain four clean, dry 150 mL beakers, and label them 1, 2, 3, and 4.

3. If you are using the Vernier temperature probe and CBL unit, refer to pages 700–701 for equipment setup.

4. Set up your filtering apparatus. If you are using a Büchner funnel for vacuum filtration or a glass funnel for gravity filtration, follow the setup procedure on page 714.

Technique

5. Measure the mass of beaker 1 to the nearest 0.01 g, and record the mass in your data table.

6. Measure about 50 mL of the NaCl–KNO$_3$ solution into a graduated cylinder. Record the exact volume in your data table. Pour this mixture into beaker 1.

7. Using a thermometer or a temperature probe, measure the temperature of the mixture. Record this temperature in your data table.

8. Measure the mass of a piece of filter paper to the nearest 0.01 g, and record the mass in your data table.

Data Table
Mass of beaker 1
Volume of NaCl–KNO$_3$ solution in beaker 1
Temperature of mixture before cooling
Mass of the filter paper
Mass of beaker 4
Mass of beaker 4 with NaCl
Mass of beaker 1 with filter paper and KNO$_3$
Temperature of mixture after cooling

9. Make an ice bath by filling a tray, tub, or trough half-full with ice. Add a handful of rock salt. The salt lowers the freezing point of water so that the ice bath can cool to a lower temperature. Fill the ice bath with water until it is three-quarters full.

10. Using a fresh supply of ice and distilled water, fill beaker 2 half-full with ice, and add water. Do not add rock salt to this ice-water mixture. You will use this water to wash your purified salt.

11. Put beaker 1 with your NaCl–KNO$_3$ solution into the ice bath. Place a thermometer or a temperature probe in the solution to monitor the temperature. Stir the solution with a stirring rod while it cools. The lower the temperature of the mixture is, the more KNO$_3$ that will crystallize out of solution. When the temperature nears 4°C, proceed with step 11a if you are using the Büchner funnel or step 11b if you are using a glass funnel. **Never stir a solution with a thermometer; the bulb is very fragile.**

a. Vacuum filtration

Prepare the filtering apparatus by pouring approximately 50 mL of ice-cold distilled water from beaker 2 through the filter paper. After the water has gone through the funnel, empty the filter flask into the sink. Reconnect the filter flask, and pour the salt-and-water mixture in beaker 1 into the funnel. Use the rubber policeman to transfer all of the cooled mixture into the funnel, especially any crystals that are visible. It may be helpful to add small amounts of ice-cold water from beaker 2 to beaker 1 to wash any crystals onto the filter paper. After all of the solution has passed through the funnel, wash the KNO$_3$ residue by pouring a very small amount of ice-cold water from beaker 2 over it. When this water has passed through the filter paper, turn off the faucet and carefully remove the tubing from the aspirator. Empty the filtrate, which has passed through the filter paper and is now in the filter flask, into beaker 3. When finished, continue with step 12.

b. Gravity filtration

Place beaker 3 under the glass funnel. Prepare the filtering apparatus by pouring approximately 50 mL of ice-cold water from beaker 2 through the filter paper. The water will pass through the filter paper and drip into beaker 3. When the dripping stops, empty beaker 3 into the sink. Place beaker 3 back under the glass funnel so that it will collect the filtrate from the funnel. Pour the salt-water mixture into the funnel. Use the rubber policeman to transfer all of the cooled mixture into the funnel, especially any visible crystals. It may be helpful to add small amounts of ice-cold water from beaker 2 to beaker 1 to wash any crystals onto the filter paper. After all of the solution has passed through the funnel, wash the KNO_3 by pouring a very small amount of ice-cold water from beaker 2 over it.

12. After you have finished filtering, use either a hot plate or a Bunsen burner, ring stand, ring, and wire gauze to heat beaker 3. When the liquid in beaker 3 begins to boil, continue heating gently until enough water has vaporized to decrease the volume to approximately 25–30 mL. **Be sure to use beaker tongs. Remember that hot glassware does not always look hot.**

13. Allow the solution in beaker 3 to cool. Then set it in the ice bath and stir until the temperature is approximately 4°C.

14. Measure the mass of beaker 4, and record the mass in your data table.

15. Repeat step 11a or step 11b, pouring the solution from beaker 3 onto the filter paper and using beaker 4 to collect the filtrate that passes through the filter.

16. Wash and dry beaker 1. Carefully remove the filter paper with the KNO_3 from the funnel, and put it in the beaker. Avoid spilling the crystals. Place the beaker in a drying oven overnight.

Figure E Use beaker tongs to move a beaker that has been heated, even if you believe that the beaker is cool.

17. Heat beaker 4 with a hot plate or Bunsen burner until the water begins to boil. Continue to heat the beaker gently until all of the water has vaporized and the salt appears dry. Turn off the hot plate or burner, and allow the beaker to cool. Use beaker tongs to move the beaker, as shown in **Figure E.** Measure the mass of beaker 4 with the NaCl to the nearest 0.01 g, and record the mass in your data table.

18. The next day, use beaker tongs to remove beaker 1 with the filter paper and KNO_3 from the drying oven. Allow the beaker to cool. Measure the mass using the same balance you used to measure the mass of the empty beaker. Record the new mass in your data table. **Be sure to use beaker tongs. Remember that hot glassware does not always look hot.**

◆ ◆ Cleanup and Disposal

19. Clean all apparatus and your lab station. Once the mass of the NaCl has been determined, add water to dissolve the NaCl, and rinse the solution down the drain. Do not wash KNO_3 down the drain. Dispose of the KNO_3 in the waste container designated by your teacher. Wash your hands thoroughly after all lab work is finished and before you leave the lab.

Analysis and Interpretation

1. Organizing Data
Find the mass of NaCl in your 50 mL sample by subtracting the mass of the empty beaker 4 from the mass of beaker 4 with NaCl.

2. Organizing Data
Find the mass of KNO_3 in your 50 mL sample by subtracting the mass of beaker 1 and the mass of the filter paper from the mass of beaker 1 with the filter paper and KNO_3.

3. Organizing Data
Determine the total mass of the two salts.

4. Analyzing Information
How many grams of KNO_3 and NaCl would be found in a 1.0 L sample of the solution? (Hint: For each substance, make a conversion factor using the mass of the compound and the volume of the solution.)

5. Interpreting Graphics
Use the graph at the beginning of this exploration to determine how much of each compound would dissolve in 100 g of water at room temperature and at the temperature of your ice-water bath.

Conclusions

6. Inferring Conclusions
Calculate the percentage by mass of NaCl in the salt mixture. Calculate the percentage by mass of KNO_3 in the salt mixture. Assume that the density of your 50 mL solution is 1.0 g/mL.

7. Applying Conclusions
The fireworks company has another 55 L of the salt mixture dissolved in water just like the sample you worked with. How many kilograms of each compound can the company expect to recover from this sample? (Hint: Use your answer from item 4 to help you answer this question.)

8. Evaluating Methods
Use the graph shown at the beginning of this exploration to estimate how much KNO_3 could still be contaminating the NaCl you recovered.

9. Relating Ideas
Use the graph shown at the beginning of this exploration to explain why it is impossible to completely separate the two compounds by fractional crystallization.

10. Evaluating Methods
Why was it important to use ice-cold water to wash the KNO_3 after filtration?

11. Evaluating Methods
If it was important to use very cold water to wash the KNO_3, why wasn't the salt-and-ice-water mixture from the bath used? After all, it had a lower temperature than the ice and distilled water from beaker 2. (Hint: Consider what is contained in rock salt.)

12. Evaluating Methods
Why was it important to keep the amount of cold water used to wash the KNO_3 as small as possible?

Extensions

1. Interpreting Graphics
Using the graph shown at the beginning of this exploration, determine the minimum mass of water necessary to dissolve the amounts of each compound from Analysis and Interpretation items 1 and 2. Calculate the mass dissolved at room temperature and at 4°C. What volumes of water would be necessary? (Hint: The density of water is about 1.0 g/mL.)

2. Designing Experiments
Describe how you could use the properties of the compounds to test the purity of your recovered samples. If your teacher approves your plan, use it to check your separation of the mixtures. (Hint: Check a chemical handbook for more information about the properties of NaCl and KNO_3.)

3. Designing Experiments
How could you improve the yield or the purity of the compounds you recovered? If you can think of ways to modify the procedure, ask your teacher to approve your plan, and run the procedure again.

2B | Separation of Mixtures
Mining Contract

THE PROBLEM

GOLDSTAKE
MINING
COMPANY

January 20, 1999

George Taylor
Director of Analytical Services
CheMystery Labs, Inc.
52 Fulton Street
Springfield, VA 22150

Dear George:

I thought of your new company when a problem came up here at Goldstake. I think I have a job for you. While performing exploratory drilling for natural gas near Afton in western Wyoming, our engineers encountered a new subterranean geothermal aquifer. We estimate the size of the aquifer to be 1×10^{12} liters.

The Bureau of Land Management advised us to alert the Environmental Protection Agency. Preliminary qualitative test of the water identified two dissolved salts: potassium nitrate and copper nitrate.

The EPA is concerned that a full-scale mining operation may harm the environment if the salts are present in large quantities. They're requiring us to halt all operations while we obtain more information for an environmental impact statement. We need your firm to separate, purify, and make a determination of the amounts of the two salts in the Afton Aquifer.

Sincerely,

Lynn L. Brown

Lynn L. Brown
Director of Operations
Goldstake Mining Corporation

References

The procedure for this Investigation is similar to one your team recently completed involving the separation of sodium chloride, NaCl and potassium nitrate, KNO_3 in Exploration 2B.

CheMystery Labs, Inc.
52 Fulton Street
Springfield, VA 22150

MEMORANDUM

Date: January 23, 1999
To: Andre Kalaviencz
From: George Taylor

We received this contract because the D.O. at Goldstake is an old friend of mine. She knows we're a new company and hungry for work. It's important that we get her an answer quickly and accurately. We can't afford to fail.

Because this is our first mining-industry contract, we need to plan carefully to get good results at minimum cost. Each research team will receive a 50.0 mL sample of the aquifer water, but that's all.

I'd like the following information from each analytical team before the work begins.
- detailed one-page plan for the procedure that you will use to accomplish the analysis, including all necessary data tables
- list of the materials and supplies you will need and their individual and total costs

(Remember, with all the costs associated with starting the company, we don't have much money—you've got to keep your cost under $200 000)

Goldstake would like the following information presented in a two-page report after the completion of all lab work.
- mass of potassium nitrate, KNO_3, and copper nitrate, $Cu(NO_3)_2$, in the 50.0 mL sample
- extrapolated mass of KNO_3 and $Cu(NO_3)_2$, in the Afton Aquifer
- summary paragraph describing the procedure used
- detailed and organized data and analysis section showing your calculations and explanations of any possible sources of error
- detailed invoice for the services rendered and the expenses incurred

Doing this job well could mean a long term contract with Goldstake.

For prices of materials, see page 692.

Required Precautions

Safety goggles and lab aprons must be worn at all times.

Before lighting the burner, remember to confine long hair and loose clothing. Use tongs at all times because heated glassware does not always look hot.

Do not touch or taste any chemicals. Wash your hands thoroughly when finished.

Spill Procedures/ Waste-Disposal Methods

- Do not try to rinse the $Cu(NO_3)_2$ and KNO_3 down the drain. Dispose of each substance in separate waste containers designated by your teacher.

3A | Flame Tests

OBJECTIVES

▶ Identify a set of flame-test color standards for selected metal ions.

▶ Relate the colors of a flame test to the behavior of excited electrons in a metal ion.

▶ Identify an unknown metal ion by using a flame test.

▶ Demonstrate proficiency in performing a flame test and in using a spectroscope.

MATERIALS

▶ 1.0 M HCl solution

▶ 250 mL beaker

▶ Bunsen burner and related equipment

▶ $CaCl_2$ solution

▶ cobalt glass plates

▶ crucible tongs

▶ distilled water

▶ flame-test wire

▶ glass test plate, or a microchemistry plate with wells

▶ K_2SO_4 solution

▶ Li_2SO_4 solution

▶ NaCl crystals

▶ NaCl solution

▶ Na_2SO_4 solution

▶ $SrCl_2$ solution

▶ spectroscope

▶ unknown solution

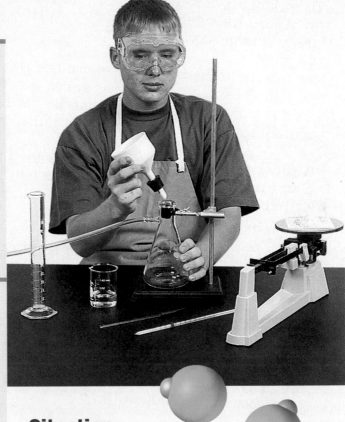

Situation

Your company has been contacted by Julius and Annette Benetti. They are worried about some abandoned, rusted barrels of chemicals that their daughter found while playing in the vacant lot behind their home. The barrels have begun to leak a colored liquid that flows through their property before emptying into a local sewer. The Benettis want your company to identify the compound in the liquid. Earlier work indicates that it is a dissolved metal compound. Many metals, such as lead, have been determined to be hazardous to our health. Many compounds of these metals are often soluble in water and are therefore easily absorbed into the body.

Always wear safety goggles and a lab apron to protect your eyes and clothing. If you get a chemical in your eyes, immediately flush the chemical out at the eyewash station while calling to your teacher. Know the location of the emergency lab shower and eyewash station and the procedures for using them.

Do not touch any chemicals. If you get a chemical on your skin or clothing, wash the chemical off at the sink while calling to your teacher. Make sure you carefully read the labels and follow the precautions on all containers of chemicals that you use. If no precautions are stated on the label, ask your teacher what precautions to follow. Do not taste any chemicals or items used in the laboratory. Never return leftover chemicals to their original containers; take only small amounts to avoid wasting supplies.

When using a Bunsen burner, confine long hair and loose clothing. If your clothing catches fire, WALK to the emergency lab shower and use it to put out the fire. Do not heat glassware that is broken, chipped, or cracked. Use tongs or a hot mitt to handle heated glassware and other equipment; heated glassware does not always look hot.

Call your teacher in the event of an acid or base spill. Acid or base spills should be cleaned up promptly according to your teacher's instructions.

Background

Electrons in atoms jump from their ground state to excited states by absorbing energy. Eventually these electrons fall back to their ground state, re-emitting the absorbed energy in the form of light. Because each atom has a unique structure and arrangement of electrons, each atom emits a unique type of light. This characteristic light is the basis for the chemical test known as a flame test. In this test the atoms are excited by being placed within a flame. As they re-emit the absorbed energy in the form of light, the color of the flame changes. For most metals, these changes are easily visible. However, even the presence of a tiny speck of another substance can interfere with the identification of the true color of a particular type of atom.

Problem

To determine what metal is contained in the barrels behind the Benettis' house, you must first perform flame tests with a variety of standard solutions of different metal compounds. Then you will perform a flame test with the unknown sample from the site to see if it matches any of the solutions you've used as standards. Be sure to keep your equipment very clean, and perform multiple trials to check your work.

Preparation

1. Organizing Data

Copy the data table below in your lab notebook. Be sure that you have plenty of room for observations about each test.

Data Table

Metal compound	Color of flame	Wavelengths (nm)
$CaCl_2$ solution		
K_2SO_4 solution		
Li_2SO_4 solution		
Na_2SO_4 solution		
$SrCl_2$ solution		
Na_2SO_4 (cobalt glass)		
K_2SO_4 (cobalt glass)		
Na_2SO_4 and K_2SO_4		
Na_2SO_4 and K_2SO_4 (cobalt glass)		
NaCl solution		
NaCl crystals		
Unknown solution		

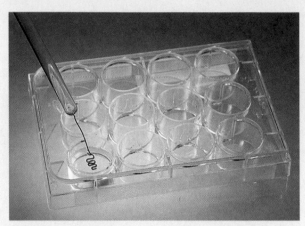

Figure A Be sure that you record the position of the various metal ion solutions in each well of the well strip.

2. Label a beaker "Waste." Thoroughly clean and dry a well strip. Fill the first well one-fourth full with 1.0 M HCl. Clean the test wire by first dipping it in the HCl and then holding it in the flame of the Bunsen burner. Repeat this procedure until the flame is not colored by the wire. When the wire is ready, rinse the well with distilled water, and collect the rinse water in the waste beaker.

3. Put 10 drops of each metal ion solution listed in the materials list except NaCl in a row in each well of the well strip. Put a row of 1.0 M HCl drops on a glass plate across from the metal ion solutions. Record the position of all of the chemicals placed in the wells. The wire will need to be cleaned thoroughly with HCl between each test solution to avoid contamination from the previous test.

Technique

4. Dip the wire into the $CaCl_2$ solution, as shown in **Figure A,** and then hold it in the Bunsen burner flame. Observe the color of the flame, and record it in the data table. Repeat the procedure again, but this time look through the spectroscope to view the results. Record the wavelengths you see

from the flame. Perform each test three times. Clean the wire with the HCl as you did in step 2.

5. Repeat step 4 with the K_2SO_4 and with each of the remaining solutions in the well strip. For each solution that you test, record the color of each flame and the wavelength observed with the spectroscope. After the solutions are tested, clean the wire thoroughly, rinse the well strip with distilled water, and collect the rinse water in the waste beaker.

6. Test another drop of Na_2SO_4, but this time view the flame through two pieces of cobalt glass. Clean the wire, and repeat the test using the K_2SO_4. View the flame through the cobalt glass. Record in your data table the colors and wavelengths of the flames. Clean the wire and the well strip, and rinse the well strip with distilled water. Pour the rinse water into the waste beaker.

7. Put a drop of K_2SO_4 in a clean well. Add a drop of Na_2SO_4. Flame-test the mixture. Observe the flame without the cobalt glass. Repeat the test, this time observing the flame through the cobalt glass. Record the colors and wavelengths of the flames in the data table. Clean the wire, and rinse the well strip with distilled water. Pour the rinse water into the waste beaker.

8. Test a drop of the NaCl solution in the flame, and then view it through the spectroscope. (Do not use the cobalt glass.) Record your observations. Clean the wire, and rinse the well strip with distilled water. Pour the rinse water into the waste beaker. Place a few crystals of NaCl in a clean well, dip the wire in the crystals, and do the flame test once more. Record the color of the flame test. Clean the wire, and rinse the well strip with distilled water. Pour the rinse water into the waste beaker.

Figure B Flame test

9. Dip the wire into the unknown solution; then hold it in the Bunsen burner flame, as shown in **Figure B.** Perform flame tests for it, both with and without the cobalt glass. Record your observations. Clean the wire, and rinse the well strip with distilled water. Pour the rinse water into the waste beaker.

Cleanup and Disposal

10. Clean all apparatus and your lab station. Dispose of the contents of the waste beaker in the container designated by your teacher. Wash your hands thoroughly after cleaning up the lab area and equipment.

Analysis and Interpretation

1. **Organizing Data**
   Examine your data table, and create a summary of the flame test for each metal ion.

2. **Analyzing Data**
   Account for any differences in the individual trials for the flame tests for the metal ions.

3. **Organizing Ideas**
   Explain how viewing the flame through cobalt glass can make it easier to analyze the ions being tested.

4. **Relating Ideas**
   Explain how the lines seen in the spectroscope relate to the position of electrons in the metal atom.

5. **Relating Ideas**
   For three of the metal ions tested, explain how the flame color you saw relates to the lines of color you saw when you looked through the spectroscope.

Conclusions

6. **Inferring Conclusions**
   What metal ions are in the unknown solution from the barrels on the vacant lot?

7. **Evaluating Methods**
   How would you characterize the flame test with respect to its sensitivity? What difficulties could there be when identifying ions by the flame test?

8. **Evaluating Methods**
   Explain how you can use a spectroscope to identify the components of solutions containing several different metal ions.

Extensions

1. **Inferring Conclusions**
   A student performed flame tests on several unknowns and observed that they all were shades of red. What should the student do to correctly identify these substances? Explain your answer.

2. **Applying Ideas**
   During a flood, the labels from three bottles of chemicals were lost. The three unlabeled bottles of white solids were known to contain the following: strontium nitrate, ammonium carbonate, and potassium sulfate. Explain how you could easily test the substances, and relabel the three bottles. (Hint: Ammonium ions do not provide a distinctive flame color.)

3. **Applying Ideas**
   Some stores sell jars of "fireplace crystals." When sprinkled on a log, these crystals make the flames blue, red, green, and violet. Explain how these crystals can change the flame's color. What ingredients would you expect them to contain?

THE PROBLEM

E·T·A
Experimental Testing Agency

January 27, 1999

Director of Investigations
CheMystery Labs, Inc.
52 Fulton Street
Springfield, VA 22150

Dear Director:

As you may have seen in news reports, one of our freelance pilots, Davin Matthews, was killed in a crash of an experimental airplane that was struck by lightning.

What the reports did not mention was that Matthews's airplane was a recently perfected new design that he'd been developing for us. The notes he left behind indicate that the coating on the nose cone was the key to the plane's speed and maneuverability. Unfortunately, he did not reveal what substances he used, and we were able to recover only flakes of material from the nose cone after the accident.

We have sent you samples of these flakes dissolved in a solution. Please identify the material Matthews used so that we can duplicate his prototype. We will pay $200,000 for this work, provided that you can identify the material within three days.

Sincerely,

Jared MacLaren

Jared MacLaren
Experimental Testing Agency

References

Review information about spectroscopic analysis. The procedure is similar to one your team recently completed to identify an unknown metal in a solution. As before, use small amounts, and clean equipment carefully to avoid contamination. Perform multiple trials for each sample.

The following information is the bright-line emission data (in nm) for the four possible metals.

- Lithium: 670, 612, 498, 462
- Potassium: 700, 695, 408, 405
- Strontium: 710, 685, 665, 500, 490, 485, 460, 420, 405
- Calcium: 650, 645, 610, 485, 460, 445, 420

THE PLAN

MEMORANDUM

CheMystery Labs, Inc.
52 Fulton Street
Springfield, VA 22150

Date: January 28, 1999
To: Edwin Thien
From: Marissa Bellinghausen

We have narrowed down the material used to four possibilities. It is a compound of either lithium, potassium, strontium, or calcium. Using flame tests and the wavelengths of spectroscopic analysis, you should be able to identify which of these is in the sample.

Because our contract depends on timeliness, give me a preliminary report that includes the following as soon as possible:
- detailed one-page summary of your plan for the procedure
- itemized list of equipment with total costs (Remember, the less you spend, the more profit for the company—provided you can get accurate results!)

After you complete your analysis, prepare a report in the form of a two-page letter to MacLaren. It must include the following:
- identity of the metal in the sample
- summary of your procedure
- detailed and organized analysis and data sections showing tests and results
- detailed invoice for all expenses and services

For prices of materials, see Page 692.

Required Precautions

Safety goggles and a lab apron must be worn at all times.

Do not touch or taste any chemicals. Wash your hands thoroughly before you leave the lab.

Confine long hair and loose clothing.

If you get acid or base on your skin or clothing, wash the chemical off at the sink while calling to your teacher. If you get acid or base in your eyes, immediately flush it out at the eyewash station while calling to your teacher.

Spill Procedures/ Waste-Disposal Methods

- In case of spills, follow your teacher's instructions.
- Place all remaining solutions in separate disposal containers as indicated by your teacher.
- Clean the area and all equipment after use.

725

4A | The Mendeleev Lab of 1869

OBJECTIVES

▶ Observe the physical properties of common elements.

▶ Observe the properties and trends in the elements on the periodic table.

▶ Identify unknown elements based on observed trends in properties.

MATERIALS

▶ blank periodic table

▶ elemental samples* of Ar, C, Cu, Sn, and Pb

▶ note cards (3 × 5)

▶ periodic table

Background

Russian chemist Dmitri Mendeleev is generally credited as being the first chemist to observe that patterns emerge when the elements are arranged according to their properties. Mendeleev's arrangement of the elements was unique because he left blank spaces for elements that he claimed were undiscovered as of 1869. Mendeleev was so confident that he even predicted the properties of these undiscovered elements. His predictions were eventually proven to be quite accurate, and these new elements fill the spaces that originally were blank in his table.

Always wear safety goggles and lab apron to protect your eyes and clothing. If you get a chemical in your eyes, immediately flush the chemical out at the eyewash station while calling to your teacher. Know the location of the emergency lab shower and eyewash station and the procedure for using them.

 Some samples may be hazardous to humans. Do not open or touch any sample unless directed to do so by your teacher.

 Call you teacher in the event of a spill. Spills should be cleaned up promptly according to your teacher's directions.

Problem

Use your knowledge of the periodic table to determine the identity of each of the nine unknown elements in this activity.

▶ The unknown elements are from the following groups in the periodic table. *Each group listed below contains at least one unknown.*

| 1 | 2 | 11 | 13 | 14 | 17 | 18 |

▶ None of the known elements serves as one of the nine unknown elements.

▶ No radioactive elements are used during this experiment. The relevant radioactive elements include Fr, Ra, At, and Rn.

▶ You may not use your textbook or other reference materials. You have been provided with enough information to determine each of the unknown elements.

Preparation

1. Organizing Data

Copy the data table below in your laboratory notebook. Be sure to add enough space for all the unknown elements.

Data Table	
Unknown	**Element**
1	
2	
3	
4	

Technique

2. Use the note cards to copy the information listed on each of the sample cards on page 728 and 729. If the word *observe* is listed, you will need to visually inspect the sample and then write the observation in the appropriate space.

3. Arrange the note cards of the known elements in a crude representation of the periodic table. In other words, all of the known elements from Group 1 should be arranged in the appropriate order. Arrange all of the other cards accordingly.

4. Once the cards of the known elements are in place, inspect the properties of the unknowns to see where their properties would best "fit" the trends of the elements of each group.

5. Assign the proper element name to each of the unknowns. Add the symbol for each one of the "unknowns" to your data table.

Cleanup and Disposal

6. Clean up your lab station, and return the leftover note cards and samples of the elements to your teacher. Do not pour any of the samples down the drain or in the trash unless your teacher directs you to do so. Wash your hands thoroughly before you leave the lab and after all your work is finished.

Conclusion

1. Summarize your group's reasoning for the assignment of each unknown. Explain in a few sentences exactly how you predicted the identity of the nine unknowns.

Li		
Physical state ....solid		
Density ....0.534 g/cm^3		
Hardness ....soft, claylike		
Conductivity ....good		
Melting point.............180°C		
Solubility (H$_2$O) ....reacts with water		
Color............................silver		

Ag		
Physical state ....solid		
Density....................10.50 g/cm^3		
Hardness......................somewhat soft		
Conductivity ....excellent		
Melting point..................961°C		
Solubility (H$_2$O)..............none		
Color..............................silver		

Cu		
Physical state...............(observe)		
Density ....8.96 g/cm^3		
Hardness....................somewhat soft		
Conductivity...................excellent		
Melting point ....1083°C		
Solubility (H$_2$O)..............none		
Color ....(observe)		

C		
Physical state...............(observe)		
Density............................2.10 g/cm^3		
Hardness........................soft yet brittle		
Conductivity ....good		
Melting point..................3550°C		
Solubility (H$_2$O)..............negligible		
Color................................(observe)		

Cl$_2$		
Physical state ....gas		
Density.........................0.00321 g/cm^3		
Hardness ....none		
Conductivity...................very poor		
Melting point ....–101°C		
Solubility (H$_2$O) ....slight		
Color............................greenish yellow		

He		
Physical state...............gas		
Density.........................0.00018 g/cm^3		
Hardness ....none		
Conductivity...................very poor		
Melting point ....–272°C		
Solubility (H$_2$O)..............none		
Color...............................colorless		

Na		
Physical state...............solid		
Density..........................0.971 g/cm^3		
Hardness........................soft, claylike		
Conductivity...................good		
Melting point..................98°C		
Solubility (H$_2$O)............reacts rapidly		
Color...............................silver		

Ca		
Physical state...............solid		
Density............................1.57 g/cm^3		
Hardness........................medium		
Conductivity...................good		
Melting point..................845°C		
Solubility (H$_2$O)..............reacts		
Color................................silvery white		

Be		
Physical state...............solid		
Density............................1.85 g/cm^3		
Hardness.........................brittle		
Conductivity...................excellent		
Melting point..................1287°C		
Solubility (H$_2$O)..............none		
Color................................gray		

Sn		
Physical state...............(observe)		
Density............................7.31 g/cm^3		
Hardness.........................somewhat soft		
Conductivity...................good		
Melting point..................232°C		
Solubility (H$_2$O)..............none		
Color................................(observe)		

Ne		
Physical state ....gas		
Density.........................0.00090 g/cm^3		
Hardness ....none		
Conductivity ....very poor		
Melting point ....–249°C		
Solubility (H$_2$O) ....none		
Color................................colorless		

Br$_2$		
Physical state...............liquid		
Density............................3.12 g/cm^3		
Hardness.........................none		
Conductivity...................very poor		
Melting point..................–7.2°C		
Solubility (H$_2$O)..............negligible		
Color................................reddish brown		

K		
Physical state...............solid		
Density............................0.86 g/cm^3		
Hardness.........................soft, claylike		
Conductivity...................good		
Melting point..................63°C		
Solubility (H$_2$O)............reacts rapidly		
Color................................silver		

Ba		
Physical state ....solid		
Density..........................3.6 g/cm^3		
Hardness ....soft		
Conductivity...................good		
Melting point ....710°C		
Solubility (H$_2$O) ....reacts strongly		
Color................................silvery white		

Xe		
Physical state ....gas		
Density.........................0.00585 g/cm^3		
Hardness ....none		
Conductivity ....very poor		
Melting point ....–111.9°C		
Solubility (H$_2$O) ....none		
Color................................colorless		

In	
Physical state	solid
Density	7.31 g/cm^3
Hardness	very soft
Conductivity	medium
Melting point	157°C
Solubility (H$_2$O)	none
Color	silvery white

I$_2$	
Physical state	solid
Density	4.93 g/cm^3
Hardness	soft
Conductivity	very poor
Melting point	113.5°C
Solubility (H$_2$O)	negligible
Color	bluish-black

Pb	
Physical state	(observe)
Density	11.35 g/cm^3
Hardness	somewhat soft
Conductivity	poor
Melting point	327.5°C
Solubility (H$_2$O)	none
Color	(observe)

Ar	
Physical state	(observe)
Density	0.00178 g/cm^3
Hardness	none
Conductivity	very poor
Melting point	−189.2°C
Solubility (H$_2$O)	none
Color	(observe)

Ga	
Physical state	solid
Density	5.904 g/cm^3
Hardness	soft
Conductivity	medium
Melting point	30°C
Solubility (H$_2$O)	none
Color	silvery

Cs	
Physical state	solid
Density	1.87 g/cm^3
Hardness	soft
Conductivity	good
Melting point	29°C
Solubility (H$_2$O)	reacts violently
Color	silvery white

Unknown #1	
Physical state	solid
Density	2.33 g/cm^3
Hardness	brittle
Conductivity	intermediate
Melting point	1410°C
Solubility (H$_2$O)	none
Color	gray

Unknown #2	
Physical state	gas
Density	0.00170 g/cm^3
Hardness	none
Conductivity	very poor
Melting point	−219.6°C
Solubility (H$_2$O)	slight
Color	pale yellow

Unknown #3	
Physical state	solid
Density	1.53 g/cm^3
Hardness	soft
Conductivity	good
Melting point	39°C
Solubility (H$_2$O)	reacts violently
Color	silvery white

Unknown #4	
Physical state	gas
Density	0.00374 g/cm^3
Hardness	none
Conductivity	very poor
Melting point	−156.6°C
Solubility (H$_2$O)	none
Color	colorless

Unknown #5	
Physical state	solid
Density	19.3 g/cm^3
Hardness	soft
Conductivity	excellent
Melting point	1064°C
Solubility (H$_2$O)	none
Color	gold

Unknown #6	
Physical state	solid
Density	2.54 g/cm^3
Hardness	somewhat soft
Conductivity	good
Melting point	769°C
Solubility (H$_2$O)	reacts rapidly
Color	silvery white

Unknown #7	
Physical state	solid
Density	5.32 g/cm^3
Hardness	fairly brittle
Conductivity	fair to poor
Melting point	937°C
Solubility (H$_2$O)	none
Color	gray

Unknown #8	
Physical state	solid
Density	1.74 g/cm^3
Hardness	medium
Conductivity	good
Melting point	651°C
Solubility (H$_2$O)	reacts slowly
Color	silvery white

Unknown #9	
Physical state	solid
Density	11.85 g/cm^3
Hardness	very soft
Conductivity	medium
Melting point	303°C
Solubility (H$_2$O)	none
Color	silvery white

5A | Percent Composition of Hydrates

EXPLORATION TECHNIQUE BUILDER

OBJECTIVES

▶ **Demonstrate** proficiency in using the balance and the Bunsen burner.

▶ **Determine** that all the water has been driven from a hydrate by heating a sample to constant mass.

▶ **Relate** results to the law of conservation of mass and the law of multiple proportions.

▶ **Perform** calculations using the molar mass.

▶ **Determine** the empirical formula of the hydrate and its percentage by mass of water.

MATERIALS

▶ balance

▶ Bunsen burner

▶ crucible and cover

▶ crucible tongs

▶ $CuSO_4$, hydrated crystals

▶ desiccator

▶ distilled water

▶ dropper or micropipet

▶ glass stirring rod

▶ ring and pipe-stem triangle

▶ ring stand

▶ spatula

▶ weighing paper

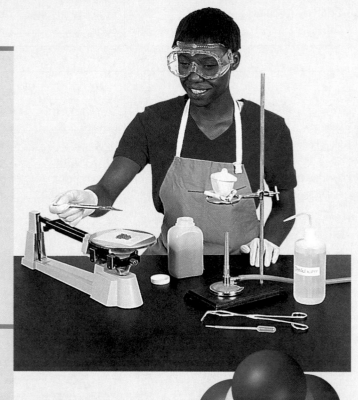

Situation

You are a research chemist working for a company that is developing a new chemical moisture absorber and indicator. The company plans to seal the moisture absorber into a transparent porous pouch attached to a cellophane window on the inside of packages for compact disc players. This way, moisture within the packages will be absorbed, and any package that has too much moisture can be quickly detected and dried out. Your company's efforts have focused on copper(II) sulfate, $CuSO_4$, which can absorb water to become a hydrate that shows a distinctive color change.

Always wear safety goggles and a lab apron to protect your eyes and clothing. If you get a chemical in your eyes, immediately flush the chemical out at the eyewash station while calling to your teacher. Know the location of the emergency lab shower and eyewash station and the procedures for using them.

Do not touch any chemicals. If you get a chemical on your skin or clothing, wash the chemical off at the sink while calling to your teacher. Make sure you carefully read the labels and follow the precautions on all containers of chemicals that you use. If no precautions are stated on the label, ask your teacher what precautions to follow. Do not taste any chemicals or items used in the laboratory. Never re-

turn leftover chemicals to their original containers; take only small amounts to avoid wasting supplies.

When using a Bunsen burner, confine long hair and loose clothing. If your clothing catches fire, WALK to the emergency lab shower and use it to put out the fire. Do not heat glassware that is broken, chipped, or cracked. Use tongs or a hot mitt to handle heated glassware and other equipment; heated glassware does not always look hot.

Never put broken glass or ceramics in a regular waste container. Broken glass and ceramics should be disposed of in a separate container designated by your teacher.

Background

When many ionic compounds are crystallized from a water solution, they include individual water molecules as part of their crystalline structure. If the substances are heated, this water of crystallization may be driven off, leaving behind the pure anhydrous form of the compound. Because the law of multiple proportions also applies to crystalline hydrates, the number of moles of water driven off per mole of the anhydrous compound should be a simple whole number ratio. You can use this information to help you determine the formula of the hydrate.

Problem

To help your company decide whether $CuSO_4$ is the right substance for the moisture absorber and indicator, you will need to examine the hydrated and anhydrous forms of the compound and determine the following:

- the empirical formula of the hydrate, including its water of crystallization
- if the compound is useful as an indicator when it changes from the hydrated to the anhydrous form
- the mass of water absorbed by the 25 g of anhydrous compound that the company proposes to use

Even if you can guess what the formula for the hydrate should be, carefully perform this exploration so that you know how well your company's supply of $CuSO_4$ absorbs moisture.

Preparation

1. Organizing Data

Copy the data table below in your lab notebook. Leave room for observations about the procedure.

2. Make sure that your equipment and tongs are very clean so that you will get the best possible results. Remember that you will need to cool the heated crucible in the desiccator before measuring its mass. **Never put a hot crucible on a balance; it will damage the balance.**

Data Table 1
Mass of empty crucible and cover
Initial mass of sample, crucible, and cover
Mass of sample, crucible, and cover after first heating
Mass of sample, crucible, and cover after second heating
Constant mass of sample, crucible, and cover

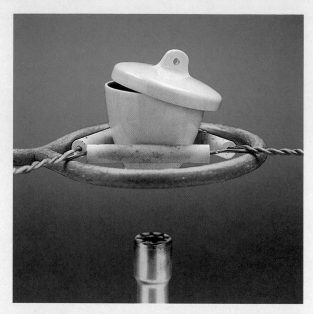

Figure A

Technique

3. Place the crucible and cover on the triangle with the lid slightly tipped, as shown in **Figure A.** The small opening will allow gases to escape. Heat the crucible and cover until the crucible glows slightly red. Use the tongs to transfer the crucible and cover to the desiccator, and allow them to cool for 5 minutes. Determine the mass of the crucible and cover to the nearest 0.01 g, and record the mass in your data table.

4. Using a spatula, add approximately 5 g of copper sulfate hydrate crystals to the crucible. Break up any large crystals before placing them in the crucible. Determine the mass of the covered crucible and crystals to the nearest 0.01 g, and record the mass in your data table.

5. Place the crucible with the copper sulfate hydrate on the triangle, and again position the cover so there is only a small opening. If the opening is too large, the crystals may spatter as they are heated. Heat the crucible very gently on a low flame to avoid spattering. Increase the temperature gradually for 2 or 3 minutes, and then heat until the crucible glows red for at least 5 minutes. Be very careful not to raise the temperature of the crucible and its contents too suddenly.

You will observe a color change, which is normal, but if the substance remains yellow after cooling, it was overheated and has begun to decompose. Allow the crucible, cover, and contents to cool for 5 minutes in the desiccator, and then measure their mass. Record the mass in your data table.

6. Heat the covered crucible and contents to redness again for 5 minutes. Allow the crucible, cover, and contents to cool in the desiccator, and then determine their mass and record it in the data table. If the two mass measurements differ by no more than 0.01 g, you may assume that all of the water has been driven off. Otherwise, repeat the process until the mass no longer changes, indicating that all of the water has evaporated. Record this constant mass in your data table.

7. After recording the constant mass, set aside a part of your sample on a piece of weighing paper. Using the dropper or pipet, as shown in **Figure B,** put a few drops of water onto this sample to rehydrate the crystals. Record your observations in your lab notebook.

⬥⬥ Cleanup and Disposal

8. Clean all apparatus and your lab station. Make sure to completely shut off the gas valve before leaving the laboratory. Remember to wash your hands thoroughly. Place the rehydrated and anhydrous chemicals in the disposal containers designated by your teacher.

Figure B

Analysis and Interpretation

1. Analyzing Methods
Why do you need to heat the clean crucible before using it in this lab? Why do the tongs used throughout this lab need to be especially clean?

2. Analyzing Methods
Why do you need to use a cover for the crucible? Could you leave the cover off each time you measure the mass of the crucible and its contents and still get accurate results? Explain your answer.

3. Analyzing Information
Calculate the mass of anhydrous copper sulfate (the residue that remains after heating to constant mass) by subtracting the mass of the empty crucible and cover from the mass of the crucible, cover, and heated $CuSO_4$. Use the molar mass for $CuSO_4$, determined from the periodic table, to calculate the number of moles present.

4. Resolving Discrepancies
Explain why the mass of the sample decreased after it was heated, despite the law of conservation of mass.

5. Analyzing Information
Calculate the mass and moles of water originally present in the hydrate using the molar mass determined from the periodic table.

Conclusions

6. Analyzing Information
Using your answers from items 3 and 5, determine the empirical formula for the copper sulfate hydrate.

7. Analyzing Information
What is the percentage by mass of water in the original hydrated compound?

8. Organizing Conclusions
How much water could 25 g of anhydrous $CuSO_4$ absorb?

9. Evaluating Conclusions
When you rehydrated the small amount of anhydrous copper sulfate, what were your observations? Explain whether this substance would make a good indicator of moisture.

Extensions

1. Applying Conclusions
Some cracker tins include a glass vial of drying material in the lid. This is often a mixture of magnesium sulfate and cobalt chloride. As the mixture absorbs moisture to form hydrated compounds, the cobalt chloride changes from blue-violet $CoCl_2 \bullet 2H_2O$ to pink $CoCl_2 \bullet 6H_2O$. When this hydrated mixture becomes totally pink, it can be restored to the dihydrate form by being heated in the oven. Write equations for the reactions that occur when this mixture is heated.

2. Applying Ideas
Three pairs of students obtained the following results when they heated a solid. In each case, the students observed that when they began to heat the solid, drops of a liquid formed on the sides of the test tube.
a. Could the solid be a hydrate? Explain how you could find out.
b. If the solid has a molar mass of 208 g/mol after heating and a formula of XY, how many formula units of water are there in one formula unit of the unheated compound?

Data Table 2		
Sample number	Mass before heating (g)	Constant mass after heating (g)
1	1.92	1.26
2	2.14	1.40
3	2.68	1.78

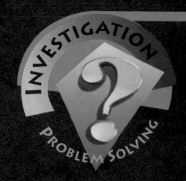

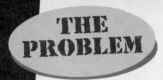

INVESTIGATION PROBLEM SOLVING

5A | Hydrates
Gypsum and Plaster of Paris

THE PROBLEM

LOST ART GYPSUM MINE

February 9, 1999

Director of Research
CheMystery Labs, Inc.
52 Fulton Street
Springfield, VA 22150

Dear Sir:

Lost Art Gypsum Mine previously sold its raw gypsum to a manufacturing company that used it to make anhydrous calcium sulfate, $CaSO_4$ (a desiccant), and plaster of Paris. That firm has now gone out of business, and we are currently negotiating the purchase of the firm's equipment to process our own gypsum into anhydrous calcium sulfate and plaster of Paris.

Your company has been recommended to plan the large-scale industrial process for our new plant. We will need a detailed report on the development of the process and formulas for these products. This report will be presented to the bank handling our loan for the new plant. As we discussed on the telephone today, we are willing to pay you $250,000 for the work, with the contract papers arriving under separate cover today.

Sincerely,

Alex Farros

Alex Farros
Vice President
Lost Art Gypsum Mine

References

Review information about hydrates and water of crystallization. Gypsum and plaster of Paris are hydrated forms of $CaSO_4$. One of the largest gypsum mines in the world is located outside Paris, France. Plaster of Paris has less water of crystallization than gypsum. Plaster of Paris is commonly used in plaster walls and art sculptures.

THE PLAN

MEMORANDUM

CheMystery Labs, Inc.
52 Fulton Street
Springfield, VA 22150

Date: February 10, 1999
To: Kenesha Smith
From: Martha Li-Hsien

Your team needs to develop a procedure to experimentally determine the correct empirical formulas for both hydrates of this anhydrous compound. You will use gypsum samples from the mine and samples of the plaster of Paris product; both are available at a cost.

Once this work is complete, our chemical engineering division will examine the most efficient way to implement the procedures for manufacturing. We're getting $250,000 from Lost Art. Your part of the job must cost less than $125,000 so that the chemical engineering division has enough money to do its job.

As soon as possible, I need a preliminary report from you that includes the following:
- detailed one-page summary of your plan for the procedure with all necessary data tables
- itemized list of equipment with total costs
  (Remember to keep costs under $125,000)

After you complete the analysis, prepare a two-page report for the chemical engineering division that includes the following information:
- formulas for anhydrous calcium sulfate, plaster of Paris, and gypsum
- summary of your procedure
- detailed and organized data and analysis sections that show calculations, along with estimates and explanations of any possible sources of error
- detailed invoice of all expenses and services

This report will become Chapter 2 of our final report to Mr. Farros.

For prices of materials, see page 692.

Required Precautions

Safety goggles and a lab apron must be worn at all times in the laboratory.

Confine long hair and loose clothing.

Do not touch or taste any chemicals. Always wash your hands thoroughly when finished in the lab.

Spill Procedures/ Waste-Disposal Methods

- Solids must go in the designated waste containers.
- Clean the lab area and all equipment after use.

EXPLORATION TECHNIQUE BUILDER

7A | Polymers and Toy Balls

OBJECTIVES

▸ Synthesize two different polymers.

▸ Prepare a small toy ball from each polymer.

▸ Observe the similarities and differences between the two types of balls.

▸ Measure the density of each polymer.

▸ Compare the bounce height of the two balls.

MATERIALS

▸ 2 L beaker, or plastic bucket or tub

▸ 3 mL 50% ethanol solution

▸ 5 oz paper cups, 2

▸ 10 mL 5% acetic acid solution (vinegar)

▸ 10 mL graduated cylinder

▸ 10 mL liquid latex

▸ 12 mL sodium silicate solution

▸ 25 mL graduated cylinder

▸ distilled water

▸ gloves

▸ meterstick

▸ paper towels

▸ wooden stick

Situation

Your company has been contacted by a toy company that specializes in toy balls made from vulcanized rubber. Recent environmental legislation has increased the cost of disposing of the sulfur and other chemical byproducts of the manufacturing process for this type of rubber. The toy company wants you to research some other materials.

Always wear safety goggles and a lab apron to protect your eyes and clothing. If you get a chemical in your eyes, immediately flush the chemical out at the eyewash station while calling to your teacher. Know the location of the emergency lab shower and eyewash station and the procedures for using them.

Do not touch any chemicals. If you get a chemical on your skin or clothing, wash the chemical off at the sink while calling to your teacher. Make sure you carefully read the labels and follow the precautions on all containers of chemicals that you use. If no precautions are stated on the label, ask your teacher what precautions to follow. Do not taste any chemicals or items used in the laboratory. Never return leftover chemicals to their original containers; take only small amounts to avoid wasting supplies.

Wear disposable plastic gloves; the sodium silicate solution and the alcohol silicate polymer are irritating to your skin.

Ethanol is flammable. Make sure there are no flames anywhere in the laboratory when you are using it. Also, keep it away from other sources of heat.

Background

Rubber is a polymer of covalently bonded atoms. When rubber is vulcanized, it is heated with sulfur. The sulfur atoms form bonds between adjacent molecules of rubber, increasing its strength and making it more elastic.

Latex rubber is a colloidal suspension that can be made synthetically or found naturally in plants such as the para rubber tree *(Hevea brasiliensis)*, in which it dries to form a waterproof layer for protection. Latex is composed of approximately 60% water, 35% hydrocarbon monomers, 2% proteins, and some sugars and inorganic salts. Commercial latex is preserved with ammonia so that it remains a liquid until it can be molded or stretched into its final form. Latex is used in paints and disposable gloves.

The polymer formed from ethanol, C_2H_5OH, and a solution of sodium silicate, mostly in the form of $Na_2Si_3O_7$, also has covalent bonds. It is known as water glass because it dissolves in water. When the polymer is formed, water is also a product.

Problem

Latex rubber and the ethanol–sodium silicate polymer are the two materials you will become familiar with as you do the following:

▶ Synthesize each polymer.

▶ Make a ball 2–3 cm in diameter from each polymer.

▶ Make observations about the physical properties of each polymer.

▶ Measure how well each ball bounces.

Preparation

1. Organizing Data

Copy the data table below in your lab notebook. Prepare one table for each polymer. Leave space to record observations about the balls.

Technique

2. Fill the 2 L beaker, bucket, or tub about half-full with distilled water.

3. Using a clean 25 mL graduated cylinder, measure 10 mL of liquid latex and pour it into one of the paper cups.

Data Table 1			
Trial	Height (cm)	Mass (g)	Diameter (cm)
1			
2			
3			

4. Thoroughly clean the 25 mL graduated cylinder with soap and water, and then rinse it with distilled water.

5. Measure 10 mL of distilled water. Pour it into the paper cup with the latex.

6. Measure 10 mL of the 5% acetic acid solution, and pour it into the paper cup with the latex and water.

7. Immediately stir the mixture with the wooden stick.

8. As you continue stirring, a polymer "lump" will form around the wooden stick. Pull the stick with the polymer lump from the paper cup and immerse the lump in the 2 L beaker, bucket, or tub.

9. While wearing gloves, gently pull the lump from the wooden stick. Be sure to keep the lump immersed in the water, as shown in **Figure A.**

10. Keep the latex rubber underwater, and use your gloved hands to mold the lump into a ball, as shown in **Figure B.** Squeeze the lump several times to remove any unused chemicals. You may remove the latex rubber from the water as you roll it in your hands to smooth the ball.

11. Set aside the latex-rubber ball to dry. While it is drying, begin to make a ball from the ethanol and sodium silicate solutions.

12. In a clean 25 mL graduated cylinder, measure 12 mL of sodium silicate solution, and pour it into the other paper cup.

13. In a clean 10 mL graduated cylinder, measure 3 mL of 50% ethanol. Pour the ethanol into the paper cup with the sodium silicate, and mix with the wooden stick until a solid substance is formed.

14. While wearing gloves, remove the polymer that forms and place it in the palm of one hand, as shown in **Figure C.** Gently press it with the palms of both your hands until a ball that does not crumble is formed. This takes a little time and patience. The liquid that comes out of the ball is a combination of ethanol and water. Occasionally moisten the ball by letting a small amount of water from a faucet run over it. When the ball no longer crumbles, you are ready to go on to the next step.

15. Observe as many physical properties of the balls as possible, and record your observations in your lab notebook.

16. Drop each ball several times, and record your observations.

17. Drop each ball from a height of 1 m, and measure its bounce. Perform three trials for each ball, and record the values in your data table.

18. Measure the diameter and the mass of each ball, and record the values in your data table.

Figure A

Figure B

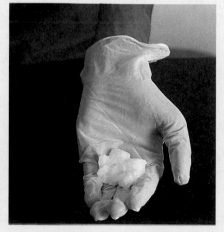
Figure C

Cleanup and Disposal

19. Clean all apparatus and your lab station. Dispose of any extra solutions in the containers indicated by your teacher. Clean up your lab area. Remember to wash your hands thoroughly when your lab work is finished.

Analysis and Interpretation

1. **Analyzing Information**
   Give the chemical formula for the latex (isoprene) monomer and the ethanol–sodium silicate polymer.

2. **Analyzing Information**
   List at least three observations you made of the properties of the two different balls.

3. **Applying Models**
   Explain how your observations in item 2 indicate that the polymers in each ball are not ionically bonded.

4. **Organizing Data**
   Calculate the average height of the bounce for each type of ball.

5. **Organizing Data**
   Calculate the volume for each ball. Even though the balls may not be perfectly spherical, assume that they are. (Hint: The volume of a sphere is equal to $4/3 \times \pi \times r^3$, where r is the radius of the sphere, which is one-half of the diameter.)

6. **Organizing Data**
   Using your measurements for the volumes from item 5 and the recorded mass, calculate the density of each ball.

Conclusions

7. **Inferring Conclusions**
   Which polymer would you recommend for the toy company's new toy balls? Explain your reasoning.

8. **Evaluating Viewpoints**
   Using the table shown below, calculate the unit cost, that is, the amount of money it costs to make a single ball. (Hint: Calculate how much of each reagent is needed to make a single ball.)

Data Table 2	
Reagent	**Price (dollars per liter)**
Acetic acid solution	1.50
Ethanol solution	9.00
Latex solution	20.00
Sodium silicate solution	10.00

9. **Evaluating Viewpoints**
   What are some other possible practical applications for each of the polymers you made?

Extensions

1. **Research and Communication**
   Polymers are used in our daily lives. Describe or list the polymers you come into contact with during a one-day period in your life.

2. **Designing Experiments**
   Design a mold for a polymer ball that will make it symmetrical and smooth. If your teacher approves of your design, try the procedure again with the mold.

3. **Predicting Outcomes**
   When a ball bounces up, kinetic energy of motion is converted into potential energy. With this in mind, explain which will bounce higher, a perfectly symmetrical, round sphere or an oblong shape that vibrates after it bounces.

4. **Predicting Outcomes**
   Explain why you didn't measure the volume of the balls by submerging them in water.

EXPLORATION TECHNIQUE BUILDER

10A | Decomposition of Baking Soda

OBJECTIVES

▶ Observe the thermal decomposition reaction of baking soda.

▶ Measure the mass of the remaining material after the reaction is complete.

▶ Calculate the expected masses of the solid products for each potential decomposition reaction.

▶ Compare the experimental mass to stoichiometric predictions to determine which reaction occurred.

MATERIALS

▶ baking soda

▶ balance

▶ Bunsen burner and sparker

▶ crucible and cover

▶ crucible tongs

▶ pipestem triangle

▶ ring clamp

▶ ring stand

▶ spatula

▶ weighing boats

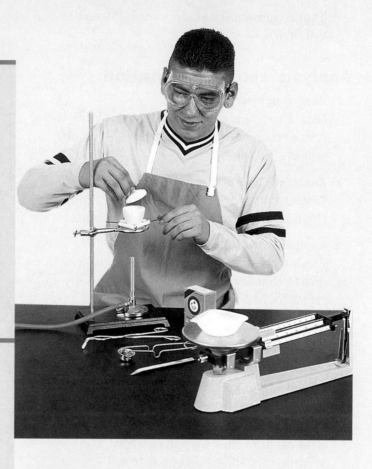

Situation

You are a food chemist working for a company that makes boxed cake mix. Your company is trying to formulate a new recipe for Black Forest cake, and every ingredient needed in the powdered cake mix has been added except sodium bicarbonate (commonly called baking soda). Sodium bicarbonate is used to ensure that breads and cakes rise during baking. Your company wants you to determine the correct decomposition reaction that baking soda undergoes. This will determine what quantity to use in the mix.

Background

Due to the widespread use of sodium bicarbonate in many food products, the thermal decomposition reaction has been studied extensively by food chemists. Baking soda is used to prepare cakes in order to ensure that cakes rise as they bake.

As the temperature of the cake batter reaches approximately 50°C, the baking soda decomposes and carbon dioxide is released. The use of baking soda is especially popular in pancakes and waffles because the high cooking temperatures of 350–450°F (175–230°C) cause the carbon dioxide to be liberated before the dough sets. Thus, the batter rises before it sets, and we get a light and tasty finished product.

Problem

The goal of this lab is for you to experimentally determine which of three possible reactions is correct. All of these equations appear to be reasonable, but only one actually occurs. On the basis of stoichiometry, you can eliminate reactions that do not fit your experimental results when you conduct the thermal decomposition of baking soda.

Possible Decomposition Reactions

sodium bicarbonate (solid) $\longrightarrow$
sodium hydroxide (solid) + carbon dioxide (gas)

sodium bicarbonate (solid) $\longrightarrow$
sodium oxide (solid) + carbon dioxide (gas)
+ water (gas)

sodium bicarbonate (solid) $\longrightarrow$
sodium carbonate (solid) + carbon dioxide (gas)
+ water (gas)

Preparation

1. Organizing Data
   Copy the data table below in your lab notebook.

2. Set up the ring stand, ring clamp and Bunsen burner setup. Place the pipestem triangle on the ring clamp.

Data Table
Mass of empty crucible (g)
Mass of baking soda (g)
Mass of crucible and baking soda (g)
Mass of crucible and product (g)

Figure A

Technique

3. Measure the mass of the empty crucible. Record this measurement in your data table.

4. Obtain 2.0 g of baking soda in a clean, dry plastic weighing boat, as shown in **Figure A.** Record the exact mass, and include all decimal places. Record this measurement in your data table.

5. Transfer the solid material to the crucible, being careful to ensure the complete transfer to the small crucible, as shown in **Figure B.**

Figure B

6. Measure the total mass of the crucible and the baking soda. Record this measurement in your data table.

7. Place the crucible directly into the small pipestem triangle.

8. Heat the crucible and its contents with the Bunsen burner for 10 minutes. The bottom of the crucible should become bright orange, as shown in **Figure C.** Use a spatula to carefully break up any clumps that form as the heating proceeds.

9. Once the crucible has cooled to room temperature, measure the mass of the crucible and the remaining solid material. Record this measurement in your data table.

Cleanup and Disposal

10. Clean all apparatus and your lab station. Return equipment to its proper place. Dispose of chemicals and solutions in the containers designated by your teacher. Do not pour any chemicals down the drain or in the trash unless your teacher directs you to do so. Wash your hands thoroughly after all work is finished and before you leave the lab.

Figure C

Analysis and Interpretation

1. Organizing Ideas
Translate each of the three possible word equations in the Problem section of the lab into balanced chemical equations.

2. Organizing Ideas
What was the mass of the remaining solid product that was formed in this chemical reaction?

3. Applying Ideas
Calculate the number of moles of baking soda that were present in your crucible.

4. Applying Ideas
Look at each of your balanced chemical equations. How many moles of the three different solid products would be formed from the number of moles of baking soda? (Hint: Use the mole ratios.)

5. Applying Ideas
How are most decomposition reactions initiated?

Conolusions

6. Applying Conclusions
Use your answers from item 4 to determine the predicted mass of the solid product in each of the three possible chemical reactions.

7. Applying Conclusions
Which chemical reaction occurred inside the crucible?

8. Evaluating Methods
If the crucible were not heated long enough, would you expect the mass of the solid material inside the crucible to have a higher or lower mass than what stoichiometry would predict?

9. Apply Ideas
A student adds 0.40 g of sodium hydroxide to a clean, dry 250 mL beaker and leaves the beaker on the lab table. The mass of the empty beaker is 112.58 g. After 24 hours, the student observes that the beaker contains a dry, solid white residue. The total mass of the beaker and its contents is 113.09 g. Following are three possible chemical reactions that could have occurred:

Reaction A

sodium hydroxide (s) + carbon dioxide $(g)\longrightarrow$
$$\text{sodium bicarbonate } (s)$$

Reaction B

sodium hydroxide (s) + carbon dioxide $(g)\longrightarrow$
$$\text{sodium carbonate } (s) + \text{water } (g)$$

Reaction C

sodium hydroxide $(s)\longrightarrow$
$$\text{sodium oxide } (s) + \text{water } (g)$$

Use your knowledge of stoichiometry to determine which chemical reaction occurred. Show your work, and explain your reasoning whenever needed.

Extensions

1. Designing Experiments
What possible sources of error can you identify with this procedure? If you can think of ways to eliminate them, ask your teacher to approve your plans, and run the procedure again.

10B | Stoichiometry and Gravimetric Analysis

OBJECTIVES

▶ Observe the double-displacement reaction between solutions of strontium chloride and sodium carbonate.

▶ Demonstrate proficiency with gravimetric methods.

▶ Measure the mass of insoluble precipitate formed.

▶ Relate the mass of precipitate formed to the mass of reactants before the reaction.

▶ Calculate the mass of sodium carbonate in a solution of unknown concentration.

MATERIALS

▶ 0.30 M $SrCl_2$ solution, 45 mL

▶ 15 mL Na_2CO_3 solution of unknown concentration

▶ 100 mL graduated cylinder

▶ 250 mL beakers, 3

▶ balance

▶ beaker tongs

▶ distilled water

▶ drying oven

▶ filter paper

▶ glass funnel or Büchner funnel with related equipment

▶ glass stirring rod

▶ paper towels

▶ ring and ring stand

▶ rubber policeman

▶ spatula

▶ water bottle

Situation

You are working for a company that makes water-softening agents for homes with hard water. Recently, there was a mix-up on the factory floor, and sodium carbonate solution was mistakenly mixed in a vat with an unknown quantity of distilled water. You must determine the amount of Na_2CO_3 in the vat in order to properly predict the percentage yield of the water-softening product. You have been given a small sample from the 575 L of new solution.

Background

When chemists are faced with problems that require them to determine the quantity of a substance by mass, they often use a technique called gravimetric analysis. In this technique, a small sample of the material undergoes a reaction with an excess of another reactant. The chosen reaction is one that almost always provides a yield near 100%. In other words, all of the reactant of unknown amount will be converted into product. If the mass of the product is carefully measured, you can use stoichiometry calculations to determine how much of the reactant of unknown amount was involved in the reaction. Then by comparing the size of the analysis sample with the size of the original material, you can determine exactly how much of the substance is present.

This procedure involves a double-displacement reaction between strontium chloride, $SrCl_2$, and sodium carbonate, Na_2CO_3. In general, this reaction can be used to determine the amount of any carbonate compound in a solution.

Problem

Remember that accurate results depend on precise mass measurements, so keep all glassware very clean and do not lose any reactants or products during your lab work. You will react an unknown amount of sodium carbonate with

an excess of strontium chloride. After purifying the product, you will determine the following:

◗ how much product is present
◗ how much Na_2CO_3 must have been present to produce that amount of product
◗ how much Na_2CO_3 is contained in the 575 L of solution

Preparation

1. **Organizing Data**
   Copy the data table below in your lab notebook.

2. Clean all of the necessary lab equipment with soap and water. Rinse each piece of equipment with distilled water.

3. Measure the mass of a piece of filter paper to the nearest 0.01 g, and record this value in your data table.

Data Table	
Volume of Na_2CO_3 solution added	
Volume of $SrCl_2$ solution added	
Mass of dry filter paper	
Mass of beaker with paper towel	
Mass of beaker with paper towel, filter paper, and precipitate	

4. Refer to page 714 to set up a filtering apparatus, either a Büchner funnel or a gravity filtration, depending on what equipment is available.

5. Label a paper towel with your name, your class, and the date. Place the towel in a clean, dry 250 mL beaker, and measure and record the mass of the towel and beaker to the nearest 0.01 g.

Technique

6. Measure about 15 mL of the Na_2CO_3 solution into the graduated cylinder. Record this volume to the nearest 0.5 mL in your data table. Pour the Na_2CO_3 solution into a clean, empty 250 mL beaker. Carefully wash the graduated cylinder, and rinse it with distilled water.

7. Measure about 25 mL of the 0.30 M $SrCl_2$ solution into the graduated cylinder. Record this volume to the nearest 0.5 mL in your data table. Pour the $SrCl_2$ solution into the beaker with the Na_2CO_3 solution, as shown in **Figure A.** Gently stir the solution and precipitate with a glass stirring rod.

8. Carefully measure another 10 mL of $SrCl_2$ into the graduated cylinder. Record the volume to the nearest 0.5 mL in your data table. Slowly add it to the beaker. Repeat this step until no more precipitate forms.

Figure A

Figure B

9. Once the precipitate has settled, slowly pour the mixture into the funnel. Be careful not to overfill the funnel because some of the precipitate could be lost between the filter paper and the funnel. Use the rubber policeman to transfer as much of the precipitate into the funnel as possible.

10. Rinse the rubber policeman into the beaker with a small amount of distilled water, and pour this solution into the funnel. Rinse the beaker several more times with small amounts of distilled water, as shown in **Figure B.** Pour the rinse water into the funnel each time.

11. After all of the solution and rinses have drained through the funnel, slowly rinse the precipitate on the filter paper in the funnel with distilled water to remove any soluble impurities.

12. Carefully remove the filter paper from the funnel, and place it on the paper towel that you have labeled with your name. Unfold the filter paper, and place the paper towel, filter paper, and precipitate in the rinsed beaker. Then place the beaker in the drying oven. For best results, allow the precipitate to dry overnight.

13. Using beaker tongs, remove your sample from the drying oven, and allow it to cool.

Measure and record the mass of the beaker with paper towel, filter paper, and precipitate to the nearest 0.01 g.

 Cleanup and Disposal

14. Dispose of the precipitate in a designated waste container. Pour the filtrate in the other 250 mL beaker into the designated waste container. Clean up the lab and all equipment after use, and dispose of substances according to your teacher's instructions. Wash your hands thoroughly after all lab work is finished and before you leave the lab.

Analysis and Interpretation

1. Organizing Ideas
Write a balanced equation for the reaction. What is the precipitate? Write its empirical formula. (Hint: It was a double-displacement reaction.)

2. Applying Ideas
Calculate the mass of the dry precipitate. Calculate the number of moles of precipitate produced in the reaction. (Hint: Use the results from step 13.)

3. Applying Ideas
How many moles of Na_2CO_3 were present in the 15 mL sample?

4. Evaluating Methods
There was 0.30 mol of $SrCl_2$ in every liter of solution. Calculate the number of moles of $SrCl_2$ that were added. Determine whether $SrCl_2$ or Na_2CO_3 was the limiting reactant. Would this experiment have worked if the other reactant had been chosen as the limiting reactant? Explain why or why not.

5. Evaluating Methods
Why was the precipitate rinsed in step 11? What soluble impurities could have been on the filter paper along with the precipitate? How would the calculated results vary if the precipitate had not been completely dry? Explain your answer.

Conclusions

6. Inferring Conclusions
How many grams of Na_2CO_3 were present in the 15 mL sample?

7. Applying Conclusions
How many grams of Na_2CO_3 are present in the 575 L? (Hint: Create a conversion factor to convert from the sample, with a volume of 15 mL, to the entire solution, with a volume of 575 L.)

Extensions

1. Evaluating Methods
Ask your teacher for the theoretical mass of Na_2CO_3 in the sample, and calculate your percentage error.

2. Designing Experiments
What possible sources of error can you identify with your procedure? If you can think of ways to eliminate them, ask your teacher to approve your plan, and run the procedure again.

10B | Gravimetric Analysis
Hard Water Testing

EDWARD F. QUIMBY, MAYOR
DANA RUBIO, CITY MANAGER

March 3, 1999

George Taylor, Director of Analysis
CheMystery Labs, Inc.
52 Fulton Street
Springfield, VA 22150

Dear Mr. Taylor:

The city's Public Works Department is investigating new sources of water. One proposal involves drilling wells into a nearby aquifer that is protected from brackish water by a unique geological formation. Unfortunately, this formation is made of calcium minerals. If the concentration of calcium ions in the water is too high, the water will be "hard," and treating it to meet local water standards would be too expensive for us.

Water containing more than 120 mg of calcium per liter is considered hard. Enclosed is a sample that has been distilled from 1.0 L to its present volume. Please determine whether it is of suitable quality.

We are seeking a firm to be our consultant for the entire testing process. Interested firms will be evaluated based on this analysis. We look forward to receiving your report.

Sincerely,

Dana Rubio

Dana Rubio
City Manager

References

Review Chapter 10 for information about mass-mass stoichiometry. In this investigation, you will use a double-displacement reaction, but Na_2CO_3 will be used as a reagent to identify how much calcium is present in a sample. Like strontium and other Group 2 metals, calcium salts react with carbonate-containing salts to produce an insoluble precipitate.

CheMystery Labs, Inc.
52 Fulton Street
Springfield, VA 22150

MEMORANDUM

Date: March 4, 1999
To: Shane Thompson
From: George Taylor

We must do a very accurate and efficient job on this analysis because this contract could be valuable for us in terms of both income and prestige. Besides, losing the contract to some out-of-town analysis firm would be awful!

We still don't have any capital expenditure funds for elaborate equipment purchases, but we can solve the city's problem with some careful gravimetric analysis because calcium salts and carbonate compounds undergo double-displacement reactions to give insoluble calcium carbonate as a precipitate.

Before you begin your work, I will need the following information from you so that I can put together our bid:
- detailed one-page summary of your plan for the procedure along with all necessary data tables
- description of necessary calculations
- itemized list of equipment with total costs. (Our financial planner tells me that even though we will bill the city for this work, we can afford to spend only $200,000 on this project.)

After you complete the analysis, prepare a two-page report for Dana Rubio. Remember that this report will be seen by a variety of city officials, so be certain it projects the image we want to present. Make sure the following items are included:
- calculation of calcium concentration in mg/L for the aquifer water
- explanation of how you determined the amount of calcium in the sample, including measurements and calculations
- balanced chemical equation for the reaction
- explanations and estimations for any possible sources of error
- detailed invoice for services rendered and expenses incurred

For prices of materials, see page 692.

Required Precautions

Safety goggles and a lab apron must be worn at all times.

Do not touch or taste any chemicals. Wash your hands thoroughly when finished.

Use beaker tongs to remove glassware from the drying oven.

Spill Procedures/ Waste-Disposal Methods

- Solids must go in the trash can. Do not wash them down the sink.
- Liquids may be washed down the sink with an excess of water.
- Clean the area and all equipment after use.

10C | Stoichiometry of Reactions

OBJECTIVES

▶ Demonstrate proficiency in measuring masses.

▶ Determine the number of moles of reactants and products in a reaction experimentally.

▶ Use the mass and mole relationships of a chemical reaction in calculations.

▶ Perform calculations that involve density and stoichiometry.

MATERIALS

▶ 1.0 M acetic acid

▶ 2–3 g NaHCO$_3$

▶ 100 mL graduated cylinder

▶ balance

▶ beaker tongs

▶ Bunsen burner and related equipment, or hot plate

▶ dropper or pipet

▶ evaporating dish

▶ ring stand and ring (for use with Bunsen burner)

▶ spatula

▶ watch glass

▶ wire gauze with ceramic center (for use with Bunsen burner)

Situation

Your company has a contract to determine the reaction requirements for a large-scale baking operation. The bakery purchases large quantities of ingredients and needs to know the correct proportions to avoid waste or inferior quality. The bakery needs to produce 425 mL of carbon dioxide, CO$_2$, for every cake during the rising step, which takes place just before baking. The bakery needs you to determine the exact amount of ingredients necessary to provide this amount of CO$_2$.

Always wear safety goggles and a lab apron to protect your eyes and clothing. If you get a chemical in your eyes, immediately flush the chemical out at the eyewash station while calling to your teacher. Know the locations of the emergency lab shower and eyewash and the procedure for using them.

Do not touch any chemicals. If you get a chemical on your skin or clothing, wash the chemical off at the sink while calling to your teacher. Make sure you carefully read the labels and follow the precautions on all containers of chemicals that you use. If there are no precautions stated on the label, ask your teacher what precautions to follow. Do not taste any chemicals or items used in the laboratory. Never return leftovers to their original containers; take only small amounts to avoid wasting supplies.

Confine long hair and loose clothing. If your clothing catches fire, WALK to the emergency lab shower and use it to put out the fire. Do not heat glassware that is broken, chipped, or cracked. Use tongs or a hot mitt to handle heated glassware and other equipment; heated glassware does not always look hot.

Never put broken glass or ceramics in a regular waste container. Broken glass or ceramics should be disposed of in a separate container designated by your teacher.

Call your teacher in the event of an acid or base spill. Acid or base spills should be cleaned up promptly according to your teacher's instructions.

Background

Some recipes use baking soda, $NaHCO_3$, to make cakes rise. When you add a weak acid, such as vinegar, which contains acetic acid, CH_3COOH, or buttermilk, which contains lactic acid, CH_3COOH, to baking soda, bubbles of carbon dioxide gas are produced. The word equation for the reaction with vinegar is as follows: acetic acid and sodium hydrogen carbonate yields sodium acetate, water, and carbon dioxide. But you can't merely add an excess of baking soda to be sure enough CO_2 is formed because too much baking soda can make the cakes crumbly and bitter. Similarly, too much acid can cause a cake to taste sour. The amount of each reactant must be perfectly measured to produce the correct amount of CO_2, which has a density of 1.25 g/L at baking temperature.

Problem

To figure out the solution for the bakery, you will need to do the following:

▶ React a carefully measured mass of the reactant, $NaHCO_3$.
▶ Measure the mass of the product, $NaCH_3COOH$.

▶ Determine the mass and mole relationships for the other reactants and products.
▶ Calculate the number of moles and mass of each reactant required to produce 425 mL of CO_2.

Preparation

1. Organizing Data

Copy the data table below in your lab notebook.

Data Table

Material	Mass (g)
Empty evaporating dish and watch glass	
Empty evaporating dish, watch glass, and $NaHCO_3$	
Heating 1, evaporating dish, watch glass, and $NaCH_3COO$	
Heating 2, evaporating dish, watch glass, and $NaCH_3COO$	
Heating 3, evaporating dish, watch glass, and $NaCH_3COO$	

Technique

2. Measure the mass of a clean, dry evaporating dish and watch glass to the nearest 0.01 g. Record this mass in your data table.

3. Add 2–3 g $NaHCO_3$ to your evaporating dish. Measure the exact mass, with the cover glass, to the nearest 0.01 g. Record this mass in your data table.

4. Slowly add 30 mL of the acetic acid solution to the $NaHCO_3$ in the evaporating dish. Add more acetic acid with a dropper or pipet until the bubbling stops.

5. If you are using a Bunsen burner, place the evaporating dish and its contents on a ceramic-centered wire gauze placed on an iron ring attached to the ring stand, as shown in **Figure A.** Place the watch glass, concave side up, on top of the dish, making sure that there is a slight opening for steam to escape. If you are using a hot plate, position the watch glass the same way.

6. Gently heat the evaporating dish until only a dry solid remains. Make sure that no water droplets remain on the underside of the watch glass. **Do not heat too rapidly, or the material will boil, and the product will spatter out of the evaporating dish.**

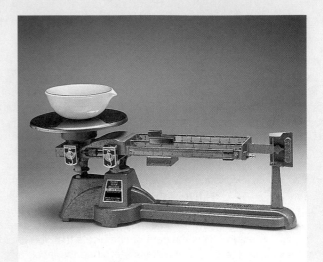

Figure B

7. Turn off the gas burner or hot plate. Allow the apparatus to cool for at least 15 minutes. Determine the mass of the cooled equipment to the nearest 0.01 g, as shown in **Figure B.** Record the mass of the dish, residue, and watch glass in your data table.

8. If time permits, reheat the evaporating dish and contents for 2 minutes. Let it cool, and measure its mass again. The sample will be dry when you can make two successive measurements within 0.02 g of each other.

Cleanup and Disposal

9. Clean up the lab and all equipment after use. Dispose of any unused chemicals in the containers designated by your teacher. Wash your hands thoroughly before you leave the lab and after all lab work is finished. Make sure to turn off all gas valves.

Analysis and Interpretation

1. Analyzing Results
Write a balanced equation for the reaction of baking soda and acetic acid. Be sure to include states of matter for all of the reactants and products.

2. Organizing Data
Use the periodic table to calculate the molar mass for each of the reactants and products.

Figure A

3. Analyzing Results

Explain what caused the bubbling when the reaction took place.

4. Analyzing Methods

How do you know that all of the residue is actually sodium acetate rather than a mixture of sodium bicarbonate and sodium acetate?

5. Organizing Data

Calculate the mass of $NaHCO_3$, the number of moles of $NaHCO_3$, the mass of $NaC_2H_3O_2$, and the number of moles of $NaC_2H_3O_2$.

6. Evaluating Data

Using the balanced equation and the amount of $NaHCO_3$, determine the theoretical yield of $NaC_2H_3O_2$ in moles and grams. (Hint: See Chapter 10 for a discussion of theoretical yield, and assume the acetic acid was present in excess.)

Conclusions

7. Analyzing Conclusions

What is the percentage yield for your reaction? (Hint: See Chapter 10 for a discussion of percentage yield.)

8. Inferring Conclusions

What is the theoretical yield for CO_2? Using the density value given, 1.25 g/L, calculate the volume of CO_2 that would be produced by this reaction in an oven. Show your calculations.

9. Applying Conclusions

How many moles of $NaHCO_3$ and CH_3COOH are necessary to produce 425 mL of CO_2 at baking temperature? Show your calculations. (Hint: Be sure to include your percentage yield for this reaction in your calculations.)

Extensions

1. Designing Experiments

If your percentage yield is less than 100%, explain why. If you can think of ways to eliminate any problems, ask your teacher to approve your plan, and run the procedure again.

2. Research and Communication

Many recipes for breads use yeast instead of baking soda as a source of CO_2. Research the use of yeast, and explain what ingredients are necessary for the yeast to produce carbon dioxide. What is the balanced chemical equation for the reaction that yeast use to produce CO_2?

DPC
DISEASE PREVENTION CENTER
1600 BROADCLIFT ROAD ATLANTA, GA 30333

March 7, 1999

Ms. Sandra Fernandez
Director of Development
CheMystery Labs, Inc.
52 Fulton Street
Springfield, VA 22150

Dear Ms. Fernandez:

The DPC has been monitoring reports of a cluster of illnesses near the town of Grover's Corner, New Jersey. Toxicology reports indicate that the disease is spread much like viral meningitis, only more quickly. We estimate that irreparable harm to the nervous system occurs in victims approximately 12 hours after their initial exposure to the virus. It is imperative that we find a treatment soon.

Preliminary research indicates that zinc chloride acts as an inhibitor to the reproduction of this unidentified virus. For this reason, several companies, including yours, have been contacted to produce a large quantity of zinc chloride quickly and economically.

Sincerely,

Rhonda Baclig

Rhonda Baclig, M.D.
Disease Prevention Center
Special Pathogens Branch

References

Review Chapter 10 for information on stoichiometric calculations. You will also need to review theoretical yield, actual yield, and percentage yield. The methods used in this procedure are very dependent on using clean and dry equipment. Remember that 1.0 M HCl contains 1.0 mol of HCl formula units in every liter.

CheMystery Labs, Inc.
52 Fulton Street
Springfield, VA 22150

MEMORANDUM

Date: March 8, 1999
To: Michael Belan
From: Sandra Fernandez

A rush job! If the disease spreads past this town and toward larger cities, an uncontrollable situation will develop very soon. Dr. Baclig has asked several companies to develop procedures for making small amounts of $ZnCl_2$ for $200,000. Based on the DPC's evaluation, a primary subcontractor will be chosen to prepare the inhibitor in bulk. She needs a preliminary report tomorrow that includes the following:
- detailed one-page summary of your plan for the procedure, including a suggested synthesis reaction
- itemized list of equipment with total costs

After you receive her approval, go ahead. When the work is complete, prepare a two-page letter and a minimum sample of 1.5 g of the inhibitor to go to Dr. Baclig. She will present them at a joint Disease Prevention Center/New Jersey Health Department meeting. Your letter must include the following:
- balanced chemical equation of the reaction you chose for producing the antidote
- molar masses and moles of the reactants and products
- theoretical and actual yield of the product
- percentage yield for your antidote, along with a discussion of what you did to keep the yield as high as possible and the cost as low as possible
- description of a procedure and cost for producing 37.50 kg of $ZnCl_2$
- detailed analysis and data sections showing calculations along with estimates and explanations of any possible sources of error
- detailed invoice for all expenses and services

For prices of materials, see page 692.

For prices of materials, see page 692.

Required Precautions

Safety goggles and a lab apron must be worn at all times.

Do not touch or taste any chemicals. Always wash your hands thoroughly when finished.

If you get acid or base on your skin or clothing, wash it off at the sink while calling to your teacher. If you get acid or base in your eyes, immediately flush it out at the eyewash station while calling to your teacher.

Spill Procedures/ Waste-Disposal Methods

- In case of spills, follow your teacher's instructions.
- Dispose of all solid and liquid wastes in the containers designated by your teacher.
- Clean the area and all equipment after use.
- Wash your hands when you are finished working in the lab.

11A | Calorimetry and Hess's Law

OBJECTIVES

▶ Demonstrate proficiency in the use of calorimeters and related equipment.

▶ Relate temperature changes to enthalpy changes.

▶ Determine the heat of reaction for several reactions.

▶ Demonstrate that the heat of reaction can be additive.

MATERIALS

▶ 0.50 M HCl solution, 100 mL

▶ 1.0 M HCl solution, 50 mL

▶ 1.0 M NaOH solution, 50 mL

▶ 4 g NaOH pellets

▶ 100 mL graduated cylinder

▶ balance

▶ distilled water

▶ glass stirring rod

▶ plastic-foam cups (or calorimeters)

▶ spatula

▶ thermometer

▶ watch glass

OPTIONAL EQUIPMENT

▶ CBL unit

▶ graphing calculator with link cable

▶ Vernier temperature probe

Situation

A man working for a cleaning firm was told by his employer to pour some old cleaning supplies into a glass container for disposal. Some of the supplies included muriatic (hydrochloric) acid, HCl(aq), and a drain cleaner containing lye, NaOH(s). When the substances were mixed, the container shattered, spilling the contents onto the worker's arms and legs. The worker claims that the hot spill caused burns, and he is therefore suing his employer. The employer claims that the worker is lying because the solutions were at room temperature before they were mixed. The employer says that a chemical burn is unlikely because tests after the accident revealed that the mixture had a neutral pH, indicating that the HCl and NaOH were neutralized. The court has asked you to evaluate whether the worker's story is supported by scientific evidence.

Always wear safety goggles and a lab apron to protect your eyes and clothing. If you get a chemical in your eyes, immediately flush the chemical out at the eyewash station while calling to your teacher. Know the locations of the emergency lab shower and eyewash station and the procedure for using them.

Do not touch any chemicals. If you get a chemical on your skin or clothing, wash the chemical off at the sink while calling to your teacher. Make sure you carefully read the labels and follow the precautions on all containers of chemicals that you use. If there are no precautions stated on the label, ask your teacher what precautions to follow. Do not taste any chemicals or items used in the laboratory. Never return leftovers to their original containers; take only small amounts to avoid wasting supplies.

Never put broken glass in a regular waste container. Broken glass should be disposed of separately in the container designated by your teacher.

Call your teacher in the event of an acid or base spill. Acid or base spills should be cleaned up promptly according to your teacher's instructions.

Background

Chemicals can be dangerous because of their special storage needs. Acids cannot be stored in metal containers, and organic solvents cannot be kept in plastic ones. Chemicals that are mixed and react are even more dangerous because many reactions release large amounts of heat. Glass, although relatively nonreactive with solutions of pure substances, is heat-sensitive and can shatter if there is a sudden change in temperature due to a reaction. Some glassware, such as Pyrex, is heat-conditioned but can still fracture under extreme heat conditions, especially if scratched.

Problem

You will measure the amount of heat released by mixing the chemicals in two ways. First you will break the reaction into steps and measure the heat change of each step. Then you will measure the heat change of the reaction when it takes place all at once. When you are finished, you will be able to use the calorimetry equation from Chapter 11 to determine the following:

- the amount of heat evolved during the overall reaction
- the amount of heat for each step
- the amount of heat for the reaction in kilojoules per mole
- whether this heat could have raised the temperature of the water in the solution high enough to cause a burn

Preparation

1. Organizing Data

Copy the data table below in your lab notebook. Reactions 1 and 3 will each require two additional spaces to record the mass of the empty watch glass and the mass of the watch glass with NaOH.

Data Table			
	Reaction 1	**Reaction 2**	**Reaction 3**
Total volumes of liquid(s)			
Initial temperature			
Final temperature			
Mass of empty watch glass			
Mass of watch glass with NaOH			

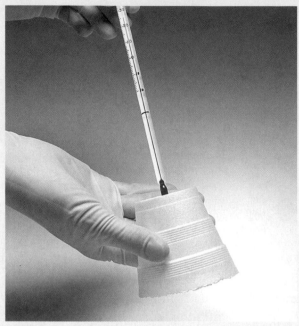

Figure A

2. If you are not using a plastic-foam cup as a calorimeter, ask your teacher for instructions on using the calorimeter. At various points in steps 3 through 13, you will need to measure the temperature of the solution within the calorimeter.

3. Measure the temperature by gently inserting the thermometer or Vernier temperature probe into the hole in the calorimeter lid, as shown in **Figure A.** If you are using the Vernier probe and CBL unit, refer to page 700 for equipment setup. The thermometer takes time to reach the same temperature as the solution inside the calorimeter, so wait to be sure you have an accurate reading. **Thermometers break easily, so be careful with them, and do not use them to stir a solution.**

Technique

Reaction 1: Dissolving NaOH
4. Pour about 100 mL of distilled water into a graduated cylinder. Measure and record the volume of the water to the nearest 0.1 mL. Pour the water into your calorimeter. Measure and record the water temperature to the nearest 0.1°C.

5. Determine and record the mass of a clean and dry watch glass to the nearest 0.01 g. Remove the watch glass from the balance. While wearing gloves, obtain about 2 g of NaOH pellets, and put them on the watch glass. Use forceps when handling NaOH pellets. Measure and record the mass of the watch glass and the pellets to the nearest 0.01 g. **It is important that this step be done quickly because NaOH is hygroscopic. It absorbs moisture from the air, and increases its mass as long as it remains exposed to the air.**

6. Immediately place the NaOH pellets in the calorimeter cup, and gently stir the solution with a stirring rod. **Do not stir with a thermometer.** Place the lid on the calorimeter. Watch the thermometer or CBL unit, and record the highest temperature in the data table. When the reaction is finished, pour the solution into the container designated by your teacher for disposal of basic solutions.

7. Be sure to clean all equipment and rinse it with distilled water before continuing with the next procedure.

Reaction 2: NaOH and HCl in solution
8. Pour about 50 mL of 1.0 M HCl into a graduated cylinder. Measure and record the volume of the HCl solution to the nearest 0.1 mL. Pour the HCl solution into your calorimeter. Measure and record the temperature of the HCl solution to the nearest 0.1°C.

9. Pour about 50 mL of 1.0 M NaOH into a graduated cylinder. Measure and record the volume of the NaOH solution to the nearest 0.1 mL. **For this step only, rinse the thermometer or probe in distilled water, and measure the temperature of the NaOH solution in the graduated cylinder to the nearest 0.1°C. Record the temperature in your data table, and then replace the thermometer in the calorimeter.**

10. Pour the NaOH solution into the calorimeter cup, and stir gently. Place the lid on the calorimeter. Watch the thermometer or CBL unit, and record the highest temperature in the data table. When finished with

this reaction, pour the solution into the container designated by your teacher for disposal of mostly neutral solutions.

11. Clean and rinse all equipment before continuing with the next procedure.

Reaction 3: Solid NaOH and HCl in solution

12. Pour about 100 mL of 0.50 M HCl into a graduated cylinder. Measure and record the volume to the nearest 0.1 mL. Pour the HCl solution into your calorimeter, as shown in **Figure B.** Measure and record the temperature of the HCl solution to the nearest 0.1°C.

13. Measure the mass of a clean and dry watch glass, and record it in your data table. Obtain approximately 2 g of NaOH. Place it on the watch glass, and record the total mass to the nearest 0.01 g. **It is important that this step be done quickly because NaOH is hygroscopic.**

14. Immediately place the NaOH pellets in the calorimeter, and gently stir the solution. Place the lid on the calorimeter. Watch the thermometer, and record the highest temperature in the data table. When finished with this reaction, pour the solution into the container designated by your teacher for disposal of mostly neutral solutions.

Figure B

Cleanup and Disposal

15. Clean all apparatus and your lab station. Check with your teacher for the proper disposal procedures. Any excess NaOH pellets should be disposed of in the designated container. Always wash your hands thoroughly after cleaning up the lab area and equipment.

Analysis and Interpretation

1. **Organizing Ideas**
   Write a balanced chemical equation for each of the three reactions that you performed. (Hint: Be sure to include states of matter for all substances in each equation.)

2. **Organizing Ideas**
   Find a way to get the equation for the total reaction by adding two of the equations from Analysis and Interpretation item 1 and then canceling out substances that appear in the same form on both sides of the new equation. (Hint: Start with the equation whose product is a reactant in a second equation. Add those two equations together.)

3. **Analyzing Methods**
   Explain why a plastic-foam cup makes a better calorimeter than a paper cup does.

4. **Organizing Data**
   Calculate the change in temperature (Δt) for each of the reactions.

5. **Organizing Data**
   Assuming that the density of the water and the solutions is 1.00 g/mL, calculate the mass, m, of liquid present for each of the reactions.

6. **Analyzing Results**
   Using the calorimeter equation, calculate the heat released by each reaction. (Hint: Use the specific heat capacity of water in your calculations; $c_{p,H_2O} = 4.180$ J/g•°C.)

$$\text{Heat} = m \times \Delta t \times c_{p,H_2O}$$

7. Organizing Data

Calculate the moles of NaOH used in each of the reactions. (Hint: To find the number of moles in a solution, multiply the volume in liters by the molar concentration.)

8. Analyzing Results

Calculate the ΔH value in terms of kilojoules per mole of NaOH for each of the three reactions.

9. Organizing Ideas

Using your answer to Analysis and Interpretation item 2 and your knowledge of Hess's law from Chapter 11, explain how the enthalpies for the three reactions should be mathematically related.

10. Organizing Ideas

Which of the following types of heat of reaction apply to the enthalpies calculated in Analysis and Interpretation item 8: heat of combustion, heat of solution, heat of reaction, heat of fusion, heat of vaporization, and heat of formation?

Conclusions

11. Evaluating Methods

Use your answers from Analysis and Interpretation items 7 and 8 to determine the ΔH value for the reaction of solid NaOH with HCl solution by direct measurement and by indirect calculation.

12. Inferring Conclusions

Third-degree burns can occur if skin comes into contact for more than 4 seconds with water that is hotter than 60°C (140°F). Suppose someone accidentally poured hydrochloric acid into a glass-disposal container that already contained the drain cleaner NaOH and the container shattered. The solution in the container was approximately 55 g of NaOH and 450 mL of muriatic acid solution containing 1.35 mol of HCl (a 3.0 M HCl solution). If the initial temperature of the solutions was 25°C, could a mixture hot enough to cause burns have resulted?

13. Applying Conclusions

For the reaction between the drain cleaner and HCl described in item 12, which chemical is the limiting reactant? How many moles of the other reactant remained unreacted?

Extensions

1. Applying Ideas

When chemists make solutions from NaOH pellets, they often keep the solution in an ice bath. Explain why.

2. Applying Ideas

When a strongly acidic or basic solution is spilled on a person, the first step is to dilute it by washing the area of the spill with a lot of water. Explain why adding an acid or base to neutralize the solution immediately is not a good idea.

3. Evaluating Methods

You have worked with heats of solution for exothermic reactions. Could the same type of procedure be used to determine the temperature changes for endothermic reactions? How would the procedure stay the same? What would change about the procedure and the data?

4. Applying Ideas

A chemical supply company is going to ship NaOH pellets to a very humid place, and you have been asked to give advice on packaging. Design a package for the NaOH pellets. Explain the advantages of your package's design and materials. (Hint: Remember that the reaction in which NaOH absorbs moisture from the air is exothermic and that NaOH reacts exothermically with other compounds as well.)

5. Inferring Conclusions

Which is more stable, solid NaOH or NaOH solution? Explain your answer.

EXPLORATION

TECHNIQUE BUILDER

CONSUMER ACTIVITY

11B | Kitchen Calorimetry

OBJECTIVES

- Construct a functional calorimeter from an empty soda can.

- Observe the combustion of several different food samples.

- Apply the law of conservation of energy to a simple heat-exchange process.

- Measure the change in temperature of the water inside the calorimeter.

- Measure the change in mass caused by the burning process.

- Calculate the heat energy lost by the burning food sample.

- Evaluate the experimental design to identify sources of heat loss.

MATERIALS

- 100 mL graduated cylinder
- balance
- empty soda can
- food samples*
- large cork
- large paper clips, 4
- matches
- ring stand
- small nail
- small ring clamp
- tap water
- thermometer
- weighing boats

* Potato chips, tortilla chips, walnuts, pecans, and peanuts are suggested for this activity.

Background

The law of conservation of energy states that energy cannot be created or destroyed. Energy can, however, be transferred from one object to another. This experiment involves the transfer of energy from a given food sample to a known quantity of water.

heat lost by the food sample =
heat gained by the water

All of the food samples chosen for this experiment can be ignited with a match. Once they begin burning, they will continue to burn for several minutes, causing the temperature of the water in the calorimeter to rise. Knowing the mass of the water, the water's specific heat capacity, and the change in temperature of the

Always wear safety goggles and a lab apron to protect your eyes and clothing. If you get a chemical in your eyes, immediately flush the chemical out at the eyewash station while calling to your teacher. Know the location of the emergency lab shower and the eyewash station and the procedure for using them.

Although there are no chemicals required for this lab, there may be chemicals stored in the laboratory room. Do not touch any chemicals. If you get a chemical on your skin or clothing, wash the chemical off at the sink while calling to your

teacher. Make sure you carefully read the labels and follow the precautions on all containers of chemicals that you use. If there are no precautions stated on the label, ask your teacher what precautions you should follow. Do not taste any chemicals or items used in the laboratory. Never return leftover chemicals to their original containers; take only small amounts to avoid wasting supplies.

When you use a match, confine long hair and loose clothing. If your clothing catches fire, WALK to the emergency lab shower, and use it to put out the fire.

water will allow you to calculate the amount of heat energy that was released from the burning food sample.

heat gained by the water =
temperature change of water × mass of water × specific heat capacity of water

The calorimeter that will be used in this experiment will be constructed from an empty soda can. Due to heat loss to the surroundings, the heat-transfer process will not be perfect, but good results can still be obtained.

Problem

You will burn four different food samples in this activity. Your goal is to measure the change in temperature of the water inside the calorimeter.

To do this, you will need to know the initial and final temperatures of the water. Because the masses of the food samples are different, the mass of each food sample must be measured. The residual mass of the food sample (ash) will also be measured. To determine the mass of the food sample that actually burned, you can subtract the residual mass from the initial mass of the food sample.

Preparation

1. Organizing Data
   Copy the data table below in your lab notebook.

2. If you are using the Vernier probe and CBL unit refer to page 700 for equipment setup.

Data Table

Food sample	Initial mass (g)	Final mass (g)	Initial temp (°C)	Final temp (°C)	Mass of water (g)

(Note: If the known density of water is 1.00 g/mL, what will be the mass of the 200.0 mL of water that is used in each trial? You can add this value to your data table for the mass of the water.)

Figure A

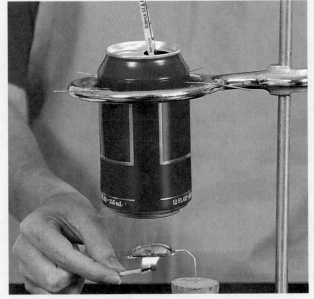

Figure B

Assembly of Calorimeter

3. To prepare a calorimeter using a soda can, as shown in **Figure A,** start by removing the tab from the top of the empty soda can.

4. Use a small nail to poke four holes into the sides of the can near the top. From the top of the can, the holes should appear in the 3, 6, 9, and 12 o'clock positions.

5. Straighten two large paper clips, and insert them into the can's holes. The wires should form a cross hair in the center of the can with the wires extending from the can.

6. Suspend the calorimeter from a ring clamp that has been fastened to a ring stand.

7. Make a stand for the food sample by straightening all but one section of another paper clip. Bend the straightened section downward, and insert it into the cork. Some food samples may need a second paper clip for more support. The food sample should now rest easily on this paper-clip stand.

Technique

8. Slowly add exactly 200.0 mL of water to the calorimeter.

9. Carefully lower the thermometer or temperature probe into the can.

10. Read the initial temperature of the water. Record this in your data table.

11. Measure the mass of the food sample. Record this in your data table.

12. Place the sample to be burned on the paper clip stand.

13. Ignite the sample with a match, as shown in **Figure B.** Be patient, and avoid moving the cork even slightly to prevent the sample from falling off.

14. Monitor the change in temperature of the water. You are measuring in the *highest temperature* of the water. Record this in your data table.

15. Allow the sample to burn out. After it has cooled to room temperature, measure its *final mass.* (Not all of the sample will have burned.) Do not place the burned sample directly on the balance. Record this in your data table.

16. After all measurements have been recorded, discard the burned sample in the wastebasket. **After each trial, pour the water from the calorimeter down the drain.**

17. Repeat with a different food sample.

Cleanup and Disposal

18. Clean all apparatus and your lab station. Return equipment to its proper place. The used soda cans can be recycled. The corks and paper clips can be kept for future use. Dispose of items in the containers designated by your teacher. Wash your hands thoroughly after all work is finished and before you leave the lab.

Analyzing Data

1. Analyzing Results

Calculate the change in temperature of the water for each sample tested.

2. Analyzing Results

Determine the mass of the sample that actually burned in each trial you conducted.

3. Applying Ideas

Use the heat equation to determine the amount of heat energy (calories) that was absorbed by the water in each trial.

4. Applying Ideas

Consider two potato chips: one is large, and the other is small. If used in this experiment, the larger chip will contain more energy. Therefore, the mass of the food samples must also be considered. For each trial, determine the number of calories per gram of food sample. Use the formula listed below.

$$\frac{\text{calories of energy released from the food sample}}{\text{mass of sample that was actually burned}}$$

Conclusions

5. Evaluating Methods

Would you expect the vertical distance from the burning food sample to the calorimeter to be important? Predict what would happen if the calorimeter were placed too far above the burning sample. Explain.

6. Applying Ideas

Explain how the conservation of energy relates to this activity. Be specific.

7. Evaluating Methods

What are several sources of error in this experiment? Be specific.

8. Applying Conclusions

Why are the experimental heat energy values (calories) for these food products always lower than what the food companies list? Explain why we never obtain experimental values that exceed the food companies' values.

9. Applying Ideas

How do food Calories differ from the calorie units that scientists use? What is the connection between these two similar units of measurement?

Extension

1. Designing Experiments

Refer to your answer for Conclusions item 6. Can you think of a way to eliminate your sources of error? If so, ask your teacher to approve your plan and run the procedure again.

13A | Paper Chromatography of Colored Markers

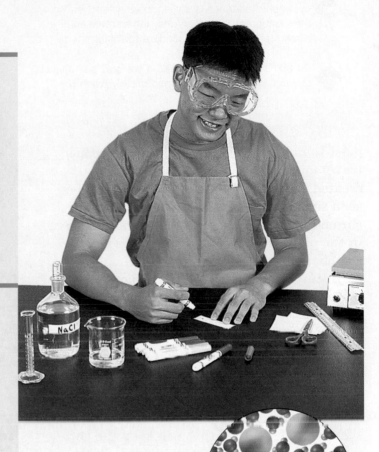

OBJECTIVES

▶ Design a successful method to ensure that the chromatography paper remains vertical throughout the experiment.

▶ Conduct a paper chromatography experiment with three different water-soluble colored markers.

▶ Observe the dye components of three different water-soluble markers.

MATERIALS

▶ 10 mL graduated cylinder

▶ 250 mL beaker

▶ chromatography paper

▶ developing solution: NaCl solution (0.1% by mass)

▶ hot plate

▶ markers

▶ paper clips

▶ pencils

▶ ruler

▶ scissors

Background

There is a wide variety of marker products on the market today ranging in color and function. All of these markers contain different dye components that are responsible for their color.

Paper chromatography is an analytical technique that uses paper as a medium to separate the different dye components dissolved in a mixture. In this process, the mixture to be separated is placed on a piece of chromatography paper. A solvent is then allowed to soak up into the paper. As the solvent travels across the paper, some of the components of the mixture are carried with it. Particles of the same component group together. The components that are

Always wear safety goggles and a lab apron to protect your eyes and clothing. If you get a chemical in your eyes, immediately flush the chemical out at the eyewash station while calling to your teacher. Know the location of the emergency lab shower and eyewash station and the procedure for using them.

Do not touch any chemicals. If you get a chemical on your skin or clothing, immediately wash the chemical off at the sink while calling to your teacher. Make sure you carefully read the labels and follow the precautions on all containers of chemicals that you use. If no precautions are stated on the label, ask your teacher what precautions to follow. Do not taste any chemicals or items used in the laboratory. Never return leftover chemicals to their original containers; take only small amounts to avoid wasting supplies.

most soluble and least attracted to the paper travel farther than others. A color band is created and the different components can be seen separated on the paper. The success of chromatography hinges on the slight difference in the physical properties of the individual components.

In this activity you will use a paper chromatography to determine the components of the dyes found in water-soluble markers.

Problem

Your goal is to use paper chromatography to determine the dye components of three different water-soluble markers. You will also need to design a simple method that will keep the chromatography paper vertical while it is in the developing solution.

Preparation

1. Organizing Data
Copy the data table below in your lab notebook.

Data Table

Marker color	Dye components

2. Obtain a clean 250 mL beaker and a 7.0 × 2.5 cm piece of chromatography paper.

3. Choose three different markers for this activity. Write the color of each marker in your data table.

4. Using a ruler, draw a horizontal line in pencil approximately 1.0 cm from one of the ends of the paper. Mark three small dots on this line, using a different marker for each dot.

5. Using a pencil, label each of the dots on the chromatography paper according to the color of the markers.

Technique

6. Measure out 7.0 mL of the developing solution in a 10 mL graduated cylinder.

7. Pour the 7.0 mL of solution in a 250 mL beaker, as shown in **Figure A** on the next page. Make sure the bottom of the beaker is completely covered. **The level of the liquid must be below the marks on your chromatography paper.**

8. You will need to design an experimental technique to ensure that your paper sample does not slide into the developing solution. The chromatography paper must remain vertical as the developing solution rises into the paper.

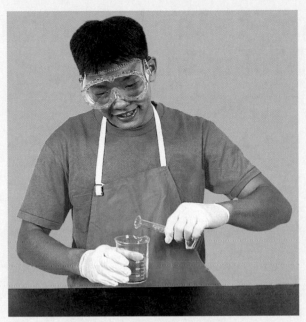

Figure A

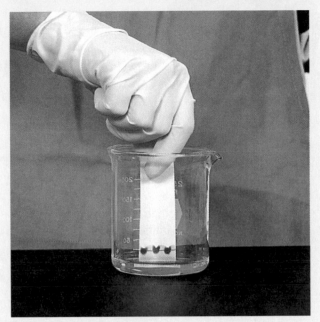

Figure B

9. Carefully place your paper (with the dots at the bottom) into the liquid, as shown in **Figure B.**

10. When the level of the liquid has advanced through most of the paper, remove the paper from the developing solution. Hold up the paper and observe the colors.

11. The chromatography samples can be carefully dried on a hot plate.

12. You may repeat this process using overwrite or color-change markers.

 **Cleanup and Disposal**

13. Clean all apparatus and your lab station. Return equipment to its proper place. Dispose of chemicals and solutions in the containers designated by your teacher. Do not pour any chemicals down the drain or in the trash unless your teacher directs you to do so.

Analysis and Interpretation

1. Organizing Ideas
What was the purpose of this experiment?

2. Evaluating Methods
Why shouldn't you use a ballpoint pen when marking the initial line and spots on the chromatography paper? Explain.

3. Evaluating Methods
Why were only water-soluble markers used in this experiment? Could permanent markers be used?

4. Evaluating Methods
Why must the spotted marks remain above the level of the liquid in the beaker?

Conclusions

5. Interpreting Results
Make observations about the dye components (colors) of each marker based on your results.

6. Applying Conclusions
Explain how law enforcement officials could use paper chromatography to identify a pen that was used in a ransom note.

7. List some other applications for using paper chromatography.

Extensions

1. Evaluating Methods
Compare your results with those of another lab group. Were the dye components found in other markers different from those found in yours?

13B | Boiling-Point Elevation and Molar Mass

OBJECTIVES

▶ Demonstrate proficiency in measuring masses, temperatures, and boiling points.

▶ Relate the concentration of a solution to boiling-point elevation data.

▶ Determine the molar mass of a solute from experimental data.

MATERIALS

▶ distilled water

▶ $MgSO_4 \cdot 7H_2O$, 10.0 g

▶ NaCl, 10.0 g

▶ sucrose, 10.0 g

▶ unknown sample, 10.0 g

▶ balance

▶ beaker tongs

▶ Bunsen burner and related equipment, or hot plate

▶ 125 mL Erlenmeyer flask

▶ ring stand and ring

▶ thermometer (nonmercury with 0.1°C markings) or Vernier temperature probe

▶ thermometer clamp

▶ wire gauze with ceramic center

OPTIONAL EQUIPMENT

▶ CBL unit

▶ graphing calculator with link cable

▶ Vernier temperature probe

Situation

Your company needs to determine the identity of a white powder that a young boy has swallowed. Doctors need to know the powder's identity to treat him. The substance must be one of the following: sodium chloride, NaCl; sugar (sucrose), $C_{12}H_{22}O_{11}$; or hydrated magnesium sulfate (Epsom salts), $MgSO_4 \cdot 7H_2O$. Along with the unknown, you have pure samples of the three substances.

Background

The boiling point of a solution is always higher than that of a pure liquid because the attraction of the solute for individual water molecules hinders their ability to move into the gaseous state. *Colligative properties* are properties of solutes that affect solutions. When dealing with

Always wear safety goggles and a lab apron to protect your eyes and clothing. If you get a chemical in your eyes, immediately flush the chemical out at the eyewash station while calling to your teacher. Know the locations of the emergency lab shower and eyewash station and the procedure for using them.

Do not touch any chemicals. If you get a chemical on your skin or clothing, wash the chemical off at the sink while calling to your teacher. Make sure you carefully read the labels and follow the precautions on all containers of chemicals that you use. If there are no precautions stated on the label, ask your teacher what precautions to follow. Do not taste any chemicals or items used in the laboratory. Never return leftovers to their original containers; take only small amounts to avoid wasting supplies.

When you use a Bunsen burner, confine any long hair and loose clothing. If your clothing catches on fire, WALK to the emergency lab shower, and use it to put out the fire. Do not heat glassware that is broken, chipped, or cracked. Use tongs or a hot mitt to handle heated glassware and other equipment because hot glassware does not always look hot.

colligative properties, the concentration units of *molality* (*m*) are used instead of *molarity* (M). Molality is defined as the number of moles of solute per kilogram of the solvent.

$$m = \frac{\text{moles solute}}{\text{kilograms solvent}}$$

Experiments have determined that the boiling-point elevation of a 1.00 *m* solution for any molecular solute in water is 0.51°C. This value is known as the molal boiling-point constant, K_b. The constant has the units °C/*m*.

Problem

To identify the unknown, you must do the following.

▶ make solutions using the same solute mass for each standard and for the unknown

▶ compare the boiling points of the resulting solutions to determine which matches that of the unknown

Calculate the molality of each solution based on the value of the boiling point. Then use the amount of solute you added and the number of moles (from the molality) to determine the molar mass.

$$\frac{\text{molar mass}}{\text{of solute}} = \frac{\text{g of solute}}{\text{kg of solvent} \times \text{molal conc.}}$$

Preparation

1. **Organizing Data**
   Prepare a data table in your lab notebook like the one below.
2. Measure the mass of the Erlenmeyer flask. Record this mass in your lab notebook.

Data Table

Solution	Mass of solute (g)	Mass of flask and water (g)	Boiling point
Water			
NaCl			
Sucrose			
$MgSO_4 \bullet 7H_2O$			
Unknown			

Figure A

3. If you are using the Vernier temperature probe and CBL unit refer to pages 700–701 for equipment setup.

Technique

4. Add distilled water to the Erlenmeyer flask until the total mass is as close as possible to 50.0 g more than the amount recorded in your lab notebook for the mass of the flask. Record this mass in your data table.

5. Place the flask of water on the wire gauze on the ring stand. Using the thermometer clamp, suspend the thermometer or probe in the water so that it does not touch the sides or bottom of the flask as shown in **Figure A.** Do not use a one-hole stopper to hold the thermometer or probe because the solution will be boiled.

6. Heat the water until it boils vigorously and the temperature remains constant. This temperature is the boiling point. Record it in your data table. (Note: Leave the box in your data table for *Mass of solute* (g) blank for this trial involving only water.)

7. Pour the contents of the flask into the sink. Then add distilled water to the flask until the total mass is as close as possible to 50.0 g more than the mass of the flask. Record this mass in your data table. Add 10.0 g of NaCl to this water, and swirl the flask gently until the salt dissolves completely. Record the mass of solute in your data table. **Do not allow the water to splash out of the flask because it will cause inaccuracy in your results.**

8. Place your flask on the wire gauze, and suspend the thermometer or probe in the water as before. Heat the solution to boiling, and record the boiling point in your data table.

9. Pour the contents of the flask into the sink. Rinse the flask three times with distilled water. Repeat steps 7 and 8 for sucrose, $MgSO_4 \cdot 7H_2O$, and for the unknown sample.

Cleanup and Disposal

10. Clean all apparatus and your lab station. Solutions may be rinsed down the sink. Check with your teacher for the proper disposal of other chemicals. Be certain all gas valves are turned off. Wash your hands thoroughly after cleaning up the area and equipment.

Analysis and Interpretation

1. Organizing Data

For the trials with solutes including the unknown, calculate the solution's change in boiling point, Δt_b. (Hint: Use the boiling point you measured for the pure water as the solvent's boiling point.)

2. Analyzing Information

Given that similar masses of each substance were used, do the data for the unknown most closely match NaCl, sucrose, or $MgSO_4 \cdot 7H_2O$?

3. Analyzing Data

Calculate the approximate molalities of dissolved particles for the known and unknown solutes using the following equation and your answers to item 1. (Hint: $K_b = 0.51°C/m$)

$$m = \frac{\Delta t_b}{K_b}$$

4. Organizing Data

For each trial, calculate the mass of water in the flask in kilograms.

5. Analyzing Data

Using your answers from Analysis and Interpretation items 3 and 4 and your data, calculate an experimental value for the molar mass of each solute.

Conclusions

6. Evaluating Conclusions

How close is the estimated molar mass of the unknown solute to the estimated molar mass of the solute chosen in Analysis and Interpretation item 2? Calculate the percentage error using the unknown solute's molar mass estimate as the experimental value.

7. Evaluating Methods

Determine the molar mass of NaCl, sucrose, and $MgSO_4 \cdot 7H_2O$ from the periodic table. Calculate the percentage error for your experimental molar-mass values.

8. Evaluating Methods

How accurate do you think it is to identify the unknown substance using this procedure? Can you explain any deviations that occur?

9. Applying Ideas

Explain in your own words why adding a solute raises the temperature at which a substance boils. (Hint: Consider what you know about bonding, phase changes, and kinetic-molecular theory.)

10. Analyzing Methods

Why do you need to determine the boiling point of water without a solute dissolved in it? Explain your answer.

Extensions

1. Designing Experiments

Obtain a water-soluble unknown from your teacher, and determine whether it is NaCl, sucrose, or $MgSO_4 \cdot 7H_2O$ by using the freezing-point depression method. (As determined by experimentation, the freezing-point depression of a 1.00 m solution of any molecular solute in water is $-1.86°C$.)

2. Research and Communication

Consult chemical handbooks and other reference works to determine the possible health hazards of these solutes. For each solute, what should be done if someone swallows it?

3. Applying Ideas

Find out how much and what type of salt a large northern city such as New York or Chicago uses on icy roads in the winter. What problems result from use of this salt? What salt substitutes can melt ice and snow? Which would be safest for our environment?

4. Research and Communication

What are some of the primary uses of $MgSO_4 \cdot 7H_2O$, and how is it produced for commercial use?

15A | Drip-Drop Acid-Base Experiment

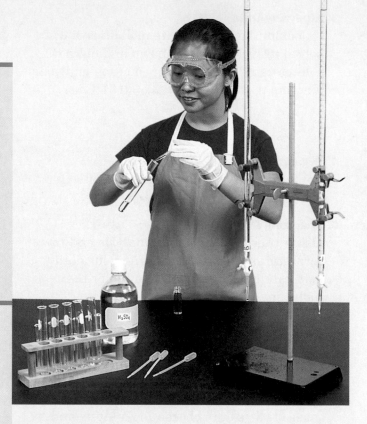

OBJECTIVES

▶ Translate word equations into chemical formulas.

▶ Count the number of drops of sodium hydroxide needed to completely react with different acid samples.

▶ Calculate the average number of drops of sodium hydroxide needed for each acid.

▶ Relate the number of drops to the coefficients in the balanced chemical equations.

MATERIALS

▶ 0.1 M H_2SO_4

▶ 0.1 M HCl

▶ 0.3 M NaOH

▶ burets, 2

▶ buret clamps

▶ phenolphthalein indicator

▶ pipets

▶ ring stands

▶ test-tube rack

▶ test tubes

Background

The purpose of this lab is to investigate the simple reaction between two different acids and a base. We will be counting the number of drops of sodium hydroxide that are needed to react completely with all of the acid. The starting acid and base solutions are colorless and clear, and the final products are colorless and clear. To monitor the progress of the chemical reaction, the acid-base indicator phenolphthalein will be used. Phenolphthalein is colorless when acidic and pink in color when neutral or basic. In this activity, we will know that all of the acid has been consumed by the base when the test-tube solution starts to turn pink. We can monitor the progress of the reaction so that a single drop of the base results in a sudden change from colorless to pink. At that point, we will know that all of the acid has reacted with the base.

Always wear safety goggles and a lab apron to protect your eyes and clothing. If you get a chemical in your eyes, immediately flush the chemical out at the eyewash station while calling to your teacher. Know the location of the emergency lab shower and eyewash station and the procedure for using them.

Do not touch any chemicals. If you get a chemical on your skin or clothing, wash the chemical off at the sink while calling to your teacher. Make sure you carefully read the labels and follow the precautions on all containers of chemicals that you use.

If there are no precautions, ask your teacher what precautions to follow. Do not taste any chemicals or items used in the laboratory. Never return leftovers to their original containers; take only small amounts to avoid wasting supplies.

Never put broken glassware in a regular waste container. Broken glass should be disposed of separately in a container designated by your teacher.

Call your teacher in the event of an acid or base spill. Acid or base spills should be cleaned up promptly according to your teacher's instructions.

Problem

You will need to count the number of drops of sodium hydroxide that are necessary to neutralize two different acids. Find the relationship between the sodium hydroxide drops necessary and the coefficients in the balanced chemical equation.

Preparation

1. Translate each of the word equations shown below into chemical equations.

   hydrochloric acid + sodium hydroxide $\longrightarrow$
   sodium chloride + water

   sulfuric acid + sodium hydroxide $\longrightarrow$
   sodium sulfate + water

2. **Organizing Data**
   Copy the two data tables in your laboratory notebook.

3. Clean six test tubes, and rinse them with distilled water. They do not need to be dry.

4. Obtain approximately 10 mL of sodium hydroxide solution in a small beaker.

Technique

Part I

5. Use a buret to put exactly 2.00 mL of hydrochloric acid directly into your test tube, as shown in **Figure A** on the next page.

6. Add two drops of phenolphthalein indicator solution to the test tube.

7. Use a pipet to add the sodium hydroxide solution dropwise to the test tube. Count the number of drops of sodium hydroxide as you add them. Gently shake the test tube from side to side after adding each drop. **Continue adding drops until the color just changes from colorless to pink.**

8. Record in your data table the total number of drops of sodium hydroxide needed to reach the color change. To obtain consistent results, repeat this trial.

Part II

9. Use a buret to add exactly 4.00 mL of hydrochloric acid directly into a clean test tube.

Data Table 1	
HCl volume (mL)	**NaOH (drops)**
2.00	
2.00	
4.00	
4.00	

Data Table 2	
H_2SO_4 Volume (mL)	**NaOH (drops)**
2.00	
2.00	

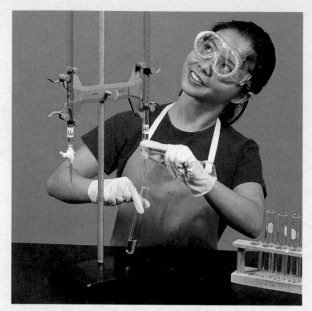

Figure A

10. Add two drops of phenolphthalein indicator solution to the test tube.

11. Using a pipet, add one drop of sodium hydroxide solution at a time to the test tube. Count the number of drops of sodium hydroxide as you add them. Gently swirl the test tube after adding each drop. **Continue adding drops until the color just changes from colorless to a pink.**

12. Record in your data table the total number of drops of sodium hydroxide needed to reach the color change. Repeat this trial.

Part III: Sulfuric Acid

13. Use a buret to add exactly 2.00 mL of sulfuric acid directly into your test tube.

14. Add two drops of phenolphthalein indicator solution to the test tube.

15. Using a pipet, add one drop of sodium hydroxide solution at a time to the test tube. Count the number of drops of sodium hydroxide as you add them. Gently swirl the test tube after adding each drop. **Continue adding drops until the color just changes from colorless to pink.**

16. Record in your data table the total number of drops of sodium hydroxide needed to reach the color change. Repeat this trial.

 Cleanup and Disposal

17. Clean all apparatus and your lab station. Return equipment to its proper place. Dispose of chemicals and solutions in the containers designated by your teacher. Do not pour any chemicals down the drain or in the trash unless your teacher directs you to do so. Wash your hands thoroughly after all work is finished and before you leave the lab.

Analysis and Interpretation

1. **Analyzing Results**
   What was the average number of drops of sodium hydroxide required to consume 2.00 mL of HCl? Show your work. 4.00 mL of HCl? Show your work.

2. **Analyzing Results**
   What was the average number of drops of sodium hydroxide required to consume 2.00 mL of H_2SO_4? Show your work.

3. **Analyzing Results**
   Compare your responses to Analysis and Interpretation item 1. Is there a difference in the average number of drops? What is the ratio between these two numbers? Is it 1:1, 1:2, 2:1, or 1:3? Explain the "chemistry" behind this ratio.

4. **Analyzing Results**
   Now compare your responses to Analysis and Interpretation items 1 and 2. Is there a difference in the average number of drops? What is the ratio between these two numbers? Is it 1:1, 1:2, 1:3, etc? Explain the "chemistry" behind this ratio.

Conclusion

5. **Applying Conclusions**
   Based on your observed results, how many drops of sodium hydroxide would be needed to react completely with a 2.00 mL sample of HNO_3?

   $$HNO_3 + NaOH \longrightarrow NaNO_3 + H_2O$$

EXPLORATION
TECHNIQUE BUILDER

15B | Acid-Base Titration of an Eggshell

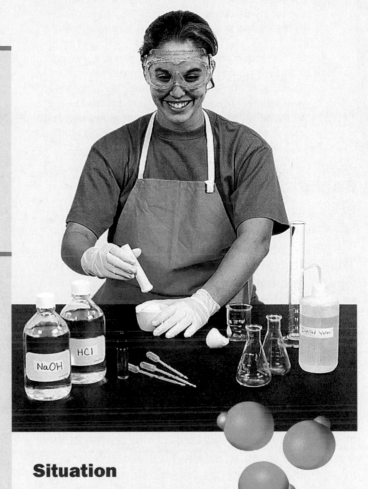

OBJECTIVES

▶ Determine the amount of calcium carbonate present in an eggshell.

▶ Relate experimental titration measurements to a balanced chemical equation.

▶ Infer a conclusion from experimental data.

▶ Apply reaction-stoichiometry concepts.

MATERIALS

▶ 1.00 M HCl

▶ 1.00 M NaOH

▶ 10 mL graduated cylinder

▶ 50 mL bottle or small Erlenmeyer flask

▶ 100 mL beaker

▶ balance

▶ desiccator (optional)

▶ distilled water

▶ drying oven

▶ eggshell

▶ forceps

▶ mortar and pestle

▶ medicine droppers or thin-stemmed pipets, 3

▶ phenolphthalein solution

▶ weighing paper

▶ white paper or white background

Situation

You are a research scientist working with the Department of Agriculture. A farmer from a nearby ranch has brought a problem to you. In the past 10 years, his hens' eggs have become increasingly fragile. So many of them have been breaking that he is beginning to lose money on the operation. The farmer believes his problems are linked to a landfill upstream, which is being investigated for illegal dumping of PCBs and other hazardous chemicals. Your job is to find out if the PCBs are the cause of the hens' fragile eggs.

Always wear safety goggles and a lab apron to protect your eyes and clothing. If you get a chemical in your eyes, immediately flush the chemical out at the eyewash station while calling to your teacher. Know the locations of the emergency lab shower and eyewash station and the procedure for using them.

Do not touch any chemicals. If you get a chemical on your skin or clothing, wash the chemical off at the sink while calling to your teacher. Make sure you carefully read the labels and follow the precautions on all containers of chemicals that you use. If no precautions are stated on the label, ask your teacher what precautions to follow. Do not taste any chemicals or items used in the laboratory. Never return leftovers to their original containers; take only small amounts to avoid wasting supplies.

The oven used in this Exploration is hot; use tongs to remove beakers from the oven because heated glassware does not always look hot.

Call your teacher in the event of an acid or base spill. Acid or base spills should be cleaned up promptly according to your teacher's instructions.

Background

Birds have evolved a chemical process that allows them to rapidly produce the calcium carbonate, $CaCO_3$, required for eggshell formation. The shell provides a strong protective covering for the developing embryo. Research has shown that some chemicals, like DDT and PCBs, can decrease the amount of calcium carbonate in the eggshell, resulting in shells that are thin and fragile.

Problem

You need to determine how much calcium carbonate is in sample eggshells from chickens that were not exposed to PCBs. The farmer's eggshells contain about 78% calcium carbonate. The calcium carbonate content of eggshells can easily be determined by means of an acid-base back-titration. A carefully measured excess of a strong acid will react with the calcium carbonate. Because the acid is in excess, there will be some left over at the end of the reaction. The resulting solution will be titrated with a strong base to determine how much acid remained unreacted. Phenolphthalein will be used as an indicator to signal the endpoint of the titration. From this measurement, you can determine the following:

▶ the amount of excess acid that reacted with the eggshell
▶ the amount of calcium carbonate that was present to react with this acid

Preparation

1. Organizing Data

Make data and calculation tables like those below and on page 777 in your lab notebook.

Data Table 1

Total volume of acid drops	
Average volume of each drop	
Total volume of base drops	
Average volume of each drop	

Data Table 2

Titration steps	
Mass of entire eggshell	
Mass of ground eggshell sample	
Number of drops of 1.00 M HCl added	150
Volume of 1.00 M HCl added	
Number of drops of 1.00 M NaOH added	
Volume of 1.00 M NaOH added	
Volume of 1.00 HCl reacting with NaOH	
Volume of 1.00 HCl reacting with eggshell	
Number of moles of HCl reacting with eggshell	
Number of moles of $CaCO_3$ reacting with HCl	
Mass of $CaCO_3$ in eggshell sample	
Percentage of $CaCO_3$ in eggshell sample	

Figure A

Figure B

2. Remove the white and the yolk from the egg, as shown in **Figure A.** Dispose of these according to your teacher's directions. Wash the shell with distilled water, and carefully peel all the membranes from the inside of the shell. Discard the membranes. Place ALL of the shell in a premassed beaker, and dry the shell in the drying oven at 110°C for about 15 minutes.

3. Put exactly 5.0 mL of water in the 10.0 mL graduated cylinder. Record this volume in the data table in your lab notebook. Fill the first dropper or pipet with water. This dropper should be labeled "Acid." **Do not use this dropper for the base solution.** Holding the dropper vertical, add 20 drops of water to the cylinder. **For the best results, keep the sizes of the drops as even as possible throughout this investigation.** Record the new volume of water in the first data table as Trial 1.

4. Without emptying the graduated cylinder, add an additional 20 drops from the dropper,

as you did in step 3, and record the new volume as the final volume for Trial 2. Repeat this procedure once more for Trial 3.

5. Repeat steps 3 and 4 for the second thin-stemmed dropper. Label this dropper "Base." **Do not use this dropper for the acid solution.**

6. Make sure that the three trials produce data that are similar to each other. If one is greatly different from the others, perform steps 3–5 over again. If you're still waiting for the eggshell in the drying oven, calculate and record in the first data table the total volume of the drops and the average volume per drop.

7. Remove the eggshell and beaker from the oven. Cool them in a desiccator. Record the mass of the entire eggshell in the second data table. Place half the shell in a clean mortar, and grind it to a very fine powder, as shown in **Figure B.** This will save time when dissolving the eggshell. (If time permits, dry the crushed eggshell again, and cool it in the desiccator.)

Graduated Cylinder Readings (Pipet Calibration: Steps 3–5)				
Trial	Initial acid pipet	Final acid pipet	Initial base pipet	Final base pipet
1				
2				
3				

Figure C

Figure D

Technique

8. Measure the mass of a piece of weighing paper. Transfer about 0.1 g of ground eggshell to a piece of weighing paper, and measure the eggshell's mass as accurately as possible. Record the mass in the second data table. Place this eggshell sample in a clean 50 mL bottle or Erlenmeyer flask. A flask will make it easier to swirl the mixture when needed.

9. Fill the acid dropper with the 1.00 M HCl acid solution, and then empty the dropper into an extra 100 mL beaker. Label the beaker "Waste." Fill the base dropper with the 1.00 M NaOH base solution, and then empty the dropper into the 100 mL beaker.

10. Fill the acid dropper once more with 1.00 M HCl. Using the acid dropper, add exactly 150 drops of 1.00 M HCl to the bottle (or flask) with the eggshell, as shown in **Figure C.** Swirl gently for 3–4 minutes. Rinse the sides of the flask with about 10 mL of distilled water. Using a third dropper, add two drops of phenolphthalein solution. Record the number of drops of HCl used in the second data table.

11. Fill the base dropper with the 1.00 M NaOH. Slowly add NaOH from the base dropper into the bottle or flask with the eggshell mixture until a faint pink color persists, even after it is swirled gently, as shown in **Figure D.** It may help to use a white piece of paper as a background so you will be able to see the color as soon as possible. **Be sure to add the base drop by drop, and be certain the drops end up in the reaction mixture and not on the side of the bottle or flask. Keep a careful count of the number of drops used.** Record the number of drops of base used in the second data table.

Cleanup and Disposal

12. Clean all apparatus and your lab station. Return the equipment to its proper place. Dispose of chemicals and solutions in the containers designated by your teacher. Do not pour any chemicals down the drain or in the trash unless your teacher directs you to do so. Wash your hands thoroughly before you leave the lab and after all work is finished.

Analysis and Interpretation

1. Organizing Ideas

The calcium carbonate in the eggshell sample undergoes a double-replacement reaction with the hydrochloric acid in step 10. Then the carbonic acid that was formed decomposes. Write a balanced chemical equation for these reactions. (Hint: The gas observed was carbon dioxide.)

2. Organizing Ideas

Write the balanced chemical equation for the acid-base neutralization of the excess unreacted HCl with the NaOH.

3. Organizing Data

Make the necessary calculations from the first data table to find the number of milliliters in each drop. Using this milliliter/drop ratio, convert the number of drops of each solution in the second data table to volumes in milliliters.

4. Organizing Data

Using the relationship between the molarity and volume of acid and the molarity and volume of base needed to neutralize the acid, calculate the volume of the HCl solution that was neutralized by the NaOH. Then subtract this amount from the initial volume of HCl to determine how much HCl reacted with $CaCO_3$.

Conclusions

5. Organizing Data

Use the stoichiometry of the reaction in Analysis and Interpretation item 1 to calculate the number of moles of $CaCO_3$ that reacted with the HCl, and record this number in your table.

6. Evaluating Methods

Workers in a lab in another city have also tested eggs, and they found that a normal eggshell is about 97% $CaCO_3$. Calculate the percent error for your measurement.

Extensions

1. Inferring Conclusions

Calculate an estimate of the mass of $CaCO_3$ present in the entire eggshell, based on your results. (Hint: Apply the percent composition of your sample to the mass of the entire eggshell.)

2. Designing Experiments

What possible sources of error can you identify in this procedure? If you can think of ways to eliminate them, ask your teacher to approve your plan, and run the procedure again.

BLEACHEX

**Vacaville Bleachex
Production Facility**
3617 Industrial Parkway
Vacaville, CA 90627

DELIVER BY OVERNIGHT COURIER
Date: April 21, 1999
To: EPA National Headquarters
From: Anthony Wong, Plant Supervisor
Re: Vacaville Bleachex Corp. Plant Spill

As a result of last night's earthquake, the Bleachex plant in the industrial park south of Vacaville was severely damaged. The safety control measures failed because of the magnitude of the earthquake.

Bleachex manufactures a variety of products using concentrated acids and bases. Plant officials noticed a large quantity of liquid, believed to be either sodium hydroxide or hydrochloric acid solution, flowing through the loading bay doors. An Emergency Toxic Spill Response Team attempted to determine the source and identity of the unknown liquid. A series of explosions and the presence of chlorine gas forced the team to abandon their efforts. The unknown liquid continues to flow into the nearly full containment ponds.

We are sending a sample of the liquid to you by overnight courier and hope that you can quickly and accurately identify the liquid and notify us of the proper method for cleanup and disposal. We need your answer as soon as possible.

Anthony Wong

Anthony Wong

References

Review titration methods using a buret. Before filling the buret, be sure it is clean. Then rinse the buret three times with 5 mL of the standard solution each time before filling the buret. The equivalence point of the titration can be determined using an indicator or pH probe. This is a simple titration, not a back-titration, in which the unknown reacts with an excess of acid and the excess acid is titrated to determine how much must have reacted.

CheMystery Labs, Inc.
52 Fulton Street
Springfield, VA 22150

MEMORANDUM

Date: April 22, 1999
To: Cicely Jackson
From: Marissa Bellinghausen

This is a rush job from the EPA. We have been promised $300,000, three times their normal fee of $100,000, so give this project top priority!

First we must determine the pH of the unknown so that we know whether it is an acid or a base. Then titrate the unknown using a standard solution to determine its concentration so that we can advise Bleachex on the amount of neutralizing agents that will be needed for the three 1.75×10^7 L containment ponds.

Because we have a limited sample, I need to approve your plans before you begin your lab work. Therefore, I need the following items:
- detailed one-page plan for your procedure with all necessary data tables (include multiple trials)
- detailed list of the equipment and materials you will need with itemized and total costs

When you are finished, prepare a report in the form of a two-page letter that we can fax to Anthony Wong. The letter must include the following:
- identity of the unknown and its concentration
- pH of the unknown and how you determined it
- paragraph summarizing how you titrated the sample to determine its concentration
- detailed and organized data table
- detailed analysis section with calculations, a discussion of the multiple trials, and a statistical analysis of your precision
- your proposed method for cleanup and disposal, including amount of neutralizing agents necessary
- detailed invoice showing all costs, services, and time for this work

For prices of materials, see page 692.

Required Precautions

Safety goggles and a lab apron must be worn at all times.

Do not touch or taste any chemicals. Always wash your hands thoroughly when finished.

If you get acid or base on your skin or clothing, wash the chemical off at the sink while calling to your teacher. If you get acid or base in your eyes, immediately flush it out at the eyewash station while calling to your teacher.

Spill Procedures/ Waste-Disposal Methods

- In case of a spill, follow your teacher's instructions.
- Put excess chemicals and solutions in the containers designated by your teacher. Do not pour them down the sink or place them in the trash can.

CONSUMER ACTIVITY

15C | Measuring the pH of Household Products

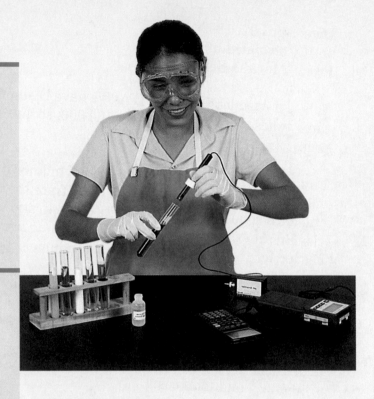

OBJECTIVES

▶ Relate the concepts of acid and base to household products.

▶ Determine if a solution is an acid or a base.

▶ Determine the pH of a solution.

▶ Demonstrate proficiency in the using litmus paper and a pH probe.

MATERIALS

▶ blue litmus paper

▶ distilled water

▶ large test tubes, 10

▶ red litmus paper

▶ small microtip pipets, 10

▶ test-tube rack

▶ wash bottle

TEST SOLUTIONS, 10

▶ 1.0 M NaOH

▶ apple juice

▶ baking soda

▶ clear soft drink

▶ detergent

▶ drain cleaner

▶ lemon juice

▶ milk

▶ vinegar

▶ tap water

OPTIONAL EQUIPMENT

▶ CBL

▶ graphing calculator with link cable

▶ Vernier pH probe with amplifier

Background

Have you ever wondered how many household products contain an acid or a base? A simple pH test can determine whether something is acidic or basic. A pH of 7 indicates a solution is neutral. Acidic solutions have pH values less than 7, and basic solutions have pH values greater than 7.

Problem

You will use what you know about acids and bases to predict which household solutions from the materials list are acidic and which are basic. Then you will measure the pH value of the 10 household solutions. To be sure your results are accurate, you will measure the pH value in two ways. First you will test each solution with a strip of red litmus paper and a strip of blue litmus paper. Then you will measure the pH value with a pH probe.

SAFETY

Always wear safety goggles and an apron to protect your eyes and clothing. If you get a chemical in your eyes, immediately flush the chemical out at the eyewash station while calling to your teacher. Know the location of the emergency lab shower and eyewash station and the procedure for using them.

Do not touch any chemicals. If you get a chemical on your skin or clothing, wash the chemical off at the sink while calling to your teacher. Make sure you carefully read the labels and follow the precautions on all containers of chemicals that you use. If there are no precautions stated on the label, ask your teacher what precautions you should follow. Do not taste any chemicals or items used in the laboratory. Never return leftovers to their original containers; take only small amounts to avoid wasting supplies.

Call your teacher in the event of an acid or base spill. Acid or base spills should be cleaned up promptly according to your teacher's instructions.

Never put broken glass into a regular waste container. Broken glass should be disposed of properly according to your teacher's instructions.

Preparation

1. Predict which solutions are acidic and which are basic, and write your predictions in your data table.

2. Obtain samples of each solution from your teacher, and label the test tubes 1–10. Label the pipets 1–10.

3. Fill each test tube with 3 mL of a different solution. Be sure to record the position of each solution in your data table.

Technique

pH test with litmus paper

4. Use pipet 1 to transfer one drop of Solution 1 to a strip of blue litmus paper. Record the result in your data table.

5. Using the same pipet, transfer one drop of Solution 1 to a strip of red litmus paper. Record the result in your data table.

6. Repeat steps 4 and 5 with the remaining solutions. Use the appropriate pipet for each pH test.

pH probe

7. Refer to page 698 for pH probe, CBL, and graphing calculator setup.

8. When you are ready to use the Vernier pH probe, take it out of the electrode solution. Rinse the probe thoroughly with distilled water, and pour the water in a waste beaker.

9. Insert the pH probe into solution 1, and swirl the solution around the probe. When the reading on the CBL unit remains constant, record this value in your data table.

10. Rinse the probe with distilled water, and then place the pH probe in the electrode solution. Make sure you swirl the solution around the probe.

11. Repeat steps 9 and 10 with the remaining solutions.

 **Cleanup and Disposal**

12. Clean all apparatus and your lab station. Return equipment to its proper place. Dispose of chemicals and solutions in the containers designated by your teacher. Do not pour any chemicals down the drain or in the trash unless your teacher directs you to do so. Wash your hands thoroughly.

Analysis and Interpretation

1. Organizing Data
List the acidic solutions in order of decreasing acid strength. List the basic solutions in order of decreasing base strength.

2. Evaluating Methods
Explain why it was important to rinse the probe after measuring the pH of each solution. What would have happened to the pH value if the probe had not been rinsed with distilled water?

16A | Reaction Rates

OBJECTIVES

▶ Prepare and observe several different reaction mixtures.

▶ Demonstrate proficiency in measuring reaction rates.

▶ Relate experimental results to a rate law that you can use to predict the results of various combinations of reactants.

MATERIALS

▶ 8-well microscale reaction strips, 2

▶ distilled or deionized water

▶ fine-tipped dropper bulbs or small micro-tip pipets, 3

▶ solution A

▶ solution B

▶ stopwatch or clock with second hand

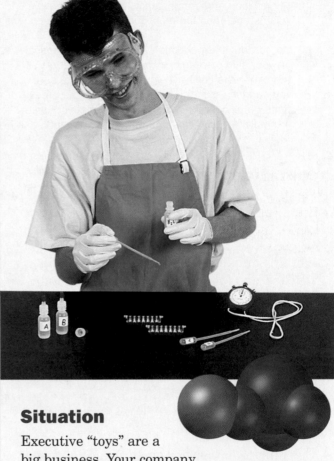

Situation

Executive "toys" are a big business. Your company has been contacted by a toy company that wants technical assistance in designing a new executive desk gadget. The company wants to investigate a reaction that turns a distinctive color in a specific amount of time. Although it will not be easy to determine the precise combination of chemicals that will work, the profit the company stands to make would be worthwhile in the end.

Always wear safety goggles and a lab apron to protect your eyes and clothing. If you get a chemical in your eyes, immediately flush the chemical out at the eyewash station while calling to your teacher. Know the location of the emergency lab shower and eyewash station and the procedure for using them.

Do not touch any chemicals. If you get a chemical on your skin or clothing, wash the chemical off at the sink while calling to your teacher. Make sure you carefully read the labels and follow the precautions on all containers of chemicals that you use.

If no precautions are stated on the label, ask your teacher what precautions to follow. Do not taste any chemicals or items used in the laboratory. Never return leftovers to their original containers; take only small amounts to avoid wasting supplies.

Always clean up the lab and all equipment after use, and dispose of substances according to proper disposal methods. Wash your hands thoroughly before you leave the lab and after all lab work is finished.

Background

In this experiment you will determine the rate of an *oxidation-reduction,* or *redox,* reaction. Reactions of this type will be discussed in Chapter 17. The net equation for the reaction you will study is as follows:

$$3Na_2S_2O_5(aq) + 2KIO_3(aq) + 3H_2O(l) \xrightarrow{H^+}$$
$$2KI(aq) + 6NaHSO_4(aq)$$

One way to study the rate of this reaction is to observe how fast $Na_2S_2O_5$ is used up. After all the $Na_2S_2O_5$ solution has reacted, the concentration of iodine, I_2, an intermediate in the reaction, builds up. A starch indicator solution added to the reaction mixture will signal when this happens. The colorless starch will change to a blue-black color in the presence of I_2.

In the experiment, the concentrations of the reactants are given in terms of drops of Solution A and drops of Solution B. Solution A contains $Na_2S_2O_5$, the starch-indicator solution, and dilute sulfuric acid to supply the hydrogen ions needed to catalyze the reaction. Solution B

contains KIO_3. You will run the reaction with several different concentrations of the reactants and record the time it takes for the blue-black color to appear.

Problem

To determine the best conditions and concentrations for the reaction, you will determine the following:

▶ how changes in reactant concentrations affect the reaction outcome
▶ how much time elapses for each reaction
▶ a rate law for the reaction that will allow you to predict the results with other combinations

Preparation

1. Organizing Data
Copy the data table below in your lab notebook.

Data Table

	Well 1	Well 2	Well 3	Well 4	Well 5
Time reaction began					
Time reaction stopped					
Drops of A					
Drops of B					
Drops of H_2O					

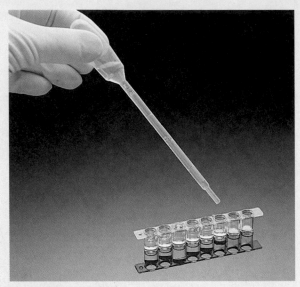

Figure A

2. Obtain three dropper bulbs or small microtip pipets, and label them "A," "B," and "H$_2$O."

3. Fill bulb or pipet A with solution A, fill bulb or pipet B with solution B, and fill the bulb or pipet for H$_2$O with distilled water.

Technique

4. Using the first 8-well strip, place five drops of Solution A into each of the first five wells, as shown in **Figure A.** (Disregard the remaining three wells.) Record the number of drops in the appropriate places in your data table. **For best results, try to make all of the drops about the same size.**

5. In the second 8-well reaction strip, place one drop of Solution B in the first well, two drops in the second well, three drops in the third well, four drops in the fourth well, and five drops in the fifth well. Record the number of drops in the appropriate places in your data table.

6. In the second 8-well strip that contains drops of Solution B, add four drops of water to the first well, three drops to the second well, two drops to the third well, and one drop to the fourth well. Do not add any water to the fifth well.

7. Carefully invert the second strip. The surface tension should keep the solutions from falling out of the wells. Place the second strip well-to-well on top of the first strip, as shown in **Figure B.**

8. Holding the strips tightly together, record the exact time or set the stopwatch as you shake the strips. This procedure should effectively mix the upper solutions with each of the corresponding lower ones.

9. Observe the lower wells. Note the sequence in which the solutions react, and record the number of seconds it takes for each solution to turn a blue-black color.

Cleanup and Disposal

10. Dispose of the solutions in the container designated by your teacher. Wash your hands thoroughly after cleaning up the area and equipment.

Analysis and Interpretation

1. **Organizing Data**
   Calculate the time elapsed for the complete reaction of each combination of Solution A and Solution B.

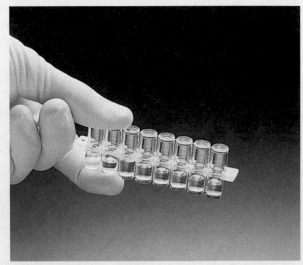

Figure B

2. Evaluating Data

Make a graph of your results. Label the *x*-axis "Number of drops of Solution B." Label the *y*-axis "Time elapsed." Make a similar graph for drops of Solution B versus rate (1/time elapsed).

3. Analyzing Information

Which mixture reacted the fastest? Which mixture reacted the slowest?

4. Evaluating Methods

Why was it important to add the drops of water to the wells that contained fewer than five drops of Solution B? (Hint: Figure out the total number of drops in each of the reaction wells.)

Conclusions

5. Analyzing Methods

How can you be sure that each of the chemical reactions began at about the same time? Why is this important?

6. Evaluating Conclusions

Of the following variables that can affect the rate of a reaction, which is tested in this experiment: temperature, catalyst, concentration, surface area, or nature of reactants? Explain your answer.

7. Applying Ideas

Use your data and graphs to determine the relationship between the concentration of Solution B and the rate of the reaction. Describe this relationship in terms of a rate law.

Extensions

1. Evaluating Data

Share your data with other lab groups, and calculate a class average for the rate of the reaction for each concentration of B. Compare the results from other groups with your results. Explain why there are differences in the results.

2. Analyzing Methods

What are some possible sources of error in this procedure? If you can think of ways to eliminate them, ask your teacher to approve your plan and run your procedure again.

3. Predicting Outcomes

What combination of drops of Solutions A and B would you use if you wanted the reaction to last exactly 2.5 minutes? Design an experiment to test your answer. If your teacher approves your plan, perform the experiment, and record these results. Make another graph that includes both the old and new data.

4. Predicting Outcomes

How would your data be different if the experiment were repeated but Solution A was diluted with one part solution for every seven parts distilled water?

5. Designing Experiments

How would you determine the smallest interval of time during which you could distinguish a clock reaction? Design an experiment to find out. If your teacher approves your plan, perform your experiment.

6. Designing Experiments

How would the results of this experiment be affected if the reaction took place in a cold environment? Design an experiment to test your answer using materials available. If your teacher approves your plan, perform your experiment and record the results. Make another graph, and compare it with your old data.

7. Designing Experiments

Devise a plan to determine the effect of Solution A on the rate law. If your teacher approves your plan, perform your experiment, and determine the rate law for this reaction.

8. Relating Ideas

If Solution B contains 0.02 M KIO_3, calculate the value for the constant, *k*, in the expression below. (Hint: Remember that Solution B is diluted when it is added to Solution A.)

$$rate = k[KIO_3]$$

17A | Redox Titration

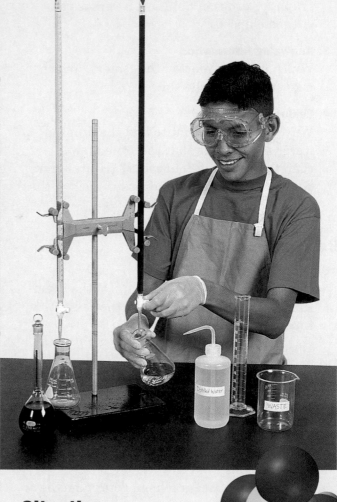

OBJECTIVES

▶ Demonstrate proficiency in performing redox titrations and recognizing the end point of a redox reaction.

▶ Determine the concentration of a solution using stoichiometry and volume data from a titration.

MATERIALS

▶ 0.0200 M KMnO$_4$

▶ 1.0 M H$_2$SO$_4$

▶ 100 mL graduated cylinder

▶ 125 mL Erlenmeyer flask, 4

▶ 250 mL beaker, 2

▶ 400 mL beaker

▶ burets, 2

▶ distilled water

▶ double buret clamp

▶ FeSO$_4$ solution

▶ ring stand

▶ wash bottle

Situation

You are a chemist working for a chemical analysis firm. A large pharmaceutical company has hired you to help salvage some products that were damaged by a small fire in their warehouse. Although there was only minimal smoke and fire damage to the warehouse and products, the sprinkler system ruined the labeling on many of the pharmaceuticals. The firm's best-selling products are iron tonics used to treat low-level anemia. The tonics are produced from hydrated iron(II) sulfate, FeSO$_4$•7H$_2$O. The different types of tonics contain different concentrations of FeSO$_4$. You have been hired to help the pharmaceutical company figure out the proper label for each bottle of tonic.

Background

In Chapter 15 you studied acid-base titrations in which an unknown amount of acid is titrated with a carefully measured amount of base. In this procedure a similar approach called a redox titration is used. In a redox titration, the reducing agent, Fe^{2+}, is oxidized to Fe^{3+} by the oxidizing agent, MnO_4^-. When this process occurs, the Mn in MnO_4^- changes from a +7 to a +2 oxidation state and has a noticeably different color. You can use this color change in the same way that you used the color change of phenolphthalein in acid-base titrations—to signify a redox reaction end point. When the reaction is complete, any excess MnO_4^- added to the reaction mixture will give the solution a pink or purple color. The volume data from the titration, the known molarity of the $KMnO_4$ solution, and the mole ratio from the following balanced redox equation will give you the information you need to calculate the molarity of the $FeSO_4$ solution.

$$5Fe^{2+} + MnO_4^- + 8H^+ \longrightarrow 5Fe^{3+} + Mn^{2+} + 4H_2O$$

Problem

To determine how to label the bottles, you must determine the concentration of iron(II) ions in the sample from an unlabeled bottle from the warehouse by answering the following questions:

▶ How can the volume data obtained from the titration and the mole ratios from the balanced redox reaction be used to determine the concentration of the sample?
▶ Which tonic is in the sample, given information about the concentration of each tonic?

Preparation

1. **Organizing Data**
   Copy the data table below in your lab notebook.

2. Clean two 50 mL burets with a buret brush and distilled water. Rinse each buret at least three times with distilled water to remove any contaminants.

Data Table

Trial	Initial KMnO₄ volume	Final KMnO₄ volume	Initial FeSO₄ volume	Final FeSO₄ volume
1				
2				
3				

3. Label two 250 mL beakers "0.0200 M $KMnO_4$," and "$FeSO_4$ solution." Label three of the flasks 1, 2, and 3. Label the 400 mL beaker "Waste." Label one buret "$KMnO_4$" and the other "$FeSO_4$."

4. Measure approximately 75 mL of 0.0200 M $KMnO_4$, and pour it into the appropriately labeled beaker. Obtain approximately 75 mL of $FeSO_4$ solution, and pour it into the appropriately labeled beaker.

5. Rinse one buret three times with a few milliliters of 0.0200 M $KMnO_4$ from the appropriately labeled beaker. Collect these rinses in the waste beaker. Rinse the other buret three times with small amounts of $FeSO_4$ solution from the appropriately labeled beaker. Collect these rinses in the waste beaker.

6. Set up the burets as shown in **Figure A.** Fill one buret with approximately 50 mL of the 0.0200 M $KMnO_4$ from the beaker, and fill the other buret with approximately 50 mL of the $FeSO_4$ solution from the other beaker.

7. With the waste beaker underneath its tip, open the $KMnO_4$ buret long enough to be

Figure B

sure the buret tip is filled. Repeat for the $FeSO_4$ buret.

8. Add 50 mL of distilled water to one of the 125 mL Erlenmeyer flasks, and add one drop of 0.0200 M $KMnO_4$ to the flask. Set this aside to use as a color standard, as shown in **Figure B,** to compare with the titration and to determine the end point.

Technique

9. Record the initial buret readings for both solutions in your data table. Add 10.0 mL of the hydrated iron(II) sulfate, $FeSO_4 \cdot 7H_2O$, solution to flask 1. Add 5 mL of 1.0 M H_2SO_4 to the $FeSO_4$ solution in this flask. The acid will help keep the Fe^{2+} ions in the reduced state, allowing you time to titrate.

10. Slowly add $KMnO_4$ from the buret to the $FeSO_4$ in the flask while swirling the flask, as shown in **Figure C.** When the color of the solution matches the color standard you prepared in step 8, record the final readings of the burets in your data table.

11. Empty the titration flask into the waste beaker. Repeat the titration procedure in steps 9 and 10 with flasks 2 and 3.

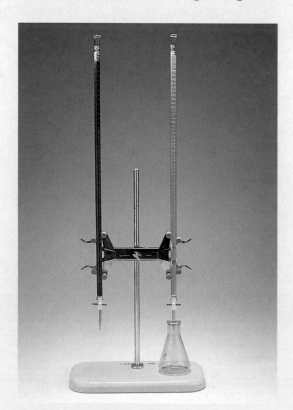

Figure A

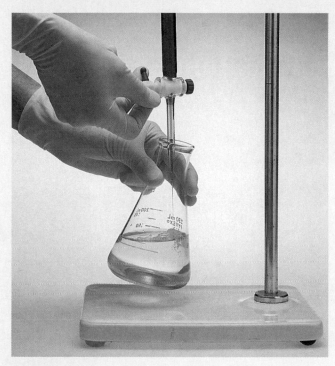

Figure C

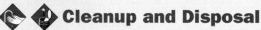 **Cleanup and Disposal**

12. Always clean up the lab and all equipment after use. Dispose of the contents of the waste beaker in the container designated by your teacher. Also pour the contents of the color-standard flask into this container. Wash your hands thoroughly after cleaning up the area and equipment.

Analysis and Interpretation

1. Evaluating Data
Calculate the number of moles of MnO_4^- reduced in each trial.

2. Analyzing Information
Calculate the number of moles of Fe^{2+} oxidized in each trial.

3. Applying Conclusions
Calculate the average concentration (molarity) of the iron tonic.

4. Analyzing Methods
Explain why it was important to rinse the burets with $KMnO_4$ or $FeSO_4$ before adding the solutions. (Hint: Consider what would happen to the concentration of each solution

if it were added to a buret that had been rinsed only with distilled water.)

Conclusions

5. Inferring Conclusions
The company makes three different types of iron tonics: Feravide A, with a concentration of 0.145 M $FeSO_4$; Feravide Extra-Strength, with 0.225 M $FeSO_4$; and Feravide Jr., with 0.120 M $FeSO_4$. Which tonic is your sample?

Extensions

1. Evaluating Methods
What possible sources of error can you identify with this procedure? If you can think of ways to eliminate them, ask your teacher to approve your plan, and run the procedure again.

2. Research and Communication
Blueprints are based on a photochemical reaction. The paper is treated with a solution of iron(III) ammonium citrate and potassium hexacyanoferrate(III) and dried in the dark. When a tracing-paper drawing is placed on the blueprint paper and exposed to light, Fe^{3+} ions are reduced to Fe^{2+} ions, which react with hexacyanoferrate(III) ions in the moist paper to form the blue color on the paper. The lines of the drawing block the light and prevent the reduction of Fe^{3+} ions, resulting in white lines. Find out how sepia prints are made, and report on this information.

3. Relating Ideas
Electrochemical cells are based on the process of electron flow in a system with varying potential differences. Batteries are composed of such systems and contain different chemicals for different purposes and price ranges. You can make simple experimental batteries using metal wires and items such as lemons, apples, and potatoes. What are some other "homemade" battery sources, and what is the role of these food items in producing electrical energy that can be measured as battery power? Explain your answers.

17A | Redox Titration
Mining Feasibility Study

GOLDSTAKE
MINING
COMPANY

May 11, 1999

George Taylor
Director of Analytical Services
CheMystery Labs, Inc.
52 Fulton Street
Springfield, VA 22150

Dear Mr. Taylor:

Because of the high quality of your firm's work in the past, Goldstake is again asking that you submit a bid for a mining feasibility study. A study site in New Mexico has yielded some promising iron ore deposits, and we are evaluating the potential yield.

Your bid should include the cost of evaluating the sample we're sending with this letter and the fees for 20 additional analyses to be completed over the next year. The sample is a slurry extracted from the mine using a special process that converts the iron ore into $FeSO_4$ dissolved in water. The mine could produce up to 1.0×10^5 L of this slurry daily, but we need to know how much iron is in that amount of slurry before we proceed.

The contract for the other analyses will be awarded based on the accuracy of this analysis and the quality of the accompanying report. Your report will be used for two purposes: to evaluate the site for quantity of iron and to determine who our analytical consultant will be if the site is developed into a mining operation. I look forward to reviewing your bid proposal.

Sincerely,

Lynn L. Brown

Lynn L. Brown
Director of Operations
Goldstake Mining Company

References

Review more information on redox reactions. Remember to add a small amount of H_2SO_4 so the iron will stay in the Fe^{2+} form. Calculate your disposal costs based on the mass of $KMnO_4$ and $FeSO_4$ in your solutions, plus the mass of the H_2SO_4 solution.

CheMystery Labs, Inc.
52 Fulton Street
Springfield, VA 22150

MEMORANDUM

Date: May 12, 1999
To: Crystal Sievers
From: George Taylor

Good news! It looks as though the quality of our work has earned us a repeat customer, Goldstake Mining Company. We've done work for them in the past, and they pay their bills on time. This analysis could turn into a long-term arrangement, so when bonus time arrives, I'll be looking favorably on lab teams that produce accurate, high-quality reports for this job. Perform the analysis more than once so that we can be confident of our accuracy.

Before you begin, send Ms. Brown the following items:
- detailed one-page plan for the procedure and all necessary data tables
- detailed bid sheet that lists all of the equipment and materials you plan to use, including individual and total costs

As soon as you have completed the laboratory work, please prepare a report in the form of a two-page letter to Ms. Brown, and include the following information.
- moles and grams of $FeSO_4$ in 10 mL of sample
- moles, grams, and percentage of iron(II) in 10 mL of the sample
- kilograms of iron that the company could extract from the mine each year, assuming that 1.0×10^5 L of slurry could be mined per day, year round
- balanced equation for the redox equation
- detailed and organized data and analysis section showing calculations of how you determined the moles, grams, and percentage of iron(II) in the sample (include calculations of the mean, or average, of the multiple trials)
- detailed invoice for this analysis that includes our equipment and labor costs (and a small amount of profit)
- bid for 20 additional analyses based on the costs incurred for this one

For prices of materials, see page 692.

For prices of materials, see page 692.

Required Precautions

Safety goggles and lab aprons must be worn at all times.

If you get acid, base, or permanganate on your skin or clothing, wash the chemical off at the sink while calling to your teacher. If you get acid, base, or permanganate in your eyes, immediately flush it out at the eyewash station while calling to your teacher.

Do not touch or taste any chemicals. Wash your hands thoroughly when finished.

Spill Procedures/ Waste-Disposal Methods

- In case of spills, follow your teacher's instructions.
- Dispose of solutions from the waste beaker and other leftover reagents in the disposal container designated by your teacher.

REFERENCE TABLES

TABLE A-1 SI Measurements

Metric Prefixes

Prefix	Symbol	Factor of base unit
giga-	G	1 000 000 000
mega-	M	1 000 000
kilo-	k	1 000
hecto-	h	100
deka-	da	10
deci-	d	0.1
centi-	c	0.01
milli-	m	0.001
micro-	μ	0.000 001
nano-	n	0.000 000 001
pico-	p	0.000 000 000 001

Mass

1 kilogram (kg)	= SI base unit of mass
1 gram (g)	= 0.001 kg
1 milligram (mg)	= 0.000 001 kg
1 microgram (μg)	= 0.000 000 001 kg

Lengths

1 kilometer (km)	= 1000 m
1 meter (m)	= SI base unit of length
1 centimeter (cm)	= 0.01 m
1 millimeter (mm)	= 0.001 m
1 micrometer (μm)	= 0.000 001 m
1 nanometer (nm)	= 0.000 000 001 m
1 picometer (pm)	= 0.000 000 000 001 m

Area

1 square kilometer (km^2)	= 100 hectares (ha)
1 hectare (ha)	= 10 000 square meters (m^2)
1 square meter (m^2)	= 10 000 square centimeters (cm^2)
1 square centimeter (cm^2)	= 100 square millimeters (mm^2)

Volume

1 liter (L)	= common unit for liquid volume (not SI)
1 cubic meter (m^3)	= 1000 L
1 kiloliter (kL)	= 1000 L
1 milliliter (mL)	= 0.001 L
1 milliliter (mL)	= 1 cubic centimeter (cm^3)

TABLE A-2 Abbreviations

amu	= atomic mass unit (mass)		mol	= mole (quantity)
atm	= atmosphere (pressure, non-SI)		M	= molarity (concentration)
Bq	= becquerel (nuclear activity)		N	= newton (force)
°C	= degree Celsius (temperature)		Pa	= pascal (pressure)
J	= joule (energy)		s	= second (time)
K	= kelvin (temperature, thermodynamic)		V	= volt (electric potential difference)

TABLE A-3 Symbols

Symbol	Meaning	Symbol	Meaning
α	= helium nucleus (also $^4_2$He) emission from radioactive materials	ΔH^0_f	= standard molar enthalpy of formation
β	= electron (also $^0_{-1}e$) emission from radioactive materials	K_a	= ionization constant (acid)
		K_{eq}	= equilibrium constant
γ	= high-energy photon emission from radioactive materials	K_{sp}	= solubility-product constant
		KE	= kinetic energy
Δ	= change in a given quantity (e.g., ΔH for change in enthalpy)	m	= mass
		N_A	= Avogadro's number
c	= speed of light in a vacuum	n	= number of moles
c_p	= specific heat capacity (at constant pressure)	P	= pressure
		pH	= measure of acidity ($-\log[H_3O^+]$)
D	= density	R	= ideal gas law constant
E_a	= activation energy	S	= entropy
E^0	= standard electrode potential	S^0	= standard molar entropy
G	= Gibbs free energy	T	= temperature (thermodynamic, in kelvins)
ΔG^0	= standard free energy of reaction	t	= temperature ($\pm$ degrees Celsius)
ΔG^0_f	= standard molar free energy of formation	V	= volume
H	= enthalpy	v	= velocity
ΔH^0	= standard enthalpy of reaction		

TABLE A-4 Water-Vapor Pressure

Temperature (°C)	Pressure (mm Hg)	Pressure (kPa)	Temperature (°C)	Pressure (mm Hg)	Pressure (kPa)	Temperature (°C)	Pressure (mm Hg)	Pressure (kPa)
0.0	4.6	0.61	19.5	17.0	2.27	27.0	26.7	3.57
5.0	6.5	0.87	20.0	17.5	2.34	28.0	28.3	3.78
10.0	9.2	1.23	20.5	18.1	2.41	29.0	30.0	4.01
12.5	10.9	1.45	21.0	18.6	2.49	30.0	31.8	4.25
15.0	12.8	1.71	21.5	19.2	2.57	35.0	42.2	5.63
15.5	13.2	1.76	22.0	19.8	2.64	40.0	55.3	7.38
16.0	13.6	1.82	22.5	20.4	2.72	50.0	92.5	12.34
16.5	14.1	1.88	23.0	21.1	2.81	60.0	149.4	19.93
17.0	14.5	1.94	23.5	21.7	2.90	70.0	233.7	31.18
17.5	15.0	2.00	24.0	22.4	2.98	80.0	355.1	47.37
18.0	15.5	2.06	24.5	23.1	3.10	90.0	525.8	70.12
18.5	16.0	2.13	25.0	23.8	3.17	95.0	633.9	84.53
19.0	16.5	2.19	26.0	25.2	3.36	100.0	760.0	101.32

TABLE A-5 The Elements—Symbols, Atomic Numbers, and Atomic Masses

Name of element	Symbol	Atomic number	Atomic mass	Name of element	Symbol	Atomic number	Atomic mass
actinium	Ac	89	[227.0278]	holmium	Ho	67	164.93032
aluminum	Al	13	26.981539	hydrogen	H	1	1.00794
americium	Am	95	[243.0614]	indium	In	49	114.818
antimony	Sb	51	121.757	iodine	I	53	126.90447
argon	Ar	18	39.948	iridium	Ir	77	192.22
arsenic	As	33	74.92159	iron	Fe	26	55.847
astatine	At	85	[209.9871]	krypton	Kr	36	83.80
barium	Ba	56	137.327	lanthanum	La	57	138.9055
berkelium	Bk	97	[247.0703]	lawrencium	Lr	103	[262.11]
beryllium	Be	4	9.012182	lead	Pb	82	207.2
bismuth	Bi	83	208.98037	lithium	Li	3	6.941
bohrium	Bh	107	[262.12]	lutetium	Lu	71	174.967
boron	B	5	10.811	magnesium	Mg	12	24.3050
bromine	Br	35	79.904	manganese	Mn	25	54.93805
cadmium	Cd	48	112.411	meitnerium	Mt	109	[266]
calcium	Ca	20	40.078	mendelevium	Md	101	[258.10]
californium	Cf	98	[251.0796]	mercury	Hg	80	200.59
carbon	C	6	12.011	molybdenum	Mo	42	95.94
cerium	Ce	58	140.115	neodymium	Nd	60	144.24
cesium	Cs	55	132.90543	neon	Ne	10	20.1797
chlorine	Cl	17	35.4527	neptunium	Np	93	[237.0482]
chromium	Cr	24	51.9961	nickel	Ni	28	58.6934
cobalt	Co	27	58.93320	niobium	Nb	41	92.90638
copper	Cu	29	63.546	nitrogen	N	7	14.00674
curium	Cm	96	[247.0703]	nobelium	No	102	[259.1009]
dubnium	Db	105	[262.114]	osmium	Os	76	190.23
dysprosium	Dy	66	162.50	oxygen	O	8	15.9994
einsteinium	Es	99	[252.083]	palladium	Pd	46	106.42
erbium	Er	68	167.26	phosphorus	P	15	30.973762
europium	Eu	63	151.965	platinum	Pt	78	195.08
fermium	Fm	100	[257.0951]	plutonium	Pu	94	[244.0642]
fluorine	F	9	18.9984032	polonium	Po	84	[208.9824]
francium	Fr	87	[223.0197]	potassium	K	19	39.0983
gadolinium	Gd	64	157.25	praseodymium	Pr	59	140.90765
gallium	Ga	31	69.723	promethium	Pm	61	[144.9127]
germanium	Ge	32	72.61	protactinium	Pa	91	231.03588
gold	Au	79	196.96654	radium	Ra	88	[226.0254]
hafnium	Hf	72	178.49	radon	Rn	86	[222.0176]
hassium	Hs	108	[265]	rhenium	Re	75	186.207
helium	He	2	4.002602	rhodium	Rh	45	102.90550

A value given in brackets denotes the mass number of the most stable or most common isotope. The atomic masses of most of these elements are believed to have an error no greater than ±1 in the last digit given.

The Elements—Symbols, Atomic Numbers, and Atomic Masses

Name of element	Symbol	Atomic number	Atomic mass	Name of element	Symbol	Atomic number	Atomic mass
rubidium	Rb	37	85.4678	thallium	Tl	81	204.3833
ruthenium	Ru	44	101.07	thorium	Th	90	232.0381
rutherfordium	Rf	104	[261.11]	thulium	Tm	69	168.93421
samarium	Sm	62	150.36	tin	Sn	50	118.710
scandium	Sc	21	44.955910	titanium	Ti	22	47.88
seaborgium	Sg	106	[263.118]	tungsten	W	74	183.84
selenium	Se	34	78.96	ununnilium	Uun	110	[269]
silicon	Si	14	28.0855	unununium	Uuu	111	[272]
silver	Ag	47	107.8682	uranium	U	92	238.0289
sodium	Na	11	22.989768	vanadium	V	23	50.9415
strontium	Sr	38	87.62	xenon	Xe	54	131.29
sulfur	S	16	32.066	ytterbium	Yb	70	173.04
tantalum	Ta	73	180.9479	yttrium	Y	39	88.90585
technetium	Tc	43	[97.9072]	zinc	Zn	30	65.39
tellurium	Te	52	127.60	zirconium	Zr	40	91.224
terbium	Tb	65	158.92534				

A value given in brackets denotes the mass number of the most stable or most common isotope. The atomic masses of most of these elements are believed to have an error no greater than ±1 in the last digit given.

TABLE A-6 **Physical Constants**

Quantity	Symbol	Value
Atomic mass unit	amu	$1.660\,5402 \times 10^{-27}$ kg
Avogadro's number	N_A	$6.022\,137 \times 10^{23}$/mol
Electron rest mass	m_e	$9.109\,3897 \times 10^{-31}$ kg 5.4858×10^{-4} amu
Ideal gas law constant	R	8.314 L•kPa/mol•K 0.0821 L•atm/mol•K
Molar volume of ideal gas at STP	V_M	22.414 10 L/mol
Neutron rest mass	m_n	$1.674\,9286 \times 10^{-27}$ kg 1.008 665 amu
Normal boiling point of water	T_b	373.15 K = 100.0°C
Normal freezing point of water	T_f	273.15 K = 0.00°C
Planck's constant	h	$6.626\,076 \times 10^{-34}$ J•s
Proton rest mass	m_p	$1.672\,6231 \times 10^{-27}$ kg 1.007 276 amu
Speed of light in a vacuum	c	$2.997\,924\,58 \times 10^8$ m/s
Temperature of triple point of water		273.16 K = 0.01°C

Name	Form/color at room temperature	Density† (g/cm³)	Melting point (°C)	Boiling point (°C)	Common oxidation states
aluminum	silver metal	2.702	660.37	2467	3+
antimony	blue-white metalloid	6.684[25]	630.5	1750	3–, 3+, 5+
argon	colorless gas	1.784*	–189.2	–185.7	0
arsenic	gray metalloid	5.727[14]	817 (28 atm)	613 (*sublimes*)	3–, 3+, 5+
barium	bluish white metal	3.51	725	1640	2+
beryllium	gray metal	1.85	1278 ± 5	2970 (0.0066 atm)	2+
bismuth	white metal	9.80	271.3	1560 ± 5	3+
boron	black metalloid	2.34	2300	2550	3+
bromine	red-brown liquid	3.119	–7.2	58.78	1–, 1+, 3+, 5+, 7+
calcium	silver metal	1.54	839 ± 2	1484	2+
carbon	diamond	3.51	3500 (63.5 atm)	3930	2+, 4+
	graphite	2.25	3652 (*sublimes*)	—	
chlorine	green-yellow gas	3.214*	–100.98	–34.6	1–, 1+, 3+, 5+, 7+
chromium	gray metal	7.2028	1857 ± 20	2672	2+, 3+, 6+
cobalt	gray metal	8.9	1495	2870	2+, 3+
copper	red metal	8.92	1083.4 ± 0.2	2567	1+, 2+
fluorine	yellow gas	1.69‡	–219.62	–188.14	1–
germanium	gray metalloid	5.323[25]	937.4	2830	4+
gold	yellow metal	19.31	1064.43	2808 ± 2	1+, 3+
helium	colorless gas	0.1785*	–272.2 (26 atm)	–268.9	0
hydrogen	colorless gas	0.0899*	–259.34	–252.8	1–, 1+
iodine	blue-black solid	4.93	113.5	184.35	1–, 1+, 3+, 5+, 7+
iron	silver metal	7.86	1535	2750	2+, 3+
lead	bluish white metal	11.3437[16]	327.502	1740	2+, 4+
lithium	silver metal	0.534	180.54	1342	1+
magnesium	silver metal	1.74[5]	648.8	1107	2+
manganese	gray-white metal	7.20	1244 ± 3	1962	2+, 3+, 4+, 6+, 7+
mercury	silver liquid metal	13.5462	–38.87	356.58	1+, 2+
neon	colorless gas	0.9002*	–248.67	–245.9	0
nickel	silver metal	8.90	1455	2730	2+, 3+
nitrogen	colorless gas	1.2506*	–209.86	–195.8	3–, 3+, 5+
oxygen	colorless gas	1.429*	–218.4	–182.962	2–
phosphorus	yellow solid	1.82	44.1	280	3–, 3+, 5+
platinum	silver metal	21.45	1772	3827 ± 100	2+, 4+
plutonium	silver metal	19.84	641	3232	3+, 4+, 5+, 6+
potassium	silver metal	0.86	63.25	760	1+
radon	colorless gas	9.73*	–71	–61.8	0
silicon	gray metalloid	2.33 ± 0.01	1410	2355	2+, 4+
silver	white metal	10.5	961.93	2212	1+
sodium	silver metal	0.97	97.8	882.9	1+

†Densities obtained at 20°C unless otherwise noted (superscript)

‡Density of fluorine given in g/L at 1 atm and 15°C

*Densities of gases given in g/L at STP

TABLE A-7 *CONTINUED* **Properties of Common Elements**

Name	Form/color at room temperature	Density† (g/cm³)	Melting point (°C)	Boiling point (°C)	Common oxidation states
strontium	silver metal	2.6	769	1384	2+
sulfur	yellow solid	1.96	119.0	444.674	2–, 4+, 6+
tin	white metal	7.28	231.88	2260	2+, 4+
titanium	white metal	4.5	1660 ± 10	3287	2+, 3+, 4+
tungsten	gray metal	19.35	3410 ± 20	5660	6+
uranium	silver metal	19.05 ± 0.0225	1132.3 ± 0.8	3818	3+, 4+, 6+
zinc	blue-white metal	7.14	419.58	907	2+

†Densities obtained at 20°C unless otherwise noted (superscript)

TABLE A-8 **Common Ions**

Cation	Symbol	Anion	Symbol
aluminum	Al^{3+}	acetate	CH_3COO^-
ammonium	NH_4^+	bromide	Br^-
arsenic(III)	As^{3+}	carbonate	CO_3^{2-}
barium	Ba^{2+}	chlorate	ClO_3^-
calcium	Ca^{2+}	chloride	Cl^-
chromium(II)	Cr^{2+}	chlorite	ClO_2^-
chromium(III)	Cr^{3+}	chromate	CrO_4^{2-}
cobalt(II)	Co^{2+}	cyanide	CN^-
cobalt(III)	Co^{3+}	dichromate	$Cr_2O_7^2$
copper(I)	Cu^+	fluoride	F^-
copper(II)	Cu^{2+}	hexacyanoferrate(II)	$Fe(CN)_6^{4-}$
hydronium	H_3O^+	hexacyanoferrate(III)	$Fe(CN)_6^{3-}$
iron(II)	Fe^{2+}	hydride	H^-
iron(III)	Fe^{3+}	hydrogen carbonate	HCO_3^-
lead(II)	Pb^{2+}	hydrogen sulfate	HSO_4^-
magnesium	Mg^{2+}	hydroxide	OH^-
mercury(I)	Hg_2^{2+}	hypochlorite	ClO^-
mercury(II)	Hg^{2+}	iodide	I^-
nickel(II)	Ni^{2+}	nitrate	NO_3^-
potassium	K^+	nitrite	NO_2^-
silver	Ag^+	oxide	O^{2-}
sodium	Na^+	perchlorate	ClO_4^-
strontium	Sr^{2+}	permanganate	MnO_4^-
tin(II)	Sn^{2+}	peroxide	O_2^{2-}
tin(IV)	Sn^{4+}	phosphate	PO_4^{3-}
titanium(III)	Ti^{3+}	sulfate	SO_4^{2-}
titanium(IV)	Ti^{4+}	sulfide	S^{2-}
zinc	Zn^{2+}	sulfite	SO_3^{2-}

TABLE A-9 Densities of Gases at STP

Gas	Density (g/L)	Gas	Density (g/L)
air, dry	1.293	hydrogen	0.0899
ammonia	0.771	hydrogen chloride	1.639
carbon dioxide	1.997	hydrogen sulfide	1.539
carbon monoxide	1.250	methane	0.7168
chlorine	3.214	nitrogen	1.2506
dinitrogen monoxide	1.977	nitrogen monoxide (at 10°C)	1.340
ethyne (acetylene)	1.165	oxygen	1.429
helium	0.1785	sulfur dioxide	2.927

TABLE A-10 Density of Water

Temperature (°C)	Density (g/cm^3)	Temperature (°C)	Density (g/cm^3)
0	0.999 84	25	0.997 05
2	0.999 94	30	0.995 65
3.98 (maximum)	0.999 973	40	0.992 22
4	0.999 97	50	0.988 04
6	0.999 94	60	0.983 20
8	0.999 85	70	0.977 77
10	0.999 70	80	0.971 79
14	0.999 24	90	0.965 31
16	0.998 94	100	0.958 36
20	0.998 20		

TABLE A-11 Solubilities of Gases in Water

Volume of gas (in L) at STP that can be dissolved in 1 L of water at the temperature indicated.

Gas	0°C	10°C	20°C	60°C
air	0.029 18	0.022 84	0.018 68	0.012 16
ammonia	1130	870	680	200
carbon dioxide	1.713	1.194	0.878	0.359
carbon monoxide	0.035 37	0.028 16	0.023 19	0.014 88
chlorine	—	3.148	2.299	1.023
hydrogen	0.021 48	0.019 55	0.018 19	0.016 00
hydrogen chloride	512	475	442	339
hydrogen sulfide	4.670	3.399	2.582	1.190
methane	0.055 63	0.041 77	0.033 08	0.019 54
nitrogen*	0.023 54	0.018 61	0.015 45	0.010 23
nitrogen monoxide	0.073 81	0.057 09	0.047 06	0.029 54
oxygen	0.048 89	0.038 02	0.031 02	0.019 46
sulfur dioxide	79.789	56.647	39.374	—

*Atmospheric nitrogen—98.815% N_2, 1.185% inert gases

TABLE A-12 Solubilities of Compounds

Solubilities are given in grams of solute dissolved in 100 g of water at the temperature indicated.

Compound	Formula	0°C	20°C	60°C	100°C
aluminum sulfate	$Al_2(SO_4)_3$	31.2	36.4	59.2	89.0
ammonium chloride	NH_4Cl	29.4	37.2	55.3	77.3
ammonium nitrate	NH_4NO_3	118	192	421	871
ammonium sulfate	$(NH_4)_2SO_4$	70.6	75.4	88	103
barium carbonate	$BaCO_3$	—*	$0.0022^{18°}$	—*	0.0065
barium hydroxide	$Ba(OH)_2$	1.67	3.89	20.94	$101.40^{80°}$
barium nitrate	$Ba(NO_3)_2$	4.95	9.02	20.4	34.4
barium sulfate	$BaSO_4$	—*	$0.000\,246^{25°}$	—*	0.000\,413
cadmium sulfate	$CdSO_4$	75.4	76.6	81.8	60.8
calcium carbonate	$CaCO_3$	—*	$0.0014^{25°}$	—*	$0.0018^{75°}$
calcium fluoride	CaF_2	$0.0016^{18°}$	$0.0017^{26°}$	—*	—*
calcium hydrogen carbonate	$Ca(HCO_3)_2$	16.15	16.60	17.50	18.40
calcium hydroxide	$Ca(OH)_2$	0.189	0.173	0.121	0.076
calcium sulfate	$CaSO_4$	—*	$0.209^{30°}$	—*	0.1619
copper(II) chloride	$CuCl_2$	68.6	73.0	96.5	120
copper(II) sulfate pentahydrate	$CuSO_4 \cdot 5H_2O$	23.1	32.0	61.8	114
lead(II) chloride	$PbCl_2$	0.67	1.00	1.94	3.20
lead(II) nitrate	$Pb(NO_3)_2$	37.5	54.3	91.6	133
lithium chloride	$LiCl$	69.2	83.5	98.4	128
lithium sulfate	Li_2SO_4	36.1	34.8	32.6	$30.9^{90°}$
magnesium hydroxide	$Mg(OH)_2$	—*	$0.0009^{18°}$	—*	0.004
magnesium sulfate	$MgSO_4$	22.0	33.7	54.6	68.3
mercury(I) chloride	Hg_2Cl_2	—*	$0.000\,20^{25°}$	$0.001^{43°}$	—*
mercury(II) chloride	$HgCl_2$	3.63	6.57	16.3	61.3
potassium aluminum sulfate	$KAl(SO_4)_2$	3.00	5.90	24.8	$109^{90°}$
potassium bromide	KBr	53.6	65.3	85.5	104
potassium chlorate	$KClO_3$	3.3	7.3	23.8	56.3
potassium chloride	KCl	28.0	34.2	45.8	56.3
potassium chromate	K_2CrO_4	56.3	63.7	70.1	$74.5^{90°}$
potassium iodide	KI	128	144	176	206
potassium nitrate	KNO_3	13.9	31.6	106	245
potassium permanganate	$KMnO_4$	2.83	6.34	22.1	—*
potassium sulfate	K_2SO_4	7.4	11.1	18.2	24.1
silver acetate	$AgC_2H_3O_2$	0.73	1.05	1.93	$2.59^{80°}$
silver chloride	$AgCl$	$0.000\,089^{10°}$	—*	—*	0.0021
silver nitrate	$AgNO_3$	122	216	440	733
sodium acetate	$NaC_2H_3O_2$	36.2	46.4	139	170
sodium chlorate	$NaClO_3$	79.6	95.9	137	204
sodium chloride	$NaCl$	35.7	35.9	37.1	39.2
sodium nitrate	$NaNO_3$	73.0	87.6	122	180
sucrose	$C_{12}H_{22}O_{11}$	179.2	203.9	287.3	487.2

*Dashes indicate that values are not available.

TABLE A-13 Standard Thermodynamic Properties

Substance	ΔH_f^o (kJ/mol)	S^o (J/mol·K)	ΔG_f^o (kJ/mol)	Substance	ΔH_f^o (kJ/mol)	S^o (J/mol·K)	ΔG_f^o (kJ/mol)
Aluminum				**Fluorine**			
Al(s)	0.0	28.3	0	$F_2(g)$	0.0	202.8	0
$AlCl_3(s)$	−705.6	110.7	−628.9	HF(g)	−272.5	173.8	−273.2
Al_2O_3(s, corundum)	−1676.0	51.0	−1582.4	**Hydrogen**			
Bromine				$H_2(g)$	0.0	130.7	0
$Br_2(l)$	0.0	152.2	0	$H_2O(l)$	−285.8	70.0	−237.2
$Br_2(g)$	30.9	245.5	30.9	$H_2O(g)$	−241.8	188.7	−228.6
HBr(g)	−36.4	198.6	−53.4	$H_2O_2(l)$	−187.8	109.6	−120.4
Calcium				HCN(g)	135.1	201.7	124.7
Ca(s)	0.0	41.6	0	**Iron**			
$CaCO_3$(s, calcite)	−1206.9	92.9	−1128.8	Fe(s)	0.0	27.3	0
$CaCl_2(s)$	−795.8	108.4	−748.1	$FeCl_3(s)$	−399.4	142.3	−334.05
CaO(s)	−634.9	38.2	−604.04	Fe_2O_3(s, hematite)	−824.8	87.4	−742.2
$Ca(OH)_2(s)$	−986.1	83.4	−898.6	Fe_3O_4(s, magnetite)	−1120.9	145.3	−1015.5
Carbon				**Lead**			
C(s, graphite)	0.0	5.7	0	Pb(s)	0.0	64.8	0
C(s, diamond)	1.9	2.4	2.90	$PbCl_2(s)$	−359.4	136.2	−317.9
$CCl_4(l)$	−132.8	216.2	−65.3	PbO(s, red)	−219.0	66.3	−188.95
$CCl_4(g)$	−95.8	309.9	−60.2	**Lithium**			
$CH_4(g)$	−74.9	186.3	−50.8	Li(s)	0.0	29.1	0
$CH_3OH(l)$	−239.1	127.2	−166.4	LiOH(s)	−484.9	42.8	−439.0
$C_2H_4(g)$	52.5	219.3	68.1	LiCl(s)	−408.6	59.3	−384.4
$C_2H_6(g)$	−83.8	229.1	32.9	**Magnesium**			
$C_2H_5OH(l)$	−277.0	161.0	−174.9	Mg(s)	0.0	32.7	0
$C_3H_8(g)$	−104.7	270.2	−24.3	$MgCl_2(s)$	−641.6	89.6	−591.8
C_4H_{10}(g, n-butane)	−125.6	310.1	−16.7	**Mercury**			
C_4H_{10}(g, isobutane)	−134.2	294.6	−20.9	Hg(l)	0.0	76.0	0
C_6H_{14}(g, n-hexane)	−167.1	388.4	0	$Hg_2Cl_2(s)$	−264.2	192.5	−210.8
C_7H_{16}(g, n-heptane)	−187.7	427.9	8.0	HgO(s, red)	−90.8	70.3	−55.6
C_8H_{18}(g, n-octane)	−208.6	466.7	16.3	**Nitrogen**			
C_8H_{18}(g, isooctane)	−224.0	423.2	12.6	$N_2(g)$	0.0	191.6	0
CO(g)	−110.5	197.6	−137.2	$NH_3(g)$	−45.9	192.8	−16.5
$CO_2(g)$	−393.5	213.8	−394.4	$NH_4Cl(s)$	−314.4	94.6	−203.0
$CS_2(g)$	117.1	237.8	67.2	NO(g)	90.3	210.8	86.6
HCOOH(l)	−425.1	129.0	−361.4	$NO_2(g)$	33.1	240.0	51.3
Chlorine				$N_2O(g)$	82.4	220.0	104.2
$Cl_2(g)$	0.0	223.1	0	$N_2O_4(g)$	9.1	304.4	97.8
HCl(g)	−92.3	186.8	−95.3	$HNO_3(g)$	−134.3	266.4	−74.8
Copper				**Oxygen**			
Cu(s)	0.0	33.2	0	$O_2(g)$	0.0	205.0	0
$CuCl_2(s)$	−220.1	108.1	−175.7	$O_3(g)$	142.7	238.9	163.2
$CuSO_4(s)$	−770.0	109.3	−661.9				

Standard Thermodynamic Properties

Substance	ΔH_f^o (kJ/mol)	S^o (J/mol•K)	ΔG_f^o (kJ/mol)	Substance	ΔH_f^o (kJ/mol)	S^o (J/mol•K)	ΔG_f^o (kJ/mol)
Potassium				NaOH(s)	−425.9	64.4	−379.5
K(s)	0.0	64.7	0	**Sulfur**			
KCl(s)	−436.7	82.6	−409.2	S(s)	0.0	32.1	0
KNO₃(s)	−494.6	133.0	−394.9	SO₂(g)	−296.8	248.1	−300.2
KOH(s)	−424.7	78.9	−379.1	SO₃(g)	−395.8	256.8	−371.1
Silicon				H₂S(g)	−20.5	205.7	−33.6
Si(s)	0.0	18.8	0	H₂SO₄(l)	−814.0	156.9	−690.1
SiCl₄(g)	−657.0	330.9	−617.0	**Tin**			
SiO₂(s, quartz)	−910.9	41.5	−856.7	Sn(s, white)	0.0	51.6	0
Silver				Sn(s, gray)	−2.1	44.1	0.13
Ag(s)	0.0	42.7	0	SnCl₄(l)	−511.3	258.6	−440.2
AgCl(s)	−127.1	96.2	−109.8	**Zinc**			
AgNO₃(s)	−124.4	140.9	−33.5	Zn(s)	0.0	41.6	0
Sodium				ZnCl₂(s)	−415.0	111.5	−369.4
Na(s)	0.0	51.5	0	ZnO(s)	−348.3	43.6	−318.32
NaCl(s)	−411.2	72.1	−384.2				

TABLE A-14 **Heat of Combustion**

Substance	Formula	State	ΔH_c	Substance	Formula	State	ΔH_c
hydrogen	H₂	g	−285.8	propene (propylene)	C₃H₆	g	−2058.0
graphite	C	s	−393.5	ethyne (acetylene)	C₂H₂	g	−1301.1
carbon monoxide	CO	g	−283.0	benzene	C₆H₆	l	−3267.6
methane	CH₄	g	−890.8	toluene	C₇H₈	l	−3910.3
ethane	C₂H₆	g	−1560.7	naphthalene	C₁₀H₈	s	−5156.3
propane	C₃H₈	g	−2219.2	anthracene	C₁₄H₁₀	s	−7076.5
butane	C₄H₁₀	g	−2877.6	methanol	CH₃OH	l	−726.1
pentane	C₅H₁₂	g	−3535.6	ethanol	C₂H₅OH	l	−1366.8
hexane	C₆H₁₄	l	−4163.2	ether	(C₂H₅)₂O	l	−2751.1
heptane	C₇H₁₆	l	−4817.0	formaldehyde	CH₂O	g	−570.7
octane	C₈H₁₈	l	−5470.5	glucose	C₆H₁₂O₆	s	−2803.0
ethene (ethylene)	C₂H₄	g	−1411.2	sucrose	C₁₂H₂₂O₁₁	s	−5640.9

ΔH_c = heat of combustion of the given substance. All values of ΔH_c are expressed as kJ/mol of substance oxidized to $H_2O(l)$ and/or $CO_2(g)$ at constant pressure and 25°C.

s = solid, l = liquid, g = gas

TABLE A-15 Comparison of Ionic and Atomic Radii

Legend:
- Atomic number
- Relative atomic size
- Ionic symbol
- Relative ionic size
- Ionic radius (pm)

6 — C⁴⁻ 260 (C^{4-} 260)

Period

Period	Group 1	Group 2	Group 3	Group 4	Group 5	Group 6	Group 7	Group 8	Group 9	Group 10	Group 11	Group 12	Group 13	Group 14	Group 15	Group 16	Group 17	Group 18
1	1 H^- 154																	2 He —
2	3 Li^+ 76	4 Be^{2+} 45											5 B —	6 C^{4-} 260	7 N^{3-} 146	8 O^{2-} 140	9 F^- 133	10 Ne —
3	11 Na^+ 102	12 Mg^{2+} 72											13 Al^{3+} 54	14 Si —	15 P^{3-} 212	16 S^{2-} 184	17 Cl^- 181	18 Ar —
4	19 K^+ 138	20 Ca^{2+} 100	21 Sc^{3+} 75	22 Ti^{2+} 86	23 V^{2+} 79	24 Cr^{2+} 80	25 Mn^{2+} 83	26 Fe^{2+} 78	27 Co^{2+} 65	28 Ni^{2+} 69	29 Cu^{2+} 73	30 Zn^{2+} 74	31 Ga^{3+} 62	32 Ge —	33 As —	34 Se^{2-} 198	35 Br^- 196	36 Kr —
5	37 Rb^+ 152	38 Sr^{2+} 118	39 Y^{3+} 90	40 Zr —	41 Nb —	42 Mo —	43 Tc —	44 Ru —	45 Rh^{3+} 67	46 Pd^{2+} 86	47 Ag^+ 115	48 Cd^{2+} 95	49 In^{3+} 80	50 Sn^{2+} 118	51 Sb^{3+} 76	52 Te^{2-} 221	53 I^- 220	54 Xe —
6	55 Cs^+ 167	56 Ba^{2+} 136	57 La^{3+} 116	72 Hf —	73 Ta —	74 W —	75 Re —	76 Os —	77 Ir —	78 Pt^{2+} 80	79 Au^+ 137	80 Hg^{2+} 137	81 Tl^{3+} 89	82 Pb^{2+} 119	83 Bi^{3+} 103	84 Po —	85 At —	86 Rn —
7	87 Fr^+ 180	88 Ra^{2+} 148	89 Ac^{3+} 111	104 Rf —	105 Db —	106 Sg —	107 Bh —	108 Hs —	109 Mt —	110 Uun —	111 Uuu —							

TABLE A-16 **Agencies Regulating Chemicals in the United States**

Agency	Purpose	Significant activities related to chemistry
Food and Drug Administration (FDA)	develops and enforces regulations regarding impurities and other hazards in foods, drugs, and cosmetics	▶ approves new drugs for public release ▶ sets labeling standards for drugs and food (except meat and poultry) ▶ sets regulations for the use of additives ▶ inspects food manufacturers for sanitary conditions ▶ validates product claims
Environmental Protection Agency	works with state and local governments to enforce laws enacted by Congress regarding control of air and water pollution, solid wastes, pesticides, radiation, and toxic substances	▶ sets limits for pollutants ▶ sets restrictions on use of hazardous substances ▶ sets tolerance levels for pesticides in foods; monitors those levels in humans, animals, and food plants
Occupational Health and Safety Administration (OSHA)	develops and enforces regulations regarding safe and healthy work environments	▶ conducts site inspections to ensure safe conditions ▶ imposes citations and penalties for noncompliance
Agency for Toxic Substances and Disease Registry	works with state and federal information regarding adverse agencies to collect and disseminate health effects of hazardous substances in storage or of accidental release of hazardous substances through fire, explosions, or transportation accidents	▶ maintains list of areas closed because of toxic contamination ▶ assists in treatment of individuals exposed to hazardous substances
Consumer Product Safety Commission	evaluates safety of consumer products	▶ enforces labeling of hazards on products ▶ bans highly hazardous products
Department of Agriculture	works to maintain and improve agricultural productivity while protecting natural resources; ensures quality of food supply	▶ analyzes foods for contaminants and pesticides ▶ provides information on nutrient values in foods

READING AND STUDY SKILLS

Power notes help you organize the chemical concepts you are studying by distinguishing main ideas from details. Similar to outlines, power notes are linear in form and provide you with a framework of important concepts. Power notes are easier to use than outlines because their structure is simpler. Using the power notes numbering system you assign a *1* to each main idea and a *2*, *3*, or *4* to each detail.

Power notes are an invaluable asset to the learning process, and they can be used frequently throughout your chemistry course. You can use power notes to organize ideas while reading your text or to restructure your class notes for studying purposes.

To learn to make power notes, practice first by using single-word concepts and a subject you are especially interested in, such as animals, sports, or movies. As you become comfortable with structuring power notes, integrate their use into your study of chemistry. For an easier transition, start with a few boldfaced vocabulary terms. Later you can strengthen your notes by expanding these single-word concepts into more-detailed phrases and sentences. Use the following general format to help you structure your power notes.

    Power 1: Main idea
      Power 2: Detail or support for power 1
        Power 3: Detail or support for power 2
          Power 4: Detail or support for power 3

1   Pick a Power 1 word from the text

The text you choose does not have to come straight from your chemistry textbook. You may be making power notes from your lecture notes or from an outside source. We'll use the italicized term *electrode* found in Section 3-2 of this book.

    Power 1: Electrode

2   Using the text, select some Power 2 words to support your Power 1 word

We'll use the boldfaced terms *anode* and *cathode,* which are two types of electrodes.

    Power 1: Electrode
      Power 2: Anode
      Power 2: Cathode

3   Select some Power 3 words to support your Power 2 words

We'll use the terms *oxidation* and *reduction,* two terms that describe the Power 2 words.

Power 1: Electrode
    Power 2: Anode
        Power 3: Oxidation
    Power 2: Cathode
        Power 3: Reduction

4 Continue to add powers to support and detail the main idea as necessary

There are no restrictions on how many power numbers you can use in your notes. If you have a main idea that requires a lot of support, add more powers to help you extend and organize your ideas. Be sure that words having the same power number have a similar relationship to the power above. Power 1 terms do not have to be related to each other. You can use power notes to organize the material in an entire section or chapter of your text. Doing so will provide you with an invaluable study guide for your classroom quizzes and tests.

Power 1: Electrode
    Power 2: Anode
        Power 3: Oxidation
            Power 4: Lose electrons
    Power 2: Cathode
        Power 3: Reduction
            Power 4: Gain electrons

PRACTICE

1. Use a periodic table and the power notes structure below to organize the following terms: *alkaline-earth metals, nonmetals, calcium, sodium, halogens, metals, alkali metals, chlorine, barium,* and *iodine.*

1 _____
  2 _____
    3 _____
  2 _____
    3 _____
    3 _____
1 _____
  2 _____
    3 _____
    3 _____

You can use pattern puzzles to help you remember sequential information. Pattern puzzles are not just a tool for memorization. They also promote a greater understanding of a variety of chemical processes, from the steps in solving a mass-mass stoichiometry problem to the procedure for making a solution of specified molarity.

1 Write down the steps of a process in your own words

We'll use the How To feature on preparing a 0.5000 M solution from Section 13-1. On a sheet of notebook paper, write down one step per line, and do not number the steps. Also, do not copy the process straight from your text. Copying encourages strict memorization, whereas writing the steps in your own words promotes a more thorough understanding of the process. You may want to divide the longer steps into two or three shorter steps.

- Calculate the mass of solute needed to make 1 L of a 0.5000 M solution.
- Measure out the correct mass of solute in a beaker.
- Add some of the solvent to the beaker in order to dissolve the solute.
- Pour the solute/solvent mixture into a 1 L volumetric flask.
- Rinse the beaker with more solvent and pour it into the flask until the solution nears the neck of the flask.
- Stopper the flask and gently swirl the mixture.
- Fill the flask to its mark with solvent.
- Stopper the flask and invert it several times to ensure complete mixing.

2 Cut the sheet of paper into strips with only one step per strip of paper

Shuffle the strips of paper so that they are out of sequence.

- Rinse the beaker with more solvent and pour it into the flask until the solution nears the neck of the flask.

- Measure out the correct mass of solute in a beaker.

- Fill the flask to its mark with solvent.

- Calculate the mass of solute needed to make 1 L of a 0.5000 M solution.

- Pour the solute/solvent mixture into a 1 L volumetric flask.

- Stopper the flask and and invert it several times to ensure complete mixing.

- Stopper the flask and gently swirl the mixture.

- Add some of the solvent to the beaker in order to dissolve the solute.

3 Place the strips in their proper sequence

Confirm the order of the process by checking your text or your class notes.

- Calculate the mass of solute needed to make 1 L of a 0.5000 M solution.

- Measure out the correct mass of solute in a beaker.

- Add some of the solvent to the beaker in order to dissolve the solute.

- Pour the solute/solvent mixture into a 1 L volumetric flask.

- Rinse the beaker with more solvent and pour it into the flask until the solution nears the neck of the flask.

- Stopper the flask and gently swirl the mixture.

- Fill the flask to its mark with solvent.

- Stopper the flask and and invert it several times to ensure complete mixing.

Pattern puzzles are especially helpful when you are studying for your chemistry tests. Before tests, use your puzzles to practice sequencing and to review the steps of chemistry processes. You and a classmate can also take turns creating your own pattern puzzles of different chemical processes and putting each other's puzzles in the correct sequence. Studying with a classmate in this manner will help make studying fun and will enable you to help each other.

PRACTICE

1. Rewrite the following sentences, which describe the process of making pattern puzzles, in the correct order.

Place the strips in their proper sequence.

Write down the steps of the process in your own words.

Shuffle the strips of paper.

Choose a multiple-step process from your text.

Using your text, confirm the order of the process.

Cut the paper into strips so that there is one step per strip.

The KWL strategy, an exciting and helpful approach to learning, is somewhat different from the other learning strategies you have seen in this appendix. This strategy, which stands for "what I **K**now—what I **W**ant to know—what I **L**earned," differs in that it prompts you to brainstorm about the subject matter before reading the assigned material. Relating your new ideas and concepts with those you have previously learned will help you to more readily understand and apply the new knowledge you obtain in this course. The section objectives throughout your text are ideal for using the KWL strategy. Just read the objectives before reading each section, and follow the instructions in the example below.

1 Read the section objectives

You may also want to scan headings, boldface terms, and illustrations in the section. We'll use a few of the objectives from Section 12-1.

- Describe the general properties of gases.
- Define pressure, and give the SI unit for pressure.
- Describe the causes of global warming.

2 Divide a sheet of paper into three columns, and label the columns "What I know," "What I want to know," and "What I learned"

What I know	What I want to know	What I learned

3 Brainstorm about what you know about the information in the objectives, and write these ideas in the first column

Because this chart is designed primarily to help you integrate your own knowledge with new information, it is not necessary to write complete sentences.

4 Think about what you want to know about the information in the objectives, and write these ideas in the second column

You'll want to know the information you will be tested over, so include information from both the section objectives and any other objectives your teacher has given you.

5 While reading the section or afterwards, use the third column to write down the information you learned

While reading, pay close attention to any information about the topics you wrote in the "What I want to know" column. If you do not find all of the answers you are looking for, you may need to reread the section or reference a second source. Be sure to ask your teacher if you still cannot find the information after reading the section a second time.

It is also important to review your brainstormed ideas when you have completed reading the section. Compare your ideas in the first column with the information you wrote down in the third column. If you find that some of your brainstormed ideas are incorrect, cross them out. It is extremely important to identify and correct any misconceptions you had prior to reading before you begin studying for your test.

What I know	What I want to know	What I learned
▶ gases are invisible and flow through the air casily ▶ gases don't have a definite volume	▶ general properties of gases	▶ gases are fluids ▶ gas molecules are in constant motion ▶ collisions between gas molecules are elastic ▶ low densities ▶ highly compressible ▶ made of tiny particles far apart from each other ▶ fill the entire container ▶ exert pressure equally in all directions
▶ pressure is when one thing pushes on something else ▶ you apply pressure to stop a wound from bleeding	▶ definition of pressure and SI unit of pressure	▶ pressure is the force on a surface divided by the area of that surface ▶ SI pressure unit is pascal
▶ CFCs in atmosphere from aerosol cans, refrigerators, and air conditioners ▶ hole in the ozone layer above Antarctica ▶ car pollution ▶ temperatures get warmer ▶ skin cancer gets worse	▶ causes of global warming	▶ increase in concentration of greenhouse gases (gases in the atmosphere that reflect infrared radiation back to Earth's surface) ▶ increased levels of carbon dioxide from fuels for driving cars and using electricity ▶ increase in artificial greenhouse gases (CFCs from air conditioning)

PRACTICE

1. Use column 3 from the table above to identify and correct any misconceptions in the following brainstorm list.

   a. The gasoline used in cars is in a gaseous state.

   b. Car pooling may help reduce global warming.

   c. The SI unit of pressure is the pascal.

   d. Global warming is solely caused by the accumulation of CFCs in the atmosphere.

   e. Gases are extremely dense.

Two-column notes can be used to learn and review definitions of vocabulary terms, examples of multiple-step processes, or details of specific concepts. The two-column-note strategy is simple: write the term, main idea, step-by-step process, or concept in the left-hand column, and the definition, example, or detail on the right.

One strategy for using two-column notes is to organize main ideas and their details. The main ideas from your reading are written in the left-hand column of your paper and can be written as questions, key words, or a combination of both. Details describing these main ideas are then written in the right-hand column of your paper.

1 Identify the main ideas

The main ideas for a chapter are listed in the section objectives. However, you decide which ideas to include in your notes. Here are the main ideas from the objectives in Section 4-1 as an example.

Describe characteristic properties of the alkali metals, alkaline-earth metals, halogens, noble gases, lanthanides, and actinides.

2 Divide a blank sheet of paper into two columns, and write the main ideas in the left-hand column

Remind yourself that your two-column notes are precisely that—notes. Do not copy ideas straight out of the book or waste your time writing them in complete sentences. Summarize your ideas using quick phrases that are easy for you to understand and remember. Decide how many details you need for each main idea, and write that number in parentheses under the main idea. Using the example from Section 4–1, you will list the number of characteristic properties you need to know for each group of the periodic table.

Main idea	
▶ Alkali metals (3 characteristic properties)	
▶ Alkaline-earth metals (2 characteristic properties)	
▶ Halogens (2 characteristic properties)	
▶ Noble gases (2 characteristic properties)	
▶ Lanthanides (2 characteristic properties)	
▶ Actinides (2 characteristic properties)	

3 Write the detail notes in the right-hand column

Be sure you list as many details as you designated in the main-idea column.

Main idea	Detail notes
▶ Alkali metals (3 characteristic properties)	▶ highly reactive ▶ good conductors of electricity ▶ soft
▶ Alkaline-earth metals (2 characteristic properties)	▶ reactive ▶ harder than alkali metals
▶ Halogens (2 characteristic properties)	▶ reactive ▶ nonmetallic
▶ Noble gases (2 characteristic properties)	▶ low reactivity ▶ gaseous
▶ Lanthanides (2 characteristic properties)	▶ reactive ▶ metallic
▶ Actinides (2 characteristic properties)	▶ radioactive ▶ metallic

The two-column method of review is perfect whether you use it to study for a short quiz or for a test on the material in an entire chapter. Just cover the information in the right-hand column with a sheet of paper, and after reciting what you know, uncover the notes to check your answers. Then ask yourself what else you know about that topic. Linking ideas in this way will help you to gain a more complete picture of chemistry.

PRACTICE

1. Make your own two-column notes using the periodic table. Your notes should include details such as the symbol and the atomic number of each of the following elements.

   a. neon   **c.** calcium   **e.** oxygen

   b. lead   **d.** copper   **f.** sodium

Making concept maps can help you decide what material in a chapter is important and how to efficiently learn that material. A concept map presents key ideas, meanings, and relationships for the concepts being studied. It can be thought of as a visual road map of the chapter. Learning happens efficiently when you use concept maps because you work with only the key ideas and how they fit together.

The concept map shown as **Map A** was made from vocabulary terms in Chapter 1. Vocabulary terms are generally labels for concepts, and concepts are generally nouns. Linking words are used to form propositions that connect concepts and give them meaning in context. For example, on the map below, "matter is described by physical properties" is a proposition.

Studies show that people are better able to remember materials presented visually. The concept map is better than an outline because you can see the relationships among many ideas. Because outlines are linear, there is no way of linking the ideas from various sections of the outline. Read through the map to become familiar with the information presented. Then look at the map in relation to all of the text pages in Chapter 1; which gives a better picture of the important concepts—the map or the full chapter?

Map A

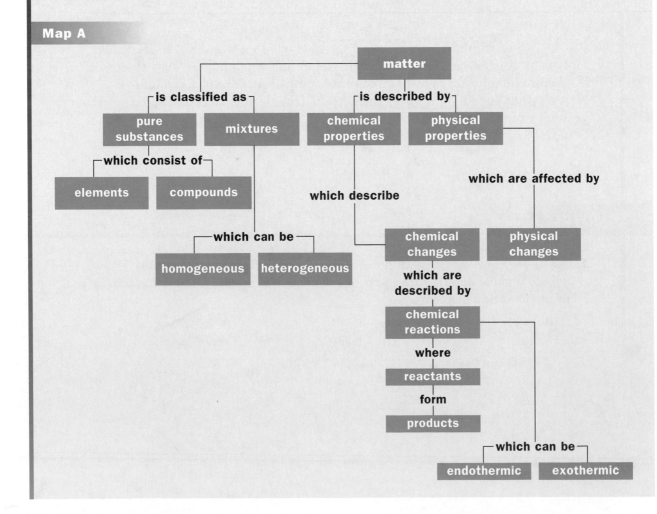

1 List all the important concepts

We'll use some of the boldface terms in Chapter 1.

allotropes

compound

element

heterogeneous mixture

homogenous mixture

inorganic compound

mixture

organic compound

pure substance

▶ From this list, group similar concepts together. For example, one way to group these concepts would be into two groups—one that is related to mixtures and one that is related to pure substances.

mixture	*pure substance*
heterogeneous mixture	compound
homogenous mixture	element
	allotrope
	inorganic compound
	organic compound

2 Select a main concept for the map

We will use *matter* as the main concept for this map.

3 Build the map by placing the concepts according to their importance under the main concept, *matter*

One way of arranging the concepts is shown in **Map B.**

Map B

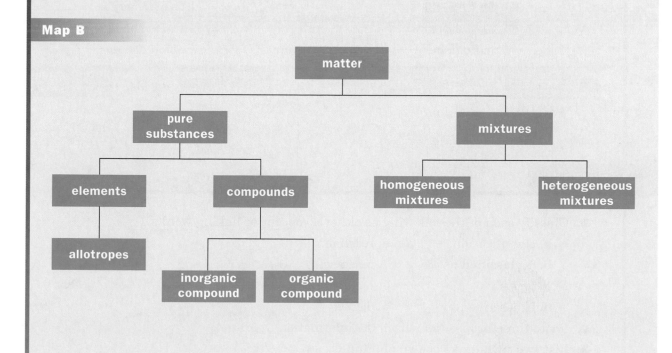

4 Add linking words to give meaning to the arrangement of concepts

When adding the links, be sure that each proposition makes sense. To distinguish concepts from links, place your concepts in circles, ovals, or rectangles, as shown in the maps. Then make cross-links. Cross-links are made of propositions and lines connecting concepts across the map. Links that apply in only one direction are indicated with an arrowhead. **Map C** is a finished map covering the main ideas found in the vocabulary listed in Step 1.

Making maps might seem difficult at first, but the process forces you to think about the meanings and relationships among the concepts. If you do not understand those relationships, you can get help early on.

Practice mapping by making concept maps about topics you know. For example, if you know a lot about a particular sport, such as basketball, or if you have a particular hobby, such as playing a musical instrument, you can use that topic to make a practice map. By perfecting your skills with information that you know very well, you will begin to feel more confident about making maps from the information in a chapter.

Remember, the time you devote to mapping will pay off when it is time to review for an exam.

Map C

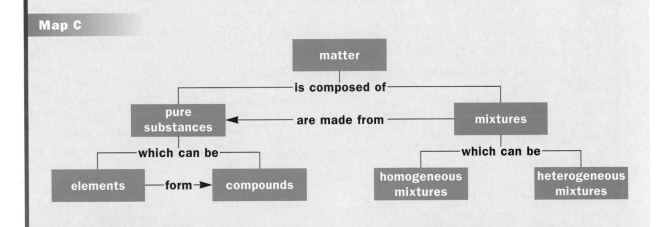

PRACTICE

1. Classify each of the following as either a concept or linking word(s).
   - **a.** classification
   - **b.** is classified as
   - **c.** forms
   - **d.** is described by
   - **e.** reaction
   - **f.** reacts with
   - **g.** metal
   - **h.** defines

2. Write three propositions from the information in **Map A.**

3. List two cross-links shown on **Map C.**

ANSWERS TO SELECTED PROBLEMS

CHAPTER 1

Practice problems, page 19

8. a. $21.59 \text{ L} \times \dfrac{1000 \text{ mL}}{1 \text{ L}} = 21\,590 \text{ mL, or } 2.159 \times 10^4 \text{ mL}$

b. 162 cm, or 1.62×10^2 cm

c. 6.4×10^4 nm   d. 0.02648 kg, or 2.648×10^{-2} kg

CHAPTER 2

Practice problems, page 47

9. a. $T(\text{K}) = 373 \text{ K}$ c. $T(\text{K}) = 273 \text{ K}$

b. $T(\text{K}) = 1058 \text{ K}$ d. $T(\text{K}) = 236 \text{ K}$

10. a. $t(^\circ\text{C}) = 0^\circ\text{C}$ c. $t(^\circ\text{C}) = -273^\circ\text{C}$

b. $t(^\circ\text{C}) = 927^\circ\text{C}$ d. $t(^\circ\text{C}) = -173^\circ\text{C}$

11. $KE = \dfrac{(1300 \text{ kg})(50 \text{ m/s})^2}{2} = 1\,625\,000 \text{ J}$

Practice problems, page 64

8. a. 3   c. 6   e. unlimited

b. 3   d. 4

9. a. 47.10 g   c. 3.424×10^5 g   e. 28.62 mi/h

b. 32.86 L   d. 0.123 cm^2

10. a. $\dfrac{129 \text{ g}}{29.2 \text{ mL}} = 4.42 \text{ g/mL}$

b. $(1.551 \text{ mm})(3.260 \text{ mm})(4.9001 \text{ mm}) = 24.78 \text{ mm}^3$

c. 1.4×10^5 kJ/s   d. $0.367 \text{ L} + 2.51 \text{ L} + 1.6004 \text{ L} = 4.48 \text{ L}$

11. 4593 kJ/min

12. a. $277\,088\,000\,000\,000 \text{ atoms} = 2.770\,88 \times 10^{14} \text{ atoms}$

b. $0.000\,000\,000\,000\,839\,602 \text{ g} = 8.396\,02 \times 10^{-13}$ g

c. $700\,004 \text{ mm} = 7.000\,04 \times 10^5$ mm

13. $2300 \text{ metric tons} \times \dfrac{1000 \text{ kg}}{1 \text{ metric ton}} \times \dfrac{1000 \text{ g}}{1 \text{ kg}} = 2.3 \times 10^9$ g

CHAPTERS 3, 4, 5

CHAPTER 6

Practice problems, page 201

6. a. ionic   d. polar covalent

b. nonpolar covalent   e. nonpolar covalent

c. ionic   f. polar covalent

7. a. Br   c. O   e. neither

b. S   d. Cl   f. Br

8. polar covalent; electronegativity difference = 1.2

Practice problems, page 213

7. a. 2   b. 5   c. 4   d. 1

8. a. Be·   b. ·N̈·   c. ·S̈i·   d. K·

9. a. :B̈r–B̈r: e. :B̈r–F̈:

b.
H
H H–C–H H
H–C———N–C–H
H   H

f.
H H
:N–N:
H H

c. Ö=O–Ö: ⟷ :Ö–O=Ö

d. $\left[\text{H–Ö–H}\right]^+$

g. $\left[\text{Ö–N–Ö:}\right]^- \longleftrightarrow \left[\text{:Ö–N=Ö}\right]^-$

10. a. silicon dioxide   c. tin tetraiodide

b. phosphorus tribromide   d. dinitrogen trioxide

11. a. PBr$_5$ b. B$_5$H$_9$ c. P$_2$O$_3$ d. N$_2$O$_4$

12. H–Ö–H

Practice problems, page 217

1. a. trigonal pyramidal   b. bent

:C̈l:
H–N–H

Ö=N–C̈l:

2. a. trigonal planar

$\left[\text{Ö=N–Ö:}\right]^- \longleftrightarrow \left[\text{:Ö–N–Ö:}\right]^- \longleftrightarrow \left[\text{:Ö–N=Ö}\right]^-$

b. tetrahedral

$\left[\begin{array}{c} \text{H} \\ \text{H–N–H} \\ \text{H} \end{array}\right]^+$

Practice problems, page 218

5. Both are linear. Br$_2$ is nonpolar. HBr is polar because H and Br have an electronegativity difference of 0.8.

6. SCl$_2$ is bent.
PF$_3$ is trigonal pyramidal.
NCl$_3$ is trigonal pyramidal.
PF$_3$ is the most polar. The electronegativity difference is greatest between P and F, and the bond angles of all three molecules are similar.

CHAPTER 7

Practice problems, page 243

9. a.
O
‖
–C–H

b. –OH;
O
‖
–C–OH

10. a. carboxylic acid   c. ketone   e. halide

b. ether   d. amine

11. in order: alkane, alcohol, carboxylic acid, ketone, ether

Practice problems, page 252

11. a.
$$Cl-\overset{\overset{\displaystyle H}{|}}{\underset{\underset{\displaystyle H}{|}}{C}}-\overset{\overset{\displaystyle H}{|}}{\underset{\underset{\displaystyle H}{|}}{C}}-\overset{\overset{\displaystyle H}{|}}{\underset{\underset{\displaystyle H}{|}}{C}}-\overset{\overset{\displaystyle H}{|}}{\underset{\underset{\displaystyle Cl}{|}}{C}}-\overset{\overset{\displaystyle H}{|}}{\underset{\underset{\displaystyle H}{|}}{C}}-\overset{\overset{\displaystyle H}{|}}{\underset{\underset{\displaystyle H}{|}}{C}}-H$$

b.
$$H-\overset{\overset{\displaystyle H}{|}}{\underset{\underset{\displaystyle H}{|}}{C}}-\overset{\overset{\displaystyle O}{|}}{\underset{}{C}}-\overset{\overset{\displaystyle H}{|}}{\underset{\underset{\displaystyle H}{|}}{C}}-\overset{\overset{\displaystyle H}{|}}{\underset{\underset{\displaystyle H}{|}}{C}}-\overset{\overset{\displaystyle H}{|}}{\underset{\underset{\displaystyle H}{|}}{C}}-H$$

c.
$$H-\overset{\overset{\displaystyle H}{|}}{\underset{\underset{\displaystyle H}{|}}{C}}-\overset{\overset{\displaystyle Br}{|}}{\underset{\underset{\displaystyle H}{|}}{C}}-\overset{\overset{\displaystyle H}{|}}{\underset{\underset{\displaystyle H}{|}}{C}}-\overset{\overset{\displaystyle H}{|}}{\underset{\underset{\displaystyle Cl}{|}}{C}}-\overset{\overset{\displaystyle H}{|}}{\underset{\underset{\displaystyle H}{|}}{C}}-\overset{\overset{\displaystyle H}{|}}{\underset{\underset{\displaystyle H}{|}}{C}}-\overset{\overset{\displaystyle H}{|}}{\underset{\underset{\displaystyle H}{|}}{C}}-H$$

d.
$$H-\overset{\overset{\displaystyle Cl}{|}}{\underset{\underset{\displaystyle H}{|}}{C}}-\overset{\overset{\displaystyle H}{|}}{\underset{\underset{\displaystyle H}{|}}{C}}-C\equiv C-\overset{\overset{\displaystyle H}{|}}{\underset{\underset{\displaystyle H}{|}}{C}}-\overset{\overset{\displaystyle H}{|}}{\underset{\underset{\displaystyle H}{|}}{C}}-\overset{\overset{\displaystyle H}{|}}{\underset{\underset{\displaystyle H}{|}}{C}}-\overset{\overset{\displaystyle H}{|}}{\underset{\underset{\displaystyle H}{|}}{C}}-H$$

12. a. 2, 4-dimethylpentane   **b.** 1, 2-dibromobutane

CHAPTER 8

Practice problems, page 278

1. $3.7 \text{ mol Na} \times \dfrac{6.022 \times 10^{23} \text{ Na atoms}}{\text{mol}} = 2.2 \times 10^{24} \text{ Na atoms}$

2. 9.33×10^{25} As atoms

3. $5.66 \times 10^{26} \text{ Xe atoms} \times \dfrac{1 \text{ mol Xe}}{6.022 \times 10^{23} \text{ Xe atoms}} = 940. \text{ mol Xe}$

4. 4.796×10^{-9} mol Ag

Practice problems, page 279

1. (27.98 amu)(0.9221) + (28.98 amu)(0.047) +
$$(29.97 \text{ amu})(0.0309) = 28.09 \text{ amu}$$

2. 15.99 amu   **3.** 55.84 amu

Practice problems, page 283

9. $8.6 \text{ mol Br} \times \dfrac{79.90 \text{ g Br}}{\text{mol Br}} = 690 \text{ g Br}$ **10.** 212 g Si

11. $38 \text{ g C} \times \dfrac{1 \text{ mol C}}{12.01 \text{ g C}} = 3.2 \text{ mol C}$ **12.** 2.0 mol H

13. a. 0.0100 mol Cl   **c.** 5.03×10^{-3} mol Cu
b. 8.012 mol Na   **d.** 5.056 mol Fe

14. (0.20)(10 amu) + (0.80)(11 amu) = 10.8 amu, 5, boron

15. a. $1.38 \text{ mol N} \times \dfrac{14.01 \text{ g N}}{\text{mol N}} = 19.3 \text{ g N}$
b. 6.022×10^{23} Ag atoms = 1 mol Ag = 107.9 g Ag
c. 8.24×10^9 g S
d. 3.19×10^{-8} g O

16. a. $2 \text{ mol Fe} \times \dfrac{6.022 \times 10^{23} \text{ Fe atoms}}{\text{mol Fe}} = 1 \times 10^{24} \text{ atoms}$

b. $40.1 \text{ g Ca} \times \dfrac{1 \text{ mol Ca}}{40.08 \text{ g Ca}} \times \dfrac{6.022 \times 10^{23} \text{ atoms Ca}}{\text{mol Ca}} =$
$$6.02 \times 10^{23} \text{ atoms}$$

c. 2.7×10^{24} atoms   **d.** 4.825×10^{24} atoms

17. a. $\dfrac{1.01 \text{ g H}}{6.022 \times 10^{23} \text{ H atoms}} = 1.68 \times 10^{-24} \text{ g/H atoms}$
b. 2.523×10^{-22} g/Eu atom   **c.** 3.239×10^{-22} g/Pt atom

Practice problems, page 288

1. a. 122.55 g/mol   **e.** 60.06 g/mol   **i.** 131.07 g/mol
b. 234.06 g/mol   **f.** 74.14 g/mol   **j.** 92.15 g/mol
c. 158.04 g/mol   **g.** 206.31 g/mol   **k.** 300.06 g/mol
d. 72.17 g/mol   **h.** 58.32 g/mol

2. a. $NaHCO_3$, 84.01 g/mol   **e.** $Fe(OH)_3$, 106.88 g/mol
b. $K_2Cr_2O_7$, 294.20 g/mol   **f.** $SnCl_2$, 189.61 g/mol
c. $Mg(ClO_4)_2$, 223.20 g/mol   **g.** $HClO_4$, 100.46 g/mol
d. $Al_2(SO_4)_3$, 342.17 g/mol   **h.** $NiCl_2 \bullet 6H_2O$, 237.71 g/mol

Practice problems, page 292

1. $70.0 \text{ g Mn} \times \dfrac{1 \text{ mol Mn}}{54.94 \text{ g Mn}} = 1.27 \text{ mol Mn}$

$30.0 \text{ g O} \times \dfrac{1 \text{ mol Cl}}{16.00 \text{ g O}} = 1.875 \text{ mol O}$

$\dfrac{1.27 \text{ mol Mn}}{1.27} = 1 \times 2 = 2$

$\dfrac{1.875 \text{ mol O}}{1.27} = 1.56 \times 2 \approx 3, \; Mn_2O_3$

2. Cl_2O_7

Practice problems, page 294

1. $\dfrac{78 \text{ g/mol}}{13.02 \text{ g/mol}} = 6, \; C_6H_6$ **2.** $\dfrac{214 \text{ g/mol}}{70.11 \text{ g/mol}} = 3.1, \; C_9H_{18}N_6$

Practice problems, page 295

1. $\dfrac{72.06 \text{ g C}}{180.18 \text{ g } C_6H_{12}O_6} \times 100 = 39.99\% \text{ C}$

$\dfrac{12.12 \text{ g H}}{180.18 \text{ g } C_6H_{12}O_6} \times 100 = 6.73\% \text{ H}$

$\dfrac{96.00 \text{ g O}}{180.18 \text{ g } C_6H_{12}O_6} \times 100 = 53.28\% \text{ O}$

2. 42.10% C, 6.49% H, 51.41% O

Practice problems, page 297

7. a. 158.18 g/mol   **c.** 183.2 g/mol   **e.** 86.20 g/mol
b. 357.49 g/mol   **d.** 180.17 g/mol

8. a. $\dfrac{87.42 \text{ g N}}{14.01 \text{ g/mol}} = 6.24 \text{ mol N}$ $\dfrac{12.58 \text{ g H}}{1.01 \text{ g/mol}} = 12.46 \text{ mol H}$
$\dfrac{6.24 \text{ mol N}}{6.24} = 1$ $\dfrac{12.46 \text{ mol H}}{6.24} = 2$
NH_2
b. BCl_2 **c.** CO_2F_2 **d.** $ZnMn_2O_8$ **e.** $C_5H_{14}N_2$

9. a. $\dfrac{116.1 \text{ g/mol}}{29.02 \text{ g/mol}} = 4, \; C_4H_4O_4$ **b.** B_2Cl_4 **c.** $N_3P_3Cl_6$

10. a. 35.41% Sr, 64.59% Br
b. 29.44% Ca, 23.55% S, 47.01% O
c. 31.83% Mg, 31.46% C, 36.70% N
d. 63.70% Pb, 14.77% C, 1.86% H, 19.67% O

11. a. SrS, 119.69 g/mol   **c.** $Zn(CH_3COO)_2$, 183.49 g/mol
b. NH_4F, 37.05 g/mol   **d.** $Hg(BrO_3)_2$, 456.39 g/mol

12. a. 55.39% Pb, 18.95% Cl, 25.66% O
  b. 25.94% N, 74.06% O
  c. 27.93% Fe, 24.05% S, 48.00% O
  d. 25.45% Cu, 12.84% S, 57.66% O, 4.04% H
  e. 68.27% C, 5.74% H, 25.98% O

13. $\dfrac{33.5 \text{ g H}_2\text{O}}{18.02 \text{ g/mol}} = 1.86 \text{ mol H}_2\text{O}$

  $1.86 \text{ mol H}_2\text{O} \times \dfrac{1 \text{ mol CaCl}_2}{6 \text{ mol H}_2\text{O}} = 0.310 \text{ mol CaCl}_2$

  $0.310 \text{ mol CaCl}_2 \times \dfrac{110.98 \text{ g CaCl}_2}{1 \text{ mol}} = 34.4 \text{ g CaCl}_2$

CHAPTER 9

Practice problems, page 316

1. a. $2\text{ZnS} + 3\text{O}_2 \longrightarrow 2\text{ZnO} + 2\text{SO}_2$ **c.** $\text{CS}_2 + 3\text{O}_2 \longrightarrow \text{CO}_2 + 2\text{SO}_2$
  b. $2\text{C}_2\text{H}_2 + 5\text{O}_2 \longrightarrow 4\text{CO}_2 + 2\text{H}_2\text{O}$ **d.** $\text{N}_2\text{O}_5 + \text{NO} \longrightarrow 3\text{NO}_2$

Practice problems, page 317

7. a. hydrogen + chlorine $\longrightarrow$ hydrogen chloride;
    $\text{H}_2 + \text{Cl}_2 \longrightarrow \text{HCl}$
  b. aluminum + iron(III) oxide $\longrightarrow$ aluminum oxide + iron;
    $\text{Al} + \text{Fe}_2\text{O}_3 \longrightarrow \text{Al}_2\text{O}_3 + \text{Fe}$
  c. potassium chlorate $\longrightarrow$ potassium chloride + oxygen;
    $\text{KClO}_3 \longrightarrow \text{KCl} + \text{O}_2$
  d. calcium hydroxide + hydrochloric acid $\longrightarrow$
                    calcium chloride + water;
    $\text{Ca(OH)}_2 + \text{HCl} \longrightarrow \text{CaCl}_2 + \text{H}_2\text{O}$

8. a. $\text{H}_2 + \text{Cl}_2 \longrightarrow 2\text{HCl}$ **c.** $2\text{KClO}_3 \longrightarrow 2\text{KCl} + 3\text{O}_2$
  b. $2\text{Al} + \text{Fe}_2\text{O}_3 \longrightarrow \text{Al}_2\text{O}_3 + 2\text{Fe}$
  d. $\text{Ca(OH)}_2 + 2\text{HCl} \longrightarrow \text{CaCl}_2 + 2\text{H}_2\text{O}$

9. a. $3\text{CaSi}_2 + 2\text{SbCl}_3 \longrightarrow 6\text{Si} + 2\text{Sb} + 3\text{CaCl}_2$
  b. $2\text{Al} + 6\text{CH}_3\text{OH} \longrightarrow 2(\text{CH}_3\text{O})_3\text{Al} + 3\text{H}_2$
  c. $\text{P}_4 + 5\text{O}_2 \longrightarrow 2\text{P}_2\text{O}_5$ **d.** $4\text{Fe} + 3\text{O}_2 \longrightarrow 2\text{Fe}_2\text{O}_3$

10. a. $2\text{Cu} + \text{O}_2 \longrightarrow 2\text{CuO}$ **b.** $2\text{Fe} + \text{O}_2 \longrightarrow 2\text{FeO}$

Practice problems, page 324

8. a. 16 mol of KCl, 24 mol of O_2 **b.** 6 mol of CaO, 6 mol of CO_2
  c. 7 mol of N_2O, 14 mol of H_2O
  d. 6 mol of NH_3, assuming sufficient N_2 is present

9. a. $16.0 \text{ mol KClO}_3 \times \dfrac{78 \text{ kJ}}{2 \text{ mol KClO}_3} = -624 \text{ kJ}$; exothermic
  b. +1070 kJ; endothermic
  c. −252 kJ; exothermic   **d.** −276 kJ; exothermic

Practice problems, page 328

1. copper, iron, zinc, aluminum, barium

2. a. $\text{Cu}(s) + \text{Zn}^{2+}(aq)$ **c.** no reaction
  b. $\text{Pb}(s) + \text{Mg}^{2+}(aq)$ **d.** $\text{Ag}(s) + \text{Cu}^{2+}(aq)$

Practice problems, page 330

8. a. $\text{H}_2\text{O}(l) + \text{SO}_3(g) \longrightarrow \text{H}_2\text{SO}_4(aq)$
  b. $2\text{C}_4\text{H}_{10}(g) + 13\text{O}_2(g) \longrightarrow 8\text{CO}_2(g) + 10\text{H}_2\text{O}(l)$
  c. $2\text{KClO}_3(s) \longrightarrow 2\text{KCl}(g) + 3\text{O}_2(g)$
  d. $\text{Zn}(s) + \text{CuSO}_4(aq) \longrightarrow \text{ZnSO}_4(aq) + \text{Cu}(s)$
  e. $\text{Ag}^+(aq) + \text{Cl}^-(aq) \longrightarrow \text{AgCl}(s)$

---

9. a. no reaction
  b. $\text{Mg}(s) + \text{Cu}^{2+}(aq) \longrightarrow \text{Mg}^{2+}(aq) + \text{Cu}(s)$
  c. $2\text{Ba}(s) + \text{O}_2(g) \longrightarrow 2\text{BaO}(s)$
  d. $\text{H}^+(aq) + \text{OH}^-(aq) \longrightarrow \text{H}_2\text{O}(l)$

CHAPTER 10

Practice problems, page 351

1. $55.0 \text{ g HF} \times \dfrac{1 \text{ mol HF}}{20.01 \text{ g HF}} \times \dfrac{1 \text{ mol SnF}_2}{2 \text{ mol HF}} \times \dfrac{156.7 \text{ g SnF}_2}{1 \text{ mol SnF}_2} =$
                    215 g SnF_2

2. $57.6 \text{ g C}_6\text{H}_5\text{Cl}$

3. $38.00 \text{ kg C}_{20}\text{H}_{12}\text{O}_5$

Practice problems, page 353

1. $0.0103 \text{ mol O}_2 \times \dfrac{31.999 \text{ g O}_2}{1 \text{ mol O}_2} = 0.3296 \text{ g O}_2$

  $0.3296 \text{ g O}_2 \times \dfrac{1 \text{ mol O}_2}{31.999 \text{ g O}_2} \times \dfrac{6 \text{ mol CO}_2}{6 \text{ mol O}_2} \times \dfrac{44.01 \text{ g CO}_2}{1 \text{ mol CO}_2} =$
                    0.453 g CO_2

2. $0.186 \text{ g H}_2\text{O}$

3. $6 \text{ mol CH}_3\text{COOH} \times \dfrac{60.05 \text{ g CH}_3\text{COOH}}{1 \text{ mol CH}_3\text{COOH}} = 360.3 \text{ g CH}_3\text{COOH}$

  $360.3 \text{ g CH}_3\text{COOH} \times \dfrac{1 \text{ mol CH}_3\text{COOH}}{60.05 \text{ g CH}_3\text{COOH}} \times$

  $\dfrac{6 \text{ mol CH}_3\text{COOC}_5\text{H}_{11}}{6 \text{ mol CH}_3\text{COOH}} \times \dfrac{130.2 \text{ g CH}_3\text{COOC}_5\text{H}_{11}}{1 \text{ mol CH}_3\text{COOC}_5\text{H}_{11}} =$
                    $781 \text{ g CH}_3\text{COOC}_5\text{H}_{11}$

Practice problems, page 355

1. $1.5 \text{ L H}_2\text{O} \times \dfrac{1000 \text{ mL}}{1 \text{ L}} \times \dfrac{1.00 \text{ g H}_2\text{O}}{1 \text{ mL H}_2\text{O}} \times \dfrac{1 \text{ mol H}_2\text{O}}{18.015 \text{ g H}_2\text{O}} \times$

  $\dfrac{2 \text{ mol LiOH}}{1 \text{ mol H}_2\text{O}} \times \dfrac{23.95 \text{ g LiOH}}{1 \text{ mol LiOH}} = 4.0 \times 10^3 \text{ g LiOH}$

2. $15 \text{ g NaHCO}_3 \times \dfrac{1 \text{ mol NaHCO}_3}{84.01 \text{ g NaHCO}_3} \times \dfrac{1 \text{ mol CO}_2}{1 \text{ mol NaHCO}_3} \times$

  $\dfrac{44.01 \text{ g CO}_2}{1 \text{ mol CO}_2} \times \dfrac{1 \text{ L CO}_2}{1.10 \text{ g CO}_2} = 7.14 \text{ L CO}_2$

Practice problems, page 360

1. No, there is not enough Al(OH)_3.
  $34.0 \text{ g HCl} \times \dfrac{1 \text{ mol HCl}}{36.46 \text{ g HCl}} \times \dfrac{1 \text{ mol Al(OH)}_3}{1 \text{ mol HCl}} \times$

  $\dfrac{78.004 \text{ g Al(OH)}_3}{1 \text{ mol Al(OH)}_3} = 78.0 \text{ g Al(OH)}_3$

2. N_2 is the limiting reactant.
  $92.7 \text{ kg N}_2 \times \dfrac{1000 \text{ g}}{1 \text{ kg}} \times \dfrac{1 \text{ mol N}_2}{28.01 \text{ g N}_2} = 3.31 \times 10^3 \text{ mol N}_2$

  $265.8 \text{ kg H}_2 \times \dfrac{1000 \text{ g}}{1 \text{ kg}} \times \dfrac{1 \text{ mol H}_2}{2.0159 \text{ g H}_2} = 1.319 \times 10^5 \text{ mol H}_2$

  $131\,900 \text{ mol H}_2 \times \dfrac{1 \text{ mol N}_2}{3 \text{ mol H}_2} = 4.397 \times 10^4 \text{ mol N}_2 \text{ needed}$

Practice problems, page 364

1. $550 \text{ g } C_7H_8 \times \dfrac{1 \text{ mol } C_7H_8}{92.141 \text{ g } C_7H_8} \times \dfrac{1 \text{ mol } C_7H_7NO_2}{1 \text{ mol } C_7H_8} \times$

$$\dfrac{137.14 \text{ g } C_7H_7NO_2}{1 \text{ mol } C_7H_7NO_2} = 818.6 \text{ g } C_7H_7NO_2$$

$\dfrac{305 \text{ g actual}}{819 \text{ g theoretical}} \times 100 = 37.2\% \text{ yield}$

2. 57.1% yield

Practice problems, page 366

4. a. $TiCl_4$ is the limiting reactant.
   O_2 is the excess reactant.

   $4.5 \text{ mol } O_2 \times \dfrac{1 \text{ mol } TiCl_4}{1 \text{ mol } O_2} = 4.5 \text{ mol } TiCl_4$

   b. 992 mol O_2 will remain.

   $3.5 \text{ mol } TiCl_4 \times \dfrac{189.7 \text{ g } TiCl_4}{1 \text{ mol } TiCl_4} = 663.95 \text{ g } TiCl_4$

   $663.95 \text{ g } TiCl_4 \times \dfrac{1 \text{ mol } TiCl_4}{189.69 \text{ g } TiCl_4} \times \dfrac{1 \text{ mol } O_2}{1 \text{ mol } TiCl_4} \times$

   $$\dfrac{32.100 \text{ g } O_2}{1 \text{ mol } O_2} = 112.36 \text{ g } O_2$$

   $4.5 \text{ mol } O_2 \times \dfrac{31.999 \text{ g } O_2}{1 \text{ mol } O_2} = 144.10 \text{ g } O_2$

   $144.10 \text{ g } O_2 - 112.35 \text{ g } O_2 = 31.75 \text{ g } O_2$

   $31.75 \text{ g } O_2 \times \dfrac{1 \text{ mol } O_2}{31.999 \text{ g } O_2} = 0.992 \text{ mol } O_2$

   c. $3.5 \text{ mol } TiCl_4 \times \dfrac{1 \text{ mol } O_2}{1 \text{ mol } TiCl_4} = 3.5 \text{ mol } O_2$

   $3.5 \text{ mol } TiCl_4 \times \dfrac{2 \text{ mol } Cl_2}{1 \text{ mol } TiCl_4} = 7 \text{ mol } Cl_2$

5. a. $P_4O_{10}(g) + 6H_2O(l) \longrightarrow 4H_3PO_4(aq)$

   b. $100 \text{ g } P_4O_{10} \times \dfrac{1 \text{ mol } P_4O_{10}}{283.9 \text{ g } P_4O_{10}} \times \dfrac{4 \text{ mol } H_3PO_4}{1 \text{ mol } P_4O_{10}} \times$

   $$\dfrac{97.995 \text{ g } H_3PO_4}{1 \text{ mol } H_3PO_4} = 138.1 \text{ g } H_3PO_4 \text{ theoretical yield}$$

   c. $\dfrac{126.2 \text{ g } H_3PO_4 \text{ actual}}{138.1 \text{ g } H_3PO_4 \text{ theoretical}} \times 100 = 91.4\% \text{ yield}$

6. 93.8%

7. $2Al(s) + 3CuSO_4(aq) \longrightarrow 3Cu(s) + Al_2(SO_4)_3(aq)$

   $1.85 \text{ g } Al \times \dfrac{1 \text{ mol } Al}{26.98 \text{ g } Al} \times \dfrac{3 \text{ mol } Cu}{2 \text{ mol } Al} \times \dfrac{63.55 \text{ g } Cu}{1 \text{ mol } Cu} = 6.53 \text{ g } Cu$

   $6.53 \text{ g } Cu \times \dfrac{56.6\%}{100\%} = 3.70 \text{ g } Cu$

8. $58.8 \text{ g } C_9H_8O$

9. $10.1 \text{ g } Mg \times \dfrac{1 \text{ mol } Mg}{24.31 \text{ g } Mg} \times \dfrac{2 \text{ mol } H_2O}{1 \text{ mol } Mg} \times \dfrac{18.02 \text{ g } H_2O}{1 \text{ mol } H_2O} \times$

$$\dfrac{1 \text{ mL } H_2O}{1.0 \text{ g } H_2O} = 15.0 \text{ mL } H_2O$$

10. Mg is the limiting reactant.

   $10.1 \text{ g } Mg \times \dfrac{1 \text{ mol } Mg}{24.31 \text{ g } Mg} = 0.415 \text{ mol } Mg$

   $15.0 \text{ g } H_2O \times \dfrac{1 \text{ mol } H_2O}{18.02 \text{ g } H_2O} = 0.832 \text{ mol } H_2O$

   $0.832 \text{ mol } H_2O \times \dfrac{1 \text{ mol } Mg}{2 \text{ mol } H_2O} = 0.416 \text{ mol } Mg$

Practice problems, page 369

1. $65.1 \text{ L N} \times \dfrac{0.916 \text{ g } N_2}{1 \text{ L } N_2} \times \dfrac{1 \text{ mol } N_2}{28.02 \text{ g } N_2} \times \dfrac{2 \text{ mol } Na}{3 \text{ mol } N_2} \times$

$$\dfrac{22.9898 \text{ g } Na}{1 \text{ mol } Na} = 32.6 \text{ g } Na$$

$32.6 \text{ g } Na \times \dfrac{1 \text{ mol } Na}{22.9898 \text{ g } Na} \times \dfrac{1 \text{ mol } Fe_2O_3}{6 \text{ mol } Na} \times$

$$\dfrac{159.89 \text{ g } Fe_2O_3}{1 \text{ mol } Fe_2O_3} = 37.8 \text{ g } Fe_2O_3$$

2. $32.6 \text{ g } Na \times \dfrac{1 \text{ mol } Na}{22.9898 \text{ g } Na} \times \dfrac{3 \text{ mol } Na_2O}{6 \text{ mol } Na} \times$

$$\dfrac{61.98 \text{ g } Na_2O}{1 \text{ mol } Na_2O} = 43.9 \text{ g } Na_2O$$

$43.9 \text{ g } Na_2O \times \dfrac{1 \text{ mol } Na_2O}{61.98 \text{ g } Na_2O} \times \dfrac{2 \text{ mol } NaHCO_3}{1 \text{ mol } Na_2O} \times$

$$\dfrac{84.007 \text{ g } NaHCO_3}{1 \text{ mol } NaHCO_3} = 119 \text{ g } NaHCO_3$$

3. $119 \text{ g } NaHCO_3 \times \dfrac{1 \text{ mL } NaHCO_3}{2.20 \text{ g } NaHCO_3} = 54.1 \text{ mL } NaHCO_3$

4. $325 \text{ g } CH_3COONa$

Practice problems, page 371

1. a. $3.00 \text{ L } C_8H_{18} \times \dfrac{1000 \text{ mL}}{1 \text{ L}} \times \dfrac{0.692 \text{ g } C_8H_{18}}{1 \text{ mL } C_8H_{18}} = 2076 \text{ g } C_8H_{18}$

   $2076 \text{ g } C_8H_{18} \times \dfrac{1 \text{ mol } C_8H_{18}}{114 \text{ g } C_8H_{18}} = 18.21 \text{ mol } C_8H_{18}$

   $35\,000 \text{ L air} \times \dfrac{21 \text{ L } O_2}{100 \text{ L air}} \times \dfrac{1.33 \text{ g } O_2}{1 \text{ L } O_2} = 9775.5 \text{ g } O_2$

   $9775.5 \text{ g } O_2 \times \dfrac{1 \text{ mol } O_2}{31.999 \text{ g } O_2} = 305 \text{ mol } O_2$

   $305 \text{ mol } O_2 \times \dfrac{2 \text{ mol } C_8H_{18}}{25 \text{ mol } O_2} \times \dfrac{114 \text{ g } C_8H_{18}}{1 \text{ mol } C_8H_{18}} \times$

   $$\dfrac{1 \text{ mL } C_8H_{18}}{0.692 \text{ g } C_8H_{18}} \times \dfrac{1 \text{ L}}{1000 \text{ mL}} = 3.95 \text{ L } C_8H_{18}$$

   $3.95 \text{ L } C_8H_{18} - 3.00 \text{ L } C_8H_{18} = 9.50 \times 10^{-1} \text{ L } C_8H_{18}$

   b. $1.5 \times 10^4 \text{ L air}$

   c. 98.4 L air

2. $984 \text{ mL } H_2O$

Practice problems, page 374

4. $22.4 \text{ g } NaN_3 \times \dfrac{1 \text{ mol } NaN_3}{65.01 \text{ g } NaN_3} \times \dfrac{3 \text{ mol } N_2}{2 \text{ mol } NaN_3} \times \dfrac{28.01 \text{ g } N_2}{1 \text{ mol } N_2} \times$

$$\dfrac{1 \text{ L } N_2}{0.916 \text{ g } N_2} = 15.8 \text{ L } N_2$$

5. $18.3 \text{ g O} \times \dfrac{1 \text{ mol O}}{15.999 \text{ g O}} \times \dfrac{1 \text{ mol O}_2}{1 \text{ mol O}} \times \dfrac{31.999 \text{ g O}_2}{1 \text{ mol O}_2} = 36.6 \text{ g O}_2$

6. $36.6 \text{ g O}_2 \times \dfrac{1 \text{ mol O}_2}{32.0 \text{ g O}_2} \times \dfrac{1 \text{ mol O}_3}{1 \text{ mol O}_2} \times \dfrac{48.0 \text{ g O}_3}{1 \text{ mol O}_3} = 54.9 \text{ g O}_3$

7. $74.0 \text{ g C}_8\text{H}_{18} \times \dfrac{1 \text{ mol C}_8\text{H}_{18}}{114 \text{ g C}_8\text{H}_{18}} \times \dfrac{16 \text{ mol CO}}{2 \text{ mol C}_8\text{H}_{18}} \times$
$$\dfrac{28.01 \text{ g CO}}{1 \text{ mol CO}} = 145 \text{ g CO}$$

CHAPTER 11

Practice problems, page 388

1. $90.0 \text{ g H}_2\text{O} \times \dfrac{1 \text{ mol H}_2\text{O}}{18.02 \text{ g H}_2\text{O}} \times \dfrac{76 \text{ J}}{\text{mol} \cdot \text{K}} \times 10 \text{ K} = 3800 \text{ J}$

2. 530 J

Practice problems, page 391

12. The value will be approximately 4×25 J/K•mol, or 100 J/K•mol.

13. $142 \text{ kJ/g} \times \dfrac{2.02 \text{ g H}_2}{1 \text{ mol H}_2} = 286.84 \text{ kJ}$

14. $260 \text{ g Al} \times \dfrac{1 \text{ mol Al}}{26.98 \text{ g Al}} \times \dfrac{24.2 \text{ J}}{\text{mol} \cdot \text{K}} \times 125 \text{ K} = 29\,000 \text{ J, or } 29 \text{ kJ}$

15. 15 000 J, or 15 kJ

Practice problems, page 394

1. $100. \text{ g H}_2\text{O} \times \dfrac{1 \text{ mol}}{18.02 \text{ g H}_2\text{O}} \times \dfrac{75.3 \text{ J}}{\text{K} \cdot \text{mol}} \times 34.5 \text{ K} = 14.4 \text{ kJ}$

2. $1 \text{ mol Al} \times \dfrac{24.2 \text{ J}}{\text{K} \cdot \text{mol}} \times -105.9 \text{ K} = -2.56 \text{ kJ}$

3. $\dfrac{618 \text{ J}}{\text{mol}} \times \dfrac{1 \text{ K} \cdot \text{mol}}{420 \text{ J}} = 1.47 \text{ K}$

Practice problems, page 395

8. $\Delta T = -9.6\ ^\circ\text{C} = -9.6 \text{ K}$

9. $80.2 \text{ g H}_2\text{O} \times \dfrac{1 \text{ mol H}_2\text{O}}{18.02 \text{ g H}_2\text{O}} \times \dfrac{37.4 \text{ J}}{\text{K} \cdot \text{mol}} \times 3.2 \text{ K} = 0.533 \text{ kJ}$

10. –2.17 kJ   **11.** 0.727 kJ

12. $\dfrac{-186.9 \text{ J}}{\text{mol}} \times \dfrac{1 \text{ K} \cdot \text{mol}}{172 \text{ J}} = -1.09\ ^\circ\text{C}$

13. $1 \text{ mol H}_2 \times \dfrac{28.8 \text{ J}}{\text{K} \cdot \text{mol}} \times 25 \text{ K} = 0.72 \text{ kJ}$

Practice problem, page 401

17. $\dfrac{29.5 \text{ kJ}}{\text{mol}} \times \dfrac{1 \text{ mol}}{88.6 \text{ J} \cdot \text{K}} \times \dfrac{1000 \text{ J}}{1 \text{ kJ}} = 333 \text{ K}$

Practice problem, page 405

1. $[(-241.8 \text{ kJ} \cdot \text{mol}) + (-1206.9 \text{ kJ} \cdot \text{mol})] - [(-986.1 \text{ kJ} \cdot \text{mol}) +$
$(-393.5 \text{ kJ} \cdot \text{mol})] = -69.1 \text{ kJ/mol}$

Practice problems, page 406

1. –141.2 J/K, more order   **2.** 159.1 J/K

3. ΔS for the conversion of 1 mol of C_{diamond} to 1 mol of C_{graphite} is 3.3 J/K. You cannot determine that the reaction is spontaneous from entropy data alone. You must also know the enthalpy change and calculate the Gibbs energy change to determine spontaneity. In this case, ΔG is negative, and the reaction is spontaneous.

Practice problems, page 408

1. $\Delta G = -58.0$ kJ The reaction is spontaneous.

2. $\Delta G = -39.0$ kJ at 900°C

3. $T = 911 \text{ K} = 638\ ^\circ\text{C}$

Practice problems, page 413

3. Reaction 1: $\Delta G = 115$ kJ, not spontaneous
Reaction 2: $\Delta G = -244$ kJ, spontaneous
Reaction 3: $\Delta G = -623$ kJ, spontaneous

4. The reaction using H_2O is not spontaneous at 25°C because $\Delta G = 474$ kJ. The reaction using HCl is likewise not spontaneous at 25°C because $\Delta G = 134$ kJ. It would be spontaneous at temperatures above 830°C.

CHAPTER 12

Practice problems, page 436

1. $P_2 = \dfrac{(22.5 \text{ kPa})(155 \text{ cm}^3)}{90.0 \text{ cm}^3} = 38.8 \text{ kPa}$

2. $V_2 = \dfrac{(0.500 \text{ atm})(300.0 \text{ mL})}{0.750 \text{ atm}} = 200. \text{ mL}$

3. 10. L   **4.** 142 mL

Practice problems, page 440

1. $V_2 = \dfrac{(80.0 \text{ K})(2.5 \text{ L})}{300.0 \text{ K}} = 0.67 \text{ L}$

2. $P_2 = \dfrac{(325 \text{ K})(3.00 \text{ atm})}{298 \text{ K}} = 3.27 \text{ atm}$

Practice problems, page 444

5. $V_2 = \dfrac{(101\,325 \text{ Pa})(30.0 \text{ m}^3)}{2.87 \times 10^2 \text{ Pa}} = 1.06 \times 10^4 \text{ m}^3$

6. $v_{\text{SO}_2} = 0.380 \text{ km/s} \sqrt{\dfrac{70.90 \text{ g/mol}}{64.07 \text{ g/mol}}} = 0.400 \text{ km/s}$

7. 471 m/s   **8.** 397 m/s

9. $\dfrac{v_{\text{H}_2\text{O}}}{v_{\text{CO}_2}} = \sqrt{\dfrac{44.01 \text{ g/mol}}{18.02 \text{ g/mol}}} = 1.56$

Molecules of water vapor effuse at 1.56 times the rate that carbon dioxide molecules do.

10. $M_{\text{H}_2\text{S}} = (2 \times 1.01 \text{ g/mol}) + 32.07 \text{ g/mol} = 34.09 \text{ g/mol}$
$M_{\text{C}_7\text{H}_6\text{O}} = (7 \times 12.01 \text{ g/mol}) + (6 \times 1.01 \text{ g/mol}) + 16.00 \text{ g/mol} =$
106.13 g/mol
$M_{\text{C}_8\text{H}_{10}\text{O}_3} = (8 \times 12.01 \text{ g/mol}) + (10 \times 1.01 \text{ g/mol}) +$
$(3 \times 16.00 \text{ g/mol}) = 154.18 \text{ g/mol}$
H_2S is the lightest molecule, so you would smell it first.

Practice problems, page 447

1. $500. \text{ g } CO_2 \times \dfrac{1 \text{ mol } CO_2}{44.01 \text{ g } CO_2} = 11.36 \text{ mol } CO_2$

$V = \dfrac{(11.36 \text{ mol } CO_2)\left(8.314\dfrac{L\cdot kPa}{mol\cdot K}\right)(298 \text{ K})}{975 \text{ kPa}} = 28.9 \text{ L } CO_2$

2. $22.4 \text{ L } CO_2$

3. $n = \dfrac{(110 \text{ kPa})(4.0 \text{ L})}{\left(8.314\dfrac{L\cdot kPa}{mol\cdot K}\right)(310 \text{ K})} = 0.17 \text{ mol } O_2$

4. $101 \text{ g } Cl_2$

Practice problems, page 449

1. $V_2 = \dfrac{(400.0 \text{ K})(2.0 \text{ m}^3)(100.0 \text{ kPa})}{(100.0 \text{ K})(200.0 \text{ kPa})} = 4.0 \text{ m}^3$

2. $6.06 \times 10^3 \text{ kPa}$ **3.** 164.7 K **4.** 81 m^3

Practice problems, page 451

5. $35.0 \text{ g } CO_2 \times \dfrac{1 \text{ mol } CO_2}{44.01 \text{ g } CO_2} = 0.7953 \text{ mol } CO_2$

$P = \dfrac{(0.7953 \text{ mol } CO_2)\left(8.314\dfrac{L\cdot kPa}{mol\cdot K}\right)(400 \text{ K})}{2.5 \text{ L}} = 1100 \text{ kPa}$

6. $0.39 \text{ L } N_2$

7. a. $n = \dfrac{(2.5 \text{ atm})(1 \text{ L})}{\left(0.0821\dfrac{L\cdot atm}{mol\cdot K}\right)(250 \text{ K})} = 0.122 \text{ mol } N_2$

$0.122 \text{ mol } N_2 \times \dfrac{28.02 \text{ g } N_2}{1 \text{ mol } N_2} = 3.4 \text{ g } N_2$

$D = \dfrac{m}{V} = \dfrac{3.4 \text{ g } N_2}{1 \text{ L}} = 3.4 \text{ g/L}$

b. 1.3 g/L

8. $5.3 \times 10^{-3} \text{ mol } SO_2$

9. $400 \text{ psi} \times \dfrac{6.892\,86 \times 10^3 \text{ Pa}}{1 \text{ psi}} \times \dfrac{1 \text{ kPa}}{1000 \text{ Pa}} = 2757 \text{ kPa}$

$V_2 = \dfrac{(2757 \text{ kPa})(10.0 \text{ L He})}{100 \text{ kPa}} = 275.7 \text{ L He}$

$275.7 \text{ L He} \times \dfrac{1 \text{ balloon}}{4 \text{ L He}} = 68.9 \text{ balloons}$

You could fill 68 balloons.

10. $2Fe(OH)_3 \xrightarrow{\Delta} Fe_2O_3 + 3H_2O$

a. $n = \dfrac{(1 \text{ atm})(0.75 \text{ L})}{\left(0.0821\dfrac{L\cdot atm}{mol\cdot K}\right)(500 \text{ K})} = 0.0183 \text{ mol } H_2O$

$0.0183 \text{ mol } H_2O \times \dfrac{2 \text{ mol } Fe(OH)_3}{3 \text{ mol } H_2O} \times \dfrac{106.88 \text{ g } Fe(OH)_3}{1 \text{ mol } Fe(OH)_3} = $
$1.3 \text{ g } Fe(OH)_3$

b. $0.0183 \text{ mol } H_2O \times \dfrac{1 \text{ mol } Fe_2O_3}{3 \text{ mol } H_2O} \times \dfrac{159.70 \text{ g } Fe_2O_3}{1 \text{ mol } Fe_2O_3} = $
$0.97 \text{ g } Fe_2O_3$

11. $3.0 \text{ L } H_2 \times \dfrac{2 \text{ L HCl}}{1 \text{ L } H_2} = 6.0 \text{ L HCl}$

Assume that the volume of HCl is measured at the same conditions of temperature and pressure under which the H_2 was measured.

12. $15 \text{ L } NH_3 \times \dfrac{5 \text{ L } O_2}{4 \text{ L } NH_3} = 19 \text{ L } O_2$

13. $V = 4.0 \times 10^2 \text{ cm} \times 2.5 \times 10^2 \text{ cm} \times 8.0 \times 10^2 \text{ cm} = $
$8.0 \times 10^7 \text{ cm}^3$

$8.0 \times 10^7 \text{ cm}^3 \times \dfrac{1 \text{ mL}}{1 \text{ cm}^3} \times \dfrac{1 \text{ L}}{1000 \text{ mL}} = 8.0 \times 10^4 \text{ L}$

$n = \dfrac{(5.0 \text{ kPa})(8.0 \times 10^4 \text{ L})}{\left(8.314\dfrac{L\cdot kPa}{mol\cdot K}\right)(288 \text{ K})} = 167 \text{ mol } CO_2$

$167 \text{ mol } CO_2 \times \dfrac{2 \text{ mol LiOH}}{1 \text{ mol } CO_2} \times \dfrac{23.95 \text{ g LiOH}}{1 \text{ mol LiOH}} = 8.0 \times 10^3 \text{ g LiOH}$

CHAPTER 13

Practice problems, page 475

1. $\dfrac{125 \text{ g}}{2.0 \text{ L}} \times \dfrac{1 \text{ mol NaClO}}{74.44 \text{ g}} = 0.840 \text{ M NaClO}$

2. $\dfrac{1 \text{ L}}{0.375 \text{ mol}} \times \dfrac{1 \text{ mol}}{84.01 \text{ g } NaHCO_3} \times 15.3 \text{ g } NaHCO_3 \times$
$\dfrac{1000 \text{ mL}}{L} = 486 \text{ mL}$

3. 1.70 L

4. $\dfrac{0.2500 \text{ mol}}{L} \times 0.0750 \text{ L} \times \dfrac{249.72 \text{ g } CuSO_4\bullet5H_2O}{mol} = $
$4.67 \text{ g } CuSO_4\bullet5H_2O$

5. $1.38 \text{ kg } C_{12}H_{22}O_{11}$

6. $\dfrac{5.00 \text{ mol } H_3PO_4}{L} \times 7.5 \text{ L} \times \dfrac{1 \text{ mol } Ca_3(PO_4)_2}{2 \text{ mol } H_3PO_4} \times$
$\dfrac{310.18 \text{ g}}{mol \text{ } Ca_3(PO_4)_2} = 5.8 \times 10^3 \text{ g } Ca_3(PO_4)_2$

$\dfrac{5.00 \text{ mol } H_3PO_4}{L} \times 7.5 \text{ L} \times \dfrac{6 \text{ mol } H_2O}{2 \text{ mol } H_3PO_4} \times \dfrac{18.02 \text{ g}}{mol \text{ } H_2O} = $
$2.0 \times 10^3 \text{ g } H_2O$

7. 0.571 M HCl

8. $0.0100 \text{ M } C_4H_4Au_2CaO_4S_2 \times \dfrac{1 \text{ L}}{1000 \text{ mL}} \times 10.0 \text{ mL} \times$
$\dfrac{614.24 \text{ g}}{mol} \times \dfrac{1000 \text{ mg}}{g} = 61.4 \text{ mg}$

9. 0.28 M KI

10. a. $2.2 \text{ M NaOH} \times 65.0 \text{ mL} \times \dfrac{1 \text{ L}}{1000 \text{ mL}} = 0.14 \text{ mol}$

b. $0.143 \text{ mol (from calculator)} \times \dfrac{40.00 \text{ g}}{mol} = 5.7 \text{ g}$

11. $146.3 \text{ g NaCl} \times \dfrac{1 \text{ mol}}{58.44 \text{ g}} \times \dfrac{1 \text{ L}}{1.50 \text{ mol}} = 1.67 \text{ L}$

12. 0.0846 M

Practice problems, page 478

6. a. $\dfrac{0.0750 \text{ mol}}{115 \text{ mL}} \times \dfrac{1000 \text{ mL}}{\text{L}} = 0.652 \text{ M}$ b. 6.52 M

7. a. 1.5 M   b. $1.5 \text{ M} \times 350 \text{ mL} \times \dfrac{1 \text{ L}}{1000 \text{ mL}} = 0.525 \text{ mol}$

8. 0.282 M

9. Weigh a clean empty beaker, and record its mass. Pour NaCl into the beaker until the mass is increased by 49.7 g, the mass of 0.85 mol of sodium chloride. Use a funnel to pour the salt into a 1 L volumetric flask. Rinse the beaker and funnel with plenty of distilled water. Add more distilled water to the beaker and swirl until thoroughly dissolved. Add more water one drop at a time until the flask is filled to the mark. Invert the flask, and swirl several times to ensure thorough mixing.

10. $35 \text{ g bear fat} \times \dfrac{8 \text{ g PCB}}{10^6 \text{ g bear fat}} \times \dfrac{1000 \text{ mg}}{\text{g}} = 0.28 \text{ mg}$

CHAPTER 14

Practice problems, page 526

1. $K_{eq} = \dfrac{[\text{CO}][\text{H}_2\text{O}]}{[\text{CO}_2][\text{H}_2]} = \dfrac{(0.019)^2}{(0.012)(0.014)} = 2.1$

2. 2.0   **3.** 1.28×10^4

Practice problems, page 527

1. $K_{eq} - 290 - \dfrac{[\text{CH}_3\text{OH}]}{[\text{CO}][\text{H}_2]^2}; [\text{CH}_3\text{OH}]$
$= (290)(0.025)(0.080)^2 = 0.046 \text{ mol/L}$

2. 3.5×10^{-5} mol/L   **3.** 0.59 mol/L

Practice problems, page 532

1. $K_{sp} = [\text{Ca}^{2+}]^3[\text{PO}_4^{3-}]^2 = (3.42 \times 10^{-7})^3(2.28 \times 10^{-7})^2$
$= 2.08 \times 10^{-33}$

2. 2.6×10^{-4} M   **4.** 1.43×10^{-2} M   **6.** 4.15×10^{-4} M

3. 6.2×10^{-9} **5.** 2.9×10^{-3} g Ag$^+$

Practice problems, page 533

6. $K_{sp} = 1.3 \times 10^{-36} = [\text{Cu}^{2+}][\text{S}^{2-}]; [\text{Cu}^{2+}] = 1.1 \times 10^{-18}$ M

7. $K_{eq} = 54.3 = \dfrac{[\text{HI}]^2}{[\text{H}_2][\text{I}_2]}; [\text{HI}]^2 = (54.3)(4.79 \times 10^{-4})^2;$
$[\text{HI}] = 3.53 \times 10^{-3}$ M

8. 2.5×10^{-2}

CHAPTER 15

Practice problems, page 549

7. $[\text{H}_3\text{O}^+] = \dfrac{86.5 \text{ g}}{2.3 \text{ L}} \times \dfrac{1 \text{ mol}}{63.02 \text{ g}} = 0.60 \text{ M};$

$[\text{OH}^-] = \dfrac{K_w}{[\text{H}_3\text{O}^+]} = 1.7 \times 10^{-14}$ M

8. $[\text{H}_3\text{O}^+] = [\text{OH}^-] = \sqrt{2.50 \times 10^{-14}} = 1.58 \times 10^{-7}$ M

Practice problems, page 562

1. a. pH = $-\log 0.010 = 2.00$ c. 2.41
     b. 1.33   d. 3.26

2. $10^{-2.50} = 0.0032$ M HNO$_3$

3. $[\text{H}_3\text{O}^+] = \dfrac{10.0 \text{ mL} \times 2.00 \text{ M}}{500.0 \text{ mL}} = 0.0400 \text{ M};$
     pH = $-\log 0.0400 = 1.398$

Practice problems, page 563

1. pH = $-\log\left(\dfrac{1.00 \times 10^{-14}}{0.00256}\right) = 11.408$

2. $[\text{OH}^-] = 0.0350$ M; pH = 12.544   **3.** 7.415

Practice problems, page 567

7. Solution 1: pH = 8; $[\text{OH}^-] = 10^{-6}$ M; $[\text{H}_3\text{O}^+] = 10^{-8}$ M
    Solution 2: pH = 11; $[\text{OH}^-] = 10^{-3}$ M; $[\text{H}_3\text{O}^+] = 10^{-11}$ M

8. pH = 3.10; $[\text{H}_3\text{O}^+] = 7.9 \times 10^{-4}$ M; $[\text{OH}^-] = 1.3 \times 10^{-11}$ M

9. 3×10^{-8} M   **10.** 3.51

Practice problems, page 577

9. $\dfrac{20.6 \text{ mL} \times 0.010 \text{ M HCl}}{30.0 \text{ mL}} = 0.0069 \text{ M NaOH}$

10. 0.585 M NaOH

11. $\dfrac{46.0 \text{ mL} \times 0.407 \text{ M HClO}_4}{0.256 \text{ M Ba(OH)}_2} \times \dfrac{1 \text{ mol Ba(OH)}_2}{2 \text{ mol HClO}_4} = 36.6 \text{ mL}$

12. $\dfrac{2.00 \text{ g} \times \dfrac{1 \text{ mol}}{204.23 \text{ g}}}{0.0347 \text{ L}} = 0.282 \text{ M}$

CHAPTER 16

Practice problems, page 596

1. $\dfrac{\text{rate}_1}{\text{rate}_2} = \dfrac{3.3 \times 10^{-2} \text{ M/s}}{8.2 \times 10^{-3} \text{ M/s}} = \dfrac{k[0.020 \text{ M}]^n}{k[0.010 \text{ M}]^n} = 4.0 = 2^n$
    rate = k[HI]^2

2. a. $k[2x]^0 = 2^0 k[x]^0 = 1k[x]^0 = 1 \times$ rate
    b. $k[2x]^3 = 2^3 k[x]^3 = 8k[x]^3 = 8 \times$ rate
    c. $k[2x]^4 = 2^4 k[x]^4 = 16k[x]^4 = 16 \times$ rate

Practice problems, page 598

7. a. rate $= \dfrac{-1}{4} \times \dfrac{\Delta[\text{PH}_3]}{\Delta t} = \dfrac{\Delta[\text{P}_4]}{\Delta t} = \dfrac{1}{6} \times \dfrac{\Delta[\text{H}_2]}{\Delta t}$

    b. rate $= \dfrac{-1}{1} \times \dfrac{\Delta[\text{S}^{2-}]}{\Delta t} = \dfrac{-1}{1} \dfrac{\Delta[\text{I}_3^-]}{\Delta t} = \dfrac{\Delta[\text{S}]}{\Delta t} = \dfrac{1}{3} \dfrac{\Delta[\text{I}^-]}{\Delta t}$

    c. rate $= \dfrac{-1}{1} \times \dfrac{\Delta[\text{C}_2\text{H}_4]}{\Delta t} = \dfrac{-1}{1} \dfrac{\Delta[\text{Br}_2]}{\Delta t} = \dfrac{\Delta[\text{C}_2\text{H}_4\text{Br}_2]}{\Delta t}$

8. a. $\dfrac{5}{4}\text{rate}_{\text{NH}_3} = \text{rate}_{\text{O}_2} = \dfrac{5}{4}(0.80 \text{ M/min}) = 1.0 \text{ M/min}$

    b. rate$_{\text{NO}}$ = 0.80 M/min
      rate$_{\text{H}_2\text{O}}$ = 1.2 M/min

9. with respect to NO: second order; with respect to Cl$_2$: first order; overall: third order

10. $k[1.41 \times \text{B}]^2 = 1.41^2 k[\text{B}]^2 = 1.99k[\text{B}]^2 \approx 2 \times$ rate

    $k[0.5 \times \text{B}]^2 = 0.5^2 k[\text{B}]^2 = 0.25k[\text{B}]^2 = \dfrac{1}{4} \times$ rate

CHAPTER 17

Practice problems, page 626

1. energy = $(0.25 \text{ V})(3.037 \times 10^6 \text{ C}) = 7.6 \times 10^5 \text{ J}$

2. $30.0 \text{ min} \times \dfrac{1.50 \text{ C}}{1 \text{ s}} \times \dfrac{60 \text{ s}}{1 \text{ min}} \times \dfrac{1 \text{ mol } e^-}{96\,485 \text{ C}} \times \dfrac{1 \text{ mol Ag}}{1 \text{ mol } e^-} \times$

$\dfrac{107.87 \text{ g Ag}}{1 \text{ mol Ag}} = 3.02 \text{ g Ag}$

Practice problems, page 627

5. $2.5 \text{ mol } e^- \times \dfrac{96\,485 \text{ C}}{1 \text{ mol } e^-} = 2.4 \times 10^5 \text{ C}$

6. $1.0 \text{ min} \times \dfrac{60 \text{ s}}{1 \text{ min}} \times \dfrac{5.0 \text{ C}}{1 \text{ s}} = 3.0 \times 10^2 \text{ C}$

energy = $(12.0 \text{ V})(3.0 \times 10^2 \text{ C}) = 3.6 \times 10^3 \text{ J}$

7. a. $Pt^{2+} + 2e^- \longrightarrow Pt$ d. $Br_2 + 2e^- \longrightarrow 2Br^-$

b. $Fe^{2+} \longrightarrow Fe^{3+} + e^-$ e. $Au \longrightarrow Au^{3+} + 3e^-$

c. $S + 2e^- \longrightarrow S^{2-}$

8. $\dfrac{1.00 \text{ C}}{1 \text{ s}} \times \dfrac{1 \text{ s}}{300 \text{ discharges}} = 3.33 \times 10^{-3} \text{ C}$

energy = $(0.1000 \text{ V})(3.33 \times 10^{-3} \text{ C}) = 3.33 \times 10^{-4} \text{ J}$

9. $600.0 \text{ V} \times \dfrac{1 \text{ plate}}{0.1500 \text{ V}} = 4.000 \times 10^3 \text{ plates}$

Practice problems, page 631

1. $n = \dfrac{(101 \text{ kPa})(1.000 \text{ L})}{(8.314 \text{ kPa} \cdot \text{L/K} \cdot \text{mol})(298 \text{ K})} = 4.08 \times 10^{-2} \text{ mol O}_2$

charge $= 4.08 \times 10^{-2} \text{ mol O}_2 \times \dfrac{4 \text{ mol } e^-}{1 \text{ mol O}_2} \times \dfrac{96\,485 \text{ C}}{1 \text{ mol } e^-} = 1.57 \times 10^4 \text{ C}$

energy = $(2.0 \text{ V})(1.57 \times 10^4 \text{ C}) = 3.1 \times 10^4 \text{ J}$

2. $1.0 \text{ h} \times \dfrac{3600 \text{ s}}{1 \text{ h}} \times \dfrac{3.0 \times 10^4 \text{ C}}{1 \text{ s}} \times \dfrac{1 \text{ mol } e^-}{96\,485 \text{ C}} \times \dfrac{1 \text{ mol Cl}_2}{2 \text{ mol } e^-} = 560 \text{ mol Cl}_2$

Practice problem, page 633

6. $100.0 \text{ g Al} \times \dfrac{1 \text{ mol Al}}{26.98 \text{ g Al}} \times \dfrac{12 \text{ mol } e^-}{4 \text{ mol Al}} \times \dfrac{96\,485 \text{ C}}{1 \text{ mol } e^-} = 1.07 \times 10^6 \text{ C}$

energy = $(6.2 \text{ V})(1.07 \times 10^6 \text{ C}) = 6.7 \times 10^6 \text{ J}$

Practice problems, page 639

1. $1.33 \times 10^5 \text{ C} \times \dfrac{1 \text{ mol } e^-}{96\,485 \text{ C}} \times \dfrac{1 \text{ mol Pb}}{2 \text{ mol } e^-} \times \dfrac{207.2 \text{ g}}{1 \text{ mol Pb}} = 140 \text{ g Pb}$

2. charge $= \dfrac{1300 \text{ J}}{1.54 \text{ V}} = 844 \text{ C}$

$844 \text{ C} \times \dfrac{1 \text{ mol } e^-}{96\,485 \text{ C}} \times \dfrac{1 \text{ mol Zn(OH)}_2}{2 \text{ mol } e^-} \times \dfrac{99.41 \text{ g Zn(OH)}_2}{1 \text{ mol Zn(OH)}_2} = 0.43 \text{ g}$

Practice problems, page 648

6. Magnesium has a greater tendency to give up electrons than does lead. Therefore, only the reverse reaction will occur spontaneously.

7. $Ce^{4+}(aq) + Ag(s) + Cl^-(aq) \longrightarrow Ce^{3+}(aq) + AgCl(s)$

8. Yes; calcium has a greater tendency to give up electrons than does lead sulfate.

9. $I_2(s) + Pb(s) \longrightarrow 2I^-(aq) + Pb^{2+}(aq)$

10. $2Fe^{3+}(aq) + 3H_2(g) + 6OH^-(aq) \longrightarrow 2Fe(s) + 6H_2O(l)$

CHAPTER 18

APPENDIX B

Practice, page 807

1. **1** metals   **1** nonmetals

     2 alkali metals   **2** halogens

        3 sodium   **3** chlorine

     2 alkaline-earth metals   **3** iodine

        3 calcium

        3 barium

Practice, page 809

1. Choose a multiple-step process from your text.

Write down the steps of the process in your own words.
Cut the paper into strips so that there is one step per strip.
Shuffle the strips of paper.
Place the strips in their proper sequence.
Using your text, confirm the order of the process.

Practice, page 811

1. a. The gasoline used in cars is not in a gaseous state; it is a liquid.

b. no misconception

c. no misconception

d. Global warming is not solely caused by the accumulation of CFCs in the atmosphere. It is also caused by the increased levels of carbon dioxide from the combustion of fossil fuels.

e. Gases are the least dense of the three states of matter.

Practice, page 813

1.

Main idea	Detail notes
▸ neon	▸ Ne, 10
▸ lead	▸ Pb, 82
▸ calcium	▸ Ca, 20
▸ copper	▸ Cu, 29
▸ oxygen	▸ O, 8
▸ sodium	▸ Na, 11

Practice, page 816

1. a. concept   d. linking words   g. concept

b. linking words   e. concept   h. linking word

c. linking word   f. linking words

2. Some possible responses are the following: *matter is described by chemical properties*, and *matter is classified as mixtures*.

3. *mixtures are made from pure substances*, and *elements form compounds*

A

accuracy: the extent to which a measurement approaches the true value of a quantity **(57)**

acid: a class of compounds whose water solutions taste sour, turn blue litmus paper red, and react with bases to form salts **(26)**

acid-ionization constant: the equilibrium constant for a reaction in which an acid donates a proton to water **(556)**

actinides: shiny, metallic transition metals with atomic numbers 90 through 103 in which electrons are added to 5f orbitals **(121)**

activated complex: a temporary combination of high-energy reactant atoms or molecules that decomposes into products; also called a transition state **(602)**

activation energy: the least amount of energy needed to permit a particular chemical reaction **(602)**

activity series: an arrangement of elements in the order of their tendency to react with water and acids **(327)**

actual yield: the measured amount of product experimentally produced from a given amount of reactant **(361)**

addition polymer: a polymer formed by chain addition reactions between monomers that contain a double bond **(256)**

adiabatic calorimetry: a method of measuring the heat absorbed or released in a chemical or physical change in which no heat is allowed to enter or leave the system **(403)**

alkali metals: highly reactive metallic elements in Group 1 that react rapidly with water to form hydrogen and alkaline solutions and that burn in air **(119)**

alkaline-earth metals: reactive metallic elements in Group 2 with two electrons in the outermost energy level **(120)**

alkane: a hydrocarbon that contains only single bonds **(236)**

alkene: a hydrocarbon that contains one or more double bonds **(237)**

alkyne: a hydrocarbon with one or more triple bonds **(238)**

allotrope: one of a number of different molecular or crystalline forms of an element **(23)**

alloy: a solid or liquid solution of two or more metals **(129)**

alpha particle: a positively charged particle produced by some nuclear disintegrations **(84)**

amine: an organic compound that contains a nitrogen atom and that can be considered a derivative of ammonia **(547)**

ampere: the SI unit of electric current; equal to 1 C/s **(621)**

amphoteric: any molecule or ion that can act either as an acid or as a base **(553)**

anhydrous: without water **(183)**

anion: an ion that has a negative charge **(159)**

annihilation of matter: the event that occurs when a particle collides with its antiparticle and both are changed into electromagnetic energy **(666)**

anode: an electrode through which electrons enter a metal **(82)**

antioxidant: a substance that can prevent chain reactions involving O_2 and O_3 **(608)**

aqueous: describing a solution in which the solvent is water **(470)**

aromatic compound: a compound containing a ring of carbon atoms pictured with alternating single and double bonds with delocalized electrons that provide great stability **(239)**

atom: the basic unit of matter **(20)**

atomic mass: the mass of an atom in atomic mass units **(80)**

atomic mass unit: one-twelfth the mass of the carbon-12 isotope **(80)**

atomic number: the number of protons in the nucleus of an atom **(86)**

atomic theory: the theory that all matter is composed of indivisible particles called atoms **(74)**

aufbau principle: electrons in an atom will occupy the lowest-energy orbitals available **(99)**

average rate: the change in a measured property (usually concentration) divided by the total time elapsed **(590)**

Avogadro's constant: the number of particles in 1 mol, 6.022×10^{23}/mol **(81)**

Avogadro's law: equal volumes of different gases under the same conditions of temperature and pressure have the same number of molecules **(441)**

B

band of stability: the area on a graph of neutron number versus proton number in which all stable nuclei lie **(662)**

base: a class of compounds that taste bitter, feel slippery in water solution, turn red litmus to blue, and react with acids to form salts **(27)**

battery: a group of self-contained galvanic cells that convert chemical energy into electrical energy **(636)**

benzene: a six-membered ring of carbon atoms pictured with alternating double and single bonds, indicating delocalized electrons **(238)**

beta particle: a high-energy electron emitted from the nucleus when a neutron changes to a proton **(665)**

binary ionic compound: an ionic compound that consists of the cations of one element and the anions of another element **(162)**

boiling-point elevation: the difference between the boiling point of a solution and that of the pure solvent **(495)**

bond energy: the energy required to break a chemical bond between two atoms and separate them **(197)**

bond length: the distance between two bonded atoms at their minimum potential energy; the average distance between two bonded atoms **(196)**

bond radius: one-half the distance from center to center of two like atoms bonded together **(135)**

Boyle's law: the volume of a given amount of gas at constant temperature is inversely proportional to the pressure **(435)**

Brønsted-Lowry acid: any ion or molecule that can donate a proton to another species **(550)**

Brønsted-Lowry base: any atom, ion, or molecule that can accept a proton from another species **(552)**

buffer solution: a solution that resists changes in pH **(565)**

C

calorimeter: a device used to measure the heat absorbed or released in a chemical or physical change **(402)**

carboxylic acid: an organic compound that contains the carboxyl functional group **(545)**

catalysis: the process by which reaction rates are increased by the addition of a catalyst **(604)**

catalyst: a substance added to a chemical reaction to increase the rate that is not itself changed in the reaction **(604)**

cathode: an electrode through which electrons leave a metal **(82)**

cation: an ion that has a positive charge **(159)**

chain reaction: a self-sustaining nuclear or chemical reaction in which the product from one step acts as a reactant for the next step **(431)**

Charles's law: the volume of a sample of gas at constant pressure is directly proportional to the absolute temperature **(438)**

chemical: any substance with a definite composition **(4)**

chemical bond: a mutual attraction between different atoms that binds the atoms together **(40)**

chemical change: a change that produces one or more new substances **(18)**

chemical energy: the energy that matter possesses because of its chemical makeup **(40)**

chemical equation: an expression showing the formulas and the relative amounts of the reactants and products in a chemical reaction **(312)**

chemical equilibrium: a condition where the forward reaction occurs at the same speed as the reverse reaction, and all reactants and products are present **(361)**

chemical kinetics: the branch of chemistry concerned with reaction rates and how reactions occur **(589)**

chemical property: a property of matter that can be observed only when substances interact with one another **(18)**

chemical reaction: the process by which elements and/or compounds interact with one another to form new substances **(7)**

chromatography: a technique for separating components of a mixture by placing the mixture in a mobile phase that is passed over a stationary phase **(477)**

coefficient: a numeral used in a chemical equation to indicate relative amounts of reactants or products **(313)**

colligative property: a physical property that is dependent on the number of solute particles present rather than on the identity of those particles **(496)**

colloid: a mixture in which small particles are suspended throughout a solvent **(469)**

combined gas law: the gas law for a given quantity of gas that is changed from one set of P, V, or T conditions to another **(448)**

combustion: a violently exothermic reaction with oxygen to form oxide(s) **(325)**

common ion: an ion that is present in two or more substances involved in an ionic chemical equilibrium **(533)**

common ion effect: the reduction in the solubility of an ionic compound by the addition of a soluble compound that provides an ion in common with it **(533)**

complex ion: an ion that has a structure in which a central atom or ion is bonded by coordinate covalent bonds to other ions or molecules **(519)**

compound: the product that results when two or more different elements are chemically combined **(26)**

concentration: the quantity of solute in a specific quantity of solvent or solution **(470)**

condensation: the process by which a gas changes to a liquid **(455)**

condensation polymer: a polymer formed by reactions in which water or another small molecule is a byproduct **(258)**

conduction band: a band within (or into which) electrons must move to allow electrical conduction **(127)**

conductivity: the ability to conduct an electric current **(487)**

conjugate acid: the acid formed when a base accepts a proton **(554)**

conjugate base: the base formed when an acid donates a proton **(554)**

conversion factor: a mathematical expression that relates two units **(13)**

corrosion: the deterioration of metals due to oxidation reactions with their environment **(640)**

coulomb: the SI unit of electric charge **(621)**

coulombic force: the attraction or repulsion between two objects that have electric charges **(168)**

Coulomb's law: the force between two charged particles is inversely proportional to the square of the distance between them **(88)**

covalent bond: the bond formed when two or more valence electrons are attracted by the positively charged nuclei of two atoms and are thus shared between both atoms **(195)**

covalent network solid: a solid composed of atoms covalently bonded in a network in two or three dimensions **(235)**

critical mass: the smallest mass of radioactive material needed to sustain a chain reaction **(670)**

critical point: the temperature and pressure at and above which the properties of the vapor phase of a substance cannot be distinguished from those of the liquid phase (458)

crystal: a substance in which the atoms or molecules are arranged in an orderly, geometric, repeating pattern (126)

crystal lattice: a repetitive geometric arrangement of points in space about which atoms, ions, or molecules are arranged to form a crystal structure (168)

D

Dalton's law of partial pressures: the total pressure in a gas mixture is the sum of the partial pressures of the individual components, each behaving as if the other gases were absent (436)

decomposition: a chemical reaction in which a single compound is broken down to produce two or more simpler substances (327)

density: the ratio of mass to volume (16)

detergent: a surfactant other than soap (501)

diffusion: the process by which particles mix by dispersing from regions of higher concentration to regions of lower concentration (443)

dipole: a molecule in which one end has a partial positive charge and the other end has a partial negative charge (200)

diprotic acid: an acid that can donate two hydrogen ions per molecule (551)

displacement reaction: a chemical reaction in which one element replaces another element in a compound that is in solution (327)

dissociation: a process in which a compound separates into fragments, such as simpler molecules, atoms, radicals, or ions (491)

distillation: a separation process in which a liquid component is evaporated from a solution and the vapor is condensed to liquid, usually for the purpose of purification (478)

double-displacement reaction: a chemical reaction in which ions from two compounds interact in solution to form a product (329)

Downs cell: an electrolytic cell that uses a graphite anode and an iron cathode to produce sodium metal (629)

E

effusion: the motion of a gas through a small opening (442)

elastomer: a polymer that has elastic properties similar to rubber (259)

electrochemical cell: an apparatus through which electricity can flow that includes at least two electrodes and at least one electrolyte solution (624)

electrochemical series: a table in which the elements are listed in order of increasing standard electrode potential (646)

electrode: the junction between a metallic conductor and an ionic conductor, often an electrolyte solution (622)

electrolysis: the decomposition of a substance by an electric current (630)

electrolyte: a substance that, when dissolved in a solvent, increases the solvent's conductivity (488)

electrolytic cell: an electrochemical cell in which electrical energy is used to drive two electrode reactions and bring about chemical changes (625)

electromagnetic spectrum: the total range of electromagnetic radiation, ranging from the longest radio waves to the shortest gamma waves (93)

electron: a small, negatively charged particle found in atoms (83)

electron affinity: the energy emitted upon the addition of an electron to an atom or group of atoms while in the gas phase (139)

electron configuration: a description of the occupied electron orbitals in an atom (98)

electron shielding: the reduction of the attractive force between a posi-

tively charged nucleus and its outermost electrons due to the cancellation of some of the positive charge by the negative charge of the other electrons (136)

electronegativity: the tendency of an atom to attract bonding electrons to itself when it bonds with another atom (198)

electroneutrality: the condition of having an equal number of positive and negative charges (159)

electroplating: an electrochemical process in which a metal ion is reduced and solid metal is deposited on a surface (622)

electrosynthesis: a synthesis reaction that is carried out in an electrochemical cell using an electric current (630)

element: one of the 111 simplest substances from which more complex materials are made (20)

elementary step: a single step in the mechanism of a reaction (597)

empirical formula: a formula that represents the simplest ratio among the elements in a compound (289)

emulsifier: a substance that stabilizes an emulsion by forming a layer between two immiscible liquids (499)

emulsion: colloidal-sized droplets (about 100 nm wide) of one liquid suspended in another liquid (498)

end point: the point in a titration at which the indicator changes color (573)

endothermic reaction: a reaction in which energy is absorbed (8)

energy: the capacity to do work (42)

enthalpy: the total energy content of a system (322)

entropy: a measure of the randomness or disorder of a system (390)

enzyme: a large protein molecule that catalyzes chemical reactions in living things (606)

equilibrium cell: an electrochemical cell in which no electric current flows (627)

equilibrium constant: for a reversible reaction in equilibrium, an expression that relates the concentrations of the reactants and products at a specific temperature to a constant (524)

equilibrium voltage: the voltage of a cell as measured by a voltmeter when no current is flowing (644)

equivalence point: the point in a titration when the amount of added base or acid exactly equals the amount of acid or base originally in solution (571)

ester: an organic compound often responsible for the aromas and flavors of fruits (345)

evaporation: the process by which molecules in a nonboiling liquid escape the liquid surface and enter the gas phase (399)

excess reactant: a reactant that will not be used up in a reaction that goes to completion (358)

excited state: the condition of an atom in a state higher than the ground state (94)

exothermic reaction: a reaction in which energy is released (8)

extensive property: a property that depends on the amount of material present (392)

F

fiber: a polymer that has a thread-like structure and is highly resistant to being stretched (259)

formula unit: the unit of an ionic compound that represents the simplest ratio of cations to anions (286)

free radical: an atom or molecule that has one or more unpaired electrons and is therefore very reactive (431)

freezing-point depression: the difference between the freezing point of a pure solvent and that of a solution (495)

fuel cell: a galvanic cell in which electricity is produced using reactants supplied from outside the cell (635)

functional group: a group of atoms that give characteristic properties to organic compounds (239)

G

galvanic cell: an electrochemical cell in which two electrode reactions occur spontaneously and produce electric energy (625)

gamma ray: high-energy electromagnetic radiation produced by decaying nuclei (666)

Gay-Lussac's law of combining volumes: at constant temperature and pressure, gases react in volume proportions that are whole numbers (equivalent to the coefficients in the balanced chemical equation) (441)

Gibbs energy: a thermodynamic property incorporating both enthalpy and entropy (400)

Graham's law of effusion: the rates of effusion for two gases are inversely proportional to the square roots of their molar masses at the same temperature and pressure (443)

greenhouse effect: an increase in the temperature of Earth caused by reflected solar radiation that is trapped in the atmosphere (430)

ground state: the lowest energy state of a quantized system (94)

group: a series of elements that form a vertical column in the periodic table (117)

H

half-life: the time required for half of a sample of radioactive atoms to decay (676)

halide: a salt that is composed of cations combined with anions of one of the halogen elements (168)

halogen: a nonmetallic element in Group 17 of the periodic table that has seven electrons in the outermost energy level and that combines with many metals to form salts (121)

heat: the sum total of kinetic energy of the particles in a sample of matter (43)

Henry's law: the solubility of a gas in a liquid is directly proportional to the partial pressure of that gas on the surface of the liquid (481)

Hess's law: the overall enthalpy change in a reaction is equal to the sum of the enthalpy changes of the individual steps in the process (403)

heterogeneous catalyst: a catalyst whose phase is different from that of the reactants (605)

heterogeneous mixture: a mixture containing substances that are not uniformly distributed (29)

homogeneous catalyst: a catalyst that is in the same phase as all of the reactants and products in a system (605)

homogeneous mixture: a mixture containing substances that are uniformly distributed (29)

Hund's rule: the most stable arrangement of electrons is that with the maximum number of unpaired electrons, all with the same spin quantum number (100)

hydrate: an ionic compound that contains precise numbers of water molecules in its crystal lattice (183)

hydration: the process by which water molecules surround each ion as it moves into solution (491)

hydrocarbon: the simplest class of organic compounds, consisting of only hydrogen and carbon atoms (236)

hydrogen bond: a form of dipole attraction in which a hydrogen atom bonded to a strongly electronegative atom is attracted to another electron-rich atom (221)

hydronium ion: a hydrogen ion covalently bonded to a water molecule, written as H_3O^+ (489)

hypothesis: a reasonable and testable explanation of observations (52)

I

ideal gas: a model that effectively describes the behavior of gases under most conditions (424)

ideal gas law: the equation of state for an ideal gas in which the product of the pressure and volume is proportional to the product of the absolute temperature and the amount of gas expressed in moles **(446)**

immiscible: describes liquids that will not dissolve appreciably in each other **(482)**

indicator: a dye that changes to different colors in solutions of different pII **(563)**

inhibitor: a substance added to a chemical reaction to slow the reaction down **(608)**

inorganic compound: all compounds outside the organic family of compounds **(28)**

insoluble: does not dissolve appreciably in a particular solvent **(480)**

intensive property: a property that does not depend on the amount of material present **(393)**

intermediate: a structure formed in one elementary step but consumed in a later step of a mechanism **(597)**

intermolecular force: an attraction that exists between molecules **(220)**

ion: an atom or group of atoms with an electrical charge **(26)**

ionic bond: the coulombic force of attraction between ions of opposite charge **(167)**

ionic compound: chemical compound composed of oppositely charged ions **(162)**

ionization energy: the amount of energy needed to remove an outer electron from a specific atom or ion in its ground state and in the gas phase **(137)**

isoelectronic: having the same electron configuration as another atom **(160)**

isomers: compounds with the same number and types of atoms but differing geometric arrangements **(237)**

isotope: one of two or more atoms of the same element with different numbers of neutrons **(89)**

K

kinetic energy: the energy a moving object has because of its motion **(41)**

kinetic-molecular theory: the theory that explains the behavior of gases at the molecular level **(424)**

L

lanthanides: shiny, metallic transition metals with atomic numbers 58 through 71 in which electrons are added to $4f$ orbitals **(120)**

lattice energy: the energy released when well-separated atoms, ions, or molecules come together to form a crystal **(172)**

law of conservation of energy: in any chemical or physical process, energy is neither created nor destroyed **(42)**

law of conservation of mass: the products of a chemical reaction have the same mass as the reactants **(54)**

law of definite proportions: any sample of a compound always has the same composition **(75)**

law of multiple proportions: the mass ratio for one of the elements that combines with a fixed mass of another element can be expressed in small whole numbers **(77)**

Le Châtelier's principle: if a system at equilibrium is disturbed by applying stress, the system attains a new equilibrium position to accommodate the change and tends to relieve the stress **(516)**

Lewis structure: a structure in which atomic symbols represent nuclei and inner-shell electrons, and dots are used to represent valence electrons **(203)**

ligand: a molecule or ion that is bonded to the central atom of a complex ion **(520)**

limiting reactant: a reactant that is consumed completely in a reaction that goes to completion **(358)**

line-emission spectrum: distinct lines of colored light that are produced when the light produced by excited atoms of an element is passed through a prism **(94)**

London force: an attraction between atoms and molecules caused by the formation of instantaneous dipoles in the atoms and molecules **(223)**

M

main-group elements: elements belonging to Groups 1 and 2 and Groups 13–18 in the periodic table and having very regular electron configurations **(118)**

mass: the quantity of matter in an object **(11)**

mass defect: the mass lost by conversion to energy when a nucleus forms from separated nucleons **(659)**

mass number: the total number of protons and neutrons in the nucleus of an atom **(87)**

matter: anything that has mass and volume **(10)**

mechanism: a proposed sequence of steps that describes how reactants are changed into products **(597)**

metal: any element that is a good conductor of electricity **(117)**

micelle: a spherical arrangement formed by molecules of fat or fat-like substances in an aqueous environment **(500)**

mineral: a naturally occurring inorganic substance that has a definite composition and an ordered structure **(182)**

miscible: describes liquids that will dissolve in each other **(482)**

mixture: a collection of two or more pure substances physically mixed together **(29)**

molar enthalpy of fusion: the heat absorbed when 1 mol of a substance melts **(397)**

molar enthalpy of vaporization: the heat absorbed when 1 mol of a liquid vaporizes **(397)**

molar heat capacity: the heat required to increase the temperature of 1 mol of a substance by 1 K (387)

molar mass: the mass in grams equal to the sum of all the atomic masses of the component atoms of a substance (280)

molarity: a concentration unit expressed as moles of solute per liter of solution (470)

mole: the SI unit for measuring the amount of a substance (81)

mole fraction: the number of moles of one component compared with the total number of moles in the mixture expressed as a ratio (437)

molecular formula: the type and actual number of atoms in a covalent compound (292)

molecular orbital: a region where an electron pair is most likely to exist as it travels in the three-dimensional space around two nuclei (195)

molecule: a neutral group of atoms held together by chemical bonds (23)

monomer: the small unit from which polymers form (256)

monoprotic acid: an acid that can donate one hydrogen ion per molecule (551)

N

net ionic equation: an equation that includes only those compounds and ions that are involved in a chemical change in a reaction (330)

neutral: describes a solution that contains equal concentrations of hydronium ions and hydroxide ions (560)

neutralization reaction: a reaction in which hydronium ions from an acid and hydroxide ions from a base react to produce water molecules (548)

neutron: a particle with no electric charge found in atomic nuclei (86)

newton: the force that will increase the speed of a 1 kg mass by 1 m/s each second that force is applied (427)

noble gas: elements in Group 18 of the periodic table that are characterized by low reactivity (122)

nonelectrolyte: a substance that, when dissolved in a solvent, will not enhance that solvent's conductivity (489)

nonmetal: an element that is a poor conductor of electricity (117)

nonpolar covalent bond: an attraction between two atoms in which bonding electrons are shared equally between the atoms (198)

normal boiling point: the temperature at which a substance boils at 1.0000 atm of pressure (457)

nuclear binding energy: the energy emitted when nucleons come together to form a nucleus; also the energy needed to break a nucleus into individual separated nucleons (660)

nuclear fission: a nuclear reaction in which a very heavy nucleus splits into two smaller nuclei of approximately equal mass (669)

nuclear fusion: the combining of two small nuclei to form a larger, more stable nucleus with the release of energy (671)

nuclear reaction: a reaction that involves a change in the composition of the nucleus of an atom (144)

nucleons: the protons and neutrons that make up the nucleus of an atom (658)

nucleus: the central region of an atom; made up of protons and neutrons (84)

nuclide: any combination of protons and neutrons in a nucleus (658)

O

octet rule: the tendency of atoms of elements to gain or lose electrons so that their outer *s* and *p* orbitals are full with eight electrons (161)

orbital: a region of an atom in which there is a high probability of finding one or more electrons (96)

order: the exponent on the concentration for a specified reactant in a rate law expression (594)

organic compound: any covalently bonded compound containing carbon (except carbonates and oxides) (28)

overall reaction order: the sum of all the exponents in a rate law expression (596)

oxidation: any chemical reaction in which the reactant loses electrons (623)

oxidation number: a number assigned to an atom in a polyatomic ion or molecular compound based on the assumption of complete transfer of electrons (180)

oxyanion: a negative polyatomic ion containing oxygen (177)

P

partial pressure: the pressure of an individual gas in a gas mixture that contributes to the total pressure of the mixture (436)

pascal: a unit of pressure equal to the force of 1 N on 1 m^2 (427)

Pauli exclusion principle: a maximum of two electrons can occupy each orbital, and these electrons must have different spin quantum numbers (98)

peptide bond: the bond formed between the carboxylic acid group of one amino acid and the amine group of another amino acid (258)

percentage composition: the percentage by mass of each element in a compound (289)

percentage yield: the ratio of actual yield to theoretical yield, multiplied by 100 (362)

period: a series of elements that form a horizontal row in the periodic table (117)

periodic law: the physical and chemical properties of elements are periodic functions of their atomic numbers (116)

pH: the negative logarithm of the hydronium ion concentration in a solution (27)

pH meter: an electronic device that measures pH (564)

phase: any part of a system that has uniform composition and properties **(457)**

phase diagram: a graphic representation of the relationships between the physical states (phases) of a substance at different pressures and temperatures **(457)**

physical change: a change that affects only physical properties **(17)**

physical property: any property of matter that can be measured without changing its chemical nature **(17)**

physical state: the form matter takes as a result of the arrangement of its particles **(6)**

plasma: a gas composed of ions, electrons, and neutral particles **(119)**

plastic: a polymer that is able to be shaped or molded without destroying the molecule **(259)**

polar covalent bond: an attraction between two atoms in which bonding electrons are localized on the more electronegative atom **(199)**

polyatomic ion: an electrically charged group of two or more chemically bonded atoms that function as a single ion **(176)**

polymer: a large organic molecule composed of smaller units bonded together **(51)**

potential energy: the energy an object has because of its position **(41)**

precision: the extent to which a series of measurements of the same quantity made in the same way agree with one another **(57)**

pressure: the force exerted per unit area **(427)**

primary cell: a galvanic cell that converts chemical energy to electrical energy; cannot be recharged **(635)**

product: a chemical produced as a result of a chemical reaction **(7)**

proton: a particle with a positive charge; found in atomic nuclei **(85)**

Q

quantity: something that has magnitude or size **(12)**

quantum number: a number with certain definite values **(95)**

R

radioactivity: the process during which unstable nuclei undergo spontaneous nuclear decay and emit particles and electromagnetic waves **(664)**

radioisotope: an unstable atom that undergoes radioactive decay **(90)**

rate-determining step: the slowest elementary step in a reaction mechanism **(597)**

rate law: an expression for the rate of a reaction as a function of the concentration of one or more reactants **(594)**

reactant: a chemical that is present at the beginning of a chemical reaction and that takes part in the reaction **(7)**

reaction rate: the decrease in reactant concentration or increase in product concentration per unit of time as a reaction proceeds **(589)**

redox reaction: any chemical process in which both oxidation and reduction occur **(623)**

reduction: a chemical reaction in which the reactant gains electrons **(622)**

resonance structure: a possible Lewis dot structure of a molecule for which more than one Lewis structure can be written **(208)**

S

sacrificial anode: metal attached to a metallic structure that serves as an anode preventing the corrosion of the structural metal **(641)**

salt: an ionic compound that is composed of cations bonded to anions, other than oxide or hydroxide anions; arranged in a regular three-dimensional pattern **(121)**

saturated: containing the amount of solute specified by the solubility **(481)**

saturated fat: a fat primarily containing saturated fatty acids **(249)**

scientific law: a description of the natural world that has proven reliable over time **(54)**

secondary cell: an electrochemical cell that can act as a galvanic cell or, on recharge as an electrolytic cell **(635)**

semiconductor: a crystalline material with intermediate electrical conductivity **(118)**

significant figure: any digit in a measurement that is known with certainty plus one final digit, which is somewhat uncertain or estimated **(58)**

silicate: any of the compounds containing silicon, oxygen, one or more metals, and possibly hydrogen **(182)**

single bond: a covalent bond in which one pair of electrons is shared between two atoms **(204)**

soap: a sodium or potassium salt of a long-chain fatty acid **(500)**

solubility: the maximum amount of a chemical that will dissolve in a given quantity of a solvent at a specified temperature while the solution is in contact with undissolved solute **(479)**

solubility product constant: the equilibrium constant for a slightly soluble ionic solid in equilibrium with its ions in a saturated solution **(529)**

soluble: can be dissolved in a particular solvent **(480)**

solute: the substance dissolved in a solution **(470)**

solvent: the substance in which the solute dissolves to make the solution **(470)**

specific heat capacity: the amount of heat energy required to raise the temperature of 1 g of a substance by 1 K **(45)**

spectator ion: an ion that remains unchanged in a chemical reaction (330)

standard electrode potential: the measured voltage when an electrode under standard conditions of temperature, pressure, and concentration is paired with a standard hydrogen electrode in an equilibrium cell (645)

standard enthalpy of formation: the amount of heat released or absorbed when 1 mol of compound is made from its elements under standard conditions (404)

standard hydrogen electrode: an electrode used as a reference for measuring other electrode potentials; it is arbitrarily assigned an electrode potential of 0.00 V (645)

standard solution: a solution whose concentration is accurately known (571)

standard temperature and pressure (STP): standard conditions for a gas at 0°C and 1 atm (428)

stoichiometry: mass and amount relationships between reactants and products in a chemical reaction (344)

strong acid: an acid that ionizes completely in aqueous solution (542)

strong nuclear force: the force of attraction among the particles of a nucleus that overcomes electrostatic repulsion and holds the nucleus together (659)

sublimation: a change of state in which a solid is transformed directly to a gas without going through the liquid state (458)

subscript: a whole number written below and to the right of an element's symbol that is used to denote the number of atoms in a formula (163)

substrate: the molecule or molecules with which an enzyme interacts (606)

superheavy element: an element with an atomic number greater than 106 (148)

supersaturated: containing more than the standard amount of

solute specified by the solubility at a given set of conditions (481)

surfactant: a class of salts, valued for their cleansing properties, whose anions possess a negatively charged "head" and a long nonpolar "tail" (500)

suspension: a mixture that appears uniform while being stirred but separates into different phases when agitation ceases (468)

synthesis: a chemical reaction in which atoms or simple molecules combine to form a compound that is more complex (326)

system: a specific portion of matter in a given region of space that has been selected for study during an experiment or observation (43)

T

temperature: a measure of the average kinetic energy of the particles in a sample of matter (44)

theoretical yield: the calculated maximum amount of product possible from a given amount of reactant (361)

theory: a well-tested explanation of observations (53)

thermodynamics: the branch of science concerned with the energy changes that accompany physical and chemical processes (390)

titrant: the solution added to another solution in a titration (571)

titration: the operation of gradually adding one solution to another to reach an equivalence point (571)

transition metals: elements in Groups 3 through 12 (117)

transition range: the pH range through which an indicator changes color (572)

transmutation: the process of changing one nucleus into another by radioactive disintegration or bombardment with other particles (145)

triple point: the temperature and pressure at which three phases of a substance exist in equilibrium (458)

triprotic acid: an acid that can donate three hydrogen ions per molecule (551)

U

unit: a standard used when measuring a quantity (12)

unit cell: the simplest repeating unit of a crystal lattice (169)

unsaturated fat: a fat primarily containing unsaturated fatty acids (249)

unsaturated hydrocarbon: a hydrocarbon that has at least one double or triple bond between carbon atoms (245)

unshared pair: a pair of valence electrons not involved in bonding to another atom (203)

V

valence electron: an electron in the outermost energy level of an atom, where it can participate in bonding (202)

van der Waals radius: half the distance between the nuclei in adjacent non-bonded molecules (135)

vapor pressure: the pressure exerted by a vapor in equilibrium with its liquid state at a given temperature (455)

volt: the SI unit of voltage (620)

voltage: an electric potential difference (620)

volume: the amount of space an object occupies (10)

VSEPR (valence shell electron pair repulsion) theory: a simple model that predicts the general shape of a molecule based on the repulsion between both bonding and nonbonding electron clouds (215)

W

weak acid: an acid that is a weak electrolyte (542)

weight: the force produced by gravity acting on mass (11)

Boldfaced page references denote illustrations; *t* references denote information in tables.

A

carbonic acid, **542**

carbon monoxide, *t* 372

carbon tetrachloride, *t* 173, 234, 338, 459

carbonate(s), 519, 526, 541, 567, 578

carboxylic acid(s), *t* 248, 545. *See also* acids, organic.

career application(s), 133, 333, 453, 643, 675

Carothers, Wallace, 254

casein, 469

catalase, 605

catalysis, definition, 604

catalyst(s), **604**, 604–609, 611

catalytic converter(s), **373**, 608–609

CAT (computerized axial tomography) scan(s), 674–675

cat fur, **606**

cathode(s), 82, 622, **622**, 624, **640**, 650

cathode ray tube(s), **82**, 82–83, **83**

cathodic protection, 641, **641**

cation(s), 159, 160–161. *See also* ion(s).

Cavendish, Henry, 124, 414, **445**

cellulose, **236**, 255, **255**

Celsius scale, 44–45, **45**, 385

cement, 336

centrifuge(s), **476**

ceramic conductor(s), 132

cesium, 119, **119**, *t* 119, 128

cesium chloride, 169, **169**

CFCs (chlorofluorocarbon compounds), **430**, 430–432, 459, 608

Chadwick, James, 86

chain reaction(s), 431, 608–609, 670–671

chalcocite, 295

change of state, **396**, 396–401, 416

Charles, Jacques, 414, 438

Charles's law, 438–439, 460

chemical(s), 4, *t* 5, 31

chemical bond(s)
    bond energy, 197, *t* 197, *t* 201, *t* 230, 237, **237**
    bond length, 196–197, *t* 197
    bond radii, 135
    bond spring analogy, 196, **196**
    bond strength, 234

    definition, 40
    hydrogen, 221–222

chemical change(s), 18, **19**, 308–309

chemical energy, 40–44, 310–311, 321–325

chemical engineer(s), 643

chemical equation(s), 308–335
    balancing, *t* 313, 313–316, **314,** *t* 314, **315**
    constructing, 312–316
    definition, 312
    energy changes, 321–325
    interpreting, 320, *t* 320, 335
    ionic, 317
    nuclear, 668
    predictions, 360–361
    recipes and, 318–319
    symbols in, 319, *t* 319

chemical equilibrium, definition, 361. *See also* equilibrium system(s).

chemical formula(s). *See* formula(s).

chemical kinetics, 589. *See also* rate(s) of reaction.

chemical producer(s), 5, *t* 5

chemical production, 345–346, 361–364

chemical property, definition, 18

chemical reaction(s)
    calculating energy in, 321–325
    catalysts and, 604–609
    chain reactions, 431, 608–609, 670–671
    completion, 512, 535
    driving forces, 384–389
    galvanic, 639
    leftover reactants, 357–365
    mechanisms, 597, 611
    orientation and, 602–603, **603**
    overview, 7, 308–311, 335
    oxidation, 623, **623**
    redox, 623, 629, 646–648
    reversible, 512–513, 535
    spontaneity, 310, 400–401, 407–409, *t* 409
    types of, 325–330, 335

chemical reactivity, **134**, 234, 307

chemistry, science of, 4–5, 34

Chernobyl, Ukraine, 671

chlorine
    free radicals, 431
    in human health, *t* 91
    molar heat capacity, *t* 389
    oxyanions, *t* 177
    properties, **121**
    uses, 634

chloroethene, *t* 262

chlorofluorocarbon compound(s). *See* CFCs.

chlorophyll, 593

chloroplast(s), 410

chromatography, 477

chromium, *t* 45, 99, 101

cinnamaldehyde, 366

cisplatin, **51**, 51–53, 288

citric acid, **236**, 542

Clean Air Act Standards, *t* 372

cleaner(s), enzymatic, 607

cloud chamber(s), 146

coefficient(s), 313

coffee, decaffeination, 452–453

collagen, 485

colligative properties
    dipole forces, 220
    ionic and molecular substances, *t* 219, 219–222
    solutes and, **495**, 495–498, 503

colloid(s), 469, **469**, 498

color
    cat fur, **606**
    changes in, 19, **19**
    fireworks, 73, 90, 102
    as indicator of chemical reaction, **520,** **563**, 563–564, **564**
    wavelengths, 102

combined gas law, 448, 460

combustion reaction(s), 325, **325**, 331

common ion effect, 532–533, 535, 566

composting, 233

compound(s), 26, 28. *See also* covalent compound(s), ionic compound(s).

compressibility of gases, **425**, 425–426

computer microprocessor chip(s), 298

computerized axial tomography (CAT) scan(s), 674–675

concentration, 470–475, *t* 471, 576–577, 594–598. *See also* mole(s).

condensation
    of gases, **399**, 454–456, 460
    of polymers, 258–259

conduction band(s), 126–129, **127**

conservation of energy, 42, 67

conservation of mass, **54**, 67, 76, **76**

contact lens(es), 607

Coulomb's law and, **88,** 88–90
overview, 85–88
properties, *t* 86, *t* 664

pure substance(s), 23

PVC (polyvinyl chloride), 263, **263,** 264

pyridine, 547

pyrotechnics, 73

Q

quantity, 12

quantum number(s), 95, 96–97, *t* 97, **98**

quantum theory, 96

quark(s), **53**

quicklime, 366

R

radiation exposure, *t* 680, 680–681

radioactivity
artificial transmutations, 669–673
dating, **676,** 676–679, **678, 679,** 682
detection of, 680
discovery, 674
half-lives, 676–680, *t* 677, 683
types of processes, 664–668, 683
uses, 674–675

radioisotope(s), 90, 121

radiological technician(s), 675

radiology, 674–675

radium, 120, **120,** *t* 677

radon, 122, *t* 677, 685

Ramsay, Malcolm, 467, 502

Ramsay, William, *t* 65

raspberry ketone, 346

rate(s) of reaction
average, 590
concentration and, 594–598
definition, 589
dynamic, 514, **514**
factors affecting, 598–601, 611
Le Chatelier's principle, 517
measurement, 590–592
modeling, 601–603
overview, 588–592, 611
rate-determining steps, 597
rate laws, 594–598, 611
temperature and, 599, 601, 610

Rayleigh, Lord, *t* 65

reactant(s)
definition, 7
excess, 358
leftover, 357–365

limiting, 358–360
overview, 308–309

reaction(s). *See* chemical reaction(s).

reactivity, 134, 234, 307

reagent-grade chemical(s), **31**

ream(s), *t* 275

recycling, 30, 263–264

red giant(s), 144–145

red tide(s), 587, 610

redox reaction(s), 623, 629, 646–648

reduction, 622

refrigerant(s), 432

relative atomic mass, 278–282

relativity, theory of, 46, 55

rem(s), 680, *t* 680

resonance structure(s), 208–209, 238

respiration, 9

resting metabolic rate, 411

retinol (vitamin A), **485,** 485–486

retrovirus(es), 332

Reye's syndrome, 9

rocket fuel, 377

Rosenberg, Barnett, 51–53

Royds, Thomas, *t* 65

rubber, 253, 259–260

rubidium, 119, **119,** *t* 119

Rutherford, Daniel, 445

Rutherford, Ernest
alpha particles, *t* 65, 145–146
atomic nucleus, 658
atomic theory, 84, 93, 96
hydrogen, 414
transmutation, 672

Rutherfordium, 147

S

sacrificial anode(s), 641

Salix, 3

salt(s). *See also* ionic compound(s).
binary, 162–164, 172–175
definition, 177
energy and formation, 170–171
hydrates, 183–184
ionic bonding in, 166–169
melting and boiling points, 173, *t* 173
names, 162–164
overview, 186

salt water, 25, **468,** 490, 628, 649

saturated fat(s), 249, 266

saturation, 481

SBR (polystyrene butadiene) rubber, 260, **326**

scandium, 113, *t* 116

Scheele, Carl, 445, 634

schizophrenia, 675

scientific discovery, 49–50

scientific law(s), **54,** 54–55, 67

scientific method, 48, 48–55, 67

scientific notation, *t* 63, 63–64, *t* 64

score(s), *t* 275

scurvy, 484

Seaborg, G. T., 147

seashell(s), 529

sea water, 25, 628, 649. *See also* salt water.

secondary amine(s), 547

secondary cell(s), 635

selenium, 608

self-ionization, 548

semiconductor(s), 118, 127, **127,** 131

Semon, Waldo, 263

serine, 236, 258

SHE (standard hydrogen electrode), 645, **645**

shellfish toxin, 587, 610

sickle cell anemia, 214, **214**

significant figure(s)
definition, 58
exact numbers, 61
rules for, 5, *t* 59, 59–62, *t* 60
scientific notation, *t* 64

silicate(s), **182,** 182–184

silicon, 126, 282, 298

silver, *t* 16, 17, 111, 149, 301, *t* 389

silver chloride, 8, 157, 185

silver iodide, 157, 185

silver rubidium iodide, 175

Simon, Helmut and Erika, 657

skeletal formula(s), *t* 250, 250–252

smelling salt(s), **209**

smog, 209, 372, 372–373. *See also* air pollution.

smoke detector(s), **679,** 679–680

soap, 500, 500–501, **559**

sodium
dietary, 165, **165, 412**
electrosynthesis, 628–630
enthalpy and entropy of, *t* 398
in human health, *t* 91

ART CREDITS

Abbreviated as follows: (t) top; (b) bottom; (l) left; (r) right; (c) center.

All art, unless otherwise noted, by Holt, Rinehart, and Winston.

Front Cover and Master Items: Leslie Kell. **Front Matter:** Page II, (tl), J/B Woolsey Associates; V (tl), J/B Woolsey Associates; V (cl), David Uhl Studio; VIII (bl), Michael Morrow; XV (tl), David Uhl Studio. **Chapter One:** 5, (br), Leslie Kell; 24, (tl), J/B Woolsey Associates; 28, (tl), J/B Woolsey Associates; 28, (tc), J/B Woolsey Associates; 28, (c), J/B Woolsey Associates; 33, (br), J/B Woolsey Associates. **Chapter Two:** Page 40, (br), J/B Woolsey Associates; 45, (tr), Foca; 48, (b) Leslie Kell; 57, (t) David Uhl Illustrations. **Chapter Three:** Page 75, (br), Leslie Kell; 77, (t) Stephen Durke/Dick Washington; 78, (cl), J/B Woolsey Associates; 82, (b) David Uhl Studio; 84, (bl) David Uhl Studio; 92, (b) David Uhl Studio; 98, (tl), J/B Woolsey Associates; 98, (tr), J/B Woolsey Associates; 98, (cr) J/B Woolsey Associates; 106, (tl), Foca; 106, (tr), Foca; 106, (tr), Foca; 107, (tl), Foca. **Chapter Four:** Page 113, (c), Jack Scott; 126, (bl) J/B Woolsey Associates; 126, (br), J/B Woosley Associates. **Chapter Five:** Page 171, (all) Leslie Kell; 173, (tl), David Uhl Studio. **Chapter Six:** Page 195, (tl), J/B Woolsey Associates; 216, (tr), J/B Woolsey Associates; 217, (bc) J/B Woolsey Associates; 217, (c), J/B Woolsey Associates; 218, (tl), J/B Woolsey Associates; 223, (b) J/B Woolsey Associates. **Chapter Seven:** Page 234, (tr), J/B Woolsey Associates; 235 (tl), J/B Woolsey Associates. **Chapter Eight:** Page 285, (t) Kristy Sprott; 286, (b) Kristy Sprott; 286, (b) Kristy Sprott; 286, (b) Kristy Sprott; 293, (tr), J/B Woolsey Associates. **Chapter Nine:** Page 333, (tr), Morgan Cain Associates. **Chapter Ten:** Page 358, (t) Leslie Kell; 368, (t) Peter Bollinger; 370, (cl), Peter Bollinger; 370, (c), Peter Bollinger; 370, (cr) Peter Bollinger. **Chapter Eleven:** Page 385, (bl) Leslie Kell; 402, (b) David Uhl Illustrations; 410, (t) Kristy Sprott. **Chapter Twelve:** Page 429, (b) David Uhl Studio; 430, (bl) J/B Woolsey Associates; 430, (br) J/B Woolsey Associates; 435, (bl) David Uhl Studio; 435, (b) David Uhl Studio; 445, (tr), David Uhl Studio; 452, (b) David Uhl Studio; 455, (tr), Stephen Durke/Dick Washington. **Chapter Thirteen:** Page 469, (c), Stephen Durke/Dick Washington; 469, (c), Stephen Durke/Dick Washington; 469, (br), Stephen Durke/Dick Washington; 488, (tc), Stephen Durke/Dick Washington; 488, (tc), Stephen Durke/Dick Washington; 489, (b) Stephen Durke/Dick Washington; 491, (b) Stephen Durke/Dick Washington; 497, (bc) Stephen Durke/Dick Washington; 497, (br), Stephen Durke/Dick Washington; 498, (bl) Stephen Durke/Dick Washington; 499, (tr), Stephen Durke/Dick Washington; 500, (br), Stephen Durke/Dick Washington. **Chapter Fourteen:** Page 518, (b) Christy Krames. **Chapter Fifteen:** Page 546, (bl) Kristy Sprott; 547, (tr), J/B Woolsey Associates; 550, (b) Kristy Sprott; 552 (bl) Kristy Sprott; 552, (t) Kristy Sprott; 552, (cr) Kristy Sprott; 553, (t) Leslie Kell; 578, (br), Leslie Kell. **Chapter Sixteen:** Page 589, (b) Stephen Durke/Dick Washington; 589, (b) Stephen Durke/Dick Washington; 589, (b) Stephen Durke/Dick Washington; 606, (bc) Christy Krames; 606, (bc) Christy Krames. **Chapter Seventeen:** Page 620, (b) David Uhl Studio; 623, (tr), Kristy Sprott; 623, (tr), Kristy Sprott; 624, (tr), David Uhl Studio; 624, (bl) David Uhl Studio; 629, (b) David Uhl Studio; 632, (br), David Uhl Studio; 635, (b) David Uhl Studio; 637, (bl) David Uhl Studio; 637, (br), David Uhl Studio; 638, (b) David Uhl Studio; 640, (b) David Uhl Studio; 640, (br), Kristy Sprott; 644 (bl) David Uhl Studio; 644, (bl) David Uhl Studio; 644, (bl) David Uhl Studio; 645, (tr), David Uhl Studio; 645, (br), David Uhl Studio. **Chapter Eighteen:** Page 671, (t) David Uhl Studio; 677, (b) Leslie Kell; 714, (tl), David Uhl Studio; 756, (tr), David Uhl Studio; 780, (tl), David Uhl Studio.

PHOTO CREDITS

Abbreviated as follows: (t) top; (b) bottom; (l) left; (r) right; (c) center.

All photos, unless otherwise noted, by HRW Staff Photographer, Sam Dudgeon. Acknowledgments:

Quick Lab Icon (watch) - Image copyright © 2000 Photodisc, Inc.
Lab Program Safety Icon (test tubes) - Image Copyright © 2000 Photodisc, Inc.
Inquiry Lab Icon (glassware) - Image copyright © 1997 Photodisc, Inc.

Table of Contents: II (br) Dennis Fagan/HRW; III (br) Charlie Winters; IV (tr) Douglas Struthers/Tony Stone Images; (bl) Tony Freeman/PhotoEdit; V (tr) EdPritchard/Tony Stone Images; (br) Charlie Winters; VI (tc) Andrew Syred/Tony Stone Images; (cl) Charlie Winters/Photo Researchers, Inc.; VII (tr) Charlie Westerman/Liaison International; (cl) Ken Whitmore/Tony Stone Images; (bl) John Langford/HRW Photo; VIII (tr) Vladimir Pcholkin/FPG International; (cl) Charlie Winters; (cr) Sergio Purtell/Foca; (bl) Matthew Stockman/Allsport; (br) Courtesy of Ford Motor Co.; IX (tr) Jenny Hager/Adventure Photo; (bl) Ozone Processing Team Code 916/NASA Goddard Space Flight Center; (tl) Westlight; X (tc) Dr. E.R. Degginger; (bl) Peter Van Steen/HRW Photo; (br, bc, c) Charlie Winters; XI (tr) Tony Stone Images; (c) Sergio Purtell/Foca; (bl) Rod Planck/Photo Researchers, Inc.; (cl) Randal Alhadeff/HRW Photo; XII (t) William Warren/Westlight; (cl) Peter Van Steen/HRW Photo; (bl) Frank Rossotto/The Stock Market; XIII (tr) Sergio Purtell/Foca; (cl) Dennis Fagan/HRW Photo; XIV (bl) Phil Degginger/Bruce Coleman, Inc.; XV (t) Harry Giglio Photography, Inc.; XVI (tr) Sergio Purtell/Foca. **Chapter 1:** 2 (all) SuperStock; 4 (b) Image Bank; 6 (br) Randal Alhadeff/HRW Photo; 7 (bc) Charlie Winters; 8 (tr) Charlie Winters; (tc) Richard Megna/Fundamental Photographs; 11 (tr) Charlie Winters; 12 (tl) Andrew Brookes Creative/The Stock Market; 16 (bl) Dennis Fagan/HRW Photo; 18 (bc) Charlie Winters; 19 (all) Sergio Purtell/Foca; 23 (tl) Sergio Purtell/Foca; 24 (tr) John Neubauer/Rainbow, Inc.; 25 (cr) Tom Pantages Photography; 26 (b) Peter Van Steen/HRW Photo; 27 (tl, tc) Charlie Winters; 29 (bl) Neal Mishler/FPG International; (br) Sergio Purtell/Foca; (tr) Jenny Hager/Adventure Photo; 31 (all) Charlie Winters; 33 (br) Sergio Purtell/Foca. **Chapter 2:** 38 (all) Paul & Lindamarie/FPG International; 41 (tc) Visuals Unlimited; 42 (bc) Tony Freeman/PhotoEdit; 43 (tl) Peter Van Steen/HRW Photo; (tc) Sergio Purtell/Foca/Prism Technologies, Inc.; 44 (tl) Sergio Purtell/Foca; 50 (b) Andre Jenny/Stock South/PNI; 52 (tl, br) Sergio Purtell/Foca; (bc) Digital Stock Corp.; 53 (tr) © 1994 by The New York Times Co. Reprinted by Permission.; 54 (tr) Image Copyright © 1996 Photodisc, Inc.; (tl) Sergio Purtell/Foca; 56 (all) Kristen Brochmann/Fundamental Photographs; 65 (tr) Scoones/SIPA Press; 66 (tr) Corbis-Bettmann. **Chapter 3:** 72 (all) Ed Pritchard/Tony Stone Images; 74 (br) Giraudon/Art Resource/NY; 75 (bl) Peter Van Steen/HRW Photo; 77 (tr) Sergio Purtell/Foca; 81 (tr) Corbis-Bettmann; 83 (br) Richard Megna/Fundamental Photographs; (tr) Sergio Purtell/Foca; 85 (tl) David Sailors/The Stock Market; (tr) Sergio Purtell/Foca; 96 (bl) Image used with permission of IMS Properties, Inc.; 102 (tr) Ed Pritchard/Tony Stone Images; 103 (cr) Dr. E.R. Degginger; (c) Carl Frank/Photo Researchers, Inc. **Chapter 4:** 110 (all) Charlie Winters; 112 (all) Charlie Winters; 117 (bl, bc) Charlie Winters; (br) Dr. E.R. Degginger; 120 (bl) Vanni/Art Resource/NY; 124 (cr) Terry Donnelly/Tony Stone Images; 125 (br) Bruce Iverson; 126 (bl) J & L Weber/Peter Arnold, Inc.; (br) Charles D. Winters; 128 (bl) Telegraph Colour Library/FPG International; 132 (cr) Wesley Hitt/Tony Stone Images; 133 (tr) Gabe Palmer/The Stock Market; 134 (b) Peter Cade/Tony Stone Images; (all others) Charlie Winters/HRW Photo; 143 (br) HST image: Hui Yang (U. of Illinois Jeff J. Hester and NASA); 144 (tl) Roger Ressmeyer/Corbis; 149 (tr) Alfred Pasieka/Peter Arnold, Inc. **Chapter 5:** 156 (all) Charlie Winters/Photo Researchers, Inc.; 163 (all) Charlie Winters; 165 (tr) Rick Lance/PhotoTake; 166 (bl) Charlie Winters; (bc) Andrew Syred/Tony Stone Images; 169 (c) Paul Silverman/Fundamental Photographs; 170 (bl) Charlie Winters; 174 (all) Charlie Winters; 182 (bc) Tom Pantages Photography; (br) Lafaille/Gamma Liaison; 183 (tl) Sergio Purtell/Foca; (tc, tr) Charlie Winters. **Chapter 6:** 192 (all) Douglas Struthers/Tony Stone Images; 194 (bc) T. McCarthy/Custom Medical Stock Photo; 195 (bc) Victoria Smith/HRW Photo; 202 (br) Courtesy of Edgar Fahs Smith Collection, University of Pennsylvania

Periodic Table of the Elements

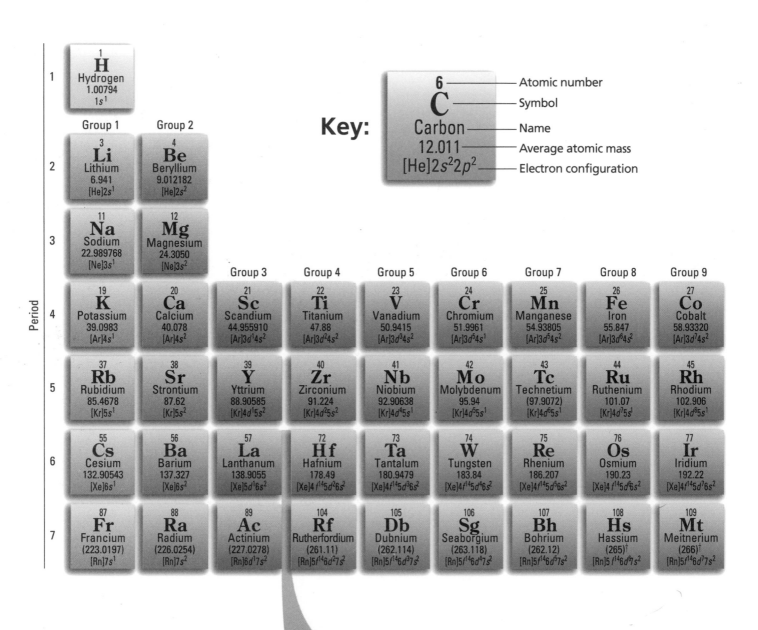

Key:

6	Atomic number
C	Symbol
Carbon	Name
12.011	Average atomic mass
$[He]2s^2 2p^2$	Electron configuration

Period

Period 1

1		
H		
Hydrogen		
1.00794		
$1s^1$		

Group 1 — **Group 2**

Period 2

3	4
Li	**Be**
Lithium	Beryllium
6.941	9.012182
$[He]2s^1$	$[He]2s^2$

Period 3

11	12
Na	**Mg**
Sodium	Magnesium
22.989768	24.3050
$[Ne]3s^1$	$[Ne]3s^2$

Group 3	Group 4	Group 5	Group 6	Group 7	Group 8	Group 9

Period 4

19	20	21	22	23	24	25	26	27
K	**Ca**	**Sc**	**Ti**	**V**	**Cr**	**Mn**	**Fe**	**Co**
Potassium	Calcium	Scandium	Titanium	Vanadium	Chromium	Manganese	Iron	Cobalt
39.0983	40.078	44.955910	47.88	50.9415	51.9961	54.93805	55.847	58.93320
$[Ar]4s^1$	$[Ar]4s^2$	$[Ar]3d^1 4s^2$	$[Ar]3d^2 4s^2$	$[Ar]3d^3 4s^2$	$[Ar]3d^5 4s^1$	$[Ar]3d^5 4s^2$	$[Ar]3d^6 4s^2$	$[Ar]3d^7 4s^2$

Period 5

37	38	39	40	41	42	43	44	45
Rb	**Sr**	**Y**	**Zr**	**Nb**	**Mo**	**Tc**	**Ru**	**Rh**
Rubidium	Strontium	Yttrium	Zirconium	Niobium	Molybdenum	Technetium	Ruthenium	Rhodium
85.4678	87.62	88.90585	91.224	92.90638	95.94	(97.9072)	101.07	102.906
$[Kr]5s^1$	$[Kr]5s^2$	$[Kr]4d^1 5s^2$	$[Kr]4d^2 5s^2$	$[Kr]4d^4 5s^1$	$[Kr]4d^5 5s^1$	$[Kr]4d^6 5s^1$	$[Kr]4d^7 5s^1$	$[Kr]4d^8 5s^1$

Period 6

55	56	57	72	73	74	75	76	77
Cs	**Ba**	**La**	**Hf**	**Ta**	**W**	**Re**	**Os**	**Ir**
Cesium	Barium	Lanthanum	Hafnium	Tantalum	Tungsten	Rhenium	Osmium	Iridium
132.90543	137.327	138.9055	178.49	180.9479	183.84	186.207	190.23	192.22
$[Xe]6s^1$	$[Xe]6s^2$	$[Xe]5d^1 6s^2$	$[Xe]4f^{14}5d^2 6s^2$	$[Xe]4f^{14}5d^3 6s^2$	$[Xe]4f^{14}5d^4 6s^2$	$[Xe]4f^{14}5d^5 6s^2$	$[Xe]4f^{14}5d^6 6s^2$	$[Xe]4f^{14}5d^7 6s^2$

Period 7

87	88	89	104	105	106	107	108	109
Fr	**Ra**	**Ac**	**Rf**	**Db**	**Sg**	**Bh**	**Hs**	**Mt**
Francium	Radium	Actinium	Rutherfordium	Dubnium	Seaborgium	Bohrium	Hassium	Meitnerium
(223.0197)	(226.0254)	(227.0278)	(261.11)	(262.114)	(263.118)	(262.12)	(265)†	(266)†
$[Rn]7s^1$	$[Rn]7s^2$	$[Rn]6d^1 7s^2$	$[Rn]5f^{14}6d^2 7s^2$	$[Rn]5f^{14}6d^3 7s^2$	$[Rn]5f^{14}6d^4 7s^2$	$[Rn]5f^{14}6d^5 7s^2$	$[Rn]5f^{14}6d^6 7s^2$	$[Rn]5f^{14}6d^7 7s^2$

† Estimated from currently available IUPAC data.

* The systematic names and symbols for elements greater than 109 will be used until the approval of trivial names by IUPAC.

58	59	60	61	62
Ce	**Pr**	**Nd**	**Pm**	**Sm**
Cerium	Praseodymium	Neodymium	Promethium	Samarium
140.115	140.908	144.24	(144.9127)	150.36
$[Xe]4f^1 5d^1 6s^2$	$[Xe]4f^3 6s^2$	$[Xe]4f^4 6s^2$	$[Xe]4f^5 6s^2$	$[Xe]4f^6 6s^2$

90	91	92	93	94
Th	**Pa**	**U**	**Np**	**Pu**
Thorium	Protactinium	Uranium	Neptunium	Plutonium
232.0381	231.03588	238.0289	(237.0482)	244.0642
$[Rn]6d^2 7s^2$	$[Rn]5f^2 6d^1 7s^2$	$[Rn]5f^3 6d^1 7s^2$	$[Rn]5f^4 6d^1 7s^2$	$[Rn]5f^6 7s^2$